Jean-Claude **Corbeil**
Ariane **Archambault**

VISUAL
FIVE-LANGUAGE
DICTIONARY

ACKNOWLEDGEMENTS FROM QA INTERNATIONAL

Our deepest gratitude to the individuals, institutions, companies and businesses that have provided us with the latest technical documentation for use in preparing the *Visual Five-Language Dictionary*.

Arcand, Denis (réalisateur); Association Internationale de Signalisation Maritime; Association canadienne des paiements (Charlie Clarke); Association des banquiers canadiens (Lise Provost); Automobiles Citroën; Automobiles Peugeot; Banque du Canada (Lyse Brousseau); Banque Royale du Canada (Raymond Chouinard, Francine Morel, Carole Trottier); Barrett Xplore inc.; Bazarin, Christine;Bibliothèque du Parlement canadien (Service de renseignements); Bibliothèque nationale du Québec (Jean-François Palomino); Bluechip Kennels (Olga Gagne); Bombardier Aéronautique; Bridgestone-Firestone; Brother (Canada); Canadien National; Casavant Frères ltée; C.O.J.O. ATHENES 2004 (Bureau des Médias Internationaux); Centre Eaton de Montréal; Centre national du Costume (Recherche et de Diffusion); Cetacean Society International (William R. Rossiter); Chagnon, Daniel (architecte D.E.S. – M.E.Q.); Cohen et Rubin Architectes (Maggy Cohen); Commission Scolaire de Montréal (École St-Henri); Compagnie de la Baie d'Hudson (Nunzia Iavarone, Ron Oyama); Corporation d'hébergement du Québec (Céline Drolet); École nationale de théâtre du Canada (Bibliothèque); Élevage Le Grand Saphir (Stéphane Ayotte); Énergie atomique du Canada ltée; Eurocopter; Famous Players; Fédération bancaire française (Védi Hékiman); Fontaine, PierreHenry (biologiste); Future Shop; Garaga; Groupe Jean Coutu; Hôpital du Sacré-Cœur de Montréal; Hôtel Inter-Continental; Hydro-Québec; I.P.I.Q. (Serge Bouchard); IGA Barcelo; International Entomological Society (Dr. Michael Geisthardt); Irisbus; Jérôme, Danielle (O.D.); La Poste (Colette Gouts); Le Groupe Canam Manac inc.; Lévesque, Georges (urgentologue); Lévesque, Robert (chef machiniste); Manutan; Marriot Spring Hill suites; MATRA S.A.; Métro inc.; ministère canadien de la Défense nationale (Affaires publiques); ministère de la Défense, République Française; ministère de la Justice du Québec (Service de la gestion immobilière – Carol Sirois); ministère de l'Éducation du Québec (Direction de l'équipement scolaire-Daniel Chagnon); Muse Productions (Annick Barbery); National Aeronautics and Space Administration; National Oceanic and Atmospheric Administration; Nikon Canada inc.; Normand, Denis (consultant en télécommunications); Office de la langue française du Québec (Chantal Robinson); Paul Demers & Fils inc.; Phillips (France); Pratt & Whitney Canada inc.; Prévost Car inc.; Radio Shack Canada ltée; Réno-Dépôt inc.; Robitaille, Jean-François (Département de biologie, Université Laurentienne); Rocking T Ranch and Poultry Farm (Pete and Justine Theer); RONA inc.; Sears Canada inc.; Secrétariat d'État du Canada : Bureau de la traduction ; Service correctionnel du Canada; Société d'Entomologie Africaine (Alain Drumont); Société des musées québécois (Michel Perron); Société Radio-Canada; Sony du Canada ltée; Sûreté du Québec; Théâtre du Nouveau Monde; Transports Canada (Julie Poirier); Urgences-Santé (Éric Berry); Ville de Longueuil (Direction de la Police); Ville de Montréal (Service de la prévention des incendies); Vimont Lexus Toyota; Volvo Bus Corporation; Yamaha Motor Canada Ltd.

Visual Five-Language Dictionary is created and produced by
QA International, a division of
Les Éditions Québec Amérique inc.
329, rue de la Commune Ouest, 3ᵉ étage
Montréal (Québec) H2Y 2E1 Canada
T 514.499.3000 F 514.499.3010

British Library Cataloguing In Publication Data
Data available
Library of Congress Cataloging In Publication Data
Data available

Printed and bound in Singapore.
www.qa-international.com

Staff – QA International

EDITORIAL STAFF

Publisher: Jacques Fortin

Authors: Jean-Claude Corbeil et Ariane Archambault

Editorial Director: François Fortin

Editor-in-Chief: Serge D'Amico

Graphic Design: Anne Tremblay

PRODUCTION

Mac Thien Nguyen Hoang

Guylaine Houle

TERMINOLOGICAL RESEARCH

Jean Beaumont

Catherine Briand

Nathalie Guillo

ILLUSTRATION

Art Direction: Jocelyn Gardner

Jean-Yves Ahern

Rielle Lévesque

Alain Lemire

Mélanie Boivin

Yan Bohler

Claude Thivierge

Pascal Bilodeau

Michel Rouleau

Anouk Noël

Carl Pelletier

LAYOUT

Pascal Goyette

Janou-Ève LeGuerrier

Véronique Boisvert

Josée Gagnon

Karine Raymond

Geneviève Théroux Béliveau

DOCUMENTATION

Gilles Vézina

Kathleen Wynd

Stéphane Batigne

Sylvain Robichaud

Jessie Daigle

DATA MANAGEMENT

Programmer : Daniel Beaulieu

Nathalie Fréchette

REVISION

Marie-Nicole Cimon

PREPRESS

Karine Lévesque

Tony O'Riley

Sophie Pellerin

Kien Tang

Staff – Oxford University Press

EDITORIAL STAFF

Natalie Pomier

Catherine Soanes

CONTRIBUTIONS

QA International wishes to thank the following for their contribution to the *Visual Five-Language Dictionary* :

Jean-Louis Martin, Marc Lalumière, Jacques Perrault, Stéphane Roy, Alice Comtois, Michel Blais, Christiane Beauregard, Mamadou Togola, Annie Maurice, Charles Campeau, Mivil Deschênes, Jonathan Jacques, Martin Lortie, Raymond Martin, Frédérick Simard, Yan Tremblay, Mathieu Blouin, Sébastien Dallaire, Hoang Khanh Le, Martin Desrosiers, Nicolas Oroc, François Escalmel, Danièle Lemay, Pierre Savoie, Benoît Bourdeau, Marie-Andrée Lemieux, Caroline Soucy, Yves Chabot, Anne-Marie Ouellette, Anne-Marie Villeneuve, Anne-Marie Brault, Nancy Lepage, Daniel Provost, François Vézina.

Introduction to the
Visual Five-Language Dictionary

The *Visual Five-Language Dictionary* is the result of a collaboration between QA International and Oxford University Press. With over 3,600 illustrations combined with thousands of specialist and general terms, the *Visual Five-Language Dictionary* provides a rich source of knowledge that is both clear and attractive to use.

EDITORIAL POLICY

The *Visual Five-Language Dictionary* takes an inventory of the physical environment of a person who is part of today's technological age and who knows and uses a large number of specialized terms in a wide variety of fields.

Designed for the general public, it responds to the needs of anyone seeking the precise, correct terms for a wide range of personal or professional reasons: finding an unknown term, checking the meaning of a word, advertising, additional teaching material, etc.

The target user has guided the choice of contents for the *Visual Five-Language Dictionary*, which aims to bring together in one volume the technical terms required to express in English, French, German, Italian, or Spanish the contemporary world, in the specialized fields that shape our daily experience.

STRUCTURE OF THE VISUAL FRENCH DICTIONARY

This book has three sections: the preliminary pages, including the list of themes and table of contents; the body of the text, i.e. the detailed treatment of each theme; the index.

Information is presented moving from the most abstract to the most concrete: theme, sub-theme, title, subtitle, illustration, terminology.

The content of the dictionary is divided into 17 THEMES, from Astronomy to Sports. More complex themes are divided into SUB-THEMES. For example, the theme Earth is divided into Geography, Geology, Meteorology, and Environment.

The TITLE has a variety of functions: to name the illustration of a unique object, of which the principal parts are identified (for example, glacier, window); to bring together under one designation illustrations that belong to the same conceptual sphere, but that represent a variety of elements, each

with its own designations and terminology (e.g. configuration of the continents, household appliances).

At times, the chief members of a class of objects are brought together under the same SUB-TITLE, each with its own name but without a detailed terminological analysis (e.g. under space probe, examples of space probes).

The ILLUSTRATION shows realistically and precisely an object, a process or a phenomenon, and the most significant details from which they are constructed. It serves as a visual definition for each of the terms presented.

TERMINOLOGY

Each word in the *Visual Five-Language Dictionary* has been carefully selected following examination of high-quality documentation, at the required level of specialization.

There may be cases where different terms are used to name the same item. In such instances, the word most frequently used by the most highly regarded authors has been chosen.

The *Visual Five-Language Dictionary* contains 13,750 index entries, or more than 23,700 English words with their French, German, Italian, and Spanish equivalents.

The INDEXES list all words in the dictionary in alphabetical order.

METHODS OF CONSULTATION

One may gain access to the contents of the *Visual Five-Language Dictionary* in a variety of ways:

• from the list of THEMES on the back of the book and at the end of the preliminary pages;

• with the INDEX the user can consult the *Visual Five-Language Dictionary* from a word, so as to see what it corresponds to, or to verify accuracy by examining the illustration that depicts it;

• the most original aspect of the *Visual Five-Language Dictionary* is the fact that the illustrations enable the user to find a word even if he or she only has a vague idea of what it is. The dictionary is unique in this feature, as consultation of any other dictionary requires the user first to know the word.

COLOUR REFERENCE

On the spine and back of the book this identifies and accompanies each theme to facilitate quick access to the corresponding section in the book.

TITLE

It is highlighted in English, and the other language equivalents are placed underneath in smaller characters. If the title runs over a number of pages, it is printed in grey on the pages subsequent to the first page on which it appears.

SUB-THEME

Most themes are subdivided into sub-themes. The sub-theme is given in all five languages.

NARROW LINES

These link the word to the item indicated. Where too many lines would make reading difficult, they have been replaced by colour codes with captions or, in rare cases, by numbers.

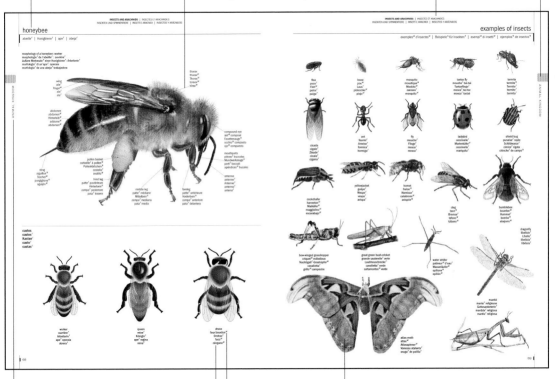

THEME

It is always in English.

ILLUSTRATION

It serves as the visual definition for the terms associated with it.

GENDER INDICATION

F: feminine M: masculine N: neuter

The gender of each word in a term is indicated.

The characters shown in the dictionary are men or women when the function illustrated can be fulfilled by either. In these cases, the gender assigned to the word depends on the illustration.

TERM

Each term appears in the index with a reference to the pages on which it appears. It is given in all languages, with English as the main index entry.

Contents

ASTRONOMY   **2**

Celestial bodies 2
Astronomical observation 7
Astronautics 10

EARTH   **14**

Geography 14
Geology 26
Meteorology 37
Environment 44

PLANT KINGDOM   **50**

ANIMAL KINGDOM   **66**

Simple organisms and echinoderms 66
Insects and arachnids 67
Crustaceans 71
Molluscs 72
Fishes 74
Amphibians 75
Reptiles 76
Birds 78
Rodents and lagomorphs 82
Ungulate mammals 83
Carnivorous mammals 86
Marine mammals 90
Primate mammals 91

HUMAN BEING   **92**

Human body 92
Anatomy 96
Sense organs 114

FOOD AND KITCHEN   **120**

Food 120
Kitchen 162

HOUSE   **182**

Location 182
Elements of a house 185
Structure of a house 187
Heating 192
Plumbing 194
Electricity 198
House furniture 200

DO-IT-YOURSELF AND GARDENING   **216**

Do-it-yourself 216
Gardening 230

CLOTHING   **238**

PERSONAL ADORNMENT AND ARTICLES   **264**

Personal adornment 264
Personal articles 271

ARTS AND ARCHITECTURE   **278**

Architecture 278
Performing arts 290
Music 295

COMMUNICATIONS AND OFFICE AUTOMATION   **312**

Communications 312
Office automation 329

TRANSPORT AND MACHINERY   **342**

Road transport 342
Rail transport 374
Maritime transport 381
Air transport 388
Handling 396
Heavy machinery 398

ENERGY   **402**

Geothermy and fossil energy 402
Hydroelectricity 406
Nuclear energy 408
Solar energy 410
Wind energy 412

SCIENCE   **414**

Chemistry 414
Physics: electricity and magnetism 416
Physics: optics 418
Measuring devices 422
Scientific symbols 426

SOCIETY   **430**

City 430
Justice 440
Economy and finance 441
Education 444
Religion 446
Politics 448
Safety 454
Health 460

SPORTS AND GAMES   **468**

Games 468
Track and field 472
Ball sports 474
Racket sports 490
Gymnastics 496
Combat sports 498
Strength sports 500
Precision and accuracy sports 502
Winter sports 506
Aquatic and nautical sports 516
Cycling 522
Motor sports 523
Sports on wheels 526
Outdoor leisure 528

List of chapters

2 **ASTRONOMY**

14 **EARTH**

50 **PLANT KINGDOM**

66 **ANIMAL KINGDOM**

92 **HUMAN BEING**

120 **FOOD AND KITCHEN**

182 **HOUSE**

216 **DO-IT-YOURSELF AND GARDENING**

238 **CLOTHING**

264 **PERSONAL ADORNMENT AND ARTICLES**

278 **ARTS AND ARCHITECTURE**

312 **COMMUNICATIONS AND OFFICE AUTOMATION**

342 **TRANSPORT AND MACHINERY**

402 **ENERGY**

414 **SCIENCE**

430 **SOCIETY**

468 **SPORTS AND GAMES**

539 **INDEX**

ASTRONOMY

solar system

système^M solaire | Sonnensystem^N | sistema^M solare | sistema^M solar

outer planets
planètes^F externes
äußere Planeten^M
pianeti^M esterni
planetas^M externos

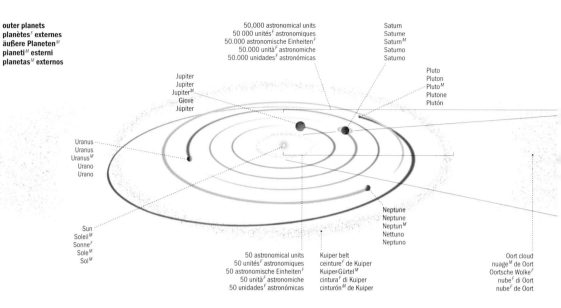

50,000 astronomical units
50 000 unités^F astronomiques
50.000 astronomische Einheiten^F
50.000 unità^F astronomiche
50.000 unidades^F astronómicas

Saturn
Saturne
Saturn^M
Saturno
Saturno

Jupiter
Jupiter
Jupiter^M
Giove
Júpiter

Pluto
Pluton
Pluto^M
Plutone
Plutón

Uranus
Uranus
Uranus^M
Urano
Urano

Sun
Soleil^M
Sonne^F
Sole^M
Sol^M

Neptune
Neptune
Neptun^M
Nettuno
Neptuno

50 astronomical units
50 unités^F astronomiques
50 astronomische Einheiten^F
50 unità^F astronomiche
50 unidades^F astronómicas

Kuiper belt
ceinture^F de Kuiper
Kuiper-Gürtel^M
cintura^F di Kuiper
cinturón^M de Kuiper

Oort cloud
nuage^M de Oort
Oortsche Wolke^F
nube^F di Oort
nube^F de Oort

planets and moons

planètes^F et satellites^M | Planeten^M und Monde^M | pianeti^M e satelliti^M | planetas^M y satélites^M

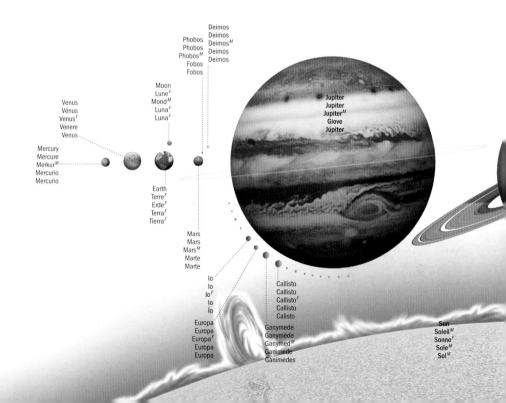

Deimos
Deimos
Deimos^M
Deimos
Deimos

Phobos
Phobos
Phobos^M
Fobos
Fobos

Moon
Lune^F
Mond^M
Luna^F
Luna^F

Jupiter
Jupiter
Jupiter^M
Giove
Júpiter

Venus
Vénus
Venus^F
Venere
Venus

Mercury
Mercure
Merkur^M
Mercurio
Mercurio

Earth
Terre^F
Erde^F
Terra^F
Tierra^F

Mars
Mars
Mars^M
Marte
Marte

Io
Io
Io^F
Io
Io

Callisto
Callisto
Callisto^F
Callisto
Calisto

Europa
Europe
Europa^F
Europa
Europa

Ganymede
Ganymède
Ganymed^M
Ganimede
Ganimedes

Sun
Soleil^M
Sonne^F
Sole^M
Sol^M

solar system

ASTRONOMY

inner planets
planètes^F internes
innere Planeten^M
pianeti^M interni
planetas^M internos

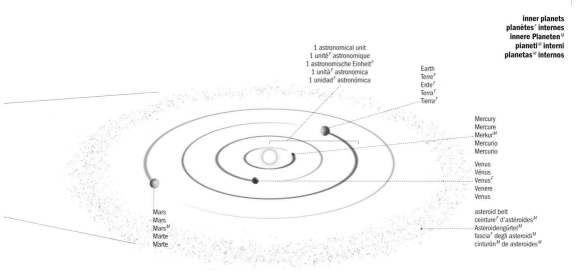

1 astronomical unit
1 unité^F astronomique
1 astronomische Einheit^F
1 unità^F astronomica
1 unidad^F astronómica

Earth
Terre^F
Erde^F
Terra^F
Tierra^F

Mercury
Mercure
Merkur^M
Mercurio
Mercurio

Venus
Vénus
Venus^F
Venere
Venus

asteroid belt
ceinture^F d'astéroïdes^M
Asteroidengürtel^M
fascia^F degli asteroidi^M
cinturón^M de asteroides^M

Mars
Mars
Mars^M
Marte
Marte

planets and moons

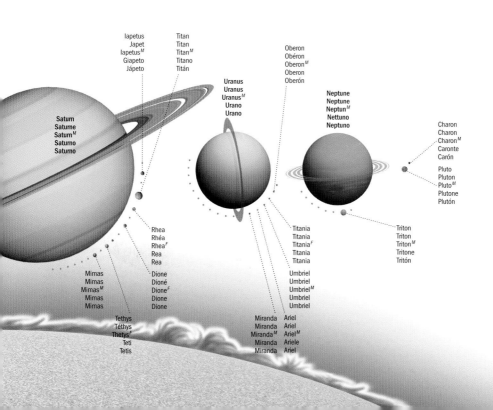

Iapetus
Japet
Iapetus^M
Giapeto
Jápeto

Titan
Titan
Titan^M
Titano
Titán

Oberon
Obéron
Oberon^M
Oberon
Oberón

Uranus
Uranus
Uranus^M
Urano
Urano

Neptune
Neptune
Neptun^M
Nettuno
Neptuno

Saturn
Saturne
Saturn^M
Saturno
Saturno

Charon
Charon
Charon^M
Caronte
Carón

Pluto
Pluton
Pluto^M
Plutone
Plutón

Rhea
Rhéa
Rhea^F
Rea
Rea

Titania
Titania
Titania^F
Titania
Titania

Triton
Triton
Triton^M
Tritone
Tritón

Mimas
Mimas
Mimas^M
Mimas
Mimas

Dione
Dioné
Dione^F
Dione
Dione

Umbriel
Umbriel
Umbriel^M
Umbriel
Umbriel

Tethys
Téthys
Thetys^F
Teti
Tetis

Miranda
Miranda
Miranda^M
Miranda
Miranda

Ariel
Ariel
Ariel^M
Ariele
Ariel

ASTRONOMY

Sun

Soleil^M | Sonne^F | Sole^M | Sol^M

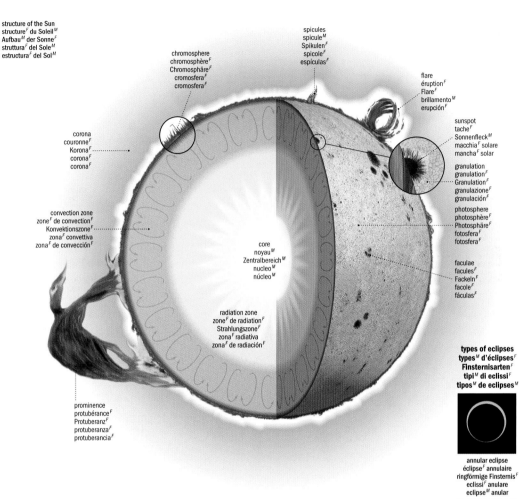

structure of the Sun
structure^F du Soleil^M
Aufbau^M der Sonne^F
struttura^F del Sole^M
estructura^F del Sol^M

spicules
spicule^M
Spikulen^F
spicole^F
espículas^F

chromosphere
chromosphère^F
Chromosphäre^F
cromosfera^F
cromosfera^F

flare
éruption^F
Flare^F
brillamento^M
erupción^F

corona
couronne^F
Korona^F
corona^F
corona^F

sunspot
tache^F
Sonnenfleck^M
macchia^F solare
mancha^F solar

granulation
granulation^F
Granulation^F
granulazione^F
granulación^F

convection zone
zone^F de convection^F
Konvektionszone^F
zona^F convettiva
zona^F de convección^F

photosphere
photosphère^F
Photosphäre^F
fotosfera^F
fotosfera^F

core
noyau^M
Zentralbereich^M
nucleo^M
núcleo^M

faculae
facules^F
Fackeln^F
facole^F
fáculas^F

radiation zone
zone^F de radiation^F
Strahlungszone^F
zona^F radiativa
zona^F de radiación^F

types of eclipses
types^M d'éclipses^F
Finsternisarten^F
tipi^M di eclissi^F
tipos^M de eclipses^M

prominence
protubérance^F
Protuberanz^F
protuberanza^F
protuberancia^F

annular eclipse
éclipse^F annulaire
ringförmige Finsternis^F
eclissi^F anulare
eclipse^M anular

solar eclipse
éclipse^F de Soleil^M
Sonnenfinsternis^F
eclissi^F di Sole^M
eclipse^M solar

Earth's orbit
orbite^F terrestre
Erdbahn^F
orbita^F della Terra^F
órbita^F terrestre

umbra
cône^M d'ombre^F
Kernschatten^M
cono^M d'ombra^F
cono^M de sombra^M

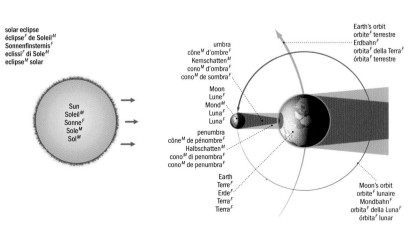

Moon
Lune^F
Mond^M
Luna^F
Luna^F

Sun
Soleil^M
Sonne^F
Sole^M
Sol^M

penumbra
cône^M de pénombre^F
Halbschatten^M
cono^M di penombra^F
cono^M de penumbra^F

Earth
Terre^F
Erde^F
Terra^F
Tierra^F

Moon's orbit
orbite^F lunaire
Mondbahn^F
orbita^F della Luna^F
órbita^F lunar

partial eclipse
éclipse^F partielle
partielle Finsternis^F
eclissi^F parziale
eclipse^M parcial

total eclipse
éclipse^F totale
totale Finsternis^F
eclissi^F totale
eclipse^M total

Moon

Lune^F | Mond^M | Luna^F | Luna^F

types of eclipses
types^M d'éclipses^F
Finsternisarten^F
tipi^M di eclissi^F
tipos^M de eclipses^M

partial eclipse
éclipse^F partielle
partielle Finsternis^F
eclissi^F parziale
eclipse^M parcial

total eclipse
éclipse^F totale
totale Finsternis^F
eclissi^F totale
eclipse^M total

lake
lac^M
See^M
lago^M
lago^M

lunar features
relief^M lunaire
Oberflächenformationen^F des Mondes^M
caratteristiche^F della Luna^F
superficie^F lunar

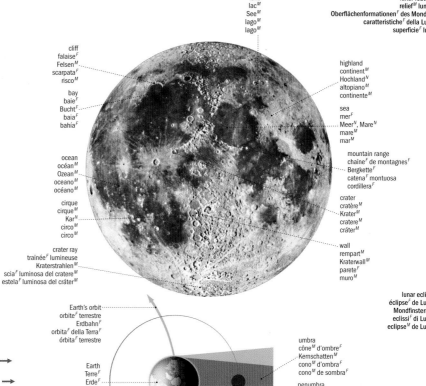

cliff
falaise^F
Felsen^M
scarpata^F
risco^M

bay
baie^F
Bucht^F
baia^F
bahía^F

ocean
océan^M
Ozean^M
oceano^M
océano^M

cirque
cirque^M
Kar^N
circo^M
circo^M

crater ray
traînée^F lumineuse
Kraterstrahlen^M
scia^F luminosa del cratere^M
estela^F luminosa del cráter^M

highland
continent^M
Hochland^N
altopiano^M
continente^M

sea
mer^F
Meer^N, Mare^N
mare^M
mar^M

mountain range
chaîne^F de montagnes^F
Bergkette^F
catena^F montuosa
cordillera^F

crater
cratère^M
Krater^M
cratere^M
cráter^M

wall
rempart^M
Kraterwall^M
parete^F
muro^M

Earth's orbit
orbite^F terrestre
Erdbahn^F
orbita^F della Terra^F
órbita^F terrestre

Sun
Soleil^M
Sonne^F
Sole^M
Sol^M

Earth
Terre^F
Erde^F
Terra^F
Tierra^F

Moon's orbit
orbite^F lunaire
Mondbahn^F
orbita^F della Luna^F
órbita^F lunar

lunar eclipse
éclipse^F de Lune^F
Mondfinsternis^F
eclissi^F di Luna^F
eclipse^M de Luna^F

umbra
cône^M d'ombre^F
Kernschatten^M
cono^M d'ombra^F
cono^M de sombra^F

penumbra
cône^M de pénombre^F
Halbschatten^M
cono^M di penombra^F
cono^M de penumbra^F

Moon
Lune^F
Mond^M
Luna^F
Luna^F

phases of the Moon
phases^F de la Lune^F
Mondphasen^F
fasi^F della Luna^F
fases^F de la Luna^F

new moon
nouvelle Lune^F
Neumond^M
Luna^F nuova
Luna^F nueva

new crescent
premier croissant^M
Mondsichel^F (zunehmender Mond^M)
Luna^F crescente
Luna^F creciente

first quarter
premier quartier^M
Halbmond^M (erstes Viertel^N)
primo quarto^M
cuarto^M creciente

waxing gibbous
gibbeuse^F croissante
zunehmender Mond^M
Luna^F gibbosa crescente
quinto octante^M

full moon
pleine Lune^F
Vollmond^M
Luna^F piena
Luna^F llena

waning gibbous
gibbeuse^F décroissante
abnehmender Mond^M
Luna^F gibbosa calante
tercer octante^M

last quarter
dernier quartier^M
Halbmond^M (letztes Viertel^N)
ultimo quarto^M
cuarto^M menguante

old crescent
dernier croissant^M
Mondsichel^F (abnehmender Mond^M)
Luna^F calante
Luna^F menguante

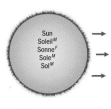

ASTRONOMY

galaxy

galaxie^F | Galaxie^F | galassia^F | galaxia^F

Milky Way
Voie^F lactée
Milchstraße^F
Via^F Lattea
Vía^F Láctea

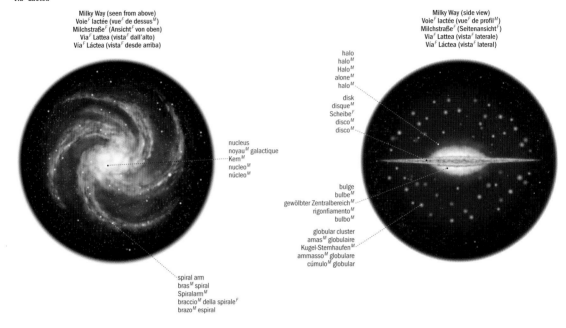

Milky Way (seen from above)
Voie^F lactée (vue^F de dessus^M)
Milchstraße^F (Ansicht^F von oben)
Via^F Lattea (vista^F dall'alto)
Vía^F Láctea (vista^F desde arriba)

Milky Way (side view)
Voie^F lactée (vue^F de profil^M)
Milchstraße^F (Seitenansicht^F)
Via^F Lattea (vista^F laterale)
Vía^F Láctea (vista^F lateral)

halo
halo^M
Halo^M
alone^M
halo^M

disk
disque^M
Scheibe^F
disco^M
disco^M

nucleus
noyau^M galactique
Kern^M
nucleo^M
núcleo^M

bulge
bulbe^F
gewölbter Zentralbereich^M
rigonfiamento^M
bulbo^M

globular cluster
amas^M globulaire
Kugel-Sternhaufen^M
ammasso^M globulare
cúmulo^M globular

spiral arm
bras^M spiral
Spiralarm^M
braccio^M della spirale^F
brazo^M espiral

comet

comète^F | Komet^M | cometa^F | cometa^M

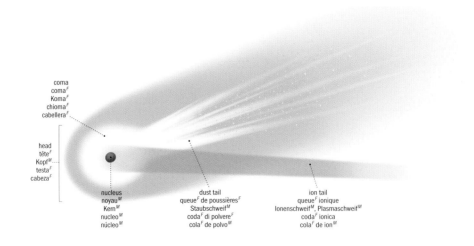

coma
coma^F
Koma^F
chioma^F
cabellera^F

head
tête^F
Kopf^M
testa^F
cabeza^F

nucleus
noyau^M
Kern^M
nucleo^M
núcleo^M

dust tail
queue^F de poussières^F
Staubschweif^M
coda^F di polvere^F
cola^F de polvo^M

ion tail
queue^F ionique
Ionenschweif^M, Plasmaschweif^M
coda^F ionica
cola^F de ion^M

Hubble space telescope

télescope[M] spatial Hubble | Hubble-Weltraumteleskop[N] | telescopio[M] spaziale Hubble | telescopio[M] espacial Hubble

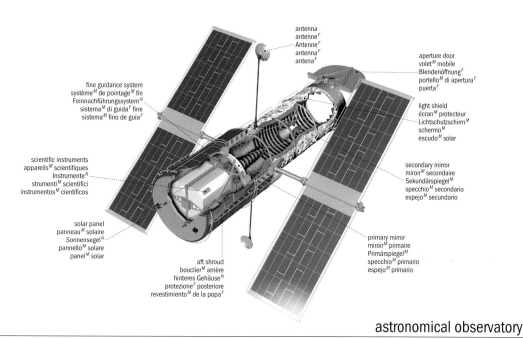

antenna
antenne[F]
Antenne[F]
antenna[F]
antena[F]

aperture door
volet[M] mobile
Blendenöffnung[F]
portello[M] di apertura[F]
puerta[F]

fine guidance system
système[M] de pointage[M] fin
Feinnachführungssystem[N]
sistema[M] di guida[F] fine
sistema[M] fino de guía[F]

light shield
écran[M] protecteur
Lichtschutzschirm[M]
schermo[M]
escudo[M] solar

scientific instruments
appareils[M] scientifiques
Instrumente[N]
strumenti[M] scientifici
instrumentos[M] científicos

secondary mirror
miroir[M] secondaire
Sekundärspiegel[M]
specchio[M] secondario
espejo[M] secundario

solar panel
panneau[M] solaire
Sonnensegel[N]
pannello[M] solare
panel[M] solar

primary mirror
miroir[M] primaire
Primärspiegel[M]
specchio[M] primario
espejo[M] primario

aft shroud
bouclier[M] arrière
hinteres Gehäuse[N]
protezione[F] posteriore
revestimiento[M] de la popa[F]

astronomical observatory

observatoire[M] astronomique | Sternwarte[F] | osservatorio[M] astronomico | observatorio[M] astronómico

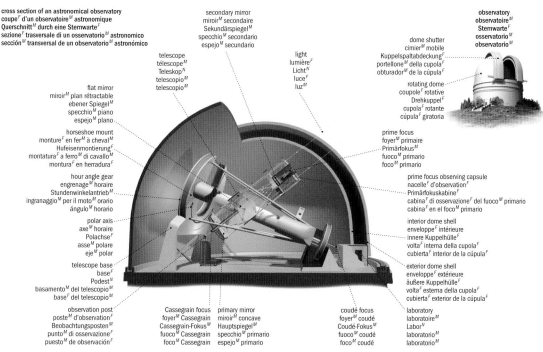

cross section of an astronomical observatory
coupe[F] d'un observatoire[M] astronomique
Querschnitt[M] durch eine Sternwarte[F]
sezione[F] trasversale di un osservatorio[M] astronomico
sección[M] transversal de un observatorio[M] astronómico

secondary mirror
miroir[M] secondaire
Sekundärspiegel[M]
specchio[M] secondario
espejo[M] secundario

observatory
observatoire[M]
Sternwarte[F]
osservatorio[M]
observatorio[M]

telescope
télescope[M]
Teleskop[N]
telescopio[M]
telescopio[M]

light
lumière[F]
Licht[N]
luce[F]
luz[M]

dome shutter
cimier[M] mobile
Kuppelspaltabdeckung[F]
portellone[F] della cupola[F]
obturador[M] de la cúpula[F]

flat mirror
miroir[M] plan rétractable
ebener Spiegel[M]
specchio[M] piano
espejo[M] plano

rotating dome
coupole[F] rotative
Drehkuppel[F]
cupola[F] rotante
cúpula[F] giratoria

horseshoe mount
monture[F] en fer[M] à cheval[M]
Hufeisenmontierung[F]
montatura[F] a ferro[M] di cavallo[M]
montura[F] en herradura[F]

prime focus
foyer[M] primaire
Primärfokus[M]
fuoco[M] primario
foco[M] primario

hour angle gear
engrenage[M] horaire
Stundenwinkelantrieb[M]
ingranaggio[M] per il moto[M] orario
ángulo[M] horario

prime focus observing capsule
nacelle[F] d'observation[F]
Primärfokuskabine[F]
cabina[F] di osservazione[F] del fuoco[M] primario
cabina[F] en el foco[M] primario

polar axis
axe[M] horaire
Polachse[F]
asse[M] polare
eje[M] polar

interior dome shell
enveloppe[F] intérieure
innere Kuppelhülle[F]
volta[F] interna della cupola[F]
cubierta[F] interior de la cúpula[F]

telescope base
base[F]
Podest[N]
basamento[M] del telescopio[M]
base[F] del telescopio[M]

exterior dome shell
enveloppe[F] extérieure
äußere Kuppelhülle[F]
volta[F] esterna della cupola[F]
cubierta[F] exterior de la cúpula[F]

observation post
poste[M] d'observation[F]
Beobachtungsposten[M]
punto[M] di osservazione[F]
puesto[M] de observación[F]

Cassegrain focus
foyer[M] Cassegrain
Cassegrain-Fokus[M]
fuoco[M] Cassegrain
foco[M] Cassegrain

primary mirror
miroir[M] concave
Hauptspiegel[M]
specchio[M] primario
espejo[M] primario

coudé focus
foyer[M] coudé
Coudé-Fokus[M]
fuoco[M] coudé
foco[M] coudé

laboratory
laboratoire[M]
Labor[N]
laboratorio[M]
laboratorio[M]

ASTRONOMY

refracting telescope

lunette^F astronomique | Linsenfernrohr^N | cannocchiale^M | telescopio^M refractor

finderscope
chercheur^M
Suchfernrohr^N
cannocchiale^M cercatore
anteojo^M buscador

cradle
bride^F de fixation^F
Wiege^F
giogo^M di supporto^M
abrazadera^F

main tube
tube^M
Tubus^M
tubo^M principale
tubo^M principal

lens hood
pare-soleil^M
Sonnenblende^F
paraluce^M
parasol^M

eyepiece
oculaire^M
Okular^N
oculare^M
ocular^M

eyepiece holder
tube^M porte-oculaire^M
Okularhalterung^F
portaoculare^M
portaocular^M

star diagonal
oculaire^M coudé
Zenitprisma^N
prisma^M astronomico
ocular^M acodado

declination setting scale
cercle^M de déclinaison^F
Einstellung^F der Deklinationsachse^F
cerchio^M graduato della declinazione^F
círculo^M graduado de declinación^F

focusing knob
bouton^M de mise^F au point^M
Scharfeinstellung^F
manopola^F della messa^F a fuoco^M
botón^M de enfoque^M

azimuth clamp
vis^F de blocage^M (azimut^M)
Azimutfesteller^M
leva^F di bloccaggio^M dell'asse^M orizzontale
palanca^F de bloqueo^M del acimut^M

azimuth fine adjustment
réglage^M micrométrique (azimut^M)
Azimutfeineinstellung^F
regolazione^F micrometrica dell'asse^M orizzontale
ajuste^M fino del acimut^M

altitude clamp
vis^F de blocage^M (latitude^F)
Höhenfesteller^M
leva^F di bloccaggio^M dell'altezza^F
palanca^F de bloqueo^M de la altura^F

altitude fine adjustment
réglage^M micrométrique (latitude^F)
Höhenfeineinstellung^F
regolazione^F micrometrica dell'altezza^F
ajuste^M fino de la altura^F

right ascension setting scale
cercle^M d'ascension^F droite
Einstellung^F der Rektaszensionsachse^F
cerchio^M graduato dell'ascensione^F retta
anillo^M graduado de ascensión^F recta

fork
fourche^F
Gabel^F
forcella^F
horquilla^F

counterweight
contrepoids^M
Gegengewicht^N
contrappeso^M
contrapeso^M

tripod accessories shelf
plateau^M pour accessoires^M
Stativablage^F
mensola^F portaccessori
repisa^F para accesorios^M

tripod
trépied^M
Stativ^N
treppiede^M
trípode^M

cross section of a refracting telescope
coupe^F d'une lunette^F astronomique
Linsenfernrohr^N im Querschnitt^M
sezione^F di un cannocchiale^M
sección^F transversal de un telescopio^M refractor

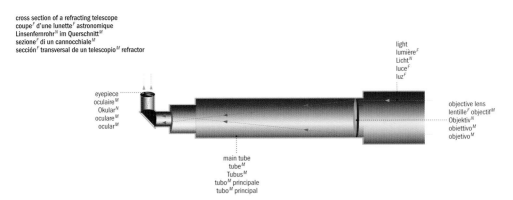

light
lumière^F
Licht^N
luce^F
luz^F

eyepiece
oculaire^M
Okular^N
oculare^M
ocular^M

objective lens
lentille^F objectif^M
Objektiv^N
obiettivo^M
objetivo^M

main tube
tube^M
Tubus^M
tubo^M principale
tubo^M principal

reflecting telescope

télescope^M | Spiegelteleskop^N | telescopio^M | telescopio^M reflector

ASTRONOMY

find
finderscope
chercheur^M
Suchfernrohr^N
cannocchiale^M cercatore
anteojo^M buscador

support
support^M de fixation^F
Halterung^F
supporto^M
soporte^M

eyepiece
oculaire^M
Okular^N
oculare^M
ocular^M

cradle
bride^F de fixation^F
Wiege^F
giogo^M di supporto^M
abrazadera^F

main tube
tube^M
Tubus^M
tubo^M principale
tubo^M principal

focusing knob
bouton^M de mise^F au point^M
Scharfeinstellung^F
manopola^F della messa^F a fuoco^M
botón^M de enfoque^M

declination setting scale
cercle^M de déclinaison^F
Einstellung^F der Deklinationsachse^F
cerchio^M graduato della declinazione^F
anillo^M graduado de declinación^F

azimuth clamp
vis^F de blocage^M (azimuth^M)
Azimutfeststeller^M
leva^F di bloccaggio^M dell'asse^M orizzontale
palanca^F de bloqueo^M del acimut^M

altitude clamp
vis^F de blocage^M (latitude^F)
Höhenfeststeller^M
leva^F di bloccaggio^M dell'altezza^F
palanca^F de bloqueo^M de la altura^F

right ascension setting scale
cercle^M d'ascension^F droite
Einstellung der Rektaszensionsachse^F
cerchio^M graduato dell'ascensione^F retta
anillo^M graduado de ascensión^F recta

azimuth fine adjustment
réglage^M micrométrique (azimut^M)
Azimutfeineinstellung^F
regolazione^F micrometrica dell'asse^M orizzontale
ajuste^M fino del acimut^M

altitude fine adjustment
réglage^M micrométrique (latitude^F)
Höhenfeineinstellung^F
regolazione^F micrometrica dell'altezza^F
ajuste^M fino de la altura^F

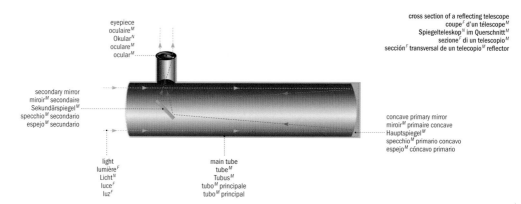

cross section of a reflecting telescope
coupe^F d'un télescope^M
Spiegelteleskop^N im Querschnitt^M
sezione^F di un telescopio^M
sección^F transversal de un telecopio^M reflector

eyepiece
oculaire^M
Okular^N
oculare^M
ocular^M

secondary mirror
miroir^M secondaire
Sekundärspiegel^M
specchio^M secondario
espejo^M secundario

concave primary mirror
miroir^M primaire concave
Hauptspiegel^M
specchio^M primario concavo
espejo^M cóncavo primario

light
lumière^F
Licht^N
luce^F
luz^F

main tube
tube^M
Tubus^M
tubo^M principale
tubo^M principal

ASTRONOMY

spacesuit

scaphandre^M spatial | Raumanzug^M | tuta^F spaziale | traje^M espacial

35 mm still camera
appareil^M photographique 35 mm
35mm-Fotoapparat^M
fotocamera^F 35 mm
cámara^F rígida de 35 mm

life support system
équipement^M de survie^F
Lebenserhaltungssystem^N
sistema^M di sopravvivenza^F
sistema^M de soporte^M vital

solar shield
visière^F antisolaire
Sonnenschutzschicht^F
visiera^F antisolare
protector^M solar

helmet
casque^M
Helm^M
casco^M
casco^M

helmet ring
collier^M de serrage^M du casque^M
Ringverschluss^M
collare^F di chiusura^F del casco^M
anillo^M de unión^F del casco^M

colour television camera
caméra^F de télévision^F couleur^F
Farbfernsehkamera^F
telecamera^F a colori^M
cámara^F de televisión^F en color^M

computer screen
écran^M de l'ordinateur^M
Computerbildschirm^M
schermo^F del computer^M
pantalla^F del ordenador^M

procedure checklist
aide-mémoire^M des procédures^F
Checkliste^F
lista^F di controllo^M delle procedure^F
lista^F de procedimientos^M

communications volume controls
réglage^M du volume^M des communications^F
Lautstärkeregler^M des Funkübertragungssystems^N
regolazione^F del livello^M sonoro delle comunicazioni^F
controles^M de volumen^M de comunicaciones^F

tool tether
attache^F pour outils^M
Werkzeughalter^M
attacco^M per attrezzi^M
correa^F para herramientas^F

glove
gant^M
Handschuh^M
guanto^M
guante^M

safety tether
attache^F de sécurité^F
Sicherheitsriemen^M
attacco^M di sicurezza^F
correa^F de seguridad^F

reading mirror
miroir^M de lecture^F
Spiegel^M
specchio^M di lettura^F
espejo^M de lectura^F

life support system controls
contrôles^M de l'équipement^M de survie^F
Steuerung^F des Lebenserhaltungssystems^N
regolazione^F del sistema^M di sopravvivenza^F
controles^M del sistema^M de soporte^M vital

body temperature control unit
contrôle^M de la température^F du corps^M
Körpertemperaturregelung^F
regolazione^F della temperatura^F corporea
unidad^F de control^M de la temperatura^F del cuerpo^M

thruster
propulseur^M
Schubdüse^F
propulsore^M
propulsor^M

oxygen pressure actuator
réglage^M de la pression^F d'oxygène^M
Sauerstoffdruck-Stelleinrichtung^F
regolazione^F della pressione^F dell'ossigeno^M
accionador^M de presión^F del oxigeno^M

manned manœuvring unit
véhicule^M spatial autonome
bemannte Manövriereinheit^F
unità^F individuale di propulsione^F e manovra^F
unidad^F para maniobras^F en el espacio^M

protection layer
revêtement^M de sécurité^F
Schutzschicht^F
strato^M protettivo
capa^F protectora

international space station

station^F spatiale internationale | internationale Raumstation^F | stazione^F spaziale internazionale | estación^F espacial internacional

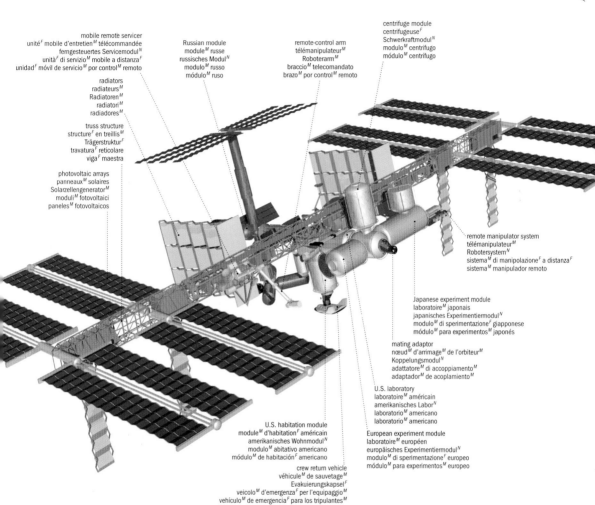

centrifuge module
centrifugeuse^F
Schwerkraftmodul^N
módulo^M centrifugo
módulo^M centrifugo

mobile remote servicer
unité^F mobile d'entretien^M télécommandée
ferngesteuertes Servicemodul^N
unità^F di servizio^M mobile a distanza^F
unidad^F móvil de servicio^M por control^M remoto

Russian module
module^M russe
russisches Modul^N
modulo^M russo
módulo^M ruso

remote-control arm
télémanipulateur^M
Roboterarm^M
braccio^M telecomandato
brazo^M por control^M remoto

radiators
radiateurs^M
Radiatoren^M
radiatori^M
radiadores^M

truss structure
structure^F en treillis^M
Trägerstruktur^F
travatura^F reticolare
viga^F maestra

photovoltaic arrays
panneaux^M solaires
Solarzellengenerator^M
moduli^M fotovoltaici
paneles^M fotovoltaicos

remote manipulator system
télémanipulateur^M
Robotersystem^N
sistema^M di manipolazione^F a distanza^F
sistema^M manipulador remoto

Japanese experiment module
laboratoire^M japonais
japanisches Experimentiermodul^N
modulo^M di sperimentazione^F giapponese
módulo^M para experimentos^M japonés

mating adaptor
nœud^M d'arrimage^M de l'orbiteur^M
Koppelungsmodul^N
adattatore^M di accoppiamento^M
adaptador^M de acoplamiento^M

U.S. laboratory
laboratoire^M américain
amerikanisches Labor^N
laboratorio^M americano
laboratorio^M americano

U.S. habitation module
module^M d'habitation^F américain
amerikanisches Wohnmodul^N
modulo^M abitativo americano
módulo^M de habitación^F americano

European experiment module
laboratoire^M européen
europäisches Experimentiermodul^N
modulo^M di sperimentazione^F europeo
módulo^M para experimentos^M europeo

crew return vehicle
véhicule^M de sauvetage^M
Evakuierungskapsel^F
veicolo^M d'emergenza^F per l'equipaggio^M
vehículo^M de emergencia^F para los tripulantes^M

ASTRONOMY

space shuttle

navette^F spatiale | Raumfähre^F | navetta^F spaziale | transbordador^M espacial

space shuttle at takeoff
navette^F spatiale au décollage^M
Raumfähre^F beim Start^M
navetta^F spaziale al decollo^M
transbordador^M espacial en posición^F de lanzamiento^M

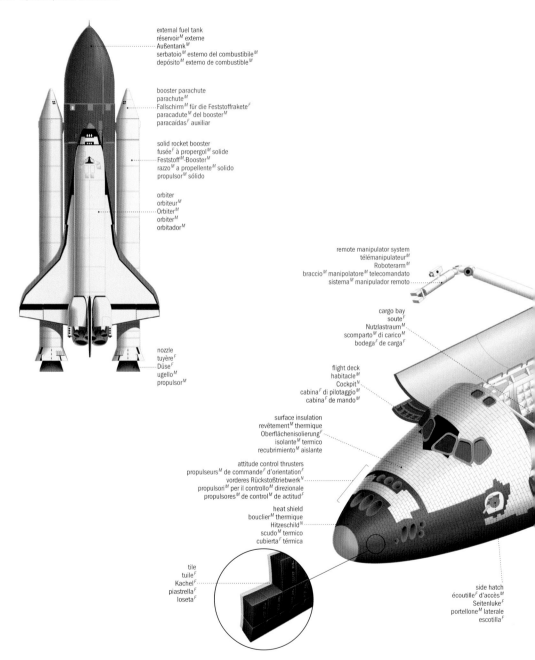

external fuel tank
réservoir^M externe
Außentank^M
serbatoio^M esterno del combustibile^M
depósito^M externo de combustible^M

booster parachute
parachute^M
Fallschirm^M für die Feststoffrakete^F
paracadute^M del booster^M
paracaidas^F auxiliar

solid rocket booster
fusée^F à propergol^M solide
Feststoff^M-Booster^M
razzo^M a propellente^M solido
propulsor^M sólido

orbiter
orbiteur^M
Orbiter^M
orbiter^M
orbitador^M

remote manipulator system
télémanipulateur^M
Roboterarm^M
braccio^M manipolatore^M telecomandato
sistema^M manipulador remoto

cargo bay
soute^F
Nutzlastraum^M
scomparto^M di carico^M
bodega^F de carga^F

nozzle
tuyère^F
Düse^F
ugello^M
propulsor^M

flight deck
habitacle^M
Cockpit^N
cabina^F di pilotaggio^M
cabina^F de mando^M

surface insulation
revêtement^M thermique
Oberflächenisolierung^F
isolante^M termico
recubrimiento^M aislante

attitude control thrusters
propulseurs^M de commande^F d'orientation^F
vorderes Rückstoßtriebwerk^N
propulsori^M per il controllo^M direzionale
propulsores^M de control^M de actitud^F

heat shield
bouclier^M thermique
Hitzeschild^N
scudo^M termico
cubierta^F térmica

tile
tuile^F
Kachel^F
piastrella^F
loseta^F

side hatch
écoutille^F d'accès^M
Seitenluke^F
portellone^M laterale
escotilla^F

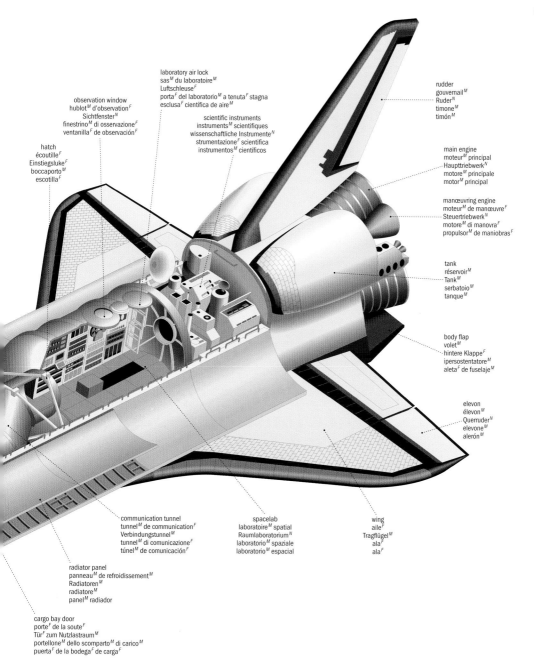

orbiter
orbiteur^M
Orbiter^M
orbiter^M
orbitador^M

laboratory air lock
sas^M du laboratoire^M
Luftschleuse^F
porta^F del laboratorio^M a tenuta^F stagna
esclusa^F científica de aire^M

observation window
hublot^M d'observation^F
Sichtfenster^N
finestrino^M di osservazione^F
ventanilla^F de observación^F

scientific instruments
instruments^M scientifiques
wissenschaftliche Instrumente^N
strumentazione^F scientifica
instrumentos^M científicos

hatch
écoutille^F
Einstiegsluke^F
boccaporto^M
escotilla^F

rudder
gouvernail^M
Ruder^N
timone^M
timón^M

main engine
moteur^M principal
Haupttriebwerk^N
motore^M principale
motor^M principal

manœuvring engine
moteur^M de manœuvre^F
Steuertriebwerk^N
motore^M di manovra^F
propulsor^M de maniobras^F

tank
réservoir^M
Tank^M
serbatoio^M
tanque^M

body flap
volet^M
hintere Klappe^F
ipersostentatore^M
aleta^F de fuselaje^M

elevon
élevon^M
Querruder^N
elevone^M
alerón^M

communication tunnel
tunnel^M de communication^F
Verbindungstunnel^M
tunnel^M di comunicazione^F
túnel^M de comunicación^F

spacelab
laboratoire^M spatial
Raumlaboratorium^N
laboratorio^M spaziale
laboratorio^M espacial

wing
aile^F
Tragflügel^M
ala^F
ala^F

radiator panel
panneau^M de refroidissement^M
Radiatoren^M
radiatore^M
panel^M radiador

cargo bay door
porte^F de la soute^F
Tür^F zum Nutzlastraum^M
portellone^M dello scomparto^M di carico^M
puerta^F de la bodega^F de carga^F

configuration of the continents

configuration[F] des continents[M] | Lage[F] der Kontinente[M] | carta[F] dei continenti[M] | configuración[F] de los continentes[M]

planisphere
planisphère[M]
Erdoberfläche[F]
planisfero[M]
planisferio[M]

North Sea
mer[F] du Nord[M]
Nordsee[F]
Mare[M] del Nord[M]
mar[M] del Norte

Mediterranean Sea
mer[F] Méditerranée[F]
Mittelmeer[N]
Mar[M] Mediterraneo
mar[M] Mediterráneo

Bering Sea
mer[F] de Béring
Beringsee[F]
Mar[M] di Bering
mar[M] de Bering

Arctic
Arctique[F]
Arktis[F]
Artide[F]
Ártico[M]

Greenland Sea
mer[F] du Groenland[M]
Grönlandsee[F]
Mar[M] di Groenlandia[F]
mar[M] de Groenlandia[F]

Black Sea
mer[F] Noire
Schwarzes Meer[N]
Mar[M] Nero
mar[M] Negro

South China Sea
mer[F] de Chine[F] méridionale
Südchinesisches Meer[N]
Mar[M] Cinese Meridionale
mar[M] de la China[F] Meridional

Caspian Sea
mer[F] Caspienne
Kaspisches Meer[N]
Mar[M] Caspio
mar[M] Caspio

Arctic Ocean
océan[M] Arctique
Nordpolarmeer[N]
Mar[M] Glaciale Artico
océano[M] Glacial Ártico

Atlantic Ocean
océan[M] Atlantique
Atlantik[M]
Oceano[M] Atlantico
océano[M] Atlántico

Pacific Ocean
océan[M] Pacifique
Pazifik[M]
Oceano[M] Pacifico
océano[M] Pacifico

Indian Ocean
océan[M] Indien
Indischer Ozean[M]
Oceano[M] Indiano
océano[M] Índico

Central America
Amérique[F] centrale
Mittelamerika[N]
America[F] Centrale
América[F] Central

Caribbean Sea
mer[F] des Antilles[F]
Karibik[F]
Mar[M] Caribico
mar[M] Caribe

Red Sea
mer[F] Rouge
Rotes Meer[N]
Mar[M] Rosso
mar[M] Rojo

Australia
Australie[F]
Australien[N]
Australia[F]
Australia[F]

Antarctica
Antarctique[F]
Antarktis[F]
Antartide[F]
Antártica[F]

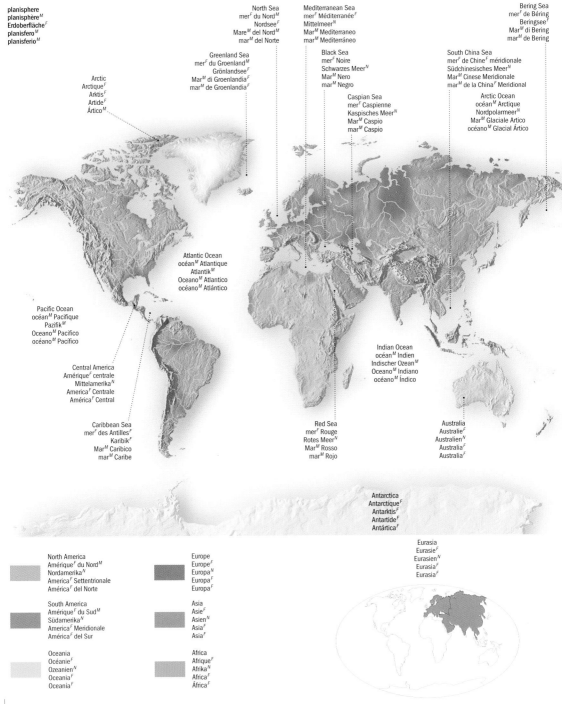

North America
Amérique[F] du Nord[M]
Nordamerika[N]
America[F] Settentrionale
América[F] del Norte

Europe
Europe[F]
Europa[N]
Europa[F]
Europa[F]

Eurasia
Eurasie[F]
Eurasien[N]
Eurasia[F]
Eurasia[F]

South America
Amérique[F] du Sud[M]
Südamerika[N]
America[F] Meridionale
América[F] del Sur

Asia
Asie[F]
Asien[N]
Asia[F]
Asia[F]

Oceania
Océanie[F]
Ozeanien[N]
Oceania[F]
Oceanía[F]

Africa
Afrique[F]
Afrika[N]
Africa[F]
África[F]

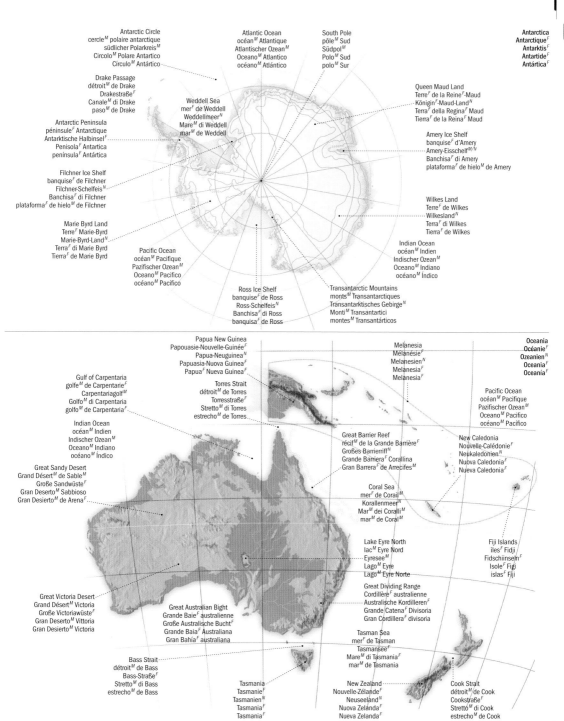

Antarctic Circle
cercle^M polaire antarctique
südlicher Polarkreis^M
Circolo^M Polare Antartico
Círculo^M Antártico

Atlantic Ocean
océan^M Atlantique
Atlantischer Ozean^M
Oceano^M Atlantico
océano^M Atlántico

South Pole
pôle^M Sud
Südpol^M
Polo^M Sud
polo^M Sur

Antarctica
Antarctique^F
Antarktis^F
Antartide^F
Antártica^F

Drake Passage
détroit^M de Drake
Drakestraße^F
Canale^M di Drake
paso^M de Drake

Weddell Sea
mer^F de Weddell
Weddellmeer^N
Mare^M di Weddell
mar^M de Weddell

Queen Maud Land
Terre^F de la Reine^F-Maud
Königin^F-Maud-Land^N
Terra^F della Regina^F Maud
Tierra^F de la Reina^F Maud

Antarctic Peninsula
péninsule^F Antarctique
Antarktische Halbinsel^F
Penisola^F Antartica
península^F Antártica

Amery Ice Shelf
banquise^F d'Amery
Amery-Eisschelf^{M/N}
Banchisa^F di Amery
plataforma^F de hielo^M de Amery

Filchner Ice Shelf
banquise^F de Filchner
Filchner-Schelfeis^N
Banchisa^F di Filchner
plataforma^F de hielo^M de Filchner

Marie Byrd Land
Terre^F Marie-Byrd
Marie-Byrd-Land^N
Terra^F di Marie Byrd
Tierra^F de Marie Byrd

Wilkes Land
Terre^F de Wilkes
Wilkesland^N
Terra^F di Wilkes
Tierra^F de Wilkes

Pacific Ocean
océan^M Pacifique
Pazifischer Ozean^M
Oceano^M Pacifico
océano^M Pacífico

Indian Ocean
océan^M Indien
Indischer Ozean^M
Oceano^M Indiano
océano^M Índico

Ross Ice Shelf
banquise^F de Ross
Ross-Schelfeis^N
Banchisa^F di Ross
banquisa^F de Ross

Transantarctic Mountains
monts^M Transantarctiques
Transantarktisches Gebirge^N
Monti^M Transantartici
montes^M Transantárticos

Papua New Guinea
Papouasie-Nouvelle-Guinée^F
Papua-Neuguinea^N
Papuasia-Nuova Guinea^F
Papua^F Nueva Guinea^F

Melanesia
Mélanésie^F
Melanesien^N
Melanesia^F
Melanesia^F

Oceania
Océanie^F
Ozeanien^N
Oceania^F
Oceanía^F

Gulf of Carpentaria
golfe^M de Carpentarie^F
Carpentariagolf^M
Golfo^M di Carpentaria
golfo^M de Carpentaria^F

Torres Strait
détroit^M de Torres
Torresstraße^F
Stretto^M di Torres
estrecho^M de Torres

Pacific Ocean
océan^M Pacifique
Pazifischer Ozean^M
Oceano^M Pacifico
océano^M Pacífico

Indian Ocean
océan^M Indien
Indischer Ozean^M
Oceano^M Indiano
océano^M Índico

Great Barrier Reef
récif^M de la Grande Barrière^F
Großes Barrierriff^N
Grande Barriera^F Corallina
Gran Barrera^F de Arrecifes^M

New Caledonia
Nouvelle-Calédonie^F
Neukaledonien^N
Nuova Caledonia^F
Nueva Caledonia^F

Great Sandy Desert
Grand Désert^M de Sable^M
Große Sandwüste^F
Gran Deserto^M Sabbioso
Gran Desierto^M de Arena^F

Coral Sea
mer^F de Corail^M
Korallenmeer^N
Mar^M dei Coralli^M
mar^M de Coral^M

Lake Eyre North
lac^M Eyre Nord
Eyresee^M
Lago^M Eyre
Lago^M Eyre Norte

Fiji Islands
îles^F Fidji
Fidschiinseln^F
Isole^F Figi
islas^F Fiji

Great Victoria Desert
Grand Désert^M Victoria
Große Victoriawüste^F
Gran Deserto^M Vittoria
Gran Desierto^M Victoria

Great Australian Bight
Grande Baie^F australienne
Große Australische Bucht^F
Grande Baia^F Australiana
Gran Bahía^F australiana

Great Dividing Range
Cordillère^F australienne
Australische Kordilleren^F
Grande Catena^F Divisoria
Gran Cordillera^F divisoria

Tasman Sea
mer^F de Tasman
Tasmansee^F
Mare^M di Tasmania^F
mar^M de Tasmania

Bass Strait
détroit^M de Bass
Bass-Straße^F
Stretto^M di Bass
estrecho^M de Bass

Tasmania
Tasmanie^F
Tasmanien^N
Tasmania^F
Tasmania^F

New Zealand
Nouvelle-Zélande^F
Neuseeland^N
Nuova Zelanda^F
Nueva Zelanda^F

Cook Strait
détroit^M de Cook
Cookstraße^F
Stretto^M di Cook
estrecho^M de Cook

configuration of the continents

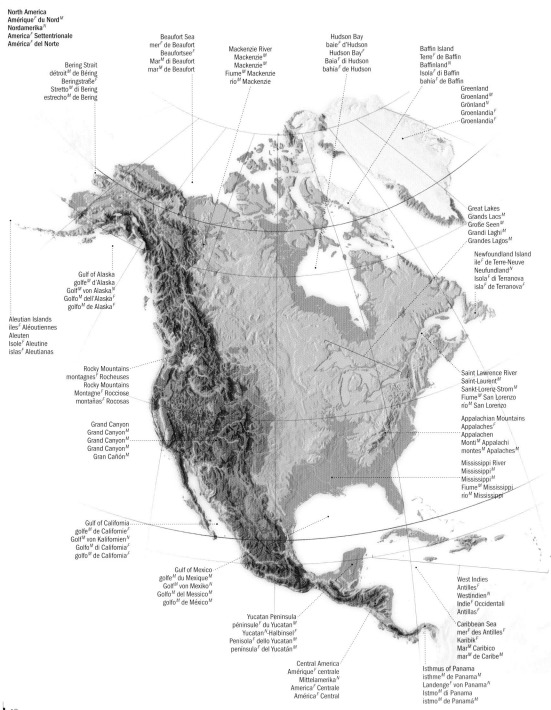

North America
Amérique^F du Nord^M
Nordamerika^N
America^F Settentrionale
América^F del Norte

Beaufort Sea
mer^F de Beaufort
Beaufortsee^F
Mar^M di Beaufort
mar^M de Beaufort

Mackenzie River
Mackenzie^M
Mackenzie^M
Fiume^M Mackenzie
río^M Mackenzie

Hudson Bay
baie^F d'Hudson
Hudson Bay^F
Baia^F di Hudson
bahía^F de Hudson

Baffin Island
Terre^F de Baffin
Baffinland^N
Isola^F di Baffin
bahía^F de Baffin

Bering Strait
détroit^M de Béring
Beringstraße^F
Stretto^M di Bering
estrecho^M de Bering

Greenland
Groenland^M
Grönland^N
Groenlandia^F
Groenlandia^F

Great Lakes
Grands Lacs^M
Große Seen^M
Grandi Laghi^M
Grandes Lagos^M

Newfoundland Island
île^F de Terre-Neuve
Neufundland^N
Isola^F di Terranova
isla^F de Terranova^F

Gulf of Alaska
golfe^M d'Alaska
Golf^M von Alaska^N
Golfo^M dell'Alaska^F
golfo^M de Alaska^F

Aleutian Islands
îles^F Aléoutiennes
Aleuten
Isole^F Aleutine
islas^F Aleutianas

Rocky Mountains
montagnes^F Rocheuses
Rocky Mountains
Montagne^F Rocciose
montañas^F Rocosas

Saint Lawrence River
Saint-Laurent^M
Sankt-Lorenz-Strom^M
Fiume^M San Lorenzo
río^M San Lorenzo

Grand Canyon
Grand Canyon^M
Grand Canyon^M
Grand Canyon^M
Gran Cañón^M

Appalachian Mountains
Appalaches^F
Appalachen
Monti^M Appalachi
montes^M Apalaches^M

Mississippi River
Mississippi^M
Mississippi^M
Fiume^M Mississippi
río^M Mississippi

Gulf of California
golfe^M de Californie^F
Golf^M von Kalifornien^N
Golfo^M di California^F
golfo^M de California^F

Gulf of Mexico
golfe^M du Mexique^M
Golf^M von Mexiko^N
Golfo^M del Messico^M
golfo^M de México^M

West Indies
Antilles^F
Westindien^N
Indie^F Occidentali
Antillas^F

Yucatan Peninsula
péninsule^F du Yucatan^M
Yucatan^N-Halbinsel^F
Penisola^F dello Yucatan^M
peninsula^F del Yucatán^M

Caribbean Sea
mer^F des Antilles^F
Karibik^F
Mar^M Caribico
mar^M de Caribe^M

Central America
Amérique^F centrale
Mittelamerika^N
America^F Centrale
América^F Central

Isthmus of Panama
isthme^M de Panama^M
Landenge^F von Panama^N
Istmo^M di Panama
istmo^M de Panamá^M

South America
Amérique^F du Sud^M
Südamerika^N
America^F Meridionale
América^F del Sur

Orinoco River
Orénoque^M
Orinoko^M
Fiume^M Orinoco
rio^M Orinoco

Amazon River
Amazone^F
Amazonas^M
Rio^M delle Amazzoni^F
rio^M Amazonas

Gulf of Panama
golfe^M de Panama^M
Golf^M von Panama^N
Golfo^M di Panama
golfo^M de Panamá^M

equator
équateur^M
Äquator^M
Equatore^M
ecuador^M

Andes Cordillera
cordillère^F des Andes
Anden
Cordigliera^F delle Ande^F
cordillera^F de los Andes^M

Lake Titicaca
lac^M Titicaca
Titicacasee^M
Lago^M Titicaca
lago^M Titicaca

Atacama Desert
désert^M d'Atacama
Atacama-Wüste^F
Deserto^M di Atacama
desierto^M de Atacama

Paraná River
Paraná^M
Paraná^M
Fiume^M Paranà
rio^M Paraná

Patagonia
Patagonie^F
Patagonien^N
Patagonia^F
Patagonia^F

Falkland Islands
îles^F Falkland
Falkland-Inseln^F
Isole^F Falkland
islas^F Malvinas

Tierra del Fuego
Terre^F de Feu^M
Feuerland^N
Terra^F del Fuoco^M
Tierra^F del Fuego^M

Cape Horn
cap^M Horn
Kap^N Horn
Capo^M Horn
cabo^M de Hornos

Drake Passage
détroit^M de Drake
Drakestraße^F
Canale^M di Drake
paso^M de Drake

configuration of the continents

EARTH

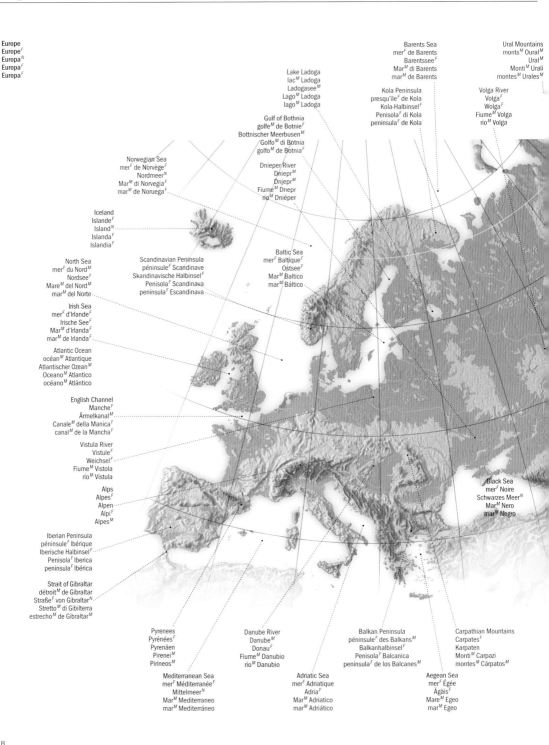

Europe
Europe[F]
Europa[N]
Europa[F]
Europa[F]

Barents Sea
mer[F] de Barents
Barentssee[F]
Mar[M] di Barents
mar[M] de Barents

Ural Mountains
monts[M] Oural[M]
Ural[M]
Monti[M] Urali
montes[M] Urales[F]

Lake Ladoga
lac[M] Ladoga
Ladogasee[M]
Lago[M] Ladoga
lago[M] Ladoga

Kola Peninsula
presqu'île[F] de Kola
Kola-Halbinsel[F]
Penisola[F] di Kola
península[F] de Kola

Volga River
Volga[F]
Wolga[F]
Fiume[M] Volga
río[M] Volga

Gulf of Bothnia
golfe[M] de Botnie[F]
Bottnischer Meerbusen[M]
Golfo[M] di Botnia
golfo[M] de Botnia[F]

Dnieper River
Dniepr[M]
Dnjepr[M]
Fiume[M] Dnepr
río[M] Dniéper

Norwegian Sea
mer[F] de Norvège[F]
Nordmeer[N]
Mar[M] di Norvegia[F]
mar[M] de Noruega[F]

Iceland
Islande[F]
Island[N]
Islanda[F]
Islandia[F]

North Sea
mer[F] du Nord[M]
Nordsee[F]
Mare[M] del Nord[M]
mar[M] del Norte

Scandinavian Peninsula
péninsule[F] Scandinave
Skandinavische Halbinsel[F]
Penisola[F] Scandinava
península[F] Escandinava

Baltic Sea
mer[F] Baltique[F]
Ostsee[F]
Mar[M] Baltico
mar[M] Báltico

Irish Sea
mer[F] d'Irlande[F]
Irische See[F]
Mar[M] d'Irlanda[F]
mar[M] de Irlanda[F]

Atlantic Ocean
océan[M] Atlantique
Atlantischer Ozean[M]
Oceano[M] Atlantico
océano[M] Atlántico

English Channel
Manche[F]
Ärmelkanal[M]
Canale[M] della Manica[F]
canal[M] de la Mancha[F]

Vistula River
Vistule[F]
Weichsel[F]
Fiume[M] Vistola
río[M] Vístula

Black Sea
mer[F] Noire
Schwarzes Meer[N]
Mar[M] Nero
mar[M] Negro

Alps
Alpes[F]
Alpen
Alpi[F]
Alpes[M]

Iberian Peninsula
péninsule[F] Ibérique
Iberische Halbinsel[F]
Penisola[F] Iberica
península[F] Ibérica

Strait of Gibraltar
détroit[M] de Gibraltar
Straße[F] von Gibraltar[N]
Stretto[M] di Gibilterra
estrecho[M] de Gibraltar[M]

Pyrenees
Pyrénées[F]
Pyrenäen
Pirenei
Pirineos[M]

Danube River
Danube[M]
Donau[F]
Fiume[M] Danubio
río[M] Danubio

Balkan Peninsula
péninsule[F] des Balkans[M]
Balkanhalbinsel[F]
Penisola[F] Balcanica
península[F] de los Balcanes[M]

Carpathian Mountains
Carpates[F]
Karpaten
Monti[M] Carpazi
montes[M] Cárpatos[M]

Mediterranean Sea
mer[F] Méditerranée[F]
Mittelmeer[N]
Mar[M] Mediterraneo
mar[M] Mediterráneo

Adriatic Sea
mer[F] Adriatique
Adria[F]
Mar[M] Adriatico
mar[M] Adriático

Aegean Sea
mer[F] Égée
Ägäis[F]
Mare[M] Egeo
mar[M] Egeo

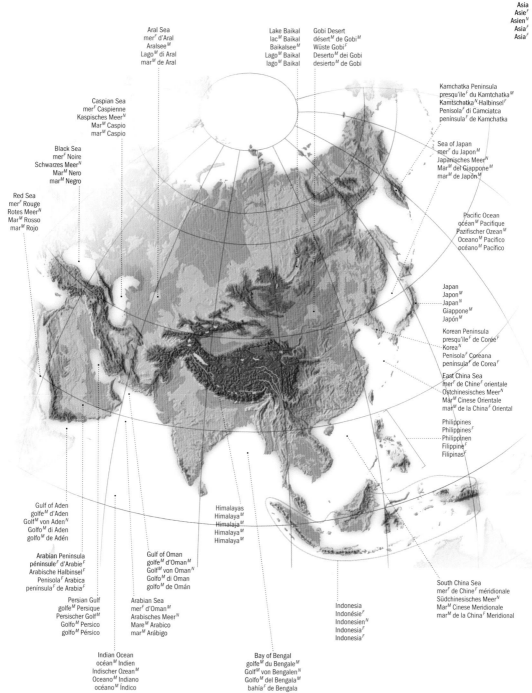

Asia
Asie^F
Asien^N
Asia^F
Asia^F

Aral Sea
mer^F d'Aral
Aralsee^M
Lago^M di Aral
mar^M de Aral

Lake Baikal
lac^M Baikal
Baikalsee^M
Lago^M Baikal
lago^M Baikal

Gobi Desert
désert^M de Gobi^M
Wüste Gobi^F
Deserto^M dei Gobi
desierto^M de Gobi

Kamchatka Peninsula
presqu'île^F du Kamtchatka^M
Kamtschatka^N-Halbinsel^F
Penisola^F di Camciatca
península^F de Kamchatka

Caspian Sea
mer^F Caspienne
Kaspisches Meer^N
Mar^M Caspio
mar^M Caspio

Sea of Japan
mer^F du Japon^M
Japanisches Meer^N
Mar^M del Giappone^M
mar^M de Japón^M

Black Sea
mer^F Noire
Schwarzes Meer^N
Mar^M Nero
mar^M Negro

Pacific Ocean
océan^M Pacifique
Pazifischer Ozean^M
Oceano^M Pacifico
océano^M Pacífico

Red Sea
mer^F Rouge
Rotes Meer^N
Mar^M Rosso
mar^M Rojo

Japan
Japon^M
Japan^N
Giappone^M
Japón^M

Korean Peninsula
presqu'île^F de Corée^F
Korea^N
Penisola^F Coreana
península^F de Corea^F

East China Sea
mer^F de Chine^F orientale
Ostchinesisches Meer^N
Mar^M Cinese Orientale
mar^M de la China^F Oriental

Philippines
Philippines^F
Philippinen
Filippine^F
Filipinas^F

Gulf of Aden
golfe^M d'Aden
Golf^M von Aden^N
Golfo^M di Aden
golfo^M de Adén

Himalayas
Himalaya^M
Himalaja^M
Himalaya^M
Himalaya^M

Gulf of Oman
golfe^M d'Oman^M
Golf^M von Oman^N
Golfo^M di Oman
golfo^M de Omán

South China Sea
mer^F de Chine^F méridionale
Südchinesisches Meer^N
Mar^M Cinese Meridionale
mar^M de la China^F Meridional

Arabian Peninsula
péninsule^F d'Arabie^F
Arabische Halbinsel^F
Penisola^F Arabica
península^F de Arabia^F

Persian Gulf
golfe^M Persique
Persischer Golf^M
Golfo^M Persico
golfo^M Pérsico

Arabian Sea
mer^F d'Oman^M
Arabisches Meer^N
Mare^M Arabico
mar^M Arábigo

Indonesia
Indonésie^F
Indonesien^N
Indonesia^F
Indonesia^F

Indian Ocean
océan^M Indien
Indischer Ozean^M
Oceano^M Indiano
océano^M Índico

Bay of Bengal
golfe^M du Bengale^M
Golf^M von Bengalen^N
Golfo^M del Bengala^M
bahía^F de Bengala

configuration of the continents

Africa
Afrique^F
Afrika^N
Africa^F
África^F

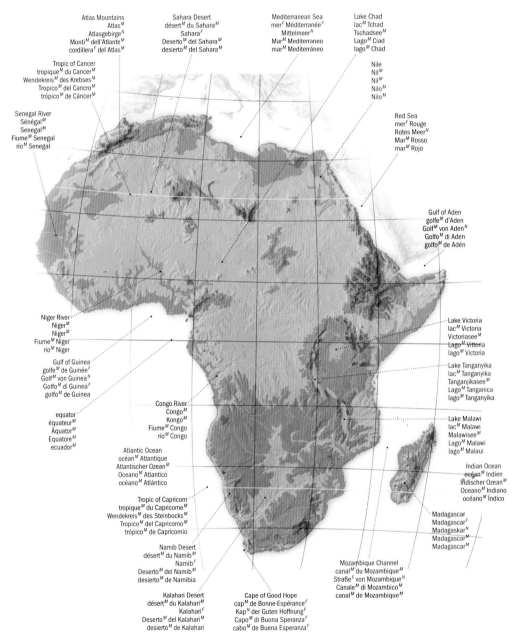

Atlas Mountains
Atlas^M
Atlasgebirge^N
Monti^M dell'Atlante^M
cordillera^F del Atlas^M

Sahara Desert
désert^M du Sahara^M
Sahara^F
Deserto^M del Sahara^M
desierto^M del Sahara^M

Mediterranean Sea
mer^F Méditerranée^F
Mittelmeer^N
Mar^M Mediterraneo
mar^M Mediterráneo

Lake Chad
lac^M Tchad
Tschadsee^M
Lago^M Ciad
lago^M Chad

Tropic of Cancer
tropique^M du Cancer^M
Wendekreis^M des Krebses^M
Tropico^M del Cancro^M
trópico^M de Cáncer^M

Nile
Nil^M
Nil^M
Nilo^M
Nilo^M

Senegal River
Sénégal^M
Senegal^M
Fiume^M Senegal
río^M Senegal

Red Sea
mer^F Rouge
Rotes Meer^N
Mar^M Rosso
mar^M Rojo

Gulf of Aden
golfe^M d'Aden
Golf^M von Aden^N
Golfo^M di Aden
golfo^M de Adén

Niger River
Niger^M
Niger^M
Fiume^M Niger
río^M Niger

Lake Victoria
lac^M Victoria
Victoriasee^M
Lago^M Vittoria
lago^M Victoria

Gulf of Guinea
golfe^M de Guinée^F
Golf^M von Guinea^N
Golfo^M di Guinea^F
golfo^M de Guinea

Lake Tanganyika
lac^M Tanganyika
Tanganjikasee^M
Lago^M Tanganica
lago^M Tanganyika

equator
équateur^M
Äquator^M
Equatore^M
ecuador^M

Congo River
Congo^M
Kongo^M
Fiume^M Congo
río^M Congo

Lake Malawi
lac^M Malawi
Malawisee^M
Lago^M Malawi
lago^M Malawi

Atlantic Ocean
océan^M Atlantique
Atlantischer Ozean^M
Oceano^M Atlantico
océano^M Atlántico

Indian Ocean
océan^M Indien
Indischer Ozean^M
Oceano^M Indiano
océano^M Índico

Tropic of Capricorn
tropique^M du Capricorne^M
Wendekreis^M des Steinbocks^M
Tropico^M del Capricorno^M
trópico^M de Capricornio

Madagascar
Madagascar^F
Madagaskar^N
Madagascar^M
Madagascar^M

Namib Desert
désert^M du Namib^M
Namib^F
Deserto^M del Namib^M
desierto^M de Namibia

Mozambique Channel
canal^M du Mozambique^M
Straße^F von Mozambique^N
Canale^M di Mozambico^M
canal^M de Mozambique^M

Kalahari Desert
désert^M du Kalahari^M
Kalahari^F
Deserto^M del Kalahari^M
desierto^M de Kalahari

Cape of Good Hope
cap^M de Bonne-Espérance^F
Kap^N der Guten Hoffnung^F
Capo^M di Buona Speranza^F
cabo^M de Buena Esperanza^F

cartography

cartographie^F | Kartographie^F | cartografia^F | cartografía^F

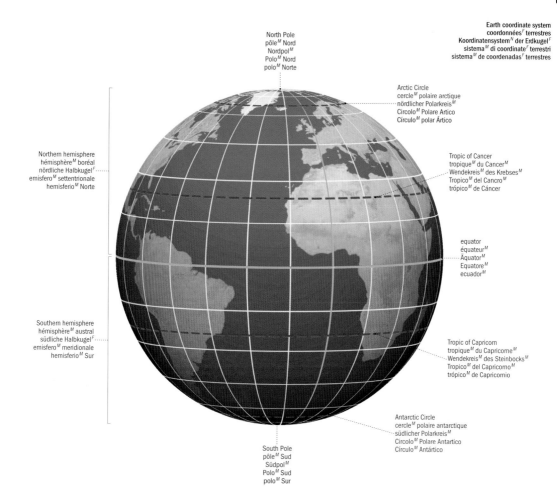

Earth coordinate system
coordonnées^F terrestres
Koordinatensystem^N der Erdkugel
sistema^M di coordinate^F terrestri
sistema^M de coordenadas^F terrestres

North Pole
pôle^M Nord
Nordpol^M
Polo^M Nord
polo^M Norte

Arctic Circle
cercle^M polaire arctique
nördlicher Polarkreis^M
Circolo^M Polare Artico
Círculo^M polar Ártico

Northern hemisphere
hémisphère^M boréal
nördliche Halbkugel^F
emisfero^M settentrionale
hemisferio^M Norte

Tropic of Cancer
tropique^M du Cancer^M
Wendekreis^M des Krebses^M
Tropico^M del Cancro^M
trópico^M de Cáncer

equator
équateur^M
Äquator^M
Equatore^M
ecuador^M

Southern hemisphere
hémisphère^M austral
südliche Halbkugel^F
emisfero^M meridionale
hemisferio^M Sur

Tropic of Capricorn
tropique^M du Capricorne^M
Wendekreis^M des Steinbocks^M
Tropico^M del Capricorno^M
trópico^M de Capricornio

Antarctic Circle
cercle^M polaire antarctique
südlicher Polarkreis^M
Circolo^M Polare Antartico
Círculo^M Antártico

South Pole
pôle^M Sud
Südpol^M
Polo^M Sud
polo^M Sur

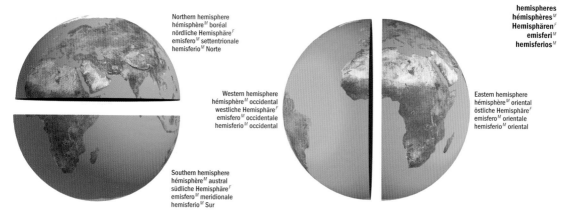

hemispheres
hémisphères^M
Hemisphären^F
emisferi^M
hemisferios^M

Northern hemisphere
hémisphère^M boréal
nördliche Hemisphäre^F
emisfero^M settentrionale
hemisferio^M Norte

Western hemisphere
hémisphère^M occidental
westliche Hemisphäre^F
emisfero^M occidentale
hemisferio^M occidental

Eastern hemisphere
hémisphère^M oriental
östliche Hemisphäre^F
emisfero^M orientale
hemisferio^M oriental

Southern hemisphere
hémisphère^M austral
südliche Hemisphäre^F
emisfero^M meridionale
hemisferio^M Sur

cartography

EARTH

grid system
divisions^F **cartographiques**
Gradnetz^N
reticolato^M **geografico**
sistema^M **de retícula**^{F}

lines of latitude
latitude^F
Breitengrade^M
latitudine^F
líneas^F de latitud^F

Arctic Circle
cercle^M polaire arctique
nördlicher Polarkreis^M
Circolo^M Polare Ártico
Círculo^M polar Ártico

lines of longitude
longitude^F
Längengrade^M
longitudine^F
líneas^F de longitud^F

Tropic of Cancer
tropique^M du Cancer^M
Wendekreis^M des Krebses^M
Tropico^M del Cancro^M
trópico^M de Cáncer

Eastern meridian
méridien^M est
östlicher Meridian^M
meridiano^M orientale
meridiano^M oriental

prime meridian
méridien^M de Greenwich
Nullmeridian^M
meridiano^M fondamentale
meridiano^M principal

Equator
équateur^M
Äquator^M
Equatore^M
Ecuador^M

Western meridian
méridien^M ouest
westlicher Meridian^M
meridiano^M occidentale
meridiano^M occidental

Tropic of Capricorn
tropique^M du Capricorne^M
Wendekreis^M des Steinbocks^M
Tropico^M del Capricorno^M
trópico^M de Capricornio

Antarctic Circle
cercle^M polaire antarctique
südlicher Polarkreis^M
Circolo^M Polare Antartico
Círculo^M Antártico

parallel
parallèle^M
Breitenkreis^M
parallelo^M
paralelo^M

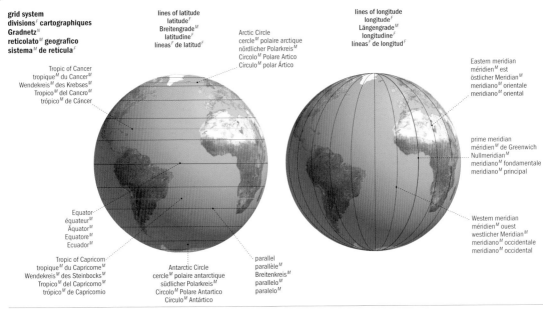

map projections
projections^F **cartographiques**
Kartendarstellungen^F
proiezioni^F **cartografiche**
proyecciones^F **cartográficas**

plane projection
projection^F horizontale
Azimutalprojektion^F
proiezione^F piana
proyección^F plana

conic projection
projection^F conique
Kegelprojektion^F
proiezione^F conica
proyección^F cónica

cylindrical projection
projection^F cylindrique
Zylinderprojektion^F
proiezione^F cilindrica
proyección^F cilíndrica

interrupted projection
projection^F interrompue
zerlappte Projektion^F
proiezione^F interrotta
proyección^F interrumpida

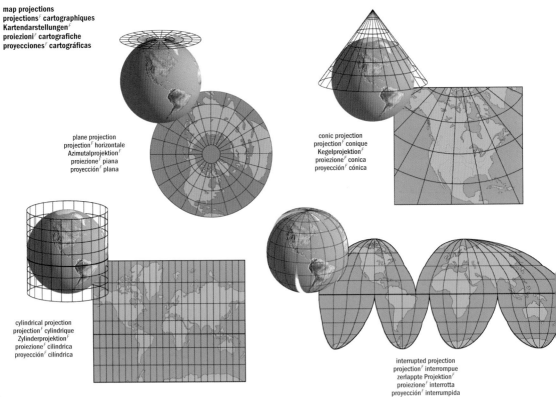

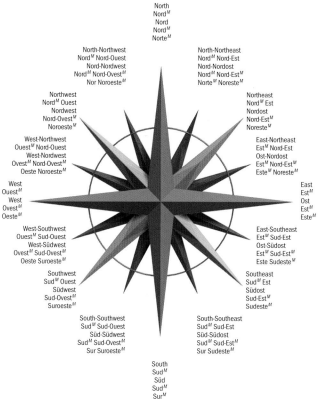

compass card
rose^F des vents^M
Windrose^F
rosa^F dei venti^M
rosa^F de los vientos^M

North
Nord^M
Nord
Nord^M
Norte^M

North-Northwest
Nord^M Nord-Ouest
Nord-Nordwest
Nord^M Nord-Ovest^M
Nor Noroeste^M

North-Northeast
Nord^M Nord-Est
Nord-Nordost
Nord^M Nord-Est^M
Norte^M Noreste^M

Northwest
Nord^M Ouest
Nordwest
Nord-Ovest^M
Noroeste^M

Northeast
Nord^M Est
Nordost
Nord-Est^M
Noreste^M

West-Northwest
Ouest^M Nord-Ouest
West-Nordwest
Ovest^M Nord-Ovest^M
Oeste Noroeste^M

East-Northeast
Est^M Nord-Est
Ost-Nordost
Est^M Nord-Est^M
Este^M Noreste^M

West
Ouest^M
West
Ovest^M
Oeste^M

East
Est^M
Ost
Est^M
Este^M

West-Southwest
Ouest^M Sud-Ouest
West-Südwest
Ovest^M Sud-Ovest^M
Oeste Suroeste^M

East-Southeast
Est^M Sud-Est
Ost-Südost
Est^M Sud-Est^M
Este Sudeste^M

Southwest
Sud^M Ouest
Südwest
Sud-Ovest^M
Suroeste^M

Southeast
Sud^M Est
Südost
Sud-Est^M
Sudeste^M

South-Southwest
Sud^M Sud-Ouest
Süd-Südwest
Sud^M Sud-Ovest^M
Sur Suroeste^M

South-Southeast
Sud^M Sud-Est
Süd-Südost
Sud^M Sud-Est^M
Sur Sudeste^M

South
Sud^M
Süd
Sud^M
Sur^M

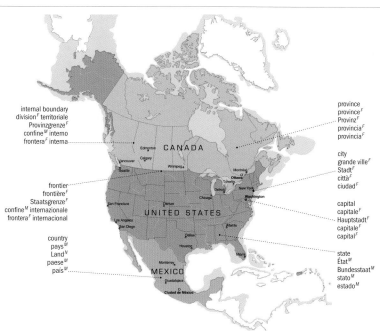

political map
carte^F politique
politische Karte^F
carta^F politica
mapa^M político

internal boundary
division^F territoriale
Provinzgrenze^F
confine^M interno
frontera^F interna

province
province^F
Provinz^F
provincia^F
provincia^F

frontier
frontière^F
Staatsgrenze^F
confine^M internazionale
frontera^F internacional

city
grande ville^F
Stadt^F
città^F
ciudad^F

capital
capitale^F
Hauptstadt^F
capitale^F
capital^F

country
pays^M
Land^N
paese^M
país^M

state
État^M
Bundesstaat^M
stato^M
estado^M

CANADA
Edmonton
Vancouver
Calgary
Seattle
Winnipeg
Montréal
Ottawa
Toronto
Detroit
New York
Chicago
San Francisco
Denver
Washington
UNITED STATES
Los Angeles
San Diego
Atlanta
Dallas
Houston
Miami
Monterrey
MEXICO
Guadalajara
Ciudad de México

cartography

EARTH

physical map
carte[F] physique
physische Karte[F]
carta[F] fisica
mapa[M] físico

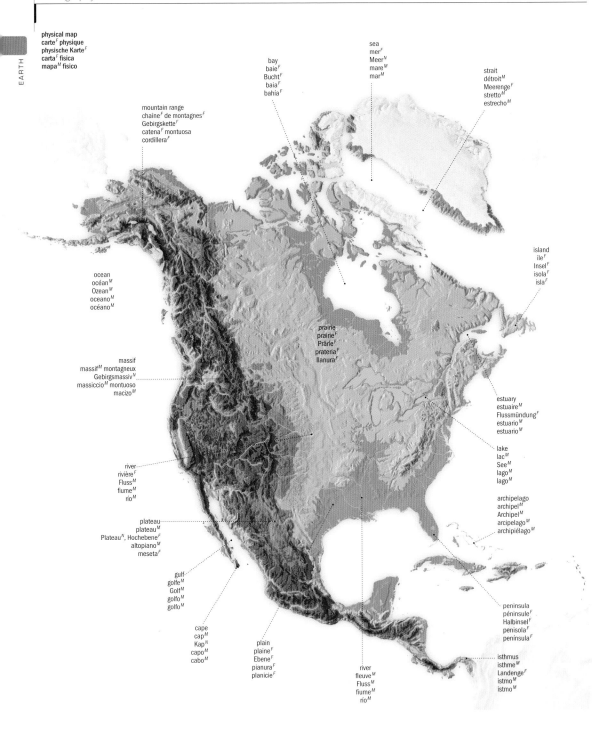

sea
mer[F]
Meer[N]
mare[M]
mar[M]

bay
baie[F]
Bucht[F]
baia[F]
bahía[F]

strait
détroit[M]
Meerenge[F]
stretto[M]
estrecho[M]

mountain range
chaîne[F] de montagnes[F]
Gebirgskette[F]
catena[F] montuosa
cordillera[F]

island
île[F]
Insel[F]
isola[F]
isla[F]

ocean
océan[M]
Ozean[M]
oceano[M]
océano[M]

prairie
prairie[F]
Prärie[F]
prateria[F]
llanura[F]

estuary
estuaire[M]
Flussmündung[F]
estuario[M]
estuario[M]

massif
massif[M] montagneux
Gebirgsmassiv[N]
massiccio[M] montuoso
macizo[M]

lake
lac[M]
See[M]
lago[M]
lago[M]

river
rivière[F]
Fluss[M]
fiume[M]
río[M]

archipelago
archipel[M]
Archipel[M]
arcipelago[M]
archipiélago[M]

plateau
plateau[M]
Plateau[N], Hochebene[F]
altopiano[M]
meseta[F]

peninsula
péninsule[F]
Halbinsel[F]
penisola[F]
península[F]

gulf
golfe[M]
Golf[M]
golfo[M]
golfo[M]

cape
cap[M]
Kap[N]
capo[M]
cabo[M]

plain
plaine[F]
Ebene[F]
pianura[F]
planicie[F]

isthmus
isthme[M]
Landenge[F]
istmo[M]
istmo[M]

river
fleuve[M]
Fluss[M]
fiume[M]
río[M]

railway
chemin^M de fer^M
Eisenbahn^F
ferrovia^F
via^F férrea

railway station
gare^F
Bahnhof^M
stazione^F ferroviaria
estación^F del ferrocarril^M

bridge
pont^M
Brücke^F
ponte^M
puente^M

urban map
plan^M urbain
Stadtplan^M
pianta^F di città^F
mapa^M urbano

suburbs
banlieue^F
Vororte^M
sobborghi^M
zona^F residencial (de las afueras^F)

river
fleuve^M
Fluss^M
fiume^M
río^M

woods
bois^M
Wald^M
bosco^M
bosques^M

ring road
boulevard^M périphérique
Umgehungsstraße^F
circonvallazione^F
circunvalación^F

roundabout
rond-point^M
Kreisverkehr^M
rotatoria^F
rotonda^F

street
rue^F
Straße^F
via^F
calle^F

park
parc^M
Park^M
parco^M
parque^M

cemetery
cimetière^M
Friedhof^M
cimitero^M
cementerio^M

monument
monument^M
Denkmal^N
monumento^M
monumento^M

motorway
autoroute^F
Autobahn^F
autostrada^F
autopista^F

district
arrondissement^M
Stadtteil^M
quartiere^M
distrito^M

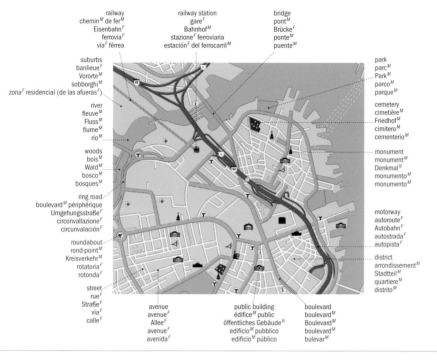

avenue
avenue^F
Allee^F
avenue^F
avenida^F

public building
édifice^M public
öffentliches Gebäude^N
edificio^M pubblico
edificio^M público

boulevard
boulevard^M
Boulevard^M
boulevard^M
bulevar^M

---

road map
carte^F routière
Straßenkarte^F
carta^F stradale
mapa^M de carreteras^F

motorway number
numéro^M d'autoroute^F
Autobahnnummer^F
numero^M di autostrada^F
número^M de la autopista^F

road
route^F
Straße^F
strada^F
carretera^F

motorway
autoroute^F
Autobahn^F
autostrada^F
autopista^F

rest area
aire^F de repos^M
Rastplatz^M
area^F di sosta^F
área^F de descanso^M

service area
aire^F de service^M
Raststätte^F
area^F di servizio^M
área^F de servicio^M

ring motorway
autoroute^F de ceinture^F
Umgehungsstraße^F
tangenziale^F
carretera^F de circunvalación^F

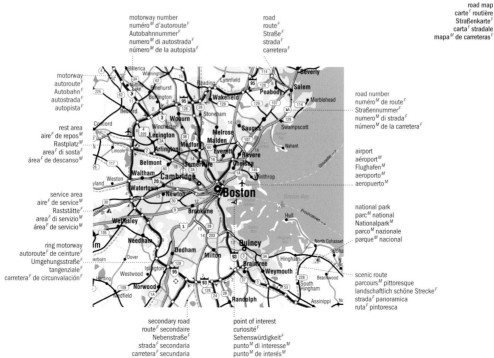

road number
numéro^M de route^F
Straßennummer^F
numero^M di strada^F
número^M de la carretera^F

airport
aéroport^M
Flughafen^M
aeroporto^M
aeropuerto^M

national park
parc^M national
Nationalpark^M
parco^M nazionale
parque^M nacional

scenic route
parcours^M pittoresque
landschaftlich schöne Strecke^F
strada^F panoramica
ruta^F pintoresca

secondary road
route^F secondaire
Nebenstraße^F
strada^F secondaria
carretera^F secundaria

point of interest
curiosité^F
Sehenswürdigkeit^F
punto^M di interesse^M
punto^M de interés^M

section of the Earth's crust

coupe^F de la croûte^F terrestre | Erdkruste^F im Querschnitt^M | sezione^F della crosta^F terrestre | corte^M de la corteza^F terrestre

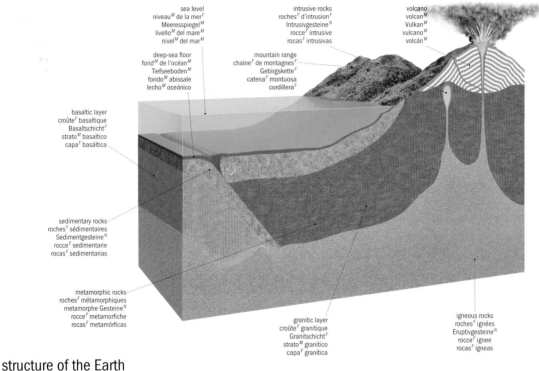

sea level
niveau^M de la mer^F
Meeresspiegel^M
livello^M del mare^M
nivel^M del mar^M

intrusive rocks
roches^F d'intrusion^F
Intrusivgesteine^N
rocce^F intrusive
rocas^F intrusivas

volcano
volcan^M
Vulkan^M
vulcano^M
volcán^M

deep-sea floor
fond^M de l'océan^M
Tiefseeboden^M
fondo^M abissale
lecho^M oceánico

mountain range
chaîne^F de montagnes^F
Gebirgskette^F
catena^F montuosa
cordillera^F

basaltic layer
croûte^F basaltique
Basaltschicht^F
strato^M basaltico
capa^F basáltica

sedimentary rocks
roches^F sédimentaires
Sedimentgesteine^N
rocce^F sedimentarie
rocas^F sedimentarias

metamorphic rocks
roches^F métamorphiques
metamorphe Gesteine^N
rocce^F metamorfiche
rocas^F metamórficas

granitic layer
croûte^F granitique
Granitschicht^F
strato^M granitico
capa^F granítica

igneous rocks
roches^F ignées
Eruptivgesteine^N
rocce^F ignee
rocas^F ígneas

structure of the Earth

structure^F de la Terre^F | Erdaufbau^M | struttura^F della Terra^F | estructura^F de la Tierra^F

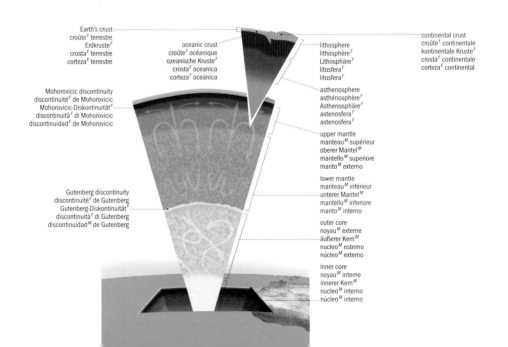

Earth's crust
croûte^F terrestre
Erdkruste^F
crosta^F terrestre
corteza^F terrestre

oceanic crust
croûte^F océanique
ozeanische Kruste^F
crosta^F oceanica
corteza^F oceánica

lithosphere
lithosphère^F
Lithosphäre^F
litosfera^F
litosfera^F

continental crust
croûte^F continentale
kontinentale Kruste^F
crosta^F continentale
corteza^F continental

Mohorovicic discontinuity
discontinuité^F de Mohorovicic
Mohorovicic-Diskontinuität^F
discontinuità^F di Mohorovicic
discontinuidad^F de Mohorovicic

asthenosphere
asthénosphère^F
Asthenosphäre^F
astenosfera^F
astenosfera^F

upper mantle
manteau^M supérieur
oberer Mantel^M
mantello^M superiore
manto^M externo

lower mantle
manteau^M inférieur
unterer Mantel^M
mantello^M inferiore
manto^M interno

Gutenberg discontinuity
discontinuité^F de Gutenberg
Gutenberg-Diskontinuität^F
discontinuità^F di Gutenberg
discontinuidad^M de Gutenberg

outer core
noyau^M externe
äußerer Kern^M
nucleo^M esterno
núcleo^M externo

inner core
noyau^M interne
innerer Kern^M
nucleo^M interno
núcleo^M interno

tectonic plates

plaques[F] tectoniques | tektonische Platten[F] | placche[F] tettoniche | placas[F] tectónicas

EARTH

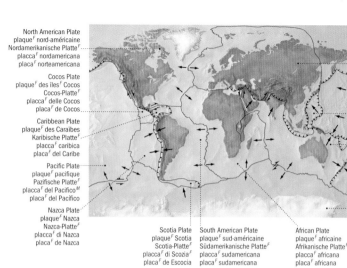

North American Plate
plaque[F] nord-américaine
Nordamerikanische Platte[F]
placca[F] nordamericana
placa[F] norteamericana

Cocos Plate
plaque[F] des îles[F] Cocos
Cocos-Platte[F]
placca[F] delle Cocos
placa[F] de Cocos

Caribbean Plate
plaque[F] des Caraïbes
Karibische Platte[F]
placca[F] caribica
placa[F] del Caribe

Pacific Plate
plaque[F] pacifique
Pazifische Platte[F]
placca[F] del Pacifico[M]
placa[F] del Pacífico

Nazca Plate
plaque[F] Nazca
Nazca-Platte[F]
placca[F] di Nazca
placa[F] de Nazca

Eurasian Plate
plaque[F] eurasiatique
Eurasiatische Platte[F]
placca[F] euroasiatica
placa[F] euroasiática

Philippine Plate
plaque[F] philippine
Philippinen-Platte[F]
placca[F] filippina
placa[F] de Filipinas

Australian-Indian Plate
plaque[F] indo-australienne
Indisch-Australische Platte[F]
placca[F] indoaustraliana
placa[F] indoaustraliana

Antarctic Plate
plaque[F] antarctique
Antarktische Platte[F]
placca[F] antartica
placa[F] antártica

Scotia Plate
plaque[F] Scotia
Scotia-Platte[F]
placca[F] di Scozia
placa[F] de Escocia

South American Plate
plaque[F] sud-américaine
Südamerikanische Platte[F]
placca[F] sudamericana
placa[F] sudamericana

African Plate
plaque[F] africaine
Afrikanische Platte[F]
placca[F] africana
placa[F] africana

subduction
subduction[F]
Subduktionszone[F]
subduzione[F]
subducción[M]

divergent plate boundaries
plaques[F] divergentes
divergierende Plattengrenzen[F]
placche[F] divergenti
placas[F] divergentes

convergent plate boundaries
plaques[F] convergentes
konvergierende Plattengrenzen[F]
placche[F] convergenti
placas[F] convergentes

transform plate boundaries
plaques[F] transformantes
Transformstörungen[F]
placche[F] trasformi
fallas[F] transformantes

earthquake

séisme[M] | Erdbeben[N] | terremoto[M] | terremoto[M]

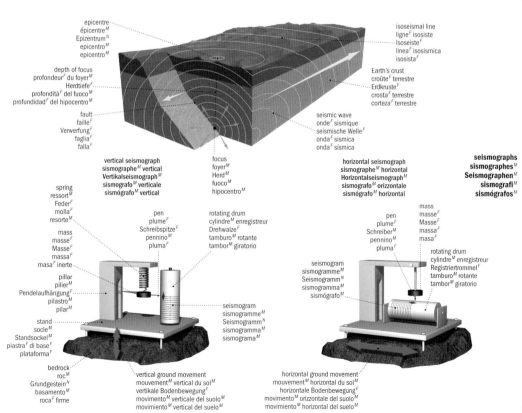

epicentre
épicentre[M]
Epizentrum[N]
epicentro[M]
epicentro[M]

depth of focus
profondeur[F] du foyer[M]
Herdtiefe[F]
profondità[F] del fuoco[M]
profundidad[F] del hipocentro[M]

fault
faille[F]
Verwerfung[F]
faglia[F]
falla[F]

isoseismal line
ligne[F] isosiste
Isoseiste[F]
linea[F] isosismica
isosista[F]

Earth's crust
croûte[F] terrestre
Erdkruste[F]
crosta[F] terrestre
corteza[F] terrestre

seismic wave
onde[F] sismique
seismische Welle[F]
onda[F] sismica
onda[F] sísmica

vertical seismograph
sismographe[M] vertical
Vertikalseismograph[M]
sismografo[M] verticale
sismógrafo[M] vertical

focus
foyer[M]
Herd[M]
fuoco[M]
hipocentro[M]

horizontal seismograph
sismographe[M] horizontal
Horizontalseismograph[M]
sismografo[M] orizzontale
sismógrafo[M] horizontal

**seismographs
sismographes[M]
Seismographen[M]
sismografi[M]
sismógrafos[M]**

spring
ressort[M]
Feder[F]
molla[F]
resorte[M]

mass
masse[F]
Masse[F]
massa[F]
masa[F] inerte

pillar
pilier[M]
Pendelaufhängung[F]
pilastro[M]
pilar[M]

stand
socle[M]
Standsockel[M]
piastra[F] di base[F]
plataforma[F]

bedrock
roc[M]
Grundgestein[N]
basamento[M]
roca[F] firme

pen
plume[M]
Schreibspitze[F]
pennino[M]
pluma[F]

rotating drum
cylindre[M] enregistreur
Drehwalze[F]
tamburo[M] rotante
tambor[M] giratorio

seismogram
sismogramme[M]
Seismogramm[N]
sismogramma[M]
sismograma[M]

seismogram
sismogramme[M]
Seismogramm[N]
sismogramma[M]
sismógrafo[M]

pen
plume[F]
Schreiber[F]
pennino[M]
pluma[F]

mass
masse[F]
Masse[F]
massa[F]
masa[F]

rotating drum
cylindre[M] enregistreur
Registriertrommel[F]
tamburo[M] rotante
tambor[M] giratorio

vertical ground movement
mouvement[M] vertical du sol[M]
vertikale Bodenbewegung[F]
movimento[M] verticale del suolo[M]
movimiento[M] vertical del suelo[M]

horizontal ground movement
mouvement[M] horizontal du sol[M]
horizontale Bodenbewegung[F]
movimento[M] orizzontale del suolo[M]
movimiento[M] horizontal del suelo[M]

volcano

volcan^M | Vulkan^M | vulcano^M | volcán^M

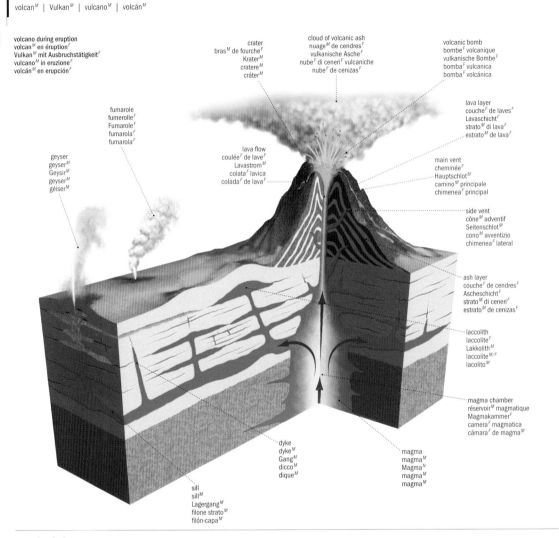

volcano during eruption
volcan^M en éruption^F
Vulkan^M mit Ausbruchstätigkeit^F
vulcano^M in eruzione^F
volcán^M en erupción^F

crater
bras^M de fourche^F
Krater^M
cratere^M
cráter^M

cloud of volcanic ash
nuage^M de cendres^F
vulkanische Asche^F
nube^F di ceneri^F vulcaniche
nube^F de cenizas^F

volcanic bomb
bombe^F volcanique
vulkanische Bombe^F
bomba^F vulcanica
bomba^F volcánica

lava layer
couche^F de laves^F
Lavaschicht^F
strato^M di lava^F
estrato^M de lava^F

fumarole
fumerolle^F
Fumarole^F
fumarola^F
fumarola^F

lava flow
coulée^F de lave^F
Lavastrom^M
colata^F lavica
colada^F de lava^F

main vent
cheminée^F
Hauptschlot^M
camino^M principale
chimenea^F principal

geyser
geyser^M
Geysir^M
geyser^M
géiser^M

side vent
cône^M adventif
Seitenschlot^M
cono^M avventizio
chimenea^F lateral

ash layer
couche^F de cendres^F
Ascheschicht^F
strato^M di ceneri^F
estrato^M de cenizas^F

laccolith
laccolite^F
Lakkolith^M
laccolite$^{M/F}$
lacolito^M

magma chamber
réservoir^M magmatique
Magmakammer^F
camera^F magmatica
cámara^F de magma^M

dyke
dyke^M
Gang^M
dicco^M
dique^M

magma
magma^M
Magma^N
magma^M
magma^M

sill
sill^M
Lagergang^M
filone strato^M
filón-capa^M

examples of volcanoes
exemples^M de volcans^M
Vulkantypen^M
esempi^M di vulcani^M
ejemplos^M de volcanes^M

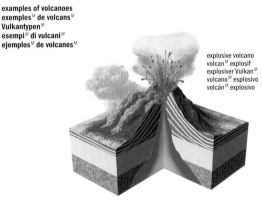

explosive volcano
volcan^M explosif
explosiver Vulkan^M
vulcano^M esplosivo
volcán^M explosivo

effusive volcano
volcan^M effusif
effusiver Vulkan^M
vulcano^M effusivo
volcán^M efusivo

mountain

montagne[F] | Berg[M] | montagna[F] | montaña[F]

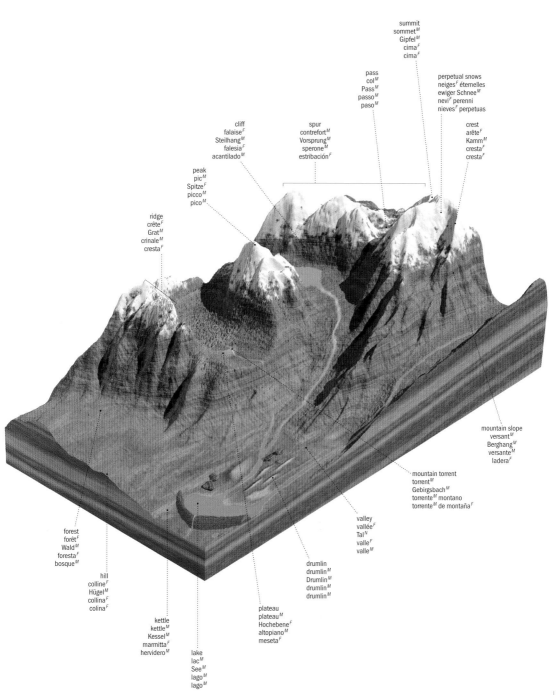

summit
sommet[M]
Gipfel[M]
cima[F]
cima[F]

pass
col[M]
Pass[M]
passo[M]
paso[M]

perpetual snows
neiges[F] éternelles
ewiger Schnee[M]
nevi[F] perenni
nieves[F] perpetuas

cliff
falaise[F]
Steilhang[M]
falesia[F]
acantilado[M]

spur
contrefort[M]
Vorsprung[M]
sperone[M]
estribación[F]

crest
arête[F]
Kamm[M]
cresta[F]
cresta[F]

peak
pic[M]
Spitze[F]
picco[M]
pico[M]

ridge
crête[F]
Grat[M]
crinale[M]
cresta[F]

mountain slope
versant[M]
Berghang[M]
versante[M]
ladera[F]

mountain torrent
torrent[M]
Gebirgsbach[M]
torrente[M] montano
torrente[M] de montaña[F]

valley
vallée[F]
Tal[N]
valle[F]
valle[M]

forest
forêt[F]
Wald[M]
foresta[F]
bosque[M]

drumlin
drumlin[M]
Drumlin[M]
drumlin[M]
drumlin[M]

hill
colline[F]
Hügel[M]
collina[F]
colina[F]

kettle
kettle[M]
Kessel[M]
marmitta[F]
hervidero[M]

plateau
plateau[M]
Hochebene[F]
altopiano[M]
meseta[F]

lake
lac[M]
See[M]
lago[M]
lago[M]

glacier

glacier[M] | Gletscher[M] | ghiacciaio[M] | glaciar[M]

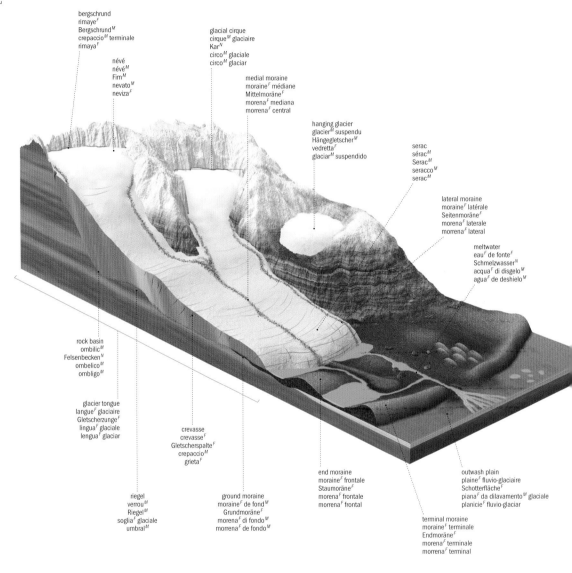

bergschrund
rimaye[F]
Bergschrund[M]
crepaccio[M] terminale
rimaya[F]

névé
névé[M]
Firn[M]
nevato[M]
neviza[F]

glacial cirque
cirque[M] glaciaire
Kar[N]
circo[M] glaciale
circo[M] glaciar

medial moraine
moraine[F] médiane
Mittelmoräne[F]
morena[F] mediana
morrena[F] central

hanging glacier
glacier[M] suspendu
Hängegletscher[M]
vedretta[F]
glaciar[M] suspendido

serac
sérac[M]
Serac[M]
seracco[M]
serac[M]

lateral moraine
moraine[F] latérale
Seitenmoräne[F]
morena[F] laterale
morrena[F] lateral

meltwater
eau[F] de fonte[F]
Schmelzwasser[N]
acqua[F] di disgelo[M]
agua[F] de deshielo[M]

rock basin
ombilic[M]
Felsenbecken[N]
ombelico[M]
ombligo[M]

glacier tongue
langue[F] glaciaire
Gletscherzunge[F]
lingua[F] glaciale
lengua[F] glaciar

crevasse
crevasse[F]
Gletscherspalte[F]
crepaccio[M]
grieta[F]

end moraine
moraine[F] frontale
Staumoräne[F]
morena[F] frontale
morrena[F] frontal

outwash plain
plaine[F] fluvio-glaciaire
Schotterfläche[F]
piana[F] da dilavamento[M] glaciale
planicie[F] fluvio-glaciar

riegel
verrou[M]
Riegel[M]
soglia[F] glaciale
umbral[M]

ground moraine
moraine[F] de fond[M]
Grundmoräne[F]
morena[F] di fondo[M]
morrena[F] de fondo[M]

terminal moraine
moraine[F] terminale
Endmoräne[F]
morena[F] terminale
morrena[F] terminal

cave

grotte[F] | Höhle[F] | grotta[F] | gruta[F]

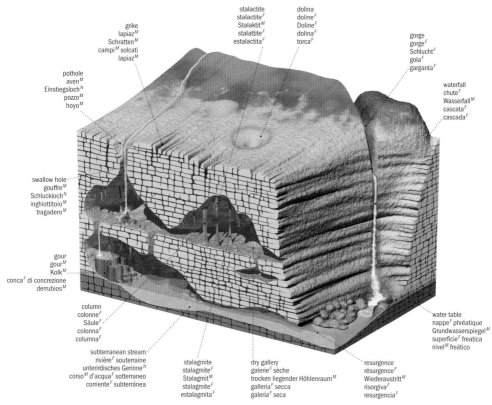

grike
lapiaz[M]
Schratten[M]
campi[M] solcati
lapiaz[M]

stalactite
stalactite[F]
Stalaktit[M]
stalattite[F]
estalactita[F]

dolina
doline[F]
Doline[F]
dolina[F]
torca[F]

gorge
gorge[F]
Schlucht[F]
gola[F]
garganta[F]

waterfall
chute[F]
Wasserfall[M]
cascata[F]
cascada[F]

pothole
aven[M]
Einstiegsloch[N]
pozzo[M]
hoyo[M]

swallow hole
gouffre[M]
Schluckloch[N]
inghiottitoio[M]
tragadero[M]

gour
gour[M]
Kolk[M]
conca[F] di concrezione
derrubios[M]

water table
nappe[F] phréatique
Grundwasserspiegel[M]
superficie[F] freatica
nivel[M] freático

column
colonne[F]
Säule[F]
colonna[F]
columna[F]

subterranean stream
rivière[F] souterraine
unterirdisches Gerinne[N]
corso[M] d'acqua[F] sotterraneo
corriente[F] subterránea

stalagmite
stalagmite[F]
Stalagmit[M]
stalagmite[F]
estalagmita[F]

dry gallery
galerie[F] sèche
trocken liegender Höhlenraum[M]
galleria[F] secca
galería[F] seca

resurgence
résurgence[F]
Wiederaustritt[M]
risorgiva[F]
resurgencia[F]

landslides

mouvements[M] de terrain[M] | Bodenbewegungen[F] | movimenti[M] del terreno[M] | desprendimientos[M] de tierras[F]

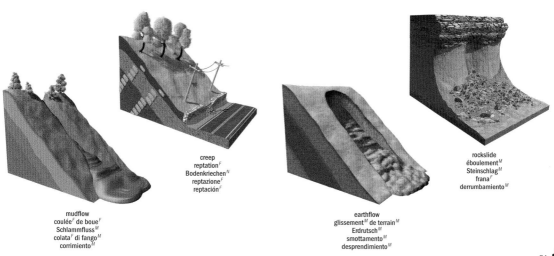

creep
reptation[F]
Bodenkriechen[N]
reptazione[F]
reptación[F]

rockslide
éboulement[M]
Steinschlag[M]
frana[F]
derrumbamiento[M]

mudflow
coulée[F] de boue[F]
Schlammfluss[M]
colata[F] di fango[M]
corrimiento[M]

earthflow
glissement[M] de terrain[M]
Erdrutsch[M]
smottamento[M]
desprendimiento[M]

watercourse

cours^M d'eau^F | Flusslandschaft^F | corso^M d'acqua^F | corriente^F de agua^F

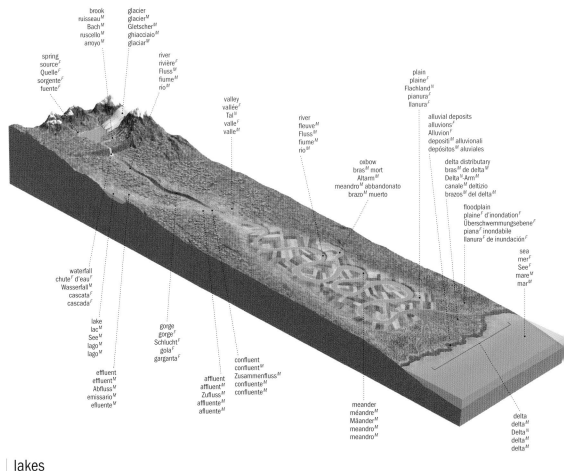

brook
ruisseau^M
Bach^M
ruscello^M
arroyo^M

glacier
glacier^M
Gletscher^M
ghiacciaio^M
glaciar^M

spring
source^F
Quelle^F
sorgente^F
fuente^F

river
rivière^F
Fluss^M
fiume^M
río^M

valley
vallée^F
Tal^N
valle^F
valle^M

river
fleuve^M
Fluss^M
fiume^M
río^M

plain
plaine^F
Flachland^N
pianura^F
llanura^F

alluvial deposits
alluvions^F
Alluvion^F
depositi^M alluvionali
depósitos^M aluviales

oxbow
bras^M mort
Altarm^M
meandro^M abbandonato
brazo^M muerto

delta distributary
bras^M de delta^M
Delta^N-Arm^M
canale^M deltizio
brazos^M del delta^M

floodplain
plaine^F d'inondation^F
Überschwemmungsebene^F
piana^F inondabile
llanura^F de inundación^F

sea
mer^F
See^F
mare^M
mar^M

waterfall
chute^F d'eau^F
Wasserfall^M
cascata^F
cascada^F

lake
lac^M
See^M
lago^M
lago^M

gorge
gorge^F
Schlucht^F
gola^F
garganta^F

confluent
confluent^M
Zusammenfluss^M
confluente^M
confluente^M

effluent
effluent^M
Abfluss^M
emissario^M
efluente^M

affluent
affluent^M
Zufluss^M
affluente^M
afluente^M

meander
méandre^M
Mäander^M
meandro^M
meandro^M

delta
delta^M
Delta^N
delta^M
delta^M

lakes

lacs^M | Seen^M | laghi^M | lagos^M

oxbow lake
lac^M en croissant^M
Altarm^M
lago^M di meandro^M abbandonato
lago^M de brazo^M muerto

glacial lake
lac^M d'origine^F glaciaire
Gletschersee^M
lago^M glaciale
lago^M glaciar

oasis
oasis^F
Oase^F
oasi^F
oasis^M

volcanic lake
lac^M d'origine^F volcanique
vulkanischer See^M
lago^M vulcanico
lago^M volcánico

artificial lake
lac^M artificiel
künstlicher See^M
lago^M artificiale
embalse^M

tectonic lake
lac^M d'origine^F tectonique
tektonischer See^M
lago^M tettonico
lago^M tectónico

wave

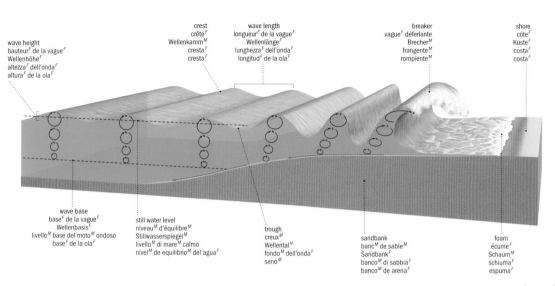

crest
crête[F]
Wellenkamm[M]
cresta[F]
cresta[F]

wave length
longueur[F] de la vague[F]
Wellenlänge[F]
lunghezza[F] dell'onda[F]
longitud[F] de la ola[F]

breaker
vague[F] déferlante
Brecher[M]
frangente[M]
rompiente[M]

shore
côte[F]
Küste[F]
costa[F]
costa[F]

wave height
hauteur[F] de la vague[F]
Wellenhöhe[F]
altezza[F] dell'onda[F]
altura[F] de la ola[F]

wave base
base[F] de la vague[F]
Wellenbasis[F]
livello[M] base del moto[M] ondoso
base[F] de la ola[F]

still water level
niveau[M] d'équilibre[M]
Stillwasserspiegel[M]
livello[M] di mare[M] calmo
nivel[M] de equilibrio[M] del agua[F]

trough
creux[M]
Wellental[N]
fondo[M] dell'onda[F]
seno[M]

sandbank
banc[M] de sable[M]
Sandbank[F]
banco[M] di sabbia[F]
banco[M] de arena[F]

foam
écume[F]
Schaum[M]
schiuma[F]
espuma[F]

ocean floor

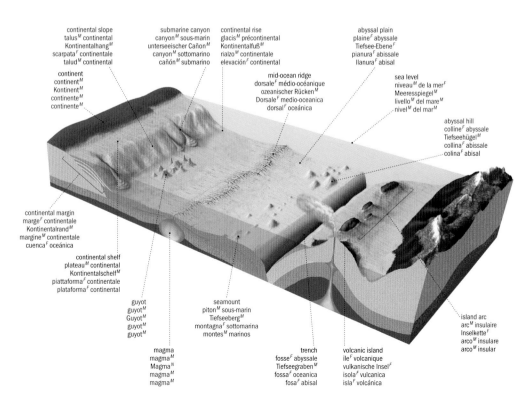

continental slope
talus[M] continental
Kontinentalhang[M]
scarpata[F] continentale
talud[M] continental

submarine canyon
canyon[M] sous-marin
unterseeischer Cañon[M]
canyon[M] sottomarino
cañón[M] submarino

continental rise
glacis[M] précontinental
Kontinentalfuß[M]
rialzo[M] continentale
elevación[F] continental

abyssal plain
plaine[F] abyssale
Tiefsee-Ebene[F]
pianura[F] abissale
llanura[F] abisal

continent
continent[M]
Kontinent[M]
continente[M]
continente[M]

mid-ocean ridge
dorsale[F] médio-océanique
ozeanischer Rücken[M]
Dorsale[F] medio-oceanica
dorsal[F] oceánica

sea level
niveau[M] de la mer[F]
Meeresspiegel[M]
livello[M] del mare[M]
nivel[M] del mar[M]

abyssal hill
colline[F] abyssale
Tiefseehügel[M]
collina[F] abissale
colina[F] abisal

continental margin
marge[F] continentale
Kontinentalrand[M]
margine[M] continentale
cuenca[F] oceánica

continental shelf
plateau[M] continental
Kontinentalschelf[M]
piattaforma[F] continentale
plataforma[F] continental

guyot
guyot[M]
Guyot[M]
guyot[M]
guyot[M]

seamount
piton[M] sous-marin
Tiefseeberg[M]
montagna[F] sottomarina
montes[M] marinos

magma
magma[M]
Magma[N]
magma[M]
magma[M]

trench
fosse[F] abyssale
Tiefseegraben[M]
fossa[F] oceanica
fosa[F] abisal

volcanic island
île[F] volcanique
vulkanische Insel[F]
isola[F] vulcanica
isla[F] volcánica

island arc
arc[M] insulaire
Inselkette[F]
arco[M] insulare
arco[M] insular

ocean trenches and ridges

fosses[F] et dorsales[F] océaniques | ozeanische Rücken[M] und Gräben[M] | fosse[F] e dorsali[F] oceaniche | fosas[F] y dorsales[F] oceánicas

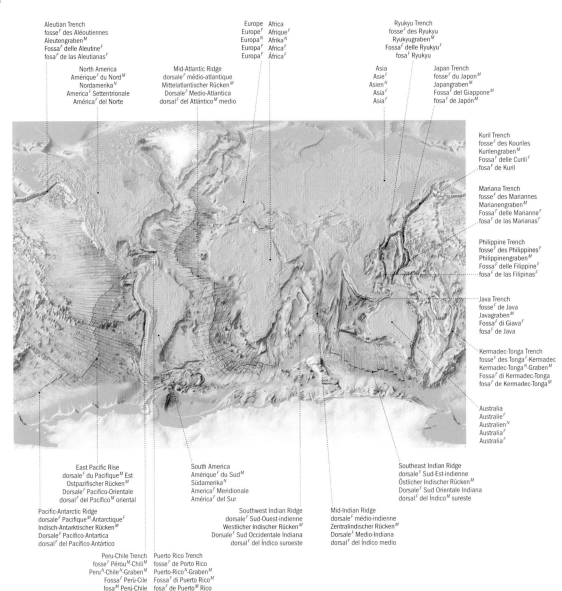

Aleutian Trench
fosse[F] des Aléoutiennes
Aleutengraben[M]
Fossa[F] delle Aleutine[F]
fosa[F] de las Aleutianas[F]

North America
Amérique[F] du Nord[M]
Nordamerika[N]
America[F] Settentrionale
América[F] del Norte

Mid-Atlantic Ridge
dorsale[F] médio-atlantique
Mittelatlantischer Rücken[M]
Dorsale[F] Medio-Atlantica
dorsal[F] del Atlántico[M] medio

Europe   Africa
Europe[F]   Afrique[F]
Europa[N]   Afrika[N]
Europa[F]   Africa[F]
Europa[F]   África[F]

Ryukyu Trench
fosse[F] des Ryukyu
Ryukyugraben[M]
Fossa[F] delle Ryukyu[F]
fosa[F] Ryukyu

Asia   Japan Trench
Asie[F]   fosse[F] du Japon[M]
Asien[N]   Japangraben[M]
Asia[F]   Fossa[F] del Giappone[M]
Asia[F]   fosa[F] de Japón[M]

Kuril Trench
fosse[F] des Kouriles
Kurilengraben[M]
Fossa[F] delle Curili[F]
fosa[F] de Kuril

Mariana Trench
fosse[F] des Mariannes
Marianengraben[M]
Fossa[F] delle Marianne[F]
fosa[F] de las Marianas[F]

Philippine Trench
fosse[F] des Philippines[F]
Philippinengraben[M]
Fossa[F] delle Filippine[F]
fosa[F] de las Filipinas[F]

Java Trench
fosse[F] de Java
Javagraben[M]
Fossa[F] di Giava[F]
fosa[F] de Java

Kermadec-Tonga Trench
fosse[F] des Tonga[F]-Kermadec
Kermadec-Tonga[N]-Graben[M]
Fossa[F] di Kermadec-Tonga
fosa[F] de Kermadec-Tonga[M]

Australia
Australie[F]
Australien[N]
Australia[F]
Australia[F]

East Pacific Rise
dorsale[F] du Pacifique[M] Est
Ostpazifischer Rücken[M]
Dorsale[F] Pacifico-Orientale
dorsal[F] del Pacífico[M] oriental

South America
Amérique[F] du Sud[M]
Südamerika[N]
America[F] Meridionale
América[F] del Sur

Southeast Indian Ridge
dorsale[F] Sud-Est-indienne
Östlicher Indischer Rücken[M]
Dorsale[F] Sud Orientale Indiana
dorsal[F] del Índico[M] sureste

Pacific-Antarctic Ridge
dorsale[F] Pacifique[M]-Antarctique[F]
Indisch-Antarktischer Rücken[M]
Dorsale[F] Pacifico-Antartica
dorsal[F] del Pacífico-Antártico

Southwest Indian Ridge
dorsale[F] Sud-Ouest-indienne
Westlicher Indischer Rücken[M]
Dorsale[F] Sud Occidentale Indiana
dorsal[F] del Índico suroeste

Mid-Indian Ridge
dorsale[F] médio-indienne
Zentralindischer Rücken[M]
Dorsale[F] Medio-Indiana
dorsal[F] del Índico medio

Peru-Chile Trench
fosse[F] Pérou[M]-Chili[M]
Peru[N]-Chile[N]-Graben[M]
Fossa[F] Perù-Cile
fosa[M] Perú-Chile

Puerto Rico Trench
fosse[F] de Porto Rico
Puerto-Rico[N]-Graben[M]
Fossa[F] di Puerto Rico[M]
fosa[F] de Puerto[M] Rico

common coastal features

configuration^F du littoral^M | typische Küstenformen^F | caratteristiche^F della costa^F | configuración^F del litoral^M

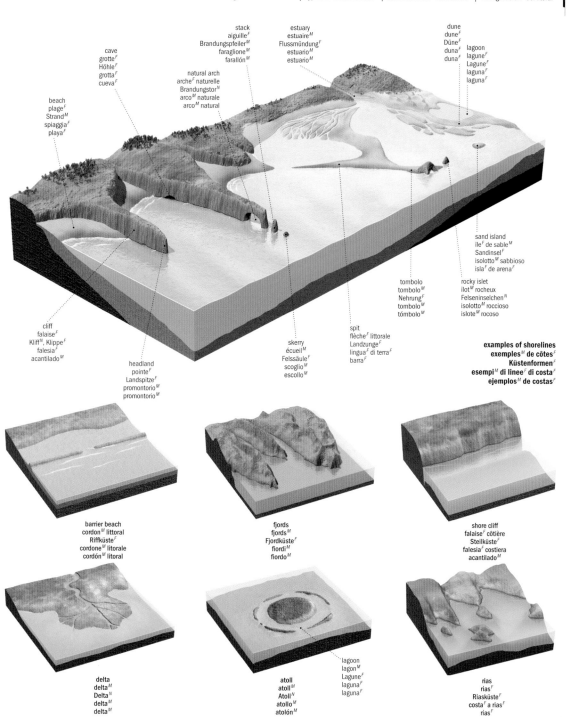

stack
aiguille^F
Brandungspfeiler^M
faraglione^M
farallón^M

estuary
estuaire^M
Flussmündung^F
estuario^M
estuario^M

dune
dune^F
Düne^F
duna^F
duna^F

lagoon
lagune^F
Laguna^F
laguna^F
laguna^F

cave
grotte^F
Höhle^F
grotta^F
cueva^F

natural arch
arche^F naturelle
Brandungstor^N
arco^M naturale
arco^M natural

beach
plage^F
Strand^M
spiaggia^F
playa^F

sand island
île^F de sable^M
Sandinsel^F
isolotto^M sabbioso
isla^F de arena^F

rocky islet
îlot^M rocheux
Felseninselchen^N
isolotto^M roccioso
islote^M rocoso

tombolo
tombolo^M
Nehrung^F
tombolo^M
tómbolo^M

cliff
falaise^F
Kliff^N, Klippe^F
falesia^F
acantilado^M

headland
pointe^F
Landspitze^F
promontorio^M
promontorio^M

skerry
écueil^M
Felssäule^F
scoglio^M
escollo^M

spit
flèche^F littorale
Landzunge^F
lingua^F di terra^F
barra^F

examples of shorelines
exemples^M de côtes^F
Küstenformen^F
esempi^M di linee^F di costa^F
ejemplos^M de costas^F

barrier beach
cordon^M littoral
Riffküste^F
cordone^M litorale
cordón^M litoral

fjords
fjords^M
Fjordküste^F
fiordi^M
fiordo^M

shore cliff
falaise^F côtière
Steilküste^F
falesia^F costiera
acantilado^M

delta
delta^M
Delta^N
delta^M
delta^M

atoll
atoll^M
Atoll^N
atollo^M
atolón^M

lagoon
lagon^M
Lagune^F
laguna^F
laguna^F

rias
rias^F
Riasküste^F
costa^F a rias^F
rias^F

desert

désert[M] | Wüste[F] | deserto[M] | desierto[M]

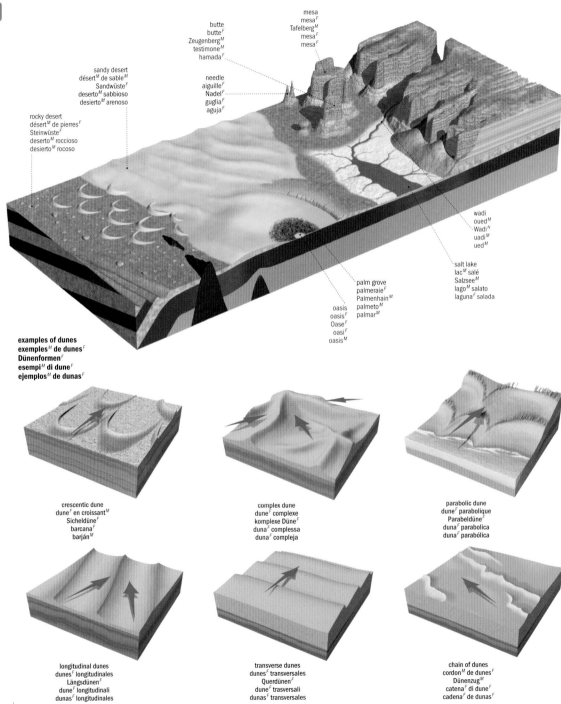

mesa
mesa[F]
Tafelberg[M]
mesa[F]
mesa[F]

butte
butte[F]
Zeugenberg[M]
testimone[M]
hamada[F]

sandy desert
désert[M] de sable[M]
Sandwüste[F]
deserto[M] sabbioso
desierto[M] arenoso

needle
aiguille[F]
Nadel[F]
guglia[F]
aguja[F]

rocky desert
désert[M] de pierres[F]
Steinwüste[F]
deserto[M] roccioso
desierto[M] rocoso

wadi
oued[M]
Wadi[N]
uadi[M]
ued[M]

salt lake
lac[M] salé
Salzsee[M]
lago[M] salato
laguna[F] salada

palm grove
palmeraie[F]
Palmenhain[M]
palmeto[M]
palmar[M]

oasis
oasis[F]
Oase[F]
oasi[F]
oasis[M]

examples of dunes
exemples[M] de dunes[F]
Dünenformen[F]
esempi[M] di dune[F]
ejemplos[M] de dunas[F]

crescentic dune
dune[F] en croissant[M]
Sicheldüne[F]
barcana[F]
barján[M]

complex dune
dune[F] complexe
komplexe Düne[F]
duna[F] complessa
duna[F] compleja

parabolic dune
dune[F] parabolique
Parabeldüne[F]
duna[F] parabolica
duna[F] parabólica

longitudinal dunes
dunes[F] longitudinales
Längsdünen[F]
dune[F] longitudinali
dunas[F] longitudinales

transverse dunes
dunes[F] transversales
Querdünen[F]
dune[F] trasversali
dunas[F] transversales

chain of dunes
cordon[M] de dunes[F]
Dünenzug[M]
catena[F] di dune[F]
cadena[F] de dunas[F]

profile of the Earth's atmosphere

coupe^F de l'atmosphère^F terrestre | Erdatmosphäre^F im Querschnitt^M | profilo^M dell'atmosfera^F terrestre | corte^M de la atmósfera^F terrestre

EARTH

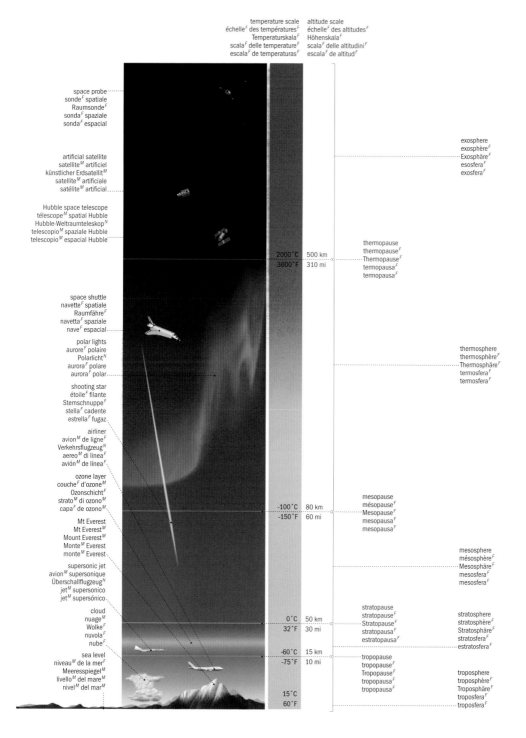

temperature scale
échelle^F des températures^F
Temperaturskala^F
scala^F delle temperature^F
escala^F de temperaturas^F

altitude scale
échelle^F des altitudes^F
Höhenskala^F
scala^F delle altitudini^F
escala^F de altitud^F

space probe
sonde^F spatiale
Raumsonde^F
sonda^F spaziale
sonda^F espacial

artificial satellite
satellite^M artificiel
künstlicher Erdsatellit^M
satellite^M artificiale
satélite^M artificial

Hubble space telescope
télescope^M spatial Hubble
Hubble-Weltraumteleskop^N
telescopio^M spaziale Hubble
telescopio^M espacial Hubble

space shuttle
navette^F spatiale
Raumfähre^F
navetta^F spaziale
nave^F espacial

polar lights
aurore^F polaire
Polarlicht^N
aurora^F polare
aurora^F polar

shooting star
étoile^F filante
Sternschnuppe^F
stella^F cadente
estrella^F fugaz

airliner
avion^M de ligne^F
Verkehrsflugzeug^N
aereo^M di linea^F
avión^M de línea^F

ozone layer
couche^F d'ozone^M
Ozonschicht^F
strato^M di ozono^M
capa^F de ozono^M

Mt Everest
Mt Everest^M
Mount Everest^M
Monte^M Everest
monte^M Everest

supersonic jet
avion^M supersonique
Überschallflugzeug^N
jet^M supersonico
jet^M supersónico

cloud
nuage^M
Wolke^F
nuvola^F
nube^F

sea level
niveau^M de la mer^F
Meeresspiegel^M
livello^M del mare^M
nivel^M del mar^M

2000˚C   500 km
3600˚F   310 mi

-100˚C   80 km
-150˚F   60 mi

0˚C   50 km
32˚F   30 mi

-60˚C   15 km
-75˚F   10 mi

15˚C
60˚F

exosphere
exosphère^F
Exosphäre^F
esosfera^F
exosfera^F

thermopause
thermopause^F
Thermopause^F
termopausa^F
termopausa^F

thermosphere
thermosphère^F
Thermosphäre^F
termosfera^F
termosfera^F

mesopause
mésopause^F
Mesopause^F
mesopausa^F
mesopausa^F

mesosphere
mésosphère^F
Mesosphäre^F
mesosfera^F
mesosfera^F

stratopause
stratopause^F
Stratopause^F
stratopausa^F
estratopausa^F

stratosphere
stratosphère^F
Stratosphäre^F
stratosfera^F
estratosfera^F

tropopause
tropopause^F
Tropopause^F
tropopausa^F
tropopausa^F

troposphere
troposphère^F
Troposphäre^F
troposfera^F
troposfera^F

EARTH

seasons of the year

cycle^M des saisons^F | Jahreszeiten^F | stagioni^F dell'anno^M | estaciones^F del año^M

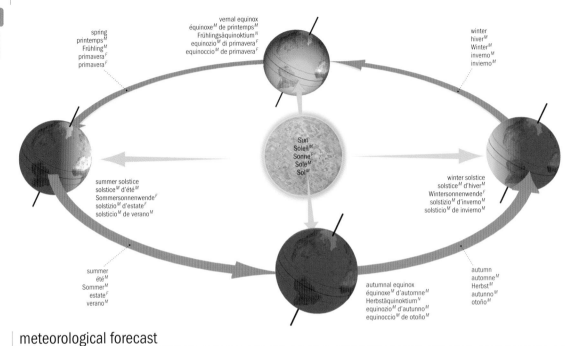

spring
printemps^M
Frühling^M
primavera^F
primavera^F

vernal equinox
équinoxe^M de printemps^M
Frühlingsäquinoktium^N
equinozio^M di primavera^F
equinoccio^M de primavera^F

winter
hiver^M
Winter^M
inverno^M
invierno^M

Sun
Soleil^M
Sonne^F
Sole^M
Sol^M

summer solstice
solstice^M d'été^M
Sommersonnenwende^F
solstizio^M d'estate^F
solsticio^M de verano^M

winter solstice
solstice^M d'hiver^M
Wintersonnenwende^F
solstizio^M d'inverno^M
solsticio^M de invierno^M

summer
été^M
Sommer^M
estate^F
verano^M

autumn
automne^M
Herbst^M
autunno^M
otoño^M

autumnal equinox
équinoxe^M d'automne^M
Herbstäquinoktium^N
equinozio^M d'autunno^M
equinoccio^M de otoño^M

meteorological forecast

prévisions^F météorologiques | Wettervorhersage^F | previsioni^F meteorologiche | previsión^F meteorológica

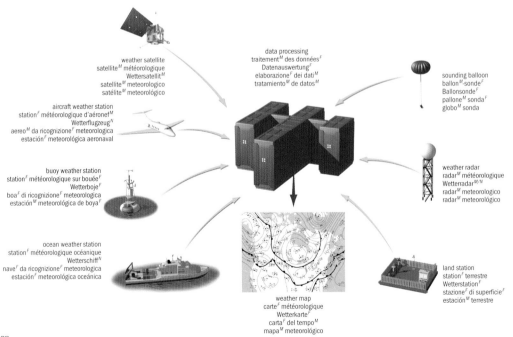

weather satellite
satellite^M météorologique
Wettersatellit^M
satellite^M meteorologico
satélite^M meteorológico

data processing
traitement^M des données^F
Datenauswertung^F
elaborazione^F dei dati^M
tratamiento^M de datos^M

sounding balloon
ballon^M-sonde^F
Ballonsonde^F
pallone^M sonda^F
globo^M sonda

aircraft weather station
station^F météorologique d'aéronef^M
Wetterflugzeug^N
aereo^M da ricognizione^F meteorologica
estación^F meteorológica aeronaval

buoy weather station
station^F météorologique sur bouée^F
Wetterboje^F
boa^F di ricognizione^F meteorologica
estación^M meteorológica de boya^F

weather radar
radar^M météorologique
Wetterradar^M/N
radar^M meteorologico
radar^M meteorológico

ocean weather station
station^F météorologique océanique
Wetterschiff^N
nave^F da ricognizione^F meteorologica
estación^F meteorológica oceánica

land station
station^F terrestre
Wetterstation^F
stazione^F di superficie^F
estación^F terrestre

weather map
carte^F météorologique
Wetterkarte^F
carta^F del tempo^M
mapa^M meteorológico

weather map

carte^F météorologique | Wetterkarte^F | carta^F del tempo^M | mapa^M meteorológico

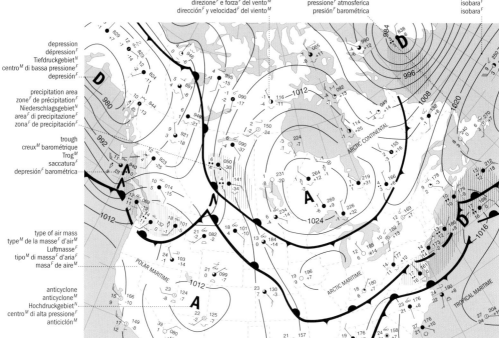

wind direction and speed
direction^F et force^F du vent^M
Windrichtung^F und Windgeschwindigkeit^F
direzione^F e forza^F del vento^M
dirección^F y velocidad^F del viento^M

barometric pressure
pression^F barométrique
Luftdruck^M
pressione^F atmosferica
presión^F barométrica

isobar
isobare^F
Isobare^F
isobara^F
isobara^F

depression
dépression^F
Tiefdruckgebiet^N
centro^M di bassa pressione^F
depresión^F

precipitation area
zone^F de précipitation^F
Niederschlagsgebiet^N
area^F di precipitazione^F
zona^F de precipitación^F

trough
creux^M barométrique
Trog^M
saccatura^F
depresión^F barométrica

type of air mass
type^M de la masse^F d'air^M
Luftmasse^F
tipo^M di massa^F d'aria^F
masa^F de aire^M

anticyclone
anticyclone^M
Hochdruckgebiet^N
centro^M di alta pressione^F
anticiclón^M

station model

disposition^F des informations^F d'une station^F | Stationsmodell^N | modello^M di stazione^F | modelo^M de estación^F

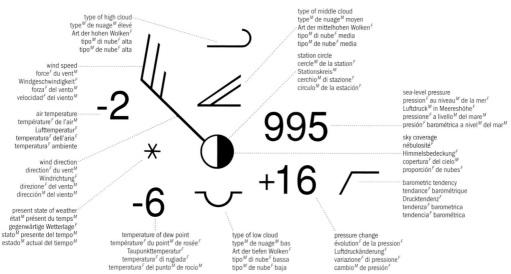

type of high cloud
type^M de nuage^M élevé
Art der hohen Wolken^F
tipo^M di nube^F alta
tipo^M de nube^F alta

type of middle cloud
type^M de nuage^M moyen
Art der mittelhohen Wolken^F
tipo^M di nube^F media
tipo^M de nube^F media

station circle
cercle^M de la station^F
Stationskreis^M
cerchio^M di stazione^F
círculo^M de la estación^F

wind speed
force^F du vent^M
Windgeschwindigkeit^F
forza^F del vento^M
velocidad^F del viento^M

air temperature
température^F de l'air^M
Lufttemperatur^F
temperatura^F dell'aria^F
temperatura^F ambiente

wind direction
direction^F du vent^M
Windrichtung^F
direzione^F del vento^M
dirección^M del viento^M

present state of weather
état^M présent du temps^M
gegenwärtige Wetterlage^F
stato^M presente del tempo^M
estado^M actual del tiempo^M

sea-level pressure
pression^F au niveau^M de la mer^F
Luftdruck^M in Meereshöhe^F
pressione^F a livello^M del mare^M
presión^F barométrica a nivel^M del mar^M

sky coverage
nébulosité^F
Himmelsbedeckung^F
copertura^F del cielo^M
proporción^F de nubes^F

barometric tendency
tendance^F barométrique
Drucktendenz^F
tendenza^F barometrica
tendencia^F barométrica

temperature of dew point
température^F du point^M de rosée^F
Taupunkttemperatur^F
temperatura^F di rugiada^F
temperatura^F del punto^M de rocío^M

type of low cloud
type^M de nuage^M bas
Art der tiefen Wolken^F
tipo^M di nube^F bassa
tipo^M de nube^F baja

pressure change
évolution^F de la pression^F
Luftdruckänderung^F
variazione^F di pressione^F
cambio^M de presión^F

climates of the world

climats^M du monde^M | Klimate^N der Welt^F | climi^M del mondo^M | climas^M del mundo^M

tropical climates
climats^M tropicaux
tropische Klimate^N
climi^M tropicali
climas^M tropicales

tropical rain forest
tropical humide
tropischer Regenwald^M
tropicale della foresta^F pluviale
tropical^M lluvioso

tropical wet-and-dry (savanna)
tropical humide et sec (savane^F)
tropisch feucht und trocken (Savanne^F)
tropicale umido e secco (savana^F)
tropical^M húmedo y seco (sabana^F)

dry climates
climats^M arides
Trockenklimate^N
climi^M aridi
climas^M áridos

steppe
steppe^F
Steppe^F
steppico
estepario

desert
désert^M
Wüste^F
desertico
desértico

cold temperate climates
climats^M tempérés froids
kaltgemäßigte Klimate^N
climi^M temperati freddi
climas^M templados fríos

humid continental - hot summer
continental humide, à été^M chaud
feucht-kontinental - heißer Sommer^M
continentale umido - estate^F torrida
continental^M húmedo - verano^M tórrido

humid continental - warm summer
continental humide, à été^M frais
feucht-kontinental - warmer Sommer^M
continentale umido - estate^F calda
continental^M húmedo - verano^M fresco

subarctic
subarctique
subarktisch
subartico
subártico

warm temperate climates
climats^M tempérés chauds
warmgemäßigte Klimate^N
climi^M temperati caldi
climas^M templados cálidos

humid subtropical
subtropical humide
feuchte Subtropen
subtropicale umido
subtropical húmedo

Mediterranean subtropical
méditerranéen
mediterrane Subtropen
subtropicale mediterraneo
subtropical mediterráneo

marine
océanique
maritim
marino
maritimo

polar climates
climats^M polaires
Polarklimate^N
climi^M polari
climas^M polares

polar tundra
toundra^F
Polartundra^F
della tundra^F polare
tundra^F

polar ice cap
calotte^F glaciaire
Eiskappe^F
della calotta^F polare
hielos^M perpetuos

highland climates
climats^M de montagne^F
Hochlandklimate^N
climi^M di montagna^F
climas^M de alta montaña^F

highland
climats^M de montagne^F
Hochgebirge^N
di montagna^F
climas^M de montaña^F

precipitations

précipitations[F] | Niederschläge[M] | precipitazioni[F] | precipitaciones[F]

EARTH

warm air air[M] chaud warme Luft[F] aria[F] calda aire[M] caliente	cold air air[M] froid kalte Luft[F] aria[F] fredda aire[M] frío

winter precipitations
précipitations[F] hivernales
Winterniederschläge[M]
precipitazioni[F] invernali
precipitaciones[F] invernales

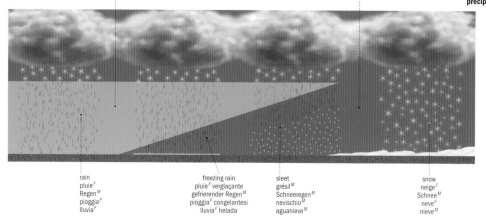

rain pluie[F] Regen[M] pioggia[F] lluvia[F]	freezing rain pluie[F] verglaçante gefrierender Regen[M] pioggia[F] congelantesi lluvia[F] helada	sleet grésil[M] Schneeregen[M] nevischio[M] aguanieve[M]	snow neige[F] Schnee[M] neve[F] nieve[M]

stormy sky
ciel[M] d'orage[M]
stürmischer Himmel[M]
cielo[M] tempestoso
cielo[M] turbulento

cloud
nuage[M]
Wolke[F]
nube[F]
nube[F]

lightning
éclair[M]
Blitz[M]
fulmine[M]
rayo[M]

rainbow
arc-en-ciel[M]
Regenbogen[M]
arcobaleno[M]
arco[M] iris

rain
pluie[F]
Regen[M]
pioggia[F]
lluvia[F]

dew
rosée[F]
Tau[M]
rugiada[F]
rocío[M]

rime
givre[M]
Reif[M]
brina[F]
escarcha[F]

mist
brume[F]
Dunst[M]
foschia[F]
neblina[F]

glazed frost
verglas[M]
Raureif[M]
vetrone[M]
hielo[M]

fog
brouillard[M]
Nebel[M]
nebbia[F]
niebla[F]

clouds

nuages^M | Wolken^F | nuvole^F | nubes^F

EARTH

high clouds
nuages^M de haute altitude^F
hohe Wolken^F
nubi^F alte
nubes^F altas

cirrostratus
cirro-stratus^M
Zirrostratus^M
cirrostrato^M
cirrostratos^M

cirrocumulus
cirro-cumulus^M
Zirrokumulus^M
cirrocumulo^M
cirrocúmulos^M

cirrus
cirrus^M
Zirrus^M
cirro^M
cirros^M

middle clouds
nuages^M de moyenne altitude^F
mittelhohe Wolken^F
nubi^F medie
nubes^F medias

altostratus
alto-stratus^M
Altostratus^M
altostrato^M
altostratos^M

altocumulus
alto-cumulus^M
Altokumulus^M
altocumulo^M
altocúmulos^M

low clouds
nuages^M de basse altitude^F
tiefe Wolken^F
nubi^F basse
nubes^F bajas

stratocumulus
strato-cumulus^M
Stratokumulus^M
stratocumulo^M
estratocúmulos^M

nimbostratus
nimbo-stratus^M
Nimbostratus^M
nembostrato^M
nimbostratos^M

cumulus
cumulus^M
Kumulus^M
cumulo^M
cúmulos^M

stratus
stratus^M
Stratus^M
strato^M
estratos^M

clouds with vertical development
nuages^M à développement^M vertical
Quellwolken^F
nubi^F a sviluppo^M verticale
nubes^F de desarrollo^M vertical

cumulonimbus
cumulo-nimbus^M
Kumulonimbus^M
cumulonembo^M
cumulonimbos^M

tornado and waterspout

tornade^F et trombe^F marine | Tornado^M und Wasserhose^F | tornado^M e tromba^F marina | tornado^M y tromba^F marina

wall cloud
mur^M de nuages^M
Gewitterwolken^F
parete^F di nuvole^F
muro^M de nubes^F

funnel cloud
nuage^M en entonnoir^M
Wolkentrichter^M
nube^F a proboscide^F
nube^F en forma^F de embudo^M

debris
buisson^M
aufgewirbelter Staub^M
detriti^M
detritos^M

waterspout
trombe^F marine
Wasserhose^F
tromba^F marina
tromba^F marina

tornado
tornade^F
Tornado^M
tornado^M
tornado^M

tropical cyclone

cyclone^M tropical | tropischer Wirbelsturm^M | ciclone^M tropicale | ciclón^M tropical

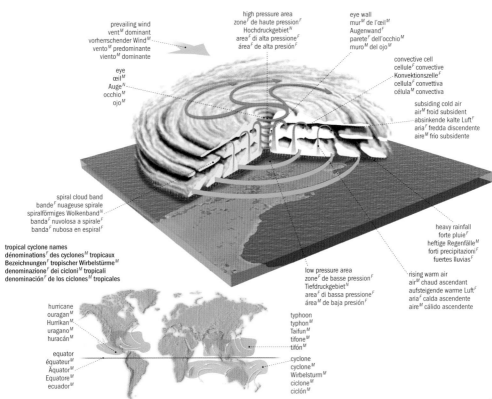

prevailing wind
vent^M dominant
vorherrschender Wind^M
vento^M predominante
viento^M dominante

high pressure area
zone^F de haute pression^F
Hochdruckgebiet^N
area^F di alta pressione^F
área^F de alta presión^F

eye wall
mur^M de l'œil^M
Augenwand^F
parete^F dell'occhio^M
muro^M del ojo^M

convective cell
cellule^F convective
Konvektionszelle^F
cellula^F convettiva
célula^M convectiva

eye
œil^M
Auge^N
occhio^M
ojo^M

subsiding cold air
air^M froid subsident
absinkende kalte Luft^F
aria^F fredda discendente
aire^M frío subsidente

spiral cloud band
bande^F nuageuse spirale
spiralförmiges Wolkenband^N
banda^F nuvolosa a spirale^F
banda^F nubosa en espiral^F

heavy rainfall
forte pluie^F
heftige Regenfälle^M
forti precipitazioni^F
fuertes lluvias^F

tropical cyclone names
dénominations^F des cyclones^M tropicaux
Bezeichnungen^F tropischer Wirbelstürme^M
denominazione^F dei cicloni^M tropicali
denominación^F de los ciclones^M tropicales

low pressure area
zone^F de basse pression^F
Tiefdruckgebiet^N
area^F di bassa pressione^F
área^F de baja presión^F

rising warm air
air^M chaud ascendant
aufsteigende warme Luft^F
aria^F calda ascendente
aire^M cálido ascendente

hurricane
ouragan^M
Hurrikan^M
uragano^M
huracán^M

typhoon
typhon^M
Taifun^M
tifone^M
tifón^M

equator
équateur^M
Äquator^M
Equatore^M
ecuador^M

cyclone
cyclone^M
Wirbelsturm^M
ciclone^M
ciclón^M

vegetation and biosphere

végétation^F et biosphère^F | Vegetation^F und Biosphäre^F | vegetazione^F e biosfera^F | vegetación^F y biosfera^F

EARTH

vegetation regions
distribution^F de la végétation^F
Vegetationszonen^F
distribuzione^F della vegetazione^F
distribución^F de la vegetación^F

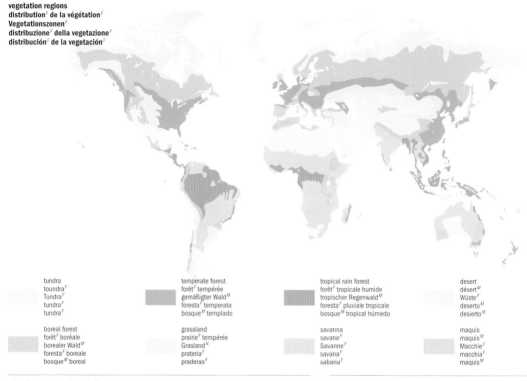

tundra
toundra^F
Tundra^F
tundra^F
tundra^F

boreal forest
forêt^F boréale
borealer Wald^M
foresta^F boreale
bosque^M boreal

temperate forest
forêt^F tempérée
gemäßigter Wald^M
foresta^F temperata
bosque^M templado

grassland
prairie^F tempérée
Grasland^N
prateria^F
praderas^F

tropical rain forest
forêt^F tropicale humide
tropischer Regenwald^M
foresta^F pluviale tropicale
bosque^M tropical húmedo

savanna
savane^F
Savanne^F
savana^F
sabana^F

desert
désert^M
Wüste^F
deserto^M
desierto^M

maquis
maquis^M
Macchie^F
macchia^F
maquis^M

elevation zones and vegetation
paysage^M végétal selon l'altitude^F
Vegetationsbild^N nach Höhenlagen^F
altitudine^F e vegetazione^F
altitud^F y vegetación^F

glacier
glacier^M
Gletscher^M
ghiacciaio^M
glaciar^M

tundra
toundra^F
Tundra^F
tundra^F
tundra^F

coniferous forest
forêt^F de conifères^M
Nadelwald^M
foresta^F di conifere^F
bosque^M de coníferas^F

mixed forest
forêt^F mixte
Mischwald^M
foresta^F mista
bosque^M mixto

deciduous forest
forêt^F de feuillus^M
Laubwald^M
foresta^F di caducifoglie^F
bosque^M de hoja^F caduca

tropical forest
forêt^F tropicale
Tropenwald^M
foresta^F tropicale
bosque^M tropical

structure of the biosphere
structure^F de la biosphère^F
Aufbau^M der Biosphäre^F
struttura^F della biosfera^F
estructura^F de la biosfera^F

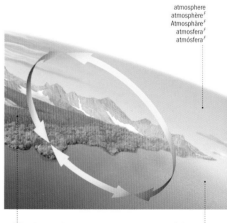

atmosphere
atmosphère^F
Atmosphäre^F
atmosfera^F
atmósfera^F

lithosphere
lithosphère^F
Lithosphäre^F
litosfera^F
litosfera^F

hydrosphere
hydrosphère^F
Hydrosphäre^F
idrosfera^F
hidrosfera^F

food chain

chaîne^F alimentaire | Nahrungskette^F | catena^F alimentare | cadena^F alimentaria

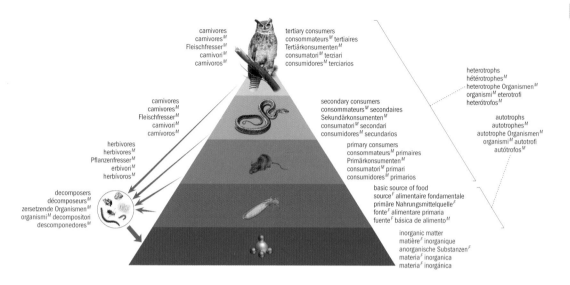

carnivores
carnivores^M
Fleischfresser^M
carnivori^M
carnívoros^M

tertiary consumers
consommateurs^M tertiaires
Tertiärkonsumenten^M
consumatori^M terziari
consumidores^M terciarios

heterotrophs
hétérotrophes^M
heterotrophe Organismen^M
organismi^M eterotrofi
heterótrofos^M

carnivores
carnivores^M
Fleischfresser^M
carnivori^M
carnívoros^M

secondary consumers
consommateurs^M secondaires
Sekundärkonsumenten^M
consumatori^M secondari
consumidores^M secundarios

autotrophs
autotrophes^M
autotrophe Organismen^M
organismi^M autotrofi
autótrofos^M

herbivores
herbivores^M
Pflanzenfresser^M
erbivori^M
herbívoros^M

primary consumers
consommateurs^M primaires
Primärkonsumenten^M
consumatori^M primari
consumidores^M primarios

decomposers
décomposeurs^M
zersetzende Organismen^M
organismi^M decompositori
descomponedores^M

basic source of food
source^F alimentaire fondamentale
primäre Nahrungsmittelquelle^F
fonte^F alimentare primaria
fuente^F básica de alimento^M

inorganic matter
matière^F inorganique
anorganische Substanzen^F
materia^F inorganica
materia^F inorgánica

hydrologic cycle

cycle^M de l'eau^F | Wasserkreislauf^M | ciclo^M idrologico | ciclo^M hidrológico

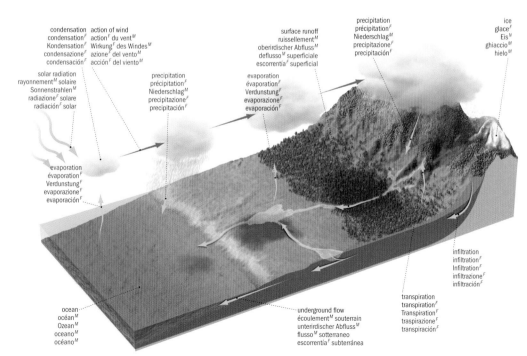

condensation
condensation^F
Kondensation^F
condensazione^F
condensación^F

action of wind
action^F du vent^M
Wirkung^F des Windes^M
azione^F del vento^M
acción^F del viento^M

surface runoff
ruissellement^M
oberirdischer Abfluss^M
deflusso^M superficiale
escorrentía^F superficial

precipitation
précipitation^F
Niederschlag^M
precipitazione^F
precipitación^F

ice
glace^F
Eis^N
ghiaccio^M
hielo^M

solar radiation
rayonnement^M solaire
Sonnenstrahlen^M
radiazione^F solare
radiación^F solar

precipitation
précipitation^F
Niederschlag^M
precipitazione^F
precipitación^F

evaporation
évaporation^F
Verdunstung^F
evaporazione^F
evaporación^F

evaporation
évaporation^F
Verdunstung^F
evaporazione^F
evaporación^F

infiltration
infiltration^F
Infiltration^F
infiltrazione^F
infiltración^F

ocean
océan^M
Ozean^M
oceano^M
océano^M

underground flow
écoulement^M souterrain
unterirdischer Abfluss^M
flusso^M sotterraneo
escorrentía^F subterránea

transpiration
transpiration^F
Transpiration^F
traspirazione^F
transpiración^F

45

greenhouse effect

effet^M de serre^F | Treibhauseffekt^M | effetto^M serra^F | efecto^M invernadero

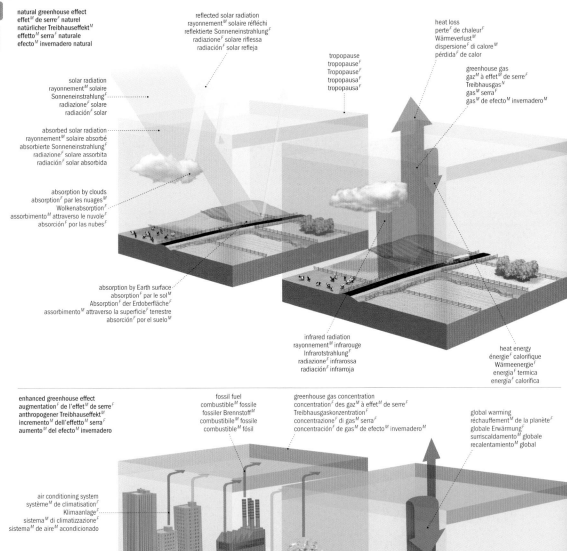

natural greenhouse effect
effet^M de serre^F naturel
natürlicher Treibhauseffekt^M
effetto^M serra^F naturale
efecto^M invernadero natural

reflected solar radiation
rayonnement^M solaire réfléchi
reflektierte Sonneneinstrahlung^F
radiazione^F solare riflessa
radiación^F solar refleja

heat loss
perte^F de chaleur^F
Wärmeverlust^M
dispersione^F di calore^M
pérdida^F de calor

tropopause
tropopause^F
Tropopause^F
tropopausa^F
tropopausa^F

greenhouse gas
gaz^M à effet^M de serre^F
Treibhausgas^N
gas^M serra^F
gas^M de efecto^M invernadero^M

solar radiation
rayonnement^M solaire
Sonneneinstrahlung^F
radiazione^F solare
radiación^F solar

absorbed solar radiation
rayonnement^M solaire absorbé
absorbierte Sonneneinstrahlung^F
radiazione^F solare assorbita
radiación^F solar absorbida

absorption by clouds
absorption^F par les nuages^M
Wolkenabsorption^F
assorbimento^M attraverso le nuvole^F
absorción^F por las nubes^F

absorption by Earth surface
absorption^F par le sol^M
Absorption^F der Erdoberfläche^F
assorbimento^M attraverso la superficie^F terrestre
absorción^F por el suelo^M

infrared radiation
rayonnement^M infrarouge
Infrarotstrahlung^F
radiazione^F infrarossa
radiación^F infrarroja

heat energy
énergie^F calorifique
Wärmeenergie^F
energia^F termica
energía^F calorífica

enhanced greenhouse effect
augmentation^F de l'effet^M de serre^F
anthropogener Treibhauseffekt^M
incremento^M dell'effetto^M serra^F
aumento^M del efecto^M invernadero

fossil fuel
combustible^M fossile
fossiler Brennstoff^M
combustibile^M fossile
combustible^M fósil

greenhouse gas concentration
concentration^F des gaz^M à effet^M de serre^F
Treibhausgaskonzentration^F
concentrazione^F di gas^M serra^F
concentración^F de gas^M de efecto^M invernadero

global warming
réchauffement^M de la planète^F
globale Erwärmung^F
surriscaldamento^M globale
recalentamiento^M global

air conditioning system
système^M de climatisation^F
Klimaanlage^F
sistema^M di climatizzazione^F
sistema^M de aire^M acondicionado

intensive husbandry
élevage^M intensif
intensive Kultur^F
allevamento^M intensivo
ganadería^F intensiva

intensive farming
agriculture^F intensive
intensive Landwirtschaft^F
agricoltura^F intensiva
agricultura^F intensiva

air pollution

pollution^F de l'air^M | Luftverschmutzung^F | inquinamento^M dell'aria^F | contaminación^F del aire^M

air pollutants
polluants^M atmosphériques
Luftschadstoffe^M
inquinanti^M atmosferici
contaminantes^M del aire^M

smog
smog^M
Smog^M
smog^M
smog^M/niebla^F tóxica

wind
vent^M
Wind^M
vento^M
viento^M

polluting gas emission
émission^F de gaz^M polluants
Emission^F schädlicher Gase^N
emissione^F di gas^M inquinanti
emisión^F de gases^M contaminantes

authorized landfill site
site^M d'enfouissement^M
Mülldeponie^F
discarica^F autorizzata
vertedero^M autorizado

acid rain
pluies^F acides
saurer Regen^M
piogge^F acide
lluvia^F ácida

forest fire
incendie^M de forêt^F
Waldbrand^M
incendio^M delle foreste^F
incendio^M forestal

industrial waste
rejets^M industriels
Industrieabfälle^M
rifiuti^M industriali
residuos^M industriales

motor vehicle pollution
pollution^F automobile
Verschmutzung^F durch Autoabgase^N
inquinamento^M da gas^M di scarico^M delle automobili^F
contaminación^F de automóviles^M

deforestation
déforestation^F
Entwaldung^F
deforestazione^F
deforestación^F

paddy field
rizière^F
Reisfeld^N
risaia^F
arrozal^M

soil fertilization
fertilisation^F des sols^M
Bodendüngung^F
fertilizzazione^F del suolo^M
fertilización^F del suelo^M

intensive husbandry
élevage^M intensif
intensive Kultur^F
allevamento^M intensivo
ganadería^F intensiva

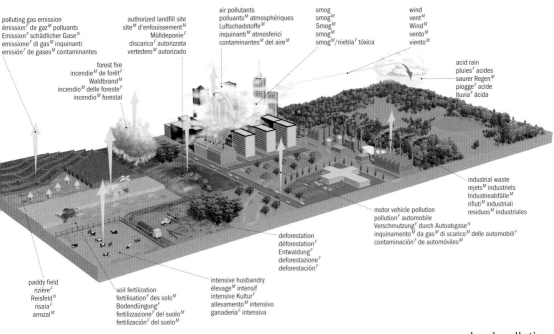

land pollution

pollution^F du sol^M | Bodenverschmutzung^F | inquinamento^M del suolo^M | contaminación^F del suelo^M

industrial pollution
pollution^F industrielle
industrielle Verschmutzung^F
inquinamento^M industriale
contaminación^F industrial

non-biodegradable pollutants
polluants^M non biodégradables
biologisch nicht abbaubare Schadstoffe^M
inquinanti^M non biodegradabili
contaminantes^M no biodegradables

intensive husbandry
élevage^M intensif
intensive Kultur^F
allevamento^M intensivo
ganadería^F intensiva

domestic pollution
pollution^F domestique
Verschmutzung^F durch Haushalte^M
inquinamento^M domestico
contaminación^F doméstica

agricultural pollution
pollution^F agricole
landwirtschaftliche Verschmutzung^F
inquinamento^M agricolo
contaminación^F agrícola

industrial waste
déchets^M industriels
Industrieabfälle^M
rifiuti^M industriali
residuos^M industriales

fertilizer application
épandage^M d'engrais^M
Einsatz^M von Düngemitteln^N
distribuzione^F del fertilizzante^M
esparcimiento^M de fertilizante^M

household waste
ordures^F ménagères
Hausmüll^M
rifiuti^M domestici
residuos^M domésticos

authorized landfill site
site^M d'enfouissement^M
Mülldeponie^F
discarica^F autorizzata
vertedero^M autorizado

herbicide
herbicide^F
Herbizid^N
erbicida^M
herbicida^M

waste layers
couches^F de déchets^M
Müllschichten^F
strati^M di rifiuti^M
capas^F de residuos^M

intrusive filtration
infiltration^F
Infiltration^F
infiltrazione^F
infiltración^F

fungicide
fongicide^F
Fungizid^N
fungicida^M
funguicida^M

pesticide
pesticide^M
Pestizid^N
pesticida^M
pesticida^M

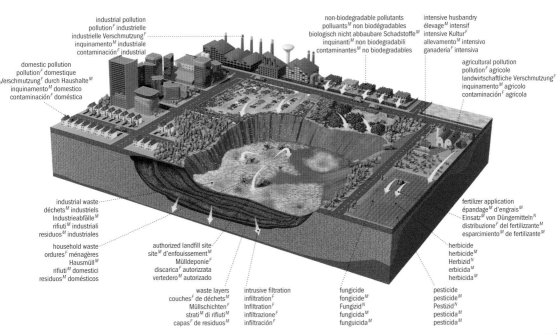

water pollution

pollution^F de l'eau^F | Wasserverschmutzung^F | inquinamento^M dell'acqua^F | contaminación^F del agua^F

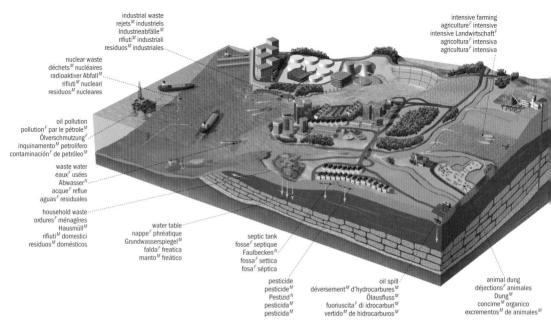

industrial waste
rejets^M industriels
Industrieabfälle^M
rifiuti^M industriali
residuos^M industriales

intensive farming
agriculture^F intensive
intensive Landwirtschaft^F
agricoltura^F intensiva
agricultura^F intensiva

nuclear waste
déchets^M nucléaires
radioaktiver Abfall^M
rifiuti^M nucleari
residuos^M nucleares

oil pollution
pollution^F par le pétrole^M
Ölverschmutzung^F
inquinamento^M petrolifero
contaminación^F de petróleo^M

waste water
eaux^F usées
Abwasser^N
acque^F reflue
aguas^F residuales

household waste
ordures^F ménagères
Hausmüll^M
rifiuti^M domestici
residuos^M domésticos

water table
nappe^F phréatique
Grundwasserspiegel^M
falda^F freatica
manto^M freático

septic tank
fosse^F septique
Faulbecken^N
fossa^F settica
fosa^F séptica

pesticide
pesticide^M
Pestizid^N
pesticida^M
pesticida^M

oil spill
déversement^M d'hydrocarbures^M
Ölausfluss^M
fuoriuscita^F di idrocarburi^M
vertido^M de hidrocarburos^M

animal dung
déjections^F animales
Dung^M
concime^M organico
excrementos^M de animales^M

acid rain

pluies^F acides | saurer Regen^M | piogge^F acide | lluvia^F ácida

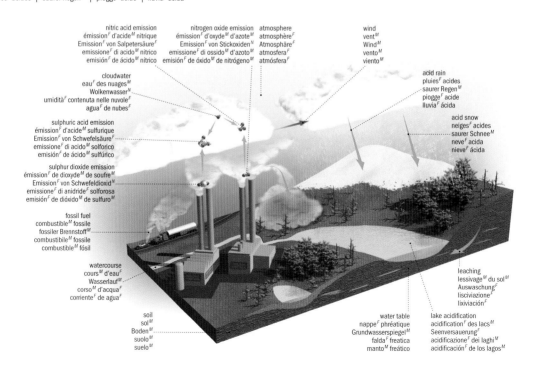

nitric acid emission
émission^F d'acide^M nitrique
Emission^F von Salpetersäure^F
emissione^F di acido^M nitrico
emisión^F de ácido^M nítrico

nitrogen oxide emission
émission^F d'oxyde^M d'azote^M
Emission^F von Stickoxiden^N
emissione^F di ossido^M d'azoto^M
emisión^F de óxido^M de nitrógeno^M

atmosphere
atmosphère^F
Atmosphäre^F
atmosfera^F
atmósfera^F

wind
vent^M
Wind^M
vento^M
viento^M

cloudwater
eau^F des nuages^M
Wolkenwasser^N
umidità^F contenuta nelle nuvole^F
agua^F de nubes^F

acid rain
pluies^F acides
saurer Regen^M
piogge^F acide
lluvia^F ácida

acid snow
neiges^F acides
saurer Schnee^M
neve^F acida
nieve^F ácida

sulphuric acid emission
émission^F d'acide^M sulfurique
Emission^F von Schwefelsäure^F
emissione^F di acido^M solforico
emisión^F de ácido^M sulfúrico

sulphur dioxide emission
émission^F de dioxyde^M de soufre^M
Emission^F von Schwefeldioxid^N
emissione^F di anidride^F solforosa
emisión^F de dióxido^M de sulfuro^M

fossil fuel
combustible^M fossile
fossiler Brennstoff^M
combustibile^M fossile
combustible^M fósil

watercourse
cours^M d'eau^F
Wasserlauf^M
corso^M d'acqua^F
corriente^F de agua^F

leaching
lessivage^M du sol^M
Auswaschung^F
lisciviazione^F
lixiviación^F

soil
sol^M
Boden^M
suolo^M
suelo^M

water table
nappe^F phréatique
Grundwasserspiegel^M
falda^F freatica
manto^M freático

lake acidification
acidification^F des lacs^M
Seenversauerung^F
acidificazione^F dei laghi^M
acidificación^F de los lagos^M

selective sorting of waste

tri^M sélectif des déchets^M | Mülltrennung^F | smistamento^M selettivo dei rifiuti^M | separación^F selectiva de residuos^M

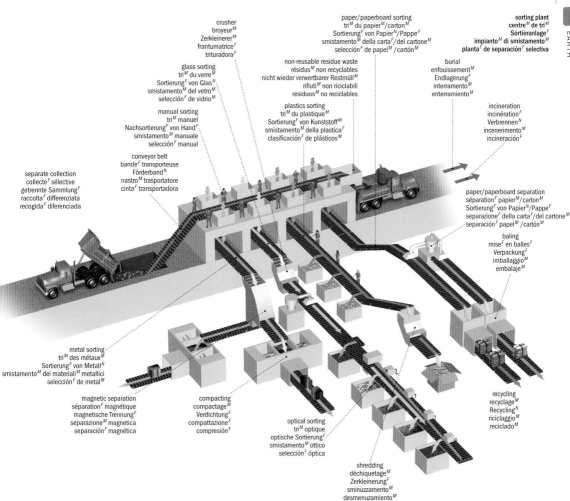

crusher
broyeur^M
Zerkleinerer^M
frantumatrice^F
trituradora^F

glass sorting
tri^M du verre^M
Sortierung^F von Glas^N
smistamento^M del vetro^M
selección^F de vidrio^M

manual sorting
tri^M manuel
Nachsortierung^F von Hand^F
smistamento^M manuale
selección^F manual

conveyor belt
bande^F transporteuse
Förderband^N
nastro^M trasportatore
cinta^F transportadora

separate collection
collecte^F sélective
getrennte Sammlung^F
raccolta^F differenziata
recogida^F diferenciada

paper/paperboard sorting
tri^M du papier^M/carton^M
Sortierung^F von Papier^N/Pappe^F
smistamento^M della carta^F/del cartone^M
selección^F de papel^M/cartón^M

non-reusable residue waste
résidus^M non recyclables
nicht wieder verwertbarer Restmüll^M
rifiuti^M non riciclabili
residuos^M no reciclables

plastics sorting
tri^M du plastique^M
Sortierung^F von Kunststoff^M
smistamento^M della plastica^F
clasificación^F de plásticos^M

sorting plant
centre^M de tri^M
Sortieranlage^F
impianto^M di smistamento^M
planta^F de separación^F selectiva

burial
enfouissement^M
Endlagerung^F
interramento^M
enterramiento^M

incineration
incinération^F
Verbrennen^N
incenerimento^M
incineración^F

paper/paperboard separation
séparation^F papier^M/carton^M
Sortierung^F von Papier^N/Pappe^F
separazione^F della carta^F/del cartone^M
separación^F papel^M/cartón^M

baling
mise^F en balles^F
Verpackung^F
imballaggio^M
embalaje^M

metal sorting
tri^M des métaux^M
Sortierung^F von Metall^N
smistamento^M dei materiali^M metallici
selección^F de metal^M

magnetic separation
séparation^F magnétique
magnetische Trennung^F
separazione^M magnetica
separación^F magnética

compacting
compactage^M
Verdichtung^F
compattazione^F
compresión^F

optical sorting
tri^M optique
optische Sortierung^F
smistamento^M ottico
selección^F óptica

shredding
déchiquetage^M
Zerkleinerung^F
sminuzzamento^M
desmenuzamiento^M

recycling
recyclage^M
Recycling^N
riciclaggio^M
reciclado^M

recycling containers
conteneurs^M de collecte^F sélective
Wertstoff^N-Sammelbehälter^M
contenitori^M per la raccolta^F
differenziata
contenedores^M de reciclaje^M

paper recycling container
conteneur^M à papier^M
Altpapier^N-Sammelbehälter^M
bidone^M carrellato per il riciclaggio^M
della carta^F
contenedor^M de reciclado^M de papel^M

glass recycling container
conteneur^M à verre^M
Altglas^N-Sammelbehälter^M
bidone^M carrellato per il riciclaggio^M del vetro^M
contenedor^M de reciclado^M de vidrio^M

aluminium recycling container
conteneur^M à boîtes^F métalliques
Altaluminium^N-Sammelbehälter^M
bidone^M carrellato per il riciclaggio^M
dell'alluminio^M
contenedor^M de reciclado^M de aluminio^M

paper collection unit
colonne^F de collecte^F du papier^M
Altpapier^N-Container^M
campana^F per la raccolta^F della carta^F
contenedor^M de recogida^F de papel^M

glass collection unit
colonne^F de collecte^F du verre^M
Altglas^N-Container^M
campana^F per la raccolta^F del vetro^M
contenedor^M de recogida^F de vidrio^M

recycling bin
bac^M de recyclage^M
Bioabfallbehälter^M
contenitore^M per il riciclaggio^M
cubo^M de basura^F reciclable

plant cell

cellule^F végétale | Pflanzenzelle^F | cellula^F vegetale | célula^F vegetal

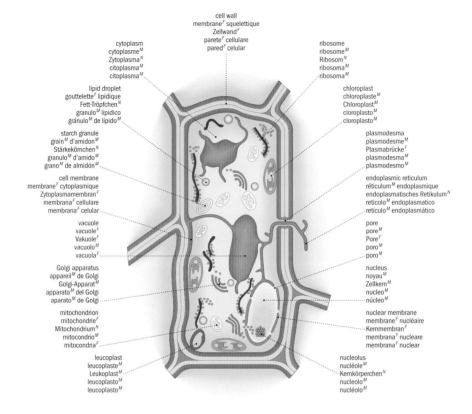

cell wall
membrane^F squelettique
Zellwand^F
parete^F cellulare
pared^F celular

cytoplasm
cytoplasme^M
Zytoplasma^N
citoplasma^M
citoplasma^M

ribosome
ribosome^M
Ribosom^N
ribosoma^M
ribosoma^M

lipid droplet
gouttelette^F lipidique
Fett-Tröpfchen^N
granulo^M lipidico
gránulo^M de lípido^M

chloroplast
chloroplaste^M
Chloroplast^M
cloroplasto^M
cloroplasto^M

starch granule
grain^M d'amidon^M
Stärkekörnchen^N
granulo^M d'amido^M
grano^M de almidón^M

plasmodesma
plasmodesme^M
Plasmabrücke^F
plasmodesma^M
plasmodesmo^M

cell membrane
membrane^F cytoplasmique
Zytoplasmamembran^F
membrana^F cellulare
membrana^F celular

endoplasmic reticulum
réticulum^M endoplasmique
endoplasmatisches Retikulum^N
reticolo^M endoplasmatico
retículo^M endoplasmático

vacuole
vacuole^F
Vakuole^F
vacuolo^M
vacuola^F

pore
pore^M
Pore^F
poro^M
poro^M

Golgi apparatus
appareil^M de Golgi
Golgi-Apparat^M
apparato^M del Golgi
aparato^M de Golgi

nucleus
noyau^M
Zellkern^M
nucleo^M
núcleo^M

mitochondrion
mitochondrie^F
Mitochondrium^N
mitocondrio^M
mitocondria^F

nuclear membrane
membrane^F nucléaire
Kernmembran^F
membrana^F nucleare
membrana^F nuclear

leucoplast
leucoplaste^M
Leukoplast^M
leucoplasto^M
leucoplasto^M

nucleolus
nucléole^M
Kernkörperchen^N
nucleolo^M
nucléolo^M

lichen

lichen^M | Flechte^F | lichene^M | liquen

structure of a lichen
structure^F d'un lichen^M
Aufbau^M einer Flechte^F
struttura^F di un lichene^M
estructura^F de un liquen^M

examples of lichens
exemples^M de lichens^M
Beispiele^N für Flechten^F
esempi^M di licheni^M
ejemplos^M de líquenes^M

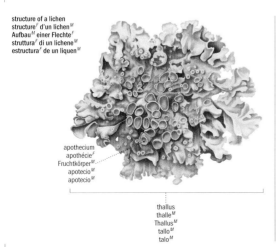

apothecium
apothécie^F
Fruchtkörper^M
apotecio^M
apotecio^M

crustose lichen
lichen^M crustacé
Krustenflechte^F
lichene^M crostoso
liquen^M custráceo

thallus
thalle^M
Thallus^M
tallo^M
talo^M

fruticose lichen
lichen^M fruticuleux
Strauchflechte^F
lichene^M fruticoso
liquen^M fruticuloso

foliose lichen
lichen^M foliacé
Laubflechte^F
lichene^M fogliaceo
liquen^M foliáceo

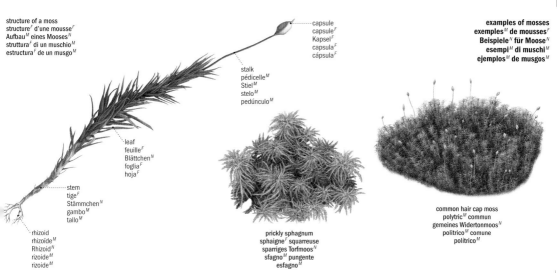

structure of a moss
structure[F] d'une mousse[F]
Aufbau[M] eines Mooses[N]
struttura[F] di un muschio[M]
estructura[F] de un musgo[M]

capsule
capsule[F]
Kapsel[F]
capsula[F]
cápsula[F]

stalk
pédicelle[M]
Stiel[M]
stelo[M]
pedúnculo[M]

examples of mosses
exemples[M] de mousses[F]
Beispiele[N] für Moose[N]
esempi[M] di muschi[M]
ejemplos[M] de musgos[M]

leaf
feuille[F]
Blättchen[N]
foglia[F]
hoja[F]

stem
tige[F]
Stämmchen[N]
gambo[M]
tallo[M]

rhizoid
rhizoïde[M]
Rhizoid[N]
rizoide[M]
rizoide[M]

prickly sphagnum
sphaigne[F] squarreuse
sparriges Torfmoos[N]
sfagno[M] pungente
esfagno[M]

common hair cap moss
polytric[M] commun
gemeines Widertonmoos[N]
politrico[M] comune
politrico[M]

alga

algue[F] | Alge[F] | alga[F] | alga[F]

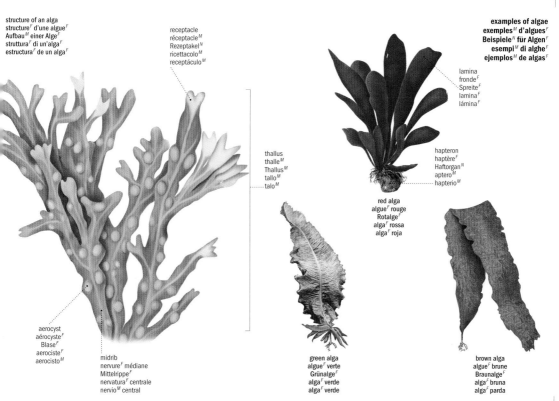

structure of an alga
structure[F] d'une algue[F]
Aufbau[M] einer Alge[F]
struttura[F] di un'alga[F]
estructura[F] de un alga[F]

receptacle
réceptacle[M]
Rezeptakel[N]
ricettacolo[M]
receptáculo[M]

examples of algae
exemples[M] d'algues[F]
Beispiele[N] für Algen[F]
esempi[M] di alghe[F]
ejemplos[M] de algas[F]

lamina
fronde[F]
Spreite[F]
lamina[F]
lámina[F]

thallus
thalle[M]
Thallus[M]
tallo[M]
talo[M]

hapteron
haptère[F]
Haftorgan[N]
aptero[M]
hapterio[M]

red alga
algue[F] rouge
Rotalge[F]
alga[F] rossa
alga[F] roja

aerocyst
aérocyste[F]
Blase[F]
aerociste[F]
aerocisto[M]

midrib
nervure[F] médiane
Mittelrippe[F]
nervatura[F] centrale
nervio[M] central

green alga
algue[F] verte
Grünalge[F]
alga[F] verde
alga[F] verde

brown alga
algue[F] brune
Braunalge[F]
alga[F] bruna
alga[F] parda

mushroom

champignon^M | Pilz^M | fungo^M | hongo^M

structure of a mushroom
structure^F d'un champignon^M
Aufbau^M eines Pilzes^M
struttura^F di un fungo^M
anatomía^F de un hongo^M

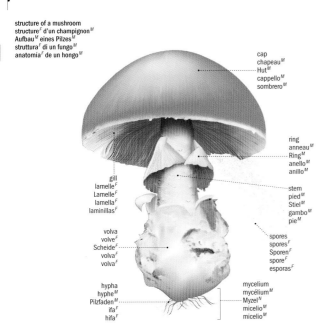

cap
chapeau^M
Hut^M
cappello^M
sombrero^M

ring
anneau^M
Ring^M
anello^M
anillo^M

gill
lamelle^F
Lamelle^F
lamella^F
laminillas^F

stem
pied^M
Stiel^M
gambo^M
pie^M

volva
volve^F
Scheide^F
volva^F
volva^F

spores
spores^F
Sporen^F
spore^F
esporas^F

hypha
hyphe^M
Pilzfaden^M
ifa^F
hifa^F

mycelium
mycélium^M
Myzel^N
micelio^M
micelio^M

deadly poisonous mushroom
champignon^M mortel
tödlich giftiger Pilz^M
fungo^M velenoso e mortale
hongo^M mortal

destroying angel
amanite^F vireuse
Knollenblätterpilz^M
amanita^F virosa
amanita^F virosa

poisonous mushroom
champignon^M vénéneux
Giftpilz^M
fungo^M velenoso
hongo^M venenoso

fly agaric
fausse oronge^F
Fliegenpilz^M
amanita^F muscaria
falsa oronja^F

fern

fougère^F | Farn^M | felce^F | helecho^M

structure of a fern
structure^F d'une fougère^F
Aufbau^M eines Farns^M
struttura^F di una felce^F
estructura^F de un helecho^M

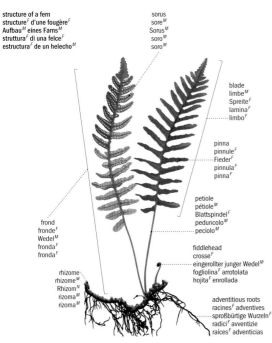

sorus
sore^M
Sorus^M
soro^M
soro^M

blade
limbe^M
Spreite^F
lamina^F
limbo^F

pinna
pinnule^F
Fieder^F
pinnula^F
pinna^F

petiole
pétiole^M
Blattspindel^F
peduncolo^M
peciolo^M

fiddlehead
crosse^F
eingerollter junger Wedel^M
fogliolina^F arrotolata
hojita^F enrollada

frond
fronde^F
Wedel^M
fronda^F
fronda^F

rhizome
rhizome^M
Rhizom^N
rizoma^M
rizoma^M

adventitious roots
racines^F adventives
sproßbürtige Wurzeln^F
radici^F avventizie
raíces^F adventicias

examples of ferns
exemples^M de fougères^F
Beispiele^N für Farne^M
esempi^M di felci^F
ejemplos^M de helechos^M

tree fern
fougère^F arborescente
Baumfarn^M
felce^F arborea
helecho^M arbóreo

trunk
tronc^M
Stamm^M
tronco^M
tronco^M

common polypody
polypode^M commun
gemeiner Tüpfelfarn^M
polipodio^M comune
polipodio^M común

bird's nest fern
fougère^F nid^M d'oiseau^M
Nestfarn^M
lingua^F di cervo^M
helecho^M nido^M de pájaro^M

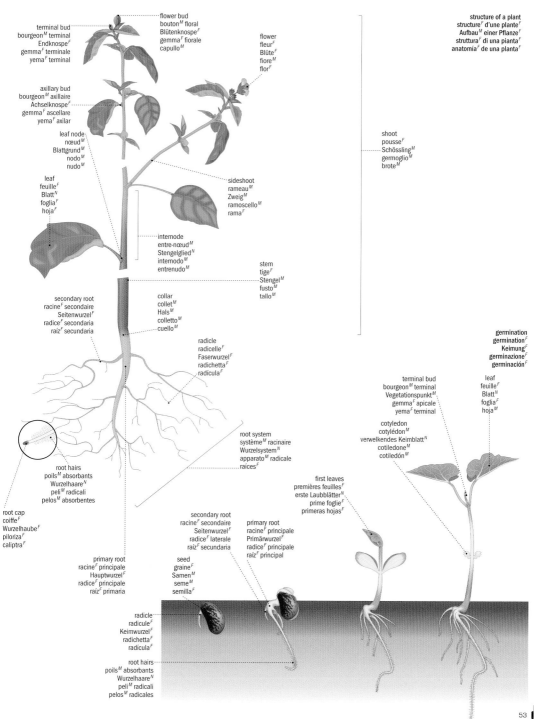

structure of a plant
structure^F d'une plante^F
Aufbau^M einer Pflanze^F
struttura^F di una pianta^F
anatomía^F de una planta^F

flower bud
bouton^M floral
Blütenknospe^F
gemma^F fiorale
capullo^M

terminal bud
bourgeon^M terminal
Endknospe^F
gemma^F terminale
yema^F terminal

flower
fleur^F
Blüte^F
fiore^M
flor^F

axillary bud
bourgeon^M axillaire
Achselknospe^F
gemma^F ascellare
yema^F axilar

shoot
pousse^F
Schössling^M
germoglio^M
brote^M

leaf node
nœud^M
Blattgrund^M
nodo^M
nudo^M

sideshoot
rameau^M
Zweig^M
ramoscello^M
rama^F

leaf
feuille^F
Blatt^N
foglia^F
hoja^F

internode
entre-nœud^M
Stengelglied^N
internodo^M
entrenudo^M

stem
tige^F
Stengel^M
fusto^M
tallo^M

secondary root
racine^F secondaire
Seitenwurzel^F
radice^F secondaria
raíz^F secundaria

collar
collet^M
Hals^M
colletto^M
cuello^M

radicle
radicelle^F
Faserwurzel^F
radichetta^F
radícula^F

germination
germination^F
Keimung^F
germinazione^F
germinación^F

terminal bud
bourgeon^M terminal
Vegetationspunkt^M
gemma^F apicale
yema^F terminal

leaf
feuille^F
Blatt^N
foglia^F
hoja^M

cotyledon
cotylédon^M
verwelkendes Keimblatt^N
cotiledone^M
cotiledón^M

root system
système^M racinaire
Wurzelsystem^N
apparato^M radicale
raíces^F

root hairs
poils^M absorbants
Wurzelhaare^N
peli^M radicali
pelos^M absorbentes

first leaves
premières feuilles^F
erste Laubblätter^N
prime foglie^F
primeras hojas^F

root cap
coiffe^F
Wurzelhaube^F
piloriza^F
caliptra^F

secondary root
racine^F secondaire
Seitenwurzel^F
radice^F laterale
raíz^F secundaria

primary root
racine^F principale
Primärwurzel^F
radice^F principale
raíz^F principal

primary root
racine^F principale
Hauptwurzel^F
radice^F principale
raíz^F primaria

seed
graine^F
Samen^M
seme^M
semilla^F

radicle
radicule^F
Keimwurzel^F
radichetta^F
radicula^F

root hairs
poils^M absorbants
Wurzelhaare^N
peli^M radicali
pelos^M radicales

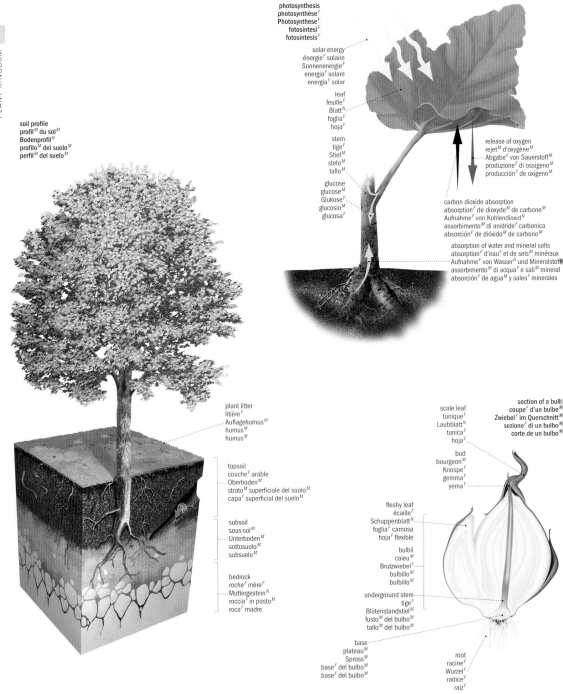

photosynthesis
photosynthèse^F
Photosynthese^F
fotosintesi^F
fotosintesis^F

solar energy
énergie^F solaire
Sonnenenergie^F
energia^F solare
energía^F solar

leaf
feuille^F
Blatt^N
foglia^F
hoja^F

stem
tige^F
Stiel^M
stelo^M
tallo^M

glucose
glucose^M
Glukose^F
glucosio^M
glucosa^F

release of oxygen
rejet^M d'oxygène^M
Abgabe^F von Sauerstoff^M
produzione^F di ossigeno^M
producción^F de oxígeno^M

carbon dioxide absorption
absorption^F de dioxyde^M de carbone^M
Aufnahme^F von Kohlendioxid^N
assorbimento^M di anidride^F carbonica
absorción^F de dióxido^M de carbono^M

absorption of water and mineral salts
absorption^F d'eau^F et de sels^M minéraux
Aufnahme^F von Wasser^N und Mineralstoff
assorbimento^M di acqua^F e sali^M mineral
absorción^F de agua^M y sales^F minerales

soil profile
profil^M du sol^M
Bodenprofil^N
profilo^M del suolo^M
perfil^M del suelo^M

plant litter
litière^F
Auflagehumus^M
humus^M
humus^M

topsoil
couche^F arable
Oberboden^M
strato^M superficiale del suolo^M
capa^F superficial del suelo^M

subsoil
sous-sol^M
Unterboden^M
sottosuolo^M
subsuelo^M

bedrock
roche^F mère^F
Muttergestein^N
roccia^F in posto^M
roca^F madre

scale leaf
tunique^F
Laubblatt^N
tunica^F
hoja^F

section of a bulb
coupe^F d'un bulbe
Zwiebel^F im Querschnitt
sezione^F di un bulbo
corte de un bulbo

bud
bourgeon^M
Knospe^F
gemma^F
yema^F

fleshy leaf
écaille^F
Schuppenblatt^N
foglia^F carnosa
hoja^F flexible

bulbil
caïeu^M
Brutzwiebel^F
bulbillo^M
bulbillo^M

underground stem
tige
Blütenstandstiel^M
fusto^M del bulbo^M
tallo^M del bulbo^M

base
plateau^M
Spross^M
base^F del bulbo^M
base^F del bulbo^M

root
racine^F
Wurzel^F
radice^F
raíz^F

PLANT KINGDOM

simple leaves
feuilles^F simples
einfache Blätter^N
foglie^F semplici
hojas^F simples

cordate
cordée
Herzförmig
cordata
acorazonada

reniform
réniforme
nierenförmig
reniforme
reniforme

orbiculate
arrondie
rund
orbicolare
orbicular

spatulate
spatulée
spatelförmig
spatolata
espatulada

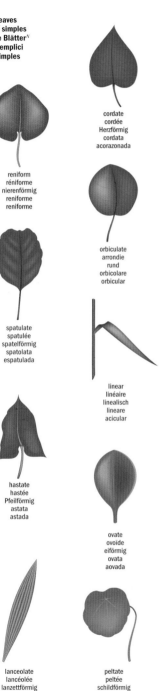

linear
linéaire
linealisch
lineare
acicular

hastate
hastée
Pfeilförmig
astata
astada

ovate
ovoide
eiförmig
ovata
aovada

lanceolate
lancéolée
lanzettförmig
lanceolata
lanceolada

peltate
peltée
schildförmig
peltata
peltada

structure of a leaf
structure^F d'une feuille^F
Aufbau^M eines Blatts^N
struttura^F di una foglia^F
estructura^F de una hoja^F

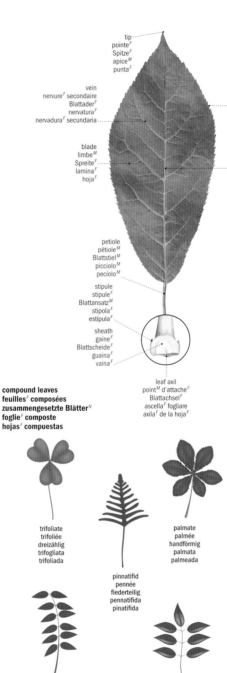

tip
pointe^F
Spitze^F
apice^M
punta^F

vein
nervure^F secondaire
Blattader^F
nervatura^F
nervadura^F secundaria

margin
bord^M
Blattrand^M
margine^M
borde^M

midrib
nervure^F principale
Mittelrippe^F
nervatura^F centrale
nervadura^F principal

blade
limbe^M
Spreite^F
lamina^F
hoja^F

petiole
pétiole^M
Blattstiel^M
picciolo^M
pecíolo^M

stipule
stipule^F
Blattansatz^M
stipola^F
estipula^F

sheath
gaine^F
Blattscheide^F
guaina^F
vaina^F

leaf axil
point^M d'attache^F
Blattachsel^F
ascella^F fogliare
axila^F de la hoja^F

leaf margins
bord^M d'une feuille^F
Blattrand^M
margine^M fogliare
la hoja^F según su borde^M

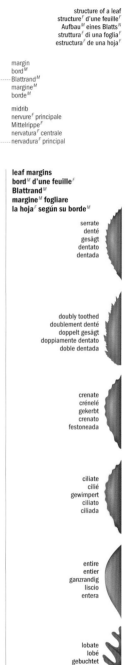

serrate
denté
gesägt
dentato
dentada

doubly toothed
doublement denté
doppelt gesägt
doppiamente dentato
doble dentada

crenate
crénelé
gekerbt
crenato
festoneada

ciliate
cilié
gewimpert
ciliato
ciliada

entire
entier
ganzrandig
liscio
entera

lobate
lobé
gebuchtet
lobato
lobulada

compound leaves
feuilles^F composées
zusammengesetzte Blätter^N
foglie^F composte
hojas^F compuestas

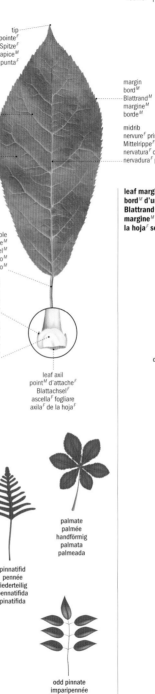

trifoliate
trifoliée
dreizählig
trifogliata
trifoliada

palmate
palmée
handförmig
palmata
palmeada

pinnatifid
pennée
fiederteilig
pennatifida
pinatifida

paripinnate
paripennée
paarig gefiedert
paripennata
paripinnada

odd pinnate
imparipennée
unpaarig gefiedert
imparipennata
imparipinnada

55

flower

fleur^F | Blüte^F | fiore^M | flor^F

structure of a flower
structure^F d'une fleur^F
Aufbau^M einer Blume^F
struttura^F di un fiore^M
estructura^F de una flor^F

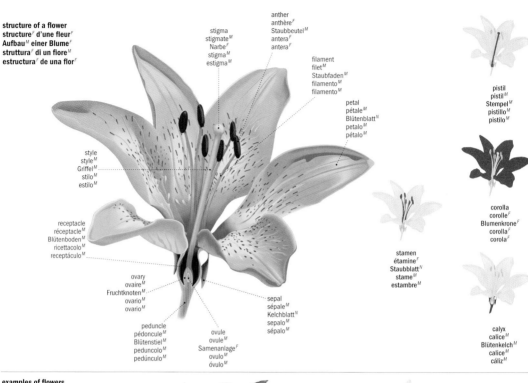

anther
anthère^F
Staubbeutel^M
antera^F
antera^F

stigma
stigmate^M
Narbe^F
stigma^M
estigma^M

filament
filet^M
Staubfaden^M
filamento^M
filamento^M

petal
pétale^M
Blütenblatt^N
petalo^M
pétalo^M

style
style^M
Griffel^M
stilo^M
estilo^M

receptacle
réceptacle^M
Blütenboden^M
ricettacolo^M
receptáculo^M

ovary
ovaire^M
Fruchtknoten^M
ovario^M
ovario^M

peduncle
pédoncule^M
Blütenstiel^M
peduncolo^M
pedúnculo^M

ovule
ovule^M
Samenanlage^F
ovulo^M
óvulo^M

sepal
sépale^F
Kelchblatt^N
sepalo^M
sépalo^M

pistil
pistil^M
Stempel^M
pistillo^M
pistilo^M

corolla
corolle^F
Blumenkrone^F
corolla^F
corola^F

stamen
étamine^F
Staubblatt^N
stame^M
estambre^M

calyx
calice^M
Blütenkelch^M
calice^M
cáliz^M

examples of flowers
exemples^M de fleurs^F
Beispiele^N für Blumen^F
esempi^M di fiori^M
ejemplos^M de flores^F

orchid
orchidée^F
Orchidee^F
orchidea^F
orquidea^F

daffodil
jonquille^F
Narzisse^F
trombone^M
narciso^M

poppy
coquelicot^M
Mohn^M
papavero^M
amapola^F

tulip
tulipe^F
Tulpe^F
tulipano^M
tulipán^M

lily of the valley
muguet^M
Maiglöckchen^N
mughetto^M
muguete^M

carnation
œillet^M
Nelke^F
garofano^M
clavel^M

rose
rose^F
Rose^F
rosa^F
rosa^F

begonia
bégonia^M
Begonie^F
begonia^F
begonia^F

lily
lis^M
Lilie^F
giglio^M
azucena^F

violet
violette^F
Veilchen^N
viola^F
violeta^F

crocus
crocus^M
Krokus^M
croco^M
croco^M

sunflower
tournesol^M
Sonnenblume^F
girasole^M
girasol^M

types of inflorescence
modes^M **d'inflorescence**^{F}
Arten^F von Blütenständen^M
tipi^M **di inflorescenze**^{F}
variedades^F de inflorescencias^F

raceme
grappe^F
geschlossene Traube^F
racemo^M
racimo^M

uniparous cyme
cyme^F unipare
eingliedrige Trugdolde^F
cima^F unipara
cima^F unipara

umbel
ombelle^F
Dolde^F
ombrella^F
umbela^F

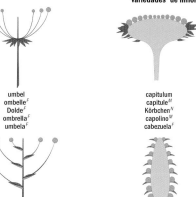

capitulum
capitule^M
Körbchen^N
capolino^M
cabezuela^F

spike
épi^M
Ähre^F
spiga^F
espiga^F

biparous cyme
cyme^F bipare
zweigliedrige Trugdolde^F
cima^F bipara
cima^F bípara

corymb
corymbe^M
Doldentraube^F
corimbo^M
corimbo^M

spadix
spadice^M
Kolben^M
spadice^M
espádice^M

fruits

fruits^M | Früchte^F | frutti^M | frutos^M

fleshy stone fruit
fruit^M **charnu à noyau**^{M}
fleischige Steinfrucht^F
drupa^F
drupa^F

technical terms
termes^M techniques
wissenschaftliche Bezeichnungen^F
termini^M tecnici
términos^M técnicos

section of a peach
coupe^F d'une pêche^F
Pfirsich^M im Querschnitt^M
sezione^F di una pesca^F
corte^M de un melocotón^M

usual terms
termes^M familiers
gebräuchliche Bezeichnungen^F
termini^M comuni
términos^M familiares

peduncle
pédoncule^M
Stiel^M
peduncolo^M
pedúnculo^M

stalk
queue^F
Stiel^M
picciolo^M
rabillo^M

exocarp
épicarpe^M
Exokarp^N
esocarpo^M
epicarpio^M

skin
peau^F
Haut^F
buccia^F
piel^F

mesocarp
mésocarpe^M
Mesokarp^N
mesocarpo^M
mesocarpio^M

flesh
pulpe^F
Fruchtfleisch^N
polpa^F
pulpa^F

seed coat
tégument^M de la graine^F
Samenmantel^M
tegumento^M del seme^M
tegumento^M de la semilla^F

almond
amande^F
Kern^M
mandorla^F
almendra^F

seed
graine^F
Samen^M
seme^M
semilla^F

stone
noyau^M
Stein^M
nocciolo^M
hueso^M

endocarp
endocarpe^M
Endokarp^N
endocarpo^M
endocarpio^M

style
style^M
Griffel^M
stilo^M
estilo^M

fleshy pome fruit
fruit^M **charnu à pépins**^{M}
fleischige Apfelfrucht^F
frutto^M **carnoso: mela**^{F}
pomo^M **carnoso**

scientific terms
termes^M techniques
wissenschaftliche Bezeichnungen^F
termini^M tecnici
términos^M técnicos

section of an apple
coupe^F d'une pomme^F
Apfel^M im Querschnitt^M
sezione^F di una mela^F
corte^M de una manzana^F

popular terms
termes^M familiers
gebräuchliche Bezeichnungen^F
termini^M comuni
términos^M familiares

peduncle
pédoncule^M
Stiel^M
peduncolo^M
pedúnculo^M

loculus
loge^F
Fruchtknotenfach^N
loculo^M
lóculo^M

seed
graine^F
Samen^M
seme^M
semilla^F

mesocarp
mésocarpe^M
Mesokarp^N
mesocarpo^M
mesocarpio^M

endocarp
endocarpe^M
Endokarp^N
endocarpo^M
endocarpio^M

exocarp
épicarpe^M
Exokarp^N
esocarpo^M
epicarpio^M

style
style^M
Griffel^M
stilo^M
estilo^M

stalk
queue^F
Stiel^M
picciolo^M
rabillo^M

skin
peau^F
Schale^F
buccia^F
piel^F

pip
pépin^M
Kern^M
seme^M
pepita^F

flesh
pulpe^F
Fruchtfleisch^N
polpa^F
pulpa^F

core
cœur^M
Kerngehäuse^N
torsolo^M
corazón^M

stamen   sepal
étamine^F sépale^M
Staubblatt^N Sepalum^N
stame^M sepalo^M
estambre^M sépalo^M

fleshy fruit: citrus fruit
fruit^M **charnu : agrume**^{M}
fleischige Frucht^F**: Zitrusfrucht**^{F}
frutto^M **carnoso: agrume**^{M}
fruto^M **carnoso: cítrico**^{M}

section of an orange
coupe^F d'une orange^F
Orange^F im Querschnitt^M
sezione^F di un'arancia^F
corte^M de una naranja^F

scientific terms
termes^M techniques
wissenschaftliche Bezeichnungen^F
termini^M tecnici
términos^M técnicos

popular terms
termes^M familiers
gebräuchliche Bezeichnungen^F
termini^M comuni
términos^M familiares

wall
cloison^F
Scheidewand^F
parete^F
membrana^F

seed
graine^F
Samen^M
seme^M
semilla^F

juice sac
loge^F
Fruchtfach^N
cellula^F del succo^M
celdilla^F

mesocarp
mésocarpe^M
Mesokarp^N
mesocarpo^M
mesocarpio^M

exocarp
épicarpe^M
Exokarp^N
epicarpo^M
epicarpio^M

rind
écorce^F
Fruchtwand^F
scorza^F
corteza^F

pulp
pulpe^F
Fruchtfleisch^N
polpa^F
pulpa^F

peel
zeste^M
Schale^F
scorzetta^F
piel^F

segment
quartier^M
Spalt^M
spicchio^M
gajo^M

pip
pépin^M
Kern^M
seme^M
pepita^F

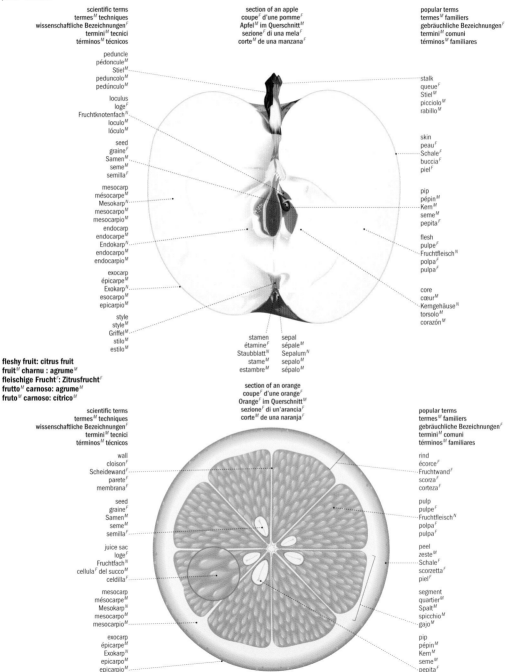

fleshy fruit: berry fruit
fruit^M **charnu : baie**^{F}
fleischige Frucht^F**: Beere**^{F}
frutto^M **carnoso: bacca**^{F}
fruto^F **carnoso: baya**^{F}

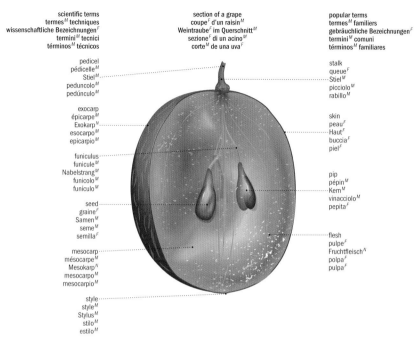

scientific terms
termes^M techniques
wissenschaftliche Bezeichnungen^F
termini^M tecnici
términos^M técnicos

section of a grape
coupe^F d'un raisin^M
Weintraube^F im Querschnitt^M
sezione^F di un acino^M
corte^M de una uva^F

popular terms
termes^M familiers
gebräuchliche Bezeichnungen^F
termini^M comuni
términos^M familiares

pedicel
pédicelle^M
Stiel^M
peduncolo^M
pedúnculo^M

stalk
queue^F
Stiel^M
picciolo^M
rabillo^M

exocarp
épicarpe^M
Exokarp^N
esocarpo^M
epicarpio^M

skin
peau^F
Haut^F
buccia^F
piel^F

funiculus
funicule^M
Nabelstrang^M
funicolo^M
funículo^M

pip
pépin^M
Kern^M
vinacciolo^M
pepita^F

seed
graine^F
Samen^M
seme^M
semilla^F

flesh
pulpe^F
Fruchtfleisch^N
polpa^F
pulpa^F

mesocarp
mésocarpe^M
Mesokarp^N
mesocarpo^M
mesocarpio^M

style
style^M
Stylus^M
stilo^M
estilo^M

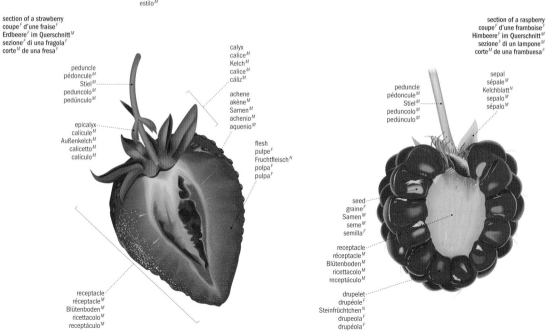

section of a strawberry
coupe^F d'une fraise^F
Erdbeere^F im Querschnitt^M
sezione^F di una fragola^F
corte^M de una fresa^F

section of a raspberry
coupe^F d'une framboise^F
Himbeere^F im Querschnitt^M
sezione^F di un lampone^M
corte^M de una frambuesa^F

peduncle
pédoncule^M
Stiel^M
peduncolo^M
pedúnculo^M

calyx
calice^M
Kelch^M
calice^M
cáliz^M

sepal
sépale^M
Kelchblatt^N
sepalo^M
sépalo^M

peduncle
pédoncule^M
Stiel^M
peduncolo^M
pedúnculo^M

achene
akène^M
Samen^M
achenio^M
aquenio^M

epicalyx
calicule^M
Außenkelch^M
calicetto^M
caliculo^M

flesh
pulpe^F
Fruchtfleisch^N
polpa^F
pulpa^F

seed
graine^F
Samen^M
seme^M
semilla^F

receptacle
réceptacle^M
Blütenboden^M
ricettacolo^M
receptáculo^M

drupelet
drupéole^F
Steinfrüchtchen^N
drupeola^F
drupéola^F

receptacle
réceptacle^M
Blütenboden^M
ricettacolo^M
receptáculo^M

dry fruits
fruits^M **secs**
Trockenfrüchte^F
frutti^M **secchi**
frutos^M **secos**

husk
brou^M
Hülle^F
mallo^M
cáscara^F

section of a follicle: star anise
coupe^F d'un follicule^M : anis^M étoilé
Balg^M im Querschnitt^M: Sternanis^M
sezione^F di un follicolo^M: anice^M stellato
corte^M de un folículo^M : anís^M estrellado

seed
graine^F
Samen^M
seme^M
semilla^F

follicle
follicule^M
Fruchtkapsel^F
follicolo^M
folículo^M

suture
suture^F
Naht^F
sutura^F
sutura^F

septum
membrane^F médiane
Scheidewand^F
replo^M
septum^M

valve
valve^F
Fruchtblatt^N
valva^F
ventalla^F

section of a silique: mustard
coupe^F d'une silique^F : moutarde^F
Schote^F im Querschnitt^M: Senf^M
sezione^F di una siliqua^F: senape^F nera
corte^M de una silicua^F : mostaza^F

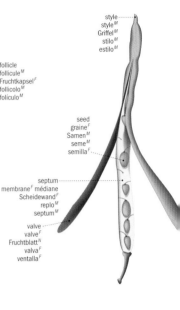

style
style^M
Griffel^M
stilo^M
estilo^M

seed
graine^F
Samen^M
seme^M
semilla^F

section of a hazelnut
coupe^F d'une noisette^F
Längsschnitt^M durch eine Haselnuss^F
sezione^F di una nocciola^F
corte^M de una avellana^F

cupule
cupule^F
Fruchtbecher^M
cupola^F
cúpula^F

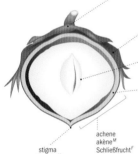

bract
bractée^F
Deckblatt^N
brattea^F
bráctea^F

seed
graine^F
Samen^M
seme^M
semilla^F

pericarp
péricarpe^M
Fruchtwand^F
pericarpo^M
pericarpio^M

stigma
stigmate^M
Narbe^F
stigma^M
estigma^M

achene
akène^M
Schließfrucht^F
achenio^M
aquenio^M

section of a legume: pea
coupe^F d'une gousse^F : pois^M
Hülsenfrucht^F im Querschnitt^M: Erbse^F
sezione^F di un legume^M: pisello^M
corte^M de una legumbre^F : guisante^M

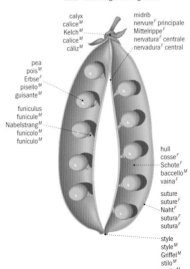

calyx
calice^F
Kelch^M
calice^M
cáliz^M

midrib
nervure^F principale
Mittelrippe^F
nervatura^F centrale
nervadura^F central

section of a walnut
coupe^F d'une noix^F
Längsschnitt^M durch eine Walnuss^F
sezione^F di una noce^F
corte^M de una nuez^F

pea
pois^M
Erbse^F
pisello^M
guisante^M

funiculus
funicule^M
Nabelstrang^M
funicolo^M
funículo^M

section of a capsule: poppy
coupe^F d'une capsule^F : pavot^M
Fruchtkapsel^F im Querschnitt^M: Mohn^M
sezione^F di una capsula^F: papavero^M
corte^M de una cápsula^F : amapola^F

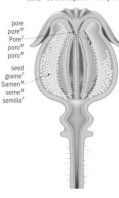

pore
pore^M
Pore^F
poro^M
poro^M

seed
graine^F
Samen^M
seme^M
semilla^F

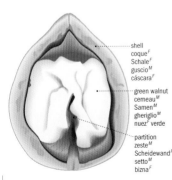

shell
coque^F
Schale^F
guscio^M
cáscara^F

green walnut
cerneau^M
Samen^M
gheriglio^M
nuez^F verde

partition
zeste^M
Scheidewand^F
setto^M
bizna^F

hull
cosse^F
Schote^F
baccello^M
vaina^F

suture
suture^F
Naht^F
sutura^F
sutura^F

style
style^M
Griffel^M
stilo^M
estilo^M

buckwheat
sarrasin^M
Buchweizen^M
grano^M saraceno
trigo^M sarraceno

buckwheat: raceme
sarrasin^M : grappe^F
Buchweizen^M: Doldenrispe^F
grano^M saraceno: racemo^M
trigo^M sarraceno: racimo^M

wheat
blé^M
Weizen^M
grano^M
trigo^M

wheat: spike
blé^M : épi^M
Weizen^M: Ähre^F
grano^M: spiga^F
trigo^M : espiga^F

section of a grain of wheat
coupe^F d'un grain^M de blé^M
Längsschnitt^M durch ein Weizenkorn^N
sezione^F di un chicco^M di grano^M
corte^M de un grano^M de trigo^M

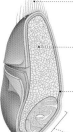

brush
brosse^F
Granne^F
barbetta^F
brocha^F

starch
albumen^M farineux
Stärke^F
amido^M
almidón^M

seed coat
tégument^M
Samenschale^F
tegumento^M seminale
cáscara^F

germ
germe^M
Keim^M
germe^M
germen^M

barley
orge^F
Gerste^F
orzo^M
cebada^F

barley: spike
orge^F : épi^M
Gerste^F: Ähre^F
orzo^M: spiga^F
cebada^F : espiga^F

rice
riz^M
Reis^M
riso^M
arroz^M

rice: panicle
riz^M : panicule^F
Reis^M: Rispe^F
riso^M: pannocchia^F
arroz^M: panicula^F

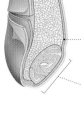

oats
avoine^F
Hafer^M
avena^F
avena^F

oats: panicle
avoine^F : panicule^F
Hafer^M: Ährchen^N
avena^F: pannocchia^F
avena^F : panicula^F

rye
seigle^M
Roggen^M
segale^F
centeno^M

rye: spike
seigle^M : épi^M
Roggen^M: Ähre^F
segale^F: spiga^F
centeno^M : espiga^F

sorghum
sorgho^M
Mohrenhirse^F
sorgo^M
sorgo^M

sorghum: panicle
sorgho^M : panicule^F
Mohrenhirse^F: Rispe^F
sorgo^M: pannocchia^F
sorgo^M : panicula^F

sweetcorn
maïs^M
Mais^M
mais^M
maíz^M

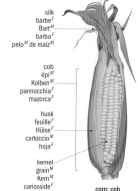

silk
barbe^F
Bart^M
barba^F
pelo^M de maíz^M

cob
épi^M
Kolben^M
pannocchia^F
mazorca^F

husk
feuille^F
Hülse^F
cartoccio^M
hoja^F

kernel
grain^M
Kern^M
cariosside^F
grano^M

corn: cob
maïs^M : épi^M
Mais^M: Kolben^M
mais^M: pannocchia^F
maíz^M : mazorca^F

millet
millet^M
Hirse^F
miglio^M
mijo^M

millet: spike
millet^M : épi^M
Hirse^F: Ährenrispe^F
miglio^M: spiga^F
mijo^M : espiga^F

grape

vigne^F | Rebe^F | vite^F | uva^F

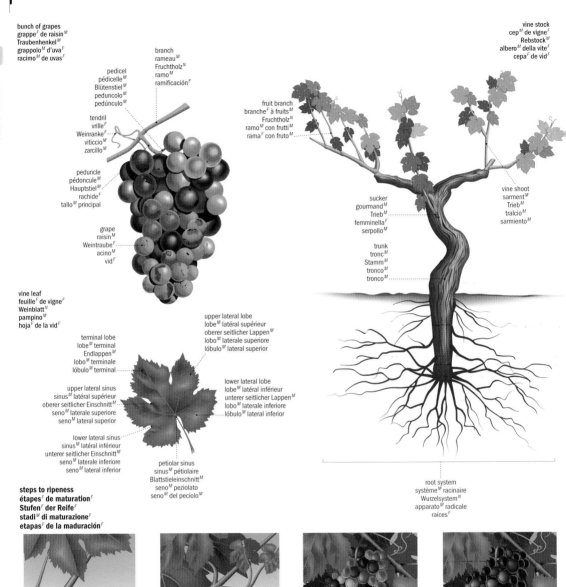

bunch of grapes
grappe^F de raisin^M
Traubenhenkel^M
grappolo^M d'uva^F
racimo^M de uvas^F

branch
rameau^M
Fruchtholz^N
ramo^M
ramificación^F

pedicel
pédicelle^M
Blütenstiel^M
peduncolo^M
pedúnculo^M

tendril
vrille^F
Weinranke^F
viticcio^M
zarcillo^M

peduncle
pédoncule^M
Hauptstiel^M
rachide^F
tallo^M principal

grape
raisin^M
Weintraube^F
acino^M
vid^F

vine leaf
feuille^F de vigne^F
Weinblatt^N
pampino^M
hoja^F de la vid^F

terminal lobe
lobe^M terminal
Endlappen^M
lobo^M terminale
lóbulo^M terminal

upper lateral sinus
sinus^M latéral supérieur
oberer seitlicher Einschnitt^M
seno^M laterale superiore
seno^M lateral superior

lower lateral sinus
sinus^M latéral inférieur
unterer seitlicher Einschnitt^M
seno^M laterale inferiore
seno^M lateral inferior

upper lateral lobe
lobe^M latéral supérieur
oberer seitlicher Lappen^M
lobo^M laterale superiore
lóbulo^M lateral superior

lower lateral lobe
lobe^M latéral inférieur
unterer seitlicher Lappen^M
lobo^M laterale inferiore
lóbulo^M lateral inferior

petiolar sinus
sinus^M pétiolaire
Blattstieleinschnitt^M
seno^M peziolato
seno^M del peciolo^M

fruit branch
branche^F à fruits^M
Fruchtholz^N
ramo^M con frutti^M
rama^F con fruto^M

vine stock
cep^M de vigne^F
Rebstock^M
albero^M della vite^F
cepa^F de vid^F

vine shoot
sarment^M
Trieb^M
tralcio^M
sarmiento^M

sucker
gourmand^M
Trieb^M
femminella^F
serpollo^M

trunk
tronc^M
Stamm^M
tronco^M
tronco^M

root system
système^M racinaire
Wurzelsystem^N
apparato^M radicale
raíces^F

steps to ripeness
étapes^F de maturation^F
Stufen^F der Reife^F
stadi^M di maturazione^F
etapas^F de la maduración^F

flowering
floraison^F
Blüte^F
fioritura^F
floración^F

fruiting
nouaison^F
Fruchtbildung^F
fruttificazione^F
fructificación^F

ripening
véraison^F
Reifeprozess^M
maturazione^F
envero^M

ripeness
maturité^F
Vollreife^F
maturità^F
madurez^F

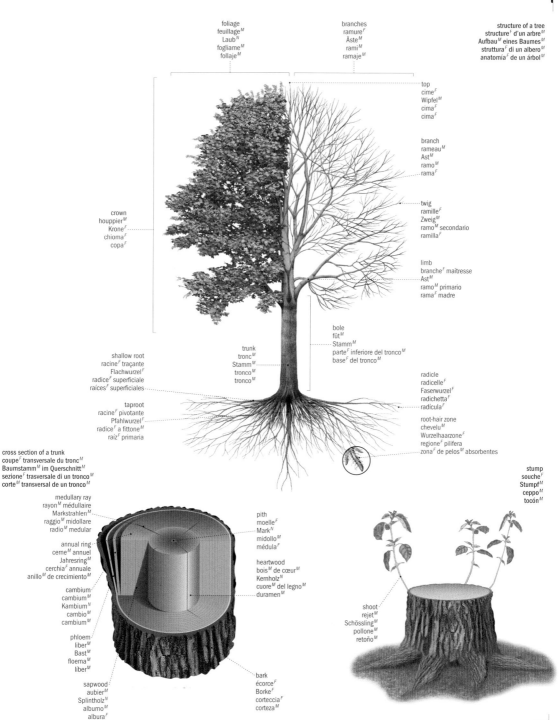

structure of a tree
structure^F d'un arbre^M
Aufbau^M eines Baumes^M
struttura^F di un albero^M
anatomía^F de un árbol^M

foliage
feuillage^M
Laub^N
fogliame^M
follaje^M

branches
ramure^F
Äste^M
rami^M
ramaje^M

top
cime^F
Wipfel^M
cima^F
cima^F

branch
rameau^M
Ast^M
ramo^M
rama^F

twig
ramille^F
Zweig^M
ramo^M secondario
ramilla^F

crown
houppier^M
Krone^F
chioma^F
copa^F

limb
branche^F maitresse
Ast^M
ramo^M primario
rama^F madre

bole
fût^M
Stamm^M
parte^F inferiore del tronco^M
base^F del tronco^M

trunk
tronc^M
Stamm^M
tronco^M
tronco^M

radicle
radicelle^F
Faserwurzel^F
radichetta^F
radícula^F

shallow root
racine^F traçante
Flachwurzel^F
radice^F superficiale
raíces^F superficiales

taproot
racine^F pivotante
Pfahlwurzel^F
radice^F a fittone^M
raíz^F primaria

root-hair zone
chevelu^M
Wurzelhaarzone^F
regione^F pilifera
zona^F de pelos^M absorbentes

cross section of a trunk
coupe^F transversale du tronc^M
Baumstamm^M im Querschnitt^M
sezione^F trasversale di un tronco^M
corte^M transversal de un tronco^M

stump
souche^F
Stumpf^M
ceppo^M
tocón^M

medullary ray
rayon^M médullaire
Markstrahlen^M
raggio^M midollare
radio^M medular

pith
moelle^F
Mark^N
midollo^M
médula^F

annual ring
cerne^M annuel
Jahresring^M
cerchia^F annuale
anillo^M de crecimiento^M

heartwood
bois^M de cœur^M
Kernholz^N
cuore^M del legno^M
duramen^M

cambium
cambium^M
Kambium^N
cambio^M
cambium^M

shoot
rejet^M
Schössling^M
pollone^M
retoño^M

phloem
liber^M
Bast^M
floema^M
liber^M

sapwood
aubier^M
Splintholz^N
alburno^M
albura^F

bark
écorce^F
Borke^F
corteccia^F
corteza^M

examples of broadleaved trees
exemples^{*M*} **d'arbres**^{*M*} **feuillus**
Beispiele^{*N*} **für Laubhölzer**^{*N*}
esempi^{*M*} **di latifoglie**^{*F*}
ejemplos^{*M*} **de latifolios**^{*M*}

oak
chêne^{*M*}
Eiche^{*F*}
quercia^{*F*}
roble^{*M*}

birch
bouleau^{*M*}
Birke^{*F*}
betulla^{*F*}
abedul^{*M*}

weeping willow
saule^{*M*} pleureur
Trauerweide^{*F*}
salice^{*M*} piangente
sauce^{*M*} llorón

poplar
peuplier^{*M*}
Pappel^{*F*}
pioppo^{*M*}
álamo^{*M*}

palm tree
palmier^{*M*}
Palme^{*F*}
palma^{*F*}
palmera^{*F*}

maple
érable^{*M*}
Ahorn^{*M*}
acero^{*M*}
arce^{*M*}

beech
hêtre^{*M*}
Buche^{*F*}
faggio^{*M*}
haya^{*F*}

walnut
noyer^{*M*}
Walnuss^{*F*}
noce^{*M*}
nogal^{*M*}

conifère^M | Nadelbaum^M | conifera^F | conifera^F

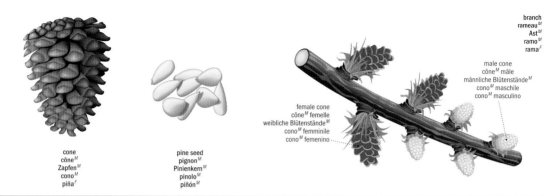

cone
cône^M
Zapfen^M
cono^M
piña^F

pine seed
pignon^M
Pinienkern^M
pinolo^M
piñón^M

branch
rameau^M
Ast^M
ramo^M
rama^F

male cone
cône^M mâle
männliche Blütenstände^M
cono^M maschile
cono^M masculino

female cone
cône^M femelle
weibliche Blütenstände^M
cono^M femminile
cono^M femenino

fir needles
aiguilles^F de sapin^M
Tannennadeln^F
aghi^M d'abete^M
agujas^F del abeto^M

pine needles
aiguilles^F de pin^M
Kiefernnadeln^F
aghi^M di pino^M
agujas^F del pino^M

scalelike leaves of the cypress
écailles^F de cyprès^M
Zypressennadeln^F
foglie^F squamiformi del cipresso^M
hojas^F escamadas del ciprés^M

examples of leaves
exemples^M de feuilles^F
Beispiele^N für Nadelblätter^N
esempi^M di foglie^F
ejemplos^M de hojas^F

examples of conifers
exemples^M de conifères^M
Beispiele^N für Nadelhölzer^N
esempi^M di conifere^F
ejemplos^M de coníferas^F

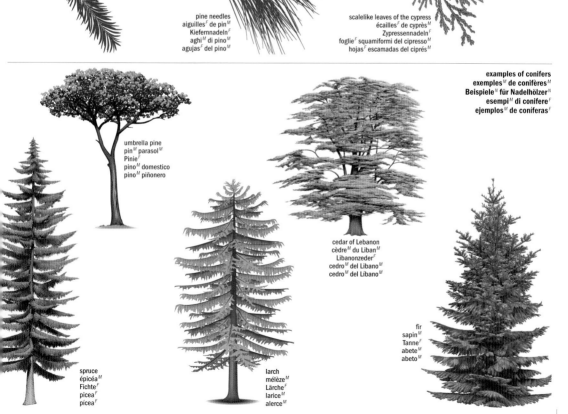

umbrella pine
pin^M parasol^M
Pinie^F
pino^M domestico
pino^M piñonero

cedar of Lebanon
cèdre^M du Liban^M
Libanonzeder^F
cedro^M del Libano^M
cedro^M del Líbano^M

fir
sapin^M
Tanne^F
abete^M
abeto^M

spruce
épicéa^M
Fichte^F
picea^F
picea^F

larch
mélèze^M
Lärche^F
larice^M
alerce^M

animal cell

cellule^F animale | tierische Zelle^F | cellula^F animale | célula^F animal

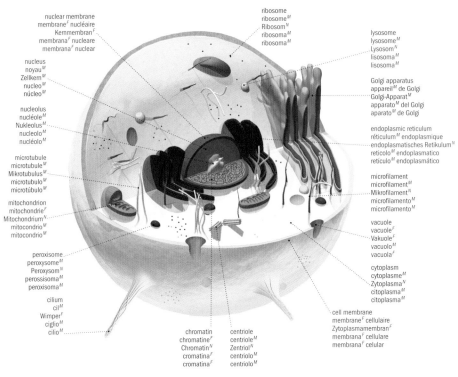

nuclear membrane
membrane^F nucléaire
Kernmembran^F
membrana^F nucleare
membrana^F nuclear

nucleus
noyau^M
Zellkern^M
nucleo^M
núcleo^M

nucleolus
nucléole^M
Nukleolus^M
nucleolo^M
nucléolo^M

microtubule
microtubule^M
Mikrotubulus^M
microtubulo^M
microtúbulo^M

mitochondrion
mitochondrie^F
Mitochondrium^N
mitocondrio^M
mitocondrio^M

peroxisome
peroxysome^M
Peroxysom^N
perossisoma^M
peroxisoma^M

cilium
cil^M
Wimper^F
ciglio^M
cilio^M

ribosome
ribosome^M
Ribosom^N
ribosoma^M
ribosoma^M

lysosome
lysosome^M
Lysosom^N
lisosoma^M
lisosoma^M

Golgi apparatus
appareil^M de Golgi
Golgi-Apparat^M
apparato^M del Golgi
aparato^M de Golgi

endoplasmic reticulum
réticulum^M endoplasmique
endoplasmatisches Retikulum^N
reticolo^M endoplasmatico
retículo^M endoplasmático

microfilament
microfilament^M
Mikrofilament^N
microfilamento^M
microfilamento^M

vacuole
vacuole^F
Vakuole^F
vacuolo^M
vacuola^F

cytoplasm
cytoplasme^M
Zytoplasma^N
citoplasma^M
citoplasma^M

cell membrane
membrane^F cellulaire
Zytoplasmamembran^F
membrana^F cellulare
membrana^F celular

chromatin
chromatine^F
Chromatin^N
cromatina^F
cromatina^F

centriole
centriole^M
Zentriol^N
centriolo^M
centriolo^M

unicellulars

unicellulaires^M | Einzeller^M | unicellulari^M | unicelulares^M

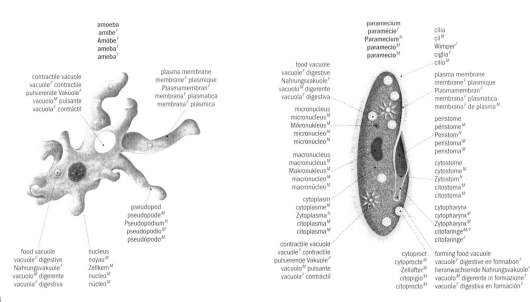

amoeba
amibe^F
Amöbe^F
ameba^F
ameba^F

contractile vacuole
vacuole^F contractile
pulsierende Vakuole^F
vacuolo^M pulsante
vacuola^F contráctil

plasma membrane
membrane^F plasmique
Plasmamembran^F
membrana^F plasmatica
membrana^F plásmica

food vacuole
vacuole^F digestive
Nahrungsvakuole^F
vacuolo^M digerente
vacuola^F digestiva

nucleus
noyau^M
Zellkern^M
nucleo^M
núcleo^M

pseudopod
pseudopode^M
Pseudopodium^N
pseudopodio^M
pseudópodo^M

paramecium
paramécie^F
Paramecium^N
paramecio^M
paramecio^M

cilia
cil^M
Wimper^F
ciglia^F
cilio^M

food vacuole
vacuole^F digestive
Nahrungsvakuole^F
vacuolo^M digerente
vacuola^F digestiva

micronucleus
micronucleus^M
Mikronukleus^M
micronucleo^M
micronúcleo^M

macronucleus
macronucleus^M
Makronukleus^M
macronucleo^M
macronúcleo^M

cytoplasm
cytoplasme^M
Zytoplasma^N
citoplasma^M
citoplasma^M

contractile vacuole
vacuole^F contractile
pulsierende Vakuole^F
vacuolo^M pulsante
vacuola^F contráctil

plasma membrane
membrane^F plasmique
Plasmamembran^F
membrana^F plasmatica
membrana^F de plasma^M

peristome
péristome^M
Peristom^N
peristoma^M
peristoma^M

cytostome
cytostome^M
Zytostom^N
citostoma^M
citostoma^M

cytopharynx
cytopharynx^M
Zytopharynx^M
citofaringe^{M/F}
citofaringe^F

cytoproct
cytoprocte^M
Zellafter^M
citopigio^M
citoprocto^M

forming food vacuole
vacuole^F digestive en formation^F
heranwachsende Nahrungsvakuole^F
vacuolo^M digerente in formazione^F
vacuola^F digestiva en formación^F

butterfly

papillon^M | Schmetterling^M | farfalla^F | mariposa^F

morphology of a butterfly
morphologie^F du papillon^M
äußere Merkmale^N eines Schmetterlings^M
morfologia^F di una farfalla^F
morfología^F de una mariposa^F

cell
cellule^F
Zelle^F
cella^F
celda^F

head
tête^F
Kopf^M
capo^M
cabeza^F

compound eye
œil^M composé
Facettenauge^N
occhio^M composto
ojo^M compuesto

labial palp
palpe^M labial
Lippentaster^M
palpo^M labiale
palpo^M labial

antenna
antenne^F
Antenne^F
antenna^F
antena^F

proboscis
trompe^F
Rüssel^M
proboscide^F
probóscide^M

thorax
thorax^M
Thorax^M
torace^M
tórax^M

foreleg
patte^F antérieure
Vorderbein^N
zampa^F anteriore
pata^F delantera

forewing
aile^F antérieure
Vorderflügel^M
ala^F anteriore
ala^F delantera

wing vein
nervure^F
Flügelader^F
nervatura^F alare
nervio^M

hind wing
aile^F postérieure
Hinterflügel^M
ala^F posteriore
ala^F trasera

spiracle
stigmate^M
Stigma^N
stigma^M
estigma^M

abdomen
abdomen^M
Hinterleib^M
addome^M
abdomen^M

middle leg
patte^F médiane
Mittelbein^N
zampa^F mediana
pata^F media

hind leg
patte^F postérieure
Hinterbein^N
zampa^F posteriore
pata^F trasera

chrysalis
chrysalide^F
Puppe^F
crisalide^F
crisálida^F

caterpillar
chenille^F
Raupe^F
bruco^M
oruga^F

simple eye
œil^M simple
Punktauge^N
occhio^M semplice
ocelo^M

head
tête^F
Kopf^M
capo^M
cabeza^F

mandible
mandibule^F
Unterkiefer^M
mandibola^F
mandibula^F

thorax
thorax^M
Thorax^M
torace^M
tórax^M

walking leg
patte^F ambulatoire
Laufbein^N
arto^M locomotorio
pata^F torácica

abdominal segment
segment^M abdominal
Hinterleibssegment^N
segmento^M addominale
segmento^M abdominal

proleg
patte^F ventouse
Bauchfuß^M
falsa zampa^F
pata^F ventosa

anal proleg
patte^F anale
Analfuß^M
falsa zampa^F anale
pata^F anal

honeybee

abeille^F | Honigbiene^F | ape^F | abeja^F

ANIMAL KINGDOM

morphology of a honeybee: worker
morphologie^F de l'abeille^F : ouvrière^F
äußere Merkmale^N einer Honigbiene^F: Arbeiterin^F
morfologia^F di un'ape^F: operaia
morfología^F de una abeja^F trabajadora

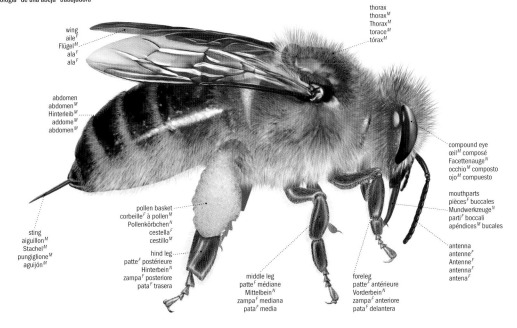

thorax
thorax^M
Thorax^M
torace^M
tórax^M

wing
aile^F
Flügel^M
ala^F
ala^F

abdomen
abdomen^M
Hinterleib^M
addome^M
abdomen^M

compound eye
œil^M composé
Facettenauge^N
occhio^M composto
ojo^M compuesto

mouthparts
pièces^F buccales
Mundwerkzeuge^N
parti^F boccali
apéndices^M bucales

sting
aiguillon^M
Stachel^M
pungiglione^M
aguijón^M

pollen basket
corbeille^F à pollen^M
Pollenkörbchen^N
cestella^F
cestillo^M

hind leg
patte^F postérieure
Hinterbein^N
zampa^F posteriore
pata^F trasera

middle leg
patte^F médiane
Mittelbein^N
zampa^F mediana
pata^F media

foreleg
patte^F antérieure
Vorderbein^N
zampa^F anteriore
pata^F delantera

antenna
antenne^F
Antenne^F
antenna^F
antena^F

castes
castes^F
Kasten^F
caste^F
castas^F

worker
ouvrière^F
Arbeiterin^F
ape^F operaia
obrera^F

queen
reine^F
Königin^F
ape^F regina
reina^F

drone
faux bourdon^M
Drohne^F
fuco^M
zángano^M

examples of insects

exemples^M d'insectes^M | Beispiele^N für Insekten^N | esempi^M di insetti^M | ejemplos^M de insectos^M

ANIMAL KINGDOM

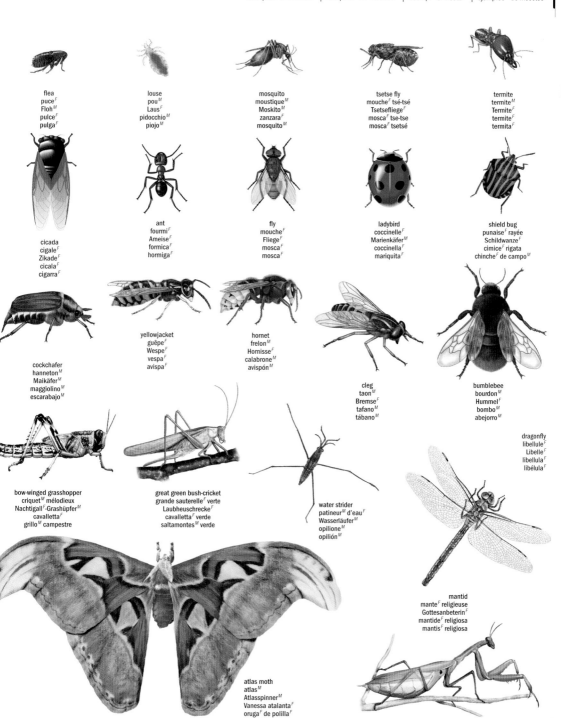

flea
puce^F
Floh^M
pulce^F
pulga^F

louse
pou^M
Laus^F
pidocchio^M
piojo^M

mosquito
moustique^M
Moskito^M
zanzara^F
mosquito^M

tsetse fly
mouche^F tsé-tsé
Tsetsefliege^F
mosca^F tse-tse
mosca^F tsetsé

termite
termite^M
Termite^F
termite^F
termita^F

cicada
cigale^F
Zikade^F
cicala^F
cigarra^F

ant
fourmi^F
Ameise^F
formica^F
hormiga^F

fly
mouche^F
Fliege^F
mosca^F
mosca^F

ladybird
coccinelle^F
Marienkäfer^M
coccinella^F
mariquita^F

shield bug
punaise^F rayée
Schildwanze^F
cimice^F rigata
chinche^F de campo^M

cockchafer
hanneton^M
Maikäfer^M
maggiolino^M
escarabajo^M

yellowjacket
guêpe^F
Wespe^F
vespa^F
avispa^F

hornet
frelon^M
Hornisse^F
calabrone^M
avispón^M

cleg
taon^M
Bremse^F
tafano^M
tábano^M

bumblebee
bourdon^M
Hummel^F
bombo^M
abejorro^M

bow-winged grasshopper
criquet^M mélodieux
Nachtigall^F-Grashüpfer^M
cavalletta^F
grillo^M campestre

great green bush-cricket
grande sauterelle^F verte
Laubheuschrecke^F
cavalletta^F verde
saltamontes^M verde

water strider
patineur^M d'eau^F
Wasserläufer^M
opilione^M
opilión^M

dragonfly
libellule^F
Libelle^F
libellula^F
libélula^F

atlas moth
atlas^M
Atlasspinner^M
Vanessa atalanta^F
oruga^F de polilla^F

mantid
mante^F religieuse
Gottesanbeterin^F
mantide^F religiosa
mantis^F religiosa

spider

araignée^F | Spinne^F | ragno^M | araña^F

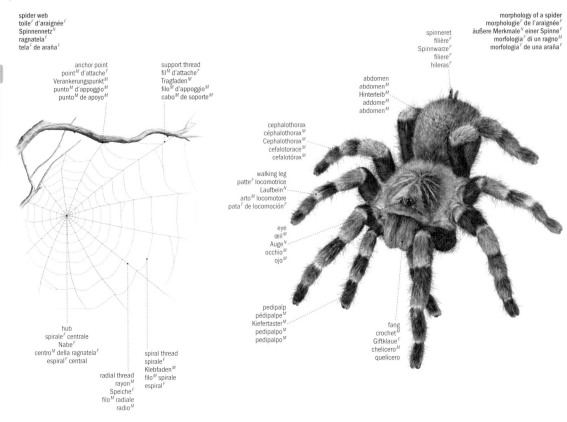

spider web
toile^F d'araignée^F
Spinnennetz^N
ragnatela^F
tela^F de araña^F

morphology of a spider
morphologie^F de l'araignée^F
äußere Merkmale^N einer Spinne^F
morfologia^F di un ragno^M
morfología^F de una araña^F

anchor point
point^M d'attache^F
Verankerungspunkt^M
punto^M d'appoggio^M
punto^M de apoyo^M

support thread
fil^M d'attache^F
Tragfaden^M
filo^M d'appoggio^M
cabo^M de soporte^M

spinneret
filière^F
Spinnwarze^F
filiere^F
hileras^F

abdomen
abdomen^M
Hinterleib^M
addome^M
abdomen^M

cephalothorax
céphalothorax^M
Cephalothorax^M
cefalotorace^M
cefalotórax^M

walking leg
patte^F locomotrice
Laufbein^N
arto^M locomotore
pata^F de locomoción^F

eye
œil^M
Auge^N
occhio^M
ojo^M

pedipalp
pédipalpe^M
Kiefertaster^M
pedipalpo^M
pedipalpo^M

fang
crochet^M
Giftklaue^F
chelicero^M
quelicero

hub
spirale^F centrale
Nabe^F
centro^M della ragnatela^F
espiral^F central

spiral thread
spirale^F
Klebfaden^M
filo^M spirale
espiral^F

radial thread
rayon^M
Speiche^F
filo^M radiale
radio^M

examples of arachnids

exemples^M d'arachnides^M | Beispiele^N für Spinnentiere^N | esempi^M di aracnidi^M | ejemplos^M de arácnidos^M

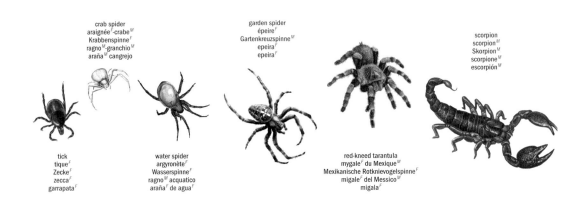

crab spider
araignée^F-crabe^M
Krabbenspinne^F
ragno^M-granchio^M
araña^M cangrejo

garden spider
épeire^F
Gartenkreuzspinne^M
epeira^F
epeira^F

scorpion
scorpion^M
Skorpion^M
scorpione^M
escorpión^M

tick
tique^F
Zecke^F
zecca^F
garrapata^F

water spider
argyronète^F
Wasserspinne^F
ragno^M acquatico
araña^F de agua^F

red-kneed tarantula
mygale^F du Mexique^M
Mexikanische Rotknievogelspinne^F
migale^F del Messico^M
migala^F

ANIMAL KINGDOM

lobster

homard^M | Hummer^M | astice^M | bogavante^M

ANIMAL KINGDOM

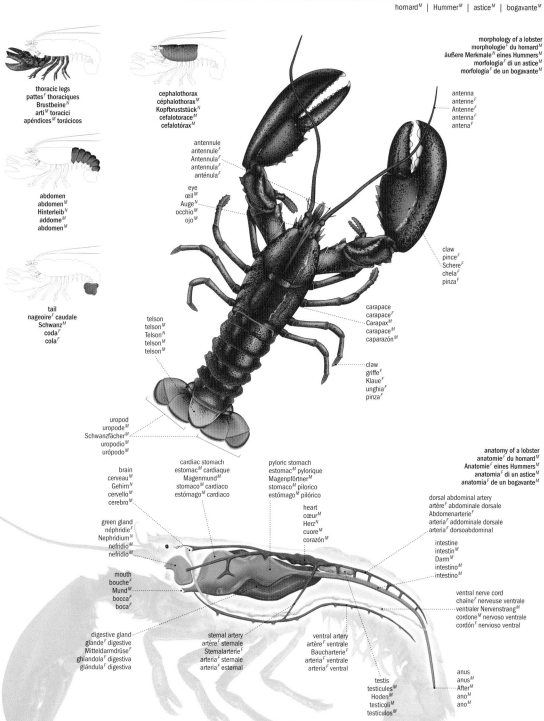

thoracic legs
pattes^F thoraciques
Brustbeine^N
arti^M toracici
apéndices^M torácicos

abdomen
abdomen
Hinterleib^N
addome^M
abdomen^M

tail
nageoire^F caudale
Schwanz^M
coda^F
cola^F

cephalothorax
céphalothorax^M
Kopfbruststück^N
cefalotorace^M
cefalotórax^M

antennule
antennule^F
Antennula^F
antennula^F
anténula^F

eye
œil^M
Auge^N
occhio^M
ojo^M

telson
telson^M
Telson^N
telson^M
telson^M

uropod
uropode^M
Schwanzfächer^M
uropodio^M
urópodo^M

morphology of a lobster
morphologie^F du homard^M
äußere Merkmale^N eines Hummers^M
morfologia^F di un astice^M
morfologia^F de un bogavante^M

antenna
antenne^F
Antenne^F
antenna^F
antena^F

claw
pince^F
Schere^F
chela^F
pinza^F

carapace
carapace^F
Carapax^M
carapace^M
caparazón^M

claw
griffe^F
Klaue^F
unghia^F
pinza^F

anatomy of a lobster
anatomie^F du homard^M
Anatomie^F eines Hummers^M
anatomia^F di un astice^M
anatomía^F de un bogavante^M

brain
cerveau^M
Gehirn^N
cervello^M
cerebro^M

cardiac stomach
estomac^M cardiaque
Magenmund^M
stomaco^M cardiaco
estómago^M cardiaco

pyloric stomach
estomac^M pylorique
Magenpförtner^M
stomaco^M pilorico
estómago^M pilórico

heart
cœur^M
Herz^N
cuore^M
corazón^M

green gland
néphridie^F
Nephridium^N
nefridio^M
nefridio^M

dorsal abdominal artery
artère^F abdominale dorsale
Abdomenarterie^F
arteria^F addominale dorsale
arteria^F dorsoabdominal

intestine
intestin^M
Darm^M
intestino^M
intestino^M

mouth
bouche^F
Mund^M
bocca^F
boca^F

ventral nerve cord
chaine^F nerveuse ventrale
ventraler Nervenstrang^M
cordone^M nervoso ventrale
cordón^F nervioso ventral

digestive gland
glande^F digestive
Mitteldarmdrüse^F
ghiandola^F digestiva
glándula^F digestiva

sternal artery
artère^F sternale
Sternalarterie^F
arteria^F sternale
arteria^F esternal

ventral artery
artère^F ventrale
Baucharterie^F
arteria^F ventrale
arteria^F ventral

testis
testicules^M
Hoden^M
testicoli^M
testículos^M

anus
anus^M
After^M
ano^M
ano^M

snail

escargot^M | Schnecke^F | chiocciola^F | caracol^M

morphology of a snail
morphologie^F de l'escargot^M
äußere Merkmale^N einer Schnecke^F
morfologia^F di una chiocciola^F
morfología^F de un caracol^M

whorl
tour^M de coquille^F
Windung^F
giro^M
espira^F

shell
coquille^F
Gehäuse^N
conchiglia^F
concha^F

growth line
ligne^F de croissance^F
Zuwachsstreifen^M
linea^F di accrescimento^M
línea^F de crecimiento^M

apex
apex^M
Apex^M
apice^M
ápice^M

head
tête^F
Kopf^M
capo^M
cabeza^F

foot
pied^M
Fuß^M
piede^M
pie^M

eye
œil^M
Auge^N
occhio^M
ojo^M

eyestalk
tentacule^M oculaire
Augenträger^M
tentacolo^M oculare
tentáculo^M ocular

mouth
bouche^F
Mund^M
bocca^F
boca^F

tentacle
tentacule^M tactile
kleiner Tentakel^M
tentacolo^M
tentáculo^M táctil

octopus

pieuvre^F | Tintenfisch^M | polpo^M | pulpo^M

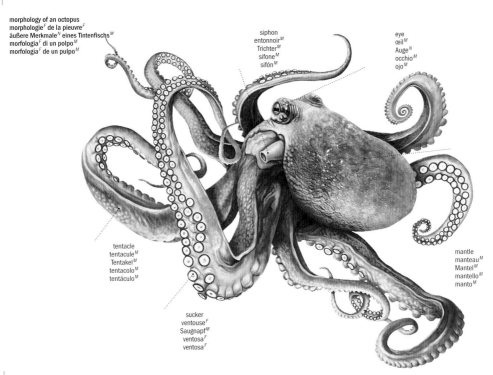

morphology of an octopus
morphologie^F de la pieuvre^F
äußere Merkmale^N eines Tintenfischs^M
morfologia^F di un polpo^M
morfología^F de un pulpo^M

siphon
entonnoir^M
Trichter^M
sifone^M
sifón^M

eye
œil^M
Auge^N
occhio^M
ojo^M

tentacle
tentacule^M
Tentakel^M
tentacolo^M
tentáculo^M

mantle
manteau^M
Mantel^M
mantello^M
manto^M

sucker
ventouse^F
Saugnapf^M
ventosa^F
ventosa^F

univalve shell

coquille^M univalve | einschalige Muschel^F | conchiglia^F univalve | concha^F univalva

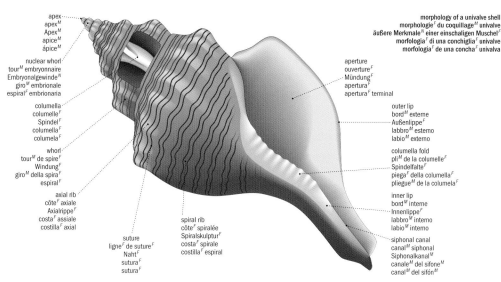

morphology of a univalve shell
morphologie^F du coquillage^M univalve
äußere Merkmale^N einer einschaligen Muschel^F
morfologia^F di una conchiglia^F univalve
morfología^F de una concha^F univalva

apex
apex^M
Apex^M
apice^M
ápice^M

nuclear whorl
tour^M embryonnaire
Embryonalgewinde^N
giro^M embrionale
espiral^F embrionaria

columella
columelle^F
Spindel^F
columella^F
columela^F

whorl
tour^M de spire^F
Windung^F
giro^M della spira^F
espiral^F

axial rib
côte^F axiale
Axialrippe^F
costa^F assiale
costilla^F axial

suture
ligne^F de suture^F
Naht^F
sutura^F
sutura^F

spiral rib
côte^F spiralée
Spiralskulptur^F
costa^F spirale
costilla^F espiral

aperture
ouverture^F
Mündung^F
apertura^F
apertura^F terminal

outer lip
bord^M externe
Außenlippe^F
labbro^M estemo
labio^M externo

columella fold
pli^M de la columelle^F
Spindelfalte^F
piega^F della columella^F
pliegue^M de la columela^F

inner lip
bord^M interne
Innenlippe^F
labbro^M interno
labio^M interno

siphonal canal
canal^M siphonal
Siphonalkanal^M
canale^M del sifone^M
canal^M del sifón^M

bivalve shell

coquillage^M bivalve | zweischalige Muschel^F | conchiglia^F bivalve | concha^F bivalva

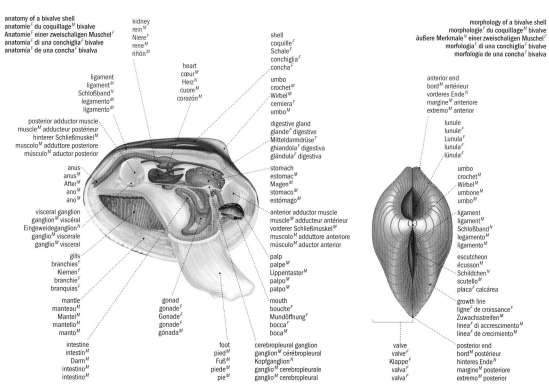

anatomy of a bivalve shell
anatomie^F du coquillage^M bivalve
Anatomie^F einer zweischaligen Muschel^F
anatomia^F di una conchiglia^F bivalve
anatomía^F de una concha^F bivalva

kidney
rein^M
Niere^F
rene^M
riñón^M

heart
cœur^M
Herz^N
cuore^M
corazón^M

shell
coquille^F
Schale^F
conchiglia^F
concha^F

ligament
ligament^M
Schloßband^N
legamento^M
ligamento^M

posterior adductor muscle
muscle^M adducteur postérieur
hinterer Schließmuskel^M
muscolo^M adduttore posteriore
músculo^M aductor posterior

anus
anus^M
After^M
ano^M
ano^M

visceral ganglion
ganglion^M viscéral
Eingeweideganglion^N
ganglio^M viscerale
ganglio^M visceral

gills
branchies^F
Kiemen^F
branchie^F
branquias^F

mantle
manteau^M
Mantel^M
mantello^M
manto^M

intestine
intestin^M
Darm^M
intestino^M
intestino^M

gonad
gonade^F
Gonade^F
gonade^F
gónada^M

foot
pied^M
Fuß^M
piede^M
pie^M

umbo
crochet^M
Wirbel^M
cerniera^F
umbo^M

digestive gland
glande^F digestive
Mitteldarmdrüse^F
ghiandola^F digestiva
glándula^F digestiva

stomach
estomac^M
Magen^M
stomaco^M
estómago^M

anterior adductor muscle
muscle^M adducteur antérieur
vorderer Schließmuskel^M
muscolo^M adduttore anteriore
músculo^M aductor anterior

palp
palpe^M
Lippentaster^M
palpo^M
palpo^M

mouth
bouche^F
Mundöffnung^F
bocca^F
boca^M

cerebropleural ganglion
ganglion^M cérébropleural
Kopfganglion^N
ganglio^M cerebropleurale
ganglio^M cerebropleural

morphology of a bivalve shell
morphologie^F du coquillage^M bivalve
äußere Merkmale^N einer zweischaligen Muschel^F
morfologia^F di una conchiglia^F bivalve
morfología de una concha^F bivalva

anterior end
bord^M antérieur
vorderes Ende^N
margine^M anteriore
extremo^M anterior

lunule
lunule^F
Lunula^F
lunula^F
lúnula^F

umbo
crochet^M
Wirbel^M
umbone^M
umbo^M

ligament
ligament^M
Schloßband^N
legamento^M
ligamento^M

escutcheon
écusson^M
Schildchen^N
scutello^M
placa^F calcárea

growth line
ligne^F de croissance^F
Zuwachsstreifen^M
linea^F di accrescimento^M
línea^F de crecimiento^M

posterior end
bord^M postérieur
hinteres Ende^N
margine^M posteriore
extremo^M posterior

valve
valve^F
Klappe^F
valva^F
valva^F

73

cartilaginous fish

poisson^M cartilagineux | Knorpelfisch^M | pesce^M cartilagineo | pez^M cartilaginoso

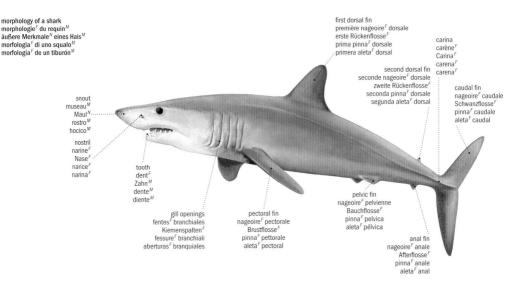

morphology of a shark
morphologie^F du requin^M
äußere Merkmale^N eines Hais^M
morfologia^F di uno squalo^M
morfología^F de un tiburón^M

first dorsal fin
première nageoire^F dorsale
erste Rückenflosse^F
prima pinna^F dorsale
primera aleta^F dorsal

carina
carène^F
Carina^F
carena^F
carena^F

second dorsal fin
seconde nageoire^F dorsale
zweite Rückenflosse^F
seconda pinna^F dorsale
segunda aleta^F dorsal

caudal fin
nageoire^F caudale
Schwanzflosse^F
pinna^F caudale
aleta^F caudal

snout
museau^M
Maul^N
rostro^M
hocico^M

nostril
narine^F
Nase^F
narice^F
narina^F

tooth
dent^F
Zahn^M
dente^M
diente^M

gill openings
fentes^F branchiales
Kiemenspalten^F
fessure^F branchiali
aberturas^F branquiales

pectoral fin
nageoire^F pectorale
Brustflosse^F
pinna^F pettorale
aleta^F pectoral

pelvic fin
nageoire^F pelvienne
Bauchflosse^F
pinna^F pelvica
aleta^F pélvica

anal fin
nageoire^F anale
Afterflosse^F
pinna^F anale
aleta^F anal

bony fish

poisson^M osseux | Knochenfisch^M | pesce^M osseo | pez^M óseo

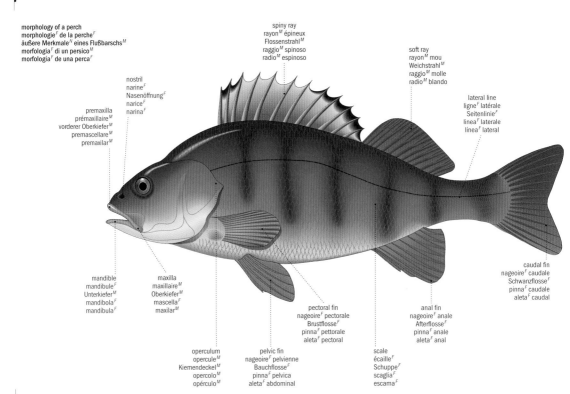

morphology of a perch
morphologie^F de la perche^F
äußere Merkmale^N eines Flußbarschs^M
morfologia^F di un persico^M
morfología^F de una perca^F

spiny ray
rayon^M épineux
Flossenstrahl^M
raggio^M spinoso
radio^M espinoso

soft ray
rayon^M mou
Weichstrahl^M
raggio^M molle
radio^M blando

nostril
narine^F
Nasenöffnung^F
narice^F
narina^F

premaxilla
prémaxillaire^M
vorderer Oberkiefer^M
premascellare^M
premaxilar^M

lateral line
ligne^F latérale
Seitenlinie^F
linea^F laterale
línea^F lateral

mandible
mandibule^F
Unterkiefer^M
mandibola^F
mandíbula^F

maxilla
maxillaire^M
Oberkiefer^M
mascella^F
maxilar^M

pectoral fin
nageoire^F pectorale
Brustflosse^F
pinna^F pettorale
aleta^F pectoral

anal fin
nageoire^F anale
Afterflosse^F
pinna^F anale
aleta^F anal

caudal fin
nageoire^F caudale
Schwanzflosse^F
pinna^F caudale
aleta^F caudal

operculum
opercule^M
Kiemendeckel^M
opercolo^M
opérculo^M

pelvic fin
nageoire^F pelvienne
Bauchflosse^F
pinna^F pelvica
aleta^F abdominal

scale
écaille^F
Schuppe^F
scaglia^F
escama^F

frog

grenouille^F | Frosch^M | rana^F | rana^F

ANIMAL KINGDOM

morphology of a frog
morphologie^F de la grenouille^F
äußere Merkmale^N eines Froschs^M
morfologia^F di una rana^F
morfología^F de una rana^F

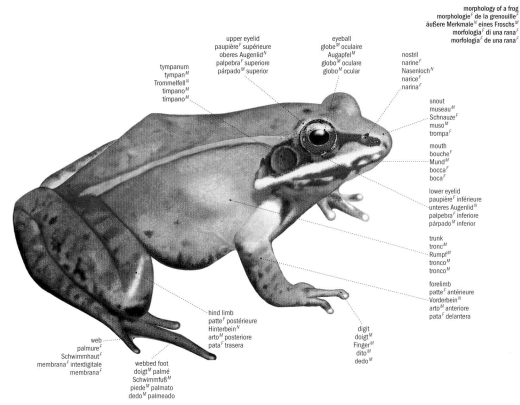

upper eyelid
paupière^F supérieure
oberes Augenlid^N
palpebra^F superiore
párpado^M superior

eyeball
globe^M oculaire
Augapfel^M
globo^M oculare
globo^M ocular

tympanum
tympan^M
Trommelfell^N
timpano^M
tímpano^M

nostril
narine^F
Nasenloch^N
narice^F
narina^F

snout
museau^M
Schnauze^F
muso^M
trompa^F

mouth
bouche^F
Mund^M
bocca^F
boca^F

lower eyelid
paupière^F inférieure
unteres Augenlid^N
palpebra^F inferiore
párpado^M inferior

trunk
tronc^M
Rumpf^M
tronco^M
tronco^M

forelimb
patte^F antérieure
Vorderbein^N
arto^M anteriore
pata^F delantera

hind limb
patte^F postérieure
Hinterbein^N
arto^M posteriore
pata^F trasera

digit
doigt^M
Finger^M
dito^M
dedo^M

web
palmure^F
Schwimmhaut^F
membrana^F interdigitale
membrana^F

webbed foot
doigt^M palmé
Schwimmfuß^M
piede^M palmato
dedo^M palmeado

examples of amphibians

exemples^M d'amphibiens^M | Beispiele^N für Amphibien^F | esempi^M di anfibi^M | ejemplos^M de anfibios^M

salamander
salamandre^F
Salamander^M
salamandra^F
salamandra^F

common frog
grenouille^F rousse
Wasserfrosch^M
rana^F comune
rana^F bermeja

tree frog
rainette^F
Laubfrosch^M
raganella^F
rana^F arboricola

wood frog
grenouille^F des bois^M
Waldfrosch^M
rana^F dei boschi^M
rana^F de bosque^M

adhesive disc
ventouse^F
Haftscheibe^F
disco^M adesivo
ventosa^F

newt
triton^M
Molch^M
tritone^M
tritón^M

common toad
crapaud^M commun
gemeine Erdkröte^F
rospo^M comune
sapo^M común

Northern leopard frog
grenouille^F léopard^M
Leopardfrosch^M
rana^F leopardo^M
rana^F leopardo

snake

serpent[M] | Schlange[F] | serpente[M] | serpiente[F]

morphology of a venomous snake: head
morphologie[F] du serpent[M] venimeux : tête[F]
äußere Merkmale[N] einer Giftschlange[F]: Kopf[M]
morfologia[F] di un serpente[M] velenoso: testa[F]
morfología[F] de una serpiente[F] venenosa: cabeza[F]

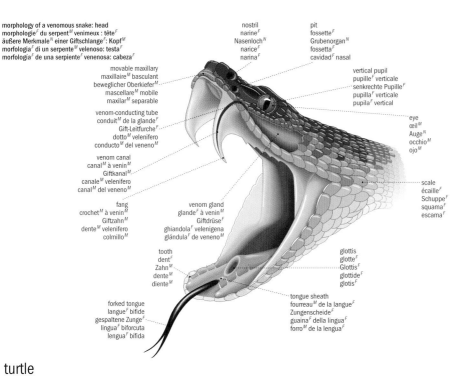

nostril
narine[F]
Nasenloch[N]
narice[F]
narina[F]

pit
fossette[F]
Grubenorgan[N]
fossetta[F]
cavidad[F] nasal

movable maxillary
maxillaire[M] basculant
beweglicher Oberkiefer[M]
mascellare[M] mobile
maxilar[M] separable

vertical pupil
pupille[F] verticale
senkrechte Pupille[F]
pupilla[F] verticale
pupila[F] vertical

venom-conducting tube
conduit[M] de la glande[F]
Gift-Leitfurche[F]
dotto[M] velenifero
conducto[M] del veneno[M]

eye
œil[M]
Auge[N]
occhio[M]
ojo[M]

venom canal
canal[M] à venin[M]
Giftkanal[M]
canale[M] velenifero
canal[M] del veneno[M]

scale
écaille[F]
Schuppe[F]
squama[F]
escama[F]

fang
crochet[M] à venin[M]
Giftzahn[M]
dente[M] velenifero
colmillo[M]

venom gland
glande[F] à venin[M]
Giftdrüse[F]
ghiandola[F] velenigena
glándula[F] de veneno[M]

tooth
dent[F]
Zahn[M]
dente[M]
diente[M]

glottis
glotte[F]
Glottis[F]
glottide[F]
glotis[F]

forked tongue
langue[F] bifide
gespaltene Zunge[F]
lingua[F] biforcuta
lengua[F] bifida

tongue sheath
fourreau[M] de la langue[F]
Zungenscheide[F]
guaina[F] della lingua[F]
forro[M] de la lengua[F]

turtle

tortue[F] | Schildkröte[F] | tartaruga[F] | tortuga[F]

morphology of a turtle
morphologie[F] de la tortue[F]
äußere Merkmale[N] einer Schildkröte[F]
morfologia[F] di una tartaruga[F]
morfología[F] de una tortuga[F]

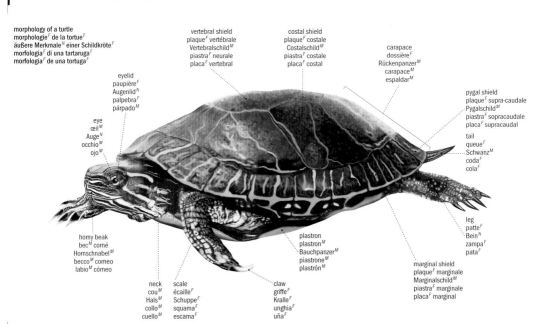

vertebral shield
plaque[F] vertébrale
Vertebralschild[M]
piastra[F] neurale
placa[F] vertebral

costal shield
plaque[F] costale
Costalschild[M]
piastra[F] costale
placa[F] costal

carapace
dossière[F]
Rückenpanzer[M]
carapace[M]
espaldar[M]

eyelid
paupière[F]
Augenlid[N]
palpebra[F]
párpado[M]

pygal shield
plaque[F] supra-caudale
Pygalschild[M]
piastra[F] sopracaudale
placa[F] supracaudal

eye
œil[M]
Auge[N]
occhio[M]
ojo[M]

tail
queue[F]
Schwanz[M]
coda[F]
cola[F]

leg
patte[F]
Bein[N]
zampa[F]
pata[F]

horny beak
bec[M] corné
Hornschnabel[M]
becco[M] corneo
labio[M] córneo

plastron
plastron[M]
Bauchpanzer[M]
piastrone[M]
plastrón[M]

marginal shield
plaque[F] marginale
Marginalschild[M]
piastra[F] marginale
placa[F] marginal

neck
cou[M]
Hals[M]
collo[M]
cuello[M]

scale
écaille[F]
Schuppe[F]
squama[F]
escama[F]

claw
griffe[F]
Kralle[F]
unghia[F]
uña[F]

examples of reptiles

exemples^M de reptiles^M | Beispiele^N für Reptilien^N | esempi^M di rettili^M | ejemplos^M de reptiles^M

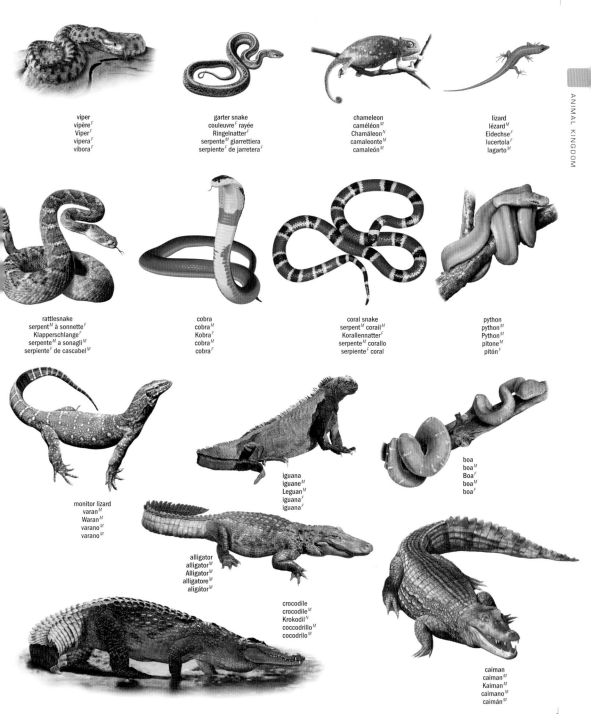

viper
vipère^F
Viper^F
vipera^F
vibora^F

garter snake
couleuvre^F rayée
Ringelnatter^F
serpente^M giarrettiera
serpiente^F de jarretera^F

chameleon
caméléon^M
Chamäleon^N
camaleonte^M
camaleón^M

lizard
lézard^M
Eidechse^F
lucertola^F
lagarto^M

rattlesnake
serpent^M à sonnette^F
Klapperschlange^F
serpente^M a sonagli^M
serpiente^F de cascabel^M

cobra
cobra^M
Kobra^F
cobra^M
cobra^F

coral snake
serpent^M corail^M
Korallennatter^F
serpente^M corallo
serpiente^F coral

python
python^M
Python^M
pitone^M
pitón^F

monitor lizard
varan^M
Waran^M
varano^M
varano^M

iguana
iguane^M
Leguan^M
iguana^F
iguana^F

boa
boa^M
Boa^F
boa^M
boa^F

alligator
alligator^M
Alligator^M
alligatore^M
aligátor^M

crocodile
crocodile^M
Krokodil^N
coccodrillo^M
cocodrilo^M

caiman
caiman^M
Kaiman^M
caimano^M
caimán^M

ANIMAL KINGDOM

bird

oiseau^M | Vogel^M | uccello^M | ave^F

morphology of a bird
morphologie^F de l'oiseau^M
äußere Merkmale^N eines Vogels^M
morfologia^F di un uccello^M
morfología^F de un pájaro^M

wing
aile^F
Flügel^M
ala^F
ala^F

back
dos^M
Rücken^M
dorso^M
lomo^M

nape
nuque^F
Nacken^M
nuca^F
cerviz^F

bill
bec^M
Schnabel^M
becco^M
pico^M

chin
menton^M
Kinn^N
mento^M
mentón^M

throat
gorge^F
Kehle^F
gola^F
garganta^F

tail feather
rectrice^F
Schwanzfeder^F
penna^F timoniera
plumas^F timoneras

rump
croupion^M
Bürzel^M
codrione^M
obispillo^M

wing covert
tectrice^F sus-alaire
Deckfeder^F
penna^F copritrice
coberteras^F

upper tail covert
tectrice^F sus-caudale
Oberschwanzdecken^F
penna^F copritrice superiore della coda^F
cobertera^F superior de la cola^F

breast
poitrine^F
Brust^F
petto^M
pechuga^F

under tail covert
tectrice^F sous-caudale
Unterschwanzdecken^F
penna^F copritrice inferiore della coda^F
cobertera^F inferior de la cola^F

flank
flanc^M
Flanke^F
fianco^M
flanco^M

abdomen
abdomen^M
Bauch^M
addome^M
abdomen^M

thigh
tibia^M
Schenkel^M
tibia^F
muslo^M

tarsus
tarse^M
Lauf^M
tarso^M
tarso^M

hind toe
doigt^M postérieur
Hinterzehe^F
dito^M posteriore
dedo^M posterior

inner toe
doigt^M interne
zweite Zehe^F
dito^M interno
dedo^M interno

outer toe
doigt^M externe
vierte Zehe^F
dito^M esterno
dedo^M externo

middle toe
doigt^M médian
dritte Zehe^F
dito^M medio
dedo^M medio

claw
ongle^M
Kralle^F
unghia^F
uña^F

head
tête^F
Kopf^M
capo^M
cabeza^F

forehead
front^M
Stim^F
fronte^F
frente^F

nostril
narine^F
Nasenloch^N
narice^F
narina^F

crown
calotte^F
Scheitel^M
vertice^M
penacho^M

upper mandible
maxillaire^M supérieur
Oberschnabel^M
mandibola^F superiore
mandibula^F superior

eyebrow stripe
raie^F sourcilière
Augenstreif^M
fascia^F sopracigliare
lista^F superciliar

lower mandible
mandibule^F
Unterschnabel^M
mandibola^F inferiore
mandibula^F inferior

auriculars
région^F auriculaire
Ohrdecken^F
regione^F auricolare
auriculares^M

malar region
région^F malaire
Bartregion^F
regione^F malare
región^F malar

eye ring
anneau^M oculaire
Augenring^M
anello^M oculare
anillo^M ocular

lore
lorum^M
Zügel^M
redine^F
puente^M

wing
aile^F
Flügel^M
ala^F
ala^F

primary covert
tectrice^F primaire
große Handdecken^F
copritrice^F primaria
coberteras^F primarias

alula
alule^F
Daumenfittich^M
alula^F
álula^F

middle covert
moyenne sus-alaire^F
mittlere Armdecken^F
copritrice^F secondaria mediana
coberteras^F medias

primaries
rémige^F primaire
Handschwingen^F
remigante^F primaria
remeras^F primarias

lesser covert
petite sus-alaire^F
kleine Armdecken^F
piccola copritrice^F secondaria
coberteras^F menores

middle primary covert
moyenne tectrice^F primaire
mittlere Handdecken^F
copritrice^F primaria media
coberteras^F primarias medias

scapular
scapulaire^F
Schulterfeder^F
scapolare^F
escapulares^M

greater covert
grande sus-alaire^F
große Armdecken^F
grande copritrice^F secondaria
coberteras^F mayores

secondaries
rémige^F secondaire
Armschwingen^F
remigante^F secondaria
remeras^F secundarias

tertial
rémige^F tertiaire
Schirmfeder^F
remigante^F terziaria
remeras^F terciarias

ANIMAL KINGDOM

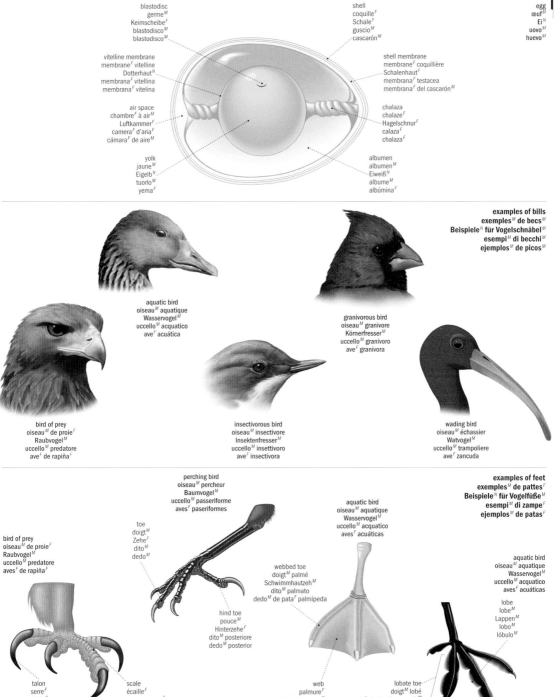

blastodisc
germe^M
Keimscheibe^F
blastodisco^M
blastodisco^M

shell
coquille^F
Schale^F
guscio^M
cascarón^M

egg
œuf^M
Ei^N
uovo^M
huevo^M

vitelline membrane
membrane^F vitelline
Dotterhaut^N
membrana^F vitellina
membrana^F vitelina

shell membrane
membrane^F coquillière
Schalenhaut^F
membrana^F testacea
membrana^F del cascarón^M

air space
chambre^F à air^M
Luftkammer^F
camera^F d'aria^F
cámara^F de aire^M

chalaza
chalaze^F
Hagelschnur^F
calaza^F
chalaza^F

yolk
jaune^M
Eigelb^N
tuorlo^M
yema^F

albumen
albumen^M
Eiweiß^N
albume^M
albúmina^F

examples of bills
exemples^M de becs^M
Beispiele^N für Vogelschnäbel^M
esempi^M di becchi^M
ejemplos^M de picos^M

aquatic bird
oiseau^M aquatique
Wasservogel^M
uccello^M acquatico
ave^F acuática

granivorous bird
oiseau^M granivore
Körnerfresser^M
uccello^M granivoro
ave^F granivora

bird of prey
oiseau^M de proie^F
Raubvogel^M
uccello^M predatore
ave^F de rapiña^F

insectivorous bird
oiseau^M insectivore
Insektenfresser^M
uccello^M insettivoro
ave^F insectivora

wading bird
oiseau^M échassier
Watvogel^M
uccello^M trampoliere
ave^F zancuda

perching bird
oiseau^M percheur
Baumvogel^M
uccello^M passeriforme
aves^F paseriformes

aquatic bird
oiseau^M aquatique
Wasservogel^M
uccello^M acquatico
aves^F acuáticas

examples of feet
exemples^M de pattes^F
Beispiele^N für Vogelfüße^M
esempi^M di zampe^F
ejemplos^M de patas^F

bird of prey
oiseau^M de proie^F
Raubvogel^M
uccello^M predatore
aves^F de rapiña^F

toe
doigt^M
Zehe^F
dito^M
dedo^M

aquatic bird
oiseau^M aquatique
Wasservogel^M
uccello^M acquatico
aves^F acuáticas

webbed toe
doigt^M palmé
Schwimmhautzeh^M
dito^M palmato
dedo^M de pata^F palmípeda

hind toe
pouce^M
Hinterzehe^F
dito^M posteriore
dedo^M posterior

lobe
lobe^M
Lappen^M
lobo^M
lóbulo^M

talon
serre^F
Kralle^F
artiglio^M
garra^F

scale
écaille^F
Hornschuppe^F
squama^F
escama^F

web
palmure^F
Schwimmhaut^F
membrana^F interdigitale
membrana^F interdigital

lobate toe
doigt^M lobé
Schwimmlappenzeh^M
dito^M lobato
dedo^M de pata^F lobulada

examples of birds

exemples^M d'oiseaux^M | unterschiedliche Vogeltypen^M | esempi^M di uccelli^M | ejemplos^M de pájaros^M

ANIMAL KINGDOM

hummingbird
colibri^M
Kolibri^M
colibri^M
colibri^M

European robin
rouge-gorge^M
Rotkehlchen^N
pettirosso^M
petirrojo^M

finch
pinson^M
Fink^M
fringuello^M
pinzón^M

kingfisher
martin-pêcheur^M
Eisvogel^M
martin pescatore^M
martín^M pescador

nightingale
rossignol^M
Nachtigall^F
usignolo^M
ruiseñor^M

sparrow
moineau^M
Sperling^M
passerotto^M
gorrión^M

swallow
hirondelle^F
Schwalbe^F
rondine^F
golondrina^F

starling
étourneau^M
Star^M
stornello^M
estornino^M

jay
geai^M
Eichelhäher^M
ghiandaia^F
arrendajo^M

cardinal
cardinal^M
Kardinal^M
cardinale^M
cardenal^M

swift
martinet^M
Mauersegler^M
rondone^M
vencejo^M

partridge
perdrix^F
Rebhuhn^N
pernice^F
perdiz^F

condor
condor^M
Kondor^M
condor^M
cóndor^M

macaw
ara^M
Ara^M
macao^M
guacamayo^M

woodpecker
pic^M
Specht^M
picchio^M
pájaro^M carpintero

raven
corbeau^M
Rabe^M
corvo^M
cuervo^M

toucan
toucan^M
Tukan^M
tucano^M
tucán^M

vulture
vautour^M
Geier^M
avvoltoio^M
buitre^M

penguin
manchot^M
Pinguin^M
pinguino^M
pingüino^M

albatross
albatros^M
Albatros^M
albatros^M
albatros^M

heron
héron^M
Reiher^M
airone^M
garza^F

pelican
pélican^M
Pelikan^M
pellicano^M
pelicano^M

stork
cigogne^F
Storch^M
cicogna^F
cigüeña^F

ANIMAL KINGDOM

pheasant
faisan^M
Fasan^M
fagiano^M
faisán^M

great horned owl
grand duc^M d'Amérique^F
Uhu^M
gufo^M reale
búho^M real

falcon
faucon^M
Falke^M
falco^M
halcón^M

quail
caille^F
Wachtel^F
quaglia^F
codorniz^F

eagle
aigle^M
Adler^M
aquila^F
águila^F

duck
canard^M
Ente^F
anatra^F
pato^M

pigeon
pigeon^M
Taube^F
piccione^M
paloma^F

hen
poule^F
Huhn^N
gallina^F
gallina^F

goose
oie^F
Gans^F
oca^F
oca^M

turkey
dindon^M
Truthahn^M
tacchino^M
pavo^M

guinea fowl
pintade^F
Perlhuhn^N
faraona^F
pintada^F

rooster
coq^M
Hahn^M
gallo^M
gallo^M

ostrich
autruche^F
Strauß^M
struzzo^M
avestruz^F

peacock
paon^M
Pfau^M
pavone^M
pavo^M real

flamingo
flamant^M
Flamingo^M
fenicottero^M
flamenco^M

ANIMAL KINGDOM

rodent

rongeur^M | Nagetier^N | roditore^M | roedor^M

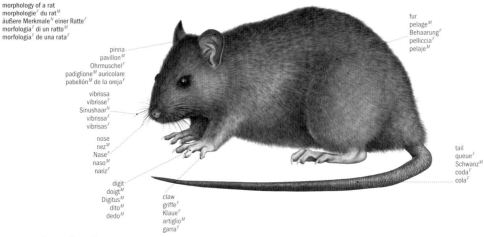

morphology of a rat
morphologie^F du rat^M
äußere Merkmale^N einer Ratte^F
morfologia^F di un ratto^M
morfologia^F de una rata^F

pinna
pavillon^M
Ohrmuschel^F
padiglione^M auricolare
pabellón^M de la oreja^F

vibrissa
vibrisse^F
Sinushaar^N
vibrissa^F
vibrisas^F

nose
nez^M
Nase^F
naso^M
nariz^F

digit
doigt^M
Digitus^M
dito^M
dedo^M

claw
griffe^F
Klaue^F
artiglio^M
garra^F

fur
pelage^M
Behaarung^F
pelliccia^F
pelaje^M

tail
queue^F
Schwanz^M
coda^F
cola^F

examples of rodents

exemples^M de mammifères^M rongeurs^M | Beispiele^N für Nagetiere^N | esempi^M di roditori^M | ejemplos^M de roedores^M

field mouse
mulot^M
Feldmaus^F
topo^M campagnolo
ratón^M de campo^M

chipmunk
tamia^M
Backenhörnchen^N
tamia^M
ardilla^M listada

jerboa
gerboise^F
Wüstenspringmaus^F
gerboa^M
jerbo^M

hamster
hamster^M
Hamster^M
criceto^M
hámster^M

squirrel
écureuil^M
Eichhörnchen^N
scoiattolo^M
ardilla^F

rat
rat^M
Ratte^F
ratto^M
rata^F

guinea pig
cobaye^M
Meerschweinchen^N
cavia^F
cobaya^F

porcupine
porc-épic^M
Stachelschwein^N
porcospino^M
puerco^M espin

groundhog
marmotte^F
Waldmurmeltier^N
marmotta^F
marmota^F

beaver
castor^M
Biber^M
castoro^M
castor^M

examples of lagomorphs

exemples^M de mammifères^M lagomorphes^M | Beispiele^N für Hasentiere^N | esempi^M di lagomorfi^M | ejemplos^M de lagomorfos^M

pika
pika^M
Pfeifhase^M
lepre^F fischiante
pica^F

rabbit
lapin^M
Kaninchen^N
coniglio^M
conejo^M

hare
lièvre^M
Hase^M
lepre^F
liebre^F

horse

cheval[M] | Pferd[N] | cavallo[M] | caballo[M]

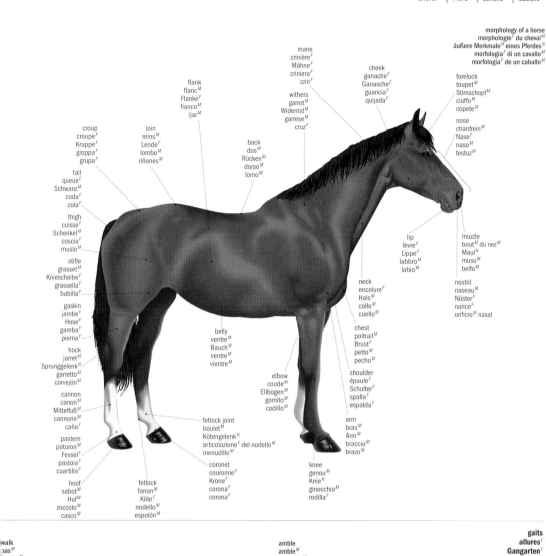

morphology of a horse
morphologie[F] du cheval[M]
äußere Merkmale[N] eines Pferdes[N]
morfologia[F] di un cavallo[M]
morfología[F] de un caballo[M]

mane
crinière[F]
Mähne[F]
criniera[F]
crin[F]

cheek
ganache[F]
Ganasche[F]
guancia[F]
quijada[F]

forelock
toupet[M]
Stirnschopf[M]
ciuffo[M]
copete[M]

flank
flanc[M]
Flanke[F]
fianco[M]
ijar[M]

withers
garrot[M]
Widerrist[M]
garrese[M]
cruz[F]

nose
chanfrein[M]
Nase[F]
naso[M]
testuz[M]

croup
croupe[F]
Kruppe[F]
groppa[F]
grupa[F]

loin
reins[M]
Lende[F]
lombo[M]
riñones[M]

back
dos[M]
Rücken[M]
dorso[M]
lomo[M]

tail
queue[F]
Schwanz[M]
coda[F]
cola[F]

lip
lèvre[F]
Lippe[F]
labbro[M]
labio[M]

muzzle
bout[M] du nez[M]
Maul[N]
muso[M]
belfo[M]

thigh
cuisse[F]
Schenkel[M]
coscia[F]
muslo[M]

stifle
grasset[M]
Kniescheibe[F]
grassella[F]
babilla[F]

neck
encolure[F]
Hals[M]
collo[M]
cuello[M]

nostril
naseau[M]
Nüster[F]
narice[F]
orificio[M] nasal

gaskin
jambe[F]
Hose[F]
gamba[F]
pierna[F]

belly
ventre[M]
Bauch[M]
ventre[M]
vientre[M]

chest
poitrail[M]
Brust[F]
petto[M]
pecho[M]

hock
jarret[M]
Sprunggelenk[N]
garretto[M]
corvejón[M]

shoulder
épaule[F]
Schulter[F]
spalla[F]
espalda[F]

cannon
canon[M]
Mittelfuß[M]
cannone[M]
caña[F]

elbow
coude[M]
Ellbogen[M]
gomito[M]
codillo[M]

arm
bras[M]
Arm[M]
braccio[M]
brazo[M]

pastern
paturon[M]
Fessel[F]
pastoia[F]
cuartilla[F]

fetlock joint
boulet[M]
Kötengelenk[N]
articolazione[F] del nodello[M]
menudillo[M]

coronet
couronne[F]
Krone[F]
corona[F]
corona[F]

knee
genou[M]
Knie[N]
ginocchio[M]
rodilla[F]

hoof
sabot[M]
Huf[M]
zoccolo[M]
casco[M]

fetlock
fanon[M]
Köte[F]
nodello[M]
espolón[M]

gaits
allures[F]
Gangarten[F]
andature[F]
andaduras[F]

walk
pas[M]
Schritt[M]
passo[M]
paso[M]

amble
amble[M]
Paßgang[M]
ambio[M]
portante[M]

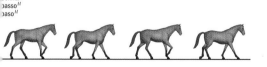

trot
trot[M]
Trab[M]
trotto[M]
trote[M]

gallop
galop[M]
Galopp[M]
galoppo[M]
galope[M]

examples of ungulate mammals

exemples^M de mammifères^M ongulés | Beispiele^N für Huftiere^N | esempi^M di mammiferi^M ungulati | ejemplos^M de mamíferos^M ungulados

ANIMAL KINGDOM

peccary
pécari^M
Nabelschwein^N
pecari^M
pécari^M

wild boar
sanglier^M
Wildschwein^N
cinghiale^M
jabalí^M

pig
porc^M
Schwein^N
maiale^M
cerdo^M

goat
chèvre^F
Ziege^F
capra^F
cabra^F

antelope
antilope^F
Antilope^F
antilope^F
antilope^M

sheep
mouton^M
Schaf^N
pecora^F
oveja^F

calf
veau^M
Kalb^N
vitello^M
ternero^M

white-tailed deer
cerf^M de Virginie
Reh^N
cervo^M dalla coda^F bianca
ciervo^M de Virginia^F

mouflon
mouflon^M
Mufflon^M
muflone^M
muflón^M

reindeer
renne^M
Rentier^N
renna^F
reno^M

Canadian elk
cerf^M du Canada
Wapitihirsch^M
wapiti^M
uapiti^M

okapi
okapi^M
Okapi^N
okapi^M
okapi^M

ass
âne^M
Esel^M
asino^M
asno^M

mule
mulet^M
Maultier^N
mulo^M
mula^F

cow
vache^F
Kuh^F
mucca^F
vaca^F

llama
lama^M
Lama^N
lama^M
llama^F

zebra
zèbre^M
Zebra^N
zebra^F
cebra^F

bison
bison^M
Bison^M
bisonte^M
bisonte^M

buffalo
buffle^M
Büffel^M
bufalo^M
búfalo^M

ANIMAL KINGDOM

ox
bœuf [M]
Ochse [M]
bue [M]
buey [M]

yak
yack [M]
Yak [M]
yak [M]
yak [M]

horse
cheval [M]
Pferd [N]
cavallo [M]
caballo [M]

elk
élan [M]
Elch [M]
alce [F]
alce [M]

camel
chameau [M]
Kamel [N]
cammello [M]
camello [M]

dromedary
dromadaire [M]
Dromedar [N]
dromedario [M]
dromedario [M]

rhinoceros
rhinocéros [M]
Nashorn [N]
rinoceronte [M]
rinoceronte [M]

hippopotamus
hippopotame [M]
Nilpferd [N]
ippopotamo [M]
hipopótamo [M]

giraffe
girafe [F]
Giraffe [F]
giraffa [F]
jirafa [F]

elephant
éléphant [M]
Elefant [M]
elefante [M]
elefante [M]

ANIMAL KINGDOM

dog

chien^M | Hund^M | cane^M | perro^M

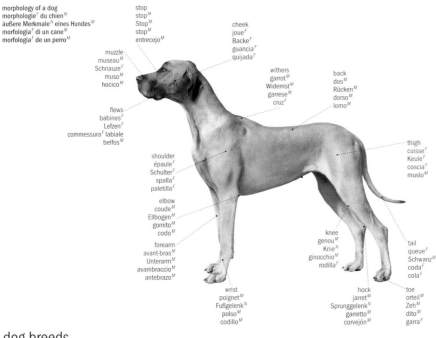

morphology of a dog
morphologie^F du chien^M
äußere Merkmale^N eines Hundes^M
morfologia^F di un cane^M
morfología^F de un perro^M

stop
stop^M
Stop^M
stop^M
entrecejo^M

cheek
joue^F
Backe^F
guancia^F
quijada^F

muzzle
museau^M
Schnauze^F
muso^M
hocico^M

withers
garrot^M
Widerrist^M
garrese^M
cruz^F

back
dos^M
Rücken^M
dorso^M
lomo^M

flews
babines^F
Lefzen^F
commessura^F labiale
belfos^M

thigh
cuisse^F
Keule^F
coscia^F
muslo^M

shoulder
épaule^F
Schulter^F
spalla^F
paletilla^F

elbow
coude^M
Ellbogen^M
gomito^M
codo^M

knee
genou^M
Knie^N
ginocchio^M
rodilla^F

tail
queue^F
Schwanz^M
coda^F
cola^F

forearm
avant-bras^M
Unterarm^M
avambraccio^M
antebrazo^M

wrist
poignet^M
Fußgelenk^N
polso^M
codillo^M

hock
jarret^M
Sprunggelenk^N
garretto^M
corvejón^M

toe
orteil^M
Zeh^M
dito^M
garra^F

dog breeds

races^F de chiens^M | Hunderassen^F | razze^F canine | razas^F de perros^M

bulldog
bouledogue^M
Bulldogge^F
bulldog^M
buldog^M

poodle
caniche^M
Pudel^M
barbone^M
caniche^M

schnauzer
schnauzer^M
Schnauzer^M
schnauzer^M
schnauzer^M

collie
colley^M
Collie^M
collie^M
collie^M

dalmatian
dalmatien^M
Dalmatiner^M
dalmata^M
dálmata^M

Saint Bernard
saint-bernard^M
Bernhardiner^M
sanbernardo^M
San Bernardo^M

Great Dane
danois^M
Dänische Dogge^F
alano^M
Gran Danés^M

German shepherd
berger^M allemand
Deutscher Schäferhund^M
pastore^M tedesco
pastor^M alemán

cat

chat^M | Katze^F | gatto^M | gato^M doméstico

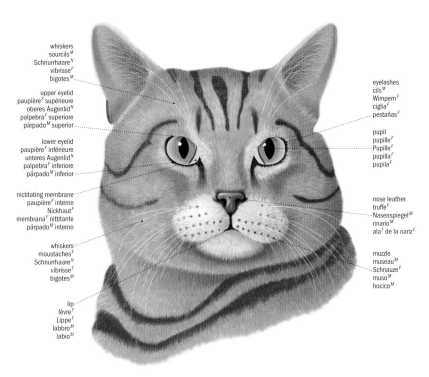

cat's head
tête^F
Kopf^M der Katze^F
testa^F di gatto^M
cabeza^F

whiskers
sourcils^M
Schnurrhaare^N
vibrisse^F
bigotes^M

upper eyelid
paupière^F supérieure
oberes Augenlid^N
palpebra^F superiore
párpado^M superior

lower eyelid
paupière^F inférieure
unteres Augenlid^N
palpebra^F inferiore
párpado^M inferior

nictitating membrane
paupière^F interne
Nickhaut^F
membrana^F nittitante
párpado^M interno

whiskers
moustaches^F
Schnurrhaare^N
vibrisse^F
bigotes^M

lip
lèvre^F
Lippe^F
labbro^M
labio^M

eyelashes
cils^M
Wimpern^F
ciglia^F
pestañas^F

pupil
pupille^F
Pupille^F
pupilla^F
pupila^F

nose leather
truffe^F
Nasenspiegel^M
rinario^M
ala^F de la nariz^F

muzzle
museau^M
Schnauze^F
muso^M
hocico^M

cat breeds

races^F de chats^M | Katzenrassen^F | razze^F di gatti^M | razas^F de gatos^M

Siamese
siamois^M
Siamkatze^F
siamese^M
siamés^M

Abyssinian
abyssin^M
Abessinierkatze^F
abissino^M
abisinio^M

Persian
persan^M
Perserkatze^F
persiano^M
persa^M

Maine Coon
Maine coon^M
Maine Coon^F
gatto^M del Maine^M
Maine Coon^M

Manx
chat^M de l'île^F de Man
Manxkatze^F
gatto^M dell'isola^F di Man
Manx^M

examples of carnivorous mammals

exemples^M de mammifères^M carnivores | Beispiele^N für Raubtiere^N | esempi^M di mammiferi^M carnivori | ejemplos^M de mamíferos^M carnívoros

ANIMAL KINGDOM

mink
vison^M
Nerz^M
visone^M
visón^M

stone marten
fouine^F
Steinmarder^M
faina^F
garduña^F

marten
martre^F
Marder^M
martora^F
marta^F

weasel
belette^F
Wiesel^N
donnola^F
comadreja^F

fox
renard^M
Fuchs^M
volpe^F
zorro^M

raccoon
raton^M laveur
Waschbär^M
procione^M
mapache^M

fennec
fennec^M
Wüstenfuchs^M
volpe^F del deserto^M
fenec^M

river otter
loutre^F de rivière^F
Seeotter^M
lontra^F comune
nutria^F de rio^M

mongoose
mangouste^F
Mungo^M
mangusta^F
mangosta^F

badger
blaireau^M
Dachs^M
tasso^M
tejón^M

skunk
moufette^F
Stinktier^N
moffetta^F
mofeta^M

hyena
hyène^F
Hyäne^F
iena^F
hiena^F

lynx
lynx^M
Luchs^M
lince^F
lince^M

wolf
loup^M
Wolf^M
lupo^M
lobo^M

cougar
puma^M
Puma^M
puma^M
puma^M

ANIMAL KINGDOM

cheetah
guépard[M]
Gepard[M]
ghepardo[M]
guepardo[M]

leopard
léopard[M]
Leopard[M]
leopardo[M]
leopardo[M]

lion
lion[M]
Löwe[M]
leone[M]
león[M]

jaguar
jaguar[M]
Jaguar[M]
giaguaro[M]
jaguar[M]

tiger
tigre[M]
Tiger[M]
tigre[F]
tigre[M]

polar bear
ours[M] polaire
Eisbär[M]
orso[M] polare
oso[M] polar

black bear
ours[M] noir
Schwarzbär[M]
orso[M] bruno
oso[M] negro

89

ANIMAL KINGDOM

dolphin

dauphin^M | Delphin^M | delfino^M | delfín^M

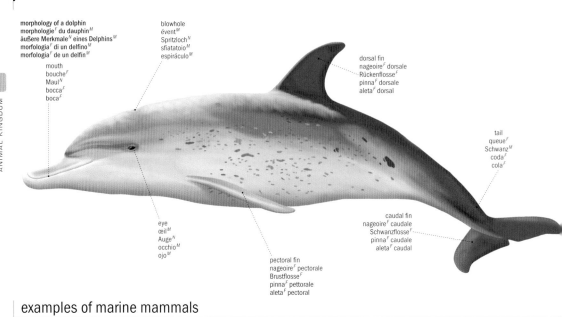

morphology of a dolphin
morphologie^F du dauphin^M
äußere Merkmale^N eines Delphins^M
morfologia^F di un delfino^M
morfologia^F de un delfín^M

mouth
bouche^F
Maul^N
bocca^F
boca^F

blowhole
évent^M
Spritzloch^N
sfiatatoio^M
espiráculo^M

dorsal fin
nageoire^F dorsale
Rückenflosse^F
pinna^F dorsale
aleta^F dorsal

tail
queue^F
Schwanz^M
coda^F
cola^F

eye
œil^M
Auge^N
occhio^M
ojo^M

pectoral fin
nageoire^F pectorale
Brustflosse^F
pinna^F pettorale
aleta^F pectoral

caudal fin
nageoire^F caudale
Schwanzflosse^F
pinna^F caudale
aleta^F caudal

examples of marine mammals

exemples^M de mammifères^M marins | Beispiele^N für Meeressäugetiere^N | esempi^M di mammiferi^M marini | ejemplos^M de mamíferos^M marinos

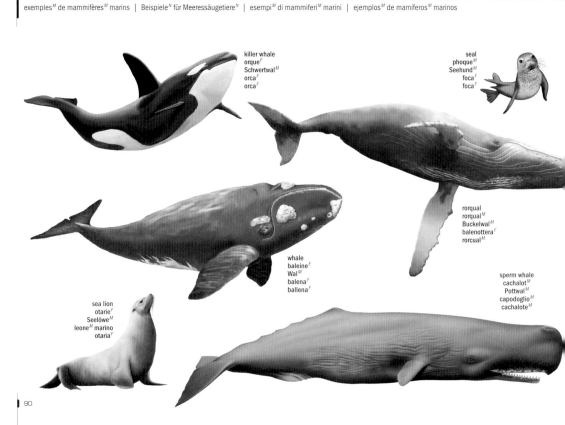

killer whale
orque^F
Schwertwal^M
orca^F
orca^F

seal
phoque^M
Seehund^M
foca^F
foca^F

whale
baleine^F
Wal^M
balena^F
ballena^F

rorqual
rorqual^M
Buckelwal^M
balenottera^F
rorcual^M

sperm whale
cachalot^M
Pottwal^M
capodoglio^M
cachalote^M

sea lion
otarie^F
Seelöwe^M
leone^M marino
otaria^F

gorilla

gorille^M | Gorilla^M | gorilla^M | gorila^M

morphology of a gorilla
morphologie^F du gorille^M
äußere Merkmale^N eines Gorillas^M
morfologia^F di un gorilla^M
morfología^F de un gorila^M

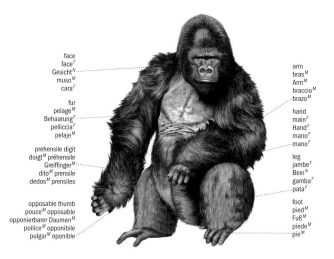

face
face^F
Gesicht^N
muso^M
cara^F

fur
pelage^M
Behaarung^F
pelliccia^F
pelaje^M

prehensile digit
doigt^M préhensile
Greiffinger^M
dito^M prensile
dedos^M prensiles

opposable thumb
pouce^M opposable
opponierbarer Daumen^M
pollice^M opponibile
pulgar^M oponible

arm
bras^M
Arm^M
braccio^M
brazo^M

hand
main^F
Hand^F
mano^F
mano^F

leg
jambe^F
Bein^N
gamba^F
pata^F

foot
pied^M
Fuß^M
piede^M
pie^M

examples of primates

exemples^M de mammifères^M primates | Beispiele^N für Primaten^M | esempi^M di primati^M | ejemplos^M de primates^M

tamarin
tamarin^M
Tamarin^M
tamarino^M
tamarino^M

marmoset
ouistiti^M
Pinseläffchen^N
uistiti^M
titi^M

baboon
babouin^M
Pavian^M
babbuino^M
babuino^M

macaque
macaque^M
Makak^M
macaco^M
macaco^M

orangutan
orang-outan^M
Orang-Utan^M
orangotango^M
orangután^M

chimpanzee
chimpanzé^M
Schimpanse^M
scimpanzé^M
chimpancé^M

lemur
lémurien^M
Lemure^M
lemure^M
lémur^M

gibbon
gibbon^M
Gibbon^M
gibbone^M
gibón^M

91

man

homme^M | Mann^M | uomo^M | hombre^M

anterior view
face^F antérieure
Vorderansicht^F
vista^F anteriore
vista^F anterior

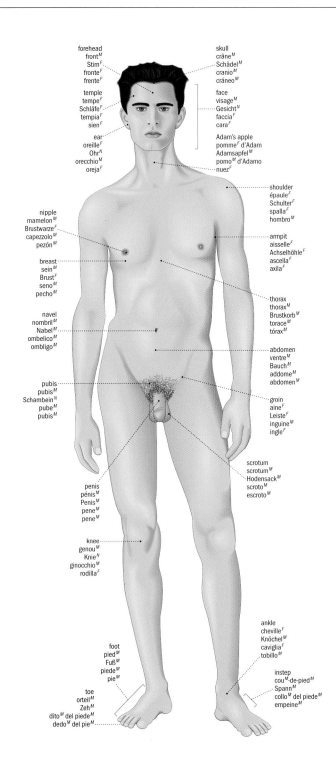

forehead
front^M
Stirn^F
fronte^F
frente^F

temple
tempe^F
Schläfe^F
tempia^F
sien^F

ear
oreille^F
Ohr^N
orecchio^M
oreja^F

skull
crâne^M
Schädel^M
cranio^M
cráneo^M

face
visage^M
Gesicht^N
faccia^F
cara^F

Adam's apple
pomme^F d'Adam
Adamsapfel^M
pomo^M d'Adamo
nuez^F

shoulder
épaule^F
Schulter^F
spalla^F
hombro^M

nipple
mamelon^M
Brustwarze^F
capezzolo^M
pezón^M

armpit
aisselle^F
Achselhöhle^F
ascella^F
axila^F

breast
sein^M
Brust^F
seno^M
pecho^M

thorax
thorax^M
Brustkorb^M
torace^M
tórax^M

navel
nombril^M
Nabel^M
ombelico^M
ombligo^M

abdomen
ventre^M
Bauch^M
addome^M
abdomen^M

pubis
pubis^M
Schambein^N
pube^M
pubis^M

groin
aine^F
Leiste^F
inguine^M
ingle^F

scrotum
scrotum^M
Hodensack^M
scroto^M
escroto^M

penis
pénis^M
Penis^M
pene^M
pene^M

knee
genou^M
Knie^N
ginocchio^M
rodilla^F

ankle
cheville^F
Knöchel^M
caviglia^F
tobillo^M

instep
cou^M-de-pied^M
Spann^M
collo^M del piede^M
empeine^M

foot
pied^M
Fuß^M
piede^M
pie^M

toe
orteil^M
Zeh^M
dito^M del piede^M
dedo^M del pie^M

posterior view
face^F postérieure
Rückenansicht^F
vista^F posteriore
vista^F posterior

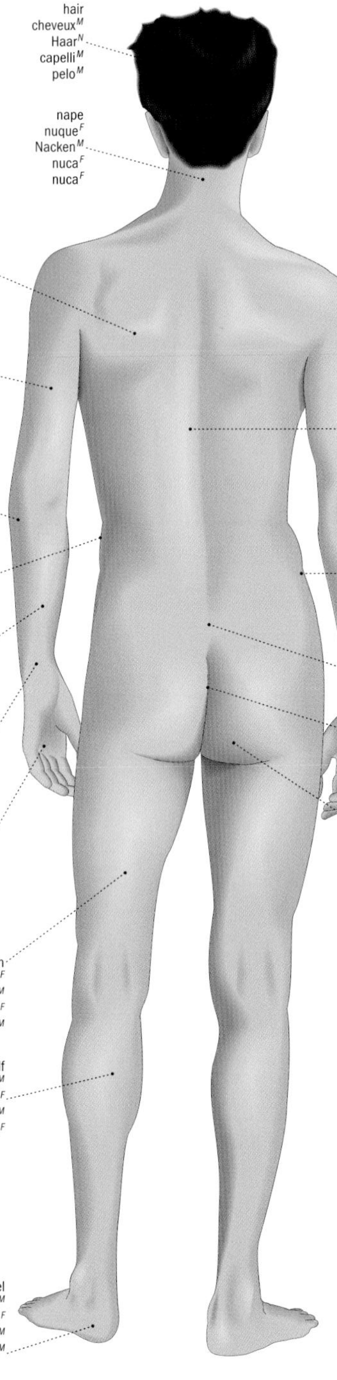

hair
cheveux^M
Haar^N
capelli^M
pelo^M

nape
nuque^F
Nacken^M
nuca^F
nuca^F

shoulder blade
omoplate^F
Schulterblatt^N
scapola^F
omoplato^M /escápula^F

arm
bras^M
Arm^M
braccio^M
brazo^M

elbow
coude^M
Ellbogen^M
gomito^M
codo^M

waist
taille^F
Taille^F
vita^F
cintura^F

forearm
avant-bras^M
Unterarm^M
avambraccio^M
antebrazo^M

wrist
poignet^M
Handgelenk^N
polso^M
muñeca^F

hand
main^F
Hand^F
mano^F
mano^F

thigh
cuisse^F
Oberschenkel^M
coscia^F
muslo^M

calf
mollet^M
Wade^F
polpaccio^M
pantorrilla^F

heel
talon^M
Ferse^F
tallone^M
talón^M

head
tête^F
Kopf^M
testa^F
cabeza^F

neck
cou^M
Hals^M
collo^M
cuello^M

back
dos^M
Rücken^M
schiena^F
espalda^F

trunk
tronc^M
Rumpf^M
tronco^M
tronco^M

hip
hanche^F
Hüfte^F
fianco^M
cadera^F

loin
reins^M
Lende^F
lombo^M
región^F lumbar

anal cleft
raie^F des fesses^F
Afterfurche^F
fessura^F
pliegue^M anal

buttock
fesse^F
Gesäß^N
natica^F
nalga^F

leg
jambe^F
Bein^N
gamba^F
pierna^F

foot
pied^M
Fuß^M
piede^M
pie^M

woman

femme[F] | Frau[F] | donna[F] | mujer[F]

anterior view
face[F] antérieure
Vorderansicht[F]
vista[F] anteriore
vista[F] anterior

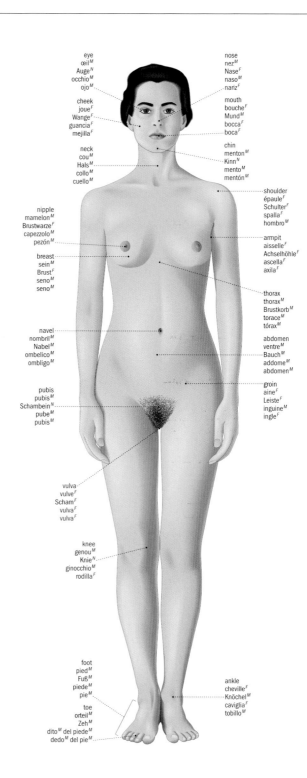

eye
œil[M]
Auge[N]
occhio[M]
ojo[M]

cheek
joue[F]
Wange[F]
guancia[F]
mejilla[F]

neck
cou[M]
Hals[M]
collo[M]
cuello[M]

nipple
mamelon[M]
Brustwarze[F]
capezzolo[M]
pezón[M]

breast
sein[M]
Brust[F]
seno[M]
seno[M]

navel
nombril[M]
Nabel[M]
ombelico[M]
ombligo[M]

pubis
pubis[M]
Schambein[N]
pube[M]
pubis[M]

vulva
vulve[F]
Scham[F]
vulva[F]
vulva[F]

knee
genou[M]
Knie[N]
ginocchio[M]
rodilla[F]

foot
pied[M]
Fuß[M]
piede[M]
pie[M]

toe
orteil[M]
Zeh[M]
dito[M] del piede[M]
dedo[M] del pie[M]

nose
nez[M]
Nase[F]
naso[M]
nariz[F]

mouth
bouche[F]
Mund[M]
bocca[F]
boca[F]

chin
menton[M]
Kinn[N]
mento[M]
mentón[M]

shoulder
épaule[F]
Schulter[F]
spalla[F]
hombro[M]

armpit
aisselle[F]
Achselhöhle[F]
ascella[F]
axila[F]

thorax
thorax[M]
Brustkorb[M]
torace[M]
tórax[M]

abdomen
ventre[M]
Bauch[M]
addome[M]
abdomen[M]

groin
aine[F]
Leiste[F]
inguine[M]
ingle[F]

ankle
cheville[F]
Knöchel[M]
caviglia[F]
tobillo[M]

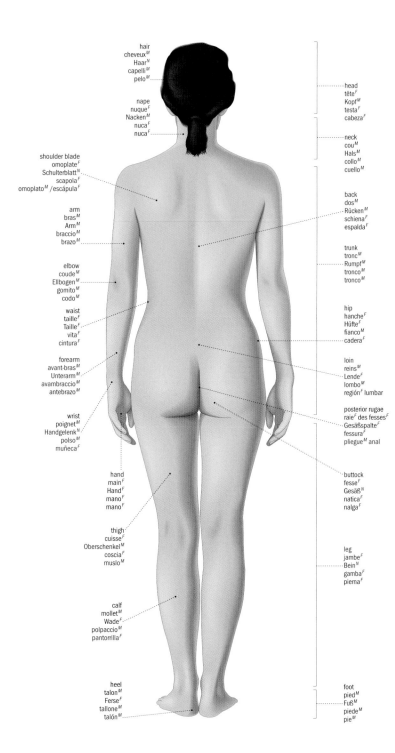

posterior view
face^F postérieure
Rückenansicht^F
vista^F posteriore
vista^F posterior

hair
cheveux^M
Haar^N
capelli^M
pelo^M

head
tête^F
Kopf^M
testa^F
cabeza^F

nape
nuque^F
Nacken^M
nuca^F
nuca^F

neck
cou^M
Hals^M
collo^M
cuello^M

shoulder blade
omoplate^F
Schulterblatt^N
scapola^F
omoplato^M /escápula^F

back
dos^M
Rücken^M
schiena^F
espalda^F

arm
bras^M
Arm^M
braccio^M
brazo^M

trunk
tronc^M
Rumpf^M
tronco^M
tronco^M

elbow
coude^M
Ellbogen^M
gomito^M
codo^M

waist
taille^F
Taille^F
vita^F
cintura^F

hip
hanche^F
Hüfte^F
fianco^M
cadera^F

forearm
avant-bras^M
Unterarm^M
avambraccio^M
antebrazo^M

loin
reins^M
Lende^F
lombo^M
región^F lumbar

wrist
poignet^M
Handgelenk^N
polso^M
muñeca^F

posterior rugae
raie^F des fesses^F
Gesäßspalte^F
fessura^F
pliegue^M anal

hand
main^F
Hand^F
mano^F
mano^F

buttock
fesse^F
Gesäß^N
natica^F
nalga^F

thigh
cuisse^F
Oberschenkel^M
coscia^F
muslo^M

leg
jambe^F
Bein^N
gamba^F
pierna^F

calf
mollet^M
Wade^F
polpaccio^M
pantorrilla^F

heel
talon^M
Ferse^F
tallone^M
talón^M

foot
pied^M
Fuß^M
piede^M
pie^M

muscles

muscles^M | Muskeln^M | muscoli^M | músculos^M

anterior view
face^F antérieure
Vorderansicht^F
vista^F anteriore
vista^F anterior

orbicularis oculi
orbiculaire^M des paupières^F
Augenringmuskel^M
orbicolare^M dell'occhio^M
orbicular^M de los párpados^M

masseter
masséter^M
Kaumuskel^M
massetere^M
masetero^M

deltoid
deltoide^M
Deltamuskel^M
deltoide^M
deltoides^M

external oblique
grand oblique^M de l'abdomen^M
äußerer schräger Bauchmuskel^M
obliquo^M esterno dell'addome^M
oblicuo^M mayor del abdomen^M

abdominal rectus
grand droit^M de l'abdomen^M
gerader Bauchmuskel^M
retto^M dell'addome^M
recto^M del abdomen^M

brachioradialis
huméro-stylo-radial^M
Oberarmspeichenmuskel^M
brachioradiale^M
supinador^M largo

tensor of fascia lata
tenseur^M du fascia lata^M
Schenkelbindenspanner^M
tensore^M della fascia^F lata
tensor^M de la fascia lata^F

long adductor
moyen adducteur^M
langer Oberschenkelanzieher^M
adduttore^M lungo
aductor^M del muslo^M

sartorius
couturier^M
Schneidermuskel^M
sartorio^M
sartorio^M

rectus femoris
droit^M antérieur de la cuisse^F
gerader Schenkelmuskel^M
retto^M della coscia^F
recto^M anterior

vastus medialis
vaste^M interne du membre^M inférieur
innerer Schenkelmuskel^M
vasto^M mediale
vasto^M externo

long peroneal
long péronier^M latéral
langer Wadenbeinmuskel^M
peroneo^M lungo
peroneo^M largo

anterior tibial
jambier^M antérieur
vorderer Schienbeinmuskel^M
tibiale^M anteriore
tibial^M anterior

short extensor of toes
pédieux^M
kurzer Zehenstrecker^M
estensore^M breve delle dita^F
pedio^M

frontal
frontal^M
Stirn^F
frontale^M
frontal^M

sternocleidomastoid
sterno-cléido-mastoïdien^M
Kopfnicker^M
sternocleidomastoideo^M
esternocleidomastoideo^M

trapezius
trapèze^M
Kapuzenmuskel^M
trapezio^M
trapecio^M

greater pectoral
grand pectoral^M
großer Brustmuskel^M
grande pettorale^M
pectoral^M mayor

biceps of arm
biceps^M brachial
zweiköpfiger Armstrecker^M
bicipite^M brachiale
bíceps^M braquial

brachial
brachial^M antérieur
Armbeuger^M
brachiale^M
braquial^M anterior

round pronator
rond pronateur^M
runder Einwärtsdreher^M
pronatore^M rotondo
pronador^M redondo

long palmar
grand palmaire^M
langer Hohlhandmuskel^M
palmare^M lungo
palmar^M mayor

ulnar flexor of wrist
cubital^M antérieur
Handbeuger^M der Ellenseite^F
flessore^M ulnare del carpo^M
cubital^M anterior

short palmar
petit palmaire^M
kurzer Hohlhandmuskel^M
palmare^M breve
palmar^M menor

vastus lateralis
vaste^M externe du membre^M inférieur
äußerer Schenkelmuskel^M
vasto^M laterale
vasto^M interno

gastrocnemius
jumeau^M
Zwillingswadenmuskel^M
gastrocnemio^M
gemelos^M

soleus
soléaire^M
Schollenmuskel^M
soleo^M
sóleo^M

long extensor of toes
extenseur^M commun des orteils^M
langer Zehenstrecker^M
estensore^M lungo delle dita^F
extensor^M largo de los dedos^M del pie^M

plantar interosseous
interosseux^M
Zwischenknochenmuskel^M
interosseo^M plantare
interóseos^M del pie^M

occipital
occipital^M
Hinterhauptmuskel^M
occipitale^M
occipital^M

posterior view
face^F postérieure
Rückansicht^F
vista^F posteriore
vista^F posterior

splenius muscle of head
splénius^M de la tête^F
Riemenmuskel^M
splenio^M
esplenio^M

complexus
grand complexus^M
Bauschmuskel^M
grande complesso^M
complexo^M mayor

trapezius
trapèze^M
Kapuzenmuskel^M
trapezio^M
trapecio^M

infraspinatus
sous-épineux^M
Untergrätenmuskel^M
infraspinato^M
infraspinoso^M

teres minor
petit rond^M
kleiner Rundmuskel^M
piccolo rotondo^M
redondo^M menor

latissimus dorsi
grand dorsal^M
breiter Rückenmuskel^M
gran dorsale^M
dorsal^M ancho

teres major
grand rond^M
großer Rundmuskel^M
grande rotondo^M
redondo^M mayor

triceps of arm
triceps^M brachial
dreiköpfiger Armstrecker^M
tricipite^M brachiale
tríceps^M braquial

brachioradialis
long supinateur^M
Oberarmspeichenmuskel^M
brachioradiale^M
supinador^M largo

long radial extensor of wrist
premier radial^M externe
langer Handstrecker^M der Speichenseite^F
estensore^M radiale lungo del carpo^M
radial^M externo primero

short radial extensor of wrist
deuxième radial^M externe
kurzer Handstrecker^M der Speichenseite^F
estensore^M radiale breve del carpo^M
radial^M externo segundo

anconeus
anconé^M
Knorrenmuskel^M
anconeo^M
ancóneo^M

ulnar flexor of wrist
cubital^M antérieur
Handbeuger^M der Ellenseite^F
flessore^M ulnare del carpo^M
cubital^M anterior

common extensor of fingers
extenseur^M commun des doigts^M
gemeinsamer Fingerstrecker^M
estensore^M comune delle dita^F
extensor^M común de los dedos^M

gluteus maximus
grand fessier^M
großer Gesäßmuskel^M
grande gluteo^M
glúteo^M mayor

ulnar extensor of wrist
cubital^M postérieur
Handstrecker^M der Ellenseite^F
estensore^M ulnare del carpo^M
cubital^M posterior

semitendinosus
demi-tendineux^M
Halbsehnenmuskel^M
semitendinoso^M
semitendinoso^M

external oblique
grand oblique^M de l'abdomen^M
äußerer schräger Bauchmuskel^M
obliquo^M esterno dell'addome^M
oblicuo^M mayor del abdomen^M

biceps of thigh
biceps^M crural
zweiköpfiger Schenkelmuskel^M
bicipite^M femorale
biceps^M femoral

vastus lateralis
vaste^M externe du membre^M inférieur
äußerer Schenkelmuskel^M
vasto^M laterale
vasto^M interno

semimembranosus
demi-membraneux^M
Plattsehnenmuskel^M
semimembranoso^M
semimembranoso^M

great adductor
grand adducteur^M
großer Oberschenkelanzieher^M
grande adduttore^M
aductor^M mayor

gracile
droit^M interne
Schlankmuskel^M
gracile^M
recto^M interno del muslo^M

plantar
plantaire^M grêle
Sohlenspanner^M
plantare^M
plantar^M delgado

short peroneal
court péronier^M latéral
kurzer Wadenbeinmuskel^M
peroneo^M breve
peroneo^M corto

gastrocnemius
jumeau^M
Zwillingswadenmuskel^M
gastrocnemio^M
gemelos^M

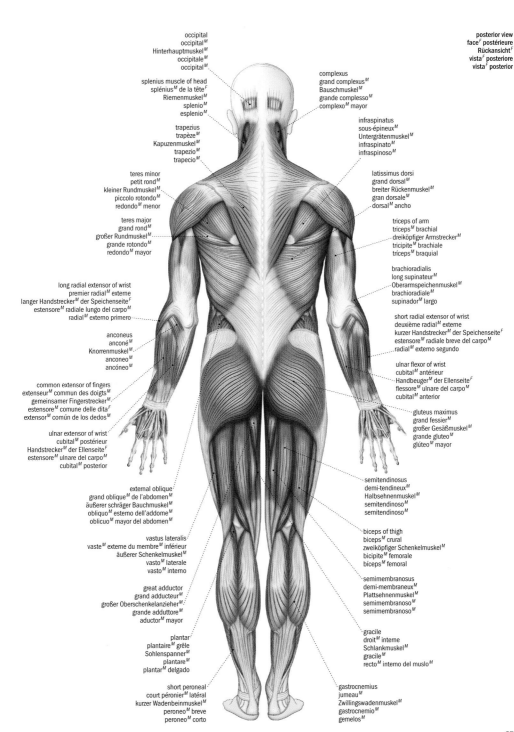

97

skeleton

squelette^M | Skelett^N | scheletro^M | esqueleto^M

HUMAN BEING

anterior view
vue^F antérieure
Vorderansicht^F
vista^F anteriore
vista^F anterior

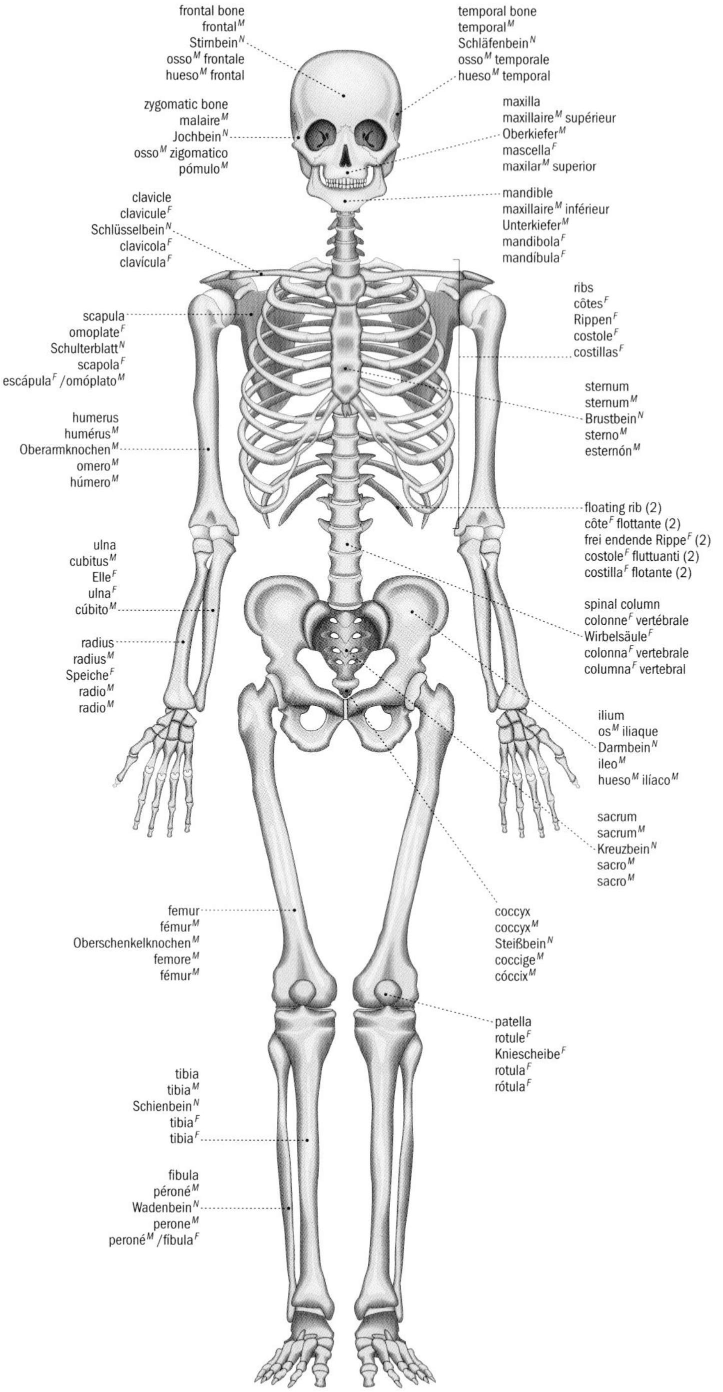

frontal bone
frontal^M
Stirnbein^N
osso^M frontale
hueso^M frontal

temporal bone
temporal^M
Schläfenbein^N
osso^M temporale
hueso^M temporal

zygomatic bone
malaire^M
Jochbein^N
osso^M zigomatico
pómulo^M

maxilla
maxillaire^M supérieur
Oberkiefer^M
mascella^F
maxilar^M superior

clavicle
clavicule^F
Schlüsselbein^N
clavicola^F
clavícula^F

mandible
maxillaire^M inférieur
Unterkiefer^M
mandibola^F
mandíbula^F

ribs
côtes^F
Rippen^F
costole^F
costillas^F

scapula
omoplate^F
Schulterblatt^N
scapola^F
escápula^F/omóplato^M

sternum
sternum^M
Brustbein^N
sterno^M
esternón^M

humerus
humérus^M
Oberarmknochen^M
omero^M
húmero^M

floating rib (2)
côte^F flottante (2)
frei endende Rippe^F (2)
costole^F fluttuanti (2)
costilla^F flotante (2)

ulna
cubitus^M
Elle^F
ulna^F
cúbito^M

spinal column
colonne^F vertébrale
Wirbelsäule^F
colonna^F vertebrale
columna^F vertebral

radius
radius^M
Speiche^F
radio^M
radio^M

ilium
os^M iliaque
Darmbein^N
ileo^M
hueso^M ilíaco^M

sacrum
sacrum^M
Kreuzbein^N
sacro^M
sacro^M

femur
fémur^M
Oberschenkelknochen^M
femore^M
fémur^M

coccyx
coccyx^M
Steißbein^N
coccige^M
cóccix^M

patella
rotule^F
Kniescheibe^F
rotula^F
rótula^F

tibia
tibia^M
Schienbein^N
tibia^F
tibia^F

fibula
péroné^M
Wadenbein^N
perone^M
peroné^M/fibula^F

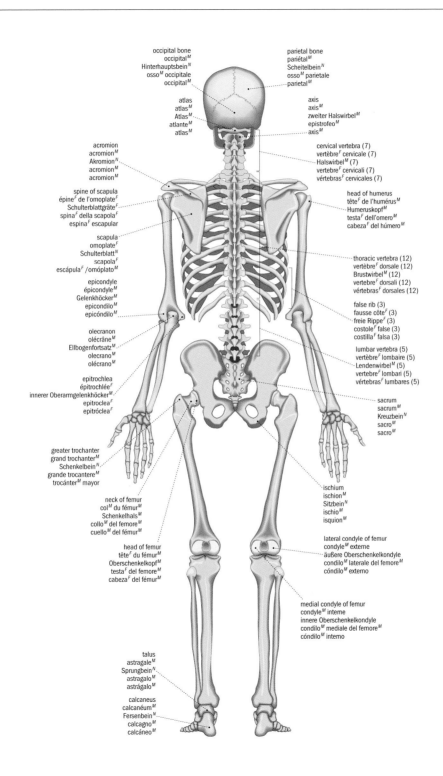

occipital bone
occipital^M
Hinterhauptsbein^N
osso^M occipitale
occipital^M

parietal bone
pariétal^M
Scheitelbein^N
osso^M parietale
parietal^M

atlas
atlas^M
Atlas^M
atlante^M
atlas^M

axis
axis^M
zweiter Halswirbel^M
epistrofeo^M
axis^M

acromion
acromion^M
Akromion^N
acromion^M
acromion^M

cervical vertebra (7)
vertèbre^F cervicale (7)
Halswirbel^M (7)
vertebre^F cervicali (7)
vértebras^F cervicales (7)

spine of scapula
épine^F de l'omoplate^F
Schulterblattgräte^F
spina^F della scapola^F
espina^F escapular

head of humerus
tête^F de l'humérus^M
Humeruskopf^M
testa^F dell'omero^M
cabeza^F del húmero^M

scapula
omoplate^F
Schulterblatt^N
scapola^F
escápula^F /omóplato^M

thoracic vertebra (12)
vertèbre^F dorsale (12)
Brustwirbel^M (12)
vertebre^F dorsali (12)
vértebras^F dorsales (12)

epicondyle
épicondyle^M
Gelenkhöcker^M
epicondilo^M
epicóndilo^M

false rib (3)
fausse côte^F (3)
freie Rippe^F (3)
costole^F false (3)
costilla^F falsa (3)

olecranon
olécrâne^M
Ellbogenfortsatz^M
olecrano^M
olécrano^M

lumbar vertebra (5)
vertèbre^F lombaire (5)
Lendenwirbel^M (5)
vertebre^F lombari (5)
vértebras^F lumbares (5)

epitrochlea
épitrochlée^F
innerer Oberarmgelenkhöcker^M
epitroclea^F
epitróclea^F

sacrum
sacrum^M
Kreuzbein^N
sacro^M
sacro^M

greater trochanter
grand trochanter^M
Schenkelbein^N
grande trocantere^M
trocánter^M mayor

ischium
ischion^M
Sitzbein^N
ischio^M
isquion^M

neck of femur
col^M du fémur^M
Schenkelhals^M
collo^M del femore^M
cuello^M del fémur^M

lateral condyle of femur
condyle^M externe
äußere Oberschenkelkondyle
condilo^M laterale del femore^M
cóndilo^M externo

head of femur
tête^F du fémur^M
Oberschenkelkopf^M
testa^F del femore^M
cabeza^F del fémur^M

medial condyle of femur
condyle^M interne
innere Oberschenkelkondyle
condilo^M mediale del femore^M
cóndilo^M interno

talus
astragale^M
Sprungbein^N
astragalo^M
astrágalo^M

calcaneus
calcanéum^M
Fersenbein^N
calcagno^M
calcáneo^M

posterior view
vue^F postérieure
Rückansicht^F
vista^F posteriore
vista^F posterior

HUMAN BEING

skeleton

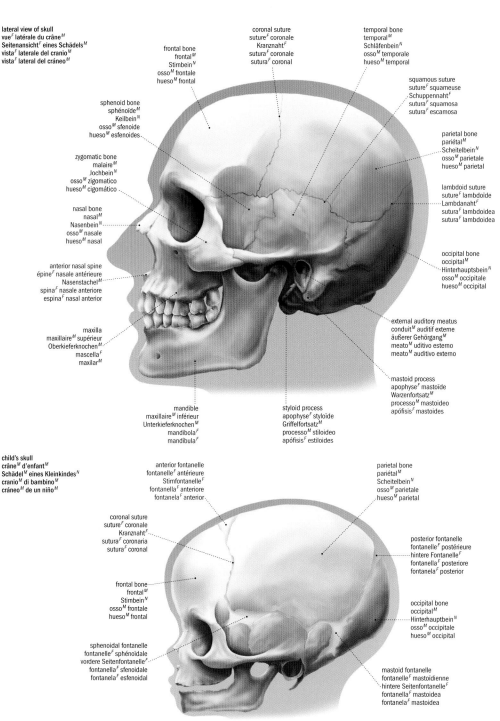

lateral view of skull
vue^F latérale du crâne^M
Seitenansicht^F eines Schädels^M
vista^F laterale del cranio^M
vista^F lateral del cráneo^M

frontal bone
frontal^M
Stirnbein^N
osso^M frontale
hueso^M frontal

coronal suture
suture^F coronale
Kranznaht^F
sutura^F coronale
sutura^F coronal

temporal bone
temporal^M
Schläfenbein^N
osso^M temporale
hueso^M temporal

squamous suture
suture^F squameuse
Schuppennaht^F
sutura^F squamosa
sutura^F escamosa

sphenoid bone
sphénoïde^M
Keilbein^N
osso^M sfenoide
hueso^M esfenoides

parietal bone
pariétal^M
Scheitelbein^N
osso^M parietale
hueso^M parietal

zygomatic bone
malaire^M
Jochbein^N
osso^M zigomatico
hueso^M cigomático

lambdoid suture
suture^F lambdoïde
Lambdanaht^F
sutura^F lambdoidea
sutura^F lambdoidea

nasal bone
nasal^M
Nasenbein^N
osso^M nasale
hueso^M nasal

occipital bone
occipital^M
Hinterhauptsbein^N
osso^M occipitale
hueso^M occipital

anterior nasal spine
épine^F nasale antérieure
Nasenstachel^M
spina^F nasale anteriore
espina^F nasal anterior

external auditory meatus
conduit^M auditif externe
äußerer Gehörgang^M
meato^M uditivo esterno
meato^M auditivo externo

maxilla
maxillaire^M supérieur
Oberkieferknochen^M
mascella^F
maxilar^M

mastoid process
apophyse^F mastoïde
Warzenfortsatz^M
processo^M mastoideo
apófisis^F mastoides

mandible
maxillaire^M inférieur
Unterkieferknochen^M
mandibola^F
mandíbula^F

styloid process
apophyse^F styloïde
Griffelfortsatz^M
processo^M stiloideo
apófisis^F estiloides

child's skull
crâne^M d'enfant^M
Schädel^M eines Kleinkindes^N
cranio^M di bambino^M
cráneo^M de un niño^M

anterior fontanelle
fontanelle^F antérieure
Stirnfontanelle^F
fontanella^F anteriore
fontanela^F anterior

parietal bone
pariétal^M
Scheitelbein^N
osso^M parietale
hueso^M parietal

coronal suture
suture^F coronale
Kranznaht^F
sutura^F coronaria
sutura^F coronal

posterior fontanelle
fontanelle^F postérieure
hintere Fontanelle^F
fontanella^F posteriore
fontanela^F posterior

frontal bone
frontal^M
Stirnbein^N
osso^M frontale
hueso^M frontal

occipital bone
occipital^M
Hinterhauptbein^N
osso^M occipitale
hueso^M occipital

sphenoidal fontanelle
fontanelle^F sphénoïdale
vordere Seitenfontanelle^F
fontanella^F sfenoidale
fontanela^F esfenoidal

mastoid fontanelle
fontanelle^F mastoïdienne
hintere Seitenfontanelle^F
fontanella^F mastoidea
fontanela^F mastoidea

teeth

dents^F | Zähne^M | denti^M | dientes^M

incisors
incisives^F
Schneidezähne^M
incisivi^M
incisivos^M

human denture
denture^F humaine
menschliches Gebiss^N
dentatura^F nell'uomo^M
dentadura^F humana

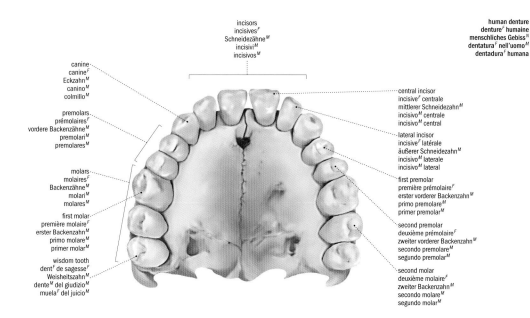

canine
canine^F
Eckzahn^M
canino^M
colmillo^M

premolars
prémolaires^F
vordere Backenzähne^M
premolari^M
premolares^M

molars
molaires^F
Backenzähne^M
molari^M
molares^M

first molar
première molaire^F
erster Backenzahn^M
primo molare^M
primer molar^M

wisdom tooth
dent^F de sagesse^F
Weisheitszahn^M
dente^M del giudizio^M
muela^F del juicio^M

central incisor
incisive^F centrale
mittlerer Schneidezahn^M
incisivo^M centrale
incisivo^M central

lateral incisor
incisive^F latérale
äußerer Schneidezahn^M
incisivo^M laterale
incisivo^M lateral

first premolar
première prémolaire^F
erster vorderer Backenzahn^M
primo premolare^M
primer premolar^M

second premolar
deuxième prémolaire^F
zweiter vorderer Backenzahn^M
secondo premolare^M
segundo premolar^M

second molar
deuxième molaire^F
zweiter Backenzahn^M
secondo molare^M
segundo molar^M

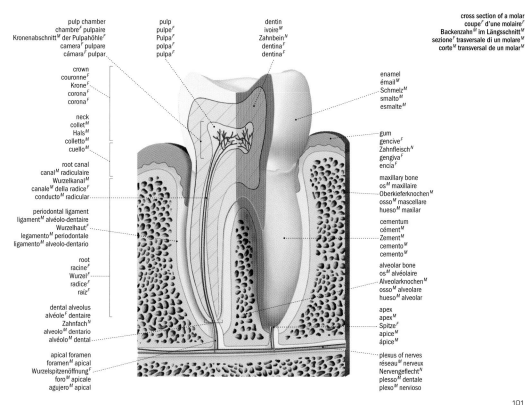

pulp chamber
chambre^F pulpaire
Kronenabschnitt^M der Pulpahöhle^F
camera^F pulpare
cámara^F pulpar

pulp
pulpe^F
Pulpa^F
polpa^F
pulpa^F

dentin
ivoire^M
Zahnbein^N
dentina^F
dentina^F

cross section of a molar
coupe^F d'une molaire^F
Backenzahn^M im Längsschnitt^M
sezione^F trasversale di un molare^M
corte^M transversal de un molar^M

crown
couronne^F
Krone^F
corona^F
corona^F

neck
collet^M
Hals^M
colletto^M
cuello^M

root canal
canal^M radiculaire
Wurzelkanal^M
canale^M della radice^F
conducto^M radicular

periodontal ligament
ligament^M alvéolo-dentaire
Wurzelhaut^F
legamento^M periodontale
ligamento^M alveolo-dentario

root
racine^F
Wurzel^F
radice^F
raíz^F

dental alveolus
alvéole^F dentaire
Zahnfach^N
alveolo^M dentario
alvéolo^M dental

apical foramen
foramen^M apical
Wurzelspitzenöffnung^F
foro^M apicale
agujero^M apical

enamel
émail^M
Schmelz^M
smalto^M
esmalte^M

gum
gencive^F
Zahnfleisch^N
gengiva^F
encía^F

maxillary bone
os^M maxillaire
Oberkieferknochen^M
osso^M mascellare
hueso^M maxilar

cementum
cément^M
Zement^M
cemento^M
cemento^M

alveolar bone
os^M alvéolaire
Alveolarknochen^M
osso^M alveolare
hueso^M alveolar

apex
apex^M
Spitze^F
apice^M
ápice^M

plexus of nerves
réseau^M nerveux
Nervengeflecht^N
plesso^M dentale
plexo^M nervioso

blood circulation

circulation^F sanguine | Blutkreislauf^M | circolazione^F del sangue^M | circulación^F sanguínea

HUMAN BEING

principal veins and arteries
principales veines^F et artères^F
die wichtigsten Venen^F und Arterien^F
principali vene^F e arterie^F
principales venas^F y arterias^F

common carotid artery
artère^F carotide primitive
Halsschlagader^F
arteria^F carotide comune
arteria^F carótida primitiva

subclavian artery
artère^F sous-clavière
Schlüsselbeinarterie^F
arteria^F succlavia
arteria^F subclavia

axillary artery
artère^F axillaire
Achselarterie^F
arteria^F ascellare
arteria^F axilar

superior vena cava
veine^F cave supérieure
obere Hohlvene^F
vena^F cava superiore
vena^F cava superior

brachial artery
artère^F brachiale
Oberarmarterie^F
arteria^F brachiale
arteria^F braquial

pulmonary vein
veine^F pulmonaire
Lungenvene^F
vena^F polmonare
vena^F pulmonar

inferior vena cava
veine^F cave inférieure
untere Hohlvene^F
vena^F cava inferiore
vena^F cava inferior

superior mesenteric vein
veine^F mésentérique supérieure
obere Mesenterialvene^F
vena^F mesenterica superiore
vena^F mesentérica superior

abdominal aorta
aorte^F abdominale
Bauchaorta^F
aorta^F addominale
aorta^F abdominal

common iliac artery
artère^F iliaque commune
gemeinsame Hüftarterie^F
arteria^F iliaca comune
arteria^F ilíaca común

internal iliac artery
artère^F iliaque interne
innere Hüftarterie^F
arteria^F iliaca interna
arteria^F ilíaca interna

femoral artery
artère^F fémorale
Oberschenkelarterie^F
arteria^F femorale
arteria^F femoral

anterior tibial artery
artère^F tibiale antérieure
vordere Schienbeinarterie^F
arteria^F tibiale anteriore
arteria^F tibial anterior

dorsalis pedis artery
artère^F dorsale du pied^M
Fußrückenarterie^F
arteria^F dorsale del piede^M
arteria^F dorsal del pie^M

arch of foot artery
artère^F arquée
Fußgewölbearterie^F
arteria^F dell'arco^M del piede^M
arteria^F arcuata

external jugular vein
veine^F jugulaire externe
äußere Drosselvene^F
vena^F giugulare esterna
vena^F yugular externa

internal jugular vein
veine^F jugulaire interne
innere Drosselvene^F
vena^F giugulare interna
vena^F yugular interna

subclavian vein
veine^F sous-clavière
Schlüsselbeinvene^F
vena^F succlavia
vena^F subclavia

axillary vein
veine^F axillaire
Achselvene^F
vena^F ascellare
vena^F axilar

arch of aorta
arc^M de l'aorte^F
Aortenbogen^M
arco^M aortico
cayado^M de la aorta^F

pulmonary artery
artère^F pulmonaire
Lungenarterie^F
arteria^F polmonare
arteria^F pulmonar

cephalic vein
veine^F céphalique
Cephalica^F
vena^F cefalica
vena^F cefálica

basilic vein
veine^F basilique
königliche Vene^F
vena^F basilica
vena^F basilica

renal vein
veine^F rénale
Nierenvene^F
vena^F renale
vena^F renal

renal artery
artère^F rénale
Nierenarterie^F
arteria^F renale
arteria^F renal

superior mesenteric artery
artère^F mésentérique supérieure
obere Mesenterialarterie^F
arteria^F mesenterica superiore
arteria^F mesentérica superior

femoral vein
veine^F fémorale
Oberschenkelvene^F
vena^F femorale
vena^F femoral

great saphenous vein
veine^F saphène interne
große Rosenvene^F
grande safena^F
vena^F safena interna

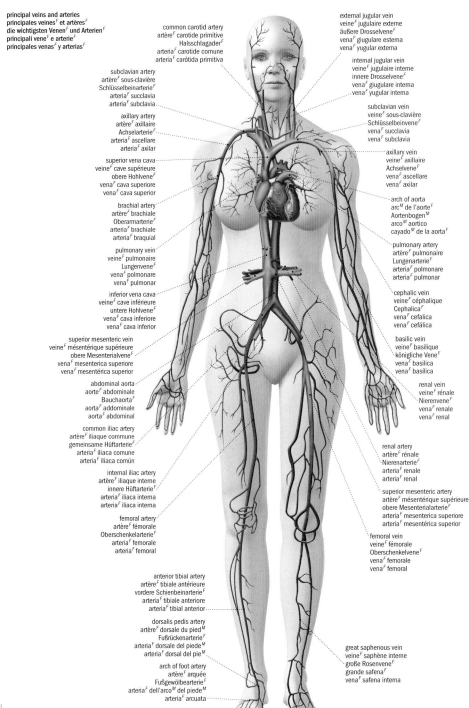

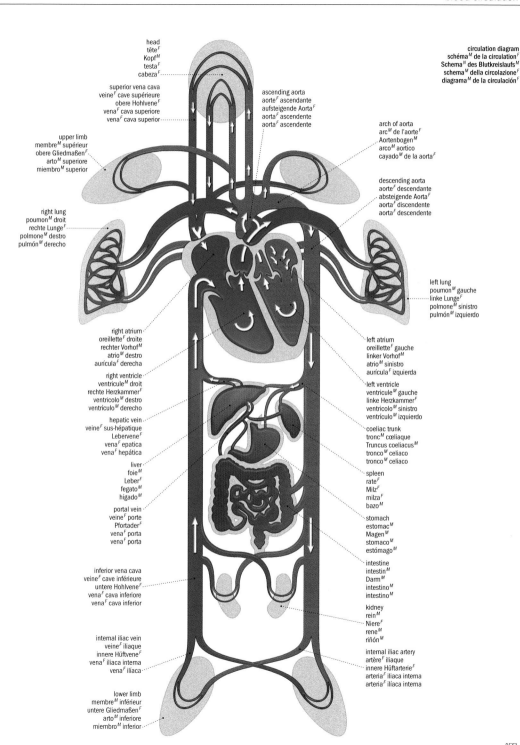

circulation diagram
schéma ^{M} de la circulation ^{F}
Schema ^{N} des Blutkreislaufs ^{M}
schema ^{M} della circolazione ^{F}
diagrama ^{M} de la circulación ^{F}

head
tête ^{F}
Kopf ^{M}
testa ^{F}
cabeza ^{F}

superior vena cava
veine ^{F} cave supérieure
obere Hohlvene ^{F}
vena ^{F} cava superiore
vena ^{F} cava superior

ascending aorta
aorte ^{F} ascendante
aufsteigende Aorta ^{F}
aorta ^{F} ascendente
aorta ^{F} ascendente

arch of aorta
arc ^{M} de l'aorte ^{F}
Aortenbogen ^{M}
arco ^{M} aortico
cayado ^{M} de la aorta ^{F}

upper limb
membre ^{M} supérieur
obere Gliedmaßen ^{F}
arto ^{M} superiore
miembro ^{M} superior

descending aorta
aorte ^{F} descendante
absteigende Aorta ^{F}
aorta ^{F} discendente
aorta ^{F} descendente

right lung
poumon ^{M} droit
rechte Lunge ^{F}
polmone ^{M} destro
pulmón ^{M} derecho

left lung
poumon ^{M} gauche
linke Lunge ^{F}
polmone ^{M} sinistro
pulmón ^{M} izquierdo

right atrium
oreillette ^{F} droite
rechter Vorhof ^{M}
atrio ^{M} destro
aurícula ^{F} derecha

left atrium
oreillette ^{F} gauche
linker Vorhof ^{M}
atrio ^{M} sinistro
aurícula ^{F} izquierda

right ventricle
ventricule ^{M} droit
rechte Herzkammer ^{F}
ventricolo ^{M} destro
ventrículo ^{M} derecho

left ventricle
ventricule ^{M} gauche
linke Herzkammer ^{F}
ventricolo ^{M} sinistro
ventrículo ^{M} izquierdo

hepatic vein
veine ^{F} sus-hépatique
Lebervene ^{F}
vena ^{F} epatica
vena ^{F} hepática

coeliac trunk
tronc ^{M} cœliaque
Truncus coeliacus ^{M}
tronco ^{M} celiaco
tronco ^{M} celiaco

liver
foie ^{M}
Leber ^{F}
fegato ^{M}
hígado ^{M}

spleen
rate ^{F}
Milz ^{F}
milza ^{F}
bazo ^{M}

portal vein
veine ^{F} porte
Pfortader ^{F}
vena ^{F} porta
vena ^{F} porta

stomach
estomac ^{M}
Magen ^{M}
stomaco ^{M}
estómago ^{M}

inferior vena cava
veine ^{F} cave inférieure
untere Hohlvene ^{F}
vena ^{F} cava inferiore
vena ^{F} cava inferior

intestine
intestin ^{M}
Darm ^{M}
intestino ^{M}
intestino ^{M}

kidney
rein ^{M}
Niere ^{F}
rene ^{M}
riñón ^{M}

internal iliac vein
veine ^{F} iliaque
innere Hüftvene ^{F}
vena ^{F} iliaca interna
vena ^{F} ilíaca

internal iliac artery
artère ^{F} iliaque
innere Hüftarterie ^{F}
arteria ^{F} iliaca interna
arteria ^{F} ilíaca interna

lower limb
membre ^{M} inférieur
untere Gliedmaßen ^{F}
arto ^{M} inferiore
miembro ^{M} inferior

blood circulation

HUMAN BEING

composition of the blood
composition^F du sang^M
Blutbestandteile^M
composizione^F del sangue^M
composición^F de la sangre^F

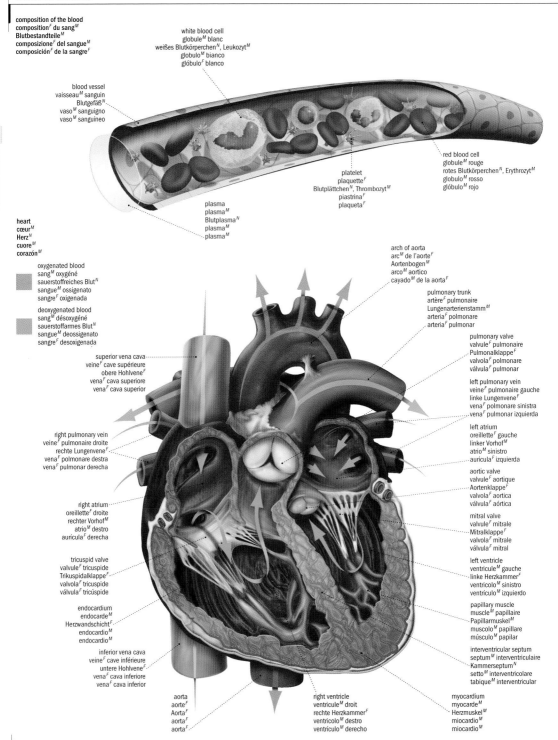

white blood cell
globule^M blanc
weißes Blutkörperchen^N, Leukozyt^M
globulo^M bianco
glóbulo^F blanco

blood vessel
vaisseau^M sanguin
Blutgefäß^N
vaso^M sanguigno
vaso^M sanguíneo

red blood cell
globule^M rouge
rotes Blutkörperchen^N, Erythrozyt^M
globulo^M rosso
glóbulo^M rojo

platelet
plaquette^F
Blutplättchen^N, Thrombozyt^M
piastrina^F
plaqueta^F

plasma
plasma^M
Blutplasma^N
plasma^M
plasma^M

heart
cœur^M
Herz^N
cuore^M
corazón^M

oxygenated blood
sang^M oxygéné
sauerstoffreiches Blut^N
sangue^M ossigenato
sangre^F oxigenada

deoxygenated blood
sang^M désoxygéné
sauerstoffarmes Blut^N
sangue^M deossigenato
sangre^F desoxigenada

arch of aorta
arc^M de l'aorte^F
Aortenbogen^M
arco^M aortico
cayado^M de la aorta^F

pulmonary trunk
artère^F pulmonaire
Lungenarterienstamm^M
arteria^F polmonare
arteria^F pulmonar

pulmonary valve
valvule^F pulmonaire
Pulmonalklappe^F
valvola^F polmonare
válvula^F pulmonar

superior vena cava
veine^F cave supérieure
obere Hohlvene^F
vena^F cava superiore
vena^F cava superior

left pulmonary vein
veine^F pulmonaire gauche
linke Lungenvene^F
vena^F polmonare sinistra
vena^F pulmonar izquierda

left atrium
oreillette^F gauche
linker Vorhof^M
atrio^M sinistro
auricula^F izquierda

right pulmonary vein
veine^F pulmonaire droite
rechte Lungenvene^F
vena^F polmonare destra
vena^F pulmonar derecha

aortic valve
valvule^F aortique
Aortenklappe^F
valvola^F aortica
válvula^F aórtica

right atrium
oreillette^F droite
rechter Vorhof^M
atrio^M destro
auricula^F derecha

mitral valve
valvule^F mitrale
Mitralklappe^F
valvola^F mitrale
válvula^F mitral

left ventricle
ventricule^M gauche
linke Herzkammer^F
ventricolo^M sinistro
ventrículo^M izquierdo

tricuspid valve
valvule^F tricuspide
Trikuspidalklappe^F
valvola^F tricuspide
válvula^F tricúspide

papillary muscle
muscle^M papillaire
Papillarmuskel^M
muscolo^M papillare
músculo^M papilar

endocardium
endocarde^M
Herzwandschicht^F
endocardio^M
endocardio^M

interventricular septum
septum^M interventriculaire
Kammerseptum^N
setto^M interventricolare
tabique^M interventricular

inferior vena cava
veine^F cave inférieure
untere Hohlvene^F
vena^F cava inferiore
vena^F cava inferior

aorta
aorte^F
Aorta^F
aorta^F
aorta^F

right ventricle
ventricule^M droit
rechte Herzkammer^F
ventricolo^M destro
ventrículo^M derecho

myocardium
myocarde^M
Herzmuskel^M
miocardio^M
miocardio^M

respiratory system

appareil^M respiratoire | Luftwege^M | apparato^M respiratorio | aparato^M respiratorio

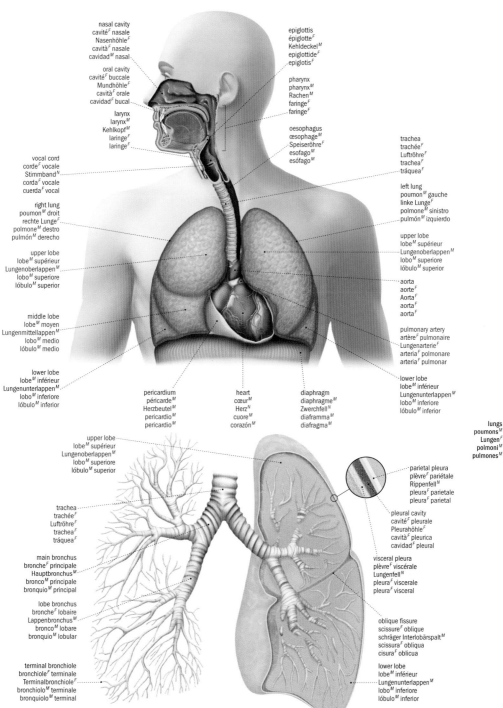

nasal cavity
cavité^F nasale
Nasenhöhle^F
cavità^F nasale
cavidad^M nasal

oral cavity
cavité^F buccale
Mundhöhle^F
cavità^F orale
cavidad^F bucal

larynx
larynx^M
Kehlkopf^M
laringe^F
laringe^F

vocal cord
corde^F vocale
Stimmband^N
corda^F vocale
cuerda^F vocal

right lung
poumon^M droit
rechte Lunge^F
polmone^M destro
pulmón^M derecho

upper lobe
lobe^M supérieur
Lungenoberlappen^M
lobo^M superiore
lóbulo^M superior

middle lobe
lobe^M moyen
Lungenmittellappen^M
lobo^M medio
lóbulo^M medio

lower lobe
lobe^M inférieur
Lungenunterlappen^M
lobo^M inferiore
lóbulo^M inferior

epiglottis
épiglotte^F
Kehldeckel^M
epiglottide^F
epiglotis^F

pharynx
pharynx^M
Rachen^M
faringe^F
faringe^F

oesophagus
œsophage^M
Speiseröhre^F
esofago^M
esófago^M

trachea
trachée^F
Luftröhre^F
trachea^F
tráquea^F

left lung
poumon^M gauche
linke Lunge^F
polmone^M sinistro
pulmón^M izquierdo

upper lobe
lobe^M supérieur
Lungenoberlappen^M
lobo^M superiore
lóbulo^M superior

aorta
aorte^F
Aorta^F
aorta^F
aorta^F

pulmonary artery
artère^F pulmonaire
Lungenarterie^F
arteria^F polmonare
arteria^F pulmonar

lower lobe
lobe^M inférieur
Lungenunterlappen^M
lobo^M inferiore
lóbulo^M inferior

pericardium
péricarde^M
Herzbeutel^M
pericardio^M
pericardio^M

heart
cœur^M
Herz^N
cuore^M
corazón^M

diaphragm
diaphragme^M
Zwerchfell^N
diaframma^M
diafragma^M

lungs
poumons^M
Lungen^F
polmoni^M
pulmones^M

upper lobe
lobe^M supérieur
Lungenoberlappen^M
lobo^M superiore
lóbulo^M superior

trachea
trachée^F
Luftröhre^F
trachea^F
tráquea^F

main bronchus
bronche^F principale
Hauptbronchus^M
bronco^M principale
bronquio^M principal

lobe bronchus
bronche^F lobaire
Lappenbronchus^M
bronco^M lobare
bronquio^M lobular

terminal bronchiole
bronchiole^F terminale
Terminalbronchiole^F
bronchiolo^M terminale
bronquiolo^M terminal

parietal pleura
plèvre^F pariétale
Rippenfell^N
pleura^F parietale
pleura^F parietal

pleural cavity
cavité^F pleurale
Pleurahöhle^F
cavità^F pleurica
cavidad^F pleural

visceral pleura
plèvre^F viscérale
Lungenfell^N
pleura^F viscerale
pleura^F visceral

oblique fissure
scissure^F oblique
schräger Interlobärspalt^M
scissura^F obliqua
cisura^F oblicua

lower lobe
lobe^M inférieur
Lungenunterlappen^M
lobo^M inferiore
lóbulo^M inferior

digestive system

appareil^M digestif | Verdauungsapparat^M | apparato^M digerente | aparato^M digestivo

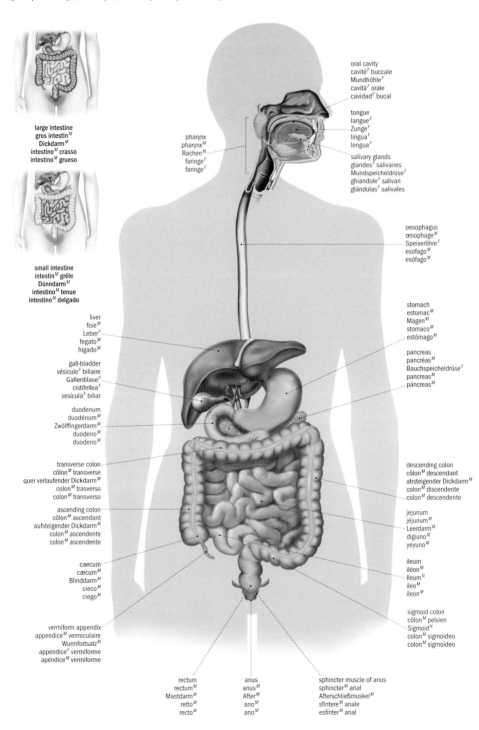

large intestine
gros intestin^M
Dickdarm^M
intestino^M crasso
intestino^M grueso

small intestine
intestin^M grêle
Dünndarm^M
intestino^M tenue
intestino^M delgado

oral cavity
cavité^F buccale
Mundhöhle^F
cavità^F orale
cavidad^F bucal

tongue
langue^F
Zunge^F
lingua^F
lengua^F

pharynx
pharynx^M
Rachen^M
faringe^F
faringe^F

salivary glands
glandes^F salivaires
Mundspeicheldrüse^F
ghiandole^F salivari
glándulas^F salivales

oesophagus
œsophage^M
Speiseröhre^F
esofago^M
esófago^M

stomach
estomac^M
Magen^M
stomaco^M
estómago^M

pancreas
pancréas^M
Bauchspeicheldrüse^F
pancreas^M
páncreas^M

liver
foie^M
Leber^F
fegato^M
hígado^M

gall-bladder
vésicule^F biliaire
Gallenblase^F
cistifellea^F
vesícula^F biliar

duodenum
duodénum^M
Zwölffingerdarm^M
duodeno^M
duodeno^M

transverse colon
côlon^M transverse
quer verlaufender Dickdarm^M
colon^M trasverso
colon^M transverso

descending colon
côlon^M descendant
absteigender Dickdarm^M
colon^M discendente
colon^M descendente

ascending colon
côlon^M ascendant
aufsteigender Dickdarm^M
colon^M ascendente
colon^M ascendente

jejunum
jéjunum^M
Leerdarm^M
digiuno^M
yeyuno^M

caecum
cæcum^M
Blinddarm^M
cieco^M
ciego^M

ileum
iléon^M
Ileum^N
ileo^M
íleon^M

sigmoid colon
côlon^M pelvien
Sigmoid^N
colon^M sigmoideo
colon^M sigmoideo

vermiform appendix
appendice^M vermiculaire
Wurmfortsatz^M
appendice^F vermiforme
apéndice^M vermiforme

rectum
rectum^M
Mastdarm^M
retto^M
recto^M

anus
anus^M
After^M
ano^M
ano^M

sphincter muscle of anus
sphincter^M anal
Afterschließmuskel^M
sfintere^M anale
esfínter^M anal

urinary system

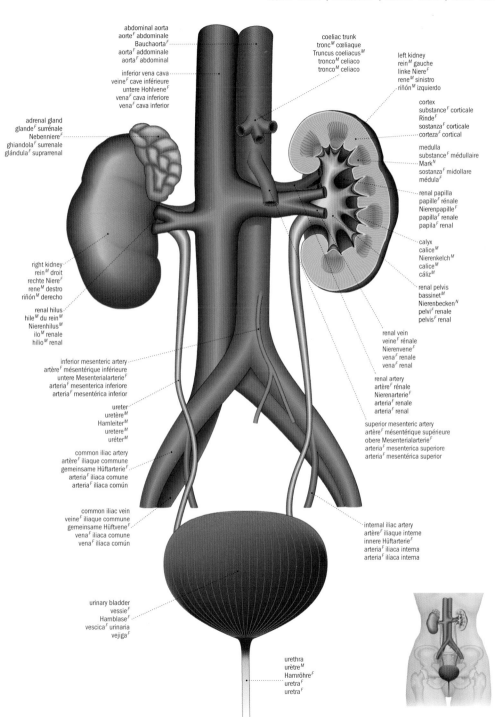

abdominal aorta
aorte^F abdominale
Bauchaorta^F
aorta^F addominale
aorta^F abdominal

inferior vena cava
veine^F cave inférieure
untere Hohlvene^F
vena^F cava inferiore
vena^F cava inferior

coeliac trunk
tronc^M cœliaque
Truncus coeliacus^M
tronco^M celiaco
tronco^M celiaco

left kidney
rein^M gauche
linke Niere^F
rene^M sinistro
riñón^M izquierdo

cortex
substance^F corticale
Rinde^F
sostanza^F corticale
corteza^F cortical

adrenal gland
glande^F surrénale
Nebenniere^F
ghiandola^F surrenale
glándula^F suprarrenal

medulla
substance^F médullaire
Mark^N
sostanza^F midollare
médula^F

renal papilla
papille^F rénale
Nierenpapille^F
papilla^F renale
papila^F renal

calyx
calice^M
Nierenkelch^M
calice^M
cáliz^M

right kidney
rein^M droit
rechte Niere^F
rene^M destro
riñón^M derecho

renal pelvis
bassinet^M
Nierenbecken^N
pelvi^F renale
pelvis^F renal

renal hilus
hile^M du rein^M
Nierenhilus^M
ilo^M renale
hilio^M renal

renal vein
veine^F rénale
Nierenvene^F
vena^F renale
vena^F renal

inferior mesenteric artery
artère^F mésentérique inférieure
untere Mesenterialarterie^F
arteria^F mesenterica inferiore
arteria^F mesentérica inferior

renal artery
artère^F rénale
Nierenarterie^F
arteria^F renale
arteria^F renal

ureter
uretère^M
Harnleiter^M
uretere^M
uréter^M

superior mesenteric artery
artère^F mésentérique supérieure
obere Mesenterialarterie^F
arteria^F mesenterica superiore
arteria^F mesentérica superior

common iliac artery
artère^F iliaque commune
gemeinsame Hüftarterie^F
arteria^F iliaca comune
arteria^F iliaca común

common iliac vein
veine^F iliaque commune
gemeinsame Hüftvene^F
vena^F iliaca comune
vena^F iliaca común

internal iliac artery
artère^F iliaque interne
innere Hüftarterie^F
arteria^F iliaca interna
arteria^F iliaca interna

urinary bladder
vessie^F
Harnblase^F
vescica^F urinaria
vejiga^F

urethra
urètre^M
Harnröhre^F
uretra^F
uretra^F

HUMAN BEING

nervous system

système^M nerveux | Nervensystem^N | sistema^M nervoso | sistema^M nervioso

peripheral nervous system
système^M nerveux périphérique
peripheres Nervensystem^N
sistema^M nervoso periferico
sistema^M nervioso periférico

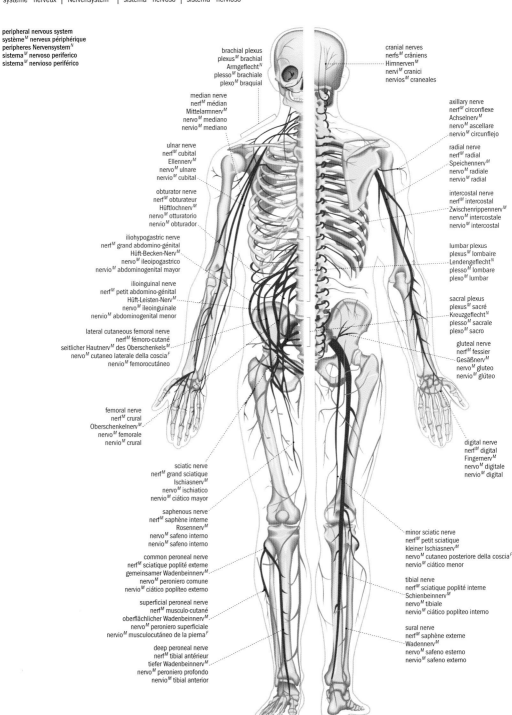

brachial plexus
plexus^M brachial
Armgeflecht^N
plesso^M brachiale
plexo^M braquial

cranial nerves
nerfs^M crâniens
Hirnnerven^M
nervi^M cranici
nervios^M craneales

median nerve
nerf^M médian
Mittelarmnerv^M
nervo^M mediano
nervio^M mediano

axillary nerve
nerf^M circonflexe
Achselnerv^M
nervo^M ascellare
nervio^M circunflejo

ulnar nerve
nerf^M cubital
Ellennerv^M
nervo^M ulnare
nervio^M cubital

radial nerve
nerf^M radial
Speichennerv^M
nervo^M radiale
nervio^M radial

obturator nerve
nerf^M obturateur
Hüftlochnerv^M
nervo^M otturatorio
nervio^M obturador

intercostal nerve
nerf^M intercostal
Zwischenrippennerv^M
nervo^M intercostale
nervio^M intercostal

iliohypogastric nerve
nerf^M grand abdomino-génital
Hüft-Becken-Nerv^M
nervo^M ileoipogastrico
nervio^M abdominogenital mayor

lumbar plexus
plexus^M lombaire
Lendengeflecht^N
plesso^M lombare
plexo^M lumbar

ilioinguinal nerve
nerf^M petit abdomino-génital
Hüft-Leisten-Nerv^M
nervo^M ileoinguinale
nervio^M abdominogenital menor

sacral plexus
plexus^M sacré
Kreuzgeflecht^N
plesso^M sacrale
plexo^M sacro

lateral cutaneous femoral nerve
nerf^M fémoro-cutané
seitlicher Hautnerv^M des Oberschenkels^M
nervo^M cutaneo laterale della coscia^F
nervio^M femorocutáneo

gluteal nerve
nerf^M fessier
Gesäßnerv^M
nervo^M gluteo
nervio^M glúteo

femoral nerve
nerf^M crural
Oberschenkelnerv^M
nervo^M femorale
nervio^M crural

digital nerve
nerf^M digital
Fingernerv^M
nervo^M digitale
nervio^M digital

sciatic nerve
nerf^M grand sciatique
Ischiasnerv^M
nervo^M ischiatico
nervio^M ciático mayor

saphenous nerve
nerf^M saphène interne
Rosennerv^M
nervo^M safeno interno
nervio^M safeno interno

minor sciatic nerve
nerf^M petit sciatique
kleiner Ischiasnerv^M
nervo^M cutaneo posteriore della coscia^F
nervio^M ciático menor

common peroneal nerve
nerf^M sciatique poplité externe
gemeinsamer Wadenbeinnerv^M
nervo^M peroniero comune
nervio^M ciático poplíteo externo

tibial nerve
nerf^M sciatique poplité interne
Schienbeinnerv^M
nervo^M tibiale
nervio^M ciático poplíteo interno

superficial peroneal nerve
nerf^M musculo-cutané
oberflächlicher Wadenbeinnerv^M
nervo^M peroniero superficiale
nervio^M musculocutáneo de la pierna^F

sural nerve
nerf^M saphène externe
Wadennerv^M
nervo^M safeno esterno
nervio^M safeno externo

deep peroneal nerve
nerf^M tibial antérieur
tiefer Wadenbeinnerv^M
nervo^M peroniero profondo
nervio^M tibial anterior

HUMAN BEING

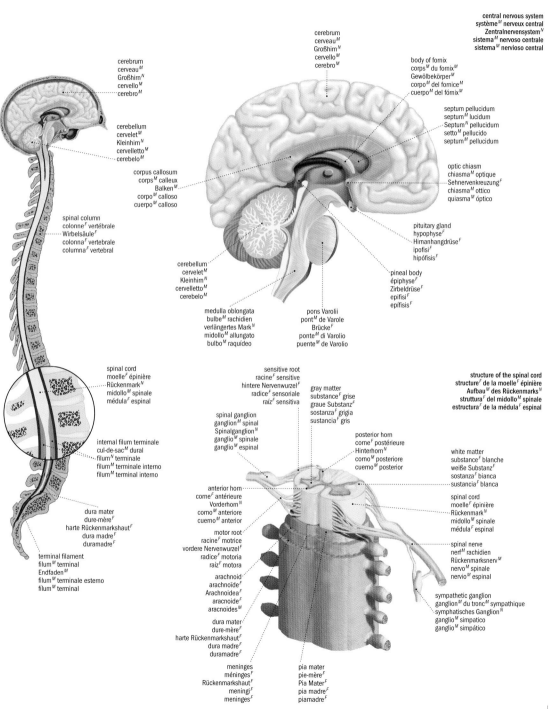

central nervous system
système^M nerveux central
Zentralnervensystem^N
sistema^M nervoso centrale
sistema^M nervioso central

cerebrum
cerveau^M
Großhirn^N
cervello^M
cerebro^M

body of fornix
corps^M du fornix^M
Gewölbekörper^M
corpo^M del fornice^M
cuerpo^M del fórnix^M

cerebrum
cerveau^M
Großhirn^N
cervello^M
cerebro^M

septum pellucidum
septum^M lucidum
Septum^N pellucidum
setto^M pellucido
septum^M pellucidum

cerebellum
cervelet^M
Kleinhirn^N
cervelletto^M
cerebelo^M

optic chiasm
chiasma^M optique
Sehnervenkreuzung^F
chiasma^M ottico
quiasma^M óptico

corpus callosum
corps^M calleux
Balken^M
corpo^M calloso
cuerpo^M calloso

spinal column
colonne^F vertébrale
Wirbelsäule^F
colonna^F vertebrale
columna^F vertebral

pituitary gland
hypophyse^F
Himanhangdrüse^F
ipofisi^F
hipófisis^F

cerebellum
cervelet^M
Kleinhirn^N
cervelletto^M
cerebelo^M

pineal body
épiphyse^F
Zirbeldrüse^F
epifisi^F
epífisis^F

medulla oblongata
bulbe^M rachidien
verlängertes Mark^N
midollo^M allungato
bulbo^M raquídeo

pons Varolii
pont^M de Varole
Brücke^F
ponte^M di Varolio
puente^M de Varolio

spinal cord
moelle^F épinière
Rückenmark^N
midollo^M spinale
médula^F espinal

sensitive root
racine^F sensitive
hintere Nervenwurzel^F
radice^F sensoriale
raíz^F sensitiva

gray matter
substance^F grise
graue Substanz^F
sostanza^F grigia
sustancia^F gris

structure of the spinal cord
structure^F de la moelle^F épinière
Aufbau^M des Rückenmarks^N
struttura^F del midollo^M spinale
estructura^F de la médula^F espinal

spinal ganglion
ganglion^M spinal
Spinalganglion^N
ganglio^M spinale
ganglio^M espinal

posterior horn
corne^F postérieure
Hinterhorn^N
corno^M posteriore
cuerno^M posterior

white matter
substance^F blanche
weiße Substanz^F
sostanza^F bianca
sustancia^F blanca

internal filum terminale
cul-de-sac^M dural
filum^N terminale
filum^M terminale interno
filum^M terminal interno

anterior horn
corne^F antérieure
Vorderhorn^N
corno^M anteriore
cuerno^M anterior

spinal cord
moelle^F épinière
Rückenmark^N
midollo^M spinale
médula^F espinal

dura mater
dure-mère^F
harte Rückenmarkshaut^F
dura madre^F
duramadre^F

motor root
racine^F motrice
vordere Nervenwurzel^F
radice^F motoria
raíz^F motora

spinal nerve
nerf^M rachidien
Rückenmarksnerv^M
nervo^M spinale
nervio^M espinal

terminal filament
filum^M terminal
Endfaden^M
filum^M terminale esterno
filum^M terminal

arachnoid
arachnoïde^F
Arachnoidea^F
aracnoide^F
aracnoides^M

sympathetic ganglion
ganglion^M du tronc^M sympathique
symphatisches Ganglion^N
ganglio^M simpatico
ganglio^M simpático

dura mater
dure-mère^F
harte Rückenmarkshaut^F
dura madre^F
duramadre^F

meninges
méninges^F
Rückenmarkshaut^F
meningi^F
meninges^F

pia mater
pie-mère^F
Pia Mater^F
pia madre^F
piamadre^F

nervous system

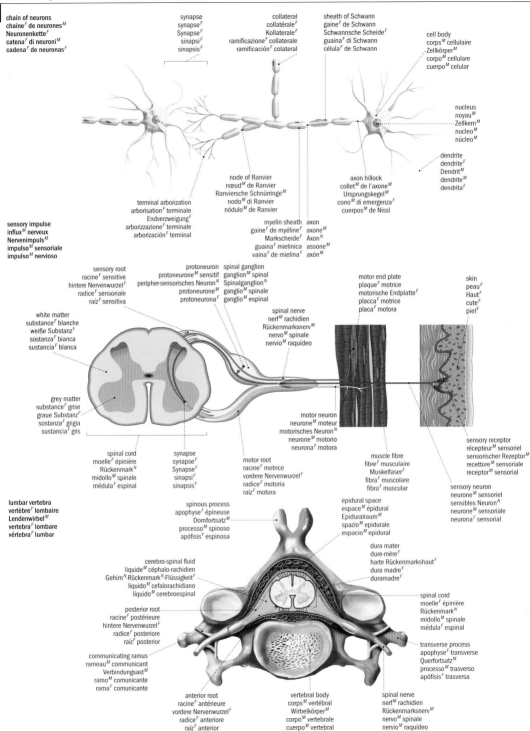

chain of neurons
chaîne^F de neurones^M
Neuronenkette^F
catena^F di neuroni^M
cadena^F de neuronas^F

synapse
synapse^F
Synapse^F
sinapsi^F
sinapsis^F

collateral
collatérale^F
Kollaterale^F
ramificazione^F collaterale
ramificación^F colateral

sheath of Schwann
gaine^F de Schwann
Schwannsche Scheide^F
guaina^F di Schwann
célula^F de Schwann

cell body
corps^M cellulaire
Zellkörper^M
corpo^M cellulare
cuerpo^M celular

nucleus
noyau^M
Zellkern^M
nucleo^M
núcleo^M

dendrite
dendrite^F
Dendrit^M
dendrite^M
dendrita^F

node of Ranvier
nœud^M de Ranvier
Ranviersche Schnürringe^M
nodo^M di Ranvier
nódulo^M de Ranvier

axon hillock
collet^M de l'axone^M
Ursprungskegel^M
cono^M di emergenza^F
cuerpos^M de Nissl

terminal arborization
arborisation^F terminale
Endverzweigung^F
arborizzazione^F terminale
arborización^F terminal

myelin sheath
gaine^F de myéline^F
Markscheide^F
guaina^F mielinica
vaina^F de mielina^F

axon
axone^M
Axon^N
assone^M
axón^M

sensory impulse
influx^M nerveux
Nervenimpuls^M
impulso^M sensoriale
impulso^M nervioso

sensory root
racine^F sensitive
hintere Nervenwurzel^F
radice^F sensoriale
raíz^F sensitiva

protoneuron
protoneurone^M sensitif
peripher-sensorisches Neuron^N
protoneurone^M
protoneurona^F

spinal ganglion
ganglion^M spinal
Spinalganglion^N
ganglio^M spinale
ganglio^M espinal

spinal nerve
nerf^M rachidien
Rückenmarksnerv^M
nervo^M spinale
nervio^M raquídeo

motor end plate
plaque^F motrice
motorische Endplatte^F
placca^F motrice
placa^F motora

skin
peau^F
Haut^F
cute^F
piel^F

white matter
substance^F blanche
weiße Substanz^F
sostanza^F bianca
sustancia^F blanca

grey matter
substance^F grise
graue Substanz^F
sostanza^F grigia
sustancia^F gris

spinal cord
moelle^F épinière
Rückenmark^N
midollo^M spinale
médula^F espinal

synapse
synapse^F
Synapse^F
sinapsi^F
sinapsis^F

motor root
racine^F motrice
vordere Nervenwurzel^F
radice^F motoria
raíz^F motora

motor neuron
neurone^M moteur
motorisches Neuron^N
neurone^M motorio
neurona^F motora

muscle fibre
fibre^F musculaire
Muskelfaser^F
fibra^F muscolare
fibra^F muscular

sensory receptor
récepteur^M sensoriel
sensorischer Rezeptor^M
recettore^M sensoriale
receptor^M sensorial

sensory neuron
neurone^M sensoriel
sensibles Neuron^N
neurone^M sensoriale
neurona^F sensorial

lumbar vertebra
vertèbre^F lombaire
Lendenwirbel^M
vertebra^F lombare
vértebra^F lumbar

spinous process
apophyse^F épineuse
Dornfortsatz^M
processo^M spinoso
apófisis^F espinosa

epidural space
espace^M épidural
Epiduralraum^M
spazio^M epidurale
espacio^M epidural

dura mater
dure-mère^F
harte Rückenmarkshaut^F
dura madre^F
duramadre^F

cerebro-spinal fluid
liquide^M céphalo-rachidien
Gehirn^N-Rückenmark^N-Flüssigkeit^F
liquido^M cefalorachidiano
liquido^M cerebroespinal

posterior root
racine^F postérieure
hintere Nervenwurzel^F
radice^F posteriore
raíz^F posterior

spinal cord
moelle^F épinière
Rückenmark^N
midollo^M spinale
médula^F espinal

transverse process
apophyse^F transverse
Querfortsatz^M
processo^M trasverso
apófisis^F trasversa

communicating ramus
rameau^M communicant
Verbindungsast^M
ramo^M comunicante
rama^F comunicante

anterior root
racine^F antérieure
vordere Nervenwurzel^F
radice^F anteriore
raíz^F anterior

vertebral body
corps^M vertébral
Wirbelkörper^M
corpo^M vertebrale
cuerpo^M vertebral

spinal nerve
nerf^M rachidien
Rückenmarksnerv^M
nervo^M spinale
nervio^M raquídeo

male genital organs

organes^M génitaux masculins | männliche Geschlechtsorgane^N | organi^M genitali maschili | órganos^M genitales masculinos

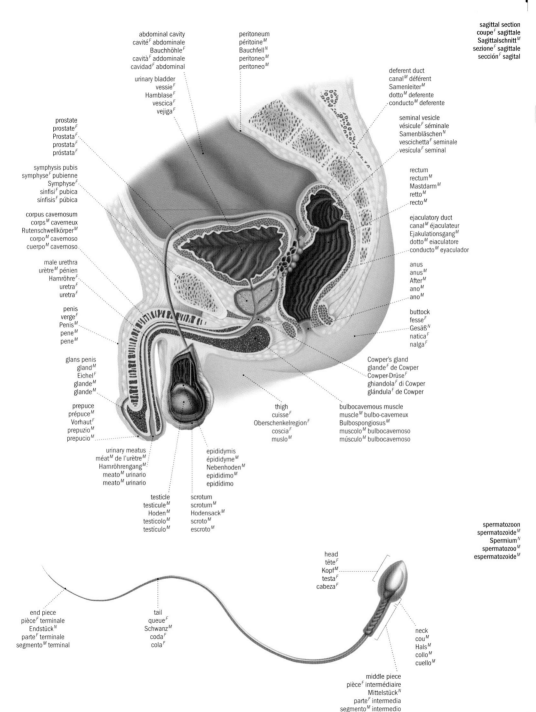

sagittal section
coupe^F sagittale
Sagittalschnitt^M
sezione^F sagittale
sección^F sagital

HUMAN BEING

abdominal cavity
cavité^F abdominale
Bauchhöhle^F
cavità^F addominale
cavidad^F abdominal

peritoneum
péritoine^M
Bauchfell^N
peritoneo^M
peritoneo^M

urinary bladder
vessie^F
Harnblase^F
vescica^F
vejiga^F

deferent duct
canal^M déférent
Samenleiter^M
dotto^M deferente
conducto^M deferente

prostate
prostate^F
Prostata^F
prostata^F
próstata^F

seminal vesicle
vésicule^F séminale
Samenbläschen^N
vescichetta^F seminale
vesícula^F seminal

symphysis pubis
symphyse^F pubienne
Symphyse^F
sinfisi^F pubica
sinfisis^F púbica

rectum
rectum^M
Mastdarm^M
retto^M
recto^M

corpus cavernosum
corps^M caverneux
Rutenschwellkörper^M
corpo^M cavernoso
cuerpo^M cavernoso

ejaculatory duct
canal^M éjaculateur
Ejakulationsgang^M
dotto^M eiaculatore
conducto^M eyaculador

male urethra
urètre^M pénien
Harnröhre^F
uretra^F
uretra^F

anus
anus^M
After^M
ano^M
ano^M

penis
verge^F
Penis^M
pene^M
pene^M

buttock
fesse^F
Gesäß^N
natica^F
nalga^F

glans penis
gland^M
Eichel^F
glande^M
glande^M

Cowper's gland
glande^F de Cowper
Cowper-Drüse^F
ghiandola^F di Cowper
glándula^F de Cowper

prepuce
prépuce^M
Vorhaut^F
prepuzio^M
prepucio^M

thigh
cuisse^F
Oberschenkelregion^F
coscia^F
muslo^M

bulbocavernous muscle
muscle^M bulbo-caverneux
Bulbospongiosus^M
muscolo^M bulbocavernoso
músculo^M bulbocavernoso

urinary meatus
méat^M de l'urètre^M
Harnröhrengang^M
meato^M urinario
meato^M urinario

epididymis
épididyme^M
Nebenhoden^M
epididimo^M
epididimo^M

testicle
testicule^M
Hoden^M
testicolo^M
testículo^M

scrotum
scrotum^M
Hodensack^M
scroto^M
escroto^M

spermatozoon
spermatozoïde^M
Spermium^N
spermatozoo^M
espermatozoide^M

head
tête^F
Kopf^M
testa^F
cabeza^F

end piece
pièce^F terminale
Endstück^N
parte^F terminale
segmento^M terminal

tail
queue^F
Schwanz^M
coda^F
cola^F

neck
cou^M
Hals^M
collo^M
cuello^M

middle piece
pièce^F intermédiaire
Mittelstück^N
parte^F intermedia
segmento^M intermedio

female genital organs

organes^M génitaux féminins | weibliche Geschlechtsorgane^N | organi^M genitali femminili | órganos^M genitales femeninos

HUMAN BEING

sagittal section
coupe^F sagittale
Sagittalschnitt^M
sezione^F sagittale
sección^F sagital

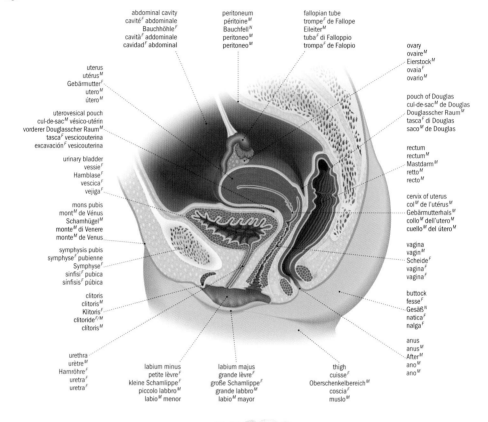

abdominal cavity
cavité^F abdominale
Bauchhöhle^F
cavità^F addominale
cavidad^F abdominal

peritoneum
péritoine^M
Bauchfell^N
peritoneo^M
peritoneo^M

fallopian tube
trompe^F de Fallope
Eileiter^M
tuba^F di Falloppio
trompa^F de Falopio

ovary
ovaire^M
Eierstock^M
ovaia^F
ovario^M

uterus
utérus^M
Gebärmutter^F
utero^M
útero^M

pouch of Douglas
cul-de-sac^M de Douglas
Douglasscher Raum^M
tasca^F di Douglas
saco^M de Douglas

uterovesical pouch
cul-de-sac^M vésico-utérin
vorderer Douglasscher Raum^M
tasca^F vescicouterina
excavación^F vesicouterina

rectum
rectum^M
Mastdarm^M
retto^M
recto^M

urinary bladder
vessie^F
Harnblase^F
vescica^F
vejiga^F

cervix of uterus
col^M de l'utérus^M
Gebärmutterhals^M
collo^M dell'utero^M
cuello^M del útero^M

mons pubis
mont^M de Vénus
Schamhügel^M
monte^M di Venere
monte^M de Venus

vagina
vagin^M
Scheide^F
vagina^F
vagina^F

symphysis pubis
symphyse^F pubienne
Symphyse^F
sinfisi^F pubica
sinfisis^F púbica

buttock
fesse^F
Gesäß^N
natica^F
nalga^F

clitoris
clitoris^M
Klitoris^F
clitoride^{F/M}
clítoris^M

anus
anus^M
After^M
ano^M
ano^M

urethra
urètre^M
Harnröhre^F
uretra^F
uretra^F

labium minus
petite lèvre^F
kleine Schamlippe^F
piccolo labbro^M
labio^M menor

labium majus
grande lèvre^F
große Schamlippe^F
grande labbro^M
labio^M mayor

thigh
cuisse^F
Oberschenkelbereich^M
coscia^F
muslo^M

egg
ovule^M
Eizelle^F
ovulo^M
óvulo^M

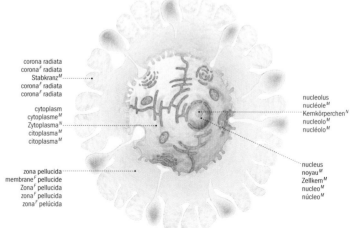

corona radiata
corona^F radiata
Stabkranz^M
corona^F radiata
corona^F radiata

nucleolus
nucléole^M
Kernkörperchen^N
nucleolo^M
nucléolo^M

cytoplasm
cytoplasme^M
Zytoplasma^N
citoplasma^M
citoplasma^M

zona pellucida
membrane^F pellucide
Zona^F pellucida
zona^F pellucida
zona^F pelúcida

nucleus
noyau^M
Zellkern^M
nucleo^M
núcleo^M

HUMAN BEING

posterior view
vue^F postérieure
Rückansicht^F
vista^F posteriore
vista^F posterior

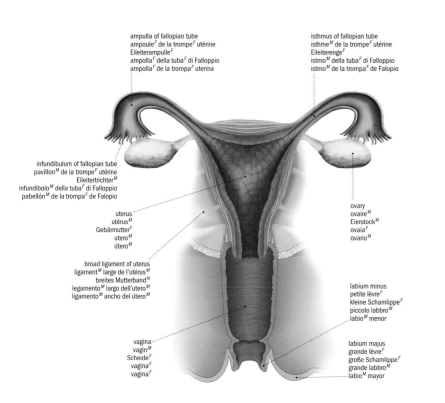

ampulla of fallopian tube
ampoule^F de la trompe^F utérine
Eileiterampulle^F
ampolla^F della tuba^F di Falloppio
ampolla^F de la trompa^F uterina

isthmus of fallopian tube
isthme^M de la trompe^F utérine
Eileiterenge^F
istmo^M della tuba^F di Falloppio
istmo^M de la trompa^F de Falopio

infundibulum of fallopian tube
pavillon^M de la trompe^F utérine
Eileitertrichter^M
infundibolo^M della tuba^F di Falloppio
pabellón^M de la trompa^F de Falopio

ovary
ovaire^M
Eierstock^M
ovaia^F
ovario^M

uterus
utérus^M
Gebärmutter^F
utero^M
útero^M

broad ligament of uterus
ligament^M large de l'utérus^M
breites Mutterband^N
legamento^M largo dell'utero^M
ligamento^M ancho del útero^M

labium minus
petite lèvre^F
kleine Schamlippe^F
piccolo labbro^M
labio^M menor

vagina
vagin^M
Scheide^F
vagina^F
vagina^F

labium majus
grande lèvre^F
große Schamlippe^F
grande labbro^M
labio^M mayor

fallopian tubes
trompes^F de Fallope
Eileiter^M
tube^F di Falloppio
trompa^F de Falopio

vulva
vulve^F
Scham^F
vulva^F
vulva^F

breast

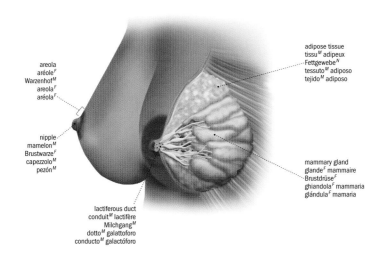

areola
aréole^F
Warzenhof^M
areola^F
aréola^F

adipose tissue
tissu^M adipeux
Fettgewebe^N
tessuto^M adiposo
tejido^M adiposo

nipple
mamelon^M
Brustwarze^F
capezzolo^M
pezón^M

mammary gland
glande^F mammaire
Brustdrüse^F
ghiandola^F mammaria
glándula^F mamaria

lactiferous duct
conduit^M lactifère
Milchgang^M
dotto^M galattoforo
conducto^M galactóforo

touch

toucher[M] | Tastsinn[M] | tatto[M] | tacto[M]

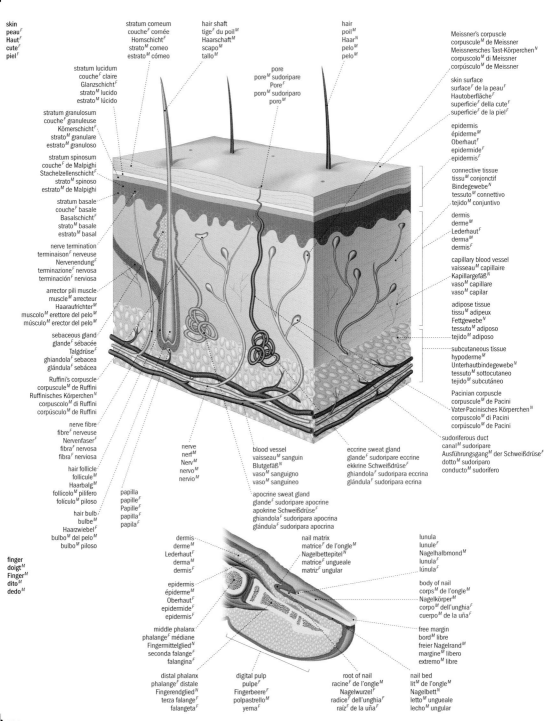

skin
peau[F]
Haut[F]
cute[F]
piel[F]

stratum corneum
couche[F] cornée
Hornschicht[F]
strato[M] corneo
estrato[M] córneo

hair shaft
tige[F] du poil[M]
Haarschaft[M]
scapo[M]
tallo[M]

hair
poil[M]
Haar[N]
pelo[M]
pelo[M]

Meissner's corpuscle
corpuscule[M] de Meissner
Meissnersches Tast-Körperchen[N]
corpuscolo[M] di Meissner
corpúsculo[M] de Meissner

stratum lucidum
couche[F] claire
Glanzschicht[F]
strato[M] lucido
estrato[M] lúcido

pore
pore[M] sudoripare
Pore[F]
poro[M] sudoriparo
poro[M]

skin surface
surface[F] de la peau[F]
Hautoberfläche[F]
superficie[F] della cute[F]
superficie[F] de la piel[F]

stratum granulosum
couche[F] granuleuse
Körnerschicht[F]
strato[M] granulare
estrato[M] granuloso

epidermis
épiderme[F]
Oberhaut[F]
epidermide[F]
epidermis[F]

stratum spinosum
couche[F] de Malpighi
Stachelzellenschicht[F]
strato[M] spinoso
estrato[M] de Malpighi

connective tissue
tissu[M] conjonctif
Bindegewebe[N]
tessuto[M] connettivo
tejido[M] conjuntivo

stratum basale
couche[F] basale
Basalschicht[F]
strato[M] basale
estrato[M] basal

dermis
derme[M]
Lederhaut[F]
derma[M]
dermis[F]

nerve termination
terminaison[F] nerveuse
Nervenendung[F]
terminazione[F] nervosa
terminación[F] nerviosa

capillary blood vessel
vaisseau[M] capillaire
Kapillargefäß[N]
vaso[M] capillare
vaso[M] capilar

arrector pili muscle
muscle[M] arrecteur
Haaraufrichter[M]
muscolo[M] erettore del pelo[M]
músculo[M] erector del pelo[M]

adipose tissue
tissu[M] adipeux
Fettgewebe[N]
tessuto[M] adiposo
tejido[M] adiposo

sebaceous gland
glande[F] sébacée
Talgdrüse[F]
ghiandola[F] sebacea
glándula[F] sebácea

subcutaneous tissue
hypoderme[M]
Unterhautbindegewebe[N]
tessuto[M] sottocutaneo
tejido[M] subcutáneo

Ruffini's corpuscle
corpuscule[M] de Ruffini
Ruffinisches Körperchen[N]
corpuscolo[M] di Ruffini
corpúsculo[M] de Ruffini

Pacinian corpuscle
corpuscule[M] de Pacini
Vater-Pacinisches Körperchen[N]
corpuscolo[M] di Pacini
corpúsculo[M] de Pacini

nerve fibre
fibre[F] nerveuse
Nervenfaser[F]
fibra[F] nervosa
fibra[F] nerviosa

nerve
nerf[M]
Nerv[M]
nervo[M]
nervio[M]

blood vessel
vaisseau[M] sanguin
Blutgefäß[N]
vaso[M] sanguigno
vaso[M] sanguineo

eccrine sweat gland
glande[F] sudoripare eccrine
ekkrine Schweißdrüse[F]
ghiandola[F] sudoripara eccrina
glándula[F] sudoripara ecrina

soudoriferous duct
canal[M] sudoripare
Ausführungsgang[M] der Schweißdrüse[F]
dotto[M] sudoriparo
conducto[M] sudorifero

hair follicle
follicule[M]
Haarbalg[M]
follicolo[M] pilifero
folículo[M] piloso

papilla
papille[F]
Papille[F]
papilla[F]
papila[F]

apocrine sweat gland
glande[F] sudoripare apocrine
apokrine Schweißdrüse[F]
ghiandola[F] sudoripara apocrina
glándula[F] sudoripara apocrina

hair bulb
bulbe[M]
Haarzwiebel[F]
bulbo[M] del pelo[M]
bulbo[M] piloso

finger
doigt[M]
Finger[M]
dito[M]
dedo[M]

dermis
derme[M]
Lederhaut[F]
derma[M]
dermis[F]

nail matrix
matrice[F] de l'ongle[M]
Nagelbettepitel[N]
matrice[F] ungueale
matriz[F] ungular

lunula
lunule[F]
Nagelhalbmond[M]
lunula[F]
lúnula[F]

epidermis
épiderme[M]
Oberhaut[F]
epidermide[F]
epidermis[F]

body of nail
corps[M] de l'ongle[M]
Nagelkörper[M]
corpo[M] dell'unghia[F]
cuerpo[M] de la uña[F]

middle phalanx
phalange[F] médiane
Fingermittelglied[N]
seconda falange[F]
falangina[F]

free margin
bord[M] libre
freier Nagelrand[M]
margine[M] libero
extremo[M] libre

distal phalanx
phalange[F] distale
Fingerendglied[N]
terza falange[F]
falangeta[F]

digital pulp
pulpe[F]
Fingerbeere[F]
polpastrello[M]
yema[F]

root of nail
racine[F] de l'ongle[M]
Nagelwurzel[F]
radice[F] dell'unghia[F]
raíz[F] de la uña[F]

nail bed
lit[M] de l'ongle[M]
Nagelbett[N]
letto[M] ungueale
lecho[M] ungular

touch

hand
main[F]
Hand[F]
mano[F]
mano[F]

HUMAN BEING

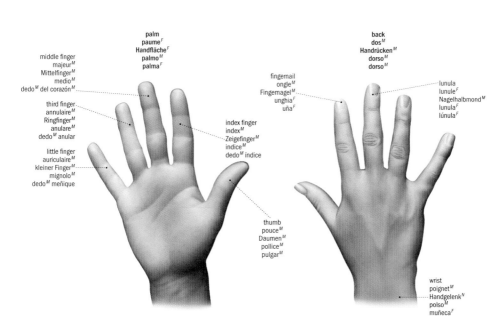

palm
paume[F]
Handfläche[F]
palmo[M]
palma[F]

middle finger
majeur[M]
Mittelfinger[M]
medio[M]
dedo[M] del corazón[M]

third finger
annulaire[M]
Ringfinger[M]
anulare[M]
dedo[M] anular

little finger
auriculaire[M]
kleiner Finger[M]
mignolo[M]
dedo[M] meñique

index finger
index[M]
Zeigefinger[M]
indice[M]
dedo[M] índice

thumb
pouce[M]
Daumen[M]
pollice[M]
pulgar[M]

back
dos[M]
Handrücken[M]
dorso[M]
dorso[M]

fingernail
ongle[M]
Fingernagel[M]
unghia[F]
uña[F]

lunula
lunule[F]
Nagelhalbmond[M]
lunula[F]
lúnula[F]

wrist
poignet[M]
Handgelenk[N]
polso[M]
muñeca[F]

hearing

ouïe[F] | Gehör[N] | udito[M] | oído[M]

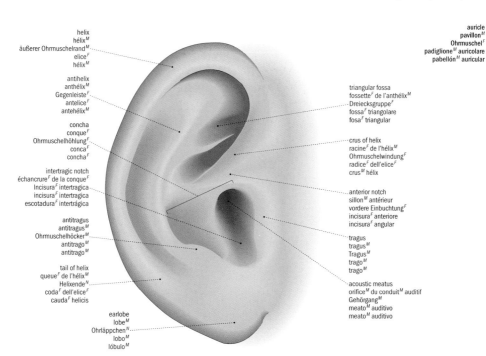

helix
hélix[M]
äußerer Ohrmuschelrand[M]
elice[F]
hélix[M]

antihelix
anthélix[M]
Gegenleiste[F]
antelice[F]
antehélix[M]

concha
conque[F]
Ohrmuschelhöhlung[F]
conca[F]
concha[F]

intertragic notch
échancrure[F] de la conque[F]
Incisura[F] intertragica
incisura[F] intertragica
escotadura[F] intertrágica

antitragus
antitragus[M]
Ohrmuschelhöcker[M]
antitrago[M]
antitrago[M]

tail of helix
queue[F] de l'hélix[M]
Helixende[N]
coda[F] dell'elice[F]
cauda[F] helicis

earlobe
lobe[M]
Ohrläppchen[N]
lobo[M]
lóbulo[M]

auricle
pavillon[M]
Ohrmuschel[F]
padiglione[M] auricolare
pabellón[M] auricular

triangular fossa
fossette[F] de l'anthélix[M]
Dreiecksgruppe[F]
fossa[F] triangolare
fosa[F] triangular

crus of helix
racine[F] de l'hélix[M]
Ohrmuschelwindung[F]
radice[F] dell'elice[F]
crus[M] hélix

anterior notch
sillon[M] antérieur
vordere Einbuchtung[F]
incisura[F] anteriore
incisura[F] angular

tragus
tragus[M]
Tragus[M]
trago[M]
trago[M]

acoustic meatus
orifice[M] du conduit[M] auditif
Gehörgang[M]
meato[M] auditivo
meato[M] auditivo

hearing

HUMAN BEING

structure of the ear
structure^F de l'oreille^F
Aufbau^M des Ohres^N
struttura^F dell'orecchio^M
estructura^F del oido^M

external ear
oreille^F externe
äußeres Ohr^N
orecchio^M esterno
oreja^F

middle ear
oreille^F moyenne
Mittelohr^N
orecchio^M medio
oido^M medio

internal ear
oreille^F interne
Innenohr^N
orecchio^M interno
oido^M interno

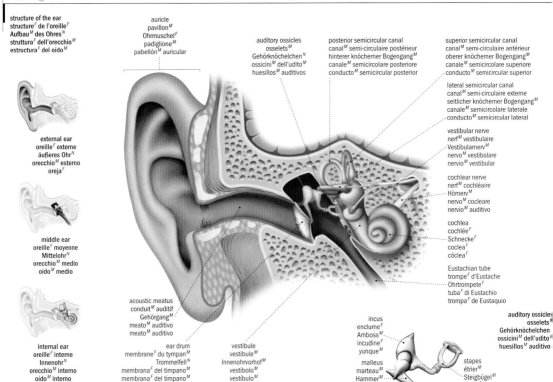

auricle
pavillon^M
Ohrmuschel^F
padiglione^M
pabellón^M auricular

auditory ossicles
osselets^M
Gehörknöchelchen^N
ossicini^M dell'udito^M
huesillos^M auditivos

posterior semicircular canal
canal^M semi-circulaire postérieur
hinterer knöcherner Bogengang^M
canale^M semicircolare posteriore
conducto^M semicircular posterior

superior semicircular canal
canal^M semi-circulaire antérieur
oberer knöcherner Bogengang^M
canale^M semicircolare superiore
conducto^M semicircular superior

lateral semicircular canal
canal^M semi-circulaire externe
seitlicher knöcherner Bogengang^M
canale^M semicircolare laterale
conducto^M semicircular lateral

vestibular nerve
nerf^M vestibulaire
Vestibularnerv^M
nervo^M vestibolare
nervio^M vestibular

cochlear nerve
nerf^M cochléaire
Hörnerv^M
nervo^M cocleare
nervio^M auditivo

cochlea
cochlée^F
Schnecke^F
coclea^F
cóclea^F

Eustachian tube
trompe^F d'Eustache
Ohrtrompete^F
tuba^F di Eustachio
trompa^F de Eustaquio

acoustic meatus
conduit^M auditif
Gehörgang^M
meato^M auditivo
meato^M auditivo

ear drum
membrane^F du tympan^M
Trommelfell^N
membrana^F del timpano^M
membrana^F del timpano^M

vestibule
vestibule^M
Innenohrvorhof^M
vestibolo^M
vestibulo^M

incus
enclume^F
Amboss^M
incudine^F
yunque^M

malleus
marteau^M
Hammer^M
martello^M
martillo^M

auditory ossicles
osselets^M
Gehörknöchelchen^N
ossicini^M dell'udito^M
huesillos^M auditivos

stapes
étrier^M
Steigbügel^M
staffa^F
estribo^M

smell and taste

odorat^M et goût^M | Geruchs-^M und Geschmackssinn^M | olfatto^M e gusto^M | olfato^M y gusto^M

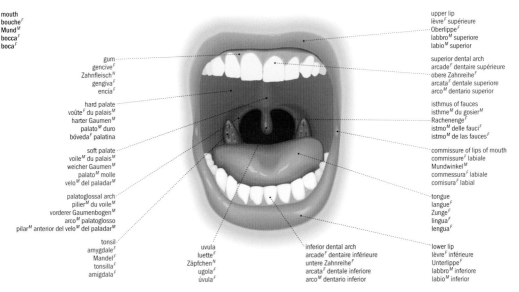

mouth
bouche^F
Mund^M
bocca^F
boca^F

gum
gencive^F
Zahnfleisch^N
gengiva^F
encia^F

hard palate
voûte^F du palais^M
harter Gaumen^M
palato^M duro
bóveda^F palatina

soft palate
voile^M du palais^M
weicher Gaumen^M
palato^M molle
velo^M del paladar^M

palatoglossal arch
pilier^M du voile^M
vorderer Gaumenbogen^M
arco^M palatoglosso
pilar^M anterior del velo^M del paladar^M

tonsil
amygdale^F
Mandel^F
tonsilla^F
amígdala^F

uvula
luette^F
Zäpfchen^N
ugola^F
úvula^F

upper lip
lèvre^F supérieure
Oberlippe^F
labbro^M superiore
labio^M superior

superior dental arch
arcade^F dentaire supérieure
obere Zahnreihe^F
arcata^F dentale superiore
arco^M dentario superior

isthmus of fauces
isthme^M du gosier^M
Rachenenge^F
istmo^F delle fauci^F
istmo^M de las fauces^F

commissure of lips of mouth
commissure^F labiale
Mundwinkel^M
commessura^F labiale
comisura^F labial

tongue
langue^F
Zunge^F
lingua^F
lengua^F

inferior dental arch
arcade^F dentaire inférieure
untere Zahnreihe^F
arcata^F dentale inferiore
arco^M dentario inferior

lower lip
lèvre^F inférieure
Unterlippe^F
labbro^M inferiore
labio^M inferior

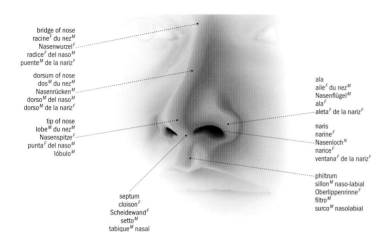

bridge of nose
racine^F du nez^M
Nasenwurzel^F
radice^F del naso^M
puente^M de la nariz^F

dorsum of nose
dos^M du nez^M
Nasenrücken^M
dorso^M del naso^M
dorso^M de la nariz^F

tip of nose
lobe^M du nez^M
Nasenspitze^F
punta^F del naso^M
lóbulo^M

septum
cloison^F
Scheidewand^F
setto^M
tabique^M nasal

external nose
parties^F externes du nez^M
äußere Nase^F
naso^M estemo
nariz^F

ala
aile^F du nez^M
Nasenflügel^M
ala^F
aleta^F de la nariz^F

naris
narine^F
Nasenloch^N
narice^F
ventana^F de la nariz^F

philtrum
sillon^M naso-labial
Oberlippenrinne^F
filtro^M
surco^M nasolabial

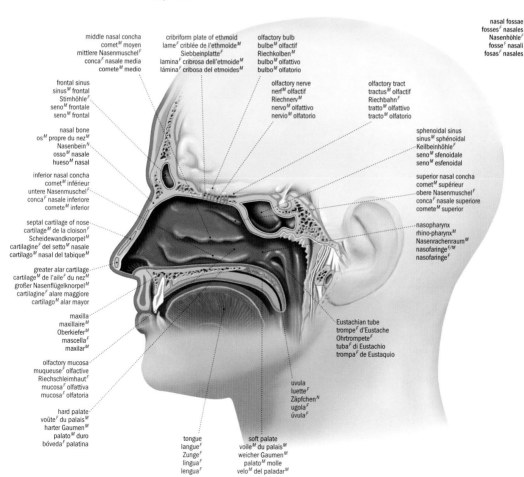

middle nasal concha
cornet^M moyen
mittlere Nasenmuschel^F
conca^F nasale media
cornete^M medio

cribriform plate of ethmoid
lame^F criblée de l'ethmoïde^M
Siebbeinplatte^F
lamina^F cribrosa dell'etmoide^M
lámina^F cribrosa del etmoides^M

olfactory bulb
bulbe^M olfactif
Riechkolben^M
bulbo^M olfattivo
bulbo^M olfatorio

nasal fossae
fosses^F nasales
Nasenhöhle^F
fosse^F nasali
fosas^F nasales

frontal sinus
sinus^M frontal
Stirnhöhle^F
seno^M frontale
seno^M frontal

olfactory nerve
nerf^M olfactif
Riechnerv^M
nervo^M olfattivo
nervio^M olfatorio

olfactory tract
tractus^M olfactif
Riechbahn^F
tratto^M olfattivo
tracto^M olfatorio

nasal bone
os^M propre du nez^M
Nasenbein^N
osso^M nasale
hueso^M nasal

sphenoidal sinus
sinus^M sphénoïdal
Keilbeinhöhle^F
seno^M sfenoidale
seno^M esfenoidal

inferior nasal concha
cornet^M inférieur
untere Nasenmuschel^F
conca^F nasale inferiore
cornete^M inferior

superior nasal concha
cornet^M supérieur
obere Nasenmuschel^F
conca^F nasale superiore
cornete^M superior

septal cartilage of nose
cartilage^M de la cloison^F
Scheidewandknorpel^M
cartilagine^F del setto^M nasale
cartílago^M nasal del tabique^M

nasopharynx
rhino-pharynx^M
Nasenrachenraum^M
nasofaringe^{F/M}
nasofaringe^F

greater alar cartilage
cartilage^M de l'aile^F du nez^M
großer Nasenflügelknorpel^M
cartilagine^F alare maggiore
cartílago^M alar mayor

maxilla
maxillaire^M
Oberkiefer^M
mascella^F
maxilar^M

Eustachian tube
trompe^F d'Eustache
Ohrtrompete^F
tuba^F di Eustachio
trompa^F de Eustaquio

olfactory mucosa
muqueuse^F olfactive
Riechschleimhaut^F
mucosa^F olfattiva
mucosa^F olfatoria

uvula
luette^F
Zäpfchen^N
ugola^F
úvula^F

hard palate
voûte^F du palais^M
harter Gaumen^M
palato^M duro
bóveda^F palatina

tongue
langue^F
Zunge^F
lingua^F
lengua^F

soft palate
voile^M du palais^M
weicher Gaumen^M
palato^M molle
velo^M del paladar^M

smell and taste

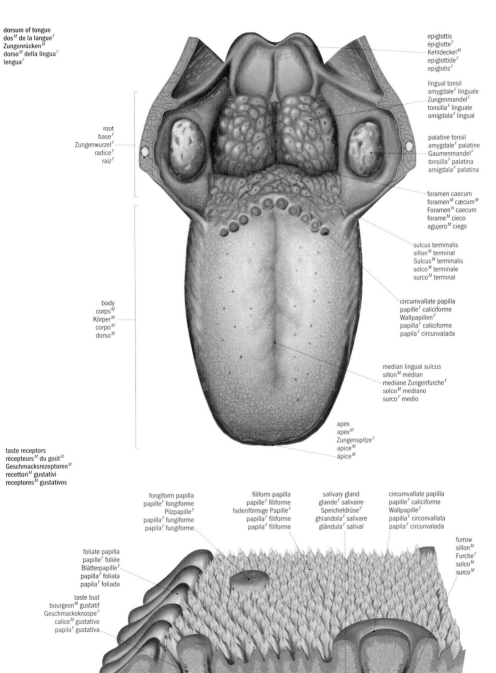

dorsum of tongue
dos^M de la langue^F
Zungenrücken^M
dorso^M della lingua^F
lengua^F

root
base^F
Zungenwurzel^F
radice^F
raíz^F

body
corps^M
Körper^M
corpo^M
dorso^M

taste receptors
récepteurs^M du goût^M
Geschmacksrezeptoren^M
recettori^M gustativi
receptores^M gustativos

epiglottis
épiglotte^F
Kehldeckel^M
epiglottide^F
epiglotis^F

lingual tonsil
amygdale^F linguale
Zungenmandel^F
tonsilla^F linguale
amígdala^F lingual

palatine tonsil
amygdale^F palatine
Gaumenmandel^F
tonsilla^F palatina
amígdala^F palatina

foramen caecum
foramen^M cæcum^M
Foramen^N caecum
forame^M cieco
agujero^M ciego

sulcus terminalis
sillon^M terminal
Sulcus^M terminalis
solco^M terminale
surco^M terminal

circumvallate papilla
papille^F caliciforme
Wallpapillen^F
papilla^F caliciforme
papila^F circunvalada

median lingual sulcus
sillon^M médian
mediane Zungenfurche^F
solco^M mediano
surco^F medio

apex
apex^M
Zungenspitze^F
apice^M
ápice^M

fongiform papilla
papille^F fongiforme
Pilzpapille^F
papilla^F fungiforme
papila^F fungiforme

filiform papilla
papille^F filiforme
fadenförmige Papille^F
papilla^F filiforme
papila^F filiforme

salivary gland
glande^F salivaire
Speicheldrüse^F
ghiandola^F salivare
glándula^F salival

circumvallate papilla
papille^F caliciforme
Wallpapille^F
papilla^F circonvallata
papila^F circonvalada

furrow
sillon^M
Furche^F
solco^M
surco^M

foliate papilla
papille^F foliée
Blätterpapille^F
papilla^F foliata
papila^F foliada

taste bud
bourgeon^M gustatif
Geschmacksknospe^F
calice^M gustativo
papila^F gustativa

sight

vue^F | Sehsinn^N | vista^F | vista^F

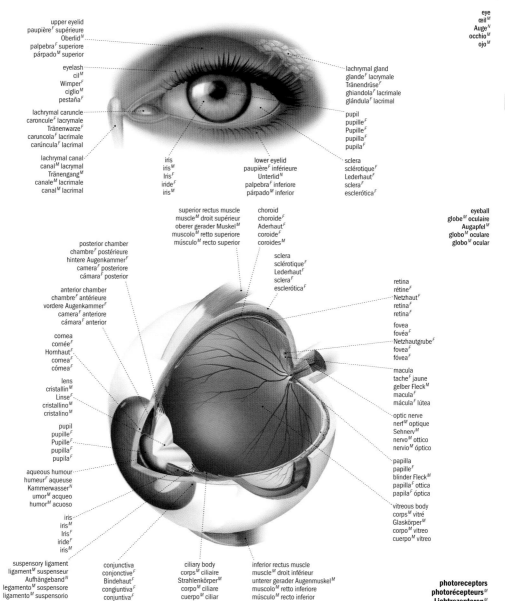

eye
œil^M
Auge^N
occhio^M
ojo^M

upper eyelid
paupière^F supérieure
Oberlid^N
palpebra^F superiore
párpado^M superior

eyelash
cil^M
Wimper^F
ciglio^M
pestaña^F

lachrymal caruncle
caroncule^F lacrymale
Tränenwarze^F
caruncola^F lacrimale
carúncula^F lacrimal

lachrymal canal
canal^M lacrymal
Tränengang^M
canale^M lacrimale
canal^M lacrimal

lachrymal gland
glande^F lacrymale
Tränendrüse^F
ghiandola^F lacrimale
glándula^F lacrimal

pupil
pupille^F
Pupille^F
pupilla^F
pupila^F

sclera
sclérotique^F
Lederhaut^F
sclera^F
esclerótica^F

iris
iris^M
Iris^F
iride^F
iris^M

lower eyelid
paupière^F inférieure
Unterlid^N
palpebra^F inferiore
párpado^M inferior

superior rectus muscle
muscle^M droit supérieur
oberer gerader Muskel^M
muscolo^M retto superiore
músculo^M recto superior

choroid
choroïde^F
Aderhaut^F
coroide^F
coroides^M

eyeball
globe^M oculaire
Augapfel^M
globo^M oculare
globo^M ocular

posterior chamber
chambre^F postérieure
hintere Augenkammer^F
camera^F posteriore
cámara^F posterior

sclera
sclérotique^F
Lederhaut^F
sclera^F
esclerótica^F

anterior chamber
chambre^F antérieure
vordere Augenkammer^F
camera^F anteriore
cámara^F anterior

retina
rétine^F
Netzhaut^F
retina^F
retina^F

fovea
fovéa^F
Netzhautgrube^F
fovea^F
fóvea^F

cornea
cornée^F
Hornhaut^F
cornea^F
córnea^F

macula
tache^F jaune
gelber Fleck^M
macula^F
mácula^F lútea

lens
cristallin^M
Linse^F
cristallino^M
cristalino^M

optic nerve
nerf^M optique
Sehnerv^M
nervo^M ottico
nervio^M óptico

pupil
pupille^F
Pupille^F
pupilla^F
pupila^F

papilla
papille^F
blinder Fleck^M
papilla^F ottica
papila^F óptica

aqueous humour
humeur^F aqueuse
Kammerwasser^N
umor^M acqueo
humor^M acuoso

vitreous body
corps^M vitré
Glaskörper^M
corpo^M vitreo
cuerpo^M vítreo

iris
iris^M
Iris^F
iride^F
iris^M

suspensory ligament
ligament^M suspenseur
Aufhängeband^N
legamento^M sospensore
ligamento^M suspensorio

conjunctiva
conjonctive^F
Bindehaut^F
congiuntiva^F
conjuntiva^F

ciliary body
corps^M ciliaire
Strahlenkörper^M
corpo^M ciliare
cuerpo^M ciliar

inferior rectus muscle
muscle^M droit inférieur
unterer gerader Augenmuskel^M
muscolo^M retto inferiore
músculo^M recto inferior

photoreceptors
photorécepteurs^M
Lichtrezeptoren^M
fotorecettori^M
fotorreceptores^M

cone
cône^M
Zapfen^M
cono^M
cono^M

rod
bâtonnet^M
Stäbchen^N
bastoncello^M
bastoncillo^M

supermarket

supermarché^M | Supermarkt^M | supermercato^M | supermercado^M

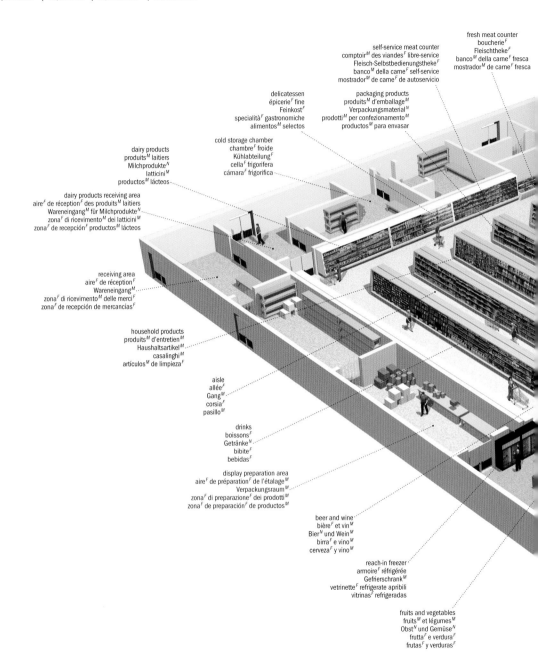

fresh meat counter
boucherie^F
Fleischtheke^F
banco^M della carne^F fresca
mostrador^M de carne^F fresca

self-service meat counter
comptoir^M des viandes^F libre-service
Fleisch-Selbstbedienungstheke^F
banco^M della carne^F self-service
mostrador^M de carne^F de autoservicio

delicatessen
épicerie^F fine
Feinkost^F
specialità^F gastronomiche
alimentos^M selectos

packaging products
produits^M d'emballage^M
Verpackungsmaterial^N
prodotti^M per confezionamento^M
productos^M para envasar

cold storage chamber
chambre^F froide
Kühlabteilung^F
cella^F frigorifera
cámara^F frigorifica

dairy products
produits^M laitiers
Milchprodukte^N
latticini^M
productos^M lácteos

dairy products receiving area
aire^F de réception^F des produits^M laitiers
Wareneingang^M für Milchprodukte^N
zona^F di ricevimento^M dei latticini^M
zona^F de recepción^F productos^M lácteos

receiving area
aire^F de réception^F
Wareneingang^M
zona^F di ricevimento^M delle merci^F
zona^F de recepción de mercancías^F

household products
produits^M d'entretien^M
Haushaltsartikel^M
casalinghi^M
artículos^M de limpieza^F

aisle
allée^F
Gang^M
corsia^F
pasillo^M

drinks
boissons^F
Getränke^N
bibite^F
bebidas^F

display preparation area
aire^F de préparation^F de l'étalage^M
Verpackungsraum^M
zona^F di preparazione^F dei prodotti^M
zona^F de preparación^F de productos^M

beer and wine
bière^F et vin^M
Bier^N und Wein^M
birra^F e vino^M
cerveza^F y vino^M

reach-in freezer
armoire^F réfrigérée
Gefrierschrank^M
vetrinette^F refrigerate apribili
vitrinas^F refrigeradas

fruits and vegetables
fruits^M et légumes^M
Obst^N und Gemüse^N
frutta^F e verdura^F
frutas^F y verduras^F

FOOD AND KITCHEN

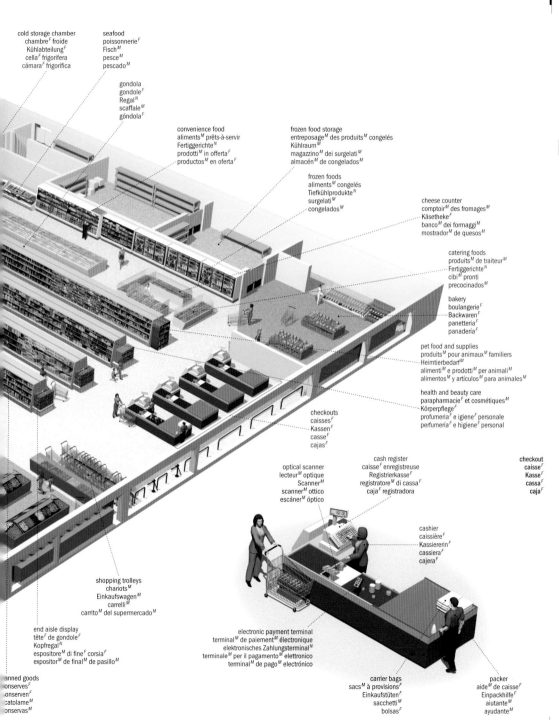

cold storage chamber
chambre^F froide
Kühlabteilung^F
cella^F frigorifera
cámara^F frigorífica

seafood
poissonnerie^F
Fisch^M
pesce^M
pescado^M

gondola
gondole^F
Regal^N
scaffale^M
góndola^F

convenience food
aliments^M prêts-à-servir
Fertiggerichte^N
prodotti^M in offerta^F
productos^M en oferta^F

frozen food storage
entreposage^M des produits^M congelés
Kühlraum^M
magazzino^M dei surgelati^M
almacén^M de congelados^M

frozen foods
aliments^M congelés
Tiefkühlprodukte^N
surgelati^M
congelados^M

cheese counter
comptoir^M des fromages^M
Käsetheke^F
banco^M dei formaggi^M
mostrador^M de quesos^M

catering foods
produits^M de traiteur^M
Fertiggerichte^N
cibi^M pronti
precocinados^M

bakery
boulangerie^F
Backwaren^F
panetteria^F
panadería^F

pet food and supplies
produits^M pour animaux^M familiers
Heimtierbedarf^M
alimenti^M e prodotti^M per animali^M
alimentos^M y artículos^M para animales^M

health and beauty care
parapharmacie^F et cosmétiques^M
Körperpflege^F
profumeria^F e igiene^F personale
perfumería^F e higiene^F personal

checkouts
caisses^F
Kassen^F
casse^F
cajas^F

optical scanner
lecteur^M optique
Scanner^M
scanner^M ottico
escáner^M óptico

cash register
caisse^F enregistreuse
Registrierkasse^F
registratore^M di cassa^F
caja^F registradora

checkout
caisse^F
Kasse^F
cassa^F
caja^F

cashier
caissière^F
Kassiererin^F
cassiera^F
cajera^F

shopping trolleys
chariots^M
Einkaufswagen^M
carrelli^M
carrito^M del supermercado^M

end aisle display
tête^F de gondole^F
Kopfregal^N
espositore^M di fine^M corsia^F
expositor^M de final^M de pasillo^M

electronic payment terminal
terminal^M de paiement^M électronique
elektronisches Zahlungsterminal^N
terminale^M per il pagamento^M elettronico
terminal^M de pago^M electrónico

canned goods
conserves^F
Konserven^F
scatolame^M
conservas^M

carrier bags
sacs^M à provisions^F
Einkaufstüten^F
sacchetti^M
bolsas^F

packer
aide^M de caisse^F
Einpackhilfe^F
aiutante^M
ayudante^M

farmstead

ferme^F | Bauernhof^M | fattoria^F | granja^F

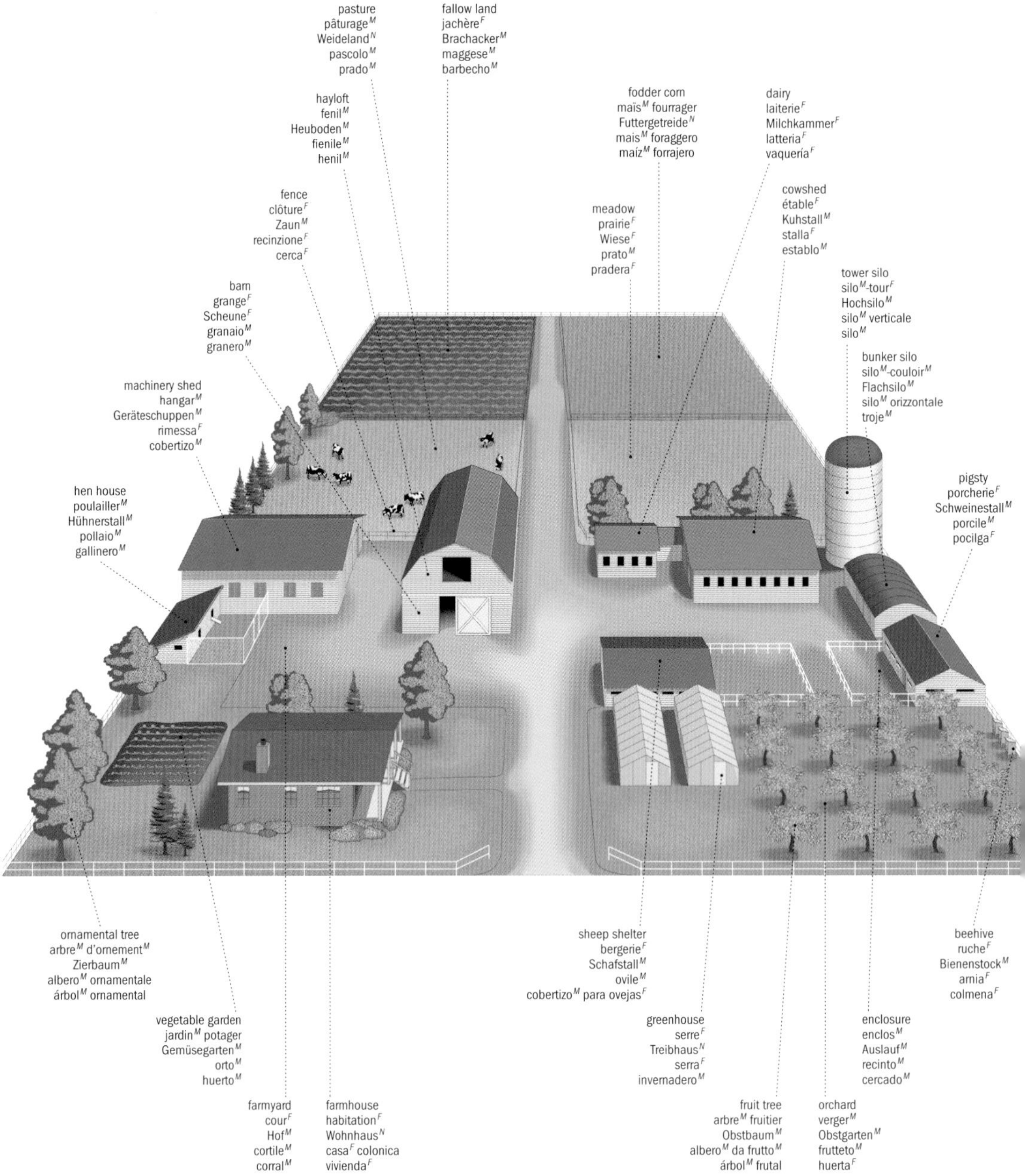

pasture
pâturage^M
Weideland^N
pascolo^M
prado^M

fallow land
jachère^F
Brachacker^M
maggese^M
barbecho^M

fodder corn
maïs^M fourrager
Futtergetreide^N
mais^M foraggero
maíz^M forrajero

dairy
laiterie^F
Milchkammer^F
latteria^F
vaquería^F

hayloft
fenil^M
Heuboden^M
fienile^M
henil^M

cowshed
étable^F
Kuhstall^M
stalla^F
establo^M

fence
clôture^F
Zaun^M
recinzione^F
cerca^F

meadow
prairie^F
Wiese^F
prato^M
pradera^F

tower silo
silo^M-tour^F
Hochsilo^M
silo^M verticale
silo^M

barn
grange^F
Scheune^F
granaio^M
granero^M

bunker silo
silo^M-couloir^M
Flachsilo^M
silo^M orizzontale
troje^M

machinery shed
hangar^M
Geräteschuppen^M
rimessa^F
cobertizo^M

pigsty
porcherie^F
Schweinestall^M
porcile^M
pocilga^F

hen house
poulailler^M
Hühnerstall^M
pollaio^M
gallinero^M

ornamental tree
arbre^M d'ornement^M
Zierbaum^M
albero^M ornamentale
árbol^M ornamental

sheep shelter
bergerie^F
Schafstall^M
ovile^M
cobertizo^M para ovejas^F

beehive
ruche^F
Bienenstock^M
arnia^F
colmena^F

vegetable garden
jardin^M potager
Gemüsegarten^M
orto^M
huerto^M

greenhouse
serre^F
Treibhaus^N
serra^F
invernadero^M

enclosure
enclos^M
Auslauf^M
recinto^M
cercado^M

farmyard
cour^F
Hof^M
cortile^M
corral^M

farmhouse
habitation^F
Wohnhaus^N
casa^F colonica
vivienda^F

fruit tree
arbre^M fruitier
Obstbaum^M
albero^M da frutto^M
árbol^M frutal

orchard
verger^M
Obstgarten^M
frutteto^M
huerta^F

mushrooms

champignons[M] | Pilze[M] | funghi[M] | hongos[M]

truffle
truffe[F]
Trüffel[F]
tartufo[M]
trufa[F]

wood ear
oreille-de-Judas[F]
Holzohr[N]
orecchio[M] di Giuda
oreja[F] de Judas

royal agaric
oronge[F] vraie
Kaiserling[M]
ovolo[M] buono
oronja[F]

delicious lactarius
lactaire[M] délicieux
echter Reizker[M]
agarico[M] delizioso
mizcalo[M]

enoki mushroom
collybie[F] à pied[M] velouté
Enoki[M]
collibia[F]
seta[F] enoki

oyster mushroom
pleurote[M] en forme[F] d'huitre[F]
Austernseitling[M]
gelone[M]
orellana[F]

cultivated mushroom
champignon[M] de couche[F]
Zuchtchampignon[M]
fungo[M] coltivato
champiñón[M]

green russula
russule[F] verdoyante
grasgrüner Täubling[M]
verdone[M]
rusula[F] verde

morel
morille[F]
Morchel[F]
spugnola[F]
morilla[F]

edible boletus
cèpe[M]
Steinpilz[M]
porcino[M]
boleto[M] comestible

shiitake
shiitake[M]
Schiitakepilz[M]
shiitake[M]
shiitake[M]

chanterelle
chanterelle[F] commune
Pfifferling[M]
cantarello[M]
rebozuelo[M]

seaweed

algues[F] | Meeresalgen[F] | alga[F] marina | algas[F]

arame
aramé[M]
Arame[F]
arame[F]
arame[M]

wakame
wakamé[M]
Wakame[F]
wakame[F]
wakame[M]

kombu
kombu[M]
Kombu[F]
kombu[F]
kombu[M]

spirulina
spiruline[F]
Spirulina[F]
spirulina[F]
espirulina[F]

Irish moss
mousse[F] d'Irlande[F]
Irisch Moos[N]
muschio[M] d'Irlanda[F]
Irish moss[M]

hijiki
hijiki[M]
Hijiki[F]
hijiki[F]
hijiki[M]

sea lettuce
laitue[F] de mer[F]
Meersalat[M]
lattuga[F] marina
lechuga[F] marina

agar-agar
agar-agar[M]
Agar-Agar[M/N]
agar-agar[M]
agar-agar[M]

nori
nori[M]
Nori[N]
nori[F]
nori[M]

dulse
rhodyménie[M] palmé
Dulse[F]
dulse[F]
dulse[M]

vegetables

légumes^M | Gemüse^N | ortaggi^M | hortalizas^F

bulb vegetables
légumes^M bulbes^M
Zwiebelgemüse^N
ortaggi^M da bulbo^M
bulbos^M

shallot
échalote^F
Schalotte^F
scalogno^M
chalote^M

water chestnut
châtaigne^F d'eau^F
Wassernuss^F
castagna^F d'acqua^F
castaña^F de agua

green onion
oignon^M vert
Frühlingszwiebel^F
cipolla^F verde
cebolla^F tierna

spring onion
ciboule^F
Frühlingszwiebel^F
cipolla^F d'inverno^M
cebolla^F tierna

garlic
ail^M
Knoblauch^M
aglio^M
ajo^M

chive
ciboulette^F
Schnittlauch^M
erba^F cipollina
cebollino^M

leek
poireau^M
Lauch^M
porro^M
puerro^M

yellow onion
oignon^M jaune
Gemüsezwiebel^F
cipolla^F di Spagna^F
cebolla^F amarilla

red onion
oignon^M rouge
rote Zwiebel^F
cipolla^F rossa
cebolla^F roja

white onion
oignon^M blanc
weiße Zwiebel^F
cipolla^F bianca
cebolla^F blanca

pickling onion
oignon^M à mariner
Perlzwiebel^F
cipollina^F
cebolleta^F

tuber vegetables
légumes^M tubercules^M
Knollengemüse^N
ortaggi^M da tubero^M
tubérculos^M

cassava
manioc^M
Maniok^M
manioca^F
mandioca^F

crosne
crosne^M
Knollenziest^M
crosne^M
crosne^M

taro
taro^M
Taro^M
taro^M
taro^M

jicama
jicama^M
Jicama^F
jicama^F
jicama^F

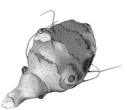

sweet potato
igname^F
Süßkartoffel^F
patata^F americana
batata^F

Jerusalem artichoke
topinambour^M
Topinambur$^{M/F}$
topinambur^M
aguaturma^F

sweet potato
patate^F
Süßkartoffel^F
patata^F americana
batata^F

potato
pomme^F de terre^F
Kartoffel^F
patata^F
patata^F

asparagus
asperge F
Spargel M
asparago M
espárrago M

tip
pointe F
Spitze F
punta F
punta F

spear
turion M
Stange F
turione M
turión M

bundle
botte F
Bund N
mazzo M
manojo M

bamboo shoot
pousse F de bambou M
Bambussprosse F
germoglio M di bambù M
brote M de bambú M

stalk vegetables
légumes M tiges F
Stengel- und Sprossengemüse N
ortaggi M da fusto M
hortalizas F de tallos M

Swiss chard
bette F à carde F
Mangold M
bietola F da coste F
acelga F

leaf
feuille F
Blatt N
foglia F
hoja F

fennel
fenouil M
Fenchel M
finocchio M
hinojo M

stalk
tige F
Stiel M
fusto M
tallo M

bulb
bulbe M
Knolle F
bulbo M
bulbo M

rib
carde F
Rippe F
costa F
tallo M

kohlrabi
chou M-rave F
Kohlrabi M
cavolo M rapa F
colinabo M

cardoon
cardon M
Kardone F
cardo M
cardo M

celery
céleri M
Stangensellerie M/F
sedano M
apio M

branch
branche F
Stange F
costa F
tallo M

fiddlehead fern
crosse F de fougère F
Farnspitze F
fronda F arrotolata
helecho M canela

head
pied M
Stielgrund M
cespo M
base F

rhubarb
rhubarbe F
Rhabarber M
rabarbaro M
ruibarbo M

vegetables

leaf vegetables
légumes^M feuilles^F
Blattgemüse^N
ortaggi^M da foglia^F
verduras^F de hojas^F

leaf lettuce
laitue^F frisée
Friséesalat^M
insalata^F riccia
lechuga^F rizada

cos lettuce
romaine^F
Romagna-Salat^M
lattuga^F romana
lechuga^F romana

celtuce
laitue^F asperge^F
Spargelsalat^M
lattuga^F asparago^M
lechuga^F de tallo^M

sea kale
chou^M marin
Meerkohl^M
cavolo^M marittimo
col^F marina

collards
chou^M cavalier^M
Riesenkohl^M
gramigna^F crestata
berza^F

escarole
scarole^F
Eskariol^M
scarola^F
escarola^F

butterhead lettuce
laitue^F pommée
Kopfsalat^M
lattuga^F cappuccina
lechuga^F de cogollo^M

iceberg lettuce
laitue^F iceberg^M
Eisbergsalat^M
lattuga^F iceberg^M
lechuga^F iceberg

radicchio
chicorée^F de Trévise
Radicchio^M
radicchio^M
achicoria^F de Treviso

ornamental kale
chou^M laitue^F
Zierkohl^M
cavolo^M ornamentale
col^F ornamental

curly kale
chou^M frisé
Grünkohl^M
cavolo^M riccio
col^F rizada

vine leaf
feuille^F de vigne^F
Weinblatt^N
pampino^M
hoja^F de parra^F

Brussels sprouts
choux^M de Bruxelles
Rosenkohl^M
cavolini^F di Bruxelles
coles^F de Bruselas

red cabbage
chou^M pommé rouge
Rotkohl^M
cavolo^M rosso
col^F lombarda

white cabbage
chou^M pommé blanc
Weißkohl^M
cavolo^M bianco
col^F/repollo^M

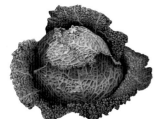

savoy cabbage
chou^M de Milan
Wirsing^M
cavolo^M verzotto
col^F rizada de otoño^M

green cabbage
chou^M pommé vert
Kohl^M
cavolo^M verza^F
col^F verde/repollo^M verde

pe-tsai
pe-tsai^M
Chinakohl^M
pe-tsai^M
col^M china

pak-choi
pak-choi^M
Pak-Choi^M
pak-choi^M
pak-choi^M

purslane
pourpier^M
Portulak^M
porcellana^F
verdolaga^F

nettle
ortie^F
Nessel^F
ortica^F
ortiga^F

watercress
cresson^M de fontaine^F
Brunnenkresse^F
crescione^M
berro^M

dandelion
pissenlit^M
Löwenzahn^M
dente^M di leone^M
diente^M de león

corn salad
mâche^F
Feldsalat^M
valerianella^F
colleja^F

rocket
roquette^F
Rauke^F
rucola^F
ruqueta^F

spinach
épinard^M
Spinat^M
spinacio^M
espinaca^F

garden cress
cresson^M alénois
Gartenkresse^F
crescione^M d'orto^M
berros^M de jardín

garden sorrel
oseille^F
Garten-Sauerampfer^M
acetosa^F
acedera^F

curly endive
chicorée^F frisée
krause Endivie^F
indivia^F riccia
escarola^F rizada

chicory
endive^F
Chicorée^{M/F}
insalata^F belga
endivia^F

inflorescent vegetables
légumes^M fleurs^F
Blütengemüse^N
ortaggi^M da infiorescenza^F
inflorescencias^F

cauliflower
chou^M-fleur^F
Blumenkohl^M
cavolfiore^M
coliflor^F

broccoli
brocoli^M
Broccoli^M
broccolo^M
brécol^M

Gai-lohn
Gai lon^M
China-Broccoli^M
Gai-lohn^M
brécol^M chino

broccoli raab
brocoli^M italien
Rübenspross^M
cime^F di rapa^F
nabiza^F

artichoke
artichaut^M
Artischocke^F
carciofo^M
alcachofa^F

vegetables

fruit vegetables
légumes^M **fruits**^{M}
Fruchtgemüse^N
ortaggi^M **da frutto**^{M}
hortalizas^F **de fruto**^{M}

avocado
avocat^M
Avocado^F
avocado^M
aguacate^M

tomato
tomate^F
Tomate^F
pomodoro^M
tomate^M

currant tomato
tomate^F en grappe^F
Kirschtomate^F
pomodorini^M a grappolo^M
tomate^M en rama^F

tomatillo
tomatille^F
Tomatillo^F
tomatillo^M
tomatillo^M

olive
olive^F
Olive^F
oliva^F
aceituna^F

yellow sweet pepper
poivron^M jaune
gelber Paprika^M
peperone^M giallo
pimiento^M dulce amarillo

green sweet pepper
poivron^M vert
grüner Paprika^M
peperone^M verde
pimiento^M dulce verde

red sweet pepper
poivron^M rouge
roter Paprika^M
peperone^M rosso
pimiento^M dulce rojo

chilli
piment^M
Pfefferschote^F
peperoncino^M
chile^M

okra
gombo^M
Okraschote^F
gombo^M
gombo^M, quingombó^M

gherkin
cornichon^M
Einlegegurke^F
cetriolino^M
pepinillo^M

cucumber
concombre^M
Gurke^F
cetriolo^M
pepino^M

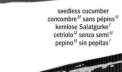

seedless cucumber
concombre^M sans pépins^M
kernlose Salatgurke^F
cetriolo^M senza semi^M
pepino^M sin pepitas^F

wax gourd
melon^M d'hiver^M chinois
Wachskürbis^M
zucca^F bianca
calabaza^F de China

aubergine
aubergine^F
Aubergine^F
melanzana^F
berenjena^F

marrow
courge^F
Gartenkürbis^M
zucca^F di Napoli
calabacín^M

courgette
courgette^F
Zucchini^F
zucchina^F
calabacín^M

bitter melon
margose^F
Bittermelone^F
melone^M amaro
pepino^M amargo

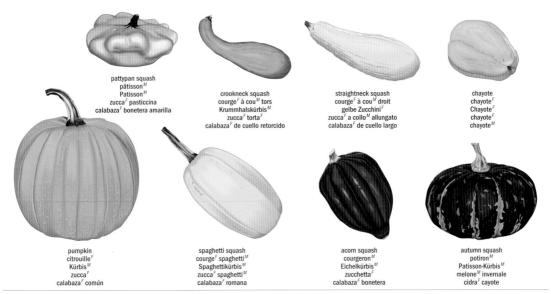

pattypan squash
pâtisson[M]
Patisson[M]
zucca[F] pasticcina
calabaza[F] bonetera amarilla

crookneck squash
courge[F] à cou[M] tors
Krummhalskürbis[M]
zucca[F] torta
calabaza[F] de cuello retorcido

straightneck squash
courge[F] à cou[M] droit
gelbe Zucchini[F]
zucca[F] a collo[M] allungato
calabaza[F] de cuello largo

chayote
chayote[F]
Chayote[F]
chayote[F]
chayote[M]

pumpkin
citrouille[F]
Kürbis[M]
zucca[F]
calabaza[F] común

spaghetti squash
courge[F] spaghetti[M]
Spaghettikürbis[M]
zucca[F] spaghetti[M]
calabaza[F] romana

acorn squash
courgeron[M]
Eichelkürbis[M]
zucchetta[F]
calabaza[F] bonetera

autumn squash
potiron[M]
Patisson-Kürbis[M]
melone[M] invernale
cidra[F] cayote

root vegetables
légumes[M] racines[F]
Wurzelgemüse[N]
ortaggi[M] da radice[F]
raices[F]

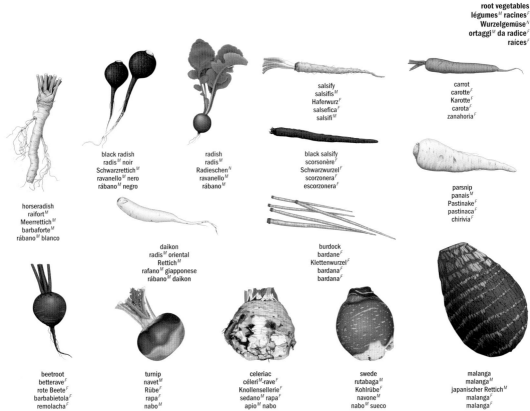

salsify
salsifis[M]
Haferwurz[F]
salsefica[F]
salsifí[M]

carrot
carotte[F]
Karotte[F]
carota[F]
zanahoria[F]

black radish
radis[M] noir
Schwarzrettich[M]
ravanello[M] nero
rábano[M] negro

radish
radis[M]
Radieschen[N]
ravanello[M]
rábano[M]

black salsify
scorsonère[F]
Schwarzwurzel[F]
scorzonera[F]
escorzonera[F]

parsnip
panais[M]
Pastinake[F]
pastinaca[F]
chirivía[F]

horseradish
raifort[M]
Meerrettich[M]
barbaforte[M]
rábano[M] blanco

daikon
radis[M] oriental
Rettich[M]
rafano[M] giapponese
rábano[M] daikon

burdock
bardane[F]
Klettenwurzel[F]
bardana[F]
bardana[F]

beetroot
betterave[F]
rote Beete[F]
barbabietola[F]
remolacha[F]

turnip
navet[M]
Rübe[F]
rapa[F]
nabo[M]

celeriac
céleri[M]-rave[F]
Knollensellerie[F]
sedano[M] rapa[F]
apio[M] nabo

swede
rutabaga[M]
Kohlrübe[F]
navone[M]
nabo[M] sueco

malanga
malanga[M]
japanischer Rettich[M]
malanga[F]
malanga[F]

legumes

légumineuses^F | Hülsenfrüchte^F | legumi^M | legumbres^F

lupine
lupin^M
Lupine^F
lupino^M
altramuz^M

peanut
cacahuète^F
Erdnuss^F
arachide^F
cacahuete^M

alfalfa
luzerne^F
blaue Luzerne^F
erba^F medica
alfalfa^F

lentils
lentilles^F
Linsen^F
lenticchie^F
lentejas^F

broad beans
fèves^F
dicke Bohnen^F
fave^F
habas^F

peas
pois^M
Erbsen^F
piselli^M
guisantes^M

dolichos beans
doliques^M
Bohnen^F
dolichi^M
dolichos^M

chick peas
pois^M chiches
Kichererbsen^F
ceci^M
garbanzos^M

split peas
pois^M cassés
gespaltene Erbsen^F
piselli^M secchi spaccati
guisantes^M partidos

black-eyed pea
dolique^M à œil^M noir
schwarzäugige Bohne^F
fagiolo^M dall'occhio^M nero
judías^F de ojo

lablab bean
dolique^M d'Égypte^F
Helmbohne^F
fagiolo^M egiziano
judía^F de Egipto

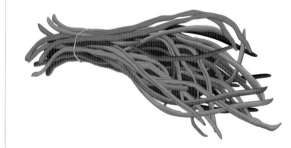

green peas
petits pois^M
grüne Erbsen^F
piselli^M
guisantes^M

mangetout
pois^M mange-tout^M
Zuckererbsen^F
piselli^M mangiatutto
guisantes^M mollares

yard-long bean
dolique^M asperge^F
Spargelbohne^F
fagiolo^M asparagio^M
judía^F china larga

beans
haricots^M
Bohnen^F
fagioli^M
judías^F

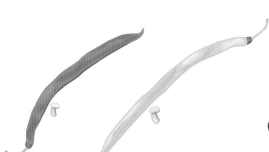

green bean
haricot^M vert
grüne Bohne^F
fagiolino^M
judías^F verdes

wax bean
haricot^M jaune
Wachsbohne^F
fagiolino^M giallo
judía^F amarilla

roman bean
haricot^M romain
römische Bohne^F
fagiolo^M romano
judía^F romana

adzuki bean
haricot^M adzuki
Asukibohne^F
fagiolo^M adzuki
judía^F adzuki

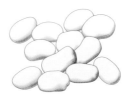

scarlet runner bean
haricot^M d'Espagne^F
Feuerbohne^F
fagiolo^M di Spagna^F
judía^F pinta

mung bean
haricot^M mungo
Mungobohne^F
fagiolo^M mungo
judía^F mungo

Lima bean
haricot^M de Lima
Limabohne^F
fagiolo^M di Lima
judía^F de Lima

pinto bean
haricot^M pinto
Pintobohne^F
fagiolo^M pinto
judía^F roja

red kidney bean
haricot^M rouge
rote Kidneybohne^F
fagiolo^M borlotto
judía^F roja

black gram
haricot^M mungo à grain^M noir
schwarze Mungobohne^F
fagiolo^M mungo nero
judía^F mungo negra

black bean
haricot^M noir
schwarze Bohne^F
fagiolo^M nero
judía^F negra

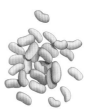

soybeans
graine^F de soja^M
Sojabohnen^F
semi^M di soia^F
semillas^F de soja^F

soybean sprouts
germes^M de soja^M
Sojasprossen^F
germogli^M di soia^F
brotes^M de soja^F

flageolet
flageolet^M
Flageolet-Bohne^F
fagiolo^M cannellino
frijol^M

fruits

fruits^M | Obst^N | frutti^M | frutas^F

berries
baies^F
Beeren^F
bacche^F
bayas^F

redcurrant
groseille^F à grappes^F
Johannisbeere^F
ribes^M
grosella^F

blackcurrant
cassis^M
schwarze Johannisbeere^F
ribes^M nero
grosella^F negra

gooseberry
groseille^F à maquereau^M
Stachelbeere^F
uvaspina^F
grosella^F espinosa

grape
raisin^M
Weintraube^F
uva^F
uva^F

blueberry
myrtille^F d'Amérique^F
Heidelbeere^F
mirtillo^M
arándano^M

bilberry
myrtille^F
Heidelbeere^F
mirtillo^M
arándano^M negro

red whortleberry
airelle^F
rote Heidelbeere^F
mirtillo^M rosso
arándano^M rojo

alkekengi
alkékenge^M
Physalis^F
alchechengi^M
alquequenje^M

cranberry
canneberge^F
Preiselbeere^F
mirtillo^M palustre
arándano^M agrio

raspberry
framboise^F
Himbeere^F
lampone^M
frambuesa^F

blackberry
mûre^F
Brombeere^F
mora^F
moras^F

strawberry
fraise^F
Erdbeere^F
fragola^F
fresa^F

stone fruits
fruits^M à noyau^M
Steinfrüchte^F
drupe^F
drupas^F

apricot
abricot^M
Aprikose^F
albicocca^F
albaricoque^M

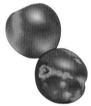

plum
prune^F
Pflaume^F
prugna^F
ciruela^F

peach
pêche^F
Pfirsich^M
pesca^F
melocotón^M

nectarine
nectarine^F
Nektarine^F
nettarina^F
nectarina^F

cherry
cerise^F
Kirsche^F
ciliegia^F
cereza^F

date
datte^F
Dattel^F
dattero^M
dátil^M

dry fruits
fruits^M **secs**
Trockenfrüchte^F
frutti^M **secchi**
frutas^F **secas**

macadamia nut
noix^F de macadamia^M
Macadamianuss^F
noce^F di macadamia^F
nuez^F de macadamia^F

ginkgo nut
noix^F de ginkgo^M
Ginkgonuss^F
noce^F di ginco^M
nuez^F de ginkgo

pistachio nut
pistache^F
Pistazie^F
pistacchio^M
pistacho^M

pine nut
pignon^M
Pinienkern^M
pinolo^M
piñón^M

cola nut
noix^F de cola^M
Kolanuss^F
noce^F di cola^F
nuez^F de cola

pecan nut
noix^F de pécan^M
Pecannuss^F
noce^F di pecan^M
pacana^F

cashew
noix^F de cajou^M
Cashewkern^M
noce^F di acagiù^M
anacardo^M

almond
amande^F
Mandel^F
mandorla^F
almendra^F

hazelnut
noisette^F
Haselnuss^F
nocciola^F
avellana^F

walnut
noix^F
Walnuss^F
noce^F
nuez^F

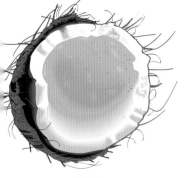

chestnut
marron^M
Esskastanie^F
castagna^F
castaña^F

beechnut
faîne^F
Buchecker^F
faggiola^F
hayuco^M

Brazil nut
noix^F du Brésil^M
Paranuss^F
noce^F del Brasile^M
nuez^F del Brasil^M

coconut
noix^F de coco^M
Kokosnuss^F
noce^F di cocco^M
coco^M

pome fruits
fruits^M **à pépins**^{M}
Apfelfrüchte^F
pomi^M
frutas^F **pomo**

pear
poire^F
Birne^F
pera^F
pera^F

quince
coing^M
Quitte^F
mela^F cotogna
membrillo^M

apple
pomme^F
Apfel^M
mela^F
manzana^F

medlar
nèfle^F du Japon^M
Mispel^F
nespola^F del Giappone^M
níspero^M

fruits

citrus fruits
agrumes^M
Zitrusfrüchte^F
agrumi^M
cítricos^M

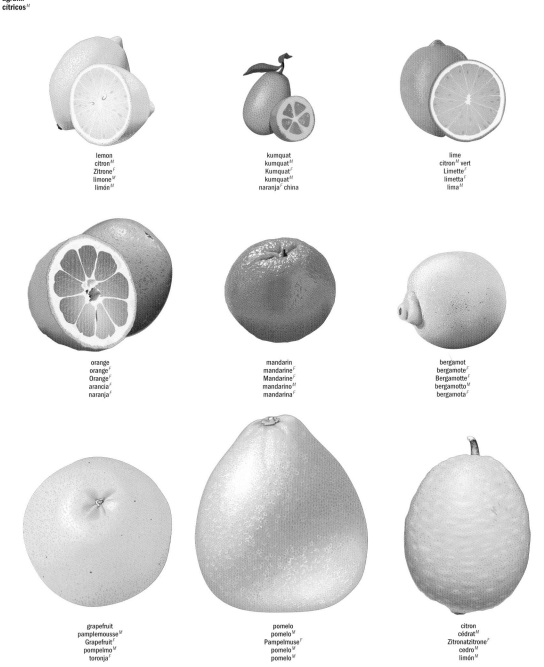

lemon
citron^M
Zitrone^F
limone^M
limón^M

kumquat
kumquat^M
Kumquat^F
kumquat^M
naranja^F china

lime
citron^M vert
Limette^F
limetta^F
lima^M

orange
orange^F
Orange^F
arancia^F
naranja^F

mandarin
mandarine^F
Mandarine^F
mandarino^M
mandarina^F

bergamot
bergamote^F
Bergamotte^F
bergamotto^M
bergamota^F

grapefruit
pamplemousse^M
Grapefruit^F
pompelmo^M
toronja^F

pomelo
pomelo^M
Pampelmuse^F
pomelo^M
pomelo^M

citron
cédrat^M
Zitronatzitrone^F
cedro^M
limón^M

fruits

melons
melons^M
Melonen^F
meloni^M
melones^M

cantaloupe
cantaloup^M
Honigmelone^F
cantalupo^M
melón^M cantalupo

casaba melon
melon^M Casaba
Casabamelone^F
melone^M invernale
melón^M invernal

honeydew melon
melon^M miel^M
Honigmelone^F
melone^M mieloso
melón^M de miel

muskmelon
melon^M brodé
Zuckermelone^F
melone^M retato
melón^M escrito

canary melon
melon^M d'Espagne^F
kanarische Melone^F
melone^M giallo canario
melón^M amarillo

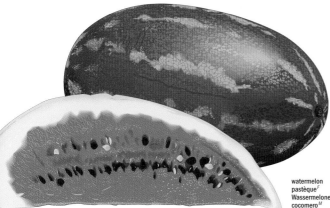

watermelon
pastèque^F
Wassermelone^F
cocomero^M
sandía^F

Ogen melon
melon^M d'Ogen
Ogenmelone^F
melone^M Ogen
melón^M de Ogen

FOOD AND KITCHEN

135

fruits

tropical fruits
fruits^M **tropicaux**
Südfrüchte^F
frutti^M **tropicali**
frutas^F **tropicales**

plantain
banane^F plantain^M
Plantainbanane^F
banana^F plantain
plátano^M

banana
banane^F
Banane^F
banana^F
banana^F

longan
longane^M
Longanfrucht^F
longan^M
longan^M

tamarillo
tamarillo^M
Baumtomate^F
tamarillo^M
tamarillo^M

passion fruit
fruit^M de la Passion^F
Passionsfrucht^F
maracuja^F
fruta^F de la pasión^F

horned melon
melon^M à cornes^F
Kiwano^F
kiwano^M
kiwano^M

mangosteen
mangoustan^M
Mangostane^F
mangostano^M
mangostán^M

kiwi
kiwi^M
Kiwi^F
kiwi^M
kiwi^M

pomegranate
grenade^F
Granatapfel^M
melograno^M
granada^F

cherimoya
chérimole^F
Chirimoya^F
cerimolia^F
chirimoya^F

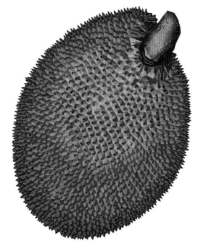

jackfruit
jaque^M
Jackfrucht^F
frutto^M del jack
fruta^F de jack

pineapple
ananas^M
Ananas^F
ananas^M
piña^F

jaboticaba
jaboticaba^M
Jaboticaba^F
jaboticaba^F
jaboticaba^F

litchi; lychee
litchi^M
Litchi^F
litchi^M
lichi^M

fig
figue^F
Feige^F
fico^M
higo^M

jujube
jujube^M
chinesische Dattel^F
giuggiola^F
jojoba^F

sapodilla
sapotille^F
Breiapfel^M
sapotiglia^F
zapote^M

guava
goyave^F
Guave^F
guaiava^F
guayaba^F

rambutan
rambutan^M
Rambutan^F
rambutan^M
rambután^M

Japanese persimmon
kaki^M
Kaki^F
cachi^M
caqui^M

prickly pear
figue^F de Barbarie
Kaktusfeige^F
fico^M d'India^F
higo^M chumbo

carambola
carambole^F
Sternfrucht^F
carambola^F
carambola^F

Asian pear
pomme^F poire^F
asiatische Birne^F
nashi^M
pera^F asiática

mango
mangue^F
Mango^F
mango^M
mango^M

durian
durian^M
Durianfrucht^F
durian^M
durión^M

papaya
papaye^F
Papaya^F
papaia^F
papaya^F

pepino
pepino^M
Birnenmelone^F
pepino^M
pepino^M dulce

feijoa
feijoa^M
Ananasguave^F
feijoa^F
feijoa^F

spices

épices^F | Gewürze^N | spezie^F | especias^F

juniper berry
baie^F de genièvre^M
Wacholderbeere^F
bacca^F di ginepro^M
bayas^F de enebro^M

clove
clou^M de girofle^M
Gewürznelke^F
chiodo^M di garofano^M
clavo^M

allspice
piment^M de la Jamaique^F
Jamaikapfeffer^M
pepe^M della Giamaica^F
pimienta^F de Jamaica

white mustard
moutarde^F blanche
weiße Senfkörner^N
senape^F bianca
mostaza^F blanca

black mustard
moutarde^F noire
schwarze Senfkörner^N
senape^F nera
mostaza^F negra

black pepper
poivre^M noir
schwarzer Pfeffer^M
pepe^M nero
pimienta^F negra

white pepper
poivre^M blanc
weißer Pfeffer^M
pepe^M bianco
pimienta^F blanca

pink pepper
poivre^M rose
rosa Pfeffer^M
pepe^M rosa
pimienta^F rosa

green pepper
poivre^M vert
grüner Pfeffer^M
pepe^M verde
pimienta^F verde

nutmeg
noix^F de muscade^F
Muskatnuss^F
noce^F moscata
nuez^F moscada

caraway
carvi^M
Kümmel^M
carvi^M
alcaravea^F

cardamom
cardamome^F
Kardamom$^{M/N}$
cardamomo^M
cardamomo^M

cinnamon
cannelle^F
Zimtstangen^M
cannella^F
canela^F

saffron
safran^M
Safran^M
zafferano^M
azafrán^M

cumin
cumin^M
Kreuzkümmel^M
cumino^M
comino^M

curry
curry^M
Curry^N
curry^M
curry^M

turmeric
curcuma^M
Kurkuma^N
curcuma^F
cúrcuma^F

fenugreek
fenugrec^M
Bockshornkleesamen^M
fieno^M greco
fenogreco^M

jalapeño chilli
piment^M Jalapeño
Jalapeño-Chili^M
peperoncino^M
chile^M jalapeño

bird's eye chilli
piment^M oiseau^M
Vogelaugenchili^M
peperoncino^M rosso
guindilla^F

crushed chillis
piments^M broyés
zerstoßene Chilis^M
peperoncino^M tritato
guindilla^F triturada

dried chillis
piments^M séchés
getrocknete Chilis^M
peperoncini^M secchi
guindilla^F seca^M

cayenne
piment^M de Cayenne
Cayennepfeffer^M
pepe^M di Cayenna
pimienta^F de cayena^F

paprika
paprika^M
Paprika^M
paprika^F
pimentón^M

ajowan
ajowan^M
Ajowan^N
ajowan^N
ajowán^M

asafœtida
asa-fœtida^F
Teufelsdreck^M
assafetida^F
asafétida^F

garam masala
garam masala^M
Garam Masala^N
garam masala^M
garam masala^M

cajun spice seasoning
mélange^M d'épices^F cajun
Cajun-Gewürzmischung^F
condimento^M alle spezie^F cajun
condimento^M de especias^F cajún

marinade spices
épices^F à marinade^F
Mariniergewürze^N
spezie^F marinate
especias^F para salmuera^F

five spice powder
cinq-épices^M chinois
Fünf-Kräuter^N-Gewürz^N
miscela^F di cinque spezie^F
cinco especias^F chinas

chilli powder
assaisonnement^M au chili^M
Chilipulver^N
peperoncino^M in polvere^F
guindilla^F molida

ground pepper
poivre^M moulu
gemahlener Pfeffer^M
pepe^M macinato
pimienta^F molida

ras el hanout
ras-el-hanout^M
Ras-El-Hanout^N
ras el hanout^M
ras el hanout^M

sumac
sumac^M
Sumach^M
sumac^M
zumaque^M

poppy seeds
graines^F de pavot^M
Mohnsamen^M
semi^M di papavero^M
semillas^F de adormidera^F

ginger
gingembre^M
Ingwer^M
zenzero^M
jengibre^M

condiments

condiments^M | Würzen^F | condimenti^M | condimentos^M

Tabasco™ sauce
sauce^F Tabasco$^®$
Tabasco™-Soße^F
salsa^F tabasco^M
salsa^F Tabasco^M

Worcestershire sauce
sauce^F Worcestershire
Worcestershire-Soße^F
salsa^F Worcestershire
salsa^F Worcertershire

tamarind paste
pâte^F de tamarin^M
Tamarindenmark^N
pasta^F di tamarindo^M
salsa^F de tamarindo^M

vanilla extract
extrait^M de vanille^F
Vanille-Extrakt^M
estratto^M di vaniglia^F
extracto^M de vainilla^F

tomato paste
concentré^M de tomate^F
Tomatenmark^N
concentrato^M di pomodoro^M
concentrado^M de tomate^M

tomato coulis
coulis^M de tomate^F
Passierte Tomaten^F
passata^F di pomodoro^M
salsa^F de tomate^M

hummus
hoummos^M
Hummus^M
hummus^M
hummus^M

tahini
tahini^M
Tahinisoße^F
tahini^M
tajín^M

hoisin sauce
sauce^F hoisin
Hoisinsoße^F
salsa^F hoisin
salsa^F hoisin

soy sauce
sauce^F soja^M
Sojasoße^F
salsa^F di soia^F
salsa^F de soja^F

powdered mustard
moutarde^F en poudre^F
Senfpulver^N
senape^F in polvere^F
mostaza^F en polvo^M

wholegrain mustard
moutarde^F à l'ancienne^F
Senfkörner^N
senape^F in granuli^M
mostaza^F en grano^M

Dijon mustard
moutarde^F de Dijon
Dijon-Senf^M
senape^F di Digione
mostaza^F de Dijon

German mustard
moutarde^F allemande
deutscher Senf^M
senape^F tedesca
mostaza^F alemana

English mustard
moutarde^F anglaise
englischer Senf^M
senape^F inglese
mostaza^F inglesa

American mustard
moutarde^F américaine
amerikanischer Senf^M
senape^F americana
mostaza^F americana

FOOD AND KITCHEN

plum sauce
sauce^F aux prunes^F
Pflaumensoße^F
salsa^F di prugne^F
salsa^F de ciruelas^F

mango chutney
chutney^M à la mangue^F
Mangochutney^N
chutney^M al mango^M
chutney^M de mango^M

harissa
harissa^F
Harissasoße^F
harissa^F
harissa^F

sambal oelek
sambal oelek^M
Sambal Oelek^M
sambal oelek^M
sambal oelek^M

ketchup
ketchup^M
Ketchup^M
ketchup^M
ketchup^M

wasabi
wasabi^M
Wasabipaste^F
wasabi^M
wasabi^M

table salt
sel^M fin
Tafelsalz^N
sale^M fino
sal^F de mesa^F

coarse salt
gros sel^M
grobes Salz^N
sale^M grosso
sal^F gorda

sea salt
sel^M marin
Meersalz^N
sale^M marino
sal^F marina

balsamic vinegar
vinaigre^M balsamique
Balsamessig^M
aceto^M balsamico
vinagre^M balsámico

rice vinegar
vinaigre^M de riz^M
Reisessig^M
aceto^M di riso^M
vinagre^M de arroz^M

cider vinegar
vinaigre^M de cidre^M
Apfelessig^M
aceto^M di mele^F
vinagre^M de manzana^F

malt vinegar
vinaigre^M de malt^M
Malzessig^M
aceto^M di malto^M
vinagre^M de malta^F

wine vinegar
vinaigre^M de vin^M
Weinessig^M
aceto^M di vino^M
vinagre^M de vino^M

herbs

fines herbes^F | Kräuter^N | piante^F aromatiche | hierbas^F aromáticas

dill
aneth^M
Dill^M
aneto^M
eneldo^M

anise
anis^M
Anis^M
anice^M
anís^M

bay
laurier^M
Lorbeer^M
alloro^M
laurel^M

oregano
origan^M
Origano^M
origano^M
orégano^M

tarragon
estragon^M
Estragon^M
dragoncello^M
estragón^M

basil
basilic^M
Basilikum^N
basilico^M
albahaca^F

sage
sauge^F
Salbei^M
salvia^F
salvia^F

thyme
thym^M
Thymian^M
timo^M
tomillo^M

mint
menthe^F
Minze^F
menta^F
hierbabuena^F

parsley
persil^M
Petersilie^F
prezzemolo^M
perejil^M

chervil
cerfeuil^M
Kerbel^M
cerfoglio^M
perifollo^M

coriander
coriandre^F
Koriander^M
coriandolo^M
cilantro^M

rosemary
romarin^M
Rosmarin^M
rosmarino^M
romero^M

hyssop
hysope^F
Ysop^M
issopo^M
hisopo^M

borage
bourrache^F
Boretsch^M
borragine^F
borraja^F

lovage
livèche^F
Liebstöckel$^{M/N}$
sedano^M di monte^M
alheña^F

savory
sarriette^F
Bohnenkraut^N
santoreggia^F
ajedrea^F

lemon balm
mélisse^F
Zitronenmelisse^F
melissa^F
melisa^F

cereals

rice
riz^M
Reis^M
riso^M
arroz^M

wild rice
riz^M sauvage
Wildreis^M
riso^M nero selvatico
arroz^M silvestre

spelt wheat
épeautre^M
Dinkel^M
farro^M
escanda^F común

wheat
blé^M
Weizen^M
frumento^M
trigo^M

oats
avoine^F
Hafer^M
avena^F
avena^F

rye
seigle^M
Roggen^M
segale^F
centeno^M

millet
millet^M
Hirse^F
miglio^M
mijo^M

corn
mais^M
Mais^M
mais^M
maíz^M

barley
orge^F
Gerste^F
orzo^M
cebada^F

buckwheat
sarrasin^M
Buchweizen^M
grano^M saraceno
trigo^M sarraceno

quinoa
quinoa^M
Reismelde^F
quinoa^M
quinua^F

amaranth
amarante^F
Amarant^M
amaranto^M
amaranto^M

triticale
triticale^M
Triticale^M
triticale^M
triticale^M

cereal products

produits^M céréaliers | Getreideprodukte^N | prodotti^M cerealicoli | cereales^M

flour and semolina
farine^F et semoule^F
Mehl^N und Grieß^M
farina^F e semolino^M
harina^F y sémola^F

FOOD AND KITCHEN

semolina
semoule^F
Grieß^M
semolino^M
sémola^F

whole wheat flour
farine^F de blé^M complet
Vollkornmehl^N
farina^F integrale
harina^F integral

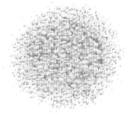

couscous
couscous^M
Couscous^N
cuscus^M
cuscús^M

plain flour
farine^F tout usage^M
Haushaltsmehl^N
farina^F semplice
harina^F común

unbleached flour
farine^F non blanchie
ungebleichtes Mehl^N
farina^F non trattata
harina^F sin blanquear

oat flour
farine^F d'avoine^F
Hafermehl^N
farina^F di avena^F
harina^F de avena^F

cornflour
farine^F de maïs^M
Maismehl^N
farina^F di mais^M
harina^F de maíz^M

bread
pain^M
Brot^N
pane^M
pan^M

croissant
croissant^M
Croissant^N
croissant^M
cruasán^M

black bread
pain^M de seigle^M noir
dunkles Roggenbrot^N
pane^M nero di segale^F
pan^M de centeno^M negro

bagel
bagel^M
Kringel^M
ciambella^F
rosquilla^F

ear loaf
baguette^F épi^M
Ährenbrot^N
spiga^F
pan^M espiga^F

French bread
pain^M parisien
Baguette^N
baguette^F
baguette^F

Greek bread
pain^M grec
griechisches Brot^N
pane^F greco
pan^M griego

French loaf
baguette^F parisienne
französisches Weißbrot^N
filone^M francese
barra^F de pan^M

Indian chapati bread
pain^M chapati indien
indisches Fladenbrot^N
pane^M chapati indiano
pan^M indio chapatí

tortilla
tortilla^F
Tortilla^F
tortilla^F
tortilla^F

pitta bread
pain^M pita
Pittabrot^N
pane^M pita
pan^M de pita^F

Indian naan bread
pain^M naan indien
indisches Naanbrot^N
pane^M naan indiano
pan^M indio naan

rye crispbread
cracker^M de seigle^M
Roggenknäckebrot^N
galletta^F di segale^F
galleta^F de centeno^M

filo dough
pâte^F phyllo^F
Blätterteig^M
pasta^F sfoglia^F
pasta^F de hojaldre^M

unleavened bread
pain^M azyme
ungesäuertes Brot^N
pane^M azzimo
pan^M ácimo

Danish rye bread
pain^M de seigle^M danois
dänisches Roggenbrot^N
pane^M di segale^F danese
pan^M danés de centeno^M

white bread
pain^M blanc
Weißbrot^N
pane^M bianco
pan^M blanco

multigrain bread
pain^M multicéréales
Mehrkornbrot^N
pane^M multicereali
pan^M multicereales

Scandinavian crispbread
cracker^M scandinave
skandinavisches Knäckebrot^N
galletta^F scandinava
galleta^F escandinava

Jewish challah
pain^M tchallah juif
jüdisches Weißbrot^N
pane^M ebraico
pan^M judío hallah

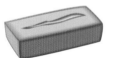

American corn bread
pain^M de mais^M américain
amerikanisches Maisbrot^N
pane^M di mais^M americano
pan^M americano de maíz^M

German rye bread
pain^M de seigle^M allemand
deutsches Roggenbrot^N
pane^M di segale^F tedesco
pan^M alemán de centeno^M

Russian black bread
pain^M noir russe
russischer Pumpernickel^M
Pumpernickel^M russo
pan^M negro ruso

farmhouse loaf
pain^M de campagne^F
Bauernbrot^N
pane^M casereccio
pan^M campesino

wholemeal bread
pain^M complet
Vollkornbrot^N
pane^M integrale
pan^M integral

Irish soda bread
pain^M irlandais
irisches Brot^N
pane^M irlandese
pan^M irlandés

cottage loaf
pain^M de mie^F
englisches Weißbrot^N
pagnottella^F inglese
pan^M de flor^F

cereal products

pasta
pâtes^F **alimentaires**
Teigwaren^F
pasta^F
pasta^F

rigatoni
rigatoni^M
Rigatoni^M
rigatoni^M
rigatoni^M

rotini
rotini^M
Rotini^M
eliche^F
sacacorchos^M

conchiglie
conchiglie^F
Conchiglie^F
conchiglie^F
conchitas^F

fusilli
fusilli^M
Fusilli^M
fusilli^M
fusilli^M

spaghetti
spaghetti^M
Spaghetti^M
spaghetti^M
espagueti^M

ditali
ditali^M
Ditali^M
ditali^M
dedalitos^M

gnocchi
gnocchi^M
Gnocchi^M
gnocchi^M
ñoquis^M

tortellini
tortellini^M
Tortellini^M
tortellini^M
tortellini^M

spaghettini
spaghettini^M
Spaghettini^M
spaghettini^M
fideos^M

elbows
coudes^M
Hörnchennudeln^F
gomiti^M
tiburones^M

penne
penne^M
Penne^F
penne^F
macarrones^M

cannelloni
cannelloni^M
Cannelloni^M
cannelloni^M
canelones^M

lasagne
lasagne^F
Lasagne^F
lasagne^F
lasañas^F

ravioli
ravioli^M
Ravioli^M
ravioli^M
raviolis^M

spinach tagliatelle
tagliatelle^M aux épinards^M
grüne Tagliatelle^F
tagliatelle^F verdi
tallarines^M de espinacas^F

fettucine
fettucine^M
Fettuccine^F
fettuccine^F
fetuchinas^F

Asian noodles
nouilles^F **asiatiques**
asiatische Teigwaren^F
spaghetti^M **asiatici**
fideos^M **asiáticos**

soba noodles
nouilles^F soba
Sobanudeln^F
spaghetti^M soba
fideos^M de soba^F

somen noodles
nouilles^F somen
Somennudeln^F
spaghetti^M somen
fideos^M de somen^M

udon noodles
nouilles^F udon
Udonnudeln^F
spaghetti^M udon
fideos^M de udon^M

rice papers
galettes^F de riz^M
Reispapier^N
gallette^F di riso^M
galletas^F de arroz^M

rice noodles
nouilles^F de riz^M
Reisnudeln^F
spaghetti^M di riso^M
fideos^M de arroz^M

bean thread cellophane noodles
nouilles^F de haricots^M mungo
Glasnudeln^F
spaghetti^M di fagioli^M mungo
fideos^M de judías^F mungo

egg noodles
nouilles^F aux œufs^M
asiatische Eiernudeln^F
spaghetti^M all'uovo^M
fideos^M de huevo^M

rice vermicelli
vermicelles^M de riz^M
Reisfadennudeln^F
vermicelli^M di riso^M
vermicelli^M de arroz^M

won ton skins
pâtes^F won-ton
Wan-tan-Teigblätter^N
pasta^F won ton
pasta^F won ton

rice
riz^M
Reis^M
riso^M
arroz^M

white rice
riz^M blanc
weißer Reis^M
riso^M bianco
arroz^M blanco

brown rice
riz^M complet
Braunreis^M
riso^M integrale
arroz^M integral

parboiled rice
riz^M étuvé
Parboiled Reis^M
riso^M parboiled
arroz^M vaporizado

basmati rice
riz^M basmati
Basmatireis^M
riso^M basmati
arroz^M basmati

coffee and infusions

café^M et infusions^F | Kaffee^M und Tee^M | caffè^M e infusi^M | café^M e infusiones^F

coffee
café^M
Kaffee^M
caffè^M
café^M

herbal teas
tisanes^F
Kräutertees^M
tisane^F
tisanas^F

green coffee beans
grains^M de café^M verts
Rohkaffee^F
chicchi^M di caffè^M verdi
granos^M verdes de café^M

roasted coffee beans
grains^M de café^M torréfiés
geröstete Kaffeebohnen^F
chicchi^M di caffè^M tostati
granos^M torrefactos de café^M

linden
tilleul^M
Linde^F
tiglio^M
tila^F

chamomile
camomille^F
Kamille^F
camomilla^F
manzanilla^F

verbena
verveine^F
Verbene^F
verbena^F
verbena^F

tea
thé^M
Tee^M
tè^M
té^M

green tea
thé^M vert
grüner Tee^M
tè^M verde
té^M verde

black tea
thé^M noir
schwarzer Tee^M
tè^M nero
té^M negro

oolong tea
thé^M oolong
Oolong-Tee^M
tè^M oolong
té^M oolong

tea bag
thé^M en sachet^M
Teebeutel^M
bustina^F di tè^M
bolsita^F de té^M

chocolate

chocolat^M | Schokolade^F | cioccolato^M | chocolate^M

dark chocolate
chocolat^M noir
Bitterschokolade^F
cioccolato^M fondente
chocolate^M amargo

milk chocolate
chocolat^M au lait^M
Milchschokolade^F
cioccolato^M al latte^M
chocolate^M con leche^F

cocoa
cacao^M
Kakao^M
cacao^M
cacao^M

white chocolate
chocolat^M blanc
weiße Schokolade^F
cioccolato^M bianco
chocolate^M blanco

FOOD AND KITCHEN

sugar

sucre^M | Zucker^M | zucchero^M | azúcar^M

granulated sugar
sucre^M granulé
Kristallzucker^M
zucchero^M in grani^M
azúcar^M granulado

powdered sugar
sucre^M glace^F
Puderzucker^M
zucchero^M a velo^M
azúcar^M glas

brown sugar
cassonade^F
brauner Zucker^M
zucchero^M di canna^F
azúcar^M moreno

rock candy
sucre^M candi
Kandiszucker^M
zucchero^M candito
azúcar^M candi

molasses
mélasse^F
Melasse^F
melassa^F
melazas^F

corn syrup
sirop^M de mais^M
Maissirup^M
sciroppo^M di mais^M
jarabe^M de maíz^M

maple syrup
sirop^M d'érable^M
Ahornsirup^M
sciroppo^M d'acero^M
jarabe^M de arce^M

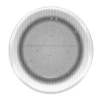

honey
miel^M
Honig^M
miele^M
miel^M

fats and oils

huiles^F et matières^F grasses | Fette^N und Öle^N | grassi^M e oli^M | grasas^F y aceites^M

corn oil
huile^F de mais^M
Maisöl^N
olio^M di mais^M
aceite^M de maíz^M

olive oil
huile^F d'olive^F
Olivenöl^N
olio^M d'oliva^F
aceite^M de oliva^F

sunflower-seed oil
huile^F de tournesol^M
Sonnenblumenöl^N
olio^M di semi^M di girasole^M
aceite^M de girasol^M

peanut oil
huile^F d'arachide^F
Erdnussöl^N
olio^M di arachidi^F
aceite^M de cacahuete^M

sesame oil
huile^F de sésame^M
Sesamöl^N
olio^M di sesamo^M
aceite^M de sésamo^M

shortening
saindoux^M
Backfett^N
grasso^M alimentare
grasa^F para cocinar

lard
lard^M
Schweinespeck^M
lardo^M
manteca^F de cerdo^M

margarine
margarine^F
Margarine^F
margarina^F
margarina^F

dairy products

produits^M laitiers | Milchprodukte^N | prodotti^M caseari | productos^M lácteos

yogurt
yaourt^M
Joghurt^M
yogurt^M
yogur^M

ghee
ghee^M
Ghee^N
ghi^M
mantequilla^F clarificada

butter
beurre^M
Butter^F
burro^M
mantequilla^M

cream
crème^F
Sahne^F
panna^F
nata^F

whipping cream
crème^F épaisse
Schlagsahne^F
panna^F da montare
nata^F de montar

sour cream
crème^F aigre
saure Sahne^F
panna^F acida
nata^F agria

milk
lait^M
Milch^F
latte^M
leche^M

homogenized milk
lait^M homogénéisé
homogenisierte Milch^F
latte^M omogeneizzato
leche^F homogeneizada

goat's milk
lait^M de chèvre^F
Ziegenmilch^F
latte^M di capra^F
leche^F de cabra

evaporated milk
lait^M concentré
Kondensmilch^F
latte^M evaporato
leche^F evaporada

buttermilk
babeurre^M
Buttermilch^F
latticello^M
suero^M de la leche^F

powdered milk
lait^M en poudre^F
Milchpulver^N
latte^M in polvere^F
leche^F en polvo^M

fresh cheeses
fromages^M **frais**
Frischkäse^M
formaggi^M **freschi**
quesos^M **frescos**

goat's-milk cheeses
fromages^M **de chèvre**^F
Ziegenkäse^M
formaggi^M **di capra**^F
quesos^M **de cabra**^F

cottage cheese
cottage^M
Hüttenkäse^M
cottage cheese^M
queso^M cottage

mozzarella
mozzarella^F
Mozzarella^M
mozzarella^F
mozzarella^F

Chèvre cheese
chèvre^M frais
Ziegenfrischkäse^M
formaggio^M fresco di capra^F
queso^M chèvre

ricotta
ricotta^F
Ricotta^M
ricotta^F
ricotta^F

cream cheese
fromage^M à tartiner
Streichkäse^M
formaggio^M cremoso
queso^M cremoso

Crottin de Chavignol
crottin^M de Chavignol
Crottin de Chavignol^M
crottin^M de chavignol
Crottin^M de Chavignol

pressed cheeses
fromages^M **à pâte**^{F} **pressée**
Hartkäse^M
formaggi^M **a pasta**^{F} **dura**
quesos^M **prensados**

Jarlsberg
jarlsberg^M
Jarlsberg^M
jarlsberg^M
jarlsberg^M

Emmenthal
emmenthal^M
Emmentaler^M
emmental^M
emmenthal^M

Raclette
raclette^F
Raclette^M
raclette^F
raclette^F

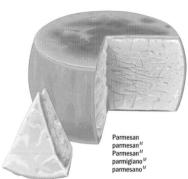

Parmesan
parmesan^M
Parmesan^M
parmigiano^M
parmesano^M

Gruyère
gruyère^M
Gruyèrekäse^M
groviera$^{M/F}$
gruyère^M

Romano
romano^M
Pecorino Romano^M
pecorino^M romano
pecorino romano^M

blue-veined cheeses
fromages^M **à pâte**^{F} **persillée**
Edelpilzkäse^M
formaggi^M **erborinati**
quesos^M **azules**

Roquefort
roquefort^M
Roquefort^M
roquefort^M
roquefort^M

Stilton
stilton^M
Stilton^M
stilton^M
stilton^M

Gorgonzola
gorgonzola^M
Gorgonzola^M
gorgonzola^M
gorgonzola^M

Danish Blue
bleu^M danois
Danish Blue^M
danish blue^M
azul danés^M

soft cheeses
fromages^M **à pâte**^{F} **molle**
Weichkäse^M
formaggi^M **a pasta**^{F} **molle**
quesos^M **blandos**

Pont-l'Évêque
pont-l'évêque^M
Pont-l'Évêque^M
pont-l'évêque^M
Pont-l'Éveque^M

Coulommiers
coulommiers^M
Coulommiers^M
coulommiers^M
coulommiers^M

Munster
munster^M
Munster^M
munster^M
munster^M

Camembert
camembert^M
Camembert^M
camembert^M
camembert^M

Brie
brie^M
Brie^M
brie^M
brie^M

FOOD AND KITCHEN

meat

viande^F | Fleisch^N | carne^F | carne^F

cuts of beef
découpes^F de bœuf^M
Rindfleisch^N
tagli^M di manzo^M
cortes^M de vacuno^M

steak
bifteck^M
Steak^N
bistecca^F
bistec^M

diced beef
cubes^M de bœuf^M
Rindfleischwürfel^M
spezzatino^M
carne^F de vacuno^M troceada

minced beef
bœuf^M haché
Rinderhackfleisch^N
macinato^M
carne^F picada

shank
jarret^M
Hachse^F
ossobuco^M
morcillo^M

fillet roast
filet^M de bœuf^M
Rinderfilet^N
filetto^M
lomo^M

rib roast
rôti^M de côtes^F
hohe Rippe^F
costate^F
chuletón^M

back ribs
côtes^F levées de dos^M
Querrippe^F
costine^F
costillar^M

cuts of veal
découpes^F de veau^M
Kalbfleisch^N
tagli^M di vitello^M
cortes^M de ternera^F

diced veal
cubes^M de veau^M
Kalbfleischwürfel^M
spezzatino^M
carne^F de ternera^F troceada

minced veal
veau^M haché
Kalbshackfleisch^N
macinato^M
carne^F picada de vacuno^M

shank
jarret^M
Hachse^F
ossobuco^M
paleta^F

roast
rôti^M
Rollbraten^M
arrotolato^M
asado^M

steak
bifteck^M
Schnitzel^N
bistecca^F
bistec^M

chop
côte^F
Kotelett^N
braciola^F
chuleta^F

cuts of lamb
découpes^F d'agneau^M
Lammfleisch^N
tagli^M **di agnello**^M
cortes^M **de cordero**^M

chop
côte^F
Kotelett^N
braciola^F
chuleta^F

minced lamb
agneau^M haché
Lammhackfleisch^N
macinato^M
carne^F picada de cordero^M

diced lamb
cubes^M d'agneau^M
Lammfleischwürfel^M
spezzatino^M
carne^F de cordero^M troceada

leg of lamb
gigot^M
Braten^M
arrosto^M
pierna^F de cordero^M

shank
jarret^M
Hachse^F
stinco^M
paletilla^F

cuts of pork
découpes^F de porc^M
Schweinefleisch^N
tagli^M **di maiale**^M
cortes^M **de cerdo**^M

spareribs
travers^M
Spareribs/Schälrippchen^N
costolette^F
costillar^M

minced pork
porc^M haché
Schweinehackfleisch^N
macinato^M
carne^F picada de cerdo^M

hock
jarret^M
Eisbein^N
piedino^M
codillo^M

loin chop
côtelette^F
Kotelett^N
lonza^F
chuleta^F

smoked ham
jambon^M fumé
Räucherschinken^M
prosciutto^M affumicato
jamón^M ahumado

roast
rôti^M
Braten^M
arrosto^M
asado^M de cerdo^M

FOOD AND KITCHEN

offal

abats^M | Innereien^F | interiora^F | despojos^M

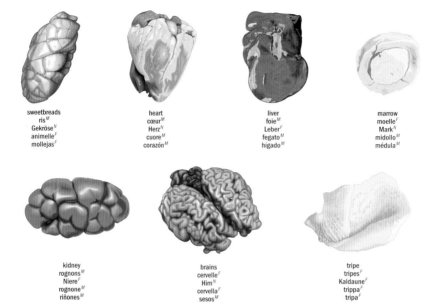

sweetbreads
ris^M
Gekröse^N
animelle^F
mollejas^F

heart
cœur^M
Herz^N
cuore^M
corazón^M

liver
foie^M
Leber^F
fegato^M
higado^M

marrow
moelle^F
Mark^N
midollo^M
médula^M

kidney
rognons^M
Niere^F
rognone^M
riñones^M

brains
cervelle^F
Hirn^N
cervella^F
sesos^M

tripe
tripes^F
Kaldaune^F
trippa^F
tripa^F

tongue
langue^F
Zunge^F
lingua^F
lengua^F

game

gibier^M | Wild^N | selvaggina^F | caza^F

quail
caille^F
Wachtel^F
quaglia^F
codorniz^F

pigeon
pigeon^M
Taube^F
piccione^M
pichón^M

guinea fowl
pintade^F
Perlhuhn^N
faraona^F
pintada^F

pheasant
faisan^M
Fasan^M
fagiano^M
faisán^M

hare
lièvre^M
Hase^M
lepre^F
liebre^F

rabbit
lapin^M
Kaninchen^N
coniglio^M
conejo^M

FOOD AND KITCHEN

poultry

volaille^F | Geflügel^N | volatili^M | aves^F de corral^M

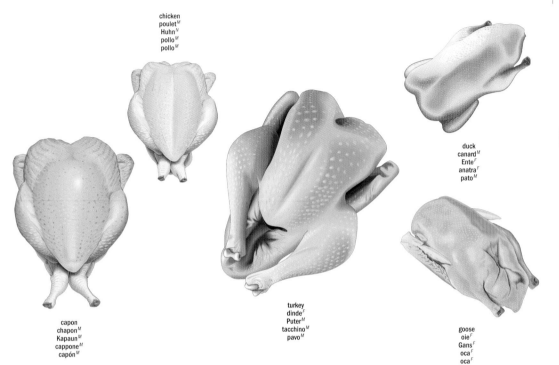

chicken
poulet^M
Huhn^N
pollo^M
pollo^M

duck
canard^M
Ente^F
anatra^F
pato^M

capon
chapon^M
Kapaun^M
cappone^M
capón^M

turkey
dinde^F
Puter^M
tacchino^M
pavo^M

goose
oie^F
Gans^F
oca^F
oca^F

eggs

œufs^M | Eier^N | uova^F | huevos^M

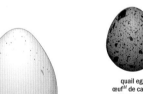

quail egg
œuf^M de caille^F
Wachtelei^N
uovo^M di quaglia^F
huevo^F de codorniz^F

pheasant egg
œuf^M de faisane^F
Fasanenei^N
uovo^M di fagiano^M
huevo^M de faisán^M

goose egg
œuf^M d'oie^F
Gänseei^N
uovo^M di oca^F
huevo^M de oca^F

ostrich egg
œuf^M d'autruche^F
Straußenei^N
uovo^M di struzzo^M
huevo^M de avestruz^M

duck egg
œuf^M de cane^F
Entenei^N
uovo^M di anatra^F
huevo^M de pato^M

hen egg
œuf^M de poule^F
Hühnerei^N
uovo^M di gallina^F
huevo^M de gallina^F

delicatessen

charcuterie^F | Spezialitäten^F | gastronomia^F | charcutería^F

rillettes
rillettes^F
Rillettes^F
ciccioli^M
rillettes^F

foie gras
foie^M gras
Stopfleber^F
foie-gras^M
foie gras

prosciutto
prosciutto^M
roher Schinken^M
prosciutto^M
jamón^M serrano

kielbasa sausage
saucisson^M kielbasa
Kielbasa-Wurst^F
salsiccia^F kielbasa
salchicha^F kielbasa

mortadella
mortadelle^F
Mortadella^F
mortadella^F
mortadela^F

black pudding
boudin^M
Blutwurst^F
sanguinaccio^M
morcilla^F

chorizo
chorizo^M
Chorizo-Wurst^F
chorizo^M
chorizo^M

pepperoni
pepperoni^M
Pepperoniwurst^F
salsiccia^F piccante
pepperoni^M

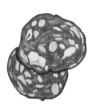

Genoa salami
salami^M de Gênes
grobe Salami^F
salame^M di Genova
salami^M de Génova

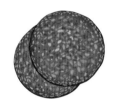

German salami
salami^M allemand
feine Salami^F
salame^M tedesco
salami^M alemán

Toulouse sausage
saucisse^F de Toulouse
Toulouser Wurst^F
salame^M di Tolosa
salchicha^F de Toulouse

merguez sausage
merguez^F
Merguez-Wurst^F
merguez^F
salchicha^F merguez

andouillette
andouillette^F
Kuttelwurst^F
salsiccia^F di trippa^F
andouillete^F

chipolata sausage
chipolata^F
Bratwurst^F
salsiccia^F alle cipolle^F
salchicha^F chipolata

frankfurter
saucisse^F de Francfort
Frankfurter Würstchen^N
salsiccia^F di Francoforte
salchicha^F de Frankfurt

pancetta
pancetta^F
Bauchspeck^M
pancetta^F
panceta^F

cooked ham
jambon^M cuit
gekochter Schinken^M
prosciutto^M cotto
jamón^M de York

American bacon
bacon^M américain
amerikanischer Bacon^M
bacon^M americano
bacón^M americano

Canadian bacon
bacon^M canadien
kanadischer Bacon^M
bacon^M canadese
bacón^M canadiense

molluscs

octopus
pieuvre^F
Krake^M
polpo^M
pulpo^M

cuttlefish
seiche^F
Tintenfisch^M
seppia^F
sepia^F

squid
calmar^M
Kalmar^M
calamaro^M
calamar^M

scallop
pétoncle^M
Kammmuschel^F
pettine^M
venera^F

hard-shell clam
palourde^F
Kreuzmuster^N-Teppichmuschel^F
tartufo^M di mare^M
almeja^F

soft shell clam
mye^F
Klaffmuschel^F
vongola^F molle
coquina^F

abalone
ormeau^M
Meerohr^N
orecchia^F di mare^M
oreja^F de mar^M

great scallop
coquille^F Saint-Jacques
Jakobsmuschel^F
capasanta^F
vieira^F

snail
escargot^M
Schnecke^F
chiocciola^F
caracol^M terrestre

limpet
patelle^F
Napfschnecke^F
patella^F
lapa^F

common periwinkle
bigorneau^M
Strandschnecke^F
littorina^F
bigaro^M

clam
praire^F
Venusmuschel^F
vongola^F
almeja^F

cockle
coque^F
Herzmuschel^F
cardio^M
berberecho^M

razor clam
couteau^M
Messermuschel^F
cannolicchio^M
navaja^F

oyster
huitre^F plate
Auster^F
ostrica^F
ostra^F

oyster
huitre^F creuse du Pacifique^M
Auster^F
ostrica^F
ostra^F

blue mussel
moule^F
Miesmuschel^F
mitilo^M
mejillón^M

whelk
buccin^M
Wellhornschnecke^F
buccino^M
buccino^M

crustaceans

crustacés ^M | Krebstiere ^N | crostacei ^M | crustáceos ^M

FOOD AND KITCHEN

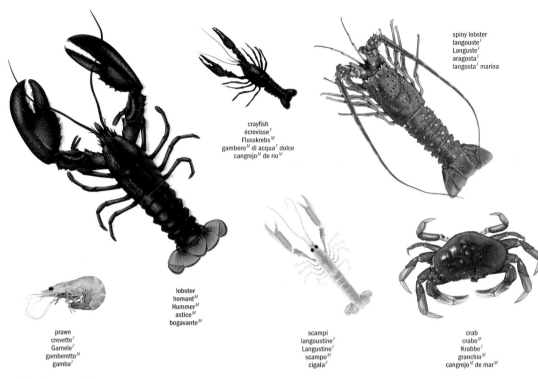

spiny lobster
langouste^F
Languste^F
aragosta^F
langosta^F marina

crayfish
écrevisse^F
Flusskrebs^M
gambero^M di acqua^F dolce
cangrejo^M de rio^M

lobster
homard^M
Hummer^M
astice^M
bogavante^M

prawn
crevette^F
Garnele^F
gamberetto^M
gamba^F

scampi
langoustine^F
Langustine^F
scampo^M
cigala^F

crab
crabe^M
Krabbe^F
granchio^M
cangrejo^M de mar^M

cartilaginous fishes

poissons^M cartilagineux | Knorpelfische^M | pesci^M cartilaginei | peces^M cartilaginosos

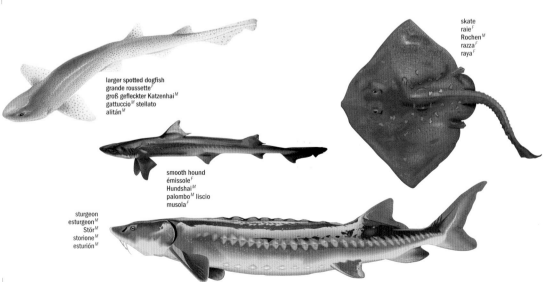

skate
raie^F
Rochen^M
razza^F
raya^F

larger spotted dogfish
grande roussette^F
groß gefleckter Katzenhai^M
gattuccio^M stellato
alitán^M

smooth hound
émissole^F
Hundshai^M
palombo^M liscio
musola^F

sturgeon
esturgeon^M
Stör^M
storione^M
esturión^M

bony fishes

poissons^M osseux | Knochenfische^M | pesci^M ossei | peces^M óseos

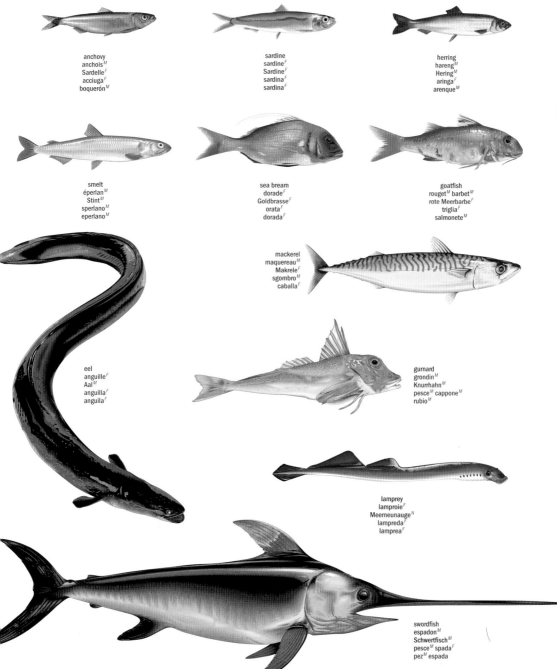

anchovy
anchois^M
Sardelle^F
acciuga^F
boquerón^M

sardine
sardine^F
Sardine^F
sardina^F
sardina^F

herring
hareng^M
Hering^M
aringa^F
arenque^M

smelt
éperlan^M
Stint^M
sperlano^M
eperlano^M

sea bream
dorade^F
Goldbrasse^F
orata^F
dorada^F

goatfish
rouget^M barbet^M
rote Meerbarbe^F
triglia^F
salmonete^M

mackerel
maquereau^M
Makrele^F
sgombro^M
caballa^F

eel
anguille^F
Aal^M
anguilla^F
anguila^F

gurnard
grondin^M
Knurrhahn^M
pesce^M cappone^M
rubio^M

lamprey
lamproie^F
Meerneunauge^N
lampreda^F
lamprea^F

swordfish
espadon^M
Schwertfisch^M
pesce^M spada^F
pez^M espada

FOOD AND KITCHEN

bony fishes

bass
perche[F] truitée
Barsch[M]
persico[M] trota[F]
róbalo[M]

mullet
mulet[M]
Meeräsche[F]
cefalo[M]
mújol[M]

carp
carpe[F]
Karpfen[M]
carpa[F]
carpa[F]

perch
perche[F]
Flussbarsch[M]
persico[M]
perca[F]

shad
alose[F]
Alse[F]
alosa[F]
sábalo[M]

pike
brochet[M]
Hecht[M]
luccio[M]
lucio[M]

pike perch
sandre[M]
Zander[M]
lucioperca[F]
lucioperca[M]

bluefish
tassergal[M]
Blaufisch[M]
ballerino[M]
anjova[F]

sea bass
bar[M] commun
Seebarsch[M]
branzino[M]
lubina[F]

monkfish
baudroie[F]
Seeteufel[M]
pesce[M] rospo[M]
rape[M]

tuna
thon[M]
Thunfisch[M]
tonno[M]
atún[M]

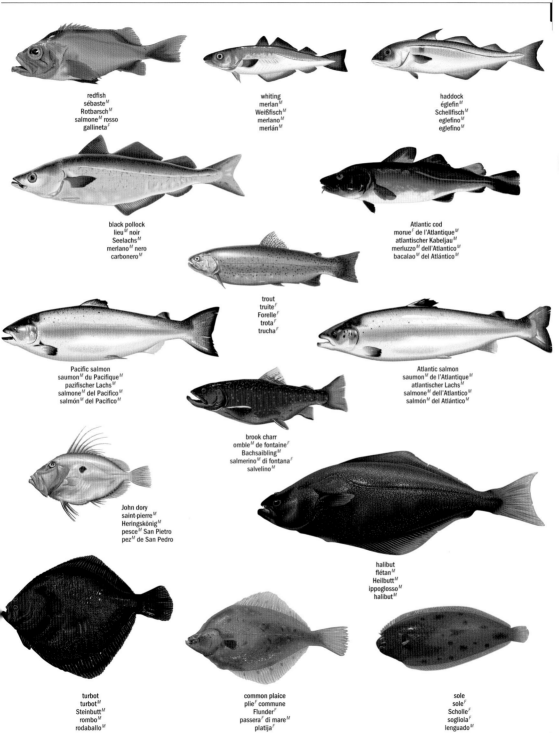

redfish
sébaste[M]
Rotbarsch[M]
salmone[M] rosso
gallineta[F]

whiting
merlan[M]
Weißfisch[M]
merlano[M]
merlán[M]

haddock
églefin[M]
Schellfisch[M]
eglefino[M]
eglefino[M]

black pollock
lieu[M] noir
Seelachs[M]
merlano[M] nero
carbonero[M]

Atlantic cod
morue[F] de l'Atlantique[M]
atlantischer Kabeljau[M]
merluzzo[M] dell'Atlantico[M]
bacalao[M] del Atlántico[M]

trout
truite[F]
Forelle[F]
trota[F]
trucha[F]

Pacific salmon
saumon[M] du Pacifique[M]
pazifischer Lachs[M]
salmone[M] del Pacifico[M]
salmón[M] del Pacífico[M]

Atlantic salmon
saumon[M] de l'Atlantique[M]
atlantischer Lachs[M]
salmone[M] dell'Atlantico[M]
salmón[M] del Atlántico[M]

brook charr
omble[M] de fontaine[F]
Bachsaibling[M]
salmerino[M] di fontana[F]
salvelino[M]

John dory
saint-pierre[M]
Heringskönig[M]
pesce[M] San Pietro
pez[M] de San Pedro

halibut
flétan[M]
Heilbutt[M]
ippoglosso[M]
halibut[M]

turbot
turbot[M]
Steinbutt[M]
rombo[M]
rodaballo[M]

common plaice
plie[F] commune
Flunder[F]
passera[F] di mare[M]
platija[F]

sole
sole[F]
Scholle[F]
sogliola[F]
lenguado[M]

packaging

emballage^M | Verpackungen^F | confezioni^F | envases^M

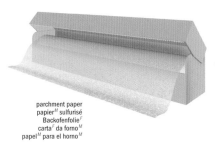

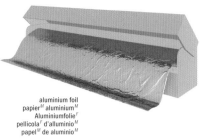

pouch
sachet^M
Beutel^M
sacchetto^M
bolsa^F

parchment paper
papier^M sulfurisé
Backofenfolie^F
carta^F da forno^M
papel^M para el horno^M

aluminium foil
papier^M aluminium^M
Aluminiumfolie^F
pellicola^F d'alluminio^M
papel^M de aluminio^M

waxed paper
papier^M paraffiné
Wachspapier^N
carta^F cerata
papel^M encerado

plastic film
pellicule^F plastique
Frischhaltefolie^F
pellicola^F trasparente
papel^M de celofán

freezer bag
sac^M de congélation^F
Gefrierbeutel^M
sacchetto^M per freezer^M
bolsa^F para congelados^M

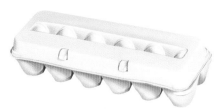

egg carton
boite^F à œufs^M
Eierkarton^M
confezione^F in cartone^M per uova^F
cajas^F de cartón^M para huevos^M

mesh bag
sac^M-filet^M
Netz^N
rete^F per alimenti^M
bolsa^F de malla^F

canisters
boites^F alimentaires
Vorratsdosen^F
barattoli^M
botes^M herméticos

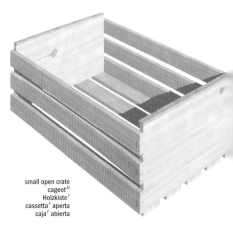

food tray
barquette^F
Schale^F
vaschetta^F per alimenti^M
barqueta^F

small crate
caissette^F
Kiste^F
cassetta^F
caja^F

small open crate
cageot^M
Holzkiste^F
cassetta^F aperta
caja^F abierta

packaging

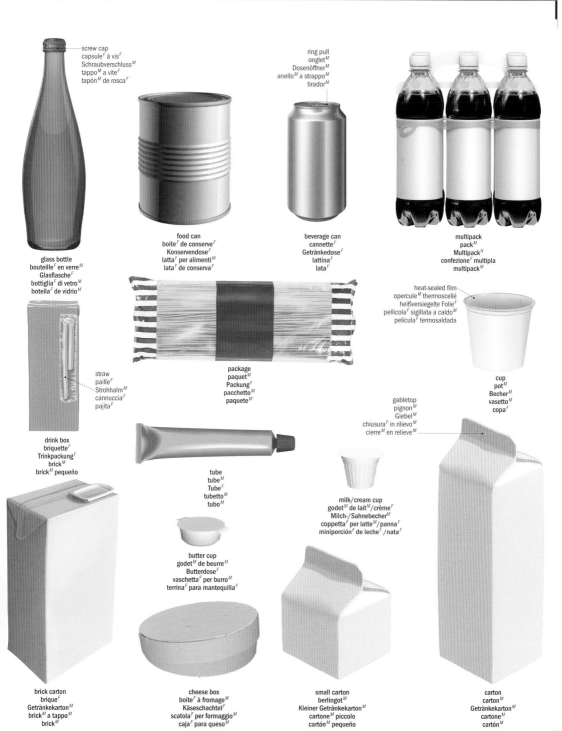

screw cap
capsule^F à vis^F
Schraubverschluss^M
tappo^M a vite^F
tapón^M de rosca^F

glass bottle
bouteille^F en verre^M
Glasflasche^F
bottiglia^F di vetro^M
botella^F de vidrio^M

food can
boîte^F de conserve^F
Konservendose^F
latta^F per alimenti^M
lata^F de conserva^F

ring pull
onglet^M
Dosenöffner^M
anello^M a strappo^M
tirador^M

beverage can
cannette^F
Getränkedose^F
lattina^F
lata^F

multipack
pack^M
Multipack^N
confezione^F multipla
multipack^M

straw
paille^F
Strohhalm^M
cannuccia^F
pajita^F

package
paquet^M
Packung^F
pacchetto^M
paquete^M

heat-sealed film
opercule^M thermoscellé
heißversiegelte Folie^F
pellicola^F sigillata a caldo^M
película^F termosaldada

cup
pot^M
Becher^M
vasetto^M
copa^F

drink box
briquette^F
Trinkpackung^F
brick^M
brick^M pequeño

tube
tube^M
Tube^F
tubetto^M
tubo^M

gabletop
pignon^M
Giebel^M
chiusura^F in rilievo^M
cierre^F en relieve^M

milk/cream cup
godet^M de lait^M/crème^F
Milch-/Sahnebecher^M
coppetta^F per latte^M/panna^F
miniporción^F de leche^F /nata^F

butter cup
godet^M de beurre^M
Butterdose^F
vaschetta^F per burro^M
terrina^F para mantequilla^F

brick carton
brique^F
Getränkekarton^M
brick^M a tappo^M
brick^M

cheese box
boîte^F à fromage^M
Käseschachtel^F
scatola^F per formaggio^M
caja^F para queso^M

small carton
berlingot^M
Kleiner Getränkekarton^M
cartone^M piccolo
cartón^M pequeño

carton
carton^M
Getränkekarton^M
cartone^M
cartón^M

kitchen

cuisine[F] | Küche[F] | cucina[F] | cocina[F]

cooker hood
hotte[F]
Dunstabzugshaube[F]
cappa[F]
campana[F] de cocina[F]

drawer
tiroir[M]
Schublade[F]
cassetto[M]
cajón[M]

hob
table[F] de cuisson[F]
Kochmulde[F]
piano[M] di cottura[F]
placa[F]

wall cabinet
armoire[F] supérieure
Oberschrank[M]
pensile[M]
armario[M] alto

ice cube dispenser
distributeur[M] de glaçons[M]
Eiswürfelspender[M]
distributore[M] di ghiaccio[M] in cubetti[M]
distribuidor[M] de hielos[M]

oven
four[M]
Backofen[M]
forno[M]
horno[M]

freezer
congélateur[M]
Gefrierschrank[M]
congelatore[M]
congelador[M]

work surface
plan[M] de travail[M]
Arbeitsplatte[F]
piano[M] di lavoro[M]
encimera[F]

refrigerator
réfrigérateur[M]
Kühlschrank[M]
frigorifero[M]
frigorífico[M]

sink
évier[M]
Spüle[F]
lavello[M]
fregadero[M]

cupboard
garde-manger[M]
Hochschrank[M]
dispensa[F]
armario[M]

patio door
porte[F]-fenêtre[F]
Verandatür[F]
porta[F]-finestra[F]
puerta ventana[F]

island
îlot[M]
Kücheninsel[F]
isola[F]
isla[F]

dinette
coin[M]-repas[M]
Esecke[F]
zona[F] pranzo[M]
mesa[F]

microwave oven
four[M] à micro-ondes[F]
Mikrowellenherd[M]
forno[M] a microonde[F]
horno[M] microondas

dishwasher
lave-vaisselle[M]
Geschirrspüler[F]
lavastoviglie[F]
lavavajillas[F]

base cabinet
armoire[F] inférieure
Unterschrank[M]
base[F]
armario[M] bajo

footstool
tabouret[M]
Hocker[M]
sgabello[M]
taburete[M]

glassware

liqueur glass
verre^M à liqueur^F
Likörglas^N
bicchierino^M da liquore^M
copa^F para licores^M

port glass
verre^M à porto^M
Portweinglas^N
bicchiere^M da porto^M
copa^F para oporto^M

champagne glass
coupe^F à mousseux^M
Sektschale^F
coppa^F da spumante^M
copa^F de champaña^F

brandy glass
verre^M à cognac^M
Kognakschwenker^M
bicchiere^M da brandy^M
copa^F para brandy^M

hock glass
verre^M à vin^M d'Alsace^F
Elsassglas^N
bicchiere^M da vino^M alsaziano
copa^F para vino^M de Alsacia

burgundy glass
verre^M à bourgogne^M
Rotweinglas^N
bicchiere^M da Borgogna^M
copa^F para vino^M de Borgoña

bordeaux glass
verre^M à bordeaux^M
Bordeauxglas^N
bicchiere^M da Bordeaux^M
copa^F para vino^M de Burdeos

white wine glass
verre^M à vin^M blanc
Weißweinglas^N
bicchiere^M da vino^M bianco
copa^F para vino^M blanco

water goblet
verre^M à eau^F
Wasserglas^N
bicchiere^M da acqua^F
copa^F de agua^F

cocktail glass
verre^M à cocktail^M
Cocktailglas^N
calice^M da cocktail^M
copa^F de cóctel^M

tall tumbler
verre^M à gin^M
Longdrinkglas^N
bicchiere^M da bibita^F
vaso^M largo

whisky tumbler
verre^M à whisky^M
Whiskyglas^M
tumbler^M
vaso^M corto

beer glass
chope^F à bière^F
Bierkrug^M
boccale^M da birra^F
jarra^M de cerveza^F

champagne flute
flûte^F à champagne^M
Sektkelch^M
flûte^M
copa^F de flauta^F

carafe
carafon^M
kleine Karaffe^F
caraffa^F
decantador^M

decanter
carafe^F
Karaffe^F
bottiglia^F da tavola^F
garrafa^F

crockery

vaisselle^F | Geschirr^N | vasellame^M da tavola^F | vajilla^F y servicio^M de mesa^F

demitasse
tasse^F à café^M
Mokkatasse^F
tazzina^F da caffè^M
tacita^F de café^M

tea cup
tasse^F à thé^M
Tasse^F
tazza^F da tè^M
taza^F

coffee mug
chope^F à café^M
Becher^M
tazza^F alta da caffè^M
jarra^F para café^M

cream jug
crémier^M
Milchkännchen^N
bricco^M del latte^M
jarrita^F de leche^F

sugar bowl
sucrier^M
Zuckerdose^F
zuccheriera^F
azucarero^M

saltcellar
salière^F
Salzstreuer^M
saliera^F
salero^M

pepperpot
poivrière^F
Pfefferstreuer^M
pepaiola^F
pimentero^M

gravy boat
saucière^F
Sauciere^F
salsiera^F
salsera^F

butter dish
beurrier^M
Butterdose^F
burriera^F
mantequera^F

ramekin
ramequin^M
Auflaufförmchen^N
formina^F da forno^M
cuenco^M de queso^M blando

soup bowl
bol^M
Suppenschale^F
scodella^F
escudilla^F

rim soup bowl
assiette^F creuse
Suppenteller^M
piatto^M fondo
plato^M sopero

dinner plate
assiette^F plate
flacher Teller^M
piatto^M piano
plato^M llano

salad plate
assiette^F à salade^F
Salatteller^M
piatto^M frutta^F / insalata^F
plato^M de postre^M

side plate
assiette^F à dessert^M
kleiner Teller^M
piattino^M per pane^M e burro^M
platito^M para el pan^M

teapot
théière^F
Teekanne^F
teiera^F
tetera^F

serving dish
plat^M ovale
Servierplatte^F
piatto^M da portata^F
fuente^F de servir

vegetable dish
légumier^M
Gemüseterrine^F
legumiera^F
fuente^F de verdura^F

fish dish
plat^M à poisson^M
Fischplatte^F
piatto^M per il pesce^M
fuente^F para pescado^M

hors d'oeuvre dish
ravier^M
Hors-d'Oeuvre-Schale^F
antipastiera^F
bandeja^F para los entremeses^M

water jug
pichet^M
Wasserkrug^M
caraffa^F
jarra^F de agua^F

salad bowl
saladier^M
Salatschüssel^F
insalatiera^F
ensaladera^F

salad dish
bol^M à salade^F
Salatschale^F
coppetta^F per l'insalata^F
bol^M para ensalada^F

soup tureen
soupière^F
Suppenterrine^F
zuppiera^F
sopera^F

cutlery

couverts^M | Silberbesteck^N | posateria^F | cubertería^F

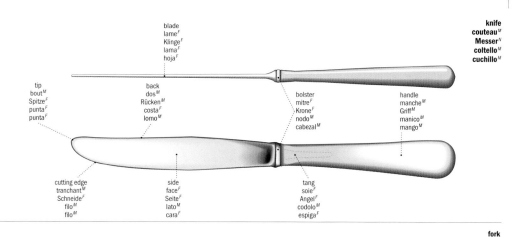

knife
couteau^M
Messer^N
coltello^M
cuchillo^M

blade
lame^F
Klinge^F
lama^F
hoja^F

tip
bout^M
Spitze^F
punta^F
punta^F

back
dos^M
Rücken^M
costa^F
lomo^M

bolster
mitre^F
Krone^F
nodo^M
cabezal^M

handle
manche^M
Griff^M
manico^M
mango^M

cutting edge
tranchant^M
Schneide^F
filo^M
filo^M

side
face^F
Seite^F
lato^M
cara^F

tang
soie^F
Angel^F
codolo^M
espiga^F

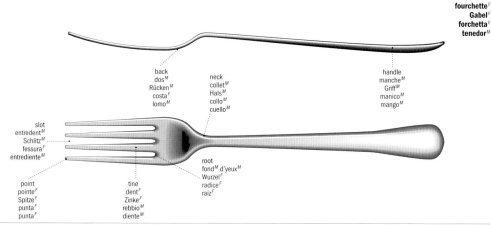

fork
fourchette^F
Gabel^F
forchetta^F
tenedor^M

back
dos^M
Rücken^M
costa^F
lomo^M

neck
collet^M
Hals^M
collo^M
cuello^M

handle
manche^M
Griff^M
manico^M
mango^M

slot
entredent^M
Schlitz^M
fessura^F
entrediente^M

point
pointe^F
Spitze^F
punta^F
punta^F

tine
dent^F
Zinke^F
rebbio^M
diente^M

root
fond^M d'yeux^M
Wurzel^F
radice^F
raíz^F

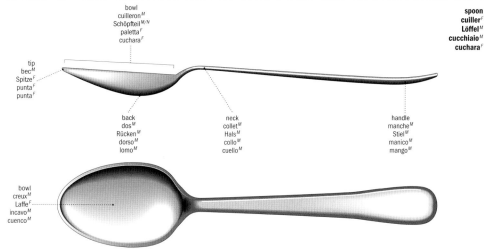

spoon
cuiller^F
Löffel^M
cucchiaio^M
cuchara^F

bowl
cuilleron^M
Schöpfteil^{M/N}
paletta^F
cuchara^F

tip
bec^M
Spitze^F
punta^F
punta^F

back
dos^M
Rücken^M
dorso^M
lomo^M

neck
collet^M
Hals^M
collo^M
cuello^M

handle
manche^M
Stiel^M
manico^M
mango^M

bowl
creux^M
Laffe^F
incavo^M
cuenco^M

FOOD AND KITCHEN

167

cutlery

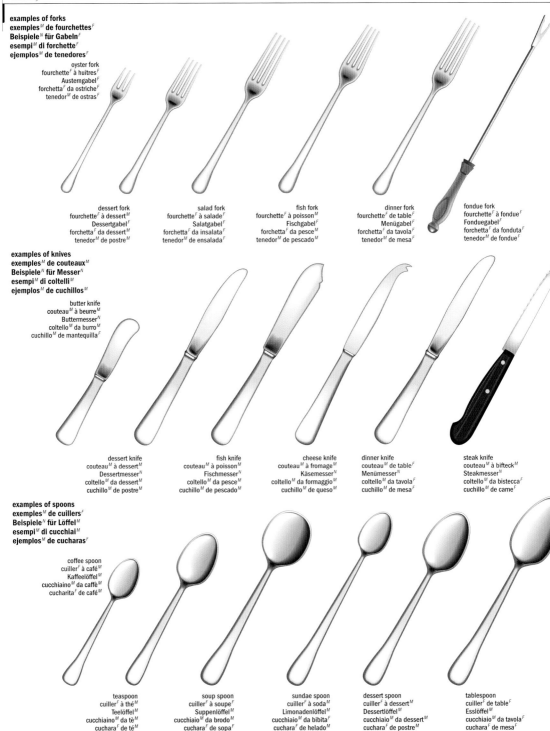

examples of forks
exemples^M **de fourchettes**^{F}
Beispiele^N **für Gabeln**^{F}
esempi^M **di forchette**^{F}
ejemplos^M **de tenedores**^{F}

oyster fork
fourchette^F à huitres^F
Austerngabel^F
forchetta^F da ostriche^F
tenedor^M de ostras^F

dessert fork
fourchette^F à dessert^M
Dessertgabel^F
forchetta^F da dessert^M
tenedor^M de postre^M

salad fork
fourchette^F à salade^F
Salatgabel^F
forchetta^F da insalata^F
tenedor^M de ensalada^F

fish fork
fourchette^F à poisson^M
Fischgabel^F
forchetta^F da pesce^M
tenedor^M de pescado^M

dinner fork
fourchette^F de table^F
Menügabel^F
forchetta^F da tavola^F
tenedor^M de mesa^F

fondue fork
fourchette^F à fondue^F
Fonduegabel^F
forchetta^F da fonduta^F
tenedor^M de fondue^F

examples of knives
exemples^M **de couteaux**^{M}
Beispiele^N **für Messer**^{N}
esempi^M **di coltelli**^{M}
ejemplos^M **de cuchillos**^{M}

butter knife
couteau^M à beurre^M
Buttermesser^N
coltello^M da burro^M
cuchillo^M de mantequilla^F

dessert knife
couteau^M à dessert^M
Dessertmesser^N
coltello^M da dessert^M
cuchillo^M de postre^M

fish knife
couteau^M à poisson^M
Fischmesser^N
coltello^M da pesce^M
cuchillo^M de pescado^M

cheese knife
couteau^M à fromage^M
Käsemesser^N
coltello^M da formaggio^M
cuchillo^M de queso^M

dinner knife
couteau^M de table^F
Menümesser^N
coltello^M da tavola^F
cuchillo^M de mesa^F

steak knife
couteau^M à bifteck^M
Steakmesser^N
coltello^M da bistecca^F
cuchillo^M de carne^F

examples of spoons
exemples^M **de cuillers**^{F}
Beispiele^N **für Löffel**^{M}
esempi^M **di cucchiai**^{M}
ejemplos^M **de cucharas**^{F}

coffee spoon
cuiller^F à café^M
Kaffeelöffel^M
cucchiaino^M da caffè^M
cucharita^F de café^M

teaspoon
cuiller^F à thé^M
Teelöffel^M
cucchiaino^M da tè^M
cuchara^F de té^M

soup spoon
cuiller^F à soupe^F
Suppenlöffel^M
cucchiaio^M da brodo^M
cuchara^F de sopa^F

sundae spoon
cuiller^F à soda^F
Limonadenlöffel^M
cucchiaio^M da bibita^F
cuchara^F de helado^M

dessert spoon
cuiller^F à dessert^M
Dessertlöffel^M
cucchiaio^M da dessert^M
cuchara^F de postre^M

tablespoon
cuiller^F de table^F
Esslöffel^M
cucchiaio^M da tavola^F
cuchara^F de mesa^F

FOOD AND KITCHEN

kitchen utensils

ustensiles^M de cuisine^F | Küchenutensilien^N | utensili^M da cucina^F | utensilios^M de cocina^F

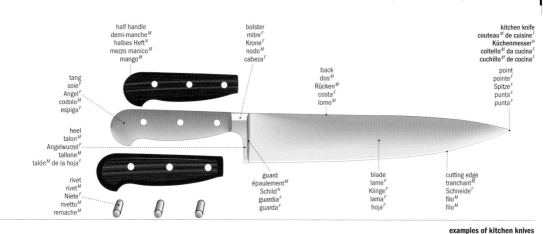

kitchen knife
couteau^M de cuisine^F
Küchenmesser^N
coltello^M da cucina^F
cuchillo^M de cocina^F

half handle
demi-manche^M
halbes Heft^N
mezzo manico^M
mango^M

bolster
mitre^F
Krone^F
nodo^M
cabeza^F

tang
soie^F
Angel^F
codolo^M
espiga^F

back
dos^M
Rücken^M
costa^F
lomo^M

point
pointe^F
Spitze^F
punta^F
punta^F

heel
talon^M
Angelwurzel^F
tallone^M
talón^M de la hoja^F

rivet
rivet^M
Niete^F
rivetto^M
remache^M

guard
épaulement^M
Schild^N
guardia^F
guarda^F

blade
lame^F
Klinge^F
lama^F
hoja^F

cutting edge
tranchant^M
Schneide^F
filo^M
filo^M

FOOD AND KITCHEN

examples of kitchen knives
exemples^M de couteaux^M de cuisine^F
Beispiele^N für Küchenmesser^N
esempi^M di coltelli^M da cucina^F
ejemplos^M de cuchillos^M de cocina^F

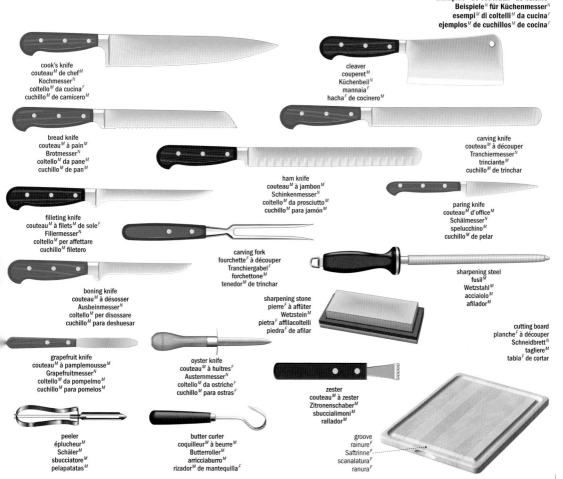

cook's knife
couteau^M de chef^M
Kochmesser^M
coltello^M da cucina^F
cuchillo^M de carnicero^M

cleaver
couperet^M
Küchenbeil^N
mannaia^F
hacha^F de cocinero^M

bread knife
couteau^M à pain^M
Brotmesser^M
coltello^M da pane^M
cuchillo^M de pan^M

carving knife
couteau^M à découper
Tranchiermesser^N
trinciante^M
cuchillo^M de trinchar

ham knife
couteau^M à jambon^M
Schinkenmesser^N
coltello^M da prosciutto^M
cuchillo^M para jamón^M

filleting knife
couteau^M à filets^M de sole^F
Filiermesser^N
coltello^M per affettare
cuchillo^M filetero

paring knife
couteau^M d'office^M
Schälmesser^N
spelucchino^M
cuchillo^M de pelar

carving fork
fourchette^F à découper
Tranchiergabel^F
forchettone^M
tenedor^M de trinchar

sharpening steel
fusil^M
Wetzstahl^M
acciaiolo^M
afilador^M

boning knife
couteau^M à désosser
Ausbeinmesser^N
coltello^M per disossare
cuchillo^M para deshuesar

sharpening stone
pierre^F à affûter
Wetzstein^M
pietra^F affilacoltelli
piedra^F de afilar

cutting board
planche^F à découper
Schneidbrett^N
tagliere^M
tabla^F de cortar

grapefruit knife
couteau^M à pamplemousse^M
Grapefruitmesser^N
coltello^M da pompelmo^M
cuchillo^M para pomelos^M

oyster knife
couteau^M à huitres^F
Austernmesser^N
coltello^M da ostriche^F
cuchillo^M para ostras^F

zester
couteau^M à zester
Zitronenschaber^M
sbuccialimoni^M
rallador^M

peeler
éplucheur^M
Schäler^M
sbucciatore^M
pelapatatas^M

butter curler
coquilleur^M à beurre^M
Butterroller^M
arricciaburro^M
rizador^M de mantequilla^F

groove
rainure^F
Saftrinne^F
scanalatura^F
ranura^F

kitchen utensils

for opening
pour ouvrir
zum Öffnen[N]
per aprire
utensilios[M] **para abrir y descorchar**

tin opener
ouvre-boîtes[M]
Büchsenöffner[M]
apriscatole[M]
abrelatas[M]

bottle opener
décapsuleur[M]
Flaschenöffner[M]
apribottiglie[M]
abrebotellas[M]

wine waiter corkscrew
tire-bouchon[M] de sommelier[M]
Kellnerbesteck[N]
cavatappi[M] da cameriere[M]
sacacorchos[M]

lever corkscrew
tire-bouchon[M] à levier[M]
Hebel-Korkenzieher[M]
cavatappi[M] a leva[F]
sacacorchos[M] con brazos[M]

for grinding and grating
pour broyer et râper
zum Zerkleinern[N] **und Zerreiben**[N]
per macinare e grattugiare
para moler y rallar

nutcracker
casse-noix[M]
Nussknacker[M]
schiaccianoci[M]
cascanueces[M]

mortar
mortier[M]
Mörser[M]
mortaio[M]
almirez[M]

pestle
pilon[M]
Stößel[M]
pestello[M]
mano[M]

mincer
hachoir[M]
Fleischwolf[M]
tritacarne[M]
picadora[F] de carne[F]

garlic press
presse-ail[M]
Knoblauchpresse[F]
spremiaglio[M]
triturador[M] de ajos[M]

lemon squeezer
presse-agrumes[M]
Zitronenpresse[F]
spremiagrumi[M]
exprimidor[M]

nutmeg grater
râpe[F] à muscade[F]
Muskatnussreibe[F]
grattugia[F] per noce[F] moscata
rallador[M] de nuez[F] moscada

rotary cheese grater
râpe[F] à fromage[M] cylindrique
Käsereibe[F]
grattugiaformaggio[M]
rallador[M] cilindrico de queso[M]

pusher
poussoir[M]
Presshebel[M]
pigiatore[M]
empujador[M]

grater
râpe[F]
Reibe[F]
grattugia[F]
rallador[M]

crank
manivelle[F]
Kurbel[F]
levetta[F]
manivela[F]

drum
tambour[M]
Trommel[F]
tamburo[M]
tambor[M]

handle
poignée[F]
Griff[M]
impugnatura[F]
mango[M]

pasta maker
machine[F] à faire les pâtes[F]
Nudelmaschine[F]
macchina[F] per fare la pasta[F]
máquina[F] para hacer pasta[F] italiana

food mill
moulin[M] à légumes[M]
Passiergerät[N]
passaverdure[M]
pasapurés[M]

mandoline
mandoline[F]
Küchenreibe[F]
affettaverdure[M]
mandolina[F]

**for measuring
pour mesurer
zum Messen**[N]
**per misurare
utensilios**[M] **para medir**

measuring spoons
cuillers[F] doseuses
Messlöffel[M]
cucchiai[M] dosatori
cucharas[F] dosificadoras

measuring cups
mesures[F]
Messbecher[M]
misurini[M]
tazas[F] medidoras

sugar thermometer
thermomètre[M] à sucre[M]
Einmachthermometer[N]
termometro[M] per zucchero[M]
termómetro[M] de azúcar[M]

instant-read thermometer
thermomètre[M] à mesure[F] instantanée
digitales Bratenthermometer[N]
termometro[M] a lettura[F] istantanea
termómetro[M] de medida[F] instantánea

measuring jug
tasse[F] à mesurer
Maß[N]
tazza[F] graduata
jarra[F] medidora

meat thermometer
thermomètre[M] à viande[F]
Fleischthermometer[N]
termometro[M] per carne[F]
termómetro[M] para carne[F]

oven thermometer
thermomètre[M] de four[M]
Backofenthermometer[N]
termometro[M] del forno[M]
termómetro[M] de horno[M]

measuring beaker
verre[M] à mesurer
Messbecher[M]
recipiente[M] graduato
vaso[M] medidor

kitchen timer
minuteur[M]
Küchenuhr[F]
contaminuti[M]
minutero[M]

egg timer
sablier[M]
Eieruhr[F]
clessidra[F] per uova[F] alla coque
reloj[M] de arena[F]

kitchen scale
balance[F] de cuisine[F]
Küchenwaage[F]
bilancia[F] da cucina[F]
báscula[F] de cocina[F]

FOOD AND KITCHEN

**for straining and draining
pour passer et égoutter
zum Sieben**[N] **und Abtropfen**[N]
**per scolare e filtrare
coladores**[M] **y escurridores**[M]

mesh strainer
passoire[F] fine
Passiersieb[N]
colino[M]
colador[M] fino

muslin
mousseline[F]
Musselin[M]
mussolina[F]
muselina[F]

chinois
chinois[M]
Spitzsieb[N]
chinois[M]
chino[M]

funnel
entonnoir[M]
Trichter[M]
imbuto[M]
embudo[M]

colander
passoire[F]
Seiher[M]
colapasta[M]
escurridor[M]

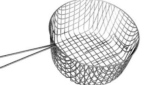

frying basket
panier[M] à friture[F]
Frittierkorb[M]
cestello[M] per friggere
cesta[F] de freir

sieve
tamis[M]
Mehlsieb[N]
setaccio[M]
tamiz[M]

salad spinner
essoreuse[F] à salade[F]
Salatschleuder[F]
centrifuga[F] scolainsalata
secadora[F] de ensalada[F]

kitchen utensils

baking utensils
pour la pâtisserie[F]
Backgerät[N]
utensili[M] **per dolci**[M]
utensilios[M] **para repostería**

icing syringe
piston[M] à décorer
Garnierspritze[F]
siringa[F] per decorazioni[F]
jeringa[F] de decoración[F]

pastry cutting wheel
roulette[F] de pâtissier[M]
Kuchenrad[N]
rotella[F] tagliapasta
cortapastas[M]

pastry brush
pinceau[M] à pâtisserie[F]
Kuchenpinsel[M]
pennello[M] per dolci[M]
pincel[M] de repostería[F]

egg beater
batteur[M] à œufs[M]
Rad-Schneeschläger[M]
frullino[M]
batidor[M] mecánico

whisk
fouet[M]
Schneebesen[M]
frusta[F]
batidor[M]

pastry bag and nozzles
poche[F] à douilles[F]
Spritzbeutel[M] mit Tüllen[F]
tasca[F] e bocchette[F]
manga[F] y boquillas[F]

sifter
tamis[M] à farine[F]
Mehlsieb[N]
setaccio[M]
tamiz[M]

biscuit cutters
emporte-pièces[M]
Ausstechformen[F]
tagliabiscotti[M]
moldes[M] de pastas[F]

dredger
saupoudreuse[F]
Streuer[M]
spolverino[M]
espolvoreador[M]

pastry blender
mélangeur[M] à pâtisserie[F]
Teigmischer[M]
miscelatore[M] per dolci[M]
mezclador[M] de pastelería[F]

mixing bowls
bols[M] à mélanger
Rührschüsseln[F]
ciotole[F] per mescolare
boles[M] para batir

rolling pin
rouleau[M] à pâtisserie[F]
Nudelholz[N]
matterello[M]
rodillo[M]

baking sheet
plaque[F] à pâtisserie[F]
Backblech[N]
teglia[F] da forno[M]
bandeja[F] de pastelería[F]

bun tin
moule[M] à muffins[M]
Muffinform[F]
stampini[M] per dolci[M]
molde[M] para magdalenas[F]

soufflé dish
moule[M] à soufflé[M]
Souffléform[F]
tegamino[M] per sufflè[M]
molde[M] de soufflé[M]

charlotte mould
moule[M] à charlotte[F]
Charlottenform[F]
stampo[M] per charlotte[F]
molde[M] de carlota[F]

removable-bottomed tin
moule[M] à fond[M] amovible
Springform[F]
teglia[F] con fondo[M] staccabile
molde[M] redondo con muelles[M]

pie tin
moule[M] à tarte[F]
flache Kuchenform[F]
teglia[F] per torta[F]
molde[M] para tartas[F]

quiche tin
moule[M] à quiche[F]
Quicheform[F]
stampo[M] per crostata[F]
molde[M] acanalado

cake tin
moule[M] à gâteau[M]
Kuchenform[F]
tortiera[F]
molde[M] para bizcocho[M]

kitchen utensils

FOOD AND KITCHEN

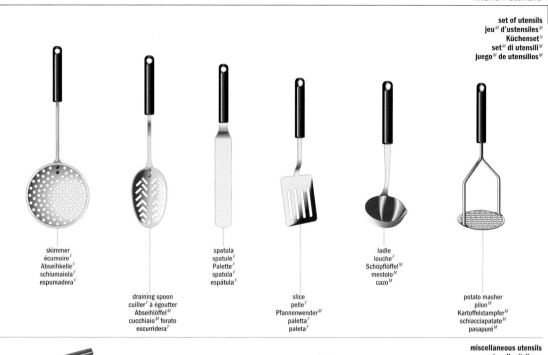

set of utensils
jeu^M d'ustensiles^M
Küchenset^N
set^M di utensili^M
juego^M de utensilios^M

skimmer
écumoire^F
Abseihkelle^F
schiumaiola^F
espumadera^F

spatula
spatule^F
Palette^F
spatola^F
espátula^F

ladle
louche^F
Schöpflöffel^M
mestolo^M
cazo^M

draining spoon
cuiller^F à égoutter
Abseihlöffel^M
cucchiaio^M forato
escurridera^F

slice
pelle^F
Pfannenwender^M
paletta^F
paleta^F

potato masher
pilon^M
Kartoffelstampfer^M
schiacciapatate^M
pasapuré^M

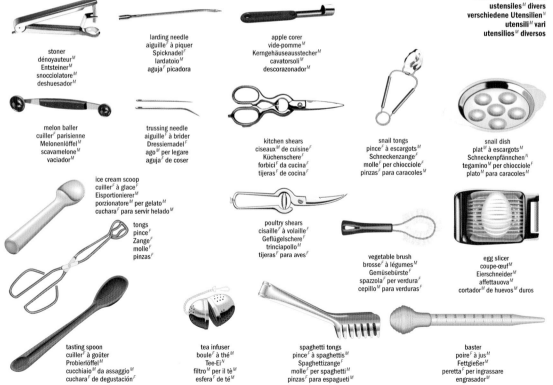

miscellaneous utensils
ustensiles^M divers
verschiedene Utensilien^N
utensili^M vari
utensilios^M diversos

stoner
dénoyauteur^M
Entsteiner^M
snocciolatore^M
deshuesador^M

larding needle
aiguille^F à piquer
Spicknadel^F
lardatoio^M
aguja^F picadora

apple corer
vide-pomme^M
Kerngehäuseausstecher^M
cavatorsoli^M
descorazonador^M

melon baller
cuiller^F parisienne
Melonenlöffel^M
scavamelone^M
vaciador^M

trussing needle
aiguille^F à brider
Dressiernadel^F
ago^M per legare
aguja^F de coser

kitchen shears
ciseaux^F de cuisine^F
Küchenschere^F
forbici^F da cucina^F
tijeras^F de cocina^F

snail tongs
pince^F à escargots^M
Schneckenzange^F
molle^F per chiocciole^F
pinzas^F para caracoles^M

snail dish
plat^F à escargots^M
Schneckenpfännchen^N
tegamino^M per chiocciole^F
plato^M para caracoles^M

ice cream scoop
cuiller^F à glace^F
Eisportionierer^M
porzionatore^M per gelato^M
cuchara^F para servir helado^M

tongs
pince^F
Zange^F
molle^F
pinzas^F

poultry shears
cisaille^F à volaille^F
Geflügelschere^F
trinciapollo^M
tijeras^F para aves^F

vegetable brush
brosse^F à légumes^M
Gemüsebürste^F
spazzola^F per verdura^F
cepillo^M para verduras^F

egg slicer
coupe-œuf^M
Eierschneider^M
affettauova^M
cortador^M de huevos^M duros

tasting spoon
cuiller^F à goûter
Probierlöffel^M
cucchiaio^M da assaggio^M
cuchara^F de degustación^F

tea infuser
boule^F à thé^M
Tee-Ei^N
filtro^M per il tè^M
esfera^F de té^M

spaghetti tongs
pince^F à spaghettis^M
Spaghettizange^F
molle^F per spaghetti^M
pinzas^F para espagueti^M

baster
poire^F à jus^M
Fettgießer^M
peretta^F per ingrassare
engrasador^M

cooking utensils

batterie^F de cuisine^F | Kochgeräte^N | utensili^M per cucinare | utensilios^M de cocina^F

wok set
wok^M
Wok-Set^N
servizio^M da wok^M
wok^M

lid
couvercle^M
Deckel^M
coperchio^M
tapa^F

rack
grille^F
Gittereinsatz^M
griglia^F
rejilla^F

tajine
tajine^M
Tajine^F
tajina^F
tajina^F

wok
wok^M
Wok^M
wok^M
wok^M

burner ring
collier^M
Aufsatz^M
bruciatore^M a corona^F
quemador^M

fondue set
service^M à fondue^F
Fondue-Set^N
servizio^M da fonduta^F
servicio^M para fondue^F

fish kettle
poissonnière^F
Fischkochtopf^M
pesciera^F
besuguera^F

fondue pot
caquelon^M
Fonduetopf^M
tegame^M per fonduta^F
cacerola^F para fondue^F

strainer
grille^F
Gittereinsatz^M
griglia^F
rejilla^F desmontable

stand
support^M
Ständer^M
base^F
soporte^M

lid
couvercle^M
Deckel^M
coperchio^M
tapa^F

burner
réchaud^M
Brenner^M
fornellino^M
quemador^M

dripping pan
lèchefrite^F
Fettpfanne^F
leccarda^F
grasera^F

terrine
terrine^F
Terrine^F
terrina^F
terrina^F

roasting pans
plats^M à rôtir
Bräter^M
teglie^F da forno^M
asadores^M

pressure cooker
autocuiseur^M
Schnellkochtopf^M
pentola^F a pressione^F
olla^F a presión^F

pressure regulator
régulateur^M de pression^F
Überdruckventil^N
regolatore^M di pressione^F
regulador^M de presión^F

safety valve
soupape^F
Sicherheitsventil^N
valvola^F di sicurezza^F
válvula^F de seguridad^F

Dutch oven
faitout^M
flacher Bratentopf^M
casseruola^F
cacerola^F refractaria

stock pot
marmite^F
Suppentopf^M
pentola^F
olla^F

couscous kettle
couscoussier^M
Couscoustopf^M
pentola^F per cuscus^M
olla^F para cuscús^M

frying pan
poêle^F à frire
Bratpfanne^F
padella^F per friggere
sartén^F

steamer
cuit-vapeur^M
Dampfkochtopf^M
pentola^F a vapore^M
cazuela^F vaporera

egg poacher
pocheuse^F
Eipochierer^M
tegame^M per uova^F in camicia^F
escalfador^M de huevos^M

sauté pan
sauteuse^F
Schmorpfanne^F
padella^F per rosolare
sartén^F honda

small saucepan
poêlon^M
Pfanne^F
piccolo tegame^M
sartén^F pequeña

diable
diable^M
Römertopf^M
padella^F doppia
sartén^F doble

pancake pan
poêle^F à crêpes^F
Crêpe-Pfanne^F
padella^F per crêpe^F
sartén^F para crepes^M

steamer basket
panier^M cuit-vapeur^M
Dämpfeinsatz^M
cestello^M per la cottura^F a vapore^M
cesto^M de cocción^M al vapor^M

double boiler
bain-marie^M
Wasserbadtopf^M
pentola^F per cucinare a bagnomaria
cacerola^F para baño^M de María

saucepan
casserole^F
Stielkasserolle^F
tegame^M
cacerola^F

FOOD AND KITCHEN

domestic appliances

appareils^M électroménagers | Haushaltsgeräte^N | elettrodomestici^M | aparatos^M electrodomésticos

FOOD AND KITCHEN

for mixing and blending
pour mélanger et battre
zum Mixen^N und Kneten^N
per frullare e miscelare
para mezclar y batir

hand mixer
batteur^M à main^F
Handrührgerät^N
frullatore^M elettrico a mano^F
batidora^F de mano^F

blender
mélangeur^M
Mixer^M
frullatore^M
batidora^F de vaso^M

cap
bouchon^M
Deckelknopf^M
tappo^M
tapa^M

container
récipient^M
Behälter^M
bicchiere^M
vaso^M mezclador

cutting blade
couteau^M
Schneidmesser^N
coltello^M
cuchilla^F

motor unit
bloc^M-moteur^M
Motorblock^M
blocco^M motore^M
motor^M

push button
bouton^M-poussoir^M
Drucktaste^F
interruttore^M
botón^M de velocidades^F

beater ejector
éjecteur^M de fouets^M
Auswurftaste^F
espulsore^M degli accessori^M
eyector de las varillas^F

speed selector
sélecteur^M de vitesse^F
Geschwindigkeitswähler^M
selettore^M di velocità^F
selector^M de velocidad^F

beater
fouet^M
Rührbesen^M
frusta^F
varilla^F de batir

handle
poignée^F
Griff^M
impugnatura^F
asa^F

heel rest
talon^M d'appui^M
Heck^N
tallone^M d'appoggio^M
talón de apoyo^M

hand blender
mélangeur^M à main^F
Stabmixer^M
frullatore^M a immersione^F
batidora^F de pie^M

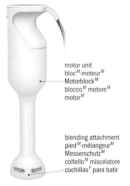

motor unit
bloc^M-moteur^M
Motorblock^M
blocco^M motore^M
motor^M

blending attachment
pied^M-mélangeur^M
Messerschutz^M
coltello^M miscelatore
cuchillas^F para batir

table mixer
batteur^M sur socle^M
Tischrührgerät^N
impastatrice^F
batidora^F de mesa^F

beater ejector
éjecteur^M de fouets^M
Auswurftaste^F
espulsore^M degli accessori^M
eyector de las varillas^F

beater
fouet^M
Rührbesen^M
frusta^F
varilla^F de batir

speed control
commande^F de vitesse^F
Geschwindigkeitsregelung^F
regolatore^M di velocità^F
selector^M de velocidades^F

tilt-back head
tête^F basculante
Schwenkarm^M
testa^F ribaltabile
cabeza^F móvil

mixing bowl
bol^M
Rührschüssel^F
ciotola^F
bol^M mezclador

turntable
plateau^M tournant
Drehscheibe^F
piattaforma^F girevole
disco^M giratorio

stand
socle^M
Ständer^M
base^F
pie^M

beaters
fouets^M
Rührbesen^M
fruste^F
tipos^M de varillas^F

four-blade beater
fouet^M quatre pales^F
Rührbesen^M
frusta^F a quattro bracci^M
de aspas^F

spiral beater
fouet^M en spirale^F
Spiralkneter^M
frusta^F a spirale^F
en espiral^F

wire beater
fouet^M à fil^M
Drahtbesen^M
frusta^F ad anello^M
circular

dough hook
crochet^M pétrisseur
Knethaken^M
gancio^M per l'impasto^M
de gancho^M

domestic appliances

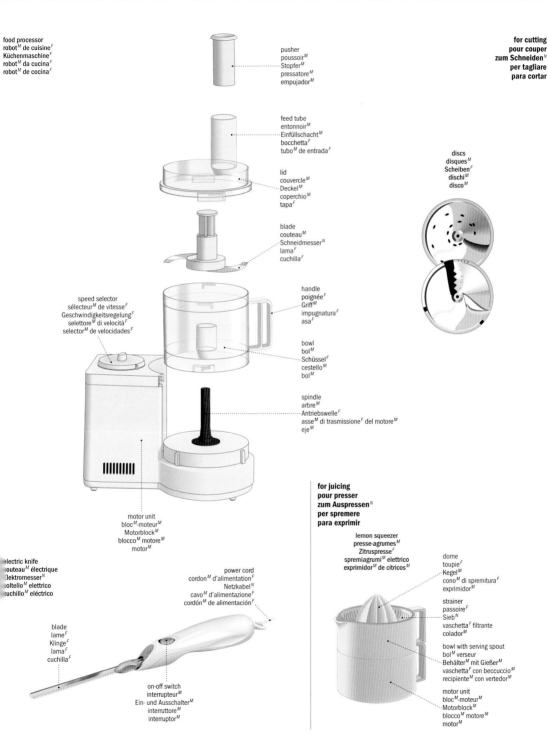

food processor
robot^M de cuisine^F
Küchenmaschine^F
robot^M da cucina^F
robot^M de cocina^F

pusher
poussoir^M
Stopfer^M
pressatore^M
empujador^M

for cutting
pour couper
zum Schneiden^N
per tagliare
para cortar

feed tube
entonnoir^M
Einfüllschacht^M
bocchetta^F
tubo^M de entrada^F

discs
disques^M
Scheiben^F
dischi^M
disco^M

lid
couvercle^M
Deckel^M
coperchio^M
tapa^F

blade
couteau^M
Schneidmesser^N
lama^F
cuchilla^F

handle
poignée^F
Griff^M
impugnatura^F
asa^F

speed selector
sélecteur^M de vitesse^F
Geschwindigkeitsregelung^F
selettore^M di velocità^F
selector^M de velocidades^F

bowl
bol^M
Schüssel^F
cestello^M
bol^M

spindle
arbre^M
Antriebswelle^F
asse^M di trasmissione^F del motore^M
eje^M

motor unit
bloc^M-moteur^M
Motorblock^M
blocco^M motore^M
motor^M

for juicing
pour presser
zum Auspressen^N
per spremere
para exprimir

lemon squeezer
presse-agrumes^M
Zitruspresse^F
spremiagrumi^M elettrico
exprimidor^M de cítricos^M

dome
toupie^F
Kegel^M
cono^M di spremitura^F
exprimidor^M

strainer
passoire^F
Sieb^N
vaschetta^F filtrante
colador^M

electric knife
couteau^M électrique
Elektromesser^N
coltello^M elettrico
cuchillo^M eléctrico

power cord
cordon^M d'alimentation^F
Netzkabel^N
cavo^M d'alimentazione^F
cordón^M de alimentación^F

bowl with serving spout
bol^M verseur
Behälter^M mit Gießer^M
vaschetta^F con beccuccio^M
recipiente^M con vertedor^M

blade
lame^F
Klinge^F
lama^F
cuchilla^F

on-off switch
interrupteur^M
Ein- und Ausschalter^M
interruttore^M
interruptor^M

motor unit
bloc^M-moteur^M
Motorblock^M
blocco^M motore^M
motor^M

FOOD AND KITCHEN

177

domestic appliances

for cooking
pour cuire
zum Kochen^N
per cucinare
para cocinar

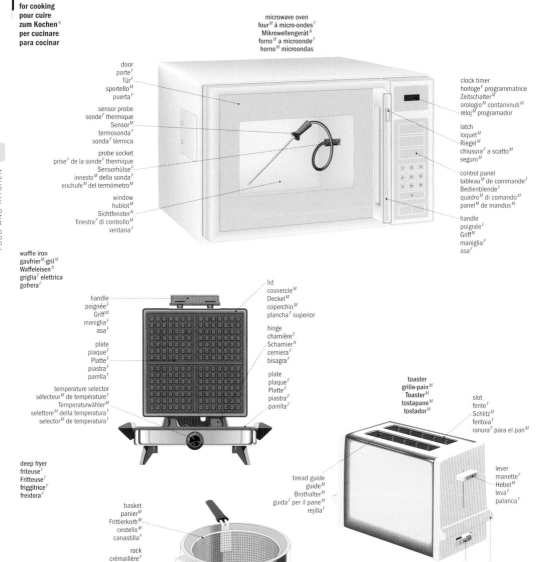

microwave oven
four^M à micro-ondes^F
Mikrowellengerät^N
forno^M a microonde^F
horno^M microondas

door
porte^F
Tür^F
sportello^M
puerta^F

sensor probe
sonde^F thermique
Sensor^M
termosonda^F
sonda^F térmica

probe socket
prise^F de la sonde^F thermique
Sensorhülse^F
innesto^M della sonda^F
enchufe^M del termómetro^M

window
hublot^M
Sichtfenster^N
finestra^F di controllo^M
ventana^F

clock timer
horloge^F programmatrice
Zeitschalter^M
orologio^M contaminuti^M
reloj^M programador

latch
loquet^M
Riegel^M
chiusura^F a scatto^M
seguro^M

control panel
tableau^M de commande^F
Bedienblende^F
quadro^M di comando^M
panel^M de mandos^M

handle
poignée^F
Griff^M
maniglia^F
asa^F

waffle iron
gaufrier^M-gril^M
Waffeleisen^N
griglia^F elettrica
gofrera^F

handle
poignée^F
Griff^M
maniglia^F
asa^F

plate
plaque^F
Platte^F
piastra^F
parrilla^F

temperature selector
sélecteur^M de température^F
Temperaturwähler^M
selettore^M della temperatura^F
selector^M de temperatura^F

lid
couvercle^M
Deckel^M
coperchio^M
plancha^F superior

hinge
charnière^F
Scharnier^N
cerniera^F
bisagra^F

plate
plaque^F
Platte^F
piastra^F
parrilla^F

toaster
grille-pain^M
Toaster^M
tostapane^M
tostador^M

slot
fente^F
Schlitz^M
feritoia^F
ranura^F para el pan^M

lever
manette^F
Hebel^M
leva^F
palanca^F

deep fryer
friteuse^F
Fritteuse^F
friggitrice^F
freidora^F

basket
panier^M
Frittierkorb^M
cestello^M
canastilla^F

rack
crémaillère^F
Regler^M
dispositivo^M di espulsione^F del cestello^M
selector^M

timer
minuterie^F
Zeituhr^F
contaminuti^M
reloj^M

thermostat
thermostat^M
Thermostat^M
termostato^M
termostato^M

pilot light
voyant^M lumineux
Kontrollleuchte^F
spia^F luminosa
piloto^M

bread guide
guide^M
Brothalter^M
guida^F per il pane^M
rejilla^F

temperature control
thermostat^M
Temperaturregler^M
termostato^M
selector^M de tostado^M

handle
poignée^F
Griff^M
impugnatura^F
asa^F

filter
filtre^M
Filter^M
filtro^M
filtro^M

lid
couvercle^M
Deckel^M
coperchio^M
tapa^F

FOOD AND KITCHEN

raclette with grill
raclette^F-grill^M
Raclette^F-Grill^M
griglia^F per raclette^F
raclette-grill^M

electric steamer
cuit-vapeur^M électrique
elektrischer Schnellkocher^M
pentola^F a vapore^M elettrica
vaporera^F eléctrica

dish
poêlon^M
Pfännchen^N
piatto^M
bandeja^F

cooking plate
surface^F de cuisson^F
Grillplatte^F
piastra^F di cottura^F
placa^F de cocción^F

base
socle^M
Unterteil$^{M/N}$
base^F
base^F

cooking dishes
bols^M de cuisson^F
Einsätze^M
piatti^M di cottura^F
platos^M de cocción^F

water level indicator
indicateur^M de niveau^M d'eau^F
Wasserstandsanzeiger^M
indicatore^M del livello^M d'acqua^F
indicador^M del nivel^M del agua^F

signal lamp
voyant^M lumineux
Kontrollleuchte^F
spia^F luminosa
indicador^M luminoso

timer
minuterie^F
Zeitschaltuhr^F
contaminuti^M
minutero^M

indoor electric grill
gril^M barbecue^M
Elektrischer Tischgrill^M
griglia^F elettrica per interni^M
parrilla^F eléctrica

insulated handle
poignée^F isolante
wärmeisolierter Griff^M
maniglia^F isolata
asa^F aislante

dripping pan
bac^M ramasse-jus^M
Fettpfanne^F
leccarda^F
grasera^F

cooking surface
surface^F de cuisson^F
Grillfläche^F
piano^M di cottura^F
superficie^F de cocción^F

adjustable thermostat
thermostat^M réglable
regelbarer Thermostat^M
termostato^M regolabile
termostato^M regulable

bread maker
robot^M boulanger^M
Brotbackautomat^M
impastatrice^F
amasadora^F

lid
couvercle^M
Deckel^M
coperchio^M
tapa^F

control panel
tableau^M de commande^F
Bedienungsfeld^N
quadro^M di comando^M
panel^M de mandos^M

window
hublot^M
Sichtfenster^N
finestra^F di controllo^M
ventana^F

loaf pan
moule^M à pain^M
Backform^F
stampo^M per pane^M
molde^M de pan^M

griddle
gril^M électrique
Grillplatte^F
piastra^F elettrica
plancha^F eléctrica

cooking surface
surface^F de cuisson^F
Kochfeld^N
piano^M di cottura^F
plancha^F

handle
poignée^F
Griff^M
maniglia^F
asa^F

detachable control
commande^F amovible
abziehbarer Temperaturregler^M
regolatore^M staccabile
enchufe^M y selector^M desmontables

grease well
collecteur^M de graisse^F
Fettauffangschale^F
bacinella^F raccogligrasso
colector^M de grasa^F

miscellaneous domestic appliances

appareils^M électroménagers divers | verschiedene Haushaltsgeräte^N | elettrodomestici^M vari | varios aparatos^M electrodomésticos

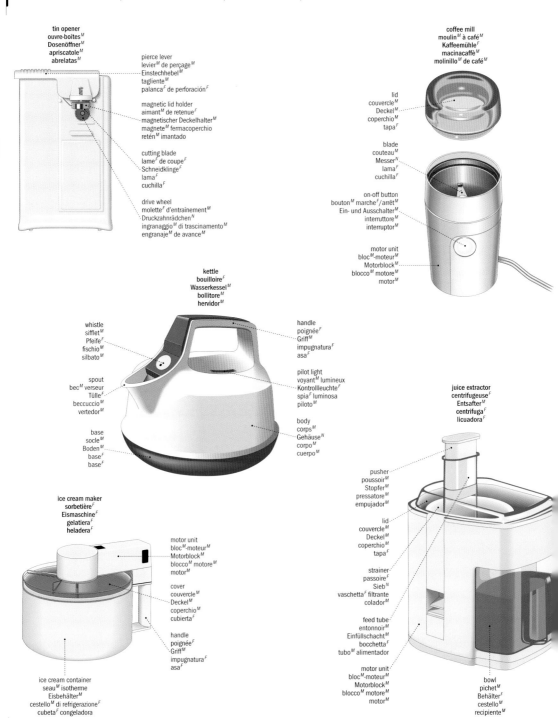

tin opener
ouvre-boites^M
Dosenöffner^M
apriscatole^M
abrelatas^M

pierce lever
levier^M de perçage^M
Einstechhebel^M
tagliente^M
palanca^F de perforación^F

magnetic lid holder
aimant^M de retenue^F
magnetischer Deckelhalter^M
magnete^M fermacoperchio
retén^M imantado

cutting blade
lame^F de coupe^F
Schneidklinge^F
lama^F
cuchilla^F

drive wheel
molette^F d'entraînement^M
Druckzahnrädchen^N
ingranaggio^M di trascinamento^M
engranaje^M de avance^M

coffee mill
moulin^M à café^M
Kaffeemühle^F
macinacaffè^M
molinillo^M de café^M

lid
couvercle^M
Deckel^M
coperchio^M
tapa^F

blade
couteau^M
Messer^N
lama^F
cuchilla^F

on-off button
bouton^M marche^F/arrêt^M
Ein- und Ausschalter^M
interruttore^M
interruptor^M

motor unit
bloc^M-moteur^M
Motorblock^M
blocco^M motore^M
motor^M

kettle
bouilloire^F
Wasserkessel^M
bollitore^M
hervidor^M

whistle
sifflet^M
Pfeife^F
fischio^M
silbato^M

spout
bec^M verseur
Tülle^F
beccuccio^M
vertedor^M

base
socle^M
Boden^M
base^F
base^F

handle
poignée^F
Griff^M
impugnatura^F
asa^F

pilot light
voyant^M lumineux
Kontrollleuchte^F
spia^F luminosa
piloto^M

body
corps^M
Gehäuse^N
corpo^M
cuerpo^M

juice extractor
centrifugeuse^F
Entsafter^M
centrifuga^F
licuadora^F

pusher
poussoir^M
Stopfer^M
pressatore^M
empujador^M

lid
couvercle^M
Deckel^M
coperchio^M
tapa^F

strainer
passoire^F
Sieb^N
vaschetta^F filtrante
colador^M

feed tube
entonnoir^M
Einfüllschacht^M
bocchetta^F
tubo^M alimentador

motor unit
bloc^M-moteur^M
Motorblock^M
blocco^M motore^M
motor^M

bowl
pichet^M
Behälter^F
cestello^M
recipiente^M

ice cream maker
sorbetière^F
Eismaschine^F
gelatiera^F
heladera^F

motor unit
bloc^M-moteur^M
Motorblock^M
blocco^M motore^M
motor^M

cover
couvercle^M
Deckel^M
coperchio^M
cubierta^F

handle
poignée^F
Griff^M
impugnatura^F
asa^F

ice cream container
seau^M isotherme
Eisbehälter^M
cestello^M di refrigerazione^F
cubeta^F congeladora

coffee makers

automatic filter coffee maker
cafetière^F filtre^M
Kaffeemaschine^F
macchina^F da caffè^M a filtro^M
cafetera^F de filtro^M automática

reservoir
réservoir^M
Wasserbehälter^M
serbatoio^M
depósito^M de agua^F

water level
niveau^M d'eau^F
Wasserstand^M
livello^M dell'acqua^F
nivel^M de agua^F

pilot light
voyant^M lumineux
Kontrollleuchte^F
spia^F luminosa
piloto^M

on-off switch
interrupteur^M
Ein- und Ausschalter^M
interruttore^M
interruptor^M

lid
couvercle^M
Deckel^M
coperchio^M
tapa^F

filter
panier^M
Filterhalter^M
cassetta^F filtro^M
filtro^M

jug
verseuse^F
Kanne^F
caraffa^F
cafetera^F

warming plate
plaque^F chauffante
Warmhalteplatte^F
piastra^F riscaldante
placa^F térmica

Neapolitan coffee maker
cafetière^F napolitaine
Neapolitanische Tropfkanne^F
caffettiera^F napoletana
cafetera^F napolitana

espresso machine
machine^F à espresso^M
Espressomaschine^F
macchina^F per espresso^M
máquina^F de café^M exprés

on-off switch
interrupteur^M
Ein- und Ausschalter^M
interruttore^M
interruptor^M

tamper
presse-café^M
Kaffeepresser^M
pressacaffè^M
prensa-café^M

drip tray
cuvette^F ramasse-gouttes^M
Auffangschale^F
vaschetta^F di raccolta^F
cubeta^F colectora de gotas^F

steam nozzle
buse^F vapeur^F
Aufschäumdüse^F
ugello^M vaporizzatore^M
tubo^M de vapor^M

steam control knob
manette^F vapeur^F
Dampfregler^M
regolazione^F del vapore^M
manecilla^F de vapor^M

filter holder
porte-filtre^M
Filterhalter^M
portafiltro^M
porta-filtro^M

water tank
réservoir^M d'eau^F
Wassertank^M
serbatoio^M dell'acqua^F
depósito^M de agua^M

vacuum coffee maker
cafetière^F à infusion^F
Vakuum-Kaffeemaschine^F
caffettiera^F a infusione^F
cafetera^F de infusión^F

upper bowl
tulipe^F
oberer Glaskolben^M
coppa^F superiore
recipiente^M superior

stem
tige^F
Röhre^F
gambo^M
tubo^M de subida^F del agua^F

lower bowl
ballon^M
unterer Glaskolben^M
coppa^F inferiore
recipiente^M inferior

percolator
percolateur^M
Kaffee-Filterkanne^M
caffettiera^F a filtro^M
percoladora^F

cafetière with plunger
cafetière^F à piston^M
Pressfilterkanne^F
caffettiera^F a pistone^M
cafetera^F de émbolo^M

espresso coffee maker
cafetière^F espresso^M
Espresso-Maschine^F
caffettiera^F per espresso^M
cafetera^F italiana

spout
bec^M verseur
Tülle^F
beccuccio^M
pitorro^M

pilot light
voyant^M lumineux
Kontrollleuchte^F
spia^F luminosa
piloto^M

exterior of a house

extérieur^M d'une maison^F | Außenansicht^F eines Hauses^N | esterno^M di una casa^F | exterior^M de una casa^F

elevation
élévation^F
Ansicht^F
prospetto^M
alzado^M

mezzanine floor
mezzanine^F
Zwischengeschoß^N
piano^M mansardato
entresuelo^M

first floor
étage^M
erster Stock^M
primo piano^M
planta^F alta

ground floor
rez-de-chaussée^M
Erdgeschoß^N
pianterreno^M
planta^F baja

basement
sous-sol^M
Keller^M
seminterrato^M
semisótano^M

gable vent
évent^M de pignon^M
Belüftungsfenster^N
griglia^F di aerazione^F
respiradero^M

gable
pignon^M
Giebel^M
timpano^M
hastial^M

vegetable garden
jardin^M potager
Gemüsegarten^M
orto^M
huerto^M

patio
terrasse^F
Terrasse^F
patio^M
terraza^F

ornamental tree
arbre^M d'ornement^M
Zierbaum^M
pianta^F ornamentale
árbol^M ornamental

property line
limite^F du terrain^M
Grundstücksgrenze^F
confine^M di proprietà^F
lindero^M

fence
clôture^F
Zaun^M
staccionata^F
vallado^M

shed
remise^F
Schuppen^M
rimessa^F
cobertizo^M

bank
déclivité^F du terrain^M
Böschung^F
scarpata^F
desnivel^M

garden path
allée^F de jardin^M
Gartenweg^M
vialetto^M del giardino^M
enlosado^M del jardín^M

border
bordure^F
Rabatte^F
bordura^F
arriate^M

dormer window
lucarne^F
Mansardenfenster^N
abbaino^M
tragaluz^M

gutter
gouttière^F
Dachrinne^F
grondaia^F
canalón^M

downpipe
descente^F de gouttière^F
Regenrohr^N
pluviale^M
bajada^F de aguas^F

garage
garage^M
Garage^F
garage^M
garaje^M

HOUSE

HOUSE

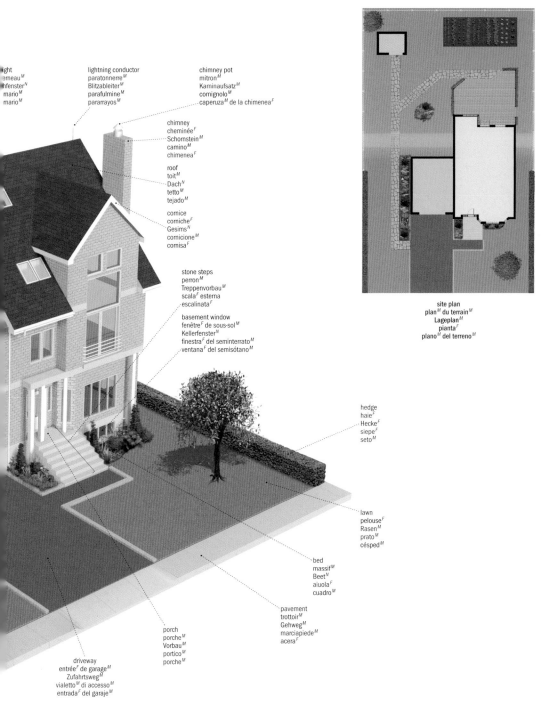

ight
emeau^M
hfenster^N
mario^M
mario^M

lightning conductor
paratonnerre^M
Blitzableiter^M
parafulmine^M
pararrayos^M

chimney pot
mitron^M
Kaminaufsatz^M
comignolo^M
caperuza^M de la chimenea^F

chimney
cheminée^F
Schornstein^M
camino^M
chimenea^F

roof
toit^M
Dach^N
tetto^M
tejado^M

cornice
corniche^F
Gesims^N
cornicione^M
cornisa^F

stone steps
perron^M
Treppenvorbau^M
scala^F esterna
escalinata^F

basement window
fenêtre^F de sous-sol^M
Kellerfenster^N
finestra^F del seminterrato^M
ventana^F del semisótano^M

site plan
plan^M du terrain^M
Lageplan^M
pianta^F
plano^M del terreno^M

hedge
haie^F
Hecke^F
siepe^F
seto^M

lawn
pelouse^F
Rasen^M
prato^M
césped^M

bed
massif^M
Beet^N
aiuola^F
cuadro^M

pavement
trottoir^M
Gehweg^M
marciapiede^M
acera^F

porch
porche^M
Vorbau^M
portico^M
porche^M

driveway
entrée^F de garage^M
Zufahrtsweg^M
vialetto^M di accesso^M
entrada^F del garaje^M

pool

piscine^F | Schwimmbecken^N | piscina^F | piscina^F

HOUSE

above ground swimming pool
piscine^F hors sol^M
freistehendes Schwimmbecken^N
piscina^F fuori terra^F
piscina^F elevada

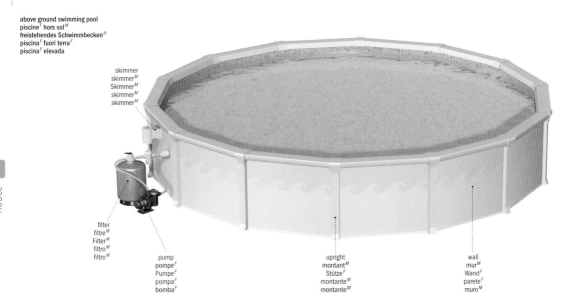

skimmer
skimmer^M
Skimmer^M
skimmer^M
skimmer^M

filter
filtre^M
Filter^M
filtro^M
filtro^M

pump
pompe^F
Pumpe^F
pompa^F
bomba^F

upright
montant^M
Stütze^F
montante^M
montante^M

wall
mur^M
Wand^F
parete^F
muro^M

sunken swimming pool
piscine^F enterrée
eingebautes Schwimmbecken^N
piscina^F interrata
piscina^F enterrada

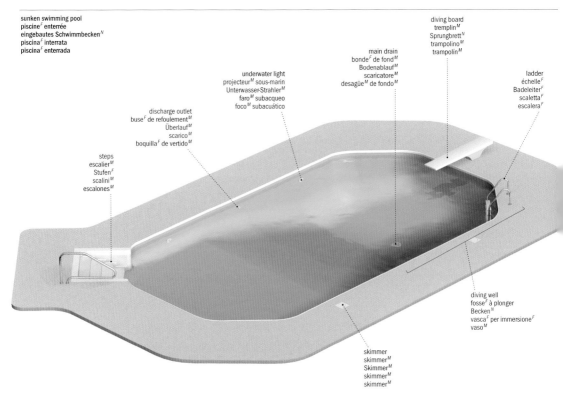

diving board
tremplin^M
Sprungbrett^N
trampolino^M
trampolin^M

main drain
bonde^F de fond^M
Bodenablauf^M
scaricatore^M
desagüe^M de fondo^M

ladder
échelle^F
Badeleiter^F
scaletta^F
escalera^F

underwater light
projecteur^M sous-marin
Unterwasser-Strahler^M
faro^M subacqueo
foco^M subacuático

discharge outlet
buse^F de refoulement^M
Überlauf^M
scarico^M
boquilla^F de vertido^M

steps
escalier^M
Stufen^F
scalini^M
escalones^M

diving well
fosse^F à plonger
Becken^N
vasca^F per immersione^F
vaso^M

skimmer
skimmer^M
Skimmer^M
skimmer^M
skimmer^M

exterior door

porte^F extérieure | Haustür^F | porta^F esterna | puerta^F de entrada^F

HOUSE

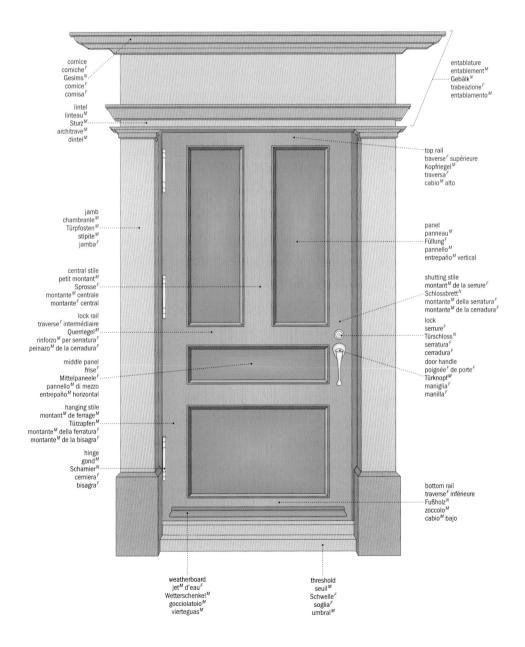

cornice
corniche^F
Gesims^N
cornice^F
cornisa^F

entablature
entablement^M
Gebälk^N
trabeazione^F
entablamento^M

lintel
linteau^M
Sturz^M
architrave^M
dintel^M

top rail
traverse^F supérieure
Kopfriegel^M
traversa^F
cabio^M alto

jamb
chambranle^M
Türpfosten^M
stipite^M
jamba^F

panel
panneau^M
Füllung^F
pannello^M
entrepaño^M vertical

central stile
petit montant^M
Sprosse^F
montante^M centrale
montante^F central

shutting stile
montant^M de la serrure^F
Schlossbrett^N
montante^M della serratura^F
montante^M de la cerradura^F

lock rail
traverse^F intermédiaire
Querriegel^M
rinforzo^M per serratura^F
peinazo^M de la cerradura^F

lock
serrure^F
Türschloss^N
serratura^F
cerradura^F

middle panel
frise^F
Mittelpaneele^F
pannello^M di mezzo
entrepaño^M horizontal

door handle
poignée^F de porte^F
Türknopf^M
maniglia^F
manilla^F

hanging stile
montant^M de ferrage^M
Türzapfen^M
montante^M della ferratura^F
montante^M de la bisagra^F

hinge
gond^M
Scharnier^N
cerniera^F
bisagra^F

bottom rail
traverse^F inférieure
Fußholz^N
zoccolo^M
cabio^M bajo

weatherboard
jet^M d'eau^F
Wetterschenkel^M
gocciolatoio^M
vierteguas^M

threshold
seuil^M
Schwelle^F
soglia^F
umbral^M

lock

serrure^F | Schloss^N | serratura^F | cerrajeria^F

HOUSE

general view
vue^F d'ensemble^M
Gesamtansicht^F
visione^F di insieme^M
vista^F general

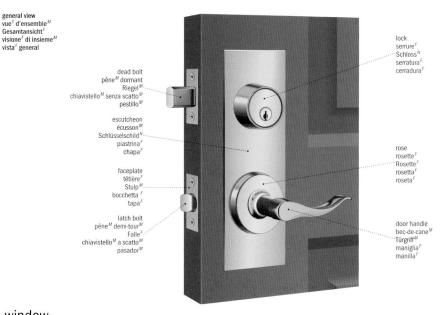

dead bolt
pêne^M dormant
Riegel^M
chiavistello^M senza scatto^M
pestillo^M

escutcheon
écusson^M
Schlüsselschild^N
piastrina^F
chapa^F

faceplate
têtière^F
Stulp^M
bocchetta^F
tapa^F

latch bolt
pêne^M demi-tour^M
Falle^F
chiavistello^M a scatto^M
pasador^M

lock
serrure^F
Schloss^N
serratura^F
cerradura^F

rose
rosette^F
Rosette^F
rosetta^F
roseta^F

door handle
bec-de-cane^M
Türgriff^M
maniglia^F
manilla^F

window

fenêtre^F | Fenster^N | finestra^F | ventana^F

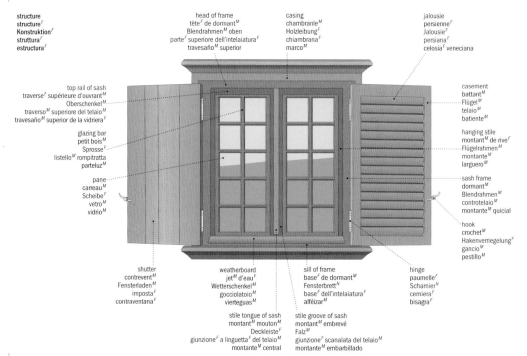

structure
structure^F
Konstruktion^F
struttura^F
estructura^F

head of frame
tête^F de dormant^M
Blendrahmen^M oben
parte^F superiore dell'intelaiatura^F
travesaño^M superior

casing
chambranle^M
Holzleibung^F
chiambrana^F
marco^M

jalousie
persienne^F
Jalousie^F
persiana^F
celosia^F veneciana

top rail of sash
traverse^F supérieure d'ouvrant^M
Oberschenkel^M
traverso^M superiore del telaio^M
travesaño^M superior de la vidriera^F

glazing bar
petit bois^M
Sprosse^F
listello^M rompitratta
parteluz^M

pane
carreau^M
Scheibe^F
vetro^M
vidrio^M

casement
battant^M
Flügel^M
telaio^M
batiente^M

hanging stile
montant^M de rive^F
Flügelrahmen^M
montante^M
larguero^M

sash frame
dormant^M
Blendrahmen^M
controtelaio^M
montante^M quicial

hook
crochet^M
Hakenverriegelung^F
gancio^M
pestillo^M

shutter
contrevent^M
Fensterladen^M
imposta^F
contraventana^F

weatherboard
jet^M d'eau^F
Wetterschenkel^M
gocciolatoio^M
vierteguas^M

sill of frame
base^F de dormant^M
Fensterbrett^N
base^F dell'intelaiatura^F
alféizar^M

hinge
paumelle^F
Scharnier^N
cerniera^F
bisagra^F

stile tongue of sash
montant^M mouton^M
Deckleiste^F
giunzione^F a linguetta^F del telaio^M
montante^M central

stile groove of sash
montant^M embrevé
Falz^M
giunzione^F scanalata del telaio^M
montante^M embarbillado

timber frame

charpente^F | Rahmen^M | struttura^F | armazón^M

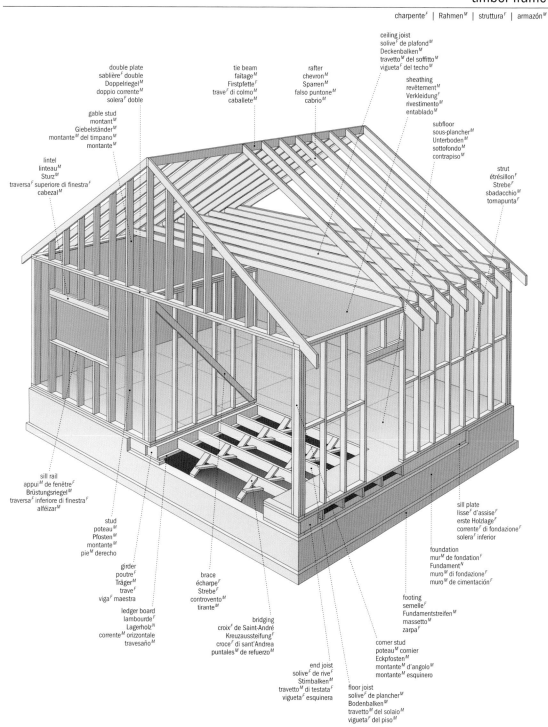

ceiling joist
solive^F de plafond^M
Deckenbalken^M
travetto^M del soffitto^M
vigueta^F del techo^M

sheathing
revêtement^M
Verkleidung^F
rivestimento^M
entablado^M

subfloor
sous-plancher^M
Unterboden^M
sottofondo^M
contrapiso^M

strut
étrésillon^F
Strebe^F
sbadacchio^M
tornapunta^F

double plate
sablière^F double
Doppelriegel^M
doppio corrente^M
solera^F doble

tie beam
faîtage^M
Firstpfette^F
trave^F di colmo^M
caballete^M

rafter
chevron^M
Sparren^M
falso puntone^M
cabrio^M

gable stud
montant^M
Giebelständer^M
montante^M del timpano^M
montante^M

lintel
linteau^M
Sturz^M
traversa^F superiore di finestra^F
cabezal^M

sill rail
appui^M de fenêtre^F
Brüstungsriegel^M
traversa^F inferiore di finestra^F
alféizar^M

sill plate
lisse^F d'assise^F
erste Holzlage^F
corrente^F di fondazione^F
solera^F inferior

stud
poteau^M
Pfosten^M
montante^M
pie^M derecho

foundation
mur^M de fondation^F
Fundament^N
muro^M di fondazione^F
muro^M de cimentación^F

girder
poutre^F
Träger^M
trave^F
viga^F maestra

brace
écharpe^F
Strebe^F
controvento^M
tirante^M

footing
semelle^F
Fundamentstreifen^M
massetto^M
zarpa^F

ledger board
lambourde^F
Lagerholz^N
corrente^M orizzontale
travesaño^M

bridging
croix^F de Saint-André
Kreuzaussteifung^F
croce^F di sant'Andrea
puntales^M de refuerzo^M

corner stud
poteau^M cornier
Eckpfosten^M
montante^M d'angolo^M
montante^M esquinero

end joist
solive^F de rive^F
Stirnbalken^M
travetto^M di testata^F
vigueta^F esquinera

floor joist
solive^F de plancher^M
Bodenbalken^M
travetto^M del solaio^M
vigueta^F del piso^M

HOUSE

187

main rooms

principales pièces^F d'une maison^F | Haupträume^M | stanze^F principali | habitaciones^F principales

ground floor
rez-de-chaussée^M
Erdgeschoß^N
pianterreno^M
planta^F baja

HOUSE

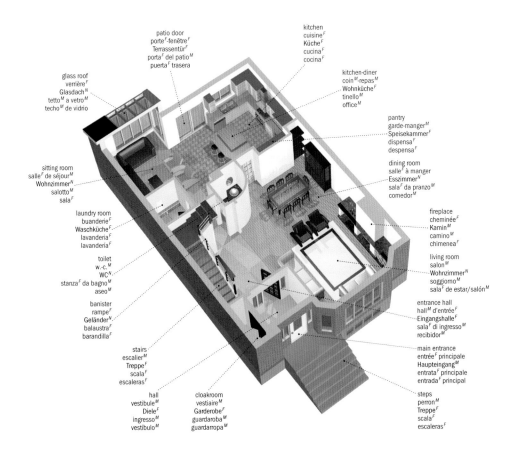

patio door
porte^F-fenêtre^F
Terrassentür^F
porta^F del patio^M
puerta^F trasera

kitchen
cuisine^F
Küche^F
cucina^F
cocina^F

kitchen-diner
coin^M-repas^M
Wohnküche^F
tinello^M
office^M

glass roof
verrière^F
Glasdach^N
tetto^M a vetro^M
techo^M de vidrio

pantry
garde-manger^M
Speisekammer^F
dispensa^F
despensa^F

sitting room
salle^F de séjour^M
Wohnzimmer^N
salotto^M
sala^F

dining room
salle^F à manger
Esszimmer^N
sala^F da pranzo^M
comedor^M

laundry room
buanderie^F
Waschküche^F
lavanderia^F
lavandería^F

fireplace
cheminée^F
Kamin^M
camino^M
chimenea^F

toilet
w.-c.^M
WC^N
stanza^F da bagno^M
aseo^M

living room
salon^M
Wohnzimmer^N
soggiorno^M
sala^F de estar/salón^M

banister
rampe^F
Geländer^N
balaustra^F
barandilla^F

entrance hall
hall^M d'entrée^F
Eingangshalle^F
sala^F di ingresso^M
recibidor^M

stairs
escalier^M
Treppe^F
scala^F
escaleras^F

main entrance
entrée^F principale
Haupteingang^M
entrata^F principale
entrada^F principal

hall
vestibule^M
Diele^F
ingresso^M
vestíbulo^M

cloakroom
vestiaire^M
Garderobe^F
guardaroba^M
guardarropa^M

steps
perron^M
Treppe^F
scala^F
escaleras^F

STRUCTURE OF A HOUSE | STRUCTURE D'UNE MAISON
KONSTRUKTION EINES HAUSES | STRUTTURA DI UNA CASA | ESTRUCTURA DE UNA CASA

main rooms

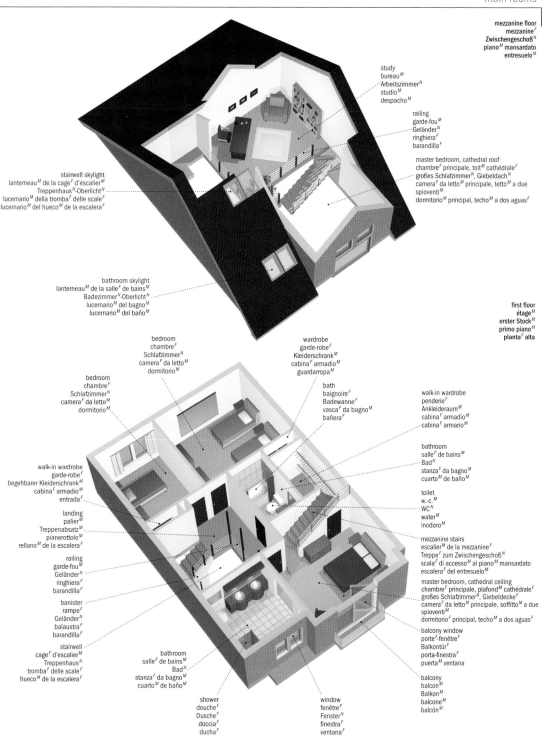

mezzanine floor^F
mezzanine^F
Zwischengeschoß^N
piano^M mansardato
entresuelo^M

study
bureau^M
Arbeitszimmer^N
studio^M
despacho^M

railing
garde-fou^M
Geländer^N
ringhiera^F
barandilla^F

master bedroom, cathedral roof
chambre^F principale, toit^M cathédrale^F
großes Schlafzimmer^N, Giebeldach^N
camera^F da letto^M principale, tetto^M a due spioventi^M
dormitorio^M principal, techo^M a dos aguas^F

stairwell skylight
lanterneau^M de la cage^F d'escalier^M
Treppenhaus^N-Oberlicht^N
lucernario^M della tromba^F delle scale^F
lucernario^M del hueco^M de la escalera^F

bathroom skylight
lanterneau^M de la salle^F de bains^M
Badezimmer^N-Oberlicht^N
lucernario^M del bagno^M
lucernario^M del baño^M

first floor
étage^M
erster Stock^M
primo piano^M
planta^F alta

bedroom
chambre^F
Schlafzimmer^N
camera^F da letto^M
dormitorio^M

wardrobe
garde-robe^F
Kleiderschrank^M
cabina^F armadio^M
guardarropa^M

bath
baignoire^F
Badewanne^F
vasca^F da bagno^M
bañera^F

walk-in wardrobe
penderie^F
Ankleideraum^M
cabina^F armadio^M
cabina^F armario^M

bedroom
chambre^F
Schlafzimmer^N
camera^F da letto^M
dormitorio^M

bathroom
salle^F de bains^M
Bad^N
stanza^F da bagno^M
cuarto^M de baño^M

toilet
w.-c.^M
WC^N
water^M
inodoro^M

walk-in wardrobe
garde-robe^F
begehbarer Kleiderschrank^M
cabina^F armadio^M
entrada^F

landing
palier^M
Treppenabsatz^M
pianerottolo^M
rellano^M de la escalera^F

mezzanine stairs
escalier^M de la mezzanine^F
Treppe^F zum Zwischengeschoß^N
scala^F di accesso^M al piano^M mansardato
escalera^F del entresuelo^M

railing
garde-fou^F
Geländer^N
ringhiera^F
barandilla^F

master bedroom, cathedral ceiling
chambre^F principale, plafond^M cathédrale^F
großes Schlafzimmer^N, Giebeldecke^F
camera^F da letto^M principale, soffitto^M a due spioventi^M
dormitorio^F principal, techo^M a dos aguas^F

banister
rampe^F
Geländer^N
balaustra^F
barandilla^F

balcony window
porte^F-fenêtre^F
Balkontür^F
porta-finestra^F
puerta^M ventana^F

stairwell
cage^F d'escalier^M
Treppenhaus^N
tromba^F delle scale^F
hueco^M de la escalera^F

bathroom
salle^F de bains^M
Bad^N
stanza^F da bagno^M
cuarto^M de baño^M

balcony
balcon^M
Balkon^M
balcone^M
balcón^M

shower
douche^F
Dusche^F
doccia^F
ducha^F

window
fenêtre^F
Fenster^N
finestra^F
ventana^F

HOUSE

wood flooring

parquet^M | Parkettboden^M | parquet^M | pisos^M de madera^F

wood flooring on cement screed
parquet^M sur chape^F de ciment^M
Parkettboden^M auf Zementestrich^M
parquet^M su sottofondo^M di cemento^M
parqué^M sobre base^F de cemento^M

wood flooring on wooden base
parquet^M sur ossature^F de bois^M
Parkettboden^M auf Holzunterbau^M
parquet^M su struttura^F lignea
entarimado^M sobre estructura^F de madera^F

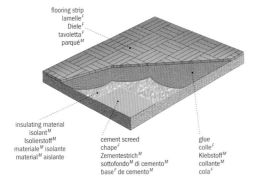

flooring strip
lamelle^F
Diele^F
tavoletta^F
parqué^M

flooring strip
lame^F
Bodendiele^F
tavoletta^F
entarimado^M

subfloor
sous-plancher^M
Unterboden^M
sottofondo^M
contrapiso^M

insulating material
isolant^M
Isolierstoff^M
materiale^M isolante
material^M aislante

cement screed
chape^F
Zementestrich^M
sottofondo^M di cemento^M
base^F de cemento^M

glue
colle^F
Klebstoff^M
collante^M
cola^F

joist
solive^F
Deckenbalken^M
travetto^M
vigueta^F

wood flooring types
arrangements^M des parquets^M
Parkettmuster^N
tipi^M di parquet^M
tipos^M de parqué^M

woodstrip flooring
parquet^M à coupe^F perdue
Stabparkett^N im Schiffsbodenverband^M
parquet^M a listoni^M
parqué^M sobrepuesto

brick-bond woodstrip flooring
parquet^M à coupe^F de pierre^F
Stabparkett^N
parquet^M a listelli^M
parqué^M alternado a la inglesa

herringbone parquet
parquet^M à bâtons^M rompus
Fischgrätparkett^N
parquet^M a spina^F di pesce^M
parqué^M espinapez^M

herringbone pattern
parquet^M en chevrons^M
Fischgrätmuster^N
parquet^M a spina^F di pesce^M
parqué^M en punta^F de Hungria

inlaid parquet
parquet^M mosaique^F
Mosaikparkett^N
parquet^M a mosaico^M
parqué^M de mosaico

basket weave pattern
parquet^M en vannerie^F
Würfelmusterparkett^N
parquet^M a tessitura^F di vimini^M
parqué^M de cesteria^F

Arenberg parquet
parquet^M d'Arenberg
Arenberg-Parkett^N
parquet^M Arenberg
parqué^M Arenberg

Chantilly parquet
parquet^M Chantilly
Chantilly-Parkett^N
parquet^M Chantilly
parqué^M Chantilly

Versailles parquet
parquet^M Versailles
Versailles-Parkett^N
parquet^M Versailles
parqué^M Versalles

textile floor coverings

revêtements^M de sol^M textiles | textile Bodenbeläge^M | rivestimenti^M in tessuto^M per pavimento^M | revestimientos^M textiles del suelo^M

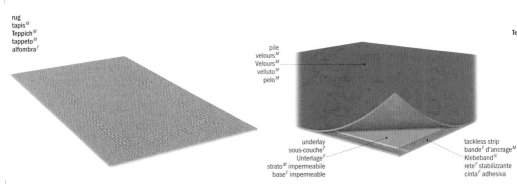

rug
tapis^M
Teppich^M
tappeto^M
alfombra^F

pile
velours^M
Velours^M
velluto^M
pelo^M

pile carpe
moquette
Teppichboden
moquette
moqueta

underlay
sous-couche^F
Unterlage^F
strato^M impermeable
base^F impermeable

tackless strip
bande^F d'ancrage^M
Klebeband^N
rete^F stabilizzante
cinta^F adhesiva

HOUSE

stairs

escalier[M] | Treppe[F] | scale[F] | escalera[F]

HOUSE

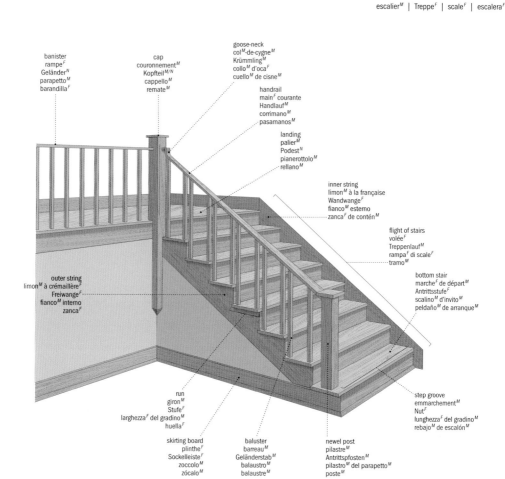

goose-neck
col[M]-de-cygne[M]
Krümmling[M]
collo[M] d'oca[F]
cuello[M] de cisne[M]

banister
rampe[F]
Geländer[N]
parapetto[M]
barandilla[F]

cap
couronnement[M]
Kopfteil[M/N]
cappello[M]
remate[M]

handrail
main[F] courante
Handlauf[M]
corrimano[M]
pasamanos[M]

landing
palier[M]
Podest[N]
pianerottolo[M]
rellano[M]

inner string
limon[M] à la française
Wandwange[F]
fianco[M] esterno
zanca[F] de contén[M]

flight of stairs
volée[F]
Treppenlauf[M]
rampa[F] di scale[F]
tramo[M]

bottom stair
marche[F] de départ[M]
Antrittsstufe[F]
scalino[M] d'invito[M]
peldaño[M] de arranque[M]

outer string
limon[M] à crémaillère[F]
Freiwange[F]
fianco[M] interno
zanca[F]

run
giron[M]
Stufe[F]
larghezza[F] del gradino[M]
huella[F]

step groove
emmarchement[M]
Nut[F]
lunghezza[F] del gradino[M]
rebajo[M] de escalón[M]

skirting board
plinthe[F]
Sockelleiste[F]
zoccolo[M]
zócalo[M]

baluster
barreau[M]
Geländerstab[M]
balaustro[M]
balaustre[M]

newel post
pilastre[M]
Antrittspfosten[M]
pilastro[M] del parapetto[M]
poste[M]

step

marche[F] | Treppenstufe[F] | gradino[M] | peldaño[M]

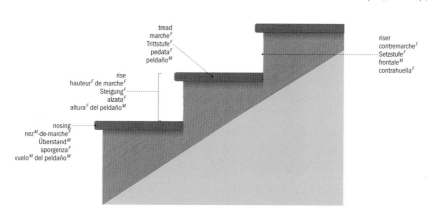

tread
marche[F]
Trittstufe[F]
pedata[F]
peldaño[M]

riser
contremarche[F]
Setzstufe[F]
frontale[M]
contrahuella[F]

rise
hauteur[F] de marche[F]
Steigung[F]
alzata[F]
altura[F] del peldaño[M]

nosing
nez[M]-de-marche[F]
Überstand[M]
sporgenza[F]
vuelo[M] del peldaño[M]

wood firing

chauffage^M au bois^M | Holzbeheizung^F | riscaldamento^M a legna^F | calefacción^F de leña^F

fireplace
cheminée^F à foyer^M ouvert
Kamin^M
camino^M
chimenea^F

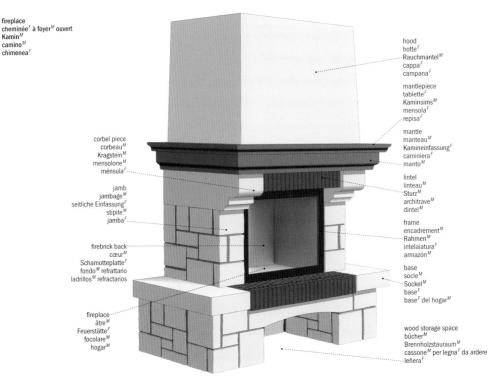

hood
hotte^F
Rauchmantel^M
cappa^F
campana^F

mantlepiece
tablette^F
Kaminsims^M
mensola^F
repisa^F

corbel piece
corbeau^M
Kragstein^M
mensolone^M
ménsula^F

mantle
manteau^M
Kamineinfassung^F
caminiera^F
manto^M

jamb
jambage^M
seitliche Einfassung^F
stipite^M
jamba^F

lintel
linteau^M
Sturz^M
architrave^M
dintel^M

frame
encadrement^M
Rahmen^M
intelaiatura^F
armazón^M

firebrick back
cœur^M
Schamotteplatte^F
fondo^M refrattario
ladrillos^M refractarios

base
socle^M
Sockel^M
base^F
base^F del hogar^M

fireplace
âtre^M
Feuerstätte^F
focolare^M
hogar^M

wood storage space
bûcher^M
Brennholzstauraum^M
cassone^M per legna^F da ardere
leñera^F

slow-burning stove
poêle^M à combustion^F lente
Dauerbrandofen^M
stufa^F a combustione^F lenta
estufa^F de leña^F a fuego^M lento

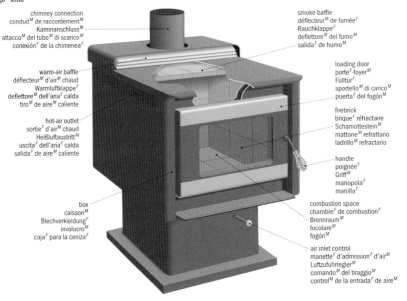

chimney connection
conduit^M de raccordement^M
Kaminanschluss^M
attacco^M del tubo^M di scarico^M
conexión^F de la chimenea^F

smoke baffle
déflecteur^M de fumée^F
Rauchklappe^F
deflettore^M del fumo^M
salida^F de humo^M

warm-air baffle
déflecteur^M d'air^M chaud
Warmluftklappe^F
deflettore^M dell'aria^F calda
tiro^M de aire^M caliente

loading door
porte^F-foyer^M
Fülltür^F
sportello^M di carico^M
puerta^F del fogón^M

hot-air outlet
sortie^F d'air^M chaud
Heißluftaustritt^M
uscita^F dell'aria^F calda
salida^F de aire^M caliente

firebrick
brique^F réfractaire
Schamottestein^M
mattone^M refrattario
ladrillo^M refractario

handle
poignée^F
Griff^M
manopola^F
manilla^F

box
caisson^M
Blechverkleidung^F
involucro^M
caja^F para la ceniza^F

combustion space
chambre^F de combustion^F
Brennraum^M
focolare^M
fogón^M

air inlet control
manette^F d'admission^F d'air^M
Luftzufuhrregler^M
comando^M del tiraggio^M
control^M de la entrada^F de aire^M

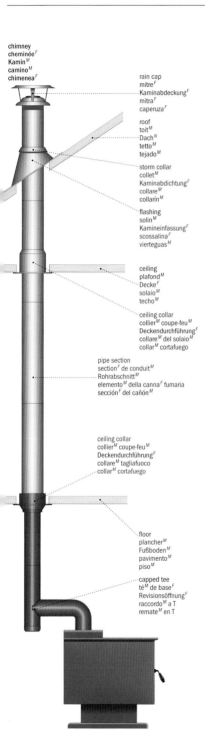

chimney
cheminée^F
Kamin^M
camino^M
chimenea^F

rain cap
mitre^F
Kaminabdeckung^F
mitra^F
caperuza^F

roof
toit^M
Dach^N
tetto^M
tejado^M

storm collar
collet^M
Kaminabdichtung^F
collare^M
collarín^M

flashing
solin^M
Kamineinfassung^F
scossalina^F
vierteguas^M

ceiling
plafond^M
Decke^F
solaio^M
techo^M

ceiling collar
collier^M coupe-feu^M
Deckendurchführung^F
collare^M del solaio^M
collar^M cortafuego

pipe section
section^F de conduit^M
Rohrabschnitt^M
elemento^M della canna^F fumaria
sección^F del cañón^M

ceiling collar
collier^M coupe-feu^M
Deckendurchführung^F
collare^M tagliafuoco
collar^M cortafuego

floor
plancher^M
Fußboden^M
pavimento^M
piso^M

capped tee
té^M de base^F
Revisionsöffnung^F
raccordo^M a T
remate^M en T

fire irons
accessoires^M de foyer^M
Kaminbesteck^N
ferri^M per il camino^M
utensilios^M para la chimenea^F

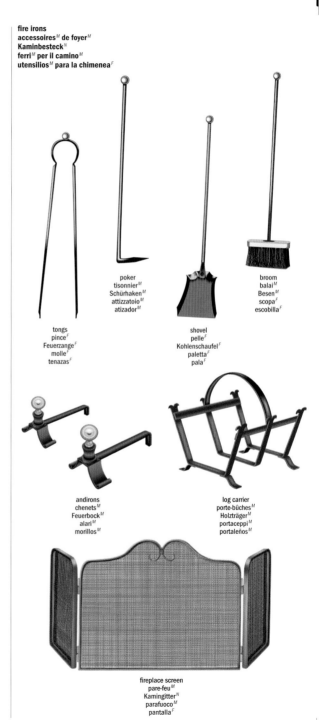

poker
tisonnier^M
Schürhaken^M
attizzatoio^M
atizador^M

broom
balai^M
Besen^M
scopa^F
escobilla^F

tongs
pince^F
Feuerzange^F
molle^F
tenazas^F

shovel
pelle^F
Kohlenschaufel^F
paletta^F
pala^F

andirons
chenets^M
Feuerbock^M
alari^M
morillos^M

log carrier
porte-bûches^M
Holzträger^M
portaceppi^M
portaleños^M

fireplace screen
pare-feu^M
Kamingitter^N
parafuoco^M
pantalla^F

plumbing system

circuit^M de plomberie^F | Sanitärinstallationssystem^N | impianto^M idraulico | cañerías^F

roof vent
chapeau^M de ventilation^F
Dunstrohrabzug^M
sfiato^M
toma^F de aire^M del tejado^M

main circuit vent
colonne^F de ventilation^F principale
Hauptentlüftungssteigrohr^N
colonna^F principale di ventilazione^F
toma^F de aire^M principal

toilet
w.-c.^M
Toilette^F
water^M
inodoro^M

circuit vent
colonne^F de ventilation^F
Entlüftungskreis^M
colonna^F di ventilazione^F
derivación^F de la toma^F de aire^M

washbasin
lavabo^M
Waschbecken^N
lavabo^M
lavabo^M

double sink
évier^M double
Doppelspüle^F
doppio lavello^M
fregadero^M doble

bath
baignoire^F
Badewanne^F
vasca^F da bagno^M
bañera^F

waste pipe
tuyau^M d'évacuation^F
Abfluss^M
tubo^M di scarico^M
desagüe^M

bath and shower mixer
mélangeur^M bain^M-douche^F
Wannen- und Brausegarmitur^F
miscelatore^M vasca^F/doccia^F
ducha^F y bañera^F

soil and waste stack
tuyau^M de chute^F
Fallstrang^M
colonna^F principale di scarico^M
desagüe^M principal

overflow
trop-plein^M
Überlauf^M
troppopieno^M
rebosadero^M

hot-water heater
chauffe-eau^M
Warmwasserbereiter^M
scaldabagno^M
calentador^M de agua^F

trap
siphon^M
Geruchsverschluss^M
sifone^M
sifón^M

main cleanout
bouchon^M de vidange^F
Reinigungsöffnung^F
tappo^M di scarico^M
tapón^M de registro^M

branch
collecteur^M d'évacuation^F
Abzweigleitung^F
collettore^M di scarico^M
cañería^F

rising main
conduite^F d'alimentation^F
Steigleitung^F
condotto^M di alimentazione^F
tubo^M de suministro^M de agua^F

waste pipe
collecteur^M d'appareil^M
Abfluss^M
tubo^M di scarico^M
conector^M del desagüe^M

stopcock
robinet^M d'arrêt^M général
Absperrventil^N
rubinetto^M generale
llave^F de paso^M

hot-water riser
colonne^F montante d'eau^F chaude
Warmwassersteigleitung^F
colonna^F montante dell'acqua^F calda
tubería^F de agua^F caliente

water service pipe
canalisation^F de branchement^M
Anschlussleitung^F
tubazione^F di allacciamento^M
tubo^M de toma^F de agua^F

cold-water riser
colonne^F montante d'eau^F froide
Kaltwassersteigleitung^F
colonna^F montante dell'acqua^F fredda
tubería^F de agua^F fría

water meter
compteur^M
Wasserzähler^M
contatore^M dell'acqua^F
contador^M de agua^F

floor drain
puisard^M
Bodenablauf^M
scarico^M
desagüe^M

main drain
collecteur^M principal
Kanalisation^F
collettore^M principale
cañería^F del desagüe^M

washing machine
lave-linge^M
Waschmaschine^F
lavatrice^F
lavadora^F

ventilating circuit
circuit^M de ventilation^F
Entlüftungskreislauf^M
rete^F di ventilazione^F
circuito^M de ventilación^F

drainage circuit
circuit^M d'évacuation^F
Abflusskreislauf^M
rete^F di scarico^M
circuito^M de desagüe^M

cold-water circuit
circuit^M d'eau^F froide
Kaltwasserkreislauf^M
rete^F di distribuzione^F dell'acqua^F fredda
circuito^M de agua^F fría

hot-water circuit
circuit^M d'eau^F chaude
Warmwasserkreislauf^M
rete^F di distribuzione^F dell'acqua^F calda
circuito^M de agua^F caliente

bathroom

HOUSE

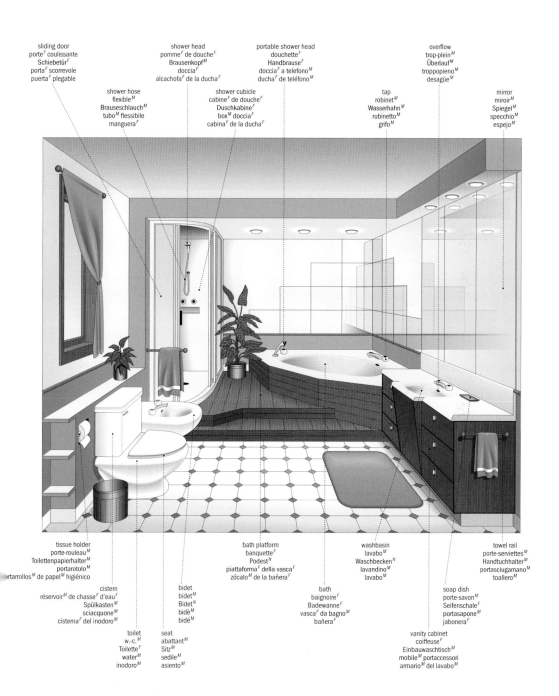

sliding door
porte^F coulissante
Schiebetür^F
porta^F scorrevole
puerta^F plegable

shower head
pomme^F de douche^F
Brausenkopf^M
doccia^F
alcachofa^F de la ducha^F

portable shower head
douchette^F
Handbrause^F
doccia^F a telefono^M
ducha^F de teléfono^M

overflow
trop-plein^M
Überlauf^M
troppopieno^M
desagüe^M

shower hose
flexible^M
Brauseschlauch^M
tubo^M flessibile
manguera^F

shower cubicle
cabine^F de douche^F
Duschkabine^F
box^M doccia^F
cabina^F de la ducha^F

tap
robinet^M
Wasserhahn^M
rubinetto^M
grifo^M

mirror
miroir^M
Spiegel^M
specchio^M
espejo^M

tissue holder
porte-rouleau^M
Toilettenpapierhalter^M
portarotolo^M
portarrollos^M de papel^M higiénico

bath platform
banquette^F
Podest^N
piattaforma^F della vasca^F
zócalo^M de la bañera^F

washbasin
lavabo^M
Waschbecken^N
lavandino^M
lavabo^M

towel rail
porte-serviettes^M
Handtuchhalter^M
portasciugamano^M
toallero^M

cistern
réservoir^M de chasse^F d'eau^F
Spülkasten^M
sciacquone^M
cisterna^F del inodoro^M

bidet
bidet^M
Bidet^N
bidè^M
bidé^M

bath
baignoire^F
Badewanne^F
vasca^F da bagno^M
bañera^F

soap dish
porte-savon^M
Seifenschale^F
portasapone^M
jabonera^F

toilet
w.-c.^M
Toilette^F
water^M
inodoro^M

seat
abattant^M
Sitz^M
sedile^M
asiento^M

vanity cabinet
coiffeuse^F
Einbauwaschtisch^M
mobile^M portaccessori
armario^M del lavabo^M

toilet

w.-c.^{M} | Toilette^F | water^M | inodoro^M

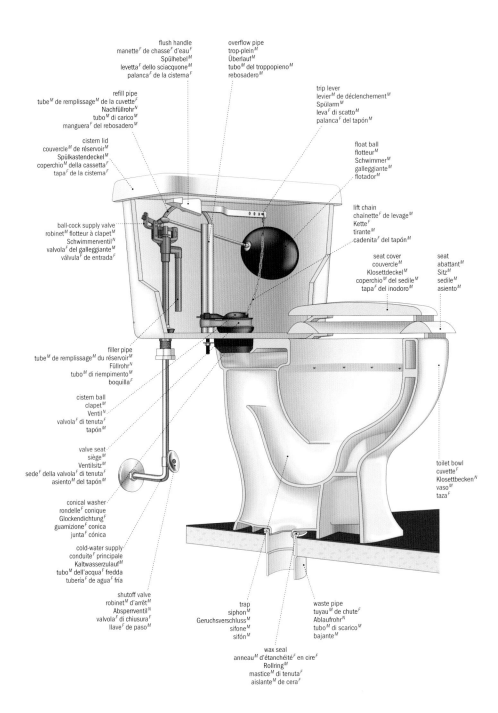

flush handle
manette^F de chasse^F d'eau^F
Spülhebel^M
levetta^F dello sciacquone^M
palanca^F de la cisterna^F

overflow pipe
trop-plein^M
Überlauf^M
tubo^M del troppopieno^M
rebosadero^M

trip lever
levier^M de déclenchement^M
Spülarm^M
leva^F di scatto^M
palanca^F del tapón^M

refill pipe
tube^M de remplissage^M de la cuvette^F
Nachfüllrohr^N
tubo^M di carico^M
manguera^F del rebosadero^M

float ball
flotteur^M
Schwimmer^M
galleggiante^M
flotador^M

cistern lid
couvercle^M de réservoir^M
Spülkastendeckel^M
coperchio^M della cassetta^F
tapa^F de la cisterna^F

lift chain
chaînette^F de levage^M
Kette^F
tirante^M
cadenita^F del tapón^M

ball-cock supply valve
robinet^M flotteur à clapet^M
Schwimmerventil^N
valvola^F del galleggiante^M
válvula^F de entrada^F

seat cover
couvercle^M
Klosettdeckel^M
coperchio^M del sedile^M
tapa^F del inodoro^M

seat
abattant^M
Sitz^M
sedile^M
asiento^M

filler pipe
tube^M de remplissage^M du réservoir^M
Füllrohr^N
tubo^M di riempimento^M
boquilla^F

cistern ball
clapet^M
Ventil^N
valvola^F di tenuta^F
tapón^M

valve seat
siège^M
Ventilsitz^M
sede^F della valvola^F di tenuta^F
asiento^M del tapón^M

toilet bowl
cuvette^F
Klosettbecken^N
vaso^M
taza^F

conical washer
rondelle^F conique
Glockendichtung^F
guarnizione^F conica
junta^F cónica

cold-water supply
conduite^F principale
Kaltwasserzulauf^M
tubo^M dell'acqua^F fredda
tubería^F de agua^F fría

shutoff valve
robinet^M d'arrêt^M
Absperrventil^N
valvola^F di chiusura^F
llave^F de paso^M

trap
siphon^M
Geruchsverschluss^M
sifone^M
sifón^M

waste pipe
tuyau^M de chute^F
Ablaufrohr^N
tubo^M di scarico^M
bajante^M

wax seal
anneau^M d'étanchéité^F en cire^F
Rollring^M
mastice^M di tenuta^F
aislante^M de cera^F

examples of branching

exemples^M de branchement^M | Beispiele^N für Anschlüsse^M | esempi^M di allacciamento^M | ejemplos^M de conexiones^F

sink with waste disposal unit
évier^M-broyeur^M
Spüle^F mit Müllschlucker^M
lavello^M con tritarifiuti^M
fregadero^M con triturador^M de basura^F

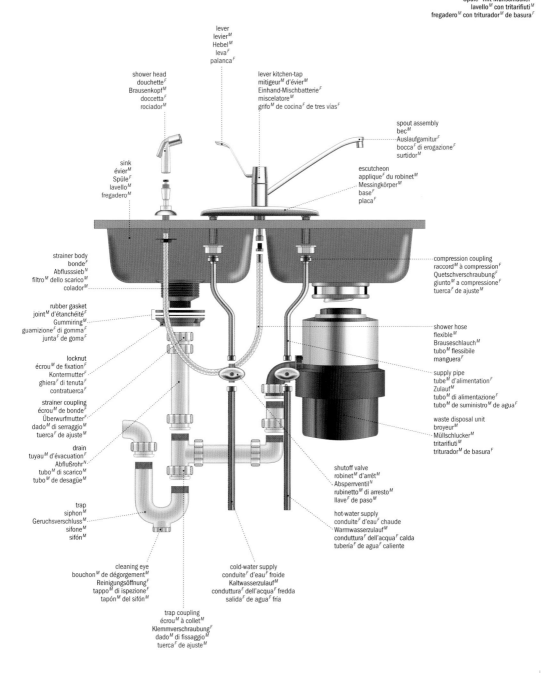

lever
levier^M
Hebel^M
leva^F
palanca^F

shower head
douchette^F
Brausenkopf^M
doccetta^F
rociador^M

lever kitchen-tap
mitigeur^M d'évier^M
Einhand-Mischbatterie^F
miscelatore^M
grifo^M de cocina^F de tres vías^F

spout assembly
bec^M
Auslaufgarnitur^F
bocca^F di erogazione^F
surtidor^M

sink
évier^M
Spüle^F
lavello^M
fregadero^M

escutcheon
applique^F du robinet^M
Messingkörper^M
base^F
placa^F

strainer body
bonde^F
Abflusssieb^N
filtro^M dello scarico^M
colador^M

compression coupling
raccord^M à compression^F
Quetschverschraubung^F
giunto^M a compressione^F
tuerca^F de ajuste^M

rubber gasket
joint^M d'étanchéité^F
Gummiring^M
guarnizione^F di gomma^F
junta^F de goma^F

shower hose
flexible^M
Brauseschlauch^M
tubo^M flessibile
manguera^F

locknut
écrou^M de fixation^F
Kontermutter^F
ghiera^F di tenuta^F
contratuerca^F

supply pipe
tube^M d'alimentation^F
Zulauf^M
tubo^M di alimentazione^F
tubo^M de suministro^M de agua^F

strainer coupling
écrou^M de bonde^F
Überwurfmutter^F
dado^M di serraggio^M
tuerca^F de ajuste^M

waste disposal unit
broyeur^M
Müllschlucker^M
tritarifiuti^M
triturador^M de basura^F

drain
tuyau^M d'évacuation^F
Abflußrohr^N
tubo^M di scarico^M
tubo^M de desagüe^M

shutoff valve
robinet^M d'arrêt^M
Absperrventil^N
rubinetto^M di arresto^M
llave^F de paso^M

trap
siphon^M
Geruchsverschluss^M
sifone^M
sifón^M

hot-water supply
conduite^F d'eau^F chaude
Warmwasserzulauf^M
conduttura^F dell'acqua^F calda
tubería^F de agua^F caliente

cleaning eye
bouchon^M de dégorgement^M
Reinigungsöffnung^F
tappo^M di ispezione^F
tapón^M del sifón^M

cold-water supply
conduite^F d'eau^F froide
Kaltwasserzulauf^M
conduttura^F dell'acqua^F fredda
salida^F de agua^F fría

trap coupling
écrou^M à collet^M
Klemmverschraubung^F
dado^M di fissaggio^M
tuerca^F de ajuste^M

HOUSE

network connection

branchement^M au réseau^M | Hausanschluss^M | allacciamento^M alla rete^F | conexión^F a la red^F

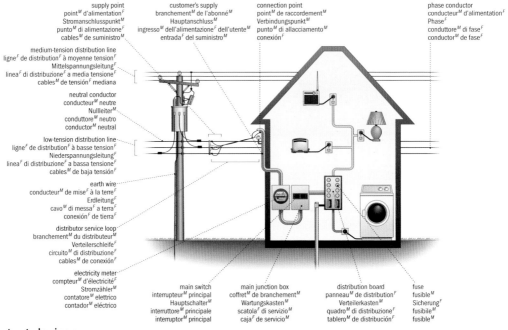

supply point
point^M d'alimentation^F
Stromanschlusspunkt^M
punto^M di alimentazione^F
cables^M de suministro^M

customer's supply
branchement^M de l'abonné^M
Hauptanschluss^M
ingresso^M dell'alimentazione^F dell'utente^M
entrada^F del suministro^M

connection point
point^M de raccordement^M
Verbindungspunkt^M
punto^M di allacciamento^M
conexión^F

phase conductor
conducteur^M d'alimentation^F
Phase^F
conduttore^M di fase^F
conductor^M de fase^F

medium-tension distribution line
ligne^F de distribution^F à moyenne tension^F
Mittelspannungsleitung^F
linea^F di distribuzione^F a media tensione^F
cables^M de tensión^F mediana

neutral conductor
conducteur^M neutre
Nullleiter^M
conduttore^M neutro
conductor^M neutral

low-tension distribution line
ligne^F de distribution^F à basse tension^F
Niederspannungsleitung^F
linea^F di distribuzione^F a bassa tensione^F
cables^M de baja tensión^F

earth wire
conducteur^M de mise^F à la terre^F
Erdleitung^F
cavo^M di messa^F a terra^F
conexión^F de tierra^F

distributor service loop
branchement^M du distributeur^M
Verteilerschleife^F
circuito^M di distribuzione^F
cables^M de conexión^F

electricity meter
compteur^M d'électricité^F
Stromzähler^M
contatore^M elettrico
contador^M eléctrico

main switch
interrupteur^M principal
Hauptschalter^M
interruttore^M principale
interruptor^M principal

main junction box
coffret^M de branchement^M
Wartungskasten^M
scatola^F di servizio^M
caja^F de servicio^M

distribution board
panneau^M de distribution^F
Verteilerkasten^M
quadro^M di distribuzione^F
tablero^M de distribución^F

fuse
fusible^M
Sicherung^F
fusibile^M
fusible^M

contact devices

dispositifs^M de contact^M | Kontaktelemente^N | dispositivi^M di contatto^M | dispositivos^M de contacto^M

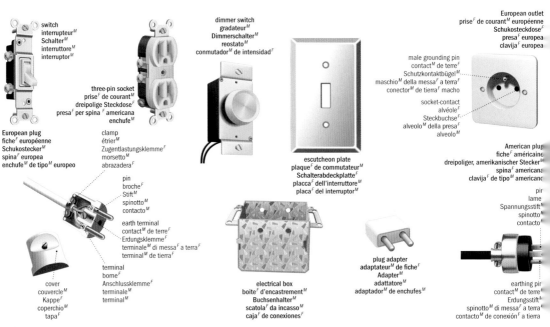

switch
interrupteur^M
Schalter^M
interruttore^M
interruptor^M

dimmer switch
gradateur^M
Dimmerschalter^M
reostato^M
conmutador^M de intensidad^F

European outlet
prise^F de courant^M européenne
Schukosteckdose^F
presa^F europea
clavija^F europea

three-pin socket
prise^F de courant^M
dreipolige Steckdose^F
presa^F per spina ^{F} americana
enchufe^M

male grounding pin
contact^M de terre^F
Schutzkontaktbügel^M
maschio^M della messa^F a terra^F
conector^M de tierra^F macho

European plug
fiche^F européenne
Schukostecker^M
spina^F europea
enchufe^M de tipo^M europeo

clamp
étrier^M
Zugentlastungsklemme^F
morsetto^M
abrazadera^F

socket-contact
alvéole^F
Steckbuchse^F
alveolo^M della presa^F
alveolo^M

American plug
fiche^F américaine
dreipoliger, amerikanischer Stecker^M
spina^F americana
clavija^F de tipo^M americano

pin
broche^F
Stift^M
spinotto^M
contacto^M

escutcheon plate
plaque^F de commutateur^M
Schalterabdeckplatte^F
placca^F dell'interruttore^M
placa^F del interruptor^M

pin
lame^F
Spannungsstift^M
spinotto^M
contacto^M

earth terminal
contact^M de terre^F
Erdungsklemme^F
terminale^M di messa^F a terra^F
terminal^M de tierra^F

terminal
borne^F
Anschlussklemme^F
terminale^M
terminal^M

cover
couvercle^M
Kappe^F
coperchio^M
tapa^F

electrical box
boîte^F d'encastrement^M
Buchsenhalter^M
scatola^F da incasso^M
caja^F de conexiones^F

plug adapter
adaptateur^M de fiche^F
Adapter^M
adattatore^M
adaptador^M de enchufes^M

earthing pin
contact^M de terre^F
Erdungsstift^M
spinotto^M di messa^F a terra^F
contacto^M de conexión^F a tierra

lighting

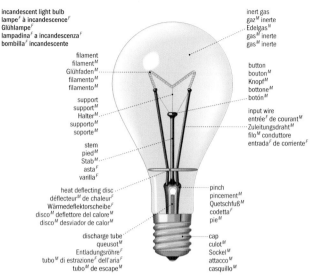

incandescent light bulb
lampe^F à incandescence^F
Glühlampe^F
lampadina^F a incandescenza^F
bombilla^F incandescente

filament
filament^M
Glühfaden^M
filamento^M
filamento^M

support
support^M
Halter^M
supporto^M
soporte^M

stem
pied^M
Stab^M
asta^F
varilla^F

heat deflecting disc
déflecteur^M de chaleur^F
Wärmedeflektorscheibe^F
disco^M deflettore del calore^M
disco^M desviador de calor^M

discharge tube
queusot^M
Entladungsröhre^F
tubo^M di estrazione^F dell'aria^F
tubo^M de escape^M

inert gas
gaz^M inerte
Edelgas^N
gas^M inerte
gas^M inerte

button
bouton^M
Knopf^M
bottone^M
botón^M

input wire
entrée^F de courant^M
Zuleitungsdraht^M
filo^M conduttore
entrada^F de corriente^F

pinch
pincement^M
Quetschfuß^M
codetta^F
pie^M

cap
culot^M
Sockel^M
attacco^M
casquillo^M

tube
ampoule^F
Kolben^M
bulbo^M
ampolla^F de vidrio^M

lampholder
douille^F de lampe^F
Lampenfassung^F
portalampada^M
portalámparas^M

screw cap
culot^M à vis^F
Schraubfassung^F
attacco^M a vite^F
bombilla^F de rosca^F

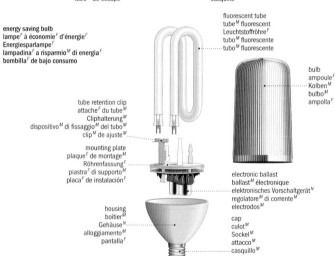

energy saving bulb
lampe^F à économie^F d'énergie^F
Energiesparlampe^F
lampadina^F a risparmio^M di energia^F
bombilla^F de bajo consumo

tube retention clip
attache^F du tube^M
Cliphalterung^M
dispositivo^M di fissaggio^M del tubo^M
clip^M de ajuste^M

mounting plate
plaque^F de montage^M
Röhrenfassung^F
piastra^F di supporto^M
placa^F de instalación^F

housing
boîtier^M
Gehäuse^N
alloggiamento^M
pantalla^F

fluorescent tube
tube^M fluorescent
Leuchtstoffröhre^F
tubo^M fluorescente
tubo^M fluorescente

bulb
ampoule^F
Kolben^M
bulbo^M
ampolla^F

electronic ballast
ballast^M électronique
elektronisches Vorschaltgerät^N
regolatore^M di corrente^M
electrodos^M

cap
culot^M
Sockel^M
attacco^M
casquillo^M

bayonet cap
culot^M à baïonnette^F
Bajonettfassung^F
attacco^M a baionetta^F
bombilla^F de bayoneta^F

tungsten-halogen bulb
lampe^F à halogène^M
Wolfram-Halogenlampe^F
lampada^F alogena al tungsteno^M
lámpara^F halógena

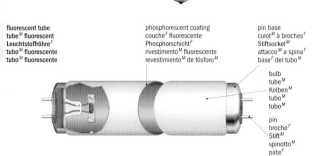

fluorescent tube
tube^M fluorescent
Leuchtstoffröhre^F
tubo^M fluorescente
tubo^M fluorescente

phosphorescent coating
couche^F fluorescente
Phosphorschicht^F
rivestimento^M fluorescente
revestimiento^M de fósforo^M

pin base
culot^M à broches^F
Stiftsockel^M
attacco^M a spina^F
base^F del tubo^M

bulb
tube^M
Kolben^M
tubo^M
tubo^M

pin
broche^F
Stift^M
spinotto^M
pata^F

pin
broche^F
Stift^M
spinotto^M
contacto^M

armchair

fauteuil^M | Armlehnstuhl^M | poltrona^F | silla^F de brazos^M

HOUSE

parts
parties^F
Teile^{M/N}
parti^F
partes^F

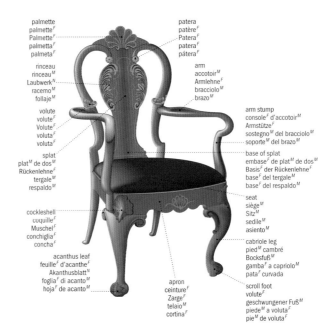

palmette
palmette^F
Palmette^F
palmetta^F
palmeta^F

patera
patère^F
Patera^F
patera^F
pátera^F

rinceau
rinceau^M
Laubwerk^N
racemo^M
follaje^M

arm
accotoir^M
Armlehne^F
bracciolo^M
brazo^M

volute
volute^F
Volute^F
voluta^F
voluta^F

arm stump
console^F d'accotoir^M
Armstütze^F
sostegno^M del bracciolo^M
soporte^M del brazo^M

splat
plat^M de dos^M
Rückenlehne^F
tergale^F
respaldo^M

base of splat
embase^F de plat^M de dos^M
Basis^F der Rückenlehne^F
base^F del tergale^M
base^F del respaldo^M

seat
siège^M
Sitz^M
sedile^M
asiento^M

cockleshell
coquille^F
Muschel^F
conchiglia^F
concha^F

cabriole leg
pied^M cambré
Bocksfuß^M
gamba^F a capriolo^M
pata^F curvada

acanthus leaf
feuille^F d'acanthe^F
Akanthusblatt^N
foglia^F di acanto^M
hoja^F de acanto^M

apron
ceinture^F
Zarge^F
telaio^M
cortina^F

scroll foot
volute^F
geschwungener Fuß^M
piede^M a voluta^F
pie^M de voluta^F

examples of armchairs
exemples^M de fauteuils^M
Beispiele^N für Armstühle^M
esempi^M di poltrone^F e divani^M
ejemplos^M de divanes^M y butacas^F

Wassily chair
fauteuil^M Wassily
Wassily-Stuhl^M
poltrona^F Wassily
silla^F Wassily

director's chair
fauteuil^M metteur^M en scène^F
Regiestuhl^M
sedia^F da regista^M
silla^F plegable de lona^F

rocking chair
fauteuil^M à bascule^F
Schaukelstuhl^M
sedia^F a dondolo^M
mecedora^F

cabriole chair
cabriolet^M
kleiner Lehnstuhl^M
cabriolet^F
silla^F cabriolé

méridienne
méridienne^F
Kanapee^N
méridienne^F
meridiana^F

chaise longue
récamier^M
Chaiselongue^N
agrippina^F
sofá^M tipo^M imperio

club chair
fauteuil^M club^M
Clubsessel^M
poltrona^F da salotto^M
butaca^F

bergère
bergère^F
Bergère^F
bergère^F
silla^F poltrona

sofa
canapé^M
Sofa^N
divano^M
sofá^M

two-seater settee
causeuse^F
Zweisitzer^M
divano^M a due posti^M
sofá^M de dos plazas^F

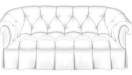

chesterfield
canapé^M capitonné
Chesterfieldsofa^N
divano^M Chesterfield
chesterfield^M

side chair

chaise^F | Stuhl^M | sedia^F | silla^F sin brazos^M

parts
parties^F
Teile^{M/N}
parti^F
partes^F

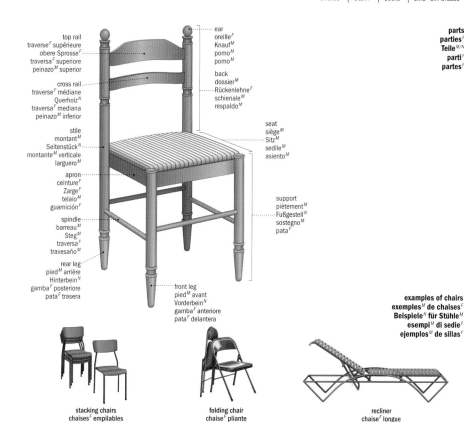

top rail
traverse^F supérieure
obere Sprosse^F
traversa^F superiore
peinazo^M superior

cross rail
traverse^F médiane
Querholz^N
traversa^F mediana
peinazo^M inferior

stile
montant^M
Seitenstück^N
montante^M verticale
larguero^M

apron
ceinture^F
Zarge^F
telaio^M
guarnición^F

spindle
barreau^M
Steg^M
traversa^F
travesaño^M

rear leg
pied^M arrière
Hinterbein^N
gamba^F posteriore
pata^F trasera

ear
oreille^F
Knauf^M
pomo^M
pomo^M

back
dossier^M
Rückenlehne^F
schienale^M
respaldo^M

seat
siège^M
Sitz^M
sedile^M
asiento^M

support
piètement^M
Fußgestell^N
sostegno^M
pata^F

front leg
pied^M avant
Vorderbein^N
gamba^F anteriore
pata^F delantera

examples of chairs
exemples^M **de chaises**^F
Beispiele^N **für Stühle**^M
esempi^M **di sedie**^F
ejemplos^M **de sillas**^F

rocking chair
chaise^F berçante
Schaukelstuhl^M
sedia^F a dondolo^M
mecedora^F

stacking chairs
chaises^F empilables
Stapelstühle^M
sedie^F impilabili
sillas^F apilables

folding chair
chaise^F pliante
Klappstuhl^M
sedia^F pieghevole
silla^F plegable

recliner
chaise^F longue
Liegestuhl^M
sedia^F a sdraio^M
tumbona^F

seats

sièges^M | Sitzmöbel^N | sedili^M | asientos^M

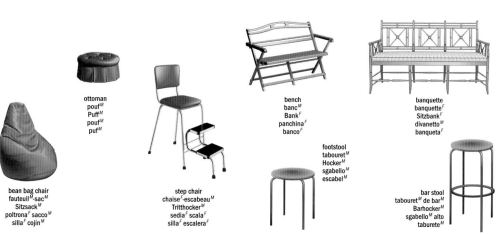

ottoman
pouf^M
Puff^M
pouf^M
puf^M

bench
banc^M
Bank^F
panchina^F
banco^F

banquette
banquette^F
Sitzbank^F
divanetto^M
banqueta^F

footstool
tabouret^M
Hocker^M
sgabello^M
escabel^M

bean bag chair
fauteuil^M-sac^M
Sitzsack^M
poltrona^F sacco^M
silla^F cojín^M

step chair
chaise^F-escabeau^M
Tritthocker^M
sedia^F scala^F
silla^F escalera^F

bar stool
tabouret^M de bar^M
Barhocker^M
sgabello^M alto
taburete^M

HOUSE

table

table^F | Tisch^M | tavolo^M | mesa^F

HOUSE

gate-leg table
table^F à abattants^M
Klapptisch^M
tavolo^M a cancello^M
mesa^F de hojas^F abatibles

drawer   knob
tiroir^M   bouton^M
Schublade^F   Knauf^M
cassetto^M   pomello^M
cajón^M   pomo^M

top
plateau^M
Tischplatte^F
piano^M
tablero^M

drop-leaf
abattant^M
Klappe^F
ribalta^F
extensión^F plegable

stretcher
traverse^F
Traverse^F
traversa^F del cancello^M
travesaño^M

leg
pied^M
Bein^N
gamba^F
pata^F

gate-leg
tréteau^M
Ausziehbein^N
cancello^M
pata^F móvil

apron
ceinture^F
Zarge^F
telaio^M
guarnición^F

crosspiece
entrejambe^F
Querstück^N
traversa^F
travesaño^M

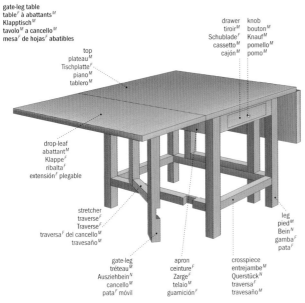

examples of tables
exemples^M de tables^F
Beispiele^N für Tische^M
esempi^M di tavoli^M
ejemplos^M de mesas^F

extending table
table^F à rallonges^F
Ausziehtisch^M
tavolo^M allungabile
mesa^F plegable

top
plateau^M
Tischplatte^F
piano^M
tablero^M

extension
rallonge^F
Auszug^M
prolunga^F
extensión^F

nest of tables
tables^F gigognes
Satztische^M
tavolini^M sovrapponibili
juego^M de mesas^F

serving trolley
desserte^F
Servierwagen^M
carrello^M portavivande
mesita^F de servicio^M

storage furniture

meubles^M de rangement^M | Aufbewahrungsmöbel^N | mobili^M contenitori | muebles^M contenedores

armoire
armoire^F
Kleiderschrank^M
armadio^M
armario^M

frame
bâti^M
Rahmen^M
telaio^M
armazón^M

door
vantail^M
Tür^F
porta^F
puerta^F

frieze
frise^F
Fries^M
cimasa^F
friso^M

top rail
traverse^F supérieure
obere Querleiste^F
traversa^F superiore
peinazo^M superior

centre post
dormant^M
Setzholz^N
montante^M centrale
montante^M central

diamond point
pointe^F de diamant^M
Rautenspitze^F
punta^F di diamante^M
punta^F de diamante^M

rail
traverse^F
Querleiste^F
traversa^F
peinazo^M

bottom rail
traverse^F inférieure
untere Querleiste^F
traversa^F inferiore
peinazo^M inferior

foot
pied^M
Fuß^M
piede^M
pata^F

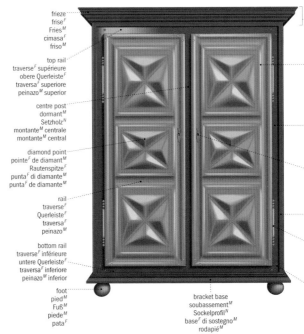

bracket base
soubassement^M
Sockelprofil^M
base^F di sostegno^M
rodapié^M

cornice
corniche^F
Kranzprofil^N
cornice^F
cornisa^F

door panel
panneau^M de vantail^M
Türfüllung^F
pannello^M dell'anta^F
entrepaño^M

hanging stile
montant^M de ferrage^M
Anschlagrahmen^M
montante^M verticale
larguero^M de la bisagra^F

lock
serrure^F
Schloss^N
serratura^F
cerradura^F

frame stile
montant^M de bâti^M
Rahmenleiste^F
montante^M del telaio^M
larguero^M del marco^M

hinge
gond^M
Scharnier^N
cerniera^F
bisagra^F

peg
cheville^F
Zapfen^M
tassello^M
espiga^F

compartment
casier^M
Fach^N
scomparto^M
casillero^M

fall front
abattant^M
herausklappbare Schreibplatte^F
ribalta^F
escritorio^M

linen chest
coffre^M
Truhe^F
cassapanca^F
baúl^M

hanging cupboard
penderie^F
Schrankteil^{M/N}
armadio^M appendiabiti
guardarropa^M

shelf
tablette^F
Fach^N
ripiano^M
anaquel^M

bureau
secrétaire^M
Sekretär^M
secrétaire^M
bufete^M

dressing table
coiffeuse^F
Kommode^F
comò^M
cómoda^F

wardrobe
armoire^F-penderie^F
Kleiderschrank^M
guardaroba^M
ropero^M

drawer
tiroir^M
Schublade^F
cassetto^M
cajón^M

chiffonier
chiffonnier^M
Chiffonière^F
cassettiera^F
chifonier^M

display cabinet
vitrine^F
Vitrine^F
vetrina^F
vitrina^F

corner cupboard
encoignure^F
Eckschrank^M
angoliera^F
rinconera^F

glass-fronted display cabinet
buffet^M-vaisselier^M
Vitrinenschrank^M
credenza^F con vetrina^F
aparador^M con vitrina^F

sideboard
buffet^M
Büfett^N
credenza^F
aparador^M

cocktail cabinet
bar^M
Cocktailbar^F
mobile^M bar^M
mueble^M bar^M

HOUSE

bed

lit^M | Bett^N | letto^M | cama^F

HOUSE

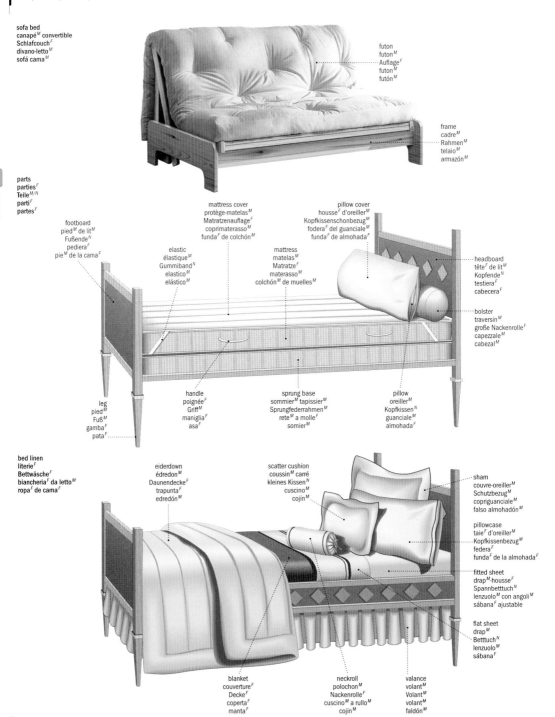

sofa bed
canapé^M convertible
Schlafcouch^F
divano-letto^M
sofá cama^M

futon
futon^M
Auflage^F
futon^M
futón^M

frame
cadre^M
Rahmen^M
telaio^M
armazón^M

parts
parties^F
Teile^M/N
parti^F
partes^F

footboard
pied^M de lit^M
Fußende^N
pediera^F
pie^M de la cama^F

mattress cover
protège-matelas^M
Matratzenauflage^F
coprimaterasso^M
funda^F de colchón^M

pillow cover
housse^F d'oreiller^M
Kopfkissenschonbezug^M
fodera^F del guanciale^M
funda^F de almohada^F

elastic
élastique^M
Gummiband^N
elastico^M
elástico^M

mattress
matelas^M
Matratze^F
materasso^M
colchón^M de muelles^M

headboard
tête^F de lit^M
Kopfende^N
testiera^F
cabecera^F

bolster
traversin^M
große Nackenrolle^F
capezzale^M
cabezal^M

leg
pied^M
Fuß^M
gamba^F
pata^F

handle
poignée^F
Griff^M
maniglia^F
asa^F

sprung base
sommier^M tapissier^M
Sprungfederrahmen^M
rete^M a molle^F
somier^M

pillow
oreiller^M
Kopfkissen^N
guanciale^M
almohada^F

bed linen
literie^F
Bettwäsche^F
biancheria^F da letto^M
ropa^F de cama^F

eiderdown
édredon^M
Daunendecke^F
trapunta^F
edredón^M

scatter cushion
coussin^M carré
kleines Kissen^N
cuscino^M
cojín^M

sham
couvre-oreiller^M
Schutzbezug^M
copriguanciale^M
falso almohadón^M

pillowcase
taie^F d'oreiller^M
Kopfkissenbezug^M
federa^F
funda^F de la almohada^F

fitted sheet
drap^M-housse^F
Spannbetttuch^N
lenzuolo^M con angoli^M
sábana^F ajustable

flat sheet
drap^M
Betttuch^N
lenzuolo^M
sábana^F

blanket
couverture^F
Decke^F
coperta^F
manta^F

neckroll
polochon^M
Nackenrolle^F
cuscino^M a rullo^M
cojín^M

valance
volant^M
Volant^M
volant^M
faldón^M

children's furniture

meubles^M d'enfants^M | Kindermöbel^N | mobili^M per bambini^M | muebles^M infantiles

nursery
lit^M pliant
Reisebett^N mit Wickelauflage^F
lettino^M pieghevole con fasciatoio^M
cuna^F plegable

changing table
plan^M à langer
Wickelauflage^F
fasciatoio^M
cambiador^M

top rail
bordure^F
oberer Abschluss^M
bordo^M
borde^M

armrest
accoudoir^M
Armlehne^F
bracciolo^M
brazos^M

booster seat
rehausseur^M
Kindersessel^M
poltroncina^F per bambini^M
silla^F alzadora

back
dossier^M
Rückenlehne^F
schienale^M
respaldo^M

seat
siège^M
Sitz^M
sedile^M
asiento^M

changing table
table^F à langer
Wickelkommode^F
fasciatoio^M
cambiador^M

mesh
filet^M
Netz^N
retina^F
red^F

mattress
matelas^M
Matratze^F
materassino^M
colchón^M

high chair
chaise^F haute
Hochstuhl^M
seggiolone^M
trona^F

back
dossier^M
Rückenlehne^F
schienale^M
respaldo^M

tray
plateau^M
Esstablett^N
vassoio^M
bandeja^F

waist belt
ceinture^F ventrale
Gurt^M
cintura^F di ritenuta^F
cinturón^F de seguridad^F

footrest
repose-pieds^M
Fußstütze^F
poggiapiedi^M
reposapies^M

leg
pied^M
Gestell^N
gamba^F
pata^F

headboard
tête^F de lit^M
Kopfteil$^{M/N}$
testiera^F
cabecera^M

barrier
barrière^F
Schutzgitter^N
sponda^F protettiva
barrera^F

cot
lit^M à barreaux^M
Gitterbett^N
lettino^M a sponde^F
cuna^F

slat
barreau^M
Sprosse^F
sbarra^F
barrote^M

caster
roulette^F
Laufrolle^F
ruota^F girevole
rueda^F giratoria

drawer
tiroir^M
Schubkasten^M
cassetto^M
cajón^M

mattress
matelas^M
Matratze^F
materasso^M
colchón^M

HOUSE

lights

luminaires^M | Lampen^F | luci^F | lámparas^F

ceiling fitting
plafonnier^M
Deckenleuchte^F
plafoniera^F
plafón^M

hanging pendant
suspension^F
Hängeleuchte^F
lampada^F a sospensione^F
lámpara^F de techo^M

clamp spotlight
spot^M à pince^F
Klemmspot^M
faretto^M a pinza^F
lámpara^F de pinza^F

halogen desk lamp
lampe^F de bureau^M halogène
Halogen^N-Tischleuchte^F
lampada^F alogena da tavolo^M
lámpara^F de despacho^M halógena

arm
bras^M
Arm^M
braccio^M
brazo^M

base
socle^M
Fuß^M
base^F
base^M

adjustable lamp
lampe^F d'architecte^M
Arbeitsleuchte^F
lampada^F a braccio^M regolabile
flexo^M

on-off switch
interrupteur^M
Ein-/Ausschalter^M
interruttore^M
interruptor^M

arm
bras^M
Arm^M
braccio^M
brazo^M

shade
abat-jour^M
Schirm^M
paralume^M
pantalla^F

spring
ressort^M
Feder^F
molla^F
resorte^M

adjustable clamp
support^M de fixation^F
verstellbare Klemme^F
morsetto^M regolabile
tornillo^M de ajuste^M

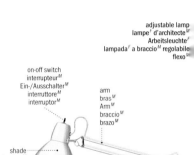

bed lamp
lampe^F liseuse
Leseleuchte^F
lampada^F da lettura^F
lámpara^F de cabecera^F

shade
abat-jour^M
Schirm^M
paralume^M
pantalla^F

base
socle^M
Sockel^M
base^F
base^F

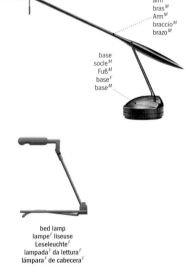

stand
pied^M
Fuß^M
base^F
pedestal^M

standard lamp
lampadaire^M
Standleuchte^F
lampada^F a stelo^M
lámpara^F de pie^M

table lamp
lampe^F de table^F
Tischleuchte^F
lampada^F da tavolo^M
lámpara^F de mesa^F

desk lamp
lampe^F de bureau^M
Schreibtischleuchte^F
lampada^F da tavolo^M
lámpara^F de escritorio^M

HOUSE

chandelier
lustre^M
Kronleuchter^M
lampadario^M
araña^F

sconce
coupelle^F
Teller^M
coppetta^F
arandela^F

crystal drop
pendeloque^F
Kristalltropfen^M
goccia^F di cristallo^M
colgante^M

crystal button
pampille^F
Koppen^M
perlina^F di cristallo^M
gota^F

column
fût^M
Mittelsäule^F
colonna^F
columna^F

track lighting
rail^M d'éclairage^M
Beleuchtungsschiene^F
faretto^M da binario^M
riel^M de iluminación^F

track frame
gouttière^F
Schiene^F
binario^M
armazón^M

contact lever
manette^F de contact^M
Befestigungshebel^M
leva^F di contatto^M
interruptor^M

transformer
transformateur^M
Transformator^M
trasformatore^M
transformador^M

spot
spot^M
Spot^M
faretto^M orientabile
foco^M

wall lantern
lanterne^F murale
Wandlaterne^F
lampione^M da parete^F
farol^M

swivel wall lamp
applique^F orientable
Scherenleuchte^F
lampada^F da parete^M con braccio^M estensibile
lámpara^F orientable de pared^F

wall light
applique^F
Wandleuchte^F
lampada^F da parete^F
aplique^M

multiple light fitting
rampe^F d'éclairage^M
Lampenreihe^F
lampade^F in serie^F
lámparas^F en serie^F

post lantern
lanterne^F de pied^M
Straßenlaterne^F
lampione^M
farola^F

domestic appliances

appareils^M électroménagers | Haushaltsgeräte^N | elettrodomestici^M | aparatos^M electrodomésticos

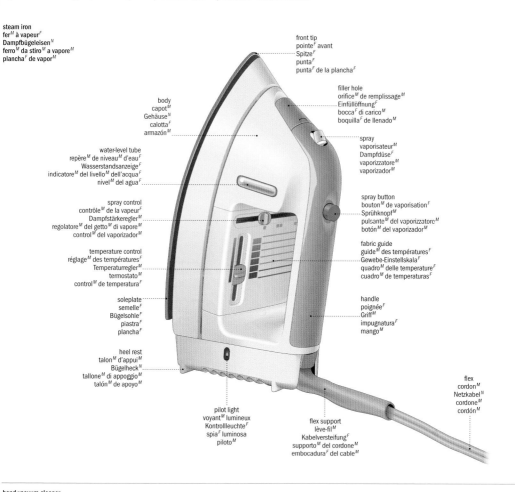

steam iron
fer^M à vapeur^F
Dampfbügeleisen^N
ferro^M da stiro^M a vapore^M
plancha^F de vapor^M

front tip
pointe^F avant
Spitze^F
punta^F
punta^F de la plancha^F

body
capot^M
Gehäuse^N
calotta^F
armazón^M

filler hole
orifice^M de remplissage^M
Einfüllöffnung^F
bocca^F di carico^M
boquilla^F de llenado^M

water-level tube
repère^M de niveau^M d'eau^F
Wasserstandsanzeige^F
indicatore^M del livello^M dell'acqua^F
nivel^M del agua^F

spray
vaporisateur^M
Dampfdüse^F
vaporizzatore^M
vaporizador^M

spray control
contrôle^M de la vapeur^F
Dampfstärkeregler^M
regolatore^M del getto^M di vapore^M
control^M del vaporizador^M

spray button
bouton^M de vaporisation^F
Sprühknopf^M
pulsante^M del vaporizzatore^M
botón^M del vaporizador^M

temperature control
réglage^M des températures^F
Temperaturregler^M
termostato^M
control^M de temperatura^F

fabric guide
guide^M des températures^F
Gewebe-Einstellskala^F
quadro^M delle temperature^F
cuadro^M de temperaturas^F

soleplate
semelle^F
Bügelsohle^F
piastra^F
plancha^F

handle
poignée^F
Griff^M
impugnatura^F
mango^M

heel rest
talon^M d'appui^M
Bügelheck^N
tallone^M di appoggio^M
talón^M de apoyo^M

flex
cordon^M
Netzkabel^N
cordone^M
cordón^M

pilot light
voyant^M lumineux
Kontrollleuchte^F
spia^F luminosa
piloto^M

flex support
lève-fil^M
Kabelversteifung^F
supporto^M del cordone^M
embocadura^F del cable^M

hand vacuum cleaner
aspirateur^M à main^F
Akku-Mini-Staubsauger^M
miniaspiratutto^M
aspirador^M manual

locking button
verrouillage^M
Entriegelungstaste^F
pulsante^M di bloccaggio^M
botón^M de cierre^M

on-off switch
interrupteur^M
Ein-/Ausschalter^M
interruttore^M
interruptor^M

dust receiver
godet^M à poussière^F
Staubbehälter^M
vano^M raccoglipolvere
depósito^M de polvo^M

recharging base
socle^M-chargeur^M
Lade-Anschlussbuchse^F
presa^F per ricarica^F
cargador^M

motor unit
bloc^M-moteur^M
Motorblock^M
blocco^M motore^M
motor^M

upright vacuum cleaner
aspirateur^M-balai^M
Handstaubsauger^M
aspirapolvere^M verticale
escoba^F eléctrica

on/off switch
interrupteur^M
Ein-/Ausschalter^M
interruttore^M
interruptor^M on/off

tool storage area
compartiment^M d'accessoires^M
Zubehörfach^N
scomparto^M degli accessori^M
cajetín^M de accesorios

hose
tuyau^M flexible
Schlauch^M
tubo^M flessibile
tubo^M flexible

bag compartment
compartiment^M de sac^M
Beutelfach^N
scomparto^M del sacchetto^M
cajetín^M portabolsa

cleaner height adjustment knob
sélecteur^M de hauteur^F
Höhenverstellung^F
opola^F di regolazione^F dell'altezza^F
alanca^F de regulación^F de altura^F

brush
brosse^F
Bürste^F
spazzola^F
cepillo^M

tools
accessoires^M
Zubehör^N
accessori^M
accesorios^M

extension tube
rallonge^F
Ansatzrohr^N
tubo^M rigido di prolunga^F
tubo^M de extensión^F

flex
cordon^M
Kabel^N
cordone^M
cordón^M

carpet and floor brush
suceur^M à tapis^M et planchers^M
Bodendüse^F
spazzola^F per tappeti^M e pavimenti^M
boquilla^F para suelos^M y alfombras^F

cylinder vacuum cleaner
aspirateur^M-traineau^F
Bodenstaubsauger^M
aspirapolvere^M
aspirador^M

locking device
système^M de verrouillage^M
Verschluss^M
dispositivo^M di bloccaggio^M
seguro^M

rigid tube
tube^M droit
Saugrohr^N
tubo^M rigido
tubo^M rígido

flexible hose
tuyau^M flexible
flexibler Schlauch^M
tubo^M flessibile
tubo^M flexible

ventilating grille
grille^F de ventilation^F
Luftaustrittsschlitz^M
griglia^F di ventilazione^F
rejilla^F del ventilador^M

on-off switch
interrupteur^M
Ein-/Ausschalter^M
interruttore^M
interruptor^M

bumper
pare-chocs^M
Stoßleiste^F
protezione^F antiurto
tope^M amortiguador

caster
roulette^F
Lenkrolle^F
ruota^F orientabile
ruedecilla^F

handle
poignée^F
Tragegriff^M
maniglia^F
asa^F

hood
capot^M
Haube^F
calotta^F
tapa^F

cleaning tools
accessoires^M
Saugzubehör^N
accessori^M di pulitura^F
accesorios^M

HOUSE

upholstery nozzle
suceur^M triangulaire à tissus^M
Polsterdüse^F
bocchetta^F per tappezzeria^F
boquilla^F para tapicería^F

dusting brush
brosse^F à épousseter
Saugbürste^F
spazzola^F a pennello^M
cepillo^M-plumero^M

crevice tool
suceur^M plat
Fugendüse^F
bocchetta^F per fessure^F
boquilla^F rinconera

floor brush
brosse^F à planchers^M
Bürste^F
spazzola^F per pavimenti^M
cepillo^M para suelos^M

domestic appliances

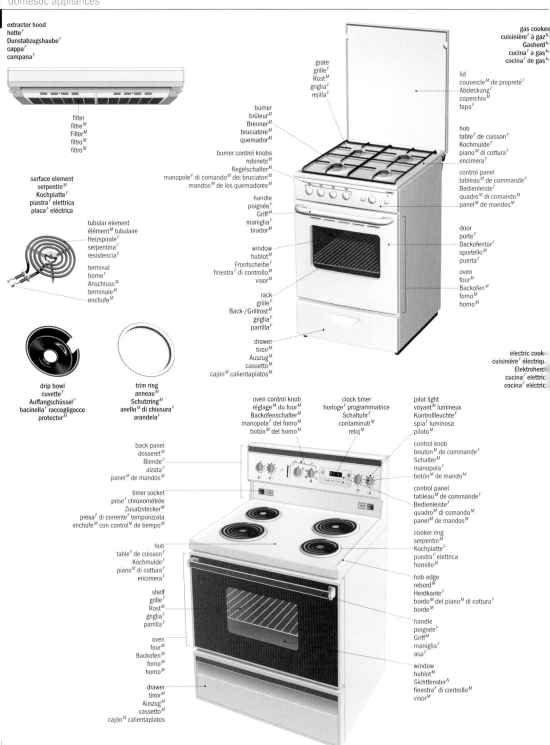

extractor hood
hotte^F
Dunstabzugshaube^F
cappa^F
campana^F

filter
filtre^M
Filter^M
filtro^M
filtro^M

surface element
serpentin^M
Kochplatte^F
piastra^F elettrica
placa^F eléctrica

tubular element
élément^M tubulaire
Heizspirale^F
serpentina^F
resistencia^F

terminal
borne^F
Anschluss^M
terminale^M
enchufe^M

drip bowl
cuvette^F
Auffangschüssel^F
bacinella^F raccogligocce
protector^M

trim ring
anneau^M
Schutzring^F
anello^M di chiusura^F
arandela^F

grate
grille^F
Rost^M
griglia^F
rejilla^F

burner
brûleur^M
Brenner^M
bruciatore^M
quemador^M

burner control knobs
Regelschalter^M
manopole^F di comando^M dei bruciatori^M
mandos^M de los quemadores^M

handle
poignée^F
Griff^M
maniglia^F
tirador^M

window
hublot^M
Frontscheibe^F
finestra^F di controllo^M
visor^M

rack
grille^F
Back-/Grillrost^M
griglia^F
parrilla^F

drawer
tiroir^M
Auszug^M
cassetto^M
cajón^M calientaplatos^M

gas cooker
cuisinière^F à gaz^M
Gasherd^M
cucina^F a gas^M
cocina^F de gas^M

lid
couvercle^M de propreté^F
Abdeckung^F
coperchio^M
tapa^F

hob
table^F de cuisson^F
Kochmulde^F
piano^M di cottura^F
encimera^F

control panel
tableau^M de commande^F
Bedienleiste^F
quadro^M di comando^M
panel^M de mandos^M

door
porte^F
Backofentür^F
sportello^M
puerta^F

oven
four^M
Backofen^M
forno^M
horno^M

electric cooker
cuisinière^F électrique
Elektroherd^M
cucina^F elettrica
cocina^F eléctrica

oven control knob
réglage^M du four^M
Backofenschalter^M
manopola^F del forno^M
botón^M del horno^M

clock timer
horloge^F programmatrice
Schaltuhr^F
contaminuti^M
reloj^M

pilot light
voyant^M lumineux
Kontrollleuchte^F
spia^F luminosa
piloto^M

back panel
dosseret^M
Blende^F
alzata^F
panel^M de mandos^M

timer socket
prise^F chronométrée
Zusatzstecker^M
presa^F di corrente^F temporizzata
enchufe^M con control^M de tiempo^M

control knob
bouton^M de commande^F
Schalter^M
manopola^F
botón^M de mando^M

control panel
tableau^M de commande^F
Bedienleiste^F
quadro^M di comando^M
panel^M de mandos^M

hob
table^F de cuisson^F
Kochmulde^F
piano^M di cottura^F
encimera^F

cooker ring
serpentin^M
Kochplatte^F
piastra^F elettrica
hornillo^M

shelf
grille^F
Rost^M
griglia^F
parrilla^F

hob edge
rebord^M
Herdkante^F
bordo^M del piano^M di cottura^F
borde^M

oven
four^M
Backofen^M
forno^M
horno^M

handle
poignée^F
Griff^M
maniglia^F
asa^F

window
hublot^M
Sichtfenster^N
finestra^F di controllo^M
visor^M

drawer
tiroir^M
Auszug^M
cassetto^M
cajón^M calientaplatos^M

HOUSE

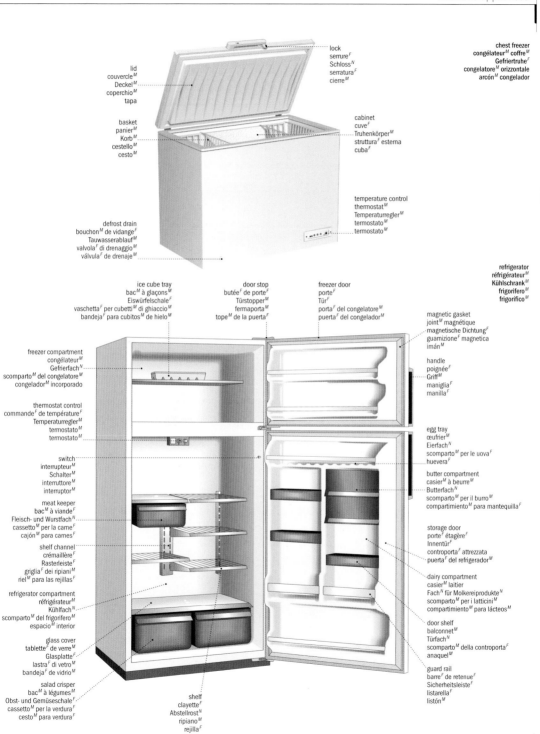

chest freezer
congélateur^M coffre^M
Gefriertruhe^F
congelatore^M orizzontale
arcón^M congelador

lock
serrure^F
Schloss^N
serratura^F
cierre^M

lid
couvercle^M
Deckel^M
coperchio^M
tapa

basket
panier^M
Korb^M
cestello^M
cesto^M

cabinet
cuve^F
Truhenkörper^M
struttura^F esterna
cuba^F

temperature control
thermostat^M
Temperaturregler^M
termostato^M
termostato^M

defrost drain
bouchon^M de vidange^F
Tauwasserablauf^M
valvola^F di drenaggio^M
válvula^F de drenaje^M

refrigerator
réfrigérateur^M
Kühlschrank^M
frigorifero^M
frigorífico^M

ice cube tray
bac^M à glaçons^M
Eiswürfelschale^F
vaschetta^F per cubetti^M di ghiaccio^M
bandeja^F para cubitos^M de hielo^M

door stop
butée^F de porte^F
Türstopper^M
fermaporta^F
tope^M de la puerta^F

freezer door
porte^F
Tür^F
porta^F del congelatore^M
puerta^F del congelador^M

magnetic gasket
joint^M magnétique
magnetische Dichtung^F
guarnizione^F magnetica
imán^M

freezer compartment
congélateur^M
Gefrierfach^N
scomparto^M del congelatore^M
congelador^M incorporado

handle
poignée^F
Griff^M
maniglia^F
manilla^F

thermostat control
commande^F de température^F
Temperaturregler^M
termostato^M
termostato^M

egg tray
œufrier^M
Eierfach^N
scomparto^M per le uova^F
huevera^F

switch
interrupteur^M
Schalter^M
interruttore^M
interruptor^M

butter compartment
casier^M à beurre^M
Butterfach^N
scomparto^M per il burro^M
compartimiento^M para mantequilla^F

meat keeper
bac^M à viande^F
Fleisch- und Wurstfach^N
cassetto^M per la carne^F
cajón^M para carnes^F

storage door
porte^F étagère^F
Innentür^F
controporta^F attrezzata
puerta^F del refrigerador^M

shelf channel
crémaillère^F
Rasterleiste^F
griglia^F dei ripiani^M
riel^M para las rejillas^F

dairy compartment
casier^M laitier
Fach^N für Molkereiprodukte^N
scomparto^M per i latticini^M
compartimiento^M para lácteos^M

refrigerator compartment
réfrigérateur^M
Kühlfach^N
scomparto^M del frigorifero^M
espacio^M interior

door shelf
balconnet^M
Türfach^N
scomparto^M della controporta^F
anaquel^M

glass cover
tablette^F de verre^F
Glasplatte^F
lastra^F di vetro^M
bandeja^F de vidrio^M

guard rail
barre^F de retenue^F
Sicherheitsleiste^F
listarella^F
listón^M

salad crisper
bac^M à légumes^M
Obst- und Gemüseschale^F
cassetto^M per la verdura^F
cesto^M para verdura^F

shelf
clayette^F
Abstellrost^N
ripiano^M
rejilla^F

HOUSE

211

domestic appliances

HOUSE

washing machine
lave-linge^M
Waschmaschine^F
lavatrice^F
lavadora^F

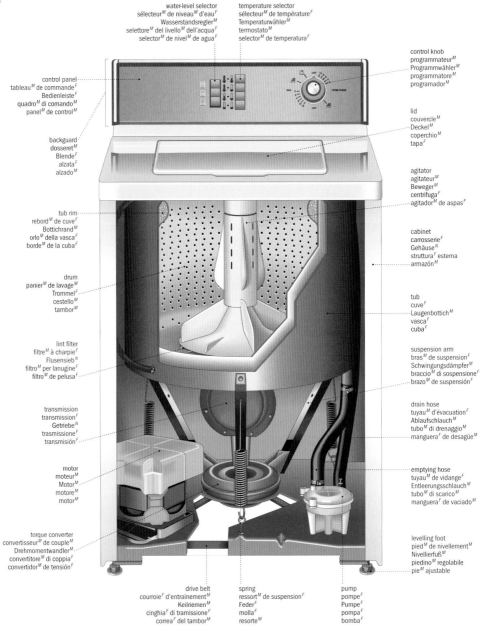

water-level selector
sélecteur^M de niveau^M d'eau^F
Wasserstandsregler^M
selettore^M del livello^M dell'acqua^F
selector^M de nivel^M de agua^F

temperature selector
sélecteur^M de température^F
Temperaturwähler^M
termostato^M
selector^M de temperatura^F

control knob
programmateur^M
Programmwähler^M
programmatore^M
programador^M

control panel
tableau^M de commande^F
Bedienleiste^F
quadro^M di comando^M
panel^M de control^M

backguard
dosseret^M
Blende^F
alzata^F
alzado^M

lid
couvercle^M
Deckel^M
coperchio^M
tapa^F

agitator
agitateur^M
Beweger^M
centrifuga^F
agitador^M de aspas^F

tub rim
rebord^M de cuve^F
Bottichrand^M
orlo^M della vasca^F
borde^M de la cuba^F

cabinet
carrosserie^F
Gehäuse^N
struttura^F esterna
armazón^M

drum
panier^M de lavage^M
Trommel^F
cestello^M
tambor^M

tub
cuve^F
Laugenbottich^M
vasca^F
cuba^F

lint filter
filtre^M à charpie^F
Flusensieb^N
filtro^M per lanugine^F
filtro^M de pelusa^F

suspension arm
bras^M de suspension^F
Schwingungsdämpfer^M
braccio^M di sospensione^F
brazo^M de suspensión^F

transmission
transmission^F
Getriebe^N
trasmissione^F
transmisión^F

drain hose
tuyau^M d'évacuation^F
Ablaufschlauch^M
tubo^M di drenaggio^M
manguera^F de desagüe^M

motor
moteur^M
Motor^M
motore^M
motor^M

emptying hose
tuyau^M de vidange^F
Entleerungsschlauch^M
tubo^M di scarico^M
manguera^F de vaciado^M

torque converter
convertisseur^M de couple^M
Drehmomentwandler^M
convertitore^M di coppia^F
convertidor^M de tensión^F

levelling foot
pied^M de nivellement^M
Nivellierfuß^M
piedino^M regolabile
pie^M ajustable

drive belt
courroie^F d'entrainement^M
Keilriemen^M
cinghia^F di tramissione^F
correa^F del tambor^M

spring
ressort^M de suspension^F
Feder^F
molla^F
resorte^M

pump
pompe^F
Pumpe^F
pompa^F
bomba^F

electric tumble dryer
sèche-linge^M électrique
Wäschetrockner^M
asciugatrice^F
secadora^F de ropa^F

HOUSE

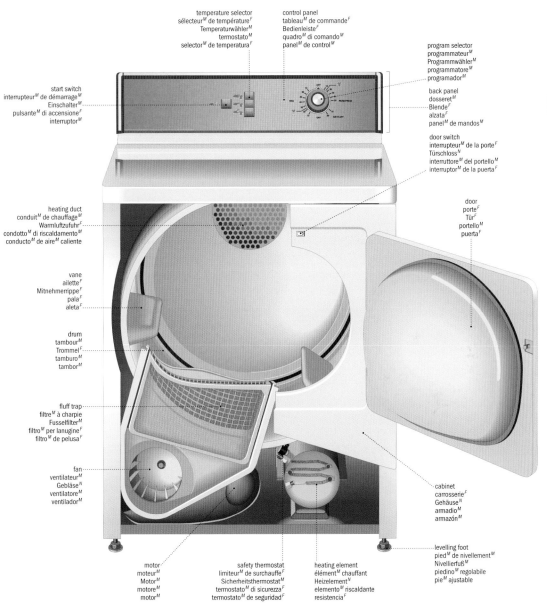

temperature selector
sélecteur^M de température^F
Temperaturwähler^M
termostato^M
selector^M de temperatura^F

control panel
tableau^M de commande^F
Bedienleiste^F
quadro^M di comando^M
panel^M de control^M

program selector
programmateur^M
Programmwähler^M
programmatore^M
programador^M

start switch
interrupteur de démarrage^M
Einschalter^M
pulsante^M di accensione^F
interruptor^M

back panel
dosseret^M
Blende^F
alzata^F
panel^M de mandos^M

door switch
interrupteur^M de la porte^F
Türschloss^N
interruttore^M del portello^M
interruptor^M de la puerta^F

heating duct
conduit^M de chauffage^M
Warmluftzufuhr^F
condotto^M di riscaldamento^M
conducto^M de aire^M caliente

door
porte^F
Tür^F
portello^M
puerta^F

vane
ailette^F
Mitnehmerrippe^F
pala^F
aleta^F

drum
tambour^M
Trommel^F
tamburo^M
tambor^M

fluff trap
filtre^M à charpie
Fusselfilter^M
filtro^M per lanugine^F
filtro^M de pelusa^F

fan
ventilateur^M
Gebläse^N
ventilatore^M
ventilador^M

cabinet
carrosserie^F
Gehäuse^N
armadio^M
armazón^M

levelling foot
pied^M de nivellement^M
Nivellierfuß^M
piedino^M regolabile
pie^M ajustable

motor
moteur^M
Motor^M
motore^M
motor^M

safety thermostat
limiteur^M de surchauffe^F
Sicherheitsthermostat^M
termostato^M di sicurezza^F
termostato^M de seguridad^F

heating element
élément^M chauffant
Heizelement^N
elemento^M riscaldante
resistencia^F

domestic appliances

HOUSE

control panel
tableau^M de commande^F
Bedienleiste^F
quadro^M di comando^M
panel^M de control^M

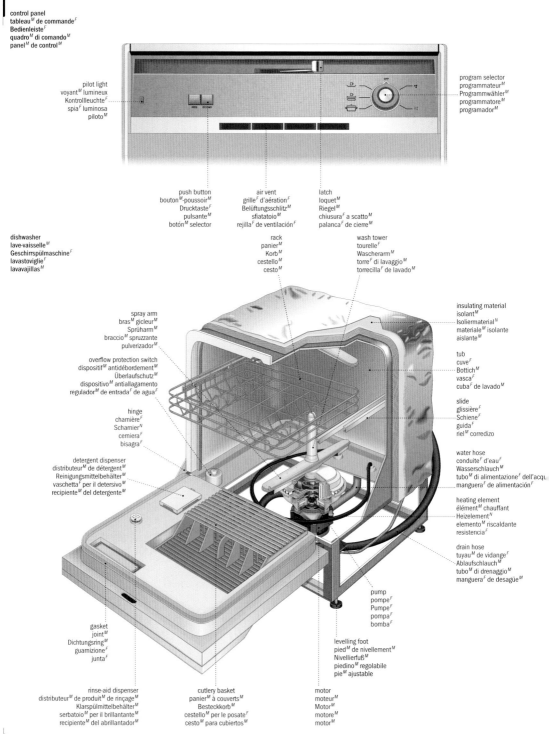

pilot light
voyant^M lumineux
Kontrollleuchte^F
spia^F luminosa
piloto^M

program selector
programmateur^M
Programmwähler^M
programmatore^M
programador^M

push button
bouton^M-poussoir^M
Drucktaste^F
pulsante^M
botón^M selector

air vent
grille^F d'aération^F
Belüftungsschlitz^M
sfiatatoio^M
rejilla^F de ventilación^F

latch
loquet^M
Riegel^M
chiusura^F a scatto^M
palanca^F de cierre^M

dishwasher
lave-vaisselle^M
Geschirrspülmaschine^F
lavastoviglie^F
lavavajillas^M

rack
panier^M
Korb^M
cestello^M
cesto^M

wash tower
tourelle^F
Wascherarm^M
torre^F di lavaggio^M
torrecilla^F de lavado^M

spray arm
bras^M gicleur^M
Sprüharm^M
braccio^M spruzzante
pulverizador^M

overflow protection switch
dispositif^M antidébordement^M
Überlaufschutz^M
dispositivo^M antiallagamento
regulador^M de entrada^F de agua^F

hinge
charnière^F
Scharnier^N
cerniera^F
bisagra^F

detergent dispenser
distributeur^M de détergent^M
Reinigungsmittelbehälter^M
vaschetta^F per il detersivo^M
recipiente^M del detergente^M

insulating material
isolant^M
Isoliermaterial^N
materiale^M isolante
aislante^M

tub
cuve^F
Bottich^M
vasca^F
cuba^F de lavado^M

slide
glissière^F
Schiene^F
guida^F
riel^M corredizo

water hose
conduite^F d'eau^F
Wasserschlauch^M
tubo^M di alimentazione^F dell'acqu
manguera^F de alimentación^F

heating element
élément^M chauffant
Heizelement^N
elemento^M riscaldante
resistencia^F

drain hose
tuyau^M de vidange^F
Ablaufschlauch^M
tubo^M di drenaggio^M
manguera^F de desagüe^M

pump
pompe^F
Pumpe^F
pompa^F
bomba^F

gasket
joint^M
Dichtungsring^M
guarnizione^F
junta^F

levelling foot
pied^M de nivellement^M
Nivellierfuß^M
piedino^M regolabile
pie^M ajustable

rinse-aid dispenser
distributeur^M de produit^M de rinçage^F
Klarspülmittelbehälter^M
serbatoio^M per il brillantante^M
recipiente^M del abrillantador^M

cutlery basket
panier^M à couverts^M
Besteckkorb^M
cestello^M per le posate^F
cesto^M para cubiertos^M

motor
moteur^M
Motor^M
motore^M
motor^M

household equipment

articles^M ménagers | Haushaltsgegenstände^M | attrezzi^M domestici | artículos^M de limpieza^F

kitchen towel
torchon^M
Geschirrtuch^N
strofinaccio^M da cucina^F
bayeta^F de cocina^F

dustpan
pelle^F à poussière^F
Kehrschaufel^F
paletta^F
recogedor^M

broom
balai^M
Besen^M
scopa^F
escoba^F

mop
balai^M à franges^F
Mop^M
scopa^F a frangia^F
fregona^F

scouring pad
éponge^F à récurer
Putzschwamm^M
spugna^F abrasiva
estropajo^M con esponja^F

brush
brosse^F
Bürste^F
spazzola^F
cepillo^M

block
monture^F
Bürstenkörper^M
dorso^M
lomo^M

fibres
fibres^F
Borsten^F
setole^F
cerdas^F

handle
manche^M
Stiel^M
manico^M
palo^M

refuse container
poubelle^F
Abfalleimer^M
bidone^M dei rifiuti^M
cubo^M de basura^F

lid
couvercle^M
Deckel^M
coperchio^M
tapa^F

fibres
fibres^F
Borsten^F
setole^F
cerdas^F

handle
poignée^F
Griff^M
manico^M
asa^F

bucket
seau^M
Eimer^M
secchio^M
cubo^M

pouring spout
bec^M verseur
Ausguss^M
beccuccio^M
pitorro^M

handle
anse^F
Henkel^M
manico^M
asa^F

HOUSE

plumbing tools

plomberie^F : outils^M | Klempnerwerkzeuge^N | attrezzi^M idraulici | fontanería^F : herramientas^F

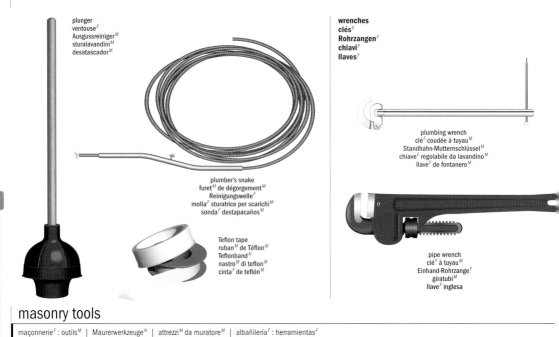

plunger
ventouse^F
Ausgussreiniger^M
sturalavandini^M
desatascador^M

wrenches
clés^F
Rohrzangen^F
chiavi^F
llaves^F

plumbing wrench
clé^F coudée à tuyau^M
Standhahn-Mutternschlüssel^M
chiave^F regolabile da lavandino^M
llave^F de fontanero^M

plumber's snake
furet^M de dégorgement^M
Reinigungswelle^F
molla^F sturatrice per scarichi^M
sonda^F destapacaños^M

Teflon tape
ruban^M de Téflon^M
Teflonband^N
nastro^M di teflon^M
cinta^F de teflón^M

pipe wrench
clé^F à tuyau^M
Einhand-Rohrzange^F
giratubi^M
llave^F inglesa

masonry tools

maçonnerie^F : outils^M | Maurerwerkzeuge^N | attrezzi^M da muratore^M | albañilería^F : herramientas^F

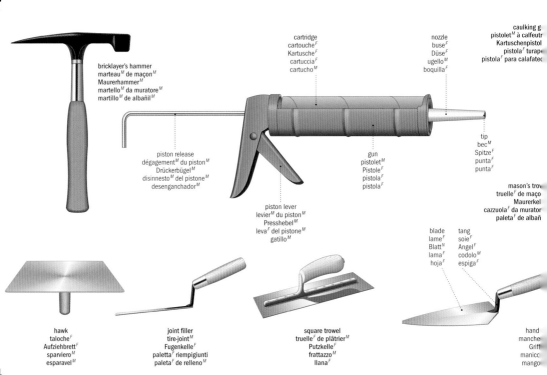

bricklayer's hammer
marteau^M de maçon^M
Maurerhammer^M
martello^M da muratore^M
martillo^M de albañil^M

cartridge
cartouche^F
Kartusche^F
cartuccia^F
cartucho^M

nozzle
buse^F
Düse^F
ugello^M
boquilla^F

caulking g
pistolet^M à calfeutr
Kartuschenpistol
pistola^F turape
pistola^F para calafatec

piston release
dégagement^M du piston^M
Drückerbügel^M
disinnesto^M del pistone^M
desenganchador^M

tip
bec^M
Spitze^F
punta^F
punta^F

gun
pistolet^M
Pistole^F
pistola^F
pistola^F

mason's trov
truelle^F de maço
Maurerkel
cazzuola^F da murator
paleta^F de albañ

piston lever
levier^M du piston^M
Presshebel^M
leva^F del pistone^M
gatillo^M

blade
lame^N
Blatt^N
lama^F
hoja^F

tang
soie^F
Angel^F
codolo^M
espiga^F

hawk
taloche^F
Aufziehbrett^F
sparviero^M
esparavel^M

joint filler
tire-joint^M
Fugenkelle^F
paletta^F riempigiunti
paleta^F de relleno^M

square trowel
truelle^F de plâtrier^M
Putzkelle^F
frattazzo^M
llana^F

hand
manche
Griff
manicc
mango

DO-IT-YOURSELF AND GARDENING

electricity tools

électricité^F : outils^M | Elektroinstallateurwerkzeuge^N | attrezzatura^F elettrica | electricidad^F : herramientas^F

inspection light
baladeuse^F
Handlampe^F
lampada^F portatile a gabbia^F
linterna^F movible

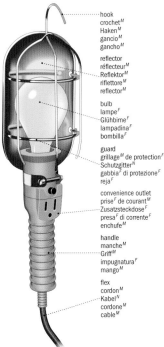

hook
crochet^M
Haken^M
gancio^M
gancho^M

reflector
réflecteur^M
Reflektor^M
riflettore^M
reflector^M

bulb
lampe^F
Glühbirne^F
lampadina^F
bombilla^F

guard
grillage^M de protection^F
Schutzgitter^N
gabbia^F di protezione^F
reja^F

convenience outlet
prise^F de courant^M
Zusatzsteckdose^F
presa^F di corrente^F
enchufe^M

handle
manche^M
Griff^M
impugnatura^F
mango^M

flex
cordon^M
Kabel^N
cordone^M
cable^M

test-lamp
vérificateur^M de circuit^M
Prüflampe^F
lampada^F provacircuiti
lámpara^F de prueba^F de neón^M

tester screwdriver
vérificateur^M de tension^F
Spannungsprüfer^M
cercafase^M
detector^M de tensión^F

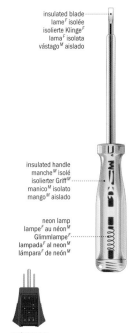

insulated blade
lame^F isolée
isolierte Klinge^F
lama^F isolata
vástago^M aislado

insulated handle
manche^M isolé
isolierter Griff^M
manico^M isolato
mango^M aislado

neon lamp
lampe^F au néon^M
Glimmlampe^F
lampada^F al neon^M
lámpara^F de neón^M

wire nut
capuchon^M de connexion^F
Kabeltülle^F
proteggicavo^M
capuchón^M de plástico^M

socket tester
vérificateur^M de prise^F de courant^M
Steckdosenprüfer^M
tester^M di presa^F
probador^M de contactos^M con tierra^F

multipurpose tool
pince^F universelle
Mehrzweckzange^F
pinza^F multiuso
pinzas^F multiuso

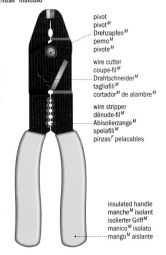

pivot
pivot^M
Drehzapfen^M
perno^M
pivote^M

wire cutter
coupe-fil^M
Drahtschneider^M
tagliafili^M
cortador^M de alambre^M

wire stripper
dénude-fil^M
Abisolierzange^M
spelafili^M
pinzas^F pelacables

insulated handle
manche^M isolant
isolierter Griff^M
manico^M isolato
mango^M aislante

needle-nose pliers
pince^F à long bec^M
Spitzzange^F
pinza^F a becchi^M lunghi
alicates^M de punta^F

combination pliers
pince^F d'électricien^M
Kombizange^F
pinza^F universale
alicates^M de electricista^M

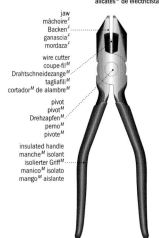

jaw
mâchoire^F
Backen^F
ganascia^F
mordaza^F

wire cutter
coupe-fil^M
Drahtschneidezange^M
tagliafili^M
cortador^M de alambre^M

pivot
pivot^M
Drehzapfen^M
perno^M
pivote^M

insulated handle
manche^M isolant
isolierter Griff^M
manico^M isolato
mango^M aislante

soldering and welding tools

soudage^M : outils^M | Löt- und Schweißwerkzeuge^N | attrezzi^M di brasatura^F e saldatura^F | herramientas^F de soldadura^F

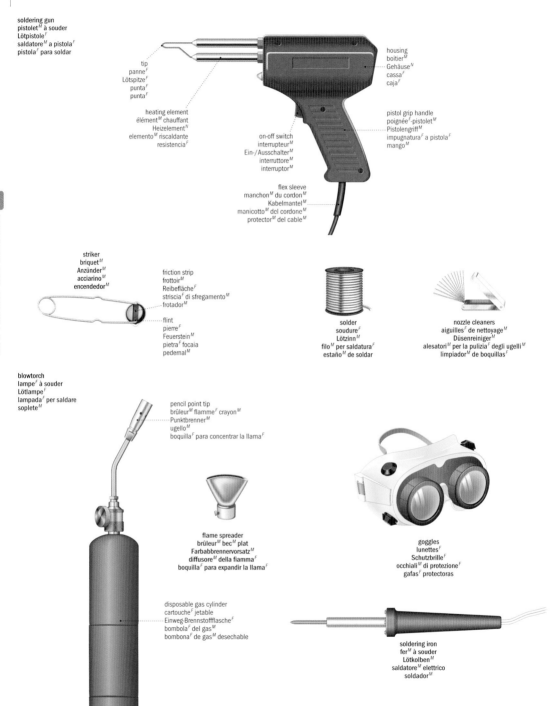

soldering gun
pistolet^M à souder
Lötpistole^F
saldatore^M a pistola^F
pistola^F para soldar

tip
panne^F
Lötspitze^F
punta^F
punta^F

heating element
élément^M chauffant
Heizelement^N
elemento^M riscaldante
resistencia^F

housing
boîtier^M
Gehäuse^N
cassa^F
caja^F

pistol grip handle
poignée^F-pistolet^M
Pistolengriff^M
impugnatura^F a pistola^F
mango^M

on-off switch
interrupteur^M
Ein-/Ausschalter^M
interruttore^M
interruptor^M

flex sleeve
manchon^M du cordon^M
Kabelmantel^M
manicotto^M del cordone^M
protector^M del cable^M

striker
briquet^M
Anzünder^M
acciarino^M
encendedor^M

friction strip
frottoir^M
Reibefläche^F
striscia^F di sfregamento^M
frotador^M

flint
pierre^F
Feuerstein^M
pietra^F focaia
pedernal^M

solder
soudure^F
Lötzinn^M
filo^M per saldatura^F
estaño^M de soldar

nozzle cleaners
aiguilles^F de nettoyage^M
Düsenreiniger^M
alesatori^M per la pulizia^F degli ugelli^M
limpiador^M de boquillas^F

blowtorch
lampe^F à souder
Lötlampe^F
lampada^F per saldare
soplete^M

pencil point tip
brûleur^M flamme^F crayon^M
Punktbrenner^M
ugello^M
boquilla^F para concentrar la llama^F

flame spreader
brûleur^M bec^M plat
Farbabbrennervorsatz^M
diffusore^M della fiamma^F
boquilla^F para expandir la llama^F

goggles
lunettes^F
Schutzbrille^F
occhiali^M di protezione^F
gafas^F protectoras

disposable gas cylinder
cartouche^F jetable
Einweg-Brennstoffflasche^F
bombola^F del gas^M
bombona^F de gas^M desechable

soldering iron
fer^M à souder
Lötkolben^M
saldatore^M elettrico
soldador^M

painting upkeep

peinture^F d'entretien^M | Anstreichen^N und Lackieren^N | verniciatura^F: manutenzione^F | mantenimiento^M de pinturas^F

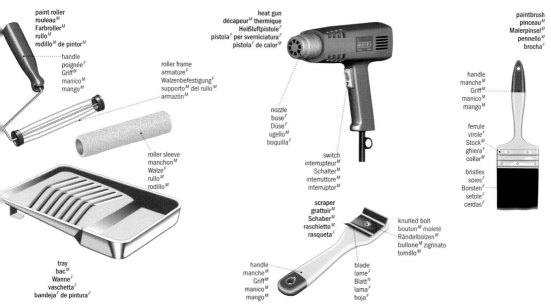

paint roller
rouleau^M
Farbroller^M
rullo^M
rodillo^M de pintor^M

handle
poignée^F
Griff^M
manico^M
mango^M

roller frame
armature^F
Walzenbefestigung^F
supporto^M del rullo^M
armazón^M

roller sleeve
manchon^M
Walze^F
rullo^M
rodillo^M

tray
bac^M
Wanne^F
vaschetta^F
bandeja^F de pintura^F

heat gun
décapeur^M thermique
Heißluftpistole^F
pistola^F per sverniciatura^F
pistola^F de calor^M

nozzle
buse^F
Düse^F
ugello^M
boquilla^F

switch
interrupteur^M
Schalter^M
interruttore^M
interruptor^M

scraper
grattoir^M
Schaber^M
raschietto^M
rasqueta^F

handle
manche^M
Griff^M
manico^M
mango^M

knurled bolt
bouton^M moleté
Rändelbolzen^M
bullone^M zigrinato
tornillo^M

blade
lame^F
Blatt^N
lama^F
hoja^F

paintbrush
pinceau^M
Malerpinsel^M
pennello^M
brocha^F

handle
manche^M
Griff^M
manico^M
mango^M

ferrule
virole^F
Stock^M
ghiera^F
collar^M

bristles
soies^F
Borsten^F
setole^F
cerdas^F

ladders and stepladders

échelles^F et escabeaux^M | Leitern^F und Stehleitern^F | scale^F e scale^F a libretto^M | escaleras^F de mano^F

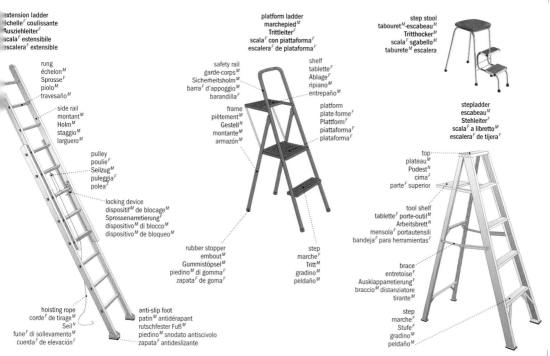

extension ladder
échelle^F coulissante
Ausziehleiter^F
scala^F estensibile
escalera^F extensible

rung
échelon^M
Sprosse^F
piolo^M
travesaño^M

side rail
montant^M
Holm^M
staggio^M
larguero^M

pulley
poulie^F
Seilzug^M
puleggia^F
polea^F

locking device
dispositif^M de blocage^M
Sprossenarretierung^F
dispositivo^M di blocco^M
dispositivo^M de bloqueo^M

hoisting rope
corde^F de tirage^M
Seil^N
fune^F di sollevamento^M
cuerda^F de elevación^F

platform ladder
marchepied^M
Trittleiter^F
scala^F con piattaforma^F
escalera^F de plataforma^F

safety rail
garde-corps^M
Sicherheitsholm^M
barra^F d'appoggio^M
barandilla^F

frame
piètement^M
Gestell^N
montante^M
armazón^M

rubber stopper
embout^M
Gummistöpsel^M
piedino^M di gomma^F
zapata^F de goma^F

anti-slip foot
patin^M antidérapant
rutschfester Fuß^M
piedino^M snodato antiscivolo
zapata^F antideslizante

shelf
tablette^F
Ablage^F
ripiano^M
entrepaño^M

platform
plate-forme^F
Plattform^F
piattaforma^F
plataforma^F

step
marche^F
Tritt^M
gradino^M
peldaño^M

step stool
tabouret^M-escabeau^M
Tritthocker^M
scala^F sgabello^M
taburete^M escalera

stepladder
escabeau^M
Stehleiter^F
scala^F a libretto^M
escalera^F de tijera^F

top
plateau^M
Podest^N
cima^F
parte^F superior

tool shelf
tablette^F porte-outil^M
Arbeitsbrett^N
mensola^F portautensili
bandeja^F para herramientas^F

brace
entretoise^F
Ausklapparretierung^F
braccio^M distanziatore
tirante^F

step
marche^F
Stufe^F
gradino^M
peldaño^M

carpentry: nailing tools

menuiserie^F : outils^M pour clouer | Bautischlerei^F: Nagelwerkzeuge^N | carpenteria^F: attrezzi^M per chiodare | carpintería: herramientas^F para clavar

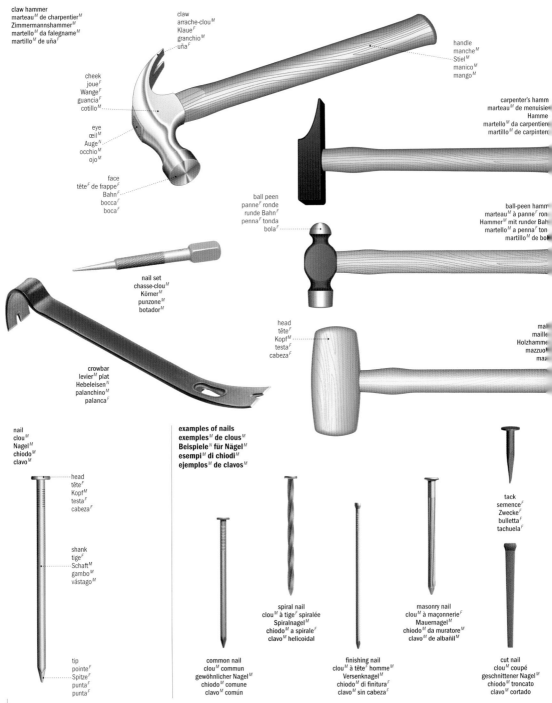

claw hammer
marteau^M de charpentier^M
Zimmermannshammer^M
martello^M da falegname^M
martillo^M de uña^F

claw
arrache-clou^M
Klaue^F
granchio^M
uña^F

handle
manche^M
Stiel^M
manico^M
mango^M

cheek
joue^F
Wange^F
guancia^F
cotillo^M

carpenter's hamm
marteau^M de menuisie
Hamme
martello^M da carpentiere
martillo^M de carpintero

eye
œil^M
Auge^N
occhio^M
ojo^M

face
tête^F de frappe^F
Bahn^F
bocca^F
boca^F

ball peen
panne^F ronde
runde Bahn^F
penna^F tonda
bola^F

ball-peen hamm
marteau^M à panne^F ron
Hammer^M mit runder Bah
martello^M a penna^F ton
martillo^M de bo

nail set
chasse-clou^M
Körner^M
punzone^M
botador^M

head
tête^F
Kopf^M
testa^F
cabeza^F

ma
maille
Holzhamme
mazzuo
maz

crowbar
levier^M plat
Hebeleisen^N
palanchino^M
palanca^F

nail
clou^M
Nagel^M
chiodo^M
clavo^M

examples of nails
exemples^M de clous^M
Beispiele^N für Nägel^M
esempi^M di chiodi^M
ejemplos^M de clavos^M

head
tête^F
Kopf^M
testa^F
cabeza^F

tack
semence^F
Zwecke^F
bulletta^F
tachuela^F

shank
tige^F
Schaft^M
gambo^M
vástago^M

spiral nail
clou^M à tige^F spiralée
Spiralnagel^M
chiodo^M a spirale^F
clavo^M helicoidal

masonry nail
clou^M à maçonnerie^F
Mauernagel^M
chiodo^M da muratore^M
clavo^M de albañil^M

tip
pointe^F
Spitze^F
punta^F
punta^F

common nail
clou^M commun
gewöhnlicher Nagel^M
chiodo^M comune
clavo^M común

finishing nail
clou^M à tête^F homme^M
Versenknagel^M
chiodo^M di finitura^F
clavo^M sin cabeza^F

cut nail
clou^M coupé
geschnittener Nagel^M
chiodo^M troncato
clavo^M cortado

carpentry: screwing tools

menuiserie^F : outils^M pour visser | Bautischlerei^F: Schraubwerkzeuge^N | carpenteria^F: utensili ^{M} per avvitare | carpintería^F : herramientas^F para atornillar

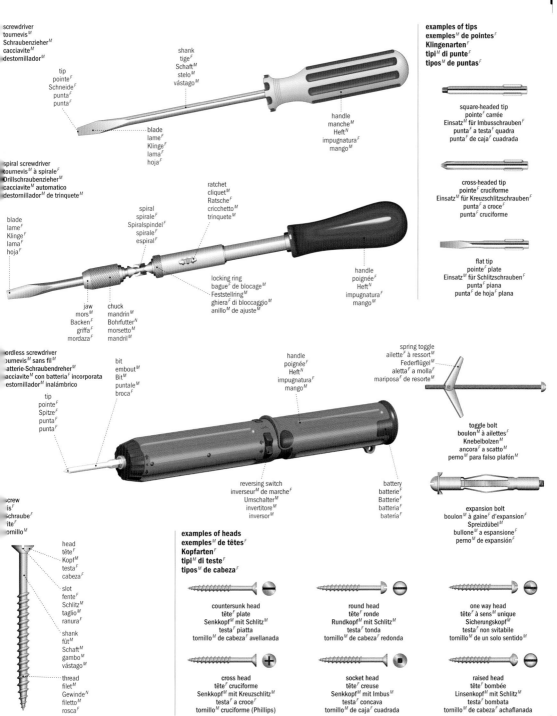

screwdriver
tournevis^M
Schraubenzieher^M
cacciavite^M
destornillador^M

tip
pointe^F
Schneide^F
punta^F
punta^F

shank
tige^F
Schaft^M
stelo^M
vástago^M

blade
lame^F
Klinge^F
lama^F
hoja^F

handle
manche^M
Heft^N
impugnatura^F
mango^M

spiral screwdriver
tournevis^M à spirale^F
Drillschraubenzieher^M
cacciavite^M automatico
destornillador^M de trinquete^M

blade
lame^F
Klinge^F
lama^F
hoja^F

spiral
spirale^F
Spiralspindel^F
spirale^F
espiral^F

ratchet
cliquet^M
Ratsche^F
cricchetto^M
trinquete^M

locking ring
bague^F de blocage^M
Feststellring^M
ghiera^F di bloccaggio^M
anillo^M de ajuste^M

handle
poignée^F
Heft^N
impugnatura^F
mango^M

jaw
mors^M
Backen^F
griffa^F
mordaza^F

chuck
mandrin^M
Bohrfutter^N
morsetto^M
mandril^M

cordless screwdriver
tournevis^M sans fil^M
Batterie-Schraubendreher^M
cacciavite^M con batteria^F incorporata
destornillador^M inalámbrico

bit
embout^M
Bit^M
puntale^M
broca^F

tip
pointe^F
Spitze^F
punta^F
punta^F

handle
poignée^F
Heft^N
impugnatura^F
mango^M

spring toggle
ailette^F à ressort^M
Federflügel^M
aletta^F a molla^F
mariposa^F de resorte^M

reversing switch
inverseur^M de marche^F
Umschalter^M
invertitore^M
inversor^M

battery
batterie^F
Batterie^F
batteria^F
batería^F

toggle bolt
boulon^M à ailettes^F
Knebelbolzen^M
ancora^F a scatto^M
perno^M para falso plafón^M

expansion bolt
boulon^M à gaine^F d'expansion^F
Spreizdübel^M
bullone^M a espansione^F
perno^M de expansión^F

screw
vis^F
Schraube^F
vite^F
tornillo^M

head
tête^F
Kopf^M
testa^F
cabeza^F

slot
fente^F
Schlitz^M
taglio^M
ranura^F

shank
fût^M
Schaft^M
gambo^M
vástago^M

thread
filet^M
Gewinde^N
filetto^M
rosca^F

examples of tips
exemples^M de pointes^F
Klingenarten^F
tipi^M di punte^F
tipos^M de puntas^F

square-headed tip
pointe^F carrée
Einsatz^M für Imbusschrauben^F
punta^F a testa^F quadra
punta^F de caja^F cuadrada

cross-headed tip
pointe^F cruciforme
Einsatz^M für Kreuzschlitzschrauben^F
punta^F a croce^F
punta^F cruciforme

flat tip
pointe^F plate
Einsatz^M für Schlitzschrauben^F
punta^F piana
punta^F de hoja^F plana

examples of heads
exemples^M de têtes^F
Kopfarten^F
tipi^M di teste^F
tipos^M de cabeza^F

countersunk head
tête^F plate
Senkkopf^M mit Schlitz^M
testa^F piatta
tornillo^M de cabeza^F avellanada

round head
tête^F ronde
Rundkopf^M mit Schlitz^M
testa^F tonda
tornillo^M de cabeza^F redonda

one way head
tête^F à sens^M unique
Sicherungskopf^M
testa^F non svitabile
tornillo^M de un solo sentido^M

cross head
tête^F cruciforme
Senkkopf^M mit Kreuzschlitz^M
testa^F a croce^F
tornillo^M cruciforme (Phillips)

socket head
tête^F creuse
Senkkopf^M mit Imbus^M
testa^F concava
tornillo^M de caja^F cuadrada

raised head
tête^F bombée
Linsenkopf^M mit Schlitz^M
testa^F bombata
tornillo^M de cabeza^F achaflanada

carpentry: gripping and tightening tools

menuiserie^F : outils^M pour serrer | Bautischlerei^F: Greif- und Spannwerkzeuge^N | carpenteria^F: attrezzi^M di serraggio^M | carpintería^F : herramientas^F para apretar

DO-IT-YOURSELF AND GARDENING

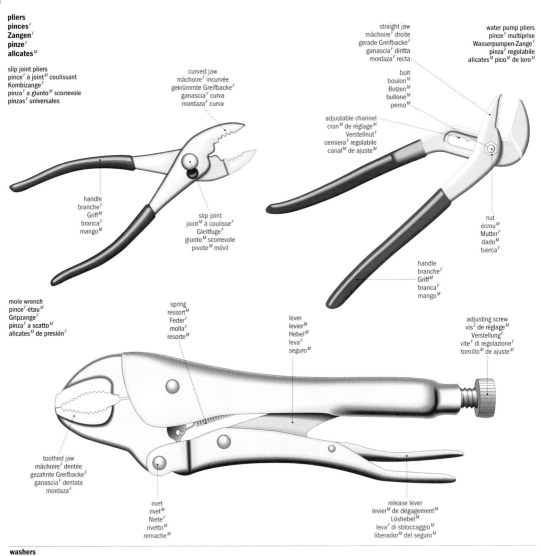

pliers
pinces^F
Zangen^F
pinze^F
alicates^M

slip joint pliers
pince^F à joint^M coulissant
Kombizange^F
pinza^F a giunto^M scorrevole
pinzas^F universales

curved jaw
mâchoire^F incurvée
gekrümmte Greifbacke^F
ganascia^F curva
mordaza^F curva

straight jaw
mâchoire^F droite
gerade Greifbacke^F
ganascia^F diritta
mordaza^F recta

water pump pliers
pince^F multiprise
Wasserpumpen-Zange^F
pinza^F regolabile
alicates^M pico^M de loro^M

bolt
boulon^M
Bolzen^M
bullone^M
perno^M

adjustable channel
cran^M de réglage^M
Verstellnut^F
cerniera^F regolabile
canal^M de ajuste^M

handle
branche^F
Griff^M
branca^F
mango^M

slip joint
joint^M à coulisse^F
Gleitfuge^F
giunto^M scorrevole
pivote^M móvil

nut
écrou^M
Mutter^F
dado^M
tuerca^F

handle
branche^F
Griff^M
branca^F
mango^M

mole wrench
pince^F-étau^M
Gripzange^F
pinza^F a scatto^M
alicates^M de presión^F

spring
ressort^M
Feder^F
molla^F
resorte^M

lever
levier^M
Hebel^M
leva^F
seguro^M

adjusting screw
vis^F de réglage^M
Verstellung^F
vite^F di regolazione^F
tornillo^M de ajuste^M

toothed jaw
mâchoire^F dentée
gezahnte Greifbacke^F
ganascia^F dentata
mordaza^F

rivet
rivet^M
Niete^F
rivetto^M
remache^M

release lever
levier^M de dégagement^M
Löshebel^M
leva^F di sbloccaggio^M
liberador^M del seguro^M

washers
rondelles^F
Unterlegscheiben^F
rosette^F
arandelas^F

flat washer
rondelle^F plate
Unterlegscheibe^F
rosetta^F piatta
arandela^F plana

spring washer
rondelle^F à ressort^M
Federring^M
rosetta^F elastica
arandela^F de presión^F

external tooth lock washer
rondelle^F à denture^F extérieure
außengezahnte Fächerscheibe^F
rosetta^F a dentatura^F esterna
arandela^F de presión^F de dientes^M externos

internal tooth lock washer
rondelle^F à denture^F intérieure
innengezahnte Fächerscheibe^F
rosetta^F a dentatura^F interna
arandela^F de presión^F de dientes^M internos

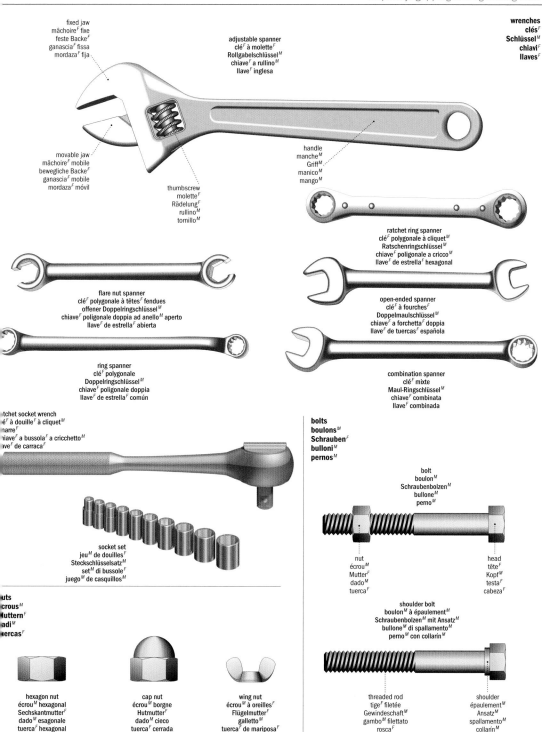

wrenches[F]
clés[F]
Schlüssel[M]
chiavi[F]
llaves[F]

fixed jaw
mâchoire[F] fixe
feste Backe[F]
ganascia[F] fissa
mordaza[F] fija

adjustable spanner
clé[F] à molette[F]
Rollgabelschlüssel[M]
chiave[F] a rullino[M]
llave[F] inglesa

handle
manche[M]
Griff[M]
manico[M]
mango[M]

movable jaw
mâchoire[F] mobile
bewegliche Backe[F]
ganascia[F] mobile
mordaza[F] móvil

thumbscrew
molette[F]
Rädelung[F]
rullino[M]
tornillo[M]

ratchet ring spanner
clé[F] polygonale à cliquet[M]
Ratschenringschlüssel[M]
chiave[F] poligonale a cricco[M]
llave[F] de estrella[F] hexagonal

flare nut spanner
clé[F] polygonale à têtes[F] fendues
offener Doppelringschlüssel[M]
chiave[F] poligonale doppia ad anello[M] aperto
llave[F] de estrella[F] abierta

open-ended spanner
clé[F] à fourches[F]
Doppelmaulschlüssel[M]
chiave[F] a forchetta[F] doppia
llave[F] de tuercas[F] española

ring spanner
clé[F] polygonale
Doppelringschlüssel[M]
chiave[F] poligonale doppia
llave[F] de estrella[F] común

combination spanner
clé[F] mixte
Maul-Ringschlüssel[M]
chiave[F] combinata
llave[F] combinada

ratchet socket wrench
clé[F] à douille[F] à cliquet[M]
narre[F]
chiave[F] a bussola[F] a cricchetto[M]
llave[F] de carraca[F]

bolts
boulons[M]
Schrauben[F]
bulloni[M]
pernos[M]

bolt
boulon[M]
Schraubenbolzen[M]
bullone[M]
perno[M]

nut
écrou[M]
Mutter[F]
dado[M]
tuerca[F]

head
tête[F]
Kopf[M]
testa[F]
cabeza[F]

socket set
jeu[M] de douilles[F]
Steckschlüsselsatz[M]
set[M] di bussole[F]
juego[M] de casquillos[M]

shoulder bolt
boulon[M] à épaulement[M]
Schraubenbolzen[M] mit Ansatz[M]
bullone[M] di spallamento[M]
perno[M] con collarín[M]

nuts
écrous[M]
Muttern[F]
dadi[M]
tuercas[F]

hexagon nut
écrou[M] hexagonal
Sechskantmutter[F]
dado[M] esagonale
tuerca[F] hexagonal

cap nut
écrou[M] borgne
Hutmutter[F]
dado[M] cieco
tuerca[F] cerrada

wing nut
écrou[M] à oreilles[F]
Flügelmutter[F]
galletto[M]
tuerca[F] de mariposa[F]

threaded rod
tige[F] filetée
Gewindeschaft[M]
gambo[M] filettato
rosca[F]

shoulder
épaulement[M]
Ansatz[M]
spallamento[M]
collarín[M]

DO-IT-YOURSELF AND GARDENING

223

carpentry: gripping and tightening tools

G-clamp
serre-joint^M
Zwinge^F
morsetto^M a C
prensa^M en C

fixed jaw
mors^M fixe
feste Backe^F
ganascia^F fissa
mordaza^F fija

movable jaw
mors^M mobile
bewegliche Backe^F
ganascia^F mobile
mordaza^F móvil

swivel head
rotule^F
Schwenkkopf^M
testa^F orientabile
plato^M giratorio

throat
gorge^F
Spannweite^F
apertura^F
boca^F

clamping screw
vis^F de serrage^M
Stellschraube^F
vite^F di serraggio^M
tornillo^M de ajuste^M

frame
monture^F
Rahmen^M
telaio^M
bastidor^M

handle
levier^M de serrage^M
Spanngriff^M
leva^F di serraggio^M
brazo^M de presión^F

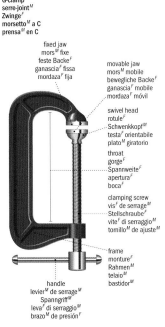

pipe clamp
serre-joint^M à tuyau^M
Rohrschraubstock^M
morsa^F serratubi^M
sargento^M

handle
levier^M de serrage^M
Knebel^M
leva^F di serraggio^M
llave^F de apriete^M

clamping screw
vis^F de serrage^M
Spannschraube^F
vite^F di serraggio^M
tornillo^M de apriete^M

jaw
mâchoire^F
bewegliche Backe^F
ganascia^F
mordaza^F

pipe
tuyau^M
Rohr^N
tubo^M
tubo^M

tail stop
sabot^M
feste Backe^F
cuneo^M
zapata^F

locking lever
levier^M de blocage^M
Arretierhebel^M
leva^F di bloccaggio^M
palanca^F de enclavamiento^M

handle
levier^M de serrage^M
Spanngriff^M
leva^F di serraggio^M
mango^M

movable jaw
mors^M mobile
bewegliche Backe^F
ganascia^F mobile
mordaza^F móvil

vice
étau^M
Schraubstock^M
morsa^F
torno^M de banco^M

fixed jaw
mors^M fixe
feste Backe^F
ganascia^F fissa
mordaza^F fija

clamping screw
vis^F de serrage^M
Stellschraube^F
vite^F di serraggio^M
tornillo^M de ajuste^M

swivel lock
blocage^M du pivot^M
Schwenkverschluss^M
bloccaggio^M della base^F
seguro^M de la base^F

bolt
boulon^M
Bolzen^M
bullone^M
perno^M

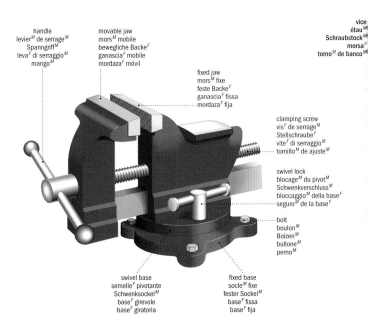

swivel base
semelle^F pivotante
Schwenksockel^M
base^F girevole
base^F giratoria

fixed base
socle^M fixe
fester Sockel^M
base^F fissa
base^F fija

peg
cale^F
Spannpratze^F
spessore^M
tope^M

jaws
mâchoires^F
Backen^F
ganasce^F
mordazas^F

work bench and vice
établi^M étau
Werkbank^F und Schraubstock
piano^M di lavoro^M a morsa
banco^M de trabajo

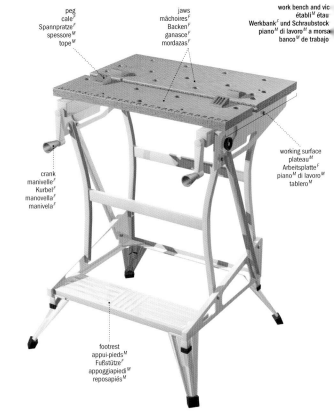

crank
manivelle^F
Kurbel^F
manovella^F
manivela^F

working surface
plateau^M
Arbeitsplatte^F
piano^M di lavoro^M
tablero^M

footrest
appui-pieds^M
Fußstütze^F
appoggiapiedi^M
reposapiés^M

carpentry: measuring and marking tools

menuiserie^F : instruments^M de traçage^M et de mesure^F | Bautischlerei^F: Mess- und Markierinstrumente^N | carpenteria^F: strumenti^M di misurazione^F e tracciamento^M | carpintería^F : instrumentos^M de trazado^M y de medición^F

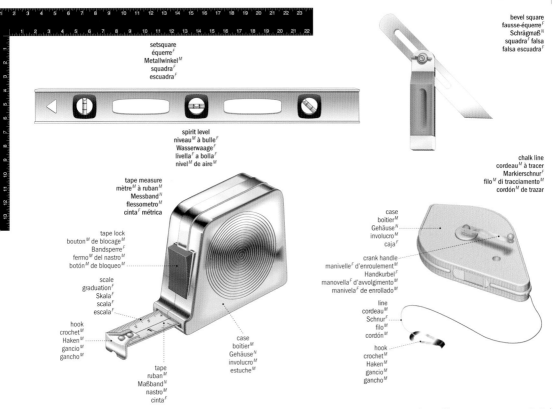

bevel square
fausse-équerre^F
Schrägmaß^N
squadra^F falsa
falsa escuadra^F

setsquare
équerre^F
Metallwinkel^M
squadra^F
escuadra^F

spirit level
niveau^M à bulle^F
Wasserwaage^F
livella^F a bolla^F
nivel^M de aire^M

chalk line
cordeau^M à tracer
Markierschnur^F
filo^M di tracciamento^M
cordón^M de trazar

tape measure
mètre^M à ruban^M
Messband^N
flessometro^M
cinta^F métrica

case
boîtier^M
Gehäuse^N
involucro^M
caja^F

tape lock
bouton^M de blocage^M
Bandsperre^F
fermo^M del nastro^M
botón^M de bloqueo^M

crank handle
manivelle^F d'enroulement^M
Handkurbel^F
manovella^F d'avvolgimento^M
manivela^F de enrollado^M

scale
graduation^F
Skala^F
scala^F
escala^F

line
cordeau^M
Schnur^F
filo^M
cordón^M

hook
crochet^M
Haken^M
gancio^M
gancho^M

case
boîtier^M
Gehäuse^N
involucro^M
estuche^M

hook
crochet^M
Haken^M
gancio^M
gancho^M

tape
ruban^M
Maßband^N
nastro^M
cinta^F

carpentry: miscellaneous material

menuiserie^F : matériel^M divers | Bautischlerei^F: verschiedenes Zubehör^N | carpenteria^F: materiale^M vario | carpintería^F : materiales^M varios

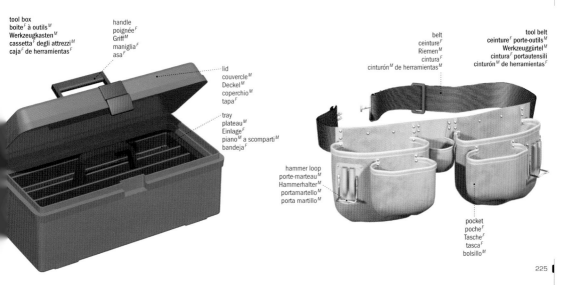

tool box
boîte^F à outils^M
Werkzeugkasten^M
cassetta^F degli attrezzi^M
caja^F de herramientas^F

handle
poignée^F
Griff^M
maniglia^F
asa^F

belt
ceinture^F
Riemen^M
cintura^F
cinturón^M de herramientas^M

tool belt
ceinture^F porte-outils^M
Werkzeuggürtel^M
cintura^F portautensili
cinturón^M de herramientas^F

lid
couvercle^M
Deckel^M
coperchio^M
tapa^F

tray
plateau^M
Einlage^F
piano^M a scomparti^M
bandeja^F

hammer loop
porte-marteau^M
Hammerhalter^M
portamartello^M
porta martillo^M

pocket
poche^F
Tasche^F
tasca^F
bolsillo^M

carpentry: sawing tools

menuiserie^F : outils^M pour scier | Bautischlerei^F: Sägewerkzeuge^N | carpenteria^F: utensili^M per segare | carpintería^F : herramientas^F para serrar

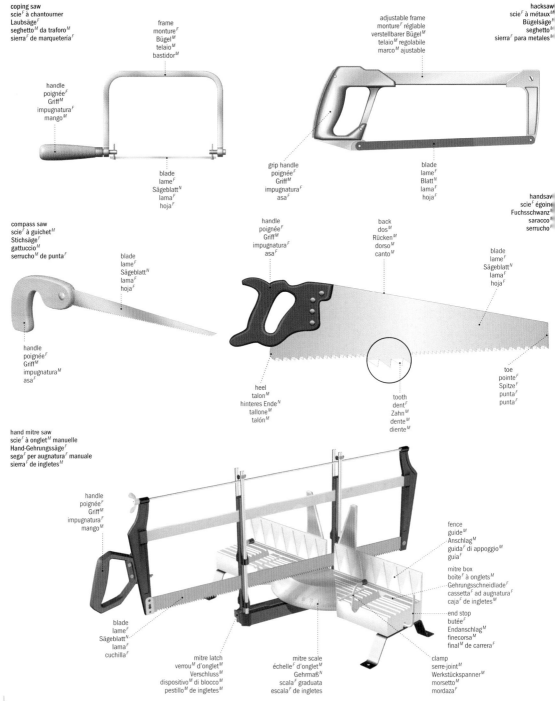

coping saw
scie^F à chantourner
Laubsäge^F
seghetto^M da traforo^M
sierra^F de marquetería^F

frame
monture^F
Bügel^M
telaio^M
bastidor^M

handle
poignée^F
Griff^M
impugnatura^F
mango^M

blade
lame^F
Sägeblatt^N
lama^F
hoja^F

adjustable frame
monture^F réglable
verstellbarer Bügel^M
telaio^M regolabile
marco^M ajustable

hacksaw
scie^F à métaux^M
Bügelsäge^F
seghetto^M
sierra^F para metales^M

grip handle
poignée^F
Griff^M
impugnatura^F
asa^F

blade
lame^F
Blatt^N
lama^F
hoja^F

compass saw
scie^F à guichet^M
Stichsäge^F
gattuccio^M
serrucho^M de punta^F

blade
lame^F
Sägeblatt^N
lama^F
hoja^F

handle
poignée^F
Griff^M
impugnatura^F
asa^F

back
dos^M
Rücken^M
dorso^M
canto^M

handsaw
scie^F égoïne
Fuchsschwanz^M
saracco^M
serrucho^M

blade
lame^F
Sägeblatt^N
lama^F
hoja^F

handle
poignée^F
Griff^M
impugnatura^M
asa^F

heel
talon^M
hinteres Ende^N
tallone^M
talón^M

tooth
dent^F
Zahn^M
dente^M
diente^M

toe
pointe^F
Spitze^F
punta^F
punta^F

hand mitre saw
scie^F à onglet^M manuelle
Hand-Gehrungssäge^F
sega^F per augnatura^F manuale
sierra^F de ingletes^M

handle
poignée^F
Griff^M
impugnatura^F
mango^M

fence
guide^F
Anschlag^M
guida^F di appoggio^M
guía^F

mitre box
boîte^F à onglets^M
Gehrungsschneidlade^F
cassetta^F ad augnatura^F
caja^F de ingletes^M

end stop
butée^F
Endanschlag^M
finecorsa^M
final^M de carrera^F

blade
lame^F
Sägeblatt^N
lama^F
cuchilla^F

mitre latch
verrou^M d'onglet^M
Verschluss^M
dispositivo^M di blocco^M
pestillo^M de ingletes^M

mitre scale
échelle^F d'onglet^M
Gehrmaß^N
scala^F graduata
escala^F de ingletes

clamp
serre-joint^M
Werkstückspanner^M
morsetto^M
mordaza^F

DO-IT-YOURSELF AND GARDENING

jigsaw
scie^F sauteuse
elektrische Stichsäge^F
seghetto^M alternativo
sierra^F de calar

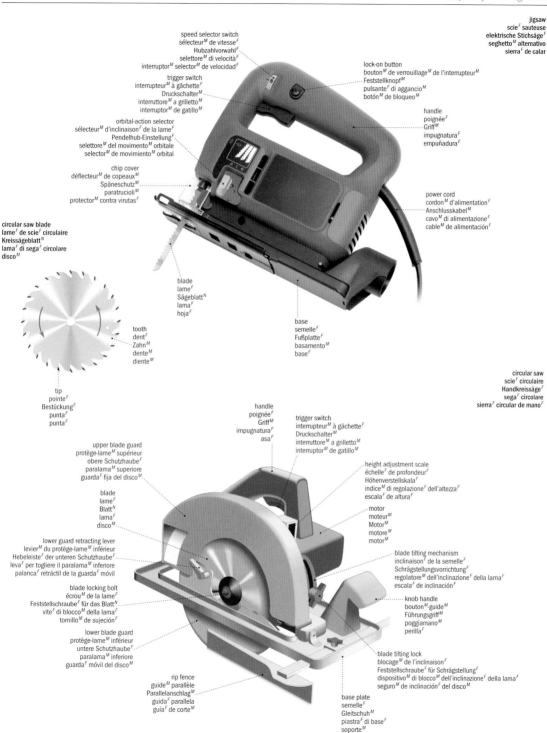

speed selector switch
sélecteur^M de vitesse^F
Hubzahlvorwahl^F
selettore^M di velocità^F
interruptor^M selector de velocidad

lock-on button
bouton^M de verrouillage^M de l'interrupteur^M
Feststellknopf^M
pulsante^M di aggancio^M
botón^M de bloqueo^M

trigger switch
interrupteur^M à gâchette^F
Druckschalter^M
interruttore^M a grilletto^M
interruptor^M de gatillo^M

handle
poignée^F
Griff^M
impugnatura^F
empuñadura^F

orbital-action selector
sélecteur^M d'inclinaison^F de la lame^F
Pendelhub-Einstellung^F
selettore^M del movimento^M orbitale
selector^M de movimiento^M orbital

chip cover
déflecteur^M de copeaux^M
Späneschutz^M
paratrucioli^M
protector^M contra virutas^F

power cord
cordon^M d'alimentation^F
Anschlusskabel^N
cavo^M di alimentazione^F
cable^M de alimentación^F

circular saw blade
lame^F de scie^F circulaire
Kreissägeblatt^N
lama^F di sega^F circolare
disco^M

blade
lame^F
Sägeblatt^N
lama^F
hoja^F

base
semelle^F
Fußplatte^F
basamento^M
base^F

tooth
dent^F
Zahn^M
dente^M
diente^M

tip
pointe^F
Bestückung^F
punta^F
punta^F

circular saw
scie^F circulaire
Handkreissäge^F
sega^F circolare
sierra^F circular de mano^F

handle
poignée^F
Griff^M
impugnatura^F
asa^F

trigger switch
interrupteur^M à gâchette^F
Druckschalter^M
interruttore^M a grilletto^M
interruptor^M de gatillo^M

upper blade guard
protège-lame^M supérieur
obere Schutzhaube^F
paralama^M superiore
guarda^F fija del disco^M

height adjustment scale
échelle^F de profondeur^F
Höhenverstellskala^F
indice^M di regolazione^F dell'altezza^F
escala^F de altura^F

motor
moteur^M
Motor^M
motore^M
motor^M

blade
lame^F
Blatt^N
lama^F
disco^M

blade tilting mechanism
inclinaison^F de la semelle^F
Schrägstellungsvorrichtung^F
regolatore^M dell'inclinazione^F della lama^F
escala^F de inclinación^F

lower guard retracting lever
levier^M du protège-lame^M inférieur
Hebeleiste^F der unteren Schutzhaube^F
leva^F per togliere il paralama^M inferiore
palanca^F retráctil de la guarda^F móvil

knob handle
bouton^M-guide^M
Führungsgriff^M
poggiamano^M
perilla^F

blade locking bolt
écrou^M de la lame^F
Feststellschraube^F für das Blatt^N
vite^F di blocco^M della lama^F
tornillo^M de sujeción^M

lower blade guard
protège-lame^M inférieur
untere Schutzhaube^F
paralama^M inferiore
guarda^F móvil del disco^M

blade tilting lock
blocage^M de l'inclinaison^F
Feststellschraube^F für Schrägstellung^F
dispositivo^M di blocco^M dell'inclinazione^F della lama^F
seguro^M de inclinación^F del disco^M

rip fence
guide^M parallèle
Parallelanschlag^M
guida^F parallela
guía^F de corte^M

base plate
semelle^F
Gleitschuh^M
piastra^F di base^F
soporte^M

carpentry: drilling tools

menuiserie^F : outils^M pour percer | Bautischlerei^F: Bohrwerkzeuge^N | carpenteria^F: attrezzi^M per trapanare | carpintería^F : herramientas^F percutoras

cordless drill-driver
perceuse^F-visseuse^F sans fil^M
Akku^M-Bohrschrauber^M
trapano^M senza fili^M
taladro^M percutor inalámbrico

keyless chuck
mandrin^M autoserrant
Schnellspannbohrfutter^N
mandrino^M autoserrante
mandril^M de sujeción^F

speed selector switch
sélecteur^M de vitesse^F de rotation^F
Drehzahlschalter^M
selettore^M di velocità^F
selector^M de velocidad^F

screwdriver bit
embout^M de vissage^M
Schrauberbit^M
mecchia^F
broca^F de atornillado

torque adjustment collar
bague^F de réglage^F du couple^M de serrage^M
Drehmoment^M-Einstellring^M
anello^M di regolazione^F della coppia^F di serraggio^M
anillo^M de reglaje^M del par^M de apriete^M

battery pack
batterie^F
Akku^M
batteria^F
batería^F

trigger switch
interrupteur^M à gâchette^F
Druckschalter^M
interruttore^M a grilletto^M
interruptor^M de gatillo^M

reversing switch
inverseur^M de marche^F
Umschalter^M
invertitore^M
inversor^M

charger
chargeur^M
Ladegerät^N
caricabatteria^M
cargador^M

battery pack
batterie^F
Akku^M
batteria^F
batería^F

electric drill
perceuse^F électrique
elektrische Bohrmaschine^F
trapano^M elettrico
taladro^M eléctrico

warning plate
plaque^F d'instructions^F
Sicherheitshinweisschild^N
targhetta^F delle avvertenze^F
placa^F de advertencias^F

specification plate
plaque^F signalétique
Typenschild^N
targhetta^F del costruttore^M
placa^F de especificaciones^F

chuck key
clé^F de mandrin^M
Bohrfutterschlüssel^M
chiave^F del mandrino^M
llave^F del mandril^M

housing
boîtier^M
Gehäuse^N
carcassa^F
cárter^M

switch lock
blocage^M de l'interrupteur^M
Feststellknopf^M
dispositivo^M di blocco^M dell'interruttore^M
seguro^M del interruptor^M

chuck
mandrin^M
Bohrfutter^N
mandrino^M
mandril^M

trigger switch
interrupteur^M à gâchette^F
Druckschalter^M
interruttore^M a grilletto^M
interruptor^M de gatillo^M

jaw
mors^M
Backen^F
griffa^F
mordaza^F

pistol grip handle
poignée^F-pistolet^M
Pistolengriff^M
impugnatura^F a pistola^F
mango^M

auxiliary handle
poignée^F auxiliaire
zusätzlicher Griff^M
impugnatura^F laterale
mango^M auxiliar

cable sleeve
manchon^M de câble^M
Kabelmuffe^F
manicotto^M del cavo^M
protector^M del cable^M

plug
fiche^F
Stecker^M
spina^F
enchufe^M

cable
câble^M
Kabel^N
cavo^M
cable^M

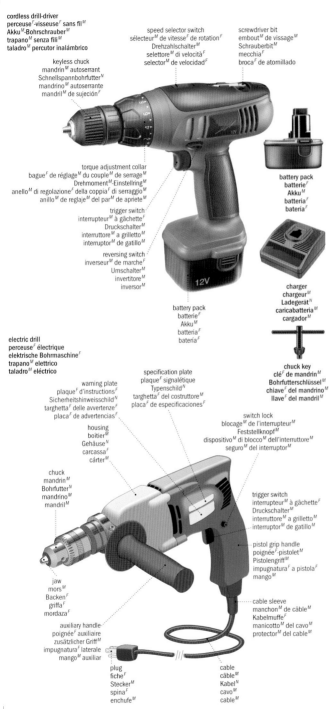

examples of bits and drills
exemples^M de mèches^F et de forets^M
Beispiele^N für Bits^M und Bohrer^M
esempi^M di mecchie^F e punte^F da trapano^M
ejemplos^M de brocas^F y barrenas^F

twist bit
mèche^F hélicoïdale
Spiralbohrer^M
mecchia^F elicoidale
broca^F helicoidal

shank
queue^F
Schaft^M
codolo^M
talón^M

flute
goujure^F
Spangang^M
scanalatura^F
canal^M

body
corps^M
Bohrkörper^M
corpo^M
cuerpo^M

fluted land
lèvre^F
Rücken^M
faccetta^F scanalata
lomo^M con canal^M

land
listel^M
Fase^F
faccetta^F
borde^M del lomo^M

centring point
pointe^F de centrage^M
Zentrierspitze^F
punta^F di centratura^F
borde^F de la punta^F

solid centre auger bit
mèche^F hélicoïdale à âme^F centrale
Schneckenbohrer^M
mecchia^F a tortiglione^M
broca^F helicoidal central

shank
queue^F
Schaft^M
codolo^M
talón^M

twist
torsade^F
Spirale^F
elica^F
torsión^F

spur
traçoir^M
Vorschneider^M
tagliente^M
espolón^M

centring point
pointe^F de centrage^M
Zentrierspitze^F
punta^F di centratura^F
tornillo^M guía

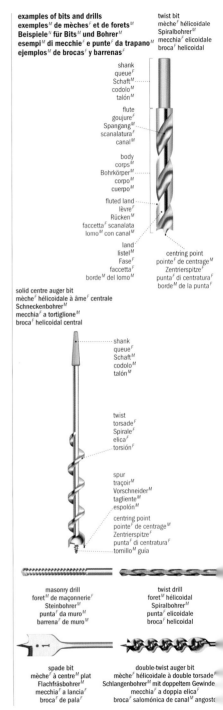

masonry drill
foret^M de maçonnerie^F
Steinbohrer^M
punta^F da muro^M
barrena^F de muro^M

twist drill
foret^M hélicoïdal
Spiralbohrer^M
punta^F elicoidale
broca^F helicoidal

spade bit
mèche^F à centre^M plat
Flachfräsbohrer^M
mecchia^F a lancia^F
broca^F de pala^F

double-twist auger bit
mèche^F hélicoïdale à double torsade^F
Schlangenbohrer^M mit doppeltem Gewinde
mecchia^F a doppia elica^F
broca^F salomónica de canal^M angosto

carpentry: shaping tools

menuiserie^F : outils^M pour façonner | Bautischlerei^F: Formwerkzeuge^N | carpenteria^F: attrezzi^M per sagomare | carpintería^F : herramientas^F de perfilado^M

lateral-adjustment lever
levier^M de réglage^M latéral
Seitenverstellhebel^M
leva^F di regolazione^F laterale
nivelador^M

wedge lever
levier^M du bloc^M
Keilhebel^M
leva^F di serraggio^M
palanca^F de la cuña^F

plane
rabot^M
Hobel^M
pialla^F
cepillo^M

handle
poignée^F
Griff^M
impugnatura^F
empuñadura^F

lever cap
bloc^M d'arrêt^M
Arretierhebel^M
blocco^M d'arresto^M
palanca^F de bloqueo^M

depth-of-cut adjustment knob
molette^F de réglage^M de la saillie^F
Hobeleisen^N-Stellschraube^F
manopola^F di regolazione^F dell'aggetto^M
calibre^M de ajuste^M de profundidad^F de corte^M

knob
pommeau^M
Handgriff^M
pomolo^M
pomo^M

heel
talon^M
hinteres Ende^N
tallone^M
talón^M

toe
nez^M
Stirn^F
punta^F
puntera^F

sole
semelle^F
Sohle^F
piastra^F d'appoggio^M
suela^F

frog-adjustment screw
réglage^M de l'angle^M
Spannschraube^F
vite^F di regolazione^F
tornillo^M de ajuste^M de ranilla^F

blade
fer^M
Hobeleisen^N
ferro^M
hoja^F

cap iron
contre-fer^M
Klappe^F
controferro^M
contrahoja^F

random orbit sander
ponceuse^F excentrique
Exzenterschleifer^M
smerigliatrice^F eccentrica
lijadora^F excéntrica

lock-on button
bouton^M de blocage^M
Arretierknopf^M
pulsante^M di arresto^M
botón^M de enclavamiento^M

power cord
cordon^M d'alimentation^F
Netzkabel^N
cavo^M d'alimentazione^F
cordón^M de alimentación^F

motor
moteur^M
Motor^M
motore^M
motor^M

router
défonceuse^F
Oberfräse^F
fresatrice^F verticale
fresadora^F

housing
boîtier^M
Gehäuse^N
carcassa^F
armazón^M

handle
poignée^F
Griff^M
impugnatura^F
empuñadura^F

head
tête^F
Kopf^M
testa^F
cabeza^F

switch
interrupteur^M
Schalter^M
interruttore^M
interruptor^M

flex sleeve
manchon^M du cordon^M
Kabelmantel^M
manicotto^M del cordone^M
protector^M del cable^M

depth adjustment
réglage^M de profondeur^F
Tiefeneinstellung^F
regolatore^M di profondità^F
ajuste^M de profundidad^F

guide handle
poignée^F de guidage^M
Führungsgriff^M
impugnatura^F
asa^F

dust canister
boîte^F à poussière^F
Staubbehälter^M
raccoglipolvere^M
caja^F colectora de polvo^M

sanding disc
disque^M abrasif
Schleifblatt^N
disco^M abrasivo
disco^M abrasivo

trigger switch
interrupteur^M à gâchette^F
Druckschalter^M
interruttore^M a grilletto^M
interruptor^M de gatillo^M

collet
écrou^M du porte-outil^M
Anlaufhülse^F
collare^M
collarín^M

sanding pad
plateau^M de ponçage^M
Schleifteller^M
supporto^M del disco^M abrasivo
plato^M lijador

sandpaper
papier^M de verre^M
Schleifpapier^N
carta^F vetrata
lija^F

base
semelle^F
Fuß^M
base^F
base^F

tool holder
porte-outil^M
Werkzeugfutter^N
portautensili^M
mordaza^F

file
lime^F
Flachfeile^F
lima^F
lima^F

wood chisel
ciseau^M à bois^M
Stemmeisen^N
scalpello^M da falegname^M
escoplo^M

DO-IT-YOURSELF AND GARDENING

pleasure garden

jardin^M d'agrément^M | Ziergarten^M | giardino^M | jardín^M

DO-IT-YOURSELF AND GARDENING

ornamental tree
arbre^M d'ornement^M
Zierbaum^M
albero^F ornamentale
árbol^M ornamental

lantern
lanterne^F
Laterne^F
lampione^M
farol^M

shed
remise^F
Schuppen^M
rimessa^F
cobertizo^M

fan trellis
treillis^M
Spalier^N
spalliera^F
encañado^M

bush
arbuste^M
Strauch^M
cespuglio^M
arbusto^M

pond
bassin^M
Gartenteich^M
laghetto^M
estanque^M

climbing plant
plante^F grimpante
Kletterpflanze^F
pianta^F rampicante
enredadera^F

patio
terrasse^F
Terrasse^F
patio^M
patio^M

pergola
pergola^F
Pergola^F
pergola^F
pérgola^F

hanging basket
corbeille^F suspendue
Ampel^F
vaso^M sospeso
maceta^F colgante

clump of flowers
massif^M de fleurs^F
Blumenrabatte^F
macchia^F di fiori^M
macizo^M de flores^F

hedge
haie^F
Hecke^F
siepe^F
seto^M

lawn
gazon^M
Rasen^M
prato^M
césped^M

stake
tuteur^M
Stab^M
tutore^M
rodrigón^M

paling fence
clôture^F en lattis^M
Lattenzaun^M
palizzata^F
empalizada^F

flower bed
plate-bande^F
Blumenbeet^N
aiuola^F
arriate^M

path
allée^F
Gartenweg^M
vialetto^M
paseo^M

flagstone
dalle^F
Pflasterstein^F
pietra^F da lastrico^M
baldosa^F

rock garden
rocaille^F
Steingarten^M
giardino^M roccioso
jardín^M de rocalla^F

edging
bordure^F d'allée^F
Einfassung^F
bordura^F
bordillo^M

garden arch
arceau^M
Spalierbogen^M
spalliera^F ad arco^M
enramada^F

tub
bac^M à plante^F
Kübel^M
vaso^M
maceta^F

miscellaneous equipment

équipement^M divers | verschiedene Geräte^N | attrezzatura^F varia | equipamiento^M vario

compost bin
bac^M à compost^M
Kompostkiste^F
contenitore^M della composta^F
cajón^M de abono^M compuesto

wheelbarrow
brouette^F
Schubkarre^F
carriola^F
carretilla^F

container
caisse^F
Mulde^F
cassone^M
caja^F

handle
brancard^M
Griff^M
stanga^F
brazo^M

leg
pied^M
Stütze^F
piede^M
pata^F

wheel
roue^F
Rad^N
ruota^F
rueda^F

seeding and planting tools

outils^M pour semer et planter | Werkzeuge^N zum Säen^N und Pflanzen^N | attrezzi^M per seminare e piantare | herramientas^F para sembrar y plantar

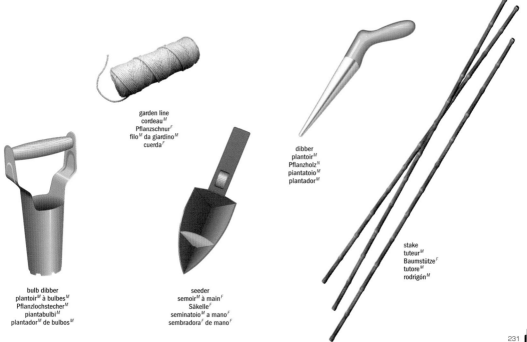

garden line
cordeau^M
Pflanzschnur^F
filo^M da giardino^M
cuerda^F

dibber
plantoir^M
Pflanzholz^N
piantatoio^M
plantador^M

stake
tuteur^M
Baumstütze^F
tutore^M
rodrigón^M

bulb dibber
plantoir^M à bulbes^M
Pflanzlochstecher^M
piantabulbi^M
plantador^M de bulbos^M

seeder
semoir^M à main^F
Säkelle^F
seminatoio^M a mano^F
sembradora^F de mano^F

hand tools

jeu^M de petits outils^M | Handwerkzeuge^N | attrezzi^M per piccoli lavori^M di giardinaggio^M | juego^M de pequeñas herramientas^F

small hand cultivator
griffe^F à fleurs^F
Kralle^F
sarchiello^M a mano^F
cultivador^M de mano^F

trowel
transplantoir^M
Pflanzkelle^F
trapiantatoio^M
desplantador^M

weeder
tire-racine^M
Unkrautstecher^M
estirpatore^M
desyerbador^M

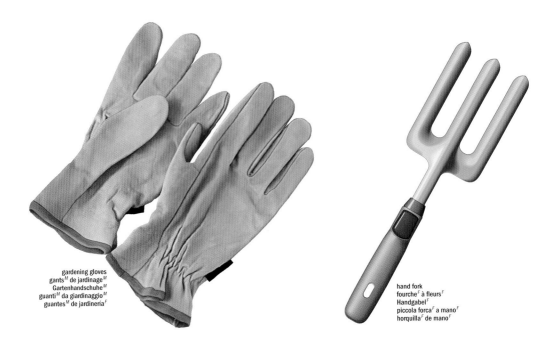

gardening gloves
gants^M de jardinage^M
Gartenhandschuhe^M
guanti^M da giardinaggio^M
guantes^M de jardinería^F

hand fork
fourche^F à fleurs^F
Handgabel^F
piccola forca^F a mano^F
horquilla^F de mano^F

tools for loosening the earth

outils^M pour remuer la terre^F | Geräte^N zur Erdbewegung^F | attrezzi^M per smuovere la terra^F | herramientas^F para remover la tierra^F

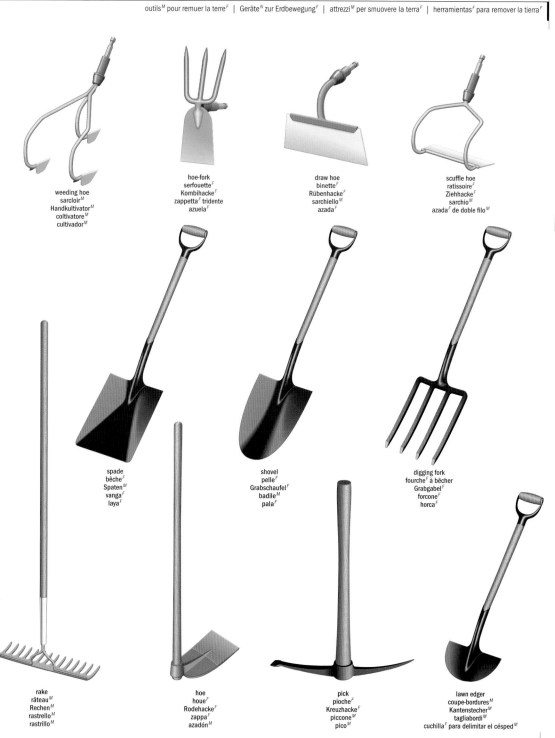

weeding hoe
sarcloir^M
Handkultivator^M
coltivatore^M
cultivador^M

hoe-fork
serfouette^F
Kombihacke^F
zappetta^F tridente
azuela^F

draw hoe
binette^F
Rübenhacke^F
sarchiello^M
azada^F

scuffle hoe
ratissoire^F
Ziehhacke^F
sarchio^M
azada^F de doble filo^M

spade
bêche^F
Spaten^M
vanga^F
laya^F

shovel
pelle^F
Grabschaufel^F
badile^M
pala^F

digging fork
fourche^F à bêcher
Grabgabel^F
forcone^F
horca^F

rake
râteau^M
Rechen^M
rastrello^M
rastrillo^M

hoe
houe^F
Rodehacke^F
zappa^F
azadón^M

pick
pioche^F
Kreuzhacke^F
piccone^M
pico^M

lawn edger
coupe-bordures^M
Kantenstecher^M
tagliabordi^M
cuchilla^F para delimitar el césped^M

DO-IT-YOURSELF AND GARDENING

pruning and cutting tools

outils^M pour couper | Schneidwerkzeuge^N | attrezzi^M per potare e tagliare | herramientas^F para cortar

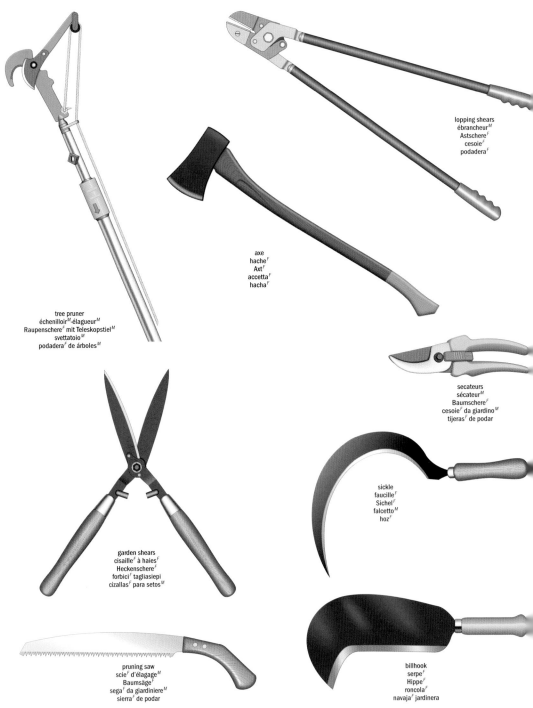

lopping shears
ébrancheur^M
Astschere^F
cesoie^F
podadera^F

axe
hache^F
Axt^F
accetta^F
hacha^F

tree pruner
échenilloir^M-élagueur^M
Raupenschere^F mit Teleskopstiel^M
svettatoio^M
podadera^F de árboles^M

secateurs
sécateur^M
Baumschere^F
cesoie^F da giardino^M
tijeras^F de podar

sickle
faucille^F
Sichel^F
falcetto^M
hoz^F

garden shears
cisaille^F à haies^F
Heckenschere^F
forbici^F tagliasiepi
cizallas^F para setos^M

pruning saw
scie^F d'élagage^M
Baumsäge^F
sega^F da giardiniere^M
sierra^F de podar

billhook
serpe^F
Hippe^F
roncola^F
navaja^F jardinera

hedge trimmer
taille-haies^M
elektrische Heckenschere^F
tagliasiepi^{M/F}
cortasetos^M eléctrico

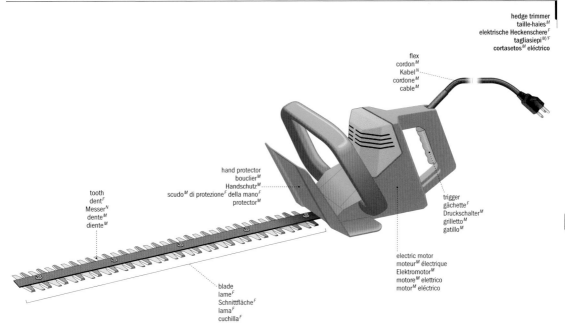

flex
cordon^M
Kabel^N
cordone^M
cable^M

hand protector
bouclier^M
Handschutz^M
scudo^M di protezione^F della mano^F
protector^M

trigger
gâchette^F
Druckschalter^M
grilletto^M
gatillo^M

tooth
dent^F
Messer^N
dente^M
diente^M

electric motor
moteur^M électrique
Elektromotor^M
motore^M elettrico
motor^M eléctrico

blade
lame^F
Schnittfläche^F
lama^F
cuchilla^F

chainsaw
tronçonneuse^F
Kettensäge^F
motosega^F
sierra^F de cadena^F

air filter
filtre^M à air^M
Luftfilter^N
filtro^M dell'aria^F
filtro^M de aire^M

anti-vibration handle
poignée^F antivibrations^F
schwingungsdämpfender Bügelgriff^M
impugnatura^F con sistema^M antivibrazione^F
barra^F antivibración

chain brake
frein^M de chaîne^F
Kettenbremse^F
freno^M della catena^F
freno^M de la cadena^F

stop button
bouton^M d'arrêt^M
Ausschalter^M
pulsante^M di arresto^M
botón^M de apagado^M

security trigger
gâchette^F de sécurité^F
Rasthebel^M
grilletto^M di sicurezza^F
gatillo^M de seguridad^F

bar nose
nez^M du guide^M
Umlenkstern^M
estremità^F della guida^F
extremo^M del brazo^M

guide bar
guide-chaîne^F
Schwert^N
guida^F della catena^F
brazo^M de la sierra^F

handle
poignée^F
Griff^M
impugnatura^F
mango^M

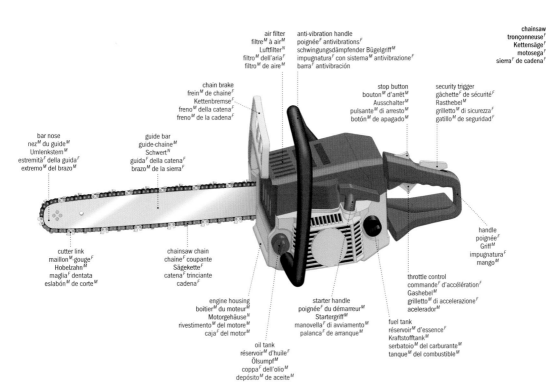

cutter link
maillon^M-gouge^F
Hobelzahn^M
maglia^F dentata
eslabón^M de corte^M

chainsaw chain
chaîne^F coupante
Sägekette^F
catena^F trinciante
cadena^F

throttle control
commande^F d'accélération^F
Gashebel^M
grilletto^M di accelerazione^F
acelerador^M

engine housing
boîtier^M du moteur^M
Motorgehäuse^N
rivestimento^M del motore^M
caja^F del motor^M

starter handle
poignée^F du démarreur^M
Startergriff^M
manovella^F di avviamento^M
palanca^F de arranque^M

fuel tank
réservoir^M d'essence^F
Kraftstofftank^M
serbatoio^M del carburante^M
tanque^M del combustible^M

oil tank
réservoir^M d'huile^F
Ölsumpf^M
coppa^F dell'olio^M
depósito^M de aceite^M

DO-IT-YOURSELF AND GARDENING

watering tools

outils^M pour arroser | Gießgeräte^N | attrezzi^M per annaffiare | herramientas^F para regar

sprayer
vaporisateur^M
Sprühflasche^F
spruzzatore^M
pulverizador^M

spray nozzle
pistolet^M arrosoir^M
Gießbrause^F
nebulizzatore^M
boquilla^F pulverizadora

pistol nozzle
pistolet^M d'arrosage^M
Gießpistole^F
polverizzatore^F a pistola^F
pistola^F pulverizadora

sprinkler hose
tuyau^M perforé
Regnerschlauch^M
tubo^M per irrigazione^F
manguera^F de riego^M

pump sprayer
pulvérisateur^M
Gartenspritze^F
atomizzatore^M
pulverizador^M

watering can
arrosoir^M
Gießkanne^F
annaffiatoio^M
regadera^F

handle
anse^F
Griff^M
manico^M
asa^F

rose
pomme^F
Brause^F
cipolla^F
roseta^F

metal arm
balancier^M
Hammer^M
braccio^M metallico
brazo^M metálico

diffuser pin
brise-jet^M
Zerstäuberstift^M
vite^F rompigetto
perno^M difusor

impulse sprinkler
arroseur^M canon^M
Impulsregner^M
irrigatore^M a impulsi
irrigador^M de impulso^M

nozzle
buse^F
Düse^F
ugello^M
boquilla^F

deflector
déflecteur^M
Strahlstörer^M
deflettore^M
deflector^M

hose connector
raccord^M de tuyau^M
Schlauchkupplung^F
attacco^M del tubo^M di
alimentazione^F dell'acqua^F
boca^F para la manguera^F

adjusting ring
bague^F de réglage^M
Stellring^M
anello^M di regolazione^F
disparador^M

sled
traineau^M
Fuß^M
slitta^F
soporte^M

oscillating sprinkler
arroseur^M oscillant
Viereckregner^M
irrigatore^M oscillante
irrigador^M oscilante

hose trolley
dévidoir^M sur roues^F
Schlauchwagen^M
carrello^M avvolgitubo
carretilla^F para manguera^F

reel
dévidoir^M
Trommel^F
carrello^M
carrete^M

garden hose
tuyau^M d'arrosage^M
Gartenschlauch^M
tubo^M flessibile
manguera^F

reel crank
manivelle^F
Kurbel^F
manovella^F
manivela^F del carrete^M

revolving sprinkler
arroseur^M rotatif
Kreisregner^M
irrigatore^M rotativo a pioggia
irrigador^M giratorio

hose connector
raccord^F de robinet^M
Schlauchkupplung^F
attacco^M del tubo^M di
alimentazione^F dell'acqua^F
toma^F

hose nozzle
lance^F d'arrosage^M
Schlauchdüse^F
lancia^F
boquilla^F

arm
bras^M
Drehdüse^F
braccio^M
brazo^M

lawn care

soins^M de la pelouse^F | Rasenpflege^F | cura^F del prato^M | cuidado^M del césped^M

trimmer
taille-bordures^M
Rasentrimmer^M
tagliabordi^M
podadora^F de bordes^M

lawn rake
balai^M à feuilles^F
Rasenbesen^M
rastrello^M scopa^F
rastrillo^M

flex
cordon^M
Kabel^N
cordone^M
cable^M

electric motor
moteur^M électrique
Elektromotor^M
motore^M elettrico
motor^M eléctrico

protective casing
carter^M de sécurité^F
Schutzgehäuse^N
calotta^F di sicurezza^F
cubierta^F de seguridad^F

lawn aerator
aérateur^M à gazon^M
Vertikutierer^M
frangizolle^M
ventilador^M de césped^M

nylon line
fil^M de nylon^M
Nylonschnur^F
filo^M di nylon^M
hilo^M de nailon^M

handle
guidon^M
Griff^M
impugnatura^F
barra^F

throttle
sélecteur^M de régime^M
Geschwindigkeitsregler^M
regolatore^M della velocità^F
control^M de velocidad^F

safety handle
poignée^F de sécurité^F
Sicherheitsgriff^M
impugnatura^F di sicurezza^F
palanca^F de seguridad^F

ignition key
clé^F de contact^M
Zündschlüssel^M
chiave^F dell'accensione^F
encendido^M

power mower
tondeuse^F à moteur^M
Motorrasenmäher^M
motofalciatrice^F
cortacésped^M con motor^M

grassbox
bac^M de ramassage^M
Grasfang^M
raccoglierba^M
recogedor^M

starter
démarreur^M manuel
Anlasser^M
motorino^M d'avviamento^M
motor^M de arranque^M

filler cap
bouchon^M de remplissage^M
Einfüllstutzen^M
bocchetta^F del serbatoio^M
boca^F del depósito^M

motor
moteur^M
Motor^M
motore^M
motor^M

throttle cable
câble^M d'accélération^F
Gaszug^M
cavo^M di accelerazione^F
cable^M del acelerador^M

deflector
déflecteur^M
Schwadenblech^N
deflettore^M
deflector^M

sparking plug
bougie^F
Zündkerze^F
candela^F di accensione^F
bujía^F

casing
carter^M
Gehäuse^N
scocca^F
caja^F

headgear

coiffure[F] | Kopfbedeckungen[F] | copricapi[M] | sombreros[M]

men's headgear
coiffures[F] d'homme[M]
Herrenkopfbedeckungen[F]
copricapi[M] maschili
sombreros[M] de hombre[M]

trilby
chapeau[M] de feutre[M]
Filzhut[M]
cappello[M] di feltro[M]
sombrero[M] de fieltro[M]

hatband
bourdalou[M]
Hutband[N]
nastro[M]
cinta[F]

binding
galon[M]
Einfassband[N]
orlo[M]
ribete[M]

crown
calotte[F]
Kopfteil[M/N]
calotta[F]
copa[F]

brim
bord[M]
Krempe[F]
tesa[F]
ala[F]

bow
nœud[M] plat
Schleife[F]
fiocco[M]
lazo[M]

boater
canotier[M]
Strohhut[M]
paglietta[F]
canotier[M]

skullcap
calotte[F]
Käppchen[N]
papalina[F]
solideo[M]

bowler
melon[M]
Melone[F]
bombetta[F]
sombrero[M] de hongo[M]

astrakhan cap
calot[M]
Fellmütze[F]
bustina[F]
gorra[F] de cuartel[M]

top hat
haut-de-forme[M]
Zylinder[M]
cilindro[M]
chistera[F]

shapka
chapska[M]
Kosakenmütze[F]
colbacco[M]
chapka[F]

hunting cap
casquette[F] norvégienne
Jagdkappe[F]
berretto[M] da cacciatore[M]
gorra[F] noruega

ear flap
cache-oreilles[M] abattant
Ohrenschützer[M]
paraorecchi[M]
orejera[F]

cap
casquette[F]
Schirmmütze[F]
berretto[M]
gorra[F]

panama
panama[M]
Panamahut[M]
panama[M]
panamá[M]

peak
visière[F]
Mützenschirm[M]
visiera[F]
visera[F]

CLOTHING

pillbox hat
tambourin^M
Pillbox^F
tocco^M
sombrero^M sin alas^F

toque
toque^F
Toque^F
toque^F
toca^F

sou'wester
suroit^M
Südwester^M
berretto^M impermeabile
sueste^M

cartwheel hat
capeline^F
Wagenradhut^M
cappello^M a falda^F larga
pamela^F

rain hat
bob^M
Regenhut^M
cappello^M da marinaio^M
gorro^M de marinero^M

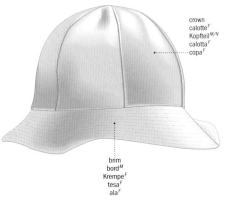

crown
calotte^F
Kopfteil$^{M/N}$
calotta^F
copa^F

brim
bord^M
Krempe^F
tesa^F
ala^F

women's headgear
coiffures^F de femme^F
Damenkopfbedeckungen^F
copricapi^M femminili
sombreros^M de mujer^F

women's headgear
coiffures^F de femme^F
Damenkopfbedeckungen^F
copricapi^M femminili
sombreros^M de mujer^F

cloche
cloche^F
Topfhut^M
cloche^F
sombrero^M de campana^F

turban
turban^M
Turban^M
turbante^M
turbante^M

CLOTHING

balaclava
cagoule^F
Kapuzenmütze^F
passamontagna^M
pasamontañas^M

peak
visière^F
Mützenschirm^M
visiera^F
visera^F

beret
béret^M
Baskenmütze^F
basco^M
boina^F

trilby
chapeau^M de feutre^M
Filzhut^M
cappello^M di feltro^M
sombrero^M de fieltro^M

unisex headgear
coiffures^F unisexes
Unisex-Kopfbedeckungen^F
copricapi^M unisex
sombreros^M unisex

bobble hat
bonnet^M à pompon^M
Pudelmütze^F
berretto^M con pompon^M
gorro^M de punto^M con borla^F

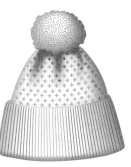

shoes

chaussures^F | Schuhe^M | scarpe^F | calzado^M

men's shoes
chaussures^F d'homme^M
Herrenschuhe^M
scarpe^F da uomo^M
zapatos^M de hombre^M

lining
doublure^F
Futter^N
fodera^F
forro^M

parts of a shoe
parties^F d'une chaussure^F
Teile^{M/N} des Schuhs^M
parti^F di una scarpa^F
partes^F de un zapato^M

shoelace
lacet^M
Schnürsenkel^M
stringa^F
cordón^M

cuff
revers^M
Einfassung^F
collo^M
ribete^M

tongue
languette^F
Zunge^F
linguetta^F
lengüeta^F

vamp
claque^F
Vorderblatt^N
tomaia^F
empella^F

heel grip
glissoir^M
Fersenhalter^M
rinforzo^M interno del calcagno^M
refuerzo^M del talón^M

stitch
surpiqûre^F
Naht^F
impuntura^F
costura^F

quarter
quartier^M
Quartier^M
quartiere^M
cuarto^M

punch hole
perforation^F
gestanztes Loch^N
foro^M
perforaciones^F

outside counter
talonnette^F de dessus^M
äußere Kappe^F
rinforzo^M esterno del calcagno^M
contrafuerte^M del talón^M

heel
talon^M
Absatz^M
tacco^M
talón^M

top lift
bonbout^M
Absatzoberflecken^M
salvatacchi^M
tapa^F

waist
cambrure^F
Gelenk^N
fiosso^M
enfranque^M

nose of the quarter
aile^F de quartier^M
Vorderteil^{M/N}
parte^F anteriore del quartiere^M
ala^F del cuarto^M

eyelet tab
garant^M
Schnürlochteil^{M/N}
lunetta^F
oreja^F

tag
ferret^M
Schnürsenkelende^N
puntale^M
herrete^M

outsole
semelle^F d'usure^F
Laufsohle^F
suola^F
suela^F

perforated toe cap
bout^M fleuri
perforierte Vorderkappe^F
mascherina^F perforata
puntera^F perforada

eyelet
œillet^M
Schnürloch^N
occhiello^M
ojete^M

welt
trépointe^F
Rahmen^M
guardolo^M
vira^F

heavy-duty boot
brodequin^M de travail^M
Arbeitsstiefel^M
scarpone^M
bota^F de trabajo^M

chukka
chukka^M
Boot^M
scarpa^F a collo^M alto
media bota^F

galosh
claque^F
Überziehschuh^M
galoscia^F
chanclo^M de goma^F

bootee
bottillon^M
Halbstiefel^M
scarponcino^M
botín^M

oxford shoe
richelieu^M
Herrenhalbschuh^M
scarpa^F oxford
zapato^M oxford

lace-up
derby^M
Schnürschuh^M
scarpa^F stringata
zapato^M de cordones^M

ankle-strap
sandale^F
Sandalette^F mit Fersenriemen^M
sandalo^M
sandalia^F

pump
ballerine^F
Ballerinaschuh^M
ballerina^F
bailarina^F

court
escarpin^M
Pumps^M
scarpa^F décolleté^M
zapato^M de salón^M

slingback shoe
escarpin^M-sandale^F
Slingpumps^M
scarpa^F chanel
zapato^M de talón abierto

one-bar shoe
Charles IX^M
Einspangenschuh^M
scarpa^F con cinturino^M
zapato^M de tacón^M con correa^F

T-strap shoe
salomé^M
Stegspangenschuh^M
scarpa^F con cinturino^M a T
zapato^M de correa^F

casual shoe
trotteur^M
Straßenschuh^M
francesina^F
zapato^M con cordones^M

thigh-boot
cuissarde^F
Schaftstiefel^M
stivale^M alla moschettiera
bota^F de medio muslo^M

boot
botte^F
Stiefel^M
stivale^M
bota^F

ankle boot
bottine^F
knöchelhohe Stiefelette^F
polacchina^F
botín^M

unisex shoes
chaussures **unisexes**
Unisex-Schuhe^M
scarpe^F **unisex**
calzado^M **unisex**

mule
mule^F
Pantoffel^M
pianella^F
pantufla^F

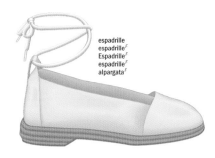

espadrille
espadrille^F
Espadrille^F
espadrille^F
alpargata^F

plimsoll
tennis^M
Tennisschuh^M
scarpa^F da tennis^M
zapatilla^F de tenis^M

slip-on
mocassin^M
Slipper^M
mocassino^M classico
mocasin^M

toe-strap
nu-pied^M
Sandale^F mit Zehenriemchen^N
sandalo^M indiano
sandalia^F

moccasin
mocassin^M
Mokassin^M
mocassino^M
mocasin^M

flip-flop
tong^M
Römerpantolette^F
infradito^M
chancleta^F playera

clog
socque^M
Pantolette^F
zoccolo^M
chancleta^F

sandal
sandalette^F
Sandale^F
sandalo^M
sandalia^F

hiking boot
brodequin^M de randonnée^F
Wanderschuh^M
pedula^F
bota^F de montaña

men's gloves
gants^M d'homme^M
Herrenhandschuhe^M
guanti^M da uomo^M
guantes^M de hombre^M

back of a glove
dos^M d'un gant^M
Handschuh^M-Außenseite^F
dorso^M del guanto^M
dorso^M de un guante^M

palm of a glove
paume^F d'un gant^M
Handschuh^M-Innenseite^F
palmo^M del guanto^M
palma^F de un guante^M

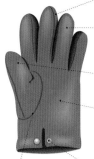

fourchette
fourchette^F
Keil^M
linguella^F
horquilla^F

glove finger
doigt^M
Finger^M
dito^M del guanto^M
dedo^M

thumb
pouce^M
Daumen^M
pollice^M
pulgar^M

palm
paume^F
Innenfläche^F
palmo^M
palma^F

snap fastener
bouton^M-pression^F
Druckknopf^M
bottone^M a pressione^F
botón^M de presión^F

stitching
baguette^F
Ziernaht^F
impuntura^F
pespunte^M

seam
couture^F d'assemblage^M
Naht^F
cucitura^F
costura^F

opening
fenêtre^F
Öffnung^F
apertura^F
aberturas^F para los nudillos^M

perforation
perforation^F
Perforierung^F
foro^M
perforaciones^F

driving glove
gant^M de conduite^F
Autohandschuh^M
guanto^M da guida^F
guante^M para conducir

mitten
moufle^F
Fäustling^M
muffola^F
manopla^F

CLOTHING

women's gloves
gants^M de femme^F
Damenhandschuhe^M
guanti^M da donna^F
guantes^M de mujer^F

short glove
gant^M court
Kurzhandschuh^M
guanto^M corto
guante^M corto

gauntlet
gant^M à crispin^M
Stulpenhandschuh^M
guanto^M alla scudiera
manopla^F

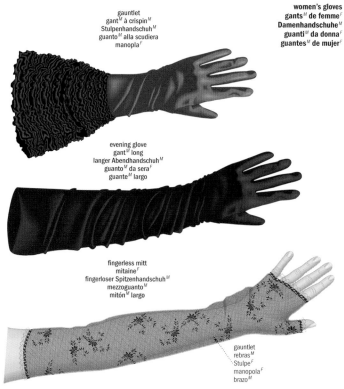

evening glove
gant^M long
langer Abendhandschuh^M
guanto^M da sera^F
guante^M largo

fingerless mitt
mitaine^F
fingerloser Spitzenhandschuh^M
mezzoguanto^M
mitón^M largo

wrist-length glove
gant^M saxe
Langhandschuh^M
guanto^M lungo
guante^M a la muñeca^F

gauntlet
rebras^M
Stulpe^F
manopola^F
brazo^M

jackets
veston^M et veste^F
Jackett^N und Weste^F
giacche^F e gilè^M
chaquetas^F y chalecos^M

CLOTHING

collar
col^M
Kragen^M
collo^M
cuello^M

double-breasted jacket
veston^M croisé
Zweireiher^M
giacca^F a doppiopetto^M
chaqueta^F cruzada

peaked lapel
revers^M à cran^M aigu
steigendes Revers^N
revers^M a punta^F
solapa^F puntiaguda

lining
doublure^F
Futter^N
fodera^F
forro^M

breast welt pocket
pochette^F
Brustleistentasche^F
taschino^M tagliato con aletta^F
bolsillo^M de ojal^M

side back vent
fente^F latérale
seitlicher Rückenschlitz^M
spacco^M laterale
abertura^F trasera lateral

sleeve
manche^F
Ärmel^M
manica^F
manga^F

flap
rabat^M
Klappe^F
aletta^F
solapa^F

outside ticket pocket
poche^F-ticket^M
Billettasche^F
taschino^M con aletta^F
bolsillo^M del cambio^M

patch pocket
poche^F plaquée
aufgesetzte Tasche^F
tasca^F applicata
bolsillo^M de parche^M

waistcoat
gilet^M
Weste^F
gilè^M
chaleco^M

V-neck
encolure^F en V
V-Ausschnitt^M
scollo^M a V
cuello^M en V

lining
doublure^F
Futter^N
fodera^F
forro^M

welt
patte^F
Patte^F
aletta^F
ribete^M

front
devant^M
Vorderseite^F
davanti^M
delantero^M

seaming
découpe^F
Teilungsnaht^F
cucitura^F
costura^F

welt pocket
poche^F gilet^M
Leistentasche^F
tasca^F interna con aletta^F
bolsillo^M de ribete^M

single-breasted jacket
veste^F droite
Einreiher^M
giacca^F a un petto^M
chaqueta^F recta

lapel
revers^M
Revers^N
revers^M
solapa^F

notch
cran^M
Crochetwinkel^M
dente^M
muesca^F

front
devant^M
Vorderseite^F
davanti^M
delantero^M

lining
doublure^F
Futter^N
fodera^F
forro^M

adjustable waist tab
tirant^M de réglage^M
Rückenspange^F
cinturino^M regolabile
trincha^F

back
dos^M
Rücken^M
dietro^M
espalda^F

pocket handkerchief
pochette^F
Einstecktuch^N
fazzoletto^M da taschino^M
pañuelo^M de bolsillo^M

sleeve
manche^F
Ärmel^M
manica^F
manga^F

flap pocket
poche^F tiroir^M
Klappentasche^F
tasca^F profilata con aletta^F
bolsillo^M con cartera^F

centre back vent
fente^F médiane
Rückenmittelschlitz^M
spacco^M centrale
abertura^F trasera central

collar
col^M
Kragen^M
colletto^M
cuello^M

set-in sleeve
manche^F montée
eingesetzter Ärmel^M
manica^F a giro^M
manga^F empotrada

breast pocket
poche^F poitrine^F
Brusttasche^F
tasca^F applicata con aletta^F
bolsillo^M superior

button facing
patte^F de boutonnage^M
Knopfleiste^F
cannoncino^M
tirilla^F

pointed tab end
patte^F capucin^M
Ärmelschlitz^M
profilo^M dello spacco^M
abertura^F con tirilla^F

cuff
poignet^M
Manschette^F
polsino^M
puño^M

yoke
empiècement^M
Sattel^M
sprone^M
canesú^M

collar point
pointe^F de col^M
Kragenspitze^F
punta^F del colletto^M
punta^F del cuello^M

front
devant^M
Vorderseite^F
davanti^M
delantero^M

button
bouton^M
Knopf^M
bottone^M
botón^M

shirttail
pan^M
Schoß^M
lembo^M della camicia^F
faldón^F de la camisa^F

shirt
chemise^F
Hemd^N
camicia^F
camisa^F

CLOTHING

collar stiffener
baleine^F de col^M
Kragenstäbchen^N
tendicollo^M
ballena^F

buttondown collar
col^M pointes^F boutonnées
Button-Down-Kragen^M
collo^M button-down
cuello^M con botones^M

cravat
ascot^F
Krawattenschal^M
lavallière^F
corbata^F inglesa

bow tie
nœud^M papillon^M
Fliege^F
papillon^M
pajarita^F

spread collar
col^M italien
gespreizter Kragen^M
collo^M a camicia^F
cuello^M italiano

necktie
cravate^F
Krawatte^F
cravalla^F
corbata^F

front apron
pan^M avant
Vorderteil^{M/N}
lembo^M anteriore
faldón^M delantero

neck end
tour^M de cou^M
Bindeteil^{M/N}
annodatura^F
contorno^M del cuello^M

rear apron
pan^M arrière
Endteil^{M/N}
lembo^M posteriore
faldón^M trasero

lining
doublure^F
Futter^N
fodera^F
forro^M

loop
passant^M
Schlaufe^F
passante^M
presilla^F

slip-stitched seam
couture^F médiane
Verziehnaht^F
cucitura^F a sottopunto^M
costura^F invisible

CLOTHING

trousers
pantalon^M
Hose^F
pantaloni^M
pantalones^M

waistband extension
patte^F boutonnée
Bundverlängerung^F
abbottonatura^F della cintura^F
trabilla^F de la pretina^F

knife pleat
pli^M plat
einfache Falte^F
piega^F piatta
pinza^F

fly
braguette^F
Hosenschlitz^M
patta^F
bragueta^F

crease
pli^M
Bügelfalte^F
piega^F
raya^F

belt loop
passant^M
Gürtelschlaufe^F
passante^M
trabilla^F

front top pocket
poche^F cavalière
Flügeltasche^F
tasca^F anteriore
bolsillo^M delantero

waistband
ceinture^F montée
Hosenbund^M
cintura^F
pretina^F

back pocket
poche^F-revolver^M
Gesäßtasche^F
tasca^F posteriore
bolsillo^M trasero

brace clip
pince^F
Klips^M
fermaglio^M
pinza^F

braces
bretelles^F
Hosenträger^M
bretelle^F
tirantes^M

elastic webbing
bande^F élastique
Gummiband^N
tessuto^M elastico
banda^F elástica

adjustment slide
coulisse^F
Versteller^M
cursore^M
corredera^F de ajuste^M

leather end
patte^F
Lederstrippe^F
laccio^M di pelle^F
lengüeta^F de cuero^M

button loop
boutonnière^F
Knopflasche^F
asola^F
presilla^F

turn-up
revers^M
Aufschlag^M
risvolto^M
vuelta^F

belt
ceinture^F
Gürtel^M
cintura^F
cinturón^M

top stitching
surpiqûre^F
Zier-Steppnaht^F
impuntura^F
pespunte^M

panel
croûte^F de cuir^M
Gürtelband^N
fascia^F di cuoio^M
cuero^M

tongue
ardillon^M
Dorn^M
ardiglione^M
pasador^M

buckle
boucle^F
Gürtelschnalle^F
fibbia^F
hebilla^F

tip
pointe^F
Gürtelspitze^F
punta^F
punta^F

punch hole
cran^M
gestanztes Loch^N
foro^M
ojete^M

belt loop
passant^M
Gürtelschlaufe^F
passante^M
trabilla^F

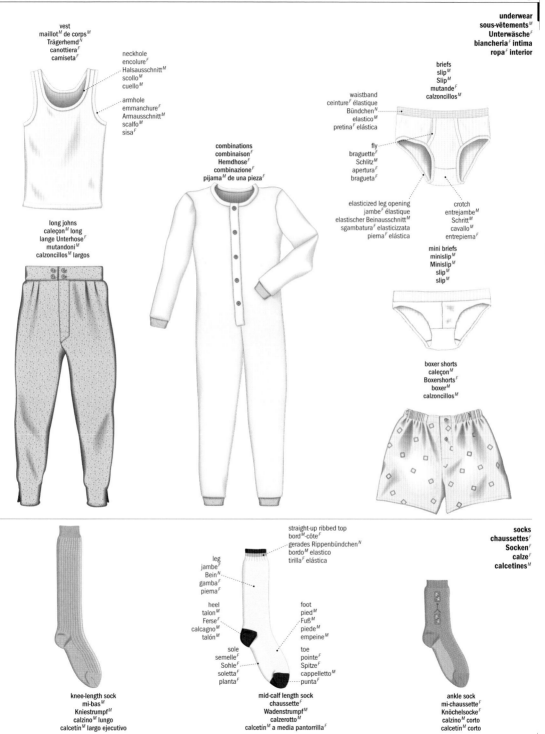

vest
maillot^M de corps^M
Trägerhemd^N
canottiera^F
camiseta^F

neckhole
encolure^F
Halsausschnitt^M
scollo^M
cuello^M

armhole
emmanchure^F
Armausschnitt^M
scalfo^M
sisa^F

underwear
sous-vêtements^M
Unterwäsche^F
biancheria^F intima
ropa^F interior

briefs
slip^M
Slip^M
mutande^F
calzoncillos^M

waistband
ceinture^F élastique
Bündchen^N
elastico^M
pretina^F elástica

fly
braguette^F
Schlitz^M
apertura^F
bragueta^F

combinations
combinaison^F
Hemdhose^F
combinazione^F
pijama^M de una pieza^F

elasticized leg opening
jambe^F élastique
elastischer Beinausschnitt^M
sgambatura^F elasticizzata
pierna^F elástica

crotch
entrejambe^M
Schritt^M
cavallo^M
entrepierna^F

long johns
caleçon^M long
lange Unterhose^F
mutandoni^M
calzoncillos^M largos

mini briefs
minislip^M
Minislip^M
slip^M
slip^M

boxer shorts
caleçon^M
Boxershorts^F
boxer^M
calzoncillos^M

socks
chaussettes^F
Socken^F
calze^F
calcetines^M

straight-up ribbed top
bord^M-côte^F
gerades Rippenbündchen^N
bordo^M elastico
tirilla^F elástica

leg
jambe^F
Bein^N
gamba^F
pierna^F

heel
talon^M
Ferse^F
calcagno^M
talón^M

foot
pied^M
Fuß^M
piede^M
empeine^M

sole
semelle^F
Sohle^F
soletta^F
planta^F

toe
pointe^F
Spitze^F
cappelletto^M
punta^F

knee-length sock
mi-bas^M
Kniestrumpf^M
calzino^M lungo
calcetín^M largo ejecutivo

mid-calf length sock
chaussette^F
Wadenstrumpf^M
calzerotto^M
calcetín^M a media pantorrilla^F

ankle sock
mi-chaussette^F
Knöchelsocke^F
calzino^M corto
calcetín^M corto

CLOTHING

coats
manteaux^M **et blousons**^{M}
Mäntel^M **und Jacken**^{F}
esempi^M **di giacconi**^{M} **e cappotti**^{M}
abrigos^M **e impermeables**^{F}

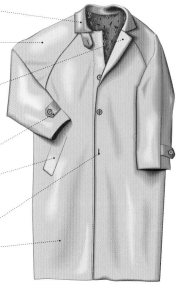

raincoat
imperméable^M
Regenmantel^M
impermeabile^M
impermeable^M

collar
col^M
Kragen^M
collo^M
cuello^M

raglan sleeve
manche^F raglan
Raglanärmel^M
manica^F alla raglan
manga^F raglán

notched lapel
revers^M cranté
abfallendes Revers^N
revers^M
solapa^F con ojal^M

tab
patte^F
Spange^F
linguetta^F
lengüeta^F

broad welt side pocket
poche^F raglan
schräge Pattentasche^F
tasca^F interna con aletta^F
bolsillo^M de ribete^M ancho

buttonhole
boutonnière^F
Knopfloch^N
occhiello^M
ojal^M

side panel
pan^M
Seitenteil$^{M/N}$
falda^F
paño^M lateral

overcoat
pardessus^M
Mantel^M
cappotto^M
abrigo^M

notched lapel
revers^M cranté
abfallendes Revers^N
revers^M
solapa^F con ojal^M

breast pocket
poche^F poitrine^F
Brusttasche^F
taschino^M
bolsillo^M superior

breast dart
pince^F de taille^F
Taillenabnäher^M
ripresa^F
pinza^F

flap pocket
poche^F à rabat^M
Klappentasche^F
tasca^F profilata con aletta^F
bolsillo^M con cartera^F

trench coat
trench^M
Trenchcoat^M
trench^M
trinchera^F

two-way collar
col^M transformable
Wendekragen^M
collo^M
cuello^M de doble vista^F

gun flap
bavolet^M
Koller^N
aletta^F staccata
protector^M

double-breasted buttoning
double boutonnage^M
zweireihig
abbottonatura^F a doppiopetto^M
botonadura^F cruzada

belt
ceinture^F
Gürtel^M
cintura^F
cinturón^M

belt loop
passant^M
Gürtelschlaufe^F
passante^M della cintura^F
presilla^F del cinturón^M

buckle
boucle^F de ceinture^F
Schnalle^F
fibbia^F
hebilla^F

epaulet
patte^F d'épaule^F
Schulterklappe^F
spallina^F
hombrera^F

raglan sleeve
manche^F raglan
Raglanärmel^M
manica^F alla raglan
manga^F raglán

sleeve strap loop
passant^M
Riegel^M
passante^M del cinturino^M
presilla^F de la manga^F

sleeve strap
patte^F de serrage^M
Ärmellasche^F
cinturino^M della manica^F
correa^F de la manga^F

broad welt side pocket
poche^F raglan
schräge Pattentasche^F
tasca^F interna con aletta^F
bolsillo^M de ribete^M ancho

three-quarter coat
paletot^M
dreiviertellange Jacke^F
trequarti^M
abrigo^M de tres cuartos

CLOTHING

parka
parka^F
Parka^M
parka^M
parka^F

sheepskin jacket
canadienne^F
Lammfelljacke^F
montone^M
zamarra^F

snap-fastening tab
patte^F à boutons^M-pression^F
Druckknopfleiste^F
allacciatura^F con bottoni^M a pressione^F
botón^M de presión^F

zip fastener
fermeture^F à glissière^F
Reißverschluss^M
chiusura^F lampo
cremallera^F

duffle coat
duffle-coat^M
Dufflecoat^M
montgomery^M
trenca^F

hood
capuchon^M
Kapuze^F
cappuccio^M
capucha^F

yoke
empiècement^M
Sattel^M
carré^M
hombrillo^M

frog
brandebourg^M
Lasche^F
alamaro^M
alamar^M

patch pocket
poche^F plaquée
aufgesetzte Tasche^F
tasca^F applicata
bolsillo^M de parche^M

toggle
bûchette^F
Knebelverschluss^M
olivetta^F
botón^M de madera^F

windcheater
blouson^M court
Blouson^M
giacca^F a vento^M
cazadora^F

windcheater
blouson^M long
Windjacke^F
giacca^F a vento^M
cazadora^F

snap fastener
bouton^M-pression^F
Druckknopf^M
bottone^M a pressione^F
botón^M de presión^M

hand-warmer pocket
poche^F repose-bras^M
Mufftasche^F
tasca^F interna con aletta^F
bolsillo^M de ojal^M

elastic waistband
ceinture^F élastique
elastischer Bund^M
fascia^F elastica
pretina^F elástica

waistband
ceinture^F montée
Bund^M
coulisse^F
pretina^F

drawstring
cordon^M coulissant
Durchziehschnur^F
cordoncino^M
cordón^M

CLOTHING

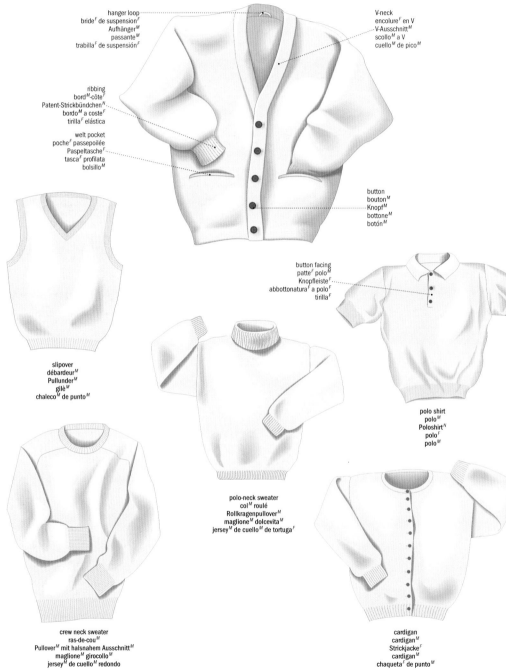

V-neck cardigan
gilet^M de laine^F
Strickjacke^F mit V-Ausschnitt^M
cardigan^M con scollo^M a V
cárdigan

hanger loop
bride^F de suspension^F
Aufhänger^M
passante^M
trabilla^F de suspensión^F

V-neck
encolure^F en V
V-Ausschnitt^M
scollo^M a V
cuello^M de pico^M

ribbing
bord^M-côte^F
Patent-Strickbündchen^N
bordo^M a coste^F
tirilla^F elástica

welt pocket
poche^F passepoilée
Paspeltasche^F
tasca^F profilata
bolsillo^M

button
bouton^M
Knopf^M
bottone^M
botón^M

button facing
patte^F polo^M
Knopfleiste^F
abbottonatura^F a polo^F
tirilla^F

slipover
débardeur^M
Pullunder^M
gilè^M
chaleco^M de punto^M

polo shirt
polo^M
Poloshirt^N
polo^F
polo^M

polo-neck sweater
col^M roulé
Rollkragenpullover^M
maglione^M dolcevita^M
jersey^M de cuello^M de tortuga^F

crew neck sweater
ras-de-cou^M
Pullover^M mit halsnahem Ausschnitt^M
maglione^M girocollo^M
jersey^M de cuello^M redondo

cardigan
cardigan^M
Strickjacke^F
cardigan^M
chaqueta^F de punto^M

CLOTHING

suit
tailleur^M
Kostüm^N
tailleur^M
traje^M de chaqueta^F

jacket
veste^F
Jacke^F
giacca^F
chaqueta^F

skirt
jupe^F
Rock^M
gonna^F
falda^F

pelerine
pèlerine^F
Pelerine^F
cappotto^M con pellegrina^F
abrigo^M con esclavina^F

pelerine
pèlerine^F
Pelerine^F
pellegrina^F
esclavina^F

seam pocket
poche^F prise dans une couture^F
Nahttasche^F
tasca^F inserita nella cucitura^F
bolsillo^M disimulado

car coat
paletot^M
Autocoat^M
giaccone^M
chaquetón^M de tres cuartos

raglan
raglan^M
Raglanmantel^M
cappotto^M alla raglan
abrigo^M raglán

raglan sleeve
manche^F raglan
Raglanärmel^M
manica^F alla raglan
manga^F raglán

fly front closing
boutonnage^M sous patte^F
verdeckte Knopfleiste^F
finta^F
pestaña^F

broad welt side pocket
poche^F raglan
schräge Pattentasche^F
tasca^F interna con aletta^F
bolsillo^M de ribete^M ancho

cape
cape^F
Cape^N
mantella^F
capa^F

arm slit
passe-bras^M
Durchgrifftasche^F
apertura^F per le braccia^F
abertura^F para el brazo^M

jacket
veste^F
Blazer^M
giacca^F
chaquetón^M

poncho
poncho^M
Poncho^M
poncho^M
poncho^M

coats
manteaux^M
Mäntel^M und Jacken^F
esempi^M di giacche^F e cappotti^M
chaquetones^M y abrigos^M

riding coat
redingote^F
Redingote^F
redingote^F
abrigo^M redingote

pea jacket
caban^M
Cabanjacke^F
giacca^F alla marinara
chaquetón^M marinero

tailored collar
col^M tailleur^M
Schneiderkragen^M
collo^M a uomo^M
cuello^M hechura^F sastre^M

hand warmer pocket
poche^F repose-bras^M
Mufftasche^F
tasca^F tagliata in verticale
bolsillo^M de ojal^M

mock pocket
fausse poche^F
blinde Tasche^F
tasca^F finta
bolsillo^M simulado

overcoat
manteau^M
Mantel^M
cappotto^M
abrigo^M

CLOTHING

251

examples of dresses
exemples *M* **de robes** *F*
Beispiele *N* **für Kleider** *N*
esempi *M* **di abiti** *M*
ejemplos *M* **de vestidos** *M*

sheath dress
robe *F* fourreau *M*
Schlauchkleid *N*
tubino *M*
recto *M* entallado

princess dress
robe *F* princesse *F*
Prinzesskleid *N*
princesse *F*
corte *M* princesa *F*

coat dress
robe *F* -manteau *M*
Mantelkleid *N*
robe-manteau *F/M*
traje *M* cruzado

polo dress
robe *F* -polo *M*
Polokleid *N*
abito *M* a polo *F*
vestido *M* de camiseta *F*

house dress
robe *F* de maison *F*
Hauskleid *N*
abito *M* da casa *F*
vestido *M* camisero sin mangas

shirtwaist dress
robe *F* chemisier *M*
Hemdblusenkleid *N*
chemisier *M*
vestido *M* camisero

drop waist dress
robe *F* taille *F* basse
Kleid *N* mit angesetztem Schoß *M*
abito *M* a vita *F* bassa
vestido de talle *M* bajo

A-line dress
robe *F* trapèze *M*
Kleid *N* in Trapez-Form *F*
abito *M* a trapezio *M*
vestido *M* acampanado

sundress
robe *F* bain *M* -de-soleil *M*
leichtes Sonnenkleid *N*
prendisole *M*
vestido *M* de tirantes *M*

wrapover dress
robe *F* enveloppe *F*
Wickelkleid *N*
abito *M* a vestaglia *F*
vestido *M* cruzado

tunic dress
robe *F* tunique *F*
Tunikakleid *N*
abito *M* a tunica *F*
túnica *F*

pinafore
chasuble *F*
Trägerrock *M*
scamiciato *M*
pichi *M*

examples of skirts
exemples[M] **de jupes**[F]
Beispiele[N] **für Röcke**[M]
esempi[M] **di gonne**[F]
ejemplos[M] **de faldas**[F]

CLOTHING

gored skirt
jupe[F] à lés[M]
Bahnenrock[M]
gonna[F] a teli[M]
falda[F] de piezas[F]

kilt
kilt[M]
Schottenrock[M]
kilt[M]
falda[F] escocesa

sarong
paréo[M]
Sarong[M]
sarong[M]
falda[F] sarong[M]

wrapover skirt
jupe[F] portefeuille[M]
Wickelrock[M]
gonna[F] a portafoglio[M]
falda[F] cruzada

sheath skirt
jupe[F] fourreau[M]
Etuirock[M]
gonna[F] ad anfora[F]
falda[F] de tubo[M]

ruffled skirt
jupe[F] à volants[M] étagés
Stufenrock[M]
gonna[F] a balze[F]
falda[F] de volantes[M]

straight skirt
jupe[F] droite
gerader Rock[M]
gonna[F] diritta
falda[F] recta

yoke skirt
jupe[F] à empiècement[M]
Sattelrock[M]
gonna[F] con baschina[F]
falda[F] acampanada

gather skirt
jupe[F] froncée
Kräuselrock[M]
gonna[F] arricciata
falda[F] fruncida

culottes
jupe[F]-culotte[F]
Hosenrock[M]
gonna[F] pantalone[M]
falda[F] pantalón[M]

examples of pleats
exemples[M] **de plis**[M]
Beispiele[N] **für Falten**[F]
esempi[M] **di pieghe**[F]
ejemplos[M] **de tablas**[F]

inverted pleat
pli[M] creux
Kellerfalte[F]
piega[F] invertita
tabla[F] delantera

kick pleat
pli[M] d'aisance[F]
Gehfalte[F]
piega[F] sovrapposta
tabla[F] abierta

accordion pleat
plissé[M] accordéon[M]
Bahnenplissee[N]
plissé[M]
plisada

top stitched pleat
pli[M] surpiqué
abgesteppte Falte[F]
piega[F] impunturata
pespunteada

knife pleat
pli[M] plat
einfache Falte[F]
piega[F] a coltello[M]
tablas[F]

CLOTHING

examples of trousers
exemples [M] **de pantalons** [M]
Beispiele [N] **für Hosen** [F]
esempi [M] **di pantaloni** [M]
ejemplos [M] **de pantalones** [M]

shorts
short [M]
Shorts [F]
shorts [M]
pantalón [M] corto

Bermuda shorts
bermuda [M]
Bermudashorts [F]
bermuda [M]
bermudas [M]

knickerbockers
knicker [M]
Kniebundhose [F]
pantaloni [M] alla zuava
bombachos [M]

pedal pushers
corsaire [M]
Caprihose [F]
pantaloni [M] alla pescatora
pirata [M]

jeans
jean [M]
Jeans [F]
jeans [M]
vaqueros [M]

ski pants
fuseau [M]
Steghose [F]
fuseau [M]
pantalones [M] de tubo [M]

footstrap
sous-pied [M]
Steg [M]
staffa [F]
trabilla [F]

jumpsuit
combinaison [F]-pantalon [M]
Overall [M]
tuta [F]
buzo [M]

dungarees
salopette [F]
Latzhose [F]
salopette [F]
pantalón [M] peto [M]

bell bottoms
pantalon [M] pattes [F] d'éléphant [M]
Schlaghose [F]
pantaloni [M] a zampa [F] di elefante [M]
pantalones [M] acampanados

waistcoats and jackets
vestes [F] **et pulls** [M]
Westen [F] **und Jacken** [F]
esempi [M] **di giacche** [F] **e pullover** [M]
chalecos [M] **, jerseys** [M] **y chaquetas** [F]

spencer
spencer [M]
Spenzer [M]
spencer [M]
bolero [M] con botones [M]

bolero
boléro [M]
Bolero [M]
bolero [M]
bolero [M]

blazer
blazer [M]
Blazer [M]
blazer [M]
americana [F]

safari jacket
saharienne^F
Safarijacke^F
sahariana^F
sahariana^F

gusset pocket
poche^F soufflet^M
Blasebalgtasche^F
tasca^F applicata a soffietto^M
bolsillo^M de fuelle^M

waistcoat
gilet^M
Weste^F
gilè^M
chaleco^M

twin-set
tandem^M
Twinset^N
twin-set^M
jerseys^M combinados

crew neck sweater
ras-de-cou^M
Pullover^M mit halsnahem Ausschnitt^M
maglia^F girocollo^M
jersey^M de cuello^M redondo

cardigan
cardigan^M
Cardigan^M
cardigan^M
chaqueta^F de punto^M

body
body^M
Bodyshirt^N
body^M
body^M

crotch piece
patte^F d'entrejambe^M
Schritt^M
cavallo^M
entrepierna^F

sailor tunic
marinière^F
Matrosenbluse^F
maglietta^F alla marinara
camisa^F marinera

examples of blouses
exemples^M de corsages^M
Beispiele^N für Blusen^F und Hemden^N
esempi^M di camicette^F
ejemplos^M de blusas^F

yoke
empiècement^M
Sattel^M
carré^M
canesú^M

gather
fronce^F
Kräuselfalte^F
arricciatura^F
fruncido^M

shirttail
pan^M
Schoß^M
lembo^M
faldón^M

classic blouse
chemisier^M classique
klassische Bluse^F
camicetta^F classica
camisera^F clásica

button-through smock
tablier^M-blouse^F
Kittelbluse^F
sopravveste^F a grembiule^M
blusón^M

overshirt
liquette^F
Hosenbluse^F
camicione^M
camisa^F

smock
tunique^F
Arbeitskittel^M
camiciotto^M
blusón^M con tirilla^F

wrapover top
cache-cœur^M
Wickelbluse^F
camicetta^F incrociata
chaqueta^F cruzada

polo shirt
polo^M
Polohemd^N
polo^F
polo^M

tunic
casaque^F
Tunika^F
casacca^F
casaca^F

nightwear
vêtements^M de nuit^F
Nachtwäsche^F
biancheria^F da notte^F
lencería^F

kimono
kimono^M
Kimono^M
kimono^M
kimono^M

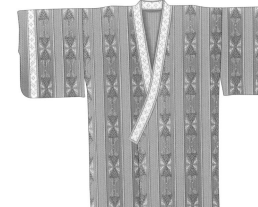

nightgown
chemise^F de nuit^F
Nachthemd^N
camicia^F da notte^F
camisón^M

baby doll
nuisette^F
Baby-Doll^N
baby-doll^M
picardía^F

pyjamas
pyjama^M
Schlafanzug^M
pigiama^M
pijama^M

negligee
déshabillé^M
Negligé^N
vestaglia^F
bata^F

bathrobe
peignoir^M
Bademantel^M
accappatoio^M
albornoz^M

CLOTHING

CLOTHING

knee sock
mi-bas^M
Kniestrumpf^M
calzettone^M
calcetín^M largo

sock
chaussette^F
Socke^F
gambaletto^M
calcetín^M

ankle sock
mi-chaussette^F
Söckchen^N
calzerotto^M
tobillera^F

short sock
socquette^F
Kurzsocke^F
calzino^M
calcetín^M

tights
collant^M
Strumpfhose^F
collant^M
pantis^M/medias^F

stocking
bas^M
Strumpf^M
calza^F
media^F

thigh stocking
bas^M-cuissarde^F
Overknee-Strumpf^M
calza^F autoreggente
media^F antideslizante

fishnet stocking
bas^M résille^F
Netzstrumpf^M
calza^F a rete^F
media^F de malla^F

underwear
sous-vêtements^M
Unterwäsche^F
biancheria^F **intima**
ropa^F **interior**

corselette
combiné^M
Korselett^N
modellatore^M aperto
faja^F con sostén^M

camisole
caraco^M
Camisol^N
top^M
camisola^F

teddy
teddy^M
Teddy^M
pagliaccetto^M
canesú^M

body
body^M
Bodysuit^M
body^M
body^M

panty corselette
combiné^M-culotte^F
Panty-Korselett^N
modellatore^M sgambato
faja^F corsé^M

half-slip
jupon^M
Unterrock^M
sottogonna^F
falda^F combinación^F

princess seaming
découpe^F princesse^F
Prinzessnaht^F
cucitura^F a princesse^F
costura^F de corte^M princesa^F

foundation slip
fond^M de robe^F
Vollachsel-Unterkleid^N
sottoveste^F
combinación^F

slip
combinaison^F-jupon^M
Unterkleid^N
sottoveste^F con reggiseno^M
combinación^F con sujetador^M

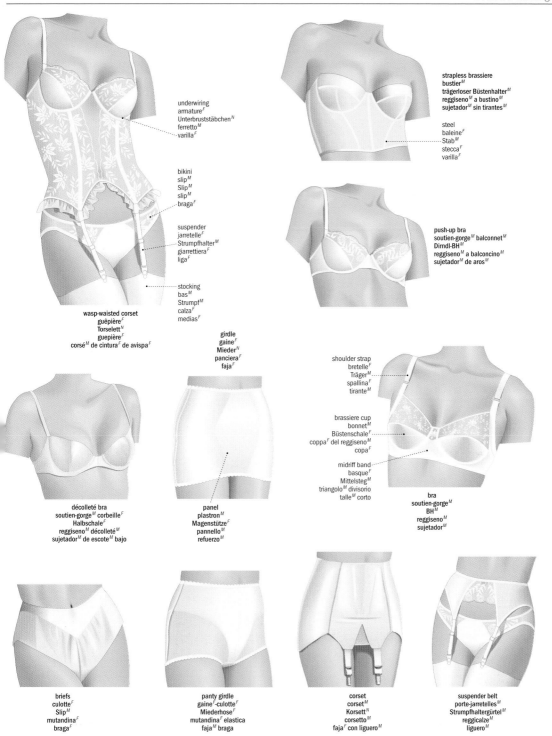

underwiring
armature^F
Unterbruststäbchen^N
ferretto^M
varilla^F

bikini
slip^M
Slip^M
slip^M
braga^F

suspender
jarretelle^F
Strumpfhalter^M
giarrettiera^F
liga^F

stocking
bas^M
Strumpf^M
calza^F
medias^F

wasp-waisted corset
guêpière^F
Torselett^N
guepière^F
corsé^M de cintura^F de avispa^F

strapless brassiere
bustier^M
trägerloser Büstenhalter^M
reggiseno^M a bustino^M
sujetador^M sin tirantes^M

steel
baleine^F
Stab^M
stecca^F
varilla^F

push-up bra
soutien-gorge^M balconnet^M
Dirndl-BH^M
reggiseno^M a balconcino^M
sujetador^M de aros^M

girdle
gaine^F
Mieder^N
panciera^F
faja^F

décolleté bra
soutien-gorge^M corbeille^F
Halbschale^F
reggiseno^M décolleté^M
sujetador^M de escote^M bajo

panel
plastron^M
Magenstütze^F
pannello^M
refuerzo^M

shoulder strap
bretelle^F
Träger^M
spallina^F
tirante^M

brassiere cup
bonnet^M
Büstenschale^F
coppa^F del reggiseno^M
copa^F

midriff band
basque^F
Mittelsteg^M
triangolo^M divisorio
talle^M corto

bra
soutien-gorge^M
BH^M
reggiseno^M
sujetador^M

briefs
culotte^F
Slip^M
mutandina^F
braga^F

panty girdle
gaine^F-culotte^F
Miederhose^F
mutandina^F elastica
faja^M braga

corset
corset^M
Korsett^N
corsetto^M
faja^F con liguero^M

suspender belt
porte-jarretelles^M
Strumpfhaltergürtel^M
reggicalze^M
liguero^M

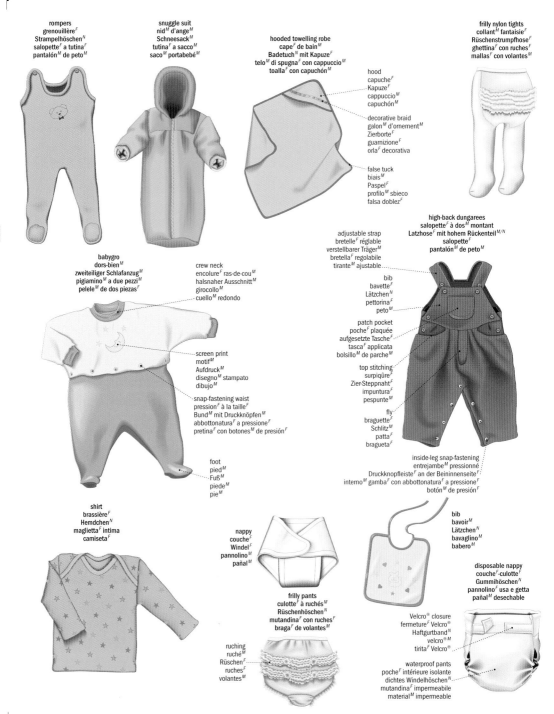

rompers
grenouillère^F
Strampelhöschen^N
salopette^F a tutina^F
pantalón^M de peto^M

snuggle suit
nid^M d'ange^M
Schneesack^M
tutina^F a sacco^M
saco^M portabebé^M

hooded towelling robe
cape^F de bain^M
Badetuch^N mit Kapuze^F
telo^M di spugna^F con cappuccio^M
toalla^F con capuchón^M

frilly nylon tights
collant^M fantaisie^F
Rüschenstrumpfhose^F
ghettina^F con ruches^F
mallas^F con volantes^M

hood
capuche^F
Kapuze^F
cappuccio^M
capuchón^M

decorative braid
galon^M d'ornement^M
Zierborte^F
guarnizione^F
orla^F decorativa

false tuck
biais^M
Paspel^F
profilo^M sbieco
falsa doblez^F

high-back dungarees
salopette^F à dos^M montant
Latzhose^F mit hohem Rückenteil^{M/N}
salopette^F
pantalón^M de peto^M

adjustable strap
bretelle^F réglable
verstellbarer Träger^M
bretella^F regolabile
tirante^M ajustable

babygro
dors-bien^M
zweiteiliger Schlafanzug^M
pigiamino^M a due pezzi^M
pelele^M de dos piezas^F

crew neck
encolure^F ras-de-cou^M
halsnaher Ausschnitt^M
girocollo^M
cuello^M redondo

bib
bavette^F
Lätzchen^N
pettorina^F
peto^M

patch pocket
poche^F plaquée
aufgesetzte Tasche^F
tasca^F applicata
bolsillo^M de parche^M

screen print
motif^M
Aufdruck^M
disegno^M stampato
dibujo^M

top stitching
surpiqûre^F
Zier-Steppnaht^F
impuntura^F
pespunte^M

snap-fastening waist
pression^F à la taille^F
Bund^M mit Druckknöpfen^M
abbottonatura^F a pressione^F
pretina^F con botones^M de presión^F

fly
braguette^F
Schlitz^M
patta^F
bragueta^F

foot
pied^M
Fuß^M
piede^M
pie^M

inside-leg snap-fastening
entrejambe^M pressionné
Druckknopfleiste^F an der Beininnenseite^F
interno^M gamba^F con abbottonatura^F a pressione^F
botón^M de presión^F

shirt
brassière^F
Hemdchen^N
maglietta^F intima
camiseta^F

nappy
couche^F
Windel^F
pannolino^M
pañal^M

bib
bavoir^M
Lätzchen^N
bavaglino^M
babero^M

disposable nappy
couche^F-culotte^F
Gummihöschen^N
pannolino^M usa e getta
pañal^M desechable

frilly pants
culotte^F à ruchés^M
Rüschenhöschen^N
mutandina^F con ruches^F
braga^F de volantes^M

Velcro® closure
fermeture^F Velcro®
Haftgurtband^N
velcro^{®M}
tirita^F Velcro®

ruching
ruché^M
Rüschen^F
ruches^F
volantes^M

waterproof pants
poche^F intérieure isolante
dichtes Windelhöschen^N
mutandina^F impermeabile
material^M impermeable

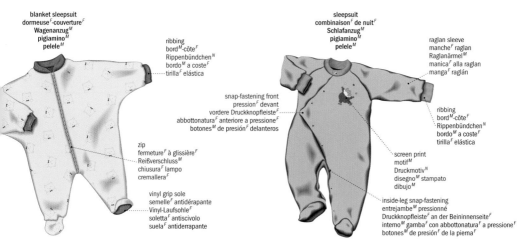

blanket sleepsuit
dormeuse^F-couverture^F
Wagenanzug^M
pigiamino^M
pelele^M

ribbing
bord^M-côte^F
Rippenbündchen^N
bordo^M a coste^F
tirilla^F elástica

zip
fermeture^F à glissière^F
Reißverschluss^M
chiusura^F lampo
cremallera^F

vinyl grip sole
semelle^F antidérapante
Vinyl-Laufsohle^F
soletta^F antiscivolo
suela^F antiderrapante

sleepsuit
combinaison^F de nuit^F
Schlafanzug^M
pigiamino^M
pelele^M

raglan sleeve
manche^F raglan
Raglanärmel^M
manica^F alla raglan
manga^F raglán

snap-fastening front
pression^F devant
vordere Druckknopfleiste^F
abbottonatura^F anteriore a pressione^F
botones^M de presión^F delanteros

ribbing
bord^M-côte^F
Rippenbündchen^N
bordo^M a coste^F
tirilla^F elástica

screen print
motif^M
Druckmotiv^N
disegno^M stampato
dibujo^M

inside-leg snap-fastening
entrejambe^F pressionné
Druckknopfleiste^F an der Beininnenseite^F
interno^M gamba^F con abbottonatura^F a pressione^F
botones^M de presión^F de la pierna^F

children's clothing

vêtements^M d'enfant^M | Kinderbekleidung^F | vestiti^M per bambini^M | ropa^F de niños^M

dungarees with crossover back straps
salopette^F à bretelles^F croisées
Latzhose^F mit gekreuzten Rückenträgern^M
salopette^F con bretelle^F incrociate
pantalones^M de peto^M

button strap
bretelle^F boutonnée
Träger^M mit Knopf^M
bretella^F abbottonabile
tirante^M con botones^M

bib
bavette^F
Lätzchen^N
pettorina^F
peto^M

snowsuit
esquimau^M
Schneeanzug^M
tuta^F da sci^M
mono^M de esqui^M con capucha^F

slip-on pyjamas
polojama^M
Schlafanzug^M in Schlupfform^F
pigiama^M
pijama^M

drawstring hood
capuchon^M coulissé
Kapuze^F mit Zugband^N
cappuccio^M con cordoncino^M
capucha^F con cordón^M

fly front closing
fermeture^F sous patte^F
Verschluss^M mit verdeckter Knopfleiste^F
finta^F
cremallera^F

T-shirt dress
robe^F tee-shirt^M
T-Shirt Kleid^N
abito^M a T-shirt^F
camiseta^F de cuerpo^M entero

rompers
barboteuse^F
Spielanzug^M
pagliaccetto^M
ranita^F

training set
tenue^F d'exercice^M
Sportset^N
completo^M da ginnastica^F
conjunto^M deportivo

vest
débardeur^M
Trägerhemdchen^N
canottiera^F
camiseta^F

shorts
short^M
kurze Hose^F
pantaloncini^M
pantalón^M corto

jumpsuit
combinaison^F
Overall^M
tuta^F
mono^M

sportswear

tenue^F d'exercice^M | Sportkleidung^F | abbigliamento^M sportivo | ropa^F deportiva

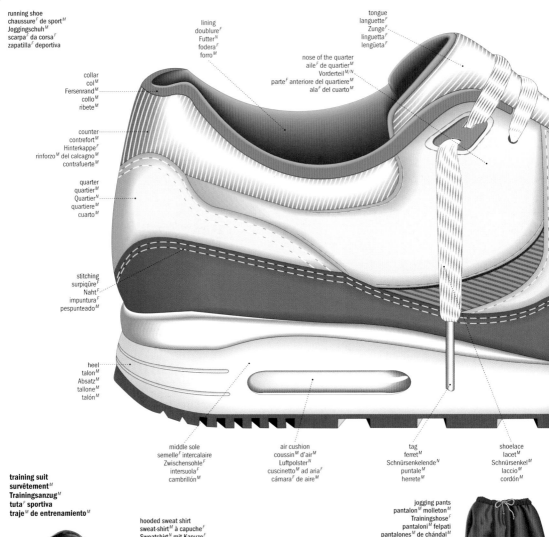

running shoe
chaussure^F de sport^M
Joggingschuh^M
scarpa^F da corsa^F
zapatilla^F deportiva

lining
doublure^F
Futter^N
fodera^F
forro^M

tongue
languette^F
Zunge^F
linguetta^F
lengüeta^F

nose of the quarter
aile^F de quartier^M
Vorderteil^{M/N}
parte^F anteriore del quartiere^M
ala^F del cuarto^M

collar
col^M
Fersenrand^M
collo^M
ribete^M

counter
contrefort^M
Hinterkappe^F
rinforzo^M del calcagno^M
contrafuerte^M

quarter
quartier^M
Quartier^N
quartiere^M
cuarto^M

stitching
surpiqûre^F
Naht^F
impuntura^F
pespunteado^M

heel
talon^M
Absatz^M
tallone^M
talón^M

middle sole
semelle^F intercalaire
Zwischensohle^F
intersuola^F
cambrillón^M

air cushion
coussin^M d'air^M
Luftpolster^N
cuscinetto^M ad aria^F
cámara^F de aire^M

tag
ferret^M
Schnürsenkelende^N
puntale^M
herrete^M

shoelace
lacet^M
Schnürsenkel^M
laccio^M
cordón^M

training suit
survêtement^M
Trainingsanzug^M
tuta^F **sportiva**
traje^M **de entrenamiento**^M

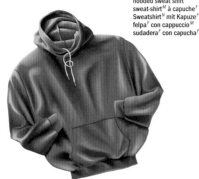

hooded sweat shirt
sweat-shirt^M à capuche^F
Sweatshirt^N mit Kapuze^F
felpa^F con cappuccio^M
sudadera^F con capucha^F

sweat shirt
sweat-shirt^M
Sweatshirt^N
felpa^F
sudadera^F

jogging pants
pantalon^M molleton^M
Trainingshose^F
pantaloni^M felpati
pantalones^M de chándal^M

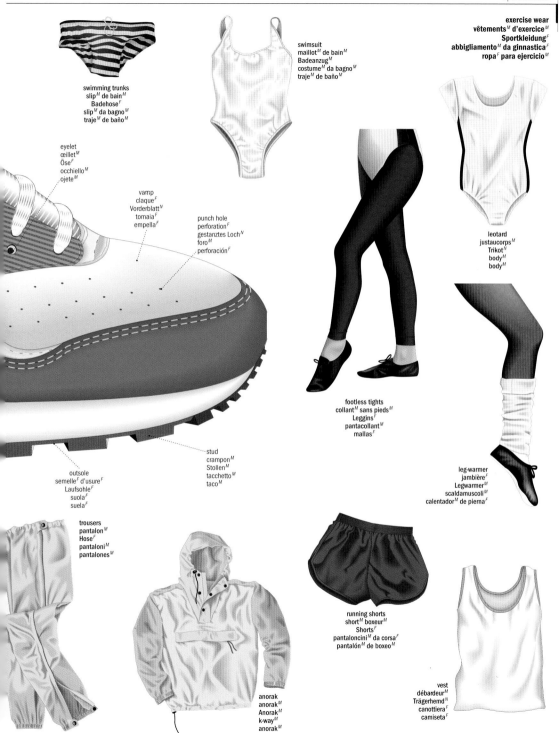

swimming trunks
slip^M de bain^M
Badehose^F
slip^M da bagno^M
traje^M de baño^M

swimsuit
maillot^M de bain^M
Badeanzug^M
costume^M da bagno^M
traje^M de baño^M

exercise wear
vêtements^M d'exercice^M
Sportkleidung^F
abbigliamento^M da ginnastica^F
ropa^F para ejercicio^M

eyelet
œillet^M
Öse^F
occhiello^M
ojete^M

vamp
claque^F
Vorderblatt^N
tomaia^F
empella^F

punch hole
perforation^F
gestanztes Loch^N
foro^M
perforación^F

leotard
justaucorps^M
Trikot^N
body^M
body^M

CLOTHING

footless tights
collant^M sans pieds^M
Leggins^F
pantacollant^M
mallas^F

stud
crampon^M
Stollen^M
tacchetto^M
taco^M

outsole
semelle^F d'usure^F
Laufsohle^F
suola^F
suela^F

leg-warmer
jambière^F
Legwarmer^M
scaldamuscoli^M
calentador^M de pierna^F

trousers
pantalon^M
Hose^F
pantaloni^M
pantalones^M

running shorts
short^M boxeur^M
Shorts^F
pantaloncini^M da corsa^F
pantalón^M de boxeo^M

anorak
anorak^M
Anorak^M
k-way^M
anorak^M

vest
débardeur^M
Trägerhemd^N
canottiera^F
camiseta^F

jewellery

bijouterie^F | Schmuck^M | gioielli^M | joyería^F

earrings
boucles^F d'oreille^F
Ohrringe^M
orecchini^M
pendientes^M

clip earrings
boucles^F d'oreille^F à pince^F
Klips^M
orecchini^M a clip^F
pendientes^M de clip^M

screw earrings
boucles^F d'oreille^F à vis^F
Ohrringe^M mit Schraubverschluss^M
orecchini^M a vite^F
pendientes^M de tornillo^M

ear studs
boucles^F d'oreille^F à tige^F
Ohrstecker^M
orecchini^M a perno^M
pendientes^M de espiga^F

drop earrings
pendants^M d'oreille^F
Ohrgehänge^N
orecchini^M pendenti
pendientes^M

hoop earrings
anneaux^F
Kreolen^F
orecchini^M ad anello^M
pendientes^M de aro^M

necklaces
colliers^M
Halsketten^F
collane^F
collares^M

matinee-length necklace
collier^M de perles^F, longueur^F matinée^F
Halskette^F in Matineelänge^F
collana^F
collar^M de una vuelta^F, matinée^F

velvet-band choker
collier^M-de-chien^M
Samtkropfband^N
collarino^M di velluto^M
gargantilla^F de terciopelo^M

pendant
pendentif^M
Anhänger^M
pendenti^M
pendiente^M

rope
sautoir^M
Endlosperlenkette^F
collana^F lunga alla vita^F
lazo^M

opera-length necklace
sautoir^M, longueur^F opéra^M
Halskette^F in Opernlänge^F
collana^F lunga
collar^M de una vuelta^F, ópera^F

bib necklace
collier^M de soirée^F
mehrreihige Halskette^F
collana^F a cinque giri^M
collar^M de 5 vueltas^M, peto^M

choker
ras-de-cou^M
Chokerkette^F
girocollo^M
gargantilla^F

locket
médaillon^M
Medaillon^N
medaglione^M
medallón^M

bracelets
bracelets^M
Armbänder^N
bracciali^M
brazaletes^M

identity bracelet
gourmette^F d'identité^F
Identitätsband^N
bracciale^M con piastrina^F
brazalete^M de identificación^F

charm bracelet
gourmette^F
Armband^N
bracciale^M con ciondoli^M
pulsera^F de dijes^M

bangle
bracelet^M tubulaire
Armreif^M
bracciale^M tubolare
brazalete^M tubular

rings
bagues^F
Ringe^M
anelli^M
anillos^M

band ring
jonc^M
Bandring^M
anello^M a fascia^F
alianza^F

signet ring
chevalière^F
Herrenring^M
anello^M con sigillo^M
sortija^F de sello^M

solitaire ring
solitaire^M
Solitärring^M
solitario^M
solitario^M

engagement ring
bague^F de fiançailles^F
Verlobungsring^M
anello^M di fidanzamento^M
anillo^M de compromiso^M

wedding ring
alliance^F
Ehering^M
fede^F nuziale
alianza^F

PERSONAL ADORNMENT AND ARTICLES

manicure

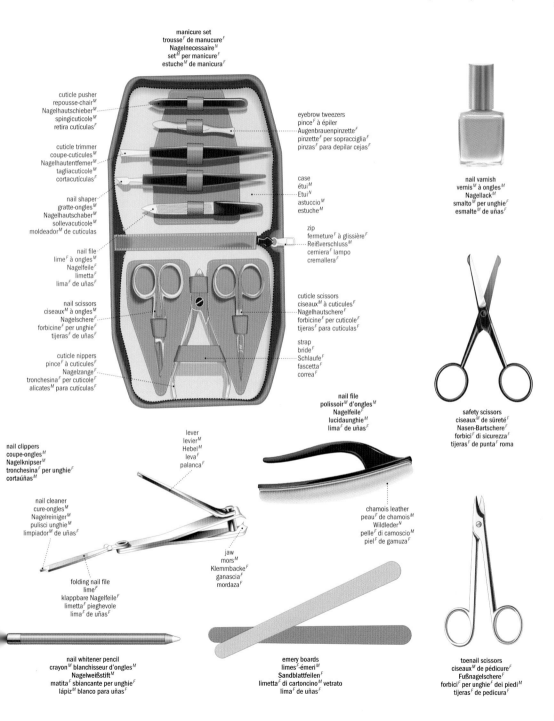

manicure set
trousse^F de manucure^F
Nagelnecessaire^N
set^M per manicure^F
estuche^M de manicura^F

cuticle pusher
repousse-chair^M
Nagelhautschieber^M
spingicuticole^M
retira cutículas^F

cuticle trimmer
coupe-cuticules^M
Nagelhautentferner^M
tagliacuticole^M
cortacuticulas^F

nail shaper
gratte-ongles^M
Nagelhautschaber^M
sollevacuticole^M
moldeador^M de cuticulas

nail file
lime^F à ongles^M
Nagelfeile^F
limetta^F
lima^F de uñas^F

nail scissors
ciseaux^M à ongles^M
Nagelschere^F
forbicine^F per unghie^F
tijeras^F de uñas^F

cuticle nippers
pince^F à cuticules^F
Nagelzange^F
tronchesina^F per cuticole^F
alicates^M para cutículas^F

eyebrow tweezers
pince^F à épiler
Augenbrauenpinzette^F
pinzette^F per sopracciglia^F
pinzas^F para depilar cejas^F

case
étui^M
Etui^N
astuccio^M
estuche^M

zip
fermeture^F à glissière^F
Reißverschluss^M
cerniera^F lampo
cremallera^F

cuticle scissors
ciseaux^M à cuticules^F
Nagelhautschere^F
forbicine^F per cuticole^F
tijeras^F para cutículas^F

strap
bride^F
Schlaufe^F
fascetta^F
correa^F

nail file
polissoir^M d'ongles^M
Nagelfeile^F
lucidaunghie^M
lima^F de uñas^F

nail varnish
vernis^F à ongles^M
Nagellack^M
smalto^M per unghie^F
esmalte^M de uñas^F

safety scissors
ciseaux^M de sûreté^F
Nasen-Bartschere^F
forbici^F di sicurezza^F
tijeras^F de punta^F roma

nail clippers
coupe-ongles^M
Nagelknipser^M
tronchesina^F per unghie^F
cortaúñas^M

nail cleaner
cure-ongles^M
Nagelreiniger^M
pulisci unghie^M
limpiador^M de uñas^F

folding nail file
lime^F
klappbare Nagelfeile^F
limetta^F pieghevole
lima^F de uñas^F

lever
levier^M
Hebel^M
leva^F
palanca^F

jaw
mors^M
Klemmbacke^F
ganascia^F
mordaza^F

chamois leather
peau^F de chamois^M
Wildleder^N
pelle^F di camoscio^M
piel^F de gamuza^F

nail whitener pencil
crayon^M blanchisseur d'ongles^M
Nagelweißstift^M
matita^F sbiancante per unghie^F
lápiz^M blanco para uñas^F

emery boards
limes^F-émeri^M
Sandblattfeilen^F
limetta^F di cartoncino^M vetrato
lima^F de uñas^F

toenail scissors
ciseaux^M de pédicure^F
Fußnagelschere^F
forbici^F per unghie^F dei piedi^M
tijeras^F de pedicura^F

make-up

maquillage^M | Make-up^N | trucco^M | maquillaje^M

make-up
maquillage^M
Make-up^N
trucco^M **per il viso**^M
maquillaje^M **facial**

compact
poudrier^M
Puderdose^F
portacipria^M
polvera^F.

blusher brush
pinceau^M pour fard^M à joues^F
Rougepinsel^M
pennello^M da fard^M
brocha^F aplicadora de colorete^M

pressed powder
poudre^F pressée
Kompaktpuder^M
cipria^F compatta
polvo^M compacto

powder puff
houppette^F
Puderkissen^N
piumino^M da cipria^F
borla^F

powder blusher
fard^M à joues^F en poudre^F
Puderrouge^M
fard^M in polvere^F
colorete^M en polvo^M

synthetic sponge
éponge^F synthétique
Kunstschwamm^M
spugna^F sintetica
esponja^F sintética

loose powder brush
pinceau^M pour poudre^F libre
Puderpinsel^M
pennello^M da cipria^F in polvere^F
brocha^F

fan brush
pinceau^M éventail^M
Fächerpinsel^M
pennello^M a ventaglio^M
brocha^F en forma^F de abanico^M

loose powder
poudre^F libre
loser Puder^M
cipria^F in polvere^F
polvos^M sueltos

liquid foundation
fond^M de teint^M liquide
flüssige Grundierung^F
fondotinta^M fluido
base^F líquida

eye make-up
maquillage^M **des yeux**^M
Augen-Make-up^N
trucco^M **per gli occhi**^M
maquillaje^M **para ojos**^M

eyelash curler
recourbe-cils^M
Wimpernzange^F
piegaciglia^M
rizador^M de pestañas^F

brow brush and lash comb
brosse^F-peigne^M pour cils^M et sourcils^M
Brauenbürstchen^N und Wimpernkämmchen^N
pettinino^M per ciglia^F e spazzolino^M per sopracciglia^F
cepillo^M para cejas^F y pestañas^F

eyebrow pencil
crayon^M à sourcils^M
Augenbrauenstift^M
matita^F per sopracciglia^F
lápiz^M de cejas^F

mascara brush
brosse^F à mascara^M
Mascarabürstchen^N
spazzolino^M per mascara^M
cepillo^M aplicador de rimel^M

liquid eyeliner
eye-liner^M liquide
flüssiger Eyeliner^M
eye-liner^M
delineador^M

sponge-tipped applicator
applicateur^M-mousse^F
Schwammstäbchen^N
applicatore^M a spugnetta^F
aplicador^M de esponja^F.

liquid mascara
mascara^M liquide
flüssiges Mascara^N
mascara^M líquido
rimel^M líquido

cake mascara
mascara^M en pain^M
Mascarastein^M
mascara^M compatto
rimel^M en pasta^F

eyeshadow
ombre^F à paupières^F
Lidschatten^M
ombretto^M
sombra^F de ojos^M

lip make-up
maquillage^M **des lèvres**^F
Lippen-Make-up^N
trucco^M **per le labbra**^F
maquillaje^M **labial**

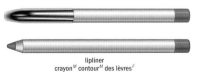

lipbrush
pinceau^M à lèvres^F
Lippenpinsel^M
pennellino^M per labbra^F
pincel^M para labios^M

lipliner
crayon^M contour^M des lèvres^F
Lippenkonturenstift^M
matite^F per il contorno^M delle labbra^F
delineador^M de labios^M

lipstick
rouge^M à lèvres^F
Lippenstift^M
rossetto^M
pintalabios^M

PERSONAL ADORNMENT AND ARTICLES

body care

soins^M du corps^M | Körperpflege^F | cura^F del corpo^M | cuidado^M personal

stopper
bouchon^M
Stopfen^M
tappo^M
tapón^M

bottle
flacon^M
Flasche^F
bottiglia^F
botella^F

eau de parfum
eau^F de parfum^M
Eau de parfum^N
profumo^M
agua^F de perfume^M

eau de toilette
eau^F de toilette^F
Eau de toilette^N
eau de toilette^F
agua^F de colonia^F

bubble bath
bain^M moussant
Schaumbad^N
bagnoschiuma^M
gel^M de baño^M

hair colour
colorant^M capillaire
Haarfärbemittel^N
tintura^F per capelli^M
tinte^M para el cabello^M

toilet soap
savon^M de toilette^F
Toilettenseife^F
saponetta^F
jabón^M de tocador^M

deodorant
déodorant^M
Deodorant^N
deodorante^M
desodorante^M

hair conditioner
revitalisant^M capillaire
Haarspülung^F
balsamo^M per capelli^M
acondicionador^M

shampoo
shampooing^M
Shampoo^N
shampoo^M
champú^M

face flannel
gant^M de toilette^F
Waschhandschuh^M
manopola^F
manopla^F de baño^M

face flannel
débarbouillette^F
Waschlappen^M
ospite^M
toalla^F para la cara^F

massage glove
gant^M de crin^M
Massagehandschuh^M
guanto^M di crine^M
guante^M de crin^M

vegetable sponge
éponge^F végétale
Luffaschwamm^M
spugna^F vegetale
esponja^F vegetal

bath sheet
drap^M de bain^M
Badetuch^N
asciugamano^M da bagno^M
toalla^F de baño^M

bath towel
serviette^F de toilette^F
Handtuch^N
asciugamano^M
toalla^F de lavabo^M

bath brush
brosse^F pour le bain^M
Badebürste^F
spazzola^F da bagno^M
cepillo^M de baño^M

natural sponge
éponge^F de mer^F
Naturschwamm^M
spugna^F naturale
esponja^F natural

back brush
brosse^F pour le dos^M
Massagebürste^F
spazzola^F per la schiena^F
cepillo^M de espalda^F

hairdressing

coiffure^F | Haarpflege^F | articoli^M per acconciatura^F | peinado^M

hairbrushes
brosses^F à cheveux^M
Haarbürsten^F
spazzole^F per capelli^M
cepillos^M

flat-back brush
brosse^F pneumatique
flache Frisierbürste^F
spazzola^F a dorso^M piatto
cepillo^M con base^F de goma^F

round brush
brosse^F ronde
Rundbürste^F
spazzola^F rotonda
cepillo^M redondo

quill brush
brosse^F anglaise
Drahtbürste^F
spazzola^F antistatica
cepillo^M de púas^F

vent brush
brosse^F-araignée^F
Skelettbürste^F
spazzola^F ragno
cepillo^M de esqueleto^M

combs
peignes^M
Kämme^M
pettini^M
peines^M

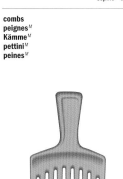

teaser comb
peigne^M à crêper
Toupierkamm^M
pettine^M per cotonare
peine^M de cardar

barber comb
peigne^M de coiffeur^M
Haarschneidekamm^M
pettine^M da barbiere^M
peine^M de peluquero^M

rake comb
démêloir^M
Griffkamm^M
pettine^M rado
peine^M para desenredar

Afro pick
peigne^M afro
Strähnenkamm^M
pettine^M afro
peine^M afro

tail comb
peigne^M à tige^F
Stielkamm^M
pettine^M a coda^F
peine^M de mango^M

pitchfork comb
combiné^M 2 dans 1
Haarliftkamm^M
pettine^M a forchetta^F
peine^M combinado

hair roller
bigoudi^M
Lockenwickler^M
bigodino^M
rulo^M para el cabello^M

roller
rouleau^M
Wickler^M
rullo^M
rulo^M

hairpin
épingle^F à cheveux^M
Lockennadel^F
forcina^F
horquilla^F de moño^M

hair grip
pince^F à cheveux^M
Haarklemme^F
molletta^F
horquilla^F

hair roller pin
épingle^F à bigoudi^M
Haarstecker^M
spillone^M
alfiler^M

wave clip
pince^F à boucles^F de cheveux^M
Abteilklammer^F
pinza^F per capelli^M
pinza^F para rizar

hair clip
pince^F de mise^F en plis^M
Haarclip^M
beccuccio^M
pinza^F para el cabello^M

hair slide
barrette^F
Haarspange^F
fermacapelli^M
pasador^M

hairdressing

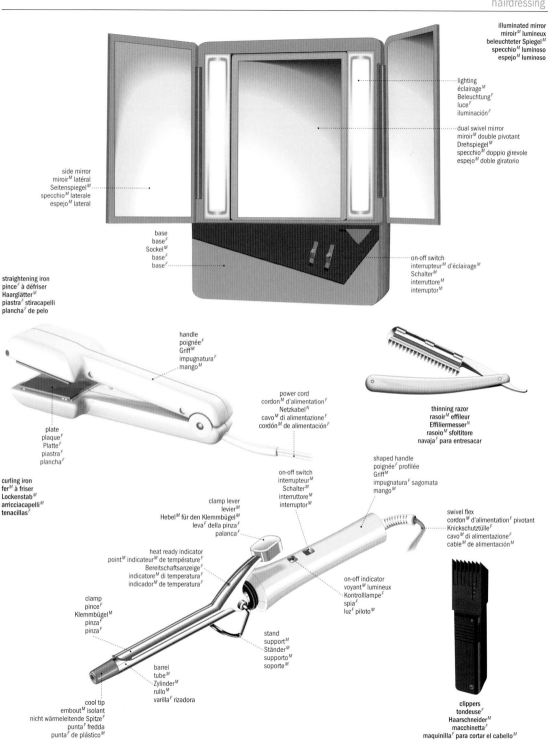

illuminated mirror
miroir^M lumineux
beleuchteter Spiegel^M
specchio^M luminoso
espejo^M luminoso

lighting
éclairage^M
Beleuchtung^F
luce^F
iluminación^F

dual swivel mirror
miroir^M double pivotant
Drehspiegel^M
specchio^M doppio girevole
espejo^M doble giratorio

side mirror
miroir^M latéral
Seitenspiegel^M
specchio^M laterale
espejo^M lateral

base
base^F
Sockel^M
base^F
base^F

on-off switch
interrupteur^M d'éclairage^M
Schalter^M
interruttore^M
interruptor^M

straightening iron
pince^F à défriser
Haarglätter^M
piastra^F stiracapelli
plancha^F de pelo

handle
poignée^F
Griff^M
impugnatura^F
mango^M

power cord
cordon^M d'alimentation^F
Netzkabel^N
cavo^M di alimentazione^F
cordón^M de alimentación^F

thinning razor
rasoir^M effileur
Effiliermesser^N
rasoio^M sfoltitore
navaja^F para entresacar

plate
plaque^F
Platte^F
piastra^F
plancha^F

curling iron
fer^M à friser
Lockenstab^M
arricciacapelli^M
tenacillas^F

on-off switch
interrupteur^M
Schalter^M
interruttore^M
interruptor^M

shaped handle
poignée^F profilée
Griff^M
impugnatura^F sagomata
mango^M

clamp lever
levier^M
Hebel^M für den Klemmbügel^M
leva^F della pinza^F
palanca^F

swivel flex
cordon^M d'alimentation^F pivotant
Knickschutztülle^F
cavo^M di alimentazione^F
cable^M de alimentación^M

heat ready indicator
point^M indicateur^M de température^F
Bereitschaftsanzeige^F
indicatore^M di temperatura^F
indicador^M de temperatura^F

clamp
pince^F
Klemmbügel^M
pinza^F
pinza^F

on-off indicator
voyant^M lumineux
Kontrolllampe^F
spia^F
luz^F piloto^M

stand
support^M
Ständer^M
supporto^M
soporte^M

barrel
tube^M
Zylinder^M
rullo^M
varilla^F rizadora

cool tip
embout^M isolant
nicht wärmeleitende Spitze^F
punta^F fredda
punta^F de plástico^M

clippers
tondeuse^F
Haarschneider^M
macchinetta^F
maquinilla^F para cortar el cabello^M

hairdressing

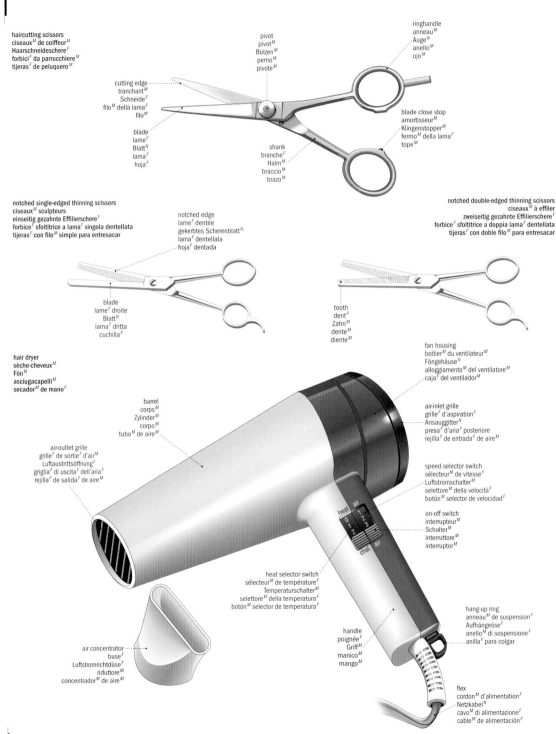

haircutting scissors
ciseaux^M de coiffeur^M
Haarschneideschere^F
forbici^F da parrucchiere^M
tijeras^F de peluquero^M

pivot
pivot^M
Bolzen^M
perno^M
pivote^M

ringhandle
anneau^M
Auge^N
anello^M
ojo^M

cutting edge
tranchant^M
Schneide^F
filo^M della lama^F
filo^M

blade close stop
amortisseur^M
Klingenstopper^M
fermo^M della lama^F
tope^M

blade
lame^F
Blatt^N
lama^F
hoja^F

shank
branche^F
Halm^M
braccio^M
brazo^M

notched single-edged thinning scissors
ciseaux^M sculpteurs
einseitig gezahnte Effilierschere^F
forbice^F sfoltitrice a lama^F singola dentellata
tijeras^F con filo^M simple para entresacar

notched edge
lame^F dentée
gekerbtes Scherenblatt^N
lama^F dentellata
hoja^F dentada

notched double-edged thinning scissors
ciseaux^M à effiler
zweiseitig gezahnte Effilierschere^F
forbice^F sfoltitrice a doppia lama^F dentellata
tijeras^F con doble filo^M para entresacar

blade
lame^F droite
Blatt^N
lama^F dritta
cuchilla^F

tooth
dent^F
Zahn^M
dente^M
diente^M

hair dryer
sèche-cheveux^M
Fön^M
asciugacapelli^M
secador^M de mano^F

fan housing
boitier^M du ventilateur^M
Föngehäuse^N
alloggiamento^M del ventilatore^M
caja^F del ventilador^M

barrel
corps^M
Zylinder^M
corpo^M
tubo^M de aire^M

air-inlet grille
grille^F d'aspiration^F
Ansauggitter^N
presa^F d'aria^F posteriore
rejilla^F de entrada^F de aire^M

air-outlet grille
grille^F de sortie^F d'air^M
Luftaustrittsöffnung^F
griglia^F di uscita^F dell'aria^F
rejilla^F de salida^F de aire^M

speed selector switch
sélecteur^M de vitesse^F
Luftstromschalter^M
selettore^M della velocità^F
botón^M selector de velocidad^F

on-off switch
interrupteur^M
Schalter^M
interruttore^M
interruptor^M

heat selector switch
sélecteur^M de température^F
Temperaturschalter^M
selettore^M della temperatura^F
botón^M selector de temperatura^F

hang-up ring
anneau^M de suspension^F
Aufhängeöse^F
anello^M di sospensione^F
anilla^F para colgar

air concentrator
buse^F
Luftstromrichtdüse^F
riduttore^M
concentrador^M de aire^M

handle
poignée^F
Griff^M
manico^M
mango^M

flex
cordon^M d'alimentation^F
Netzkabel^N
cavo^M di alimentazione^F
cable^M de alimentación^F

shaving

rasage^M | Rasur^F | rasatura^F | afeitado^M

electric razor
rasoir^M électrique
Elektrorasierer^M
rasoio^M elettrico
máquina^F de afeitar eléctrica

floating head
tête^F flottante
Scherkopf^M
testina^F rotante
cabezal^M flotante

trimmer
tondeuse^F
Langhaarschneider^M
tagliabasette^M
cortapatillas^M

screen
grille^F
Scherkopfhalter^M
griglia^F
peine^M y cuchilla^F

closeness setting
sélecteur^M de coupe^F
Justierring^M
regolatore^M delle testine^F
selector^M de corte^M

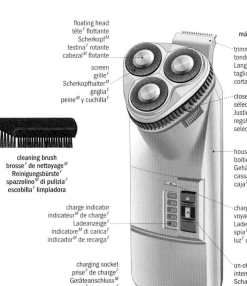

housing
boîtier^M
Gehäuse^N
cassa^F
caja^F

cleaning brush
brosse^F de nettoyage^M
Reinigungsbürste^F
spazzolino^M di pulizia^F
escobilla^F limpiadora

charge indicator
indicateur^M de charge^F
Ladeanzeige^F
indicatore^M di carica^F
indicador^M de recarga^F

charging light
voyant^M de charge^F
Ladekontrolllampe^F
spia^F luminosa di carica^F
luz^F de encendido^M

charging socket
prise^F de charge^F
Geräteanschluss^M
presa^F di ricarica^F
enchufe^M de recarga^F

on-off switch
interrupteur^M
Schalter^M
interruttore^M
interruptor^M

shaving foam
mousse^F à raser
Rasierschaum^M
schiuma^F da barba^F
espuma^F de afeitar

flex
cordon^M d'alimentation^F
Netzkabel^N
cordone^M dell'alimentazione^F
cable^M de alimentación^F

shaving brush
blaireau^M
Rasierpinsel^M
pennello^M da barba^F
brocha^F de afeitar

plug adapter
adaptateur^M de fiche^F
Adapter^M
adattatore^M
adaptador^M

cut-throat razor
rasoir^M à manche^M
Rasiermesser^N
rasoio^M a mano^F libera
navaja^F de barbero^M

blade
lame^F
Klinge^F
lama^F
hoja^F

bristle
soie^F
Borste^F
setola^F
cerdas^F

aftershave
après-rasage^M
Rasierwasser^N
dopobarba^M
loción^F para después del afeitado^M

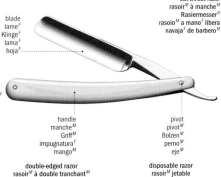

handle
manche^M
Griff^M
impugnatura^F
mango^M

pivot
pivot^M
Bolzen^M
perno^M
eje^M

shaving brush

double-edged razor
rasoir^M à double tranchant^M
zweischneidiger Rasierer^M
rasoio^M di sicurezza^F
maquinilla^F de afeitar

disposable razor
rasoir^M jetable
Einwegrasierer^M
rasoio^M usa e getta
maquinilla^F desechable

collar
anneau^M
Ring^M
colletto^M
anillo^M

head
tête^F
Kopf^M
testina^F
cabeza^F

blade dispenser
distributeur^M de lames^F
Klingendose^F
caricatore^M di lamette^F
distribuidor^M de hojas^F de afeitar

handle
manche^M
Griff^M
manico^M
mango^M

shaving mug
bol^M à raser
Seifenbecher^M
tazza^F per sapone^M da barba^F
jabonera^F

double-edged razor blade
lame^F à double tranchant^M
zweischneidige Klinge^F
lametta^F a due tagli^M
hoja^F de afeitar

dental care

hygiène^F dentaire | Zahnpflege^F | igiene^F orale | higiene^F dental

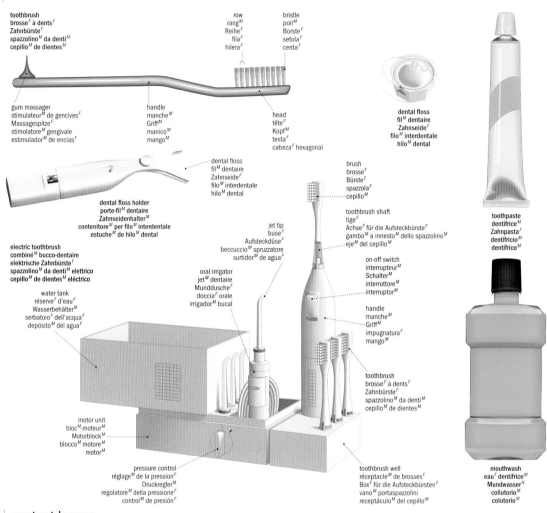

toothbrush
brosse^F à dents^F
Zahnbürste^F
spazzolino^M da denti^M
cepillo^M de dientes^M

row
rang^M
Reihe^F
fila^F
hilera^F

bristle
poil^M
Borste^F
setola^F
cerda^F

gum massager
stimulateur^M de gencives^F
Massagespitze^F
stimolatore^M gengivale
estimulador^M de encías^F

handle
manche^M
Griff^M
manico^M
mango^M

head
tête^F
Kopf^M
testa^F hexagonal
cabeza^F hexagonal

dental floss
fil^M dentaire
Zahnseide^F
filo^M interdentale
hilo^M dental

dental floss
fil^M dentaire
Zahnseide^F
filo^M interdentale
hilo^M dental

dental floss holder
porte-fil^M dentaire
Zahnseidenhalter^M
contenitore^M per filo^M interdentale
estuche^M de hilo^M dental

brush
brosse^F
Bürste^F
spazzola^F
cepillo^M

toothbrush shaft
tige^F
Achse^F für die Aufsteckbürste^F
gambo^M a innesto^M dello spazzolino^M
eje^M del cepillo^M

electric toothbrush
combiné^M bucco-dentaire
elektrische Zahnbürste^F
spazzolino^M da denti^M elettrico
cepillo^M de dientes^M eléctrico

jet tip
buse^F
Aufsteckdüse^F
beccuccio^M spruzzatore
surtidor^M de agua^F

on-off switch
interrupteur^M
Schalter^M
interruttore^M
interruptor^M

water tank
réserve^F d'eau^F
Wasserbehälter^M
serbatoio^F dell'acqua^F
depósito^M del agua^F

oral irrigator
jet^M dentaire
Munddusche^F
doccia^F orale
irrigador^M bucal

handle
manche^M
Griff^M
impugnatura^F
mango^M

toothbrush
brosse^F à dents^F
Zahnbürste^F
spazzolino^M da denti^M
cepillo^M de dientes^M

motor unit
bloc^M-moteur^M
Motorblock^M
blocco^M motore^M
motor^M

pressure control
réglage^M de la pression^F
Druckregler^M
regolatore^M della pressione^F
control^M de presión^F

toothbrush well
réceptacle^M de brosses^F
Box^F für die Aufsteckbürsten^F
vano^M portaspazzolini
receptáculo^M del cepillo^M

toothpaste
dentifrice^M
Zahnpasta^F
dentifricio^M
dentífrico^M

mouthwash
eau^F dentifrice^M
Mundwasser^N
collutorio^M
colutorio^M

contact lenses

lentilles^F de contact^M | Kontaktlinsen^F | lenti^F a contatto^M | lentes^F de contacto^M

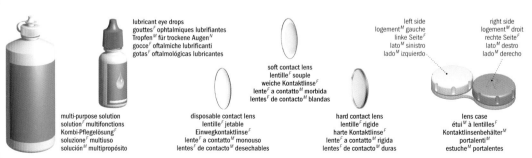

lubricant eye drops
gouttes^F ophtalmiques lubrifiantes
Tropfen^M für trockene Augen^N
gocce^F oftalmiche lubricanti
gotas^F oftalmológicas lubricantes

soft contact lens
lentille^F souple
weiche Kontaktlinse^F
lente^F a contatto^M morbida
lentes^F de contacto^M blandas

left side
logement^M gauche
linke Seite^F
lato^M sinistro
lado^M izquierdo

right side
logement^M droit
rechte Seite^F
lato^M destro
lado^M derecho

multi-purpose solution
solution^F multifonctions
Kombi-Pflegelösung^F
soluzione^F multiuso
solución^M multipropósito

disposable contact lens
lentille^F jetable
Einwegkontaktlinse^F
lente^F a contatto^M monouso
lentes^F de contacto^M desechables

hard contact lens
lentille^F rigide
harte Kontaktlinse^F
lente^F a contatto^M rigida
lentes^F de contacto^M duras

lens case
étui^M à lentilles^F
Kontaktlinsenbehälter^M
portalenti^M
estuche^M portalentes

spectacles

lunettes^F | Brille^F | occhiali^M | gafas^F

parts of spectacles
parties^F des lunettes^F
Teile$^{M/N}$ der Brille^F
parti^F degli occhiali^M
gafas^F : partes^F

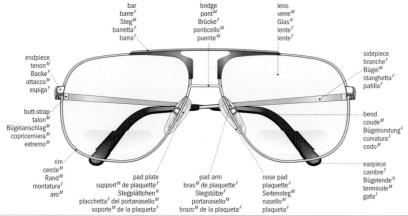

bar
barre^F
Steg^M
barretta^F
barra^F

bridge
pont^M
Brücke^F
ponticello^M
puente^M

lens
verre^M
Glas^N
lente^F
lente^F

sidepiece
branche^F
Bügel^M
stanghetta^F
patilla^F

endpiece
tenon^M
Backe^F
attacco^M
espiga^F

butt-strap
talon^M
Bügelanschlag^M
copriceniera^M
extremo^M

bend
coude^M
Bügelrundung^F
curvatura^F
codo^M

rim
cercle^M
Rand^M
montatura^F
aro^M

earpiece
cambre^F
Bügelende^N
terminale^M
gafa^F

pad plate
support^M de plaquette^F
Stegplättchen^N
placchetta^F del portanasello^M
soporte^M de la plaqueta^F

pad arm
bras^M de plaquette^F
Stegstütze^F
portanasello^M
brazo^M de la plaqueta^F

nose pad
plaquette^F
Seitensteg^M
nasello^M
plaqueta^F

examples of spectacles
exemples^M de lunettes^F
Beispiele^N für Augengläser^N
esempi^M di occhiali^M
ejemplos^M de gafas^F

opera glasses
lorgnette^F
Opernglas^N
binocolo^M da teatro^M
gemelos^M de teatro^M

sunglasses
lunettes^F de soleil^M
Sonnenbrille^F
occhiali^M da sole^M
gafas^F de sol^M

half-glasses
demi-lune^F
Halbbrille^F
mezzi occhiali^M
media luna^F

umbrella and stick

parapluie^M et canne^F | Schirm^M und Stock^M | ombrello^M e bastone^M | paraguas^M y bastones^M

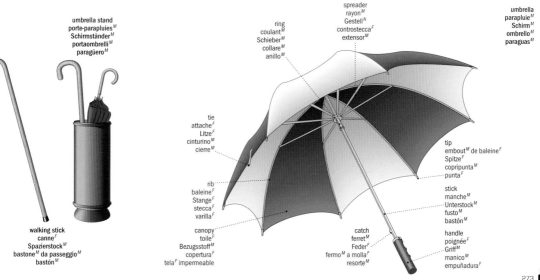

umbrella stand
porte-parapluies^M
Schirmständer^M
portaombrelli^M
paragüero^M

ring
coulant^M
Schieber^M
collare^M
anillo^M

spreader
rayon^M
Gestell^N
controstecca^F
extensor^M

umbrella
parapluie^M
Schirm^M
ombrello^M
paraguas^M

tie
attache^F
Litze^F
cinturino^M
cierre^M

tip
embout^M de baleine^F
Spitze^F
copripunta^M
punta^F

rib
baleine^F
Stange^F
stecca^F
varilla^F

stick
manche^M
Unterstock^M
fusto^M
bastón^M

canopy
toile^F
Bezugsstoff^M
copertura^F
tela^F impermeable

catch
ferret^M
Feder^F
fermo^M a molla^F
resorte^M

handle
poignée^F
Griff^M
manico^M
empuñadura^F

walking stick
canne^F
Spazierstock^M
bastone^M da passeggio^M
bastón^M

leather goods

articles^M de maroquinerie^F | Lederwaren^F | articoli^M di pelletteria^F | artículos^M de marroquinería

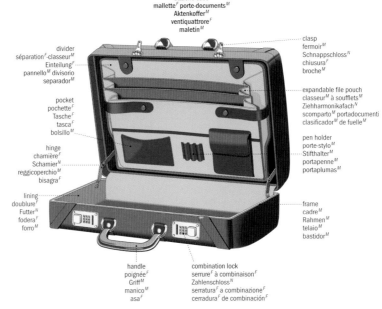

attaché case
mallette^F porte-documents^M
Aktenkoffer^M
ventiquattrore^F
maletin^M

divider
séparation^F-classeur^F
Einteilung^F
pannello^M divisorio
separador^M

pocket
pochette^F
Tasche^F
tasca^F
bolsillo^M

hinge
charnière^F
Scharnier^N
reggicoperchio^M
bisagra^F

lining
doublure^F
Futter^N
fodera^F
forro^M

clasp
fermoir^M
Schnappschloss^N
chiusura^F
broche^M

expandable file pouch
classeur^M à soufflets^M
Ziehharmonikafach^N
scomparto^M portadocumenti
clasificador^M de fuelle^M

pen holder
porte-stylo^M
Stifthalter^M
portapenne^M
portaplumas^M

frame
cadre^M
Rahmen^M
telaio^M
bastidor^M

handle
poignée^F
Griff^M
manico^M
asa^F

combination lock
serrure^F à combinaison^F
Zahlenschloss^N
serratura^F a combinazione^F
cerradura^F de combinación^F

briefcase
serviette^F
Aktentasche^F
borsa^F a soffietto^M
cartera^F

bottom-fold document case
porte-documents^M à soufflet^M
Kollegmappe^F mit Griff^M
portacarte^M a soffietto^M
cartera^F de fondo^M plegable

retractable handle
poignée^F rentrante
ausziehbarer Griff^M
manico^M a scomparsa^F
asa^F extensible

exterior pocket
poche^F extérieure
Außentasche^F
tasca^F esterna
bolsillo^M delantero

gusset
soufflet^M
Keil^M
soffietto^M
fuelle^M

tab
patte^F
Lasche^F
linguetta^F
lengüeta^F

key lock
serrure^F à clé^F
Schlüsselschloss^N
serratura^F a chiave^F
cerradura^F

calculator/cheque book holder
porte-chéquier^M
Etui^N für Taschenrechner^M und Scheckheft^N
portassegni^M/portacalcolatrice^M
chequera^F con calculadora^F

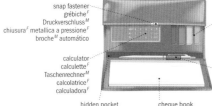

credit card wallet
porte-cartes^F
Kreditkartenetui^N
portafoglio^M per carte^F di credito^M
tarjetero^M

snap fastener
grébiche^F
Druckverschluss^M
chiusura^F metallica a pressione^F
broche^M automático

calculator
calculette^F
Taschenrechner^M
calcolatrice^F
calculadora^F

credit card wallet
porte-cartes^F
Kreditkartenfach^N
scomparto^M per carte^F di credito^M
tarjetero^M

pen holder
porte-stylo^M
Stifthalter^M
portapenne^M
portaplumas^M

wallet section
poche^F américaine
Geldscheinfach^N
scomparto^M per banconote^F
billetera^F

transparent pockets
feuillets^M
Klarsichthüllen^F
bustine^F trasparenti
plásticos^M transparentes

tab
patte^F
Lasche^F
linguetta^F
lengüeta^F

hidden pocket
poche^F secrète
Unterfach^N
tasca^F nascosta
bolsillo^M secreto

cheque book
chéquier^M
Scheckheft^N
libretto^M degli assegni^M
talonario^M de cheques^M

slot
fente^F
Fach^N
fessura^F
ranura^F

window
volet^M transparent
Klarsichtfenster^N
riquadro^M
plástico^M transparente

leather goods

wallet
portefeuille^M
Brieftasche^F
portafoglio^M
billetero^M

coin purse
porte-monnaie^M
Geldbeutel^M für Münzen^F
portamonete^M
portamonedas^M

key case
porte-clés^M
Schlüsseletui^N
portachiavi^M
llavero^M

purse
bourse^F à monnaie^F
Geldbeutel^M
borsellino^M
monedero^M

passport case
porte-passeport^M
Brieftasche^F
portapassaporto^M
porta pasaportes^M

wallet
porte-coupures^M
Brieftasche^F
portafoglio^M
billetera^F

writing case
écritoire^F
Schreibmappe^F
portablocco^M
agenda^F

cheque book cover
porte-chéquier^M
Scheckhülle^F
portassegni^M
talonario^M de cheques^M

spectacles case
étui^M à lunettes^F
Brillenetui^N
astuccio^M per occhiali^M
funda^F de gafas^F

underarm briefcase
porte-documents^M plat
Unterarmmappe^F
busta^F portadocumenti
cartera^F portadocumentos^M

handbags

sacs^M à main^F | Handtaschen^F | borse^F | bolsos^M

drawstring bag
sac^M seau^M
Beuteltasche^F
secchiello^M con cordoncino^M
bolso^M tipo cubo^M

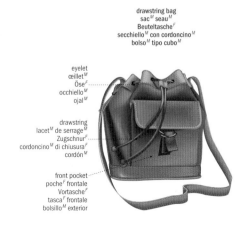

eyelet
œillet^M
Öse^F
occhiello^M
ojal^M

drawstring
lacet^M de serrage^M
Zugschnur^F
cordoncino^M di chiusura^F
cordón^M

front pocket
poche^F frontale
Vortasche^F
tasca^F frontale
bolsillo^M exterior

satchel bag
sac^M cartable^M
Aktentasche^F
cartella^F
bolso^M clásico

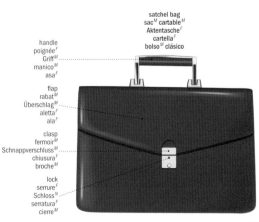

handle
poignée^F
Griff^M
manico^M
asa^F

flap
rabat^M
Überschlag^M
aletta^F
ala^F

clasp
fermoir^M
Schnappverschluss^M
chiusura^F
broche^M

lock
serrure^F
Schloss^N
serratura^F
cierre^M

handbags

box bag
sac^M boite^F
Boxtasche^F
borsa^F a telaio^M rigido
bolso^M de vestir

small drawstring bag
balluchon^M
kleine Beuteltasche^F
secchiello^M piccolo con cordoncino^M
bolso^M saco

shoulder bag
sac^M à bandoulière^F
Schultertasche^F
borsa^F a tracolla^F
bolso^M de bandolera^F

buckle
boucle^F
Schnalle^F
fibbia^F
hebilla^F

muff
manchon^M
Mufftasche^F
borsa^F a manicotto^M
bolso^M manguito^M

shoulder strap
bandoulière^F
Schulterriemen^M
tracolla^F
bandolera^F

accordion bag
sac^M accordéon^M
Umhängetasche^F mit Dehnfalte^F
borsa^F da postino^M
bolso^M de fuelle^M

shoulder bag with zip
sac^M besace^F
Umhängetasche^F mit Reißverschluss^M
sacca^F a tracolla^F
morral^M

gusset
soufflet^M
Keil^M
soffietto^M
fuelle^M

tote bag
sac^M fourre-tout^M
Einkaufstasche^F
sporta^F
bolsa^F de lona^F

men's bag
pochette^F d'homme^M
Herrentasche^F
borsello^M
bolso^M de hombre

duffle bag
sac^M marin^M)
Matchbeutel^M
sacca^F da marinaio^M
saco^M de marinero^M

holdall
sac^M à polochon^M
geräumige Tasche^F
borsone^M da viaggio^M
bolso^M de viaje^M

shopping bag
sac^M à provisions^F
Einkaufstasche^F
borsa^F della spesa^F
bolso^M de la compra^F

shopping bag
cabas^M
große Einkaufstasche^F
borsa^F della spesa^F
capazo^M

luggage

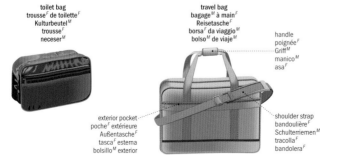

toilet bag
trousse^F de toilette^F
Kulturbeutel^M
trousse^F
neceser^M

travel bag
bagage^M à main^F
Reisetasche^F
borsa^F da viaggio^M
bolso^M de viaje^M

handle
poignée^F
Griff^M
manico^M
asa^F

flight bag
sac^M fourre-tout^M
Flugtasche^F
bagaglio^M a mano^F
maletín^M

exterior pocket
poche^F extérieure
Außentasche^F
tasca^F esterna
bolsillo^M exterior

shoulder strap
bandoulière^F
Schulterriemen^M
tracolla^F
bandolera^F

luggage

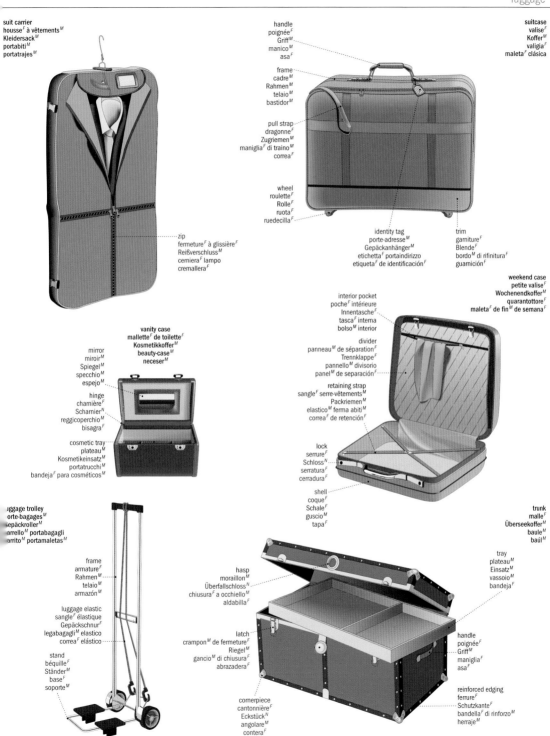

suit carrier
housse^F à vêtements^M
Kleidersack^M
portabiti^M
portatrajes^M

zip
fermeture^F à glissière^F
Reißverschluss^M
cerniera^F lampo
cremallera^F

handle
poignée^F
Griff^M
manico^M
asa^F

frame
cadre^M
Rahmen^M
telaio^M
bastidor^M

pull strap
dragonne^F
Zugriemen^M
maniglia^F di traino^M
correa^F

wheel
roulette^F
Rolle^F
ruota^F
ruedecilla^F

identity tag
porte-adresse^M
Gepäckanhänger^M
etichetta^F portaindirizzo
etiqueta^F de identificación^F

trim
garniture^F
Blende^F
bordo^M di rifinitura^F
guarnición^F

suitcase
valise^F
Koffer^M
valigia^F
maleta^F clásica

vanity case
mallette^F de toilette^F
Kosmetikkoffer^M
beauty-case^M
neceser^M

mirror
miroir^M
Spiegel^M
specchio^M
espejo^M

hinge
charnière^F
Scharnier^N
reggicoperchio^M
bisagra^F

cosmetic tray
plateau^M
Kosmetikeinsatz^M
portatrucchi^M
bandeja^F para cosméticos^M

interior pocket
poche^F intérieure
Innentasche^F
tasca^F interna
bolso^M interior

divider
panneau^M de séparation^F
Trennklappe^F
pannello^M divisorio
panel^M de separación^F

retaining strap
sangle^F serre-vêtements^M
Packriemen^M
elastico^M ferma abiti^M
correa^F de retención^F

lock
serrure^F
Schloss^N
serratura^F
cerradura^F

shell
coque^F
Schale^F
guscio^M
tapa^F

weekend case
petite valise^F
Wochenendkoffer^M
quarantottore^F
maleta^F de fin^M de semana^F

luggage trolley
porte-bagages^M
Gepäckroller^M
carrello^M portabagagli
carrito^M portamaletas^M

frame
armature^F
Rahmen^M
telaio^M
armazón^M

luggage elastic
sangle^F élastique
Gepäckschnur^F
legabagagli^M elastico
correa^F elástico

stand
béquille^F
Ständer^M
base^F
soporte^M

hasp
moraillon^M
Überfallschloss^N
chiusura^F a occhiello^M
aldabilla^F

latch
crampon^M de fermeture^F
Riegel^M
gancio^M di chiusura^F
abrazadera^F

cornerpiece
cantonnière^F
Eckstück^N
angolare^M
contera^F

trunk
malle^F
Überseekoffer^M
baule^M
baúl^M

tray
plateau^M
Einsatz^M
vassoio^M
bandeja^F

handle
poignée^F
Griff^M
maniglia^F
asa^F

reinforced edging
ferrure^F
Schutzkante^F
bandella^F di rinforzo^M
herraje^M

pyramid

pyramide^F | Pyramide^F | piramide^F | pirámide^F

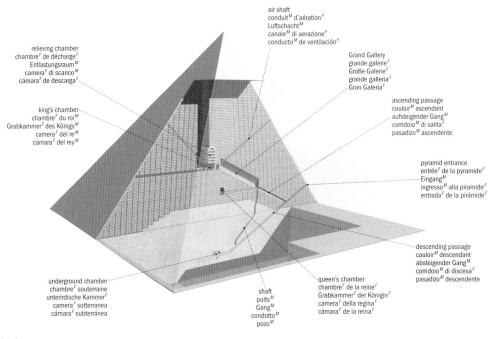

relieving chamber
chambre^F de décharge^F
Entlastungsraum^M
camera^F di scarico^M
cámara^F de descarga^F

air shaft
conduit^M d'aération^F
Luftschacht^M
canale^M di aerazione^F
conducto^M de ventilación^F

Grand Gallery
grande galerie^F
Große Galerie^F
grande galleria^F
Gran Galería^F

king's chamber
chambre^F du roi^M
Grabkammer^F des Königs^M
camera^F del re^M
cámara^F del rey^M

ascending passage
couloir^M ascendant
aufsteigender Gang^M
corridoio^M di salita^F
pasadizo^M ascendente

pyramid entrance
entrée^F de la pyramide^F
Eingang^M
ingresso^M alla piramide^F
entrada^F de la pirámide^F

descending passage
couloir^M descendant
absteigender Gang^M
corridoio^M di discesa^F
pasadizo^M descendente

underground chamber
chambre^F souterraine
unterirdische Kammer^F
camera^F sotterranea
cámara^F subterránea

shaft
puits^M
Gang^M
condotto^M
pozo^M

queen's chamber
chambre^F de la reine^F
Grabkammer^F der Königin^F
camera^F della regina^F
cámara^F de la reina^F

Greek theatre

théâtre^M grec | griechisches Theater^N | teatro^M greco | teatro^M griego

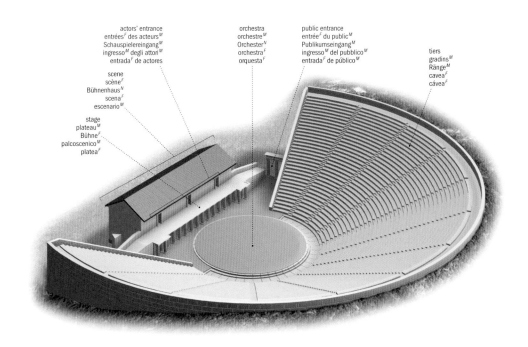

actors' entrance
entrées^F des acteurs^M
Schauspielereingang^M
ingresso^M degli attori^M
entrada^F de actores

orchestra
orchestre^M
Orchester^N
orchestra^F
orquesta^F

public entrance
entrée^F du public^M
Publikumseingang^M
ingresso^M del pubblico^M
entrada^F de público^M

tiers
gradins^M
Ränge^M
cavea^F
cávea^F

scene
scène^F
Bühnenhaus^N
scena^F
escenario^M

stage
plateau^M
Bühne^F
palcoscenico^M
platea^F

Greek temple

temple^M grec | griechischer Tempel^M | tempio^M greco | templo^M griego

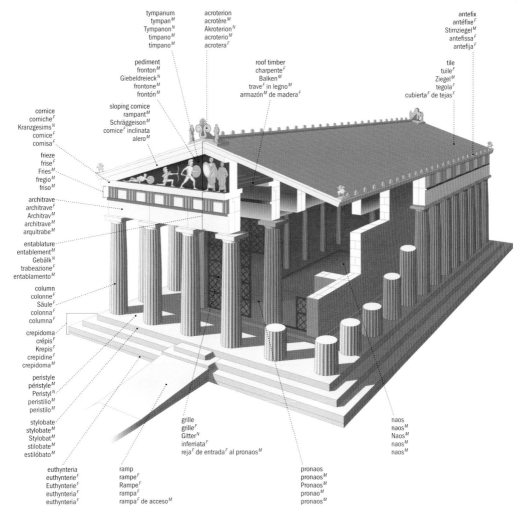

tympanum
tympan^M
Tympanon^N
timpano^M
tímpano^M

acroterion
acrotère^M
Akroterion^N
acroterio^M
acrotera^F

antefix
antéfixe^F
Stirnziegel^M
antefissa^F
antefija^F

pediment
fronton^M
Giebeldreieck^N
frontone^M
frontón^M

roof timber
charpente^F
Balken^M
trave^F in legno
armazón^M de madera^F

tile
tuile^F
Ziegel^M
tegola^F
cubierta^F de tejas^F

cornice
corniche^F
Kranzgesims^N
cornice^F
comisa^F

sloping cornice
rampant^M
Schräggeison^M
cornice^F inclinata
alero^M

frieze
frise^F
Fries^M
fregio^M
friso^M

architrave
architrave^F
Architrav^M
architrave^M
arquitrabe^M

entablature
entablement^M
Gebälk^N
trabeazione^F
entablamento^M

column
colonne^F
Säule^F
colonna^F
columna^F

crepidoma
crépis^F
Krepis^F
crepidine^F
crepidoma^M

peristyle
péristyle^M
Peristyl^N
peristilio^M
peristilo^M

stylobate
stylobate^M
Stylobat^M
stilobate^M
estilóbato^M

grille
grille^F
Gitter^N
inferriata^F
reja^F de entrada^F al pronaos^M

naos
naos^M
Naos^M
naos^M
naos^M

euthynteria
euthyntérie^F
Euthynterie^F
euthynteria^F
euthynteria^F

ramp
rampe^F
Rampe^F
rampa^F
rampa^F de acceso^M

pronaos
pronaos^M
Pronaos^M
pronao^M
pronaos^M

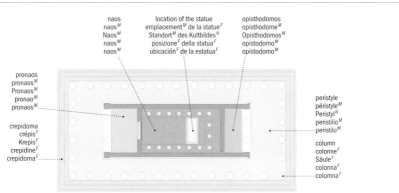

naos
naos^M
Naos^M
naos^M
naos^M

location of the statue
emplacement^M de la statue^F
Standort^M des Kultbildes^N
posizione^F della statua^F
ubicación^F de la estatua^F

opisthodomos
opisthodome^M
Opisthodomos^M
opistodomo^M
opistodomo^M

plan
plan^M
Grundriss^M
pianta^F
plano^M

pronaos
pronaos^M
Pronaos^M
pronao^M
pronaos^M

crepidoma
crépis^F
Krepis^F
crepidine^F
crepidoma^F

peristyle
péristyle^M
Peristyl^N
peristilio^M
peristilo^M

column
colonne^F
Säule^F
colonna^F
columna^F

Roman house

maison^F romaine | römisches Wohnhaus^N | casa^F romana | casa^F romana

ARTS AND ARCHITECTURE

tablinum
tablinum^M
Tablinum^N
tablino^M
tablinum^M

compluvium
compluvium^M
Compluvium^N
compluvio^M
compluvio^M

timber
charpente^F
Balken^M
trave^F in legno^M
viga^F

peristyle
péristyle^M
Peristyl^N
peristilio^M
peristilo^M

garden
jardin^M
Garten^M
giardino^M
jardín^M

fresco
fresque^F
Fresko^N
affresco^M
fresco^M

tile
tuile^F
Ziegel^M
tegola^F
teja^F

dining room
triclinium^M
Küche^F
triclinio^M
triclinio^M

kitchen
cuisine^F
Triklinium^N
cucina^F
cocina^F

latrines
latrines^F
Latrinen^F
latrine^F
letrinas^F

vestibule
vestibule^M
äußerer Hausflur^M
vestibolo^M
vestibulo^M

bed chamber
cubiculum^M
Cubiculum^N
cubicolo^M
cubículo^M

atrium
atrium^M
Atrium^N
atrio^M
atrio^M

impluvium
impluvium^M
Impluvium^N
impluvio^M
impluvio^M

shop
boutique^F
Laden^M
bottega^F
tienda^F

mosaic
mosaïque^F
Mosaik^N
mosaico^M
mosaico^M

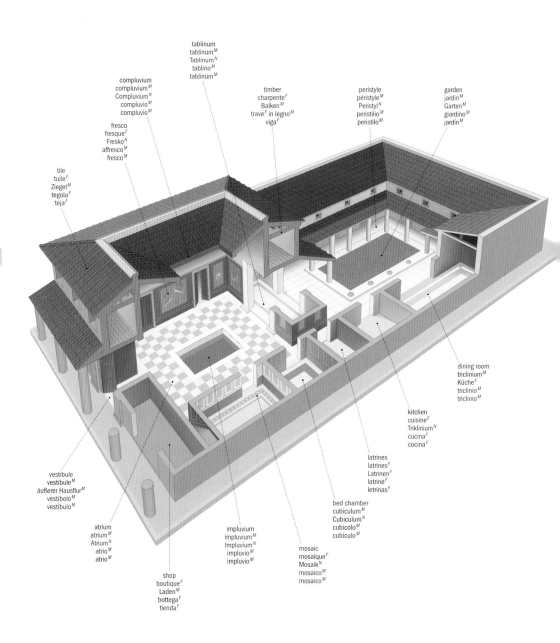

Roman amphitheatre

amphithéâtre^M romain | römisches Amphitheater^N | anfiteatro^M romano | anfiteatro^M romano

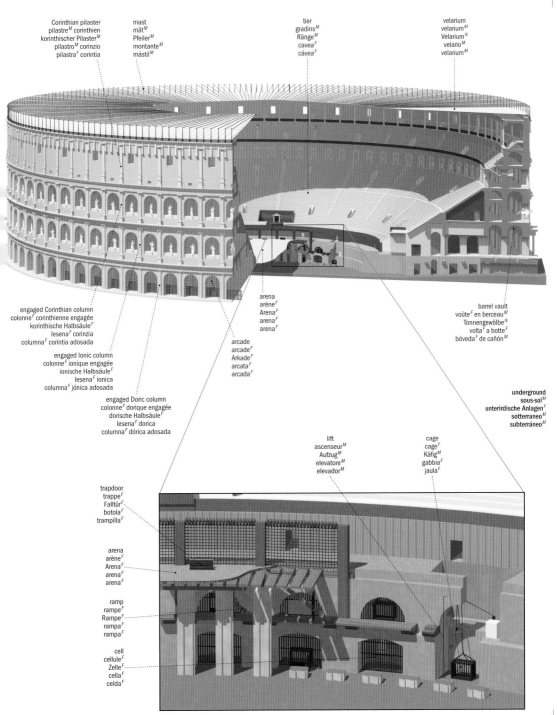

Corinthian pilaster
pilastre^M corinthien
korinthischer Pilaster^M
pilastro^M corinzio
pilastra^F corintia

mast
mât^M
Pfeiler^M
montante^M
mástil^M

tier
gradins^M
Ränge^M
cavea^F
cávea^F

velarium
velarium^M
Velarium^N
velario^M
velarium^M

engaged Corinthian column
colonne^F corinthienne engagée
korinthische Halbsäule^F
lesena^F corinzia
columna^F corintia adosada

engaged Ionic column
colonne^F ionique engagée
ionische Halbsäule^F
lesena^F ionica
columna^F jónica adosada

engaged Doric column
colonne^F dorique engagée
dorische Halbsäule^F
lesena^F dorica
columna^F dórica adosada

arena
arène^F
Arena^F
arena^F
arena^F

arcade
arcade^F
Arkade^F
arcata^F
arcada^F

barrel vault
voûte^F en berceau^M
Tonnengewölbe^N
volta^F a botte^F
bóveda^F de cañón^M

underground
sous-sol^M
unterirdische Anlagen^F
sotterraneo^M
subterráneo^M

lift
ascenseur^M
Aufzug^M
elevatore^M
elevador^M

cage
cage^F
Käfig^M
gabbia^F
jaula^F

trapdoor
trappe^F
Falltür^F
botola^F
trampilla^F

arena
arène^F
Arena^F
arena^F
arena^F

ramp
rampe^F
Rampe^F
rampa^F
rampa^F

cell
cellule^F
Zelle^F
cella^F
celda^F

castle

château^M fort | Burg^F | castello^M | castillo^M

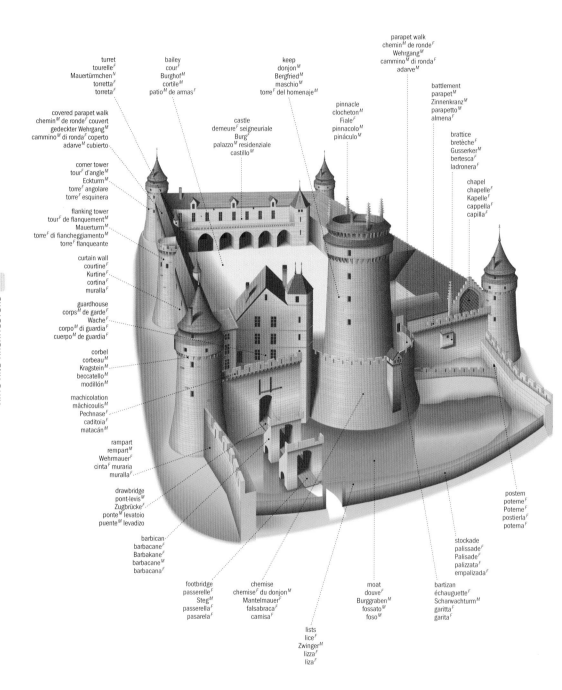

turret
tourelle^F
Mauertürmchen^N
torretta^F
torreta^F

bailey
cour^F
Burghof^M
cortile^M
patio^M de armas^F

keep
donjon^M
Bergfried^M
maschio^M
torre^F del homenaje^M

parapet walk
chemin^M de ronde^F
Wehrgang^M
cammino^M di ronda^F
adarve^M

battlement
parapet^M
Zinnenkranz^M
parapetto^M
almena^F

covered parapet walk
chemin^M de ronde^F couvert
gedeckter Wehrgang^M
cammino^M di ronda^F coperto
adarve^M cubierto

pinnacle
clocheton^M
Fiale^F
pinnacolo^M
pináculo^M

castle
demeure^F seigneuriale
Burg^F
palazzo^M residenziale
castillo^M

brattice
bretèche^F
Gusserker^M
bertesca^F
ladronera^F

chapel
chapelle^F
Kapelle^F
cappella^F
capilla^F

corner tower
tour^F d'angle^M
Eckturm^M
torre^F angolare
torre^F esquinera

flanking tower
tour^F de flanquement^M
Mauerturm^M
torre^F di fiancheggiamento^M
torre^F flanqueante

curtain wall
courtine^F
Kurtine^F
cortina^F
muralla^F

guardhouse
corps^M de garde^F
Wache^F
corpo^M di guardia^F
cuerpo^M de guardia^F

corbel
corbeau^M
Kragstein^M
beccatello^M
modillón^M

machicolation
mâchicoulis^M
Pechnase^F
caditoia^F
matacán^F

rampart
rempart^M
Wehrmauer^F
cinta^F muraria
muralla^F

drawbridge
pont-levis^M
Zugbrücke^F
ponte^M levatoio
puente^M levadizo

postern
poterne^F
Poterne^F
postierla^F
poterna^F

barbican
barbacane^F
Barbakane^F
barbacane^M
barbacana^F

stockade
palissade^F
Palisade^F
palizzata^F
empalizada^F

footbridge
passerelle^F
Steg^M
passerella^F
pasarela^F

chemise
chemise^F du donjon^M
Mantelmauer^F
falsabraca^F
camisa^F

moat
douve^F
Burggraben^M
fossato^M
foso^M

bartizan
échauguette^F
Scharwachturm^M
garitta^F
garita^F

lists
lice^F
Zwinger^M
lizza^F
liza^F

pagoda

pagode^F | Pagode^F | pagoda^F | pagoda^F

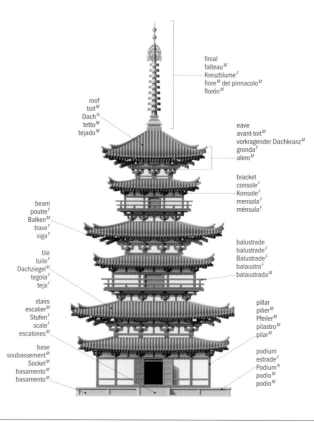

finial
faîteau^M
Kreuzblume^F
fiore^M del pinnacolo^M
florón^M

roof
toit^M
Dach^N
tetto^M
tejado^M

eave
avant-toit^M
vorkragender Dachkranz^M
gronda^F
alero^M

bracket
console^F
Konsole^F
mensola^F
ménsula^F

beam
poutre^F
Balken^M
trave^F
viga^F

balustrade
balustrade^F
Balustrade^F
balaustra^F
balaustrada^F

tile
tuile^F
Dachziegel^M
tegola^F
teja^F

stairs
escalier^M
Stufen^F
scale^F
escalones^M

pillar
pilier^M
Pfeiler^M
pilastro^M
pilar^M

base
soubassement^M
Sockel^M
basamento^M
basamento^M

podium
estrade^F
Podium^N
podio^M
podio^M

Aztec temple

temple^M aztèque | aztekischer Tempel^M | tempio^M azteco | templo^M azteca

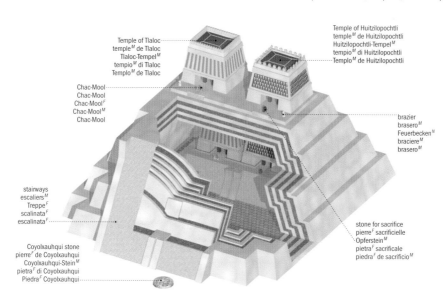

Temple of Tlaloc
temple^M de Tlaloc
Tlaloc-Tempel^M
tempio^M di Tlaloc
Templo^M de Tlaloc

Temple of Huitzilopochtli
temple^M de Huitzilopochtli
Huitzilopochtli-Tempel^M
tempio^M di Huitzilopochtli
Templo^M de Huitzilopochtli

Chac-Mool
Chac-Mool
Chac-Mool^F
Chac-Mool^M
Chac-Mool

brazier
brasero^M
Feuerbecken^N
braciere^M
brasero^M

stairways
escaliers^M
Treppe^F
scalinata^F
escalinata^F

stone for sacrifice
pierre^F sacrificielle
Opferstein^M
pietra^F sacrificale
piedra^F de sacrificio^M

Coyolxauhqui stone
pierre^F de Coyolxauhqui
Coyolxauhqui-Stein^M
pietra^F di Coyolxauhqui
Piedra^F Coyolxauhqui

ARTS AND ARCHITECTURE

cathedral

cathédrale^F | Dom^M | cattedrale^F | catedral^F

Gothic cathedral
cathédrale^F gothique
gotischer Dom^M
cattedrale^F gotica
catedral^F gótica

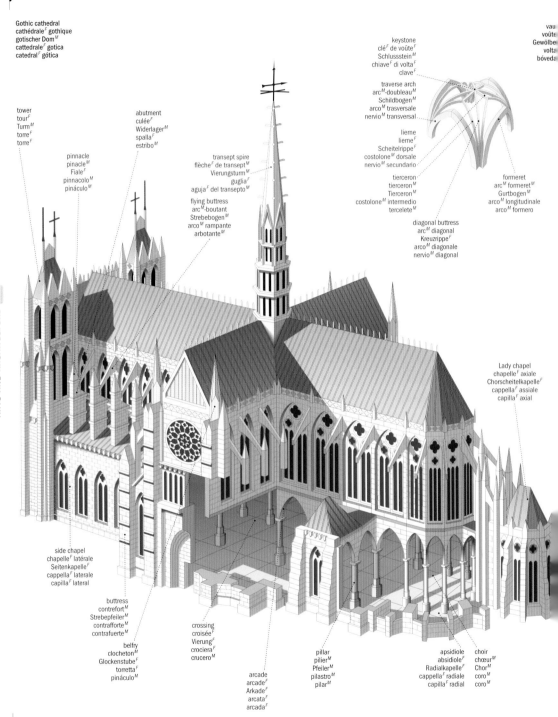

vau
voûte
Gewölbe
volta
bóveda

keystone
clé^F de voûte^F
Schlussstein^M
chiave^F di volta^F
clave^F

traverse arch
arc^M-doubleau^M
Schildbogen^M
arco^M trasversale
nervio^M transversal

lierne
lierne^F
Scheitelrippe^F
costolone^M dorsale
nervio^M secundario

tierceron
tierceron^M
Tierceron^M
costolone^M intermedio
tercelete^M

diagonal buttress
arc^M diagonal
Kreuzrippe^F
arco^M diagonale
nervio^M diagonal

formeret
arc^M formeret^M
Gurtbogen^M
arco^M longitudinale
arco^M formero

tower
tour^F
Turm^M
torre^F
torre^F

abutment
culée^F
Widerlager^M
spalla^F
estribo^M

pinnacle
pinacle^M
Fiale^F
pinnacolo^M
pináculo^M

transept spire
flèche^F de transept^M
Vierungsturm^M
guglia^F
aguja^F del transepto^M

flying buttress
arc^M-boutant
Strebebogen^M
arco^M rampante
arbotante^M

Lady chapel
chapelle^F axiale
Chorscheitelkapelle^F
cappella^F assiale
capilla^F axial

side chapel
chapelle^F latérale
Seitenkapelle^F
cappella^F laterale
capilla^F lateral

buttress
contrefort^M
Strebepfeiler^M
contrafforte^M
contrafuerte^M

belfry
clocheton^M
Glockenstube^F
torretta^F
pináculo^M

crossing
croisée^F
Vierung^F
crociera^F
crucero^M

arcade
arcade^F
Arkade^F
arcata^F
arcada^F

pillar
pilier^M
Pfeiler^M
pilastro^M
pilar^M

apsidiole
absidiole^F
Radialkapelle^F
cappella^F radiale
capilla^F radial

choir
chœur^M
Chor^M
coro^M
coro^M

cathedral

façade
façade^F
Fassade^F
facciata^F
fachada^F

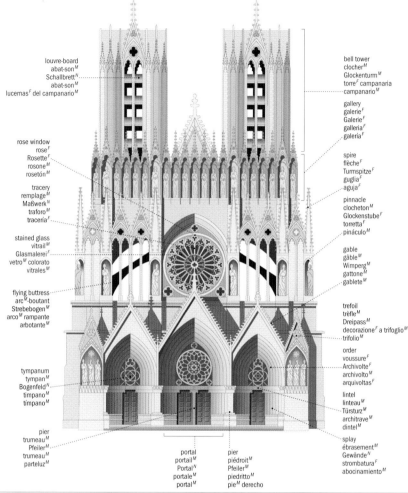

louvre-board
abat-son^M
Schallbrett^N
abat-son^M
lucernas^F del campanario^M

bell tower
clocher^M
Glockenturm^M
torre^F campanaria
campanario^M

gallery
galerie^F
Galerie^F
galleria^F
galería^F

rose window
rose^F
Rosette^F
rosone^M
rosetón^M

spire
flèche^F
Turmspitze^F
guglia^F
aguja^F

tracery
remplage^M
Maßwerk^N
traforo^M
tracería^F

pinnacle
clocheton^M
Glockenstube^F
torretta^F
pináculo^M

stained glass
vitrail^M
Glasmalerei^F
vetro^M colorato
vitrales^M

gable
gâble^M
Wimperg^M
gattone^M
gablete^M

flying buttress
arc^M-boutant
Strebebogen^M
arco^M rampante
arbotante^M

trefoil
trèfle^M
Dreipass^M
decorazione^F a trifoglio^M
trifolio^M

order
voussure^F
Archivolte^F
archivolto^M
arquivoltas^F

tympanum
tympan^M
Bogenfeld^N
timpano^M
tímpano^M

lintel
linteau^M
Türsturz^M
architrave^F
dintel^M

pier
trumeau^M
Pfeiler^M
trumeau^M
parteluz^M

splay
ébrasement^M
Gewände^N
strombatura^F
abocinamiento^M

portal
portail^M
Portal^N
portale^M
portal^M

pier
piédroit^M
Pfeiler^M
piedritto^M
pie^M derecho

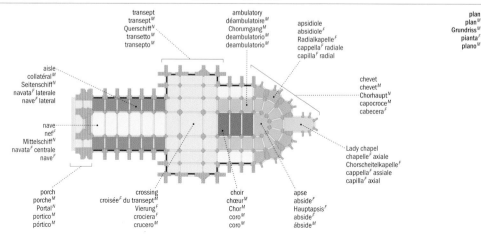

plan
plan^M
Grundriss^M
pianta^F
plano^M

transept
transept^M
Querschiff^N
transetto^M
transepto^M

ambulatory
déambulatoire^M
Chorumgang^M
deambulatorio^M
deambulatorio^M

apsidiole
absidiole^F
Radialkapelle^F
cappella^F radiale
capilla^F radial

aisle
collatéral^M
Seitenschiff^N
navata^F laterale
nave^F lateral

chevet
chevet^M
Chorhaupt^N
capocroce^M
cabecera^F

nave
nef^F
Mittelschiff^N
navata^F centrale
nave^F

Lady chapel
chapelle^F axiale
Chorscheitelkapelle^F
cappella^F assiale
capilla^F axial

porch
porche^M
Portal^N
portico^M
pórtico^M

crossing
croisée^F du transept^M
Vierung^F
crociera^F
crucero^M

choir
chœur^M
Chor^M
coro^M
coro^M

apse
abside^F
Hauptapsis^F
abside^F
ábside^M

elements of architecture

éléments^M d'architecture^F | Architekturelemente^N | elementi^M architettonici | elementos^M arquitectónicos

examples of doors
exemples^M de portes^F
Beispiele^N für Türen^F
esempi^M di porte^F
ejemplos^M de puertas^F

manual revolving door
porte^F à tambour^M manuelle
Drehtür^F
porta^F girevole manuale
puerta^F giratoria manual

canopy
couronne^F
Gehäusedach^N
cappello^M
tambor^M

wing
vantail^M
Flügel^M
battente^M
hoja^F

motion detector
détecteur^M de mouvement^M
Bewegungsmelder^M
rilevatore^M di movimento^M
sensor^M de movimiento

automatic sliding door
porte^F coulissante automatique
automatische Schiebetür^F
porta^F scorrevole automatica
puerta^F corredera automática

enclosure
sas^M
Drehgehäuse^N
alloggiamento
estructura^F interior

push bar
barre^F de poussée^F
Handgriff^M
maniglia^F di spinta^F
tirador^M

compartment
compartiment^M
Zelle^F
vano^M
compartimiento^M

wing
vantail^M
Flügel^M
battente^M
hoja^F

strip
lanière^F
Streifen^M
banda^F
tira^F

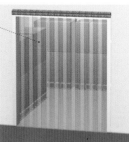

conventional door
porte^F classique
Drehflügeltür^F
porta^F a un battente^M
puerta^F convencional

folding door
porte^F pliante
Falttür^F
porta^F a libro^M
puerta^F plegable

strip door
porte^F à lanières^F
Streifenvorhang^M
porta^F a bande^F verticali
puerta^F de tiras^F

fire door
porte^F coupe-feu
Feuerschutztür^F
porta^F antincendio
puerta^F cortafuego

concertina-type folding door
porte^F accordéon^M
Harmonikatür^F
porta^F a fisarmonica^F
puerta^F de librillo^M

sliding door
porte^F coulissante
Schiebetür^F
porta^F scorrevole
puerta^F corredera

sectional garage door
porte^F de garage^M sectionnelle
Sektionalgaragentor^N
porta^F sezionale del garage^M
puerta^F de garaje^M seccional

up-and-over garage door
porte^F de garage^M basculante
Schwinggaragentor^N
porta^F basculante del garage^M
puerta^F basculante de garaje^M

ARTS AND ARCHITECTURE

examples of windows
exemples ^{M} **de fenêtres** ^{F}
Beispiele ^{N} **für Fenster** ^{N}
esempi ^{I} **di finestre** ^{F}
ejemplos ^{M} **de ventanas** ^{F}

sliding folding window
fenêtre ^{F} en accordéon ^{M}
Faltfenster ^{N}
finestra ^{F} a libro ^{M}
ventana ^{F} de librillo ^{M}

casement window opening inwards
fenêtre ^{F} à la française ^{F}
Drehflügel ^{M} nach innen
finestra ^{F} a battenti ^{M} con apertura ^{F} all'interno ^{M}
ventana ^{F} a la francesa ^{F}

casement window
fenêtre ^{F} à l'anglaise ^{F}
Drehflügel ^{M} nach außen
finestra ^{F} a battenti ^{M}
ventana ^{F} a la inglesa ^{F}

louvred window
fenêtre ^{F} à jalousies ^{F}
Jalousiefenster ^{N}
finestra ^{F} a gelosia ^{F}
ventana ^{F} de celosia ^{F}

sliding window
fenêtre ^{F} coulissante
horizontales Schiebefenster ^{N}
finestra ^{F} scorrevole
ventana ^{F} corredera

sash window
fenêtre ^{F} à guillotine ^{F}
vertikales Schiebefenster ^{N}
finestra ^{F} a ghigliottina ^{F}
ventana ^{F} de guillotina ^{F}

horizontal pivoting window
fenêtre ^{F} basculante
Schwingflügel ^{M}
finestra ^{F} a bilico ^{M} orizzontale
ventana ^{F} basculante

vertical pivoting window
fenêtre ^{F} pivotante
Wendeflügel ^{M}
finestra ^{F} a bilico ^{M} verticale
ventana ^{F} pivotante

lift

ascenseur ^{M} | Aufzug ^{M} | ascensore ^{M} | ascensor ^{M}

lift car
cabine ^{F} d'ascenseur ^{M}
Fahrkorb ^{M}
cabina ^{F} dell'ascensore ^{M}
cabina ^{F} del ascensor ^{M}

position indicator
indicateur ^{M} de position ^{F}
Standortanzeiger ^{M}
indicatore ^{M} del piano ^{M}
indicador ^{M} de posición ^{F}

winch
treuil ^{M}
Treibscheibe ^{F}
argano ^{M}
máquina ^{F}

speed governor
régulateur ^{M} de vitesse ^{F}
Geschwindigkeitsregler ^{M}
regolatore ^{M} di velocità ^{F}
limitador ^{M} de velocidad ^{F}

car ceiling
plafond ^{M} de cabine ^{F}
Fahrkorbdecke ^{F}
soffitto ^{M} della cabina ^{F}
techo ^{M} de cabina ^{F}

call button
bouton ^{M} d'appel ^{M}
Ruftaste ^{F}
pulsante ^{M} di chiamata ^{F}
pulsador ^{M} de llamada ^{F}

hoisting rope
câble ^{M} de levage ^{M}
Tragseil ^{N}
fune ^{F} di sollevamento ^{M}
cable ^{M} de tracción ^{F}

lift car
cabine ^{F} d'ascenseur ^{M}
Fahrkorb ^{M}
cabina ^{F} dell'ascensore ^{M}
cabina ^{F} del ascensor ^{M}

limit switch
interrupteur ^{M} de fin ^{F} de course ^{F}
Endschalter ^{M}
interruttore ^{M} di fine ^{F} corsa ^{F}
final ^{M} de carrera ^{F}

operating panel
tableau ^{M} de manœuvre ^{F}
Bedienungstafel ^{F}
pannello ^{M} di funzionamento ^{M}
botonera ^{F} de cabina ^{F}

car safety
parachute ^{M} de cabine ^{F}
Fahrkorb ^{M}-Fangvorrichtung ^{F}
paracadute ^{F}
paracaidas ^{M}

handrail
main ^{F} courante
Handlauf ^{M}
corrimano ^{M}
pasamanos ^{M}

car guide rail
rail ^{M}-guide ^{M} de la cabine ^{F}
Fahrkorb ^{M}-Führungsschiene ^{F}
guida ^{F} della cabina ^{F}
guia ^{F} de cabina ^{F}

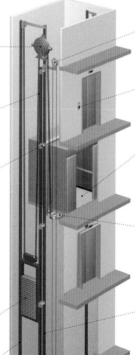

car floor
plancher ^{M} de cabine ^{F}
Fahrkorbboden ^{M}
pavimento ^{M} della cabina ^{F}
suelo ^{M} de cabina ^{F}

counterweight
contrepoids ^{M}
Gegengewicht ^{N}
contrappeso ^{M}
contrapeso ^{M}

buffer
amortisseur ^{M}
Puffer ^{M}
ammortizzatore ^{M}
amortiguador ^{M}

door
porte ^{F}
Tür ^{F}
porta ^{F}
puerta ^{F}

counterweight guide rail
rail ^{M}-guide ^{M} de contrepoids ^{M}
Gegengewichtsführung ^{F}
guida ^{F} del contrappeso ^{M}
guia ^{F} del contrapeso ^{M}

governor tension sheave
poulie ^{F} de tension ^{F} du régulateur ^{M}
Reglerspanngewicht ^{N}
puleggia ^{F} di tensione ^{F} del regolatore ^{M}
polea ^{F} tensora del limitador ^{M} de velocidad ^{F}

traditional dwellings

maisons^F traditionnelles | traditionelle Wohnhäuser^N | case^F tradizionali | viviendas^F tradicionales

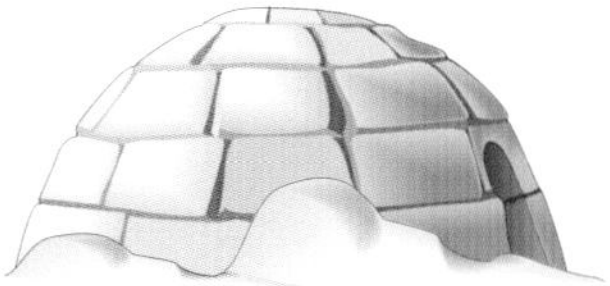

igloo
igloo^M
Iglu^M
igloo^M
iglú^M

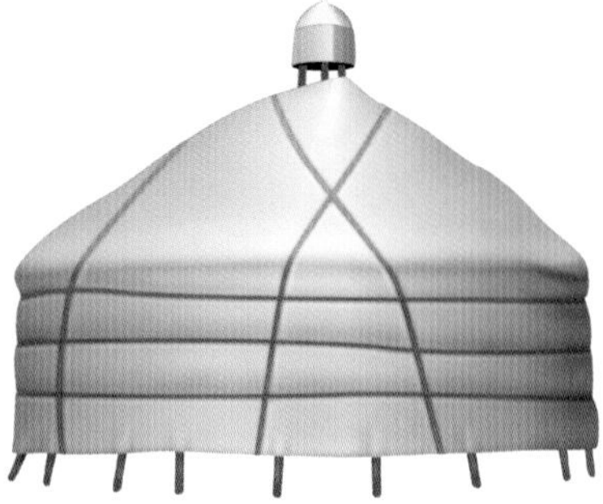

yurt
yourte^F
Jurte^F
iurta^F
yurta^F

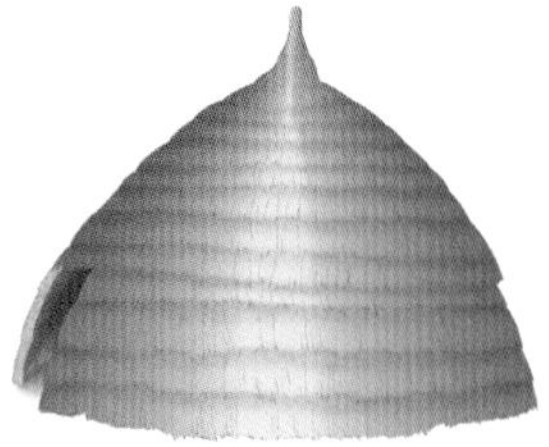

(straw) hut
hutte^F
Strohhütte^F
capanna^F di paglia^F
choza^F indigena

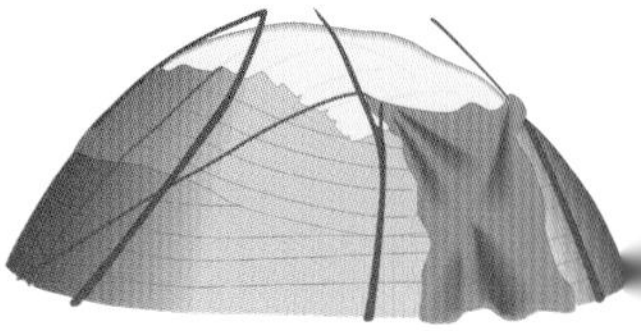

wigwam
wigwam^M
Wigwam^M
wigwam^M
wigwam^M

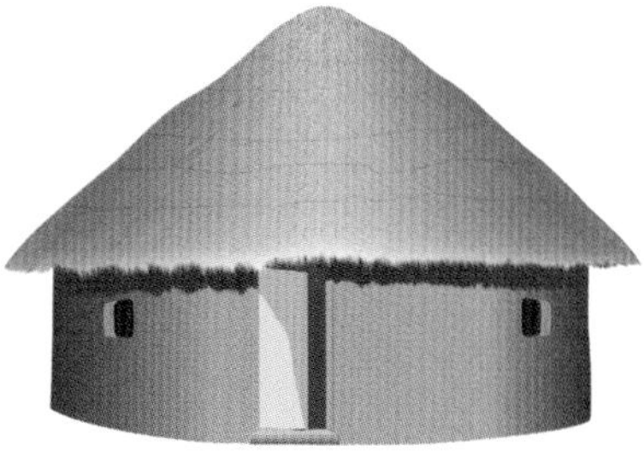

(mud) hut
case^F
Lehmhütte^F
capanna^F di fango^M
choza^F

isba
isba^F
Isba^F
isba^F
isba^F

tepee
tipi^M
Tipi^N
tepee^M
tipi^M

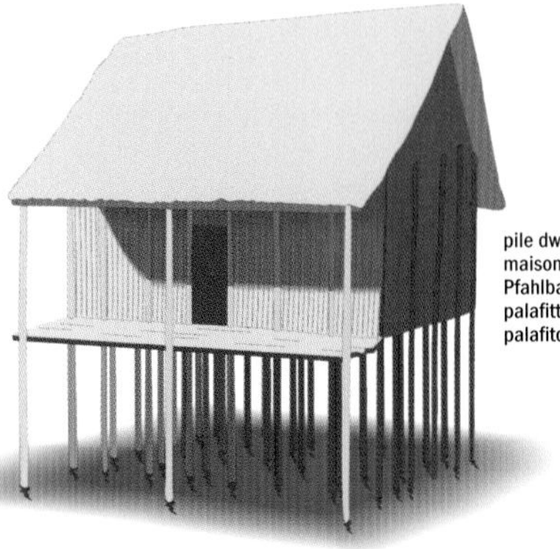

pile dwelling
maison^F sur pilotis^M
Pfahlbau^M
palafitta^F
palafito^M

beam
poutre^F
Balken^M
trave^F
viga^F

adobe house
maison^F en adobe
Backsteinhau
casa^F in mattoni^M co
casa^F de adobes

ladder
échelle^F
Leiter^F
scala^F
escalera^F

ARTS AND ARCHITECTURE

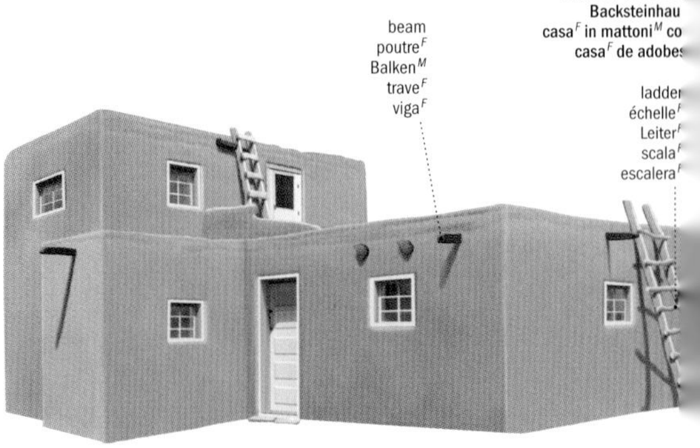

town houses

maisons^F de ville^F | Häuserformen^F in der Stadt^F | abitazioni^F urbane | viviendas^F urbanas

two-storey house
maison^F à étage^M
zweistöckiges Haus^N
casa^F a due piani^M
casa^F de dos plantas^M

one-storey-house
maison^F de plain-pied^M
einstöckiges Haus^N
casa^F a un piano^M
casa^F de una planta^F

semi-detached houses
maison^F jumelée
Doppelhaus^N
villetta^F bifamiliare
casas^F pareadas

terraced houses
maisons^F en rangée^F
Reihenhaus^N
case^F a schiera^F
casas^F adosadas

freehold flats
appartements^M en copropriété^F
Eigentumswohnungen^F
palazzo^M in condominio^M
viviendas^F plurifamiliares

high-rise block
tour^F d'habitation^F
Wohnblock^M
casatorre^F
bloque^M de apartamentos^M

shooting stage

plateau^M de tournage^M | Aufnahmebühne^F | set^M delle riprese^F | plató^M de rodaje^M

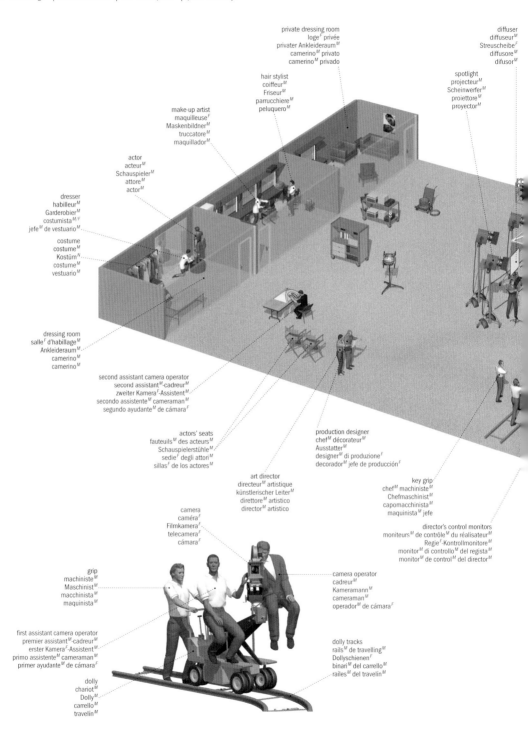

private dressing room
loge^F privée
privater Ankleideraum^M
camerino^M privato
camerino^M privado

diffuser
diffuseur^M
Streuscheibe^F
diffusore^M
difusor^M

hair stylist
coiffeur^M
Friseur^M
parrucchiere^M
peluquero^M

spotlight
projecteur^M
Scheinwerfer^M
proiettore^M
proyector^M

make-up artist
maquilleuse^F
Maskenbildner^M
truccatore^M
maquillador^M

actor
acteur^M
Schauspieler^M
attore^M
actor^M

dresser
habilleur^M
Garderobier^M
costumista^{M/F}
jefe^M de vestuario^M

costume
costume^M
Kostüm^N
costume^M
vestuario^M

dressing room
salle^F d'habillage^M
Ankleideraum^M
camerino^M
camerino^M

second assistant camera operator
second assistant^M-cadreur^M
zweiter Kamera^F-Assistent^M
secondo assistente^M cameraman^M
segundo ayudante^M de cámara^F

actors' seats
fauteuils^M des acteurs^M
Schauspielerstühle^M
sedie^F degli attori^M
sillas^F de los actores^M

production designer
chef^M décorateur^M
Ausstatter^M
designer^M di produzione^F
decorador^M jefe de producción^F

art director
directeur^M artistique
künstlerischer Leiter^M
direttore^M artistico
director^M artístico

key grip
chef^M machiniste^M
Chefmaschinist^M
capomacchinista^M
maquinista^M jefe

camera
caméra^F
Filmkamera^F
telecamera^F
cámara^F

director's control monitors
moniteurs^M de contrôle^M du réalisateur^M
Regie^F-Kontrollmonitore^M
monitor^M di controllo^M del regista^M
monitor^M de control^M del director^M

grip
machiniste^M
Maschinist^M
macchinista^M
maquinista^M

camera operator
cadreur^M
Kameramann^M
cameraman^M
operador^M de cámara^F

first assistant camera operator
premier assistant^M-cadreur^M
erster Kamera^F-Assistent^M
primo assistente^M cameraman^M
primer ayudante^M de cámara^F

dolly tracks
rails^M de travelling^M
Dollyschienen^F
binari^M del carrello^M
raíles^M del travelín^M

dolly
chariot^M
Dolly^M
carrello^M
travelín^M

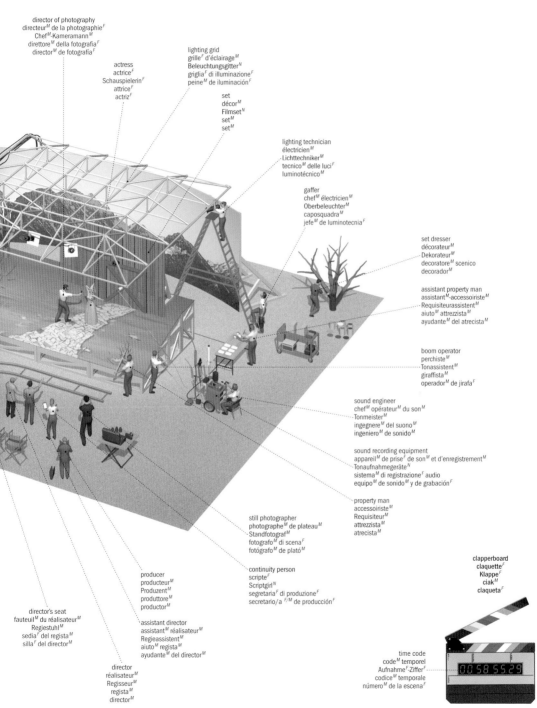

director of photography
directeur^M de la photographie^F
Chef^M-Kameramann^M
direttore^M della fotografia^F
director^M de fotografía^F

actress
actrice^F
Schauspielerin^F
attrice^F
actriz^F

lighting grid
grille^F d'éclairage^M
Beleuchtungsgitter^N
griglia^F di illuminazione^F
peine^M de iluminación^F

set
décor^M
Filmset^N
set^M
set^M

lighting technician
électricien^M
Lichttechniker^M
tecnico^M delle luci^F
luminotécnico^M

gaffer
chef^M électricien^M
Oberbeleuchter^M
caposquadra^M
jefe^M de luminotecnia^F

set dresser
décorateur^M
Dekorateur^M
decoratore^M scenico
decorador^M

assistant property man
assistant^M-accessoiriste^M
Requisiteurassistent^M
aiuto^M attrezzista^M
ayudante^M del atrecista^M

boom operator
perchiste^M
Tonassistent^M
giraffista^M
operador^M de jirafa^F

sound engineer
chef^M opérateur^M du son^M
Tonmeister^M
ingegnere^M del suono^M
ingeniero^M de sonido^M

sound recording equipment
appareil^M de prise^F de son^M et d'enregistrement^M
Tonaufnahmegeräte^N
sistema^M di registrazione^F audio
equipo^M de sonido^M y de grabación^F

property man
accessoiriste^M
Requisiteur^M
attrezzista^M
atrecista^M

still photographer
photographe^M de plateau^M
Standfotograf^M
fotografo^M di scena^F
fotógrafo^M de plató^M

continuity person
scripte^F
Scriptgirl^N
segretaria^F di produzione^F
secretario/a $^{F/M}$ de producción^F

producer
producteur^M
Produzent^M
produttore^M
productor^M

director's seat
fauteuil^M du réalisateur^M
Regiestuhl^M
sedia^F del regista^M
silla^F del director^M

assistant director
assistant^M réalisateur^M
Regieassistent^M
aiuto^M regista^M
ayudante^M del director^M

director
réalisateur^M
Regisseur^M
regista^M
director^M

clapperboard
claquette^F
Klappe^F
ciak^M
claqueta^F

time code
code^M temporel
Aufnahme^F-Ziffer^F
codice^M temporale
número^M de la escena^F

00:58:55:29

ARTS AND ARCHITECTURE

theatre

salle^F de spectacle^M | Theater^N | teatro^M | teatro^M

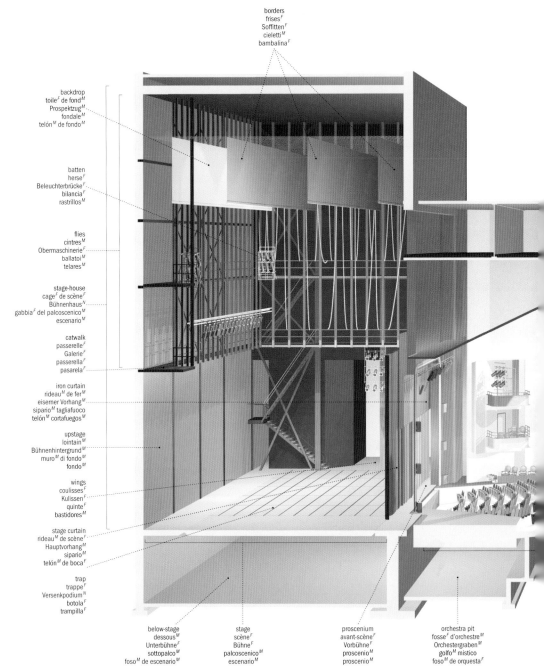

borders
frises^F
Soffitten^F
cieletti^M
bambalina^F

backdrop
toile^F de fond^M
Prospektzug^M
fondale^M
telón^M de fondo^M

batten
herse^F
Beleuchterbrücke^F
bilancia^F
rastrillos^M

flies
cintres^M
Obermaschinerie^F
ballatoi^M
telares^M

stage-house
cage^F de scène^F
Bühnenhaus^N
gabbia^F del palcoscenico^M
escenario^M

catwalk
passerelle^F
Galerie^F
passerella^F
pasarela^F

iron curtain
rideau^M de fer^M
eiserner Vorhang^M
sipario^M tagliafuoco
telón^M cortafuegos^M

upstage
lointain^M
Bühnenhintergrund^M
muro^M di fondo^M
fondo^M

wings
coulisses^F
Kulissen^F
quinte^F
bastidores^M

stage curtain
rideau^M de scène^F
Hauptvorhang^M
sipario^M
telón^M de boca^F

trap
trappe^F
Versenkpodium^N
botola^F
trampilla^F

below-stage
dessous^M
Unterbühne^F
sottopalco^M
foso^M de escenario^M

stage
scène^F
Bühne^F
palcoscenico^M
escenario^M

proscenium
avant-scène^F
Vorbühne^F
proscenio^M
proscenio^M

orchestra pit
fosse^F d'orchestre^M
Orchestergraben^M
golfo^M mistico
foso^M de orquesta^F

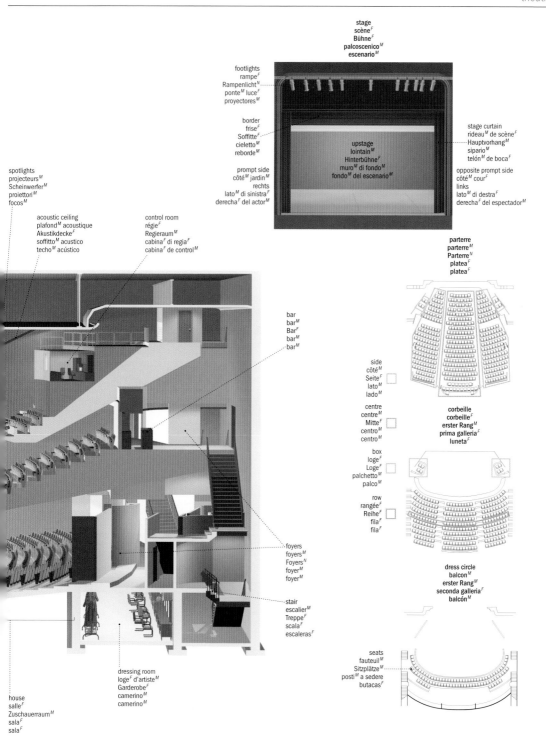

stage
scène^F
Bühne^F
palcoscenico^M
escenario^M

footlights
rampe^F
Rampenlicht^N
ponte^M luce^F
proyectores^M

border
frise^F
Soffitte^F
cieletto^M
reborde^M

stage curtain
rideau^M de scène^F
Hauptvorhang^M
sipario^M
telón^M de boca^F

upstage
lointain^M
Hinterbühne^F
muro^M di fondo^M
fondo^M del escenario^M

prompt side
côté^M jardin^M
rechts
lato^M di sinistra^F
derecha^F del actor^M

opposite prompt side
côté^M cour^F
links
lato^M di destra^F
derecha^F del espectador^M

spotlights
projecteurs^M
Scheinwerfer^M
proiettori^M
focos^M

acoustic ceiling
plafond^M acoustique
Akustikdecke^F
soffitto^M acustico
techo^M acústico

control room
régie^F
Regieraum^M
cabina^F di regia^F
cabina^F de control^M

parterre
parterre^M
Parterre^N
platea^F
platea^F

bar
bar^M
Bar^F
bar^M
bar^M

side
côté^M
Seite^F
lato^M
lado^M

centre
centre^M
Mitte^F
centro^M
centro^M

corbeille
corbeille^F
erster Rang^M
prima galleria^F
luneta^F

box
loge^F
Loge^F
palchetto^M
palco^M

row
rangée^F
Reihe^F
fila^F
fila^F

foyers
foyers^M
Foyers^N
foyer^M
foyer^M

stair
escalier^M
Treppe^F
scala^F
escaleras^F

dress circle
balcon^M
erster Rang^M
seconda galleria^F
balcón^M

dressing room
loge^F d'artiste^M
Garderobe^F
camerino^M
camerino^M

house
salle^F
Zuschauerraum^M
sala^F
sala^F

seats
fauteuil^M
Sitzplätze^M
posti^M a sedere
butacas^F

cinema

cinéma^M | Kino^N | cinema^M | cine^M

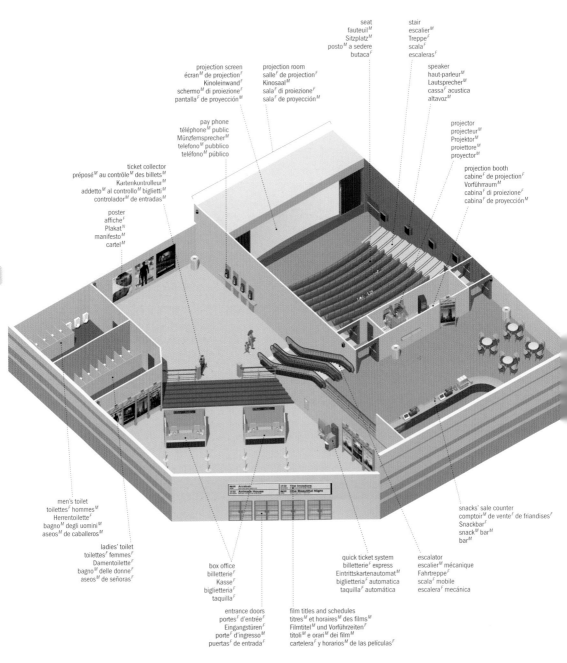

seat
fauteuil^M
Sitzplatz^M
posto^M a sedere
butaca^F

stair
escalier^M
Treppe^F
scala^F
escaleras^F

projection screen
écran^M de projection^F
Kinoleinwand^F
schermo^M di proiezione^F
pantalla^F de proyección^M

projection room
salle^F de projection^F
Kinosaal^M
sala^F di proiezione^F
sala^F de proyección^M

speaker
haut-parleur^M
Lautsprecher^M
cassa^F acustica
altavoz^M

pay phone
téléphone^M public
Münzfernsprecher^M
telefono^M pubblico
teléfono^M público

projector
projecteur^M
Projektor^M
proiettore^M
proyector^M

ticket collector
préposé^M au contrôle^M des billets^M
Kartenkontrolleur^M
addetto^M al controllo^M biglietti^M
controlador^M de entradas^M

projection booth
cabine^F de projection^F
Vorführraum^M
cabina^F di proiezione^F
cabina^F de proyección^M

poster
affiche^F
Plakat^N
manifesto^M
cartel^M

men's toilet
toilettes^F hommes^M
Herrentoilette^F
bagno^M degli uomini^M
aseos^M de caballeros^M

ladies' toilet
toilettes^F femmes^F
Damentoilette^F
bagno^M delle donne^F
aseos^M de señoras^F

snacks' sale counter
comptoir^M de vente^F de friandises^F
Snackbar^F
snack^M bar^M
bar^M

box office
billetterie^F
Kasse^F
biglietteria^F
taquilla^F

quick ticket system
billetterie^F express
Eintrittskartenautomat^M
biglietteria^F automatica
taquilla^F automática

escalator
escalier^M mécanique
Fahrtreppe^F
scala^F mobile
escalera^F mecánica

entrance doors
portes^F d'entrée^F
Eingangstüren^F
porte^F d'ingresso^M
puertas^F de entrada^F

film titles and schedules
titres^M et horaires^M des films^M
Filmtitel^M und Vorführzeiten^F
titoli^M e orari^M dei film^M
cartelera^F y horarios^M de las películas^F

symphony orchestra

orchestre^M symphonique | Sinfonieorchester^N | orchestra^F sinfonica | orquesta^F sinfónica

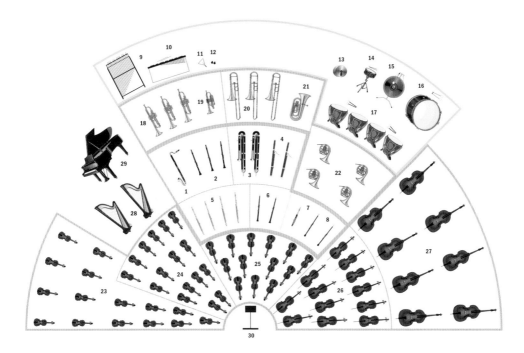

woodwind family
famille^F des bois^M
Familie^F der Holzblasinstrumente^N
famiglia^F dei legni^M
familia^F de instrumentos^M de madera^F

bass clarinet
clarinette^F basse
Bassklarinette^F
clarinetto^M basso
clarinete^M bajo

clarinets
clarinettes^F
Klarinetten^F
clarinetti^M
clarinetes^M

contrabassoons
contrabassons^M
Kontrafagotte^N
contrafagotti^M
contrafagots^M

bassoons
bassons^M
Fagotte^N
fagotti^M
fagotes^M

flutes
flûtes^F
Querflöten^F
flauti^M
flautas^F traverseras

oboes
hautbois^M
Oboen^F
oboi^M
oboes^M

piccolo
piccolo^M
7 Pikkoloflöte^F
ottavino^M
piccolo^M

cors anglais
cors^M anglais
8 Englischhörner^N
corni^M inglesi
cornos^M ingleses

percussion instruments
instruments^M à percussion^F
Schlaginstrumente^N
strumenti^M a percussione^F
instrumentos^M de percusión^F

tubular bells
carillon^M tubulaire
9 Röhrenglocken^F
campane^F tubolari
campanas^F tubulares

xylophone
xylophone^M
10 Xylophon^N
xilofono^M
xilófono^M

triangle
triangle^M
11 Triangel^M
triangolo^M
triángulo^M

castanets
castagnettes^F
12 Kastagnetten^F
nacchere^F
castañuelas^F

cymbals
cymbales^F
13 Becken^N
piatti^M
platillos^M

snare drum
caisse^F claire
14 kleine Trommel^F
cassa^F chiara
caja^F clara

gong
gong^M
15 Gong^N
gong^M
gong^M

bass drum
grosse caisse^F
16 Basstrommel^F
grancassa^F
bombo^M

timpani
timbales^F
17 Pauken^F
timpani^M
timbales^M

harps
harpes^F
28 Harfen^F
arpe^F
arpas^F

brass family
famille^F des cuivres^M
Familie^F der Blechbläser^M
famiglia^F degli ottoni^M
familia^F de los metales^M

trumpets
trompettes^F
18 Trompeten^F
trombe^F
trompetas^F

cornet
cornet^M à pistons^M
19 Kornett^N
cornetta^F
cornetín^M

trombones
trombones^M
20 Posaunen^F
tromboni^M
trombones^M

tuba
tuba^M
21 Tuba^F
tuba^F
tuba^F

French horns
cors^M d'harmonie^F
22 Waldhörner^N
corni^M
cornos^M franceses/trompas^F

piano
piano^M
29 Flügel^M
pianoforte^M
piano^M

violin family
famille^F du violon^M
Geigenfamilie^F
famiglia^F degli archi^M
familia^F de los violines^M

first violins
premiers violons^M
23 erste Violinen^F
primi violini^M
primeros violines^M

second violins
seconds violons^M
24 zweite Violinen^F
secondi violini^M
segundos violines^M

violas
altos^M
25 Bratschen^F
viole^F
violas^F

cellos
violoncelles^M
26 Celli^N
violoncelli^M
violoncelos^M

double basses
contrebasses^F
27 Kontrabässe^F
contrabbassi^M
contrabajos^M

conductor's podium
pupitre^M du chef^M d'orchestre^M
30 Dirigentenpult^N
podio^M del direttore^M d'orchestra^F
estrado^M del director^M

traditional musical instruments

instruments^M traditionnels | traditionelle Musikinstrumente^N | strumenti^M musicali tradizionali | instrumentos^M musicales tradicionales

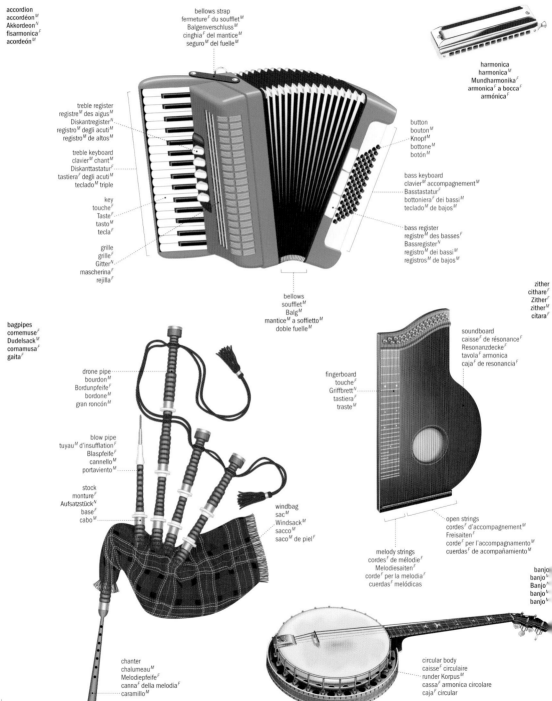

accordion
accordéon^M
Akkordeon^N
fisarmonica^F
acordeón^M

bellows strap
fermeture^F du soufflet^M
Balgenverschluss^M
cinghia^F del mantice^M
seguro^M del fuelle^M

harmonica
harmonica^M
Mundharmonika^F
armonica^F a bocca^F
armónica^F

treble register
registre^M des aigus^M
Diskantregister^N
registro^M degli acuti^M
registro^M de altos^M

treble keyboard
clavier^M chant^M
Diskanttastatur^F
tastiera^F degli acuti^M
teclado^M triple

button
bouton^M
Knopf^M
bottone^M
botón^M

key
touche^F
Taste^F
tasto^M
tecla^F

bass keyboard
clavier^M accompagnement^M
Basstastatur^F
bottoniera^F dei bassi^M
teclado^M de bajos^M

bass register
registre^M des basses^F
Bassregister^N
registro^M dei bassi^M
registros^M de bajos^M

grille
grille^F
Gitter^N
mascherina^F
rejilla^F

bellows
soufflet^M
Balg^M
mantice^M a soffietto^M
doble fuelle^M

zither
cithare^F
Zither^F
zither^M
citara^F

bagpipes
cornemuse^F
Dudelsack^M
cornamusa^F
gaita^F

drone pipe
bourdon^M
Bordunpfeife^F
bordone^M
gran roncón^M

soundboard
caisse^F de résonance^F
Resonanzdecke^F
tavola^F armonica
caja^F de resonancia^F

fingerboard
touche^F
Griffbrett^N
tastiera^F
traste^M

blow pipe
tuyau^M d'insufflation^F
Blaspfeife^F
cannello^M
portaviento^M

stock
monture^F
Aufsatzstück^N
base^F
cabo^M

windbag
sac^M
Windsack^M
sacco^M
saco^M de piel^F

open strings
cordes^F d'accompagnement^M
Freisaiten^F
corde^F per l'accompagnamento^M
cuerdas^F de acompañamiento^M

melody strings
cordes^F de mélodie^F
Melodiesaiten^F
corde^F per la melodia^F
cuerdas^F melódicas

banjo
banjo^M
Banjo^N
banjo^M
banjo^M

chanter
chalumeau^M
Melodiepfeife^F
canna^F della melodia^F
caramillo^M

circular body
caisse^F circulaire
runder Korpus^M
cassa^F armonica circolare
caja^F circular

kora
kora[F]
Kora[F]
kora[F]
kora[M]

mandolin
mandoline[F]
Mandoline[F]
mandolino[M]
mandolina[F]

balalaika
balalaika[F]
Balalaika[F]
balalaica[F]
balalaika[F]

neck
manche[M]
Hals[M]
manico[M]
mástil[M]

strings
cordes[F]
Saiten[F]
corde[F]
cuerdas[F]

hand post
support[M] de main[F]
Handgriff[M]
poggiamano[M]
soporte[M] de la mano[M]

tuning ring
attache[F] d'accordage[M]
Stimmring[M]
anello[M] d'accordatura[F]
anillos[M] de sonido[M]

triangular body
caisse[F] triangulaire
dreieckiger Korpus[M]
cassa[F] armonica triangolare
caja[F] triangular

snare head
peau[F] de timbre[M]
Klangfell[N]
pelle[F] armonica
piel[F] armónica

sound box
caisse[F] de résonance[F]
Resonanzkörper[M]
cassa[F] di risonanza[F]
caja[F] de resonancia[F]

pear-shaped body
caisse[F] bombée
bimenförmiger Korpus[M]
cassa[F] armonica piriforme
caja[F] media pera[F]

bridge
chevalet[M]
Steg[M]
ponticello[M]
puente[M]

tailpiece
cordier[M]
Saitenhalterung[F]
cordiera[F]
cordal[M]

lyre
lyre[F]
Lyra[F]
lira[F]
lira[F]

frame
cadre[M]
Rahmen[M]
telaio[M]
estructura[F]

tongue
lame[F]
Zunge[F]
linguetta[F]
lengüeta[F] de la caña[F]

crossbar
traverse[F]
Querjoch[N]
traversa[F]
travesaño[M]

drumstick
mailloche[F]
Trommelschlegel[M]
mazzuolo[M]
baqueta[F]

Jew's harp
guimbarde[F]
Maultrommel[F]
scacciapensieri[M]
birimbao[M]

arm
montant[M]
Jocharm[M]
braccio[M]
brazo[M]

plectrum
médiator[M]
Plektron[N]
plettro[M]
púa[F]

djembe
djembé[M]
Djembe[F]
djembè[M]
yembé[M]

soundboard
caisse[F] de résonance[F]
Resonanzdecke[F]
tavola[F] armonica
caja[F] de resonancia[F]

batter skin
peau[F] de batterie[F]
Trommelfell[N]
battitoia[F]
piel[F]

talking drum
tambour[M] d'aisselle[F]
Sprechtrommel[F]
tamburo[M] parlante
tambor[M] hablante

panpipe
flûte[F] de Pan
Panflöte[F]
flauto[M] di Pan
zampoña[F]

sound box
caisse[F] de résonance[F]
Resonanzkörper[M]
cassa[F] di risonanza[F]
caja[F] de resonancia[F]

tension rope
corde[F] de tension[F]
Spannschnur[F]
corda[F] di tensione[F]
cuerda[F] de tensión[F]

musical notation

notation^F musicale | Musiknotation^F | notazione^F musicale | notación^F musical

staff
portée^F
Liniensystem^N
pentagramma^M
pentagrama^F

space
interligne^M
Zwischenraum^M
spazio^M
espacio^M

line
ligne^F
Notenlinie^F
linea^F
línea^F

ledger line
ligne^F supplémentaire
Hilfslinie^F
taglio^M addizionale
línea^F suplementaria

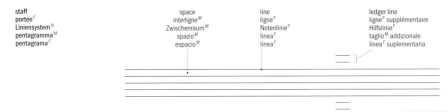

clefs
clés^F
Notenschlüssel^M
chiavi^F
claves^F

treble clef
clé^F de sol^M
Violinschlüssel^M
chiave^F di violino^M
clave^F de sol

bass clef
clé^F de fa^M
Bassschlüssel^M
chiave^F di basso^M
clave^F de fa

alto clef
clé^F d'ut^M
Altschlüssel^M
chiave^F di contralto^M
clave^F de do

time signatures
mesures^F
Taktarten^F
indicazioni^F di tempo^M
compás^M

two-two time
mesure^F à deux temps^M
Zweihalbetakt^M
tempo^M di due metà^F
de dos mitades^F

three-four time
mesure^F à trois temps^M
Dreivierteltakt^M
tempo^M di tre quarti^M
de tres cuartos^M

four-four time
mesure^F à quatre temps^M
Viervierteltakt^M
tempo^M di quattro quarti^M
de cuatro cuartos^M

bar line
barre^F de mesure^F
Taktstrich^M
stanghetta^F
barra^F de compás^M

repeat mark
barre^F de reprise^F
Wiederholungszeichen^N
ritornello^M
barra^F de repetición^F

intervals
intervalles^M
Intervalle^N
intervalli^M
intervalos^M

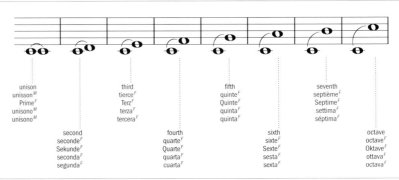

unison
unisson^M
Prime^F
unisono^M
unisono^M

second
seconde^F
Sekunde^F
seconda^F
segunda^F

third
tierce^F
Terz^F
terza^F
tercera^F

fourth
quarte^F
Quarte^F
quarta^F
cuarta^F

fifth
quinte^F
Quinte^F
quinta^F
quinta^F

sixth
sixte^F
Sexte^F
sesta^F
sexta^F

seventh
septième^F
Septime^F
settima^F
séptima^F

octave
octave^F
Oktave^F
ottava^F
octava^F

scale
gamme^F
Tonleiter^F
scala^F
escala^F

c	d	e	f	g	a	b	c
do^M	ré^M	mi^M	fa^M	sol^M	la^M	si^M	do^M
C	D	E	F	G	A	H	C
do^M	re^M	mi^M	fa^M	sol^M	la^M	si^M	do^M
do(C)	re(D)	mi(E)	fa(F)	sol(G)	la(A)	si(B)	do(C)

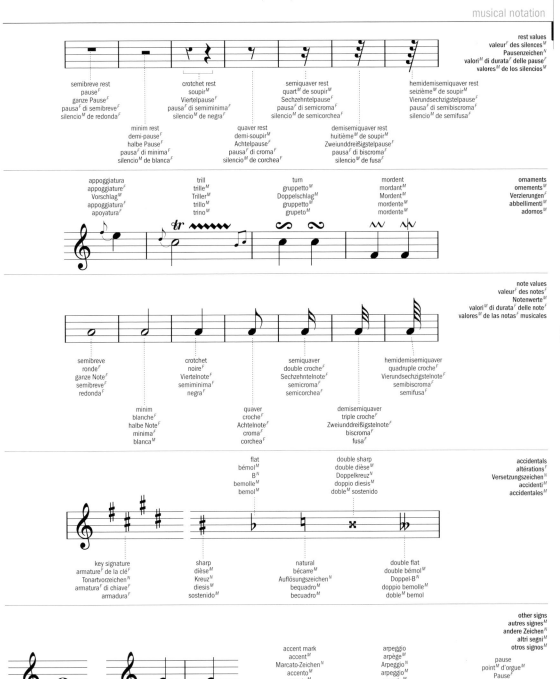

rest values
valeur[F] des silences[M]
Pausenzeichen[N]
valori[M] di durata[F] delle pause[F]
valores[M] de los silencios[M]

semibreve rest
pause[F]
ganze Pause[F]
pausa[F] di semibreve[F]
silencio[M] de redonda[F]

minim rest
demi-pause[F]
halbe Pause[F]
pausa[F] di minima[F]
silencio[M] de blanca[F]

crotchet rest
soupir[M]
Viertelpause[F]
pausa[F] di semiminima[F]
silencio[M] de negra[F]

quaver rest
demi-soupir[F]
Achtelpause[F]
pausa[F] di croma[F]
silencio[M] de corchea[F]

semiquaver rest
quart[M] de soupir[M]
Sechzehntelpause[F]
pausa[F] di semicroma[F]
silencio[M] de semicorchea[F]

demisemiquaver rest
huitième[M] de soupir[F]
Zweiunddreißigstelpause[F]
pausa[F] di biscroma[F]
silencio[M] de fusa[F]

hemidemisemiquaver rest
seizième[M] de soupir[M]
Vierundsechzigstelpause[F]
pausa[F] di semibiscroma[F]
silencio[M] de semifusa[F]

ornaments
ornements[M]
Verzierungen[F]
abbellimenti[M]
adornos[M]

appoggiatura
appoggiature[F]
Vorschlag[M]
appoggiatura[F]
apoyatura[F]

trill
trille[M]
Triller[M]
trillo[M]
trino[M]

turn
gruppetto[M]
Doppelschlag[M]
gruppetto[M]
grupeto[M]

mordent
mordant[M]
Mordent[M]
mordente[M]
mordente[M]

note values
valeur[F] des notes[F]
Notenwerte[M]
valori[M] di durata[F] delle note[F]
valores[M] de las notas[F] musicales

semibreve
ronde[F]
ganze Note[F]
semibreve[F]
redonda[F]

minim
blanche[F]
halbe Note[F]
minima[F]
blanca[M]

crotchet
noire[F]
Viertelnote[F]
semiminima[F]
negra[F]

quaver
croche[F]
Achtelnote[F]
croma[F]
corchea[F]

semiquaver
double croche[F]
Sechzehntelnote[F]
semicroma[F]
semicorchea[F]

demisemiquaver
triple croche[F]
Zweiunddreißigstelnote[F]
biscroma[F]
fusa[F]

hemidemisemiquaver
quadruple croche[F]
Vierundsechzigstelnote[F]
semibiscroma[F]
semifusa[F]

accidentals
altérations[F]
Versetzungszeichen[N]
accidenti[M]
accidentales[M]

flat
bémol[M]
B[N]
bemolle[M]
bemol[M]

double sharp
double dièse[M]
Doppelkreuz[N]
doppio diesis[M]
doble[F] sostenido

key signature
armature[F] de la clé[F]
Tonartvorzeichen[N]
armatura[F] di chiave[F]
armadura[F]

sharp
dièse[M]
Kreuz[N]
diesis[M]
sostenido[M]

natural
bécarre[M]
Auflösungszeichen[N]
bequadro[M]
becuadro[M]

double flat
double bémol[M]
Doppel-B[N]
doppio bemolle[M]
doble[M] bemol

other signs
autres signes[M]
andere Zeichen[N]
altri segni[M]
otros signos[M]

accent mark
accent[M]
Marcato-Zeichen[N]
accento[M]
acento[M]

arpeggio
arpège[M]
Arpeggio[N]
arpeggio[M]
arpegio[M]

pause
point[M] d'orgue[M]
Pause[F]
punto[M] coronato
calderón[M]

chord
accord[M]
Akkord[M]
accordo[M]
acorde[M]

tie
liaison[F]
Bindebogen[M]
legatura[F]
ligadura[F]

299

examples of instrumental groups

exemples^M de groupes^M instrumentaux | Beispiele^N für Instrumentalgruppierungen^F | esempi^M di gruppi^M strumentali | ejemplos^M de conjuntos^M instrumentales

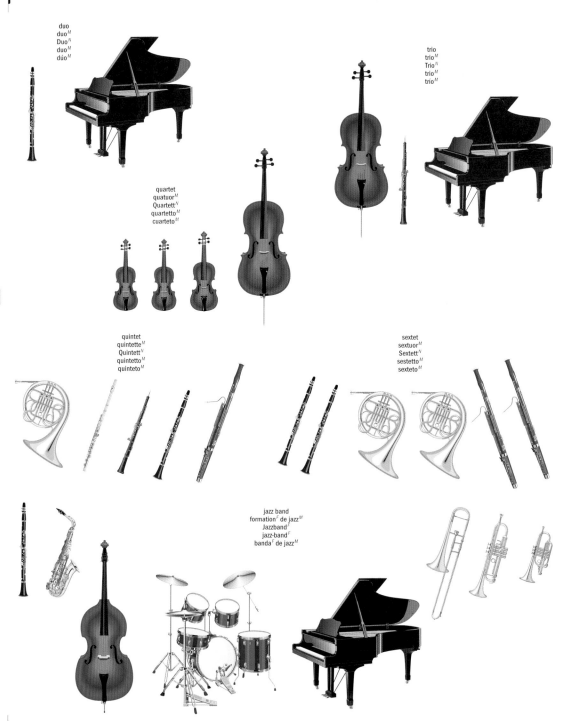

duo
duo^M
Duo^N
duo^M
dúo^M

trio
trio^M
Trio^N
trio^M
trio^M

quartet
quatuor^M
Quartett^N
quartetto^M
cuarteto^M

quintet
quintette^M
Quintett^N
quintetto^M
quinteto^M

sextet
sextuor^M
Sextett^N
sestetto^M
sexteto^M

jazz band
formation^F de jazz^M
Jazzband^F
jazz-band^F
banda^F de jazz^M

stringed instruments

instruments^M à cordes^F | Saiteninstrumente^N | strumenti^M a corde^F | instrumentos^M de cuerda^F

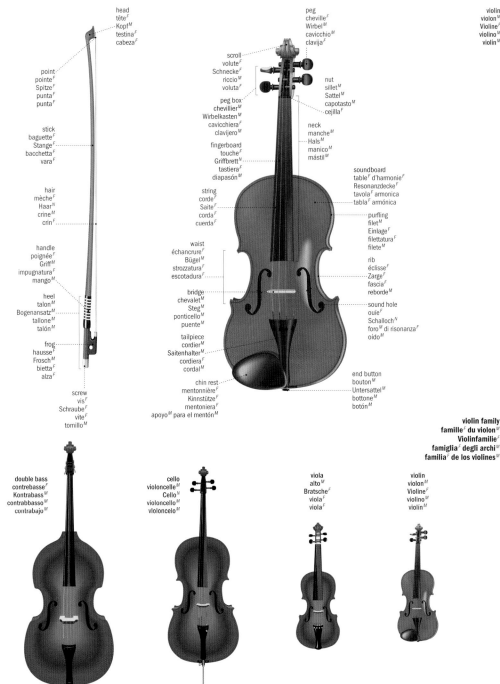

bow
archet^M
Bogen^M
archetto^M
arco^M

head
tête^F
Kopf^M
testina^F
cabeza^F

peg
cheville^F
Wirbel^M
cavicchio^M
clavija^F

violin
violon^M
Violine^F
violino^M
violín^M

scroll
volute^F
Schnecke^F
riccio^M
voluta^F

nut
sillet^M
Sattel^M
capotasto^M
cejilla^F

point
pointe^F
Spitze^F
punta^F
punta^F

peg box
chevillier^M
Wirbelkasten^M
cavicchiera^F
clavijero^M

neck
manche^M
Hals^M
manico^M
mástil^M

stick
baguette^F
Stange^F
bacchetta^F
vara^F

fingerboard
touche^F
Griffbrett^N
tastiera^F
diapasón^M

soundboard
table^F d'harmonie^F
Resonanzdecke^F
tavola^F armonica
tabla^F armónica

hair
mèche^F
Haar^N
crine^M
crin^F

string
corde^F
Saite^F
corda^F
cuerda^F

purfling
filet^M
Einlage^F
filettatura^F
filete^M

waist
échancrure^F
Bügel^M
strozzatura^F
escotadura^F

rib
éclisse^F
Zarge^F
fascia^F
reborde^M

handle
poignée^F
Griff^M
impugnatura^F
mango^M

bridge
chevalet^M
Steg^M
ponticello^M
puente^M

sound hole
ouïe^F
Schalloch^N
foro^M di risonanza^F
oído^M

heel
talon^M
Bogenansatz^M
tallone^M
talón^M

tailpiece
cordier^M
Saitenhalter^M
cordiera^F
cordal^M

frog
hausse^F
Frosch^M
bietta^F
alza^F

chin rest
mentonnière^F
Kinnstütze^F
mentoniera^F
apoyo^M para el mentón^M

end button
bouton^M
Untersattel^M
bottone^M
botón^M

screw
vis^F
Schraube^F
vite^F
tornillo^M

ARTS AND ARCHITECTURE

violin family
famille^F du violon^M
Violinfamilie^F
famiglia^F degli archi^M
familia^F de los violines^M

double bass
contrebasse^F
Kontrabass^M
contrabbasso^M
contrabajo^M

cello
violoncelle^M
Cello^N
violoncello^M
violoncelo^M

viola
alto^M
Bratsche^F
viola^F
viola^F

violin
violon^M
Violine^F
violino^M
violín^M

stringed instruments

harp
harpe^F
Harfe^F
arpa^F
arpa^F

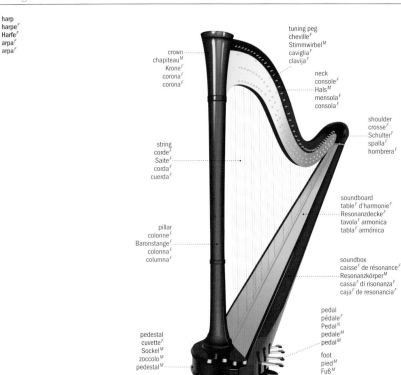

crown
chapiteau^M
Krone^F
corona^F
corona^F

tuning peg
cheville^F
Stimmwirbel^M
caviglia^F
clavija^F

neck
console^F
Hals^M
mensola^F
consola^F

shoulder
crosse^F
Schulter^F
spalla^F
hombrera^F

string
corde^F
Saite^F
corda^F
cuerda^F

soundboard
table^F d'harmonie^F
Resonanzdecke^F
tavola^F armonica
tabla^F armónica

pillar
colonne^F
Baronstange^F
colonna^F
columna^F

soundbox
caisse^F de résonance^F
Resonanzkörper^M
cassa^F di risonanza^F
caja^F de resonancia^F

pedal
pédale^F
Pedal^N
pedale^M
pedal^M

pedestal
cuvette^F
Sockel^M
zoccolo^M
pedestal^M

foot
pied^M
Fuß^M
piede^M
pie^M

acoustic guitar
guitare^F acoustique
akustische Gitarre^F
chitarra^F acustica
guitarra^F clásica

soundboard
table^F d'harmonie^F
Resonanzdecke^F
tavola^F armonica
tabla^F armónica

sound box
caisse^F de résonance^F
Resonanzkasten^M
cassa^F di risonanza^F
caja^F de resonancia^F

neck
manche^M
Hals^M
manico^M
mástil^M

head
tête^F
Kragen^M
paletta^F
cabeza^F

peg
cheville^F
Wirbel^M
cavicchio^M
clavija^F

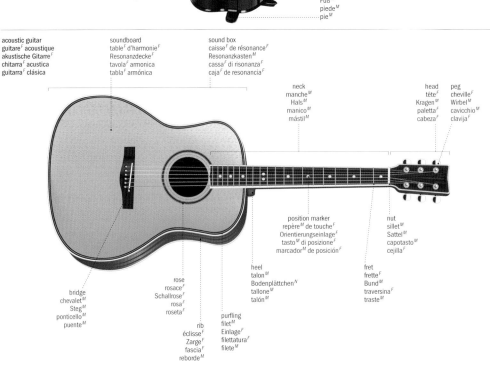

position marker
repère^M de touche^F
Orientierungseinlage^F
tasto^M di posizione^F
marcador^M de posición^F

nut
sillet^M
Sattel^M
capotasto^M
cejilla^F

fret
frette^F
Bund^M
traversina^F
traste^M

heel
talon^M
Bodenplättchen^N
tallone^M
talón^M

bridge
chevalet^M
Steg^M
ponticello^M
puente^M

rose
rosace^F
Schallrose^F
rosa^F
roseta^F

rib
éclisse^F
Zarge^F
fascia^F
reborde^M

purfling
filet^M
Einlage^F
filettatura^F
filete^M

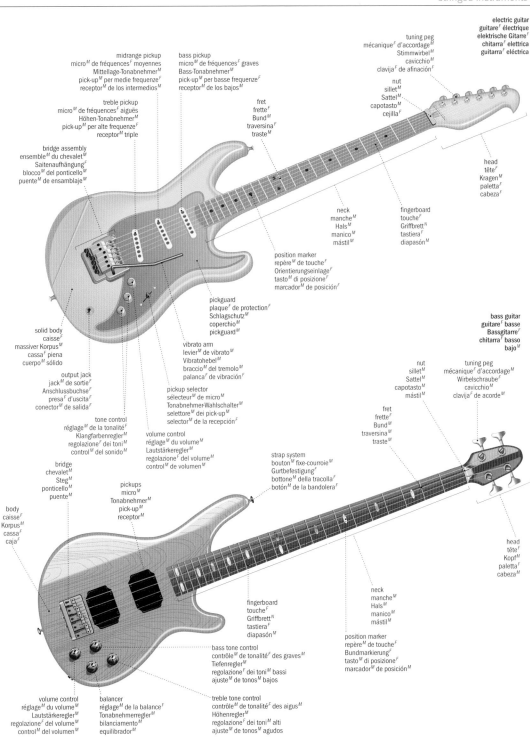

electric guitar
guitare^F électrique
elektrische Gitarre^F
chitarra^F elettrica
guitarra^F eléctrica

midrange pickup
micro^M de fréquences^F moyennes
Mittellage-Tonabnehmer^M
pick-up^M per medie frequenze^F
receptor^M de los intermedios^M

bass pickup
micro^M de fréquences^F graves
Bass-Tonabnehmer^M
pick-up^M per basse frequenze^F
receptor^M de los bajos^M

tuning peg
mécanique^M d'accordage^M
Stimmwirbel^M
cavicchio^M
clavija^F de afinación^F

nut
sillet^M
Sattel^M
capotasto^M
cejilla^F

treble pickup
micro^M de fréquences^F aiguës
Höhen-Tonabnehmer^M
pick-up^M per alte frequenze^F
receptor^M triple

fret
frette^F
Bund^M
traversina^F
traste^M

bridge assembly
ensemble^M du chevalet^M
Saitenaufhängung^F
blocco^M del ponticello^M
puente^M de ensamblaje^M

head
tête^F
Kragen^M
paletta^F
cabeza^F

neck
manche^M
Hals^M
manico^M
mástil^M

fingerboard
touche^F
Griffbrett^N
tastiera^F
diapasón^M

position marker
repère^F de touche^F
Orientierungseinlage^F
tasto^F di posizione^F
marcador^M de posición^F

solid body
caisse^F
massiver Korpus^M
cassa^F piena
cuerpo^M sólido

pickguard
plaque^F de protection^F
Schlagschutz^M
coperchio^M
pickguard^M

bass guitar
guitare^F basse
Bassgitarre^F
chitarra^F basso
bajo^M

vibrato arm
levier^M de vibrato^M
Vibratohebel^M
braccio^M del tremolo^M
palanca^F de vibración^F

nut
sillet^M
Sattel^M
capotasto^M
mástil^M

tuning peg
mécanique^M d'accordage^M
Wirbelschraube^F
cavicchio^M
clavija^F de acorde^M

output jack
jack^M de sortie^F
Anschlussbuchse^F
presa^F d'uscita^F
conector^M de salida^F

pickup selector
sélecteur^M de micro^M
Tonabnehmer-Wahlschalter^M
selettore^M dei pick-up^M
selector^M de la recepción^F

fret
frette^F
Bund^M
traversina^M
traste^M

tone control
réglage^M de la tonalité^F
Klangfarbenregler^M
regolazione^F dei toni^M
control^M del sonido^M

volume control
réglage^M du volume^M
Lautstärkeregler^M
regolazione^F del volume^M
control^M de volumen^M

strap system
bouton^M fixe-courroie^M
Gurtbefestigung^F
bottone^M della tracolla^F
botón^M de la bandolera^F

head
tête^F
Kopf^M
paletta^F
cabeza^M

bridge
chevalet^M
Steg^M
ponticello^M
puente^M

pickups
micro^M
Tonabnehmer^M
pick-up^M
receptor^M

body
caisse^F
Korpus^M
cassa^F
caja^F

fingerboard
touche^F
Griffbrett^N
tastiera^F
diapasón^M

neck
manche^M
Hals^M
manico^M
mástil^M

position marker
repère^M de touche^F
Bundmarkierung^F
tasto^M di posizione^F
marcador^M de posición^M

bass tone control
contrôle^M de tonalité^F des graves^M
Tiefenregler^M
regolazione^F dei toni^M bassi
ajuste^M de tonos^M bajos

volume control
réglage^M du volume^M
Lautstärkeregler^M
regolazione^F del volume^M
control^M del volumen^M

balancer
réglage^M de la balance^F
Tonabnehmerregler^M
bilanciamento^M
equilibrador^M

treble tone control
contrôle^M de tonalité^F des aigus^M
Höhenregler^M
regolazione^F dei toni^M alti
ajuste^M de tonos^M agudos

ARTS AND ARCHITECTURE

keyboard instruments

instruments^M à clavier^M | Tasteninstrumente^N | strumenti^M a tastiera^F | instrumentos^M de teclado^M

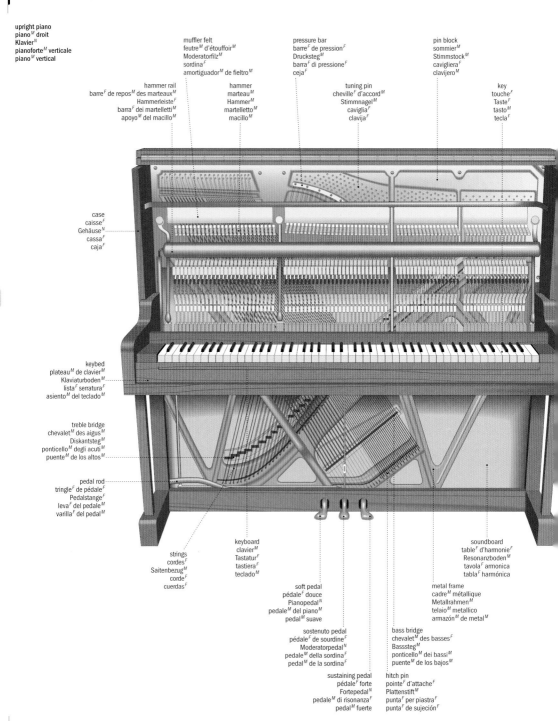

upright piano
piano^M droit
Klavier^N
pianoforte^M verticale
piano^M vertical

muffler felt
feutre^M d'étouffoir^M
Moderatorfilz^M
sordina^F
amortiguador^M de fieltro^M

pressure bar
barre^F de pression^F
Drucksteg^M
barra^F di pressione^F
ceja^F

pin block
sommier^M
Stimmstock^M
cavigliera^F
clavijero^M

hammer rail
barre^F de repos^M des marteaux^M
Hammerleiste^F
barra^F dei martelletti^M
apoyo^M del macillo^M

hammer
marteau^M
Hammer^M
martelletto^M
macillo^M

tuning pin
cheville^F d'accord^M
Stimmnagel^M
caviglia^F
clavija^F

key
touche^F
Taste^F
tasto^M
tecla^F

case
caisse^F
Gehäuse^N
cassa^F
caja^F

keybed
plateau^M de clavier^M
Klaviaturboden^M
lista^F serratura^F
asiento^M del teclado^M

treble bridge
chevalet^M des aigus^M
Diskantsteg^M
ponticello^M degli acuti^M
puente^M de los altos^M

pedal rod
tringle^F de pédale^F
Pedalstange^F
leva^F del pedale^M
varilla^F del pedal^M

strings
cordes^F
Saitenbezug^M
corde^F
cuerdas^F

keyboard
clavier^M
Tastatur^F
tastiera^F
teclado^M

soundboard
table^F d'harmonie^F
Resonanzboden^M
tavola^F armonica
tabla^F harmónica

soft pedal
pédale^F douce
Pianopedal^N
pedale^M del piano^M
pedal^M suave

metal frame
cadre^M métallique
Metallrahmen^M
telaio^M metallico
armazón^M de metal^M

sostenuto pedal
pédale^F de sourdine^F
Moderatorpedal^N
pedale^M della sordina^F
pedal^M de la sordina^F

bass bridge
chevalet^M des basses^F
Basssteg^M
ponticello^M dei bassi^M
puente^M de los bajos^M

sustaining pedal
pédale^F forte
Fortepedal^N
pedale^M di risonanza^F
pedal^M fuerte

hitch pin
pointe^F d'attache^F
Plattenstift^M
punta^F per piastra^F
punta^F de sujeción^F

organ
orgue^M
Orgel^F
organo^M
órgano^M

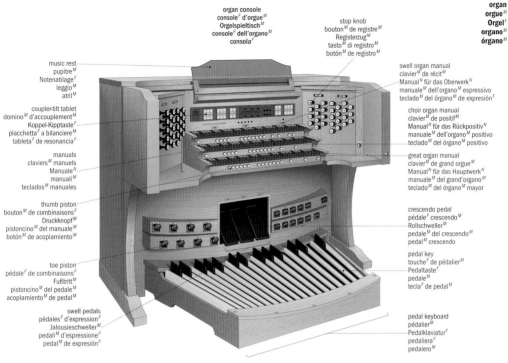

organ console
console^F d'orgue^M
Orgelspieltisch^M
console^F dell'organo^M
consola^F

stop knob
bouton^M de registre^M
Registerzug^M
tasto^M di registro^M
botón^M de registro^M

music rest
pupitre^M
Notenablage^F
leggio^M
atril^M

swell organ manual
clavier^M de récit^M
Manual^N für das Oberwerk^N
manuale^M dell'organo^M espressivo
teclado^M del órgano^M de expresión^F

coupler-tilt tablet
domino^M d'accouplement^M
Koppel-Kipptaste^F
placchetta^F a bilanciere^M
tableta^F de resonancia^F

choir organ manual
clavier^M de positif^M
Manual^N für das Rückpositiv^N
manuale^M dell'organo^M positivo
teclado^M del órgano^M positivo

manuals
claviers^M manuels
Manuale^N
manuali^M
teclados^M manuales

great organ manual
clavier^M de grand orgue^M
Manual^N für das Hauptwerk^N
manuale^M del grand'organo^M
teclado^M del órgano^M mayor

thumb piston
bouton^M de combinaisons^F
Druckknopf^M
pistoncino^M del manuale^M
botón^M de acoplamiento^M

crescendo pedal
pédale^F crescendo^M
Rollschweller^M
pedale^M del crescendo^M
pedal^M crescendo

pedal key
touche^F de pédalier^M
Pedaltaste^F
pedale^M
tecla^F de pedal^M

toe piston
pédale^F de combinaisons^F
Fußtritt^M
pistoncino^M del pedale^M
acoplamiento^M de pedal^M

swell pedals
pédales^F d'expression^F
Jalousieschweller^M
pedali^M d'espressione^F
pedal^M de expresión^F

pedal keyboard
pédalier^M
Pedalklaviatur^F
pedaliera^F
pedalero^M

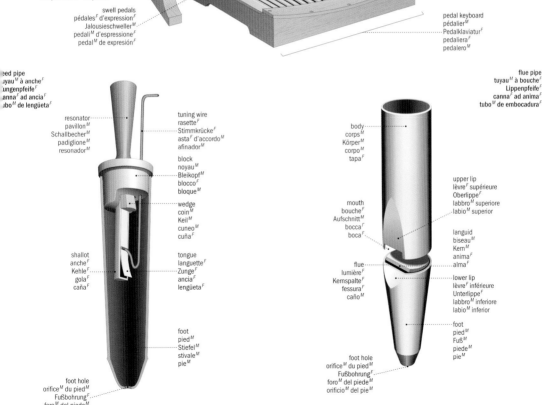

reed pipe
tuyau^M à anche^F
Zungenpfeife^F
canna^F ad ancia^F
tubo^M de lengüeta^F

flue pipe
tuyau^M à bouche^F
Lippenpfeife^F
canna^F ad anima^F
tubo^M de embocadura^F

resonator
pavillon^M
Schallbecher^M
padiglione^M
resonador^M

tuning wire
rasette^F
Stimmkrücke^F
asta^F d'accordo^M
afinador^M

block
noyau^M
Bleikopf^M
blocco^F
bloque^M

body
corps^M
Körper^M
corpo^M
tapa^F

wedge
coin^M
Keil^M
cuneo^M
cuña^F

upper lip
lèvre^F supérieure
Oberlippe^F
labbro^M superiore
labio^M superior

mouth
bouche^F
Aufschnitt^M
bocca^F
boca^F

languid
biseau^M
Kern^M
anima^F
alma^F

shallot
anche^F
Kehle^F
gola^F
caña^F

tongue
languette^F
Zunge^F
ancia^F
lengüeta^F

flue
lumière^F
Kernspalte^F
fessura^F
caño^M

lower lip
lèvre^F inférieure
Unterlippe^F
labbro^M inferiore
labio^M inferior

foot
pied^M
Stiefel^M
stivale^M
pie^M

foot
pied^M
Fuß^M
piede^M
pie^M

foot hole
orifice^M du pied^M
Fußbohrung^F
foro^M del piede^M
orificio^M del pie^M

foot hole
orifice^M du pied^M
Fußbohrung^F
foro^M del piede^M
orificio^M del pie^M

wind instruments

instruments^M à vent^M | Blasinstrumente^N | strumenti^M a fiato^M | instrumentos^M de viento^M

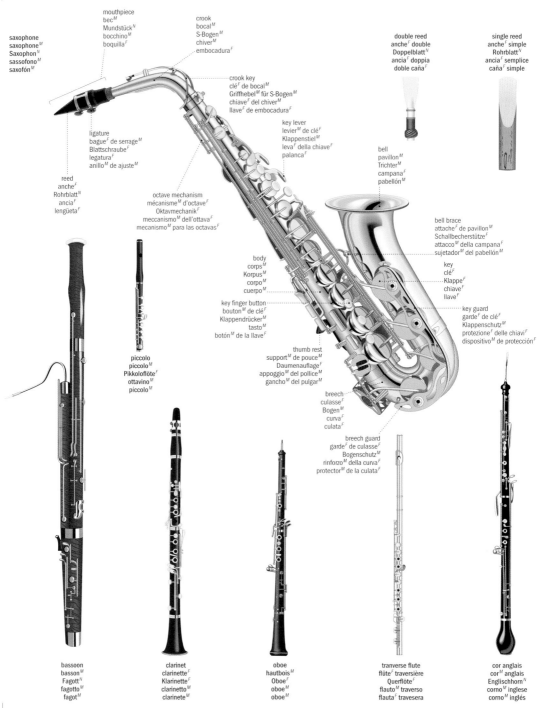

mouthpiece
bec^M
Mundstück^N
bocchino^M
boquilla^F

crook
bocal^M
S-Bogen^M
chiver^M
embocadura^F

double reed
anche^F double
Doppelblatt^N
ancia^F doppia
doble caña^F

single reed
anche^F simple
Rohrblatt^N
ancia^F semplice
caña^F simple

saxophone
saxophone^M
Saxophon^N
sassofono^M
saxofón^M

crook key
clé^F de bocal^M
Griffhebel^M für S-Bogen^M
chiave^F del chiver^M
llave^F de embocadura^F

key lever
levier^M de clé^F
Klappenstiel^M
leva^F della chiave^F
palanca^F

bell
pavillon^M
Trichter^M
campana^F
pabellón^M

ligature
bague^F de serrage^M
Blattschraube^F
legatura^F
anillo^M de ajuste^M

reed
anche^F
Rohrblatt^N
ancia^F
lengüeta^F

octave mechanism
mécanisme^M d'octave^F
Oktavmechanik^F
meccanismo^M dell'ottava^F
mecanismo^M para las octavas^F

bell brace
attache^F de pavillon^M
Schallbecherstütze^F
attacco^M della campana^F
sujetador^M del pabellón^M

body
corps^M
Korpus^M
corpo^M
cuerpo^M

key
clé^F
Klappe^F
chiave^F
llave^F

key finger button
bouton^M de clé^F
Klappendrücker^M
tasto^M
botón^M de la llave^F

key guard
garde^F de clé^F
Klappenschutz^M
protezione^F delle chiavi^F
dispositivo^M de protección^F

thumb rest
support^M de pouce^M
Daumenauflage^F
appoggio^M del pollice^M
gancho^M del pulgar^M

breech
culasse^F
Bogen^M
curva^F
culata^F

breech guard
garde^F de culasse^F
Bogenschutz^M
rinforzo^M della curva^F
protector^M de la culata^F

piccolo
piccolo^M
Pikkoloflöte^F
ottavino^M
píccolo^M

bassoon
basson^M
Fagott^N
fagotto^M
fagot^M

clarinet
clarinette^F
Klarinette^F
clarinetto^M
clarinete^M

oboe
hautbois^M
Oboe^F
oboe^M
oboe^M

tranverse flute
flûte^F traversière
Querflöte^F
flauto^M traverso
flauta^F travesera

cor anglais
cor^M anglais
Englischhorn^N
corno^M inglese
corno^M inglés

ARTS AND ARCHITECTURE

finger button
bouton^M de piston^M
Drücker^M
pistone^M
llave^F

little finger hook
crochet^M de petit doigt^M
Kleinfingerhaken^M
appoggio^M del mignolo^M
gancho^M del meñique^M

bell
pavillon^M
Trichter^M
campana^F
pabellón^M

trumpet
trompette^F
Trompete^F
tromba^F
trompeta^F

mouthpipe
branche^F d'embouchure^F
Mundrohr^N
canna^F di imboccatura^F
tubo^M

ring
bague^F
Ring^M
anello^M
anillo^M

mouthpiece receiver
boisseau^M d'embouchure^F
Mundstückaufnahme^F
alloggiamento^M del bocchino^M
empate^M de la boquilla^F

mouthpiece
embouchure^F
Mundstück^N
bocchino^M
boquilla^F

tuning slide
coulisse^F d'accord^M
Stimmzug^M
tubo^M di accordo^M
corredera^F de afinamiento^M

water key
soupape^F d'évacuation^F
Wasserklappe^F
chiave^F dell'acqua^F
llave^F para agua^F

first valve slide
coulisse^F du premier piston^M
erster Ventilzug^M
tubo^M della prima valvola^F
primer pistón^M móvil

third valve slide
coulisse^F du troisième piston^M
dritter Ventilzug^M
tubo^M della terza valvola^F
tercer pistón^M móvil

thumb hook
crochet^M de pouce^M
Daumenring^M
appoggio^M del pollice^M
gancho^M del pulgar^M

valve
piston^M
Ventil^N
valvola^F
pistón^M

mute
sourdine^F
Dämpfer^M
sordina^F
sordina^F

valve casing
corps^M de piston^M
Ventilbüchse^F
corpo^M della valvola^F
tubo^M del pistón^M

second valve slide
coulisse^F du deuxième piston^M
zweiter Ventilzug^M
tubo^M della seconda valvola^F
segundo pistón^M móvil

French horn
cor^M d'harmonie^F
Waldhorn^N
corno^M
corno^M francés/trompa^F

cornet
cornet^M à pistons^M
Kornett^N
cornetta^F
cornetín^M

bugle
clairon^M
Bügelhorn^N
tromba^F militare
clarín^M

saxhorn
saxhorn^M
Saxhorn^N
saxhorn^M
bombardino^M

tuba
tuba^M
Tuba^F
tuba^F
tuba^F

trombone
trombone^M
Posaune^F
trombone^M
trombón^M

percussion instruments

instruments^M à percussion^F | Schlaginstrumente^N | strumenti^M a percussione^F | instrumentos^M de percusión^F

drums
batterie^F
Trommeln^F
batteria^F
batería^F

tom-tom
tam-tam^M
Tomtom^N
tom tom^M
tam-tam^M

cymbal
cymbale^F suspendue
Becken^N
piatto^M
platillo^M suspendido

Charleston cymbal
cymbale^F charleston
Charlestonmaschine^F
charleston^M
platillo^M high hat

superior cymbal
cymbale^F supérieure
oberes Becken^N
piatto^M superiore
platillo^M superior

inferior cymbal
cymbale^F inférieure
unteres Becken^N
piatto^M inferiore
platillo^M inferior

drumhead
peau^F de batterie^F
Trommelfell^N
battitoia^F
parche^M superior

snare drum
caisse^F claire
kleine Trommel^F
cassa^F chiara
caja^F clara

tripod stand
trépied^M
Dreifußständer^M
treppiede^M
tripode^M

bass drum
grosse caisse^F
Basstrommel^F
grancassa^F
bombo^M

mallet
mailloche^F
Schlegel^M
mazza^F
palillo^M

tenor drum
caisse^F roulante
Standtom^N
tamburo^M tenore^M
tamboril^M

spur
éperon^M
Feststellspitze^F
piedino^M
espolón^M

pedal
pédale^F
Pedal^N
pedale^M
pedal^M

leg
pied^M
Bein^N
piedino^M
pata^F

stand
support^M
Ständer^M
supporto^M
soporte^M

tension screw
vis^F de tension^F
Stellschraube^F
tirante^M a vite^F
clavija^F de tensión^F

kettledrum
timbale
Kesselpauke
timpano
timbal

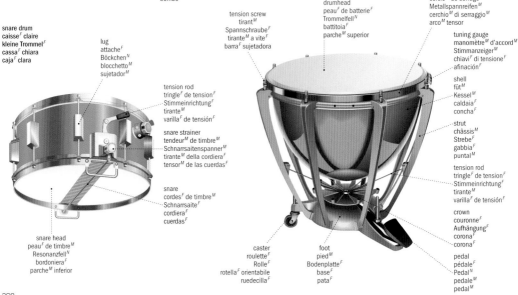

snare drum
caisse^F claire
kleine Trommel^F
cassa^F chiara
caja^F clara

lug
attache^F
Böckchen^N
blocchetto^M
sujetador^M

tension rod
tringle^F de tension^F
Stimmeinrichtung^F
tirante^M
varilla^F de tensión^F

snare strainer
tendeur^M de timbre^M
Schnarrsaitenspanner^M
tirante^M della cordiera^F
tensor^M de las cuerdas^F

snare
cordes^F de timbre^M
Schnarrsaite^F
cordiera^F
cuerdas^F

snare head
peau^F de timbre^M
Resonanzfell^N
bordoniera^F
parche^M inferior

tension screw
tirant^M
Spannschraube^F
tirante^M a vite^F
barra^F sujetadora

drumhead
peau^F de batterie^F
Trommelfell^N
battitoia^F
parche^M superior

metal counterhoop
cercle^M de serrage^M
Metallspannreifen^M
cerchio^M di serraggio^M
arco^M tensor

tuning gauge
manomètre^M d'accord^M
Stimmanzeiger^M
chiavi^F di tensione^F
afinación^F

shell
fût^M
Kessel^M
caldaia^F
concha^F

strut
chàssis^M
Strebe^F
gabbia^F
puntal^M

tension rod
tringle^F de tension^F
Stimmeinrichtung^F
tirante^M
varilla^F de tensión^F

crown
couronne^F
Aufhängung^F
corona^F
corona^F

pedal
pédale^F
Pedal^N
pedale^M
pedal^M

caster
roulette^F
Rolle^F
rotella^F orientabile
ruedecilla^F

foot
pied^M
Bodenplatte^F
base^F
pata^F

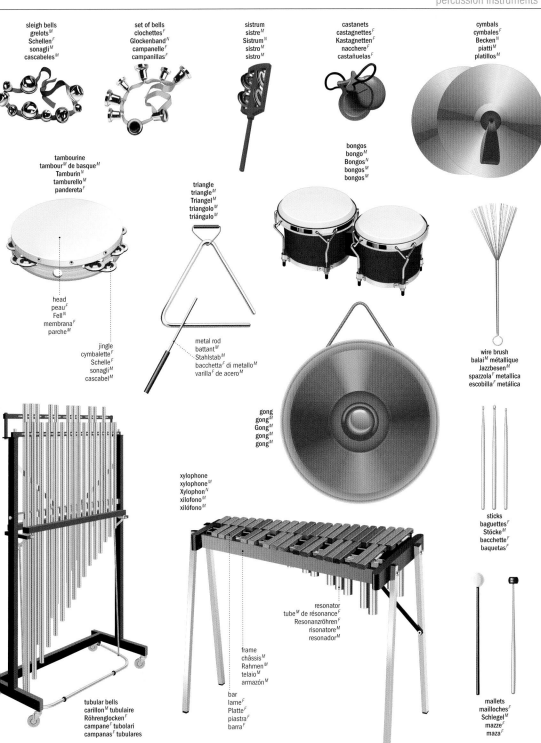

sleigh bells
grelots^M
Schellen^F
sonagli^M
cascabeles^M

set of bells
clochettes^F
Glockenband^N
campanelle^F
campanillas^F

sistrum
sistre^M
Sistrum^N
sistro^M
sistro^M

castanets
castagnettes^F
Kastagnetten^F
nacchere^F
castañuelas^F

cymbals
cymbales^F
Becken^N
piatti^M
platillos^M

bongos
bongo^M
Bongos^N
bongos^M
bongos^M

tambourine
tambour^M de basque^M
Tamburin^N
tamburello^M
pandereta^F

triangle
triangle^M
Triangel^M
triangolo^M
triángulo^M

head
peau^F
Fell^N
membrana^F
parche^M

jingle
cymbalette^F
Schelle^F
sonagli^M
cascabel^M

metal rod
battant^M
Stahlstab^M
bacchetta^F di metallo^M
varilla^F de acero^M

wire brush
balai^M métallique
Jazzbesen^M
spazzola^F metallica
escobilla^F metálica

gong
gong^M
Gong^M
gong^M
gong^M

xylophone
xylophone^M
Xylophon^N
xilofono^M
xilófono^M

sticks
baguettes^F
Stöcke^M
bacchette^F
baquetas^F

resonator
tube^M de résonance^F
Resonanzröhren^F
risonatore^M
resonador^M

frame
châssis^M
Rahmen^M
telaio^M
armazón^M

bar
lame^F
Platte^F
piastra^F
barra^F

tubular bells
carillon^M tubulaire
Röhrenglocken^F
campane^F tubolari
campanas^F tubulares

mallets
mailloches^F
Schlegel^M
mazze^F
maza^F

electronic instruments

instruments^M électroniques | elektronische Instrumente^N | strumenti^M elettronici | instrumentos^M electrónicos

sequencer
séquenceur^M
Sequencer^M
sequencer^M
secuenciador^M

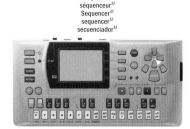

sampler
échantillonneur^M
Sampler^M
campionatore^M
muestreador^M

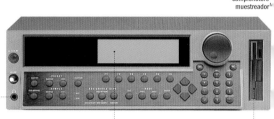

headphone jack
prise^F casque^M
Kopfhöreranschlussbuchse^F
presa^F per cuffia^F
toma^F para auriculares^M

expander
expandeur^M
Expander^M
expander^M
amplificador^M

function display
affichage^M des fonctions^F
Funktionsdisplay^N
display^M delle funzioni^F
display^M de las funciones^M

disc drive
lecteur^M de disquette^F
Diskettenlaufwerk^N
unità^F a disco^M
lector^M de CD^M

synthesizer
synthétiseur^M
Synthesizer^M
sintetizzatore^M
sintetizador^M

volume control
contrôle^M du volume^M
Lautstärkeregler^M
controllo^M del volume^M
control^M de volumen^M

fine data entry control
modification^F fine des variables^F
Feinregler^M für Dateneingabe^F
controllo^M fine dei dati^M
control^M de entrada^F de información^F fina

disc drive
lecteur^M de disquette^F
Diskettenlaufwerk^N
unità^F a disco^M
unidad^F de discos^M

system buttons
fonctions^F système^M
Systemschalter^M
tasti^M di sistema^M
sistema^M de botones^M

function display
affichage^M des fonctions^F
Funktionsanzeige^F
display^M delle funzioni^F
display^M de funciones^F

sequencer control
contrôle^M du séquenceur^M
Sequenzerregler^M
controllo^M del sequencer^M
control^M de secuencias^F

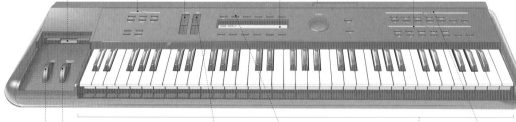

fast data entry control
modification^F rapide des variables^F
Grobregler^M für Dateneingabe^F
controllo^M veloce dei dati^M
control^M de entrada^F de información^F rápida

program selector
sélecteur^M de programme^M
Programmwahlschalter^M
selettore^M di programma^M
selector^M de programa^M

keyboard
clavier^M
Tastatur^F
tastiera^F
teclado^M

modulation wheel
modulation^F du timbre^M du son^M
Modulationsrad^N
rotella^F di modulazione^F
rueda^F de modulación^F

voice edit buttons
programmation^F des voix^F
Stimmenwahlschalter^M
tasti^M per l'editing^M del suono^M
botones^M para editar la voz^F

pitch wheel
modulation^F de la hauteur^F du son^M
Tonhöhenrad^N
rotella^F di intonazione^F
rueda^F para ajustar el tono^M

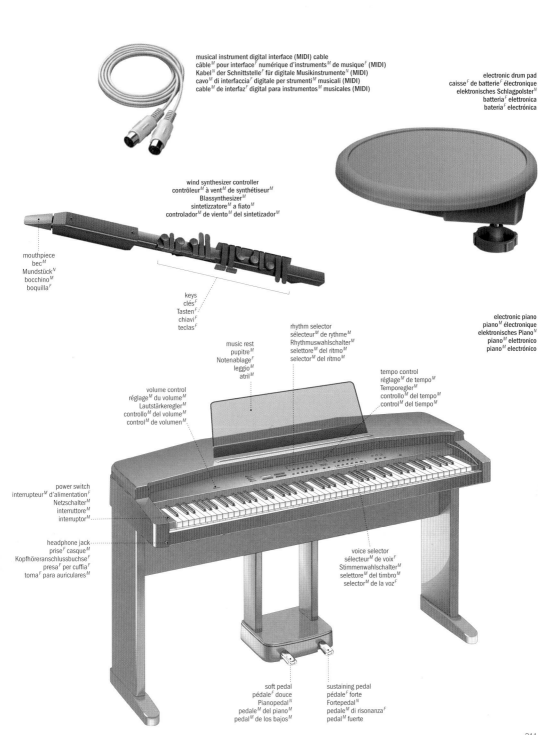

musical instrument digital interface (MIDI) cable
câble^M pour interface^F numérique d'instruments^M de musique^F (MIDI)
Kabel^N der Schnittstelle^F für digitale Musikinstrumente^N (MIDI)
cavo^M di interfaccia^F digitale per strumenti^M musicali (MIDI)
cable^M de interfaz^F digital para instrumentos^M musicales (MIDI)

electronic drum pad
caisse^F de batterie^F électronique
elektronisches Schlagpolster^N
batteria^F elettronica
batería^F electrónica

wind synthesizer controller
contrôleur^M à vent^M de synthétiseur^M
Blassynthesizer^M
sintetizzatore^M a fiato^M
controlador^M de viento^M del sintetizador^M

mouthpiece
bec^M
Mundstück^N
bocchino^M
boquilla^F

keys
clés^F
Tasten^F
chiavi^F
teclas^F

music rest
pupitre^M
Notenablage^F
leggio^M
atril^M

rhythm selector
sélecteur^M de rythme^M
Rhythmuswahlschalter^M
selettore^M del ritmo^M
selector^M del ritmo^M

tempo control
réglage^M de tempo^M
Temporegler^M
controllo^M del tempo^M
control^M del tiempo^M

electronic piano
piano^M électronique
elektronisches Piano^N
piano^M elettronico
piano^M electrónico

volume control
réglage^M du volume^M
Lautstärkeregler^M
controllo^M del volume^M
control^M de volumen^M

power switch
interrupteur^M d'alimentation^F
Netzschalter^M
interruttore^M
interruptor^M

headphone jack
prise^F casque^M
Kopfhöreranschlussbuchse^F
presa^F per cuffia^F
toma^F para auriculares^M

voice selector
sélecteur^M de voix^F
Stimmenwahlschalter^M
selettore^M del timbro^M
selector^M de la voz^F

soft pedal
pédale^F douce
Pianopedal^N
pedale^M del piano^M
pedal^M de los bajos^M

sustaining pedal
pédale^F forte
Fortepedal^N
pedale^M di risonanza^F
pedal^M fuerte

ARTS AND ARCHITECTURE

writing instruments

instruments^M d'écriture^F | Schreibgeräte^N | strumenti^M scrittori | instrumentos^M para escribir

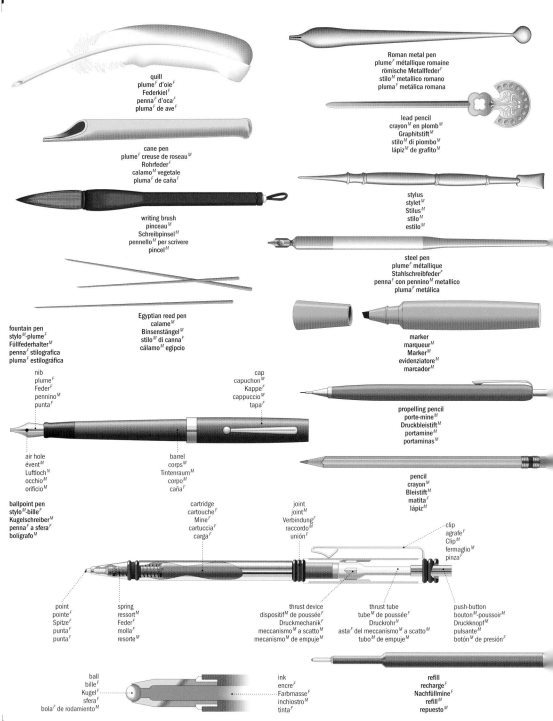

quill
plume^F d'oie^F
Federkiel^F
penna^F d'oca^F
pluma^F de ave^F

Roman metal pen
plume^F métallique romaine
römische Metallfeder^F
stilo^M metallico romano
pluma^F metálica romana

cane pen
plume^F creuse de roseau^M
Rohrfeder^F
calamo^M vegetale
pluma^F de caña^F

lead pencil
crayon^M en plomb^M
Graphitstift^M
stilo^M di piombo^M
lápiz^M de grafito^M

writing brush
pinceau^M
Schreibpinsel^M
pennello^M per scrivere
pincel^M

stylus
stylet^M
Stilus^M
stilo^M
estilo^M

steel pen
plume^F métallique
Stahlschreibfeder^F
penna^F con pennino^M metallico
pluma^F metálica

Egyptian reed pen
calame^M
Binsenstängel^M
stilo^M di canna^F
cálamo^M egipcio

marker
marqueur^M
Marker^M
evidenziatore^M
marcador^M

fountain pen
stylo^M-plume^F
Füllfederhalter^M
penna^F stilografica
pluma^F estilográfica

nib
plume^F
Feder^F
pennino^M
punta^F

cap
capuchon^M
Kappe^F
cappuccio^M
tapa^F

propelling pencil
porte-mine^M
Druckbleistift^M
portamine^M
portaminas^M

air hole
évent^M
Luftloch^N
occhio^M
orificio^M

barrel
corps^M
Tintenraum^M
corpo^M
caña^F

pencil
crayon^M
Bleistift^M
matita^F
lápiz^M

ballpoint pen
stylo^M-bille^F
Kugelschreiber^M
penna^F a sfera^F
bolígrafo^M

cartridge
cartouche^F
Mine^F
cartuccia^F
carga^F

joint
joint^M
Verbindung^F
raccordo^M
unión^F

clip
agrafe^F
Clip^M
fermaglio^M
pinza^F

point
pointe^F
Spitze^F
punta^F
punta^F

spring
ressort^M
Feder^F
molla^F
resorte^M

thrust device
dispositif^M de poussée^F
Druckmechanik^F
meccanismo^M a scatto^M
mecanismo^M de empuje^M

thrust tube
tube^M de poussée^F
Druckrohr^N
asta^F del meccanismo^M a scatto^M
tubo^M de empuje^M

push-button
bouton^M-poussoir^M
Druckknopf^M
pulsante^M
botón^M de presión^F

ball
bille^F
Kugel^F
sfera^F
bola^F de rodamiento^M

ink
encre^F
Farbmasse^F
inchiostro^M
tinta^F

refill
recharge^F
Nachfüllmine^F
refill^M
repuesto^M

COMMUNICATIONS AND OFFICE AUTOMATION

newspaper

journal^M | Zeitung^F | giornale^M | periódico^M

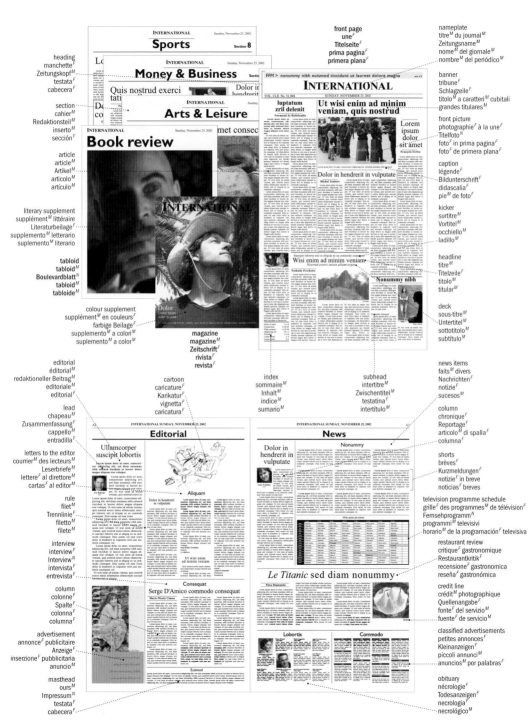

front page
une^F
Titelseite^F
prima pagina^F
primera plana^F

nameplate
titre^M du journal^M
Zeitungsname^M
nome^M del giornale^M
nombre^M del periódico^M

heading
manchette^F
Zeitungskopf^M
testata^F
cabecera^F

section
cahier^M
Redaktionsteil^M
inserto^M
sección^F

article
article^M
Artikel^M
articolo^M
artículo^M

literary supplement
supplément^M littéraire
Literaturbeilage^F
supplemento^M letterario
suplemento^M literario

tabloid
tabloid^M
Boulevardblatt^N
tabloid^M
tabloide^M

colour supplement
supplément^M en couleurs^F
farbige Beilage^F
supplemento^M a colori^M
suplemento^M a color^M

magazine
magazine^M
Zeitschrift^F
rivista^F
revista^F

banner
tribune^F
Schlagzeile^F
titolo^M a caratteri^M cubitali
grandes titulares^F

front picture
photographie^F à la une^F
Titelfoto^N
foto^F in prima pagina^F
foto^F de primera plana^F

caption
légende^F
Bildunterschrift^F
didascalia^F
pie^M de foto^F

kicker
surtitre^M
Vortitel^M
occhiello^M
ladillo^M

headline
titre^M
Titelzeile^F
titolo^M
titular^M

deck
sous-titre^M
Untertitel^M
sottotitolo^M
subtitulo^M

INTERNATIONAL
Sports
Sunday, November 25, 2002
Section 8

INTERNATIONAL
Money & Business
Sunday, November 25, 2002

INTERNATIONAL
Arts & Leisure
Sunday,

INTERNATIONAL
Book review
Sunday, November 25, 2002

FFM > nonumny nibh euismod tincidunt ut laoreet dolore, magna

INTERNATIONAL
VOL. CLII No. 51,948
SUNDAY, NOVEMBER 25, 2002

luptatum
zril delenit

Ut wisi enim ad minim
veniam, quis nostrud

Lorem
ipsum
dolor
sit amet

Dolor in hendrerit in vulputate

Wisi enim ad minim veniam

Nonummy nibh

index
sommaire^M
Inhalt^M
indice^M
sumario^M

subhead
intertitre^M
Zwischentitel^M
testatina^F
intertitulo^M

news items
faits^M divers
Nachrichten^F
notizie^F
sucesos^M

column
chronique^F
Reportage^F
articolo^M di spalla^F
columna^F

shorts
brèves^F
Kurzmeldungen^F
notizie^F in breve
noticias^F breves

television programme schedule
grille^F des programmes^M de télévision^F
Fernsehprogramm^N
programmi^M televisivi
horario^M de la programación^F televisiva

restaurant review
critique^F gastronomique
Restaurantkritik^F
recensione^F gastronomica
reseña^F gastronómica

credit line
crédit^M photographique
Quellenangabe^F
fonte^F del servizio^M
fuente^F de servicio^M

classified advertisements
petites annonces^F
Kleinanzeigen^F
piccoli annunci^M
anuncios^M por palabras^F

obituary
nécrologie^F
Todesanzeigen^F
necrologia^F
necrológico^M

editorial
éditorial^M
redaktioneller Beitrag^M
editoriale^M
editorial^F

lead
chapeau^M
Zusammenfassung^F
cappello^M
entradilla^F

letters to the editor
courrier^M des lecteurs^M
Leserbriefe^M
lettere^F al direttore^M
cartas^F al editor^M

rule
filet^M
Trennlinie^F
filetto^M
filete^M

interview
interview^F
Interview^N
intervista^F
entrevista^F

column
colonne^F
Spalte^F
colonna^F
columna^F

advertisement
annonce^F publicitaire
Anzeige^F
inserzione^F pubblicitaria
anuncio^M

masthead
ours^N
Impressum^N
testata^F
cabecera^F

INTERNATIONAL SUNDAY, NOVEMBER 25, 2002
Editorial

Ullamcorper
suscipit lobortis

Dolor in hendrerit
in hendrerit

Aliquam

Ut wisi enim
ad minim veniam

Consequat

Serge D'Amico commodo consequat

INTERNATIONAL SUNDAY, NOVEMBER 25, 2002
News

Dolor in
hendrerit in
vulputate

Nonummy

Le Titanic sed diam nonummy

Lobortis

Commodo

cartoon
caricature^F
Karikatur^F
vignetta^F
caricatura^F

313

photography

photographie^F | Fotografie^F | fotografia^F | fotografía^F

single-lens reflex (SLR) camera: front view
appareil^M à visée^F reflex mono-objectif^M : vue^F avant
einäugige Spiegelreflexkamera^F/SLR-Kamera^F: Vorderansicht^F
macchina^F fotografica reflex monoculare: vista^F frontale
cámara^F reflex monocular: vista^F frontal

film rewind knob
rebobinage^M
Rückspulknopf^M
pulsante^M di riavvolgimento^M della pellicola^F
botón^M de rebobinado^M de la película^F

accessory shoe
griffe^F porte-accessoires^M
Zubehörschuh^M
slitta^F per accessori^M
patín^M de los accesorios^M

exposure adjustment knob
correction^F d'exposition^F
Belichtungskorrekturknopf^M
pulsante^M di compensazione^F dell'esposizione^F
botón^M de compensación^M de la exposición^F

hot-shoe contact
contact^M électrique
Blitzkontakt^M
contatto^M caldo
contacto^M central

film advance mode
mode^M d'entraînement^M du film^M
Filmtransporteinstellung^F
tasto^M per l'avanzamento^M della pellicola^F
modalidad^F de avance^M de la película^F

data panel
écran^M de contrôle^M
Display^N
display^M
panel^M de controles^M

exposure mode
mode^M d'exposition^F
Belichtungseinstellung^F
tasto^M per il modo^M di esposizione^F
modalidad^F de exposición^F

program selector
sélecteur^M de fonctions^F
Programmwählscheibe^F
selettore^M dei programmi^M
selector^M de programa^M

multiple exposure mode
surimpression^F
Belichtungsmesser^M
tasto^M per le esposizioni^F multiple
modalidad^F de exposición^F múltiple

on/off switch
commutateur^M marche^F/arrêt^M
Ein-/Ausschalter^M
interruttore^M di accensione^F
interruptor^M de encendido/apagado

film speed
sensibilité^F du film^M
Filmempfindlichkeit^F
tasto^M per la sensibilità^F della pellico
indicador^M de velocidad^F

shutter release button
déclencheur^M
Auslöser^M
pulsante^M di scatto^M
disparador^M

self-timer indicator
témoin^M du retardateur^M
Selbstauslöser-Lichtsignal^N
spia^F luminosa dell'autoscatto^M
indicador^M de tiempo^M

remote control terminal
prise^F de télécommande^F
Diode^F des Selbstauslösers^M
presa^F per il comando^M a distanza^F
terminal^M del control^M remoto

focus mode selector
mode^M de mise^F au point^M
Autofocus-Umschalter^M
selettore^M della messa^F a fuoco^M
selector^M de focalización^F

camera body
boîtier^M
Kameragehäuse^N
corpo^M della macchina^F fotografica
caja^F

lens release button
déverrouillage^M de l'objectif^M
Objektivauswurf^M
pulsante^M di sblocco^M dell'obiettivo^M
botón^M de desbloqueo^M del objetivo^M

lens
objectif^M
Objektiv^N
obiettivo^M
objetivo^M

depth-of-field preview button
vérification^F de la profondeur^F de champ^M
Schärfentiefenknopf^M
pulsante^M di controllo^M della profondità^F di campo^M
botón^M de previsionado de profundidad^F de campo^M

lenses
objectifs^M
Objektive^N
obiettivi^M
objetivos^M

telephoto lens
téléobjectif^M
Teleobjektiv^N
teleobiettivo^M
teleobjetivo^M

zoom lens
objectif^M zoom^M
Zoomobjektiv^N
obiettivo^M zoom
objetivo^M zoom^M

wide-angle lens
objectif^M grand-angulaire
Weitwinkelobjektiv^N
obiettivo^M grandangolare
objetivo^M gran angular^M

macro lens
objectif^M macro
Makroobjektiv^N
obiettivo^M macro
objetivo^M macro

lens accessori⦁
accessoires^M de l'objecti⦁
Objektivzubehö⦁
accessori^M dell'obiettivo⦁
accesorios^M para el objetivo⦁

lens cap
capuchon^M d'objectif^M
Objektivschutzdeckel^M
coperchio^M di protezione^F dell'obiettivo^M
tapa^F del objetivo^M

lens hood
parasoleil^M
Gegenlichtblende^F
paraluce^M
capuchón^M

polarizing filter
filtre^M de polarisation^F
Polarisationsfilter^M
filtro^M polarizzatore
filtro^M de polarización^F

power switch
commutateur^M d'alimentation^F
Hauptschalter^M
interruttore^M di accensione^F
conmutador^M de alimentación^F

menu button
touche^F de sélection^F des menus^M
Menütaste^F
pulsante^M del menu^M
botón^M de selección^F del menú^M

liquid crystal display
écran^M à cristaux^M liquides
Flüssigkristallanzeige^F
display^M a cristalli^M liquidi
pantalla^F de cristal^M líquido

viewfinder
viseur^M
Sucherokular^N
mirino^M
visor^M

digital reflex camera: camera back
appareil^M à visée^F reflex numérique : dos^M
digitale Spiegelreflexkamera^F: Rückansicht^F
macchina^F fotografica reflex digitale: dorso^M
cámara^F réflex digital: vista^F posterior

settings display button
touche^F d'affichage^M des réglages^M
Einstellungsanzeige^F
pulsante^M di visualizzazione^F delle impostazioni^F
botón^M de visualización^F de ajustes^M

compact memory card
carte^F de mémoire^F
Speicherkarte^F
scheda^F di memoria^F
tarjeta^F de memoria^F

cover
couvercle^M
Abdeckung^F
coperchio^M
tapa^F

strap eyelet
œillet^M d'attache^F
Öse^F für Tragriemen^M
occhiello^M per la tracolla^F
ojete^M para la correa^F

multi-image jump button
touche^F de saut^M d'images^F
Bildvorlauf^M
pulsante^M per il salto^M di immagini^F
botón^M de salto^M de imágenes^F

video and digital terminals
prises^F vidéo et numérique
Anschlussbuchsen^F für Video- und Digitalübertragung^F
prese^F video e digitali
tomas^F vídeo y digital

image review button
touche^F de visualisation^F des images^F
Bildanzeige^F
pulsante^M di visualizzazione^F delle immagini^F
botón^M de visualización^F de imágenes^F

remote control terminal
prise^F de télécommande^F
Fernsteuerungsanschlussbuchse^F
presa^F per il comando^M a distanza^F
botón^M de control^M remoto

index/enlarge button
touche^F d'index^M/agrandissement^M
Indexanzeige^F-/Zoomregler^M
pulsante^M per l'indice^M e per l'ingrandimento^M
botón^M de índice^M/ampliación^F

erase button
touche^F d'effacement^M
Löschtaste^F
pulsante^M di cancellazione^F
botón^M de cancelación^F

four-way selector
sélecteur^M quadridirectionnel
Vierwegeregler^M
selettore^M quadridirezionale
selector^M cuadro-direccional

eject button
bouton^M d'éjection^F
Auswurftaste^F
pulsante^M di espulsione^F
botón^M de expulsión^M

still cameras
appareils^M photographiques
Fotoapparate^M
macchine^F fotografiche
cámaras^F fijas

Polaroid® Land camera
Polaroid®^{M}
Sofortbildkamera^F
Polaroid^F
cámara^F Polaroid Land

medium format SLR (6 x 6)
appareil^M reflex 6 X 6 mono-objectif^M
Mittelformatkamera^F SLR (6 x 6)
macchina^F fotografica reflex (6x6)
cámara^F reflex de formato^M medio SLR (6x6)

rangefinder camera
appareil^M à télémètre^M couplé
Sucherkamera^F
macchina^F fotografica autofocus
telémetro^M

digital camera
appareil^M numérique
Digitalkamera^F
macchina^F fotografica digitale
cámara^F digital

disposable camera
appareil^M jetable
Einwegkamera^F
macchina^F fotografica usa e getta
cámara^F desechable

view camera
chambre^F photographique
Großformatkamera^F
macchina^F fotografica a banco^M ottico
cámara^F de fuelle^M

satellite broadcasting

télédiffusion^F par satellite^M | Satellitenübertragungstechnik^F | trasmissione^F via satellite^M | comunicación^F vía satélite

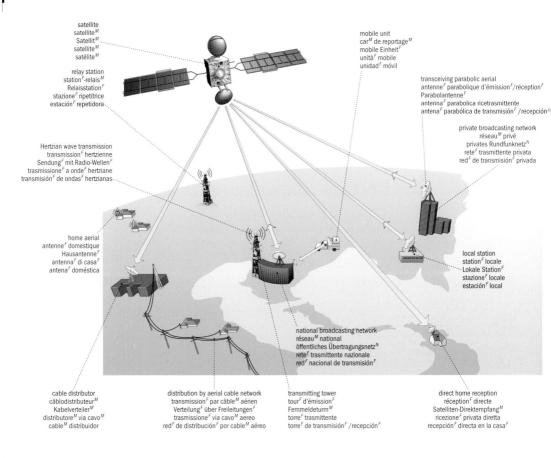

satellite
satellite^M
Satellit^M
satellite^M
satélite^M

relay station
station^F-relais^M
Relaisstation^F
stazione^F ripetitrice
estación^F repetidora

Hertzian wave transmission
transmission^F hertzienne
Sendung^F mit Radio-Wellen^F
trasmissione^F a onde^F hertziane
transmisión^F de ondas^F hertzianas

home aerial
antenne^F domestique
Hausantenne^F
antenna^F di casa^F
antena^F doméstica

mobile unit
car^M de reportage^M
mobile Einheit^F
unità^F mobile
unidad^F móvil

transceiving parabolic aerial
antenne^F parabolique d'émission^F/réception^F
Parabolantenne^F
antenna^F parabolica ricetrasmittente
antena^F parabólica de transmisión^F/recepción^F

private broadcasting network
réseau^M privé
privates Rundfunknetz^N
rete^F trasmittente privata
red^F de transmisión^F privada

local station
station^F locale
Lokale Station^F
stazione^F locale
estación^F local

cable distributor
câblodistributeur^M
Kabelverteiler^M
distributore^M via cavo^M
cable^M distribuidor

distribution by aerial cable network
transmission^F par câble^M aérien
Verteilung^F über Freileitungen^F
trasmissione^F via cavo^M aereo
red^F de distribución^F por cable^M aéreo

transmitting tower
tour^F d'émission^F
Fernmeldeturm^M
torre^F trasmittente
torre^F de transmisión^F/recepción^F

national broadcasting network
réseau^M national
öffentliches Übertragungsnetz^N
rete^F trasmittente nazionale
red^F nacional de transmisión^F

direct home reception
réception^F directe
Satelliten-Direktempfang^M
ricezione^F privata diretta
recepción^F directa en la casa^F

telecommunication satellites

satellites^M de télécommunications^F | Fernmeldesatelliten^M | satelliti^M per telecomunicazioni^F | satélites^M de telecomunicaciones^F

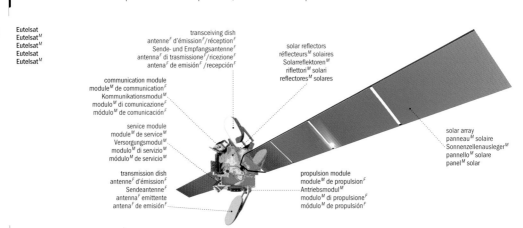

Eutelsat
Eutelsat^M
Eutelsat^M
Eutelsat^M
Eutelsat^M

transceiving dish
antenne^F d'émission^F/réception^F
Sende- und Empfangsantenne^F
antenna^F di trasmissione^F/ricezione^F
antena^F de emisión^F/recepción^F

solar reflectors
réflecteurs^M solaires
Solarreflektoren^M
riflettori^M solari
reflectores^M solares

communication module
module^M de communication^F
Kommunikationsmodul^M
modulo^M di comunicazione^F
módulo^M de comunicación^F

service module
module^M de service^M
Versorgungsmodul^M
modulo^M di servizio^M
módulo^M de servicio^M

solar array
panneau^M solaire
Sonnenzellenausleger^M
pannello^M solare
panel^M solar

transmission dish
antenne^F d'émission^F
Sendeantenne^F
antenna^F emittente
antena^F de emisión^F

propulsion module
module^M de propulsion^F
Antriebsmodul^M
modulo^M di propulsione^F
módulo^M de propulsión^F

COMMUNICATIONS AND OFFICE AUTOMATION

telecommunications by satellite

télécommunications^F par satellite^M | Telekommunikation^F über Nachrichtensatellit^M | telecomunicazioni^F via satellite^M | telecomunicaciones^F vía satélite^M

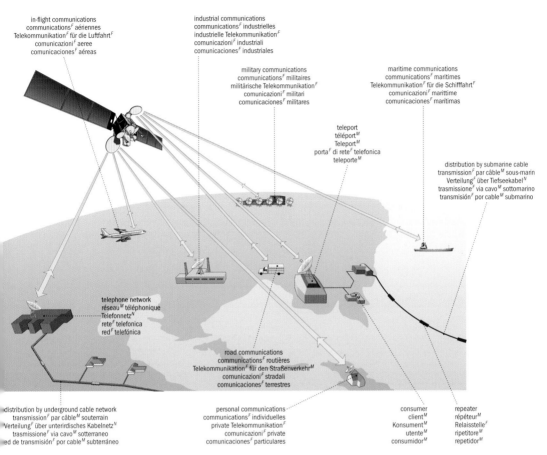

in-flight communications
communications^F aériennes
Telekommunikation^F für die Luftfahrt^F
comunicazioni^F aeree
comunicaciones^F aéreas

industrial communications
communications^F industrielles
industrielle Telekommunikation^F
comunicazioni^F industriali
comunicaciones^F industriales

military communications
communications^F militaires
militärische Telekommunikation^F
comunicazioni^F militari
comunicaciones^F militares

maritime communications
communications^F maritimes
Telekommunikation^F für die Schifffahrt^F
comunicazioni^F marittime
comunicaciones^F maritimas

teleport
téléport^M
Teleport^M
porta^F di rete^F telefonica
teleporte^M

distribution by submarine cable
transmission^F par câble^M sous-marin
Verteilung^F über Tiefseekabel^N
trasmissione^F via cavo^M sottomarino
transmisión^F por cable^M submarino

telephone network
réseau^M téléphonique
Telefonnetz^N
rete^F telefonica
red^F telefónica

road communications
communications^F routières
Telekommunikation^F für den Straßenverkehr^M
comunicazioni^F stradali
comunicaciones^F terrestres

distribution by underground cable network
transmission^F par câble^M souterrain
Verteilung^F über unterirdisches Kabelnetz^N
trasmissione^F via cavo^M sotterraneo
red de transmisión^F por cable^M subterráneo

personal communications
communications^F individuelles
private Telekommunikation^F
comunicazioni^F private
comunicaciones^F particulares

consumer
client^M
Konsument^M
utente^M
consumidor^M

repeater
répéteur^M
Relaisstelle^F
ripetitore^M
repetidor^M

telecommunication satellites

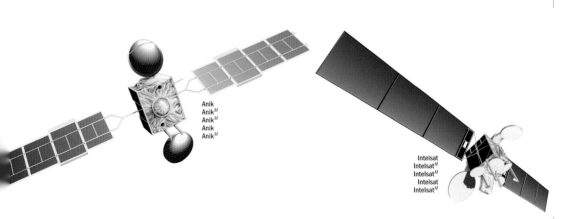

Anik
Anik^M
Anik^M
Anik
Anik^M

Intelsat
Intelsat^M
Intelsat^M
Intelsat
Intelsat^M

television

télévision^F | Fernsehen^N | televisione^F | televisión^F

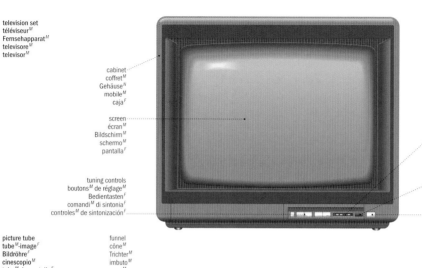

television set
téléviseur^M
Fernsehapparat^M
televisore^M
televisor^M

cabinet
coffret^M
Gehäuse^N
mobile^M
caja^F

screen
écran^M
Bildschirm^M
schermo^M
pantalla^F

indicators
lampes^F témoins^M
Betriebsanzeigen^F
spie^F luminose
indicadores^M

remote control sensor
capteur^M de télécommande^F
Sensor^M für Fernbedienung^F
sensore^M del telecomando^M
sensor^M del mando^M a distancia^F

tuning controls
boutons^M de réglage^M
Bedientasten^F
comandi^M di sintonia^F
controles^M de sintonización^F

power button
interrupteur^M d'alimentation^F
Netzschalter^M
interruttore^M di accensione^F
botón^M de encendido

picture tube
tube^M-image^F
Bildröhre^F
cinescopio^M
tubo^M de pantalla^F

funnel
cône^M
Trichter^M
imbuto^M
cono^M

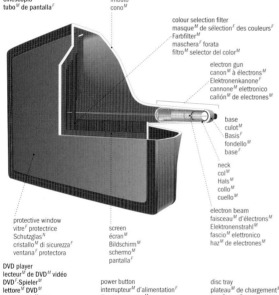

colour selection filter
masque^M de sélection^F des couleurs^F
Farbfilter^M
maschera^F forata
filtro^M selector del color^M

electron gun
canon^M à électrons^M
Elektronenkanone^F
cannone^M elettronico
cañón^M de electrones^M

base
culot^M
Basis^F
fondello^M
base^F

neck
col^M
Hals^M
collo^M
cuello^M

electron beam
faisceau^M d'électrons^M
Elektronenstrahl^M
fascio^M elettronico
haz^M de electrones^M

electron gun
canon^M à électrons
Elektronenkanone
cannone^M elettronic
cañón^M de electrones

grid
grille^F
Gitter^N
griglia^F
rejilla^F

red beam
faisceau^M rouge
Rotstrahl^M
fascio^M rosso
haz^M rojo

magnetic field
champ^M magnétique
magnetisches Feld^N
campo^M magnetico
campo^M magnético

green beam
faisceau^M vert
Grünstrahl^M
fascio^M verde
haz^M verde

blue beam
faisceau^M bleu
Blaustrahl^M
fascio^M blu
haz^M azul

protective window
vitre^F protectrice
Schutzglas^N
cristallo^M di sicurezza^F
ventana^F protectora

screen
écran^M
Bildschirm^M
schermo^M
pantalla^F

DVD player
lecteur^M de DVD^M vidéo
DVD^F-Spieler^M
lettore^M DVD^M
reproductor^M DVD

power button
interrupteur^M d'alimentation^F
Ein-/Ausschalter^M
pulsante^M di alimentazione^F
interruptor^M de alimentación^F

disc tray
plateau^M de chargement^M
DVD^F-Lade^F
vassoio^M portadischi
bandeja^F del disco

display
afficheur^M
Display^N
display^M
pantalla^F

digital versatile disc (DVD)
disque^M numérique polyvalent (DVD)
DVD^F
disco^M versatile digitale (DVD)
disco^M versátil digital (DVD)

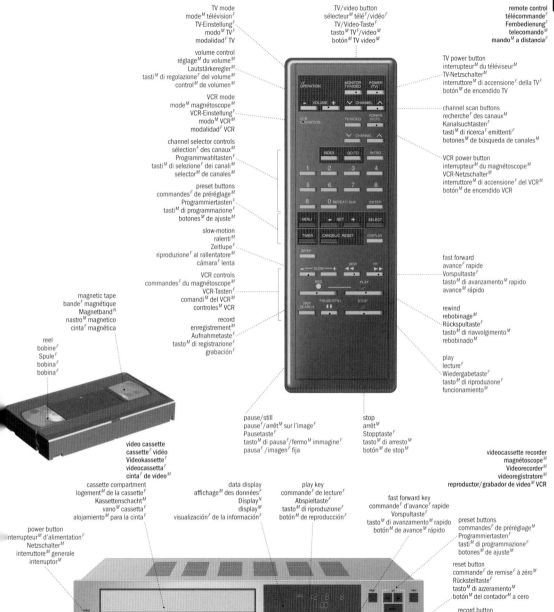

TV mode
mode^M télévision^F
TV-Einstellung^F
modo^M TV^F
modalidad^F TV

TV/video button
sélecteur^M télé^F/vidéo^F
TV/Video-Taste^F
tasto^M TV^F/video^M
botón^M TV video^M

remote control
télécommande^F
Fernbedienung^F
telecomando^M
mando^M a distancia^F

volume control
réglage^M du volume^M
Lautstärkeregler^M
tasti^M di regolazione^F del volume^M
control^M de volumen^M

TV power button
interrupteur^M du téléviseur^M
TV-Netzschalter^M
interruttore^M di accensione^F della TV^F
botón^M de encendido TV

VCR mode
mode^M magnétoscope^M
VCR-Einstellung^F
modo^M VCR^M
modalidad^F VCR

channel scan buttons
recherche^F des canaux^M
Kanalsuchtasten^F
tasti^M di ricerca^F emittenti^F
botones^M de búsqueda de canales^M

channel selector controls
sélection^F des canaux^M
Programmwahltasten^F
tasti^M di selezione^F dei canali^M
selector^M de canales^M

VCR power button
interrupteur^M du magnétoscope^M
VCR-Netzschalter^M
interruttore^M di accensione^F del VCR^M
botón^M de encendido VCR

preset buttons
commandes^F de préréglage^M
Programmiertasten^F
tasti^M di programmazione^F
botones^M de ajuste^M

slow-motion
ralenti^M
Zeitlupe^F
riproduzione^F al rallentatore^M
cámara^F lenta

fast forward
avance^F rapide
Vorspultaste^F
tasto^M di avanzamento^M rapido
avance^M rápido

VCR controls
commandes^F du magnétoscope^M
VCR-Tasten^F
comandi^M del VCR^M
controles^M VCR

magnetic tape
bande^F magnétique
Magnetband^N
nastro^M magnetico
cinta^F magnética

rewind
rebobinage^M
Rückspultaste^F
tasto^M di riavvolgimento^M
rebobinado^M

reel
bobine^F
Spule^F
bobina^F
bobina^F

record
enregistrement^M
Aufnahmetaste^F
tasto^M di registrazione^F
grabación^F

play
lecture^F
Wiedergabetaste^F
tasto^M di riproduzione^F
funcionamiento^M

pause/still
pause^F/arrêt^M sur l'image^F
Pausetaste^F
tasto^M di pausa^F/fermo^M immagine^F
pausa^F /imagen^F fija

stop
arrêt^M
Stopptaste^F
tasto^M di arresto^M
botón^M de stop^M

video cassette
cassette^F vidéo
Videokassette^F
videocassetta^F
cinta^F de video^M

videocassette recorder
magnétoscope^M
Videorecorder^M
videoregistratore^M
reproductor/grabador de video^M VCR

cassette compartment
logement^M de la cassette^F
Kassettenschacht^M
vano^M cassetta^F
alojamiento^M para la cinta^F

data display
affichage^M des données^F
Display^N
display^M
visualización^F de la información^F

play key
commande^F de lecture^F
Abspieltaste^F
tasto^M di riproduzione^F
botón^M de reproducción^F

fast forward key
commande^F d'avance^F rapide
Vorspultaste^F
tasto^M di avanzamento^M rapido
botón^M de avance^M rápido

preset buttons
commandes^F de préréglage^M
Programmiertasten^F
tasti^M di programmazione^F
botones^M de ajuste^M

power button
interrupteur^M d'alimentation^F
Netzschalter^M
interruttore^M generale
interruptor^M

reset button
commande^F de remise^F à zéro^M
Rückstelltaste^F
tasto^M di azzeramento^M
botón^M del contador^F a cero

record button
commande^F d'enregistrement^M
Aufnahmetaste^F
tasto^M di registrazione^F
botón^M de grabación^F

channel scan buttons
recherche^F des canaux^M
Kanalsuchtasten^F
tasti^M di ricerca delle emittenti^F
botones^M para búsqueda^F de canales^M

cassette eject button
commande^F d'éjection^F de la cassette^F
Kassettenauswurfschalter^M
tasto^M di espulsione^F
botón^M de expulsión^F

stop key
commande^F d'arrêt^M
Stopptaste^F
tasto^M di arresto^M
botón^M de stop^M

rewind button
commande^F de rebobinage^M
Rückspultaste^F
tasto^M di riavvolgimento^M
botón^M de rebobinado^M

pause/still key
pause^F/arrêt^M sur l'image^F
Pausetaste^F
tasto^M di pausa^F/fermo^M immagine^F
pausa^F /imagen^F fija

television

electronic viewfinder
viseur^M électronique
elektronischer Sucher^M
mirino^M elettronico
visor^M electrónico

eyecup
œilleton^M
Sonnenschutzblende^F
adattatore^M per oculare^M
ojera^F

analogue camcorder: front view
caméscope^M analogique : vue^F avant
Analog-Camcorder^M: Vorderansicht^F
videocamera^F portatile: vista^F frontale
videocámara^F analógica: vista^F frontal

edit search button
touche^F de raccord^F d'enregistrement^M
Editier-Such-Taste^F
tasto^M di selezione^F e montaggio^M
botón^M de selección^F y montaje^M

videotape operation controls
commandes^F de la bande^F vidéo
Videobandsteuerungen^F
comandi^M della videocassetta^F
mandos^M de la cinta^F de video^M

display panel
panneau^M de l'écran^M
Display^N-Panel^N
pannello^M del display^M
panel^M del display^M

zoom lens
objectif^M zoom^M
Zoomobjektiv^N
zoom^M
objetivo^M zoom

nightshot switch
commutateur^M de prise^F de vues^F nocturne
Nachtaufnahmeschalter^M
selettore^M di registrazione^F notturna
conmutador^M de grabación^F nocturna

power/functions switch
commutateur^M alimentation^F/fonctions^F
Haupt-/Funktionsschalter^M
interruttore^M di accensione^F/funzioni^F
interruptor^M alimentación^F /funciones^F

cassette compartment
logement^M de la cassette^F
Videokassettenschacht^M
vano^M della videocassetta^F
alojamiento^M de la cinta^F

microphone
microphone^M
Mikrofon^N
microfono^M
micrófono^M

focus selector
sélecteur^M de mise^F au point^M
Fokussiersteuerung^F
selettore^M della messa^F a fuoco^M
selector^M de enfoque^M

near/far dial
molette^F de réglage^M près/loin
Zoomer^M
rotella^F regolatrice vicino/lontano
ruleta^F de enfoque^M lejos/cerca

compact video cassette adapter
adaptateur^M de cassette^F vidéo compacte
Videokassettenadapter^M
adattatore^M per videocassette^F compatte
adaptador^M de cinta^F de video^M compacto

analogue camcorder: back view
caméscope^M analogique : vue^F arrière
Analog-Camcorder^M: Rückansicht^F
videocamera^F portatile: dorso^M
videocámara^F analógica: vista^F posterior

eyepiece
oculaire^M
Sucher^M
oculare^M
ocular^M

power zoom button
commande^F électrique du zoom^M
Zoomwippe^F
comando^M dello zoom^M elettrico
botón^M del zoom^M eléctrico

recording start/stop button
touche^F d'enregistrement^M
Aufnahme^F-Start^M-/Stopptaste^F
tasto^M di avvio^M/arresto^M registrazione^F
tecla^F de inicio/stop de grabación^F

rechargeable battery pack
batterie^F rechargeable
Akku^M
batteria^F ricaricabile
pila^F recargable

speaker
haut-parleur^M
Lautsprecher^M
altoparlante^M
altavoz^M

image adjustment buttons
touches^F de réglage^F de l'image^F
Bildeinstelltasten^F
tasti^M di regolazione^F dell'immagine^F
botones^M de ajuste^M de imagen^F

indicators display button
touche^F d'affichage^F des indicateurs^M
Anzeigetaste^F
tasto^M di visualizzazione^F degli indicatori^M
tecla^F de fijación^F de pantalla^F

liquid crystal display
écran^M à cristaux^M liquides
Flüssigkristallanzeige^F
display^M a cristalli^M liquidi
pantalla^F táctil LCD

end search button
touche^F de raccord^F d'enregistrement^M
End-Suchtaste^F
tasto^M di ricerca^F della fine^F
tecla^F de final^M de búsqueda^F

date display/recording button
touche^F de la date^F
Datumeinblende-/Aufnahmetaste^F
tasto^M di registrazione^F e di visualizzazione^F della data^F
botón grabación^F /visualización^F fecha^F

time display/recording button
touche^F de l'heure^F
Zeiteinblende-/Aufnahmetaste^F
tasto^M di registrazione^F e di visualizzazione^F dell'ora^F
botón grabación^F /visualización^F hora

special effects buttons
touches^F d'effets^F spéciaux
Trickeffektetasten^F
tasti^M degli effetti^M speciali
botones^M de efectos^M especiales

title display button
touche^F d'affichage^M de titre^M
Titeleinblendetaste^F
tasto^M di visualizzazione^F dei titoli^M
tecla^F de visualización^F del título^M

special effects selection dial
molette^F de sélection^F des effets^M spéciaux
Trickeffektewähler^M
rotella^F di selezione^F degli effetti^M speciali
ruleta^F de selección^F de efectos^M especiales

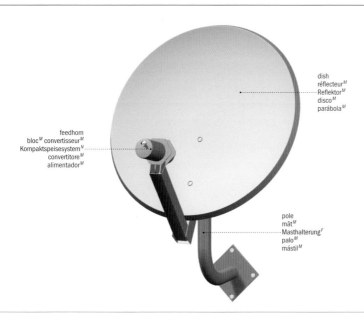

dish aerial
antenne^F parabolique
Parabolantenne^F
antenna^F parabolica
antena^F parabólica

dish
réflecteur^M
Reflektor^M
disco^M
parábola^M

feedhorn
bloc^M convertisseur^M
Kompaktspeisesystem^N
convertitore^M
alimentador^M

pole
mât^M
Masthalterung^F
palo^M
mástil^M

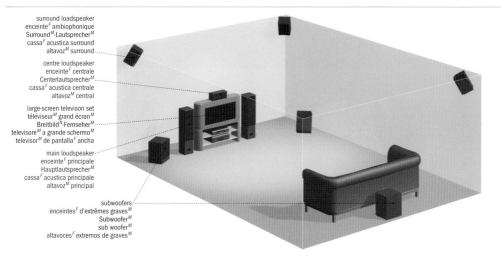

receiver
terminal^M numérique
Receiver^M
ricevitore^M
receptor^M

card reader
lecteur^M de carte^F
Kartenleser^M
lettore^M di schede^F
lector^M de tarjeta^F

remote control
télécommande^F
Fernbedienung^F
telecomando^M
mando^M a distancia^F

surround loadspeaker
enceinte^F ambiophonique
Surround^M-Lautsprecher^M
cassa^F acustica surround
altavoz^M surround

centre loudspeaker
enceinte^F centrale
Centerlautsprecher^M
cassa^F acustica centrale
altavoz^M central

large-screen televison set
téléviseur^M grand écran^M
Breitbild^N-Fernseher^M
televisore^M a grande schermo^M
televisor^M de pantalla^F ancha

main loudspeaker
enceinte^F principale
Hauptlautsprecher^M
cassa^F acustica principale
altavoz^M principal

subwoofers
enceintes^F d'extrêmes graves^M
Subwoofer^M
sub woofer^M
altavoces^F extremos de graves^M

home theatre
home cinéma^M
Heimkino^N
home theatre^M
home^M theatre

stereo sound system

chaîne^F stéréo | Tonwiedergabesystem^N | impianto^M hi-fi di riproduzione^F del suono^M | equipo^M de alta fidelidad^F

ampli-tuner: front view
ampli^M-syntoniseur^M : vue^F avant
Receiver^M: Vorderansicht^F
sintoamplificatore^M: vista^F frontale
amplificador^M /sintonizador^M : vista^F frontal

sound mode lights
voyants^M d'indication^F du mode^M sonore
Klangwahlanzeige^F
spie^F della modalità^F audio^M
indicadores^M del modo^M audio

input lights
voyants^M d'entrée^F
Kontrollleuchten^F für Tonsignalquellen^F
luci^F delle sorgenti^F
indicadores^M de entrada^F

tape recorder select button
touche^F de sélection^F du magnétophone^M
Kassettenrekorder^M-Wahltaste^F
tasto^M di selezione^F del registratore^M
tecla^F de selección^F del grabador^M

sound mode selector
sélecteur^M de mode^M sonore
Klangwahlschalter^M
selettore^M della modalità^F audio^M
selector^M del modo^M audio

sound field control
contrôle^M du champ^M sonore
Feldstärkeregler^M
controllo^M del campo^M audio^M
control^M del campo^M audio

input select button
touche^F de sélection^F d'entrée^F
Tonsignalquellen^F-Wahltaster^M
tasto^M di selezione^F delle sorgenti^F
tecla^F de selección^F de entrada^F

power button
interrupteur^M d'alimentation^F
Netzschalter^M
interruttore^M di accensione^F
botón^M de encendido

loudspeaker system select buttons
touches^F de sélection^F des enceintes^F
Kanalwahltasten^F für Lautsprecher^M
tasti^M di selezione^F delle casse^F acustiche
teclas^F de selección^F de los altavoces^M

headphone jack
prise^F casque^M
Kopfhörerbuchse^F
presa^F per cuffia^F
toma^F para los auriculares^M

tuning buttons
touches^F de sélection^F des stations^F
Sendersuchlauftasten^F
tasti^M di selezione^F della sintonia^F
teclas^F de selección^F de la sintonía^F

preset tuning button
touche^F de présélection^F
Vorwahlsender^M-Wahltaste^F
tasto^M di preselezione^F della sintonia^F
tecla^F de selección^F sintonía^F

band select button
touche^F de modulation^F
Bandwahltaste^F
tasto^M di selezione^F della banda^F
tecla^F de selección^F de banda

FM mode select button
touche^F de sélection^F du mode^M FM
UKW^F-Wahltaste^F
tasto^M di selezione^F della modalità^F FM
tecla^F de selección^F de modalidad^F FM

memory button
touche^F mémoire^F
Speichertaste^F
tasto^M di memorizzazione^F
tecla^F memoria

display
afficheur^M
Display^N
display^M
display^M

input selector
sélecteur^M d'entrée^F
Eingangsschalter^M
selettore^M di ingresso^M
selector^M de entrada^F

bass tone control
contrôle^M de tonalité^F des graves^M
Bassregler^M
regolatore^M dei bassi^M
control^M de graves^M

volume control
réglage^M du volume^M
Lautstärkeregler^M
regolatore^M di volume^M
control^M del volumen^M

balance control
équilibrage^M des haut-parleurs^M
Balanceregler^M
bilanciamento^M degli altoparlanti^M
control^M de balance^M

treble tone control
contrôle^M de tonalité^F des aigus^M
Höhenregler^M
regolatore^M degli alti^M
control^M de agudos^M

ampli-tuner: back view
ampli^M-syntoniseur^M : vue^F arrière
Amplituner^M: Rückansicht^F
sintoamplificatore^M: dorso^M
amplificador^M /sintonizador^M : vista^F posterior

ground terminal
borne^F de mise^F à la terre^F
Massekontakt^M
terminale^M della messa^F a terra^F
conector^M de puesta^F de tierra^F

cooling fan
ventilateur^M
Lüfter^M
ventola^F
ventilador^M

power cord
cordon^M d'alimentation^F
Netzkabel^N
cavo^M di alimentazione^F
cable^M de alimentación^F

aerial terminals
bornes^F de raccordement^M des antennes^F
Antennenbuchsen^F
terminali^M di collegamento^M delle antenne^F
conectores^M de antenas^F

input/output video jacks
prises^F d'entrée^F/de sortie^F audio/vidéo
Video-Ein- und -Ausgänge^M
ingressi^M uscite^F audio^M/video^M
tomas^F entrada^F /salida^F video^M

loudspeaker terminals
bornes^F de raccordement^M des enceintes^F
Lautsprecherbuchsen^F
terminali^M di collegamento^M delle casse^F acustiche
conector^M de altavoces^M

switched outlet
prise^F de courant^M commutée
geschaltete Steckdose^F
presa^F di corrente^F commutata
conmutador^M de corriente^F

counter reset button
bouton^M de remise^F à zéro^M
Rückstelltaste^F
tasto^M di azzeramento^M del contatore^M
botón^M de ajuste^M a cero^M del contador^M

tape selector
sélecteur^M de bandes^F
Bandsortenschalter^M
selettore^M del nastro^M
selector^M de tipo^M de cinta^F

fast-forward button
avance^F rapide
Schnellvorlauf-Taste^F
tasto^M di avanzamento^M rapido
botón^M de avance^M rápido

cassette tape deck
platine^F cassette^F
Kassettendeck^N
piastra^F di registrazione^F
pletina^F de casete^F

eject button
bouton^M d'éjection^F
Auswurf-Taste^F
tasto^M di espulsione^F
botón^M de expulsión^F

tape counter
compteur^M
Zählwerk^N
contatore^M
contador^M

play button
lecture^F
Play-Taste^F
tasto^M di riproduzione^F
botón^M de reproducción^F

peak level meter
indicateur^M de niveau^M
LED-Pegelanzeige^F
LED^M indicatore^M del livello^M di picco^M
medidor^M de altos niveles^M de frecuencia^F

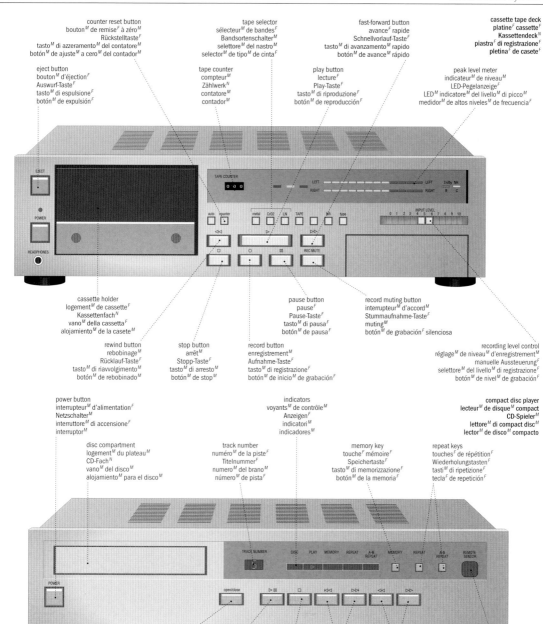

cassette holder
logement^M de cassette^F
Kassettenfach^N
vano^M della cassetta^F
alojamiento^M de la casete^F

pause button
pause^F
Pause-Taste^F
tasto^M di pausa^F
botón^M de pausa^F

record muting button
interrupteur^M d'accord^M
Stummaufnahme-Taste^F
muting^M
botón^M de grabación^F silenciosa

rewind button
rebobinage^M
Rücklauf-Taste^F
tasto^M di riavvolgimento^M
botón^M de rebobinado^M

stop button
arrêt^M
Stopp-Taste^F
tasto^M di arresto^M
botón^M de stop^M

record button
enregistrement^M
Aufnahme-Taste^F
tasto^M di registrazione^F
botón^M de inicio^M de grabación^F

recording level control
réglage^M de niveau^M d'enregistrement^M
manuelle Aussteuerung^F
selettore^M del livello^M di registrazione^F
botón^M de nivel^M de grabación^F

power button
interrupteur^M d'alimentation^F
Netzschalter^M
interruttore^M di accensione^F
interruptor^M

indicators
voyants^M de contrôle^M
Anzeigen^F
indicatori^M
indicadores^M

compact disc player
lecteur^M de disque^M compact
CD-Spieler^M
lettore^M di compact disc^M
lector^M de disco^M compacto

disc compartment
logement^M du plateau^M
CD-Fach^N
vano^M del disco^M
alojamiento^M para el disco^M

track number
numéro^M de la piste^F
Titelnummer^F
numero^M del brano^M
número^M de pista^F

memory key
touche^F mémoire^F
Speichertaste^F
tasto^M di memorizzazione^F
botón^M de la memoria^F

repeat keys
touches^F de répétition^F
Wiederholungstasten^F
tasti^M di ripetizione^F
tecla^F de repetición^F

disc compartment control
contrôle^M du plateau^M
Auswurftaste^F für das
tasto^M di espulsione^F
botón^M de control^M del alojamiento^M del disco^M

play/pause
lecture^F/pause^F
Start^M/Pause^F
tasto^M di riproduzione^F/pausa^F
lectura^F /pausa^F

track search keys
changement^M de piste^F
Titelsuchtasten^F
tasti^M di ricerca^F del brano^M
botón^M para buscar las pistas^F

scan
lecture^F rapide
Vor- und Rücklauf^M
tasti^M di ricerca^F rapida
operación^F rápida

stop/clear key
arrêt^M/effacement^M de mémoire^F
Stopp-/Löschtaste^F
tasto^M di arresto^M/cancellazione^F
botón^M para parar y borrar

remote control sensor
capteur^M de télécommande^F
Fernbedienungssensor^M
sensore^M del telecomando^M
sensor^M del mando^M a distancia^F

COMMUNICATIONS AND OFFICE AUTOMATION

stereo sound system

headphones
casque^M d'écoute^F
Kopfhörer^M
cuffia^F
auriculares^M

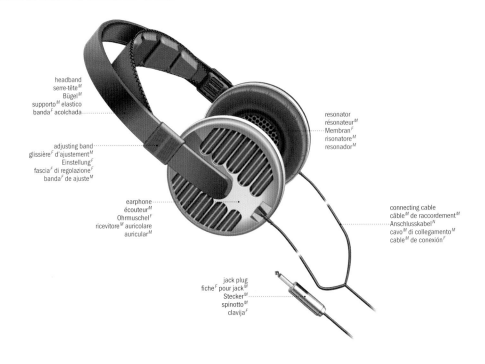

headband
serre-tête^M
Bügel^M
supporto^M elastico
banda^F acolchada

adjusting band
glissière^F d'ajustement^M
Einstellung^F
fascia^F di regolazione^F
banda^F de ajuste^M

earphone
écouteur^M
Ohrmuschel^F
ricevitore^M auricolare
auricular^M

resonator
résonateur^M
Membran^F
risonatore^M
resonador^M

connecting cable
câble^M de raccordement^M
Anschlusskabel^N
cavo^M di collegamento^M
cable^M de conexión^F

jack plug
fiche^F pour jack^M
Stecker^M
spinotto^M
clavija^F

loudspeaker
enceinte^F acoustique
Lautsprecherbox^F
cassa^F acustica
altavoz^M

right channel
canal^M droit
rechter Kanal^M
canale^M destro
canal^M derecho

left channel
canal^M gauche
linker Kanal^M
canale^M sinistro
canal^M izquierdo

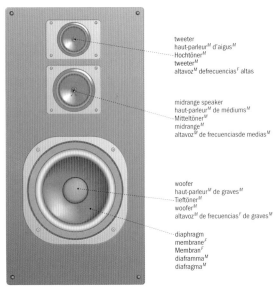

tweeter
haut-parleur^M d'aigus^M
Hochtöner^M
tweeter^M
altavoz^M defrecuencias^F altas

midrange speaker
haut-parleur^M de médiums^M
Mitteltöner^M
midrange^M
altavoz^M de frecuenciasde medias^M

speaker cover
treillis^M
Abdeckung^F
griglia^F
rejilla^F protectora

woofer
haut-parleur^M de graves^M
Tieftöner^M
woofer^M
altavoz^M de frecuencias^F de graves^M

diaphragm
membrane^F
Membran^F
diaframma^M
diafragma^M

mini stereo sound system

minichaine^F stéréo | Mini-HiFi^F-System^N | mini impianto^M hi-fi | mini-cadena^F estéreo

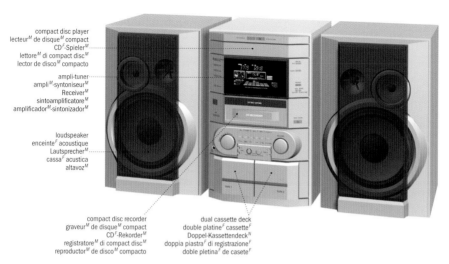

compact disc player
lecteur^M de disque^M compact
CD^F-Spieler^M
lettore^M di compact disc^M
lector de disco^M compacto

ampli-tuner
ampli^M-syntoniseur^M
Receiver^M
sintoamplificatore^M
amplificador^M-sintonizador^M

loudspeaker
enceinte^F acoustique
Lautsprecher^M
cassa^F acustica
altavoz^M

compact disc recorder
graveur^M de disque^M compact
CD^F-Rekorder^M
registratore^M di compact disc^M
reproductor^M de disco^M compacto

dual cassette deck
double platine^F cassette^F
Doppel-Kassettendeck^N
doppia piastra^F di registrazione^F
doble pletina^F de casete^F

portable sound systems

appareils^M de son^M portatifs | tragbare Tonwiedergabesysteme^N | riproduttori^M portatili | sistemas^M de sonido^M portátiles

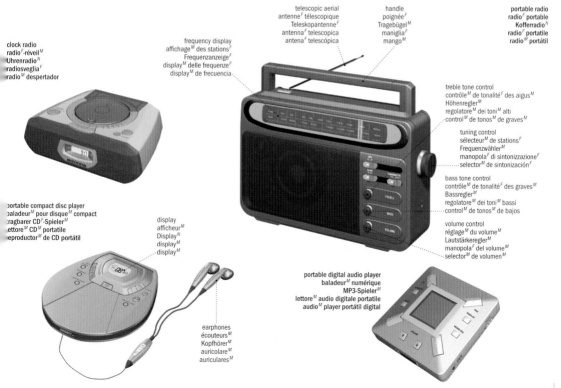

clock radio
radio^F-réveil^M
Uhrenradio^N
radiosveglia^F
radio^M despertador

frequency display
affichage^M des stations^F
Frequenzanzeige^F
display^M delle frequenze^F
display^M de frecuencia

telescopic aerial
antenne^F télescopique
Teleskopantenne^F
antenna^F telescopica
antena^F telescópica

handle
poignée^F
Tragebügel^M
maniglia^F
mango^M

portable radio
radio^F portable
Kofferradio^N
radio^F portatile
radio^M portátil

treble tone control
contrôle^M de tonalité^F des aigus^M
Höhenregler^M
regolatore^M dei toni^M alti
control^M de tonos^M de graves^M

tuning control
sélecteur^M de stations^F
Frequenzwähler^M
manopola^F di sintonizzazione^F
selector^M de sintonización^F

bass tone control
contrôle^M de tonalité^F des graves^M
Bassregler^M
regolatore^M dei toni^M bassi
control^M de tonos^M de bajos^M

portable compact disc player
baladeur^M pour disque^M compact
tragbarer CD^F-Spieler^M
lettore^M CD^M portatile
reproductor^M de CD portátil

display
afficheur^M
Display^N
display^M
display^M

volume control
réglage^M du volume^M
Lautstärkeregler^M
manopola^F del volume^M
selector^M de volumen^M

portable digital audio player
baladeur^M numérique
MP3-Spieler^M
lettore^M audio digitale portatile
audio^M player portátil digital

earphones
écouteurs^M
Kopfhörer^M
auricolare^M
auriculares^M

COMMUNICATIONS AND OFFICE AUTOMATION

portable sound systems

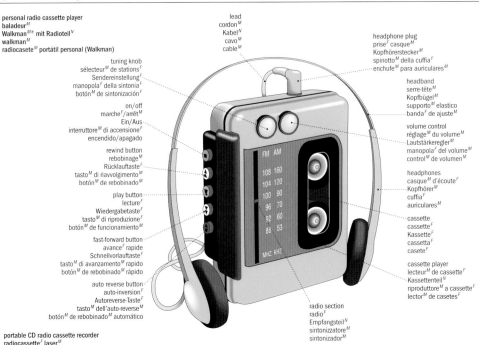

personal radio cassette player
baladeur^M
Walkman$^{M®}$ mit Radioteil^N
walkman^M
radiocasete^M portátil personal (Walkman)

lead
cordon^M
Kabel^N
cavo^M
cable^M

headphone plug
prise^F casque^M
Kopfhörerstecker^M
spinotto^M della cuffia^F
enchufe^M para auriculares^M

tuning knob
sélecteur^M de stations^F
Sendereinstellung^F
manopola^F della sintonia^F
botón^M de sintonización^F

headband
serre-tête^M
Kopfbügel^M
supporto^M elastico
banda^F de ajuste^M

on/off
marche^F/arrêt^M
Ein/Aus
interruttore^M di accensione^F
encendido/apagado

volume control
réglage^M du volume^M
Lautstärkeregler^M
manopola^F del volume^M
control^M de volumen^M

rewind button
rebobinage^M
Rücklauftaste^F
tasto^M di riavvolgimento^M
botón^M de rebobinado^M

headphones
casque^M d'écoute^F
Kopfhörer^M
cuffia^F
auriculares^M

play button
lecture^F
Wiedergabetaste^F
tasto^M di riproduzione^F
botón^M de funcionamiento^M

cassette
cassette^F
Kassette^F
cassetta^F
casete^F

fast-forward button
avance^F rapide
Schnellvorlauftaste^F
tasto^M di avanzamento^M rapido
botón^M de rebobinado^M rápido

cassette player
lecteur^M de cassette^F
Kassettenteil^N
riproduttore^M a cassette^F
lector^M de casetes^F

auto reverse button
auto-inversion^F
Autoreverse-Taste^F
tasto^M dell'auto-reverse^M
botón^M de rebobinado^M automático

radio section
radio^F
Empfangsteil^N
sintonizzatore^M
sintonizador^M

portable CD radio cassette recorder
radiocassette^F laser^M
Radiorecorder^M mit CD-Spieler^M
radioregistratore^M con compact disc^M
radiocasete^M con lector^M de disco^M compacto

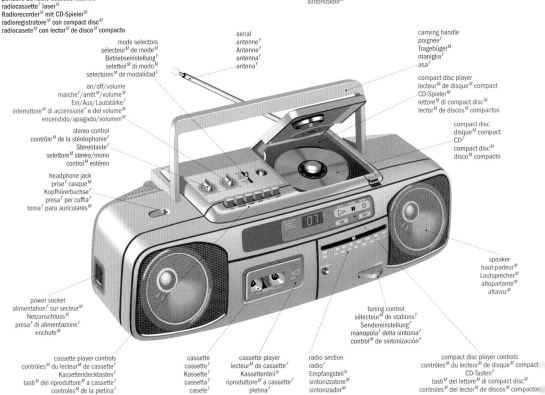

mode selectors
sélecteur^M de mode^M
Betriebseinstellung^F
selettori^M di modo^M
selectores^M de modalidad^F

aerial
antenne^F
Antenne^F
antenna^F
antena^F

carrying handle
poignée^F
Tragebügel^M
maniglia^F
asa^F

on/off/volume
marche^F/arrêt^M/volume^M
Ein/Aus/Lautstärke^F
interruttore^M di accensione^F e del volume^M
encendido/apagado/volumen^M

compact disc player
lecteur^M de disque^M compact
CD-Spieler^M
lettore^M di compact disc^M
lector^M de discos^M compactos

stereo control
contrôle^M de la stéréophonie^F
Stereotaste^F
selettore^M stereo/mono
control^M estéreo

compact disc
disque^M compact
CD^F
compact disc^M
disco^M compacto

headphone jack
prise^F casque^M
Kopfhörerbuchse^F
presa^F per cuffia^F
toma^F para auriculares^M

power socket
alimentation^F sur secteur^M
Netzanschluss^M
presa^F di alimentazione^F
enchufe^M

tuning control
sélecteur^M de stations^F
Sendereinstellung^F
manopola^F della sintonia^F
control^M de sintonización^F

speaker
haut-parleur^M
Lautsprecher^M
altoparlante^M
altavoz^M

cassette player controls
contrôles^M du lecteur^M de cassette^F
Kassettendecktasten^F
tasti^M del riproduttore^M a cassette^F
controles^M de la pletina^F

cassette
cassette^F
Kassette^F
cassetta^F
casete^F

cassette player
lecteur^M de cassette^F
Kassettenteil^N
riproduttore^M a cassette^F
pletina^F

radio section
radio^F
Empfangsteil^N
sintonizzatore^M
sintonizador^M

compact disc player controls
contrôles^M du lecteur^M de disque^M compact
CD-Tasten^F
tasti^M del lettore^M di compact disc^M
controles^M del lector^M de discos^M compactos

communication by telephone

communication^F par téléphone^M | Telefonieren^N | comunicazione^F via telefono^M | comunicación^F por teléfono^M

mobile telephone
téléphone^M portable
Handy^N
telefono^M cellulare
teléfono^M celular

display
afficheur^M
Display^N
display^M
display^M

speaker
haut-parleur^M
Lautsprecher^M
altoparlante^M
parlante^M

aerial
antenne^F
Antenne^F
antenna^F
antena^F

numeric pager
téléavertisseur^M numérique
Pager^M
cercapersone^M
buscapersonas^M

belt clip
pince^F de ceinture^F
Gürtelclip^M
gancio^M della cintura^F
pinza^F de cinturón^M

selection key
touche^F de sélection^F
Wahltaste^F
tasto^M di selezione^F
tecla^F de selección^F

talk key
touche^F d'appel^M
Ruftaste^F
tasto^M di chiamata^F
tecla^F de llamada^F

display
afficheur^M
Display^N
display^M
display^M

alphanumeric keypad
clavier^M alphanumérique
alphanumerische Tastatur^F
tastierino^M alfanumerico
teclado^M alfanumérico

power key
interrupteur^M
Ausschalter^M
interruttore^M
interruptor^M

sliding cover
clapet^M
verschiebbarer Tastaturschutz^M
coperchio^M scorrevole
tapa^F deslizante

scroll wheel
roulette^F de défilement^M
Scrollrad^N
manopola^F di scorrimento^M
rueda^F de corrimiento^M

read button
touche^F de lecture^F
Lesetaste^F
tasto^M di lettura^F
botón^M de lectura^F

microphone
microphone^M
Mikrofon^N
microfono^M
micrófono^M

end key
touche^F de fin^F d'appel^M
Ende-Taste^F
tasto^M di fine^F chiamata^F
tecla^F de final^F de llamada^F

select button
touche^F de sélection^F
Wahltaste^F
tasto^M di selezione^F
botón^M de selección^F

menu button
touche^F de menu^M
Menütaste^F
tasto^M del menu^M
botón^M del menú^M

telephone
poste^M téléphonique
Telefonapparat^M
apparecchio^M telefonico
teléfono^M

receiver
récepteur^M
Hörmuschel^F
ricevitore^M
receptor^M

display
afficheur^M
Display^N
display^M
display^M

on/off light
voyant^M de mise^F en circuit^M
An-/Aus-Kontrolllampe^F
spia^F luminosa di accensione^F/spegnimento^M
luz^F de encendido/apagado

handset
combiné^M
Hörer^M
microtelefono^M
auricular^M

receiver volume control
commande^F de volume^M du récepteur^M
Lautstärkeregler^M für den Hörer^M
regolatore^M del volume^M di ricezione^F
control^M de volumen^M del auricular^M

transmitter
microphone^M
Sprechmuschel^F
microfono^M
transmisor^M

display setting
réglage^M de l'afficheur^M
Displayeinstellung^F
regolatore^M del display^M
ajuste^M del display^M

ringing volume control
commande^F de volume^M de la sonnerie^F
Lautstärkeregler^M für den Rufton^M
regolatore^M del volume^M e della suoneria^F
control^M de volumen^M del timbre^M

handset flex
cordon^M de combiné^M
Schnur^F
cordone^M del microtelefono^M
cable^M del auricular^M

push buttons
clavier^M
Tasten^F
tastiera^F
teclado^M

telephone list
répertoire^M téléphonique
Rufnummernregister^N
rubrica^F telefonica
agenda^F telefónica

automatic dialling index
index^M de composition^F automatique
Rufnummernregister^N für automatische Wahl^F
tasti^M di chiamata^F automatica
marcador^M automático

memory button
commande^F mémoire^F
Speichertaste^F
tasto^M di memorizzazione^F
botón^M de memoria^F

function selectors
sélecteurs^M de fonctions^F
Funktionswahltaste^F
selettori^M di funzione^F
selectores^M de funciones^F

COMMUNICATIONS AND OFFICE AUTOMATION

communication by telephone

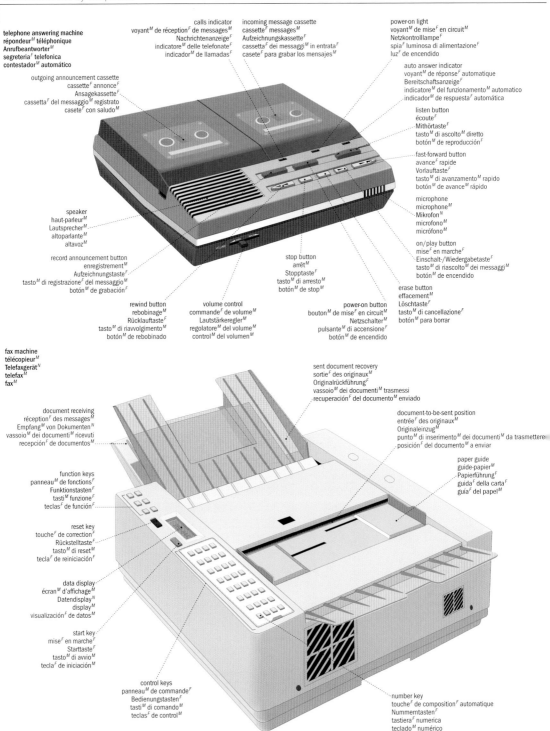

telephone answering machine
répondeur^M **téléphonique**
Anrufbeantworter^M
segreteria^F **telefonica**
contestador^M **automático**

calls indicator
voyant^M de réception^F de messages^M
Nachrichtenanzeige^F
indicatore^M delle telefonate^F
indicador^M de llamadas^F

incoming message cassette
cassette^F messages^M
Aufzeichnungskassette^F
cassetta^F dei messaggi^M in entrata^F
casete^F para grabar los mensajes^M

power-on light
voyant^M de mise^F en circuit^M
Netzkontrolllampe^F
spia^F luminosa di alimentazione^F
luz^F de encendido

outgoing announcement cassette
cassette^F annonce^F
Ansagekassette^F
cassetta^F del messaggio^M registrato
casete^F con saludo^M

auto answer indicator
voyant^M de réponse^F automatique
Bereitschaftsanzeige^F
indicatore^M del funzionamento^M automatico
indicador^M de respuesta^F automática

listen button
écoute^F
Mithörtaste^F
tasto^M di ascolto^M diretto
botón^M de reproducción^F

fast-forward button
avance^F rapide
Vorlauftaste^F
tasto^M di avanzamento^M rapido
botón^M de avance^M rápido

microphone
microphone^M
Mikrofon^N
microfono^M
micrófono^M

speaker
haut-parleur^M
Lautsprecher^M
altoparlante^M
altavoz^M

on/play button
mise^F en marche^F
Einschalt-/Wiedergabetaste^F
tasto^M di riascolto^M dei messaggi^M
botón^M de encendido

record announcement button
enregistrement^M
Aufzeichnungstaste^F
tasto^M di registrazione^F del messaggio^M
botón^M de grabación^F

stop button
arrêt^M
Stopptaste^F
tasto^M di arresto^M
botón^M de stop^M

erase button
effacement^M
Löschtaste^F
tasto^M di cancellazione^F
botón^M para borrar

rewind button
rebobinage^M
Rücklauftaste^F
tasto^M di riavvolgimento^M
botón^M de rebobinado

volume control
commande^F de volume^M
Lautstärkeregler^M
regolatore^M del volume^M
control^M del volumen^M

power-on button
bouton^M de mise^F en circuit^M
Netzschalter^M
pulsante^F di accensione^F
botón^M de encendido

fax machine
télécopieur^M
Telefaxgerät^N
telefax^M
fax^M

sent document recovery
sortie^F des originaux^M
Originalrückführung^F
vassoio^M dei documenti^M trasmessi
recuperación^F del documento^M enviado

document receiving
réception^F des messages^M
Empfang^M von Dokumenten^N
vassoio^M dei documenti^M ricevuti
recepción^F de documentos^M

document-to-be-sent position
entrée^F des originaux^M
Originaleinzug^M
punto^M di inserimento^M dei documenti^M da trasmettere
posición^F del documento^M a enviar

paper guide
guide-papier^M
Papierführung^F
guida^F della carta^F
guía^F del papel^M

function keys
panneau^M de fonctions^F
Funktionstasten^F
tasti^M funzione^F
teclas^F de función^F

reset key
touche^F de correction^F
Rückstelltaste^F
tasto^M di reset^M
tecla^F de reiniciación^F

data display
écran^M d'affichage^M
Datendisplay^N
display^M
visualización^F de datos^M

start key
mise^F en marche^F
Starttaste^F
tasto^M di avvio^M
tecla^F de iniciación^F

control keys
panneau^M de commande^F
Bedienungstasten^F
tasti^M di comando^M
teclas^F de control^M

number key
touche^F de composition^F automatique
Nummerntasten^F
tastiera^F numerica
teclado^M numérico

personal computer

micro-ordinateur^M | Personalcomputer^M | personal computer^M | ordenador^M personal

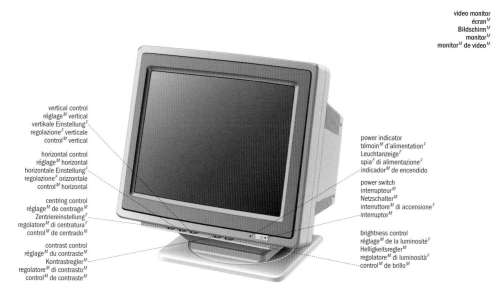

video monitor
écran^M
Bildschirm^M
monitor^M
monitor^M de vídeo^M

vertical control
réglage^M vertical
vertikale Einstellung^F
regolazione^F verticale
control^M vertical

horizontal control
réglage^M horizontal
horizontale Einstellung^F
regolazione^F orizzontale
control^M horizontal

centring control
réglage^M de centrage^M
Zentriereinstellung^F
regolatore^M di centratura^F
control^M de centrado^M

contrast control
réglage^M du contraste^M
Kontrastregler^M
regolatore^M di contrasto^M
control^M de contraste^M

power indicator
témoin^M d'alimentation^F
Leuchtanzeige^F
spia^F di alimentazione^F
indicador^M de encendido

power switch
interrupteur^M
Netzschalter^M
interruttore^M di accensione^F
interruptor^M

brightness control
réglage^M de la luminosité^F
Helligkeitsregler^M
regolatore^M di luminosità^F
control^M de brillo^M

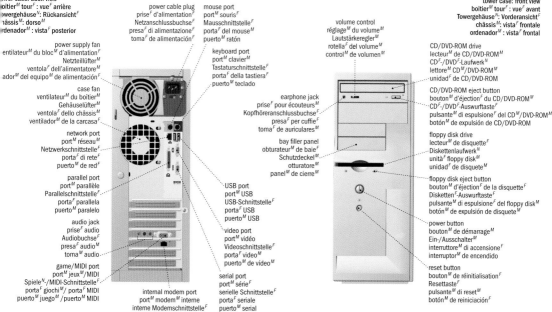

tower case: back view
boîtier^M tour^F : vue^F arrière
Towergehäuse^N: Rückansicht^F
chässis^M: dorso^M
ordenador^M : vista^F posterior

power supply fan
ventilateur^M du bloc^M d'alimentation^F
Netzteillüfter^M
ventola^F dell'alimentatore^M
ventilador^M del equipo^M de alimentación^F

case fan
ventilateur^M du boîtier^M
Gehäuselüfter^M
ventola^F dello chässis^M
ventilador^M de la carcasa^F

network port
port^M réseau^M
Netzwerkschnittstelle^F
porta^F di rete^F
puerto^M de red^F

parallel port
port^M parallèle
Parallelschnittstelle^F
porta^F parallela
puerto^M paralelo

audio jack
prise^F audio
Audiobuchse^F
presa^F audio^M
toma^M audio

game/MIDI port
port^M jeux^M/MIDI
Spiele^N-/MIDI-Schnittstelle^F
porta^F giochi^M/ porta^F MIDI
puerto^M juego^M /puerto^M MIDI

power cable plug
prise^F d'alimentation^F
Netzanschlussbuchse^F
presa^F di alimentazione^F
toma^F de alimentación^F

internal modem port
port^M modem^M interne
interne Modemschnittstelle^F
porta^F del modem^M interno
puerto^M de módem^M interno

mouse port
port^M souris^F
Mausschnittstelle^F
porta^F del mouse^M
puerto^M ratón

keyboard port
port^M clavier^M
Tastaturschnittstelle^F
porta^F della tastiera^F
puerto^M teclado

earphone jack
prise^F pour écouteurs^M
Kopfhöreranschlussbuchse^F
presa^F per cuffie^F
toma^F de auriculares^M

bay filler panel
obturateur^M de baie^F
Schutzdeckel^M
otturatore^M
panel^M de cierre^M

USB port
port^M USB
USB-Schnittstelle^F
porta^F USB
puerto^M USB

video port
port^M vidéo
Videoschnittstelle^F
porta^F video^M
puerto^M de vídeo^M

serial port
port^M série^F
serielle Schnittstelle^F
porta^F seriale
puerto^M serial

volume control
réglage^M du volume^M
Lautstärkeregler^M
rotella^F del volume^M
control^M de volumen^M

tower case: front view
boîtier^M tour^F : vue^F avant
Towergehäuse^N: Vorderansicht^F
chässis^M: vista^F frontale
ordenador^M : vista^F frontal

CD/DVD-ROM drive
lecteur^M de CD/DVD-ROM^M
CD^F-/DVD^F-Laufwerk^N
lettore^M CD^M/DVD-ROM^M
unidad^F de CD/DVD-ROM

CD/DVD-ROM eject button
bouton^M d'éjection^F du CD/DVD-ROM^M
CD^F-/DVD^F-Auswurftaste^F
pulsante^M di espulsione^F del CD^M/DVD-ROM^M
botón^M de expulsión de CD/DVD-ROM

floppy disk drive
lecteur^M de disquette^F
Diskettenlaufwerk^N
unità^F floppy disk^M
unidad^F de disquete^M

floppy disk eject button
bouton^M d'éjection^F de la disquette^F
Disketten^F-Auswurftaste^F
pulsante^M di espulsione^F del floppy disk^M
botón^M de expulsión de disquete^M

power button
bouton^M de démarrage^M
Ein-/Ausschalter^M
interruttore^M di accensione^F
interruptor^M de encendido

reset button
bouton^M de réinitialisation^F
Resettaste^F
pulsante^M di reset^M
botón^M de reiniciación^F

input devices

périphériques[M] d'entrée[F] | Eingabegeräte[N] | dispositivi[M] di entrata[F] | unidades[F] de entrada[F] de información[F]

keyboard and pictograms
clavier[M] et pictogrammes[M]
Tastatur[F] und Piktogramme[N]
tastiera[F] e pittogrammi[M]
teclado[M] y pictogramas[M]

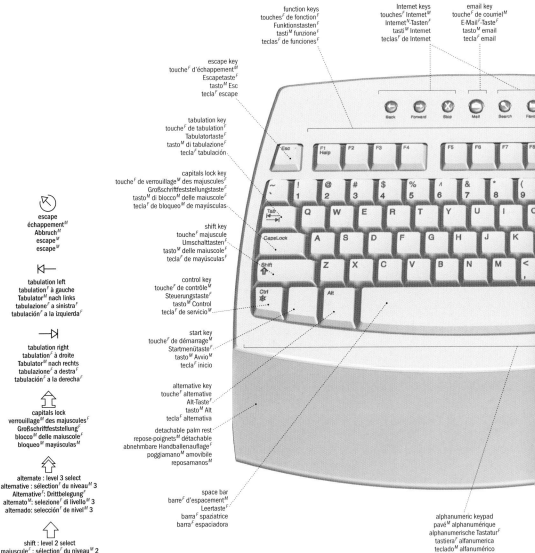

function keys
touches[F] de fonction[F]
Funktionstasten[F]
tasti[M] funzione[F]
teclas[F] de funciones[F]

Internet keys
touches[F] Internet[M]
Internet[N]-Tasten[F]
tasti[M] Internet
teclas[F] de Internet

email key
touche[F] de courriel[M]
E-Mail[F]-Taste[F]
tasto[M] email
tecla[F] email

escape key
touche[F] d'échappement[M]
Escapetaste[F]
tasto[M] Esc
tecla[F] escape

tabulation key
touche[F] de tabulation[F]
Tabulatortaste[F]
tasto[M] di tabulazione[F]
tecla[F] tabulación

capitals lock key
touche[F] de verrouillage[M] des majuscules[F]
Großschriftfeststellungstaste[F]
tasto[M] di blocco[M] delle maiuscole[F]
tecla[F] de bloqueo[M] de mayúsculas

shift key
touche[F] majuscule[F]
Umschalttasten[F]
tasto[M] delle maiuscole[F]
tecla[F] de mayúsculas[F]

control key
touche[F] de contrôle[M]
Steuerungstaste[F]
tasto[M] Control
tecla[F] de servicio[M]

start key
touche[F] de démarrage[M]
Startmenütaste[F]
tasto[M] Avvio[M]
tecla[F] inicio

alternative key
touche[F] alternative
Alt-Taste[F]
tasto[M] Alt
tecla[F] alternativa

detachable palm rest
repose-poignets[M] détachable
abnehmbare Handballenauflage[F]
poggiamano[M] amovibile
reposamanos[M]

space bar
barre[F] d'espacement[M]
Leertaste[F]
barra[F] spaziatrice
barra[F] espaciadora

alphanumeric keypad
pavé[M] alphanumérique
alphanumerische Tastatur[F]
tastiera[F] alfanumerica
teclado[M] alfanumérico

escape
échappement[M]
Abbruch[M]
escape[M]
escape[M]

tabulation left
tabulation[F] à gauche
Tabulator[M] nach links
tabulazione[F] a sinistra[F]
tabulación[F] a la izquierda[F]

tabulation right
tabulation[F] à droite
Tabulator[M] nach rechts
tabulazione[F] a destra[F]
tabulación[F] a la derecha[F]

capitals lock
verrouillage[M] des majuscules[F]
Großschriftfeststellung[F]
blocco[M] delle maiuscole[F]
bloqueo[M] mayúsculas[M]

alternate : level 3 select
alternative[F] : sélection[F] du niveau[M] 3
Alternative[F]: Drittbelegung[F]
alternato[M]: selezione[F] di livello[M] 3
alternado: selección[F] de nivel[M] 3

shift : level 2 select
majuscule[F] : sélection[F] du niveau[M] 2
Großschriftumschaltung[F]: Zweitbelegung[F]
maiuscola[F]: selezione[F] di livello[M] 2
mayúscula[F] : selección[F] de nivel[M] 2

control : group select
contrôle[M] : sélection[F] de groupe[M]
Steuerung[F]: Gruppenwahl[F]
controllo[M]: selezione[F] di gruppo[M]
control[M] : selección[F] de grupo[M]

control
contrôle[M]
Steuerung[F]
controllo[M]
control[M]

alternate
alternative
Alternative[F]
alternato[M]
alternativa[F]

space
espace[F]
Leerzeichen[N]
spazio[M]
espacio[M]

non-breaking space
espace[F] insécable
geschütztes Leerzeichen[N]
spazio[M] unificatore
espacio[M] sin pausa[F]

print screen/system request key
touche[F] d'impression[F] de l'écran[M]/d'appel[M] système[M]
Taste[F] Druck[M]/Systemabfrage[F]
tasto[M] di stampa[F]/chiamata[M] sistema[M]
tecla[F] de impresión[M] pantalla/petición[F] del sistema[F]

indicator lights
voyants[M]
Kontrollleuchten[F]
spie[F] luminose
luces[F] de estado[M]

insert key
touche[F] d'insertion[F]
Einfügetaste[F]
tasto[M] Ins
insert[M]

backspace key
touche[F] d'effacement[M]
Taste[F] löschender Rückschritt[M]
tasto[M] backspace
tecla[F] de retroceso[M]

scrolling lock key
touche[F] d'arrêt[M] du défilement[M]
Scrollen[N]-Feststelltaste[F]
tasto[M] di arresto[M] e di scorrimento[M]
bloqueo[M] corrimiento[M]

pause/break key
touche[F] de pause[F]/d'interruption[F]
Taste[F] Pause[F]/Unterbrechung[F]
tasto[M] di pausa[F]/interruzione[F]
tecla[F] pausa

home key
touche[F] début[M]
Taste[F] Cursor[M] an Zeilenanfang[M]
tasto[M] Home
inicio[M]

numeric lock key
touche[F] de verrouillage[M] numérique
Taste[F] numerischer Block[M]
tasto[M] di blocco[M] numerico
tecla[F] bloqueo[M] numérico

page up key
touche[F] page[F] précédente
Taste[F] vorherige Seite[F]
tasto[M] di pagina[F] su
página[F] atrás

page down key
touche[F] page[F] suivante
Taste[F] nächste Seite[F]
tasto[M] di pagina[F] giù
página[F] adelante

enter key
touche[F] de retour[M]
Eingabetaste[F]
tasto[M] Invio[M]
tecla[F] de enter

end key
touche[F] fin[F]
Taste[F] Ende[N]
tasto[M] Fine[F]
fin[M]

numeric keypad
pavé[M] numérique
numerisches Tastenfeld[N]
tastierino[M] numerico
teclado[M] numérico

cursor movement keys
touches[F] de déplacement[M] du curseur[M]
Richtungstasten[F]
tasti[M] del cursore[M]
teclas[F] de cursor

delete key
touche[F] de suppression[F]
Löschtaste[F]
tasto[M] di cancellazione[F]
suprimir

enter key
touche[F] de retour[M]
Eingabetaste[F]
tasto[M] Invio[M]
tecla[F] de enter

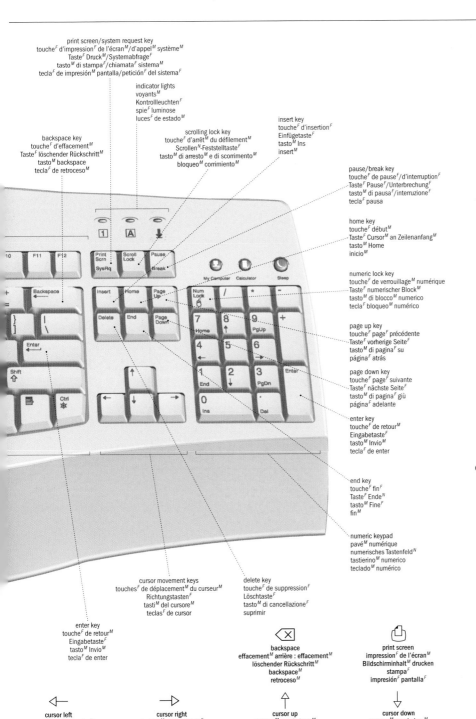

pause
pause[F]
Pause[F]
pausa[F]
pausa[F]

break
interruption[F]
Unterbrechung[F]
interruzione[F]
pausa[F]

numeric lock
verrouillage[M] numérique
numerischer Block[M]
blocco[M] numerico
bloqueo[M] numérico

scrolling
défilement[M]
Scrollen[N]
scorrimento[M]
desplazamiento[M]

insert
insertion[F]
Einfügen[N]
inserimento[M]
insertar

delete
suppression[F]
Löschen[N]
cancellazione[F]
borrar

home
début[M]
Cursor[M] an Zeilenanfang[M]
home[F]
inicio[M]

end
fin[F]
Cursor[M] an Zeilenende[N]
fine[F]
fin[M]

page up
page[F] précédente
vorherige Seite[F]
pagina[F] precedente
ventana[F] arriba

backspace
effacement[M] arrière : effacement[M]
löschender Rückschritt[M]
backspace
retroceso[M]

print screen
impression[F] de l'écran[M]
Bildschirminhalt[M] drucken
stampa[F]
impresión[F] pantalla[F]

page down
page[F] suivante
nächste Seite[F]
pagina[F] successiva
ventana[F] abajo

cursor left
curseur[M] vers la gauche[F]
Cursor[M] nach links
cursore[M] a sinistra[F]
cursor[M] hacia la izquierda[F]

cursor right
curseur[M] vers la droite[F]
Cursor[M] nach rechts
cursore[M] a destra[F]
cursor[M] hacia la derecha[F]

cursor up
curseur[M] vers le haut[M]
Cursor[M] nach oben
cursore[M] in alto[M]
cursor[M] arriba

cursor down
curseur[M] vers le bas[M]
Cursor[M] nach unten
cursore[M] in basso[M]
cursor[M] abajo

return
retour[M]
Eingabe[F]
invio[M]
retorno[M]

input devices

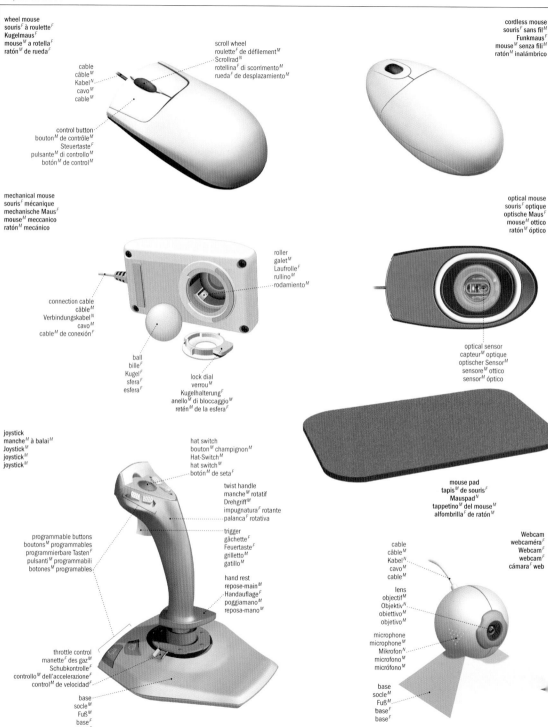

wheel mouse
souris^F à roulette^F
Kugelmaus^F
mouse^M a rotella^F
ratón^M de rueda^F

cable
câble^M
Kabel^N
cavo^M
cable^M

scroll wheel
roulette^F de défilement^M
Scrollrad^N
rotellina^F di scorrimento^M
rueda^F de desplazamiento^M

cordless mouse
souris^F sans fil^M
Funkmaus^F
mouse^M senza fili^M
ratón^M inalámbrico

control button
bouton^M de contrôle^M
Steuertaste^F
pulsante^M di controllo^M
botón^M de control^M

mechanical mouse
souris^F mécanique
mechanische Maus^F
mouse^M meccanico
ratón^M mecánico

optical mouse
souris^F optique
optische Maus^F
mouse^M ottico
ratón^M óptico

roller
galet^M
Laufrolle^F
rullino^M
rodamiento^M

connection cable
câble^M
Verbindungskabel^N
cavo^M
cable^M de conexión^F

ball
bille^F
Kugel^F
sfera^F
esfera^F

lock dial
verrou^M
Kugelhalterung^F
anello^M di bloccaggio^M
retén^M de la esfera^F

optical sensor
capteur^M optique
optischer Sensor^M
sensore^M ottico
sensor^M óptico

joystick
manche^M à balai^M
Joystick^M
joystick^M
joystick^M

hat switch
bouton^M champignon^M
Hat-Switch^M
hat switch^M
botón^M de seta^F

twist handle
manche^M rotatif
Drehgriff^M
impugnatura^F rotante
palanca^F rotativa

programmable buttons
boutons^M programmables
programmierbare Tasten^F
pulsanti^M programmabili
botones^M programables

trigger
gâchette^F
Feuertaste^F
grilletto^M
gatillo^M

hand rest
repose-main^M
Handauflage^F
poggiamano^M
reposa-mano^M

mouse pad
tapis^M de souris^F
Mauspad^N
tappetino^M del mouse^M
alfombrilla^F de ratón^M

Webcam
webcaméra^F
Webcam^F
webcam^F
cámara^F web

cable
câble^M
Kabel^N
cavo^M
cable^M

lens
objectif^M
Objektiv^N
obiettivo^M
objetivo^M

throttle control
manette^F des gaz^M
Schubkontrolle^F
controllo^M dell'accelerazione^F
control^M de velocidad^F

microphone
microphone^M
Mikrofon^N
microfono^M
micrófono^M

base
socle^M
Fuß^M
base^F
base^F

base
socle^M
Fuß^M
base^F
base^F

COMMUNICATIONS AND OFFICE AUTOMATION

output devices

périphériques^M de sortie^F | Ausgabegeräte^N | dispositivi^M di uscita^F | unidades^F de salida^F de información^F

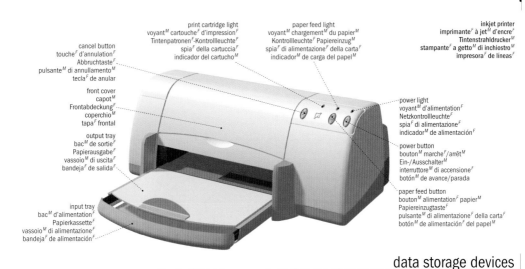

print cartridge light
voyant^M cartouche^F d'impression^F
Tintenpatronen^F-Kontrollleuchte^F
spia^F della cartuccia^F
indicador del cartucho^M

cancel button
touche^F d'annulation^F
Abbruchtaste^F
pulsante^M di annullamento^M
tecla^F de anular

front cover
capot^M
Frontabdeckung^F
coperchio^M
tapa^F frontal

output tray
bac^F de sortie^F
Papierausgabe^F
vassoio^M di uscita^F
bandeja^F de salida^F

input tray
bac^F d'alimentation^F
Papierkassette^F
vassoio^M di alimentazione^F
bandeja^F de alimentación^F

paper feed light
voyant^M chargement^M du papier^M
Kontrollleuchte^F Papiereinzug^M
spia^F di alimentazione^F della carta^F
indicador^M de carga del papel^M

inkjet printer
imprimante^F à jet^M d'encre^F
Tintenstrahldrucker^M
stampante^F a getto^M di inchiostro^M
impresora^F de líneas^F

power light
voyant^M d'alimentation^F
Netzkontrollleuchte^F
spia^F di alimentazione^F
indicador^M de alimentación^F

power button
bouton^M marche^F/arrêt^M
Ein-/Ausschalter^M
interruttore^M di accensione^F
botón^M de avance/parada

paper feed button
bouton^M alimentation^F papier^M
Papiereinzugtaste^F
pulsante^M di alimentazione^F della carta^F
botón^M de alimentación^F del papel^M

data storage devices

périphériques^M de stockage^M | Speichergeräte^N | dispositivi^M di memorizzazione^F dei dati^M | unidades^F de almacenamiento^F de información^F

removable hard disk drive
lecteur^M de disque^M dur amovible
externes Festplattenlaufwerk^N
unità^F hard disk^M estraibile
unidad^F de disco^M duro extraible

removable hard disk
disque^M dur amovible
herausnehmbare Festplatte^F
hard disk^M estraibile
disco^M duro extraible

cassette drive
lecteur^M de cassette^F
Kassettenlaufwerk^N
drive^M per cassette^F
unidad^F de casetes^F

cassette
cassette^F
Kassette^F
cassetta^F
casete^F

DVD recorder
graveur^M de DVD^M
DVD^F-Rekorder^M
registratore^M DVD^M
reproductor^M de DVD

disk
disque^M
Platte^F
disco^M
disco^M

hard disk drive
lecteur^M de disque^M dur
Festplattenlaufwerk^N
unità^F hard disk^M
unidad^F del disco^M duro

read/write head
tête^F de lecture^F/écriture^F
Schreib-/Lesekopf^M
testina^F di lettura^F/scrittura^F
cabeza^F de lectura^F/escritura^F

actuator arm
guide^M
Sucharm^M
braccio^M
brazo^M actuador

compact disc rewritable recorder
graveur^M de disque^M compact réinscriptible
Rewritable-Rekorder^M
registratore^M di compact disc^M riscrivibili
grabador^M de disco^M compacto regrabable

diskette, floppy disk
disquette^F
Diskette^F
floppy disk^M
disquete^M

access window
fenêtre^F de lecture^F
Zugriffsöffnung^F
finestra^F di accesso^M
ventana^F de acceso^M

protect tab
taquet^M de verrouillage^M
Schreibschutz^M
linguetta^F di protezione^F
lengüeta^F protectora

external floppy disk drive
lecteur^M de disquette^F externe
externes Diskettenlaufwerk^N
unità^F floppy disk^M esterna
unidad^F de disquete^M externo

shutter
volet^M
Verschluss^M
coperchio^M protettivo
obturador^M

Internet

Internet^M | Internet^N | Internet^F | Internet^M

URL (uniform resource locator)
adresse^F URL^F (localisateur^M universel de ressources^F)
URL-Adresse^F (vereinheitlichter Ressourcenzugriff^M)
URL (localizzatore^M universale di risorse^F)
URL localizador universal de recursos

communication protocol
protocole^M de communication^F
Kommunikationsprotokoll^N
protocollo^M di comunicazione^F
protocolo^M de comunicación^F

domain name
nom^M de domaine^M
Domainname^M
nome^M del dominio^M
nombre^M del dominio^M

file format
format^M du fichier^M
Dateiformat^N
formato^M del file^M
formato^M del archivo^M

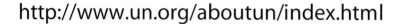

http://www.un.org/aboutun/index.html

double slash
double barre^F oblique
Doppelschrägstrich^M
doppio slash^M
doble barra^F oblicua

second-level domain
domaine^M de second niveau^M
Domain^F zweiten Grades^M
dominio^M di secondo livello^M
dominio^M de segundo nivel^M

file
fichier^M
Datei^F
file^M
archivo^M

server
serveur^M
Server^M
server^M
servidor^M

top-level domain
domaine^M de premier niveau^M
Toplevel^N-Domain^F
dominio^M di livello^M superiore
dominio^M de primer nivel^M

directory
répertoire^M
Ordner^M, Verzeichnis^N
directory^F
directorio^M

browser
navigateur^M
Browser^M
browser^M
navegador

microwave relay station
station^F-relais^M à micro-ondes^F
Mikrowellen^F-Relaisstation^F
stazione^F ripetitrice a microonde^F
estación^F repetidora de microondas^F

URL
adresse^F URL^F
URL-Adresse^F
URL
dirección URL^M

submarine line
ligne^F sous-marine
Tiefseekabel^N
linea^F sottomarina
línea^F submarina

hyperlinks
hyperliens^M
Hyperlinks^M
collegamenti^M ipertestuali
hipervínculos^M

telephone line
ligne^F téléphonique
Telefonleitung^F
linea^F telefonica
línea^F telefónica

email software
logiciel^M de courrier^M électronique
E-Mail^F-Software^F
software^M di posta^F elettronica
programa^M de correo^M electrónico

Internet user
internaute^F
Internet^N-Nutzer^M
utente^M di Internet^F
internauta^M

browser
navigateur^M
Browser^M
browser^M
navegador^M

router
routeur^M
Router^M
router^M
router^M

modem
modem^M
Modem^N
modem^M
módem^M

dedicated line
ligne^F dédiée
Standleitung^F
linea^F dedicata
línea^F reservada

desktop computer
ordinateur^M de bureau^M
Tischcomputer^M
computer^M da tavolo^M
ordenador^M de sobremesa

Internet uses

utilisations^F d'Internet^M | Internet^N-Nutzungen^F | impieghi^M di Internet^F | usos^M de Internet^M

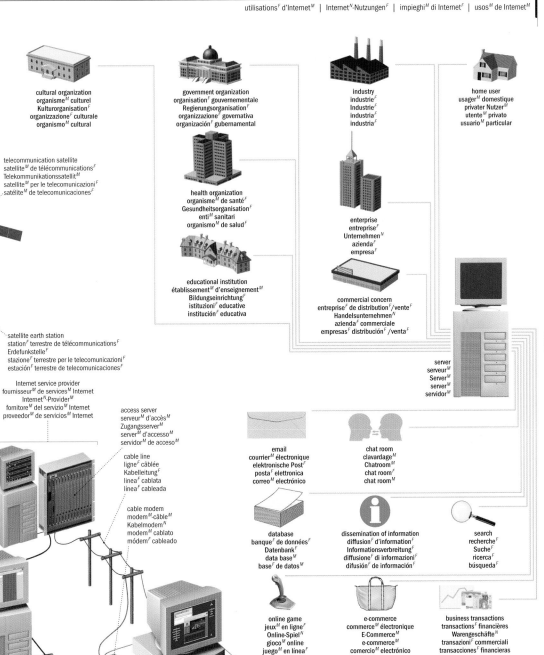

cultural organization
organisme^M culturel
Kulturorganisation^F
organizzazione^F culturale
organismo^M cultural

government organization
organisation^F gouvernementale
Regierungsorganisation^F
organizzazione^F governativa
organización^F gubernamental

industry
industrie^F
Industrie^F
industria^F
industria^F

home user
usager^M domestique
privater Nutzer^M
utente^M privato
usuario^M particular

telecommunication satellite
satellite^M de télécommunications^F
Telekommunikationssatellit^M
satellite^M per le telecomunicazioni^F
satélite^M de telecomunicaciones^F

health organization
organisme^M de santé^F
Gesundheitsorganisation^F
enti^M sanitari
organismo^M de salud^F

enterprise
entreprise^F
Unternehmen^N
azienda^F
empresa^F

educational institution
établissement^M d'enseignement^M
Bildungseinrichtung^F
istituzioni^F educative
institución^F educativa

commercial concern
entreprise^F de distribution^F/vente^F
Handelsunternehmen^N
azienda^F commerciale
empresas^F distribución^F/venta^F

satellite earth station
station^F terrestre de télécommunications^F
Erdefunkstelle^F
stazione^F terrestre per le telecomunicazioni^F
estación^F terrestre de telecomunicaciones^F

server
serveur^M
Server^M
server^M
servidor^M

Internet service provider
fournisseur^M de services^M Internet
Internet^N-Provider^M
fornitore^M del servizio^M Internet
proveedor^M de servicios^M Internet

access server
serveur^M d'accès^M
Zugangsserver^M
server^M d'accesso^M
servidor^M de acceso^M

email
courrier^M électronique
elektronische Post^F
posta^F elettronica
correo^M electrónico

chat room
clavardage^M
Chatroom^M
chat room^F
chat room^M

cable line
ligne^F câblée
Kabelleitung^F
linea^F cablata
línea^F cableada

cable modem
modem^M-câble^M
Kabelmodem^N
modem^M cablato
módem^F cableado

database
banque^F de données^F
Datenbank^F
data base^M
base^F de datos^M

dissemination of information
diffusion^F d'information^F
Informationsverbreitung^F
diffusione^F di informazioni^F
difusión^F de información^F

search
recherche^F
Suche^F
ricerca^F
búsqueda^F

online game
jeux^M en ligne^F
Online-Spiel^N
gioco^M online
juego^M en línea^F

e-commerce
commerce^M électronique
E-Commerce^M
e-commerce^M
comercio^M electrónico

business transactions
transactions^F financières
Warengeschäfte^N
transazioni^F commerciali
transacciones^F financieras

server
serveur^M
Server^M
server^M
servidor^M

laptop computer

ordinateur^M portable | Laptop^M | computer^M portatile | ordenador^M portátil

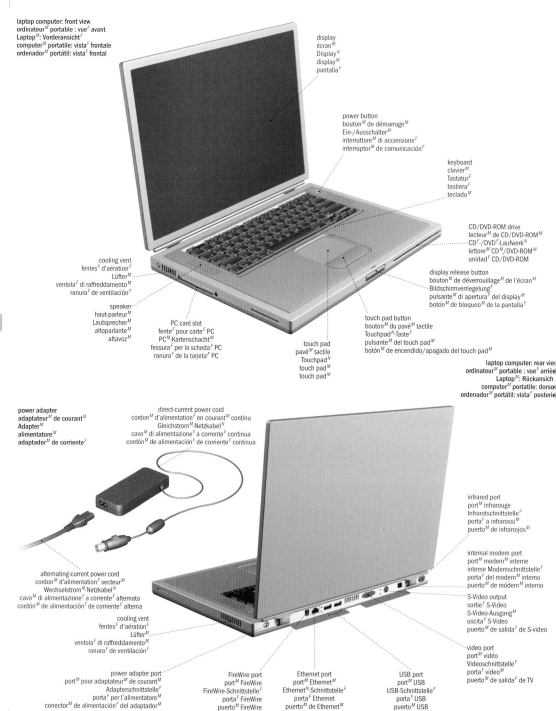

laptop computer: front view
ordinateur^M portable : vue^F avant
Laptop^M: Vorderansicht^F
computer^M portatile: vista^F frontale
ordenador^M portátil: vista^F frontal

display
écran^M
Display^N
display^M
pantalla^F

power button
bouton^M de démarrage^M
Ein-/Ausschalter^M
interruttore^M di accensione^F
interruptor^M de comunicación^F

keyboard
clavier^M
Tastatur^F
tastiera^F
teclado^M

CD/DVD-ROM drive
lecteur^M de CD/DVD-ROM^M
CD^F-/DVD^F-Laufwerk^N
lettore^M CD^M/DVD-ROM^M
unidad^F CD/DVD-ROM

cooling vent
fentes^F d'aération^F
Lüfter^M
ventola^F di raffreddamento^M
ranura^F de ventilación^F

display release button
bouton^M de déverrouillage^M de l'écran^M
Bildschirmverriegelung^F
pulsante^M di apertura^F del display^M
botón^M de bloqueo^M de la pantalla^F

speaker
haut-parleur^M
Lautsprecher^M
altoparlante^M
altavoz^M

PC card slot
fente^F pour carte^F PC
PC^M-Kartenschacht^M
fessura^F per la scheda^F PC
ranura^F de la tarjeta^F PC

touch pad button
bouton^M du pavé^M tactile
Touchpad^N-Taste^F
pulsante^M del touch pad^M
botón^M de encendido/apagado del touch pad^M

touch pad
pavé^M tactile
Touchpad^N
touch pad^M
touch pad^M

laptop computer: rear view
ordinateur^M portable : vue^F arrière
Laptop^M: Rückansicht
computer^M portatile: dorso
ordenador^M portátil: vista^F posterior

power adapter
adaptateur^M de courant^M
Adapter^M
alimentatore^M
adaptador^M de corriente^F

direct-current power cord
cordon^M d'alimentation^F en courant^M continu
Gleichstrom^M-Netzkabel^N
cavo^M di alimentazione^F a corrente^F continua
cordón^M de alimentación^F de corriente^F continua

infrared port
port^M infrarouge
Infrarotschnittstelle^F
porta^F a infrarossi^M
puerto^M de infrarrojos^M

internal modem port
port^M modem^M interne
interne Modemschnittstelle^F
porta^F del modem^M interno
puerto^M de módem^M interno

S-Video output
sortie^F S-Video
S-Video-Ausgang^M
uscita^F S-Video
puerto^M de salida^F de S-video

alternating-current power cord
cordon^M d'alimentation^F secteur^M
Wechselstrom^M-Netzkabel^N
cavo^M di alimentazione^F a corrente^F alternata
cordón^M de alimentación^F de corriente^F alterna

cooling vent
fentes^F d'aération^F
Lüfter^M
ventola^F di raffreddamento^M
ranura^F de ventilación^F

video port
port^M vidéo
Videoschnittstelle^F
porta^F video^M
puerto^M de salida^F de TV

power adapter port
port^M pour adaptateur^M de courant^M
Adapterschnittstelle^F
porta^F per l'alimentatore^M
conector^M de alimentación^F del adaptador^M

FireWire port
port^M FireWire
FireWire-Schnittstelle^F
porta^F FireWire
puerto^M FireWire

Ethernet port
port^M Ethernet^M
Ethernet^N-Schnittstelle^F
porta^F Ethernet
puerto^M de Ethernet^M

USB port
port^M USB
USB-Schnittstelle^F
porta^F USB
puerto^M USB

PDA

ordinateur^M de poche^F | Handheld-Computer^M | computer^M tascabile | ordenador^M de bolsillo^M

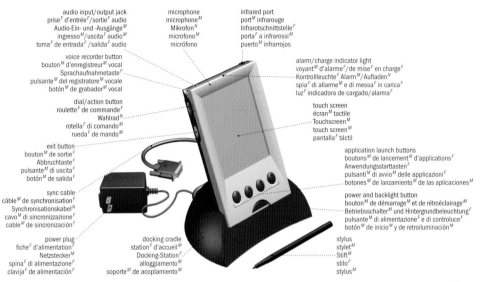

audio input/output jack
prise^F d'entrée^F/sortie^F audio
Audio-Ein- und -Ausgänge^M
ingresso^M/uscita^F audio^M
toma^F de entrada^F /salida^F audio

microphone
microphone^M
Mikrofon^N
microfono^M
micrófono

infrared port
port^M infrarouge
Infrarotschnittstelle^F
porta^F a infrarossi^M
puerto^M infrarrojos

voice recorder button
bouton^M d'enregistreur^M vocal
Sprachaufnahmetaste^F
pulsante^M del registratore^M vocale
botón^M de grabador^M vocal

alarm/charge indicator light
voyant^M d'alarme^F/de mise^F en charge^F
Kontrollleuchte^F Alarm^M/Aufladen^N
spia^F di allarme^M e di messa^F in carica^F
luz^F indicadora de cargado/alarma^F

dial/action button
roulette^F de commande^F
Wahlrad^N
rotella^F di comando^M
rueda^F de mando^M

touch screen
écran^M tactile
Touchscreen^M
touch screen^M
pantalla^F táctil

exit button
bouton^M de sortie^F
Abbruchtaste^F
pulsante^M di uscita^F
botón^M de salida^F

application launch buttons
boutons^M de lancement^M d'applications^F
Anwendungsstarttasten^F
pulsanti^M di avvio^M delle applicazioni^F
botones^M de lanzamiento^M de las aplicaciones^M

sync cable
câble^M de synchronisation^F
Synchronisationskabel^N
cavo^M di sincronizzazione^F
cable^M de sincronización^F

power and backlight button
bouton^M de démarrage^M et de rétroéclairage^M
Betriebsschalter^M und Hintergrundbeleuchtung^F
pulsante^M di alimentazione^F e di controluce^F
botón^M de inicio^M y de retroiluminación^M

power plug
fiche^F d'alimentation^F
Netzstecker^M
spina^F di alimentazione^F
clavija^F de alimentación^F

docking cradle
station^F d'accueil^M
Docking-Station^F
alloggiamento^M
soporte^M de acoplamiento^M

stylus
stylet^M
Stift^M
stilo^F
stylus^M

stationery

articles^M de bureau^M | Schreibwaren^F | articoli^M di cancelleria^F | artículos^M de escritorio^M

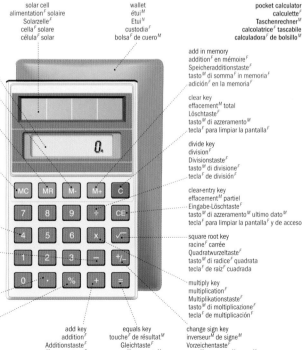

display
affichage^M
Anzeige^F
display^M
pantalla^F

solar cell
alimentation^F solaire
Solarzelle^F
cella^F solare
célula^F solar

wallet
étui^M
Etui^N
custodia^F
bolsa^F de cuero^M

pocket calculator
calculette^F
Taschenrechner^M
calcolatrice^F tascabile
calculadora^F de bolsillo^M

scientific calculator
calculatrice^F scientifique
wissenschaftlicher Taschenrechner^M
calcolatrice^F scientifica
calculadora^F científica

subtract from memory
soustraction^F en mémoire^F
Speichersubtraktionstaste^F
tasto^M di sottrazione^F in memoria^F
substracción^F de la memoria^F

add in memory
addition^F en mémoire^F
Speicheradditionstaste^F
tasto^M di somma^F in memoria^F
adición^F en la memoria^F

memory recall
rappel^M de mémoire^F
Speicheranzeigetaste^F
tasto^M di richiamo^M della memoria^F
retorno^M a la memoria^F

clear key
effacement^M total
Löschtaste^F
tasto^M di azzeramento^M
tecla^F para limpiar la pantalla^F

memory cancel
effacement^M de mémoire^F
Speicherlöschtaste^F
tasto^M di cancellazione^F della memoria^F
anulación^F de la memoria^F

divide key
division^F
Divisionstaste^F
tasto^M di divisione^F
tecla^F de división^F

printing calculator
calculatrice^F à imprimante^F
Tischrechner^M mit Druckerteil^N
calcolatrice^F da tavolo^M
calculadora^F con impresora^F

number key
touche^F numérique
Zifferntaste^F
tasto^M numerico
tecla^F de número^M

clear-entry key
effacement^M partiel
Eingabe-Löschtaste^F
tasto^M di azzeramento^M ultimo dato^M
tecla^F para limpiar la pantalla^F y de acceso

subtract key
soustraction^F
Subtraktionstaste^F
tasto^M di sottrazione^F
tecla^F de sustracción^F

square root key
racine^F carrée
Quadratwurzeltaste^F
tasto^M di radice^F quadrata
tecla^F de raíz^F cuadrada

decimal key
touche^F de décimale^F
Kommataste^F
tasto^M di punto^M decimale
tecla^F decimal

multiply key
multiplication^F
Multiplikationstaste^F
tasto^M di moltiplicazione^F
tecla^F de multiplicación^F

percent key
pourcentage^M
Prozenttaste^F
tasto^M di percentuale^F
tecla^F de porcentaje^M

add key
addition^F
Additionstaste^F
tasto^M di addizione^F
tecla^F de adición^F

equals key
touche^F de résultat^M
Gleichtaste^F
tasto^M di uguale^F
tecla^F de igualdad^F

change sign key
inverseur^M de signe^M
Vorzeichentaste^F
tasto^M di cambio^M segno^M
tecla^F de cambio^M de signo^M

stationery

for time use
pour l'emploi^M **du temps**^{M}
für die Terminplanung^F
per la gestione^F **del tempo**^{M}
para el empleo^M **del tiempo**^{M}

tear-off calendar
calendrier^M-mémorandum^M
Abreißkalender^M
calendario^M a fogli^M staccabili
calendario^M de sobremesa

calendar pad
bloc^M-éphéméride^F
Ringbuchkalender^M
calendario^M da tavolo^M
calendario^M de sobremesa

personal organizer
organiseur^M
Organizer^M
organizer^M
agenda^F electrónica

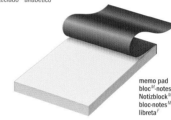

display
écran^M
Display^N
display^M
pantalla^F

appointment book
agenda^M
Terminkalender^M
agenda^F
agenda^F

alphabetical keypad
pavé^M alphabétique^F
alphabetische Tastatur^F
tastierino^M alfabetico
teclado^M alfabético

numeric keypad
pavé^M numérique^M
numerische Tastatur^F
tastierino^M numerico
teclado^M numérico

memo pad
bloc^M-notes^F
Notizblock^M
bloc-notes^M
libreta^F

---

for correspondence
pour la correspondance^F
für die Korrespondenz^F
per la corrispondenza^F
para la correspondencia^F

stamp pad
tampon^M encreur
Stempelkissen^N
tampone^M
cojín^M para sellos^M

rubber stamp
timbre^M caoutchouc^M
Stempel^M
timbro^M di gomma^F
sello^M de goma^F

numbering stamp
numéroteur^M
Nummerierstempel^M
numeratore^M
foliador^M

date stamp
timbre^M dateur
Datumstempel^M
datario^M
fechador^M

desk tray
boite^F à courrier^M
Dokumentenablage^F
vaschetta^F portacorrispondenza
bandeja^F de correspondencia^F

rotary file
fichier^M rotatif
Drehkartei^F
schedario^M rotativo
fichero^M giratorio

telephone index
répertoire^M téléphonique
Telefonnummernverzeichnis^N
rubrica^F telefonica
agenda^F telefónica

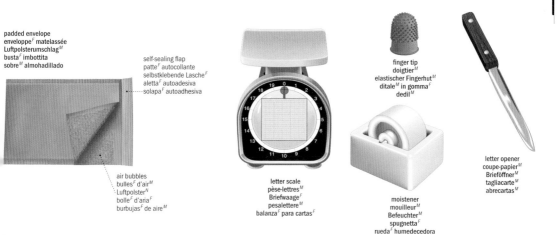

padded envelope
enveloppe^F matelassée
Luftpolsterumschlag^M
busta^F imbottita
sobre^M almohadillado

self-sealing flap
patte^F autocollante
selbstklebende Lasche^F
aletta^F autoadesiva
solapa^F autoadhesiva

finger tip
doigtier^M
elastischer Fingerhut^M
ditale^M in gomma^F
dedil^M

letter opener
coupe-papier^M
Brieföffner^M
tagliacarte^M
abrecartas^M

air bubbles
bulles^F d'air^M
Luftpolster^N
bolle^F d'aria^F
burbujas^F de aire^M

letter scale
pèse-lettres^M
Briefwaage^F
pesalettere^M
balanza^F para cartas^F

moistener
mouilleur^M
Befeuchter^M
spugnetta^F
rueda^F humedecedora

for filing
pour le classement^M
für die Ablage^F
per l'archiviazione^F
para archivar

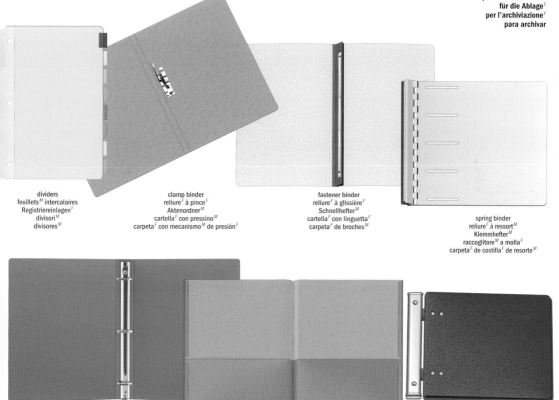

dividers
feuillets^M intercalaires
Registriereinlagen^F
divisori^M
divisores^M

clamp binder
reliure^F à pince^F
Aktenordner^M
cartella^F con pressino^M
carpeta^F con mecanismo^M de presión^F

fastener binder
reliure^F à glissière^F
Schnellhefter^M
cartella^F con linguetta^F
carpeta^F de broches^M

spring binder
reliure^F à ressort^M
Klemmhefter^M
raccoglitore^M a molla^F
carpeta^F de costilla^F de resorte^M

ring binder
classeur^M
Ringbuch^N
raccoglitore^M ad anelli^M
carpeta^F de argollas^F

document folder
pochette^F d'information^F
Dokumentenmappe^F
cartella^F per documenti^M
carpeta^F con guardas^F

post binder
reliure^F à vis^F
Hefter^M
portatabulati^M
carpeta^F de tornillos^M

COMMUNICATIONS AND OFFICE AUTOMATION

self-adhesive labels
étiquettes^F autocollantes
Selbstklebeetiketten^N
etichette^F autoadesive
etiquetas^F adhesivas

tab
onglet^M
Reiter^M
linguetta^F
indicador^M

window tab
onglet^M à fenêtre^F
durchsichtiger Reiter^M
linguetta^F con finestra^F
indicador^M transparente

folder
chemise^F
Aktenmappe^F
cartelletta^F
carpeta^F de archivo^M

file guides
guides^M de classement^M
Karteiregister^N
divisori^M alfabetici per schedario^M
guias^F de archivo^M

suspension file
dossier^M suspendu
Hängemappe^F
cartella^F sospesa
archivador^M colgante

spiral binder
reliure^F spirale^F
Spiralringbuch^N
rilegatura^F con spirale^F
carpeta^F de espiral^F

clipboard
planchette^F à pince^F
Klemmbrett^N
tavoletta^F portablocco^M
tabla^F con pinza^F

archboard
planchette^F à arches^F
Ringablage^F
portablocco^M
tabla^F con argollas^F

label maker
pince^F à étiqueter
Präger^M
etichettatrice^F
rotulador^M

filing box
boîte^F-classeur^M
Aktenbox^F
scatola^F per archivio^M
caja^F archivo^M

paper punch
perforatrice^F
Locher^M
perforatore^M
perforadora^F

comb binding
reliure^F à anneaux^M plastiques
Spiralheftung^F
rilegatura^F con spirale^F
encuadernación^F de anillas^F

concertina file
pochette^F de classement^M
Erweiterungskartei^F
classificatore^M a soffietto^M
archivador^M de fuelle^M

COMMUNICATIONS AND OFFICE AUTOMATION

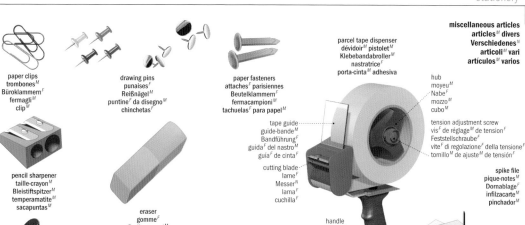

paper clips
trombones^M
Büroklammern^F
fermagli^M
clip^M

drawing pins
punaises^F
Reißnägel^M
puntine^F da disegno^M
chinchetas^F

paper fasteners
attaches^F parisiennes
Beutelklammern^F
fermacampioni^M
tachuelas^F para papel^M

parcel tape dispenser
dévidoir^M pistolet^M
Klebebandabroller^M
nastratrice^F
porta-cinta^M adhesiva

miscellaneous articles
articles^M divers
Verschiedenes^N
articoli^M vari
artículos^M varios

hub
moyeu^M
Nabe^F
mozzo^M
cubo^M

pencil sharpener
taille-crayon^M
Bleistiftspitzer^M
temperamatite^F
sacapuntas^M

tape guide
guide-bande^M
Bandführung^F
guida^F del nastro^M
guía^F de cinta^F

tension adjustment screw
vis^F de réglage^M de tension^F
Feststellschraube^F
vite^F di regolazione^F della tensione^F
tornillo^M de ajuste^M de tensión^F

cutting blade
lame^F
Messer^N
lama^F
cuchilla^F

spike file
pique-notes^M
Dornablage^F
infilzacarte^M
pinchador^M

eraser
gomme^F
Radiergummi^M
gomma^F
goma^F

handle
poignée^F
Griff^M
manico^M
empuñadura^F

staple remover
dégrafeuse^F
Entklammerer^M
levapunti^M
quitagrapas^M

tape dispenser
dévidoir^M de ruban^M adhésif
Klebefilmspender^M
chiocciola^F per nastro^M adesivo
porta-celo^M

glue stick
bâtonnet^M de colle^F
Klebestift^M
colla^F in stick^M
lápiz^M adhesivo

stapler
agrafeuse^F
Hefter^M
cucitrice^F
grapadora^F

book ends
serre-livres^M
Bücherstütze^F
reggilibri^M
sujetalibros^M

paper-clip holder
distributeur^M de trombones^M
Büroklammerhalter^M
portafermagli^M
distribuidor^M de clips^M

staples
agrafes^F
Heftklammern^F
punti^M metallici
grapas^F

pencil sharpener
taille-crayon^M
Bleistiftspitzer^M
temperamatite^F
sacapuntas^M

magnet
aimant^M
Magnet^M
calamita^F
imán^M

noticeboard
tableau^M d'affichage^M
Pinnwand^F
bacheca^F
tablero^M de anuncios^M

cutting head
tête^F de coupe^F
Schneidkopf^M
testa^F di taglio^M
cabeza^F cortadora

waste basket
corbeille^F à papier^M
Papierkorb^M
cestino^M
papelera^F

waste basket
corbeille^F à papier^M
Papierkorb^M
cestino^M
papelera

posting surface
surface^F d'affichage^M
Anschlagfläche^F
superficie^F di affissione^F
superficie^F de fijación^F

paper shredder
destructeur^M de documents^M
Aktenvernichter^M
distruggidocumenti^M
trituradora^F de documentos^M

road system

système^M routier | Straßenbau^M | sistema^M stradale | sistema^M de carreteras^F

cross section of a road
coupe^F d'une route^F
Straße^F im Querschnitt^M
sezione^F trasversale di una strada^F
sección^F transversal de una carretera^F

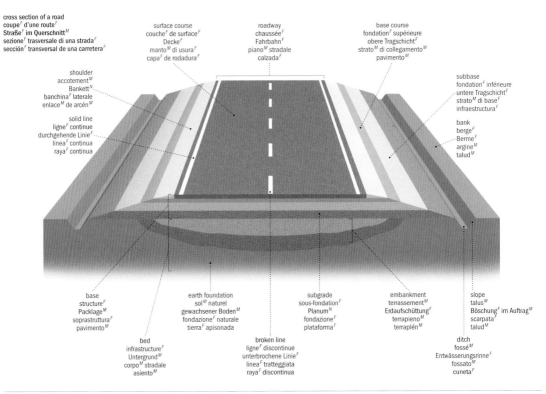

surface course
couche^F de surface^F
Decke^F
manto^M di usura^F
capa^F de rodadura^F

roadway
chaussée^F
Fahrbahn^F
piano^M stradale
calzada^F

base course
fondation^F supérieure
obere Tragschicht^F
strato^M di collegamento^M
pavimento^M

shoulder
accotement^M
Bankett^N
banchina^F laterale
enlace^F de arcén^M

solid line
ligne^F continue
durchgehende Linie^F
linea^F continua
raya^F continua

subbase
fondation^F inférieure
untere Tragschicht^F
strato^M di base^F
infraestructura^F

bank
berge^F
Berme^F
argine^M
talud^M

base
structure^F
Packlage^F
soprastruttura^F
pavimento^M

earth foundation
sol^M naturel
gewachsener Boden^M
fondazione^F naturale
tierra^F apisonada

subgrade
sous-fondation^F
Planum^N
fondazione^F
plataforma^F

embankment
terrassement^M
Erdaufschüttung^F
terrapieno^M
terraplén^M

slope
talus^M
Böschung^F im Auftrag^M
scarpata^F
talud^M

bed
infrastructure^F
Untergrund^M
corpo^M stradale
asiento^M

broken line
ligne^F discontinue
unterbrochene Linie^F
linea^F tratteggiata
raya^F discontinua

ditch
fossé^M
Entwässerungsrinne^F
fossato^M
cuneta^F

examples of interchanges
exemples^M d'échangeurs^M
Beispiele^N für Anschlussstellen^F
esempi^M di raccordo^M
ejemplos^M de enlaces^M de carreteras^F

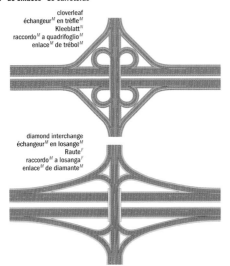

cloverleaf
échangeur^M en trèfle^M
Kleeblatt^N
raccordo^M a quadrifoglio^M
enlace^M de trébol^M

diamond interchange
échangeur^M en losange^M
Raute^F
raccordo^M a losanga^F
enlace^M de diamante^M

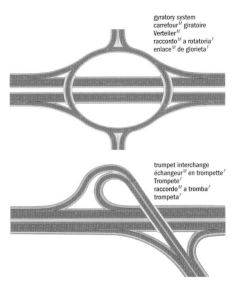

gyratory system
carrefour^M giratoire
Verteiler^M
raccordo^M a rotatoria^F
enlace^M de glorieta^F

trumpet interchange
échangeur^M en trompette^F
Trompete^F
raccordo^M a tromba^F
trompeta^F

TRANSPORT AND MACHINERY

cloverleaf
échangeur^M en trèfle^M
Kleeblatt^N
raccordo^M a quadrifoglio^M
enlace^M de trébol^M

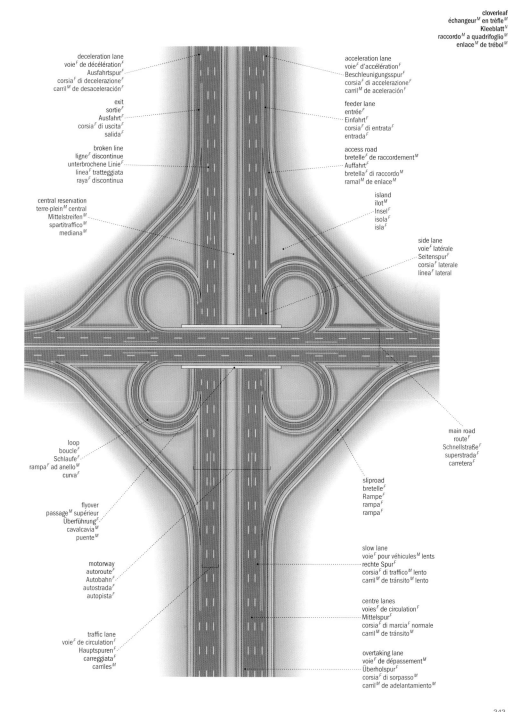

deceleration lane
voie^F de décélération^F
Ausfahrtspur^F
corsia^F di decelerazione^F
carril^M de desaceleración^F

acceleration lane
voie^F d'accélération^F
Beschleunigungsspur^F
corsia^F di accelerazione^F
carril^M de aceleración^F

exit
sortie^F
Ausfahrt^F
corsia^F di uscita^F
salida^F

feeder lane
entrée^F
Einfahrt^F
corsia^F di entrata^F
entrada^F

broken line
ligne^F discontinue
unterbrochene Linie^F
linea^F tratteggiata
raya^F discontinua

access road
bretelle^F de raccordement^M
Auffahrt^F
bretella^F di raccordo^M
ramal^M de enlace^M

central reservation
terre-plein^M central
Mittelstreifen^M
spartitraffico^M
mediana^F

island
ilot^M
Insel^F
isola^F
isla^F

side lane
voie^F latérale
Seitenspur^F
corsia^F laterale
línea^F lateral

loop
boucle^F
Schlaufe^F
rampa^F ad anello^M
curva^F

main road
route^F
Schnellstraße^F
superstrada^F
carretera^F

sliproad
bretelle^F
Rampe^F
rampa^F
rampa^F

flyover
passage^M supérieur
Überführung^F
cavalcavia^M
puente^M

motorway
autoroute^F
Autobahn^F
autostrada^F
autopista^F

slow lane
voie^F pour véhicules^M lents
rechte Spur^F
corsia^F di traffico^M lento
carril^M de tránsito^M lento

centre lanes
voies^F de circulation^F
Mittelspur^F
corsia^F di marcia^F normale
carril^M de tránsito^M

traffic lane
voie^F de circulation^F
Hauptspuren^F
carreggiata^F
carriles^M

overtaking lane
voie^F de dépassement^M
Überholspur^F
corsia^F di sorpasso^M
carril^M de adelantamiento^M

fixed bridges

ponts^M fixes | starre Brücken^F | ponti^M fissi | puentes^M fijos

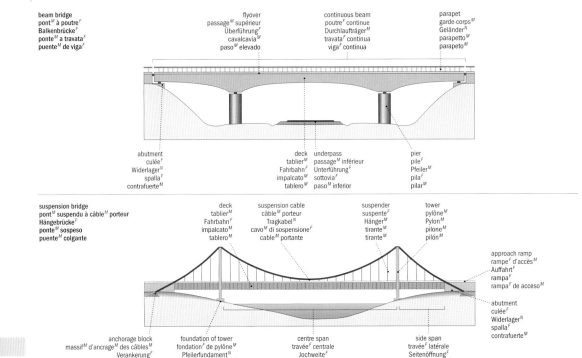

beam bridge
pont^M à poutre^F
Balkenbrücke^F
ponte^M a travata^F
puente^M de viga^F

flyover
passage^M supérieur
Überführung^F
cavalcavia^M
paso^M elevado

continuous beam
poutre^F continue
Durchlaufträger^M
travata^F continua
viga^F continua

parapet
garde-corps^M
Geländer^N
parapetto^M
parapeto^M

abutment
culée^F
Widerlager^N
spalla^F
contrafuerte^M

deck
tablier^M
Fahrbahn^F
impalcato^M
tablero^M

underpass
passage^M inférieur
Unterführung^F
sottovia^F
paso^M inferior

pier
pile^F
Pfeiler^M
pila^F
pilar^M

suspension bridge
pont^M suspendu à câble^M porteur
Hängebrücke^F
ponte^M sospeso
puente^M colgante

deck
tablier^M
Fahrbahn^F
impalcato^M
tablero^M

suspension cable
câble^M porteur
Tragkabel^N
cavo^M di sospensione^F
cable^M portante

suspender
suspente^F
Hänger^M
tirante^M
tirante^M

tower
pylône^M
Pylon^M
pilone^M
pilón^M

approach ramp
rampe^F d'accès^M
Auffahrt^F
rampa^F
rampa^F de acceso^M

abutment
culée^F
Widerlager^N
spalla^F
contrafuerte^M

anchorage block
massif^M d'ancrage^M des câbles^M
Verankerung^F
blocco^M di ancoraggio^M dei cavi^M
anclaje^M

foundation of tower
fondation^F de pylône^M
Pfeilerfundament^N
fondazione^F del pilone^M
cimiento^M del pilón^M

centre span
travée^F centrale
Jochweite^F
campata^F centrale
tramo^M central

side span
travée^F latérale
Seitenöffnung^F
campata^F laterale
tramo^M lateral

cantilever bridge
pont^M cantilever
Auslegerbrücke^F
ponte^M a cantilever^M
puente^M cantilever

suspended span
poutre^F suspendue
eingehängte Spannweite^F
travata^F appoggiata
tramo^M suspendido

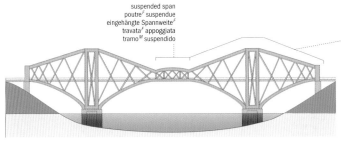

cantilever span
poutre^F cantilever
Kragträger^M
travata^F a cantilever^M
viga^F cantilever^M

movable bridges

ponts^M mobiles | bewegliche Brücken^F | ponti^M mobili | puentes^M móviles

swing bridge
pont^M tournant
Drehbrücke^F
ponte^M girevole
puente^M giratorio

turntable
plaque^F tournante
Drehkranz^M
corona^F
tramo^M giratorio

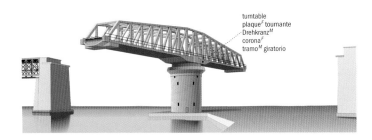

TRANSPORT AND MACHINERY

movable bridges

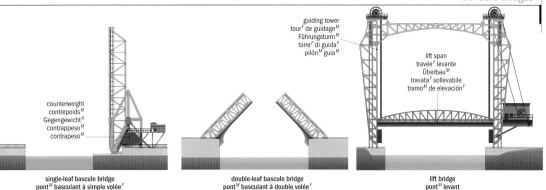

guiding tower
tour^F de guidage^M
Führungsturm^M
torre^F di guida^F
pilón^M guía^M

lift span
travée^F levante
Überbau^M
travata^F sollevabile
tramo^M de elevación^F

counterweight
contrepoids^M
Gegengewicht^N
contrappeso^M
contrapeso^M

single-leaf bascule bridge
pont^M basculant à simple volée^F
einteilige Klappbrücke^F
ponte^M ribaltabile a un'ala^F
puente^M levadizo sencillo

double-leaf bascule bridge
pont^M basculant à double volée^F
Doppelklappbrücke^F
ponte^M ribaltabile a due ali^F
puente^M levadizo doble

lift bridge
pont^M levant
Hubbrücke^F
ponte^M sollevabile
puente^M elevador

road tunnel

tunnel^M routier | Straßentunnel^M | galleria^F | túnel^M de carretera^F

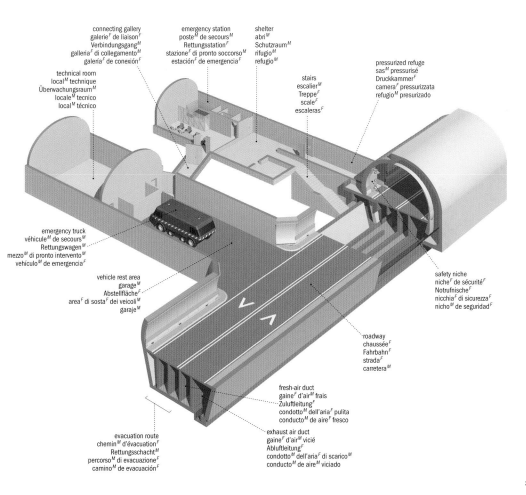

connecting gallery
galerie^F de liaison^F
Verbindungsgang^M
galleria^F di collegamento^M
galería^F de conexión^F

emergency station
poste^M de secours^M
Rettungsstation^F
stazione^F di pronto soccorso^M
estación^F de emergencia^F

shelter
abri^M
Schutzraum^M
rifugio^M
refugio^M

pressurized refuge
sas^M pressurisé
Druckkammer^F
camera^F pressurizzata
refugio^M presurizado

technical room
local^M technique
Überwachungsraum^M
locale^M tecnico
local^M técnico

stairs
escalier^M
Treppe^F
scale^F
escaleras^F

emergency truck
véhicule^M de secours^M
Rettungswagen^M
mezzo^M di pronto intervento^M
vehículo^M de emergencia^F

safety niche
niche^F de sécurité^F
Notrufnische^F
nicchia^F di sicurezza^F
nicho^M de seguridad^F

vehicle rest area
garage^M
Abstellfläche^F
area^F di sosta^F dei veicoli^M
garaje^M

roadway
chaussée^F
Fahrbahn^F
strada^F
carretera^M

fresh-air duct
gaine^F d'air^M frais
Zuluftleitung^F
condotto^M dell'aria^F pulita
conducto^M de aire^F fresco

evacuation route
chemin^M d'évacuation^F
Rettungsschacht^M
percorso^M di evacuazione^F
camino^M de evacuación^F

exhaust air duct
gaine^F d'air^M vicié
Abluftleitung^F
condotto^M dell'aria^F di scarico^M
conducto^M de aire^M viciado

service station

station^F-service^M | Tankstelle^F | stazione^F di servizio^M | estación^F de servicio^M

petrol pump
distributeur^M d'essence^F
Zapfsäule^F
pompa^F della benzina^F
surtidor^M de gasolina^F

display
écran^M
Anzeige^F
display^M
display^M

cash readout
afficheur^M totaliseur
Zahlungsbetragsanzeige^F
importo^M da pagare
indicador^M del importe^M total^M

card reader slot
fente^F du lecteur^M de carte^F
Kartenleserschlitz^M
lettore^M di carte^F
ranura^F de lectura^F de tarjeta^F

volume readout
afficheur^M volume^M
Füllmengenanzeige^F
litri^M erogati
cuentalitros^M

alphanumeric keyboard
clavier^M alphanumérique
alphanumerische Tastatur^F
tastiera^F alfanumerica
teclado^M alfanumérico

price per gallon/litre
afficheur^M prix^M
Preis^M pro Liter^M/Gallone^F
prezzo^M per litro^M/gallone^M
indicador^M del precio^M por litro^M /galón^M

slip presenter
sortie^F des tickets^M
Belegausgabe^F
emissione^F dello scontrino^M
expedidor^M de recibo^M

pump number
numéro^M de la pompe^F
Zapfsäulennummer^F
numero^M della pompa^F
número^M del surtidor^M

type of fuel
type^M de carburant^M
Treibstoffart^F
tipo^M di carburante^M
tipo^M de combustible^M

pump nozzle
pistolet^M de distribution^F
Zapfhahn^M
pistola^F di erogazione^F
pistola^F del surtidor^M

operating instructions
mode^M d'emploi^M
Bedienungsanleitung^F
istruzioni^F per l'uso^M
instrucciones^F operativas

petrol pump hose
flexible^M de distribution^F
Zapfschlauch^M
tubo^M della pompa^F
manguera^F de servicio^M

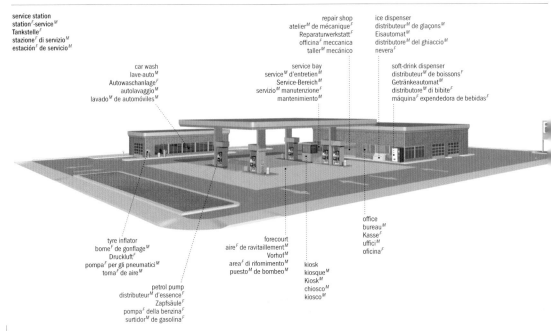

service station
station^F-service^M
Tankstelle^F
stazione^F di servizio^M
estación^F de servicio^M

repair shop
atelier^M de mécanique^F
Reparaturwerkstatt^F
officina^F meccanica
taller^M mecánico

ice dispenser
distributeur^M de glaçons^M
Eisautomat^M
distributore^M del ghiaccio^M
nevera^F

car wash
lave-auto^M
Autowaschanlage^F
autolavaggio^M
lavado^M de automóviles^M

service bay
service^M d'entretien^M
Service-Bereich^M
servizio^M manutenzione^F
mantenimiento^M

soft-drink dispenser
distributeur^M de boissons^F
Getränkeautomat^M
distributore^M di bibite^F
máquina^F expendedora de bebidas^F

office
bureau^M
Kasse^F
uffici^M
oficina^F

tyre inflator
borne^F de gonflage^M
Druckluft^F
pompa^F per gli pneumatici^M
toma^F de aire^M

forecourt
aire^F de ravitaillement^M
Vorhof^M
area^F di rifornimento^M
puesto^M de bombeo^M

kiosk
kiosque^M
Kiosk^M
chiosco^M
kiosco^M

petrol pump
distributeur^M d'essence^F
Zapfsäule^F
pompa^F della benzina^F
surtidor^M de gasolina^F

car

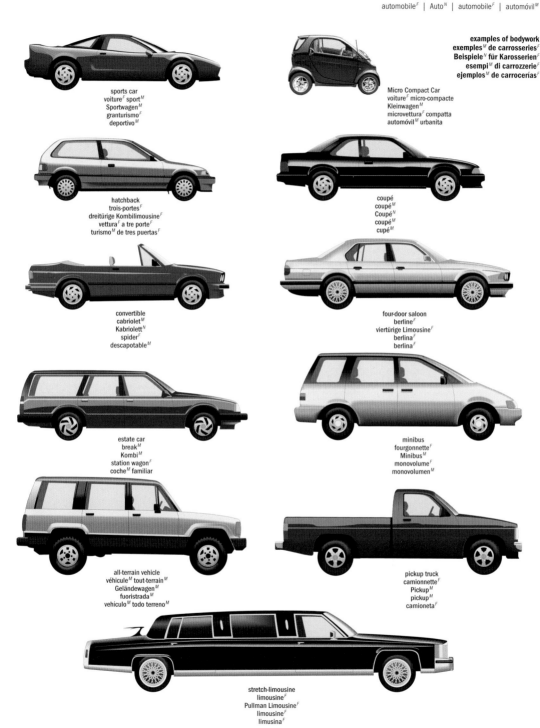

examples of bodywork
exemples^M de carrosseries^F
Beispiele^N für Karosserien^F
esempi^M di carrozzerie^F
ejemplos^M de carrocerías^F

sports car
voiture^F sport^M
Sportwagen^M
granturismo^F
deportivo^M

Micro Compact Car
voiture^F micro-compacte
Kleinwagen^M
microvettura^F compatta
automóvil^M urbanita

hatchback
trois-portes^F
dreitürige Kombilimousine^F
vettura^F a tre porte^F
turismo^M de tres puertas^F

coupé
coupé^M
Coupé^N
coupé^M
cupé^M

convertible
cabriolet^M
Kabriolett^N
spider^F
descapotable^M

four-door saloon
berline^F
viertürige Limousine^F
berlina^F
berlina^F

estate car
break^M
Kombi^M
station wagon^F
coche^M familiar

minibus
fourgonnette^F
Minibus^M
monovolume^F
monovolumen^M

all-terrain vehicle
véhicule^M tout-terrain^M
Geländewagen^M
fuoristrada^M
vehiculo^M todo terreno^M

pickup truck
camionnette^F
Pickup^M
pickup^M
camioneta^F

stretch-limousine
limousine^F
Pullman Limousine^F
limousine^F
limusina^F

TRANSPORT AND MACHINERY

347

car

body
carrosserie^F
Karosserie^F
carrozzeria^F
carrocería^F

windscreen
pare-brise^M
Windschutzscheibe^F
parabrezza^M
parabrisas^M

outside mirror
rétroviseur^M extérieur
Seitenspiegel^M
specchietto^M retrovisore esterno
espejo^M lateral

windscreen wiper
essuie-glace^M
Scheibenwischer^M
tergicristallo^M
limpiaparabrisas^M

scuttle panel
auvent^M
Windlaufquerteil^N
pannello^M di copertura^F
bóveda^F del salpicadero^M

bonnet
capot^M
Motorhaube^F
cofano^M anteriore
capó^M

washer nozzle
gicleur^M de lave-glace^M
Scheibenwaschdüse^F
ugello^M del lavaparabrezza^M
pulverizador^M de agua^F

grille
calandre^F
Kühlergrill^M
mascherina^F
calandra^F

bumper moulding
moulure^F de pare-chocs^M
kunststoffummantelter Stoßfänger^M
modanatura^F
resguardo^M del parachoques^M

headlight
phare^M
Scheinwerfer^M
proiettore^M
faro^M delantero

front fascia
carénage^M avant
Frontstoßfänger^M
fascione^M anteriore
banda^F frontal

wing
aile^F
Kotflügel^M
parafango^M
guardabarros^M

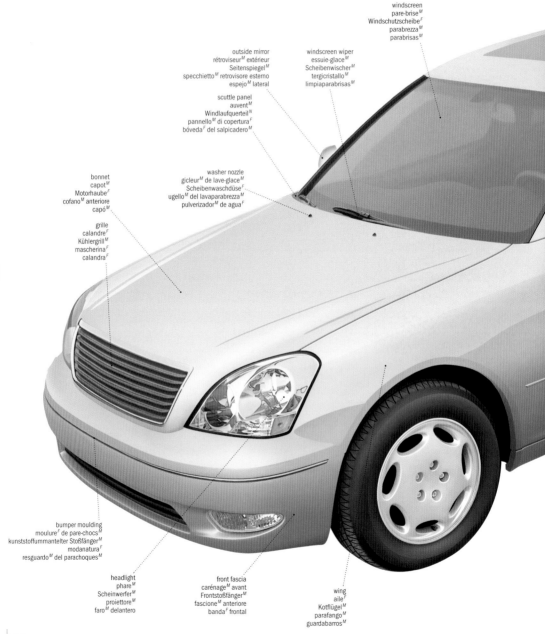

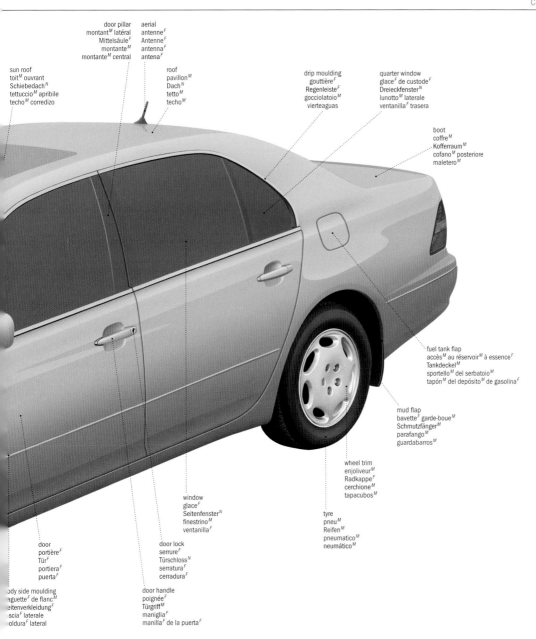

door pillar
montant^M latéral
Mittelsäule^F
montante^M
montante^M central

aerial
antenne^F
Antenne^F
antenna^F
antena^F

sun roof
toit^M ouvrant
Schiebedach^N
tettuccio^M apribile
techo^M corredizo

roof
pavillon^M
Dach^N
tetto^M
techo^M

drip moulding
gouttière^F
Regenleiste^F
gocciolatoio^M
vierteaguas

quarter window
glace^F de custode^F
Dreieckfenster^N
lunotto^M laterale
ventanilla^F trasera

boot
coffre^M
Kofferraum^M
cofano^M posteriore
maletero^M

fuel tank flap
accès^M au réservoir^M à essence^F
Tankdeckel^M
sportello^M del serbatoio^M
tapón^M del depósito^M de gasolina^F

mud flap
bavette^F garde-boue^M
Schmutzfänger^M
parafango^M
guardabarros^M

wheel trim
enjoliveur^M
Radkappe^F
cerchione^M
tapacubos^M

window
glace^F
Seitenfenster^N
finestrino^M
ventanilla^F

tyre
pneu^M
Reifen^M
pneumatico^M
neumático^M

door
portière^F
Tür^F
portiera^F
puerta^F

door lock
serrure^F
Türschloss^N
serratura^F
cerradura^F

body side moulding
baguette^F de flanc^M
Seitenverkleidung^F
fascia^F laterale
moldura^F lateral

door handle
poignée^F
Türgriff^M
maniglia^F
manilla^F de la puerta^F

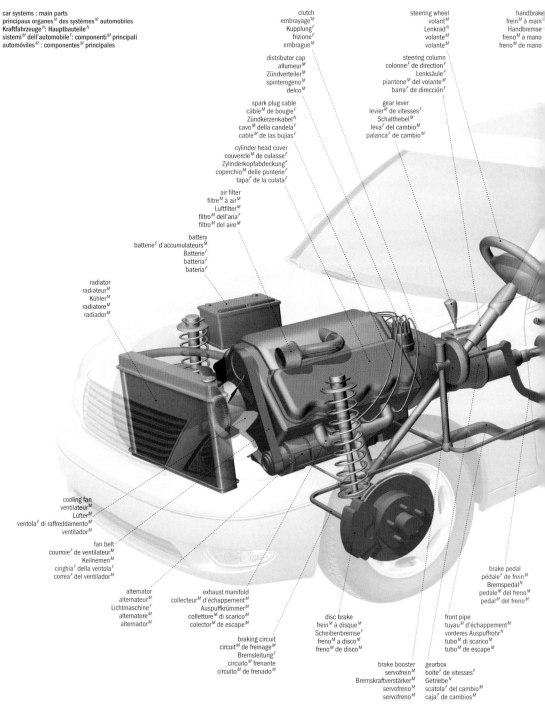

car systems : main parts
principaux organes^M des systèmes^M automobiles
Kraftfahrzeuge^N: Hauptbauteile^N
sistemi^M dell'automobile^F: componenti^M principali
automóviles^M : componentes^M principales

clutch
embrayage^M
Kupplung^F
frizione^F
embrague^M

distributor cap
allumeur^M
Zündverteiler^M
spinterogeno^M
delco^M

spark plug cable
câble^M de bougie^F
Zündkerzenkabel^N
cavo^M della candela^F
cable^M de las bujías^F

cylinder head cover
couvercle^M de culasse^F
Zylinderkopfabdeckung^F
coperchio^M delle punterie^F
tapa^F de la culata^F

air filter
filtre^M à air^M
Luftfilter^M
filtro^M dell'aria^F
filtro^M del aire^M

battery
batterie^F d'accumulateurs^M
Batterie^F
batteria^F
batería^F

radiator
radiateur^M
Kühler^M
radiatore^M
radiador^M

steering wheel
volant^M
Lenkrad^N
volante^M
volante^M

steering column
colonne^F de direction^F
Lenksäule^F
piantone^M del volante^M
barra^F de dirección^F

gear lever
levier^M de vitesses^F
Schalthebel^M
leva^F del cambio^M
palanca^F de cambio^M

handbrake
frein^M à main
Handbremse^F
freno^M a mano
freno^M de mano

cooling fan
ventilateur^M
Lüfter^M
ventola^F di raffreddamento^M
ventilador^M

fan belt
courroie^F de ventilateur^M
Keilriemen^M
cinghia^F della ventola^F
correa^F del ventilador^M

alternator
alternateur^M
Lichtmaschine^F
alternatore^M
alternador^M

exhaust manifold
collecteur^M d'échappement^M
Auspuffkrümmer^M
collettore^M di scarico^M
colector^M de escape^M

braking circuit
circuit^M de freinage^M
Bremsleitung^F
circuito^M frenante
circuito^M de frenado^M

disc brake
frein^M à disque^M
Scheibenbremse^F
freno^M a disco^M
freno^M de disco^M

brake booster
servofrein^M
Bremskraftverstärker^M
servofreno^M
servofreno^M

gearbox
boîte^F de vitesses^F
Getriebe^N
scatola^F del cambio^M
caja^F de cambios^M

front pipe
tuyau^M d'échappement^M
vorderes Auspuffrohr^N
tubo^M di scarico^M
tubo^M de escape^M

brake pedal
pédale^F de frein^M
Bremspedal^N
pedale^M del freno^M
pedal^M del freno^M

TRANSPORT AND MACHINERY

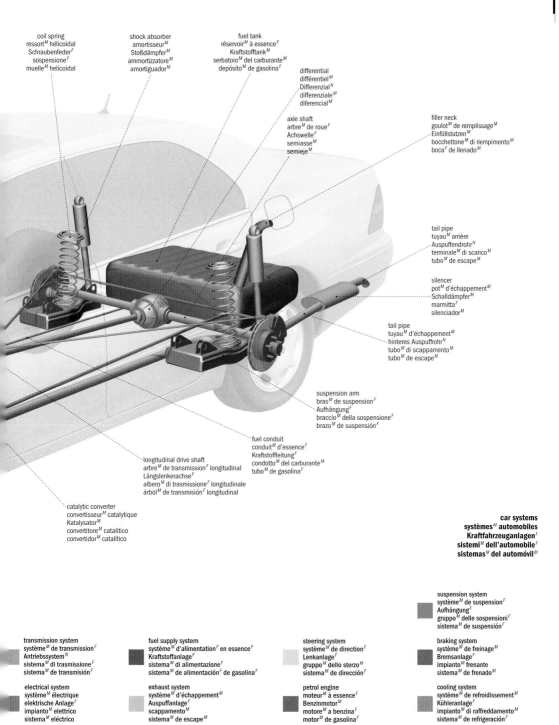

coil spring
ressort[M] hélicoïdal
Schraubenfeder[F]
sospensione[F]
muelle[M] helicoïdal

shock absorber
amortisseur[M]
Stoßdämpfer[M]
ammortizzatore[M]
amortiguador[M]

fuel tank
réservoir[M] à essence[F]
Kraftstofftank[M]
serbatoio[M] del carburante[M]
depósito[M] de gasolina[F]

differential
différentiel[M]
Differenzial[N]
differenziale[M]
diferencial[M]

axle shaft
arbre[M] de roue[F]
Achswelle[F]
semiasse[M]
semieje[M]

filler neck
goulot[M] de remplissage[M]
Einfüllstutzen[M]
bocchettone[M] di riempimento[M]
boca[F] de llenado[M]

tail pipe
tuyau[M] arrière
Auspuffendrohr[N]
terminale[M] di scarico[M]
tubo[M] de escape[M]

silencer
pot[M] d'échappement[M]
Schalldämpfer[M]
marmitta[F]
silenciador[M]

tail pipe
tuyau[M] d'échappement[M]
hinteres Auspuffrohr[N]
tubo[M] di scappamento[M]
tubo[M] de escape[M]

suspension arm
bras[M] de suspension[F]
Aufhängung[F]
braccio[M] della sospensione[F]
brazo[M] de suspensión[F]

fuel conduit
conduit[M] d'essence[F]
Kraftstoffleitung[F]
condotto[M] del carburante[M]
tubo[M] de gasolina[F]

longitudinal drive shaft
arbre[M] de transmission[F] longitudinal
Längslenkerachse[F]
albero[M] di trasmissione[F] longitudinale
árbol[M] de transmisión[F] longitudinal

catalytic converter
convertisseur[M] catalytique
Katalysator[M]
convertitore[M] catalitico
convertidor[M] catalítico

car systems
systèmes[M] automobiles
Kraftfahrzeuganlagen[F]
sistemi[M] dell'automobile[F]
sistemas[M] del automóvil[M]

suspension system
système[M] de suspension[F]
Aufhängung[F]
gruppo[M] delle sospensioni[F]
sistema[M] de suspensión[F]

transmission system
système[M] de transmission[F]
Antriebssystem[N]
sistema[M] di trasmissione[F]
sistema[M] de transmisión[F]

fuel supply system
système[M] d'alimentation[F] en essence[F]
Kraftstoffanlage[F]
sistema[M] di alimentazione[F]
sistema[M] de alimentación[F] de gasolina[F]

steering system
système[M] de direction[F]
Lenkanlage[F]
gruppo[M] dello sterzo[M]
sistema[M] de dirección[F]

braking system
système[M] de freinage[M]
Bremsanlage[F]
impianto[M] frenante
sistema[M] de frenado[M]

electrical system
système[M] électrique
elektrische Anlage[F]
impianto[M] elettrico
sistema[M] eléctrico

exhaust system
système[M] d'échappement[M]
Auspuffanlage[F]
scappamento[M]
sistema[M] de escape[M]

petrol engine
moteur[M] à essence[F]
Benzinmotor[M]
motore[M] a benzina[F]
motor[M] de gasolina[F]

cooling system
système[M] de refroidissement[M]
Kühleranlage[F]
impianto[M] di raffreddamento[M]
sistema[M] de refrigeración[F]

TRANSPORT AND MACHINERY

car

front lights
feux^M avant
Frontscheinwerfer^F
luci^F anteriori
faros^M delanteros

main beam headlight
feu^M de route^F
Fernlicht^N
proiettore^M abbagliante e anabbagliante
luz^F larga

dipped beam headlight
feu^M de croisement^F
Abblendlicht^N
luce^F di posizione^F
luz^F de cruce^M

fog lamp
feu^M antibrouillard
Nebelleuchte^F
faro^M fendinebbia
luz^F antiniebla

indicator
feu^M clignotant
Blinkleuchte^F
indicatore^M di direzione^F
intermitente^M

side marker light
feu^M de position^F
Begrenzungsleuchte^F
luce^F di ingombro^M laterale
luz^M de posición^F

rear lights
feux^M arrière
Heckleuchten^F
luci^F posteriori
luces^F traseras

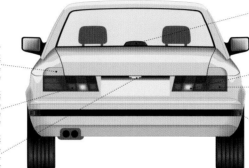

indicator
feu^M clignotant
Blinkleuchte^F
indicatore^M di direzione^F
intermitente^M

brake light
feu^M de freinage^M
Bremsleuchte^F
luce^F di arresto^M
luz^F de freno^M

number plate light
feu^M de plaque^F
Nummernschildbeleuchtung^F
luce^F della targa^F
iluminación^F de la placa^F de matrícula^F

brake light
feu^M de freinage^M
Bremsleuchte^F
luce^F di arresto^M
luz^F de freno^M

reversing light
feu^M de recul^M
Rückfahrscheinwerfer^M
luce^F di retromarcia^F
luz^F de marcha^F atrás

rear light
feu^M rouge arrière
Schlussleuchte^F
luce^F di posizione^F posteriore
luz^F trasera

side marker light
feu^M de position^F
Begrenzungsleuchte^F
luce^F di ingombro^M laterale
luz^F de posición^F

door
portière^F
Wagentür^F
portiera^F
puerta^F

interior door handle
poignée^F intérieure
Türöffnungshebel^M
maniglia^F interna
tirador^M de la puerta^F

door grip
poignée^F de maintien^M
Seitengriff^M
maniglia^F fissa
asidero^M

outside mirror control
commande^F du rétroviseur^M
Seitenspiegelverstellhebel^N
regolazione^F dello specchietto^M retrovisore esterno
control^M del espejo^M retrovisor exterior

window winder handle
manivelle^F de lève-glace^M
Fensterheber^M
manopola^F alzacristalli
manivela^F de la ventanilla^F

hinge
charnière^F
Scharnier^N
cardine^M
bisagra^F

door pocket
vide-poches^M
Seitenfach^N
tasca^F portaoggetti
bolsillo^M lateral

window
glace^F
Fenster^N
finestrino^M
ventanilla^F

interior door lock button
bouton^M de verrouillage^M
Sicherungsknopf^M
pomello^M della sicura^F
botón^M del seguro^M

armrest
appui^M-bras^M
Armstütze^F
bracciolo^M
soporte^M para el brazo^M

lock
serrure^F
Türschloss^N
serratura^F
cerradura^F

trim panel
panneau^M de garniture^F
Türverkleidung^F
pannello^M
panel^M de la puerta^F

inner door shell
caisson^M de portière^F
Türinnenverschalung^F
telaio^M interno della portiera^F
revestimiento^M interior

bucket seat : front view
siège^M-baquet^M : vue^F de face^F
Schalensitz^M: Vorderansicht^F
sedile^M: vista^F anteriore
asiento^M : vista^F frontal

bucket seat : side view
siège^M-baquet^M : vue^F de profil^M
Schalensitz^M: Seitenansicht^F
sedile^M: vista^F laterale
asiento^M : vista^F lateral

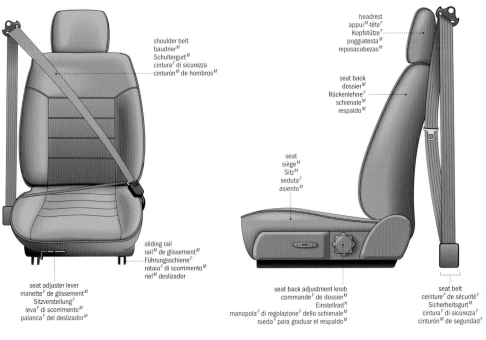

shoulder belt
baudrier^M
Schultergurt^M
cintura^F di sicurezza
cinturón^M de hombros^M

headrest
appui^M-tête^F
Kopfstütze^F
poggiatesta^M
reposacabezas^M

seat back
dossier^M
Rückenlehne^F
schienale^M
respaldo^M

seat
siège^M
Sitz^M
seduta^F
asiento^M

sliding rail
rail^M de glissement^M
Führungsschiene^F
rotaia^F di scorrimento^M
riel^M deslizador

seat adjuster lever
manette^F de glissement^M
Sitzverstellung^F
leva^F di scorrimento^M
palanca^F del deslizador^M

seat back adjustment knob
commande^F de dossier^M
Einstellrad^N
manopola^F di regolazione^F dello schienale^M
rueda^F para graduar el respaldo^M

seat belt
ceinture^F de sécurité^F
Sicherheitsgurt^M
cintura^F di sicurezza^F
cinturón^M de seguridad^F

rear seat
banquette^F arrière
Rückbank^F
divano^M posteriore
asiento^M trasero

armrest
appui^M-bras^M
Armstütze^F
bracciolo^M
reposabrazo^M

lap belt
sangle^F
Beckengurt^M
cintura^F ventrale
cinturón^M subabdominal

buckle
boucle^F
Gurtschließe^F
fibbia^F
enganche^M

bench seat
banquette^F
Sitzbank^F
seduta^F del divano^M posteriore
asiento^M

TRANSPORT AND MACHINERY

car

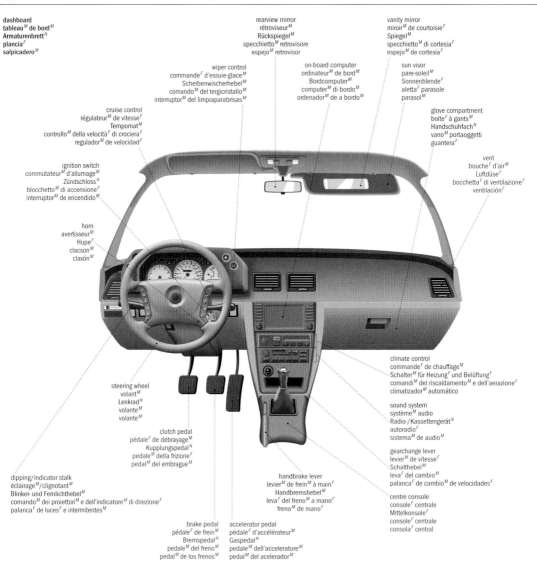

dashboard
tableau^M de bord^M
Armaturenbrett^N
plancia^F
salpicadero^M

rearview mirror
rétroviseur^M
Rückspiegel^M
specchietto^M retrovisore
espejo^M retrovisor

vanity mirror
miroir^M de courtoisie^F
Spiegel^M
specchietto^M di cortesia^F
espejo^M de cortesía^F

wiper control
commande^F d'essuie-glace^M
Scheibenwischerhebel^M
comando^M del tergicristallo^M
interruptor^M del limpiaparabrisas^M

on-board computer
ordinateur^M de bord^M
Bordcomputer^M
computer^M di bordo^M
ordenador^M de a bordo^M

sun visor
pare-soleil^M
Sonnenblende^F
aletta^F parasole
parasol^M

cruise control
régulateur^M de vitesse^F
Tempomat^M
controllo^M della velocità^F di crociera^F
regulador^M de velocidad^F

glove compartment
boîte^F à gants^M
Handschuhfach^N
vano^M portaoggetti
guantera^F

ignition switch
commutateur^M d'allumage^M
Zündschloss^N
blocchetto^M di accensione^F
interruptor^M de encendido^M

vent
bouche^F d'air^M
Luftdüse^F
bocchetta^F di ventilazione^F
ventilación^F

horn
avertisseur^M
Hupe^F
clacson^M
claxón^M

climate control
commande^F de chauffage^M
Schalter^M für Heizung^F und Belüftung^F
comandi^M del riscaldamento^M e dell'aerazione^F
climatizador^M automático

steering wheel
volant^M
Lenkrad^N
volante^M
volante^M

sound system
système^M audio
Radio-/Kassettengerät^N
autoradio^F
sistema^M de audio^M

clutch pedal
pédale^F de débrayage^M
Kupplungspedal^N
pedale^M della frizione^F
pedal^M del embrague^M

gearchange lever
levier^M de vitesse^F
Schalthebel^M
leva^F del cambio^M
palanca^F de cambio^M de velocidades^F

dipping/indicator stalk
éclairage^M/clignotant^M
Blinker- und Fernlichthebel^M
comando^M dei proiettori^M e dell'indicatore^M di direzione^F
palanca^F de luces^F e intermitentes^M

handbrake lever
levier^M de frein^M à main^F
Handbremshebel^M
leva^F del freno^M a mano^F
freno^M de mano^F

centre console
console^F centrale
Mittelkonsole^F
console^F centrale
consola^F central

brake pedal
pédale^F de frein^M
Bremspedal^N
pedale^M del freno^M
pedal^M de los frenos^M

accelerator pedal
pédale^F d'accélérateur^M
Gaspedal^N
pedale^M dell'acceleratore^M
pedal^M del acelerador^M

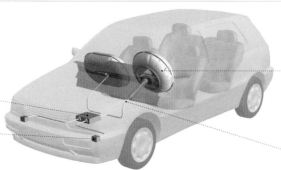

air bag restraint system
système^M de retenue^F à sacs^M gonflables
Airbag^M-Rückhaltesystem^N
sistema^M di ritenuta^F degli air bag^M
sistema^M de restricción^F del airbag^M

safing sensor
détecteur^M de sécurité^F
Sicherheitssensor^M
sensore^M di sicurezza^F
sensor^M de seguridad^F

air bag
sac^M gonflable
Airbag^M
air bag^M
airbag^M

primary crash sensor
détecteur^M d'impact^M primaire
Aufprallsensor^M
sensore^M di collisione^F principale
sensor^M de colisión^F primario

electrical cable
câble^M électrique
Elektrokabel^N
cavo^M elettrico
cable^M eléctrico

TRANSPORT AND MACHINERY

instrument panel
instruments^M de bord^M
Instrumententafel^F
quadro^M degli strumenti^M di controllo^M
instrumentos^M del salpicadero^M

battery warning light
témoin^M de charge^F
Batterieladekontrollleuchte^F
spia^F della batteria^F
luz^F de advertencia^F del alternador^M

oil warning light
témoin^M de niveau^M d'huile^F
Öldruckwarnleuchte^F
spia^F della pressione^F dell'olio^M
luz^F de advertencia^F del aceite^M

temperature gauge
indicateur^M de température^F
Temperaturanzeige^F
indicatore^M della temperatura^F del liquido^M di raffreddamento^M
indicador^M de temperatura^F

main beam indicator light
témoin^M des feux^M de route^F
Fernlichtanzeige^F
spia^F dei proiettori^M abbaglianti
luz^F indicadora de luz^F larga

low fuel warning light
témoin^M de bas niveau^M de carburant^M
Kraftstoffreserveanzeige^F
spia^F della riserva^F di carburante^M
luz^F de advertencia^F de la gasolina^F

fuel gauge
indicateur^M de niveau^M de carburant^M
Kraftstoffanzeige^F
indicatore^M del livello^M di carburante^M
indicador^M de nivel^M de gasolina^F

warning lights
lampes^F témoins^M
Warnleuchten^F
spie^F
luces^F de advertencia^F

indicator telltale
témoin^M de clignotants^M
Blinklichtkontrolle^F
spia^F dell'indicatore^M di direzione^F
intermitente^M

tachometer
compte-tours^M
Drehzahlmesser^M
contagiri^M
tacómetro^M

speedometer
indicateur^M de vitesse^F
Tachometer^M
tachimetro^M
velocímetro^M

mileometer
compteur^M kilométrique
Kilometerzähler^M
contachilometri^M totale
cuentakilómetros^M

seat-belt warning light
témoin^M de ceinture^F de sécurité^F
Anzeige^F "Sicherheitsgurte anlegen"
spia^F delle cinture^F di sicurezza^F non allacciate
luz^F de advertencia^F del cinturón^M de seguridad^F

trip mileometer
totalisateur^M journalier
Tageskilometerzähler^M
contachilometri^M parziale
odómetro^M

door open warning light
témoin^M d'ouverture^F de porte^F
Warnleuchte^F "Tür offen"
spia^F delle porte^F aperte
luz^F de advertencia^F de puerta^F abierta

windscreen wiper blade
balai^M d'essuie-glace^M
Wischblatt^N
spatola^F metallica
soporte^M

windscreen wiper
essuie-glace^M
Scheibenwischer^M
tergicristallo^M
limpiaparabrisas^M

joint
articulation^F
Gelenk^N
articolazione^F
articulación^F

wiper blade rubber
lame^F
Wischgummi^M
spazzola^F di gomma^F
limpiador^M

wiper arm
bras^M d'essuie-glace^M
Wischerarm^M
braccio^M del tergicristallo^M
brazo^M

tension spring
ressort^M de tension^F
Zugfeder^F
molla^F di tensione^F
resorte^M tensor

pivot spindle
arbre^M cannelé
Wischerachse^F
perno^M oscillante
tubo^M articulado

TRANSPORT AND MACHINERY

355

car

TRANSPORT AND MACHINERY

accessories
accessoires^M
Zubehör^N
accessori^M
accesorios^M

jumper cables
câbles^M de démarrage^M
Starthilfekabel^N
cavi^M di accoppiamento^M
cables^M de emergencia^F

black clamp
pince^F noire
schwarze Klemme^F
morsetto^M nero
pinza^F negra

floor mat
tapis^M de plancher^M
Fußraummatte^F
tappetino^M
alfombrilla^F

roller shade
store^M à enroulement^M automatique
Sonnenrollo^N
tendina^F parasole avvolgibile
cortina^F de enrollamiento automático

red clamp
pince^F rouge
rote Klemme^F
morsetto^M rosso
pinza^F roja

cable
câble^M
Kabel^N
cavo^M
cable^M

ball mount
ferrure^F d'attelage^M
Unterteil^N
supporto^M della sfera^F
enganche^M de bola^F

hitch ball
boule^F d'attelage^M
Anhängerkupplung^F
occhione^M di traino^M
gancho^M de arrastre^M

four-way lug wrench
clé^F en croix^F
Kreuzschlüssel^M
chiave^F a croce^F
llave^F en cruz^M

snow brush with scraper
balai^M à neige^F à grattoir^M
Schneefeger^M mit Eiskratzer^M
spazzola^F da neve^F con raschietto^M
escoba^F de nieve^F con rascador^M

ski rack
porte-skis^M
Skiträger^M
portasci^M
porta-esquí^M

bike carrier
porte-vélos^M
Fahrradträger^M
portabici^M
portabicicletas^M

jack
cric^M
Wagenheber^M
cric^M
gato^M

sun visor
pare-soleil^M
Windschutzscheiben^F-Sonnenschutz^M
parasole^M
parasol^M

handle
manivelle^F
Kurbel^F
manovella^F
manivela^F

car cover
housse^F pour automobile^F
Autoplane^F
telone^M proteggiauto
funda^F de automóvil^M

child seat
siège^M de sécurité^F pour enfant^M
Kindersitz^M
seggiolino^M per bambini^M
silla^F de seguridad^F para niños^M

brakes

freins ^{M} | Bremsen ^{F} | freni ^{M} | frenos ^{M}

disc brake
frein ^{M} à disque ^{M}
Scheibenbremse ^{F}
freno ^{M} a disco ^{M}
freno ^{M} de disco ^{M}

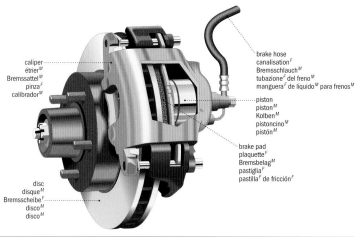

brake hose
canalisation ^{F}
Bremsschlauch ^{M}
tubazione ^{F} del freno ^{M}
manguera ^{F} de líquido ^{M} para frenos ^{M}

caliper
étrier ^{M}
Bremssattel ^{M}
pinza ^{F}
calibrador ^{M}

piston
piston ^{M}
Kolben ^{M}
pistoncino ^{M}
pistón ^{M}

brake pad
plaquette ^{F}
Bremsbelag ^{M}
pastiglia ^{F}
pastilla ^{F} de fricción ^{F}

disc
disque ^{M}
Bremsscheibe ^{F}
disco ^{M}
disco ^{M}

brake shoe
segment ^{M}
Bremsbacke ^{F}
ganascia ^{F}
zapata ^{F}

drum brake
frein ^{M} à tambour ^{M}
Trommelbremse ^{F}
freno ^{M} a tamburo ^{M}
freno ^{M} de tambor ^{M}

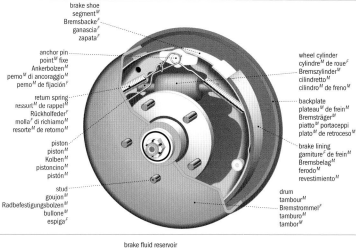

anchor pin
point ^{M} fixe
Ankerbolzen ^{M}
perno ^{M} di ancoraggio ^{M}
perno ^{M} de fijación ^{F}

wheel cylinder
cylindre ^{M} de roue ^{F}
Bremszylinder ^{M}
cilindretto ^{M}
cilindro ^{M} de freno ^{M}

return spring
ressort ^{M} de rappel ^{M}
Rückholfeder ^{F}
molla ^{F} di richiamo ^{M}
resorte ^{M} de retorno ^{M}

backplate
plateau ^{M} de frein ^{M}
Bremsträger ^{M}
piatto ^{M} portaceppi ^{M}
plato ^{M} de retroceso ^{M}

piston
piston ^{M}
Kolben ^{M}
pistoncino ^{M}
pistón ^{M}

brake lining
garniture ^{F} de frein ^{M}
Bremsbelag ^{M}
ferodo ^{M}
revestimiento ^{M}

stud
goujon ^{M}
Radbefestigungsbolzen ^{M}
bullone ^{M}
espiga ^{F}

drum
tambour ^{M}
Bremstrommel ^{F}
tamburo ^{M}
tambor ^{M}

brake fluid reservoir
réservoir ^{M} de liquide ^{M} de frein ^{M}
Bremsflüssigkeitsbehälter ^{M}
serbatoio ^{M} del liquido ^{M} dei freni ^{M}
depósito ^{M} del líquido ^{M} de frenos ^{M}

brake booster
servofrein ^{M}
Bremskraftverstärker ^{M}
servofreno ^{M}
servofreno ^{M}

antilock braking system (ABS)
système ^{M} de freinage ^{M} antiblocage
Antiblockiersystem ^{N} (ABS)
ABS ^{M}, sistema ^{M} frenante antibloccaggio
sistema ^{M} antibloqueo de frenos ^{M}

electronic control unit
module ^{M} de commande ^{F} électronique
elektrische Steuereinheit ^{F}
unità ^{F} di controllo ^{M} elettronico
unidad ^{F} de control ^{M} electrónico

master cylinder
maître ^{M}-cylindre ^{M}
Hauptzylinder ^{M}
cilindro ^{M} principale
cilindro ^{M} maestro

brake pedal
pédale ^{F} de frein ^{M}
Bremspedal ^{N}
pedale ^{M} del freno ^{M}
pedal ^{M} del freno ^{M}

wheel speed sensor
capteur ^{M} de vitesse ^{F} de roue ^{F}
Räder ^{N}-Drehgeschwindigkeitssensor ^{M}
sensore ^{M} di velocità ^{F} delle ruote ^{F}
sensor ^{M} de velocidad ^{F} de las ruedas ^{F}

pump and motor assembly
groupe ^{M} électropompe ^{F}
Elektropumpe ^{F}
gruppo ^{M} dell'elettropompa ^{F}
equipo ^{M} electrobomba ^{F}

sensor wiring circuit
circuit ^{M} capteurs ^{M}
Sensorkreis ^{M}
circuito ^{M} elettrico dei sensori ^{M}
circuito ^{M} eléctrico de los captadores ^{M}

disc brake
frein ^{M} à disque ^{M}
Scheibenbremse ^{F}
freno ^{M} a disco ^{M}
freno ^{M} de disco ^{M}

accumulator
accumulateur ^{M}
Akkumulator ^{M}
accumulatore ^{M}
acumulador ^{M}

braking circuit
circuit ^{M} de freinage ^{M}
Bremskreis ^{M}
circuito ^{M} frenante
circuito ^{M} de frenado ^{M}

brake pressure modulator
modulateur ^{M} de pression ^{F} de freinage ^{M}
Bremskraftregler ^{M}
modulatore ^{M} della pressione ^{F} dei freni ^{M}
modulador ^{M} de presión ^{F} de frenado ^{M}

TRANSPORT AND MACHINERY

tyre

pneu^M | Reifen^M | pneumatico^M | neumático^M

technical specifications
spécifications^F techniques
Kennzeichnung^F
dati^M tecnici
especificaciones^F técnicas^F

tread design
sculptures^F
Profil^N
scolpitura^F del battistrada^M
dibujo^M de la superficie^F de rodadura^F

scuff rib
bourrelet^M
Scheuerleiste^F
striscia^F antiabrasiva
banda^F protectora

sidewall
flanc^M
Reifenflanke^F
fianco^M
costado^M

bead
talon^M
Wulst^M
tallone^M
moldura^F

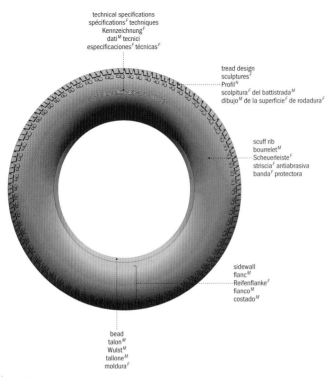

**examples of tyres
exemples^M de pneus^M
Reifenarten^F
esempi^M di pneumatici^M
ejemplos^M de neumáticos^M**

performance tyre
pneu^M de performance^F
Sportreifen^M
pneumatico^M sportivo
neumático^M de rendimiento^M

all-season tyre
pneu^M toutes saisons^F
Ganzjahresreifen^M
pneumatico^M per tutte le stagioni^F
neumático^M de todas las estaciones^F

studded tyre
pneu^M à crampons^M
Spikereifen^M
pneumatico^M chiodato
neumático^M de tacos^M

winter tyre
pneu^M d'hiver^M
Winterreifen^M
pneumatico^M invernale
neumático^M de invierno^M

touring tyre
pneu^M autoroutier
Touringreifen^M
pneumatico^M granturismo
neumático^M de turismo^M

radiator

radiateur^M | Kühler^M | radiatore^M | radiador^M

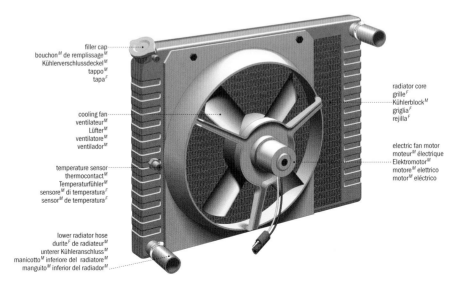

filler cap
bouchon^M de remplissage^M
Kühlerverschlussdeckel^M
tappo^M
tapa^F

cooling fan
ventilateur^M
Lüfter^M
ventilatore^M
ventilador^M

temperature sensor
thermocontact^M
Temperaturfühler^M
sensore^M di temperatura^F
sensor^M de temperatura^F

lower radiator hose
durite^F de radiateur^M
unterer Kühleranschluss^M
manicotto^M inferiore del radiatore^M
manguito^M inferior del radiador^M

radiator core
grille^F
Kühlerblock^M
griglia^F
rejilla^F

electric fan motor
moteur^M électrique
Elektromotor^M
motore^M elettrico
motor^M eléctrico

spark plug

bougie^F d'allumage^M | Zündkerze^F | candela^F | bujía^F

spark plug
borne^F
Anschluss^M für Zündkabel^N
morsetto^M terminale a spina^F
borne^M

centre electrode
électrode^F centrale
Mittelelektrode^F
elettrodo^M centrale
electrodo^M central

groove
cannelure^F
Kriechstrombarriere^F
scanalatura^F
ranura^F

insulator
isolateur^M
Isolator^M
corpo^M isolante
aislador^M

hex nut
écrou^M hexagonal
Sechskantmutter^F
dado^M esagonale
hexagonal

spark plug seat
joint^M de bougie^F
Zündkerzendichtring^M
rondella^F di tenuta^F
junta^F

spark plug body
culot^M
Zündkerzengehäuse^N
radice^F filettata
cuerpo^M metálico de la bujía^F

side electrode
électrode^F de masse^F
Masseelektrode^F
elettrodo^M di massa^F
electrodo^M de masa^F

spark plug gap
écartement^M des électrodes^F
Funkenstrecke^F
distanza^F tra le puntine^F
espacio^M para la chispa^F

battery

batterie^F d'accumulateurs^M | Batterie^F | batteria^F | batería^F

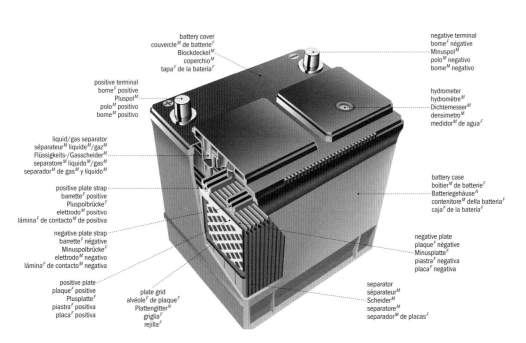

battery cover
couvercle^M de batterie^F
Blockdeckel^M
coperchio^M
tapa^F de la batería^F

negative terminal
borne^F négative
Minuspol^M
polo^M negativo
borne^M negativo

positive terminal
borne^F positive
Pluspol^M
polo^M positivo
borne^M positivo

hydrometer
hydromètre^M
Dichtemesser^M
densimetro^M
medidor^M de agua^F

liquid/gas separator
séparateur^M liquide^M/gaz^M
Flüssigkeits-/Gasscheider^M
separatore^M liquido^M/gas^M
separador^M de gas^M y líquido^M

battery case
boîtier^M de batterie^F
Batteriegehäuse^N
contenitore^M della batteria^F
caja^F de la batería^F

positive plate strap
barrette^F positive
Pluspolbrücke^F
elettrodo^M positivo
lámina^F de contacto^M de positiva

negative plate strap
barrette^F négative
Minuspolbrücke^F
elettrodo^M negativo
lámina^F de contacto^M negativa

negative plate
plaque^F négative
Minusplatte^F
piastra^F negativa
placa^F negativa

positive plate
plaque^F positive
Plusplatte^F
piastra^F positiva
placa^F positiva

plate grid
alvéole^F de plaque^F
Plattengitter^N
griglia^F
rejilla^F

separator
séparateur^M
Scheider^M
separatore^M
separador^M de placas^F

TRANSPORT AND MACHINERY

359

petrol engine

moteur^M à essence^F | Ottomotor^M | motore^M a benzina^F | motor^M de gasolina^F

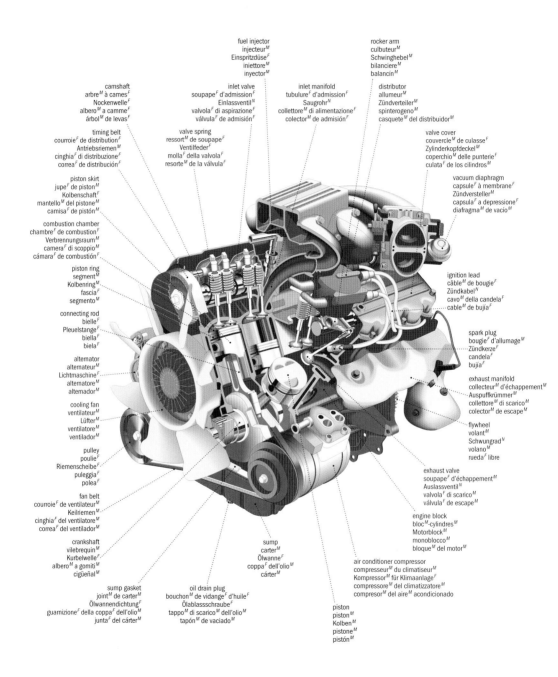

fuel injector
injecteur^M
Einspritzdüse^F
iniettore^M
inyector^M

rocker arm
culbuteur^M
Schwinghebel^M
bilanciere^M
balancín^M

camshaft
arbre^M à cames^F
Nockenwelle^F
albero^M a camme^F
árbol^M de levas^F

inlet valve
soupape^F d'admission^F
Einlassventil^N
valvola^F di aspirazione^F
válvula^F de admisión^F

inlet manifold
tubulure^F d'admission^F
Saugrohr^N
collettore^M di alimentazione^F
colector^M de admisión^F

distributor
allumeur^M
Zündverteiler^M
spinterogeno^M
casquete^M del distribuidor^M

timing belt
courroie^F de distribution^F
Antriebsriemen^M
cinghia^F di distribuzione^F
correa^F de distribución^F

valve spring
ressort^M de soupape^F
Ventilfeder^F
molla^F della valvola^F
resorte^M de la válvula^F

valve cover
couvercle^M de culasse^F
Zylinderkopfdeckel^M
coperchio^M delle punterie^F
culata^F de los cilindros^M

piston skirt
jupe^F de piston^M
Kolbenschaft^F
mantello^M del pistone^M
camisa^F de pistón^M

vacuum diaphragm
capsule^F à membrane^F
Zündversteller^M
capsula^F a depressione^F
diafragma^M de vacío^M

combustion chamber
chambre^F de combustion^F
Verbrennungsraum^M
camera^F di scoppio^M
cámara^F de combustión^F

piston ring
segment^M
Kolbenring^M
fascia^F
segmento^M

ignition lead
câble^M de bougie^F
Zündkabel^N
cavo^M della candela^F
cable^M de bujía^F

connecting rod
bielle^F
Pleuelstange^F
biella^F
biela^F

spark plug
bougie^F d'allumage^M
Zündkerze^F
candela^F
bujía^F

alternator
alternateur^M
Lichtmaschine^F
alternatore^M
alternador^M

exhaust manifold
collecteur^M d'échappement^M
Auspuffkrümmer^M
collettore^M di scarico^M
colector^M de escape^M

cooling fan
ventilateur^M
Lüfter^M
ventilatore^M
ventilador^M

flywheel
volant^M
Schwungrad^N
volano^M
rueda^F libre

pulley
poulie^F
Riemenscheibe^F
puleggia^F
polea^F

exhaust valve
soupape^F d'échappement^M
Auslassventil^N
valvola^F di scarico^M
válvula^F de escape^M

fan belt
courroie^F de ventilateur^M
Keilriemen^M
cinghia^F del ventilatore^M
correa^F del ventilador^M

engine block
bloc^M-cylindres^M
Motorblock^M
monoblocco^M
bloque^M del motor^M

crankshaft
vilebrequin^M
Kurbelwelle^F
albero^M a gomiti^M
cigüeñal^M

sump
carter^M
Ölwanne^F
coppa^F dell'olio^M
cárter^M

air conditioner compressor
compresseur^M du climatiseur^M
Kompressor^M für Klimaanlage^F
compressore^M del climatizzatore^M
compresor^M del aire^M acondicionado

sump gasket
joint^M de carter^M
Ölwannendichtung^F
guarnizione^F della coppa^F dell'olio^M
junta^F del cárter^M

oil drain plug
bouchon^M de vidange^F d'huile^F
Ölablassschraube^F
tappo^M di scarico^M dell'olio^M
tapón^M de vaciado^M

piston
piston^M
Kolben^M
pistone^M
pistón^M

TRANSPORT AND MACHINERY

caravan

caravane^F | Wohnwagen^M | rimorchi^M e autocaravan^M | caravana^F

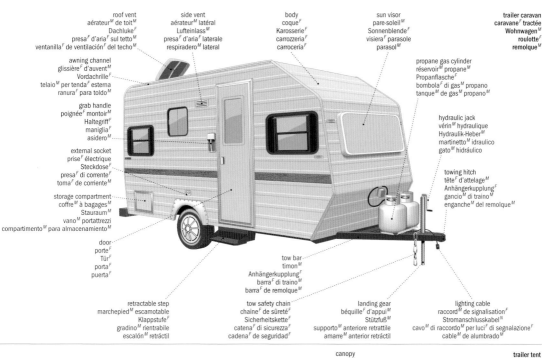

roof vent
aérateur^M de toit^M
Dachluke^F
presa^F d'aria^F sul tetto^M
ventanilla^F de ventilación^F del techo^M

side vent
aérateur^M latéral
Lufteinlass^M
presa^F d'aria^F laterale
respiradero^M lateral

body
coque^F
Karosserie^F
carrozzeria^F
carroceria^F

sun visor
pare-soleil^M
Sonnenblende^F
visiera^F parasole
parasol^M

trailer caravan
caravane^F tractée
Wohnwagen^M
roulotte^F
remolque^M

awning channel
glissière^F d'auvent^M
Vordachrille^F
telaio^M per tenda^F esterna
ranura^F para toldo^M

propane gas cylinder
réservoir^M propane^M
Propanflasche^F
bombola^F di gas^M propano
tanque^M de gas^M propano^M

grab handle
poignée^F montoir^M
Haltegriff^F
maniglia^F
asidero^M

hydraulic jack
vérin^M hydraulique
Hydraulik-Heber^M
martinetto^M idraulico
gato^M hidráulico

external socket
prise^F électrique
Steckdose^F
presa^F di corrente^F
toma^F de corriente^M

towing hitch
tête^F d'attelage^M
Anhängerkupplung^F
gancio^M di traino^M
enganche^M del remolque^M

storage compartment
coffre^M à bagages^M
Stauraum^M
vano^M portattrezzi
compartimento^M para almacenamiento^M

door
porte^F
Tür^F
porta^F
puerta^F

tow bar
timon^M
Anhängerkupplung^F
barra^F di traino^M
barra^F de remolque^M

retractable step
marchepied^M escamotable
Klappstufe^F
gradino^M rientrabile
escalón^M retráctil

tow safety chain
chaîne^F de sûreté^F
Sicherheitskette^F
catena^F di sicurezza^F
cadena^F de seguridad^F

landing gear
béquille^F d'appui^M
Stützfuß^M
supporto^M anteriore retrattile
amarre^M anterior retráctil

lighting cable
raccord^M de signalisation^F
Stromanschlusskabel^N
cavo^M di raccordo^M per luci^F di segnalazione^F
cable^F de alumbrado^M

roof
toit^M
Dach^N
tetto^M
techo^M

canopy
auvent^M
Vordach^N
tettuccio^M
toldo^M

trailer tent
caravane^F pliante
Zeltwagen^M
carrello^M tenda^F
caravana^F plegable

bunk
lit^M
Bett^N
letto^M
litera^F

window
fenêtre^F
Fenster^N
finestrino^M
ventana^F

spare tyre
roue^F de secours^M
Reserverad^N
ruota^F di scorta^F
rueda^F de repuesto^M

body
coque^F
Aufbau^M
scocca^F
carrocería^F

stabilizer jack
béquille^F d'appoint^M
Stütze^F
supporto^M stabilizzatore
gato^M estabilizador

screen door
porte^F moustiquaire^F
Fliegengittertür^F
porta^F a zanzariera^F
puerta^F mosquitera

air conditioner
climatiseur^M
Klimaanlage^F
condizionatore^M
aire^M acondicionado

camper
auto^F-caravane^F
Wohnmobil^N
autocaravan^M
autocaravana^M

luggage rack
porte-bagages^M
Gepäckträger^M
portabagagli^M
portaequipajes^M

ladder
échelle^F
Leiter^F
scala^F
escalerilla^F

bus

autobus^M | Bus^M | autobus^M | autobús^M

school bus
autobus^M scolaire
Schulbus^M
scuolabus^M
autobús^M escolar

blind spot mirror
rétroviseur^M grand-angle^M
Weitwinkelspiegel^M
specchietto^M per il punto^M cieco
retrovisor^M de gran angular^M

blinking lights
feux^M intermittents
Blinklichter^N
luci^F intermittenti
faros^M intermitentes

outside mirror
rétroviseur^M extérieur
Außenspiegel^M
specchietto^M retrovisore esterno
espejo^M retrovisor exterior

crossover mirror
miroir^M de traversée^F avant
Sicherheitsspiegel^M
specchietto^M anteriore di accostame
espejo^M de cercanías^F

city bus
autobus^M
Linienbus^M
autobus^M urbano
autobús^M urbano

air intake
prise^F d'air^M
Lufteinlass^M
presa^F d'aria^F
toma^F de aire^M

two-leaf door
porte^F à deux vantaux^M
zweiflügelige Ausgangstür^F
porta^F a due battenti^M
puerta^F de dos hojas^F

crossing arm
bras^M d'éloignement^M
Absperrarm^M
barra^F distanziatrice
barra^F distanciadora

route sign
indicateur^M de ligne^F
Linienanzeige^F
indicatore^M di linea^F
indicador^M de línea^F

coach
autocar^M
Reisebus^M
pullman^M
autocar^M

engine air intake
prise^F d'air^M du moteur^M
Motorlufteinlass^M
presa^F d'aria^F del motore^M
toma^F de aire^M del motor^M

entrance door
porte^F d'entrée^F
Einstiegstür^F
porta^F di entrata^F
puerta^F de entrada^F

engine compartment
compartiment^M moteur^M
Motorraum^M
vano^M motore^M
compartimiento^M motor

baggage compartment
soute^F à bagages^M
Gepäckraum^M
bagagliaio^M
maletero^M

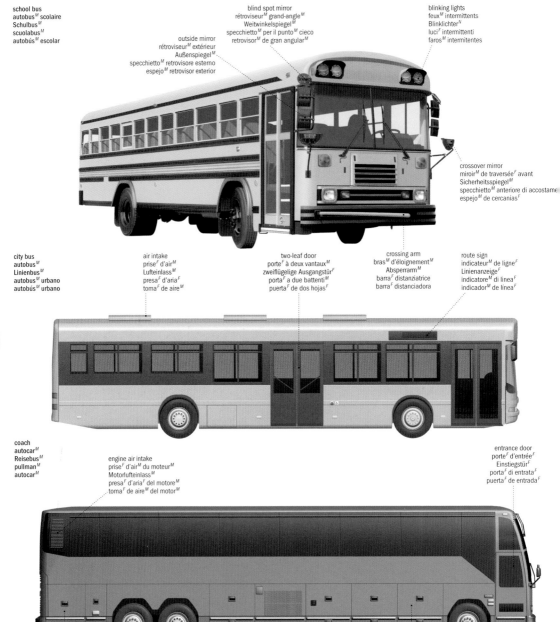

double-decker bus
autobus^M à impériale^F
Doppeldeckerbus^M
autobus^M a due piani^M
autocar^M de dos pisos^M

route sign
indicateur^M de ligne^F
Linienanzeige^F
indicatore^M di linea^F
indicador^M de línea^F

upper deck
impériale^F
Oberdeck^N
piano^M superiore
piso^M superior

minibus
minibus^M
Kleinbus^M
minibus^M
minibús^M

lift door
porte^F de l'élévateur^M
elektrische Schiebetür^F
porta^F dell'elevatore^M
puerta^F de la plataforma^F elevadora

blind spot mirror
rétroviseur^M grand-angle^M
Weitwinkelspiegel^M
specchietto^M per il punto^M cieco
retrovisor^M gran angular

West Coast mirror
rétroviseur^M
Außenspiegel^M
specchietto^M retrovisore
espejo^M retrovisor

handrail
barre^F de maintien^M
Haltegriff^M
corrimano^M
pasamano^M

wheelchair lift
élévateur^M pour fauteuils^M roulants
Rollstuhllift^M
elevatore^M per sedie^F a rotelle^F
plataforma^F elevadora para silla^F de ruedas^F

platform
plate-forme^F
Plattform^F
piattaforma^F
plataforma^F

entrance door
porte^F d'entrée^F
Einstiegstür^F
porta^F di entrata^F
puerta^F de entrada^F

articulated bus
autobus^M articulé
Gelenkbus^M
autobus^M articolato
autobús^M articulado

articulated joint
section^F articulée
Gelenk^N
passaggio^M a soffietto^M
sección^F articulada

rear rigid section
tronçon^M rigide arrière
steifer Nachläufer^M
sezione^F rigida posteriore
remolque^M rígido trasero

front rigid section
tronçon^M rigide avant
steifes Vorderteil^N
sezione^F rigida anteriore
sección^F rígida de tracción^F delantera

TRANSPORT AND MACHINERY

trucking

camionnage[M] | Lastkraftfahrzeuge[N] | autoveicoli[M] industriali | camiones[M]

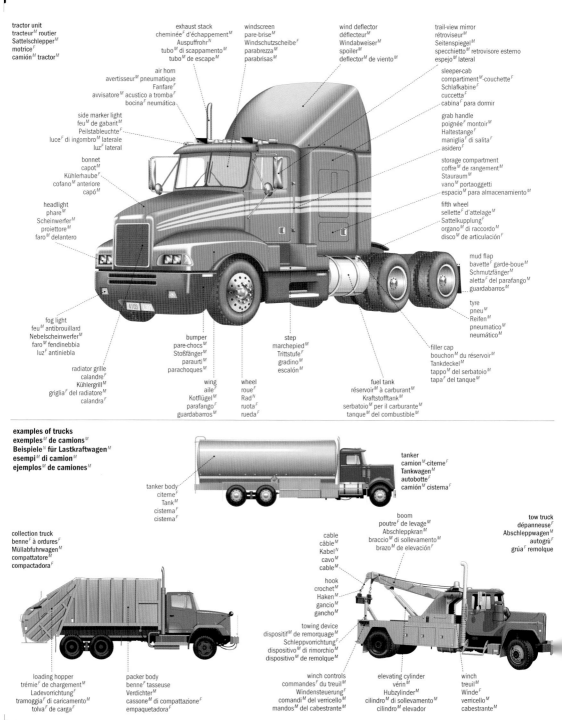

tractor unit
tracteur[M] routier
Sattelschlepper[M]
motrice[F]
camión[M] tractor[M]

exhaust stack
cheminée[F] d'échappement[M]
Auspuffrohr[N]
tubo[M] di scappamento[M]
tubo[M] de escape[M]

windscreen
pare-brise[M]
Windschutzscheibe[F]
parabrezza[M]
parabrisas[M]

wind deflector
déflecteur[M]
Windabweiser[M]
spoiler[M]
deflector[M] de viento[M]

trail-view mirror
rétroviseur[M]
Seitenspiegel[M]
specchietto[M] retrovisore esterno
espejo[M] lateral

air horn
avertisseur[M] pneumatique
Fanfare[F]
avvisatore[M] acustico a tromba[F]
bocina[F] neumática

sleeper-cab
compartiment[M]-couchette[F]
Schlafkabine[F]
cuccetta[F]
cabina[F] para dormir

side marker light
feu[M] de gabarit[M]
Peilstableuchte[F]
luce[F] di ingombro[M] laterale
luz[F] lateral

grab handle
poignée[F] montoir[M]
Haltestange[F]
maniglia[F] di salita[F]
asidero[F]

bonnet
capot[M]
Kühlerhaube[F]
cofano[M] anteriore
capó[M]

storage compartment
coffre[M] de rangement[M]
Stauraum[M]
vano[M] portaoggetti
espacio[M] para almacenamiento[M]

headlight
phare[M]
Scheinwerfer[M]
proiettore[M]
faro[M] delantero

fifth wheel
sellette[F] d'attelage[M]
Sattelkupplung[F]
organo[M] di raccordo[M]
disco[M] de articulación[F]

mud flap
bavette[F] garde-boue[M]
Schmutzfänger[M]
aletta[F] del parafango[M]
guardabarros[M]

tyre
pneu[M]
Reifen[M]
pneumatico[M]
neumático[M]

fog light
feu[M] antibrouillard
Nebelscheinwerfer[M]
faro[M] fendinebbia
luz[F] antiniebla

bumper
pare-chocs[M]
Stoßfänger[M]
paraurti[M]
parachoques[M]

step
marchepied[M]
Trittstufe[F]
gradino[M]
escalón[M]

filler cap
bouchon[M] du réservoir[M]
Tankdeckel[M]
tappo[M] del serbatoio[M]
tapa[F] del tanque[M]

radiator grille
calandre[F]
Kühlergrill[M]
griglia[F] del radiatore[M]
calandra[F]

wing
aile[F]
Kotflügel[M]
parafango[F]
guardabarros[M]

wheel
roue[F]
Rad[N]
ruota[F]
rueda[F]

fuel tank
réservoir[M] à carburant[M]
Kraftstofftank[M]
serbatoio[M] per il carburante[M]
tanque[M] del combustible[M]

examples of trucks
exemples[M] de camions[M]
Beispiele[N] für Lastkraftwagen[M]
esempi[M] di camion[M]
ejemplos[M] de camiones[M]

tanker
camion[M]-citerne[F]
Tankwagen[M]
autobotte[F]
camión[M] cisterna[F]

tanker body
citerne[F]
Tank[M]
cisterna[F]
cisterna[F]

boom
poutre[F] de levage[M]
Abschleppkran[M]
braccio[M] di sollevamento[M]
brazo[M] de elevación[F]

tow truck
dépanneuse[F]
Abschleppwagen[M]
autogrù[F]
grúa[F] remolque

collection truck
benne[F] à ordures[F]
Müllabfuhrwagen[M]
compattatore[M]
compactadora[F]

cable
câble[M]
Kabel[N]
cavo[M]
cable[M]

hook
crochet[M]
Haken[M]
gancio[M]
gancho[M]

towing device
dispositif[M] de remorquage[M]
Schleppvorrichtung[F]
dispositivo[M] di rimorchio[M]
dispositivo[M] de remolque[M]

loading hopper
trémie[F] de chargement[M]
Ladevorrichtung[F]
tramoggia[F] di caricamento[M]
tolva[F] de carga[F]

packer body
benne[F] tasseuse
Verdichter[M]
cassone[M] di compattazione[F]
empaquetadora[F]

winch controls
commandes[F] du treuil[M]
Windensteuerung[F]
comandi[M] del verricello[M]
mandos[M] del cabestrante[M]

elevating cylinder
vérin[M]
Hubzylinder[M]
cilindro[M] di sollevamento[M]
cilindro[M] elevador

winch
treuil[M]
Winde[F]
verricello[M]
cabestrante[M]

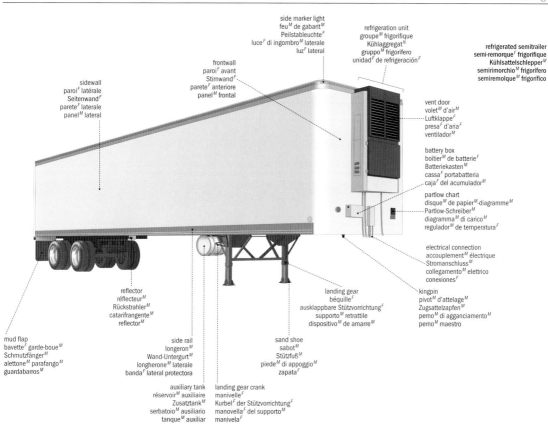

side marker light
feu^M de gabarit^M
Peilstableuchte^F
luce^F di ingombro^M laterale
luz^F lateral

refrigeration unit
groupe^M frigorifique
Kühlaggregat^N
gruppo^M frigorifero
unidad^F de refrigeración^F

refrigerated semitrailer
semi-remorque^F frigorifique
Kühlsattelschlepper^M
semirimorchio^M frigorifero
semiremolque^M frigorifico

frontwall
paroi^F avant
Stirnwand^F
parete^F anteriore
panel^M frontal

sidewall
paroi^F latérale
Seitenwand^F
parete^F laterale
panel^M lateral

vent door
volet^M d'air^M
Luftklappe^F
presa^F d'aria^F
ventilador^M

battery box
boîtier^M de batterie^F
Batteriekasten^M
cassa^F portabatteria
caja^F del acumulador^M

partlow chart
disque^M de papier^M-diagramme^M
Partlow-Schreiber^M
diagramma^M di carico^M
regulador^M de temperatura^F

electrical connection
accouplement^M électrique
Stromanschluss^M
collegamento^M elettrico
conexiones^F

reflector
réflecteur^M
Rückstrahler^M
catarifrangente^M
reflector^M

landing gear
béquille^F
ausklappbare Stützvorrichtung^F
supporto^M retrattile
dispositivo^M de amarre^M

kingpin
pivot^M d'attelage^M
Zugsattelzapfen^M
perno^M di agganciamento^M
perno^M maestro

mud flap
bavette^F garde-boue^M
Schmutzfänger^M
alettone^M parafango^M
guardabarros^M

side rail
longeron^M
Wand-Untergurt^M
longherone^M laterale
banda^F lateral protectora

sand shoe
sabot^M
Stützfuß^M
piede^M di appoggio^M
zapata^F

auxiliary tank
réservoir^M auxiliaire
Zusatztank^M
serbatoio^M ausiliario
tanque^M auxiliar

landing gear crank
manivelle^F
Kurbel^F der Stützvorrichtung^F
manovella^F del supporto^M
manivela^F

van
camion^M porteur^M fourgon^M
Transporter^M
furgone^M
camioneta^F

concrete mixer truck
camion^M-toupie^F
Transportmischer^M
betoniera^F
hormigonera^F

street sweeper
balayeuse^F
Straßenkehrmaschine^F
spazzatrice^F
barredora^F

snowblower
chasse-neige^M à soufflerie^F
Schneefräse^F
spazzaneve^M a turbina^F
quitanieves^M

collection body
réceptacle^M à déchets^M
Sammelbehälter^M
cassone^M di raccolta^F dei rifiuti^M
cajón^M de basura^F

projection device
canal^M de projection^F
Schleuder^F
tubo^M di getto^M laterale
chimenea^F de expulsión^F

central brush
brosse^F centrale
Walzenbürste^F
spazzola^F rotante centrale
escoba^F central

worm
vis^F sans fin^F
Schnecke^F
vite^F senza fine^F
tornillo^M sin fin^M

lateral brush
brosse^F latérale
Tellerbürste^F
spazzola^F rotante laterale
escoba^F lateral

watering tube
canalisation^F d'arrosage^M
Wassersprühdüse^F
tubo^M annaffiatore^M
tubo^M de irrigación^F

TRANSPORT AND MACHINERY

365

motorcycle

moto^F | Motorrad^N | motocicletta^F | motocicleta^F

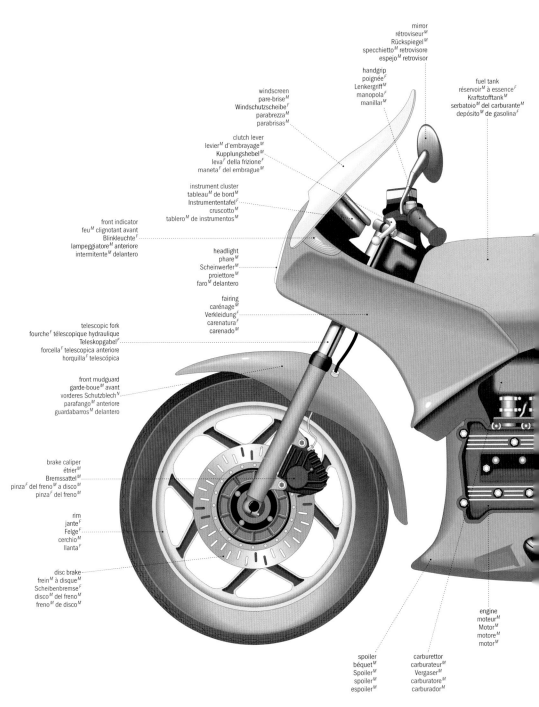

mirror
rétroviseur^M
Rückspiegel^M
specchietto^M retrovisore
espejo^M retrovisor

handgrip
poignée^F
Lenkergriff^M
manopola^F
manillar^M

fuel tank
réservoir^M à essence^F
Kraftstofftank^M
serbatoio^M del carburante^M
depósito^M de gasolina^F

windscreen
pare-brise^M
Windschutzscheibe^F
parabrezza^M
parabrisas^F

clutch lever
levier^M d'embrayage^M
Kupplungshebel^M
leva^F della frizione^F
maneta^F del embrague^M

instrument cluster
tableau^M de bord^M
Instrumententafel^F
cruscotto^M
tablero^M de instrumentos^M

front indicator
feu^M clignotant avant
Blinkleuchte^F
lampeggiatore^M anteriore
intermitente^M delantero

headlight
phare^M
Scheinwerfer^M
proiettore^M
faro^M delantero

fairing
carénage^M
Verkleidung^F
carenatura^F
carenado^M

telescopic fork
fourche^F télescopique hydraulique
Teleskopgabel^F
forcella^F telescopica anteriore
horquilla^F telescópica

front mudguard
garde-boue^M avant
vorderes Schutzblech^N
parafango^M anteriore
guardabarros^M delantero

brake caliper
étrier^M
Bremssattel^M
pinza^F del freno^M a disco^M
pinza^F del freno^M

rim
jante^F
Felge^F
cerchio^M
llanta^F

disc brake
frein^M à disque^M
Scheibenbremse^F
disco^M del freno^M
freno^M de disco^M

spoiler
béquet^M
Spoiler^M
spoiler^M
espoiler^M

carburettor
carburateur^M
Vergaser^M
carburatore^M
carburador^M

engine
moteur^M
Motor^M
motore^M
motor^M

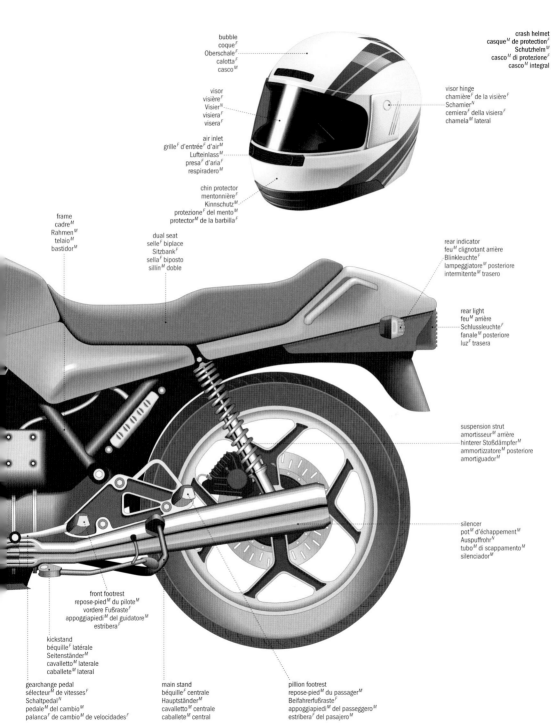

bubble
coque^F
Oberschale^F
calotta^F
casco^M

crash helmet
casque^M de protection^F
Schutzhelm^M
casco^M di protezione^F
casco^M integral

visor
visière^F
Visier^N
visiera^F
visera^F

visor hinge
charnière^F de la visière^F
Scharnier^N
cerniera^F della visiera^F
charnela^M lateral

air inlet
grille^F d'entrée^F d'air^M
Lufteinlass^M
presa^F d'aria^F
respiradero^M

chin protector
mentonnière^F
Kinnschutz^M
protezione^F del mento^M
protector^F de la barbilla^F

frame
cadre^M
Rahmen^M
telaio^M
bastidor^M

dual seat
selle^F biplace
Sitzbank^F
sella^F biposto
sillín^M doble

rear indicator
feu^M clignotant arrière
Blinkleuchte^F
lampeggiatore^M posteriore
intermitente^M trasero

rear light
feu^M arrière
Schlussleuchte^F
fanale^M posteriore
luz^F trasera

suspension strut
amortisseur^M arrière
hinterer Stoßdämpfer^M
ammortizzatore^M posteriore
amortiguador^M

silencer
pot^M d'échappement^M
Auspuffrohr^N
tubo^M di scappamento^M
silenciador^M

front footrest
repose-pied^M du pilote^M
vordere Fußraste^F
appoggiapiedi^M del guidatore^M
estribera^F

kickstand
béquille^F latérale
Seitenständer^M
cavalletto^M laterale
caballete^M lateral

gearchange pedal
sélecteur^M de vitesses^F
Schaltpedal^N
pedale^M del cambio^M
palanca^F de cambio^M de velocidades^F

main stand
béquille^F centrale
Hauptständer^M
cavalletto^M centrale
caballete^M central

pillion footrest
repose-pied^M du passager^M
Beifahrerfußraste^F
appoggiapiedi^M del passeggero^M
estribera^F del pasajero^M

motorcycle

instrument cluster
tableau^M de bord^M
Instrumententafel^F
cruscotto^M
tablero^M de instrumentos^M

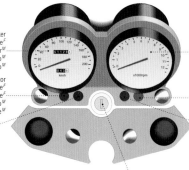

speedometer
indicateur^M de vitesse^F
Tachometer^M
tachimetro^M
velocímetro^M

tachometer
tachymètre^M
Drehzahlmesser^M
contagiri^M
tacómetro^M

oil pressure warning indicator
témoin^M de pression^F d'huile^F
Öldruckkontrollleuchte^F
spia^F della pressione^F dell'olio^M
luz^F indicadora de la presión^F del aceite^M

main beam warning light
témoin^M de phare^M
Fernlichtkontrollleuchte^F
spia^F delle luci^F abbaglianti
indicador^M de luz^F larga

neutral indicator
témoin^M de position^F neutre
Leerlaufanzeige^N
spia^F della posizione^F di folle
indicador^M de punto^M muerto

indicator telltale
témoin^M de clignotants^M
Blinkerkontrollleuchte^F
spia^F dell'indicatore^F di direzione^F
indicador^M del intermitente^M

ignition switch
commutateur^M d'allumage^M
Zündschalter^M
blocchetto^M di avviamento^M
interruptor^M de encendido^M

motorcycle : view from above
moto^F : vue^F en plongée^F
Motorrad^N: Draufsicht^F
motocicletta^F: vista^F dall'alto^M
motocicleta^F : vista^F desde lo alto^M

headlight
phare^M
Scheinwerfer^M
proiettore^M
faro^M delantero

front indicator
feu^M clignotant avant
Blinkleuchte^F
lampeggiatore^M anteriore
intermitente^M delantero

mirror
rétroviseur^M
Seitenspiegel^M
specchietto^M retrovisore
retrovisor^M

front brake lever
levier^M de frein^M avant
Hebel^M für Vorderbremse^F
leva^F del freno^M anteriore
maneta^F del freno^M delantero

clutch lever
levier^M d'embrayage^M
Kupplungshebel^M
leva^F della frizione^F
maneta^F del embrague^M

twist grip throttle
poignée^F des gaz^M
Gashebel^M
manopola^F dell'acceleratore^M
acelerador^M

dip switch
inverseur^M route^F-croisement^M
Abblendschalter^M
commutatore^M delle luci^F
interruptor^M de ráfagas^F

emergency switch
coupe-circuit^M d'urgence^F
Notschalter^M
interruttore^M di emergenza^F
interruptor^M de emergencia^F

horn
avertisseur^M
Hupe^F
clacson^M
claxon^M

starter button
bouton^M de démarreur^M
Zündschalter^M
interruttore^M di avviamento^M
interruptor^M de encendido^M

petrol tank cap
bouchon^M du réservoir^M
Benzintankverschluss^M
tappo^M del serbatoio^M
tapón^M del depósito^M de la gasolina^F

clutch housing
carter^M d'embrayage^M
Kupplungsgehäuse^N
scatola^F della frizione^F
cárter^M del embrague^M

gearchange pedal
sélecteur^M de vitesses^F
Schaltpedal^N
pedale^M del cambio^M
palanca^M de cambio^M de velocidades^F

rear brake pedal
pédale^F de frein^M arrière
Bremspedal^N
pedale^M del freno^M posteriore
pedal^M del freno^M trasero

front footrest
repose-pied^M du pilote^M
vordere Fußraste^F
appoggiapiedi^M del guidatore^M
estribera^F

pillion footrest
repose-pied^M du passager^M
Beifahrer-Fußraste^F
appoggiapiedi^M del passeggero^M
estribera^F del pasajero^M

silencer
pot^M d'échappement^M
Auspuffrohr^N
tubo^M di scappamento^M
tubo^M de escape^M

rear indicator
feu^M clignotant arrière
Blinkleuchte^F
lampeggiatore^M posteriore
intermitente^M trasero

rear light
feu^M arrière
Schlussleuchte^F
fanale^M posteriore
luz^F trasera

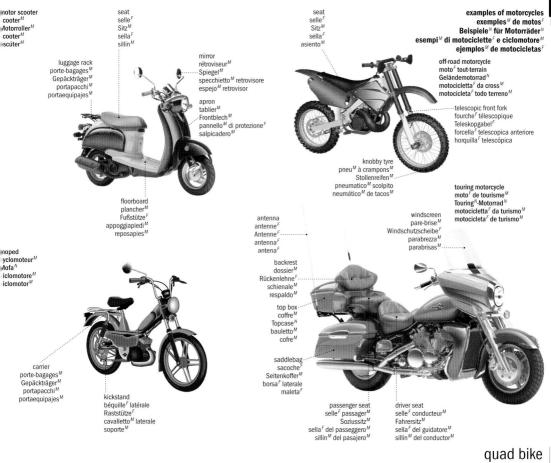

motor scooter
cooter^M
Motorroller^M
cooter^M
scúter^M

seat
selle^F
Sitz^M
sella^F
sillín^M

luggage rack
porte-bagages^M
Gepäckträger^M
portapacchi^M
portaequipajes^M

mirror
rétroviseur^M
Spiegel^M
specchietto^M retrovisore
espejo^M retrovisor

apron
tablier^M
Frontblech^M
pannello^M di protezione^F
salpicadero^M

floorboard
plancher^M
Fußstütze^F
appoggiapiedi^M
reposapies^M

moped
yclomoteur^M
Mofa^N
iclomotore^M
iclomotor^M

carrier
porte-bagages^M
Gepäckträger^M
portapacchi^M
portaequipajes^M

kickstand
béquille^F latérale
Raststütze^F
cavalletto^M laterale
soporte^M

seat
selle^F
Sitz^M
sella^F
asiento^M

examples of motorcycles
exemples^M de motos^F
Beispiele^N für Motorräder^N
esempi^M di motociclette^F e ciclomotore^M
ejemplos^M de motocicletas^F

off-road motorcycle
moto^F tout-terrain
Geländemotorrad^N
motocicletta^F da cross^M
motocicleta^F todo terreno^M

telescopic front fork
fourche^F télescopique
Teleskopgabel^F
forcella^F telescopica anteriore
horquilla^F telescópica

knobby tyre
pneu^M à crampons^M
Stollenreifen^M
pneumatico^M scolpito
neumático^M de tacos^M

touring motorcycle
moto^F de tourisme^M
Touring^N-Motorrad^N
motocicletta^F da turismo^M
motocicleta^F de turismo^M

antenna
antenne^F
Antenne^F
antenna^F
antena^F

windscreen
pare-brise^M
Windschutzscheibe^F
parabrezza^M
parabrisas^M

backrest
dossier^M
Rückenlehne^F
schienale^M
respaldo^M

top box
coffre^M
Topcase^N
bauletto^M
cofre^M

saddlebag
sacoche^F
Seitenkoffer^M
borsa^F laterale
maleta^F

passenger seat
selle^F passager^M
Soziussitz^M
sella^F del passeggero^M
sillín^M del pasajero^M

driver seat
selle^F conducteur^M
Fahrersitz^M
sella^F del guidatore^M
sillín^M del conductor^M

quad bike

quad^M | 4x4-Geländemotorrad^N | veicolo^M a trazione^F integrale 4x4 | quad^M

rear cargo rack
porte-bagages^M arrière
Gepäckträger^M
portapacchi^M posteriore
portaequipajes^M posterior

rear bumper
garde-boue^M arrière
hinterer Kotflügel^M
paraurti^M posteriore
parachoques^M posterior

silencer
pot^M d'échappement^M
Auspuffrohr^N
tubo^M di scappamento^M
silenciador^M

seat
selle^F
Sitz^M
sella^F
sillín^M

fuel tank
réservoir^M à essence^F
Kraftstofftank^M
serbatoio^M del carburante^M
depósito^M de gasolina^F

handgrip
poignée^F
Lenkergriff^M
manopola^F
manillar^M

bumper
pare-chocs^M
Stoßfänger^M
paraurti^M
parachoques^M

front shock absorber
amortisseur^M avant
Frontstoßdämpfer^M
ammortizzatore^M anteriore
amortiguador^M delantero

gear lever
sélecteur^M de vitesses^F
Schalthebel^M
pedale^M del cambio^M
palanca^F de cambio^M de velocidades^F

bicycle

bicyclette[F] | Fahrrad[N] | bicicletta[F] | bicicleta[F]

parts of a bicycle
parties[F] d'une bicyclette[F]
Teile[N] eines Fahrrads[N]
componenti[M] di una bicicletta[F]
partes[F] de una bicicleta[F]

saddle pillar
tige[F] de selle[F]
Sattelstütze[F]
cannotto[M] reggisella
poste[M] del asiento[M]

saddle
selle[F]
Sattel[M]
sella[F]
sillín[M]

tyre pump
pompe[F]
Luftpumpe[F]
pompa[F]
bomba[F] de aire[M]

cross
tube[M] horizon
Oberroh
canr
bar

seat stay
hauban[M]
hinterer Streben[M]
forcella[F] superiore
horquilla[F] trasera

seat tube
tube[M] de selle[F]
Sitzrohr[N]
tubo[M] verticale
tubo[M] del asiento[M]

rear brake
frein[M] arrière
hintere Felgenbremse[F]
freno[M] posteriore
freno[M] trasero

carrier
porte-bagages[M]
Gepäckträger[M]
portapacchi[M]
portaequipajes[M]

dynamo
dynamo[F]
Dynamo[M]
dinamo[F]
dinamo[F]

reflector
catadioptre[M]
Rückstrahler[M]
catarifrangente[M]
reflector[M]

rear light
feu[M] arrière
Rücklicht[N]
fanale[M] posteriore
luz[F] trasera

mudguard
garde-boue[M]
Schutzblech[N]
parafango[M]
guardabarros[M]

rear derailleur
dérailleur[M] arrière
hinterer Umwerfer[M]
deragliatore[M] posteriore
cambio[M] de marchas[F] trasero

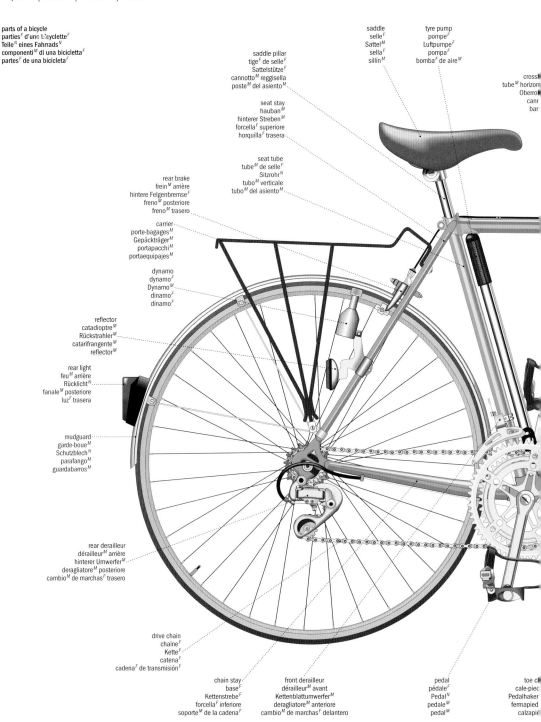

drive chain
chaine[F]
Kette[F]
catena[F]
cadena[F] de transmisión[F]

chain stay
base[F]
Kettenstrebe[F]
forcella[F] inferiore
soporte[M] de la cadena[F]

front derailleur
dérailleur[M] avant
Kettenblattumwerfer[M]
deragliatore[M] anteriore
cambio[M] de marchas[F] delantero

pedal
pédale[F]
Pedal[N]
pedale[M]
pedal[M]

toe cl
cale-pied
Pedalhaker
fermapied
calzapie

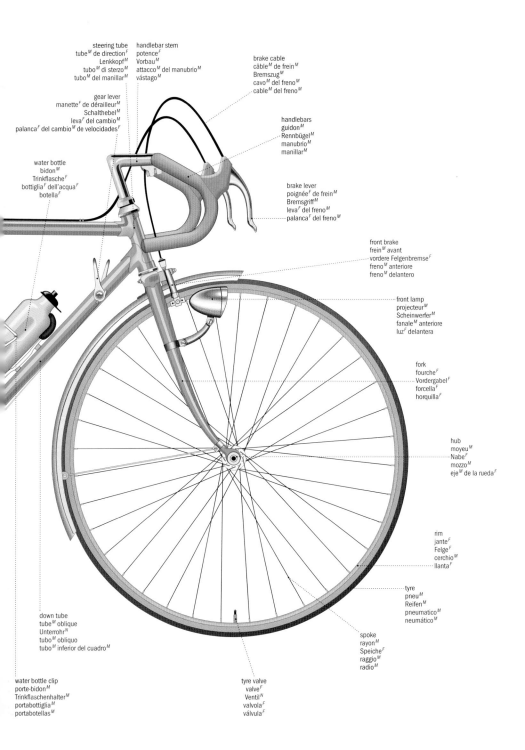

steering tube
tube^M de direction^F
Lenkkopf^M
tubo^M di sterzo^M
tubo^M del manillar^M

handlebar stem
potence^F
Vorbau^M
attacco^M del manubrio^M
vástago^M

brake cable
câble^M de frein^M
Bremszug^M
cavo^M del freno^M
cable^M del freno^M

gear lever
manette^F de dérailleur^M
Schalthebel^M
leva^F del cambio^M
palanca^F del cambio^M de velocidades^F

handlebars
guidon^M
Rennbügel^M
manubrio^M
manillar^M

water bottle
bidon^M
Trinkflasche^F
bottiglia^F dell'acqua^F
botella^F

brake lever
poignée^F de frein^M
Bremsgriff^M
leva^F del freno^M
palanca^F del freno^M

front brake
frein^M avant
vordere Felgenbremse^F
freno^M anteriore
freno^M delantero

front lamp
projecteur^M
Scheinwerfer^M
fanale^M anteriore
luz^F delantera

fork
fourche^F
Vordergabel^F
forcella^F
horquilla^F

hub
moyeu^M
Nabe^F
mozzo^M
eje^M de la rueda^F

rim
jante^F
Felge^F
cerchio^M
llanta^F

tyre
pneu^M
Reifen^M
pneumatico^M
neumático^M

down tube
tube^M oblique
Unterrohr^N
tubo^M obliquo
tubo^M inferior del cuadro^M

spoke
rayon^M
Speiche^F
raggio^M
radio^M

water bottle clip
porte-bidon^M
Trinkflaschenhalter^M
portabottiglia^M
portabotellas^M

tyre valve
valve^F
Ventil^N
valvola^F
válvula^F

TRANSPORT AND MACHINERY

bicycle

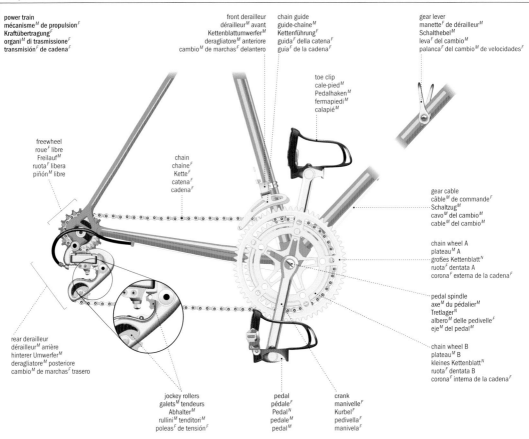

power train
mécanisme^M de propulsion^F
Kraftübertragung^F
organi^M di trasmissione^F
transmisión^F de cadena^F

front derailleur
dérailleur^M avant
Kettenblattumwerfer^M
deragliatore^M anteriore
cambio^M de marchas^F delantero

chain guide
guide-chaîne^M
Kettenführung^F
guida^F della catena^F
guía^F de la cadena^F

gear lever
manette^F de dérailleur^M
Schalthebel^M
leva^F del cambio^M
palanca^F del cambio^M de velocidades^F

toe clip
cale-pied^M
Pedalhaken^M
fermapiedi^M
calapié^M

freewheel
roue^F libre
Freilauf^M
ruota^F libera
piñón^M libre

chain
chaîne^F
Kette^F
catena^F
cadena^F

gear cable
câble^M de commande^F
Schaltzug^M
cavo^M del cambio^M
cable^M del cambio^M

chain wheel A
plateau^M A
großes Kettenblatt^N
ruota^F dentata A
corona^F externa de la cadena^F

pedal spindle
axe^M du pédalier^M
Tretlager^N
albero^M delle pedivelle^F
eje^M del pedal^M

chain wheel B
plateau^M B
kleines Kettenblatt^N
ruota^F dentata B
corona^F interna de la cadena^F

rear derailleur
dérailleur^M arrière
hinterer Umwerfer^M
deragliatore^M posteriore
cambio^M de marchas^F trasero

jockey rollers
galets^M tendeurs
Abhalter^M
rullini^M tenditori^M
poleas^F de tensión^F

pedal
pédale^F
Pedal^N
pedale^M
pedal^M

crank
manivelle^F
Kurbel^F
pedivella^F
manivela^F

accessories
accessoires^M
Zubehör^N
accessori^M
accesorios^M

cycle lock
cadenas^M
Schloss^N
lucchetto^M
candado^M para bicicleta^F

cycling helmet
casque^M de protection^F
Fahrradhelm^M
casco^M di protezione^F
casco^M protector

tool kit
trousse^F de dépannage^M
Werkzeugsatz^M
kit^M di attrezzi^M
herramientas^F

pannier bag
sacoche^F
Satteltasche^F
zaino^M
cartera^F

child carrier
siège^M de vélo^M pour enfant^M
Kindersitz^M
seggiolino^M per bambini^M
silla^F porta-niño^M

BMX bike
vélo^M cross^M
BMX-Rad^N, Mountainbike^N
mountain bike^F da cross^M
bicicleta^F BMX

child's tricycle
tricycle^M d'enfant^M
Dreirad^N
triciclo^M
triciclo^M

examples of bicycles
exemples^M de bicyclettes^F
Beispiele^N für Fahrräder^N
esempi^M di biciclette^F
ejemplos^M de bicicletas^F

all-terrain bicycle
vélo^M tout-terrain (VTT)
Mountain Bike^N
mountain bike^F
bicicleta^F todo terreno^M

Dutch bicycle
bicyclette^F hollandaise
Hollandrad^N
bicicletta^F olandese
bicicleta^F holandesa

road bicycle
bicyclette^F de course^F
Rennrad^N
bicicletta^F da corsa^F
bicicleta^F de carretera^F

city bicycle
bicyclette^F de ville^F
Stadtrad^N
city bike^F
bicicleta^F de ciudad^F

touring bicycle
bicyclette^F de tourisme^M
Tourenrad^N
bicicletta^F da turismo^M
bicicleta^F de turismo^M

tandem
tandem^M
Tandem^N
tandem^M
tándem^M

TRANSPORT AND MACHINERY

passenger station

gare^F de voyageurs^M | Bahnhof^M | stazione^F dei viaggiatori^M | estación^F de ferrocarril^M

office
locaux^M administratifs
Büro^N
uffici^M
oficina^F

timetable
panneau^M indicateur
Fahrplan^N
tabellone^M degli orari^M
tablero^M de información^F

luggage trolley
chariot^M à bagages^M
Förderwagen^M
carrello^M portabagagli
carro^M portaequipaje

luggage lockers
consigne^F automatique
Gepäckschließfächer^N
cassette^F di deposito^M per bagagli^M
taquillas^F de consigna^F automática

glass roof
verrière^F
Glasüberdachung^F
tettoia^F vetrata
techo^M de vidrio^M

metal structure
structure^F métallique
Eisenträger^M
struttura^F metallica
estructura^F de metal^M

platform number
numéro^M de quai^M
Gleisnummer^F
numero^M del binario^M
indicador^M de número^M de andén^M

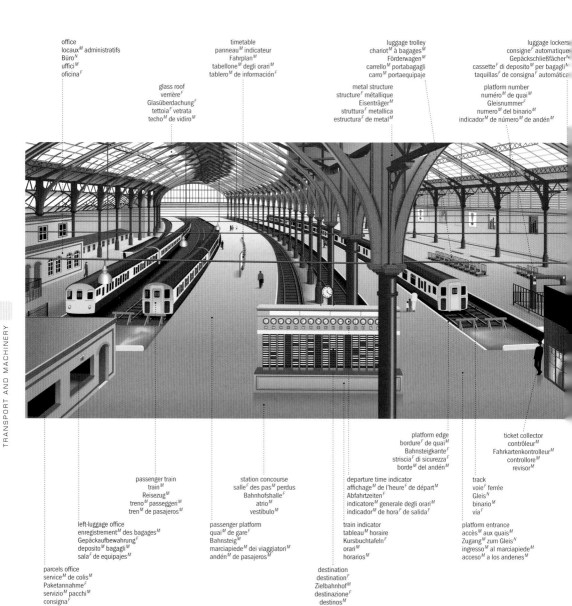

platform edge
bordure^F de quai^M
Bahnsteigkante^F
striscia^F di sicurezza^F
borde^M del andén^M

ticket collector
contrôleur^M
Fahrkartenkontrolleur^M
controllore^M
revisor^M

passenger train
train^M
Reisezug^M
treno^M passeggeri^M
tren^M de pasajeros^M

station concourse
salle^F des pas^M perdus
Bahnhofshalle^F
atrio^M
vestíbulo^M

departure time indicator
affichage^M de l'heure^F de départ^M
Abfahrtzeiten^F
indicatore^M generale degli orari^M
indicador^M de hora^F de salida^F

track
voie^F ferrée
Gleis^N
binario^M
vía^F

left-luggage office
enregistrement^M des bagages^M
Gepäckaufbewahrung^F
deposito^M bagagli^M
sala^F de equipajes^M

passenger platform
quai^M de gare^F
Bahnsteig^M
marciapiede^M dei viaggiatori^M
andén^M de pasajeros^M

train indicator
tableau^M horaire
Kursbuchtafeln^F
orari^M
horarios^M

platform entrance
accès^M aux quais^M
Zugang^M zum Gleis^N
ingresso^M al marciapiede^M
acceso^M a los andenes^M

parcels office
service^M de colis^M
Paketannahme^F
servizio^M pacchi^M
consigna^F

destination
destination^F
Zielbahnhof^M
destinazione^F
destinos^M

railway station

gare^F | Bahnhof^M | stazione^F ferroviaria | estación^F de ferrocarril^M

passenger station
gare^F de voyageurs^M
Personenbahnhof^M
stazione^F dei viaggiatori^M
estación^F de ferrocarril^M

station platform
quai^M
Bahnsteig^M
marciapiede^M
andén^M

commuter train
train^M de banlieue^F
Nahverkehrszug^M
treno^M locale
tren^M suburbano

main line
grandes lignes^F
Hauptgleis^N
linea^F ferroviaria principale
vía^F principal

suburban commuter railway
voie^F de banlieue^F
S-Bahn-Strecke^F
linea^F ferroviaria locale
vía^F de tren^M suburbano

siding
voie^F de service^M
Nebengleis^N
binario^M morto
vía^F subsidiaria

buffers
butoir^M
Prellbock^M
respingente^M
tope^M

level crossing
passage^M à niveau^M
Bahnübergang^M
passaggio^M a livello^M
paso^M a nivel^M

car park
parking^M
Parkplatz^M
parcheggio^M
estacionamiento^M

platform shelter
abri^M
Bahnsteigüberdachung^F
pensilina^F
marquesina^M del andén^M

footbridge
passerelle^F
Fußgängerbrücke^F
ponte^M pedonale
pasarela^F

semaphore signal
signal^M de voie^F
Signal^N
semaforo^M
semáforo^M

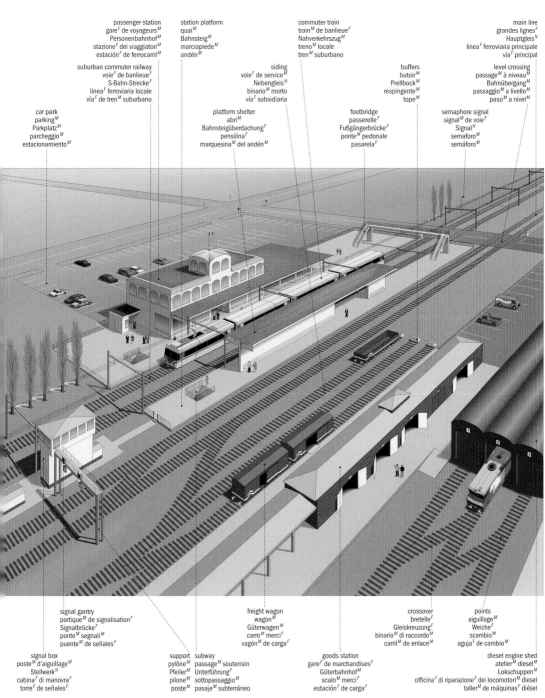

signal gantry
portique^M de signalisation^F
Signalbrücke^F
ponte^M segnali^M
puente^M de señales^F

freight wagon
wagon^M
Güterwagen^M
carro^M merci^F
vagón^M de carga^F

crossover
bretelle^F
Gleiskreuzung^F
binario^M di raccordo^M
carril^M de enlace^M

points
aiguillage^M
Weiche^F
scambio^M
aguja^F de cambio^M

signal box
poste^M d'aiguillage^M
Stellwerk^N
cabina^F di manovra^F
torre^F de señales^F

support
pylône^M
Pfeiler^M
pilone^M
poste^M

subway
passage^M souterrain
Unterführung^F
sottopassaggio^M
pasaje^M subterráneo

goods station
gare^F de marchandises^F
Güterbahnhof^M
scalo^M merci^F
estación^F de carga^F

diesel engine shed
atelier^M diesel^M
Lokschuppen^M
officina^F di riparazione^F dei locomotori^M diesel
taller^M de máquinas^F diésel

high-speed train

train^M à grande vitesse^F (T.G.V.) | Hochgeschwindigkeitszug^M | treno^M ad alta velocità^F | tren^M de alta velocidad^F

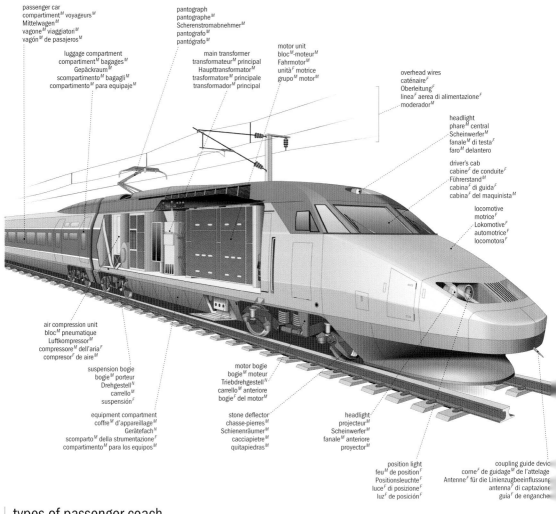

passenger car
compartiment^M voyageurs^M
Mittelwagen^M
vagone^M viaggiatori^M
vagón^M de pasajeros^M

luggage compartment
compartiment^M bagages^M
Gepäckraum^M
scompartimento^M bagagli^M
compartimento^M para equipaje^M

pantograph
pantographe^M
Scherenstromabnehmer^M
pantografo^M
pantógrafo^M

main transformer
transformateur^M principal
Haupttransformator^M
trasformatore^M principale
transformador^M principal

motor unit
bloc^M-moteur^M
Fahrmotor^M
unità^F motrice
grupo^M motor^M

overhead wires
caténaire^F
Oberleitung^F
linea^F aerea di alimentazione^F
moderador^M

headlight
phare^M central
Scheinwerfer^M
fanale^M di testa^F
faro^M delantero

driver's cab
cabine^F de conduite^F
Führerstand^M
cabina^F di guida^F
cabina^F del maquinista^M

locomotive
motrice^F
Lokomotive^F
automotrice^F
locomotora^F

air compression unit
bloc^M pneumatique
Luftkompressor^M
compressore^M dell'aria^F
compresor^F de aire^M

suspension bogie
bogie^M porteur
Drehgestell^N
carrello^M
suspensión^F

motor bogie
bogie^M moteur
Triebdrehgestell^N
carrello^M anteriore
bogie^F del motor^M

equipment compartment
coffre^M d'appareillage^M
Gerätefach^N
scomparto^M della strumentazione^F
compartimento^M para los equipos^M

stone deflector
chasse-pierres^M
Schienenräumer^M
cacciapietre^M
quitapiedras^M

headlight
projecteur^M
Scheinwerfer^M
fanale^M anteriore
proyector^M

position light
feu^M de position^F
Positionsleuchte^F
luce^F di posizione^F
luz^F de posición^F

coupling guide device
corne^F de guidage^M de l'attelage
Antenne^F für die Linienzugbeeinflussung
antenna^F di captazione
guia^F de enganche

types of passenger coach

types^M de voitures^F | Personenzüge^M: Wagentypen^M | tipi^M di vagoni^M passeggeri^M | vagones^M de pasajeros^M

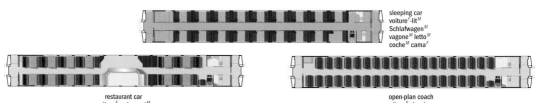

sleeping car
voiture^F-lit^M
Schlafwagen^M
vagone^M letto^M
coche^M cama^F

restaurant car
voiture^F restaurant^M
Speisewagen^M
vagone^M ristorante^M
vagón^M comedor^M

open-plan coach
voiture^F classique
Großraumwagen^M
vagone^M viaggiatori^M
vagón^M de pasajeros^M

diesel-electric locomotive

locomotive[F] diesel-électrique | dieselelektrische Lokomotive[F] | locomotiva[F] diesel-elettrica | locomotora[F] diésel eléctrica

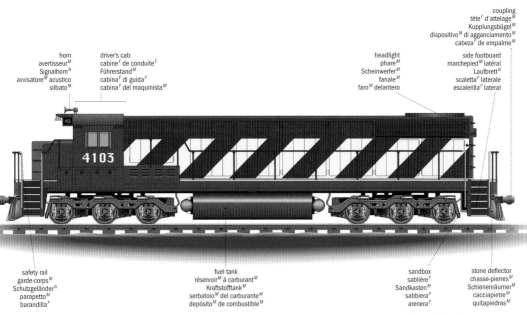

coupling
tête[F] d'attelage[M]
Kupplungsbügel[M]
dispositivo[M] di agganciamento[M]
cabeza[F] de empalme[M]

horn
avertisseur[M]
Signalhorn[N]
avvisatore[M] acustico
silbato[M]

driver's cab
cabine[F] de conduite[F]
Führerstand[M]
cabina[F] di guida[F]
cabina[F] del maquinista[M]

headlight
phare[M]
Scheinwerfer[M]
fanale[M]
faro[M] delantero

side footboard
marchepied[M] latéral
Laufbrett[N]
scaletta[F] laterale
escalerilla[F] lateral

safety rail
garde-corps[M]
Schutzgeländer[N]
parapetto[M]
barandilla[F]

fuel tank
réservoir[M] à carburant[M]
Kraftstofftank[M]
serbatoio[M] del carburante[M]
depósito[M] de combustible[M]

sandbox
sablière[F]
Sandkasten[M]
sabbiera[F]
arenera[F]

stone deflector
chasse-pierres[M]
Schienenräumer[M]
cacciapietre[M]
quitapiedras[M]

examples of freight wagons

exemples[M] de wagons[M] | Beispiele[N] für Güterwagen[M] | esempi[M] di carri[M] merci[F] | ejemplos[M] de vagones[M]

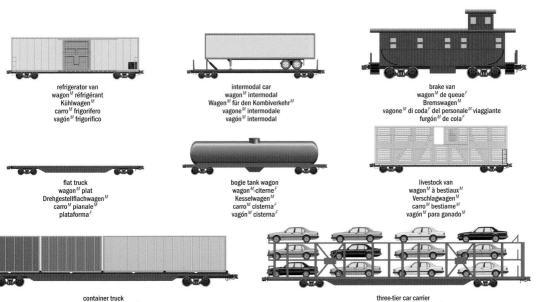

refrigerator van
wagon[M] réfrigérant
Kühlwagen[M]
carro[M] frigorifero
vagón[M] frigorífico

intermodal car
wagon[M] intermodal
Wagen[M] für den Kombiverkehr[M]
vagone[M] intermodale
vagón[M] intermodal

brake van
wagon[M] de queue[F]
Bremswagen[M]
vagone[M] di coda[F] del personale[M] viaggiante
furgón[M] de cola[F]

flat truck
wagon[M] plat
Drehgestellflachwagen[M]
carro[M] pianale[F]
plataforma[F]

bogie tank wagon
wagon[M]-citerne[F]
Kesselwagen[M]
carro[M] cisterna[F]
vagón[M] cisterna[F]

livestock van
wagon[M] à bestiaux[M]
Verschlagwagen[M]
carro[M] bestiame[M]
vagón[M] para ganado[M]

container truck
wagon[M] porte-conteneurs[M]
Containerflachwagen[M]
carro[M] pianale[F] portacontainer[M]
vagón[M] para contenedores[M]

three-tier car carrier
wagon[M] porte-automobiles[M]
Autotransportwagen[M]
carro[M] bisarca[F]
vagón[M] para automóviles[M]

underground railway

chemin^M de fer^M métropolitain | U-Bahn^F | metropolitana^F | metro^M

underground station
station^F de métro^M
U-Bahn-Station^F
stazione^F della metropolitana^F
estación^F de metro^M

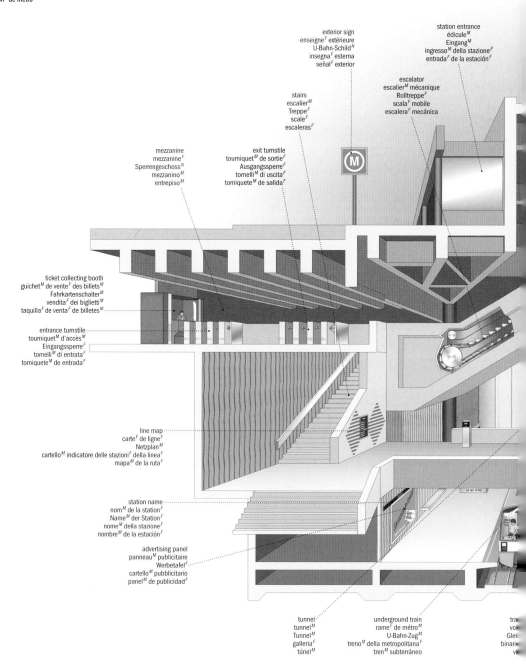

exterior sign
enseigne^F extérieure
U-Bahn-Schild^N
insegna^F esterna
señal^F exterior

station entrance
édicule^M
Eingang^M
ingresso^M della stazione^F
entrada^F de la estación^F

escalator
escalier^M mécanique
Rolltreppe^F
scala^F mobile
escalera^F mecánica

stairs
escalier^M
Treppe^F
scale^F
escaleras^F

mezzanine
mezzanine^F
Sperrengeschoss^N
mezzanino^M
entrepiso^M

exit turnstile
tourniquet^M de sortie^F
Ausgangssperre^F
tornelli^M di uscita^F
torniquete^M de salida^F

ticket collecting booth
guichet^M de vente^F des billets^M
Fahrkartenschalter^M
vendita^F dei biglietti^M
taquilla^F de venta^F de billetes^M

entrance turnstile
tourniquet^M d'accès^M
Eingangssperre^F
tornelli^M di entrata^F
torniquete^M de entrada^F

line map
carte^F de ligne^F
Netzplan^M
cartello^M indicatore delle stazioni^F della linea^F
mapa^M de la ruta^F

station name
nom^M de la station^F
Name^M der Station^F
nome^M della stazione^F
nombre^M de la estación^F

advertising panel
panneau^M publicitaire
Werbetafel^F
cartello^M pubblicitario
panel^M de publicidad^F

tunnel
tunnel^M
Tunnel^M
galleria^F
túnel^M

underground train
rame^F de métro^M
U-Bahn-Zug^M
treno^M della metropolitana^F
tren^M subterráneo

tra
voi
Glei
binari
vi

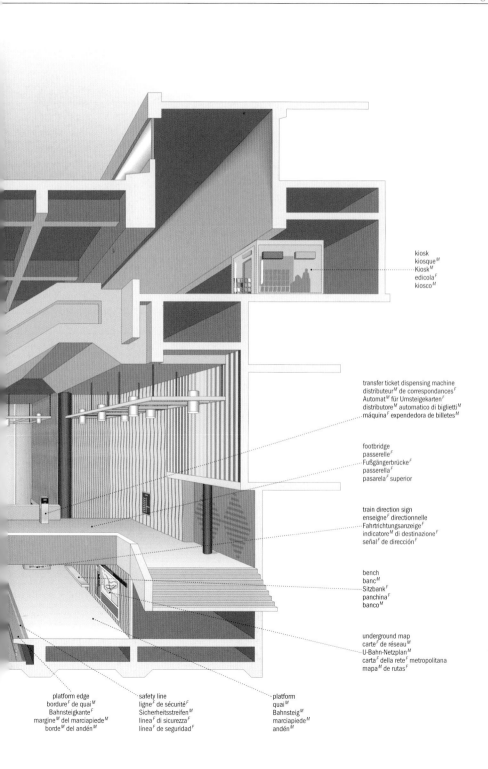

kiosk
kiosque^M
Kiosk^M
edicola^F
kiosco^M

transfer ticket dispensing machine
distributeur^M de correspondances^F
Automat^M für Umsteigekarten^F
distributore^M automatico di biglietti^M
máquina^F expendedora de billetes^M

footbridge
passerelle^F
Fußgängerbrücke^F
passerella^F
pasarela^F superior

train direction sign
enseigne^F directionnelle
Fahrtrichtungsanzeige^F
indicatore^M di destinazione^F
señal^F de dirección^F

bench
banc^M
Sitzbank^F
panchina^F
banco^M

underground map
carte^F de réseau^M
U-Bahn-Netzplan^M
carta^F della rete^F metropolitana
mapa^M de rutas^F

platform edge
bordure^F de quai^M
Bahnsteigkante^F
margine^M del marciapiede^M
borde^M del andén^M

safety line
ligne^F de sécurité^F
Sicherheitsstreifen^M
linea^F di sicurezza^F
linea^F de seguridad^F

platform
quai^M
Bahnsteig^M
marciapiede^M
andén^M

TRANSPORT AND MACHINERY

underground railway

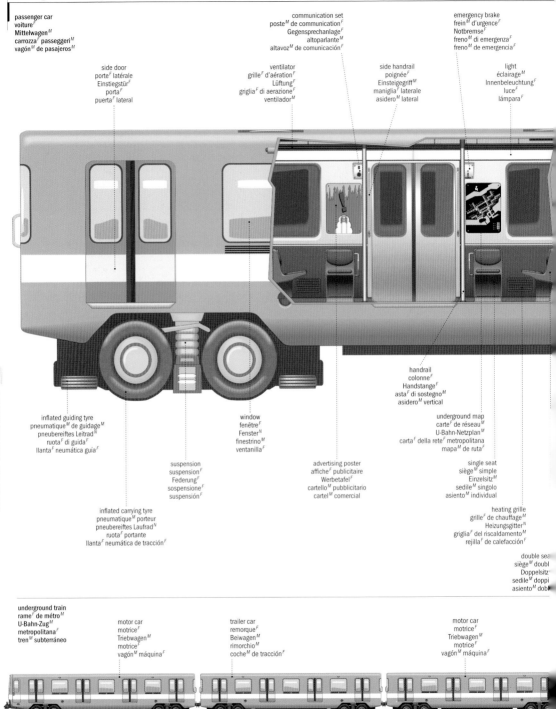

passenger car
voiture^F
Mittelwagen^M
carrozza^F passeggeri^M
vagón^M de pasajeros^M

communication set
poste^M de communication^F
Gegensprechanlage^F
altoparlante^M
altavoz^M de comunicación^F

emergency brake
frein^M d'urgence^F
Notbremse^F
freno^M di emergenza^F
freno^M de emergencia^F

side door
porte^F latérale
Einstiegstür^F
porta^F
puerta^F lateral

ventilator
grille^F d'aération^F
Lüftung^F
griglia^F di aerazione^F
ventilador^M

side handrail
poignée^F
Einsteigegriff^M
maniglia^F laterale
asidero^M lateral

light
éclairage^M
Innenbeleuchtung^F
luce^F
lámpara^F

handrail
colonne^F
Handstange^M
asta^F di sostegno^M
asidero^M vertical

inflated guiding tyre
pneumatique^M de guidage^M
pneubereiftes Leitrad^N
ruota^F di guida^F
llanta^F neumática guía^F

window
fenêtre^F
Fenster^N
finestrino^M
ventanilla^F

underground map
carte^F de réseau^M
U-Bahn-Netzplan^M
carta^F della rete^F metropolitana
mapa^M de ruta^F

suspension
suspension^F
Federung^F
sospensione^F
suspensión^F

advertising poster
affiche^F publicitaire
Werbetafel^F
cartello^M pubblicitario
cartel^M comercial

single seat
siège^M simple
Einzelsitz^M
sedile^M singolo
asiento^M individual

inflated carrying tyre
pneumatique^M porteur
pneubereiftes Laufrad^N
ruota^F portante
llanta^F neumática de tracción^F

heating grille
grille^F de chauffage^M
Heizungsgitter^N
griglia^F del riscaldamento^M
rejilla^F de calefacción^F

double sea
siège^M doubl
Doppelsitz
sedile^M doppi
asiento^M dobl

underground train
rame^F de métro^M
U-Bahn-Zug^M
metropolitana^F
tren^M subterráneo

motor car
motrice^F
Triebwagen^M
motrice^F
vagón^M máquina^F

trailer car
remorque^F
Beiwagen^M
rimorchio^M
coche^M de tracción^F

motor car
motrice^F
Triebwagen^M
motrice^F
vagón^M máquina^F

harbour

port^M maritime | Hafen^M | porto^M marittimo | puerto^M

canal lock
écluse^F
Kanalschleuse^F
chiusa^F di un canale^M
esclusa^F de canal^M

container-loading bridge
portique^M de chargement^M de conteneurs^M
Containerbrücke^F
ponte^M di caricamento^M per containers^M
puente^M de carga^F para contenedores^M

oil terminal
terminal^M pétrolier
Öllöschbrücke^F
deposito^M del petrolio^M
terminal^F de petróleo^M

dry dock
bassin^M de radoub^M
Trockendock^N
bacino^M di carenaggio^M
dique^M seco

transit shed
hangar^M de transit^M
Transitlagerschuppen^M
capannoni^M delle merci^F in transito^M
depósito^M de mercancía^F en tránsito^M

tanker
pétrolier^M
Tanker^M
petroliera^F
petrolero^M

quayside crane
grue^F à flèche^F
Werftkran^M
gru^F mobile a braccio^M
grúa^F de muelle^M

bulk terminal
terminal^M de vrac^M
Massengut-Terminal^M
deposito^M delle rinfuse^F
terminal^F de carga^F

cold store
entrepôt^M frigorifique
Kühlhaus^N
magazzino^M frigorifero
cámara^F frigorifica

ferryboat
transbordeur^M
Hafenfähre^F
traghetto^M
transbordador^M

gate
porte^F
Tor^N
porta^F del bacino^M
compuerta^F

quay
quai^M
Kai^M
banchina^F
muelle^M

lighthouse
phare^M
Leuchtturm^M
faro^M
faro^M

passenger terminal
gare^F maritime
Fahrgastanlage^F
stazione^F dei viaggiatori^M
terminal^F de pasajeros^M

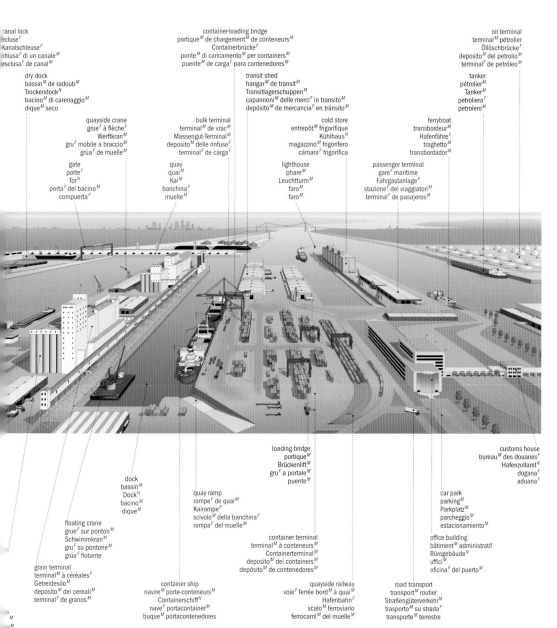

loading bridge
portique^M
Brückenlift^M
gru^F a portale^M
puente^M

customs house
bureau^M des douanes^F
Hafenzollamt^N
dogana^F
aduana^F

dock
bassin^M
Dock^N
bacino^M
dique^M

quay ramp
rampe^F de quai^M
Kairampe^F
scivolo^M della banchina^F
rampa^F del muelle^M

car park
parking^M
Parkplatz^M
parcheggio^M
estacionamiento^M

floating crane
grue^F sur ponton^M
Schwimmkran^M
gru^F su pontone^M
grúa^F flotante

container terminal
terminal^M à conteneurs^M
Containerterminal^M
deposito^M dei containers^M
depósito^M de contenedores^M

office building
bâtiment^M administratif
Bürogebäude^N
uffici^M
oficina^F del puerto^M

grain terminal
terminal^M à céréales^F
Getreidesilo^M
deposito^M dei cereali^M
terminal^F de granos^M

container ship
navire^M porte-conteneurs^M
Containerschiff^N
nave^F portacontainer^M
buque^M portacontenedores

quayside railway
voie^F ferrée bord^M à quai^M
Hafenbahn^F
scalo^M ferroviario
ferrocarril^F del muelle^M

road transport
transport^M routier
Straßengüterverkehr^M
trasporto^M su strada^F
transporte^M terrestre

^{M}
^{M}
^{M}
^{M}

examples of boats and ships

exemples^M de bateaux^M et d'embarcations^F | Beispiele^N für Boote^N und Schiffe^N | esempi^M di barche^F e navi^F | ejemplos^M de barcos^M y embarcaciones^F

drill ship
navire^M de forage^M
Bohrschiff^N
nave^F da perforazione^F
barco^M perforador

derrick
tour^F de forage^M
Derrickkran^M
derrick^M
torre^F de perforación^F

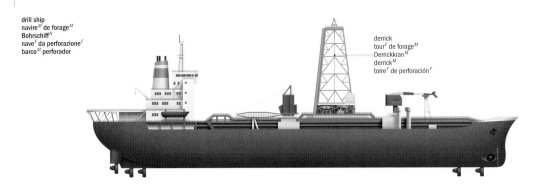

bulk carrier
vraquier^M
Frachtschiff^N
nave^F per il trasporto^M delle merci^F
buque^M de carga^F

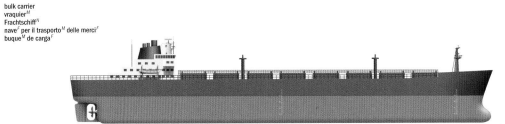

container ship
navire^M porte-conteneurs^M
Containerschiff^N
nave^F portacontainer^M
carguero^M portacontenedores^F

radar
radar^M
Radar^N
radar^M
radar^M

funnel
cheminée^F
Schornstein^M
fumaiolo^M
chimenea^F

chart room
salle^F des cartes^F
Kartenraum^M
sala^F nautica
sala^F de navegación^F

radio antenna
antenne^F radio^F
Funkantenne^F
antenna^F radio^M
antena^F de radio^F

compass bridge
passerelle^F de navigation^F
Peildeck^N
ponte^M di comando^M
puente^M de mando^M

crew quarters
locaux^M de l'équipage^M
Besatzungsunterkünfte^F
alloggi^M dell'equipaggio^M
camarotes^M de la tripulación^F

lifeboat
chaloupe^F de sauvetage^M
Rettungsboot^N
scialuppa^F di salvataggio^M
bote^M salvavidas

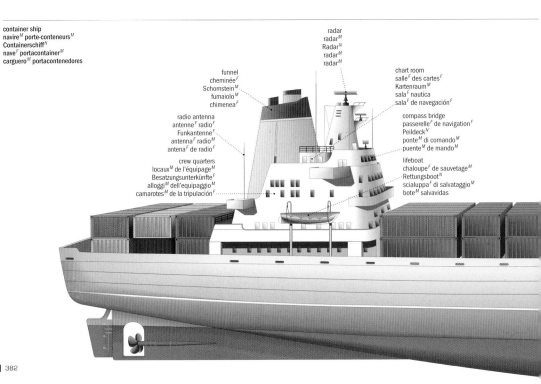

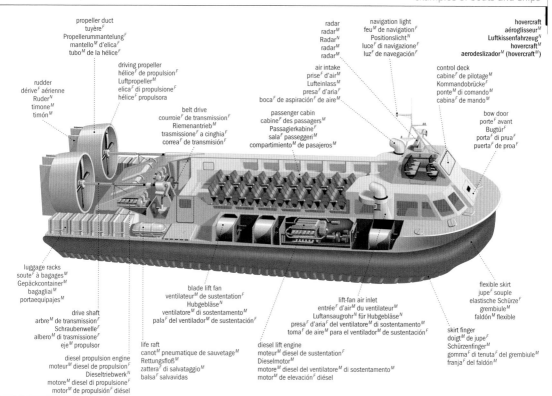

propeller duct
tuyère^F
Propellerummantelung^F
mantello^M d'elica^F
tubo^M de la hélice^F

radar
radar^M
Radar^N
radar^M
radar^M

navigation light
feu^M de navigation^F
Positionslicht^N
luce^F di navigazione^F
luz^F de navegación^F

hovercraft
aéroglisseur^M
Luftkissenfahrzeug^N
hovercraft^M
aerodeslizador^M (hovercraft^M)

driving propeller
hélice^F de propulsion^F
Luftpropeller^M
elica^F di propulsione^F
hélice^F propulsora

air intake
prise^F d'air^M
Lufteinlass^M
presa^F d'aria^F
boca^F de aspiración^F de aire^M

control deck
cabine^F de pilotage^F
Kommandobrücke^F
ponte^M di comando^M
cabina^F de mando^M

rudder
dérive^F aérienne
Ruder^N
timone^M
timón^M

belt drive
courroie^F de transmission^F
Riemenantrieb^M
trasmissione^F a cinghia^F
correa^F de transmisión^F

passenger cabin
cabine^F des passagers^M
Passagierkabine^F
sala^F passeggeri^M
compartimiento^M de pasajeros^M

bow door
porte^F avant
Bugtür^F
porta^F di prua^F
puerta^F de proa^F

luggage racks
soute^F à bagages^M
Gepäckcontainer^M
bagagliai^M
portaequipajes^M

blade lift fan
ventilateur^M de sustentation^F
Hubgebläse^N
ventilatore^M di sostentamento^M
pala^F del ventilador^M de sustentación^F

lift-fan air inlet
entrée^F d'air^M du ventilateur^M
Luftansaugrohr^N für Hubgebläse^N
presa^F d'aria^F del ventilatore^M di sostentamento^M
toma^F de aire^M para el ventilador^M de sustentación^F

flexible skirt
jupe^F souple
elastische Schürze^F
grembiule^M
faldón^M flexible

drive shaft
arbre^F de transmission^F
Schraubenwelle^F
albero^M di trasmissione^F
eje^M propulsor

life raft
canot^M pneumatique de sauvetage^M
Rettungsfloß^M
zattera^F di salvataggio^M
balsa^F salvavidas

diesel lift engine
moteur^M diesel de sustentation^F
Dieselmotor^M
motore^M diesel del ventilatore^M di sostentamento^M
motor^M de elevación^F diésel

skirt finger
doigt^M de jupe^F
Schürzenfinger^M
gomma^F di tenuta^F del grembiule^M
franja^F del faldón^M

diesel propulsion engine
moteur^M diesel de propulsion^F
Dieseltriebwerk^N
motore^M diesel di propulsione^F
motor^M de propulsión^F diésel

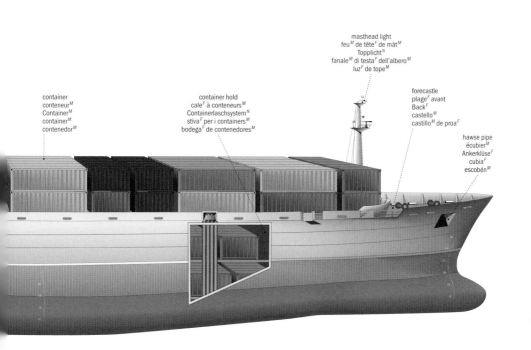

masthead light
feu^M de tête^F de mât^M
Topplicht^N
fanale^M di testa^F dell'albero^M
luz^F de tope^M

container
conteneur^M
Container^M
container^M
contenedor^M

container hold
cale^F à conteneurs^M
Containerlaschsystem^N
stiva^F per i containers^M
bodega^F de contenedores^M

forecastle
plage^F avant
Back^F
castello^M
castillo^M de proa^F

hawse pipe
écubier^M
Ankerklüse^F
cubia^F
escobén^M

examples of boats and ships

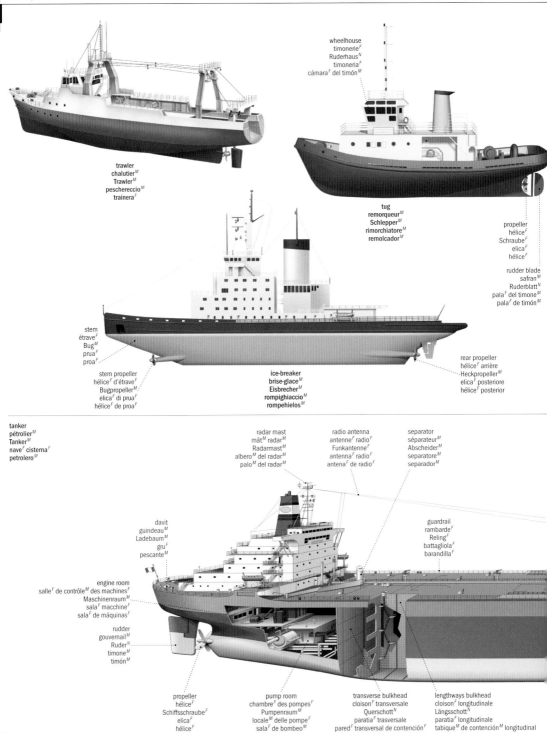

trawler
chalutier^M
Trawler^M
peschereccio^M
trainera^F

wheelhouse
timonerie^F
Ruderhaus^N
timoneria^F
cámara^F del timón^M

tug
remorqueur^M
Schlepper^M
rimorchiatore^M
remolcador^M

propeller
hélice^F
Schraube^F
elica^F
hélice^F

rudder blade
safran^M
Ruderblatt^N
pala^F del timone^M
pala^F de timón^M

stem
étrave^F
Bug^M
prua^F
proa^F

rear propeller
hélice^F arrière
Heckpropeller^M
elica^F posteriore
hélice^F posterior

stem propeller
hélice^F d'étrave^F
Bugpropeller^M
elica^F di prua^F
hélice^F de proa^F

ice-breaker
brise-glace^M
Eisbrecher^M
rompighiaccio^M
rompehielos^M

tanker
pétrolier^M
Tanker^M
nave^F cisterna^F
petrolero^M

radar mast
mât^M radar^M
Radarmast^M
albero^M del radar^M
palo^M del radar^M

radio antenna
antenne^F radio^F
Funkantenne^F
antenna^F radio^F
antena^F de radio^F

separator
séparateur^M
Abscheider^M
separatore^M
separador^M

davit
guindeau^M
Ladebaum^M
gru^F
pescante^M

guardrail
rambarde^F
Reling^F
battagliola^F
barandilla^F

engine room
salle^F de contrôle^M des machines^F
Maschinenraum^M
sala^F macchine^F
sala^F de máquinas^F

rudder
gouvernail^M
Ruder^N
timone^M
timón^M

propeller
hélice^F
Schiffsschraube^F
elica^F
hélice^F

pump room
chambre^F des pompes^F
Pumpenraum^M
locale^M delle pompe^F
sala^F de bombeo^M

transverse bulkhead
cloison^F transversale
Querschott^N
paratia^F trasversale
pared^F transversal de contención^F

lengthways bulkhead
cloison^F longitudinale
Längsschott^N
paratia^F longitudinale
tabique^M de contención^M longitudinal

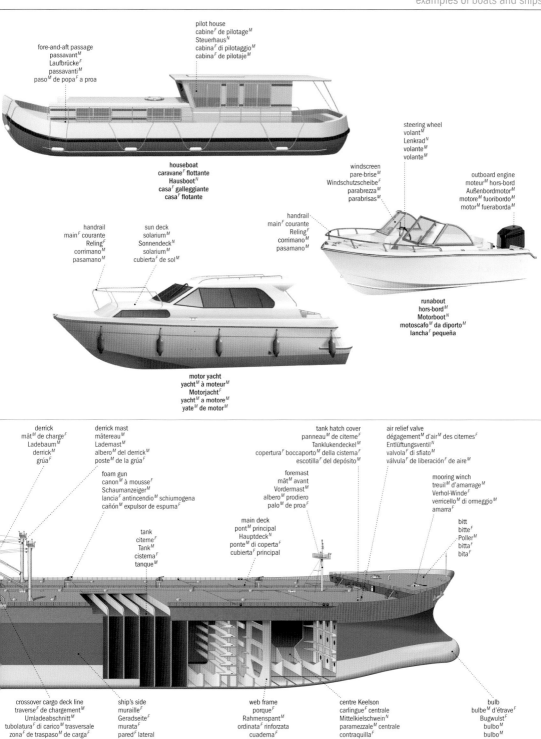

pilot house
cabine^F de pilotage^M
Steuerhaus^N
cabina^F di pilotaggio^M
cabina^F de pilotaje^M

fore-and-aft passage
passavant^M
Laufbrücke^F
passavanti^M
paso^M de popa^F a proa

steering wheel
volant^M
Lenkrad^N
volante^M
volante^M

windscreen
pare-brise^M
Windschutzscheibe^F
parabrezza^M
parabrisas^M

outboard engine
moteur^M hors-bord
Außenbordmotor^M
motore^M fuoribordo^M
motor^M fueraborda^M

houseboat
caravane^F flottante
Hausboot^N
casa^F galleggiante
casa^F flotante

handrail
main^F courante
Reling^F
corrimano^M
pasamano^M

sun deck
solarium^M
Sonnendeck^N
solarium^M
cubierta^F de sol^M

handrail
main^F courante
Reling^F
corrimano^M
pasamano^M

runabout
hors-bord^M
Motorboot^N
motoscafo^M da diporto^M
lancha^F pequeña

motor yacht
yacht^M à moteur^M
Motorjacht^F
yacht^M a motore^M
yate^M de motor^M

derrick
mât^M de charge^F
Ladebaum^M
derrick^M
grúa^F

derrick mast
mâtereau^M
Lademast^M
albero^M del derrick^M
poste^M de la grúa^F

tank hatch cover
panneau^M de citerne^F
Tanklukendeckel^M
copertura^F boccaporto^M della cisterna^F
escotilla^F del depósito^M

air relief valve
dégagement^M d'air^M des citernes^F
Entlüftungsventil^N
valvola^F di sfiato^M
válvula^F de liberación^F de aire^M

foam gun
canon^M à mousse^F
Schaumanzeiger^M
lancia^F antincendio^M schiumogena
cañón^M expulsor de espuma^F

foremast
mât^M avant
Vordermast^M
albero^M prodiero
palo^M de proa^F

mooring winch
treuil^M d'amarrage^M
Verhol-Winde^F
verricello^M di omeggio^M
amarra^F

tank
citerne^F
Tank^M
cisterna^F
tanque^M

main deck
pont^M principal
Hauptdeck^N
ponte^F di coperta^F
cubierta^F principal

bitt
bitte^F
Poller^M
bitta^F
bita^F

crossover cargo deck line
traverse^F de chargement^M
Umladeabschnitt^M
tubolatura^F di carico^M trasversale
zona^F de traspaso^M de carga^F

ship's side
muraille^F
Geradseite^F
murata^F
pared^F lateral

web frame
porque^F
Rahmenspant^M
ordinata^F rinforzata
cuaderna^F

centre Keelson
carlingue^F centrale
Mittelkielschwein^N
paramezzale^M centrale
contraquilla^F

bulb
bulbe^M d'étrave^F
Bugwulst^F
bulbo^M
bulbo^M

examples of boats and ships

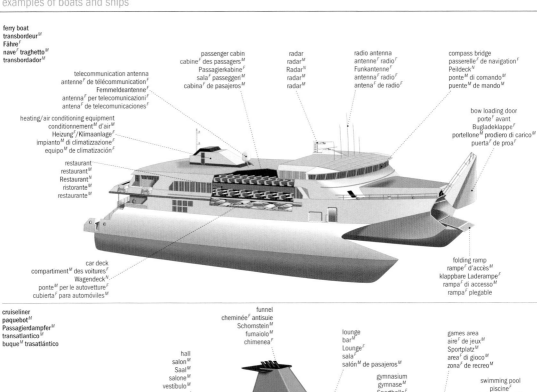

ferry boat
transbordeur^M
Fähre^F
nave^F traghetto^M
transbordador^M

passenger cabin
cabine^F des passagers^M
Passagierkabine^F
sala^F passeggeri^F
cabina^F de pasajeros^M

radar
radar^M
Radar^N
radar^M
radar^M

radio antenna
antenne^F radio^F
Funkantenne^F
antenna^F radio^F
antena^F de radio^F

compass bridge
passerelle^F de navigation^F
Peildeck^N
ponte^M di comando^M
puente^M de mando^M

telecommunication antenna
antenne^F de télécommunication^F
Fernmeldeantenne^F
antenna^F per telecomunicazioni^F
antena^F de telecomunicaciones^F

bow loading door
porte^F avant
Bugladeklappe^F
portellone^M prodiero di carico^M
puerta^F de proa^F

heating/air conditioning equipment
conditionnement^M d'air^M
Heizung^F/Klimaanlage^F
impianto^M di climatizzazione^F
equipo^M de climatización^F

restaurant
restaurant^M
Restaurant^N
ristorante^M
restaurante^M

folding ramp
rampe^F d'accès^M
klappbare Laderampe^F
rampa^F di accesso^M
rampa^F plegable

car deck
compartiment^M des voitures^F
Wagendeck^N
ponte^M per le autovetture^F
cubierta^F para automóviles^M

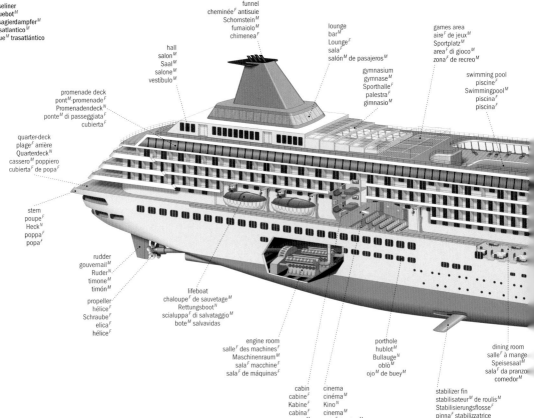

cruiseliner
paquebot^M
Passagierdampfer^M
transatlantico^M
buque^M trasatlántico

funnel
cheminée^F antisuie
Schornstein^M
fumaiolo^M
chimenea^F

lounge
bar^M
Lounge^F
sala^F
salón^M de pasajeros^M

games area
aire^F de jeux^M
Sportplatz^M
area^F di gioco^M
zona^F de recreo^M

hall
salon^M
Saal^M
salone^M
vestibulo^M

gymnasium
gymnase^M
Sporthalle^F
palestra^F
gimnasio^M

swimming pool
piscine^F
Swimmingpool^M
piscina^F
piscina^F

promenade deck
pont^M-promenade^F
Promenadendeck^N
ponte^M di passeggiata^F
cubierta^F

quarter-deck
plage^F arrière
Quarterdeck^N
cassero^M poppiero
cubierta^F de popa^F

stern
poupe^F
Heck^N
poppa^F
popa^F

rudder
gouvernail^M
Ruder^N
timone^M
timón^M

lifeboat
chaloupe^F de sauvetage^M
Rettungsboot^N
scialuppa^F di salvataggio^M
bote^M salvavidas

propeller
hélice^F
Schraube^F
elica^F
hélice^F

porthole
hublot^M
Bullauge^N
oblò^M
ojo^M de buey^M

dining room
salle^F à mange
Speisesaal^M
sala^F da pranzo
comedor^M

engine room
salle^F des machines^F
Maschinenraum^M
sala^F macchine^F
sala^F de máquinas^F

cabin
cabine^F
Kabine^F
cabina^F
camarote^M

cinema
cinéma^M
Kino^N
cinema^M
sala^F de cine^M

stabilizer fin
stabilisateur^F de roulis^M
Stabilisierungsflosse^F
pinna^F stabilizzatrice
aleta^F estabilizadora

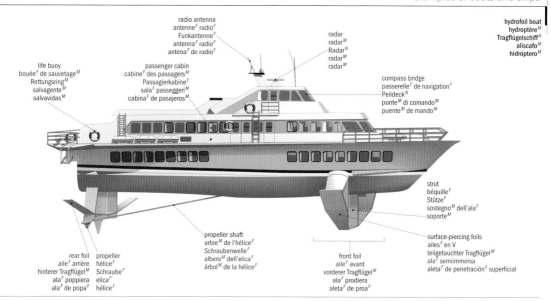

radio antenna
antenne^F radio^F
Funkantenne^F
antenna^F radio^F
antena^F de radio^F

radar
radar^M
Radar^N
radar^M
radar^M

hydrofoil boat
hydroptère^M
Tragflügelschiff^N
aliscafo^M
hidróptero^M

life buoy
bouée^F de sauvetage^M
Rettungsring^M
salvagente^M
salvavidas^M

passenger cabin
cabine^F des passagers^M
Passagierkabine^F
sala^F passeggeri^M
cabina^F de pasajeros^M

compass bridge
passerelle^F de navigation^F
Peildeck^N
ponte^M di comando^M
puente^M de mando^M

strut
béquille^F
Stütze^F
sostegno^M dell'ala^F
soporte^M

propeller shaft
arbre^M de l'hélice^F
Schraubenwelle^F
albero^M dell'elica^F
árbol^M de la hélice^F

surface-piercing foils
ailes^F en V
teilgetauchter Tragflügel^M
ala^F semiimmersa
aleta^F de penetración^F superficial

rear foil
aile^F arrière
hinterer Tragflügel^M
ala^F poppiera
ala^F de popa^F

propeller
hélice^F
Schraube^F
elica^F
hélice^F

front foil
aile^F avant
vorderer Tragflügel^M
ala^F prodiera
aleta^F de proa^F

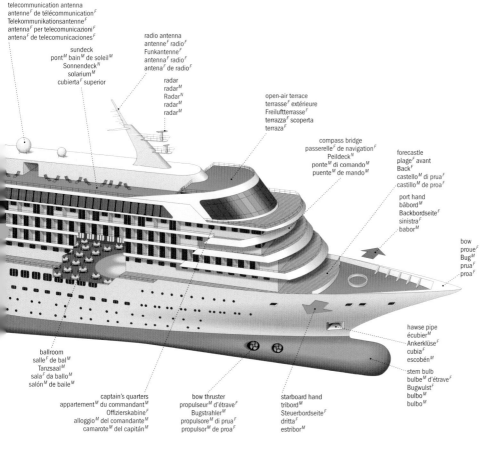

telecommunication antenna
antenne^F de télécommunication^F
Telekommunikationsantenne^F
antenna^F per telecomunicazioni^F
antena^F de telecomunicaciones^F

radio antenna
antenne^F radio^F
Funkantenne^F
antenna^F radio^F
antena^F de radio^F

sundeck
pont^M bain^M de soleil^M
Sonnendeck^N
solarium^M
cubierta^F superior

radar
radar^M
Radar^N
radar^M
radar^M

open-air terrace
terrasse^F extérieure
Freiluftterrasse^F
terrazza^F scoperta
terraza^F

compass bridge
passerelle^F de navigation^F
Peildeck^N
ponte^M di comando^M
puente^M de mando^M

forecastle
plage^F avant
Back^F
castello^M di prua^F
castillo^M de proa^F

port hand
bâbord^M
Backbordseite^F
sinistra^F
babor^M

bow
proue^F
Bug^M
prua^F
proa^F

hawse pipe
écubier^M
Ankerklüse^F
cubia^F
escobén^M

stem bulb
bulbe^F d'étrave^F
Bugwulst^F
bulbo^M
bulbo^M

ballroom
salle^F de bal^M
Tanzsaal^M
sala^F da ballo^M
salón^M de baile^M

captain's quarters
appartement^M du commandant^M
Offizierskabine^F
alloggio^M del comandante^M
camarote^M del capitán^M

bow thruster
propulseur^M d'étrave^F
Bugstrahler^M
propulsore^M di prua^F
propulsor^M de proa^F

starboard hand
tribord^M
Steuerbordseite^F
dritta^F
estribor^M

airport

aéroport[M] | Flughafen[M] | aeroporto[M] | aeropuerto[M]

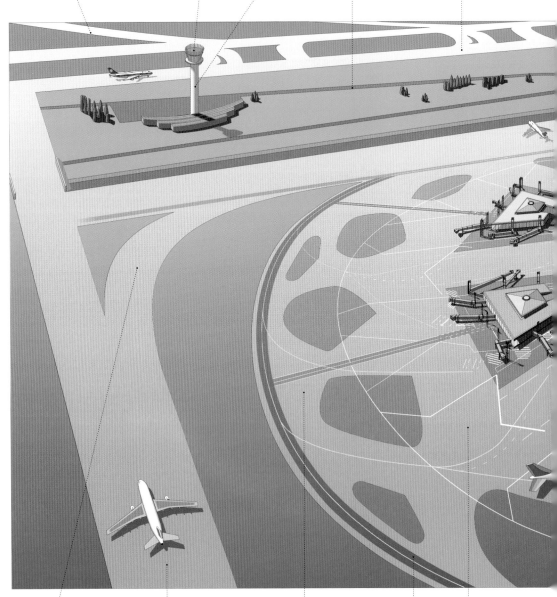

high-speed exit taxiway
sortie[F] de piste[F] à grande vitesse[F]
Schnellabrollbahn[F]
bretella[F] di uscita[F] della pista[F] ad alta velocità[F]
salida[F] de la pista[F] de alta velocidad[F]

tower control room
vigie[F]
Kontrollraum[M]
cabina[F] della torre[F] di controllo[M]
cabina[F] de la torre[F] de control[M]

control tower
tour[F] de contrôle[M]
Kontrolltower[M]
torre[F] di controllo[M]
torre[F] de control[M]

access road
route[F] d'accès[M]
Zufahrtsstraße[F]
strada[F] di accesso[M]
carretera[F] de acceso[M]

taxiway
voie[F] de circulation[F]
Rollbahn[F]
pista[F] di rullaggio[M]
pista[F] de rodaje[M]

by-pass taxiway
bretelle[F]
Überholrollbahn[F]
pista[F] di accesso[M]
pista[F] de enlace[M]

taxiway
voie[F] de circulation[F]
Rollbahn[F]
pista[F] di rullaggio[M]
pista[F] de rodaje[M]

apron
aire[F] de trafic[M]
Vorfeld[N]
piazzale[M]
pista[F] de estacionamiento[M]

service road
voie[F] de service[M]
Versorgungsstraße[F]
strada[F] di servizio[M]
ruta[F] de servicio[M]

apron
aire[F] de manœuvre[F]
Vorfeld[N]
piazzale[M]
pista[F] de estacionamiento[M]

passenger terminal
aérogare^F de passagers^M
Passagierterminal^M
terminal^M dei passeggeri^M
terminal^F de pasajeros^M

maintenance hangar
hangar^M
Flugzeugwartungshalle^F
aviorimessa^F
hangar^M de mantenimiento^M

parking area
aire^F de stationnement^M
Abstellplatz^M
area^F di parcheggio^M
parque^M de estacionamiento^M

telescopic corridor
passerelle^F télescopique
ausziehbare Fluggastbrücke^F
corridoio^M telescopico
pasarela^F telescópico

service area
aire^F de service^M
Versorgungsbereich^M
area^F di servizio^M
zona^F de servicio^M

boarding walkway
quai^M d'embarquement^M
Fluggastbrücke^F
passerella^F di imbarco^M
túnel^M de embarque^M

taxiway line
marques^F de circulation^F
Rollbahnmarkierung^F
linea^F di rullaggio^M
linea^F de pista^F

satellite terminal
aérogare^F satellite^M
radiale Einsteigestation^F
terminal^M satellite^M dei passeggeri^M
terminal^F satélite de pasajeros^M

TRANSPORT AND MACHINERY

airport

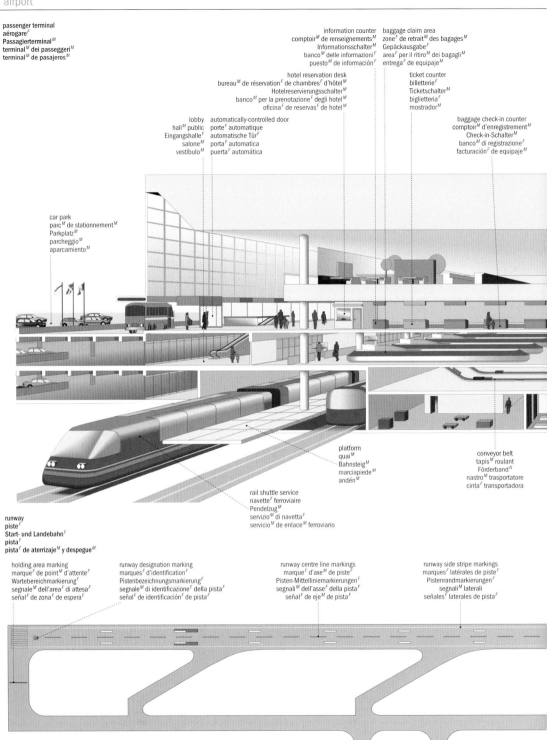

passenger terminal
aérogare^F
Passagierterminal^M
terminal^M dei passeggeri^M
terminal^M de pasajeros^M

information counter
comptoir^M de renseignements^M
Informationsschalter^M
banco^M delle informazioni^F
puesto^M de información^F

baggage claim area
zone^F de retrait^M des bagages^M
Gepäckausgabe^F
area^F per il ritiro^M dei bagagli^M
entrega^F de equipaje^M

hotel reservation desk
bureau^M de réservation^F de chambres^F d'hôtel^M
Hotelreservierungsschalter^M
banco^M per la prenotazione^F degli hotel^M
oficina^F de reservas^F de hotel^M

ticket counter
billetterie^F
Ticketschalter^M
biglietteria^F
mostrador^M

lobby
hall^M public
Eingangshalle^F
salone^M
vestibulo^M

automatically-controlled door
porte^F automatique
automatische Tür^F
porta^F automatica
puerta^F automática

baggage check-in counter
comptoir^M d'enregistrement^M
Check-in-Schalter^M
banco^M di registrazione^F
facturación^F de equipaje^M

car park
parc^M de stationnement^M
Parkplatz^M
parcheggio^M
aparcamiento^M

platform
quai^M
Bahnsteig^M
marciapiede^M
andén^M

conveyor belt
tapis^M roulant
Förderband^N
nastro^M trasportatore
cinta^F transportadora

rail shuttle service
navette^F ferroviaire
Pendelzug^M
servizio^M di navetta^F
servicio^M de enlace^M ferroviario

runway
piste^F
Start- und Landebahn^F
pista^F
pista^F de aterrizaje^M y despegue^M

holding area marking
marque^F de point^M d'attente^F
Wartebereichmarkierung^F
segnale^M dell'area^F di attesa^F
señal^F de zona^F de espera^F

runway designation marking
marques^F d'identification^F
Pistenbezeichnungsmarkierung^F
segnale^M di identificazione^F della pista^F
señal^F de identificación^F de pista^F

runway centre line markings
marque^F d'axe^M de piste^F
Pisten-Mittelliniemarkierungen^F
segnali^M dell'asse^F della pista^F
señal^F de eje^M de pista^F

runway side stripe markings
marques^F latérales de piste^F
Pistenrandmarkierungen^F
segnali^M laterali
señales^F laterales de pista^F

security check
contrôle^M de sécurité^F
Sicherheitskontrolle^F
controllo^M di sicurezza^F
control^M de seguridad^F

duty-free shop
boutique^F hors taxe^F
Duty-free-Shop^M
duty free^M
tienda^F libre de impuestos^M

observation deck
terrasse^F
Besucherterrasse^F
terrazza^F
mirador^M

flight information board
tableau^M d'affichage^M des vols^M
Fluginformationsanzeige^F
tabellone^M degli arrivi^M e delle partenze^F
tablero^M de llegadas^F y salidas^F

cargo dispatch
expédition^F du fret^M
Frachtversand^M
spedizione^F merci^F
expedición^F de carga^F

passport control
contrôle^F des passeports^M
Passkontrolle^F
controllo^M dei passaporti^M
control^M de pasaportes^M

departure lounge
salle^F d'embarquement^M
Abflugwartehalle^F
sala^F di imbarco^M
sala^F de espera^F de embarque^M

passenger transfer vehicle
transbordeur^M
Passagiertransferfahrzeug^N
navetta^F per il trasbordo^M dei passeggeri^M
transbordador^M

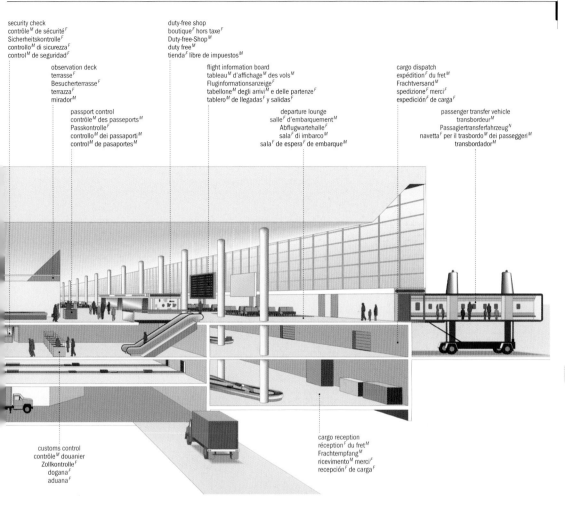

customs control
contrôle^M douanier
Zollkontrolle^F
dogana^F
aduana^F

cargo reception
réception^F du fret^M
Frachtempfang^M
ricevimento^M merci^F
recepción^F de carga^F

exit taxiway
sortie^F de piste^F
Abrollbahn^F
bretella^F di uscita^F
salida^F de la pista^F

runway touchdown zone marking
marque^F d'aire^F de prise^F de contact^M
Aufsetzzonenmarkierungen^F
segnale^M di zona^F di contatto^M
señal^F de zona^F de contacto^M de pista^F

runway threshold markings
marques^F de seuil^M de piste^F
Schwellenmarkierungen^F
segnali^M della soglia della pista^F
señales^F de límite^M de la pista^F

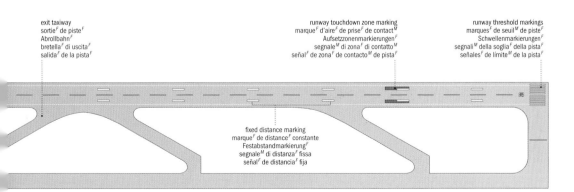

fixed distance marking
marque^F de distance^F constante
Festabstandmarkierung^F
segnale^M di distanza^F fissa
señal^F de distancia^F fija

long-range jet airliner

avion^M long-courrier^M | Langstrecken-Düsenflugzeug^N | aviogetto^M a lungo raggio^M | avión^M turborreactor de pasajeros^M

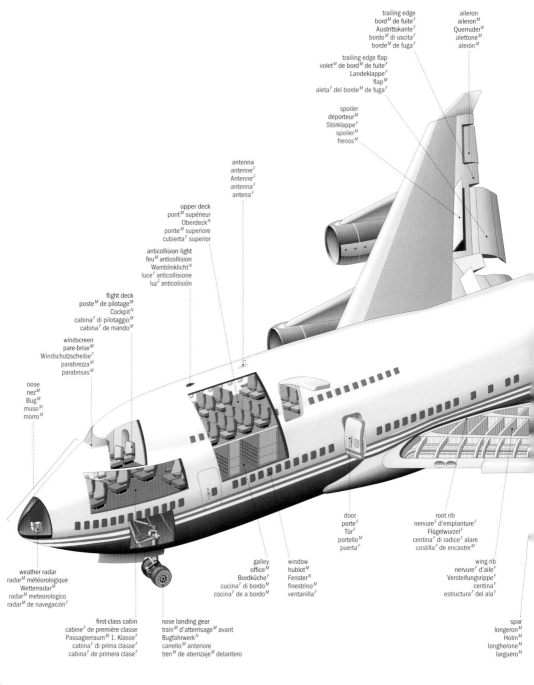

trailing edge
bord^M de fuite^F
Austrittskante^F
bordo^M di uscita^F
borde^M de fuga^F

aileron
aileron^M
Querruder^N
alettone^M
alerón^M

trailing edge flap
volet^M de bord^M de fuite^F
Landeklappe^F
flap^M
aleta^F del borde^M de fuga^F

spoiler
déporteur^M
Störklappe^F
spoiler^M
frenos^M

antenna
antenne^F
Antenne^F
antenna^F
antena^F

upper deck
pont^M supérieur
Oberdeck^N
ponte^M superiore
cubierta^F superior

anticollision light
feu^M anticollision
Wamblinklicht^N
luce^F anticollisione
luz^F anticolisión

flight deck
poste^M de pilotage^M
Cockpit^N
cabina^F di pilotaggio^M
cabina^F de mando^M

windscreen
pare-brise^M
Windschutzscheibe^F
parabrezza^M
parabrisas^M

nose
nez^M
Bug^M
muso^M
morro^M

door
porte^F
Tür^F
portello^M
puerta^F

root rib
nervure^F d'emplanture^F
Flügelwurzel^F
centina^F di radice^F alare
costilla^F de encastre^M

wing rib
nervure^F d'aile^F
Versteifungsrippe^F
centina^F
estructura^F del ala^F

weather radar
radar^M météorologique
Wetterradar^M
radar^M meteorologico
radar^M de navegación^F

galley
office^M
Bordküche^F
cucina^F di bordo^F
cocina^F de a bordo^M

window
hublot^M
Fenster^N
finestrino^M
ventanilla^F

spar
longeron^M
Holm^M
longherone^M
larguero^M

first-class cabin
cabine^F de première classe
Passagierraum^M 1. Klasse^F
cabina^F di prima classe^F
cabina^F de primera clase^F

nose landing gear
train^M d'atterrisage^M avant
Bugfahrwerk^N
carrello^M anteriore
tren^M de aterrizaje^M delantero

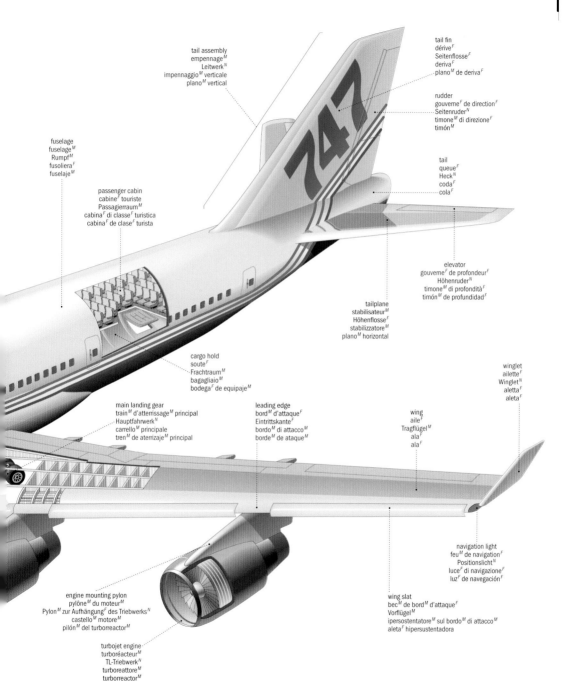

tail assembly
empennage^M
Leitwerk^N
impennaggio^M verticale
plano^M vertical

tail fin
dérive^F
Seitenflosse^F
deriva^F
plano^M de deriva^F

rudder
gouverne^F de direction^F
Seitenruder^N
timone^M di direzione^F
timón^M

fuselage
fuselage^M
Rumpf^M
fusoliera^F
fuselaje^M

tail
queue^F
Heck^N
coda^F
cola^F

passenger cabin
cabine^F touriste
Passagierraum^M
cabina^F di classe^F turistica
cabina^F de clase^F turista

elevator
gouverne^F de profondeur^F
Höhenruder^N
timone^M di profondità^F
timón^M de profundidad^F

tailplane
stabilisateur^M
Höhenflosse^F
stabilizzatore^M
plano^M horizontal

cargo hold
soute^F
Frachtraum^M
bagagliaio^M
bodega^F de equipaje^M

winglet
ailette^F
Winglet^N
aletta^F
aleta^F

main landing gear
train^M d'atterrissage^M principal
Hauptfahrwerk^N
carrello^M principale
tren^M de aterrizaje^M principal

leading edge
bord^M d'attaque^F
Eintrittskante^F
bordo^M di attacco^M
borde^M de ataque^M

wing
aile^F
Tragflügel^M
ala^F
ala^F

navigation light
feu^M de navigation^F
Positionslicht^N
luce^F di navigazione^F
luz^F de navegación^F

engine mounting pylon
pylône^M du moteur^M
Pylon^M zur Aufhängung^F des Triebwerks^N
castello^M motore^M
pilón^M del turborreactor^M

wing slat
bec^M de bord^M d'attaque^F
Vorflügel^M
ipersostentatore^M sul bordo^M di attacco^M
aleta^F hipersustentadora

turbojet engine
turboréacteur^M
TL-Triebwerk^N
turboreattore^M
turborreactor^M

examples of aircraft

exemples^M d'avions^M | Beispiele^N für Flugzeuge^N | esempi^M di aeroplani^M | ejemplos^M de aviones^M

float seaplane
hydravion^M à flotteurs^M
Wasserflugzeug^N
idrovolante^M a due galleggianti^M
hidroavión^M de flotadores^M

three-blade propeller
hélice^F tripale
dreiflügeliger Propeller^M
elica^F tripala
hélice^F de tres aspas^F

business aircraft
avion^M d'affaires^F
Privatflugzeug^N
aeroplano^M privato
avión^M particular

winglet
ailette^F
Flosse^F
aletta^F
aleta^F

high wing
aile^F haute
Tragflügel^M
ala^F alta
ala^F alta

float
flotteur^M
Schwimmkörper^M
galleggiante^M
flotador^M

cargo aircraft
avion^M-cargo^M
Frachtflugzeug^N
aeroplano^M da carico^M
avión^M de carga

high-frequency antenna cable
câble^M de l'antenne^F haute fréquence^F
Funkantenne^F
cavo^M dell'antenna^F ad alta frequenza^F
cable^M de la antena^F de alta frecuencia^F

light aircraft
avion^M léger
Leichtflugzeug^N
aeroplano^M leggero
avión^M ligero

wing strut
hauban^M
Flügelstrebe^F
montante^M dell'ala^F
montante^M

canopy
verrière^F
Kuppel^F
parabrezza^M
parabrisas^M

amphibious firefighting aircraft
avion^M-citerne^F amphibie
Amphibien^F-Löschflugzeug^N
aeroplano^M anfibio antincendio
hidroavión^M cisterna

two-blade propeller
hélice^F bipale
zweiflügeliger Propeller^M
elica^F bipala
hélice^F de dos aspas^F

three-blade propeller
hélice^F tripale
dreiflügeliger Propeller^M
elica^F tripala
hélice^F de tres aspas^F

water-tank area
compartiment^M de réservoirs^M d'eau
Wassertank^M
vano^M del serbatoio^M dell'acqua^F
compartimiento^M del depósito^M del agua^F

float
flotteur^M
Schwimmkörper^M
galleggiante^M
flotador^M

supersonic jet
avion^M de ligne^F supersonique
Überschallflugzeug^N
jet^M supersonico
avión^M supersónico

droop nose
nez^M basculant
abgesenkte Nase^F
muso^M abbassabile
morro^M abatible

variable ejector nozzle
tuyère^F à section^F variable
Verstelldüse^F
ugello^M a sezione^F variabile
tobera^F de sección^F variable

delta wing
voilure^F delta^M
Deltaflügel^M
ala^F a delta^M
ala^F delta

movements of an aircraft

mouvements^M de l'avion^M | Bewegungen^F eines Flugzeugs^N | movimenti^M di un aeroplano^M | movimientos^M de un avión^M

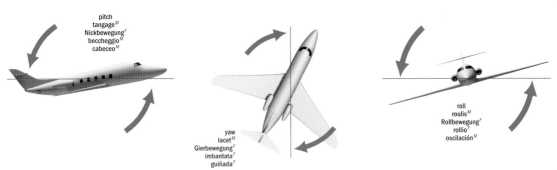

pitch
tangage^M
Nickbewegung^F
beccheggio^M
cabeceo^M

yaw
lacet^M
Gierbewegung^F
imbardata^F
guiñada^F

roll
roulis^M
Rollbewegung^F
rollio^F
oscilación^M

helicopter

hélicoptère^M | Hubschrauber^M | elicottero^M | helicóptero^M

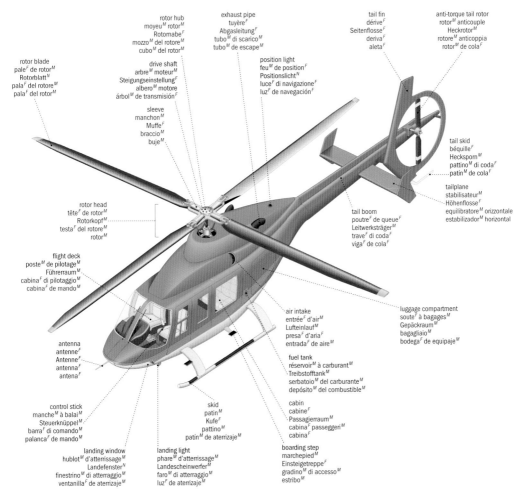

rotor hub
moyeu^M rotor^M
Rotornabe^F
mozzo^M del rotore^M
cubo^M del rotor^M

exhaust pipe
tuyère^F
Abgasleitung^F
tubo^M di scarico^M
tubo^M de escape^M

tail fin
dérive^F
Seitenflosse^F
deriva^F
aleta^F

anti-torque tail rotor
rotor^M anticouple
Heckrotor^M
rotore^M anticoppia
rotor^M de cola^M

rotor blade
pale^F de rotor^M
Rotorblatt^N
pala^F del rotore^M
pala^F del rotor^M

drive shaft
arbre^M moteur^M
Steigungseinstellung^F
albero^M motore
árbol^M de transmisión^F

position light
feu^M de position^F
Positionslicht^N
luce^F di navigazione^F
luz^F de navegación^F

tail skid
béquille^F
Hecksporn^M
pattino^M di coda^F
patín^M de cola^F

sleeve
manchon^M
Muffe^F
braccio^M
buje^M

tailplane
stabilisateur^M
Höhenflosse^F
equilibratore^M orizzontale
estabilizador^M horizontal

rotor head
tête^F de rotor^M
Rotorkopf^M
testa^F del rotore^M
rotor^M

tail boom
poutre^F de queue^F
Leitwerksträger^M
trave^F di coda^F
viga^F de cola^F

flight deck
poste^M de pilotage^M
Führerraum^M
cabina^F di pilotaggio^M
cabina^F de mando^M

luggage compartment
soute^F à bagages^M
Gepäckraum^M
bagagliaio^M
bodega^F de equipaje^M

antenna
antenne^F
Antenne^F
antenna^F
antena^F

air intake
entrée^F d'air^M
Lufteinlauf^M
presa^F d'aria^F
entrada^F de aire^M

fuel tank
réservoir^M à carburant^M
Treibstofftank^M
serbatoio^M del carburante^M
depósito^M del combustible^M

control stick
manche^M à balai^M
Steuerknüppel^M
barra^F di comando^M
palanca^F de mando^M

skid
patin^M
Kufe^F
pattino^M
patín^M de aterrizaje^M

cabin
cabine^F
Passagierraum^M
cabina^F passeggeri^M
cabina^F

landing window
hublot^M d'atterrissage^M
Landefenster^N
finestrino^M di atterraggio^M
ventanilla^F de aterrizaje^M

landing light
phare^M d'atterrissage^M
Landescheinwerfer^M
faro^M di atterraggio^M
luz^F de aterrizaje^M

boarding step
marchepied^M
Einsteigetreppe^F
gradino^M di accesso^M
estribo^M

TRANSPORT AND MACHINERY

395

material handling

manutention*F* | Lastenfortbewegung*F* | movimentazione*F* dei materiali*M* | manejo*M* de materiales*M*

forklift truck
chariot*M* élévateur
Gabelstapler*M*
carrello*M* elevatore*M*
carretilla*F* elevadora de horquilla*F*

mast
mât*M*
Führungsständer*M*
guida*F*
mástil*M*

crosshead
tête*F* du vérin*M* de levage*M*
Kreuzkopf*M*
testa*F* del martinetto*M* elevatore*M*
cabeza*F* del gato*M* elevador

lifting chain
chaîne*F* de levage*M*
Hubkette*F*
catena*F* di sollevamento*M*
cadena*F* de elevación*F*

hydraulic system
système*M* hydraulique
Hydraulik*F*
sistema*M* idraulico
sistema*M* hidráulico

carriage
tablier*M*
Träger*M*
piastra*F* portaforche
portahorquilla*M*

fork arm
bras*M* de fourche*F*
Gabelarm*M*
braccio*M* della forca*F*
brazo*M* de la horquilla*F*

fork
fourches*F*
Gabel*F*
forca*F*
horquilla*F*

overhead guard
toit*M* de protection*F*
Schutzdach*N*
tettuccio*M* di protezione*F*
techo*M* de protección*F*

mast operating lever
levier*M* de manœuvre*F* du mât*M*
Maststeuerhebel*M*
leva*F* di manovra*F* della guida*F*
palanca*F* de maniobra*F*

engine compartment
moteur*M*
Motorraum*M*
vano*M* motore*M*
hueco*M* del motor*M*

frame
châssis*M*
Rahmen*M*
telaio*M*
chasis*M*

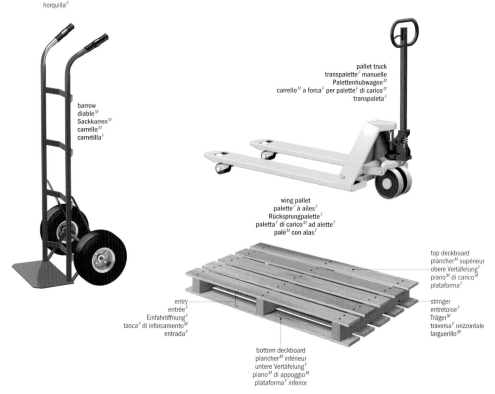

barrow
diable*M*
Sackkarren*M*
carrello*M*
carretilla*F*

pallet truck
transpalette*F* manuelle
Palettenhubwagen*M*
carrello*M* a forca*F* per palette*F* di carico*M*
transpaleta*F*

wing pallet
palette*F* à ailes*F*
Rücksprungpalette*F*
paletta*F* di carico*M* ad alette*F*
palé*M* con alas*F*

top deckboard
plancher*M* supérieur
obere Vertäfelung*F*
piano*M* di carico*M*
plataforma*F*

stringer
entretoise*F*
Träger*M*
traversa*F* orizzontale
larguerillo*M*

entry
entrée*F*
Einfahröffnung*F*
tasca*F* di inforcamento*M*
entrada*F*

bottom deckboard
plancher*M* inférieur
untere Vertäfelung*F*
piano*M* di appoggio*M*
plataforma*F* inferior

cranes

grues^F et portique^M | Kräne^M | gru^F | grúas^F

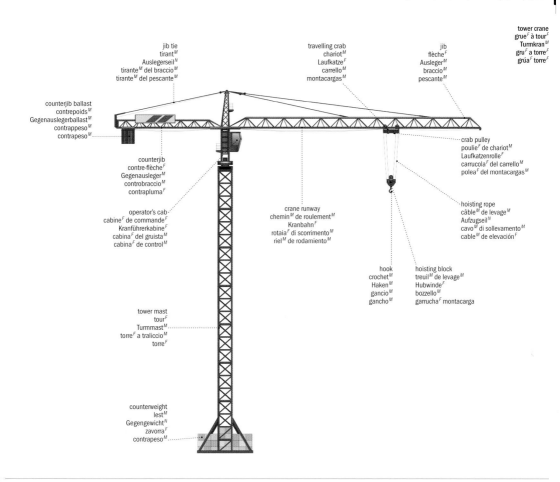

tower crane
grue^F à tour^F
Turmkran^M
gru^F a torre^F
grúa^F torre^F

jib tie
tirant^M
Auslegerseil^N
tirante^M del braccio^M
tirante^M del pescante^M

travelling crab
chariot^M
Laufkatze^F
carrello^M
montacargas^M

jib
flèche^F
Ausleger^M
braccio^M
pescante^M

counterjib ballast
contrepoids^M
Gegenauslegerballast^M
contrappeso^M
contrapeso^M

crab pulley
poulie^F de chariot^M
Laufkatzenrolle^F
carrucola^F del carrello^M
polea^F del montacargas^M

counterjib
contre-flèche^F
Gegenausleger^M
controbraccio^F
contrapluma^F

hoisting rope
câble^F de levage^M
Aufzugseil^N
cavo^M di sollevamento^M
cable^M de elevación^F

operator's cab
cabine^F de commande^F
Kranführerkabine^F
cabina^F del gruista^M
cabina^F de control^M

crane runway
chemin^M de roulement^M
Kranbahn^F
rotaia^F di scorrimento^M
riel^M de rodamiento^M

hook
crochet^M
Haken^M
gancio^M
gancho^M

hoisting block
treuil^M de levage^M
Hubwinde^F
bozzello^M
garrucha^F montacarga

tower mast
tour^F
Turmmast^M
torre^F a traliccio^M
torre^F

counterweight
lest^M
Gegengewicht^N
zavorra^F
contrapeso^M

truck crane
grue^F sur porteur^M
Fahrkran^M
autogrù^F
grúa^F móvil

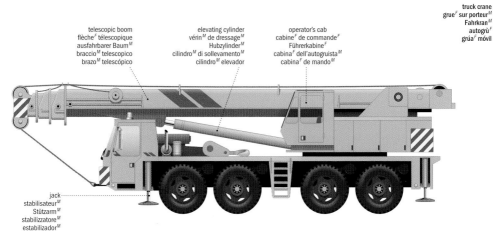

telescopic boom
flèche^F télescopique
ausfahrbarer Baum^M
braccio^M telescopico
brazo^M telescópico

elevating cylinder
vérin^M de dressage^M
Hubzylinder^M
cilindro^M di sollevamento^M
cilindro^M elevador

operator's cab
cabine^F de commande^F
Führerkabine^F
cabina^F dell'autogruista^M
cabina^F de mando^M

jack
stabilisateur^M
Stützarm^M
stabilizzatore^M
estabilizador^M

bulldozer

bouteur^M | Planierraupe^F | bulldozer^M | bulldozer^M

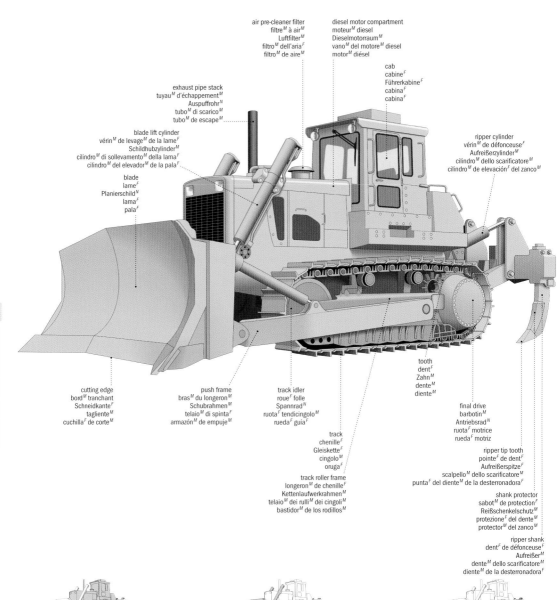

air pre-cleaner filter
filtre^M à air^M
Luftfilter^M
filtro^M dell'aria^F
filtro^M de aire^M

diesel motor compartment
moteur^M diesel
Dieselmotorraum^M
vano^M del motore^M diesel
motor^M diésel

cab
cabine^F
Führerkabine^F
cabina^F
cabina^F

exhaust pipe stack
tuyau^M d'échappement^M
Auspuffrohr^N
tubo^M di scarico^M
tubo^M de escape^M

blade lift cylinder
vérin^M de levage^M de la lame^F
Schildhubzylinder^M
cilindro^M di sollevamento^M della lama^F
cilindro^M del elevador^M de la pala^F

blade
lame^F
Planierschild^N
lama^F
pala^F

ripper cylinder
vérin^M de défonceuse^F
Aufreißerzylinder^M
cilindro^M dello scarificatore^M
cilindro^M de elevación^M del zanco^M

cutting edge
bord^M tranchant
Schneidkante^F
tagliente^M
cuchilla^F de corte^M

push frame
bras^M du longeron^M
Schubrahmen^M
telaio^M di spinta^F
armazón^M de empuje^M

track idler
roue^F folle
Spannrad^M
ruota^F tendicingolo^M
rueda^F guía^F

track
chenille^F
Gleiskette^F
cingolo^M
oruga^F

track roller frame
longeron^M de chenille^F
Kettenlaufwerkrahmen^M
telaio^M dei rulli^M dei cingoli^M
bastidor^M de los rodillos^M

tooth
dent^F
Zahn^M
dente^M
diente^M

final drive
barbotin^M
Antriebsrad^N
ruota^F motrice
rueda^F motriz

ripper tip tooth
pointe^F de dent^F
Aufreißerspitze^F
scalpello^M dello scarificatore^M
punta^F del diente^M de la desterronadora^F

shank protector
sabot^M de protection^F
Reißschenkelschutz^M
protezione^F del dente^M
protector^M del zanco^M

ripper shank
dent^F de défonceuse^F
Aufreißer^M
dente^M dello scarificatore^M
diente^M de la desterronadora^F

tracklaying tractor
tracteur^M à chenilles^F
Gleiskettenschlepper^M
trattore^M cingolato
tractor^M de orugas^F

blade
lame^F
Planierschaufel^F
lama^F
pala^F

ripper
défonceuse^F
Aufreißer^M
scarificatore^M
zanco^M

backhoe loader

chargeuse^F-pelleteuse^F | Radlader^M | terna^F | cargadora^F-retroexcavadora^F

dipper arm
bras^M
Löffelstiel^M
braccio^M della pala^F caricatrice
brazo^M del cucharón^M

dipper arm cylinder
vérin^M du bras^M
Löffelstielzylinder^M
cilindro^M della pala^F caricatrice
cilindro^M del brazo^M elevador

boom
flèche^F
Ausleger^M
braccio^M di sollevamento^M
elevador^M

bucket cylinder
vérin^M du godet^M
Schaufelzylinder^M
cilindro^M della pala^F caricatrice
cilindro^M del cucharón^M

backward bucket
godet^M rétro
hintere Schaufel^F
pala^F caricatrice posteriore
cucharón^M trasero

cab
cabine^F
Führerkabine^F
cabina^F
cabina^F

bucket lever
levier^M coudé
Schaufelarm^M
braccio^M della pala^F caricatrice
palanca^F del cucharón^M

backhoe controls
manœuvre^F de la pelleteuse^F
Tieflöffelsteuerung^F
comandi^M del retroescavatore^M
maniobra^F de la excavadora^F

bucket
godet^M
Schaufel^F
pala^F caricatrice anteriore
cucharón^M

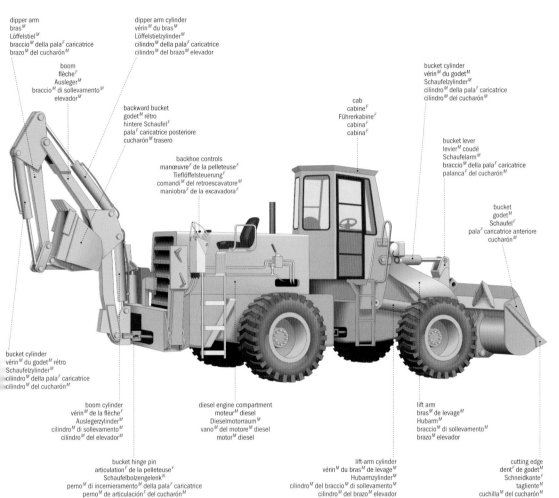

bucket cylinder
vérin^M du godet^M rétro
Schaufelzylinder^M
cilindro^M della pala^F caricatrice
cilindro^M del cucharón^M

boom cylinder
vérin^M de la flèche^F
Auslegerzylinder^M
cilindro^M di sollevamento^M
cilindro^M del elevador^M

diesel engine compartment
moteur^M diesel
Dieselmotorraum^M
vano^M del motore^M diesel
motor^M diesel

lift arm
bras^M de levage^M
Hubarm^M
braccio^M di sollevamento^M
brazo^M elevador

bucket hinge pin
articulation^F de la pelleteuse^F
Schaufelbolzengelenk^N
perno^M di incernieramento^M della pala^F caricatrice
perno^M de articulación^M del cucharón^M

lift-arm cylinder
vérin^M du bras^M de levage^M
Hubarmzylinder^M
cilindro^M del braccio^M di sollevamento^M
cilindro^M del brazo^M elevador

cutting edge
dent^F de godet^M
Schneidkante^F
tagliente^M
cuchilla^M del cucharón^M

front-end loader
chargeuse^F frontale
Schaufellader^M
pala^F caricatrice anteriore
cargador^M delantero

wheel tractor
tracteur^M
Radtraktor^M
trattore^M gommato
tractor^M de ruedas^F

backhoe
pelleteuse^F
Tieflöffel^M
retroescavatore^M
excavadora^F

scraper

décapeuse[F] | Schrapper[M] | ruspa[F] | raspador[M]

gooseneck
col[M]-de-cygne[M]
Schwanenhals[M]
collo[M] d'oca[F]
cuello[M] de ganso[M]

steering cylinder
vérin[M] de direction[F]
Lenkzylinder[M]
cilindro[M] direzionale
cilindro[M] de dirección[F]

elevator
élévateur[M]
Heber[M]
elevatore[M]
elevador[M]

tractor engine compartment
tracteur[M]-remorqueur[M]
Motorraum[M]
vano[M] del motore[M] di traino[M]
motor[M] del tractor[M]

draught tube
palonnier[M]
Saugrohr[N]
tubo[M] di posizionamento[M]
barra[F] de arrastre[M]

skip
benne[F]
Schürfkübel[M]
cassone[M]
contenedor[M]

cutting edge
lame[F] racleuse
Schneidkante[F]
tagliente[M]
cuchilla[F] de corte[M]

draught arm
brancard[M]
Saugarm[M]
braccio[M] di posizionamento[M]
brazo[M] de arrastre[M]

hydraulic shovel

pelle[F] hydraulique | Hydraulik-Hochlöffelbagger[M] | escavatore[M] idraulico | pala[F] hidráulica

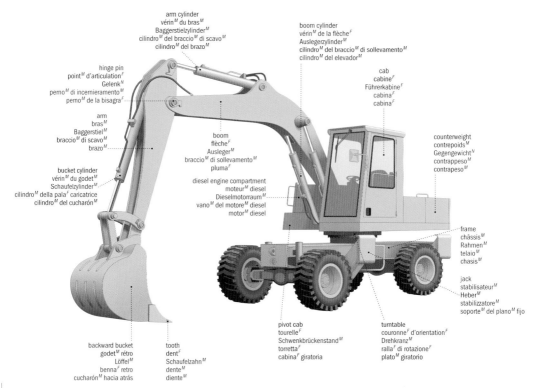

arm cylinder
vérin[M] du bras[M]
Baggerstielzylinder[M]
cilindro[M] del braccio[M] di scavo[M]
cilindro[M] del brazo[M]

boom cylinder
vérin[M] de la flèche[F]
Auslegerzylinder[M]
cilindro[M] del braccio[M] di sollevamento[M]
cilindro[M] del elevador[M]

cab
cabine[F]
Führerkabine[F]
cabina[F]
cabina[F]

hinge pin
point[M] d'articulation[F]
Gelenk[N]
perno[M] di incernieramento[M]
perno[M] de la bisagra[F]

arm
bras[M]
Baggerstiel[M]
braccio[M] di scavo[M]
brazo[M]

boom
flèche[F]
Ausleger[M]
braccio[M] di sollevamento[M]
pluma[F]

counterweight
contrepoids[M]
Gegengewicht[N]
contrappeso[M]
contrapeso[M]

bucket cylinder
vérin[M] du godet[M]
Schaufelzylinder[M]
cilindro[M] della pala[F] caricatrice
cilindro[M] del cucharón[M]

diesel engine compartment
moteur[M] diesel
Dieselmotorraum[M]
vano[M] del motore[M] diesel
motor[M] diesel

frame
châssis[M]
Rahmen[M]
telaio[M]
chasis[M]

jack
stabilisateur[M]
Heber[M]
stabilizzatore[M]
soporte[M] del plano[M] fijo

backward bucket
godet[M] rétro
Löffel[M]
benna[F] retro
cucharón[M] hacia atrás

tooth
dent[F]
Schaufelzahn[M]
dente[M]
diente[M]

pivot cab
tourelle[F]
Schwenkbrückenstand[M]
torretta[F]
cabina[F] giratoria

turntable
couronne[F] d'orientation[F]
Drehkranz[M]
ralla[F] di rotazione[F]
plato[M] giratorio

grader

niveleuse^F | Straßenhobel^M | livellatrice^F | niveladora^F

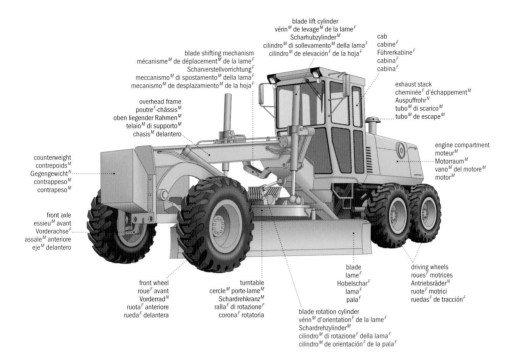

blade lift cylinder
vérin^M de levage^M de la lame^F
Scharhubzylinder^M
cilindro^M di sollevamento^M della lama^F
cilindro^M de elevación^F de la hoja^F

blade shifting mechanism
mécanisme^M de déplacement^M de la lame^F
Scharverstellvorrichtung^F
meccanismo^M di spostamento^M della lama^F
mecanismo^M de desplazamiento^M de la hoja^F

cab
cabine^F
Führerkabine^F
cabina^F
cabina^F

overhead frame
poutre^F-châssis^M
oben liegender Rahmen^M
telaio^M di supporto^M
chasis^M delantero

exhaust stack
cheminée^F d'échappement^M
Auspuffrohr^N
tubo^M di scarico^M
tubo^M de escape^M

engine compartment
moteur^M
Motorraum^M
vano^M del motore^M
motor^M

counterweight
contrepoids^M
Gegengewicht^N
contrappeso^M
contrapeso^M

front axle
essieu^M avant
Vorderachse^F
assale^M anteriore
eje^M delantero

front wheel
roue^F avant
Vorderrad^N
ruota^F anteriore
rueda^F delantera

turntable
cercle^M porte-lame^M
Schardrehkranz^M
ralla^F di rotazione^F
corona^F rotatoria

blade
lame^F
Hobelschar^F
lama^F
pala^F

driving wheels
roues^F motrices
Antriebsräder^N
ruote^F motrici
ruedas^F de tracción^F

blade rotation cylinder
vérin^M d'orientation^F de la lame^F
Schardrehzylinder^M
cilindro^M di rotazione^F della lama^F
cilindro^M de orientación^F de la pala^F

tipper truck

camion^M-benne^F | Muldenkipper^M | autocarro^M a cassone^M ribaltabile | volcadora^F

TRANSPORT AND MACHINERY

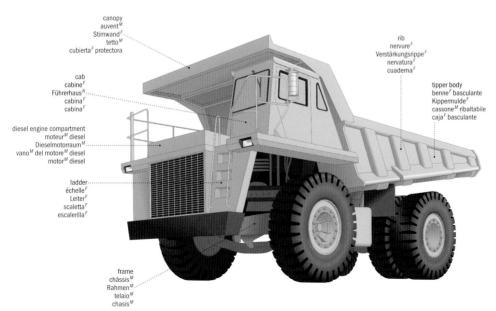

canopy
auvent^M
Stimwand^F
tetto^M
cubierta^F protectora

rib
nervure^F
Verstärkungsrippe^F
nervatura^F
cuaderna^F

cab
cabine^F
Führerhaus^N
cabina^F
cabina^F

tipper body
benne^F basculante
Kippermulde^F
cassone^M ribaltabile
caja^F basculante

diesel engine compartment
moteur^M diesel
Dieselmotorraum^M
vano^M del motore^M diesel
motor^M diesel

ladder
échelle^F
Leiter^F
scaletta^F
escalerilla^F

frame
châssis^M
Rahmen^M
telaio^M
chasis^M

production of electricity from geothermal energy

production^F d'électricité^F par énergie^F géothermique | Elektrizitätserzeugung^F aus geothermischer Energie^F | produzione^F di elettricità^F da energia^F geotermica | producción^F de electricidad^F por energía^F geotérmica

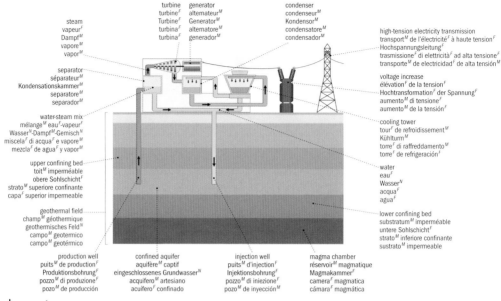

turbine
turbine^F
Turbine^F
turbina^F
turbina^F

generator
alternateur^M
Generator^M
alternatore^M
generador^M

condenser
condenseur^M
Kondensor^M
condensatore^M
condensador^M

steam
vapeur^F
Dampf^M
vapore^M
vapor^M

high-tension electricity transmission
transport^M de l'électricité^F à haute tension^F
Hochspannungsleitung^F
trasmissione^F di elettricità^F ad alta tensione^F
transporte^M de electricidad^F de alta tensión^M

separator
séparateur^M
Kondensationskammer^F
separatore^M
separador^M

voltage increase
élévation^F de la tension^F
Hochtransformation^F der Spannung^F
aumento^M di tensione^F
aumento^M de la tensión^F

water-steam mix
mélange^M eau^F-vapeur^F
Wasser^N-Dampf^M-Gemisch^N
miscela^F di acqua^F e vapore^M
mezcla^F de agua^F y vapor^M

cooling tower
tour^F de refroidissement^M
Kühlturm^M
torre^F di raffreddamento^M
torre^F de refrigeración^F

upper confining bed
toit^M imperméable
obere Sohlschicht^F
strato^M superiore confinante
capa^F superior impermeable

water
eau^F
Wasser^N
acqua^F
agua^F

geothermal field
champ^M géothermique
geothermisches Feld^N
campo^M geotermico
campo^M geotérmico

lower confining bed
substratum^M imperméable
untere Sohlschicht^F
strato^M inferiore confinante
sustrato^M impermeable

production well
puits^M de production^F
Produktionsbohrung^F
pozzo^M di produzione^F
pozo^M de producción

confined aquifer
aquifère^M captif
eingeschlossenes Grundwasser^N
acquifero^M artesiano
acuifero^F confinado

injection well
puits^M d'injection^F
Injektionsbohrung^F
pozzo^M di iniezione^F
pozo^M de inyección^M

magma chamber
réservoir^M magmatique
Magmakammer^F
camera^F magmatica
cámara^F magmática

thermal energy

énergie^F thermique | Wärmeenergie^F | energia^F termica | energía^F térmica

production of electricity from thermal energy
production^F d'électricité^F par énergie^F thermique
Elektrizitätserzeugung^F aus Wärmeenergie^F
produzione^F di elettricità^F da energia^F termica
producción^F de electricidad^F por energía^F térmica

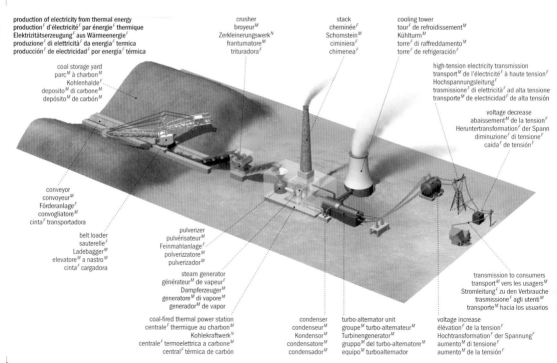

crusher
broyeur^M
Zerkleinerungswerk^N
frantumatore^M
trituradora^F

stack
cheminée^F
Schornstein^M
ciminiera^F
chimenea^F

cooling tower
tour^F de refroidissement^M
Kühlturm^M
torre^F di raffreddamento^M
torre^F de refrigeración^F

coal storage yard
parc^M à charbon^M
Kohlenhalde^F
deposito^M di carbone^M
depósito^M de carbón^M

high-tension electricity transmission
transport^M de l'électricité^F à haute tension^F
Hochspannungsleitung^F
trasmissione^F di elettricità^F ad alta tensione
transporte^M de electricidad^F de alta tensión

voltage decrease
abaissement^M de la tension^F
Heruntertransformation^F der Spann
diminuzione^F di tensione^F
caída^F de tensión^F

conveyor
convoyeur^M
Förderanlage^F
convogliatore^M
cinta^F transportadora

belt loader
sauterelle^F
Ladebagger^M
elevatore^M a nastro^M
cinta^F cargadora

pulverizer
pulvérisateur^M
Feinmahlanlage^F
polverizzatore^M
pulverizador^M

steam generator
générateur^M de vapeur^F
Dampferzeuger^M
generatore^M di vapore^M
generador^M de vapor

transmission to consumers
transport^M vers les usagers^M
Stromleitung^F zu den Verbrauche
trasmissione^F agli utenti^M
transporte^M hacia los usuarios

coal-fired thermal power station
centrale^F thermique au charbon^M
Kohlekraftwerk^N
centrale^F termoelettrica a carbone^M
central^F térmica de carbón

condenser
condenseur^M
Kondensor^M
condensatore^M
condensador^M

turbo-alternator unit
groupe^M turbo-alternateur^M
Turbinengenerator^M
gruppo^M del turbo-alternatore^M
equipo^M turboalternador

voltage increase
élévation^F de la tension^F
Hochtransformation^F der Spannung^F
aumento^M di tensione^F
aumento^M de la tensión^F

GEOTHERMY AND FOSSIL ENERGY | GÉOTHERMIE ET ÉNERGIE FOSSILE
GEOTHERMISCHE UND FOSSILE ENERGIE | ENERGIA GEOTERMICA E FOSSILE | ENERGÍA GEOTÉRMICA Y FÓSIL

oil

pétrole[M] | Erdöl[N] | petrolio[M] | petróleo[M]

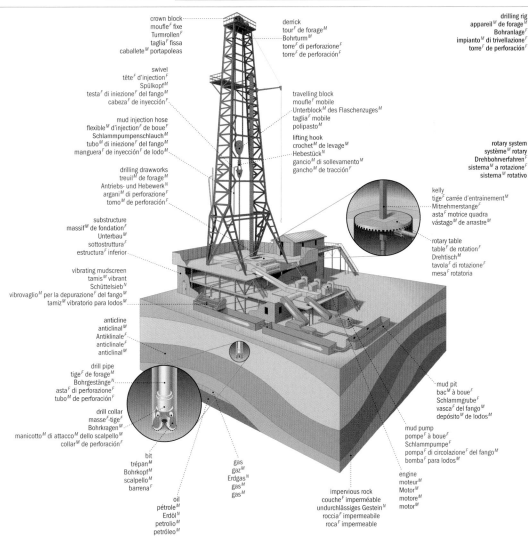

surface prospecting
prospection[F] terrestre
Oberflächenerkundung[F]
prospezione[F] terrestre
prospección[F] terrestre

seismographic recording
enregistrement[M] sismographique
seismologische Aufzeichnung[F]
registrazione[F] sismografica
registro[M] sismico

petroleum trap
gisement[M] de pétrole[M]
Erdölvorkommen[N]
trappola[F] petrolifera
trampa[F] petrolifera

shock wave
onde[F] de choc[M]
Druckwelle[F]
onda[F] d'urto[M]
onda[F] de choque[M]

crown block
moufle[F] fixe
Turmrollen[F]
taglia[F] fissa
caballete[M] portapoleas

derrick
tour[F] de forage[M]
Bohrturm[M]
torre[F] di perforazione[F]
torre[F] de perforación[F]

drilling rig
appareil[M] de forage[M]
Bohranlage[F]
impianto[M] di trivellazione[F]
torre[F] de perforación[F]

swivel
tête[F] d'injection[F]
Spülkopf[M]
testa[F] di iniezione[F] del fango[M]
cabeza[F] de inyección[F]

mud injection hose
flexible[M] d'injection[F] de boue[F]
Schlammpumpenschlauch[M]
tubo[M] di iniezione[F] del fango[M]
manguera[F] de inyección[F] de lodo[M]

travelling block
moufle[F] mobile
Unterblock[M] des Flaschenzuges[M]
taglia[F] mobile
polipasto[M]

lifting hook
crochet[M] de levage[M]
Hebestück[N]
gancio[M] di sollevamento[M]
gancho[M] de tracción[F]

rotary system
système[M] rotary
Drehbohrverfahren[N]
sistema[M] a rotazione[F]
sistema[M] rotativo

drilling drawworks
treuil[M] de forage[M]
Antriebs- und Hebewerk[N]
argani[M] di perforazione[F]
torno[M] de perforación[F]

kelly
tige[F] carrée d'entraînement[M]
Mitnehmerstange[F]
asta[F] motrice quadra
vástago[M] de arrastre[M]

substructure
massif[M] de fondation[F]
Unterbau[M]
sottostruttura[F]
estructura[F] inferior

rotary table
table[F] de rotation[F]
Drehtisch[M]
tavola[F] di rotazione[F]
mesa[F] rotatoria

vibrating mudscreen
tamis[M] vibrant
Schüttelsieb[N]
vibrovaglio[M] per la depurazione[F] del fango[M]
tamiz[M] vibratorio para lodos[M]

anticline
anticlinal[M]
Antiklinale[F]
anticlinale[F]
anticlinal[M]

drill pipe
tige[F] de forage[M]
Bohrgestänge[N]
asta[F] di perforazione[F]
tubo[M] de perforación[F]

mud pit
bac[M] à boue[F]
Schlammgrube[F]
vasca[F] del fango[M]
depósito[M] de lodos[M]

drill collar
masse[F]-tige[F]
Bohrkragen[M]
manicotto[M] di attacco[M] dello scalpello[M]
collar[M] de perforación[F]

mud pump
pompe[F] à boue[F]
Schlammpumpe[F]
pompa[F] di circolazione[F] del fango[M]
bomba[F] para lodos[M]

bit
trépan[M]
Bohrkopf[M]
scalpello[M]
barrena[F]

gas
gaz[M]
Erdgas[N]
gas[M]
gas[M]

engine
moteur[M]
Motor[M]
motore[M]
motor[M]

oil
pétrole[M]
Erdöl[N]
petrolio[M]
petróleo[M]

impervious rock
couche[F] imperméable
undurchlässiges Gestein[N]
roccia[F] impermeabile
roca[F] impermeable

ENERGY

oil

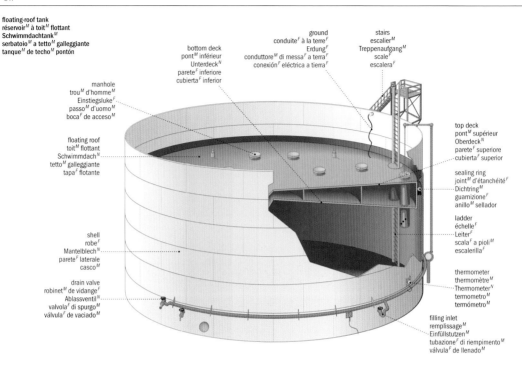

floating-roof tank
réservoir^M à toit^M flottant
Schwimmdachtank^M
serbatoio^M a tetto^M galleggiante
tanque^M de techo^M pontón

ground
conduite^F à la terre^F
Erdung^F
conduttore^M di messa^F a terra^F
conexión^F eléctrica a tierra^F

stairs
escalier^M
Treppenaufgang^M
scale^F
escalera^F

bottom deck
pont^M inférieur
Unterdeck^N
parete^F inferiore
cubierta^F inferior

manhole
trou^M d'homme^M
Einstiegsluke^F
passo^M d'uomo^M
boca^F de acceso^M

top deck
pont^M supérieur
Oberdeck^N
parete^F superiore
cubierta^F superior

floating roof
toit^M flottant
Schwimmdach^N
tetto^M galleggiante
tapa^F flotante

sealing ring
joint^F d'étanchéité^F
Dichtring^M
guarnizione^F
anillo^M sellador

ladder
échelle^F
Leiter^F
scala^F a pioli^M
escalerilla^F

shell
robe^F
Mantelblech^N
parete^F laterale
casco^M

thermometer
thermomètre^M
Thermometer^N
termometro^M
termómetro^M

drain valve
robinet^M de vidange^F
Ablassventil^N
valvola^F di spurgo^M
válvula^F de vaciado^M

filling inlet
remplissage^M
Einfüllstutzen^M
tubazione^F di riempimento^M
válvula^F de llenado^M

---

crude-oil pipeline
réseau^M d'oléoducs^M
Rohölpipeline^F
rete^F di oleodotti^M
oleoducto^M para crudo^M

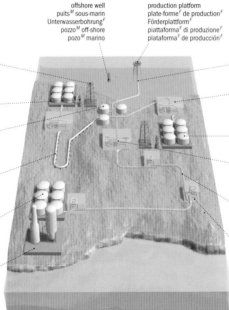

offshore well
puits^M sous-marin
Unterwasserbohrung^F
pozzo^M off-shore
pozo^M marino

production platform
plate-forme^F de production^F
Förderplattform^F
piattaforma^F di produzione^F
plataforma^F de producción^F

submarine pipeline
oléoduc^M sous-marin
Unterwasserpipeline^F
oleodotto^M sottomarino
oleoducto^M submarino

derrick
tour^F de forage^M
Bohrturm^M
torre^F di perforazione^F
torre^F de perforación^F

pumping station
station^F de pompage^F
Pumpstation^F
stazione^F di pompaggio^M
planta^F de bombeo^M

Christmas tree
arbre^M de Noël^M
Erdöleruptionskreuz^M
albero^M di Natale^M
árbol^M de Navidad^F

tank farm
parc^M de stockage^M
Tankanlage^F
serbatoi^M di stoccaggio^M
patio^M de tanques^M

buffer tank
réservoir^M tampon^M
Puffertank^M
serbatoio^M di stoccaggio^M temporaneo
tanque^M de regulación^F de presión^F

central pumping station
station^F de pompage^M principale
zentrale Pumpstation^F
stazione^F di pompaggio^M principale
estación^F central de bombeo^M

aboveground pipeline
oléoduc^M surélevé
überirdische Pipeline^F
oleodotto^M di superficie^F
oleoducto^M de superficie^F

pipeline
oléoduc^M
Pipeline^F
oleodotto^M
oleoducto^M

terminal
parc^M de stockage^M terminal
Erdölterminal^N
stazione^F terminale
terminal^M

intermediate booster station
station^F de pompage^M intermédiaire
Druckverstärkerpumpanlage^F
stazione^F di pompaggio^M intermedia
planta^F intermedia de refuerzo^M

refinery
raffinerie^F
Raffinerie^F
raffineria^F
refinería^F

ENERGY

GEOTHERMY AND FOSSIL ENERGY | GÉOTHERMIE ET ÉNERGIE FOSSILE
GEOTHERMISCHE UND FOSSILE ENERGIE | ENERGIA GEOTERMICA E FOSSILE | ENERGÍA GEOTÉRMICA Y FÓSIL

oil

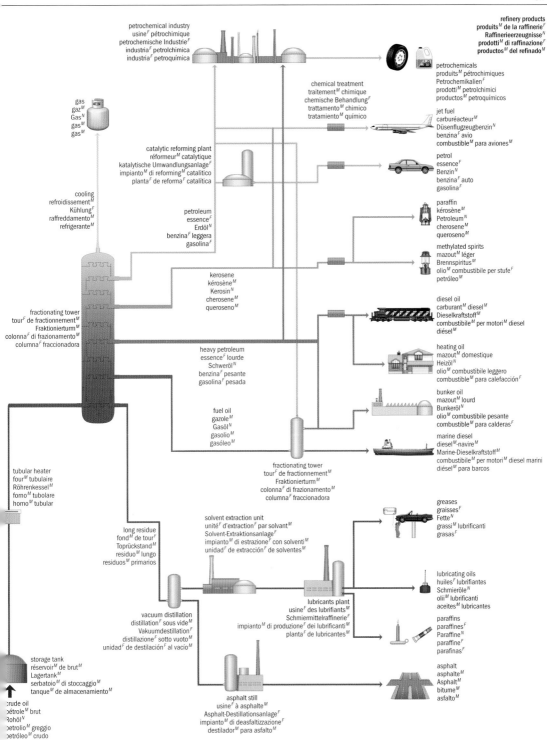

refinery products
produits^M de la raffinerie^F
Raffinerieerzeugnisse^N
prodotti^M di raffinazione^F
productos^M del refinado^M

petrochemical industry
usine^F pétrochimique
petrochemische Industrie^F
industria^F petrolchimica
industria^F petroquímica

petrochemicals
produits^M pétrochimiques
Petrochemikalien^F
prodotti^M petrolchimici
productos^M petroquímicos

chemical treatment
traitement^M chimique
chemische Behandlung^F
trattamento^M chimico
tratamiento^M químico

jet fuel
carburéacteur^M
Düsenflugzeugbenzin^N
benzina^F avio
combustibile^M para aviones^M

gas
gaz^M
Gas^N
gas^M
gas^M

catalytic reforming plant
réformeur^M catalytique
katalytische Umwandlungsanlage^F
impianto^M di reforming^M catalitico
planta^F de reforma^F catalítica

petrol
essence^F
Benzin^N
benzina^F auto
gasolina^F

cooling
refroidissement^M
Kühlung^F
raffreddamento^M
refrigerante^M

petroleum
essence^F
Erdöl^N
benzina^F leggera
gasolina^F

paraffin
kérosène^M
Petroleum^N
cherosene^M
queroseno^M

methylated spirits
mazout^M léger
Brennspiritus^M
olio^M combustibile per stufe^F
petróleo^M

kerosene
kérosène^M
Kerosin^N
cherosene^M
queroseno^M

diesel oil
carburant^M diesel^M
Dieselkraftstoff^M
combustibile^M per motori^M diesel
diésel^M

fractionating tower
tour^F de fractionnement^M
Fraktionierturm^M
colonna^F di frazionamento^M
columna^F fraccionadora

heavy petroleum
essence^F lourde
Schweröl^N
benzina^F pesante
gasolina^F pesada

heating oil
mazout^M domestique
Heizöl^N
olio^M combustibile leggero
combustible^M para calefacción^F

fuel oil
gazole^M
Gasöl^N
gasolio^M
gasóleo^M

bunker oil
mazout^M lourd
Bunkeröl^N
olio^M combustibile pesante
combustible^M para calderas^F

marine diesel
diesel^M-navire^M
Marine-Dieselkraftstoff^M
combustibile^M per motori^M diesel marini
diésel^M para barcos

tubular heater
four^M tubulaire
Röhrenkessel^M
forno^M tubolare
horno^M tubular

fractionating tower
tour^F de fractionnement^M
Fraktionierturm^M
colonna^F di frazionamento^M
columna^F fraccionadora

greases
graisses^F
Fette^N
grassi^M lubrificanti
grasas^F

solvent extraction unit
unité^F d'extraction^F par solvant^M
Solvent-Extraktionsanlage^F
impianto^M di estrazione^F con solventi^M
unidad^F de extracción^F de solventes^M

long residue
fond^M de tour^F
Toprückstand^M
residuo^M lungo
residuos^M primarios

lubricating oils
huiles^F lubrifiantes
Schmieröle^N
olii^M lubrificanti
aceites^M lubricantes

lubricants plant
usine^F des lubrifiants^M
Schmiermittelraffinerie^F
impianto^M di produzione^F dei lubrificanti^M
planta^F de lubricantes^M

paraffins
paraffines^F
Paraffine^N
paraffine^F
parafinas^F

vacuum distillation
distillation^F sous vide^M
Vakuumdestillation^F
distillazione^F sotto vuoto^M
unidad^F de destilación^F al vacío^M

asphalt
asphalte^M
Asphalt^M
bitume^M
asfalto^M

storage tank
réservoir^M de brut^M
Lagertank^M
serbatoio^M di stoccaggio^M
tanque^M de almacenamiento^M

crude oil
pétrole^M brut
Rohöl^N
petrolio^M greggio
petróleo^M crudo

asphalt still
usine^F à asphalte^M
Asphalt-Destillationsanlage^F
impianto^M di deasfaltizzazione^F
destilador^M para asfalto^M

hydroelectric complex

complexe^M hydroélectrique | Wasserkraftwerk^N | impianto^M idroelettrico | complejo^M hidroeléctrico

crest of spillway
seuil^M de l'évacuateur^M
Überlaufkrone^F
soglia^F dello sfioratore^M
cresta^F del aliviadero^M

spillway gate
vanne^F
Verschluss^F des Hochwasserentlastungswehrs^N
paratoia^F dello sfioratore^M
compuerta^F del aliviadero

top of dam
crête^F
Dammkrone^F
coronamento^M
cresta^F de la presa^F

reservoir
réservoir^M
Stausee^M
bacino^M
embalse^M

headbay
bief^M d'amont^M
Oberwasser^N
bacino^M a monte^M
embalse^M a monte^M

spillway
évacuateur^M
Hochwasserentlastungswehr^N
sfioratore^M
aliviadero^M

penstock
conduite^F forcée
Fallleitung^F
condotta^F forzata
tubería^F de carga^F

gantry crane
portique^M
Bockkran^M
grù^F a portale^M
grúa^F de caballete^M

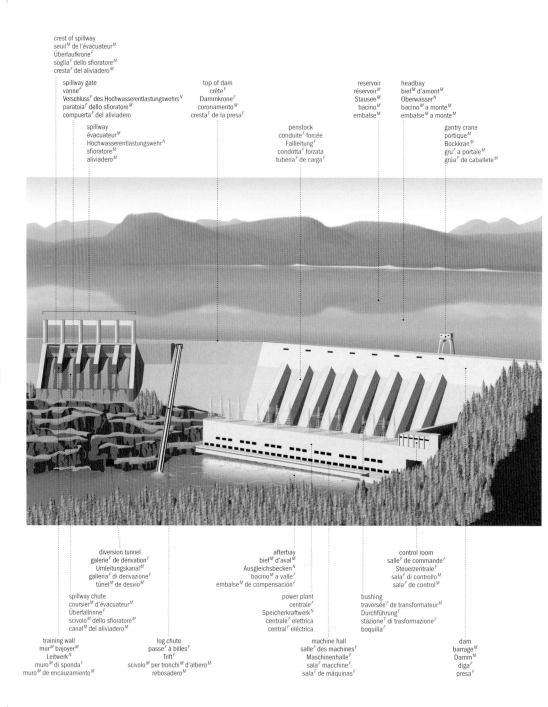

diversion tunnel
galerie^F de dérivation^F
Umleitungskanal^M
galleria^F di derivazione^F
túnel^M de desvio^M

afterbay
bief^M d'aval^M
Ausgleichsbecken^N
bacino^M a valle^F
embalse^M de compensación^F

control room
salle^F de commande^F
Steuerzentrale^F
sala^F di controllo^M
sala^F de control^M

spillway chute
coursier^M d'évacuateur^M
Überfallrinne^F
scivolo^M dello sfioratore^M
canal^M del aliviadero^M

power plant
centrale^F
Speicherkraftwerk^N
centrale^F elettrica
central^F eléctrica

bushing
traversée^F de transformateur^M
Durchführung^F
stazione^F di trasformazione^F
boquilla^F

training wall
mur^M bajoyer^M
Leitwerk^N
muro^M di sponda^F
muro^M de encauzamiento^M

log chute
passe^F à billes^F
Trift^F
scivolo^M per tronchi^M d'albero^M
rebosadero^M

machine hall
salle^F des machines^F
Maschinenhalle^F
sala^F macchine^F
sala^F de máquinas^F

dam
barrage^M
Damm^M
diga^F
presa^F

ENERGY

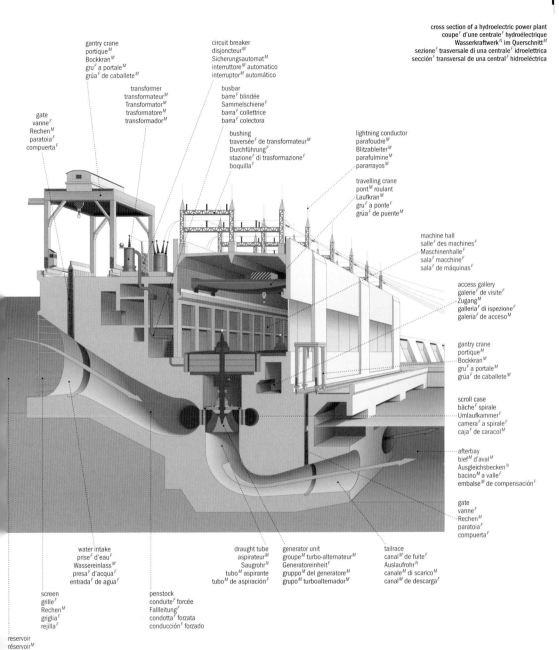

cross section of a hydroelectric power plant
coupe^F d'une centrale^F hydroélectrique
Wasserkraftwerk^N im Querschnitt^M
sezione^F trasversale di una centrale^F idroelettrica
sección^F transversal de una central^F hidroeléctrica

gantry crane
portique^M
Bockkran^M
gru^F a portale^M
grúa^F de caballete^M

circuit breaker
disjoncteur^M
Sicherungsautomat^M
interruttore^M automatico
interruptor^M automático

transformer
transformateur^M
Transformator^M
trasformatore^M
transformador^M

busbar
barre^F blindée
Sammelschiene^F
barra^F collettrice
barra^F colectora

gate
vanne^F
Rechen^M
paratoia^F
compuerta^F

bushing
traversée^F de transformateur^M
Durchführung^F
stazione^F di trasformazione^F
boquilla^F

lightning conductor
parafoudre^M
Blitzableiter^M
parafulmine^M
pararrayos^M

travelling crane
pont^M roulant
Laufkran^M
gru^F a ponte^M
grúa^F de puente^M

machine hall
salle^F des machines^F
Maschinenhalle^F
sala^F macchine^F
sala^F de máquinas^F

access gallery
galerie^F de visite^F
Zugang^M
galleria^F di ispezione^F
galería^F de acceso^M

gantry crane
portique^M
Bockkran^M
gru^F a portale^M
grúa^F de caballete^M

scroll case
bâche^F spirale
Umlaufkammer^F
camera^F a spirale^F
caja^F de caracol^M

afterbay
bief^M d'aval^M
Ausgleichsbecken^N
bacino^M a valle^F
embalse^M de compensación^F

gate
vanne^F
Rechen^M
paratoia^F
compuerta^F

water intake
prise^F d'eau^F
Wassereinlass^M
presa^F d'acqua^F
entrada^F de agua^F

draught tube
aspirateur^M
Saugrohr^N
tubo^M aspirante
tubo^M de aspiración^F

generator unit
groupe^M turbo-alternateur^M
Generatoreinheit^F
gruppo^M del generatore^M
grupo^M turboalternador^M

tailrace
canal^M de fuite^F
Auslaufrohr^N
canale^M di scarico^M
canal^M de descarga^F

screen
grille^F
Rechen^M
griglia^F
rejilla^F

penstock
conduite^F forcée
Fallleitung^F
condotta^F forzata
conducción^F forzado

reservoir
réservoir^M
Stausee^M
bacino^M
embalse^M

ENERGY

production of electricity from nuclear energy

production^F d'électricité^F par énergie^F nucléaire | Elektrizitätserzeugung^F aus Kernenergie^F | produzione^F di elettricità^F da energia^F nucleare | producción^F de electricidad^F por energía^F nuclear

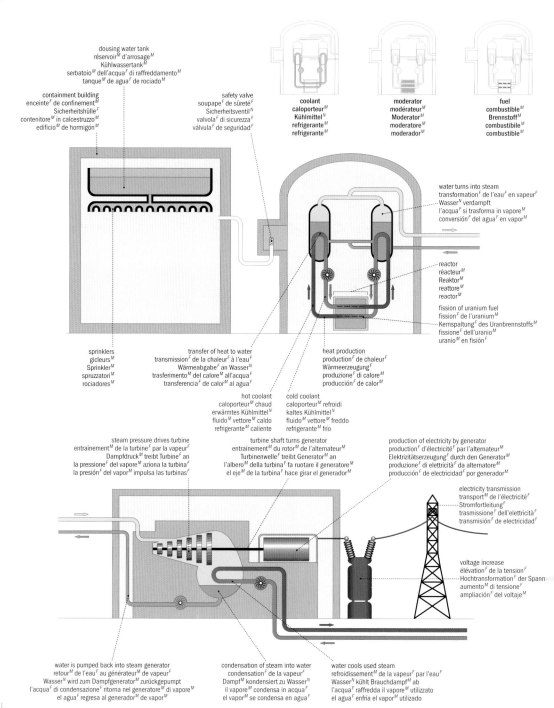

dousing water tank
réservoir^M d'arrosage^M
Kühlwassertank^M
serbatoio^M dell'acqua^F di raffreddamento^M
tanque^M de agua^F de rociado^M

containment building
enceinte^F de confinement^M
Sicherheitshülle^F
contenitore^M in calcestruzzo^M
edificio^M de hormigón^M

safety valve
soupape^F de sûreté^F
Sicherheitsventil^N
valvola^F di sicurezza^F
válvula^F de seguridad^F

coolant
caloporteur^M
Kühlmittel^N
refrigerante^M
refrigerante^M

moderator
modérateur^M
Moderator^M
moderatore^M
moderador^M

fuel
combustible^M
Brennstoff^M
combustibile^M
combustible^M

water turns into steam
transformation^F de l'eau^F en vapeur^F
Wasser^N verdampft
l'acqua^F si trasforma in vapore^M
conversión^F del agua^F en vapor^M

reactor
réacteur^M
Reaktor^M
reattore^M
reactor^M

fission of uranium fuel
fission^F de l'uranium^M
Kernspaltung^F des Uranbrennstoffs^M
fissione^F dell'uranio^M
uranio^M en fisión^F

sprinklers
gicleurs^M
Sprinkler^M
spruzzatori^M
rociadores^M

transfer of heat to water
transmission^F de la chaleur^F à l'eau^F
Wärmeabgabe^F an Wasser^N
trasferimento^M del calore^M all'acqua^F
transferencia^F de calor^F al agua^F

heat production
production^F de chaleur^F
Wärmeerzeugung^F
produzione^F di calore^M
producción^F de calor^M

hot coolant
caloporteur^M chaud
erwärmtes Kühlmittel^N
fluido^M vettore^M caldo
refrigerante^M caliente

cold coolant
caloporteur^M refroidi
kaltes Kühlmittel^N
fluido^M vettore^M freddo
refrigerante^M frío

steam pressure drives turbine
entrainement^M de la turbine^F par la vapeur^F
Dampfdruck^M treibt Turbine^F an
la pressione^F del vapore^M aziona la turbina^F
la presión^F del vapor^M impulsa las turbinas^F

turbine shaft turns generator
entrainement^M du rotor^M de l'alternateur^M
Turbinenwelle^F treibt Generator^M an
l'albero^M della turbina^F fa ruotare il generatore^M
el eje^M de la turbina^F hace girar el generador^M

production of electricity by generator
production^F d'électricité^F par l'alternateur^M
Elektrizitätserzeugung^F durch den Generator^M
produzione^F di elettricità^F da alternatore^M
producción^F de electricidad^F por generador^M

electricity transmission
transport^M de l'électricité^F
Stromfortleitung^F
trasmissione^F dell'elettricità^F
transmisión^F de electricidad^F

voltage increase
élévation^F de la tension^F
Hochtransformation^F der Spann
aumento^M di tensione^F
ampliación^F del voltaje^M

water is pumped back into steam generator
retour^M de l'eau^F au générateur^M de vapeur^F
Wasser^N wird zum Dampfgenerator^M zurückgepumpt
l'acqua^F di condensazione^F ritorna nel generatore^M di vapore^M
el agua^F regresa al generador^M de vapor^M

condensation of steam into water
condensation^F de la vapeur^F
Dampf^M kondensiert zu Wasser^N
il vapore^M condensa in acqua^F
el vapor^M se condensa en agua^F

water cools used steam
refroidissement^M de la vapeur^F par l'eau^F
Wasser^N kühlt Brauchdampf^M ab
l'acqua^F raffredda il vapore^M utilizzato
el agua^F enfría el vapor^M utilizado

ENERGY

fuel bundle

grappe^F de combustible^M | Brennstabbündel^N | elemento^M di combustibile^M | elemento^M de combustible^M

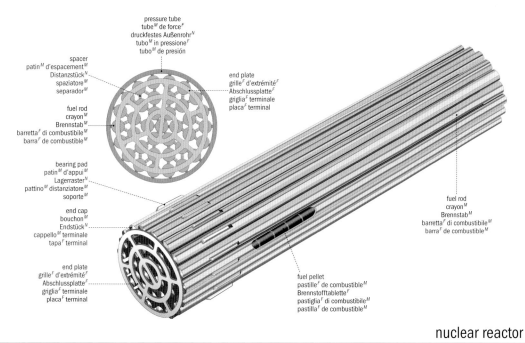

pressure tube
tube^M de force^F
druckfestes Außenrohr^N
tubo^M in pressione^F
tubo^M de presión

spacer
patin^M d'espacement^M
Distanzstück^N
spaziatore^M
separador^M

fuel rod
crayon^M
Brennstab^M
barretta^F di combustibile^M
barra^F de combustible^M

bearing pad
patin^M d'appui^M
Lagerraster^N
pattino^M distanziatore^M
soporte^M

end cap
bouchon^M
Endstück^N
cappello^M terminale
tapa^F terminal

end plate
grille^F d'extrémité^F
Abschlussplatte^F
griglia^F terminale
placa^F terminal

end plate
grille^F d'extrémité^F
Abschlussplatte^F
griglia^F terminale
placa^F terminal

fuel rod
crayon^M
Brennstab^M
barretta^F di combustibile^M
barra^F de combustible^M

fuel pellet
pastille^F de combustible^M
Brennstofftablette^F
pastiglia^F di combustibile^M
pastilla^F de combustible^M

nuclear reactor

réacteur^M nucléaire | Kernreaktor^M | reattore^M nucleare | carga^F del reactor^M nuclear

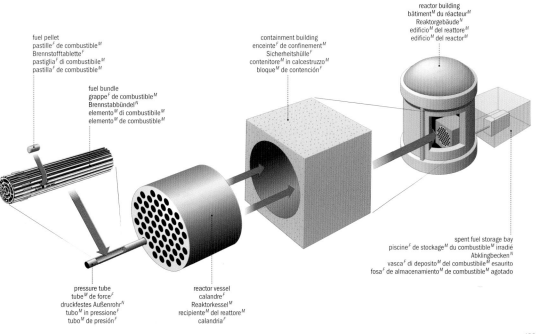

fuel pellet
pastille^F de combustible^M
Brennstofftablette^F
pastiglia^F di combustibile^M
pastilla^F de combustible^M

fuel bundle
grappe^F de combustible^M
Brennstabbündel^N
elemento^M di combustibile^M
elemento^M de combustible^M

containment building
enceinte^F de confinement^M
Sicherheitshülle^F
contenitore^M in calcestruzzo^M
bloque^M de contención^F

reactor building
bâtiment^M du réacteur^M
Reaktorgebäude^N
edificio^M del reattore^M
edificio^M del reactor^M

spent fuel storage bay
piscine^F de stockage^M du combustible^M irradié
Abklingbecken^N
vasca^F di deposito^M del combustibile^M esaurito
fosa^F de almacenamiento^M de combustible^M agotado

pressure tube
tube^M de force^F
druckfestes Außenrohr^N
tubo^M in pressione^F
tubo^M de presión^F

reactor vessel
calandre^F
Reaktorkessel^M
recipiente^M del reattore^M
calandria^F

solar cell

photopile^F | Solarzelle^F | cella^F solare | célula^F solar

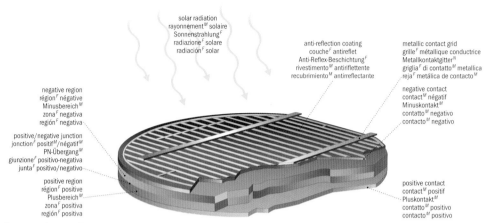

solar radiation
rayonnement^M solaire
Sonnenstrahlung^F
radiazione^F solare
radiación^F solar

anti-reflection coating
couche^F antireflet
Anti-Reflex-Beschichtung^F
rivestimento^M antiriflettente
recubrimiento^M antirreflectante

metallic contact grid
grille^F métallique conductrice
Metallkontaktgitter^N
griglia^F di contatto^M metallica
reja^F metálica de contacto^M

negative region
région^F négative
Minusbereich^M
zona^F negativa
región^F negativa

negative contact
contact^M négatif
Minuskontakt^M
contatto^M negativo
contacto^M negativo

positive/negative junction
jonction^F positif^M/négatif^M
PN-Übergang^M
giunzione^F positivo-negativa
junta^F positivo/negativo

positive region
région^F positive
Plusbereich^M
zona^F positiva
región^F positiva

positive contact
contact^M positif
Pluskontakt^M
contatto^M positivo
contacto^M positivo

flat-plate solar collector

capteur^M solaire plan | Flachkollektor^M | collettore^M solare piatto | colector^M solar plano

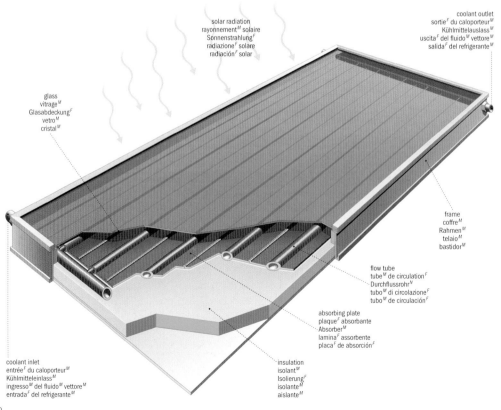

solar radiation
rayonnement^M solaire
Sonnenstrahlung^F
radiazione^F solare
radiación^F solar

coolant outlet
sortie^F du caloporteur^M
Kühlmittelauslass^M
uscita^F del fluido^M vettore^M
salida^F del refrigerante^M

glass
vitrage^M
Glasabdeckung^F
vetro^M
cristal^M

frame
coffre^M
Rahmen^M
telaio^M
bastidor^M

flow tube
tube^M de circulation^F
Durchflussrohr^N
tubo^M di circolazione^F
tubo^M de circulación^F

absorbing plate
plaque^F absorbante
Absorber^M
lamina^F assorbente
placa^F de absorción^F

coolant inlet
entrée^F du caloporteur^M
Kühlmitteleinlass^M
ingresso^M del fluido^M vettore^M
entrada^F del refrigerante^M

insulation
isolant^M
Isolierung^F
isolante^M
aislante^M

ENERGY

solar-cell system

circuit^M de photopiles^F | Solarzellensystem^N | sistema^M a celle^F solari | sistema^M de células^F solares

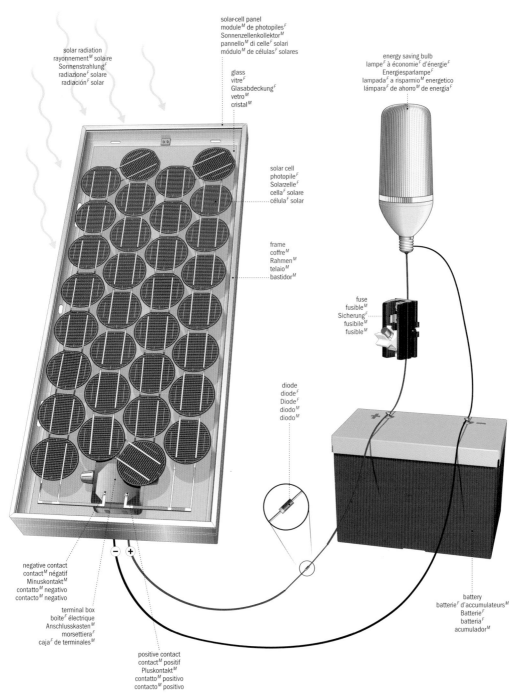

solar-cell panel
module^M de photopiles^F
Sonnenzellenkollektor^M
pannello^M di celle^F solari
módulo^M de células^F solares

energy saving bulb
lampe^F à économie^F d'énergie^F
Energiesparlampe^F
lampada^F a risparmio^M energetico
lámpara^F de ahorro^M de energía^F

solar radiation
rayonnement^M solaire
Sonnenstrahlung^F
radiazione^F solare
radiación^F solar

glass
vitre^F
Glasabdeckung^F
vetro^M
cristal^M

solar cell
photopile^F
Solarzelle^F
cella^F solare
célula^F solar

frame
coffre^M
Rahmen^M
telaio^M
bastidor^M

fuse
fusible^M
Sicherung^F
fusibile^M
fusible^M

diode
diode^F
Diode^F
diodo^M
diodo^M

negative contact
contact^M négatif
Minuskontakt^M
contatto^M negativo
contacto^M negativo

terminal box
boîte^F électrique
Anschlusskasten^M
morsettiera^F
caja^F de terminales^M

positive contact
contact^M positif
Pluskontakt^M
contatto^M positivo
contacto^M positivo

battery
batterie^F d'accumulateurs^M
Batterie^F
batteria^F
acumulador^M

ENERGY

411

windmill

moulin^M à vent^M | Windmühle^F | mulino^M a vento^M | molino^M de viento^M

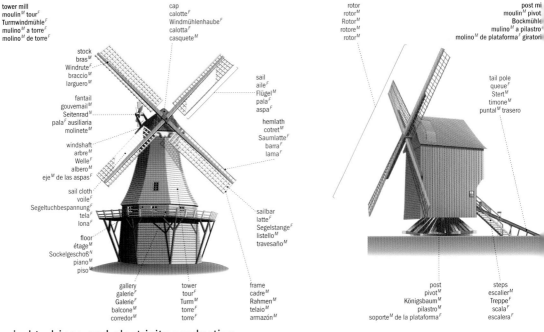

tower mill
moulin^M tour^F
Turmwindmühle^F
mulino^M a torre^F
molino^M de torre^F

cap
calotte^F
Windmühlenhaube^F
calotta^F
casquete^M

rotor
rotor^M
Rotor^M
rotore^M
rotor^M

post mi
moulin^M pivot
Bockmühle
mulino^M a pilastro
molino^M de plataforma^F giratori

stock
bras^M
Windrute^F
braccio^M
larguero^M

sail
aile^F
Flügel^M
pala^F
aspa^F

tail pole
queue^F
Stert^M
timone^M
puntal^M trasero

fantail
gouvernail^M
Seitenrad^N
pala^F ausiliaria
molinete^M

hemlath
cotret^M
Saumlatte^F
barra^F
lama^F

windshaft
arbre^M
Welle^F
albero^M
eje^M de las aspas^F

sail cloth
voile^F
Segeltuchbespannung^F
tela^F
lona^F

sailbar
latte^F
Segelstange^F
listello^M
travesaño^M

floor
étage^M
Sockelgeschoß^N
piano^M
piso^M

gallery
galerie^F
Galerie^F
balcone^M
corredor^M

tower
tour^F
Turm^M
torre^F
torre^F

frame
cadre^M
Rahmen^M
telaio^M
armazón^M

post
pivot^M
Königsbaum^M
pilastro^M
soporte^M de la plataforma^F

steps
escalier^M
Treppe^F
scala^F
escalera^F

wind turbines and electricity production

éoliennes^F et production^F d'électricité^F | Windkraftwerke^N und Elektrizitätserzeugung^F | turbine^F eoliche e produzione^F di elettricità^F | turbinas^F de viento^M y producción^F eléctrica

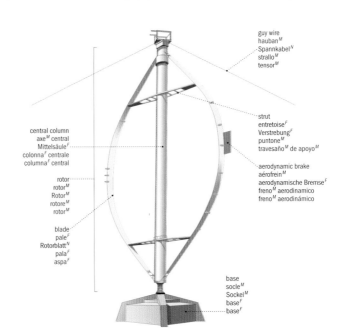

vertical-axis wind turbine
éolienne^F à axe^M vertical
Windkraftwerk mit vertikaler Achse^F
turbina^F ad asse^M verticale
turbina^F de viento^M de eje^M vertical

guy wire
hauban^M
Spannkabel^N
strallo^M
tensor^M

central column
axe^M central
Mittelsäule^F
colonna^F centrale
columna^F central

strut
entretoise^F
Verstrebung^F
puntone^M
travesaño^M de apoyo^M

aerodynamic brake
aérofrein^M
aerodynamische Bremse^F
freno^M aerodinamico
freno^M aerodinámico

rotor
rotor^M
Rotor^M
rotore^M
rotor^M

blade
pale^F
Rotorblatt^N
pala^F
aspa^F

base
socle^M
Sockel^M
base^F
base^F

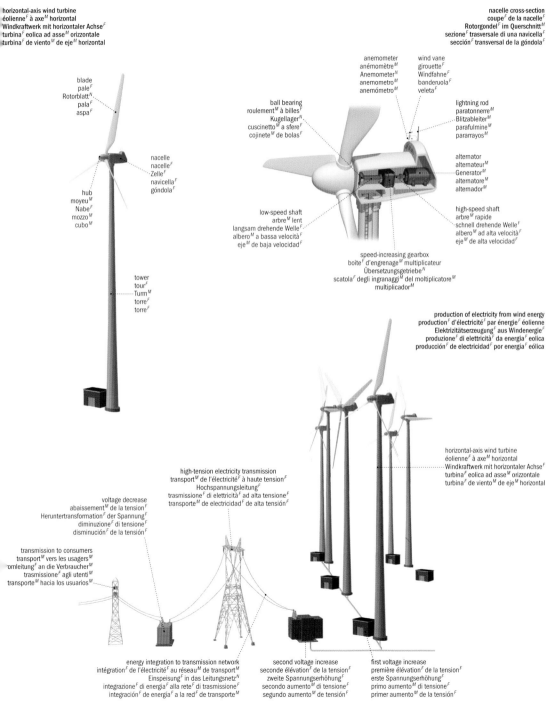

horizontal-axis wind turbine
éolienne^F à axe^M horizontal
Windkraftwerk mit horizontaler Achse^F
turbina^F eolica ad asse^M orizzontale
turbina^F de viento^M de eje^M horizontal

blade
pale^F
Rotorblatt^N
pala^F
aspa^F

nacelle
nacelle^F
Zelle^F
navicella^F
góndola^F

hub
moyeu^M
Nabe^F
mozzo^M
cubo^M

tower
tour^F
Turm^M
torre^F
torre^F

nacelle cross-section
coupe^F de la nacelle^F
Rotorgondel^F im Querschnitt^M
sezione^F trasversale di una navicella^F
sección^F transversal de la góndola^F

anemometer
anémomètre^M
Anemometer^N
anemometro^M
anemómetro^M

wind vane
girouette^F
Windfahne^F
banderuola^F
veleta^F

ball bearing
roulement^M à billes^F
Kugellager^N
cuscinetto^M a sfere^F
cojinete^M de bolas^F

lightning rod
paratonnerre^M
Blitzableiter^M
parafulmine^M
pararrayos^M

alternator
alternateur^M
Generator^M
alternatore^M
alternador^M

low-speed shaft
arbre^M lent
langsam drehende Welle^F
albero^M a bassa velocità^F
eje^M de baja velocidad^F

high-speed shaft
arbre^M rapide
schnell drehende Welle^F
albero^M ad alta velocità^F
eje^M de alta velocidad^F

speed-increasing gearbox
boîte^F d'engrenage^M multiplicateur
Übersetzungsgetriebe^N
scatola^F degli ingranaggi^M del moltiplicatore^M
multiplicador^M

production of electricity from wind energy
production^F d'électricité^F par énergie^F éolienne
Elektrizitätserzeugung^F aus Windenergie^F
produzione^F di elettricità^F da energia^F eolica
producción^F de electricidad^F por energía^F eólica

horizontal-axis wind turbine
éolienne^F à axe^M horizontal
Windkraftwerk mit horizontaler Achse^F
turbina^F eolica ad asse^M orizzontale
turbina^F de viento^M de eje^M horizontal

high-tension electricity transmission
transport^M de l'électricité^F à haute tension^F
Hochspannungsleitung^F
trasmissione^F di elettricità^F ad alta tensione^F
transporte^M de electricidad^F de alta tensión^F

voltage decrease
abaissement^M de la tension^F
Heruntertransformation^F der Spannung^F
diminuzione^F di tensione^F
disminución^F de la tensión^F

transmission to consumers
transport^M vers les usagers^M
Stromleitung^F an die Verbraucher^M
trasmissione^F agli utenti^M
transporte^M hacia los usuarios^M

energy integration to transmission network
intégration^F de l'électricité^F au réseau^M de transport^M
Einspeisung^F in das Leitungsnetz^N
integrazione^F di energia^F alla rete^F di trasmissione^F
integración^F de energía^F a la red^F de transporte^M

second voltage increase
seconde élévation^F de la tension^F
zweite Spannungserhöhung^F
secondo aumento^M di tensione^F
segundo aumento^M de tensión^F

first voltage increase
première élévation^F de la tension^F
erste Spannungserhöhung^F
primo aumento^M di tensione^F
primer aumento^M de la tensión^F

matter

matière[F] | Materie[F] | materia[F] | materia[F]

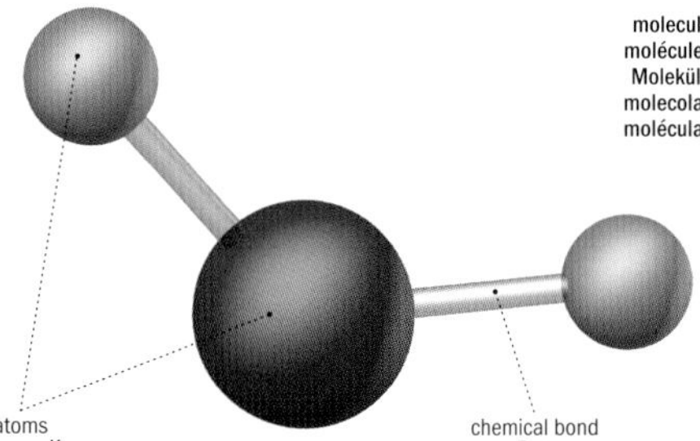

atom
atome[M]
Atom[N]
atomo[M]
átomo[M]

nucleus
noyau[M]
Atomkern[M]
nucleo[M]
núcleo[M]

d quark
quark[M] d
Down-Quark[N]
quark[M] d
quark[M] d

neutron
neutron[M]
Neutron[N]
neutrone[M]
neutrón[M]

u quark
quark[M] u
Up-Quark[N]
quark[M] u
quark[M] u

neutron
neutron[M]
Neutron[N]
neutrone[M]
neutrón[M]

proton
proton[M]
Proton[N]
protone[M]
protón[M]

molecul
molécule
Molekül
molecola
molécula

proton
proton[M]
Proton[N]
protone[M]
protón[M]

electron
électron[M]
Elektron[N]
elettrone[M]
electrón[M]

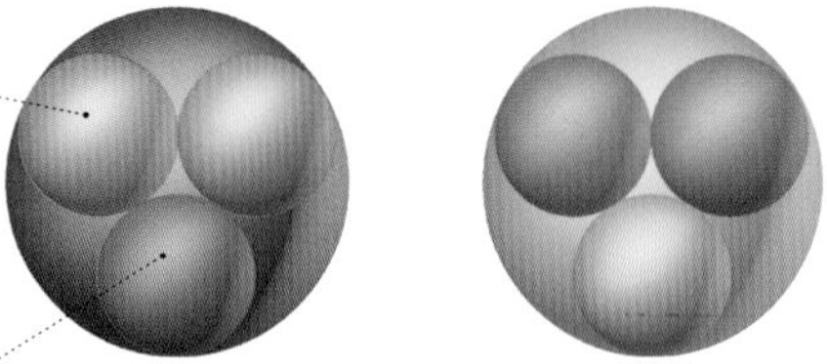

atoms
atomes[M]
Atome[N]
atomi[M]
átomos[M]

chemical bond
liaison[F] chimique
chemische Bindung[F]
legame[M] chimico
enlace[M] químico

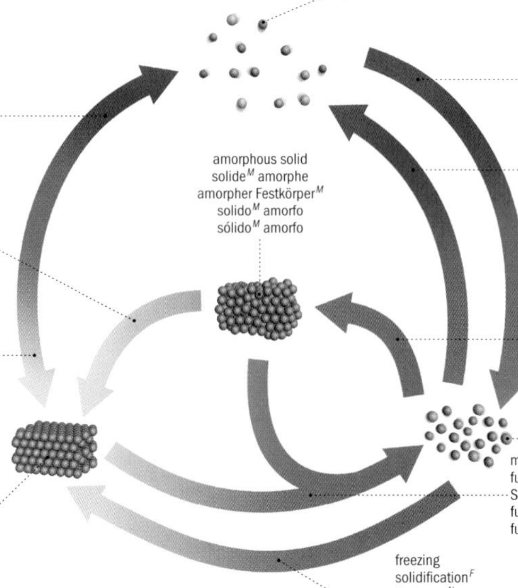

states of matter
états[M] de la matière[F]
Aggregatzustände[M]
stati[M] della materia[F]
estados[M] de la materia[F]

gas
gaz[M]
Gas[N]
gas[M]
gas[M]

sublimation
sublimation[F]
Sublimation[F]
sublimazione[F]
sublimación[F]

condensation
condensation[F]
Kondensieren[N]
condensazione[F]
condensación[F]

crystallization
cristallisation[F]
Kristallisation[F]
cristallizzazione[F]
cristalización[F]

amorphous solid
solide[M] amorphe
amorpher Festkörper[M]
solido[M] amorfo
sólido[M] amorfo

evaporation
vaporisation[F]
Verdampfen[N]
evaporazione[F]
evaporación[F]

supercooling
surfusion[F]
Unterkühlen[N]
soprafusione[F]
sobrefusión[F]

condensation
condensation[F]
Kondensieren[N]
condensazione[F]
condensación[F]

liquid
liquide[M]
Flüssigkeit[F]
liquido[M]
líquido[M]

melting
fusion[F]
Schmelzen[N]
fusione[F]
fusión[F]

solid
solide[M]
Festkörper[M]
solido[M]
sólido[M]

freezing
solidification[F]
Erstarren[N]
solidificazione[F]
solidificación[F]

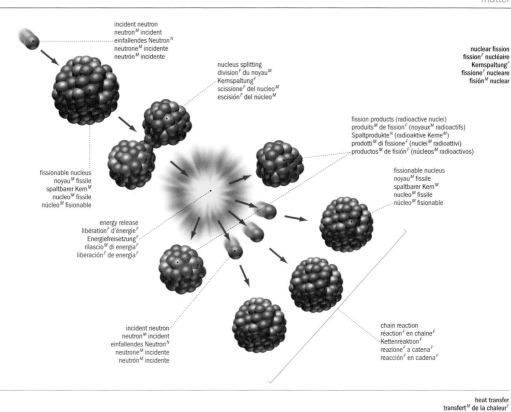

nuclear fission
fission^F nucléaire
Kernspaltung^F
fissione^F nucleare
fisión^M nuclear

incident neutron
neutron^M incident
einfallendes Neutron^N
neutrone^M incidente
neutrón^M incidente

nucleus splitting
division^F du noyau^M
Kernspaltung^F
scissione^F del nucleo^M
escisión^F del núcleo^M

fission products (radioactive nuclei)
produits^M de fission^F (noyaux^M radioactifs)
Spaltprodukte^N (radioaktive Kerne^M)
prodotti^M di fissione^F (nuclei^M radioattivi)
productos^M de fisión^F (núcleos^M radioactivos)

fissionable nucleus
noyau^M fissile
spaltbarer Kern^M
nucleo^M fissile
núcleo^M fisionable

fissionable nucleus
noyau^M fissile
spaltbarer Kern^M
nucleo^M fissile
núcleo^M fisionable

energy release
libération^F d'énergie^F
Energiefreisetzung^F
rilascio^M di energia^F
liberación^F de energia^F

incident neutron
neutron^M incident
einfallendes Neutron^N
neutrone^M incidente
neutrón^M incidente

chain reaction
réaction^F en chaîne^F
Kettenreaktion^F
reazione^F a catena^F
reacción^F en cadena^F

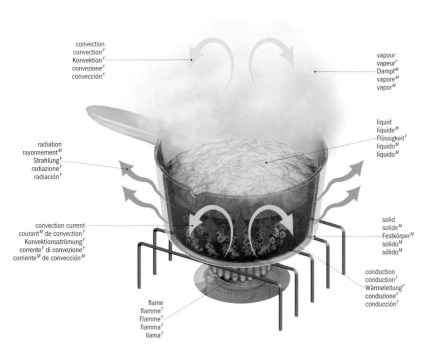

heat transfer
transfert^M de la chaleur^F
Wärmeübertragung^F
trasferimento^M di calore^M
transmisión^F de calor^M

convection
convection^F
Konvektion^F
convezione^F
convección^F

vapour
vapeur^F
Dampf^M
vapore^M
vapor^M

liquid
liquide^M
Flüssigkeit^F
liquido^M
líquido^M

radiation
rayonnement^M
Strahlung^F
radiazione^F
radiación^F

solid
solide^M
Festkörper^M
solido^M
sólido^M

convection current
courant^M de convection^F
Konvektionsströmung^F
corrente^F di convezione^F
corriente^M de convección^M

conduction
conduction^F
Wärmeleitung^F
conduzione^F
conducción^F

flame
flamme^F
Flamme^F
fiamma^F
llama^F

SCIENCE

415

magnetism

magnétisme^M | Magnetismus^M | magnetismo^M | magnetismo^M

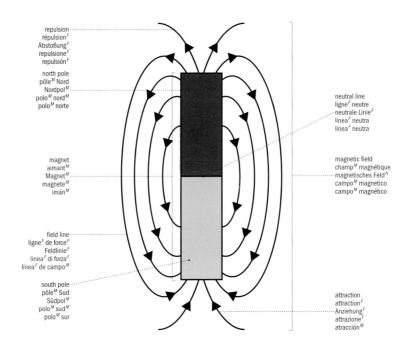

repulsion
répulsion^F
Abstoßung^F
repulsione^F
repulsión^F

north pole
pôle^M Nord
Nordpol^M
polo^M nord^M
polo^M norte

magnet
aimant^M
Magnet^M
magnete^M
imán^M

field line
ligne^F de force^F
Feldlinie^F
linea^F di forza^F
línea^F de campo^M

south pole
pôle^M Sud
Südpol^M
polo^M sud^M
polo^M sur

neutral line
ligne^F neutre
neutrale Linie^F
linea^F neutra
línea^F neutra

magnetic field
champ^M magnétique
magnetisches Feld^N
campo^M magnetico
campo^M magnético

attraction
attraction^F
Anziehung^F
attrazione^F
atracción^M

parallel electrical circuit

circuit^M électrique en parallèle^F | Parallelschaltung^F | circuito^M elettrico parallelo | circuito^M eléctrico en paralelo^M

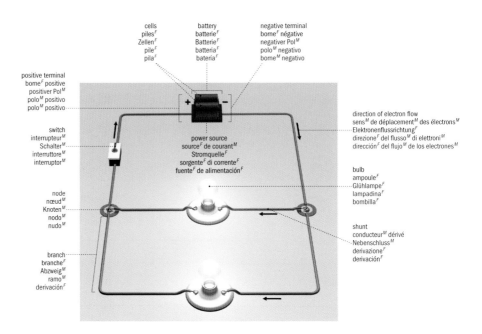

cells
piles^F
Zellen^F
pile^F
pila^F

battery
batterie^F
Batterie^F
batteria^F
batería^F

negative terminal
borne^F négative
negativer Pol^M
polo^M negativo
borne^M negativo

positive terminal
borne^F positive
positiver Pol^M
polo^M positivo
polo^M positivo

switch
interrupteur^M
Schalter^M
interruttore^M
interruptor^M

power source
source^F de courant^M
Stromquelle^F
sorgente^F di corrente^F
fuente^F de alimentación^F

direction of electron flow
sens^M de déplacement^M des électrons^M
Elektronenflussrichtung^F
direzione^F del flusso^M di elettroni^M
dirección^F del flujo^M de los electrones^M

bulb
ampoule^F
Glühlampe^F
lampadina^F
bombilla^F

node
nœud^M
Knoten^M
nodo^M
nudo^M

shunt
conducteur^M dérivé
Nebenschluss^M
derivazione^F
derivación^F

branch
branche^F
Abzweig^M
ramo^M
derivación^F

dry cells

piles[F] sèches | Trockenelemente[N] | pile[F] a secco[M] | pilas[F] secas

carbon-zinc cell
pile[F] carbone[M]-zinc[M]
Kohle[F]-Zink[N]-Zelle[F]
pila[F] a carbone[M]-zinco[M]
pila[F] de carbón-cinc

top cap
couvercle[M] supérieur
obere Abschlusskappe[F]
coperchio[M] superiore
tapa[F] superior

electrolytic separator
séparateur[M] électrolytique
Elektrolytseparator[M]
separatore[M] elettrolitico
separador[M] electrolítico

jacket
gaine[F]
Mantel[M]
rivestimento[M]
funda[F]

carbon rod (cathode)
tige[F] de carbone[M] (cathode[F])
Kohlestab[M] (Kathode[F])
astoncino[M] di carbone[M] (catodo[M])
varilla[F] de carbón[M] (cátodo[M])

depolarizing mix
mélange[M] dépolarisant
Depolarisationsgemisch[N]
miscela[F] di sostanze[F] depolarizzanti
sustancia[F] despolarizante

zinc can (anode)
boîte[F] en zinc[M] (anode[F])
Zinkzylinder[M] (Anode[F])
involucro[M] di zinco[M] (anodo[M])
caja[F] de cinc[F] (ánodo[M])

sealing plug
bouchon[M] de scellement[M]
Verschlussstopfen[M]
tappo[M] di isolamento[M]
tapa[F] de cierre[M]

positive terminal
borne[F] positive
Pluspol[M]
polo[M] positivo
borne[M] positivo

washer
rondelle[F]
Abdeckscheibe[F]
rondella[F]
arandela[F]

bottom cap
couvercle[M] inférieur
untere Abschlusskappe[F]
coperchio[M] inferiore
tapa[F] inferior

negative terminal
borne[F] négative
Minuspol[M]
polo[M] negativo
polo[M] negativo

alkaline manganese-zinc cell
pile[F] alcaline manganèse[M]-zinc[M]
alkalische Zink[N]-Mangan[N]-Zelle[F]
pila[F] alcalina a manganese[M]-zinco[M]
pila[F] alcalina de manganeso-zinc

zinc-electrolyte mix (anode)
mélange[M] de zinc[M] et d'électrolyte[M] (anode[F])
Zink[N]-Elektrolytmischung[F] (Anode[F])
miscela[F] di zinco[M] ed elettroliti[M] (anodo[M])
mezcla[F] de zinc[M] y electrolito[M] (ánodo[M])

electron collector
collecteur[M] d'électrons[M]
Elektronenkollektor[M]
collettore[M] di elettroni[M]
colector[M] de electrones[M]

steel casing
chemise[F] en acier[M]
Stahlmantel[M]
corpo[M] d'acciaio[M]
encofrado[M] metálico

separator
séparateur[M]
Separator[M]
separatore[M]
separador[M]

manganese mix (cathode)
mélange[M] au manganèse[M] (cathode[F])
Manganmischung[F] (Kathode[F])
miscela[F] di manganese[M] (catodo[M])
mezcla[F] de manganeso[M] (cátodo[M])

sealing plug
bouchon[M] de scellement[M]
Verschlussstopfen[M]
tappo[M] di isolamento[M]
tapa[F] de sellado[M]

sealing material
matériau[M] de scellement[M]
Verschlussmaterial[N]
materiale[M] isolante
material[M] de cierre[M]

bottom cap
couvercle[M] inférieur
untere Abschlusskappe[F]
coperchio[M] inferiore
tapa[F] inferior

direction of electron flow
sens[M] de déplacement[M] des électrons[M]
Elektronenflussrichtung[F]
direzione[F] del flusso[M] di elettroni[M]
dirección[F] de flujo[M] de electrones[M]

electronics

électronique[F] | Elektronik[F] | elettronica[F] | electrónica[F]

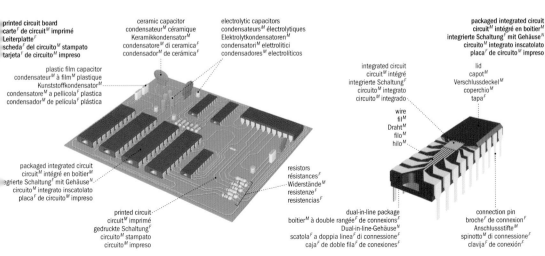

printed circuit board
carte[F] de circuit[M] imprimé
Leiterplatte[F]
scheda[F] del circuito[M] stampato
tarjeta[F] de circuito[M] impreso

plastic film capacitor
condensateur[M] à film[M] plastique
Kunststoffkondensator[M]
condensatore[M] a pellicola[F] plastica
condensador[M] de película[F] plástica

packaged integrated circuit
circuit[M] intégré en boîtier[M]
egrierte Schaltung[F] mit Gehäuse[N]
circuito[M] integrato inscatolato
placa[F] de circuito[M] impreso

printed circuit
circuit[M] imprimé
gedruckte Schaltung[F]
circuito[M] stampato
circuito[M] impreso

ceramic capacitor
condensateur[M] céramique
Keramikkondensator[M]
condensatore[M] di ceramica[F]
condensador[M] de cerámica[F]

electrolytic capacitors
condensateurs[M] électrolytiques
Elektrolytkondensatoren[M]
condensatori[M] elettrolitici
condensadores[M] electrolíticos

integrated circuit
circuit[M] intégré
integrierte Schaltung[F]
circuito[M] integrato
circuito[M] integrado

wire
fil[M]
Draht[M]
filo[M]
hilo[M]

resistors
résistances[F]
Widerstände[M]
resistenze[F]
resistencias[F]

dual-in-line package
boîtier[M] à double rangée[F] de connexions[F]
Dual-in-line-Gehäuse[N]
scatola[F] a doppia linea[F] di connessione[F]
caja[F] de doble fila[F] de conexiones[F]

packaged integrated circuit
circuit[M] intégré en boîtier[M]
integrierte Schaltung[F] mit Gehäuse[N]
circuito[M] integrato inscatolato
placa[F] de circuito[M] impreso

lid
capot[M]
Verschlussdeckel[M]
coperchio[M]
tapa[F]

connection pin
broche[F] de connexion[F]
Anschlussstifte[M]
spinotto[M] di connessione[F]
clavija[F] de conexión[F]

electromagnetic spectrum

spectre^M électromagnétique | elektromagnetisches Spektrum^N | spettro^M elettromagnetico | espectro^M electromagnético

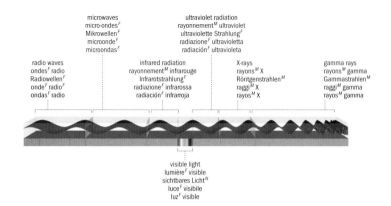

microwaves
micro-ondes^F
Mikrowellen^F
microonde^F
microondas^F

ultraviolet radiation
rayonnement^M ultraviolet
ultraviolette Strahlung^F
radiazione^F ultravioletta
radiación^F ultravioleta

radio waves
ondes^F radio
Radiowellen^F
onde^F radio^F
ondas^F radio

infrared radiation
rayonnement^M infrarouge
Infrarotstrahlung^F
radiazione^F infrarossa
radiación^F infrarroja

X-rays
rayons^M X
Röntgenstrahlen^M
raggi^M X
rayos^M X

gamma rays
rayons^M gamma
Gammastrahlen^M
raggi^M gamma
rayos^M gamma

visible light
lumière^F visible
sichtbares Licht^N
luce^F visibile
luz^F visible

wave

onde^F | Welle^F | onda^F | onda^F

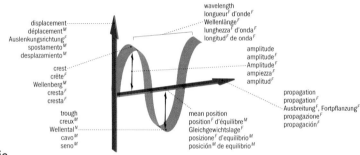

displacement
déplacement^M
Auslenkungsrichtung^F
spostamento^M
desplazamiento^M

wavelength
longueur^F d'onde^F
Wellenlänge^F
lunghezza^F d'onda^F
longitud^F de onda^F

amplitude
amplitude^F
Amplitude^F
ampiezza^F
amplitud^F

crest
crête^F
Wellenberg^M
cresta^F
cresta^F

propagation
propagation^F
Ausbreitung^F, Fortpflanzung^F
propagazione^F
propagación^F

trough
creux^M
Wellental^N
cavo^M
seno^M

mean position
position^F d'équilibre^M
Gleichgewichtslage^F
posizione^F d'equilibrio^M
posición^M de equilibrio^M

colour synthesis

synthèse^F des couleurs^F | Farbmischung^F | sintesi^F dei colori^M | síntesis^F de los colores^M

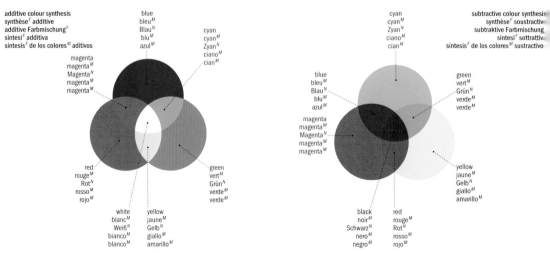

additive colour synthesis
synthèse^F additive
additive Farbmischung^F
sintesi^F additiva
sintesis^F de los colores^M aditivos

blue
bleu^M
Blau^N
blu^M
azul^M

cyan
cyan^M
Zyan^N
ciano^M
cian^M

cyan
cyan^M
Zyan^N
ciano^M
cian^M

subtractive colour synthesis
synthèse^F soustractive
subtraktive Farbmischung
sintesi^F sottrattiva
sintesis^F de los colores^M sustractivo

magenta
magenta^M
Magenta^N
magenta^M
magenta^M

blue
bleu^M
Blau^N
blu^M
azul^M

green
vert^M
Grün^N
verde^M
verde^M

magenta
magenta^M
Magenta^N
magenta^M
magenta^M

red
rouge^M
Rot^N
rosso^M
rojo^M

green
vert^M
Grün^N
verde^M
verde^M

yellow
jaune^M
Gelb^N
giallo^M
amarillo^M

white
blanc^M
Weiß^N
bianco^M
blanco^M

yellow
jaune^M
Gelb^N
giallo^M
amarillo^M

black
noir^M
Schwarz^N
nero^M
negro^M

red
rouge^M
Rot^N
rosso^M
rojo^M

SCIENCE

vision

vision[F] | Sehen[N] | vista[F] | visión[F]

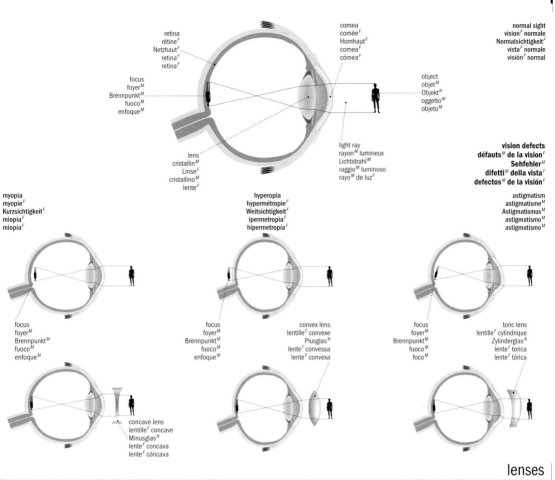

retina
rétine[F]
Netzhaut[F]
retina[F]
retina[F]

focus
foyer[M]
Brennpunkt[M]
fuoco[M]
enfoque[M]

cornea
cornée[F]
Hornhaut[F]
cornea[F]
córnea[F]

object
objet[M]
Objekt[N]
oggetto[M]
objeto[M]

lens
cristallin[M]
Linse[F]
cristallino[M]
lente[F]

light ray
rayon[M] lumineux
Lichtstrahl[M]
raggio[M] luminoso
rayo[M] de luz[F]

**normal sight
vision[F] normale
Normalsichtigkeit[F]
vista[F] normale
visión[F] normal**

**vision defects
défauts[M] de la vision[F]
Sehfehler[M]
difetti[M] della vista[F]
defectos[M] de la visión[F]**

myopia
myopie[F]
Kurzsichtigkeit[F]
miopia[F]
miopía[F]

hyperopia
hypermétropie[F]
Weitsichtigkeit[F]
ipermetropia[F]
hipermetropía[F]

**astigmatism
astigmatisme[F]
Astigmatismus[M]
astigmatismo[M]
astigmatismo[M]**

focus
foyer[M]
Brennpunkt[M]
fuoco[M]
enfoque[M]

focus
foyer[M]
Brennpunkt[M]
fuoco[M]
enfoque[M]

convex lens
lentille[F] convexe
Plusglas[N]
lente[F] convessa
lente[F] convexa

focus
foyer[M]
Brennpunkt[M]
fuoco[M]
foco[M]

toric lens
lentille[F] cylindrique
Zylinderglas[N]
lente[F] torica
lente[F] tórica

concave lens
lentille[F] concave
Minusglas[N]
lente[F] concava
lente[F] cóncava

SCIENCE

lenses

lentilles[F] | Linsen[F] | lenti[F] | lentes[F]

converging lenses
lentilles[F] convergentes
Sammellinsen[F]
lenti[F] convergenti
lentes[F] convergentes

biconvex lens
lentille[F] biconvexe
bikonvexe Linse[F]
lente[F] biconvessa
lentes[F] biconvexas

positive meniscus
ménisque[M] convergent
konkavkonvexe Linse[F]
menisco[M] convergente
menisco[M] convergente

plano-concave lens
lentille[F] plan[M]-concave
plankonkave Linse[F]
lente[F] piano-concava
lentes[F] cóncavo-planas

diverging lenses
lentilles[F] divergentes
Zerstreuungslinsen[F]
lenti[F] divergenti
lentes[F] divergentes

concave lens
lentille[F] concave
konkave Linse[F]
lente[F] concava
lentes[F] cóncavas

convex lens
lentille[F] convexe
konvexe Linse[F]
lente[F] convessa
lentes[F] convexas

plano-convex lens
lentille[F] plan[M]-convexe
plankonvexe Linse[F]
lente[F] piano-convessa
lente[F] convexo-plana

biconcave lens
lentille[F] biconcave
bikonkave Linse[F]
lente[F] biconcava
lentes[F] bicóncavas

negative meniscus
ménisque[M] divergent
konvexkonkave Linse[F]
menisco[M] divergente
menisco[M] divergente

pulsed ruby laser

laser^M à rubis^M pulsé | Rubin^M-Impulslaser^M | laser^M a rubino^M pulsato | láser^M de rubí^M pulsado

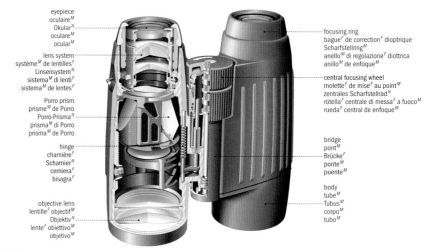

photon
photon^M
Photon^N
fotone^M
fotón^M

cooling cylinder
manchon^M refroidisseur
Kühlzylinder^M
cilindro^M di raffreddamento^M
varilla^F de refrigeración^F

reflecting cylinder
cylindre^M réflecteur
Spiegelzylinder^M
cilindro^M di riflessione^F
varilla^F reflectante

laser beam
faisceau^M laser^M
Laserstrahl^M
raggio^M laser^M
rayo^M láser

totally reflecting mirror
miroir^M à réflexion^F totale
vollreflektierender Spiegel^M
specchio^M a riflessione^F totale
espejo^M de reflexión^F total

partially reflecting mirror
miroir^M à réflexion^F partielle
teilreflektierender Spiegel^M
specchio^M a riflessione^F parziale
espejo^M de reflexión^F parcial

flash tube
tube^M à éclairs^M
Blitzröhre^F
tubo^M a flash^M
tubo^M de destellos^M

ruby cylinder
cylindre^M de rubis^M
Rubinzylinder^M
cilindro^M di rubino^M
varilla^F de rubí^M

prism binoculars

jumelles^F à prismes^M | Prismenfernglas^N | binocolo^M prismatico | prismáticos^M binoculares

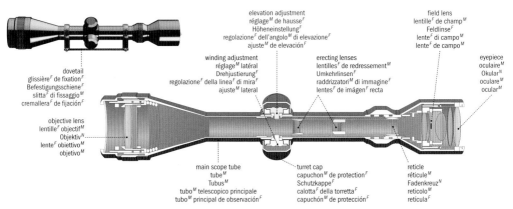

eyepiece
oculaire^M
Okular^N
oculare^M
ocular^M

focusing ring
bague^F de correction^F dioptrique
Scharfstellring^M
anello^M di regolazione^F diottrica
anillo^M de enfoque^M

lens system
système^M de lentilles^F
Linsensystem^N
sistema^M di lenti^F
sistema^M de lentes^F

central focusing wheel
molette^F de mise^F au point^M
zentrales Scharfstellrad^N
rotella^F centrale di messa^F a fuoco^M
rueda^F central de enfoque^M

Porro prism
prisme^M de Porro
Porro-Prisma^N
prisma^M di Porro
prisma^M de Porro

hinge
charnière^F
Scharnier^N
cerniera^F
bisagra^F

bridge
pont^M
Brücke^F
ponte^M
puente^M

body
tube^M
Tubus^M
corpo^M
tubo^M

objective lens
lentille^F objectif^M
Objektiv^N
lente^F obiettivo^M
objetivo^M

telescopic sight

lunette^F de visée^F | Zielfernrohr^N | cannocchiale^M di mira^F | visor^M telescópico

elevation adjustment
réglage^M de hausse^F
Höheneinstellung^F
regolazione^F dell'angolo^M di elevazione^F
ajuste^M de elevación^F

field lens
lentille^F de champ^M
Feldlinse^F
lente^F di campo^M
lente^F de campo^M

winding adjustment
réglage^M latéral
Drehjustierung^F
regolazione^F della linea^F di mira^F
ajuste^M lateral

erecting lenses
lentilles^F de redressement^M
Umkehrlinsen^F
raddrizzatori^M di immagine^F
lentes^F de imágen^F recta

eyepiece
oculaire^M
Okular^N
oculare^M
ocular^M

dovetail
glissière^F de fixation^F
Befestigungsschiene^F
slitta^F di fissaggio^M
cremallera^F de fijación^F

objective lens
lentille^F objectif^M
Objektiv^N
lente^F obiettivo^M
objetivo^M

main scope tube
tube^M
Tubus^M
tubo^M telescopico principale^F
tubo^M principal de observación^F

turret cap
capuchon^M de protection^F
Schutzkappe^F
calotta^F della torretta^F
capuchón^M de protección^F

reticle
réticule^M
Fadenkreuz^N
reticolo^M
reticula^F

magnifying glass and microscopes

loupe^F et microscopes^M | Lupe^F und Mikroskope^N | lente^F di ingrandimento^M e microscopi^M | lupa^F y microscopios^M

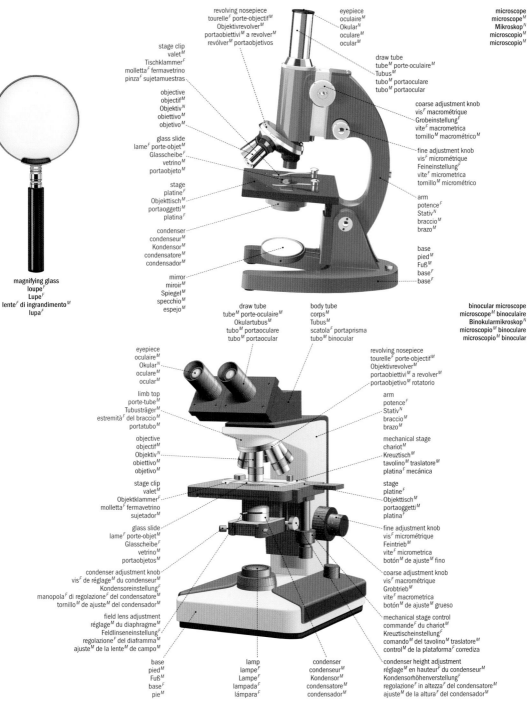

microscope
microscope^M
Mikroskop^N
microscopio^M
microscopio^M

revolving nosepiece
tourelle^F porte-objectif^M
Objektivrevolver^M
portaobiettivi^M a revolver^M
revólver^M portaobjetivos

eyepiece
oculaire^M
Okular^N
oculare^M
ocular^M

stage clip
valet^M
Tischklammer^F
molletta^F fermavetrino
pinza^F sujetamuestras

draw tube
tube^M porte-oculaire^M
Tubus^M
tubo^M portaoculare
tubo^M portaocular

objective
objectif^M
Objektiv^N
obiettivo^M
objetivo^M

coarse adjustment knob
vis^F macrométrique
Grobeinstellung^F
vite^F macrometrica
tornillo^M macrométrico^M

glass slide
lame^F porte-objet^M
Glasscheibe^F
vetrino^M
portaobjeto^M

fine adjustment knob
vis^F micrométrique
Feineinstellung^F
vite^F micrometrica
tornillo^M micrométrico

stage
platine^F
Objekttisch^M
portaoggetti^M
platina^F

arm
potence^F
Stativ^N
braccio^M
brazo^M

condenser
condenseur^M
Kondensor^M
condensatore^M
condensador^M

base
pied^M
Fuß^M
base^F
base^F

mirror
miroir^M
Spiegel^M
specchio^M
espejo^M

magnifying glass
loupe^F
Lupe^F
lente^F di ingrandimento^M
lupa^F

draw tube
tube^M porte-oculaire^M
Okulartubus^M
tubo^M portaoculare
tubo^M portaocular

body tube
corps^M
Tubus^M
scatola^F portaprisma
tubo^M binocular

binocular microscope
microscope^M binoculaire
Binokularmikroskop^N
microscopio^M binoculare
microscopio^M binocular

eyepiece
oculaire^M
Okular^N
oculare^M
ocular^M

revolving nosepiece
tourelle^F porte-objectif^M
Objektivrevolver^M
portaobiettivi^M a revolver^M
portaobjetivo^M rotatorio

limb top
porte-tube^M
Tubusträger^M
estremità^F del braccio^M
portatubo^M

arm
potence^F
Stativ^N
braccio^M
brazo^M

mechanical stage
chariot^M
Kreuztisch^M
tavolino^M traslatore^M
platina^F mecánica

objective
objectif^M
Objektiv^N
obiettivo^M
objetivo^M

stage
platine^F
Objekttisch^M
portaoggetti^M
platina^F

stage clip
valet^M
Objektklammer^F
molletta^F fermavetrino
sujetador^M

fine adjustment knob
vis^F micrométrique
Feintrieb^M
vite^F micrometrica
botón^M de ajuste^M fino

glass slide
lame^F porte-objet^M
Glasscheibe^F
vetrino^M
portaobjetos^M

coarse adjustment knob
vis^F macrométrique
Grobtrieb^M
vite^F macrometrica
botón^M de ajuste^M grueso

condenser adjustment knob
vis^F de réglage^M du condenseur^M
Kondensoreinstellung^F
manopola^F di regolazione^F del condensatore^M
tornillo^M de ajuste^M del condensador^M

mechanical stage control
commande^F du chariot^M
Kreuztischeinstellung^F
comando^M del tavolino^M traslatore^M
control^M de la plataforma^F corrediza

field lens adjustment
réglage^M du diaphragme^M
Feldlinseneinstellung^F
regolazione^F del diaframma^M
ajuste^M de la lente^M de campo^M

base
pied^M
Fuß^M
base^F
pie^M

lamp
lampe^F
Lampe^F
lampada^F
lámpara^F

condenser
condenseur^M
Kondensor^M
condensatore^M
condensador^M

condenser height adjustment
réglage^M en hauteur^F du condenseur^M
Kondensorhöhenverstellung^F
regolazione^F in altezza^F del condensatore^M
ajuste^M de la altura^F del condensador^M

SCIENCE

measurement of weight

mesure^F de la masse^F | Wiegen^N | misura^F del peso^M | medición^F del peso^M

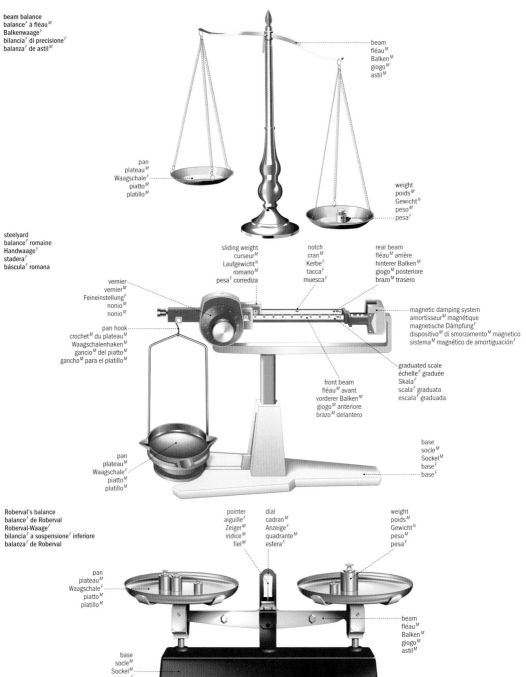

beam balance
balance^F à fléau^M
Balkenwaage^F
bilancia^F di precisione^F
balanza^F de astil^M

beam
fléau^M
Balken^M
giogo^M
astil^M

pan
plateau^M
Waagschale^F
piatto^M
platillo^M

weight
poids^M
Gewicht^N
peso^M
pesa^F

steelyard
balance^F romaine
Handwaage^F
stadera^F
báscula^F romana

sliding weight
curseur^M
Laufgewicht^N
romano^M
pesa^F corrediza

notch
cran^M
Kerbe^F
tacca^F
muesca^F

rear beam
fléau^M arrière
hinterer Balken^M
giogo^M posteriore
brazo^M trasero

vernier
vernier^M
Feineinstellung^F
nonio^M
nonio^M

magnetic damping system
amortisseur^M magnétique
magnetische Dämpfung^F
dispositivo^M di smorzamento^M magnetico
sistema^M magnético de amortiguación^F

pan hook
crochet^M du plateau^M
Waagschalenhaken^M
gancio^M del piatto^M
gancho^M para el platillo^M

graduated scale
échelle^F graduée
Skala^F
scala^F graduata
escala^F graduada

front beam
fléau^M avant
vorderer Balken^M
giogo^M anteriore
brazo^M delantero

base
socle^M
Sockel^M
base^F
base^F

pan
plateau^M
Waagschale^F
piatto^M
platillo^M

Roberval's balance
balance^F de Roberval
Roberval-Waage^F
bilancia^F a sospensione^F inferiore
balanza^F de Roberval

pointer
aiguille^F
Zeiger^M
indice^M
fiel^M

dial
cadran^M
Anzeige^F
quadrante^M
esfera^F

weight
poids^M
Gewicht^N
peso^M
pesa^F

pan
plateau^M
Waagschale^F
piatto^M
platillo^M

beam
fléau^M
Balken^M
giogo^M
astil^M

base
socle^M
Sockel^M
base^F
base^F

SCIENCE

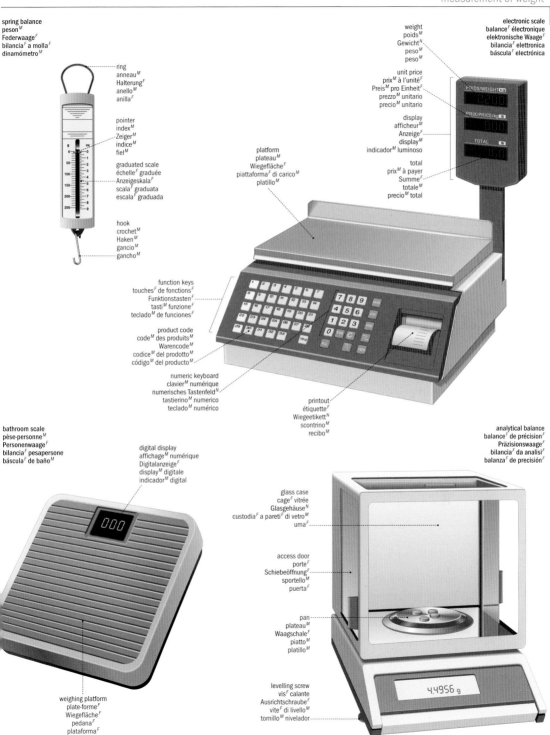

spring balance
peson^M
Federwaage^F
bilancia^F a molla^F
dinamómetro^M

ring
anneau^M
Halterung^F
anello^M
anilla^F

pointer
index^M
Zeiger^M
indice^M
fiel^M

graduated scale
échelle^F graduée
Anzeigeskala^F
scala^F graduata
escala^F graduada

hook
crochet^M
Haken^M
gancio^M
gancho^M

weight
poids^M
Gewicht^N
peso^M
peso^M

electronic scale
balance^F électronique
elektronische Waage^F
bilancia^F elettronica
báscula^F electrónica

unit price
prix^M à l'unité^F
Preis^M pro Einheit^F
prezzo^M unitario
precio^M unitario

display
afficheur^M
Anzeige^F
display^M
indicador^M luminoso

platform
plateau^M
Wiegefläche^F
piattaforma^F di carico^M
platillo^M

total
prix^M à payer
Summe^F
totale^M
precio^M total

function keys
touches^F de fonctions^F
Funktionstasten^F
tasti^M funzione^F
teclado^M de funciones^F

product code
code^M des produits^M
Warencode^M
codice^M del prodotto^M
código^M del producto^M

numeric keyboard
clavier^M numérique
numerisches Tastenfeld^N
tastierino^M numerico
teclado^M numérico

printout
étiquette^F
Wiegeetikett^N
scontrino^M
recibo^M

bathroom scale
pèse-personne^M
Personenwaage^F
bilancia^F pesapersone
báscula^F de baño^M

digital display
affichage^M numérique
Digitalanzeige^F
display^M digitale
indicador^M digital

weighing platform
plate-forme^F
Wiegefläche^F
pedana^F
plataforma^F

analytical balance
balance^F de précision^F
Präzisionswaage^F
bilancia^F da analisi^F
balanza^F de precisión^F

glass case
cage^F vitrée
Glasgehäuse^N
custodia^F a pareti^F di vetro^M
urna^F

access door
porte^F
Schiebeöffnung^F
sportello^M
puerta^F

pan
plateau^M
Waagschale^F
piatto^M
platillo^M

levelling screw
vis^F calante
Ausrichtschraube^F
vite^F di livello^M
tornillo^M nivelador

SCIENCE

measurement of temperature

mesure^F de la température^F | Temperaturmessung^F | misura^F della temperatura^F | medición^F de la temperatura^F

thermometer
thermomètre^M
Thermometer^N
termometro^M
termómetro^M

clinical thermometer
thermomètre^M médical
Fieberthermometer^N
termometro^M clinico
termómetro^M clínico

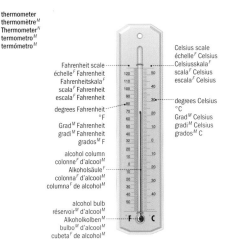

Celsius scale
échelle^F Celsius
Celsiusskala^F
scala^F Celsius
escala^F Celsius

Fahrenheit scale
échelle^F Fahrenheit
Fahrenheitskala^F
scala^F Fahrenheit
escala^F Fahrenheit

degrees Fahrenheit
°F
Grad^M Fahrenheit
gradi^M Fahrenheit
grados^M F

degrees Celsius
°C
Grad^M Celsius
gradi^M Celsius
grados^M C

alcohol column
colonne^F d'alcool^M
Alkoholsäule^F
colonna^F d'alcool^M
columna^F de alcohol^M

alcohol bulb
réservoir^M d'alcool^M
Alkoholkolben^M
bulbo^M d'alcool^M
cubeta^F de alcohol^M

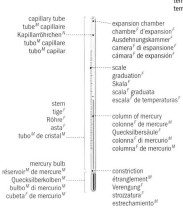

capillary tube
tube^M capillaire
Kapillarröhrchen^N
tubo^M capillare
tubo^M capilar

expansion chamber
chambre^F d'expansion^F
Ausdehnungskammer^F
camera^F di espansione^F
cámara^F de expansión^F

scale
graduation^F
Skala^F
scala^F graduata
escala^F de temperaturas^F

stem
tige^F
Röhre^F
asta^F
tubo^M de cristal

column of mercury
colonne^F de mercure^M
Quecksilbersäule^F
colonna^F di mercurio^M
columna^F de mercurio^M

mercury bulb
réservoir^M de mercure^M
Quecksilberkolben^M
bulbo^M di mercurio^M
cubeta^F de mercurio^M

constriction
étranglement^M
Verengung^F
strozzatura^F
estrechamiento^M

measurement of time

mesure^F du temps^M | Zeitmessung^F | misura^F del tempo^M | medición^F del tiempo^M

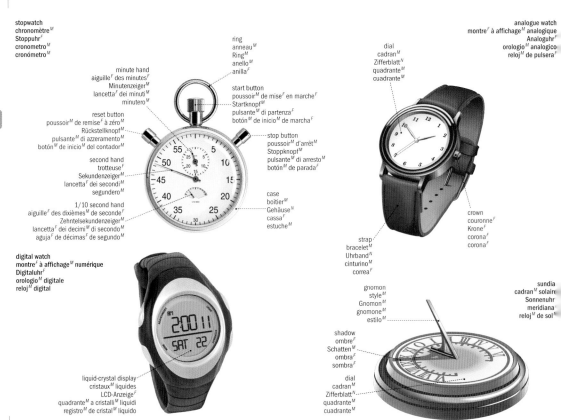

stopwatch
chronomètre^M
Stoppuhr^F
cronometro^M
cronómetro^M

analogue watch
montre^F à affichage^M analogique
Analoguhr^F
orologio^M analogico
reloj^M de pulsera^F

minute hand
aiguille^F des minutes^F
Minutenzeiger^M
lancetta^F dei minuti^M
minutero^M

ring
anneau^M
Ring^M
anello^M
anilla^F

dial
cadran^M
Zifferblatt^N
quadrante^M
cuadrante^M

start button
poussoir^M de mise^F en marche^F
Startknopf^M
pulsante^M di partenza^F
botón^M de inicio^M de marcha^F

reset button
poussoir^M de remise^F à zéro^M
Rückstellknopf^M
pulsante^M di azzeramento^M
botón^M de inicio^M del contador^M

second hand
trotteuse^F
Sekundenzeiger^M
lancetta^F dei secondi^M
segundero^M

stop button
poussoir^M d'arrêt^M
Stoppknopf^M
pulsante^M di arresto^M
botón^M de parada^F

1/10 second hand
aiguille^F des dixièmes^M de seconde^F
Zehntelsekundenzeiger^M
lancetta^F dei decimi^M di secondo^M
aguja^F de décimas^F de segundo^M

case
boîtier^M
Gehäuse^N
cassa^F
estuche^M

strap
bracelet^M
Uhrband^N
cinturino^M
correa^F

crown
couronne^F
Krone^F
corona^F
corona^F

digital watch
montre^F à affichage^M numérique
Digitaluhr^F
orologio^M digitale
reloj^M digital

gnomon
style^M
Gnomon^M
gnomone^M
estilo^M

sundial
cadran^M solaire
Sonnenuhr^F
meridiana^F
reloj^M de sol^M

shadow
ombre^F
Schatten^M
ombra^F
sombra^F

liquid-crystal display
cristaux^M liquides
LCD-Anzeige^F
quadrante^M a cristalli^M liquidi
registro^M de cristal^M líquido

dial
cadran^M
Zifferblatt^N
quadrante^M
cuadrante^M

SCIENCE

measurement of length

mesure^F de la longueur^F | Längenmessung^F | misura^F della lunghezza^F | medición^F de la longitud^F

ruler
règle^F graduée
Lineal^N
righello^M
regla^F graduada

scale
graduation^F
Skala^F
scala^F graduata
escala^F graduada

measurement of thickness

mesure^F de l'épaisseur^F | Dickemessung^F | misura^F dello spessore^M | medición^F del espesor^M

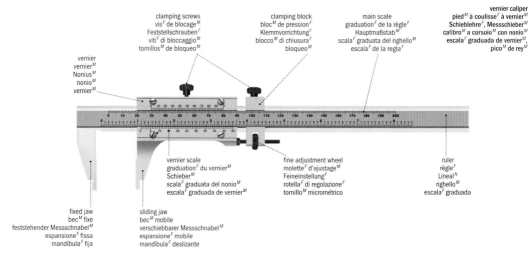

clamping screws
vis^F de blocage^M
Feststellschrauben^F
viti^F di bloccaggio^M
tornillos^M de bloqueo^M

clamping block
bloc^M de pression^F
Klemmvorrichtung^F
blocco^M di chiusura^F
bloqueo^M

main scale
graduation^F de la règle^F
Hauptmaßstab^M
scala^F graduata del righello^M
escala^F de la regla^F

vernier caliper
pied^M à coulisse^F à vernier^M
Schieblehre^F, Messschieber^M
calibro^M a corsoio^M con nonio^M
escala^F graduada de vernier^M,
pico^M de rey^M

vernier
vernier^M
Nonius^M
nonio^M
vernier^M

vernier scale
graduation^F du vernier^M
Schieber^M
scala^F graduata del nonio^M
escala^F graduada de vernier^M

fine adjustment wheel
molette^F d'ajustage^M
Feineinstellung^F
rotella^F di regolazione^F
tornillo^M micrométrico

ruler
règle^F
Lineal^N
righello^M
escala^F graduada

fixed jaw
bec^M fixe
feststehender Messschnabel^M
espansione^F fissa
mandíbula^F fija

sliding jaw
bec^M mobile
verschiebbarer Messschnabel^M
espansione^F mobile
mandíbula^F deslizante

micrometer caliper
micromètre^M palmer^M
Mikrometerschraube^F
micrometro^M a vite^F
micrómetro^M

anvil
touche^F fixe
Anschlag^M
contropunta^F
tope^M fijo

spindle
touche^F mobile
Messspindel^F
asta^F mobile
tope^M móvil

finely threaded screw
vis^F micrométrique
Filigrangewinde^N
vite^F micrometrica
rosca^F

ratchet knob
bouton^M à friction^F
Sperrdrehknopf^M
nottolino^M a scatto^M
husillo^M

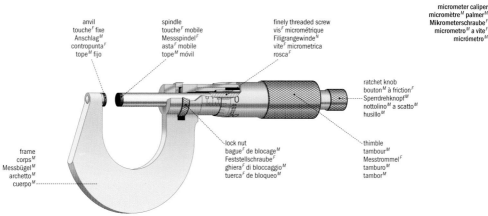

frame
corps^M
Messbügel^M
archetto^M
cuerpo^M

lock nut
bague^F de blocage^M
Feststellschraube^F
ghiera^F di bloccaggio^M
tuerca^F de bloqueo^M

thimble
tambour^M
Messtrommel^F
tamburo^M
tambor^M

international system of units

système^M international d'unités^F | internationales Einheitensystem^N | sistema^M internazionale di unità^F di misura^F | sistema^M internacional de unidades^F de medida^F

measurement of frequency	measurement of electric potential difference	measurement of electric charge	measurement of energy
mesure^F de la fréquence^F	mesure^F de la différence^F de potentiel^M électrique	mesure^F de la charge^F électrique	mesure^F de l'énergie^F
Maßeinheit^F der Frequenz^F	Maßeinheit^F der elektrischen Spannung^F	Maßeinheit^F der elektrischen Ladung^F	Maßeinheit^F der Energie^F
unità^F di misura^F della frequenza^F	unità^F di misura^F della differenza^F di potenziale^M elettrico	unità^F di misura^F della carica^F elettrica	unità^F di misura^F dell'energ
unidad^F de medida^F de frecuencia^F	unidad^F de medida^F de la diferencia^F de potencial^M eléctrico	unidad^F de medida^F de carga^F eléctrica	unidad^F de medida^F de energ

Hz
hertz
hertz^M
Hertz^N
hertz^M
hercio^M

V
volt
volt^M
Volt^N
volt^M
voltio^M , volt^M

C
coulomb
coulomb^M
Coulomb^N
coulomb^M
culombio^M

J
joule
joule^M
Joule^N
joule^M
julio^M

measurement of power	measurement of force	measurement of electric resistance	measurement of electric current
mesure^F de la puissance^F	mesure^F de la force^F	mesure^F de la résistance^F électrique	mesure^F du courant^M électrique
Maßeinheit^F der Leistung^F	Maßeinheit^F der Kraft^F	Maßeinheit^F des elektrischen Widerstands^M	Maßeinheit^F der elektrischen Stromstä
unità^F di misura^F della potenza^F elettrica	unità^F di misura^F della forza^F	unità^F di misura^F della resistenza^F elettrica	unità^F di misura^F della corrente^F elett
unidad^F de medida^F de potencia^F eléctrica	unidad^F de medida^F de fuerza^F	unidad^F de medida^F de resistencia^F eléctrica	unidad^F de medida^F de corriente^F eléct

W
watt
watt^M
Watt^N
watt^M
vatio^M

N
newton
newton^M
Newton^N
newton^M
newton^M

Ω
ohm
ohm^M
Ohm^N
ohm^M
ohmnio^M , ohm^M

A
ampere
ampère^M
Ampere^N
ampere^M
amperio^M

measurement of length	measurement of mass	measurement of Celsius temperature	measurement of thermodynamic temperature
mesure^F de la longueur^F	mesure^F de la masse^F	mesure^F de la température^F Celsius	mesure^F de la température^F thermodynamique
Maßeinheit^F der Länge^F	Maßeinheit^F der Masse^F	Maßeinheit^F der Celsius-Temperatur^F	Maßeinheit^F der thermodynamischen Temperatu
unità^F di misura^F della lunghezza^F	unità^F di misura^F della massa^F	unità^F di misura^F della temperatura^F Celsius	unità^F di misura^F della temperatura^F termodinam
unidad^F de medida^F de longitud^F	unidad^F de medida^F de masa^F	unidad^F de medida^F de la temperatura^F Celsius	unidad^F de medida^F de temperatura^F termodinám

m
metre
mètre^M
Meter^M
metro^M
metro^M

kg
kilogram
kilogramme^M
Kilogramm^N
kilogrammo^M
kilogramo^M

°C
degree Celsius
degré^M Celsius
Grad^M Celsius
grado^M Celsius
grado^M Celsius

K
kelvin
kelvin^M
Kelvin^N
kelvin^M
kelvin^M

measurement of amount of substance	measurement of radioactivity	measurement of pressure	measurement of luminous intensity
mesure^F de la quantité^F de matière^F	mesure^F de la radioactivité^F	mesure^F de la pression^F	mesure^F de l'intensité^F lumineuse
Maßeinheit^F der Stoffmenge^F	Maßeinheit^F der Radioaktivität^F	Maßeinheit^F des Drucks^M	Maßeinheit^F der Lichtstärke^F
unità^F di misura^F della quantità^F di sostanza^F	unità^F di misura^F della radioattività^F	unità^F di misura^F della pressione^F	unità^F di misura^F dell'intensità^F lumino
unidad^F de medida^F de cantidad^F de materia^F	unidad^F de medida^F de radioactividad^F	unidad^F de medida^F de presión^F	unidad^F de medida^F de intensidad^F lumin

mol
mole
mole^F
Mol^N
mole^F
mole^M

Bq
becquerel
becquerel^M
Becquerel^N
becquerel^M
becquerel^M

Pa
pascal
pascal^M
Pascal^N
pascal^M
pascal^M

cd
candela
candela^F
Candela^F
candela^F
candela^F

biology

biologie^F | Biologie^F | biologia^F | biología^F

♀
female
femelle^F
weiblich
femminile
femenino^M

♂
male
mâle^M
männlich
maschile
masculino^M

Rh-
blood factor negative
facteur^M rhésus négatif
Rhesusfaktor^M negativ
fattore^M Rh negativo
factor^M RH negativo

Rh+
blood factor positive
facteur^M rhésus positif
Rhesusfaktor^M positiv
fattore^M Rh positivo
factor^M RH positivo

†
died
mort^F
gestorben
morte^F
muerte^F

✳
born
naissance^F
geboren
nascita^F
nacimiento^M

mathematics

mathématiques[F] | Mathematik[F] | matematica[F] | matemáticas[F]

subtraction
soustraction[F]
Subtraktion[F]
sottrazione[F]
resta[F]

addition
addition[F]
Addition[F]
addizione[F]
suma[F]

multiplication
multiplication[F]
Multiplikation[F]
moltiplicazione[F]
multiplicación[F]

division
division[F]
Division[F]
divisione[F]
división[F]

is equal to
égale
ist gleich
uguale a
igual a

is not equal to
n'égale pas
ist ungleich
diverso da
no es igual a

is approximately equal to
égale à peu près
ist annähernd gleich
approssimativamente uguale a
casi igual a

is equivalent to
équivaut à
ist äquivalent mit
equivalente a
equivalente a

is identical with
est identique à
ist identisch mit
coincide con
idéntico a

is not identical with
n'est pas identique à
ist nicht identisch mit
non coincide con
no es idéntico a

plus or minus
plus ou moins
plus oder minus
più o meno
más o menos[M]

is equal to or less than
égal ou plus petit que
ist gleich oder kleiner als
minore o uguale a
igual o menor que

is greater than
plus grand que
ist größer als
maggiore di
mayor que

is equal to or greater than
égal ou plus grand que
ist gleich oder größer als
maggiore o uguale a
igual o mayor que

is less than
plus petit que
ist kleiner als
minore di
menor que

empty set
ensemble[M] vide
leere Menge[F]
insieme[M] vuoto
conjunto[M] vacío

union
réunion[F]
Mengenvereinigung[F]
unione[F]
unión[F]

intersection
intersection[F]
Mengenschnitt[M]
intersezione[F]
intersección[F]

is contained in
inclusion[F]
echte Teilmenge[F] von
contenuto in
inclusión[F]

%

percent
pourcentage[M]
Prozent[N]
percento[M]
porcentaje[M]

belongs to
appartenance[F]
Element[N] von
appartiene a
pertenece a

does not belong to
non-appartenance[F]
nicht Element[N] von
non appartiene a
no pertenece a

Σ

sum
sommation[F]
Summe[F]
sommatoria[F]
suma[F]

square root of
racine[F] carrée de
Quadratwurzel[F] aus
radice[F] quadrata di
raíz[F] cuadrada de

½

fraction
fraction[F]
Bruch[M]
frazione[F]
fracción[M]

∞

infinity
infini[M]
unendlich
infinito[M]
infinito[M]

integral
intégrale[F]
Integral[N]
integrale[M]
integral

!

factorial
factorielle[F]
Fakultät[F]
fattoriale[M]
factorial

Roman numerals
chiffres[M] romains
römische Ziffern[F]
numeri[M] romani
números[M] romanos

I

one
un[M]
Eins[F]
uno[M]
uno

V

five
cinq[M]
Fünf[F]
cinque[M]
cinco

X

ten
dix[M]
Zehn[F]
dieci[M]
diez

L

fifty
cinquante[M]
Fünfzig[F]
cinquanta[M]
cincuenta

C

one hundred
cent[M]
Hundert[F]
cento[M]
cien

D

five hundred
cinq cents[M]
Fünfhundert[F]
cinquecento[M]
quinientos

M

one thousand
mille[M]
Tausend[F]
mille[M]
mil

geometry

géométrie[F] | Geometrie[F] | geometria[F] | geometría[F]

degree degré[M] Grad[M] grado[M] grado[M]	minute minute[F] Bogenminute[F] primo[M] minuto[M]	second seconde[F] Bogensekunde[F] secondo[M] segundo[M]	pi pi[M] Pi[N] pi[N] greco pi[M]	perpendicular perpendiculaire[F] ist senkrecht zu perpendicolare perpendicular[F]

is parallel to parallèle ist parallel zu parallelo a es paralelo a	is not parallel to non-parallèle ist nicht parallel zu non parallelo a no es paralelo a	right angle angle[M] droit rechter Winkel[M] angolo[M] retto ángulo[M] recto	obtuse angle angle[M] obtus stumpfer Winkel[M] angolo[M] ottuso ángulo[M] obtuso	acute angle angle[M] aigu spitzer Winkel[M] angolo[M] acuto ángulo[M] agudo

geometrical shapes

formes[F] géométriques | geometrische Formen[F] | forme[F] geometriche | formas[F] geométricas

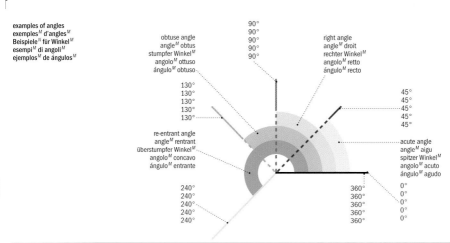

examples of angles
exemples[M] d'angles[M]
Beispiele[N] für Winkel[M]
esempi[M] di angoli[M]
ejemplos[M] de ángulos[M]

obtuse angle
angle[M] obtus
stumpfer Winkel[M]
angolo[M] ottuso
ángulo[M] obtuso

90°
90°
90°
90°
90°

right angle
angle[M] droit
rechter Winkel[M]
angolo[M] retto
ángulo[M] recto

130°
130°
130°
130°
130°

45°
45°
45°
45°
45°

re-entrant angle
angle[M] rentrant
überstumpfer Winkel[M]
angolo[M] concavo
ángulo[M] entrante

acute angle
angle[M] aigu
spitzer Winkel[M]
angolo[M] acuto
ángulo[M] agudo

240°
240°
240°
240°
240°

360°
360°
360°
360°
360°

0°
0°
0°
0°
0°

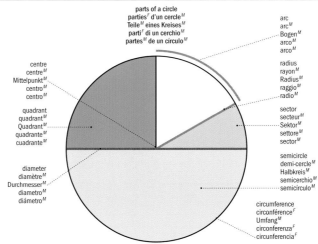

plane surfaces
surfaces[F]
ebene Flächen[F]
superfici[F]
superficies[F]

parts of a circle
parties[F] d'un cercle[M]
Teile[M] eines Kreises[M]
parti[F] di un cerchio[M]
partes[M] de un circulo[M]

arc
arc[M]
Bogen[M]
arco[M]
arco[M]

centre
centre[M]
Mittelpunkt[M]
centro[M]
centro[M]

radius
rayon[M]
Radius[M]
raggio[M]
radio[M]

quadrant
quadrant[M]
Quadrant[M]
quadrante[M]
cuadrante[M]

sector
secteur[M]
Sektor[M]
settore[M]
sector[M]

diameter
diamètre[M]
Durchmesser[M]
diametro[M]
diámetro[M]

semicircle
demi-cercle[M]
Halbkreis[M]
semicerchio[M]
semicirculo[M]

circumference
circonférence[F]
Umfang[M]
circonferenza[F]
circunferencia[F]

SCIENCE

geometrical shapes

triangle
triangle[M]
Dreieck[N]
triangolo[M]
triángulo[M]

square
carré[M]
Quadrat[N]
quadrato[M]
cuadrado[M]

rectangle
rectangle[M]
Rechteck[N]
rettangolo[M]
rectángulo[M]

rhombus
losange[M]
Rhombus[M]
rombo[M]
rombo[M]

trapezoid
trapèze[M]
unregelmäßiges Trapez[N]
trapezio[M]
trapecio[M]

parallelogram
parallélogramme[M]
Parallelogramm[N]
parallelogramma[M]
paralelogramo[M]

quadrilateral
quadrilatère[M]
Viereck[N]
quadrilatero[M]
cuadrilátero[M]

regular pentagon
pentagone[M] régulier
regelmäßiges Fünfeck[N]
pentagono[M] regolare
pentágono[M] regular

regular hexagon
hexagone[M] régulier
regelmäßiges Sechseck[N]
esagono[M] regolare
hexágono[M] regular

regular heptagon
heptagone[M] régulier
regelmäßiges Siebeneck[N]
ettagono[M] regolare
heptágono[M] regular

regular octagon
octogone[M] régulier
regelmäßiges Achteck[N]
ottagono[M] regolare
octágono[M] regular

regular nonagon
ennéagone[M] régulier
regelmäßiges Neuneck[N]
enneagono[M] regolare
nonágono[M] regular

regular decagon
décagone[M] régulier
regelmäßiges Zehneck[N]
decagono[M] regolare
decágono[M] regular

regular hendecagon
hendécagone[M] régulier
regelmäßiges Elfeck[N]
endecagono[M] regolare
endecágono[M] regular

regular dodecagon
dodécagone[M] régulier
regelmäßiges Zwölfeck[N]
dodecagono[M] regolare
dodecágono[M] regular

SCIENCE

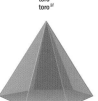
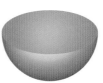

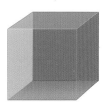

helix
hélice[F]
Helix[F]
elica[F]
hélice[F]

torus
tore[M]
Torus[M]
toro[M]
toro[M]

hemisphere
hémisphère[M]
Halbkugel[F]
semisfera[F]
hemisferio[M]

sphere
sphère[F]
Kugel[F]
sfera[F]
esfera[F]

cube
cube[M]
Würfel[M]
cubo[M]
cubo[M]

cone
cône[M]
Kegel[M]
cono[M]
cono[M]

pyramid
pyramide[F]
Pyramide[F]
piramide[F]
pirámide[M]

cylinder
cylindre[M]
Zylinder[M]
cilindro[M]
cilindro[M]

parallelepiped
parallélépipède[M]
Parallelepiped[N]
parallelepipedo[M]
paralelepípedo[M]

regular octahedron
octaèdre[M] régulier
regelmäßiges Oktaeder[N]
ottaedro[M] regolare
octaedro[M] regular

conurbation

agglomération^F | Ballungsgebiet^N | conurbazione^F | conurbación^F

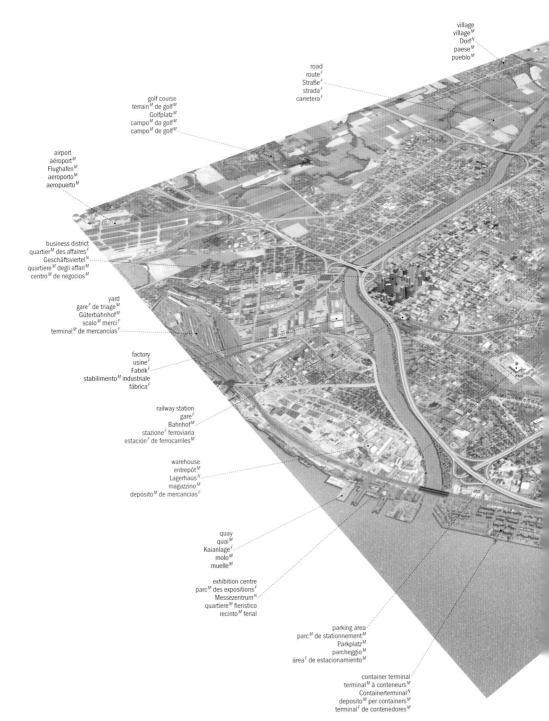

village
village^M
Dorf^N
paese^M
pueblo^M

road
route^F
Straße^F
strada^F
carretera^F

golf course
terrain^M de golf^M
Golfplatz^M
campo^M da golf^M
campo^M de golf^M

airport
aéroport^M
Flughafen^M
aeroporto^M
aeropuerto^M

business district
quartier^M des affaires^F
Geschäftsviertel^N
quartiere^M degli affari^M
centro^M de negocios^M

yard
gare^F de triage^M
Güterbahnhof^M
scalo^M merci^F
terminal^M de mercancías^F

factory
usine^F
Fabrik^F
stabilimento^M industriale
fábrica^F

railway station
gare^F
Bahnhof^M
stazione^F ferroviaria
estación^F de ferrocarriles^M

warehouse
entrepôt^M
Lagerhaus^N
magazzino^M
depósito^M de mercancías^F

quay
quai^M
Kaianlage^F
molo^M
muelle^M

exhibition centre
parc^M des expositions^F
Messezentrum^N
quartiere^M fieristico
recinto^M ferial

parking area
parc^M de stationnement^M
Parkplatz^M
parcheggio^M
área^F de estacionamiento^M

container terminal
terminal^M à conteneurs^M
Containerterminal^N
deposito^M per containers^M
terminal^F de contenedores^M

track
voie^F ferrée
Eisenbahnstrecke^F
binario^M
vía^F ferroviaria

peripheral
périphérique^M
Zubringer^M
tangenziale^F
carretera^F secundaria

motorway
autoroute^F
Autobahn^F
autostrada^F
autopista^F

landfill
décharge^F
Mülldeponie^F
discarica^F
vertedero^M

interchange
échangeur^M
Anschlussstelle^F
svincolo^M
nudo^M viario

shopping centre
centre^M commercial
Einkaufszentrum^N
centro^M commerciale
centro^M comercial

residential district
zone^F résidentielle
Wohngebiet^N
quartiere^M residenziale
zona^F residencial

country
campagne^F
Land^N
campagna^F
campo^M

commercial zone
zone^F commerciale
Gewerbegebiet^N
zona^F commerciale
zona^F comercial

suburb
banlieue^F
Vorstadt^F
suburbio^M
zona^F residencial de las afueras^F

stadium
stade^M
Stadion^N
stadio^M
estadio^M

refinery
raffinerie^F
Raffinerie^F
raffineria^F
refinería^F

city centre
centre^M-ville^F
Innenstadt^F
centro^M della città^F
centro^M ciudad^F

industrial area
zone^F industrielle
Industriegebiet^N
zona^F industriale
polígono^M industrial

port
port^M
Hafen^M
porto^M
puerto^M

sports complex
complexe^M sportif
Sportanlagen^F
complesso^M sportivo
polideportivo^M

SOCIETY

city centre

centre^M-ville^F | Innenstadt^F | centro^M della città^F | centro^M ciudad^F

courthouse
palais^M de justice^F
Gerichtsgebäude^N
palazzo^M di giustizia^F
Palacio^M de Justicia^F

business district
quartier^M des affaires^F
Geschäftsviertel^N
quartiere^M degli affari^M
centro^M de negocios^M

hotel
hôtel^M
Hotel^N
albergo^M
hotel^M

office building
édifice^M à bureaux^M
Bürogebäude^N
edificio^M per uffici^M
edificio^M de oficinas^F

railway station
gare^F
Bahnhof^M
stazione^F ferroviaria
estación^F de ferrocarriles^M

opera
opéra^M
Opernhaus^N
Opera^F
opera^F

bus station
gare^F routière
Busbahnhof^M
stazione^F degli autobus^M
estación^F de autobuses^M

railway track
voie^F ferrée
Gleis^N
binario^M ferroviario
via^F ferroviaria

pavilion
pavillon^M
Pavillon^M
padiglione^M
pabellón^M

university
université^F
Universität^F
università^F
universidad^F

town hall
hôtel^M de ville^F
Rathaus^N
municipio^M
ayuntamiento^M

theatre
salle^F de spectacle^M
Theater^N
teatro^M
teatro^M

bar
bar^M
Bar^F
bar^M
bar^M

shop
magasin^M
Geschäft^N
negozio^M
tienda^F

restaurant
restaurant^M
Restaurant^N
ristorante^M
restaurante^M

shopping street
rue^F commerçante
Einkaufsstraße^F
via^F commerciale
calle^F comercial

bank
banque^F
Bank^F
banca^F
banco^M

coffee shop
café^M
Café^N
caffè^M
cafetería^F

underground railway station
station^F de métro^M
U-Bahn^F-Station^F
stazione^F della metropolitana^F
estación^F de metro^M

cinema
cinéma^M
Kino^N
cinema^M
cine^M

SOCIETY

convention centre
palais^M des congrès^M
Kongresszentrum^N
palazzo^M dei congressi^M
palacio^M de congresos^M

educational institution
établissement^M scolaire
Bildungseinrichtung^F
complesso^M scolastico
centro^M educativo

boulevard
boulevard^M
Boulevard^M
boulevard^M
bulevar^M

street
rue^F
Straße^F
via^F
calle^F

avenue
avenue^F
Querstraße^F, Allee^F
avenue^F
avenida^F

fire station
caserne^F de pompiers^M
Feuerwache^F
caserma^F dei vigili^M del fuoco^M
parque^M de bomberos^M

cemetery
cimetière^M
Friedhof^M
cimitero^M
cementerio^M

church
église^F
Kirche^F
chiesa^F
iglesia^F

lane
ruelle^F
Gasse^F
vicolo^M
callejón^M

apartment building
immeuble^M résidentiel
Wohnblock^M
condominio^M
bloque^M de apartamentos^M

police station
poste^M de police^F
Polizeirevier^N
stazione^F di polizia^F
comisaría^F de policía^F

park
parc^M
Park^M
parco^M
parque^M

library
bibliothèque^F
Bibliothek^F
biblioteca^F
biblioteca^F

post office
bureau^M de poste^F
Postamt^N
ufficio^M postale
oficina^F de correos^M

service station
station^F-service^M
Tankstelle^F
stazione^F di servizio^M
estación^F de servicio^M

supermarket
supermarché^M
Supermarkt^M
supermercato^M
supermercado^M

museum
musée^M
Museum^N
museo^M
museo^M

theatre
théâtre^M
Theater^N
teatro^M
teatro^M

car dealer
concessionnaire^M d'automobiles^F
Autohaus^N
concessionaria^F di automobili^F
concesionario^M de automóviles

hospital
hôpital^M
Krankenhaus^N
ospedale^M
hospital^M

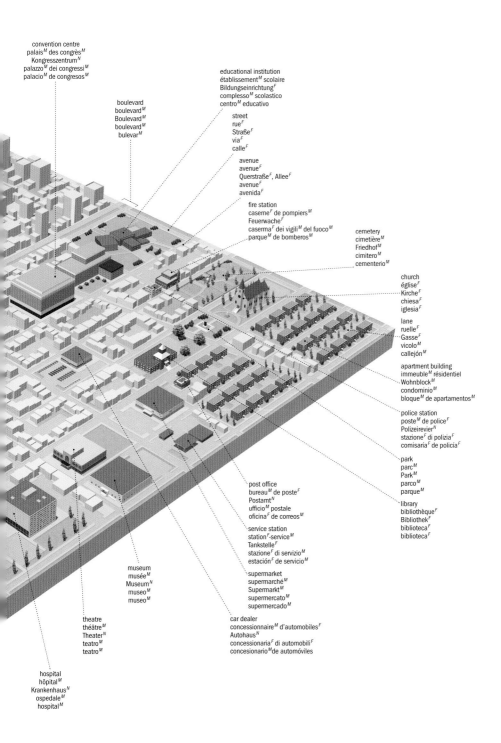

cross section of a street

coupe^F d'une rue^F | Straße^F im Querschnitt^M | sezione^F trasversale di una strada^F | vista^F transversal de una calle^F

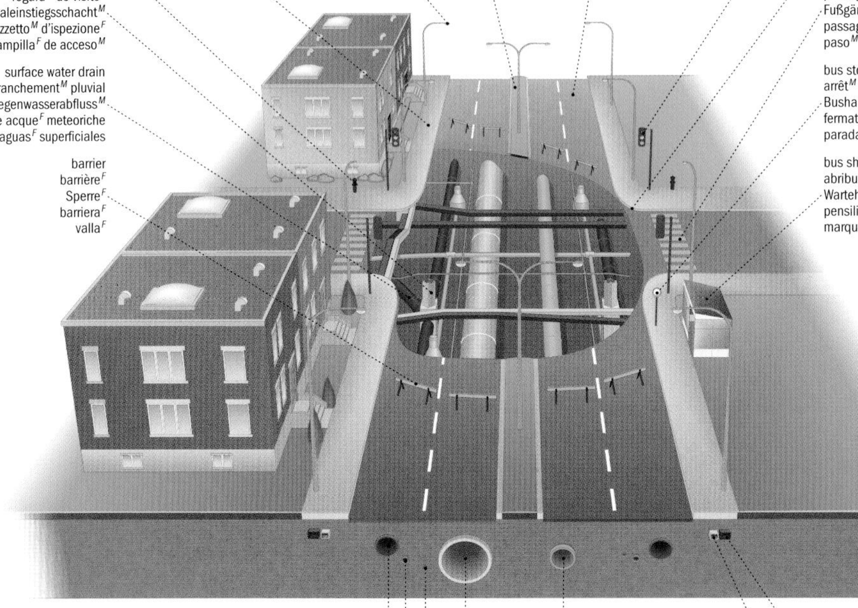

pavement
trottoir^M
Bürgersteig^M
marciapiede^M
acera^F

street light
réverbère^M
Straßenlaterne^F
lampione^M
farol^M

central reservation
terre-plein^M
Mittelstreifen^M
spartitraffico^M
mediana^F

roadway
chaussée^F
Fahrbahn^F
corsia^F
calzada^F

traffic lights
feu^M de circulation^F
Verkehrsampel^F
semaforo^M
semáforo^M

fire hydrant
borne^F d'incendie^M
Hydrant^M
idrante^M antincendio
boca^F de riego^M

kerb
bordure^F de trottoir^M
Bordstein^M
cordolo^M
bordillo^M

manhole
regard^M de visite^F
Kanaleinstiegsschacht^M
pozzetto^M d'ispezione^F
trampilla^F de acceso^M

pedestrian crossing
passage^M pour piétons^M
Fußgängerüberweg^M
passaggio^M pedonale
paso^M de peatones^M

surface water drain
branchement^M pluvial
Regenwasserabfluss^M
canale^M per le acque^F meteoriche
drenaje^M de aguas^F superficiales

bus stop
arrêt^M d'autobus^M
Bushaltestelle^F
fermata^F dell'autobus^M
parada^F de autobús^M

barrier
barrière^F
Sperre^F
barriera^F
valla^F

bus shelter
abribus^M
Wartehäuschen^N
pensilina^F
marquesina^F

sewer
égout^M
Abwasserkanal^M
condotta^F fognaria
alcantarilla^F

water main
conduite^F d'eau^F potable
Trinkwasserleitung^F
condotta^F dell'acquedotto^M
colector^M principal

electricity cable
câble^M électrique
Stromversorgungskabel^N
cavo^M dell'elettricità^F
cable^M eléctrico

main sewer
égout^M collecteur
Mischwasserkanal^M
condotta^F fognaria principale
alcantarilla^F principal

telephone cable
câble^M téléphonique
Telefonkabel^N
cavo^M telefonico
red^F de cables^M telefónicos

traffic lights
feu^M de circulation^F
Verkehrsampel^F
semaforo^M
semáforo^F

red light
feu^M rouge
rotes Licht^N
luce^F rossa
luz^F roja

amber light
feu^M jaune
gelbes Licht^N
luce^F gialla
luz^M ámbar

gas main
conduite^F de gaz^M
Gasleitung^F
conduttura^F del gas^M
conducto^M principal del gas^M

water main
conduite^F d'eau^F potable
Trinkwasserleitung^F
condotta^F dell'acquedotto^M
colector^M principal

green light
feu^M vert
grünes Licht^N
luce^F verde
luz^F verde

pedestrian lights
feu^M pour piétons^M
Fußgängerampel^F
luci^F pedonali
semáforo^M de peatones^M

pedestrian call button
bouton^M d'appel^M pour piétons^M
Fußgängerknopf^M
pulsante^M di chiamata^F pedonale
botón^M de llamada^F para peatones^M

office building

édifice^M à bureaux^M | Bürogebäude^N | edificio^M per uffici^M | edificio^M de oficinas^F

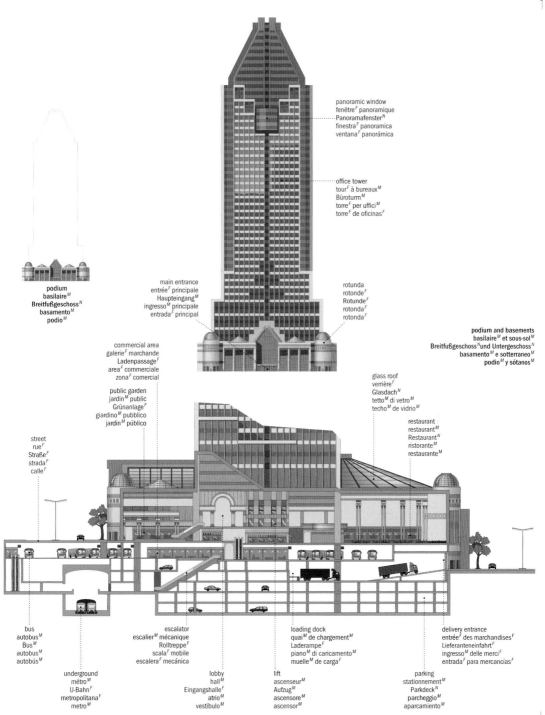

panoramic window
fenêtre^F panoramique
Panoramafenster^N
finestra^F panoramica
ventana^F panorámica

office tower
tour^F à bureaux^M
Büroturm^M
torre^F per uffici^M
torre^F de oficinas^F

rotunda
rotonde^F
Rotunde^F
rotonda^F
rotonda^F

podium
basilaire^M
Breitfußgeschoss^N
basamento^M
podio^M

main entrance
entrée^F principale
Haupteingang^M
ingresso^M principale
entrada^F principal

podium and basements
basilaire^M et sous-sol^M
Breitfußgeschoss^N und Untergeschoss^N
basamento^M e sotterraneo^M
podio^M y sótanos^M

commercial area
galerie^F marchande
Ladenpassage^F
area^F commerciale
zona^F comercial

glass roof
verrière^F
Glasdach^N
tetto^M di vetro^M
techo^M de vidrio^M

public garden
jardin^M public
Grünanlage^F
giardino^M pubblico
jardín^M público

restaurant
restaurant^M
Restaurant^N
ristorante^M
restaurante^M

street
rue^F
Straße^F
strada^F
calle^F

SOCIETY

bus
autobus^M
Bus^M
autobus^M
autobús^M

escalator
escalier^M mécanique
Rolltreppe^F
scala^F mobile
escalera^F mecánica

loading dock
quai^M de chargement^M
Laderampe^F
piano^M di caricamento^M
muelle^M de carga^F

delivery entrance
entrée^F des marchandises^F
Lieferanteneinfahrt^F
ingresso^M delle merci^F
entrada^F para mercancías^F

underground
métro^M
U-Bahn^F
metropolitana^F
metro^M

lobby
hall^M
Eingangshalle^F
atrio^M
vestíbulo^M

lift
ascenseur^M
Aufzug^M
ascensore^M
ascensor^M

parking
stationnement^M
Parkdeck^N
parcheggio^M
aparcamiento^M

435

shopping centre

centre^M commercial | Einkaufszentrum^N | centro^M commerciale | centro^M comercial

electronics shop
magasin^M d'électronique^F
Elektronikgeschäft^N
negozio^M di elettronica^F
tienda^F de electrónica^F

restaurant
restaurant^M
Restaurant^N
ristorante^M
restaurante^M

clothing shop
magasin^M de prêt-à-porter^M
Bekleidungsgeschäft^N
negozio^M di abbigliamento^M
tienda^F de ropa^F

bookshop
librairie^F
Buchhandlung^F
libreria^F
librería^F

jewellery shop
bijouterie^F
Juweliergeschäft^N
gioielleria^F
joyería^F

leather goods shop
maroquinerie^F
Lederwarengeschäft^N
pelletteria^F
peletería^F

pet shop
animalerie^F
Tierhandlung^F
negozio^M di animali^M
tienda^F de animales^M

gift shop
magasin^M de cadeaux^M
Geschenkwarenladen^M
negozio^M di articoli^M da regalo^M
tienda^F de regalos^M

do-it-yourself shop
magasin^M de bricolage^M
Heimwerkerladen^M
negozio^M di bricolage^M
tienda^F de bricolaje^M

toyshop
magasin^M de jouets^M
Spielwarengeschäft^N
negozio^M di giocattoli^M
juguetería^F

bowling
bowling^M
Bowlingbahn^F
bowling^M
bolera^F

bar
bar^M
Gaststätte^F
bar^M
bar^M

lingerie shop
magasin^M de lingerie^F
Unterwäschegeschäft^N
negozio^M di biancheria^F intima
lencería^F

perfume shop
parfumerie^F
Parfümerie^F
profumeria^F
perfumería^F

pharmacy
pharmacie^F
Apotheke^F
farmacia^F
farmacia^F

hairdresser
salon^M de coiffure^F
Friseur^M
parrucchiere^M
peluquería^F

photographer
photographe^M
Fotograf^M
fotografo^M
fotógrafo^M

travel agency
agence^F de voyages^M
Reisebüro^N
agenzia^F di viaggi^M
agencia^F de viajes^M

record shop
disquaire^M
Schallplattenladen^M
negozio^M di dischi^M
tienda^F de discos^M

tobacconist's shop
débit^M de tabac^M
Tabakwarengeschäft^N
tabaccheria^F
estanco^M

cinema
cinéma^M
Kino^N
cinema^M
cine^M

walkway
mail^M
Fußweg^M
passaggio^M pedonale
pasillo^M

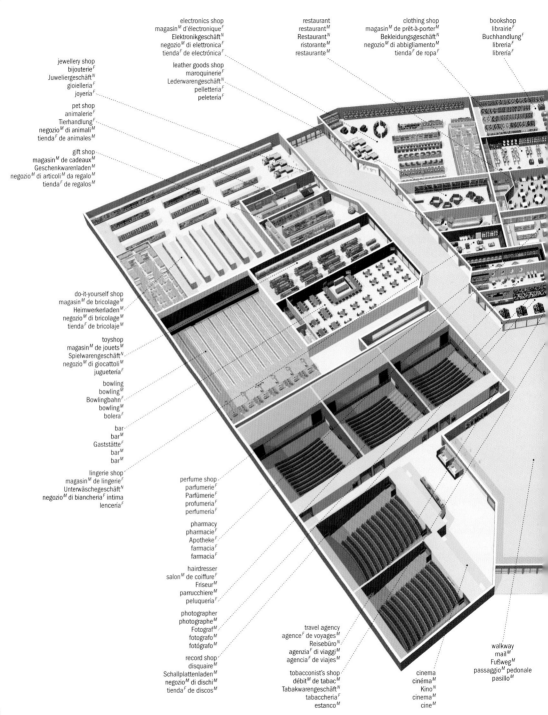

ash dispenser
stributeur^M de billets^M
eldausgabeautomat^M
ortello^M bancomat^M
ajero^M automático

bank
banque^F
Bank^F
banca^F
banco^M

dry cleaner
pressing^M
chemische Reinigung^F
lavanderia^F a secco^M
tintoreria^F

unloading dock
quai^M de déchargement^M
Entladerampe^F
banchina^F di scarico^M delle merci^F
muelle^M de carga^F

optician
opticien^M
Optiker^M
ottico^M
óptica^F

department store
magasin^M à rayons^M
Kaufhaus^N
grandi magazzini^M
grandes almacenes^M

coffee shop
café^M
Café^N
caffè^M
cafeteria^F

day-care centre
halte^F-garderie^F
Kinderbetreuung^F
servizio^M di babysitteraggio^M
guardería^F

florist
fleuriste^M
Blumenladen^M
fioraio^M
floristeria^F

supermarket
supermarché^M
Supermarkt^M
supermercato^M
supermercado^M

key cutting
reproduction^F de clés^F
Schlüsseldienst^M
negozio^M per la riproduzione^F delle chiavi^F
cerrajería^F

decorative articles shop
magasin^M de décoration^F
Dekorationsgeschäft^N
negozio^F di oggettistica^F
tienda^F de artículos^M de decoración^F

photo booth
photomaton^{®M}
Passbildautomat^M
macchina^F per fototessere^F
fotomatón^{®M}

information booth
point^M d'information^F
Informationsstand^M
banco^M delle informazioni^F
punto^M de información^F

pay phone
téléphone^M public
Münzfernsprecher^M
telefono^M pubblico
teléfono^M público

newsagent's shop
marchand^M de journaux^M
Zeitschriftenladen^M
edicola^F
quiosco^M

toilets
w.-c.^M
Toiletten^F
toilette^F
aseos^M

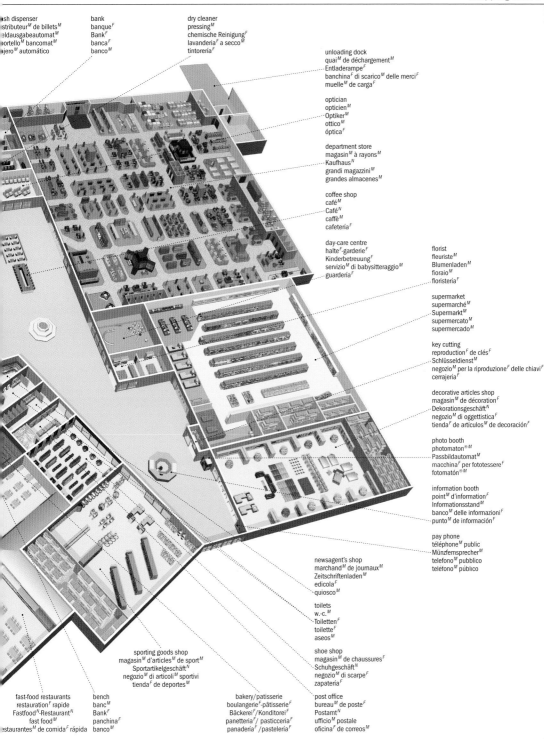

fast-food restaurants
restauration^F rapide
Fastfood^N-Restaurant^N
fast food^M
estaurantes^M de comida^F rápida

bench
banc^M
Bank^F
panchina^F
banco^M

sporting goods shop
magasin^M d'articles^M de sport^M
Sportartikelgeschäft^N
negozio^M di articoli^M sportivi
tienda^F de deportes^M

bakery/patisserie
boulangerie^F-pâtisserie^F
Bäckerei^F/Konditorei^F
panetteria^F/ pasticceria^F
panadería^F /pasteleria^F

shoe shop
magasin^M de chaussures^F
Schuhgeschäft^N
negozio^M di scarpe^F
zapatería^F

post office
bureau^M de poste^F
Postamt^N
ufficio^M postale
oficina^F de correos^M

restaurant

restaurant^M | Restaurant^M | ristorante^M | restaurante^M

storeroom
salle^F d'entreposage^M
Lagerraum^M
magazzino^M
despensa^F

office
bureau^M
Büro^N
ufficio^M
oficina^F

refrigerated display case
présentoir^M réfrigéré
Kühlvitrine^F
armadio^M frigorifero
mostrador^M frigorifico

customers' toilets
w.-c.^M
Gästetoiletten^F
toilette^F per i clienti^M
aseos^M para los clientes^M

wine waiter
sommelier^M
Weinkellner^M, Sommelier^M
sommelier^M
sumiller^M

refrigerator
réfrigérateur^M
Kühlschrank^M
frigorifero^M
frigorifico^M

wine cellar
cave^F à vins^M
Weinkeller^M
cantina^F dei vini^M
bodega^F

service table
table^F de service^M
Serviertisch^M
tavolo^M di servizio^M
mesa^F de servicio^M

customers' cloakroom
vestiaire^M des clients^M
Gästegarderobe^F
guardaroba^M dei clienti^M
guardarropa^M de los clientes^M

freezer
congélateur^M
Gefrierschrank^M
congelatore^M
congelador^M

buffet
buffet^M
Buffet^N
buffet^M
buffet^M

maitre d'hôtel
maître^M d'hôtel^M
Oberkellner^M
maître^M
maître^M

staff entrance
entrée^F du personnel^M
Personaleingang^M
ingresso^M del personale^M
entrada^F del personal^M

staff cloakroom
vestiaire^M du personnel^M
Personalgarderobe^F
guardaroba^M del personale^M
guardarropa^M del personal^M

refrigerators
réfrigérateurs^M
Kühlschränke^M
frigoriferi^M
frigorificos^M

barmaid
barmaid^F
Bardame^F
barista^{M/F}
camarera^F

bar counter
comptoir^M du bar^M
Theke^F
bancone^M del bar^M
barra^F del bar^M

bar stool
tabouret^M de bar^M
Barhocker^M
sgabello^M da bar^M
taburete^M de bar^M

bar
bar^M
Bar^F
bar^M
bar^M

pay phone
téléphone^M public
Münzfernsprecher^M
telefono^M pubblico
teléfono^M público

customers' entrance
entrée^F des clients^M
Gästeeingang^M
ingresso^M dei clienti^M
entrada^F de clientes^M

booth
box^M
Tisch^M
séparé^M
apartado^M

dining room
salle^F à manger
Speisesaal^M
sala^F da pranzo^M
comedor^M

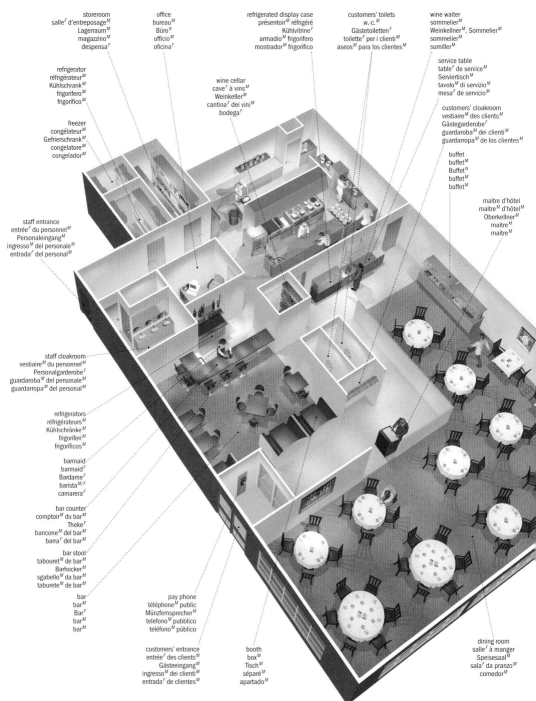

SOCIETY

hotel

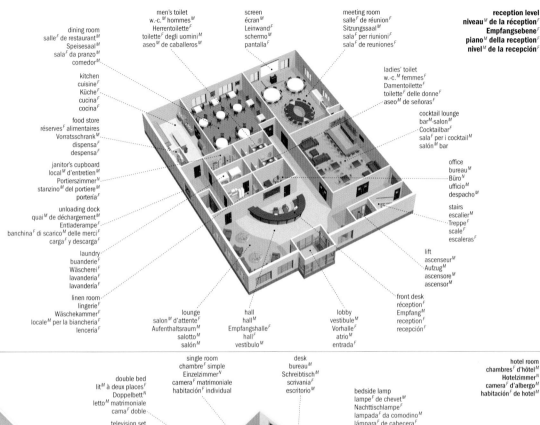

men's toilet
w.-c.^M hommes^M
Herrentoilette^F
toilette^F degli uomini^M
aseo^M de caballeros^M

screen
écran^M
Leinwand^F
schermo^M
pantalla^F

meeting room
salle^F de réunion^F
Sitzungssaal^M
sala^F per riunioni^F
sala^F de reuniones^F

reception level
niveau^M de la réception^F
Empfangsebene^F
piano^M della reception^F
nivel^M de la recepción^F

dining room
salle^F de restaurant^M
Speisesaal^M
sala^F da pranzo^M
comedor^M

ladies' toilet
w.-c.^M femmes^F
Damentoilette^F
toilette^F delle donne^F
aseo^M de señoras^F

kitchen
cuisine^F
Küche^F
cucina^F
cocina^F

cocktail lounge
bar^M-salon^M
Cocktailbar^F
sala^F per i cocktail^M
salón^M bar

food store
réserves^F alimentaires
Vorratsschrank^M
dispensa^F
despensa^F

office
bureau^M
Büro^N
ufficio^M
despacho^M

janitor's cupboard
local^M d'entretien^M
Portierszimmer^N
stanzino^M del portiere^M
portería^F

stairs
escalier^M
Treppe^F
scale^F
escaleras^F

unloading dock
quai^M de déchargement^M
Entladerampe^F
banchina^F di scarico^M delle merci^F
carga^F y descarga^F

lift
ascenseur^M
Aufzug^M
ascensore^M
ascensor^M

laundry
buanderie^F
Wäscherei^F
lavanderia^F
lavandería^F

linen room
lingerie^F
Wäschekammer^F
locale^M per la biancheria^F
lencería^F

front desk
réception^F
Empfang^M
reception^F
recepción^F

lounge
salon^M d'attente^F
Aufenthaltsraum^M
salotto^M
salón^M

hall
hall^M
Empfangshalle^F
hall^M
vestíbulo^M

lobby
vestibule^M
Vorhalle^F
atrio^M
entrada^F

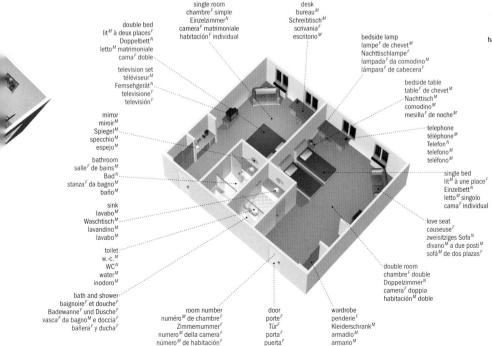

single room
chambre^F simple
Einzelzimmer^N
camera^F matrimoniale
habitación^F individual

desk
bureau^M
Schreibtisch^M
scrivania^F
escritorio^M

hotel room
chambres^F d'hôtel^M
Hotelzimmer^N
camera^F d'albergo^M
habitación^F de hotel^M

double bed
lit^M à deux places^F
Doppelbett^N
letto^M matrimoniale
cama^F doble

bedside lamp
lampe^F de chevet^M
Nachttischlampe^F
lampada^F da comodino^M
lámpara^F de cabecera^F

television set
téléviseur^M
Fernsehgerät^N
televisione^F
televisión^F

bedside table
table^F de chevet^M
Nachttisch^M
comodino^M
mesilla^F de noche^M

mirror
miroir^M
Spiegel^M
specchio^M
espejo^M

telephone
téléphone^M
Telefon^M
telefono^M
teléfono^M

bathroom
salle^F de bains^M
Bad^N
stanza^F da bagno^M
baño^M

single bed
lit^M à une place^F
Einzelbett^N
letto^M singolo
cama^F individual

sink
lavabo^M
Waschtisch^M
lavandino^M
lavabo^M

love seat
causeuse^F
zweisitziges Sofa^N
divano^M a due posti^M
sofá^M de dos plazas^F

toilet
w.-c.^M
WC^N
water^M
inodoro^M

double room
chambre^F double
Doppelzimmer^M
camera^F doppia
habitación^M doble

bath and shower
baignoire^F et douche^F
Badewanne^F und Dusche^F
vasca^F da bagno^M e doccia^F
bañera^F y ducha^F

room number
numéro^M de chambre^F
Zimmernummer^F
numero^M della camera^F
número^M de habitación^F

door
porte^F
Tür^F
porta^F
puerta^F

wardrobe
penderie^F
Kleiderschrank^M
armadio^M
armario^M

court

tribunal^M | Gericht^N | tribunale^M | tribunal^M

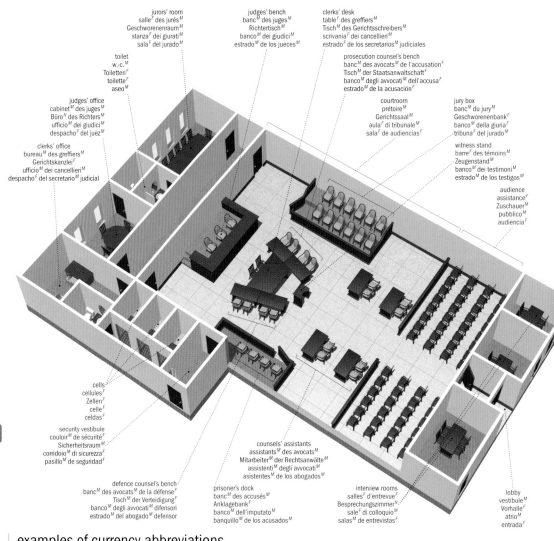

jurors' room
salle^F des jurés^M
Geschworenenraum^M
stanza^F dei giurati^M
sala^F del jurado^M

judges' bench
banc^M des juges^M
Richtertisch^M
banco^M dei giudici^M
estrado^F de los jueces^M

clerks' desk
table^F des greffiers^M
Tisch^M des Gerichtsschreibers^M
scrivania^F dei cancellieri^M
estrado^F de los secretarios^M judiciales

toilet
w.-c.^M
Toiletten^F
toilette^F
aseo^M

prosecution counsel's bench
banc^M des avocats^M de l'accusation^F
Tisch^M der Staatsanwaltschaft^F
banco^M degli avvocati^M dell'accusa^F
estrado^F de la acusación^F

judges' office
cabinet^M des juges^M
Büro^N des Richters^M
ufficio^M dei giudici^M
despacho^F del juez^M

courtroom
prétoire^M
Gerichtssaal^M
aula^F di tribunale^M
sala^F de audiencias^F

jury box
banc^M du jury^M
Geschworenenbank^F
banco^M della giuria^F
tribuna^F del jurado^M

clerks' office
bureau^M des greffiers^M
Gerichtskanzlei^F
ufficio^M dei cancellieri^M
despacho^F del secretario^M judicial

witness stand
barre^F des témoins^M
Zeugenstand^M
banco^M dei testimoni^M
estrado^M de los testigos^M

audience
assistance^F
Zuschauer^M
pubblico^M
audiencia^F

cells
cellules^F
Zellen^F
celle^F
celdas^F

security vestibule
couloir^M de sécurité^F
Sicherheitsraum^M
corridoio^M di sicurezza^F
pasillo^M de seguridad^F

counsels' assistants
assistants^M des avocats^M
Mitarbeiter^M der Rechtsanwälte^M
assistenti^M degli avvocati^M
asistentes^M de los abogados^M

defence counsel's bench
banc^M des avocats^M de la défense^F
Tisch^M der Verteidigung^F
banco^M degli avvocati^M difensori
estrado^M del abogado^M defensor

prisoner's dock
banc^M des accusés^M
Anklagebank^F
banco^M dell'imputato^M
banquillo^M de los acusados^M

interview rooms
salles^F d'entrevue^F
Besprechungszimmer^N
sale^F di colloquio^M
salas^M de entrevistas^F

lobby
vestibule^M
Vorhalle^F
atrio^M
entrada^F

examples of currency abbreviations

exemples^M d'unités^F monétaires | Beispiele^N für Währungsabkürzungen^F | esempi^M di simboli^M di valute^F | ejemplos^M de abreviaciones^F de monedas^F

cent
cent^M
Cent^M
cent^M
centavo^M

euro
euro^M
Euro^M
euro^M
euro^M

peso
peso^M
Peso^M
peso^M
peso^M

pound
livre^F
Pfund^N
sterlina^F
libra^F

dollar
dollar^M
Dollar^M
dollaro^M
dólar^M

rupee
roupie^F
Rupie^F
rupia^F
rupia^F

new shekel
nouveau shekel^M
neuer Schekel^M
nuovo shekel^M
nuevo shekel^M

yen
yen^M
Yen^M
yen^M
yen^M

money and modes of payment

monnaie^F et modes^M de paiement^M | Geld^N und Zahlungsmodalitäten^F | denaro^M e metodi^M di pagamento^M | dinero^M y modos^M de pago^M

coin: obverse
pièce^F : avers^M
Münze^F: Vorderseite^F
moneta^F: diritto^M
moneda^F : anverso^M

initials of issuing bank
initiales^F de la banque^F émettrice
Kürzel^N der Ausgabebank^F
iniziali^F della banca^F di emissione^F
iniciales^F del banco^M emisor

banknote: front
billet^M de banque^F : recto^M
Banknote^F: Vorderseite^F
banconota^F: dritto^M
billete^M: recto^M

security thread
fil^M de sécurité^F
Sicherheitsfaden^M
filo^M di sicurezza^F
hilo^M de seguridad^F

hologram foil strip
bande^F métallisée holographique
metallisiertes Hologramm^N
banda^F olografica
banda^F holográfica metalizada

date
millésime^M
Jahreszahl^F
anno^M
fecha^F

watermark
filigrane^M
Wasserzeichen^N
filigrana^F
filigrana^F

official signature
signature^F officielle
amtliche Unterschrift^F
firma^F ufficiale
firma^F oficial

colour shifting ink
encre^F à couleur^F changeante
metallische Tinte^F
inchiostro^M a colori^M cangianti
tinta^F de color^M cambiante

edge
tranche^F
Rand^M
contorno^M
canto^M

coin: reverse
pièce^F : revers^M
Münze^F: Rückseite^F
moneta^F: rovescio^M
moneda^F: reverso^M

portrait
effigie^F
Porträt^N
effigie^F
retrato^M

serial number
numéro^M de série^F
Seriennummer^F
numero^M di serie^F
número^M de serie^F

banknote: back
billet^M de banque^F : verso^M
Banknote^F: Rückseite^F
banconota^F: rovescio^M
billete^M : verso^M

European Union flag
drapeau^M de l'Union^F Européenne
Flagge^F der Europäischen Union^F
bandiera^F dell'Unione^F Europea
bandera^F de la Unión^F Europea

serial number
numéro^M de série^F
Seriennummer^F
numero^M di serie^F
número^M de serie^F

outer ring
couronne^F
Außenring^M
corona^F
cordoncillo^M

motto
devise^F
Leitspruch^M
motto^M
lema^M

denomination
valeur^F
Wertangabe^F
indicazione^F del valore^M
valor^M

denomination
valeur^F
Wertangabe^F
indicazione^F del valore^M
valor^M

currency name
nom^M de la monnaie^F
Währungsangabe^F
nome^M della valuta^F
nombre^M de la moneda^F

magnetic strip
bande^F magnétique
Magnetstreifen^M
banda^F magnetica
banda^F magnética

credit card
carte^F de crédit^M
Kreditkarte^F
carta^F di credito^M
tarjeta^M de crédito^M

holder's signature
signature^F du titulaire^M
Unterschrift^F des Inhabers^M
firma^F del titolare^M
firma^M del titular^M

card number
numéro^M de carte^F
Kartennummer^F
numero^M della carta^F
número^M de la tarjeta^F

cheques
chèques^M
Schecks^M
assegni^M
cheques^M

traveller's cheque
chèque^M de voyage^M
Travellerscheck^M
traveller's cheque^M
cheque^M de viaje^M

holder's name
nom^M du titulaire^M
Name^M des Inhabers^M
nome^M del titolare^M
nombre^M del titular^M

expiry date
date^F d'expiration^F
Verfallsdatum^N
data^F di scadenza^F
fecha^F de vencimiento^M

SOCIETY

bank

banque^F | Bank^F | banca^F | banco^M

professional training office
bureau^M de formation^F professionnelle
Fortbildungsbüro^N
ufficio^M di formazione^F professionale
oficina^F de formación^F profesional

cash dispenser
distributeur^M de billets^M
Geldausgabeautomat^M
sportello^M bancomat^M
cajero^M automático

waiting area
aire^F d'attente^F
Wartebereich^M
area^F d'attesa^F
zona^F de espera^F

insurance services
services^M d'assurance^F
Versicherungsabteilung^F
servizi^M assicurativi
servicios^M de seguros^M

brochure rack
présentoir^M de brochures^F
Prospektständer^M
espositore^M di brochure^F
expositor^M de folletos^M

reprography
reprographie^F
Fotokopiergerät^N
fotocopiatrice^F
fotocopiadora^F

financial services
services^M financiers
Finanzabteilung^F
servizi^M finanziari
servicios^M financieros

information desk
comptoir^M de renseignements^M
Informationsschalter^M
banco^M delle informazioni^F
información^F

conference room
salle^F de conférences^F
Konferenzraum^M
sala^F per conferenze^F
sala^F de conferencias^F

automatic teller machine
guichet^M automatique bancaire
automatischer Bankschalter^M
sportello^M automatico
cajero^M automático

reception desk
accueil^M
Empfang^N
banco^M della reception^F
recepción^F

operation keys
touches^F d'opérations^F
Funktionstasten^F
tasti^M funzione^F
teclas^F de operación^F

deposit slot
fente^F de dépôt^M
Einzahlungsschlitz^M
fessura^F per il deposito^M
ranura^F de depósito^M

loan services
services^M de crédit^M
Kreditabteilung^F
servizi^M di credito^M
servicios^M de crédito^M

display
écran^M
Display^N
display^M
pantalla^F

meeting room
salle^F de réunion^F
Sitzungsraum^M
sala^F per riunioni^F
sala^F de reuniones^F

card reader slot
fente^F du lecteur^M de carte^F
Kartenlesegerät^N
lettore^M di carte^F
lector^M de tarjeta^F

transaction record slot
fente^F de relevé^M d'opération^F
Quittungsausgabe^F
fessura^F di registrazione^F della transazione^F
ranura^F de registro^M de la transacción^F

alphanumeric keyboard
clavier^M alphanumérique
alphanumerische Tastatur^F
tastiera^F alfanumerica
teclado^M alfanumérico

security grille
grille^F de sécurité^F
Schutzgitter^N
griglia^F di sicurezza^F
reja^F de seguridad^F

note presenter
sortie^F des billets^M
Geldscheinausgabe^F
emissione^F di banconote^F
emisión^F de billetes^M

passbook update slot
fente^F de mise^F à jour^M du livret^M bancaire
Sparbuchnachtrag^M
fessura^F di aggiornamento^F dell'estratto conto^M
ranura^F de puesta^F al día^F de la cartilla^F

lob
vestibul
Vorhal
atri
entrac

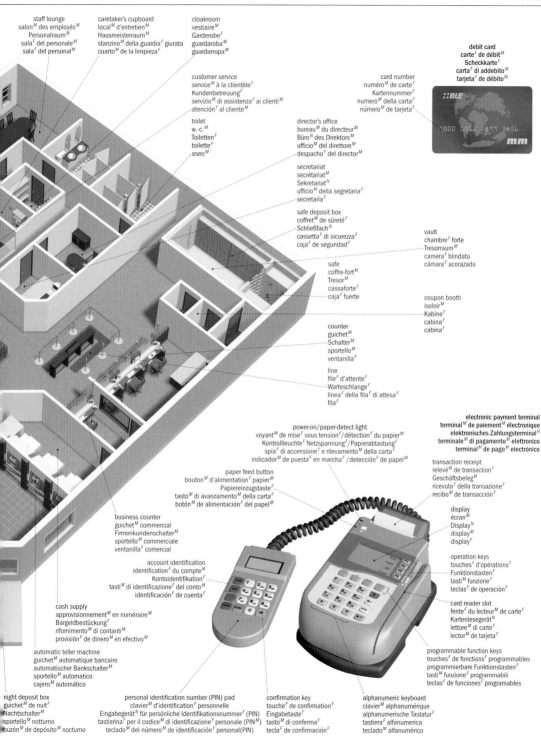

staff lounge
salon^M des employés^M
Personalraum^M
sala^F del personale^M
sala^F del personal^M

caretaker's cupboard
local^M d'entretien^M
Hausmeisterraum^M
stanzino^M della guardia^F giurata
cuarto^M de la limpieza^F

cloakroom
vestiaire^M
Garderobe^F
guardaroba^M
guardarropa^M

customer service
service^M à la clientèle^F
Kundenbetreuung^F
servizio^M di assistenza^F ai clienti^M
atención^F al cliente^M

toilet
w.-c.^{M}
Toiletten^F
toilette^F
aseo^M

director's office
bureau^M du directeur^M
Büro^N des Direktors^M
ufficio^M del direttore^M
despacho^M del director^M

secretariat
secrétariat^M
Sekretariat^N
ufficio^M della segretaria^F
secretaría^F

safe deposit box
coffret^M de sûreté^F
Schließfach^N
cassetta^F di sicurezza^F
caja^F de seguridad^F

safe
coffre-fort^M
Tresor^M
cassaforte^F
caja^F fuerte

counter
guichet^M
Schalter^M
sportello^M
ventanilla^F

line
file^F d'attente^F
Warteschlange^F
linea^F della fila^F di attesa^F
fila^F

debit card
carte^F de débit^M
Scheckkarte^F
carta^F di addebito^M
tarjeta^F de débito^M

card number
numéro^M de carte^F
Kartennummer^F
numero^M della carta^F
número^M de tarjeta^F

::BLE

4000 0012 7659 3456

mm

vault
chambre^F forte
Tresorraum^M
camera^F blindata
cámara^F acorazada

coupon booth
isoloir^M
Kabine^F
cabina^F
cabina^F

electronic payment terminal
terminal^M de paiement^M électronique
elektronisches Zahlungsterminal^N
terminale^M di pagamento^M elettronico
terminal^M de pago^M electrónico

power-on/paper-detect light
voyant^M de mise^F sous tension^F/détection^F du papier^M
Kontrollleuchte^F Netzspannung^F/Papierabtastung^F
spia^F di accensione^F e rilevamento^M della carta^F
indicador^M de puesta^F en marcha^F/detección^F de papel^M

paper feed button
bouton^M d'alimentation^F papier^M
Papiereinzugstaste^F
tasto^M di avanzamento^M della carta^F
botón^M de alimentación^F del papel^M

transaction receipt
relevé^M de transaction^F
Geschäftsbeleg^M
ricevuta^F della transazione^F
recibo^M de transacción^F

display
écran^M
Display^N
display^M
display^M

operation keys
touches^F d'opérations^F
Funktionstasten^F
tasti^M funzione^F
teclas^F de operación^F

card reader slot
fente^F du lecteur^M de carte^F
Kartenlesegerät^N
lettore^M di carte^F
lector^M de tarjeta^F

business counter
guichet^M commercial
Firmenkundenschalter^M
sportello^M commerciale
ventanilla^F comercial

account identification
identification^F du compte^M
Kontoidentifikation^F
tasti^M di identificazione^F del conto^M
identificación^F de cuenta^F

cash supply
approvisionnement^M en numéraire^M
Bargeldbestückung^F
rifornimento^M di contanti^M
provisión^F de dinero^M en efectivo^M

automatic teller machine
guichet^M automatique bancaire
automatischer Bankschalter^M
sportello^M automatico
cajero^M automático

programmable function keys
touches^F de fonctions^F programmables
programmierbare Funktionstasten^F
tasti^M funzione^F programmabili
teclas^F de funciones^F programables

night deposit box
guichet^M de nuit^F
Nachtschalter^M
sportello^M notturno
buzón^M de depósito^M nocturno

personal identification number (PIN) pad
clavier^M d'identification^F personnelle
Eingabegerät^N für persönliche Identifikationsnummer^F (PIN)
tastierina^F per il codice^M di identificazione^F personale (PIN^M)
teclado^M del número^M de identificación^F personal(PIN)

confirmation key
touche^F de confirmation^F
Eingabetaste^F
tasto^M di conferma^F
tecla^F de confirmación^F

alphanumeric keyboard
clavier^M alphanumérique
alphanumerische Tastatur^F
tastiera^F alfanumerica
teclado^M alfanumérico

school

écoleᶠ | Schuleᶠ | scuolaᶠ | colegioᴹ

equipment storage room
localᴹ d'entreposageᴹ du matérielᴹ
Materialraumᴹ
ripostiglioᴹ per l'attrezzaturaᶠ
depósitoᴹ de los utensiliosᴹ

podium
estradeᶠ
Podiumᴺ
podioᴹ
estradoᴹ

plastic arts room
salleᶠ d'artsᴹ plastiques
Kunstraumᴹ
aulaᶠ di artiᶠ plastiche
aulaᶠ de artesᶠ plásticas

music room
salleᶠ de musiqueᶠ
Musikraumᴹ
aulaᶠ di musicaᶠ
aulaᶠ de músicaᶠ

science room
salleᶠ de sciencesᶠ
Wissenschaftsraumᴹ
aulaᶠ di scienzeᶠ
aulaᶠ de cienciasᶠ

changing room
vestiaireᴹ
Umkleideraumᴹ
spogliatoioᴹ
vestuariosᴹ

gymnasium office
bureauᴹ du gymnaseᴹ
Turnhallenbüroᴺ
ufficioᴹ della palestraᶠ
despachoᴹ del gimnasioᴹ

movable stands
gradinsᴹ mobiles
bewegliche Tribünenᶠ
tribuneᶠ mobili
gradasᶠ móviles

gymnasium
gymnaseᴹ
Turnhalleᶠ
palestraᶠ
gimnasioᴹ

storeroom
localᴹ d'entretienᴹ
Geräteraumᴹ
magazzinoᴹ
almacénᴹ

computer science room
salleᶠ d'informatiqueᶠ
Computerraumᴹ
aulaᶠ di informaticaᶠ
aulaᶠ de informáticaᶠ

library
bibliothèqueᶠ
Bibliothekᶠ
bibliotecaᶠ
bibliotecaᶠ

classroom
salleᶠ de classeᶠ
Klassenzimmerᴺ
aulaᶠ
claseᶠ

classroom for students with learning disabilities
salleᶠ de classeᶠ pour élèvesᶠ en difficultésᶠ d'apprentissageᴹ
Klassenzimmerᴺ für Schülerᴹ mit Lernschwierigkeitenᶠ
aulaᶠ per studentiᶠ con difficoltàᶠ d'apprendimentoᴹ
aulaᶠ para alumnosᴹ con dificultad de aprendizajeᶠ

bulletin board
tableauᴹ d'affichageᴹ
schwarzes Brettᴺ
bachecaᶠ
tablónᴹ de anunciosᴹ

geographical map
carteᶠ géographique
Landkarteᶠ
cartaᶠ geografica
mapaᴹ geográfico

globe
globeᴹ terrestre
Globusᴹ
mappamondoᴹ
globoᴹ terráqueo

clock
penduleᶠ
Uhrᶠ
orologioᴹ
relojᴹ

teacher
enseignantᴹ
Lehrerᴹ/Lehrerinᶠ
insegnanteᶠ/ᴹ
profesorᴹ

bookcase
bibliothèqueᶠ
Bücherregalᴺ
libreriaᶠ
libreríaᶠ

computer
ordinateurᴹ
Computerᴹ
computerᴹ
ordenadorᴹ

blackboard
tableauᴹ
Tafelᶠ
lavagnaᶠ
pizarraᶠ

armchair
fauteuilᴹ
Armstuhlᴹ
sediaᶠ con braccioliᴹ
sillónᴹ

armless chair
chaiseᶠ
Stuhlᴹ
sediaᶠ senza bracciꞁiᴹ
sillaᶠ sin brazosᴹ

television set
téléviseurᴹ
Fernsehgerätᴺ
televisioneᶠ
televisiorᴹ

teacher's desk
bureauᴹ de l'enseignantᴹ
Lehrerpultᴺ
cattedraᶠ
pupitreᴹ del profesorᴹ

student's desk
bureauᴹ d'élèveᴹ
Schulbankᶠ
bancoᴹ
pupitreᴹ del alumnoᴹ

student
élèveᴹ
Schülerᴹ/Schülerinᶠ
studenteᴹ
alumnoᴹ

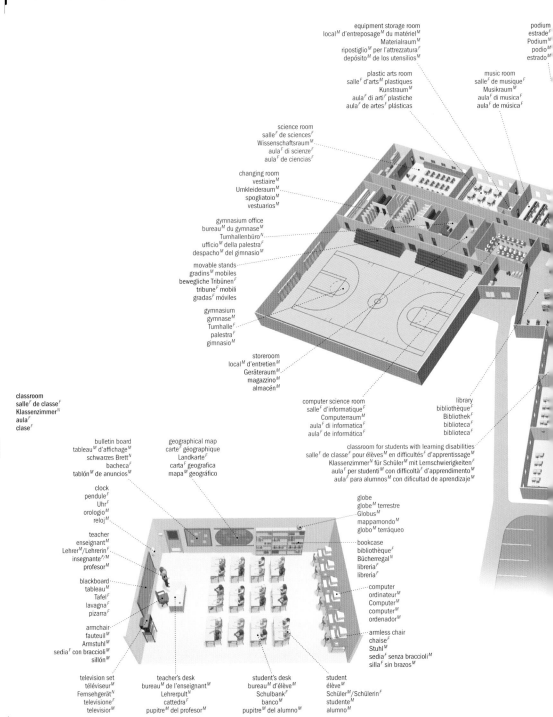

cafeteria
cafétéria^F
Cafeteria^F
caffè^M
cafeteria^F

kitchen
cuisine^F
Küche^F
cucina^F
cocina^F

proctors' office
bureau^M des surveillants^M
Büro^N der Schulaufsicht^F
ufficio^M del bidello^M
despacho^M del bedel^M

students' lockers
casiers^M des élèves^M
Schülerspinde^M
armadietti^M degli studenti^M
taquillas^F de los alumnos^M

main entrance
entrée^F principale
Haupteingang^M
ingresso^M principale
entrada^F principal

toilet
w.-c.^M
Toilette^F
toilette^F
aseos^M

playground
cour^F de récréation^F
Schulhof^M
cortile^M
patio^M

classroom
salle^F de classe^F
Klassenzimmer^N
aula^F
aula^M

students' room
foyer^M des élèves^M
Pausenraum^M
stanza^F degli studenti^M
sala^F de alumnos^M

teachers' room
salle^F des enseignants^M
Lehrerzimmer^N
stanza^F degli insegnanti^M
sala^F de profesores^M

administration
administration^F
Verwaltung^F
amministrazione^F
administración^F

parking area
parc^M de stationnement^M
Parkplatz^M
parcheggio^M
aparcamiento^M

staff entrance
entrée^F du personnel^M
Diensteingang^M
ingresso^M del personale^M
entrada^F del personal^M

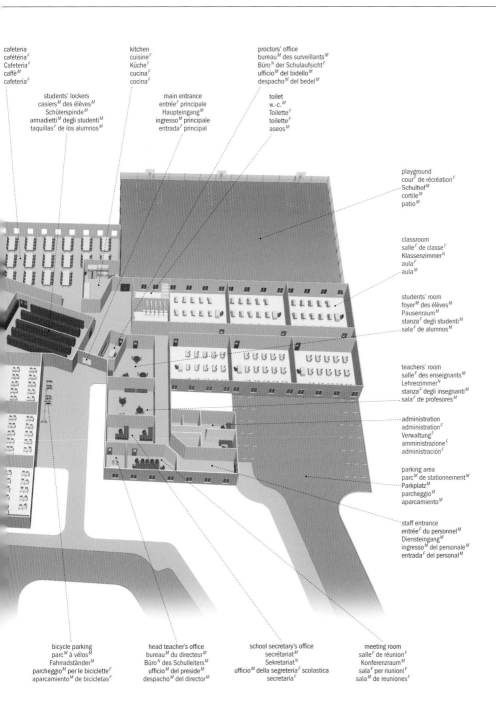

bicycle parking
parc^M à vélos^M
Fahrradständer^M
parcheggio^M per le biciclette^F
aparcamiento^M de bicicletas^F

head teacher's office
bureau^M du directeur^M
Büro^N des Schulleiters^M
ufficio^M del preside^M
despacho^M del director^M

school secretary's office
secrétariat^M
Sekretariat^N
ufficio^M della segreteria^F scolastica
secretaría^F

meeting room
salle^F de réunion^F
Konferenzraum^M
sala^F per riunioni^F
sala^M de reuniones^F

church

église^F | Kirche^F | chiesa^F | iglesia^F

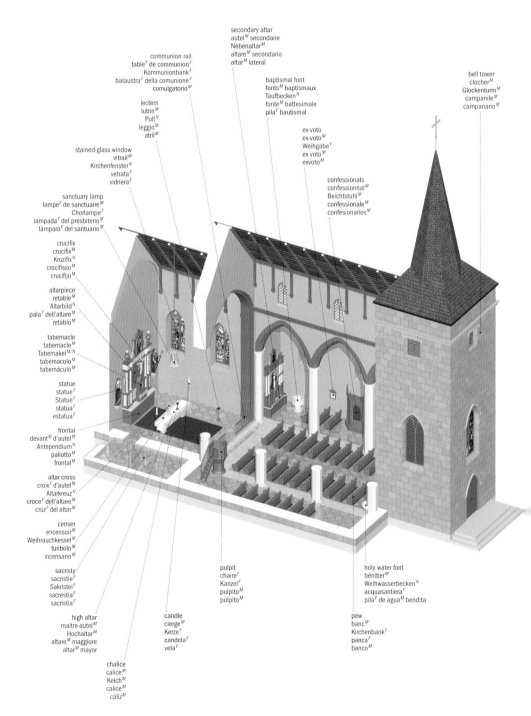

secondary altar
autel^M secondaire
Nebenaltar^M
altare^M secondario
altar^M lateral

communion rail
table^F de communion^F
Kommunionbank^F
balaustra^F della comunione^F
comulgatorio^M

baptismal font
fonts^M baptismaux
Taufbecken^N
fonte^M battesimale
pila^F bautismal

bell tower
clocher^M
Glockenturm^M
campanile^M
campanario^M

lectern
lutrin^M
Pult^N
leggio^M
atril^M

ex-voto
ex-voto^M
Weihgabe^F
ex voto^M
exvoto^M

stained-glass window
vitrail^M
Kirchenfenster^N
vetrata^F
vidriera^F

confessionals
confessionnal^M
Beichtstuhl^M
confessionale^M
confesionarios^M

sanctuary lamp
lampe^F de sanctuaire^M
Chorlampe^F
lampada^F del presbiterio^M
lámpara^F del santuario^M

crucifix
crucifix^M
Kruzifix^N
crocifisso^M
crucifijo^M

altarpiece
retable^M
Altarbild^N
pala^F dell'altare^M
retablo^M

tabernacle
tabernacle^M
Tabernakel^M/N
tabernacolo^M
tabernáculo^M

statue
statue^F
Statue^F
statua^F
estatua^F

frontal
devant^M d'autel^M
Antependium^N
paliotto^M
frontal^M

altar cross
croix^F d'autel^M
Altarkreuz^N
croce^F dell'altare^M
cruz^F del altar^M

censer
encensoir^M
Weihrauchkessel^M
turibolo^M
incensario^M

sacristy
sacristie^F
Sakristei^F
sacrestia^F
sacristía^F

pulpit
chaire^F
Kanzel^F
pulpito^M
púlpito^M

holy water font
bénitier^M
Weihwasserbecken^N
acquasantiera^F
pila^F de agua^M bendita

high altar
maître-autel^M
Hochaltar^M
altare^M maggiore
altar^M mayor

candle
cierge^M
Kerze^F
candela^F
vela^F

pew
banc^M
Kirchenbank^F
panca^F
banco^M

chalice
calice^M
Kelch^M
calice^M
cáliz^M

synagogue

synagogue^F | Synagoge^F | sinagoga^F | sinagoga^F

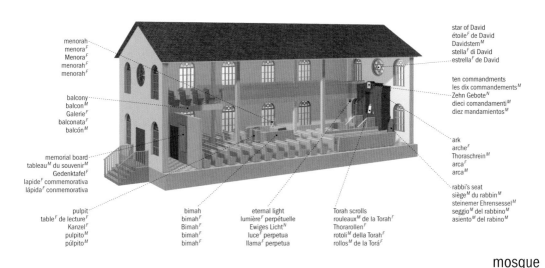

menorah
menora^F
Menora^F
menorah^F
menorah^F

star of David
étoile^F de David
Davidstern^M
stella^F di David
estrella^F de David

ten commandments
les dix commandements^M
Zehn Gebote^N
dieci comandamenti^M
diez mandamientos^M

balcony
balcon^M
Galerie^F
balconata^F
balcón^M

ark
arche^F
Thoraschrein^M
arca^F
arca^M

memorial board
tableau^M du souvenir^M
Gedenktafel^F
lapide^F commemorativa
lápida^F conmemorativa

rabbi's seat
siège^M du rabbin^M
steinerner Ehrensessel^M
seggio^M del rabbino^M
asiento^M del rabino^M

pulpit
table^F de lecture^F
Kanzel^F
pulpito^M
púlpito^M

bimah
bimah^F
Bimah^F
bimah^F
bimah^F

eternal light
lumière^F perpétuelle
Ewiges Licht^N
luce^F perpetua
llama^F perpetua

Torah scrolls
rouleaux^M de la Torah^F
Thorarollen^F
rotoli^M della Torah^F
rollos^M de la Torá^F

mosque

mosquée^F | Moschee^F | moschea^F | mezquita^F

porch dome
coupole^F du porche^M
Portalkuppel^F
cupola^F sul porticato^M
cúpula^F del pórtico^M

central nave
nef^F centrale
Mittelschiff^N
navata^F centrale
nave^F central

Mihrab dome
coupole^F du mihrab^M
Kuppel^F des Mihrab^{M/N}
cupola^F sul mihrab^M
cúpula^F del Mihrab^M

direction of Mecca
direction^F de La Mecque^F
Richtung^F Mekka
direzione^F della Mecca^F
dirección^F de la Meca^F

Mihrab
mihrab^M
Mihrab^{M/N}
mihrab^M
mihrab^M

prayer hall
salle^F de prière^F
Gebetshalle^F
sala^F della preghiera^F
sala^F de oración^F

Minbar
minbar^M
Minbar^M
minbar^M
mimbar^M

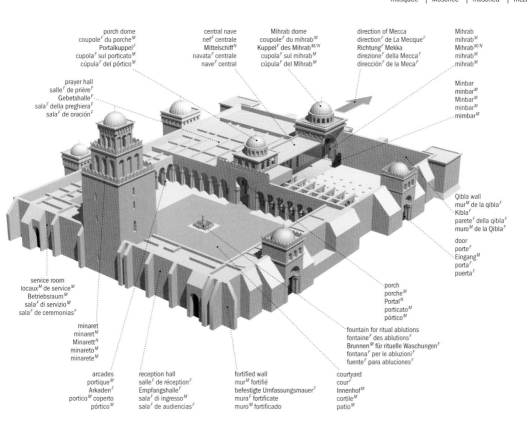

Qibla wall
mur^M de la qibla^F
Kibla^F
parete^F della qibla^F
muro^M de la Qibla^F

door
porte^F
Eingang^M
porta^F
puerta^F

service room
locaux^M de service^M
Betriebsraum^M
sala^F di servizio^M
sala^F de ceremonias^F

porch
porche^M
Portal^N
porticato^M
pórtico^M

fountain for ritual ablutions
fontaine^F des ablutions^F
Brunnen^M für rituelle Waschungen^F
fontana^F per le abluzioni^F
fuente^F para abluciones^F

minaret
minaret^M
Minarett^N
minareto^M
minarete^M

arcades
portique^M
Arkaden^F
portico^M coperto
pórtico^M

reception hall
salle^F de réception^F
Empfangshalle^F
sala^F di ingresso^M
sala^F de audiencias^F

fortified wall
mur^M fortifié
befestigte Umfassungsmauer^F
mura^F fortificate
muro^M fortificado

courtyard
cour^F
Innenhof^M
cortile^M
patio^M

SOCIETY

flags

drapeaux^M | Flaggen^F | bandiere^F | banderas^F

Americas
Amériques^F
Amerika
Americhe^F
Américas^F

1

Canada
Canada^M
Kanada
Canada^M
Canadá^M

2

United States of America
États-Unis^M d'Amérique^F
Vereinigte Staaten^M von Amerika
Stati^M Uniti d'America^F
Estados^M Unidos de América^F

3

Mexico
Mexique^M
Mexiko
Messico^M
México^M

4

Honduras
Honduras^M
Honduras
Honduras^M
Honduras^M

5

Guatemala
Guatemala^M
Guatemala
Guatemala^M
Guatemala^F

6

Belize
Belize^M
Belize
Belize^M
Belice^M

7

El Salvador
El Salvador^M
El Salvador
El Salvador^M
El Salvador^M

8

Nicaragua
Nicaragua^M
Nicaragua
Nicaragua^M
Nicaragua^F

9

Costa Rica
Costa Rica^M
Costa Rica
Costa Rica^M
Costa Rica^F

10

Panama
Panama^M
Panama
Panama^M
Panamá^M

11

Colombia
Colombie^F
Kolumbien
Colombia^F
Colombia^F

12

Venezuela
Venezuela^M
Venezuela
Venezuela^M
Venezuela^F

13

Guyana
Guyana^F
Guyana
Guyana^F
Guyana^F

14

Suriname
Suriname^M
Surinam
Suriname^M
Surinam^M

15

Ecuador
Équateur^M
Ecuador
Ecuador^M
Ecuador^M

16

Peru
Pérou^M
Peru
Perù^M
Perú^M

17

Brazil
Brésil^M
Brasilien
Brasile^M
Brasil^M

18

Bolivia
Bolivie^F
Bolivien
Bolivia^F
Bolivia^F

19

Paraguay
Paraguay^M
Paraguay
Paraguay^M
Paraguay^M

20

Chile
Chili^M
Chile
Cile^M
Chile^M

21

Argentina
Argentine^F
Argentinien
Argentina^F
Argentina^F

22

Uruguay
Uruguay^M
Uruguay
Uruguay^M
Uruguay^M

Caribbean Islands
Antilles^F
Karibische Inseln^F
Isole^F **delle Antille**^F
islas^F **del Caribe**^M

23

Bahamas
Bahamas^F
Bahamas^F
Bahama^F
Bahamas^F

24

Cuba
Cuba^F
Kuba
Cuba^F
Cuba^F

25

Jamaica
Jamaique^F
Jamaika
Giamaica^F
Jamaica^F

26

Haiti
Haiti^M
Haiti
Haiti^F
Haiti^M

SOCIETY

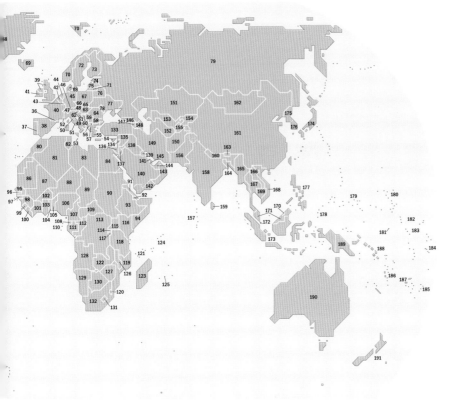

27

Saint Kitts and Nevis
Saint-Kitts-et-Nevis[M]
Saint Kitts und Nevis
Saint Kitts e Nevis[F]
Saint Kitts and Nevis[M]

28

Antigua and Barbuda
Antigua-et-Barbuda[F]
Antigua und Barbuda
Antigua[F] e Barbuda[F]
Antigua[F] y Barbuda[F]

29

Dominica
Dominique[F]
Dominica
Dominica[F]
Dominica[F]

30

Saint Lucia
Sainte-Lucie[F]
St. Lucia
Saint Lucia[F]
Santa Lucía[F]

31

Saint Vincent and the Grenadines
Saint-Vincent[M]-et-les Grenadines[F]
Saint Vincent und die Grenadinen
Saint Vincent e Grenadine[F]
San Vicente y las Granadinas[F]

32

Dominican Republic
République[F] dominicaine
Dominikanische Republik[F]
Repubblica[F] Dominicana
República[F] Dominicana

33

Barbados
Barbade[F]
Barbados
Barbados[F]
Barbados[F]

34

Grenada
Grenade[F]
Grenada
Grenada[F]
Granada[F]

35

Trinidad and Tobago
Trinité-et-Tobago[F]
Trinidad und Tobago
Trinidad[F] e Tobago[F]
Trinidad[F] y Tobago[M]

SOCIETY

36

Andorra
Andorre[F]
Andorra
Andorra[F]
Principado[M] de Andorra[F]

37

Portugal
Portugal[M]
Portugal
Portogallo[M]
Portugal[M]

38

Spain
Espagne[F]
Spanien
Spagna[F]
España[F]

Europe
Europe[F]
Europa
Europa[F]
Europa[F]

39

United Kingdom of Great Britain and Northern Ireland
Royaume-Uni[M] de Grande-Bretagne[F] et d'Irlande[F] du Nord[M]
Vereinigtes Königreich[N] von Großbritannien und Nordirland
Regno[M] Unito di Gran Bretagna[F] e Irlanda[F] del Nord[M]
Reino[M] Unido de Gran Bretaña[F] e Irlanda[F] del Norte[M]

40

France
France[F]
Frankreich
Francia[F]
Francia[F]

41

Ireland
Irlande[F]
Irland
Irlanda[F]
Irlanda[F]

42

Belgium
Belgique[F]
Belgien
Belgio[M]
Bélgica[F]

43

Luxembourg
Luxembourg[M]
Luxemburg
Lussemburgo[M]
Luxemburgo[M]

44

Netherlands
Pays-Bas[M]
Niederlande[F]
Paesi[M] Bassi
Países[M] Bajos

449

flags

45

Germany
Allemagne^F
Deutschland
Germania^F
Alemania^F

46

Liechtenstein
Liechtenstein^M
Liechtenstein
Liechtenstein^M
Liechtenstein^M

47

Switzerland
Suisse^F
Schweiz^F
Svizzera^F
Suiza^F

48

Austria
Autriche^F
Österreich
Austria^F
Austria^F

49

Italy
Italie^F
Italien
Italia^F
Italia^F

50

San Marino
Saint-Marin^M
San Marino
Repubblica^F di San Marino^M
República^F de San Marino^M

51

Vatican City State
État^M de la cité^F du Vatican^M
Vatikanstaat^M
Città^F del Vaticano^M
Ciudad^F del Vaticano^M

52

Monaco
Monaco^M
Monaco
Principato^M di Monaco^M
Principado^M de Mónaco^M

53

Malta
Malte^F
Malta
Malta^F
Malta^F

54

Cyprus
Chypre^F
Zypern
Cipro^F
Chipre^M

55

Greece
Grèce^F
Griechenland
Grecia^F
Grecia^F

56

Albania
Albanie^F
Albanien
Albania^F
Albania^F

57

Macedonia
Ex-République^F yougoslave de Macédoine^F
Mazedonien
Macedonia^F
Macedonia^F

58

Bulgaria
Bulgarie^F
Bulgarien
Bulgaria^F
Bulgaria^F

59

Yugoslavia
Yougoslavie^F
Jugoslawien
Iugoslavia^F
Yugoslavia^F

60

Bosnia-Herzegovina
Bosnie-Herzégovine^F
Bosnien und Herzegowina^F
Bosnia^F ed Erzegovina^F
Bosnia-Herzegovina^F

61

Croatia
Croatie^F
Kroatien
Croazia^F
Croacia^F

62

Slovenia
Slovénie^F
Slowenien
Slovenia^F
Eslovenia^F

63

Hungary
Hongrie^F
Ungarn
Ungheria^F
Hungria^F

64

Romania
Roumanie^F
Rumänien
Romania^F
Rumania^F

65

Slovakia
Slovaquie^F
Slowakische Republik^F
Slovacchia^F
Eslovaquia^F

66

Czech Republic
République^F tchèque
Tschechische Republik^F
Repubblica^F Ceca
República^F Checa

67

Poland
Pologne^F
Polen
Polonia^F
Polonia^F

68

Denmark
Danemark^M
Dänemark
Danimarca^F
Dinamarca^F

69

Iceland
Islande^F
Island
Islanda^F
Islandia^F

70

Norway
Norvège^F
Norwegen
Norvegia^F
Noruega^F

71

Lithuania
Lituanie^F
Litauen
Lituania^F
Lituania^F

72

Sweden
Suède^F
Schweden
Svezia^F
Suecia^F

73

Finland
Finlande^F
Finnland
Finlandia^F
Finlandia^F

74

Estonia
Estonie^F
Estland
Estonia^F
Estonia^F

75

Latvia
Lettonie^F
Lettland
Lettonia^F
Letonia^F

76

Belarus
Bélarus^M
Weißrussland
Bielorussia^F
Bielorrusia^F

77

Ukraine
Ukraine^F
Ukraine
Ucraina^F
Ucrania^F

78

Moldova
République^F de Moldova^F
Moldawien
Moldavia^F
Moldavia^F

79

Russian Federation
Fédération^F de Russie^F
Russland
Federazione^F Russa
Federación^F Rusa

flags

80

Morocco
Maroc[M]
Marokko
Marocco[M]
Marruecos[M]

81

Algeria
Algérie[F]
Algerien
Algeria[F]
Argelia[F]

82

Tunisia
Tunisie[F]
Tunesien
Tunisia[F]
Túnez[M]

83

Libya
Jamahiriya[F] arabe libyenne
Libyen
Libia[F]
Libia[F]

84

Egypt
Égypte[F]
Ägypten
Egitto[M]
Egipto[M]

85

Cape Verde Islands
Cap-Vert[M]
Kap Verde
Capo Verde[M]
islas[F] de Cabo[M] Verde

86

Mauritania
Mauritanie[F]
Mauretanien
Mauritania[F]
Mauritania[F]

87

Mali
Mali[M]
Mali
Repubblica[F] del Mali[M]
República[F] de Malí

88

Niger
Niger[M]
Niger[M]
Niger[M]
Niger[M]

89

Chad
Tchad[M]
Tschad[M]
Ciad[M]
Chad[M]

90

Sudan
Soudan[M]
Sudan[M]
Sudan[M]
Sudán[M]

91

Eritrea
Érythrée[F]
Eritrea
Eritrea[F]
Eritrea[F]

92

Djibouti
Djibouti[M]
Dschibuti
Gibuti[M]
Yibouti[F]

93

Ethiopia
Éthiopie[F]
Äthiopien
Etiopia[F]
Etiopía[F]

94

Somalia
Somalie[F]
Somalia
Somalia[F]
Somalia[F]

95

Senegal
Sénégal[M]
Senegal
Senegal[M]
Senegal[M]

96

Gambia
Gambie[F]
Gambia
Gambia[M]
Gambia[M]

97

Guinea-Bissau
Guinée-Bissau[F]
Guinea-Bissau
Guinea Bissau[F]
Guinea-Bissau[F]

98

Guinea
Guinée[F]
Guinea
Guinea[F]
Guinea[F]

99

Sierra Leone
Sierra Leone[F]
Sierra Leone
Sierra Leone[F]
Sierra[F] Leona

100

Liberia
Liberia[M]
Liberia
Liberia[F]
Liberia[F]

101

Ivory Coast
Côte d'Ivoire[F]
Elfenbeinküste[F]
Costa d'Avorio[F]
Costa de Marfil[F]

102

Burkina Faso
Burkina Faso
Burkina Faso
Burkina Faso[M]
Burkina Faso[M]

103

Ghana
Ghana[M]
Ghana
Ghana[M]
Ghana[F]

104

Togo
Togo[M]
Togo
Togo[M]
Togo[M]

105

Benin
Bénin[M]
Benin
Benin[M]
Benin[M]

106

Nigeria
Nigeria[M]
Nigeria
Nigeria[F]
Nigeria[F]

107

Cameroon
Cameroun[M]
Kamerun
Camerun[M]
Camerún[M]

108

Equatorial Guinea
Guinée[F] équatoriale
Äquatorialguinea
Guinea[F] Equatoriale
Guinea[F] Ecuatorial

109

Central African Republic
République[F] centrafricaine
Zentralafrikanische Republik[F]
Repubblica[F] Centrafricana
República[F] Centroafricana

110

Sao Tome and Principe
São Tomé-et-Príncipe[M]
São Tomé und Príncipe
São Tomé e Príncipe[M]
Santo Tomé y Príncipe[M]

111

Gabon
Gabon[M]
Gabun
Gabon[M]
Gabón[M]

112

Congo
Congo[M]
Kongo[M]
Congo[M]
Congo[M]

113

Democratic Republic of Congo
République[F] démocratique du Congo[M]
Republik[F] Kongo[M]
Repubblica[F] Democratica del Congo[M]
República[F] Democrática del Congo[M]

114

Rwanda
Rwanda[M]
Ruanda
Ruanda[M]
Ruanda[M]

115

Uganda
Ouganda[M]
Uganda
Uganda[F]
Uganda[F]

116

Kenya
Kenya[M]
Kenia
Kenya[F]
Kenia[F]

117

Burundi
Burundi[M]
Burundi
Burundi[M]
Burundi[M]

118

Tanzania
République[F]-Unie de Tanzanie[F]
Tansania
Tanzania[F]
Tanzania[F]

SOCIETY

flags

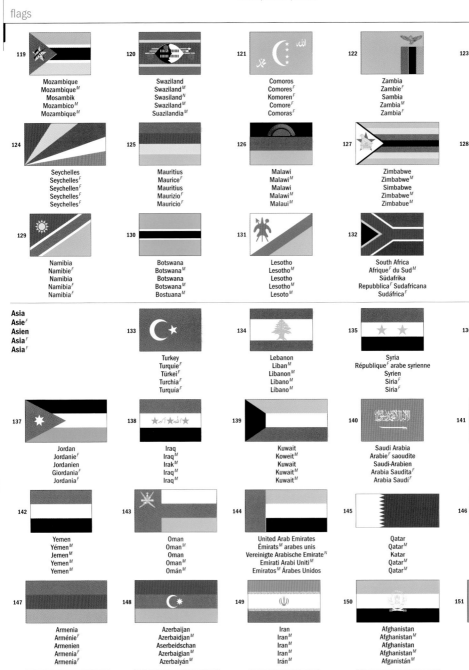

119	Mozambique / Mozambique^M / Mosambik / Mozambico^M / Mozambique^M
120	Swaziland / Swaziland^M / Swasiland^N / Swaziland^M / Suazilandia^M
121	Comoros / Comores^F / Komoren^F / Comore^F / Comoras^F
122	Zambia / Zambie^F / Sambia / Zambia^M / Zambia^F
123	Madagascar / Madagascar^F / Madagaskar / Madagascar^M / Madagascar^M
124	Seychelles / Seychelles^F / Seychellen / Seychelles^F / Seychelles^F
125	Mauritius / Maurice^F / Mauritius / Maurizio^F / Mauricio^F
126	Malawi / Malawi^M / Malawi / Malawi^M / Malaui^M
127	Zimbabwe / Zimbabwe^M / Simbabwe / Zimbabwe^M / Zimbabue^M
128	Angola / Angola^M / Angola / Angola^F / Angola^F
129	Namibia / Namibie^F / Namibia / Namibia^F / Namibia^F
130	Botswana / Botswana^F / Botswana / Botswana^M / Bostuana^M
131	Lesotho / Lesotho^M / Lesotho / Lesotho^M / Lesoto^M
132	South Africa / Afrique^F du Sud^M / Südafrika / Repubblica^F Sudafricana / Sudáfrica^F

Asia
Asie^F
Asien
Asia^F
Asia^F

133	Turkey / Turquie^F / Türkei^F / Turchia^F / Turquía^F
134	Lebanon / Liban^M / Libanon^M / Libano^M / Líbano^M
135	Syria / République^F arabe syrienne / Syrien / Siria^M / Siria^F
136	Israel / Israël^M / Israel / Israele^M / Israel^M
137	Jordan / Jordanie^F / Jordanien / Giordania^F / Jordania^F
138	Iraq / Iraq^M / Irak / Iraq^M / Iraq^M
139	Kuwait / Koweit^M / Kuwait / Kuwait^M / Kuwait^M
140	Saudi Arabia / Arabie^F saoudite / Saudi-Arabien / Arabia Saudita^F / Arabia Saudí^F
141	Bahrain / Bahrein^M / Bahrain / Bahrein^M / Bahrein^M
142	Yemen / Yémen^M / Jemen^M / Yemen^M / Yemen^M
143	Oman / Oman^M / Oman / Oman^M / Omán^M
144	United Arab Emirates / Émirats^M arabes unis / Vereinigte Arabische Emirate^N / Emirati Arabi Uniti^M / Emiratos^M Árabes Unidos
145	Qatar / Qatar^M / Katar / Qatar^M / Qatar^M
146	Georgia / Géorgie^F / Georgien / Georgia^F / Georgia^F
147	Armenia / Arménie^F / Armenien / Armenia^F / Armenia^F
148	Azerbaijan / Azerbaïdjan^M / Aserbeidschan / Azerbaigian^M / Azerbaiyán^M
149	Iran / Iran^M / Iran^M / Iran^M / Irán^M
150	Afghanistan / Afghanistan^M / Afghanistan / Afghanistan^M / Afganistán^M
151	Kazakhstan / Kazakhstan^M / Kasachstan / Kazakistan^M / Kazajistán^M
152	Turkmenistan / Turkménistan^M / Turkmenistan / Turkmenistan^M / Turkmenistán^M
153	Uzbekistan / Ouzbékistan^M / Usbekistan / Uzbekistan^M / Uzbekistán^M
154	Kyrgyzstan / Kirghizistan^M / Kirgisistan / Kirghizistan^M / Kirguizistán^M
155	Tajikistan / Tadjikistan^M / Tadschikistan / Tagikistan^M / Tajikistán^M
156	Pakistan / Pakistan^M / Pakistan / Pakistan^M / Pakistán^M

SOCIETY

452

157
Maldives
Maldives[F]
Malediven[F]
Maldive[F]
Maldivas[F]

158
India
Inde[F]
Indien
India[F]
India[F]

159
Sri Lanka
Sri Lanka[M]
Sri Lanka
Sri Lanka[M]
Sri Lanka[M]

160
Nepal
Népal[M]
Nepal
Nepal[M]
Nepal[M]

161
China
Chine[F]
China
Cina[F]
China[F]

162
Mongolia
Mongolie[F]
Mongolei[F]
Mongolia[F]
Mongolia[F]

163
Bhutan
Bhoutan[M]
Bhutan
Bhutan[M]
Bután[M]

164
Bangladesh
Bangladesh[M]
Bangladesch
Bangladesh[M]
Bangladesh[M]

165
Myanmar
Myanmar[M]
Myanmar
Myanmar[M]
Myanmar[M]

166
Laos
République[F] démocratique populaire lao
Laos
Laos[M]
Laos[M]

167
Thailand
Thailande[F]
Thailand
Tailandia[F]
Tailandia[F]

168
Vietnam
Viet Nam[M]
Vietnam
Vietnam[M]
Vietnam[M]

169
Cambodia
Cambodge[M]
Kambodscha
Cambogia[F]
Camboya[F]

170
Brunei Darussalam
Brunéi Darussalam[M]
Brunei
Brunei[M]
Brunei[M]

171
Malaysia
Malaisie[F]
Malaysia
Malaysia[F]
Malasia[F]

172
Singapore
Singapour[F]
Singapur
Singapore[F]
Singapur[M]

173
Indonesia
Indonésie[F]
Indonesien
Indonesia[F]
Indonesia[F]

174
Japan
Japon[M]
Japan
Giappone[M]
Japón[M]

175
Democratic People's Republic of Korea
République[F] populaire démocratique de Corée[F]
Nord-Korea
Repubblica[F] Democratica Popolare di Corea[F]
Republica[F] Democrática Popular de Corea[F]

176
Republic of Korea
République[F] de Corée[F]
Süd-Korea
Repubblica[F] di Corea[F]
República[F] de Corea[F]

177
Philippines
Philippines[F]
Philippinen[F]
Filippine[F]
Filipinas[F]

178
Palau
Palaos[M]
Palau
Palau[M]
Palau[M]

179
Micronesia
États[M] fédérés de Micronésie[F]
Mikronesien
Micronesia[F]
Micronesia[F]

Oceania and Polynesia
Océanie[F] et Polynésie[F]
Ozeanien und Polynesien
Oceania[F] e Polinesia[F]
Oceanía[F] y Polinesia[F]

180
Marshall Islands
Îles[F] Marshall
Marshallinseln[F]
Isole Marshall[F]
Islas[F] Marshall

181
Nauru
Nauru[F]
Nauru
Nauru[M]
Nauru[M]

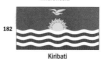

182
Kiribati
Kiribati[F]
Kiribati
Kiribati[M]
Kiribati[M]

183
Tuvalu
Tuvalu[M]
Tuvalu
Tuvalu[M]
Tuvalu[M]

184
Samoa
Samoa[F]
Samoa
Samoa[F]
Samoa[F]

185
Tonga
Tonga[F]
Tonga
Tonga[M]
Tonga[M]

186
Vanuatu
Vanuatu[M]
Vanuatu
Vanuatu[M]
Vanuatu[M]

187
Fiji
Fidji[F]
Fidschi
Figi[F]
Fiji[F]

188
Solomon Islands
Îles[F] Salomon
Salomoninseln[F]
Isole[F] Salomone
Islas Salomón[F]

189
Papua New Guinea
Papouasie-Nouvelle-Guinée[F]
Papua-Neuguinea
Papua Nuova Guinea[F]
Papua Nueva Guinea[F]

190
Australia
Australie[F]
Australien
Australia[F]
Australia[F]

191
New Zealand
Nouvelle-Zélande[F]
Neuseeland
Nuova Zelanda[F]
Nueva Zelanda[F]

SOCIETY

fire prevention

fire-fighting material
matériel^M de lutte^F contre les incendies^M
Brandbekämpfungsmaterial^N
materiale^M antincendio
material^M de lucha^F contra los incendios^M

smoke detector
détecteur^M de fumée^F
Rauchmelder^M
rilevatore^M di fumo^M
detector^M de humo^M

base
base^F
Unterteil^N
base^F
base^F

cover
couvercle^M
Abdeckung^F
coperchio^M
tapa^F

test button
bouton^M d'essai^M
Testknopf^M
pulsante^M di prova^F
botón^M de ensayo^M

indicator light
témoin^M lumineux
Kontrollleuchte^F
spia^F luminosa
testigo^M luminoso

portable fire extinguisher
extincteur^M
Handfeuerlöscher^M
estintore^M portatile
extintor^M portátil

trigger
gâchette^F
Abzug^M
grilletto^M
disparador^M

pin
goupille^F
Sicherungsstift^M
copiglia^F
clavija^F

hose
tuyau^M
Schlauch^M
tubo^M flessibile
manguera^F

tank
réservoir^M
Löschmittelbehälter^M
bombola^F
tanque^M

pike pole
gaffe^F
Einreißhaken^M
rampone^M
pica^F

hatchet
hache^F
Beil^N
piccozza^F
hacha^F

fire hose
tuyau^M de refoulement^M
Schlauchleitung^F
manichetta^F antincendio
manguera^F de incendios^M

fire hydrant
borne^F d'incendie^F
Überflurhydrant^M
idrante^M a colonna^F
boca^F de riego^M

firefighter
pompier^M
Feuerwehrmann^M
vigile^M del fuoco^M
bombero^M

helmet
casque^M
Feuerschutzhelm^M
elmo^M
casco^M

compressed-air cylinder
bouteille^F d'air^M comprimé
Druckluftflasche^F
bombola^F di aria^F compressa
bombona^F de aire^M comprimido

full face mask
masque^M complet
geschlossener Gesichtsschutz^M
maschera^F
máscara^F

self-contained breathing apparatus
appareil^M de protection^F respiratoire
geschlossenes Atemschutzsystem^N
autorespiratore^M
aparato^M de respiración^F autónomo

air-supply tube
tube^M d'alimentation^F en air^M
Atemluftzufuhrschlauch^M
tubo^M di alimentazione^F dell'aria^F
tubo^M de aire^M

pressure demand regulator
robinet^M de réglage^M de débit^M
Druckregler^M
rubinetto^M di regolazione^F della pressione^F
regulador^M de presión^F

mandown alarm
avertisseur^M de détresse^F
Funkmeldeempfänger^M
segnalatore^M di pericolo^M
avisador^M de alarma^F

turnouts
tenue^F d'intervention^F
Einsatzkleidung^F
divisa^F da incendio^M
traje^M

rubber boot
botte^F de caoutchouc^M
Gummistiefel^M
stivale^M di gomma^F
botas^F de caucho^M

SOCIETY

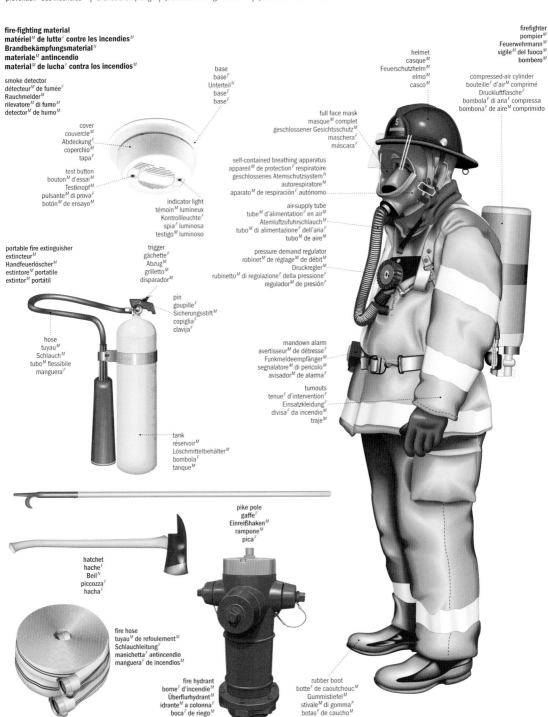

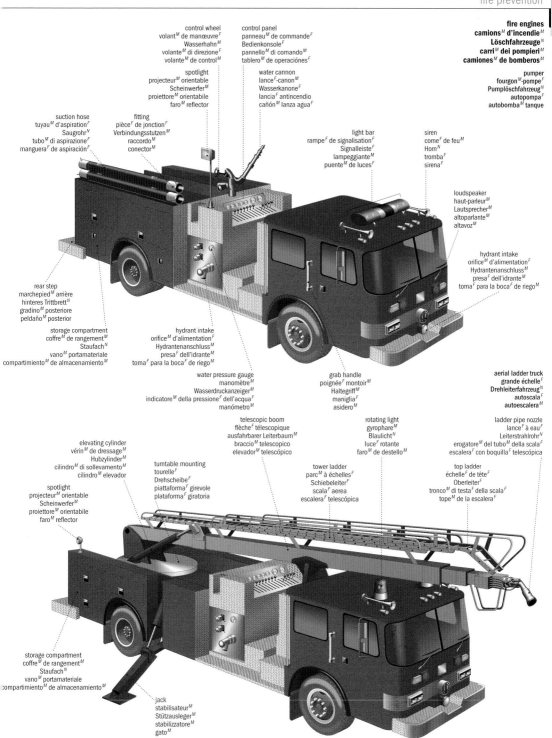

control wheel
volant^M de manœuvre^F
Wasserhahn^M
volante^M di direzione^M
volante^M de control^M

control panel
panneau^M de commande^F
Bedienkonsole^F
pannello^M di comando^M
tablero^M de operaciones^F

fire engines
camions^M d'incendie^M
Löschfahrzeuge^N
carri^M dei pompieri^M
camiones^M de bomberos^M

spotlight
projecteur^M orientable
Scheinwerfer^M
proiettore^M orientabile
faro^F reflector

water cannon
lance^F-canon^M
Wasserkanone^F
lancia^F antincendio
cañón^M lanza agua^F

pumper
fourgon^M-pompe^F
Pumplöschfahrzeug^N
autopompa^F
autobomba^M tanque

suction hose
tuyau^M d'aspiration^F
Saugrohr^N
tubo^M di aspirazione^F
manguera^F de aspiración^F

fitting
pièce^F de jonction^F
Verbindungsstutzen^M
raccordo^M
conector^M

light bar
rampe^F de signalisation^F
Signalleiste^F
lampeggiante^M
puente^M de luces^F

siren
corne^F de feu^M
Horn^N
tromba^F
sirena^F

loudspeaker
haut-parleur^M
Lautsprecher^M
altoparlante^M
altavoz^M

hydrant intake
orifice^M d'alimentation^F
Hydrantenanschluss^M
presa^F dell'idrante^M
toma^F para la boca^F de riego^M

rear step
marchepied^M arrière
hinteres Trittbrett^N
gradino^M posteriore
peldaño^M posterior

storage compartment
coffre^M de rangement^M
Staufach^N
vano^M portamateriale
compartimiento^M de almacenamiento^M

hydrant intake
orifice^M d'alimentation^F
Hydrantenanschluss^M
presa^F dell'idrante^M
toma^F para la boca^F de riego^M

water pressure gauge
manomètre^M
Wasserdruckanzeiger^M
indicatore^M della pressione^F dell'acqua^F
manómetro^M

grab handle
poignée^F montoir^M
Haltegriff^M
maniglia^F
asidero^M

aerial ladder truck
grande échelle^F
Drehleiterfahrzeug^N
autoscala^F
autoescalera^M

elevating cylinder
vérin^M de dressage^M
Hubzylinder^M
cilindro^M di sollevamento^M
cilindro^M elevador

turntable mounting
tourelle^F
Drehscheibe^F
piattaforma^F girevole
plataforma^F giratoria

telescopic boom
flèche^F télescopique
ausfahrbarer Leiterbaum^M
braccio^M telescopico
elevador^M telescópico

tower ladder
parc^M à échelles^F
Schiebeleiter^F
scala^F aerea
escalera^F telescópica

rotating light
gyrophare^M
Blaulicht^N
luce^F rotante
faro^M de destello^M

ladder pipe nozzle
lance^F à eau^F
Leiterstrahlrohr^N
erogatore^M del tubo^M della scala^F
escalera^F con boquilla^F telescópica

top ladder
échelle^F de tête^F
Oberleiter^F
tronco^M di testa^F della scala^F
tope^M de la escalera^F

spotlight
projecteur^M orientable
Scheinwerfer^M
proiettore^M orientabile
faro^M reflector

storage compartment
coffre^M de rangement^M
Staufach^N
vano^M portamateriale
compartimiento^M de almacenamiento^M

jack
stabilisateur^M
Stützausleger^M
stabilizzatore^M
gato^M

SOCIETY

crime prevention

prévention^F de la criminalité^F | vorbeugende Verbrechensbekämpfung^F | prevenzione^F del crimine^M | prevención^F de la criminalidad^F

police officer
agent^M de police^F
Polizeibeamter^M
agente^M di polizia^F
agente^M de policia^F

cap
casquette^F
Mütze^F
berretto^M
gorra^F

badge
insigne^M
Abzeichen^N
distintivo^M
insignia^F

shoulder strap
patte^F d'épaule^F
Schulterklappe^F
spallina^F
hombrera^F

rank insignia
insigne^M de grade^M
Dienstgradabzeichen^N
gradi^M
insignia^F de grado^M

identification badge
insigne^M d'identité^F
Namensschild^N
cartellino^M di identificazione^F
placa^F de identificación^F

uniform
uniforme^M
Uniform^F
uniforme^F
uniforme^M

duty belt
ceinturon^M de service^M
Dienstgürtel^M
cintura^F di servizio^M
cinturón^M de servicio^M

microphone
microphone^M
Mikrofon^N
microfono^M
micrófono^M

latex glove case
étui^M pour gants^M de latex^M
Tasche^F für Latexhandschuhe^M
astuccio^M per i guanti^M di lattice^M
funda^F de guantes^M de látex^M

handcuff case
étui^M à menottes^F
Handschellentasche^F
astuccio^M delle manette^F
estuche^M de las esposas^F

pistol
pistolet^M
Pistole^F
pistola^F
pistola^F

pepper spray
vaporisateur^M de poivre^M
Pfefferspray^N
spray^M al peperoncino^M
aerosol^M de pimienta^F

ammunition pouch
étui^M à munitions^F
Patronentasche^F
cartucciera^F
cartuchera^F

walkie-talkie
talkie-walkie^M
Hand^F-Funksprechgerät^N
radiotelefono^M portatile
walkie-talkie^M

holster
étui^M à pistolet^M
Halfter^N
fondina^F
pistolera^F

flashlight
lampe^F-torche^F
Stablampe^F
torcia^F
linterna^F

baton holder
porte-matraque^M
Schlagstockhalter^M
gancio^M del manganello^M
gancho^M para la porra^F

expandable baton
matraque^F télescopique
Teleskopschlagstock^M
bastone^M estendibile
porra^F

lightbar controller
système^M de contrôle^M de la rampe^F de signalisation^F
Lichtleistensteuerung^F
sistema^M di controllo^M del lampeggiante^M
sistema^M de control^M del puente^M de luces^F

dashboard equipment
équipement^M du tableau^M de bord^M
Armaturenbrettausrüstung^F
equipaggiamento^M del cruscotto^M
equipamiento^M del salpicadero^M

radar transceiver
émetteur^M-récepteur^M radar^M
Radaranlage^F
ricetrasmettitore^M radar^M
transmisor^M-receptor^M radar^M

reading light
lampe^F de lecture^F
Leselampe^F
luce^F di lettura^F
lámpara^F de lectura^F

microphones
microphones^M
Mikrofon^N
microfoni^M
micrófonos^M

dashboard computer
ordinateur^M de bord^M
Bordcomputer^M
computer^M di bordo^M
ordenador^M de a bordo

computer programs
programmes^M informatiques
Computerprogramme^N
programmi^M del computer^M
programas^M informáticos

radar display
affichage^M radar^M
Radaranlagendisplay^N
display^M del radar^M
pantalla^F del radar^M

radio
radio^F
Funkgerät^N
radio^F
radio^F

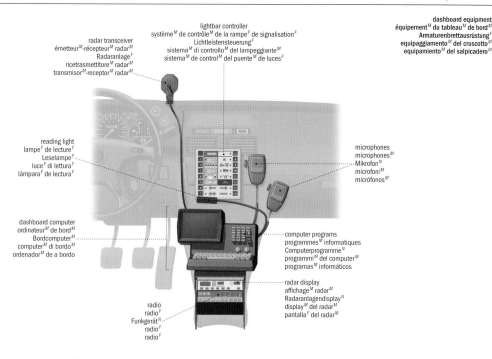

lightbar
rampe^F de signalisation^F
Lichtleiste^F
lampeggiante^M
puente^M de luces^F

antenna
antenne^F
Antenne^F
antenna^F
antena^F

safety lighting
éclairage^M de sécurité^F
Sicherheitsleuchte^F
luce^F di sicurezza^F
luces^F de seguridad^F

police car
voiture^F de police^F
Polizeifahrzeug^N
macchina^F della polizia^F
coche^M de policía^F

fire extinguisher
extincteur^M
Feuerlöscher^M
estintore^M
extintor^M

barrier barricade tape
ruban^M de bouclage^M
Absperrband^N
nastro^M di delimitazione^F
cinta^F de acordonamiento^M

partition
cloison^F
Trennwand^F
divisorio^M
divisorio^M

road flare
fusée^F éclairante
Leuchtrakete^F
razzo^M illuminante
faro^M de carretera^F

lifebuoy
bouée^F de sauvetage^M
Rettungsring^M
salvagente^M
flotador^M

first aid kit
trousse^F de secours^M
Erste-Hilfe^F-Kasten^M
cassetta^F di pronto soccorso^M
botiquín^M de urgencias^F

used syringe box
boîte^F pour seringues^F usagées
Behälter^M für gebrauchte Spritzen^F
contenitore^M delle siringhe^F usate
caja^F de jeringuillas^F usadas

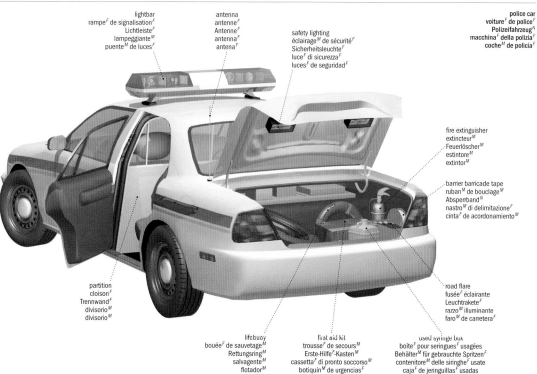

ear protection

protection^F de l'ouïe^F | Gehörschutz^M | protezione^F per le orecchie^F | protección^F para los oídos^M

safety earmuffs
casque^M antibruit
Ohrenschützer^M
cuffie^F di sicurezza^F
cascos^M de seguridad^F

headband
arceau^M
Kopfband^N
supporto^M elastico
diadema^F

earplugs
protège-tympan^M
Ohrstöpsel^M
tappi^M per le orecchie^F
tapones^M para los oídos^M

foam cushion
coussinet^M en mousse^F
Schaumgummipolsterung^F
cuscinetti^M antirumore
protector^M de espuma^F

eye protection

protection^F des yeux^M | Augenschutz^M | protezione^F per gli occhi^M | protección^F para los ojos^M

safety glasses
lunettes^F de sécurité^F
Schutzbrille^F
occhiali^M di protezione^F con ripari^M laterali
gafas^F de seguridad^F

safety goggles
lunettes^F de protection^F
Schutzmaske^F
occhiali^M di protezione^F panoramici
gafas^F protectoras

head protection

protection^F de la tête^F | Kopfschutz^M | protezione^F per la testa^F | protección^F para la cabeza^F

SOCIETY

hard hat
casque^M de sécurité^F
Schutzhelm^M
elmetto^M
casco^M de seguridad^F

suspension band
sangle^F d'amortissement^M
Trageband^N
fascia^F di sospensione^F
banda^F de suspensión^F

headband
tour^M de tête^F
Kopfband^N
fascia^F stringitesta
cinta^F

rib
nervure^F
Verstärkungsschwelle^F
nervatura^F
refuerzo^M

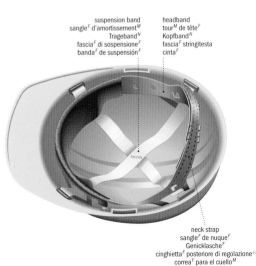

peak
visière^F
Schild^N
visiera^F
visera^F

neck strap
sangle^F de nuque^F
Genicklasche^F
cinghietta^F posteriore di regolazione
correa^F para el cuello^M

respiratory system protection

protection^F des voies^F respiratoires | Atemschutz^M | protezione^F per le vie^F respiratorie | protección^F para el sistema^M respiratorio^M

respirator
masque^M respiratoire
Gasmaske^F
maschera^F a pieno facciale^M bifiltro
máscara^F antigás^M

facepiece
jupe^F de masque^M
Gesichtsstück^N
fascia^F protettiva della fronte^F
sección^F frontal

visor
oculaire^M
Visier^N
visore^M
careta^F

head harness
jeu^M de brides^F
Kopfriemen^M
elastico^M regolabile per il capo^M
correas^F

cartridge
cartouche^F
Kartusche^F
filtro^M
cartucho^M

inhalation valve
soupape^F inspiratoire
Einatmungsventil^N
valvola^F di inspirazione^F
válvula^F de inhalación^F

filter cover
couvre-filtre^M
Filterabdeckung^F
coprifiltro^M
tapa^F del filtro^M

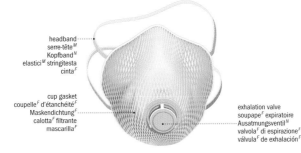

exhalation valve
soupape^F expiratoire
Ausatmungsventil^N
valvola^F di espirazione^F
válvula^F de exhalación^F

half-mask respirator
masque^M bucco-nasal
leichte Atemschutzmaske^F
mascherina^F
máscara^F para el polvo^M

headband
serre-tête^M
Kopfband^N
elastici^M stringitesta
cinta^F

cup gasket
coupelle^F d'étanchéité^F
Maskendichtung^F
calotta^F filtrante
mascarilla^F

exhalation valve
soupape^F expiratoire
Ausatmungsventil^N
valvola^F di espirazione^F
válvula^F de exhalación^F

foot protection

protection^F des pieds^M | Fußschutz^M | protezione^F per i piedi^M | protección^F para los pies^M

SOCIETY

safety boot
brodequin^M de sécurité^F
Sicherheitsschuh^M
scarponcino^M di sicurezza^F
bota^F de seguridad^F

toe guard
protège-orteils^M
Zehenschützer^M
puntale^M di protezione^F
puntera^F protectora

reinforced toe
embout^M de protection^F
Stahlkappe^F
puntale^M rinforzato
tope^M

first aid equipment

matériel^M de secours^M | Notfallausrüstung^F | strumenti^M per il pronto soccorso^M | equipo^M de primeros auxilios^M

stethoscope
stéthoscope^M
Stethoskop^N
fonendoscopio^M
fonendoscopio^M

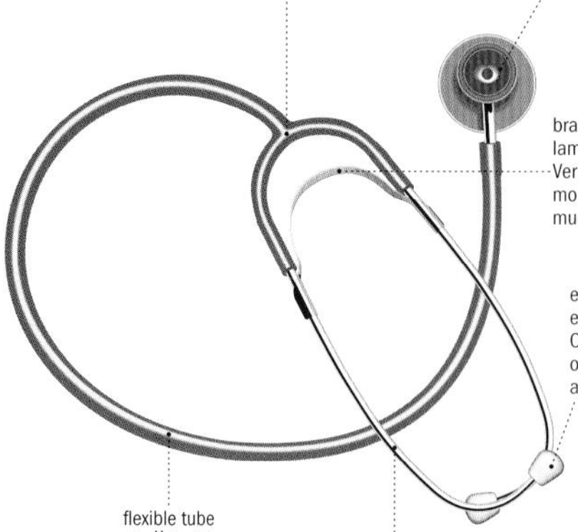

Y-tube
tube^M en Y^M
Y-Schlauch^M
raccordo^M a Y
tubo^M en Y

sound receiver
récepteur^M de son^M
Höraufsatz^M
capsula^F di risonanza^F
receptor^M del sonido^M

branch clip
lame^F-ressort^M
Verbindungsclip^M
molla^F
muelle^M

earpiece
embout^M auriculaire
Ohrstöpsel^M
oliva^F auricolare
auricular^M

flexible tube
tube^M flexible
Gummischlauch^M
tubo^M flessibile
tubo^M flexible

branch
branche^F
Rohrstück^N
archetto^M
rama^F

bevel
biseau^M
Schräge^F
punta^F
bisel^M

needle
aiguille^F
Kanüle^F
ago^M
aguja^F

Luer-Lock tip
embout^M Luer Lock
Luer-Lock-Spitze^F
punta^F Luer-Lock
jeringilla^F de Luer-Lock

hollow barrel
corps^M de pompe^F
Spritzenkörper^M
cilindro^M
cilindro^M

finger flange
anneau^M de retenue^F
Fingerrand^M
aletta^F
pestaña^F de arrojo^M

thumb rest
poussoir^M
Daumenteil^M
spingistantuffo^M
apoyo^M del pulgar^M

syringe
seringue^F
Spritze^F
siringa^F
jeringuilla^F

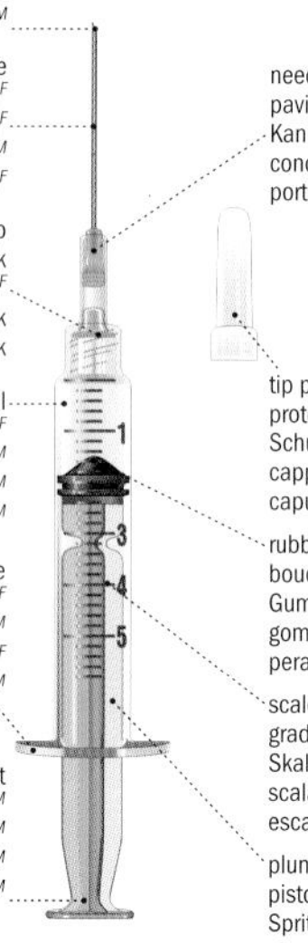

needle hub
pavillon^M
Kanülenansatz^M
cono^M
portaagujas^M

tip protector
protecteur^M d'embout^M
Schutzkappe^F
cappuccio^M di protezione^F
capuchón^M

rubber bulb
bouchon^M
Gummipfropfen^M
gommino^M
pera^F de goma^F

scale
graduation^F
Skala^F
scala^F graduata
escala^F

plunger
piston^M
Spritzenkolben^M
stantuffo^M
émbolo^M

latex glove
gant^M en latex^M
Latexhandschuh^M
guanto^M di lattice^M
guantes^M de látex^M

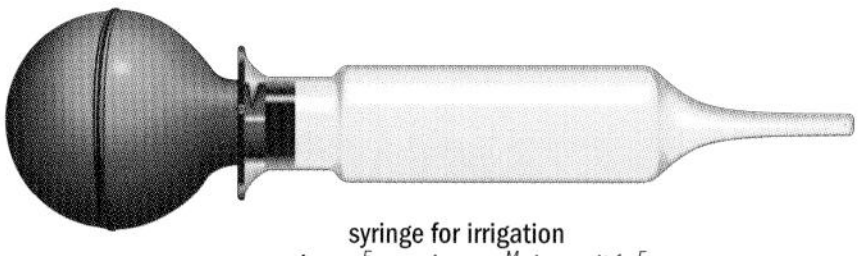

syringe for irrigation
seringue^F pour lavage^M de cavités^F
Klistierspritze^F
schizzetto^M
jeringuilla^F de irrigación^F

hospital trolley
civière^F
Fahrtrage^F
lettino^M
camilla^F

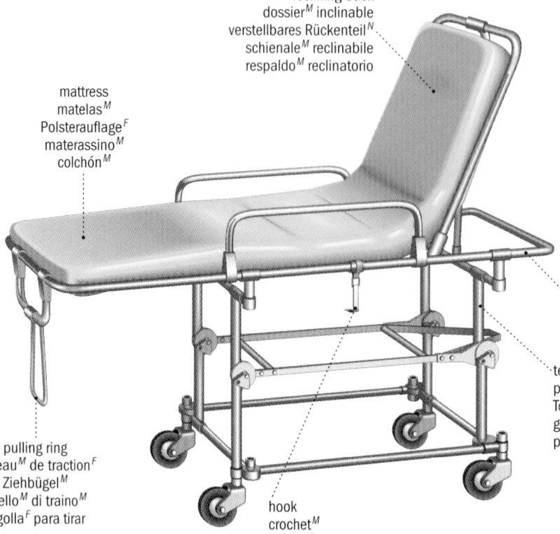

reclining back
dossier^M inclinable
verstellbares Rückenteil^N
schienale^M reclinabile
respaldo^M reclinatorio

mattress
matelas^M
Polsterauflage^F
materassino^M
colchón^M

stretcher
brancard^M
Krankentrage^F
lettiga^F
camilla^F

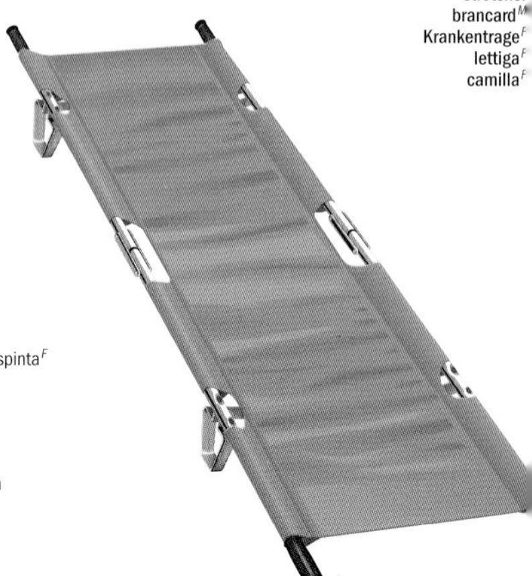

frame
cadre^M
Gestell^N
corrimano^M di spinta^F
chasis^M

telescopic leg
pied^M télescopique
Teleskoptragebein^N
gamba^F telescopica
pata^F telescópica

pulling ring
anneau^M de traction^F
Ziehbügel^M
anello^M di traino^M
argolla^F para tirar

hook
crochet^M
Haken^M
gancio^M
gancho^M de tracción^F

SOCIETY

first aid kit

trousse^F de secours^M | Erste-Hilfe-Kasten^M | cassetta^F di pronto soccorso^M | botiquín^M de primeros auxilios^M

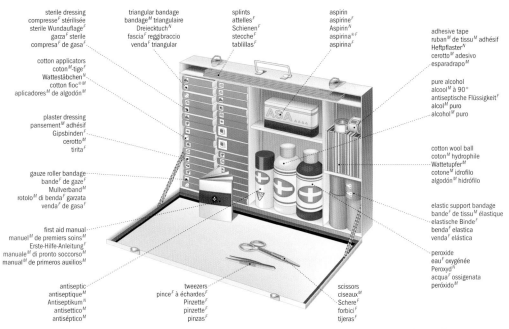

sterile dressing
compresse^F stérilisée
sterile Wundauflage^F
garza^F sterile
compresa^F de gasa^F

cotton applicators
coton^M-tige^F
Wattestäbchen^N
cotton fioc^{®M}
aplicadores^M de algodón^M

plaster dressing
pansement^M adhésif
Gipsbinden^F
cerotto^M
tirita^F

gauze roller bandage
bande^F de gaze^F
Mullverband^M
rotolo^M di benda^F garzata
venda^F de gasa^F

first aid manual
manuel^M de premiers soins^M
Erste-Hilfe-Anleitung^F
manuale^M di pronto soccorso^M
manual^M de primeros auxilios^M

antiseptic
antiseptique^M
Antiseptikum^N
antisettico^M
antiséptico^M

triangular bandage
bandage^M triangulaire
Dreiecktuch^N
fascia^F reggibraccio
venda^F triangular

tweezers
pince^F à échardes^F
Pinzette^F
pinzette^F
pinzas^F

splints
attelles^F
Schienen^F
stecche^F
tablillas^F

scissors
ciseaux^M
Schere^F
forbici^F
tijeras^F

aspirin
aspirine^F
Aspirin^N
aspirina^{®F}
aspirina^F

adhesive tape
ruban^M de tissu^M adhésif
Heftpflaster^N
cerotto^M adesivo
esparadrapo^M

pure alcohol
alcool^M à 90°
antiseptische Flüssigkeit^F
alcol^M puro
alcohol^M puro

cotton wool ball
coton^M hydrophile
Wattetupfer^M
cotone^M idrofilo
algodón^M hidrófilo

elastic support bandage
bande^F de tissu^M élastique
elastische Binde^F
benda^F elastica
venda^F elástica

peroxide
eau^F oxygénée
Peroxyd^N
acqua^F ossigenata
peróxido^M

clinical thermometers

thermomètres^M médicaux | Fieberthermometer^N | termometri^M clinici | termómetros^M clínicos

digital thermometer
thermomètre^M numérique
Digitalthermometer^N
termometro^M digitale
termómetro^M digital

mercury thermometer
thermomètre^M à mercure^M
Quecksilberthermometer^N
termometro^M a mercurio^M
termómetro^M de mercurio^M

SOCIETY

blood pressure monitor

tensiomètre^M | Blutdruckmessgerät^N | monitor^M della pressione^F sanguigna | tensiómetro^M

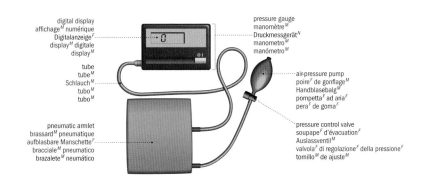

digital display
affichage^M numérique
Digitalanzeige^F
display^M digitale
display^M

tube
tube^M
Schlauch^M
tubo^M
tubo^M

pneumatic armlet
brassard^M pneumatique
aufblasbare Manschette^F
bracciale^M pneumatico
brazalete^M neumático

pressure gauge
manomètre^M
Druckmessgerät^N
manometro^M
manómetro^M

air-pressure pump
poire^F de gonflage^M
Handblasebalg^M
pompetta^F ad aria^F
pera^F de goma^F

pressure control valve
soupape^F d'évacuation^F
Auslassventil^M
valvola^F di regolazione^F della pressione^F
tornillo^M de ajuste^M

hospital

hôpital[M] | Krankenhaus[N] | ospedale[M] | hospital[M]

emergency
urgences[F]
Unfallstation[F]
pronto soccorso[M]
urgencias[F]

family waiting room
salle[F] d'attente[F] des familles[F]
Warteraum[M] für Angehörige[M]
sala[F] d'attesa[F] dei familiari[M]
sala[F] de espera[F] para la familia[F]

soiled utility room
salle[F] de stockage[M] du matériel[M] souillé
Lagerraum[M] für gebrauchtes Material[N]
ripostiglio[M] per il materiale[M] sporco
almacén[M] de material[M] sucio

clean utility room
salle[F] de stockage[M] du matériel[M] stérile
Lagerraum[M] für Sterilgut[N]
ripostiglio[M] per il materiale[M] pulito
almacén[M] de material[M] estéril

observation room
chambre[F] d'observation[F]
Beobachtungsraum[M]
stanza[F] di osservazione[F]
habitación[F] de observación[F]

nurses' station (major emergency)
poste[M] des infirmières[F] (urgence[F] majeure)
Schwesternstation[F] (Unfallstation[F])
postazione[F] degli infermieri[M] (pronto soccorso[M] principale)
puesto[M] de enfermeras[F] (urgencias[F])

pharmacy
pharmacie[F]
Medikamentenraum[M]
farmacia[F]
farmacia[F]

resuscitation room
salle[F] de réanimation[F]
Reanimationsraum[M]
sala[F] di rianimazione[F]
sala[F] de reanimación[F]

isolation room
chambre[F] d'isolement[M]
Isolierraum[M]
stanza[F] di isolamento[M]
habitación[F] de aislamiento[M]

psychiatric observation room
chambre[F] d'observation[F] psychiatrique
psychiatrischer Beobachtungsraum[M]
stanza[F] per osservazione[F] psichiatrica
sala[F] de observación[F] psiquiátrica

psychiatric examination
examen[M] psychiatrique
psychiatrischer Untersuchungsraum[M]
stanza[F] per esame[M] psichiatrico
examen[M] psiquiátrico

mobile X-ray unit
appareil[M] de radiographie[F] mobile
fahrbares Röntgengerät[N]
unità[F] radiologica mobile
unidad[F] móvil de rayos[M] X

stretcher area
secteur[M] des civières[F]
Tragen[F]-Abstellraum[M]
deposito[M] delle barelle[F]
zona[F] de camillas[F]

ambulance
ambulance[F]
Rettungswagen[M]
ambulanza[F]
ambulancia[F]

minor surgery
chirurgie[F] mineure
kleine Chirurgie[F]
sala[F] per operazioni[F] di chirurgia[F] minore
cirugía[F] menor

reception area
aire[F] d'accueil[M]
Aufnahme[F]
accettazione[F]
recepción[F]

emergency physician's office
bureau[M] de l'urgentiste[M]
Büro[N] des diensthabenden Arztes[M]
ufficio[M] del medico[M] di guardia[F]
oficina[F] de urgencias[F]

SOCIETY

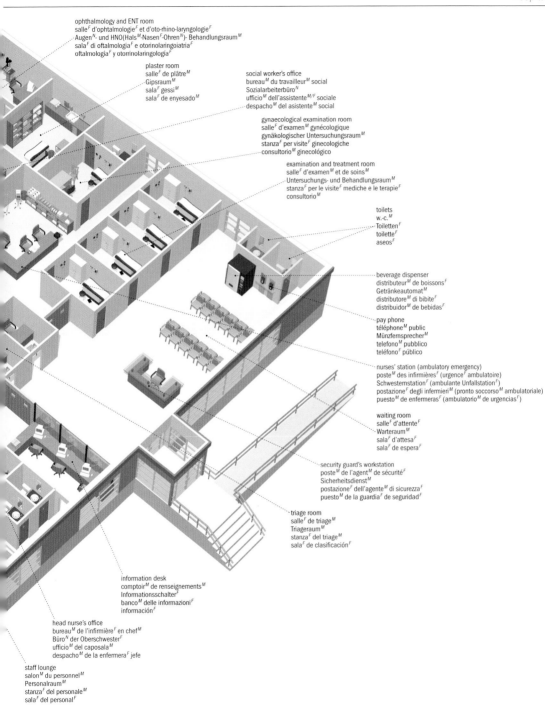

ophthalmology and ENT room
salle[F] d'ophtalmologie[F] et d'oto-rhino-laryngologie[F]
Augen[N]- und HNO(Hals[M]-Nasen[F]-Ohren[N])- Behandlungsraum[M]
sala[F] di oftalmologia[F] e otorinolaringoiatria[F]
oftalmología[F] y otorrinolaringología[F]

plaster room
salle[F] de plâtre[M]
Gipsraum[M]
sala[F] gessi[M]
sala[F] de enyesado[M]

social worker's office
bureau[M] du travailleur[M] social
Sozialarbeiterbüro[N]
ufficio[M] dell'assistente[M/F] sociale
despacho[M] del asistente[M] social

gynaecological examination room
salle[F] d'examen[M] gynécologique
gynäkologischer Untersuchungsraum[M]
stanza[F] per visite[F] ginecologiche
consultorio[M] ginecológico

examination and treatment room
salle[F] d'examen[M] et de soins[M]
Untersuchungs- und Behandlungsraum[M]
stanza[F] per le visite[F] mediche e le terapie[F]
consultorio[M]

toilets
w.-c.[M]
Toiletten[F]
toilette[F]
aseos[F]

beverage dispenser
distributeur[M] de boissons[F]
Getränkeautomat[M]
distributore[M] di bibite[F]
distribuidor[M] de bebidas[F]

pay phone
téléphone[M] public
Münzfernsprecher[M]
telefono[M] pubblico
teléfono[M] público

nurses' station (ambulatory emergency)
poste[M] des infirmières[F] (urgence[F] ambulatoire)
Schwesternstation[F] (ambulante Unfallstation[F])
postazione[F] degli infermieri[M] (pronto soccorso[M] ambulatoriale)
puesto[M] de enfermeras[F] (ambulatorio[M] de urgencias[F])

waiting room
salle[F] d'attente[F]
Warteraum[M]
sala[F] d'attesa[F]
sala[F] de espera[F]

security guard's workstation
poste[M] de l'agent[M] de sécurité[F]
Sicherheitsdienst[M]
postazione[F] dell'agente[M] di sicurezza[F]
puesto[M] de la guardia[F] de seguridad[F]

triage room
salle[F] de triage[M]
Triageraum[M]
stanza[F] del triage[M]
sala[F] de clasificación[F]

information desk
comptoir[M] de renseignements[M]
Informationsschalter[F]
banco[M] delle informazioni[F]
información[F]

head nurse's office
bureau[M] de l'infirmière[F] en chef[M]
Büro[N] der Oberschwester[F]
ufficio[M] del caposala[F]
despacho[M] de la enfermera[F] jefe

staff lounge
salon[M] du personnel[M]
Personalraum[M]
stanza[F] del personale[M]
sala[F] del personal[F]

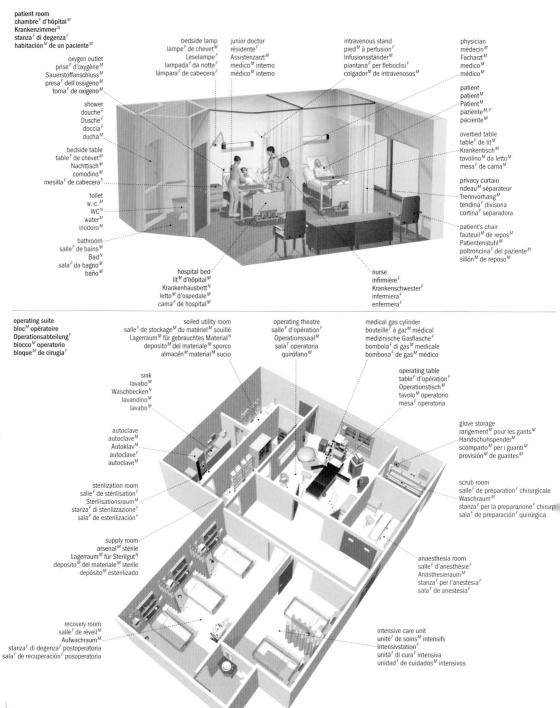

patient room
chambre^F d'hôpital^M
Krankenzimmer^N
stanza^F di degenza^F
habitación^M de un paciente^M

oxygen outlet
prise^F d'oxygène^M
Sauerstoffanschluss^M
presa^F dell'ossigeno^M
toma^F de oxigeno^M

shower
douche^F
Dusche^F
doccia^M
ducha^M

bedside table
table^F de chevet^M
Nachttisch^M
comodino^M
mesilla^F de cabecera^F

toilet
w.-c.^{M}
WC^N
water^M
inodoro^M

bathroom
salle^F de bains^M
Bad^N
sala^F da bagno^M
baño^M

bedside lamp
lampe^F de chevet^M
Leselampe^F
lampada^F da notte^F
lámpara^F de cabecera^F

junior doctor
résidente^F
Assistenzarzt^M
medico^M interno
médico^M interno

intravenous stand
pied^M à perfusion^F
Infusionsständer^M
piantana^F per fleboclisi^F
colgador^M de intravenosos^M

physician
médecin^M
Facharzt^M
medico^M
médico^M

patient
patient^M
Patient^M
paziente$^{M/F}$
paciente^M

overbed table
table^F de lit^M
Krankentisch^M
tavolino^M da letto^M
mesa^F de cama^M

privacy curtain
rideau^M séparateur
Trennvorhang^M
tendina^F divisoria
cortina^F separadora

patient's chair
fauteuil^M de repos^M
Patientenstuhl^M
poltroncina^F del paziente^M
sillón^M de reposo^M

hospital bed
lit^M d'hôpital^M
Krankenhausbett^N
letto^M d'ospedale^M
cama^F de hospital^M

nurse
infirmière^F
Krankenschwester^F
infermiera^F
enfermera^F

operating suite
bloc^M opératoire
Operationsabteilung^F
blocco^M operatorio
bloque^M de cirugía^F

sink
lavabo^M
Waschbecken^N
lavandino^M
lavabo^M

autoclave
autoclave^M
Autoklav^M
autoclave^M
autoclave^M

sterilization room
salle^F de stérilisation^F
Sterilisationsraum^M
stanza^F di sterilizzazione^F
sala^F de esterilización^F

supply room
arsenal^M stérile
Lagerraum^M für Sterilgut^N
deposito^M del materiale^M sterile
depósito^M esterilizado

recovery room
salle^F de réveil^M
Aufwachraum^M
stanza^F di degenza^F postoperatoria
sala^F de recuperación^F posoperatoria

soiled utility room
salle^F de stockage^M du matériel^M souillé
Lagerraum^M für gebrauchtes Material^N
deposito^M del materiale^M sporco
almacén^M material^M sucio

operating theatre
salle^F d'opération^F
Operationssaal^M
sala^F operatoria
quirófano^M

medical gas cylinder
bouteille^F à gaz^M médical
medizinische Gasflasche^F
bombola^F di gas^M medicale
bombona^F de gas^M médico

operating table
table^F d'opération^F
Operationstisch^M
tavolo^M operatorio
mesa^F operatoria

glove storage
rangement^M pour les gants^M
Handschuhspender^M
scomparto^M per i guanti^M
provisión^M de guantes^M

scrub room
salle^F de préparation^F chirurgicale
Waschraum^M
stanza^F per la preparazione^F chirurg
sala^F de preparación^F quirúrgica

anaesthesia room
salle^F d'anesthésie^F
Anästhesieraum^M
stanza^F per l'anestesia^F
sala^F de anestesia^F

intensive care unit
unité^F de soins^M intensifs
Intensivstation^F
unità^F di cura^F intensiva
unidad^F de cuidados^M intensivos

SOCIETY

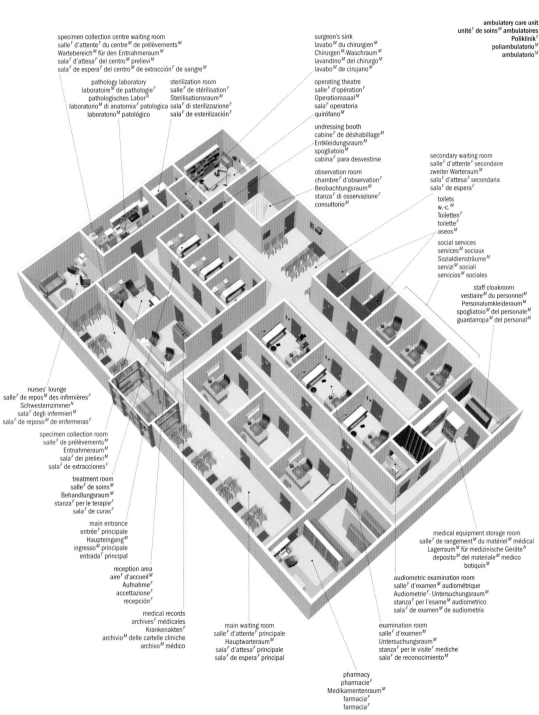

specimen collection centre waiting room
salle^F d'attente^F du centre^M de prélèvements^M
Wartebereich^M für den Entnahmeraum^M
sala^F d'attesa^F del centro^M prelievi^M
sala^F de espera^F del centro^M de extracción^F de sangre^M

pathology laboratory
laboratoire^M de pathologie^F
pathologisches Labor^N
laboratorio^M di anatomia^F patologica
laboratorio^M patológico

sterilization room
salle^F de stérilisation^F
Sterilisationsraum^M
sala^F di sterilizzazione^F
sala^F de esterilización^F

surgeon's sink
lavabo^M du chirurgien^M
Chirurgen^M-Waschraum^M
lavandino^M del chirurgo^M
lavabo^M de cirujano^M

operating theatre
salle^F d'opération^F
Operationssaal^M
sala^F operatoria
quirófano^M

ambulatory care unit
unité^F de soins^M ambulatoires
Poliklinik^F
poliambulatorio^M
ambulatorio^M

undressing booth
cabine^F de déshabillage^M
Entkleidungsraum^M
spogliatoio^M
cabina^F para desvestirse

observation room
chambre^F d'observation^F
Beobachtungsraum^M
stanza^F di osservazione^F
consultorio^M

secondary waiting room
salle^F d'attente^F secondaire
zweiter Warteraum^M
sala^F d'attesa^F secondaria
sala^F de espera^F

toilets
w.-c.^M
Toiletten^F
toilette^F
aseos^M

social services
services^M sociaux
Sozialdiensträume^M
servizi^M sociali
servicios^M sociales

staff cloakroom
vestiaire^M du personnel^M
Personalumkleideraum^M
spogliatoio^M del personale^M
guardarropa^M del personal^M

nurses' lounge
salle^F de repos^M des infirmières^F
Schwesternzimmer^N
sala^F degli infermieri^M
sala^F de reposo^M de enfermeras^F

specimen collection room
salle^F de prélèvements^M
Entnahmeraum^M
sala^F dei prelievi^M
sala^F de extracciones^F

treatment room
salle^F de soins^M
Behandlungsraum^M
stanza^F per le terapie^F
sala^F de curas^F

main entrance
entrée^F principale
Haupteingang^M
ingresso^M principale
entrada^F principal

reception area
aire^F d'accueil^M
Aufnahme^F
accettazione^F
recepción^F

medical records
archives^F médicales
Krankenakten^F
archivio^M delle cartelle cliniche
archivo^M médico

main waiting room
salle^F d'attente^F principale
Hauptwarteraum^M
sala^F d'attesa^F principale
sala^F de espera^F principal

pharmacy
pharmacie^F
Medikamentenraum^M
farmacia^F
farmacia^F

medical equipment storage room
salle^F de rangement^M du matériel^M médical
Lagerraum^M für medizinische Geräte^N
deposito^M del materiale^M medico
botiquín^M

audiometric examination room
salle^F d'examen^M audiométrique
Audiometrie^F- Untersuchungsraum^M
stanza^F per l'esame^M audiometrico
sala^F de examen^M de audiometría

examination room
salle^F d'examen^M
Untersuchungsraum^M
stanza^F per le visite^F mediche
sala^F de reconocimiento^M

SOCIETY

walking aids

aides^F à la marche^F | Gehhilfen^F | supporti^M per camminare | auxiliares^M ortopédicos para caminar

forearm crutch
béquille^F d'avant-bras^M
Gehkrücke^F
stampella^F canadese
muleta^F de antebrazo^M

forearm support
embrasse^F
Unterarmstütze^F
supporto^M per il braccio^M
soporte^M para el antebrazo^M

handgrip
poignée^F
Griff^M
impugnatura^F
empuñadura^F

adjuster
réglage^M
Längenverstellung^F
regolatore^M
tubo^M ajustable

underarm crutch
béquille^F commune
Achselkrücke^F
gruccia^F
muleta^F de sobaco^M

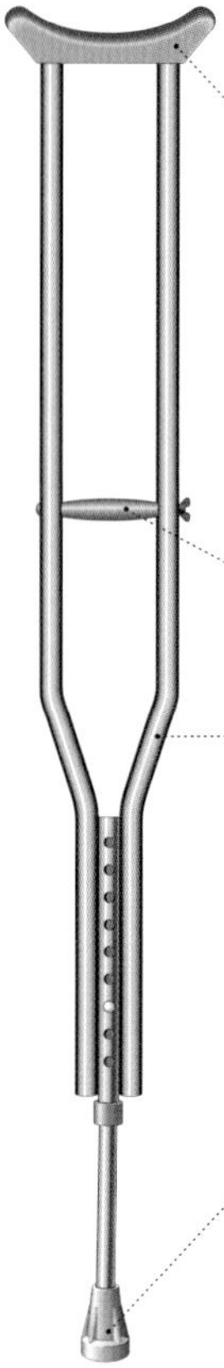

underarm rest
crosse^F
Achselstütze^F
supporto^M sottoascellare
soporte^M para el sobaco^M

crosspiece
traverse^F
Querstück^N
appoggiamano^M
travesaño^M

upright
montant^M
Holm^M
telaio^M
montante^M

rubber ferrule
embout^M de caoutchouc^M
Gummikappe^F
puntale^M
contera^F de caucho^M

English stick
canne^F en T^M
englischer Stock^M
bastone^M inglese
bastón^M inglés

walking frame
déambulateur^M
Gehgestell^N
deambulatore^M
andador^M

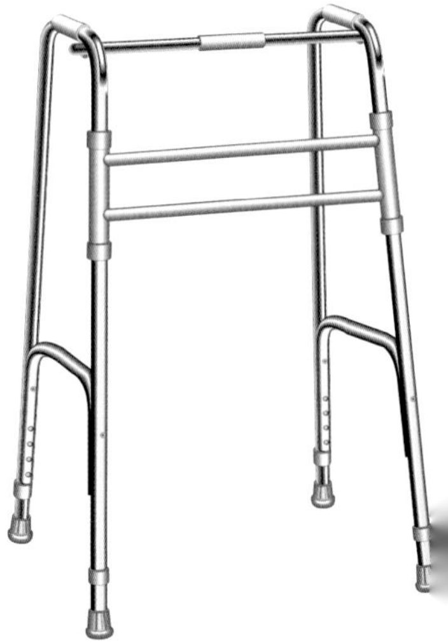

quadruped stick
canne^F avec quadripode^M
vierfüßiger Stock^M
quadripode^M
bastón^M cuadrangular

ortho-stick
canne^F avec poignée^F orthopédique
orthopädischer Stock^M
bastone^M con manico^M anatomico
bastón^M ortopédico

walking stick
canne^F en C^M
Spazierstock^M
bastone^M da passeggio^M
bastón^M para caminar

SOCIETY

wheelchair

fauteuil^M roulant | Rollstuhl^M | sedia^F a rotelle^F | silla^F de ruedas^F

handle
poignée^F de conduite^F
Schiebegriff^M
impugnatura^F
agarrador^M

spacer
barre^F d'espacement^M
Abstandstück^N
distanziatore^M
separador^M

brake
poignée^F de frein^M
Bremse^F
freno^M
freno^M

hub
moyeu^M
Nabe^F
mozzo^M
cubo^M

push rim
main^F courante
Schieberad^N
ruota^F di spinta^F
rueda^F de empuje^M

large wheel
roue^F
Großrad^N
ruota^F piena o gonfiabile
rueda^F

back
dossier^M
Rückenlehne^F
schienale^M
respaldo^M

armrest
accoudoir^M
Armstütze^F
bracciolo^M
reposabrazos^M

arm
bras^M
Arm^M
braccio^M
brazo^M

clothing guard
panneau^M de protection^F latéral
Kleiderschutz^M
fiancata^F
panel^M protector

seat
siège^M
Sitz^M
seduta^F
asiento^M

hanger bracket
potence^F
Haltebügel^M
braccio^M di sospensione^F
soporte^M colgante

heel loop
butée^F talonnière^F
Fersenstütze^F
supporto^M per il tallone^M
talón^M

front wheel
roue^F pivotante
Vorderrad^N
ruota^F pivotante
rueda^F de la dirección^F

cross brace
croisillon^M
Querstrebe^F
rinforzo^M a crociera^F
travesaño^M

stabilizer
dispositif^M anti-bascule
Kipphebel^M
pedale^M di sollevamento^M
palanca^F estabilizadora

footrest
repose-pied^M
Fußstütze^F
appoggiapiedi^M
reposapiés^M

pharmaceutical forms of medication

formes^F pharmaceutiques des médicaments^M | Arzneimittel^N-Darreichungsformen^F | confezioni^F farmaceutiche di medicinali^M | formas^F farmacéuticas de medicamentos^M

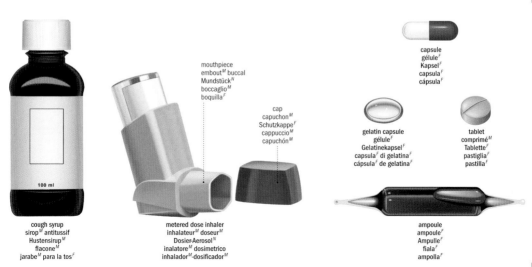

capsule
gélule^F
Kapsel^F
capsula^F
cápsula^F

mouthpiece
embout^M buccal
Mundstück^N
boccaglio^M
boquilla^F

cap
capuchon^M
Schutzkappe^F
cappuccio^M
capuchón^M

gelatin capsule
gélule^F
Gelatinekapsel^F
capsula^F di gelatina^F
cápsula^F de gelatina^F

tablet
comprimé^M
Tablette^F
pastiglia^F
pastilla^F

100 ml

cough syrup
sirop^M antitussif
Hustensirup^M
flacone^M
jarabe^F para la tos^F

metered dose inhaler
inhalateur^M doseur^M
Dosier-Aerosol^N
inalatore^M dosimetrico
inhalador^M-dosificador^M

ampoule
ampoule^F
Ampulle^F
fiala^F
ampolla^F

dice and dominoes

dés^M et dominos^M | Würfel^M und Dominosteine^M | dadi^M e domino^M | dados^M y dominós^M

ordinary die
dé^M régulier
gewöhnlicher Würfel^M
dado^M comune
dado^M común

poker die
dé^M à poker^M
Pokerwürfel^M
dado^M da poker^M
dado^M de póquer^M

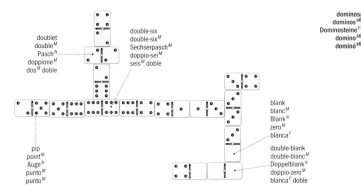

doublet
double^M
Pasch^N
doppione^M
dos^M doble

double-six
double-six^M
Sechserpasch^M
doppio-sei^M
seis^M doble

dominos
dominos^M
Dominosteine^F
domino^M
dominó^M

blank
blanc^M
Blank^N
zero^M
blanca^F

pip
point^M
Auge^N
punto^M
punto^M

double-blank
double-blanc^M
Doppelblank^N
doppio-zero^M
blanca^F doble

card games

cartes^F | Kartenspiele^N | giochi^M di carte^F | baraja^F

symbols
symboles^M
Farben^F
simboli^M
símbolos^M

heart
cœur^M
Herz^N
cuori^M
corazón^M

diamond
carreau^M
Karo^N
quadri^M
diamante^M

club
trèfle^M
Kreuz^N
fiori^M
trébol^M

spade
pique^M
Pik^N
picche^M
espada^F

Joker
Joker^M
Joker^M
jolly^M
comodín^M

Ace
As^M
Ass^N
asso^M
as^M

King
Roi^M
König^M
re^M
rey^M

Queen
Dame^F
Dame^F
donna^F
reina^F

Jack
Valet^M
Bube^M
fante^M
jota^F

standard poker hands
combinaisons^F **au poker**^{M}
normale Pokerblätter^N
combinazioni^F **del poker**^{M}
manos^F **de póquer**^{M}

high card
carte^F isolée
höchste Karte^F
carta^F più alta
cartas^F altas

one pair
paire^F
ein Pärchen^N
coppia^F
un par^M

two pairs
double paire^F
zwei Pärchen^N
doppia coppia^F
dos pares^M

three-of-a-kind
brelan^M
Drilling^M
tris^M
trio^M

straight
séquence^F
Straße^F
scala^F
escalera^F

flush
couleur^F
Flush^M
colore^M
color^M

full house
main^F pleine
Full House^N
full^M
full^M

four-of-a-kind
carré^M
Vierling^M
poker^M
póquer^M

straight flush
quinte^F
Straight Flush^M
scala^F reale
escalera^F de color^M

royal flush
quinte^F royale
Royal Flush^M
scala^F reale massima
escalera^F real

SPORTS AND GAMES

board game

jeux^M de plateau^M | Brettspiel^N | giochi^M da tavola^F | juegos^M de mesa^F

backgammon
jacquet^M
Backgammon^N
backgammon^M
backgammon^M

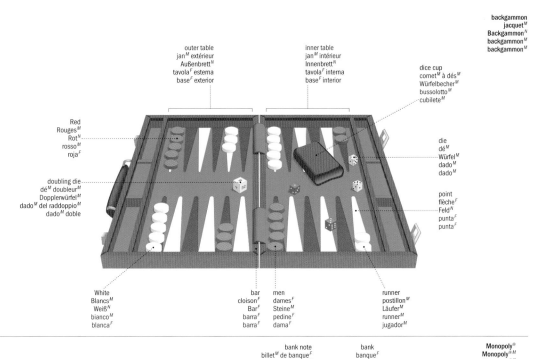

outer table
jan^M extérieur
Außenbrett^N
tavola^F esterna
base^F exterior

inner table
jan^M intérieur
Innenbrett^N
tavola^F interna
base^F interior

dice cup
cornet^M à dés^M
Würfelbecher^M
bussolotto^M
cubilete^M

Red
Rouges^M
Rot^N
rosso^M
roja^F

die
dé^M
Würfel^M
dado^M
dado^M

doubling die
dé^M doubleur^M
Dopplerwürfel^M
dado^M del raddoppio^M
dado^M doble

point
flèche^F
Feld^N
punta^F
punta^F

White
Blancs^M
Weiß^N
bianco^M
blanca^F

bar
cloison^F
Bar^F
barra^F
barra^F

men
dames^F
Steine^M
pedine^F
dama^F

runner
postillon^M
Läufer^M
runner^M
jugador^M

bank note
billet^M de banque^F
Spielgeld^N
banconota^F
billetes^M de banco^M

bank
banque^F
Bank^F
banca^F
banco^M

Monopoly®
Monopoly^{® M}
Monopoly^{® N}
Monopoli^{® M}
Monopoly^{® M}

Chance card
carte^F Chance^F
Ereigniskarte^F
carta^F delle probabilità^F
carta^F de la Suerte^F

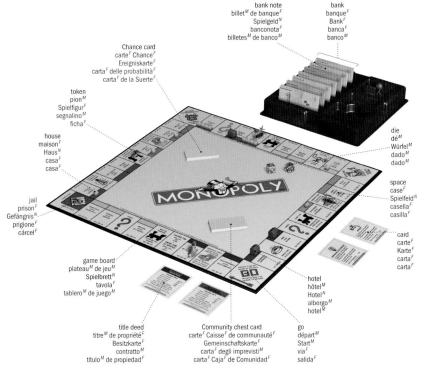

token
pion^M
Spielfigur^F
segnalino^M
ficha^F

house
maison^F
Haus^N
casa^F
casa^F

die
dé^M
Würfel^M
dado^M
dado^M

jail
prison^F
Gefängnis^N
prigione^F
cárcel^F

space
case^F
Spielfeld^N
casella^F
casilla^F

card
carte^F
Karte^F
carta^F
carta^F

game board
plateau^M de jeu^M
Spielbrett^N
tavola^F
tablero^M de juego^M

hotel
hôtel^M
Hotel^N
albergo^M
hotel^M

title deed
titre^M de propriété^F
Besitzkarte^F
contratto^M
título^M de propiedad^F

Community chest card
carte^F Caisse^F de communauté^F
Gemeinschaftskarte^F
carta^F degli imprevisti^M
carta^F Caja^F de Comunidad^F

go
départ^M
Start^M
via^F
salida^F

SPORTS AND GAMES

board game

chess
échecs^M
Schach^N
scacchi^M
ajedrez^M

chessboard
échiquier^M
Schachbrett^N
scacchiera^F
tablero^M de ajedrez^M

Queen's side
aile^F Dame^F
Damenflanke^F
lato^M della regina^F
lado^M de la reina^F

King's side
aile^F Roi^M
Königsflanke^F
lato^M del re^M
lado^M del rey^M

men
pièces^F
Schachfiguren^F
pezzi^M
piezas^F

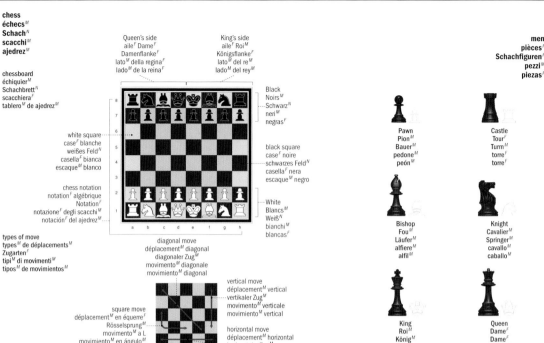

Black
Noirs^M
Schwarz^N
neri^M
negras^F

white square
case^F blanche
weißes Feld^N
casella^F bianca
escaque^M blanco

black square
case^F noire
schwarzes Feld^N
casella^F nera
escaque^M negro

chess notation
notation^F algébrique
Notation^F
notazione^F degli scacchi^M
notación^F del ajedrez^M

White
Blancs^M
Weiß^N
bianchi^M
blancas^F

Pawn
Pion^M
Bauer^M
pedone^M
peón^M

Castle
Tour^F
Turm^M
torre^F
torre^F

Bishop
Fou^M
Läufer^M
alfiere^M
alfil^M

Knight
Cavalier^M
Springer^M
cavallo^M
caballo^M

King
Roi^M
König^M
re^M
rey^M

Queen
Dame^F
Dame^F
regina^F
reina^F

types of move
types^M de déplacements^M
Zugarten^F
tipi^M di movimenti^M
tipos^M de movimientos^M

diagonal move
déplacement^M diagonal
diagonaler Zug^M
movimento^M diagonale
movimiento^M diagonal

vertical move
déplacement^M vertical
vertikaler Zug^M
movimento^M verticale
movimiento^M vertical

square move
déplacement^M en équerre^F
Rösselsprung^M
movimento^M a L
movimiento^M en ángulo^M

horizontal move
déplacement^M horizontal
horizontaler Zug^M
movimento^M orizzontale
movimiento^M horizontal

go
go^M
Go^N
go^M
go (sun-tse)^M

board
plateau^M
Spielbrett^N
scacchiera^F
tablero^M

major motion
principaux mouvements
Hauptspielzüge
mosse^F **principal**
principales movimientos

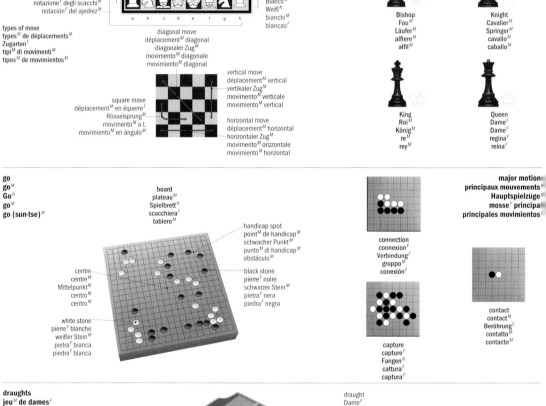

handicap spot
point^M de handicap^M
schwacher Punkt^M
punto^M di handicap^M
obstáculo^M

connection
connexion^F
Verbindung^F
gruppo^M
conexión^F

centre
centre^M
Mittelpunkt^M
centro^M
centro^M

black stone
pierre^F noire
schwarzer Stein^M
pietra^F nera
piedra^F negra

white stone
pierre^F blanche
weißer Stein^M
pietra^F bianca
piedra^F blanca

capture
capture^F
Fangen^N
cattura^F
captura^F

contact
contact^M
Berührung^F
contatto^M
contacto^M

draughts
jeu^M **de dames**^{F}
Dame^F
dama^F
damas^F

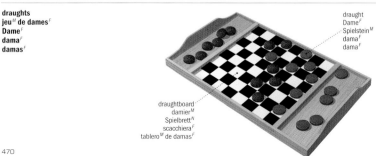

draught
Dame^F
Spielstein^M
dama^F
dama^F

draughtboard
damier^M
Spielbrett^N
scacchiera^F
tablero^M de damas^F

video entertainment system

système^M de jeux^M vidéo | Videospielsystem^N | videogioco^M | videojuego^M

game console
console^F de jeu^M
Spielekonsole^F
console^F
consola^F de juego^M

visual display
écran^M
Monitor^M
video^M
pantalla^F

memory card slots
ports^M pour carte^F mémoire^F
Speicherkartenschächte^M
porte^F per le memory card^F
puertos^M para tarjeta^F de memoria^F

CD/DVD player
lecteur^M CD^M/DVD^M
CD^F-/DVD^F-Einschub^M
lettore^M CD^M/DVD^M
lector^M CD/DVD

action buttons
touches^F d'action^F
Aktionstasten^F
pulsanti^M di azione^F
botones^M de acción^F

controller ports
ports^M pour manette^F
Controller^M-Schnittstellen^F
porte^F di controllo^M
puertos^M para el mando^M

directional buttons
touches^F directionnelles
Richtungstasten^F
pulsanti^M direzionali
botones^M de dirección^F

reset button
bouton^M de réinitialisation^F
Resettaste^F
pulsante^M di reset^M
botón^M de reset^M

controller
manette^F de jeu^M
Controller^M
manopola^F di controllo^M
mando^M

joysticks
manches^M à balai^M
Joysticks^M
joystick^M
joysticks^M

eject button
touche^F d'éjection^F
Auswurftaste^F
pulsante^M di espulsione^F
botón^M de expulsión^F

game of darts

jeu^M de fléchettes^F | Dartspiel^N | freccette^F | juego^M de dardos^M

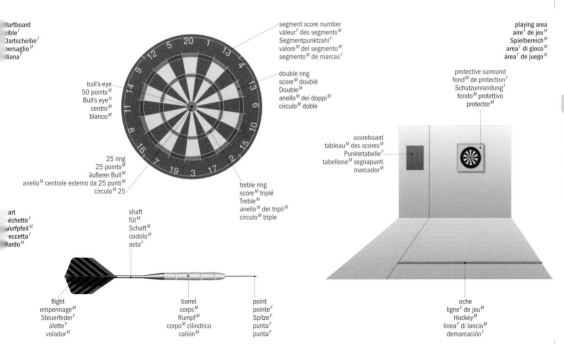

dartboard
cible^F
Dartscheibe^F
bersaglio^M
diana^F

segment score number
valeur^F des segments^M
Segmentpunktzahl^F
valore^M del segmento^M
segmento^M de marcas^F

playing area
aire^F de jeu^M
Spielbereich^M
area^F di gioco^M
área^F de juego^M

bull's-eye
50 points^M
Bull's eye^N
centro^M
blanco^M

double ring
score^M doublé
Double^M
anello^M dei doppi^M
círculo^M doble

protective surround
fond^M de protection^F
Schutzumrandung^F
fondo^M protettivo
protector^M

25 ring
25 points^M
äußerer Bull^M
anello^M centrale esterno da 25 punti^M
círculo^M 25

scoreboard
tableau^M des scores^M
Punktetabelle^F
tabellone^M segnapunti
marcador^M

treble ring
score^M triplé
Treble^M
anello^M dei tripli^M
círculo^M triple

dart
fléchette^F
Wurfpfeil^M
freccetta^F
dardo^M

shaft
fût^M
Schaft^M
codolo^M
asta^F

flight
empennage^M
Steuerfeder^F
alette^F
volador^M

barrel
corps^M
Rumpf^M
corpo^M cilindrico
cañón^M

point
pointe^F
Spitze^F
punta^F
punta^F

oche
ligne^F de jeu^M
Hockey^M
linea^F di lancio^M
demarcación^F

SPORTS AND GAMES

arena

stade^M | Stadion^N | stadio^M | estadio^M

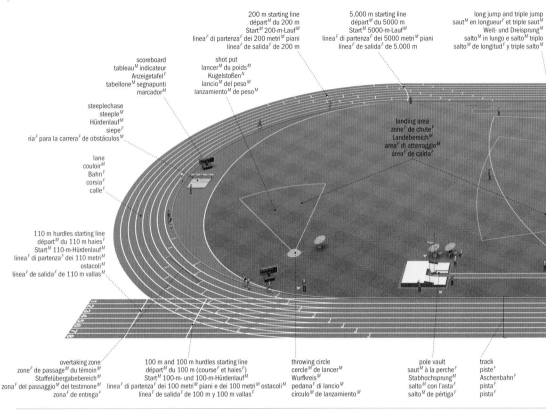

200 m starting line
départ^M du 200 m
Start^M 200-m-Lauf^M
linea^F di partenza^F dei 200 metri^M piani
linea^F de salida^F de 200 m

5,000 m starting line
départ^M du 5000 m
Start^M 5000-m-Lauf^M
linea^F di partenza^F dei 5000 metri^M piani
linea^F de salida^F de 5.000 m

long jump and triple jump
saut^M en longueur^F et triple saut^M
Weit- und Dreisprung^M
salto^M in lungo e salto^M triplo
salto^M de longitud^F y triple salto^M

scoreboard
tableau^M indicateur
Anzeigetafel^F
tabellone^M segnapunti
marcador^M

shot put
lancer^M du poids^M
Kugelstoßen^N
lancio^M del peso^M
lanzamiento^M de peso^M

landing area
zone^F de chute^F
Landebereich^M
area^F di atterraggio^M
área^F de caída^F

steeplechase
steeple^M
Hürdenlauf^M
siepe^F
ría^F para la carrera^F de obstáculos^M

lane
couloir^M
Bahn^F
corsia^F
calle^F

110 m hurdles starting line
départ^M du 110 m haies^F
Start^M 110-m-Hürdenlauf^M
linea^F di partenza^F dei 110 metri^M
ostacoli^M
linea^F de salida^F de 110 m vallas^M

overtaking zone
zone^F de passage^M du témoin^M
Staffelübergabebereich^M
zona^F del passaggio^M del testimone^M
zona^F de entrega^F

100 m and 100 m hurdles starting line
départ^M du 100 m (course^F et haies^F)
Start^M 100-m- und 100-m-Hürdenlauf^M
linea^F di partenza^F dei 100 metri^M piani e dei 100 metri^M ostacoli^M
linea^F de salida^F de 100 m y 100 m vallas^F

throwing circle
cercle^M de lancer^M
Wurfkreis^M
pedana^F di lancio^M
círculo^M de lanzamiento^M

pole vault
saut^M à la perche^F
Stabhochsprung^M
salto^M con l'asta^F
salto^M de pértiga^F

track
piste^F
Aschenbahn^F
pista^F
pista^F

equipment
équipement^M
Geräte^N
attrezzatura^F
equipamiento^M

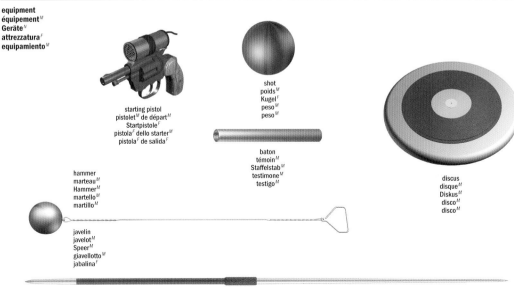

starting pistol
pistolet^M de départ^M
Startpistole^F
pistola^F dello starter^M
pistola^F de salida^F

shot
poids^M
Kugel^F
peso^M
peso^M

baton
témoin^M
Staffelstab^M
testimone^M
testigo^M

discus
disque^M
Diskus^M
disco^M
disco^M

hammer
marteau^M
Hammer^M
martello^M
martillo^M

javelin
javelot^M
Speer^M
giavellotto^M
jabalina^F

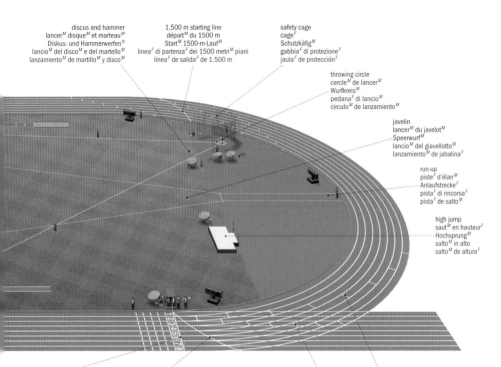

discus and hammer
lancer^M disque^M et marteau^M
Diskus- und Hammerwerfen^N
lancio^M del disco^M e del martello^M
lanzamiento^M de martillo^M y disco^M

1,500 m starting line
départ^M du 1500 m
Start^M 1500-m-Lauf^M
linea^F di partenza^F dei 1500 metri^M piani
línea^F de salida^F de 1.500 m

safety cage
cage^F
Schutzkäfig^M
gabbia^F di protezione^F
jaula^F de protección^F

throwing circle
cercle^M de lancer^M
Wurfkreis^M
pedana^F di lancio^M
círculo^M de lanzamiento^M

javelin
lancer^M du javelot^M
Speerwurf^M
lancio^M del giavellotto^M
lanzamiento^M de jabalina^F

run-up
piste^F d'élan^M
Anlaufstrecke^F
pista^F di rincorsa^F
pista^F de salto^M

high jump
saut^M en hauteur^F
Hochsprung^M
salto^M in alto
salto^M de altura^F

finish line
ligne^F d'arrivée^F
Ziellinie^F
linea^F del traguardo^M
llegada^F

10,000 m and 4 x 400 m relay starting line
départ^M du 10 000 m et du relais^M 4 x 400 m
Start^M 10000-m- und 4-x-400-m-Lauf^M
linea^F di partenza^F dei 10000 metri^M piani e della staffetta^F 4 x 400 metri^M
línea^F de salida^F de 10.000 m y de relevos^M de 4 x 400 m

800 m starting line
départ^M du 800 m
Start^M 800-m-Lauf^M
linea^F di partenza^F degli 800 metri^M piani
línea^F de salida^F 800 m

400 m, 400 m hurdles, 4 x 100 m relay starting line
départ^M des 400 m (course^F, haies^F, relais^M)
Start^M 400-m-, 400-m-Hürden^F-, 4-x-100-m-Lauf^M
linea^F di partenza^F dei 400 metri^M piani e a ostacoli^M e della
staffetta^F 4x100 metri^M
línea^F de salida^F de 400 m, 400 m vallas^F y relevos^M de 4x100 m

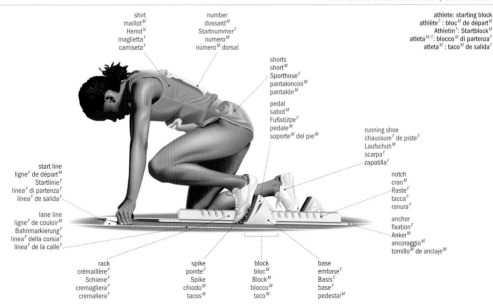

shirt
maillot^M
Hemd^N
maglietta^F
camiseta^F

number
dossard^M
Startnummer^F
numero^M
número^M dorsal

athlete: starting block
athlète^F : bloc^M de départ^M
Athletin^F: Startblock^M
atleta^{M/F}: blocco^M di partenza^F
atleta^M : taco^M de salida^F

shorts
short^M
Sporthose^F
pantaloncini^M
pantalón^M

pedal
sabot^M
Fußstütze^F
pedale^M
soporte^M del pie^M

running shoe
chaussure^F de piste^F
Laufschuh^M
scarpa^F
zapatilla^F

notch
cran^M
Raste^F
tacca^F
ranura^F

start line
ligne^F de départ^M
Startlinie^F
linea^F di partenza^F
línea^F de salida^F

anchor
fixation^F
Anker^M
ancoraggio^M
tornillo^M de anclaje^M

lane line
ligne^F de couloir^M
Bahnmarkierung^F
linea^F della corsia^F
línea^F de la calle^F

rack
crémaillère^F
Schiene^F
cremagliera^F
cremallera^F

spike
pointe^F
Spike^M
chiodo^M
tacos^M

block
bloc^M
Block^M
blocco^M
taco^M

base
embase^F
Basis^F
base^F
pedestal^M

baseball

baseball^M | Baseball^M | baseball^M | béisbol^M

player positions
position^F des joueurs^M
Spielerpositionen^F
posizioni^F dei giocatori^M
posición^F de los jugadores^M

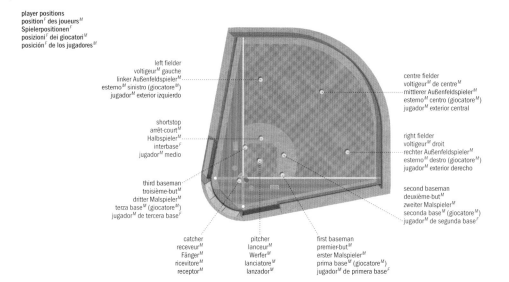

left fielder
voltigeur^M gauche
linker Außenfeldspieler^M
esterno^M sinistro (giocatore^M)
jugador^M exterior izquierdo

centre fielder
voltigeur^M de centre^M
mittlerer Außenfeldspieler^M
esterno^M centro (giocatore^M)
jugador^M exterior central

shortstop
arrêt-court^M
Halbspieler^M
interbase^F
jugador^M medio

right fielder
voltigeur^M droit
rechter Außenfeldspieler^M
esterno^M destro (giocatore^M)
jugador^M exterior derecho

third baseman
troisième-but^M
dritter Malspieler^M
terza base^M (giocatore^M)
jugador^M de tercera base^F

second baseman
deuxième-but^M
zweiter Malspieler^M
seconda base^M (giocatore^M)
jugador^M de segunda base^F

catcher
receveur^M
Fänger^M
ricevitore^M
receptor^M

pitcher
lanceur^M
Werfer^M
lanciatore^M
lanzador^M

first baseman
premier-but^M
erster Malspieler^M
prima base^M (giocatore^M)
jugador^M de primera base^F

field
terrain^M
Spielfeld^N
campo^M
campo^M

third base
troisième but^M
drittes Mal^N
terza base^F (posizione^F)
tercera base^F

dugout
abri^M des joueurs^M
Spielerbank^F
panchina^F dei giocatori^M
banquillo^M de jugadores^M

coach's box
rectangle^M des instructeurs^M
Coach-Box^F
zona^F dell'allenatore^M
banquillo^M del entrenador^M

foul line
ligne^F de jeu^M
Foullinie^F
linea^F di fuoricampo^M
línea^F de foul^M

backstop
écran^M de protection^F
Ballfangzaun^M
schermo^M di protezione^F
pantalla^F de protección^F

on-deck circle
cercle^M d'attente^F
On-Deck-Circle^M
cerchio^M del battitore^M successivo
círculo^M de espera^F

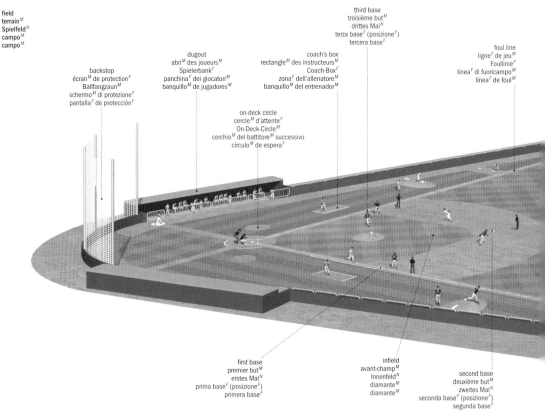

first base
premier but^M
erstes Mal^N
prima base^F (posizione^F)
primera base^F

infield
avant-champ^M
Innenfeld^N
diamante^M
diamante^M

second base
deuxième but^M
zweites Mal^N
seconda base^F (posizione^F)
segunda base^F

SPORTS AND GAMES

pitch
lancer^M
Wurf^M
lancio^M
lanzamiento^M

home-plate umpire
arbitre^M en chef^M
Hauptschiedsrichter^M
arbitro^M capo^M
árbitro^M de base^F meta^F

batter
frappeur^M
Schlagmann^M
battitore^M
bateador^M

pitcher
lanceur^M
Werfer^M
lanciatore^M
lanzador^M

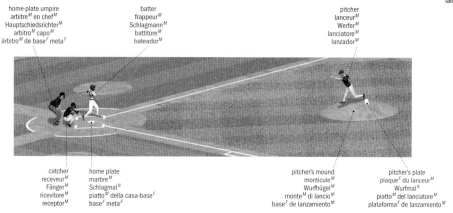

catcher
receveur^M
Fänger^M
ricevitore^M
receptor^M

home plate
marbre^M
Schlagmal^N
piatto^M della casa-base^F
base^F meta^F

pitcher's mound
monticule^M
Wurfhügel^M
monte^M di lancio^M
base^F de lanzamiento^M

pitcher's plate
plaque^F du lanceur^M
Wurfmal^N
piatto^M del lanciatore^M
plataforma^F de lanzamiento^M

outfield fence
clôture^F du champ^M extérieur
Outfieldzaun^M
recinzione^F
vallado^M del campo^M

left field
champ^M gauche
linkes Feld^N
esterno^M sinistro (posizione^F)
exterior^M izquierdo

centre field
champ^M centre^M
Mittelfeld^N
esterno^M centro (posizione^F)
exterior^M

right field
champ^M droit
rechtes Feld^N
esterno^M destro (posizione^F)
exterior^M derecho

foul line post
poteau^M de ligne^F de jeu^M
Foullinienpfosten^M
palo^M della linea^F di fuoricampo^M
poste^M de foul^M

warning track
piste^F d'avertissement^M
Zuschauergrenze^F
limite^M del campo^M
zona^F de atención^F

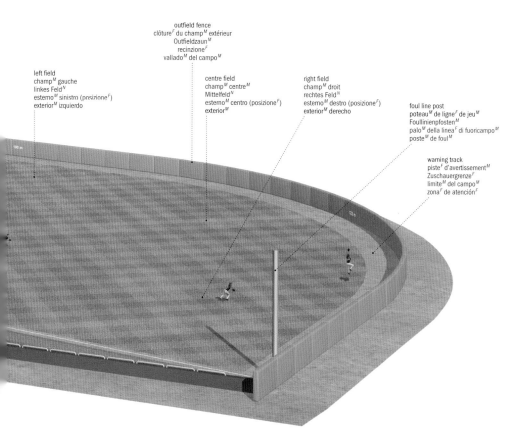

baseball

baseball
balle^F de baseball^M
Baseball^N
palla^F
béisbol^M

bat
bâton^M
Schläger^M
mazza^F
bate^M

batter's helmet
casque^M de frappeur^M
Helm^M
casco^M
casco^M del bateador^M

batter
frappeur^M
Schlagmann^M
battitore^M
bateador^M

catcher
receveur^M
Fänger^M
ricevitore^M
receptor^M

throat protector
protège-gorge^M
Halsschutz^M
paragola^M
protector^M de la garganta^F

mask
masque^M
Maske^F
maschera^F
máscara^F

frame
grille^F
Visiergestell^N
griglia^F per casco^M
armazón^M de la máscara^F

chest protector
plastron^M
Brustschutz^M
pettorina^F di protezione^F
peto^M

catcher's glove
gant^M de receveur^M
Fanghandschuh^M
guanto^M
guante^M del receptor^M

team shirt
maillot^M d'équipe^F
Mannschaftstrikot^N
maglia^F della squadra^F
camiseta^F

undershirt
maillot^M de corps^M
Unterhemd^N
prima maglia^F
camiseta^F interior

batting glove
gant^M de frappeur^M
Schlaghandschuh^M
guanto^M
guante^M de bateo^M

trousers
pantalon^M
Hose^F
pantaloni^M
pantalón^M

stirrup sock
chaussette^F-étrier^M
Stutzen^M
calza^F con reggicalze^M
calcetín^M con tirante^M

spiked shoe
chaussure^F à crampons^M
Stollenschuh^M
scarpa^F con tacchetti^M
zapatilla^F con tacos^M

toe guard
protège-orteils^M
Zehenschützer^M
parapunta^F
protector^M del pie^M

leg guard
jambière^F
Beinschutz^M
schiniere^M
espinillera^F

knee pad
genouillère^F
Knieschützer^M
ginocchiera^F
rodillera^F

ankle guard
protège-cheville^M
Knöchelschutz^M
parastinchi^M
tobillera^F

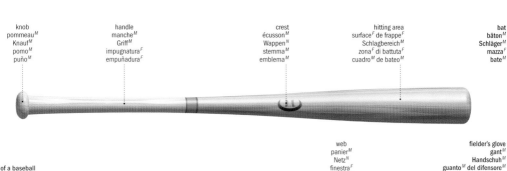

knob
pommeau^M
Knauf^M
pomo^M
puño^M

handle
manche^M
Griff^M
impugnatura^F
empuñadura^F

crest
écusson^M
Wappen^N
stemma^M
emblema^M

hitting area
surface^F de frappe^F
Schlagbereich^M
zona^F di battuta^F
cuadro^M de bateo^M

bat
bâton^M
Schläger^M
mazza^F
bate^M

web
panier^M
Netz^N
finestra^F
canasta^F

fielder's glove
gant^M
Handschuh^M
guanto^M del difensore^M
guante^M de recogida^F

cross section of a baseball
coupe^F de la balle^F
Baseball^M im Querschnitt^M
sezione^F di una palla^F
corte^M de la pelota^F de béisbol^M

strap
patte^F
Riemen^M
cinturino^M
trabilla^F

cork ball
balle^F de liège^M
Korkball^M
palla^F di sughero^M
bola^F de corcho^M

yarn ball
balle^F de fil^M
Gamball^M
palla^F di filo^M
bola^F de hilo^M

thumb
pouce^M
Daumen^M
pollice^M
pulgar^M

finger
doigt^M
Finger^M
dito^M
dedo^M

palm
paume^F
Handfläche^F
sacco^M
palma^F

heel
talon^M
Handwurzel^F
tallone^M
talón^M

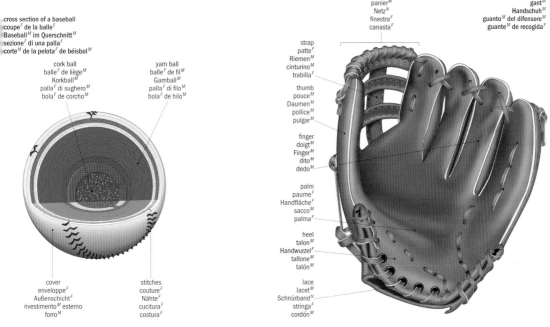

cover
enveloppe^F
Außenschicht^F
rivestimento^M esterno
forro^M

stitches
couture^F
Nähte^F
cucitura^F
costura^F

lace
lacet^M
Schnürband^N
stringa^F
cordón^M

softball

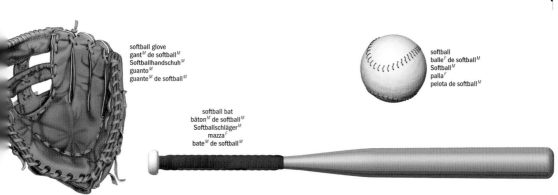

softball glove
gant^M de softball^M
Softballhandschuh^M
guanto^M
guante^M de softball^M

softball
balle^F de softball^M
Softball^M
palla^F
pelota de softball^M

softball bat
bâton^M de softball^M
Softballschläger^M
mazza^F
bate^M de softball^M

cricket

cricket^M | Cricket^N | cricket^M | cricket^M

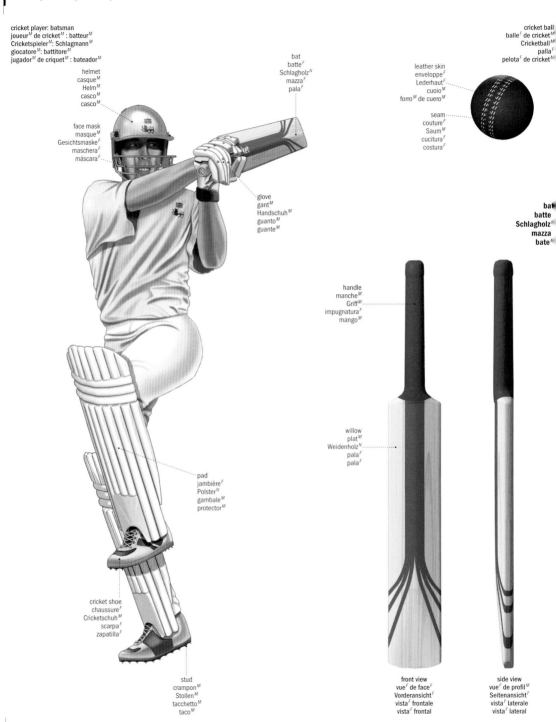

cricket player: batsman
joueur^M de cricket^M : batteur^M
Cricketspieler^M: Schlagmann^M
giocatore^M: battitore^M
jugador^M de críquet^M : bateador^M

helmet
casque^M
Helm^M
casco^M
casco^M

face mask
masque^M
Gesichtsmaske^F
maschera^F
máscara^F

bat
batte^F
Schlagholz^N
mazza^F
pala^F

glove
gant^M
Handschuh^M
guanto^M
guante^M

cricket ball
balle^F de cricket^M
Cricketball^M
palla^F
pelota^F de cricket^M

leather skin
enveloppe^F
Lederhaut^F
cuoio^M
forro^M de cuero^M

seam
couture^F
Saum^M
cucitura^F
costura^F

bat
batte
Schlagholz
mazza
bate

handle
manche^M
Griff^M
impugnatura^F
mango^M

willow
plat^M
Weidenholz^N
pala^F
pala^F

pad
jambière^F
Polster^N
gambale^M
protector^M

cricket shoe
chaussure^F
Cricketschuh^M
scarpa^F
zapatilla^F

stud
crampon^M
Stollen^M
tacchetto^M
taco^M

front view
vue^F de face^F
Vorderansicht^F
vista^F frontale
vista^F frontal

side view
vue^F de profil^M
Seitenansicht^F
vista^F laterale
vista^F lateral

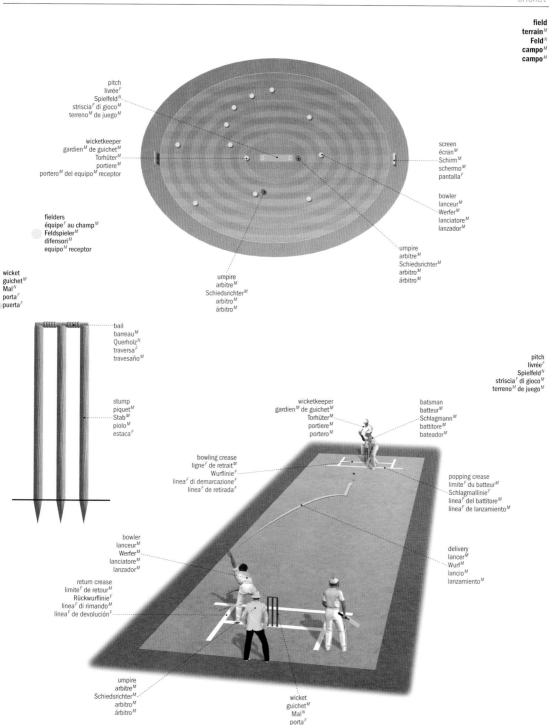

field
terrain^M
Feld^N
campo^M
campo^M

pitch
livrée^F
Spielfeld^N
striscia^F di gioco^M
terreno^M de juego^M

wicketkeeper
gardien^M de guichet^M
Torhüter^M
portiere^M
portero^M del equipo^M receptor

screen
écran^M
Schirm^M
schermo^M
pantalla^F

bowler
lanceur^M
Werfer^M
lanciatore^M
lanzador^M

umpire
arbitre^M
Schiedsrichter^M
arbitro^M
árbitro^M

fielders
équipe^F au champ^M
Feldspieler^M
difensori^M
equipo^M receptor

wicket
guichet^M
Mal^N
porta^F
puerta^F

umpire
arbitre^M
Schiedsrichter^M
arbitro^M
árbitro^M

bail
barreau^M
Querholz^N
traversa^F
travesaño^M

stump
piquet^M
Stab^M
piolo^M
estaca^F

pitch
livrée^F
Spielfeld^N
striscia^F di gioco^M
terreno^M de juego^M

wicketkeeper
gardien^M de guichet^M
Torhüter^M
portiere^M
portero^M

batsman
batteur^M
Schlagmann^M
battitore^M
bateador^M

bowling crease
ligne^F de retrait^M
Wurflinie^F
linea^F di demarcazione^F
línea^F de retirada^F

popping crease
limite^F du batteur^M
Schlagmallinie^F
linea^F del battitore^M
línea^F de lanzamiento^M

bowler
lanceur^M
Werfer^M
lanciatore^M
lanzador^M

delivery
lancer^M
Wurf^M
lancio^M
lanzamiento^M

return crease
limite^F de retour^M
Rückwurflinie^F
linea^F di rimando^M
línea^F de devolución^F

umpire
arbitre^M
Schiedsrichter^M
arbitro^M
árbitro^M

wicket
guichet^M
Mal^N
porta^F
puerta^F

association football

football[M] | Fußball[M] | calcio[M] | fútbol[M]

footballer
footballeur[M]
Fußballspieler[M]
calciatore[M]
futbolista[M/F]

team shirt
maillot[M] d'équipe[F]
Mannschaftstrikot[N]
maglia[F] della squadra[F]
camiseta[F] del equipo[M]

goalkeeper's gloves
gants[M] de gardien[M] de but[M]
Torwarthandschuhe[M]
guanti[M] del portiere[M]
guantes[M] del portero[M]

shorts
short[M]
Hose[F]
pantaloncini[M]
pantalones[M]

screw-in studs
crampons[M] interchangeables
Schraubstollen[M]
tacchetti[M] intercambiabili
tacos[M] de rosca[F]

football boot
chaussure[F] de football[M]
Fußballschuh[M]
scarpa[F]
bota[F] de fútbol[M]

shin guard
protège-tibia[M]
Schienbeinschützer[M]
parastinchi[M]
espinillera[F]

sock
chaussette[F]
Socken[M]
calzettone[M]
calcetín[M]

football
ballon[M] de football[M]
Fußball[M]
pallone[M]
balón[M] de fútbol[M]

playing field
terrain[M]
Spielfeld[N]
campo[M] di gioco[M]
campo[M]

centre flag
drapeau[M] de centre[M]
Mittelfahne[F]
bandierina[F] centrale
banderín[M] de línea[F] de centro[M]

penalty spot
point[M] de réparation[F]
Elfmeterpunkt[M]
dischetto[M] del rigore[M]
punto[M] de penalti[M]

goal area
surface[F] de but[M]
Torraum[M]
area[F] di porta[F]
área[F] pequeña

goal
but[N]
Tor[N]
porta[F]
portería[F]

penalty area
surface[F] de réparation[F]
Strafraum[M]
area[F] di rigore[M]
área[F] de penalti[M]

penalty area marking
ligne[F] de surface[F] de réparation[F]
Strafraumlinie[F]
linea[F] dell'area[F] di rigore[M]
línea[F] de área[F] de penalti[M]

penalty arc
arc[M] de cercle[M]
Strafraumbogen[M]
lunetta[F]
semicírculo[M] del área[F]

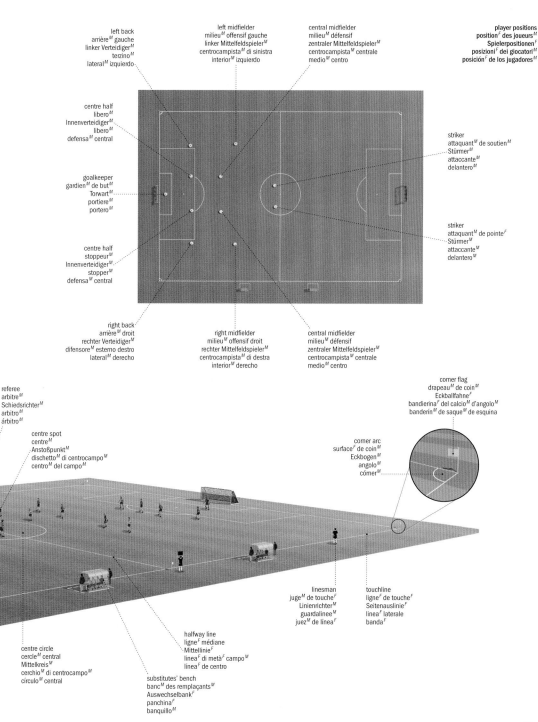

left back
arrière^M gauche
linker Verteidiger^M
terzino^M
lateral^M izquierdo

left midfielder
milieu^M offensif gauche
linker Mittelfeldspieler^M
centrocampista^M di sinistra
interior^M izquierdo

central midfielder
milieu^M défensif
zentraler Mittelfeldspieler^M
centrocampista^M centrale
medio^M centro

player positions
position^F des joueurs^M
Spielerpositionen^F
posizioni^F dei giocatori^M
posición^F de los jugadores^M

centre half
libero^M
Innenverteidiger^M
libero^M
defensa^M central

striker
attaquant^M de soutien^M
Stürmer^M
attaccante^M
delantero^M

goalkeeper
gardien^M de but^M
Torwart^M
portiere^M
portero^M

striker
attaquant^M de pointe^F
Stürmer^M
attaccante^M
delantero^M

centre half
stoppeur^M
Innenverteidiger^M
stopper^M
defensa^M central

right back
arrière^M droit
rechter Verteidiger^M
difensore^M esterno destro
lateral^M derecho

right midfielder
milieu^M offensif droit
rechter Mittelfeldspieler^M
centrocampista^M di destra
interior^M derecho

central midfielder
milieu^M défensif
zentraler Mittelfeldspieler^M
centrocampista^M centrale
medio^M centro

referee
arbitre^M
Schiedsrichter^M
arbitro^M
árbitro^M

corner flag
drapeau^M de coin^M
Eckballfahne^F
bandierina^F del calcio^M d'angolo^M
banderín^M de saque^M de esquina

centre spot
centre^M
Anstoßpunkt^M
dischetto^M di centrocampo^M
centro^M del campo^M

corner arc
surface^F de coin^M
Eckbogen^M
angolo^M
córner^M

linesman
juge^M de touche^F
Linienrichter^M
guardalinee^M
juez^M de línea^F

touchline
ligne^F de touche^F
Seitenauslinie^F
linea^F laterale
banda^F

halfway line
ligne^F médiane
Mittellinie^F
linea^F di metà^F campo^M
línea^F de centro

centre circle
cercle^M central
Mittelkreis^M
cerchio^M di centrocampo^M
círculo^M central

substitutes' bench
banc^M des remplaçants^M
Auswechselbank^F
panchina^F
banquillo^M

SPORTS AND GAMES

481

rugby

rugby^M | Rugby^N | rugby^M | rugby^M

player positions
position^F des joueurs^M
Spielerpositionen^F
posizioni^F dei giocatori^M
posición^F de los jugadores^M

right centre
centre^M droit
rechter Centre^M
trequarti^M centrodestro
centro^M derecho

full back
arrière^M
Fullback^M
estremo^M
zaguero^M

left centre
centre^M gauche
linker Centre^M
trequarti^M centrosinistro
centro^M izquierdo

fly half
demi^M d'ouverture^F
Fly-Half^M
mediano^M di apertura^F
medio^M de apertura

scrum half
demi^M de mêlée^F
Gedrängehalbspieler^M
mediano^M di mischia^F
medio de melé^M

right wing
ailier^M droit
Right-Wing^M
seconda linea^F destra
ala^M derecho

left wing
ailier^M gauche
Left-Wing^M
seconda linea^F sinistra
ala^M izquierdo

flank forward
aile^F droite
Außenstürmer^M rechts
ala^F destra
tercera linea derecho^M

no. 8 forward
centre^M
Nummer-8-Forward^M
n. 8 avanti^M
delantero^M número 8

third row
troisième ligne^F
dritte Reihe^F
terza linea^F
tercera linea^F

flank forward
aile^F gauche
Außenstürmer^M links
ala^F sinistra
tercera linea izquierdo^M

second row
deuxième ligne^F
zweite Reihe^F
seconda linea^F
segunda linea^F

lock forward
avant^M gauche
Zweite-Reihe-Stürmer^M links
avanti^M
delantero^M izquierdo

first row
première ligne^F
erste Reihe^F
prima linea^F
primera linea^F

tight head prop
pilier^M droit
Außendreiviertel^M rechts
pilone^M destro
pilar^M derecho

loose head prop
pilier^M gauche
Außendreiviertel^M links
pilone^M sinistro
pilar^M izquierdo

field
terrain^M
Spielfeld^N
campo^M
campo^M de juego^M

lock forward
avant^M droit
Zweite-Reihe-Stürmer^M rechts
avanti^M
delantero^M derecho

hooker
talonneur^M
Hakler^M
tallonatore^M
taloneador^M

10 m line
ligne^F des 10 m
10-m-Linie^F
linea^F dei 10 metri^M
línea^F de 10 m

flag
drapeau^M
Fahne^F
bandierina^F
bandera^F

goal line
ligne^F de but^M
Torlinie^F
linea^F di meta^F
línea^F de marca^F

goal
but^M
Tor^N
porta^F
palos^M

dead ball line
ligne^F de ballon^M mort
Auslinie^F
linea^F di pallone^M morto
línea^F de fondo^M

22 m line
ligne^F des 22 m
22-m-Linie^F
linea^F dei 22 metri^M
línea^F de 22 m

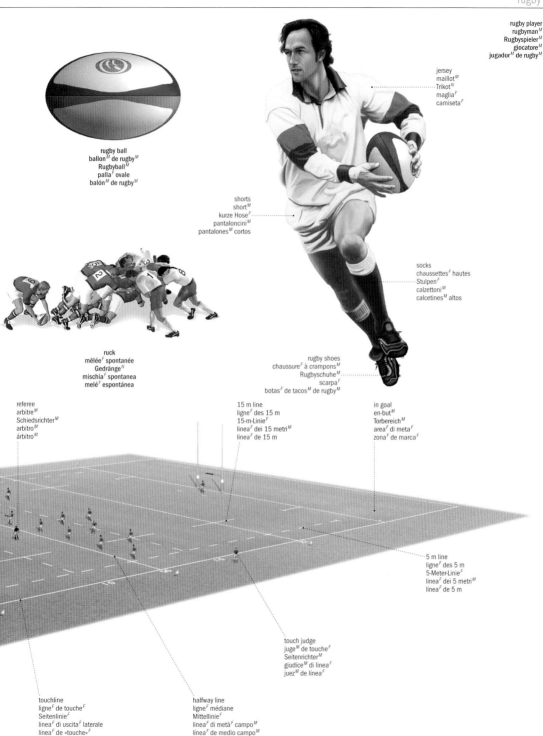

rugby player
rugbyman[M]
Rugbyspieler[M]
giocatore[M]
jugador[M] de rugby[M]

jersey
maillot[M]
Trikot[N]
maglia[F]
camiseta[F]

rugby ball
ballon[M] de rugby[M]
Rugbyball[M]
palla[F] ovale
balón[M] de rugby[M]

shorts
short[M]
kurze Hose[F]
pantaloncini[M]
pantalones[M] cortos

socks
chaussettes[F] hautes
Stulpen[F]
calzettoni[M]
calcetines[M] altos

ruck
mêlée[F] spontanée
Gedränge[N]
mischia[F] spontanea
melé[F] espontánea

rugby shoes
chaussure[F] à crampons[M]
Rugbyschuhe[M]
scarpa[F]
botas[F] de tacos[M] de rugby[M]

referee
arbitre[M]
Schiedsrichter[M]
arbitro[M]
árbitro[M]

15 m line
ligne[F] des 15 m
15-m-Linie[F]
linea[F] dei 15 metri[M]
línea[F] de 15 m

in goal
en-but[M]
Torbereich[M]
area[F] di meta[F]
zona[F] de marca[F]

5 m line
ligne[F] des 5 m
5-Meter-Linie[F]
linea[F] dei 5 metri[M]
línea[F] de 5 m

touch judge
juge[M] de touche[F]
Seitenrichter[M]
giudice[M] di linea[F]
juez[M] de línea[F]

touchline
ligne[F] de touche[F]
Seitenlinie[F]
linea[F] di uscita[F] laterale
línea[F] de «touche»[F]

halfway line
ligne[F] médiane
Mittellinie[F]
linea[F] di metà[F] campo[M]
línea[F] de medio campo[M]

American football

football^M américain | American Football^M | football^M americano | fútbol^M americano

scrimmage: defence
mêlée^F : défense^F
Gedränge^N: Verteidigung^F
mischia^F: difesa^F
melé^F: defensa^F

right defensive end
ailier^M défensif droit
rechter Defensive End^M
difensore^M ala^F destra
ala^M defensivo derecho

right cornerback
demi^M de coin^M droit
rechter Corner Back^M
terzino^M di destra
esquinero^M derecho

right defensive tackle
plaqueur^M droit
rechter Defensive Tackle^M
placcatore^M destro
tackle^M defensivo derecho

outside linebacker
secondeur^M extérieur droit
äußerer Linebacker^M
linebacker^M esterno
apoyador^M exterior

right safety
demi^M de sûreté^F droit
rechter Safety^M
estremo^M di destra
safety^M débil

left defensive tackle
plaqueur^M gauche
linker Defensive Tackle^M
placcatore^M sinistro
tackle^M defensivo izquierdo

middle linebacker
secondeur^M intérieur
mittlerer Linebacker^M
linebacker^M centrale
apoyador^M

inside linebacker
secondeur^M extérieur gauche
Middle Linebacker^M
linebacker^M interno
apoyador^M interior

left defensive end
ailier^M défensif gauche
linker Defensive End^M
difensore^M ala^F sinistra
ala^M defensivo izquierdo

neutral zone
zone^F neutre
neutrale Zone^F
zona^F neutra
zona^F neutral

left cornerback
demi^M de coin^M gauche
linker Corner Back^M
terzino^M di sinistra
esquinero^M izquierdo

left safety
demi^M de sûreté^F gauche
linker Safety^M
estremo^M di sinistra
safety^M fuerte

playing field for American football
terrain^M de football^M américain
Spielfeld^N für American Football^M
campo^M
campo^M de juego^M de fútbol^M americano

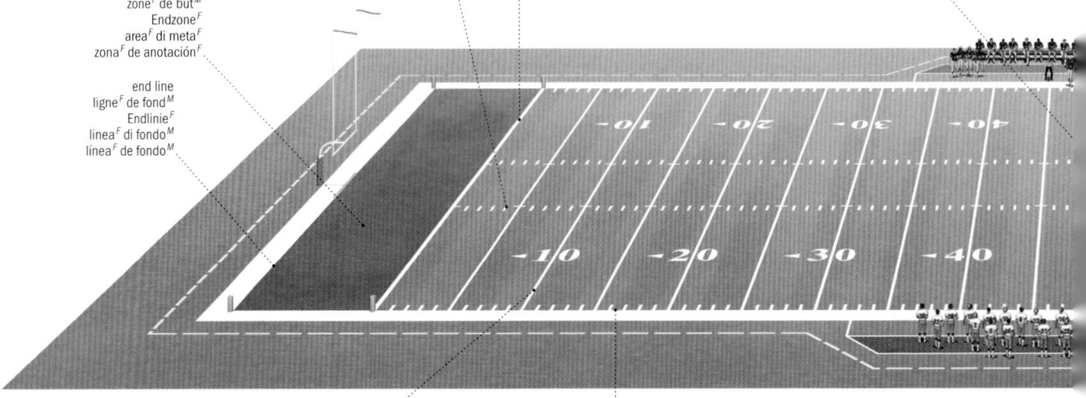

inbound line
trait^M de mise^F au jeu^M
Inbound-Linie^F
linea^F di messa^F in gioco^M
línea^F límite^M de inicio^M de jugada^F

goal line
ligne^F de but^M
Torlinie^F
linea^F di meta^F
línea^F de gol^M

centre line
ligne^F de centre^M
Mittellinie^F
linea^F di centrocampo^M
línea^F media

end zone
zone^F de but^M
Endzone^F
area^F di meta^F
zona^F de anotación^F

end line
ligne^F de fond^M
Endlinie^F
linea^F di fondo^M
línea^F de fondo^M

yard line
ligne^F des verges^F
Yardlinie^F
linea^F delle yards^F
línea^F yardas^F

sideline
ligne^F de touche^F
Seitenlinie^F
linea^F laterale
banda^F

484

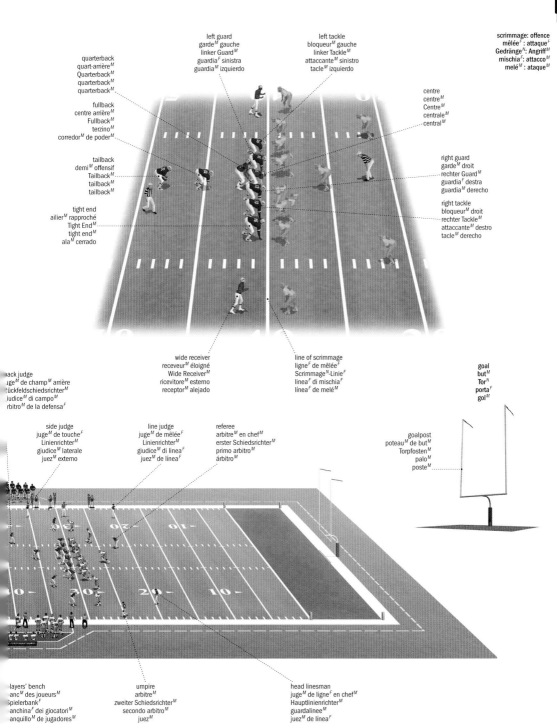

scrimmage: offence
mêlée^F : attaque^F
Gedränge^N: Angriff^M
mischia^F: attacco^M
melé^M : ataque^M

left guard
garde^M gauche
linker Guard^M
guardia^F sinistra
guardia^M izquierdo

left tackle
bloqueur^M gauche
linker Tackle^M
attaccante^M sinistro
tacle^M izquierdo

quarterback
quart-arrière^M
Quarterback^M
quarterback^M
quarterback^M

centre
centre^M
Centre^M
centrale^M
central^M

fullback
centre arrière^M
Fullback^M
terzino^M
corredor^M de poder^M

right guard
garde^M droit
rechter Guard^M
guardia^F destra
guardia^M derecho

tailback
demi^M offensif
Tailback^M
tailback^M
tailback^M

right tackle
bloqueur^M droit
rechter Tackle^M
attaccante^M destro
tacle^M derecho

tight end
ailier^M rapproché
Tight End^M
tight end^M
ala^M cerrado

back judge
juge^M de champ^M arrière
Rückfeldschiedsrichter^M
giudice^M di campo^M
arbitro^M de la defensa^F

wide receiver
receveur^M éloigné
Wide Receiver^M
ricevitore^M esterno
receptor^M alejado

line of scrimmage
ligne^F de mêlée^F
Scrimmage^N-Linie^F
linea^F di mischia^F
línea^F de melé^M

goal
but^M
Tor^N
porta^F
gol^M

side judge
juge^M de touche^F
Linienrichter^M
giudice^M laterale
juez^M externo

line judge
juge^M de mêlée^F
Linienrichter^M
giudice^M di linea^F
juez^M de línea^F

referee
arbitre^M en chef^M
erster Schiedsrichter^M
primo arbitro^M
árbitro^M

goalpost
poteau^M de but^M
Torpfosten^M
palo^M
poste^M

players' bench
banc^M des joueurs^M
Spielerbank^F
panchina^F dei giocatori^M
banquillo^M de jugadores^M

umpire
arbitre^M
zweiter Schiedsrichter^M
secondo arbitro^M
juez^M

head linesman
juge^M de ligne^F en chef^M
Hauptlinienrichter^M
guardalinee^M
juez^M de línea^F

SPORTS AND GAMES

485

American football

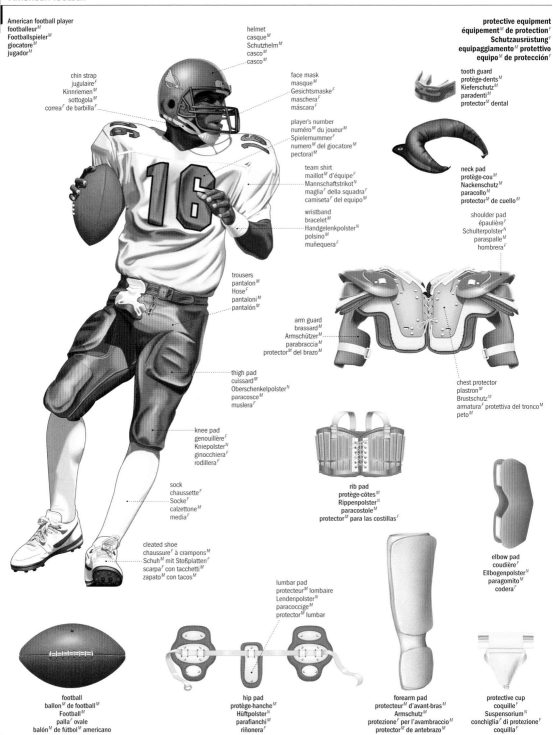

American football player
footballeur[M]
Footballspieler[M]
giocatore[M]
jugador[M]

chin strap
jugulaire[F]
Kinnriemen[M]
sottogola[M]
correa[F] de barbilla[F]

helmet
casque[M]
Schutzhelm[M]
casco[M]
casco[M]

face mask
masque[M]
Gesichtsmaske[F]
maschera[F]
máscara[F]

player's number
numéro[M] du joueur[M]
Spielernummer[F]
numero[M] del giocatore[M]
pectoral[M]

team shirt
maillot[M] d'équipe[F]
Mannschaftstrikot[N]
maglia[F] della squadra[F]
camiseta[F] del equipo[M]

wristband
bracelet[M]
Handgelenkpolster[N]
polsino[M]
muñequera[F]

trousers
pantalon[M]
Hose[F]
pantaloni[M]
pantalón[M]

arm guard
brassard[M]
Armschützer[M]
parabraccia[M]
protector[M] del brazo[M]

thigh pad
cuissard[M]
Oberschenkelpolster[N]
paracosce[M]
muslera[F]

knee pad
genouillère[F]
Kniepolster[N]
ginocchiera[F]
rodillera[F]

sock
chaussette[F]
Socke[F]
calzettone[M]
media[F]

cleated shoe
chaussure[F] à crampons[M]
Schuh[M] mit Stoßplatten[F]
scarpa[F] con tacchetti[M]
zapato[M] con tacos[M]

protective equipment
équipement[M] de protection[F]
Schutzausrüstung[F]
equipaggiamento[M] protettivo
equipo[M] de protección[F]

tooth guard
protège-dents[M]
Kieferschutz[M]
paradenti[M]
protector[M] dental

neck pad
protège-cou[M]
Nackenschutz[M]
paracollo[M]
protector[M] de cuello[M]

shoulder pad
épaulière[F]
Schulterpolster[N]
paraspalle[M]
hombrera[F]

chest protector
plastron[M]
Brustschutz[M]
armatura[F] protettiva del tronco[M]
peto[M]

rib pad
protège-côtes[M]
Rippenpolster[N]
paracostole[M]
protector[M] para las costillas[F]

elbow pad
coudière[F]
Ellbogenpolster[N]
paragomito[M]
codera[F]

lumbar pad
protecteur[M] lombaire
Lendenpolster[N]
paracoccige[M]
protector[M] lumbar

football
ballon[M] de football[M]
Football[M]
palla[F] ovale
balón[M] de fútbol[M] americano

hip pad
protège-hanche[M]
Hüftpolster[N]
parafianchi[M]
riñonera[F]

forearm pad
protecteur[M] d'avant-bras[M]
Armschutz[M]
protezione[F] per l'avambraccio[M]
protector[M] de antebrazo[M]

protective cup
coquille[F]
Suspensorium[N]
conchiglia[F] di protezione[F]
coquilla[F]

SPORTS AND GAMES

volleyball

volleyball[M] | Volleyballspiel[N] | pallavolo[F] | voleibol[M]

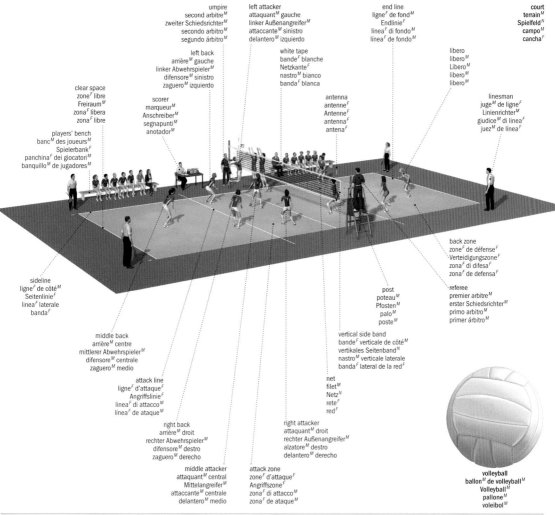

umpire
second arbitre[M]
zweiter Schiedsrichter[M]
secondo arbitro[M]
segundo árbitro[M]

left attacker
attaquant[M] gauche
linker Außenangreifer[M]
attaccante[M] sinistro
delantero[M] izquierdo

end line
ligne[F] de fond[M]
Endlinie[F]
linea[F] di fondo[M]
línea[F] de fondo[M]

court
terrain[M]
Spielfeld[N]
campo[M]
cancha[F]

left back
arrière[M] gauche
linker Abwehrspieler[M]
difensore[M] sinistro
zaguero[M] izquierdo

white tape
bande[F] blanche
Netzkante[F]
nastro[M] bianco
banda[F] blanca

libero
libero[M]
Libero[M]
libero[M]
libero[M]

clear space
zone[F] libre
Freiraum[M]
zona[F] libera
zona[F] libre

antenna
antenne[F]
Antenne[F]
antenna[F]
antena[F]

linesman
juge[M] de ligne[F]
Linienrichter[M]
giudice[M] di linea[F]
juez[M] de línea[F]

scorer
marqueur[M]
Anschreiber[M]
segnapunti[M]
anotador[M]

players' bench
banc[M] des joueurs[M]
Spielerbank[F]
panchina[F] dei giocatori[M]
banquillo[M] de jugadores[M]

back zone
zone[F] de défense[F]
Verteidigungszone[F]
zona[F] di difesa[F]
zona[F] de defensa[F]

sideline
ligne[F] de côté[M]
Seitenlinie[F]
linea[F] laterale
banda[F]

post
poteau[M]
Pfosten[M]
palo[M]
poste[M]

referee
premier arbitre[M]
erster Schiedsrichter[M]
primo arbitro[M]
primer árbitro[M]

middle back
arrière[M] centre
mittlerer Abwehrspieler[M]
difensore[M] centrale
zaguero[M] medio

vertical side band
bande[F] verticale de côté[M]
vertikales Seitenband[N]
nastro[M] verticale laterale
banda[F] lateral de la red[F]

attack line
ligne[F] d'attaque[F]
Angriffslinie[F]
linea[F] di attacco[M]
línea[F] de ataque[M]

net
filet[M]
Netz[N]
rete[F]
red[F]

right back
arrière[M] droit
rechter Abwehrspieler[M]
difensore[M] destro
zaguero[M] derecho

right attacker
attaquant[M] droit
rechter Außenangreifer[M]
alzatore[M] destro
delantero[M] derecho

middle attacker
attaquant[M] central
Mittelangreifer[M]
attaccante[M] centrale
delantero[M] medio

attack zone
zone[F] d'attaque[F]
Angriffszone[F]
zona[F] di attacco[M]
zona[F] de ataque[M]

volleyball
ballon[M] de volleyball[M]
Volleyball[M]
pallone[M]
voleibol[M]

techniques
techniques[F]
Techniken[F]
tecniche[F]
técnicas[F]

tip
touche[F]
pritschen
palleggio[M]
toque[M]

bump
manchette[F]
baggern
bagher[M]
rebote[M]

serve
service[M]
Aufschlag[M]
servizio[M]
saque[M]

basketball

basketball[M] | Basketballspiel[N] | pallacanestro[F] | baloncesto[M]

basketball player
joueur[M] de basketball[M]
Basketballspieler[M]
giocatore[M]
jugador[M] de baloncesto[M]

shirt
maillot[M]
Trikot[N]
maglia[F]
camiseta[F]

basketball
ballon[M] de basket[M]
Basketball[M]
pallone[M]
balón[M] de baloncesto[M]

player's number
numéro[M] du joueur[M]
Spielernummer[F]
numero[M] del giocatore[M]
número[M] del jugador[M]

shorts
short[M]
kurze Hose[F]
pantaloncini[M]
pantalones[M] cortos

shoe
chaussure[F]
Schuh[M]
scarpa[F]
zapatilla[F]

scorer
marqueur[M]
Anschreiber[M]
segnapunti[M]
anotador[M]

court
terrain[M]
Spielfeld[N]
campo[M]
cancha[F]

clock operator
chronométreur[M] des trente secondes[F]
Uhrenmeister[M]
addetto[M] ai 24 secondi[M]
operador[M] del reloj[M] de 30 segundos[M]

timekeeper
chronométreur[M]
Zeitnehmer[M]
cronometrista[M]
cronometrador[M]

referee
aide[M]-arbitre[M]
Schiedsrichter[M]
arbitro[M]
árbitro[M]

referee
arbitre[M]
Schiedsrichter[M]
arbitro[M]
árbitro[M]

sideline
ligne[F] de touche[F]
Seitenlinie[F]
linea[F] laterale
banda[F]

semi-circle
demi-cercle[M]
Halbkreis[M]
lunetta[F]
semicírculo[M] de la zona[F] de tiro[M] libre

restricting circle
cercle[M] restrictif
Mittelkreis[M]
cerchio[M] di centrocampo[M]
círculo[M] central

centre line
ligne[F] médiane
Mittellinie[F]
linea[F] di centrocampo[M]
línea[F] media

centre circle
cercle[M] central
Mittelkreis[M]
cerchio[M] centrale
círculo[M] central

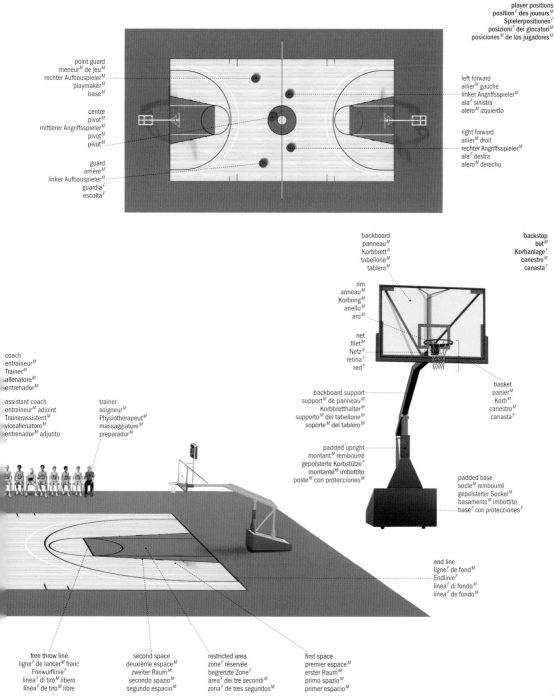

player positions
position^F des joueurs^M
Spielerpositionen^F
posizioni^F dei giocatori^M
posiciones^M de los jugadores^M

point guard
meneur^M de jeu^M
rechter Aufbauspieler^M
playmaker^M
base^M

left forward
ailier^M gauche
linker Angriffsspieler^M
ala^F sinistra
alero^M izquierdo

centre
pivot^M
mittlerer Angriffsspieler^M
pivot^M
pívot^M

right forward
ailier^M droit
rechter Angriffsspieler^M
ala^F destra
alero^M derecho

guard
arrière^F
linker Aufbauspieler^M
guardia^F
escolta^F

backboard
panneau^M
Korbbrett^N
tabellone^M
tablero^M

backstop
but^M
Korbanlage^F
canestro^M
canasta^F

rim
anneau^M
Korbring^M
anello^M
aro^M

net
filet^M
Netz^N
retina^F
red^F

basket
panier^M
Korb^M
canestro^M
canasta^F

coach
entraineur^M
Trainer^M
allenatore^M
entrenador^M

assistant coach
entraineur^M adjoint
Trainerassistent^M
viceallenatore^M
entrenador^M adjunto

trainer
soigneur^M
Physiotherapeut^M
massaggiatore^M
preparador^M

backboard support
support^M de panneau^M
Korbbretthalter^M
supporto^M del tabellone^M
soporte^M del tablero^M

padded upright
montant^M rembourré
gepolsterte Korbstütze^F
montante^M imbottito
poste^M con protecciones^M

padded base
socle^M rembourré
gepolsterter Sockel^M
basamento^M imbottito
base^F con protecciones^F

end line
ligne^F de fond^M
Endlinie^F
linea^F di fondo^M
linea^F de fondo^M

free throw line
ligne^F de lancer^M franc
Freiwurflinie^F
linea^F di tiro^M libero
línea^F de tiro^M libre

second space
deuxième espace^M
zweiter Raum^M
secondo spazio^M
segundo espacio^M

restricted area
zone^F réservée
begrenzte Zone^F
area^F dei tre secondi^M
zona^F de tres segundos^M

first space
premier espace^M
erster Raum^M
primo spazio^M
primer espacio^M

SPORTS AND GAMES

tennis

tennis^M | Tennis^N | tennis^M | tenis^M

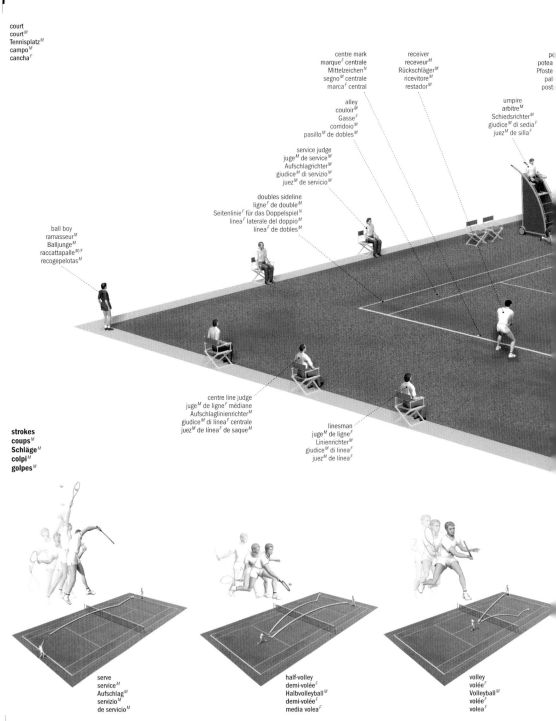

court
court^M
Tennisplatz^M
campo^M
cancha^F

centre mark
marque^F centrale
Mittelzeichen^N
segno^M centrale
marca^F central

receiver
receveur^M
Rückschläger^M
ricevitore^M
restador^M

p(
potea
Pfoste
pal
post

alley
couloir^M
Gasse^F
corridoio^M
pasillo^M de dobles^M

umpire
arbitre^M
Schiedsrichter^M
giudice^M di sedia^F
juez^M de silla^F

service judge
juge^M de service^M
Aufschlagrichter^M
giudice^M di servizio^M
juez^M de servicio^M

doubles sideline
ligne^F de double^M
Seitenlinie^F für das Doppelspiel^N
linea^F laterale del doppio^M
línea^F de dobles^M

ball boy
ramasseur^M
Balljunge^M
raccattapalle^{M/F}
recogepelotas^M

centre line judge
juge^M de ligne^F médiane
Aufschlaglinienrichter^M
giudice^M di linea^F centrale
juez^M de línea^F de saque^M

linesman
juge^M de ligne^F
Linienrichter^M
giudice^M di linea^F
juez^M de línea^F

strokes
coups^M
Schläge^M
colpi^M
golpes^M

serve
service^M
Aufschlag^M
servizio^M
de servicio^M

half-volley
demi-volée^F
Halbvolleyball^M
demi-volée^F
media volea^F

volley
volée^F
Volleyball^M
volée^F
volea^F

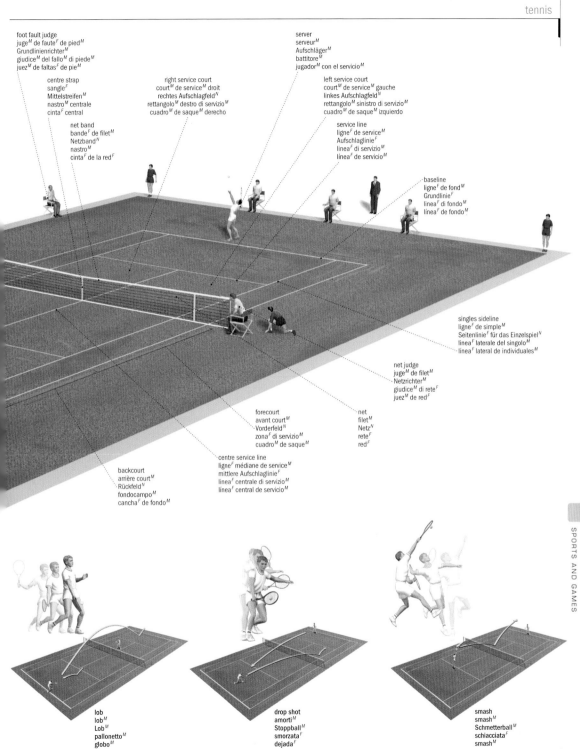

foot fault judge
juge^M de faute^F de pied^M
Grundlinienrichter^M
giudice^M del fallo^M di piede^M
juez^M de faltas^F de pie^M

server
serveur^M
Aufschläger^M
battitore^M
jugador^M con el servicio^M

centre strap
sangle^F
Mittelstreifen^M
nastro^M centrale
cinta^F central

right service court
court^M de service^M droit
rechtes Aufschlagfeld^N
rettangolo^M destro di servizio^M
cuadro^M de saque^M derecho

left service court
court^M de service^M gauche
linkes Aufschlagfeld^N
rettangolo^M sinistro di servizio^M
cuadro^M de saque^M izquierdo

net band
bande^F de filet^M
Netzband^N
nastro^M
cinta^F de la red^F

service line
ligne^F de service^M
Aufschlaglinie^F
linea^F di servizio^M
línea^F de servicio^M

baseline
ligne^F de fond^M
Grundlinie^F
linea^F di fondo^M
línea^F de fondo^M

singles sideline
ligne^F de simple^M
Seitenlinie^F für das Einzelspiel^N
linea^F laterale del singolo^M
línea^F lateral de individuales^M

net judge
juge^M de filet^M
Netzrichter^M
giudice^M di rete^F
juez^M de red^F

forecourt
avant court^M
Vorderfeld^N
zona^F di servizio^M
cuadro^M de saque^M

net
filet^M
Netz^N
rete^F
red^F

backcourt
arrière court^M
Rückfeld^N
fondocampo^M
cancha^F de fondo^M

centre service line
ligne^F médiane de service^M
mittlere Aufschlaglinie^F
linea^F centrale di servizio^M
línea^F central de servicio^M

lob
lob^M
Lob^M
pallonetto^M
globo^M

drop shot
amorti^M
Stoppball^M
smorzata^F
dejada^F

smash
smash^M
Schmetterball^M
schiacciata^F
smash^M

tennis

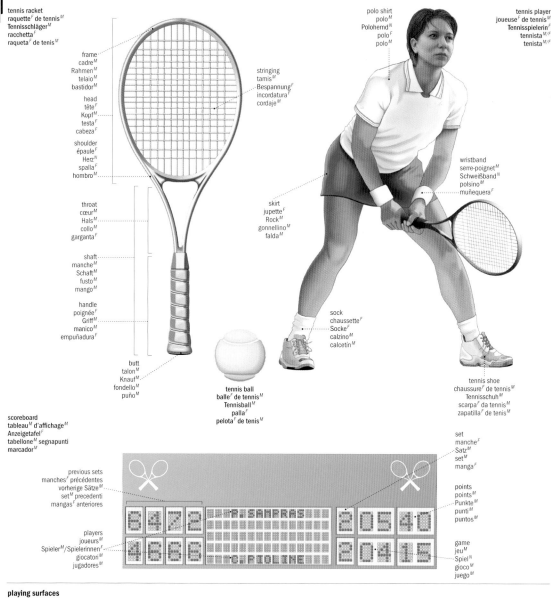

tennis racket
raquette^F de tennis^M
Tennisschläger^M
racchetta^F
raqueta^F de tenis^M

frame
cadre^M
Rahmen^M
telaio^M
bastidor^M

head
tête^F
Kopf^M
testa^F
cabeza^F

shoulder
épaule^F
Herz^N
spalla^F
hombro^M

throat
cœur^M
Hals^M
collo^M
garganta^F

shaft
manche^M
Schaft^M
fusto^M
mango^M

handle
poignée^F
Griff^M
manico^M
empuñadura^F

butt
talon^M
Knauf^M
fondello^M
puño^M

stringing
tamis^M
Bespannung^F
incordatura^F
cordaje^M

polo shirt
polo^M
Polohemd^N
polo^F
polo^M

tennis player
joueuse^F de tennis^M
Tennisspielerin^F
tennista^{M/F}
tenista^{M/F}

wristband
serre-poignet^M
Schweißband^N
polsino^M
muñequera^F

skirt
jupette^F
Rock^M
gonnellino^M
falda^M

sock
chaussette^F
Socke^F
calzino^M
calcetín^M

tennis ball
balle^F de tennis^M
Tennisball^M
palla^F
pelota^F de tenis^M

tennis shoe
chaussure^F de tennis^M
Tennisschuh^M
scarpa^F da tennis^M
zapatilla^F de tenis^M

scoreboard
tableau^M d'affichage^M
Anzeigetafel^F
tabellone^M segnapunti
marcador^M

set
manche^F
Satz^M
set^M
manga^F

previous sets
manches^F précédentes
vorherige Sätze^M
set^M precedenti
mangas^F anteriores

points
points^M
Punkte^M
punti^M
puntos^M

players
joueurs^M
Spieler^M/Spielerinnen^F
giocatori^M
jugadores^M

game
jeu^M
Spiel^N
gioco^M
juego^M

playing surfaces
surfaces^F de jeu^M
Spielfeldbeläge^M
superfici^F di gioco^M
superficies^F de juego^M

grass
gazon^M
Rasen^M
erba^F
hierba^F

clay
terre^F battue
Sand^M
terra^F battuta
tierra^F batida

hard surface (cement)
surface^F dure (ciment^M)
Hartplatz^M (Zement^M)
superficie^F dura (cemento^M)
superficie^F dura (cemento^M)

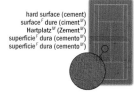

synthetic surface
revêtement^M synthétique
Kunststoffboden^M
superficie^F sintetica
superficie^F sintética

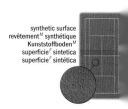

table tennis

tennis^M de table^F | Tischtennis^N | tennis^M da tavolo^M | tenis^M de mesa^F

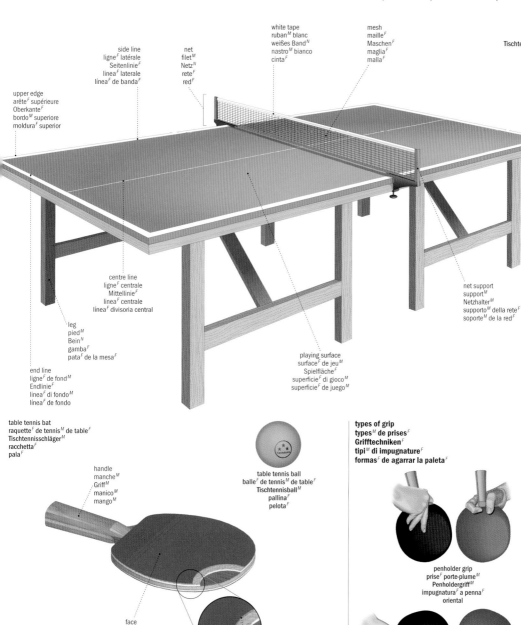

side line
ligne^F latérale
Seitenlinie^F
linea^F laterale
línea^F de banda^F

net
filet^M
Netz^N
rete^F
red^F

white tape
ruban^M blanc
weißes Band^N
nastro^M bianco
cinta^F

mesh
maille^F
Maschen^F
maglia^F
malla^F

table
table^F
Tischtennisplatte^F
tavolo^M
mesa^F

upper edge
arête^F supérieure
Oberkante^F
bordo^M superiore
moldura^F superior

centre line
ligne^F centrale
Mittellinie^F
linea^F centrale
línea^F divisoria central

net support
support^M
Netzhalter^M
supporto^M della rete^F
soporte^M de la red^F

leg
pied^M
Bein^N
gamba^F
pata^F de la mesa^F

playing surface
surface^F de jeu^M
Spielfläche^F
superficie^F di gioco^M
superficie^F de juego^M

end line
ligne^F de fond^M
Endlinie^F
linea^F di fondo^M
línea^F de fondo

table tennis bat
raquette^F de tennis^M de table^F
Tischtennisschläger^M
racchetta^F
pala^F

handle
manche^M
Griff^M
manico^M
mango^M

table tennis ball
balle^F de tennis^M de table^F
Tischtennisball^M
pallina^F
pelota^F

types of grip
types^M de prises^F
Grifftechniken^F
tipi^M di impugnature^F
formas^F de agarrar la paleta^F

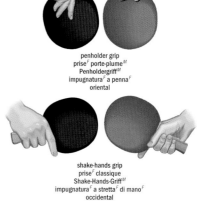

penholder grip
prise^F porte-plume^M
Penholdergriff^M
impugnatura^F a penna^F
oriental

face
face^F
Oberfläche^F
faccia^F
cara^F

blade
palette^F
Blatt^N
fusto^M
paleta^F

covering
revêtement^M
Beschichtung^F
rivestimento^M
revestimiento^M

shake-hands grip
prise^F classique
Shake-Hands-Griff^M
impugnatura^F a stretta^F di mano^F
occidental

badminton

badminton^M | Badminton^N | gioco^M del volano^M | bádminton^M

court
terrain^M
Badmintonplatz^M
campo^M
cancha^F

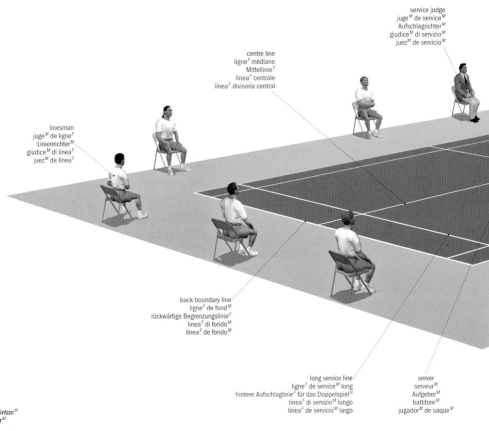

service judge
juge^M de service^M
Aufschlagrichter^M
giudice^M di servizio^M
juez^M de servicio^M

centre line
ligne^F médiane
Mittellinie^F
linea^F centrale
línea^F divisoria central

linesman
juge^M de ligne^F
Linienrichter^M
giudice^M di linea^F
juez^M de línea^F

back boundary line
ligne^F de fond^M
rückwärtige Begrenzungslinie^F
linea^F di fondo^M
línea^F de fondo^M

long service line
ligne^F de service^M long
hintere Aufschlaglinie^F für das Doppelspiel^N
linea^F di servizio^M lungo
línea^F de servicio^M largo

server
serveur^M
Aufgeber^M
battitore^M
jugador^M de saque^M

badminton racket
raquette^F de badminton^M
Badmintonschläger^M
racchetta^F
raqueta^F de bádminton^M

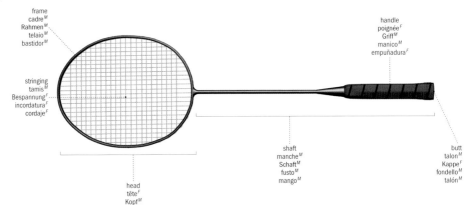

frame
cadre^M
Rahmen^M
telaio^M
bastidor^M

handle
poignée^F
Griff^M
manico^M
empuñadura^F

stringing
tamis^M
Bespannung^F
incordatura^F
cordaje^F

shaft
manche^M
Schaft^M
fusto^M
mango^M

butt
talon^M
Kappe^F
fondello^M
talón^M

head
tête^F
Kopf^M
testa^F
cabeza^F

SPORTS AND GAMES

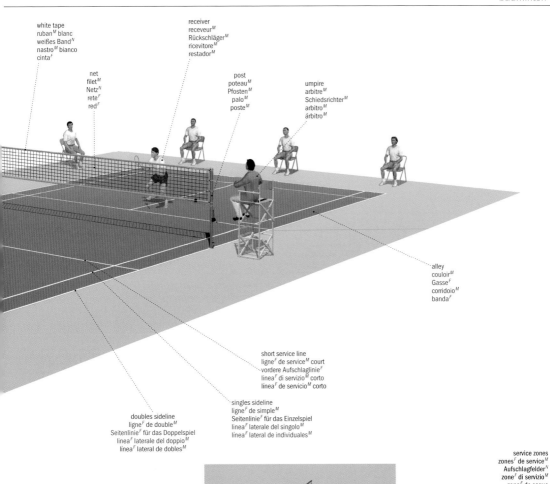

white tape
ruban^M blanc
weißes Band^N
nastro^M bianco
cinta^F

receiver
receveur^M
Rückschläger^M
ricevitore^M
restador^M

net
filet^M
Netz^N
rete^F
red^F

post
poteau^M
Pfosten^M
palo^M
poste^M

umpire
arbitre^M
Schiedsrichter^M
arbitro^M
árbitro^M

alley
couloir^M
Gasse^F
corridoio^M
banda^F

short service line
ligne^F de service^M court
vordere Aufschlaglinie^F
linea^F di servizio^M corto
línea^F de servicio^M corto

singles sideline
ligne^F de simple^M
Seitenlinie^F für das Einzelspiel
linea^F laterale del singolo^M
línea^F lateral de individuales^M

doubles sideline
ligne^F de double^M
Seitenlinie^F für das Doppelspiel
linea^F laterale del doppio^M
línea^F lateral de dobles^M

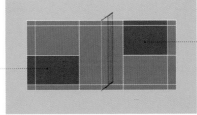

service zones
zones^F de service^M
Aufschlagfelder^N
zone^F di servizio^M
zona^F de saque

singles service court
demi-court^M de service^M en simple^M
Aufschlagfeld^N für das Einzelspiel
campo^M di servizio^M del singolo^M
cuadro^M de servicio^M de individuales^M

doubles service court
demi-court^M de service^M en double^M
Aufschlagfeld^N für das Doppelspiel
campo^M di servizio^M del doppio^M
cuadro^M de servicio^M de dobles^M

SPORTS AND GAMES

synthetic shuttlecock
volant^M synthétique
Kunststoff^M-Federball^M
volano^M sintetico
volante^M sintético

feathered shuttlecock
volant^M de plumes^F
Federball^M
volano^M a penne^F naturali
volante^M de plumas^F

feather crown
empennage^M
Federkranz^M
corona^F di penne^F
penacho^M de plumas^F

cork tip
tête^F en liège^M
Korkspitze^F
mezza sfera^F di sughero^M
corcho^M

gymnastics

gymnastique^F | Geräteturnen^N | ginnastica^F | gimnasia^F

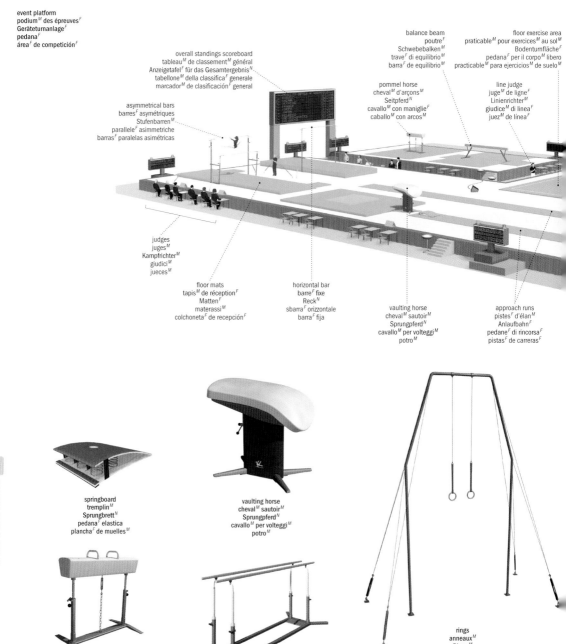

event platform
podium^M des épreuves^F
Geräteturnanlage^F
pedana^F
área^F de competición^F

balance beam
poutre^F
Schwebebalken^M
trave^F di equilibrio^M
barra^F de equilibrio^M

floor exercise area
praticable^M pour exercices^M au sol^M
Bodenturnfläche^F
pedana^F per il corpo^M libero
practicable^M para ejercicios^M de suelo^M

overall standings scoreboard
tableau^M de classement^M général
Anzeigetafel^F für das Gesamtergebnis^N
tabellone^M della classifica^F generale
marcador^M de clasificación^F general

pommel horse
cheval^M d'arçons^M
Seitpferd^N
cavallo^M con maniglie^F
caballo^M con arcos^M

line judge
juge^M de ligne^F
Linienrichter^M
giudice^M di linea^F
juez^M de linea^F

asymmetrical bars
barres^F asymétriques
Stufenbarren^M
parallele^F asimmetriche
barras^F paralelas asimétricas

judges
juges^M
Kampfrichter^M
giudici^M
jueces^M

floor mats
tapis^M de réception^F
Matten^F
materassi^M
colchoneta^F de recepción^F

horizontal bar
barre^F fixe
Reck^N
sbarra^F orizzontale
barra^F fija

vaulting horse
cheval^M sautoir^M
Sprungpferd^N
cavallo^M per volteggi^M
potro^M

approach runs
pistes^F d'élan^M
Anlaufbahn^F
pedane^F di rincorsa^F
pistas^F de carreras^F

springboard
tremplin^M
Sprungbrett^N
pedana^F elastica
plancha^F de muelles^M

vaulting horse
cheval^M sautoir^M
Sprungpferd^N
cavallo^M per volteggi^M
potro^M

pommel horse
cheval^M d'arçons^M
Seitpferd^N
cavallo^M con maniglie^F
caballo^M con aros^M

parallel bars
barres^F parallèles
Barren^M
parallele^F
barras^F paralelas

rings
anneaux^M
Ringe^M
anelli^M
anillas^M

SPORTS AND GAMES

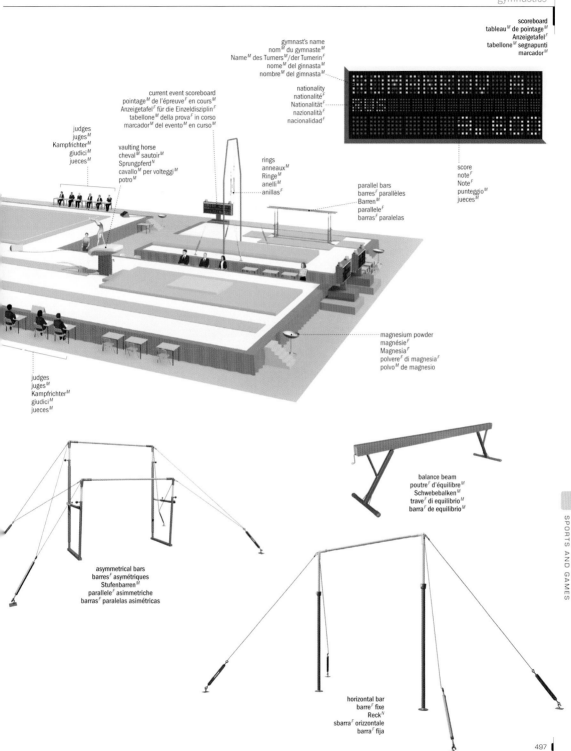

scoreboard
tableau^M de pointage^M
Anzeigetafel^F
tabellone^M segnapunti
marcador^M

gymnast's name
nom^M du gymnaste^M
Name^M des Turners^M/der Turnerin^F
nome^M del ginnasta^M
nombre^M del gimnasta^M

nationality
nationalité^F
Nationalität^F
nazionalità^F
nacionalidad^F

current event scoreboard
pointage^M de l'épreuve^F en cours^M
Anzeigetafel^F für die Einzeldisziplin^F
tabellone^M della prova^F in corso
marcador^M del evento^M en curso^M

judges
juges^M
Kampfrichter^M
giudici^M
jueces^M

vaulting horse
cheval^M sautoir^M
Sprungpferd^N
cavallo^M per volteggi^M
potro^M

rings
anneaux^M
Ringe^M
anelli^M
anillas^F

parallel bars
barres^F parallèles
Barren^M
parallele^F
barras^F paralelas

score
note^F
Note^F
punteggio^M
jueces^M

magnesium powder
magnésie^F
Magnesia^F
polvere^F di magnesia^F
polvo^M de magnesio

judges
juges^M
Kampfrichter^M
giudici^M
jueces^M

balance beam
poutre^F d'équilibre^M
Schwebebalken^M
trave^F di equilibrio^M
barra^F de equilibrio^M

asymmetrical bars
barres^F asymétriques
Stufenbarren^M
parallele^F asimmetriche
barras^F paralelas asimétricas

horizontal bar
barre^F fixe
Reck^N
sbarra^F orizzontale
barra^F fija

boxing

boxe^F | Boxen^N | pugilato^M | boxeo^M

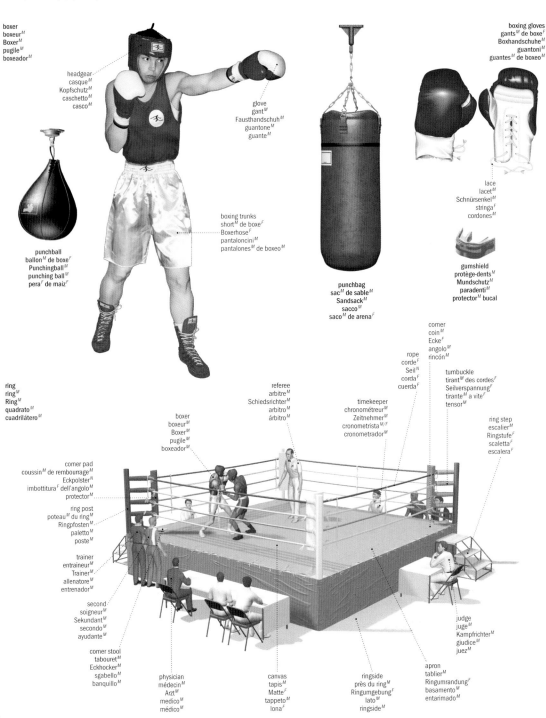

boxer
boxeur^M
Boxer^M
pugile^M
boxeador^M

boxing gloves
gants^M de boxe^F
Boxhandschuhe^M
guantoni^M
guantes^M de boxeo^M

headgear
casque^M
Kopfschutz^M
caschetto^M
casco^M

glove
gant^M
Fausthandschuh^M
guantone^M
guante^M

lace
lacet^M
Schnürsenkel^M
stringa^F
cordones^M

punchball
ballon^M de boxe^F
Punchingball^M
punching ball^M
pera^F de maíz^F

boxing trunks
short^M de boxe^F
Boxerhose^F
pantaloncini^M
pantalones^M de boxeo^M

gumshield
protège-dents^M
Mundschutz^M
paradenti^M
protector^M bucal

punchbag
sac^M de sable^M
Sandsack^M
sacco^M
saco^M de arena^F

corner
coin^M
Ecke^F
angolo^M
rincón^M

rope
corde^F
Seil^N
corda^F
cuerda^F

turnbuckle
tirant^M des cordes^F
Seilverspannung^F
tirante^M a vite^F
tensor^M

ring
ring^M
Ring^M
quadrato^M
cuadrilátero^M

referee
arbitre^M
Schiedsrichter^M
arbitro^M
árbitro^M

boxer
boxeur^M
Boxer^M
pugile^M
boxeador^M

timekeeper
chronométreur^M
Zeitnehmer^M
cronometrista$^{M/F}$
cronometrador^M

ring step
escalier^M
Ringstufe^F
scaletta^F
escalera^F

corner pad
coussin^M de rembourrage^M
Eckpolster^N
imbottitura^F dell'angolo^M
protector^M

ring post
poteau^M du ring^M
Ringpfosten^M
paletto^M
poste^M

trainer
entraineur^M
Trainer^M
allenatore^M
entrenador^M

second
soigneur^M
Sekundant^M
secondo^M
ayudante^M

judge
juge^M
Kampfrichter^M
giudice^M
juez^M

corner stool
tabouret^M
Eckhocker^M
sgabello^M
banquillo^M

physician
médecin^M
Arzt^M
medico^M
médico^M

canvas
tapis^M
Matte^F
tappeto^M
lona^F

ringside
près du ring^M
Ringumgebung^F
lato^M
ringside^M

apron
tablier^M
Ringumrandung^F
basamento^M
entarimado^M

judo

scorers and timekeepers
marqueurs^M et chronométreurs^M
Registratoren^M und Zeitnehmer^M
segnapunti^M e cronometristi
anotadores^M y cronometradores^M

mat
tapis^M
Matte^F
tappeto^M
tatami^M

medical team
équipe^F médicale
Ärzteteam^N
staff^M medico
equipo^M médico

contestant
combattant^M
Judokämpfer^M Wettkampfteilnehmer
lottatore^M
uke (defensor^M)

safety area
surface^F de sécurité^F
Sicherheitsbereich^M
area^F di sicurezza^F
zona^F de seguridad^F

danger area
zone^F de danger^M
Gefahrenbereich^M
zona^F di pericolo^M
área^F de peligro^M

scoreboard
tableau^M d'affichage^M
Anzeigetafel^F
tabellone^M segnapunti
marcador^M

contest area
surface^F de combat^M
Kampfbereich^M
area^F di combattimento^M
zona^F de combate^M

referee
arbitre^M
Schiedsrichter^M
arbitro^M
judoka^M neutral

examples of holds
exemples^M de prises^F
Griff- und Wurfbeispiele^N
esempi^M di prese^F
ejemplos^M de llaves^F

judge
juge^M
Kampfrichter^M
giudice^M
juez^M

judogi
judogi^M
Judogi^M
judogi^M
traje^M de judo: judoji^M

jacket
veste^F
Jacke^F
giacca^F
kimono^M

holding
immobilisation^F
Haltegriffe^M
presa^F a terra^F
inmovilización^F

stomach throw
projection^F en cercle^M
Kopfwurf^M
rovesciata^F all'indietro
proyección^F en círculo^M

sweeping hip throw
hanche^F ailée
Hüftwurf^M
spazzata^F d'anca^F
proyección^F primera de cadera^F

major outer reaping throw
grand fauchage^M extérieur
Große Außensichel^F
grande falciata^F esterna
osoto-gari (gran siega^F) exterior

major inner reaping throw
grand fauchage^M intérieur
Große Innensichel^F
grande falciata^F interna
gran siega^F interior

naked strangle
étranglement^M
Halsumklammerung^F
presa^F di strangolamento^M
estrangulación^F

arm lock
clé^F de bras^M
Armhebel^M
presa^F a croce^F
inmovilización^F de brazo^M

trousers
pantalon^M
Hose^F
pantaloni^M
pantalón^M

belt
ceinture^F
Gürtel^M
cintura^F
cinturón^M

one-arm shoulder throw
projection^F d'épaule^F par un côté^M
einarmiger Schulterwurf^M
proiezione^F di spalla^F e braccio^M
proyección^F por encima del hombro^M con una mano^F

weightlifting

haltérophilie[F] | Gewichtheben[N] | sollevamento[M] pesi[M] | halterofilia[F]

barbell
haltère[M] long
Scheibenhantel[F]
bilanciere[M]
barra[F] con pesas[F]

wrist band
poignet[M] de force[F]
Handgelenksbandage[F]
polsino[M]
muñequera[F]

weightlifting belt
ceinture[F] d'haltérophilie[F]
Gewichthebergürtel[M]
cintura[F] da sollevamento[M] pesi[M]
cinturón[M]

singlet
maillot[M] de corps[M]
ärmelloses Sporthemd[N]
canottiera[F]
camiseta[F] sin mangas[F]

shorts
culotte[F]
Hose[F]
pantaloncini[M]
pantalón[M]

knee wrap
genouillère[F]
Kniebandage[F]
ginocchiera[F]
rodillera[F]

strap
lanière[F]
Riemen[M]
cinturino[M]
correa[F]

weightlifting shoe
chaussure[F] d'haltérophilie[F]
Gewichtheberschuh[M]
scarpa[F]
zapatilla[F]

clean and jerk
épaulé[M]-jeté[M]
Stoßen[N]
slancio[M]
envión[M]

snatch
arraché[M]
Reißen[N]
strappo[M]
arranque[M]

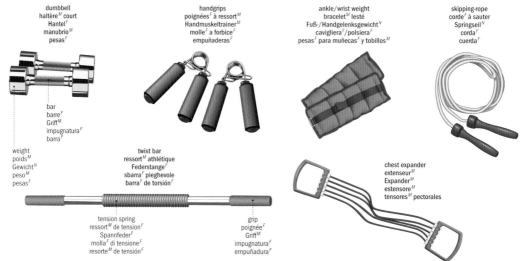

fitness equipment

appareils[M] de conditionnement[M] physique | Fitnessgeräte[N] | attrezzi[M] ginnici | aparatos[M] de ejercicios[M]

dumbbell
haltère[M] court
Hantel[F]
manubrio[M]
pesas[F]

handgrips
poignées[F] à ressort[M]
Handmuskeltrainer[M]
molle[F] a forbice[F]
empuñaderas[F]

ankle/wrist weight
bracelet[M] lesté
Fuß-/Handgelenksgewicht[N]
cavigliera[F]/polsiera[F]
pesas[F] para muñecas[F] y tobillos[M]

skipping-rope
corde[F] à sauter
Springseil[N]
corda[F]
cuerda[F]

bar
barre[F]
Griff[M]
impugnatura[F]
barra[F]

weight
poids[M]
Gewicht[N]
peso[M]
pesas[F]

twist bar
ressort[M] athlétique
Federstange[F]
sbarra[F] pieghevole
barra[F] de torsión[F]

chest expander
extenseur[M]
Expander[M]
estensore[M]
tensores[M] pectorales

tension spring
ressort[M] de tension[F]
Spannfeder[F]
molla[F] di tensione[F]
resorte[M] de tensión[F]

grip
poignée[F]
Griff[M]
impugnatura[F]
empuñadura[F]

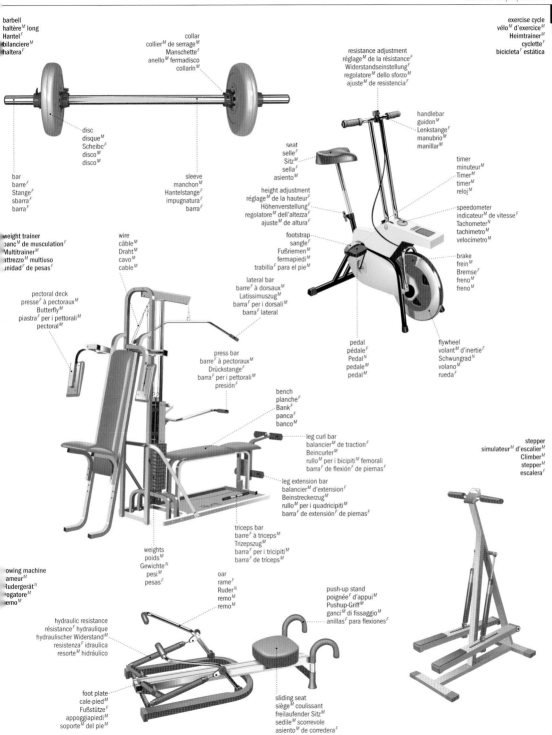

barbell
haltère^M long
Hantel^F
bilanciere^M
haltera^F

collar
collier^M de serrage^M
Manschette^F
anello^M fermadisco
collarín^M

exercise cycle
vélo^M d'exercice^M
Heimtrainer^M
cyclette^F
bicicleta^F estática

resistance adjustment
réglage^M de la résistance^F
Widerstandseinstellung^F
regolatore^M dello sforzo^M
ajuste^M de resistencia^F

disc
disque^M
Scheibe^F
disco^M
disco^M

sleeve
manchon^M
Hantelstange^F
impugnatura^F
barra^F

bar
barre^F
Stange^F
sbarra^F
barra^F

handlebar
guidon^M
Lenkstange^F
manubrio^M
manillar^M

seat
selle^F
Sitz^M
sella^F
asiento^M

timer
minuteur^M
Timer^M
timer^M
reloj^M

height adjustment
réglage^M de la hauteur^F
Höhenverstellung^F
regolatore^M dell'altezza^F
ajuste^M de altura^F

speedometer
indicateur^M de vitesse^F
Tachometer^M
tachimetro^M
velocímetro^M

weight trainer
banc^M de musculation^F
Multitrainer^M
attrezzo^M multiuso
unidad^F de pesas^F

wire
câble^M
Draht^M
cavo^M
cable^M

footstrap
sangle^F
Fußriemen^M
fermapiedi^M
trabilla^F para el pie^M

brake
frein^M
Bremse^F
freno^M
freno^M

pectoral deck
presse^F à pectoraux^M
Butterfly^M
piastra^F per i pettorali^M
pectoral^M

lateral bar
barre^F à dorsaux^M
Latissimuszug^M
barra^F per i dorsali^M
barra^F lateral

pedal
pédale^F
Pedal^N
pedale^M
pedal^M

flywheel
volant^M d'inertie^F
Schwungrad^N
volano^M
rueda^F

press bar
barre^F à pectoraux^M
Drückstange^F
barra^F per i pettorali^M
presión^F

bench
planche^F
Bank^F
panca^F
banco^M

leg curl bar
balancier^M de traction^F
Beincurler^M
rullo^M per i bicipiti^M femorali
barra^F de flexión^F de piernas^F

stepper
simulateur^M d'escalier^M
Climber^M
stepper^M
escalera^F

leg extension bar
balancier^M d'extension^F
Beinstreckerzug^M
rullo^M per i quadricipiti^M
barra^F de extensión^F de piernas^F

triceps bar
barre^F à triceps^M
Trizepszug^M
barra^F per i tricipiti^M
barra^F de triceps^M

weights
poids^M
Gewichte^N
pesi^M
pesas^F

rowing machine
rameur^M
Rudergerät^N
vogatore^M
remo^M

oar
rame^F
Ruder^N
remo^N
remo^M

push-up stand
poignée^F d'appui^M
Pushup-Griff^M
ganci^M di fissaggio^M
anillas^F para flexiones^F

hydraulic resistance
résistance^F hydraulique
hydraulischer Widerstand^M
resistenza^F idraulica
resorte^M hidráulico

foot plate
cale-pied^M
Fußstütze^F
appoggiapiedi^M
soporte^M del pie^M

sliding seat
siège^M coulissant
freilaufender Sitz^M
sedile^M scorrevole
asiento^M de corredera^F

billiards

billard^M | Billard^N | biliardo^M | billar^M

carom billiards
billard^M français
Karambolagebillard^N
biliardo^M per carambola^F
billar^M francés

poo
billard^M poo
Pool^N
pool^M
pool^M

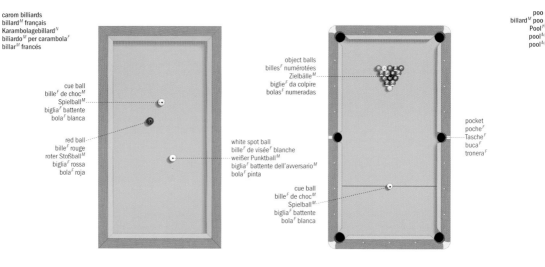

cue ball
bille^F de choc^M
Spielball^M
biglia^F battente
bola^F blanca

object balls
billes^F numérotées
Zielbälle^M
biglie^F da colpire
bolas^F numeradas

red ball
bille^F rouge
roter Stoßball^M
biglia^F rossa
bola^F roja

white spot ball
bille^F de visée^F blanche
weißer Punktball^M
biglia^F battente dell'avversario^M
bola^F pinta

pocket
poche^F
Tasche^F
buca^F
tronera^F

cue ball
bille^F de choc^M
Spielball^M
biglia^F battente
bola^F blanca

table
table^F
Billardtisch^M
tavolo^M
mesa^F

«D»
D^M
D^N
zona^F di inizio^M partita^F
D^F

baulk line spot
mouche^F de ligne^F de cadre^M
Anstoßpunkt^M
acchito^M della linea^F di battuta^F
mosca^F de la línea^F de cuadro^M

pyramid spot
mouche^F supérieure
Aufstellpunkt^M
acchito^M superiore
mosca^F superior

baize
tapis^M
Bespannung^F
panno^M
tapete^M

baulk
cadre^M
Anstoßraum^M
rettangolo^M di battuta^F
cuadro^M

bottom pocket
poche^F inférieure
untere Tasche^F
buca^F inferiore
bolsillo^M

centre spot
mouche^F centrale
Mittelpunkt^M
acchito^M centrale
mosca^F central

top pocket
poche^F supérieure
obere Tasche^F
buca^F superiore
tronera^F

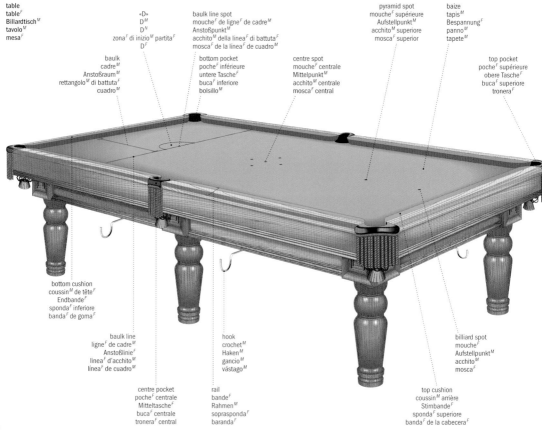

bottom cushion
coussin^M de tête^F
Endbande^F
sponda^F inferiore
banda^F de goma^F

baulk line
ligne^F de cadre^M
Anstoßlinie^F
linea^F d'acchito^M
línea^F de cuadro^M

hook
crochet^M
Haken^M
gancio^M
vástago^M

billiard spot
mouche^F
Aufstellpunkt^M
acchito^M
mosca^F

centre pocket
poche^F centrale
Mitteltasche^F
buca^F centrale
tronera^F central

rail
bande^F
Rahmen^M
soprasponda^F
baranda^F

top cushion
coussin^M arrière
Stimbande^F
sponda^F superiore
banda^F de la cabecera^F

SPORTS AND GAMES

PRECISION AND ACCURACY SPORTS | SPORTS DE PRÉCISION
PRÄZISIONSSPORT | SPORT DI PRECISIONE | DEPORTES DE PRECISIÓN Y PUNTERÍA

billiards

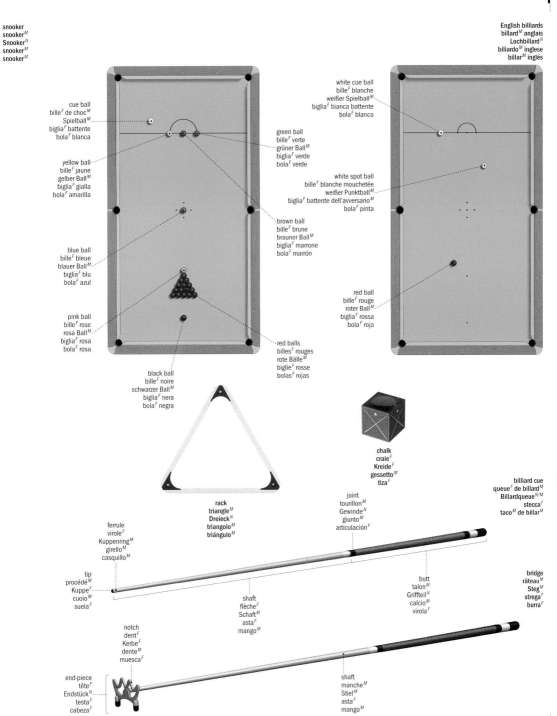

snooker
snooker^M
Snooker^N
snooker^M
snooker^M

English billiards
billard^M anglais
Lochbillard^N
biliardo^M inglese
billar^M inglés

cue ball
bille^F de choc^M
Spielball^M
biglia^F battente
bola^F blanca

white cue ball
bille^F blanche
weißer Spielball^M
biglia^F bianca battente
bola^F blanca

green ball
bille^F verte
grüner Ball^M
biglia^F verde
bola^F verde

yellow ball
bille^F jaune
gelber Ball^M
biglia^F gialla
bola^F amarilla

white spot ball
bille^F blanche mouchetée
weißer Punktball^M
biglia^F battente dell'avversario^M
bola^F pinta

brown ball
bille^F brune
brauner Ball^M
biglia^F marrone
bola^F marrón

blue ball
bille^F bleue
blauer Ball^M
biglia^F blu
bola^F azul

red ball
bille^F rouge
roter Ball^M
biglia^F rossa
bola^F roja

pink ball
bille^F rose
rosa Ball^M
biglia^F rosa
bola^F rosa

red balls
billes^F rouges
rote Bälle^M
biglie^F rosse
bolas^F rojas

black ball
bille^F noire
schwarzer Ball^M
biglia^F nera
bola^F negra

chalk
craie^F
Kreide^F
gessetto^M
tiza^F

billiard cue
queue^F de billard^M
Billardqueue$^{N/M}$
stecca^F
taco^M de billar^M

rack
triangle^M
Dreieck^N
triangolo^M
triángulo^M

joint
tourillon^M
Gewinde^N
giunto^M
articulación^F

ferrule
virole^F
Kuppenring^M
girello^M
casquillo^M

tip
procédé^M
Kuppe^F
cuoio^M
suela^F

shaft
flèche^F
Schaft^M
asta^F
mango^M

butt
talon^M
Griffteil^N
calcio^M
virola^F

bridge
râteau^M
Steg^M
strega^F
burra^F

notch
dent^F
Kerbe^F
dente^F
muesca^F

end-piece
tête^F
Endstück^N
testa^F
cabeza^F

shaft
manche^M
Stiel^M
asta^F
mango^M

golf

golf^M | Golfspiel^N | golf^M | accesorios^M de golf^M

course
parcours^M
Golfplatz^M
percorso^M
campo^M de golf^M

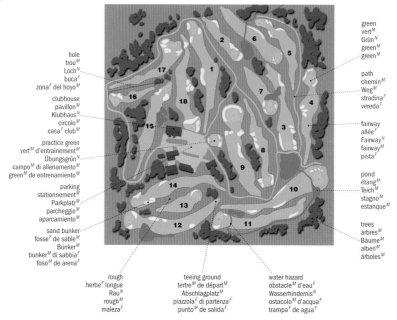

hole
trou^M
Loch^N
buca^F
zona^F del hoyo^M

clubhouse
pavillon^M
Klubhaus^N
circolo^M
casa^F club^M

practice green
vert^M d'entraînement^M
Übungsgrün^N
campo^M di allenamento^M
green^M de entrenamiento^M

parking
stationnement^M
Parkplatz^M
parcheggio^M
aparcamiento^M

sand bunker
fosse^F de sable^M
Bunker^M
bunker^M di sabbia^F
foso^M de arena^F

green
vert^M
Grün^N
green^M
green^M

path
chemin^M
Weg^M
stradina^F
vereda^F

fairway
allée^F
Fairway^N
fairway^M
pista^F

pond
étang^M
Teich^M
stagno^M
estanque^M

trees
arbres^M
Bäume^M
alberi^M
árboles^M

rough
herbe^F longue
Rau^N
rough^M
maleza^F

teeing ground
tertre^M de départ^M
Abschlagplatz^M
piazzola^F di partenza^F
punto^M de salida^F

water hazard
obstacle^M d'eau^F
Wasserhindernis^N
ostacolo^M d'acqua^F
trampa^F de agua^F

par 5 hole
trou^M de normale^F 5
Par^N-5-Loch^N
buca^F par 5
hoyo^M de par 5

water hazard
obstacle^M d'eau^F
Wasserhindernis^N
ostacolo^M d'acqua^F
fosa^F de agua

fairway
allée^F
Fairway^N
fairway^M
fairway^M

teeing ground
tertre^M de départ^M
Abschlagsbereich^M
piazzola^F di partenza^F
colina^F de salida^F

green
vert^M
Grün^N
green^M
green^M

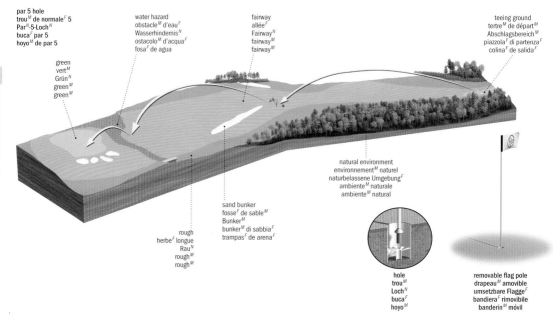

natural environment
environnement^M naturel
naturbelassene Umgebung^F
ambiente^M naturale
ambiente^M natural

rough
herbe^F longue
Rau^N
rough^M
rough^M

sand bunker
fosse^F de sable^M
Bunker^M
bunker^M di sabbia^F
trampas^F de arena^F

hole
trou^M
Loch^N
buca^F
hoyo^M

removable flag pole
drapeau^M amovible
umsetzbare Flagge^F
bandiera^F rimovibile
banderín^M móvil

PRECISION AND ACCURACY SPORTS | SPORTS DE PRÉCISION
PRÄZISIONSSPORT | SPORT DI PRECISIONE | DEPORTES DE PRECISIÓN Y PUNTERÍA

golf

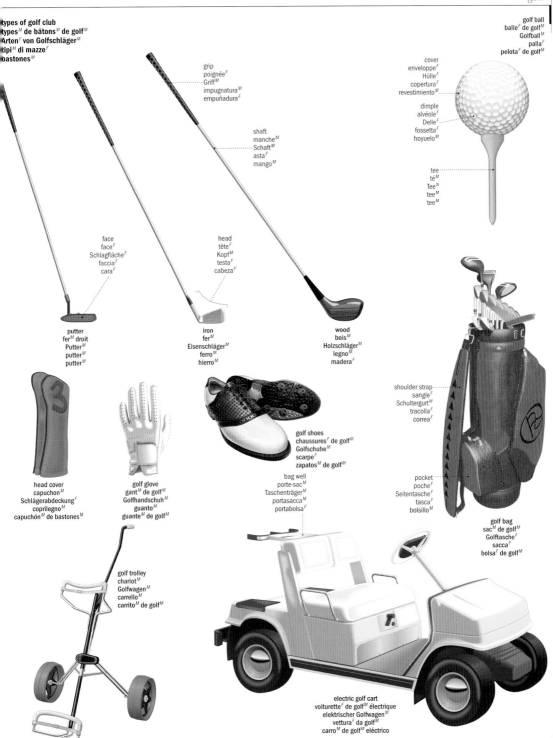

types of golf club
types^M de bâtons^M de golf^M
Arten^F von Golfschläger^M
tipi^M di mazze^F
bastones^M

golf ball
balle^F de golf^M
Golfball^M
palla^F
pelota^F de golf^M

grip
poignée^F
Griff^M
impugnatura^M
empuñadura^F

cover
enveloppe^F
Hülle^F
copertura^F
revestimiento^M

shaft
manche^M
Schaft^M
asta^F
mango^M

dimple
alvéole^F
Delle^F
fossetta^F
hoyuelo^M

tee
té^M
Tee^N
tee^M
tee^M

face
face^F
Schlagfläche^F
faccia^F
cara^F

head
tête^F
Kopf^M
testa^F
cabeza^F

putter
fer^M droit
Putter^M
putter^M
putter^M

iron
fer^M
Eisenschläger^M
ferro^M
hierro^M

wood
bois^M
Holzschläger^M
legno^M
madera^F

shoulder strap
sangle^F
Schultergurt^M
tracolla^F
correa^F

golf shoes
chaussures^F de golf^M
Golfschuhe^M
scarpe^F
zapatos^M de golf^M

head cover
capuchon^M
Schlägerabdeckung^F
coprilegno^M
capuchón^M de bastones^M

golf glove
gant^M de golf^M
Golfhandschuh^M
guanto^M
guante^M de golf^M

bag well
porte-sac^M
Taschenträger^M
portasacca^M
portabolsa^F

pocket
poche^F
Seitentasche^F
tasca^F
bolsillo^M

golf bag
sac^M de golf^M
Golftasche^F
sacca^F
bolsa^F de golf^M

golf trolley
chariot^M
Golfwagen^M
carrello^M
carrito^M de golf^M

electric golf cart
voiturette^F de golf^M électrique
elektrischer Golfwagen^M
vettura^F da golf^M
carro^M de golf^M eléctrico

SPORTS AND GAMES

505

ice hockey

hockey^M sur glace^F | Eishockey^N | hockey^M su ghiaccio^M | hockey^M sobre hielo^M

ice hockey player
hockeyeur^M
Eishockeyspieler^M
giocatore^M
jugador^M

helmet
casque^M
Schutzhelm^M
casco^M
casco^M

butt end
embout^M
Knauf^M
pomolo^M del bastone^M
pomo^M

player's stic
crosse^F de joueur
Eishockeyschläger
bastone^M del giocatore
palo^M del jugador

visor
visière^F
Gesichtsschutz^M
visiera^F
visera^F

player's number
numéro^M du joueur^M
Spielnummer^F
numero^M del giocatore^M
número^M del jugador^M

shaft
manche^M
Schaft^M
asta^F
mango^M

team's emblem
emblème^M d'équipe^F
Mannschaftsabzeichen^N
simbolo^M della squadra^F
emblema^M del equipo^M

glove
gant^M
Handschuh^M
guanto^M
guante^M

trousers
culotte^F
Hose^F
pantaloni^M
pantalón^M

heel
talon^M
Unterkante^F
tallone^M
talón^M

stocking
bas^M
Stutzen^M
calzettone^M
calcetines^M

skate
patin^M
Schlittschuh^M
pattino^M
bota^F

blade
lame^F
Kufe^F
lama^F
cuchilla^F

blade
lame^F
Blatt^N
pala^F
pala^F del stick^M

rink
patinoire^F
Eisfläche^F
campo^M
pista^F

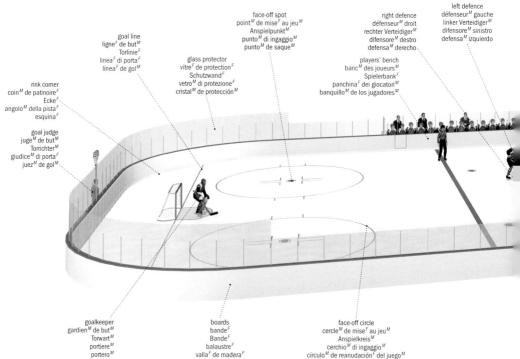

face-off spot
point^M de mise^F au jeu^M
Anspielpunkt^M
punto^M di ingaggio^M
punto^M de saque^M

right defence
défenseur^M droit
rechter Verteidiger^M
difensore^M destro
defensa^M derecho

left defence
défenseur^M gauche
linker Verteidiger^M
difensore^M sinistro
defensa^M izquierdo

goal line
ligne^F de but^M
Torlinie^F
linea^F di porta^F
línea^F de gol^M

glass protector
vitre^F de protection^F
Schutzwand^F
vetro^M di protezione^F
cristal^M de protección^M

players' bench
banc^M des joueurs^M
Spielerbank^F
panchina^F dei giocatori^M
banquillo^M de los jugadores^M

rink corner
coin^M de patinoire^F
Ecke^F
angolo^M della pista^F
esquina^F

goal judge
juge^M de but^M
Torrichter^M
giudice^M di porta^F
juez^M de gol^M

goalkeeper
gardien^M de but^M
Torwart^M
portiere^M
portero^M

boards
bande^F
Bande^F
balaustre^F
valla^F de madera^F

face-off circle
cercle^M de mise^F au jeu^M
Anspielkreis^M
cerchio^M di ingaggio^M
círculo^M de reanudación^F del juego^M

goalkeeper
gardien^M de but^M
Torwart^M
portiere^M
portero^M

face mask
masque^M
Gesichtsschutzmaske^F
maschera^F
protector^M facial

blocking glove
bouclier^M
Abwehrhandschuh^M
guanto^M da respinta^F
escudo^M

catching glove
mitaine^F
Fanghandschuh^M
guanto^M da presa^F
guante^M rígido

goalkeeper's pad
jambière^F de gardien^M de but^M
Beinpolster^N
paragambe^M
protector^M de piernas^F

goalkeeper's stick
crosse^F de gardien^M de but^M
Torwartschläger^M
bastone^M
bastón^M del portero^M

protective cup
coquille^F
Suspensorium^N
conchiglia^F di protezione^F
coquilla^F

puck
palet^M
Puck^M
dischetto^M
disco^M

goalkeeper's skate
patin^M de gardien^M de but^M
Torwartschlittschuh^M
pattino^M del portiere^M
patín^M del portero^M

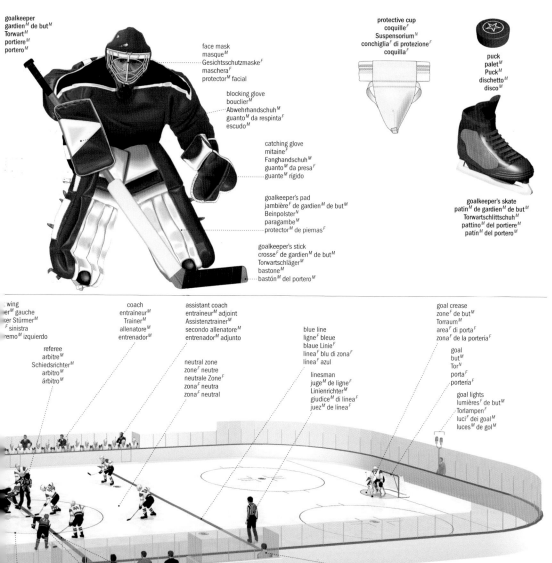

wing
er^M gauche
ker Stürmer^M
^F sinistra
remo^M izquierdo

coach
entraineur^M
Trainer^M
allenatore^M
entrenador^M

assistant coach
entraineur^M adjoint
Assistenztrainer^M
secondo allenatore^M
entrenador^M adjunto

blue line
ligne^F bleue
blaue Linie^F
linea^F blu di zona^F
línea^F azul

goal crease
zone^F de but^M
Torraum^M
area^F di porta^F
zona^F de la portería^F

referee
arbitre^M
Schiedsrichter^M
arbitro^M
árbitro^M

neutral zone
zone^F neutre
neutrale Zone^F
zona^F neutra
zona^F neutral

linesman
juge^M de ligne^F
Linienrichter^M
giudice^M di linea^F
juez^M de línea^F

goal
but^M
Tor^N
porta^F
portería^F

goal lights
lumières^F de but^M
Torlampen^F
luci^F dei goal^M
luces^M de gol^M

centre face-off circle
cercle^M central
mittlerer Anspielpunkt^M
cerchio^M di centrocampo^M
círculo^M de saque^M inicial

centre line
ligne^F centrale
Mittellinie^F
linea^F di centrocampo^M
línea^F media

penalty bench
banc^M des pénalités^F
Strafbank^F
panca^F dei puniti^M
banquillo^M de los penaltis^M

penalty bench official
préposé^M au banc^M des pénalités^F
Strafbankbetreuer^M
addetto^M alla panca^F dei puniti^M
oficial^M del banco^M de los penaltis^M

entre
entre^M
turmspitze^F
entroattacco^M
entro^M

right wing
ailier^M droit
rechter Stürmer^M
ala^F destra
extremo^M derecho

officials' bench
banc^M des officiels^M
Offiziellenbank^F
panca^F degli ufficiali^M di gara^F
mesa^F arbitral

speed skating

patinage^M de vitesse^F | Eisschnelllauf^M | pattinaggio^M di velocità^F | patinaje^M de velocidad^F

skater: long track
patineur^M : longue piste^F
Eisschnellläufer^M: Langstrecke^F
pattinatore^M: pista^F lunga
patinador^M : pista^F larga

hood
capuchon^M
Kapuze^F
cappuccio^M
capuchón^M

skater: short track
patineur^M : courte piste^F
Eisschnellläufer^M: Kurzstrecke^F
pattinatore^M: short track^M
patinador^M : pista^F corta

helmet
casque^M
Helm^M
casco^M
casco^M

glove
gant^M
Handschuh^M
guanto^M
guante^M

racing suit
combinaison^F de course^F
Rennanzug^M
tuta^F
traje^M de carrera^F

speed skates
patins^M de course^F
Eisschnelllauf^M-Schlittschuhe^M
pattini^M per velocità^F
patines^M de carreras^F

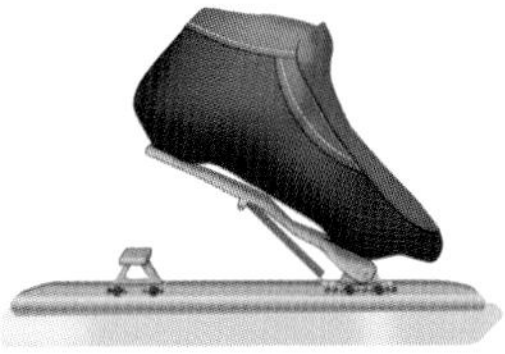

clapskate
patin^M clap
Klappschlittschuh^M
pattino^M ad incastro^M
patin^M de pista^F larga

short track skate
patin^M de courte piste^F
Kurzstreckenschlittschuh^M
pattino^M da short track^M
patin^M de pista^F corta

short track
courte piste^F
Kurzstrecke^F
short track^M
pista^F corta

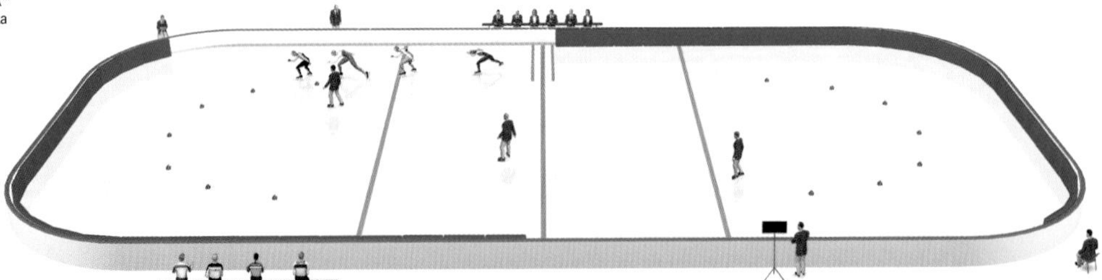

long track
longue piste^F
Eisschnelllaufbahn^F
pista^F lunga
pista^F larga

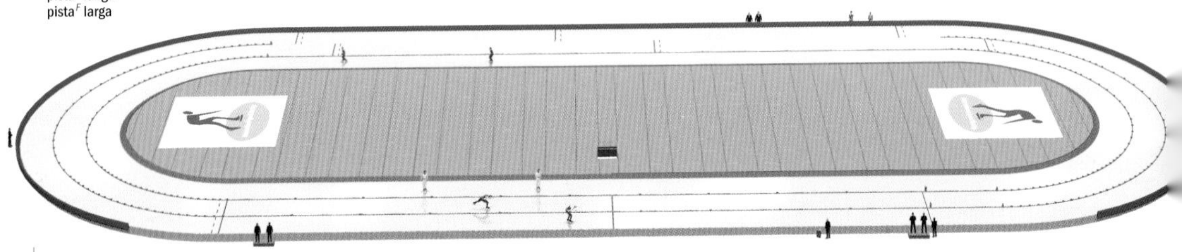

figure skating

patinage^M artistique | Eiskunstlauf^M | pattinaggio^M artistico | patinaje^M artístico

lining
doublure^F
Futter^N
fodera^F
forro^M

hook
crochet^M
Schnürhaken^M
gancio^M
corchete^M

backstay
tige^F
Rückenverstärkung^F
rinforzo^M posteriore
contrafuerte^M

boot
chaussure^F
Stiefel^M
scarpa^F
bota^F

heel
talon^M
Absatz^M
tacco^M
tacón^M

stanchion
montant^M
Träger^M
sostegno^M
montante^M

tongue
languette^F
Zunge^F
linguetta^F
lengüeta^F

lace
lacet^M
Schnürsenkel^M
stringa^F
cordón^M

eyelet
œillet^M
Schnüröse^F
occhiello^M
ojal^M

sole
semelle^F
Sohle^F
suola^F
suela^F

toe pick
dent^F
Abstoßsäge^F
punta^F dentellata
dientes^M

figure skate
patin^M de figure^F
Eiskunstlaufstiefel^M
pattino^M per pattinaggio^M artistico
patín^M para figuras^F

dance blade
lame^F de danse^F sur glace^F
Eistanzkufe^F
lama^F per danza^F
cuchilla^F de baile^M

free-skating blade
lame^F pour programme^M libre
Eiskunstlaufkufe^F
lama^F per pattinaggio^M libero
cuchilla^F de patinaje^M artístico

edge
carre^F
Schneide^F
lamina^F
canto^M

blade
lame^F
Kufe^F
lama^F
hoja^F de cuchilla^F

Axel
axel^M
Axel^M
axel^M
axel^M

Salchow
salchow^M
Salchow^M
salchow^M
salchow^M

examples of jumps
exemples^M de sauts^M
Beispiele^N für Sprünge^M
esempi^M di salti^M
ejemplos^M de piruetas^F

toe loop
boucle^F piquée
Toeloop^M
loop^M di punta^F
loop^M de puntera^F

flip
flip^M
Flip^M
flip^M
flip^M

Lutz
lutz^M
Lutz^M
lutz^M
lutz^M

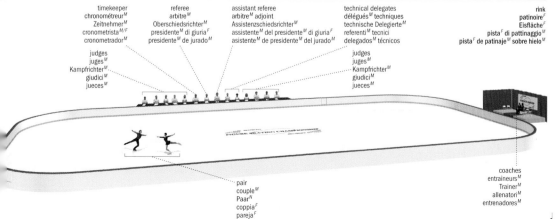

timekeeper
chronométreur^M
Zeitnehmer^M
cronometrista^{M/F}
cronometrador^M

referee
arbitre^M
Oberschiedsrichter^M
presidente^M di giuria^F
presidente^M de jurado^M

assistant referee
arbitre^M adjoint
Assistenzschiedsrichter^M
assistente^M del presidente^M di giuria^F
asistente^M de presidente^M del jurado^M

technical delegates
délégués^M techniques
technische Delegierte^M
referenti^M tecnici
delegados^M técnicos

rink
patinoire^F
Eisfläche^F
pista^F di pattinaggio^M
pista^F de patinaje^M sobre hielo^M

judges
juges^M
Kampfrichter^M
giudici^M
jueces^M

judges
juges^M
Kampfrichter^M
giudici^M
jueces^M

pair
couple^M
Paar^N
coppia^F
pareja^F

coaches
entraineurs^M
Trainer^M
allenatori^M
entrenadores^M

SPORTS AND GAMES

509

alpine skiing

ski^M alpin | alpines Skilaufen^N | sci^M alpino | esquí^M alpino

alpine skier
skieur^M alpin
alpiner Skiläufer^M
sciatore^M
esquiador^M alpino

ski goggles
lunettes^F de ski^M
Skibrille^F
occhiali^M
gafas^F de esquí^M

ski suit
combinaison^F de ski^M
Skianzug^M
tuta^F
traje^M de esquí^M

helmet
casque^M
Sturzhelm^M
casco^M
casco^M

ski glove
gant^M de ski^M
Skihandschuhe^M
guanto^M
guante^M de esquí^M

basket
rondelle^F
Stockteller^M
rotella^F
arandela^F

ski pole
bâton^M de ski^M
Skistock^M
racchetta^F
bastón^M de esquí^M

ski boot
chaussure^F de ski^M
Skistiefel^M
scarpone^M
bota^F

wrist strap
dragonne^F
Handschlaufe^F
cappio^M
correa^F para la mano^F

handle
poignée^F
Griff^M
impugnatura^F
empuñadura^F

groove
rainure^F
Führungsrille^F
scanalatura^F
ranura^F guía^F

ski
ski^M
Ski^M
sci^M
esquí^M

tip
pointe^F
Spitze^F
punta^F
punta^F

bottom face
semelle^F
Laufsohle^F
suola^F
superficie^F de deslizamiento^M

safety binding
fixation^F de sécurité^F
Sicherheitsbindung^F
attacco^M di sicurezza^F
fijaciones^F

tail
talon^M
Ende^N
coda^F
cola^F

shovel
spatule^F
Schaufel^F
spatola^F
pala^F

edge
carre^F
Stahlkante^F
lamina^F
canto^M

ski
ski^M
Ski^M
sci^M
esquí^M

examples of skis
exemples^M de skis^M
Beispiele^N für Skier^M
esempi^M di sci^M
ejemplos^M de esquís^M

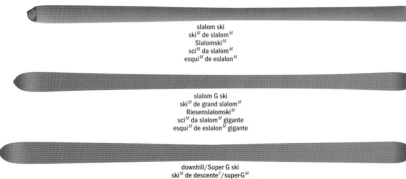

slalom ski
ski^M de slalom^M
Slalomski^M
sci^M da slalom^M
esquí^M de eslalon^M

slalom G ski
ski^M de grand slalom^M
Riesenslalomski^M
sci^M da slalom^M gigante
esquí^M de eslalon^M gigante

downhill/Super G ski
ski^M de descente^F/super-G^M
Abfahrts- und Superriesenslalom^M-Ski^M
sci^M da discesa^F libera e supergigante^M
esquí^M de descenso^M/eslalon^M

technical events
épreuves^F
Disziplinen^F
specialità^F
pruebas^F

downhill
descente^F
Abfahrtslauf^M
discesa^M libera
descenso^M

super giant slalom
super-géant^M
Superriesenslalom^M
slalom^M supergigante
eslalon^M supergigante

giant slalom
slalom^M géant
Riesenslalom^M
slalom^M gigante
eslalon^M gigante

special slalom
slalom^M spécial
Spezialslalom^M
slalom^M speciale
eslalon^M especial

ski boot
chaussure^F de ski^M
Skistiefel^M
scarpone^M
botas^F para esquiar

inner boot
chausson^M intérieur
Innenstiefel^M
scarpetta^F interna
botín^M interior

upper cuff
collier^M
obere Manschette^F
bordo^M della scarpetta^F
guarnición^F

upper
tige^F
Rücklagenstütze^F
appoggio^M del polpaccio^M
alto^M de caña^F

upper shell
coque^F supérieure
obere Schale^F
gambale^M
bota^F externa

buckle
boucle^F
Verschluss^M
gancio^M
hebilla^F

hinge
charnière^F
Gelenk^N
snodo^M
pivote^M

tongue
languette^F
Zunge^F
linguettone^M
lengüeta^F

upper strap
courroie^F de tige^F
oberes Verschlussband^N
fascia^F di chiusura^F
correa^F de ajuste^M

adjustable catch
cran^M de réglage^M
Einstellkerbe^F
dispositivo^M di regolazione^F
ajustador^M de la bota^F

sole
semelle^F
Sohle^F
suola^F
suela^F rígida

lower shell
coque^F inférieure
untere Schale^F
scafo^M
contrafuerte^M

safety binding
fixation^F de sécurité^F
Sicherheitsbindung^F
attacco^M di sicurezza^F
fijación^F de seguridad^F del esquí^M

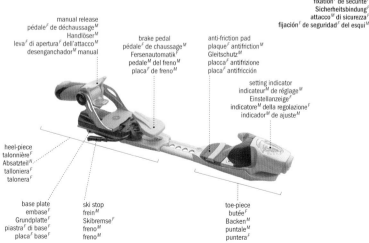

manual release
pédale^F de déchaussage^M
Handlöser^M
leva^F di apertura^F dell'attacco^M
desenganchador^M manual

brake pedal
pédale^F de chaussage^M
Fersenautomatik^F
pedale^M del freno^M
placa^F de freno^M

anti-friction pad
plaque^F antifriction^M
Gleitschutz^M
placca^F antifrizione
placa^F antifricción

setting indicator
indicateur^M de réglage^M
Einstellanzeige^F
indicatore^M della regolazione^F
indicador^M de ajuste^M

heel-piece
talonnière^F
Absatzteil^N
talloniera^F
talonera^F

base plate
embase^F
Grundplatte^F
piastra^F di base^F
placa^F base^F

ski stop
frein^M
Skibremse^F
freno^M
freno^M

toe-piece
butée^F
Backen^M
puntale^M
puntera^F

SPORTS AND GAMES

ski resort

station^F de ski^M | Skigebiet^N | stazione^F sciistica | estación^F de esquí

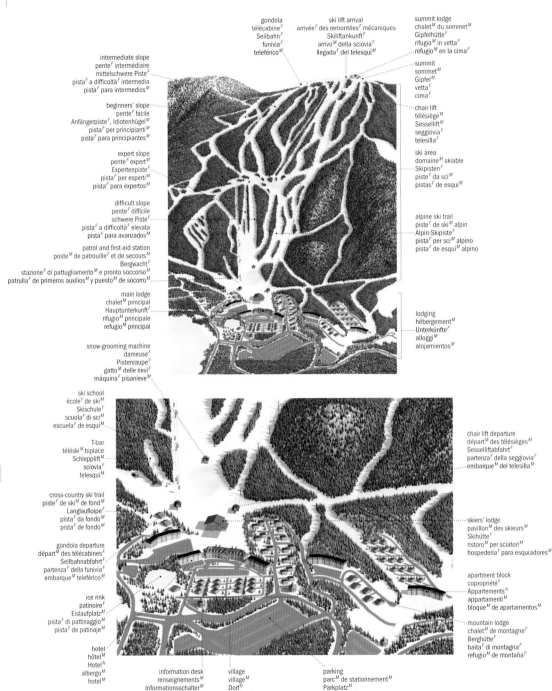

gondola
télécabine^F
Seilbahn^F
funivia^F
teleférico^M

ski lift arrival
arrivée^F des remontées^F mécaniques
Skiliftankunft^F
arrivo^M della sciovia^F
llegada^F del telesquí^M

summit lodge
chalet^M du sommet^M
Gipfelhütte^F
rifugio^M in vetta^F
refugio^M en la cima^F

intermediate slope
pente^F intermédiaire
mittelschwere Piste^F
pista^F a difficoltà^F intermedia
pista^F para intermedios^M

summit
sommet^M
Gipfel^M
vetta^F
cima^F

beginners' slope
pente^F facile
Anfängerpiste^F, Idiotenhügel^M
pista^F per principianti^M
pista^F para principiantes^M

chair lift
télésiège^M
Sessellift^M
seggiovia^F
telesilla^F

expert slope
pente^F expert^M
Expertenpiste^F
pista^F per esperti^M
pista^F para expertos^M

ski area
domaine^M skiable
Skipisten^F
piste^F da sci^M
pistas^F de esqui^M

difficult slope
pente^F difficile
schwere Piste^F
pista^F a difficoltà^F elevata
pista^F para avanzados^M

alpine ski trail
piste^F de ski^M alpin
Alpin-Skipiste^F
pista^F per sci^M alpino
pista^F de esquí^M alpino

patrol and first-aid station
poste^M de patrouille^F et de secours^M
Bergwacht^F
stazione^F di pattugliamento^M e pronto soccorso^M
patrulla^F de primeros auxilios^M y puesto^M de socorro^M

main lodge
chalet^M principal
Hauptunterkunft^F
rifugio^M principale
refugio^M principal

lodging
hébergement^M
Unterkünfte^F
alloggi^M
alojamientos^M

snow-grooming machine
dameuse^F
Pistenraupe^F
gatto^M delle nevi^F
máquina^F pisanieve^M

ski school
école^F de ski^M
Skischule^F
scuola^F di sci^M
escuela^F de esqui^M

chair lift departure
départ^M des télésièges^M
Sesselliftabfahrt^F
partenza^F della seggiovia^F
embarque^M del telesilla^M

T-bar
téléski^M biplace
Schlepplift^M
sciovia^F
telesquí^M

cross-country ski trail
piste^F de ski^M de fond^M
Langlaufloipe^F
pista^F da fondo^M
pista^F de fondo^M

skiers' lodge
pavillon^M des skieurs^M
Skihütte^F
ristoro^M per sciatori^M
hospedería^F para esquiadores^M

gondola departure
départ^M des télécabines^F
Seilbahnabfahrt^F
partenza^F della funivia^F
embarque^M teleférico^M

apartment block
copropriété^F
Appartements^N
appartamenti^M
bloque^M de apartamentos^M

ice rink
patinoire^F
Eislaufplatz^M
pista^F di pattinaggio^M
pista^F de patinaje^M

mountain lodge
chalet^M de montagne^F
Berghütte^F
baita^F di montagna^F
refugio^M de montaña^F

hotel
hôtel^M
Hotel^N
albergo^M
hotel^M

information desk
renseignements^M
Informationsschalter^M
ufficio^M delle informazioni^F
punto^M de información^F

village
village^M
Dorf^N
villaggio^M
pueblo^M

parking
parc^M de stationnement^M
Parkplatz^M
parcheggio^M
aparcamiento^M

SPORTS AND GAMES

snowboarding

surf^M des neiges^F | Snowboarden^N | snowboard^M | snowboard^M

helmet
casque^M
Helm^M
casco^M
casco^M

coveralls
combinaison^F
Skianzug^M
tuta^F
traje^M de esqui^M

goggles
lunettes^F
Skibrille^F
occhiali^M
gafas^F de esqui^M

snowboarder
surfeur^M
Snowboarder^M
snowboardista$^{M/F}$
snowboarder^M

shin guard
protège-tibia^M
Schienbeinschützer^M
parastinchi^M
tobillera^F

snowboard
surf^M des neiges^F
Snowboard^N
snowboard^M
snowboard^M

glove
gant^M
Handschuh^M
guanto^M
guante^M

hard boot
botte^F rigide
Hardboots^M
scarpone^M rigido
bota^F rigida

flexible boot
botte^F souple
Softboots^M
scarpone^M morbido
bota^F blanda

freestyle snowboard
surf^M acrobatique
Freestyleboard^N
snowboard^M per freestyle^M
tabla^F de freestyle^M

alpine snowboard
surf^M alpin
Alpinboard^N
snowboard^M per sci^M alpino
tabla^F alpina

ski jumping

saut^M à ski^M | Skispringen^N | salto^M con gli sci^M | técnica^F de salto^M

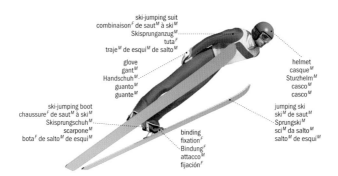

ski-jumping suit
combinaison^F de saut^M à ski^M
Skisprunganzug^M
tuta^F
traje^M de esqui^M de salto^M

glove
gant^M
Handschuh^M
guanto^M
guante^M

ski-jumping boot
chaussure^F de saut^M à ski^M
Skisprungschuh^M
scarpone^M
bota^F de salto^M de esqui^M

binding
fixation^F
Bindung^F
attacco^M
fijación^F

ski jumper
sauteur^M
Skispringer^M
saltatore^M
saltador^M

helmet
casque^M
Sturzhelm^M
casco^M
casco^M

jumping ski
ski^M de saut^M
Sprungski^M
sci^M da salto^M
salto^M de esquis^M

cross-country skiing

ski^M de fond^M | Skilanglauf^M | sci^M da fondo^M | esquí^M de fondo^M

cross-country skier
skieur^M de fond^M
Langläufer^M
fondista^{M/F}
fondista^M

polo neck
col^M roulé
Rollkragen^M
collo^M alto
jersey^M de cuello^M de cisne^M

ski hat
bonnet^M
Skimütze^F
berretto^M
gorro^M

waxing kit
trousse^F de fartage^M
Wachsausrüstung^F
accessori^M per la sciolinatura^F
estuche^M de encerado^M

pole grip
poignée^F
Stockgriff^M
impugnatura^F
puño^M

cork
liège^M
Kork^M
sughero^M
corcho^M

pole shaft
tige^F
Stockschaft^M
asta^F
fuste^M del bastón^M

ski suit
combinaison^F de ski^M
Skianzug^M
tuta^F
traje^M de esquí^M

ski pole
bâton^M
Skistock^M
racchetta^F
bastón^M de esquí^M

wrist strap
dragonne^F
Handschlaufe^F
cappio^M
correa^F para la mano^F

wax
fart^M
Wachs^N
sciolina^F
cera^F

cross-country ski
ski^M de fond^M
Langlaufski^M
sci^M da fondo^M
esquí^M de fondo^M

scraper
racloir^M
Abziehklinge^F
raschietto^M metallico
rasqueta^F

glove
gant^M
Handschuh^M
guanto^M
guante^M

boot
chaussure^F
Skistiefel^M
scarpone^M
bota^F

binding
fixation^F
Langlauf-Rattenfallbindung^F
attacco^M
fijador^M

shovel
spatule^F
Schaufel^F
spatola^F
punta^F

cross-country ski
ski^M de fond^M
Langlaufski^M
sci^M da fondo^M
esquí^M de fondo^M

ski tip
pointe^F de ski^M
Skispitze^F
punta^F dello sci^M
punta^F del esquí^M

toe binding
fixation^F à butée^F avant
Vorfußbindung^F
attacco^M
fijación^F para el pie^M

tail
talon^M
Ende^N
coda^F
cola^F

shovel
spatule^F
Schaufel^F
spatola^F
punta^F

skating step
pas^M de patineur^M
Schlittschuhschritt^M
passo^M pattinato
paso^M de patinador^M

toepiece
butée^F
Halteplatte^F
punta^F
puntera^F

heelplate
talonnière^F
Absatzplatte^F
talloniera^F
pieza^F de talón^M

diagonal step
pas^M alternatif
diagonaler Schlittschuhschritt^M
passo^M alternato
paso^M alternativo

skating kick
coup^M de patin^M
Doppelstockschub^M
colpo^M di pattino^M
golpe^M de patín^M

gliding phase
phase^F de glisse^F
Gleitphase^F
fase^F di scivolamento^M
fase^F de impulsión^F

pushing phase
phase^F de poussée^F
Schubphase^F
fase^F di spinta^F
fase^F de impulsión^F

gliding phase
phase^F de glisse^F
Gleitphase^F
fase^F di scivolamento^M
fase^F de deslizamiento^M

pushing phase
phase^F de poussée^F
Schubphase^F
fase^F di spinta^F
fase^F de impulso^M

SPORTS AND GAMES

curling

curling^M | Curling^N | curling^M | curling^M

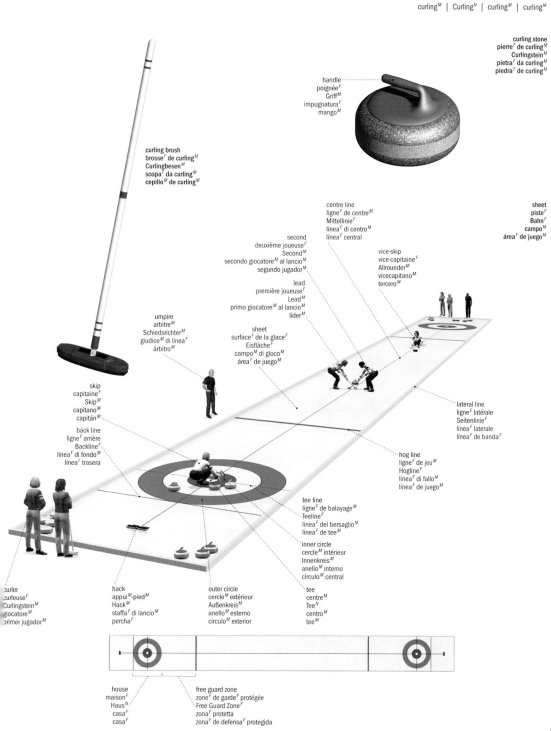

curling stone
pierre^F de curling^M
Curlingstein^M
pietra^F da curling^M
piedra^F de curling^M

handle
poignée^F
Griff^M
impugnatura^F
mango^M

curling brush
brosse^F de curling^M
Curlingbesen^M
scopa^F da curling^M
cepillo^M de curling^M

centre line
ligne^F de centre^M
Mittellinie^F
linea^F di centro^M
linea^F central

sheet
piste^F
Bahn^F
campo^M
área^F de juego^M

second
deuxième joueuse^F
Second^M
secondo giocatore^M al lancio^M
segundo jugador^M

vice-skip
vice-capitaine^F
Allrounder^M
vicecapitano^M
tercero^M

lead
première joueuse^F
Lead^M
primo giocatore^M al lancio^M
líder^M

umpire
arbitre^M
Schiedsrichter^M
giudice^M di linea^F
árbitro^M

sheet
surface^F de la glace^F
Eisfläche^F
campo^M di gioco^M
área^F de juego^M

skip
capitaine^F
Skip^M
capitano^M
capitán^M

lateral line
ligne^F latérale
Seitenlinie^F
linea^F laterale
línea^F de banda^F

back line
ligne^F arrière
Backline^F
linea^F di fondo^M
línea^F trasera

hog line
ligne^F de jeu^M
Hogline^F
linea^F di fallo^M
línea^F de juego^M

tee line
ligne^F de balayage^M
Teeline^F
linea^F del bersaglio^M
línea^F de tee^M

inner circle
cercle^M intérieur
Innenkreis^M
anello^M interno
círculo^M central

curler
curleuse^F
Curlingstein^M
giocatore^M
primer jugador^M

hack
appui^M-pied^M
Hack^M
staffa^F di lancio^M
percha^F

outer circle
cercle^M extérieur
Außenkreis^M
anello^M esterno
círculo^M exterior

tee
centre^M
Tee^N
centro^M
tee^M

house
maison^F
Haus^N
casa^F
casa^F

free guard zone
zone^F de garde^F protégée
Free Guard Zone^F
zona^F protetta
zona^F de defensa^F protegida

swimming

natation^F | Schwimmen^N | nuoto^M | natación^F

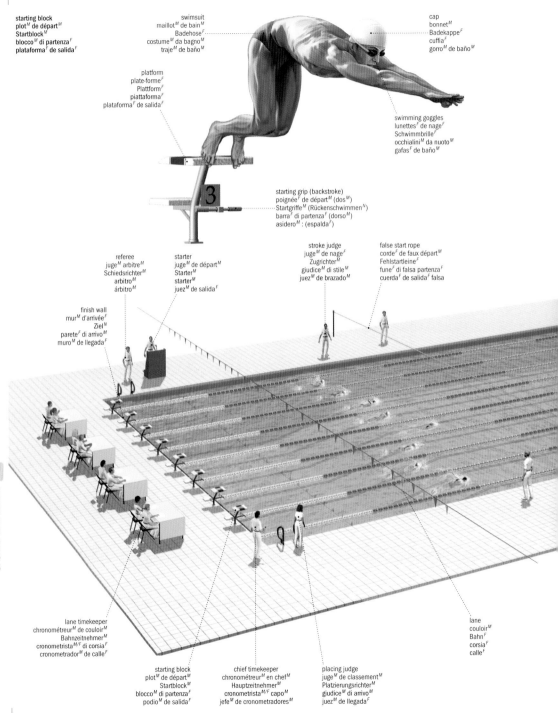

starting block
plot^M de départ^M
Startblock^M
blocco^M di partenza^F
plataforma^F de salida^F

swimsuit
maillot^M de bain^M
Badehose^F
costume^M da bagno^M
traje^M de baño^M

cap
bonnet^M
Badekappe^F
cuffia^F
gorro^M de baño^M

platform
plate-forme^F
Plattform^F
piattaforma^F
plataforma^F de salida^F

swimming goggles
lunettes^F de nage^F
Schwimmbrille^F
occhialini^M da nuoto^M
gafas^F de baño^M

starting grip (backstroke)
poignée^F de départ^M (dos^M)
Startgriffe^M (Rückenschwimmen^N)
barra^F di partenza^F (dorso^M)
asidero^M : (espalda^F)

stroke judge
juge^M de nage^F
Zugrichter^M
giudice^M di stile^M
juez^M de brazado^M

false start rope
corde^F de faux départ^M
Fehlstartleine^F
fune^F di falsa partenza^F
cuerda^F de salida^F falsa

referee
juge^M arbitre^M
Schiedsrichter^M
arbitro^M
árbitro^M

starter
juge^M de départ^M
Starter^M
starter^M
juez^M de salida^F

finish wall
mur^M d'arrivée^F
Ziel^N
parete^F di arrivo^M
muro^M de llegada^F

lane timekeeper
chronométreur^M de couloir^M
Bahnzeitnehmer^M
cronometrista^{M/F} di corsia^F
cronometrador^M de calle^F

lane
couloir^M
Bahn^F
corsia^F
calle^F

starting block
plot^M de départ^M
Startblock^M
blocco^M di partenza^F
podio^M de salida^F

chief timekeeper
chronométreur^M en chef^M
Hauptzeitnehmer^M
cronometrista^{M/F} capo^M
jefe^M de cronometradores^M

placing judge
juge^M de classement^M
Platzierungsrichter^M
giudice^M di arrivo^M
juez^M de llegada^F

swimming

crawl stroke
crawl^M
Kraulen^N
stile^M libero o crawl^M
crol^M

breaststroke
brasse^F
Brustschwimmen^N
rana^F
braza^F

butterfly stroke
papillon^M
Schmetterlingsstil^M
farfalla^F
mariposa

backstroke
nage^F sur le dos^M
Rückenschwimmen^N
dorso^M
espalda

types of stroke
types^M de nages^F
verschiedene Schwimmstile^M
stili^M di nuoto^M
estilos^M de natación^F

backstroke turn indicator
repère^M de virage^M de dos^M
Wechselanzeige^F für die Rückenlage^F
contrassegno^M per la virata^F a dorso^M
indicador^M para viraje^M en nado^M de espalda^F

side wall
mur^M latéral
Seitenwand^F
parete^F laterale
pared^F lateral

turning wall
mur^M de virage^M
Wendewand^F
parete^F di virata^F
pared^F de viraje^M

turning judges
juges^M de virages^F
Wendekampfrichter^M
giudici^M di virata^F
jueces^M de virajes^M

competitive course
bassin^M de compétition^F
Wettkampfbecken^N
piscina^F olimpionica
piscina^F olímpica

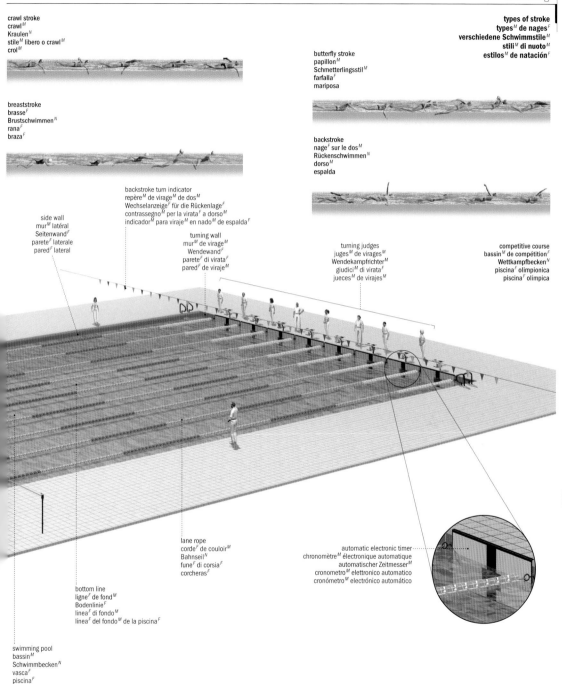

lane rope
corde^F de couloir^M
Bahnseil^N
fune^F di corsia^F
corcheras^F

automatic electronic timer
chronomètre^M électronique automatique
automatischer Zeitmesser^M
cronometro^M elettronico automatico
cronómetro^M electrónico automático

bottom line
ligne^F de fond^M
Bodenlinie^F
linea^F di fondo^M
linea^F del fondo^M de la piscina^F

swimming pool
bassin^M
Schwimmbecken^N
vasca^F
piscina^F

SPORTS AND GAMES

diving

plongeon^M | Kunstspringen^N | tuffi^M | saltos^M

starting positions
positions^F de départ^M
Startpositionen^F
posizioni^F di partenza^F
posiciones^F de salto^M

flights
vols^M
Sprungfiguren^F
voli^M
saltos^M

tuck position
position^F groupée
Saltostellung^F
posizione^F raggruppata
posición^F C - cuerpo^M encogido

reverse
renversé
auswärts
rovesciata^F
salto^M inverso

inward
retourné
einwärts
ritornata^F
salto^M interior

backward
arrière
rückwärts
all'indietro
salto^M de espalda^F

forward
avant
vorwärts
in avanti
salto^M frontal

armstand
en équilibre^M
Handstand^M
verticale^F sulle braccia^F
salto^M en equilibrio^M

straight position
position^F droite
Bohrerstellung^F
posizione^F tesa
posición^F A - en plancha^F

pike position
position^F carpée
Hechtsprungstellung^F
posizione^F carpiata
posición^F B - hacer la carpa^F

diving apparatus
plongeoir^M
Springeinrichtungen^F
strutture^F per i tuffi^M
torre^F de saltos^M

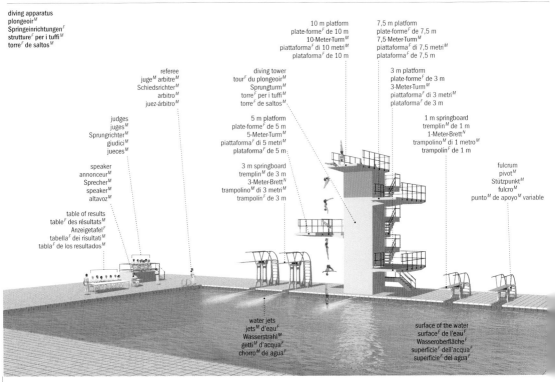

referee
juge^M arbitre^M
Schiedsrichter^M
arbitro^M
juez-árbitro^M

10 m platform
plate-forme^F de 10 m
10-Meter-Turm^M
piattaforma^F di 10 metri^M
plataforma^F de 10 m

7,5 m platform
plate-forme^F de 7,5 m
7,5 Meter-Turm^M
piattaforma^F di 7,5 metri^M
plataforma^F de 7,5 m

diving tower
tour^F du plongeoir^M
Sprungturm^M
torre^F per i tuffi^M
torre^F de saltos^M

3 m platform
plate-forme^F de 3 m
3-Meter-Turm^M
piattaforma^F di 3 metri^M
plataforma^F de 3 m

judges
juges^M
Sprungrichter^M
giudici^M
jueces^M

5 m platform
plate-forme^F de 5 m
5-Meter-Turm^M
piattaforma^F di 5 metri^M
plataforma^F de 5 m

1 m springboard
tremplin^M de 1 m
1-Meter-Brett^N
trampolino^M di 1 metro^M
trampolín^F de 1 m

speaker
annonceur^M
Sprecher^M
speaker^M
altavoz^M

3 m springboard
tremplin^M de 3 m
3-Meter-Brett^N
trampolino^M di 3 metri^M
trampolín^F de 3 m

fulcrum
pivot^M
Stützpunkt^M
fulcro^M
punto^M de apoyo^M variable

table of results
table^F des résultats^M
Anzeigetafel^F
tabella^F dei risultati^M
tabla^F de los resultados^M

water jets
jets^M d'eau^F
Wasserstrahl^M
getti^M d'acqua^F
chorro^M de agua^F

surface of the water
surface^F de l'eau^F
Wasseroberfläche^F
superficie^F dell'acqua^F
superficie^F del agua^F

sailboard

planche^F à voile^F | Surfbrett^N | windsurf^M | windsurf^M

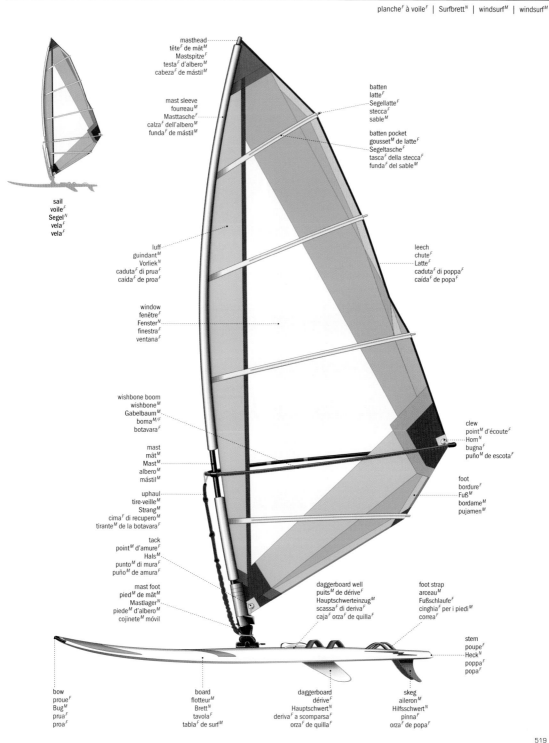

masthead
tête^F de mât^M
Mastspitze^F
testa^F d'albero^M
cabeza^F de mástil^M

batten
latte^F
Segellatte^F
stecca^F
sable^M

mast sleeve
fourreau^M
Masttasche^F
calza^F dell'albero^M
funda^F de mástil^M

batten pocket
gousset^M de latte^F
Segeltasche^F
tasca^F della stecca^F
funda^F del sable^M

sail
voile^F
Segel^N
vela^F
vela^F

luff
guindant^M
Vorliek^N
caduta^F di prua^F
caída^F de proa^F

leech
chute^F
Latte^F
caduta^F di poppa^F
caída^F de popa^F

window
fenêtre^F
Fenster^N
finestra^F
ventana^F

wishbone boom
wishbone^M
Gabelbaum^M
boma$^{M/F}$
botavara^F

clew
point^M d'écoute^F
Horn^N
bugna^F
puño^M de escota^F

mast
mât^M
Mast^M
albero^M
mástil^M

foot
bordure^F
Fuß^M
bordame^M
pujamen^M

uphaul
tire-veille^M
Strang^M
cima^F di recupero^M
tirante^M de la botavara^F

tack
point^M d'amure^F
Hals^M
punto^M di mura^F
puño^M de amura^F

mast foot
pied^M de mât^M
Mastlager^N
piede^M d'albero^M
cojinete^M móvil

daggerboard well
puits^M de dérive^F
Hauptschwerteinzug^M
scassa^F di deriva^F
caja^F orza^F de quilla^F

foot strap
arceau^M
Fußschlaufe^F
cinghia^F per i piedi^M
correa^F

stern
poupe^F
Heck^N
poppa^F
popa^F

bow
proue^F
Bug^M
prua^F
proa^F

board
flotteur^M
Brett^N
tavola^F
tabla^F de surf^M

daggerboard
dérive^F
Hauptschwert^N
deriva^F a scomparsa^F
orza^F de quilla^F

skeg
aileron^M
Hilfsschwert^N
pinna^F
orza^F de popa^F

sailing

voile^F | Segelsport^M | vela^F | vela^F

sailing boat
dériveur^M
Segelboot^N
barca^F a vela^F
velero^M

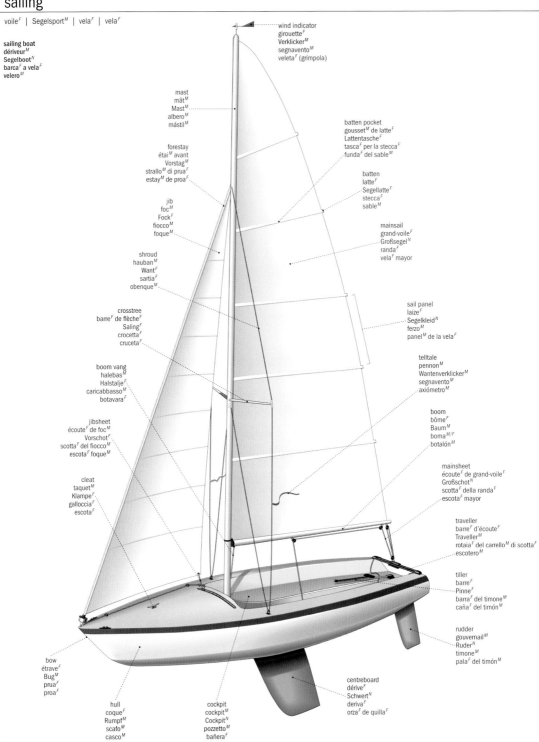

wind indicator
girouette^F
Verklicker^M
segnavento^M
veleta^F (grimpola)

mast
mât^M
Mast^M
albero^M
mástil^M

batten pocket
gousset^F de latte^F
Lattentasche^F
tasca^F per la stecca^F
funda^F del sable^M

forestay
étai^M avant
Vorstag^M
strallo^M di prua^F
estay^M de proa^F

batten
latte^F
Segellatte^F
stecca^F
sable^M

jib
foc^M
Fock^F
fiocco^M
foque^M

mainsail
grand-voile^F
Großsegel^N
randa^F
vela^F mayor

shroud
hauban^M
Want^F
sartia^F
obenque^M

sail panel
laize^F
Segelkleid^N
ferzo^M
panel^M de la vela^F

crosstree
barre^F de flèche^F
Saling^F
crocetta^F
cruceta^F

telltale
pennon^M
Wantenverklicker^M
segnavento^M
axiómetro^M

boom vang
halebas^M
Halstalje^F
caricabbasso^M
botavara^F

boom
bôme^F
Baum^M
boma^{M/F}
botalón^M

jibsheet
écoute^F de foc^M
Vorschot^F
scotta^F del fiocco^M
escota^F foque^M

mainsheet
écoute^F de grand-voile^F
Großschot^N
scotta^F della randa^F
escota^F mayor

cleat
taquet^M
Klampe^F
galloccia^F
escota^F

traveller
barre^F d'écoute^F
Traveller^M
rotaia^F del carrello^M di scotta^F
escotero^M

tiller
barre^F
Pinne^F
barra^F del timone^M
caña^F del timón^M

rudder
gouvernail^M
Ruder^N
timone^M
pala^F del timón^M

bow
étrave^F
Bug^M
prua^F
proa^F

hull
coque^F
Rumpf^M
scafo^M
casco^M

cockpit
cockpit^M
Cockpit^N
pozzetto^M
bañera^F

centreboard
dérive^F
Schwert^N
deriva^F
orza^F de quilla^F

AQUATIC AND NAUTICAL SPORTS | SPORTS AQUATIQUES ET NAUTIQUES
WASSERSPORT | SPORT ACQUATICI E NAUTICI | DEPORTES ACUÁTICOS Y NÁUTICOS

sailing

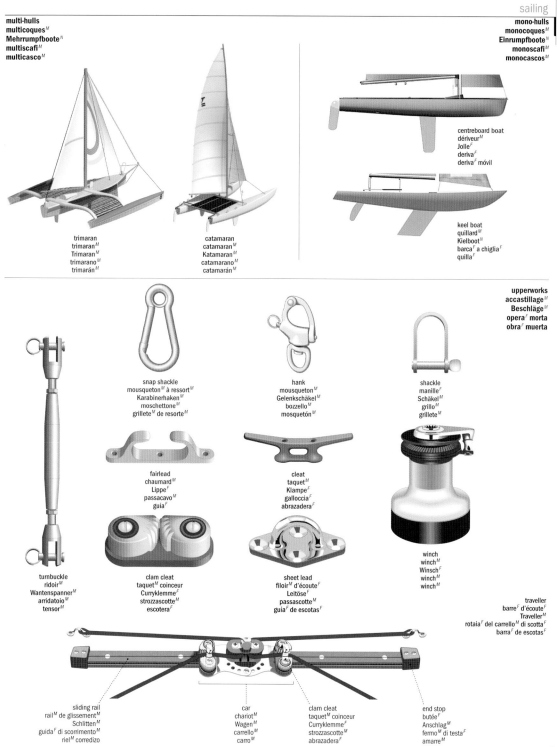

multi-hulls
multicoques^M
Mehrrumpfboote^N
multiscafi^M
multicasco^M

mono-hulls
monocoques^M
Einrumpfboote^N
monoscafi^M
monocascos^M

centreboard boat
dériveur^M
Jolle^F
deriva^F
deriva^F móvil

trimaran
trimaran^M
Trimaran^M
trimarano^M
trimarán^M

catamaran
catamaran^M
Katamaran^M
catamarano^M
catamarán^M

keel boat
quillard^M
Kielboot^N
barca^F a chiglia^F
quilla^F

upperworks
accastillage^M
Beschläge^M
opera^F **morta**
obra^F **muerta**

snap shackle
mousqueton^M à ressort^M
Karabinerhaken^M
moschettone^M
grillete^M de resorte^M

hank
mousqueton^M
Gelenkschäkel^M
bozzello^M
mosquetón^M

shackle
manille^F
Schäkel^M
grillo^M
grillete^M

fairlead
chaumard^M
Lippe^F
passacavo^M
guía^F

cleat
taquet^M
Klampe^F
galloccia^F
abrazadera^F

winch
winch^M
Winsch^F
winch^M
winch^M

turnbuckle
ridoir^M
Wantenspanner^M
arridatoio^M
tensor^M

clam cleat
taquet^M coinceur
Curryklemme^F
strozzascotte^M
escotera^F

sheet lead
filoir^M d'écoute^F
Leitöse^F
passascotte^M
guía^F de escotas^F

traveller
barre^F d'écoute^F
Traveller^M
rotaia^F del carrello^M di scotta^F
barra^F de escotas^F

sliding rail
rail^M de glissement^M
Schlitten^M
guida^F di scorrimento^M
riel^M corredizo

car
chariot^M
Wagen^M
carrello^M
carro^M

clam cleat
taquet^M coinceur
Curryklemme^F
strozzascotte^M
abrazadera^F

end stop
butée^F
Anschlag^M
fermo^M di testa^F
amarre^M

SPORTS AND GAMES

road racing

cyclisme^M sur route^F | Straßenradsport^M | ciclismo^M su strada^F | ciclismo^M por carretera^F

road-racing bicycle and cyclist
vélo^M de course^F et cycliste^M
Straßenrennrad^N und Fahrer^M
bicicletta^F da corsa^F e ciclista^{M/F}
bicicleta^F de carreras^F y ciclista^M

helmet
casque^M
Helm^M
casco^M
casco^M

jersey
maillot^M
Trikot^N
maglia^F
malla^F

shorts
cuissard^M
kurze Hose^F
pantaloncini^M
pantalones^M elásticos

glove
gant^M
Handschuh^M
guanto^M
guante^M

frame
cadre^M
Rahmen^M
telaio^M
bastidor^M

brake lever and shifter
poignée^F de frein^M et manette^F de dérailleur^M
Bremsgriff^M und Schalthebel^M
leva^F del freno^M e del cambio^M
palanca^F del freno^M y cambio^M de velocidades^F

tyre
pneu^M
Reifen^M
pneumatico^M
neumático^M

brake
frein^M
Bremse^F
freno^M
freno^M

derailleur
dérailleur^M
Umwerfer^M
deragliatore^M
cambio^M de velocidades^F

fork
fourche^F
Radgabel^F
forcella^F
horquilla^F

wheel
roue^F
Rad^N
ruota^F
rueda^F

shoe
chaussure^F
Schuh^M
scarpa^F
zapato^M

pedal
pédale^F
Pedal^N
pedale^M
pedal^M

chain wheel
plateau^M
Kettenrad^N
ruota^F della moltiplica^F
cadena^F

road cycling competition
compétition^F de cyclisme^M sur route^F
Straßenradrennen^N
gara^F di ciclismo^M su strada^F
competición^F de ciclismo^M por carretera^F

motorcycle-mounted camera
moto^F-caméra^F
Motorradkamera^F
motocicletta^F con telecamera^F
moto cámara^F

leading motorcycle
moto^F de tête^F
Führungsmotorrad^N
motocicletta^F di testa^F
moto^M de cabeza^F

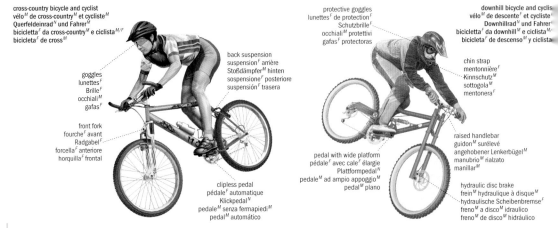

bunch
peloton^M
Hauptfeld^N
gruppo^M
pelotón^M

following car
voiture^F suiveuse
Verfolgerauto^N
ammiraglia^F
coche^M del equipo^M

race director
directeur^M de course^F
Rennleiter^M
direttore^M della corsa^F
director^M de carrera^F

leading bunch
peloton^M de tête^F
Führungsgruppe^F
gruppo^M di testa^F
pelotón^M de cabeza^F

mountain biking

vélo^M de montagne^F | Mountainbike^N | mountain bike^F | ciclismo^M de montaña^F

cross-country bicycle and cyclist
vélo^M de cross-country^M et cycliste^M
Querfeldeinrad^N und Fahrer^M
bicicletta^F da cross-country^M e ciclista^{M/F}
bicicleta^F de cross^M

protective goggles
lunettes^F de protection^F
Schutzbrille^F
occhiali^M protettivi
gafas^F protectoras

downhill bicycle and cyclis
vélo^M de descente^F et cycliste^M
Downhillrad^N und Fahrer^M
bicicleta^F da downhill^M e ciclista^{M/}
bicicleta^F de descenso^M y ciclista

back suspension
suspension^F arrière
Stoßdämpfer^M hinten
sospensione^F posteriore
suspensión^F trasera

chin strap
mentonnière^F
Kinnschutz^M
sottogola^M
mentonera^F

goggles
lunettes^F
Brille^F
occhiali^M
gafas^F

front fork
fourche^F avant
Radgabel^F
forcella^F anteriore
horquilla^F frontal

raised handlebar
guidon^M surélevé
angehobener Lenkerbügel^M
manubrio^M rialzato
manillar^F

clipless pedal
pédale^F automatique
Klickpedal^N
pedale^M senza fermapiedi^M
pedal^M automático

pedal with wide platform
pédale^F avec cale^F élargie
Plattformpedal^N
pedale^M ad ampio appoggio^M
pedal^M plano

hydraulic disc brake
frein^M hydraulique à disque^M
hydraulische Scheibenbremse^F
freno^M a disco^M idraulico
freno^M de disco^M hidráulico

personal watercraft

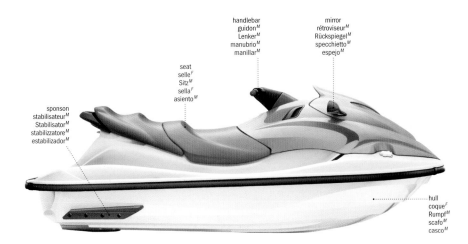

handlebar
guidon^M
Lenker^M
manubrio^M
manillar^M

mirror
rétroviseur^M
Rückspiegel^M
specchietto^M
espejo^M

seat
selle^F
Sitz^M
sella^F
asiento^M

sponson
stabilisateur^M
Stabilisator^M
stabilizzatore^M
estabilizador^M

hull
coque^F
Rumpf^M
scafo^M
casco^M

snowmobile

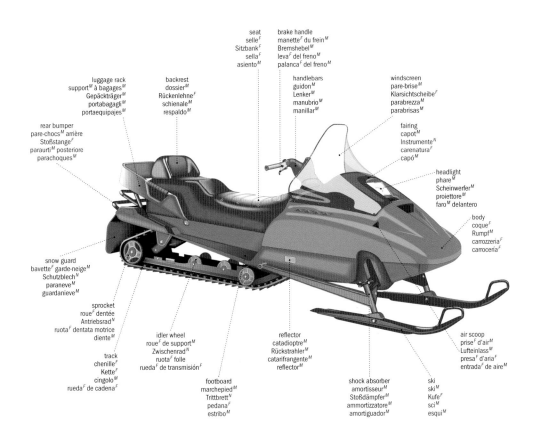

seat
selle^F
Sitzbank^F
sella^F
asiento^M

brake handle
manette^F du frein^M
Bremshebel^M
leva^F del freno^M
palanca^F del freno^M

handlebars
guidon^M
Lenker^M
manubrio^M
manillar^M

windscreen
pare-brise^M
Klarsichtscheibe^F
parabrezza^F
parabrisas^M

luggage rack
support^M à bagages^M
Gepäckträger^M
portabagagli^M
portaequipajes^M

backrest
dossier^M
Rückenlehne^F
schienale^M
respaldo^M

fairing
capot^M
Instrumente^N
carenatura^F
capó^M

rear bumper
pare-chocs^M arrière
Stoßstange^F
paraurti^M posteriore
parachoques^M

headlight
phare^M
Scheinwerfer^M
proiettore^M
faro^M delantero

body
coque^F
Rumpf^M
carrozzeria^F
carrocería^F

snow guard
bavette^F garde-neige^M
Schutzblech^N
paraneve^M
guardanieve^M

sprocket
roue^F dentée
Antriebsrad^N
ruota^F dentata motrice
diente^M

idler wheel
roue^F de support^M
Zwischenrad^N
ruota^F folle
rueda^F de transmisión^F

reflector
catadioptre^M
Rückstrahler^M
catarifrangente^M
reflector^M

air scoop
prise^F d'air^M
Lufteinlass^M
presa^F d'aria^F
entrada^F de aire^M

track
chenille^F
Kette^F
cingolo^M
rueda^F de cadena^F

footboard
marchepied^M
Trittbrett^N
pedana^F
estribo^M

shock absorber
amortisseur^M
Stoßdämpfer^M
ammortizzatore^M
amortiguador^M

ski
ski^M
Kufe^F
sci^M
esquí^M

motor racing

course^F automobile | Autorennen^N | automobilismo^M | carreras^F de coches^M

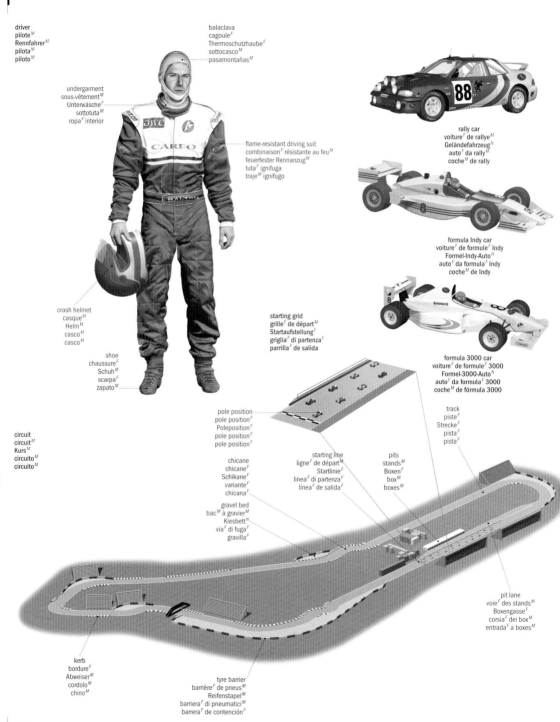

driver
pilote^M
Rennfahrer^M
pilota^M
piloto^M

balaclava
cagoule^F
Thermoschutzhaube^F
sottocasco^M
pasamontañas^M

undergarment
sous-vêtement^M
Unterwäsche^F
sottotuta^M
ropa^F interior

flame-resistant driving suit
combinaison^F résistante au feu^M
feuerfester Rennanzug^M
tuta^F ignifuga
traje^M ignifugo

rally car
voiture^F de rallye^M
Geländefahrzeug^N
auto^F da rally^M
coche^M de rally

formula Indy car
voiture^F de formule^F Indy
Formel-Indy-Auto^N
auto^F da formula^F Indy
coche^M de Indy

crash helmet
casque^M
Helm^M
casco^M
casco^M

shoe
chaussure^F
Schuh^M
scarpa^F
zapato^M

starting grid
grille^F de départ^M
Startaufstellung^F
griglia^F di partenza^F
parrilla^F de salida

formula 3000 car
voiture^F de formule^F 3000
Formel-3000-Auto^N
auto^F da formula^F 3000
coche^M de fórmula 3000

pole position
pole position^F
Poleposition^F
pole position^F
pole position^F

track
piste^F
Strecke^F
pista^F
pista^F

circuit
circuit^M
Kurs^M
circuito^M
circuito^M

chicane
chicane^F
Schikane^F
variante^F
chicana^F

starting line
ligne^F de départ^M
Startlinie^F
linea^F di partenza^F
línea^F de salida^F

pits
stands^M
Boxen^F
box^M
boxes^M

gravel bed
bac^M à gravier^M
Kiesbett^N
via^F di fuga^F
gravilla^F

pit lane
voie^F des stands^M
Boxengasse^F
corsia^F dei box^M
entrada^F a boxes^M

kerb
bordure^F
Abweiser^M
cordolo^M
chino^M

tyre barrier
barrière^F de pneus^M
Reifenstapel^M
barriera^F di pneumatici^M
barrera^F de contención^F

SPORTS AND GAMES

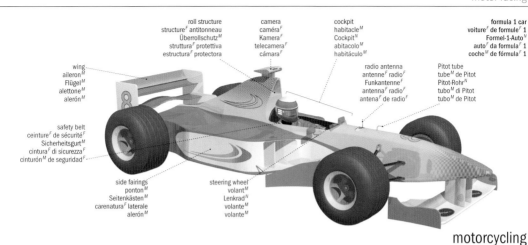

formula 1 car
voiture^F de formule^F 1
Formel-1-Auto^N
auto^F da formula^F 1
coche^M de fórmula^F 1

roll structure
structure^F antitonneau
Überrollschutz^M
struttura^F protettiva
estructura^F protectora

camera
caméra^F
Kamera^F
telecamera^F
cámara^F

cockpit
habitacle^M
Cockpit^N
abitacolo^M
habitáculo^M

radio antenna
antenne^F radio^F
Funkantenne^F
antenna^F radio^F
antena^F de radio^F

Pitot tube
tube^M de Pitot
Pitot-Rohr^N
tubo^M di Pitot
tubo^M de Pitot

wing
aileron^M
Flügel^M
alettone^M
alerón^M

safety belt
ceinture^F de sécurité^F
Sicherheitsgurt^M
cintura^F di sicurezza^F
cinturón^M de seguridad^F

side fairings
ponton^M
Seitenkästen^M
carenatura^F laterale
alerón^M

steering wheel
volant^M
Lenkrad^N
volante^M
volante^M

motorcycling

motocyclisme^M | Motorradsport^M | motociclismo^M | motocicleta^F

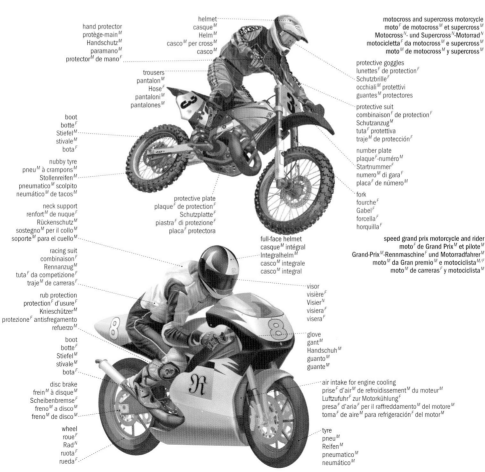

hand protector
protège-main^M
Handschutz^M
paramano^M
protector^M de mano^F

helmet
casque^M
Helm^M
casco^M per cross^M
casco^M

motocross and supercross motorcycle
moto^F de motocross^M et supercross^M
Motocross^N- und Supercross^N-Motorrad^N
motocicletta^F da motocross^M e supercross^M
moto^M de motocross^M y supercross^M

protective goggles
lunettes^F de protection^F
Schutzbrille^F
occhiali^M protettivi
guantes^M protectores

trousers
pantalon^M
Hose^F
pantaloni^M
pantalones^M

protective suit
combinaison^F de protection^F
Schutzanzug^M
tuta^F protettiva
traje^M de protección^F

boot
botte^F
Stiefel^M
stivale^M
bota^F

number plate
plaque^F-numéro^M
Startnummer^F
numero^M di gara^F
placa^F de número^M

nubby tyre
pneu^M à crampons^M
Stollenreifen^M
pneumatico^M scolpito
neumático^M de tacos^M

fork
fourche^F
Gabel^F
forcella^F
horquilla^F

protective plate
plaque^F de protection^F
Schutzplatte^F
piastra^F di protezione^F
placa^F protectora

neck support
renfort^M de nuque^F
Rückenschutz^M
sostegno^M per il collo^M
soporte^M para el cuello^M

full-face helmet
casque^M intégral
Integralhelm^M
casco^M integrale
casco^M integral

speed grand prix motorcycle and rider
moto^F de Grand Prix^M et pilote^M
Grand-Prix^M-Rennmaschine^F und Motorradfahrer^M
moto^F da Gran premio^M e motociclista^{M/F}
moto^M de carreras^F y motociclista^M

racing suit
combinaison^F
Rennanzug^M
tuta^F da competizione^F
traje^M de carreras^F

visor
visière^F
Visier^N
visiera^F
visera^F

rub protection
protection^F d'usure^F
Knieschützer^M
protezione^F antisfregamento
refuerzo^M

boot
botte^F
Stiefel^M
stivale^M
bota^F

glove
gant^M
Handschuh^M
guanto^M
guante^M

disc brake
frein^M à disque^M
Scheibenbremse^F
freno^M a disco^M
freno^M de disco^M

air intake for engine cooling
prise^F d'air^M de refroidissement^M du moteur^M
Luftzufuhr^F zur Motorkühlung^F
presa^F d'aria^F per il raffreddamento^M del motore^M
toma^F de aire^M para refrigeración^F del motor^M

wheel
roue^F
Rad^N
ruota^F
rueda^F

tyre
pneu^M
Reifen^M
pneumatico^M
neumático^M

SPORTS AND GAMES

skateboarding

planche^F à roulettes^F | Skateboarding^N | skateboard^M | skateboard^M

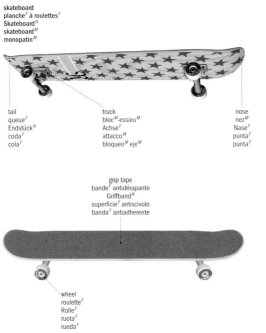

skateboard
planche^F à roulettes^F
Skateboard^N
skateboard^M
monopatin^M

tail
queue^F
Endstück^N
coda^F
cola^F

truck
bloc^M-essieu^M
Achse^F
attacco^M
bloqueo^M eje^M

nose
nez^M
Nase^F
punta^F
punta^F

grip tape
bande^F antidérapante
Griffband^N
superficie^F antiscivolo
banda^F antiadherente

wheel
roulette^F
Rolle^F
ruota^F
rueda^F

knee pad
genouillère^F
Knieschützer^M
ginocchiera^F
rodillera^F

skateboarder
planchiste^M
Skateboarder^M
skater^{M/F}
monopatin^M

elbow pad
protège-coude^M
Ellbogenschützer^M
gomitiera^F
codera^F

helmet
casque^M
Helm^M
casco^M
casco^M

coping
arête^F
Kantenschiene^F
tubo^M metallico
coping^M

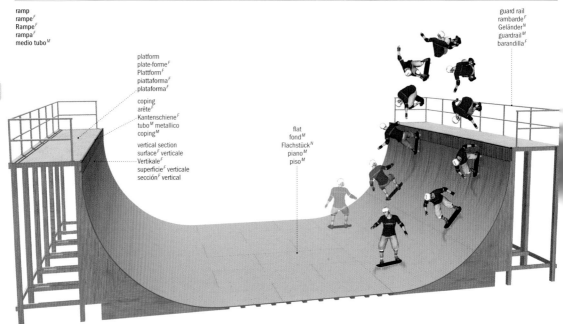

ramp
rampe^F
Rampe^F
rampa^F
medio tubo^M

guard rail
rambarde^F
Geländer^N
guardrail^M
barandilla^F

platform
plate-forme^F
Plattform^F
piattaforma^F
plataforma^F

coping
arête^F
Kantenschiene^F
tubo^M metallico
coping^M

vertical section
surface^F verticale
Vertikale^F
superficie^F verticale
sección^F vertical

flat
fond^M
Flachstück^N
piano^M
piso^M

inline skating

acrobatic skate
patin^M acrobatique
Stuntskate^M
pattino^M acrobatico
patinaje^M acrobático

inner boot
chausson^M intérieur
Innenstiefel^M
scarpetta^F interna
botín^M interior

upper shell
coque^F supérieure
Schalenschuh^M
gambale^M
bota^F externa

skater
patineuse^F
Skaterin^F
pattinatore^M
patinador^M

helmet
casque^M
Helm^M
casco^M
casco^M

elbow pad
coudière^F
Ellbogenschützer^M
gomitiera^F
codera^F

knee pad
genouillère^F
Knieschützer^M
ginocchiera^F
rodillera^F

frame
platine^F
Schiene^F
telaio^M
bastidor^M

wheel
roue^F
Rolle^F
rotella^F
rueda^F

roller speed skate
patin^M de vitesse^F
Speedskate^M
pattino^M da velocità^F
patin^M en línea^F

wrist guard
protège-poignet^M
Handgelenkschützer^M
polsiera^F
muñequera^F

roller skate
patin^M à roues^F alignées
Rollschuh^M
pattino^M a rotelle^F
patín^M en línea^F

upper shell
coque^F supérieure
Oberschale^F
gambale^M
bota^F externa

inner boot
chausson^M intérieur
Innenstiefel^M
scarpetta^F interna
botín^F interior

adjustable buckle
boucle^F de réglage^M
Einstellspanner^M
dispositivo^M di regolazione^F
hebilla^F de ajuste^M

roller hockey skate
patin^M de hockey^M
Hockeyskate^M
pattino^M da hockey^M
patin en línea^F de hockey^M

boot
chaussure^F
Stiefel^M
scarpa^F
bota^F

axle
essieu^M
Achse^F
assale^M
eje^M

heel stop
frein^M de talon^M
Absatzstopper^M
freno^M a tampone^M
freno^M trasero^M

wheel
roue^F
Rolle^F
ruota^F
rueda^F

truck
bloc^M-essieu^M
Wagen^M
carrello^M
bogie^M

camping

camping^M | Camping^N | campeggio^M | acampada^F

examples of tents
exemples^M de tentes^F
Beispiele^N für Zelte^N
esempi^M di tende^F
ejemplos^M de tiendas^F de campaña^F

flysheet
double toit^M
Überdach^N
telo^M esterno
doble techo^M

two-person tent
tente^F deux places^F
Zweipersonenzelt^N
tenda^F a due posti^M
tienda^F para dos

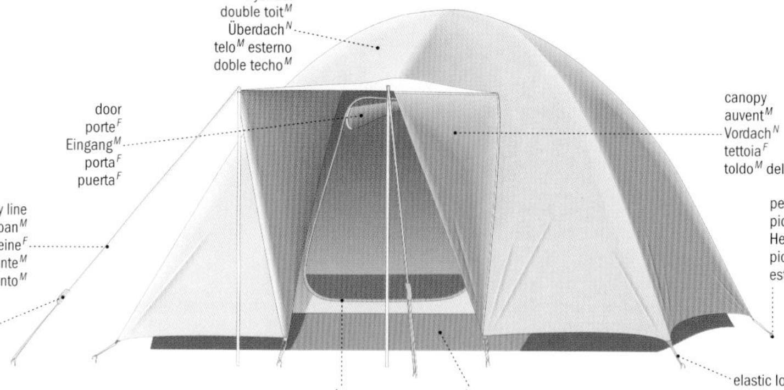

door
porte^F
Eingang^M
porta^F
puerta^F

canopy
auvent^M
Vordach^N
tettoia^F
toldo^M delantero

guy line
hauban^M
Zeltspannleine^F
tirante^M
viento^M

peg
piquet^M
Hering^M
picchetto^M
estaquilla^F

tension adjuster
tendeur^M
Spanner^M
regolatore^M del tirante^M
fiador^M

elastic loop
Sandow®^M
Gummispannring^M
elastico^M
fiador^M elástico

zip
fermeture^F à glissière^F
Reißverschluss^M
cerniera^F lampo
cierre^M

inner tent
tente^F intérieure
Innenzelt^N
tenda^F interna
tienda^F interior

family tent
tente^F familiale
Familienzelt^N
tenda^F di tipo^M familiare
tienda^F de campaña^F tamaño^M familiar

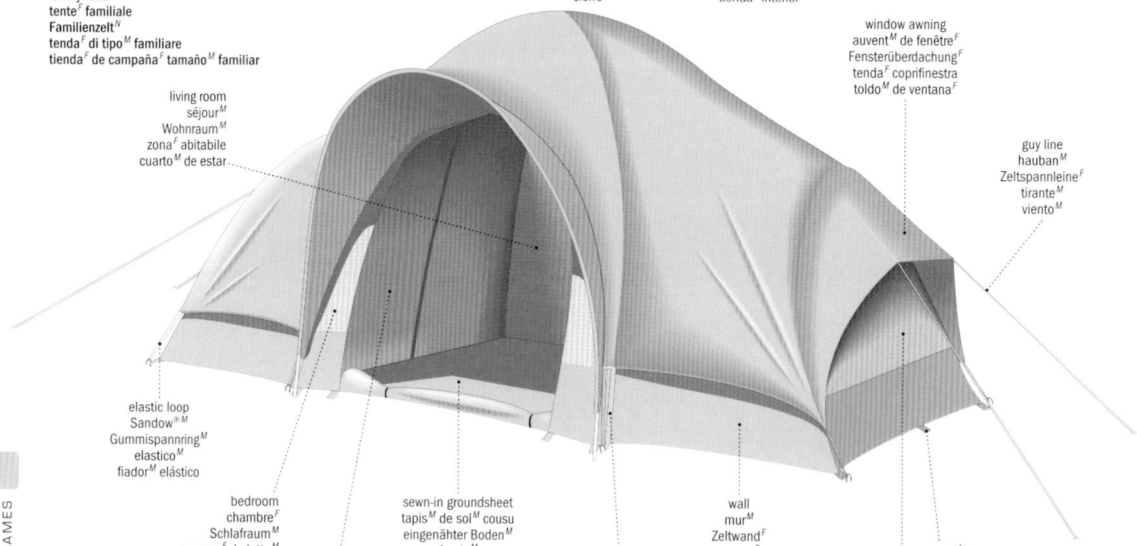

window awning
auvent^M de fenêtre^F
Fensterüberdachung^F
tenda^F coprifinestra
toldo^M de ventana^F

living room
séjour^M
Wohnraum^M
zona^F abitabile
cuarto^M de estar

guy line
hauban^M
Zeltspannleine^F
tirante^M
viento^M

elastic loop
Sandow®^M
Gummispannring^M
elastico^M
fiador^M elástico

bedroom
chambre^F
Schlafraum^M
camera^F da letto^M
dormitorio^M

sewn-in groundsheet
tapis^M de sol^M cousu
eingenähter Boden^M
fondo^M
piso^M cosido

wall
mur^M
Zeltwand^F
parete^F
muro^M

peg loop
boucle^F de piquet^M
Heringsschlaufe^F
asola^F per il picchetto^M
presilla^F de estaquilla^F

canvas divider
cloison^F
Raumteiler^M
divisorio^M di tela^F
lona^F de separación^F

frame
armature^F
Gestänge^N
intelaiatura^F
armadura^F

screen window
fenêtre^F moustiquaire^F
Fliegenfenster^N
finestra^F zanzariera
ventana^F-mosquitero^M

wagon tent
tente^F grange^F
Mannschaftszelt^N
tenda^F da cucina^F
tienda^F tipo^M vagón^M

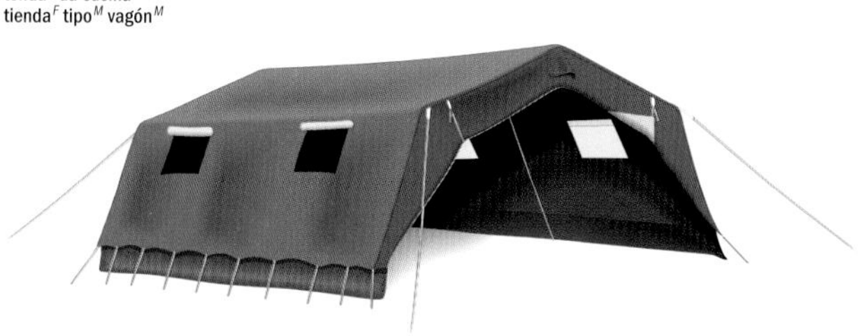

wall tent
tente^F rectangulaire
Steilwandzelt^N
tenda^F da campo^M
tienda^F rectangular

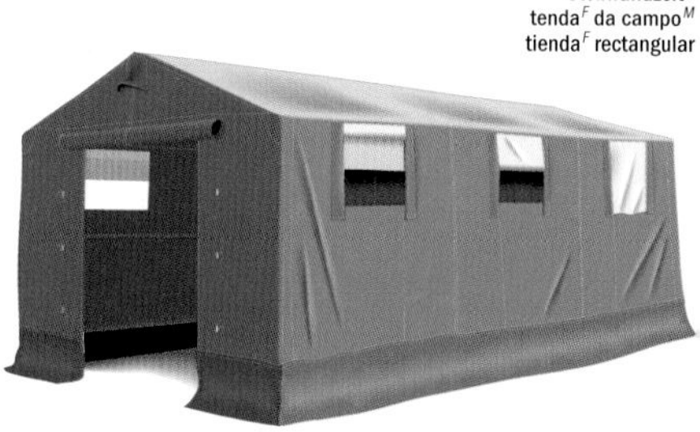

flysheet
double toit^M
Überdach^M
telo^M esterno
doble toldo^M

roof pole
mât^M de toit^M
Zeltstange^F
palo^M frontale
palo^M de la tienda^F

ridge tent
tente^F canadienne
Hauszelt^N
tenda^F canadese
tienda^F de campaña^F clásica

elastic strainer
Sandow$^{®\,M}$
Gummispannring^M
elastico^M
fiador^M elástico

inner tent
tente^F intérieure
Innenzelt^N
tenda^F interna
tienda^F interior

door
porte^F
Eingang^M
porta^F
puerta^F

peg loop
boucle^F de piquet^M
Heringsschlaufe^F
asola^F per il picchetto^M
presilla^F de estaquilla^F

sewn-in groundsheet
tapis^M de sol^M cousu
eingenähter Boden^M
fondo^M
piso^M cosido

peg
piquet^M
Hering^M
picchetto^M
estaquilla^F

one-person tent
tente^F individuelle
Einpersonenzelt^N
tenda^F a un posto^M
tienda^F unipersonal

dome tent
tente^F dôme^M
Kuppelzelt^N
tenda^F a cupola^F
tienda^F tipo^M domo^M

igloo tent
tente^F igloo^M
Igluzelt^N
tenda^F a igloo^M
tienda^F tipo^M iglú^M

lantern
lanterne^F
Lampe^F
lanterna^F
linterna^F

globe
globe^M
Glas^N
globo^M di vetro^M
globo^M

burner frame
bâti^M du brûleur^M
Brennsockel^M
telaio^M del bruciatore^M
armazón^M del quemador^M

pressure regulator
régulateur^M de pression^F
Gasstromregulierung^F
regolatore^M di luminosità^F
regulador^M de presión^F

pump
pompe^F
Pumpe^F
pompa^F
bomba^F

leakproof cap
bouchon^M antifuite
Dichtverschluss^M
capsula^F ermetica
tapón^M hermético

gas container
réservoir^M
Gasbehälter^M
bombola^F
tanque^M

propane or butane appliances
accessoires^M au propane^M ou au butane^M
Propan- oder Butangas-Geräte^N
accessori^M a propano^M o butano^M
equipos^M de gas^M

heater
chaufferette^F
Heizstrahler^M
stufa^F a gas^M
calentador^M

two-burner camp stove
réchaud^M à deux feux^M
zweiflammiger Gasbrenner^M
fornello^M da campo^M a due fuochi^M
cocina^F de campo^M

gas container
réservoir^M
Gasbehälter^M
bombola^F
bombona^F de gas^M

burner
brûleur^M
Brenner^M
bruciatore^M
quemador^M

wire frame
grille^F stabilisatrice
Metallaufsatz^M
griglia^F
parrilla^F estabilizadora

single-burner camp stove
réchaud^M à un feu^M
einflammiger Gasbrenner^M
fornello^M da campo^M con un bruciatore^M
hornillo^M

control valve
robinet^M relais^M
Reglerventil^N
manopola^F di regolazione^F del gas^M
válvula^F de control^M

camping

examples of sleeping bags
exemples^M **de sacs**^{M} **de couchage**^{M}
Beispiele^N **für Schlafsäcke**^{M}
esempi^M **di sacchi**^{M} **a pelo**^{M}
ejemplos^M **de sacos**^{M} **de dormir**

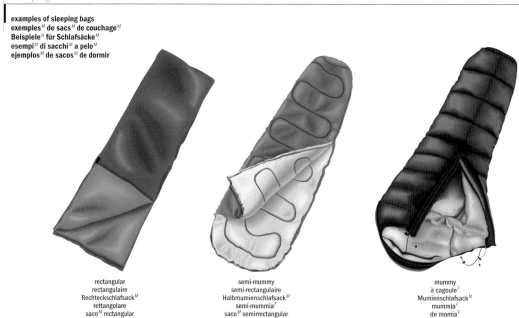

rectangular
rectangulaire
Rechteckschlafsack^M
rettangolare
saco^M rectangular

semi-mummy
semi-rectangulaire
Halbmumienschlafsack^M
semi-mummia^F
saco^M semirrectangular

mummy
à cagoule^F
Mumienschlafsack^M
mummia^F
de momia^F

bed and mattress
lit^M **et matelas**^{M}
Bett^N **mit Matratze**^{F}
branda^F **e materassino**^{M}
camas^F **y colchonetas**^{F}

camp bed
lit^M de camp^M pliant
Feldbett^N
brandina^F smontabile
catre^M desmontable

inflator-deflator
gonfleur^M-dégonfleur^M
Kombipumpe^F
gonfiatore^M a soffietto^M
muelle^M para inflar y desinflar

inflator
gonfleur^M
Blasebalg^M
gonfiatore^M
inflador^M

air mattress
matelas^M pneumatique
Luftmatratze^F
materassino^M pneumatico
colchoneta^F de aire^M

self-inflating mattress
matelas^M autogonflant
selbstaufblasbare Luftmatratze^F
materassino^M autogonfiante
colchoneta^F aislante

foam pad
matelas^M mousse^F
Schaumgummimatratze^F
materassino^M isolante
colchoneta^F de espuma^F

SPORTS AND GAMES

cutlery set
ustensiles^M de campeur^M
Essbesteck^N
posate^F
cuberteria^F

cooking set
popote^F
Kochgeschirr^N
set^M **per cucinare**
utensilios^M **de cocina**^{F}

spoon
cuiller^F
Löffel^M
cucchiaio^M
cuchara^F

belt loop
ganse^F
Gürtelschlaufe^F
asola^F
presilla^F

fork
fourchette^F
Gabel^F
forchetta^F
tenedor^M

pouch
étui^M
Hülle^F
fodero^M
funda^F

knife
couteau^M
Messer^N
coltello^M
cuchillo^M

plate
assiette^F plate
Teller^M
piatto^M
plato^M

saucepan
faitout^M
Kochtopf^M
tegame^M
cazuela^F

handle
queue^F
Griff^M
manico^M
mango^M

frying pan
poêle^F à frire
Bratpfanne^F
padella^F
sartén^F

coffee pot
cafetière^F
Kaffeekanne^F
caffettiera^F
cafetera^F

cup
tasse^F
Tasse^F
tazza^F
taza^F

---

scissors
ciseaux^M
Schere^F
forbici^F
tijeras^F

fish scaler
écailleur^M
Fischschupper^M
desquamatore^M
descamador^M

ruler
règle^F graduée
Lineal^N
righello^M
regla^F

camping equipment
matériel^M **de camping**^{M}
Campingausrüstung^F
attrezzature^F **da campeggio**^{M}
equipamiento^M **para acampar**

Swiss army knife
couteau^M suisse
schweizer Offiziersmesser^N
temperino^M multiuso
navaja^F multiusos suiza

file
lime^F
Feile^F
lima^F
lima^F

magnifier
loupe^F
Lupe^F
lente^F
lupa^F

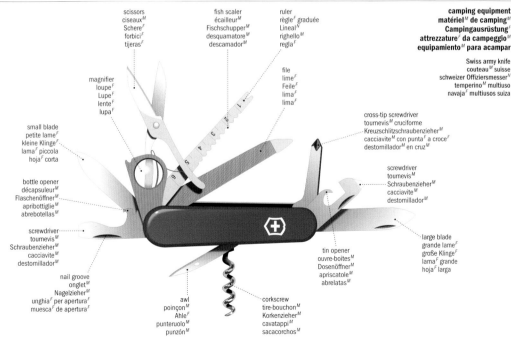

cross-tip screwdriver
tournevis^M cruciforme
Kreuzschlitzschraubenzieher^M
cacciavite^M con punta^F a croce^F
destornillador^M en cruz^M

small blade
petite lame^F
kleine Klinge^F
lama^F piccola
hoja^F corta

screwdriver
tournevis^M
Schraubenzieher^M
cacciavite^M
destornillador^M

bottle opener
décapsuleur^M
Flaschenöffner^M
apribottiglie^M
abrebotellas^M

large blade
grande lame^F
große Klinge^F
lama^F grande
hoja^F larga

screwdriver
tournevis^M
Schraubenzieher^M
cacciavite^M
destornillador^M

tin opener
ouvre-boîtes^M
Dosenöffner^M
apriscatole^M
abrelatas^M

nail groove
onglet^M
Nagelzieher^M
unghia^F per apertura^F
muesca^F de apertura^F

awl
poinçon^M
Ahle^F
punteruolo^M
punzón^M

corkscrew
tire-bouchon^M
Korkenzieher^M
cavatappi^M
sacacorchos^M

SPORTS AND GAMES

camping

backpack
sac^M à dos^M
Rucksack^M
zaino^M
mochila^F

top flap
rabat^M
Deckeltasche^F
patta^F di chiusura^F
solapa^F

shoulder strap
bretelle^F
Schultergurt^M
spallaccio^M
espaldera^F

tightening buckle
boucle^F de réglage^M
Schließe^F
fibbia^F di regolazione^F
hebilla^F de regulación^F

side compression strap
sangle^F de compression^F
seitlicher Kompressionsgurt^M
cinghia^F di compressione^F laterale
correa^F de compresión^F

front compression strap
sangle^F de fermeture^F
vorderer Straffergurt^M
cinghia^F di compressione^F frontale
correa^F de cierre^M

strap loop
passe-sangle^M
Riemenschlaufe^F
passacinghia^M
pasador^M

waist belt
ceinture^F
Hüftgurt^M
cintura^F a vita^F
cinturón^M

folding shovel
pelle^F-pioche^F pliante
Klappspaten^M
badile^M pieghevole
pala^F plegable

hurricane lamp
lampe^F-tempête^F
Sturmlampe^F
lampada^F a petrolio^M
lámpara^F de petróleo^M

vacuum flask
bouteille^F isolante
Thermosflasche^F
thermos^M
termo^M

bottle
bouteille^F
Flasche^F
bottiglia^F
botella^F del termo^M

stopper
bouchon^M
Verschluss^M
tappo^M
tapón^M

cup
tasse^F
Becher^M
bicchiere^M
taza^F

canteen
gourde^F
Feldflasche^F
borraccia^F
cantimplora^F

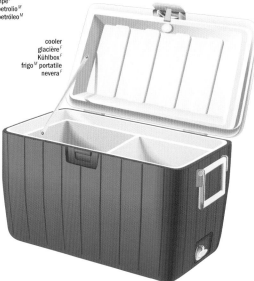

cooler
glacière^F
Kühlbox^F
frigo^M portatile
nevera^F

water carrier
bidon^M à eau^F
Wasserkanister^M
contenitore^M termico
termo^M con llave^F de servicio^M

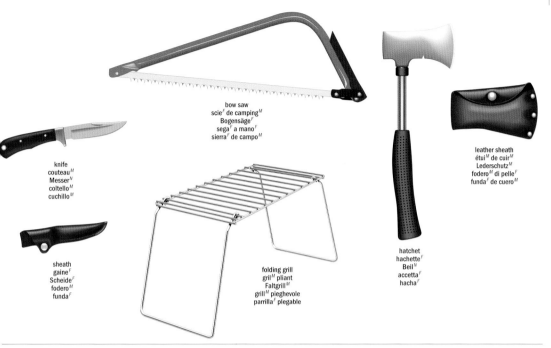

bow saw
scie^F de camping^M
Bogensäge^F
sega^F a mano^F
sierra^F de campo^M

leather sheath
étui^M de cuir^M
Lederschutz^M
fodero^M di pelle^F
funda^F de cuero^M

knife
couteau^M
Messer^N
coltello^M
cuchillo^M

sheath
gaine^F
Scheide^F
fodero^M
funda^F

folding grill
gril^M pliant
Faltgrill^M
grill^M pieghevole
parrilla^F plegable

hatchet
hachette^F
Beil^N
accetta^F
hacha^F

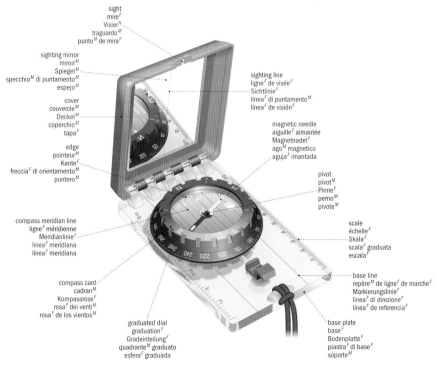

magnetic compass
boussole^F magnétique
Magnetkompass^M
bussola^F magnetica
brújula^F magnética

sight
mire^F
Visier^N
traguardo^M
punto^M de mira^F

sighting mirror
miroir^M
Spiegel^M
specchio^M di puntamento^M
espejo^M

sighting line
ligne^F de visée^F
Sichtlinie^F
linea^F di puntamento^M
línea^F de visión^F

cover
couvercle^M
Deckel^M
coperchio^M
tapa^F

magnetic needle
aiguille^F aimantée
Magnetnadel^F
ago^M magnetico
aguja^F imantada

edge
pointeur^M
Kante^F
freccia^F di orientamento^M
puntero^M

pivot
pivot^M
Pinne^F
perno^M
pivote^M

scale
échelle^F
Skala^F
scala^F graduata
escala^F

compass meridian line
ligne^F méridienne
Meridianlinie^F
linea^F meridiana
línea^F meridiana

base line
repère^M de ligne^F de marche^F
Markierungslinie^F
linea^F di direzione^F
línea^F de referencia^F

compass card
cadran^M
Kompassrose^F
rosa^F dei venti^M
rosa^F de los vientos^M

graduated dial
graduation^F
Gradeinteilung^F
quadrante^M graduato
esfera^F graduada

base plate
base^F
Bodenplatte^F
piastra^F di base^F
soporte^M

SPORTS AND GAMES

hunting

chasse^F | Jagen^N | caccia^F | caza^F

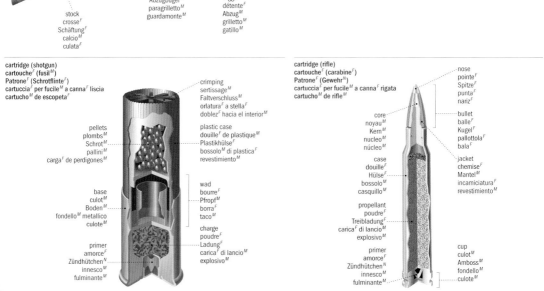

rifle (rifled bore)
carabine^F (canon^M rayé)
Gewehr^N (gezogener Lauf^M)
fucile^M a canna^F rigata
rifle^M

breechblock
bloc^M de culasse^F
Verschlussstück^N
blocco^M della culatta^F
bloque^M de cierre^M de la recámara^F

muzzle
bouche
Mündung^F
bocca
boca

pistol grip
poignée^F
Kolbenhals^M
impugnatura^F a pistola^F
empuñadura^F

hammer
chien^M
Hahn^M
cane^M
percutor^M

telescopic sight
lunette^F de visée^F
Zielfernrohr^N
mirino^M a cannocchiale^M
mira^F telescópica

rear sight
hausse^F
Kimme^F
tacca^F di mira^F
alza^F

front sight
guidon^M
Korn^N
mirino^M
punto^M de mira^F

butt plate
plaque^F de couche^F
Rückschlaghinderer^M
calciolo^M
cantonera^F

trigger guard
pontet^M
Abzugbügel^M
paragrilletto^M
guardamonte^M

barrel
canon^M
Rohr^N
canna^F
cañón^M

stock
crosse^F
Schäftung^F
calcio^M
culata^F

lever
levier^M
Bügelhebel^M
leva^F
palanca^F

trigger
détente^F
Abzug^M
grilletto^M
gatillo^M

muzzle
bouche
Mündung^F
bocca
boca

shotgun (smooth-bore)
fusil^M (canon^M lisse)
Schrotflinte^F (glatter Lauf^M)
fucile^M a canna^F liscia
escopeta^F

pistol grip
poignée^F
Pistolengriff^M
impugnatura^F a pistola^F
empuñadura^F

hammer
chien^M
Hahn^M
cane^M
percutor^M

ventilated rib
bande^F ventilée
Laufschiene^F
bindella^F ventilata
banda^F de ventilación^F

front sight
guidon^M
Korn^N
mirino^M
punto^M de mira^F

butt plate
plaque^F de couche^F
Rückschlaghinderer^M
calciolo^M
cantonera^F

breechblock
bloc^M de culasse^F
Verschlussstück^N
blocco^M della culatta^F
bloque^M de cierre^M de recámara^F

forearm
fût^M
Vorderschaft^M
asta^F
caña^F

barrel
canon^M
Rohr^N
canna^F
cañón^M

trigger guard
pontet^M
Abzugbügel^M
paragrilletto^M
guardamonte^M

trigger
détente^F
Abzug^M
grilletto^M
gatillo^M

stock
crosse^F
Schäftung^F
calcio^M
culata^F

cartridge (shotgun)
cartouche^F (fusil^M)
Patrone^F (Schrotflinte^F)
cartuccia^F per fucile^M a canna^F liscia
cartucho^M de escopeta^F

crimping
sertissage^M
Faltverschluss^M
orlatura^F a stella^F
doblez^M hacia el interior^M

pellets
plombs^M
Schrot^M
pallini^M
carga^F de perdigones^M

plastic case
douille^F de plastique^M
Plastikhülse^F
bossolo^M di plastica^F
revestimiento^M

base
culot^M
Boden^M
fondello^M metallico
culote^M

wad
bourre^F
Pfropf^M
borra^F
taco^M

charge
poudre^F
Ladung^F
carica^F di lancio^M
explosivo^M

primer
amorce^F
Zündhütchen^N
innesco^M
fulminante^M

cartridge (rifle)
cartouche^F (carabine^F)
Patrone^F (Gewehr^N)
cartuccia^F per fucile^M a canna^F rigata
cartucho^M de rifle^M

nose
pointe^F
Spitze^F
punta^F
nariz^F

core
noyau^M
Kern^M
nucleo^M
núcleo^M

bullet
balle^F
Kugel^F
pallottola^F
bala^F

case
douille^F
Hülse^F
bossolo^M
casquillo^M

jacket
chemise^F
Mantel^M
incamiciatura^F
revestimiento^M

propellant
poudre^F
Treibladung^F
carica^F di lancio^M
explosivo^M

primer
amorce^F
Zündhütchen^N
innesco^M
fulminante^M

cup
culot^M
Amboss^M
fondello^M
culote^M

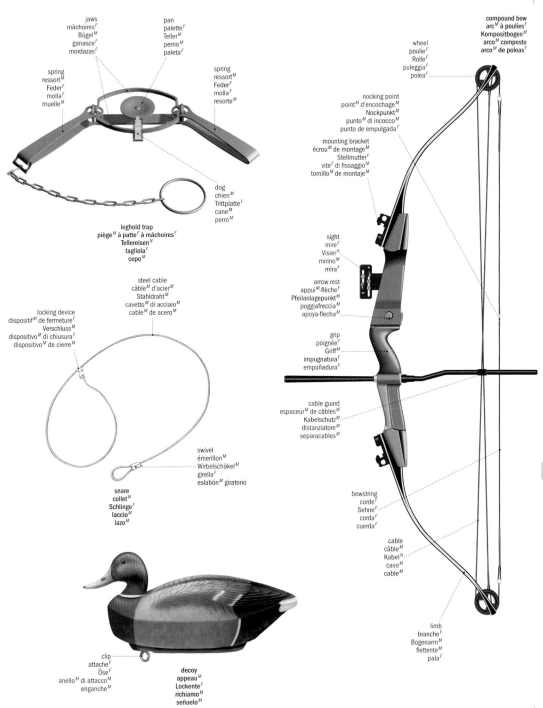

jaws
mâchoires^F
Bügel^M
ganasce^F
mordazas^F

pan
palette^F
Teller^M
perno^M
paleta^F

spring
ressort^M
Feder^F
molla^F
muelle^M

spring
ressort^M
Feder^F
molla^F
resorte^M

dog
chien^M
Trittplatte^F
cane^M
perro^M

leghold trap
piège^M à patte^F à mâchoires^F
Tellereisen^N
tagliola^F
cepo^M

compound bow
arc^M à poulies^F
Kompositbogen^M
arco^M composto
arco^M de poleas^F

wheel
poulie^F
Rolle^F
puleggia^F
polea^F

nocking point
point^M d'encochage^M
Nockpunkt^M
punto^M di incocco^M
punto de empulgada^F

mounting bracket
écrou^M de montage^M
Stellmutter^F
vite^F di fissaggio^M
tornillo^M de montaje^M

sight
mire^F
Visier^N
mirino^M
mira^F

arrow rest
appui^M-flèche^F
Pfeilanlagepunkt^M
poggiafreccia^M
apoya-flecha^M

grip
poignée^F
Griff^M
impugnatura^F
empuñadura^F

steel cable
câble^M d'acier^M
Stahldraht^M
cavetto^M di acciaio^M
cable^M de acero^M

locking device
dispositif^M de fermeture^F
Verschluss^M
dispositivo^M di chiusura^F
dispositivo^M de cierre^M

cable guard
espaceur^M de câbles^M
Kabelschutz^M
distanziatore^M
separacables^M

swivel
émerillon^M
Wirbelschäkel^M
girella^F
eslabón^M giratorio

snare
collet^M
Schlinge^F
laccio^M
lazo^M

bowstring
corde^F
Sehne^F
corda^F
cuerda^F

cable
câble^M
Kabel^N
cavo^M
cable^M

limb
branche^F
Bogenarm^M
flettente^M
pala^F

clip
attache^F
Öse^F
anello^M di attacco^M
enganche^M

decoy
appeau^M
Lockente^F
richiamo^M
señuelo^M

fishing

pêche^F | Sportfischerei^F | pesca^F | pesca^F

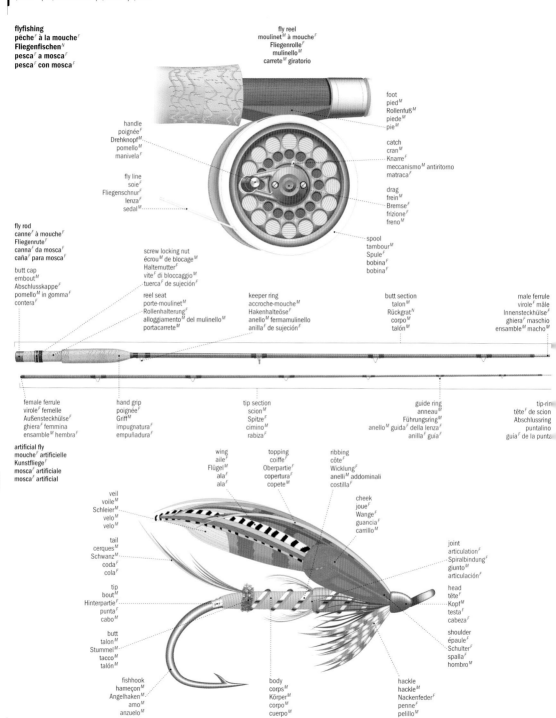

flyfishing
pêche^F **à la mouche**^F
Fliegenfischen^N
pesca^F **a mosca**^F
pesca^F **con mosca**^F

fly reel
moulinet^M à mouche^F
Fliegenrolle^F
mulinello^M
carrete^M giratorio

foot
pied^M
Rollenfuß^M
piede^M
pie^M

handle
poignée^F
Drehknopf^M
pomello^M
manivela^F

catch
cran^M
Knarre^F
meccanismo^M antiritorno
matraca^F

fly line
soie^F
Fliegenschnur^F
lenza^F
sedal^M

drag
frein^M
Bremse^F
frizione^F
freno^M

spool
tambour^M
Spule^F
bobina^F
bobina^F

fly rod
canne^F **à mouche**^F
Fliegenrute^F
canna^F **da mosca**^F
caña^F **para mosca**^F

butt cap
embout^M
Abschlusskappe^F
pomello^M in gomma^F
contera^F

screw locking nut
écrou^M de blocage^M
Haltemutter^F
vite^F di bloccaggio^M
tuerca^F de sujeción^F

reel seat
porte-moulinet^M
Rollenhalterung^F
alloggiamento^M del mulinello^M
portacarrete^F

keeper ring
accroche-mouche^M
Hakenhalteöse^F
anello^M fermamulinello
anilla^F de sujeción^F

butt section
talon^M
Rückgrat^N
corpo^M
talón^M

male ferrule
virole^F mâle
Innensteckhülse^F
ghiera^F maschio
ensamble^M macho^M

female ferrule
virole^F femelle
Außensteckhülse^F
ghiera^F femmina
ensamble^M hembra^F

hand grip
poignée^F
Griff^M
impugnatura^F
empuñadura^F

tip section
scion^M
Spitze^F
cimino^M
rabiza^F

guide ring
anneau^M
Führungsring^M
anello^M guida^F della lenza^F
anilla^F guía^F

tip-ring
tête^F de scion
Abschlussring
puntalino
guía^F de la punta

artificial fly
mouche^F **artificielle**
Kunstfliege^F
mosca^F **artificiale**
mosca^F **artificial**

wing
aile^F
Flügel^M
ala^F
ala^F

topping
coiffe^F
Oberpartie^F
copertura^F
copete^M

ribbing
côte^F
Wicklung^F
anelli^M addominali
costilla^F

cheek
joue^F
Wange^F
guancia^F
carrillo^M

veil
voile^M
Schleier^M
velo^M
velo^M

joint
articulation^F
Spiralbindung^F
giunto^M
articulación^F

tail
cerques^M
Schwanz^M
coda^F
cola^F

head
tête^F
Kopf^M
testa^F
cabeza^F

tip
bout^M
Hinterpartie^F
punta^F
cabo^M

shoulder
épaule^F
Schulter^F
spalla^F
hombro^M

butt
talon^M
Stummel^M
tacco^M
talón^M

fishhook
hameçon^M
Angelhaken^M
amo^M
anzuelo^M

body
corps^M
Körper^M
corpo^M
cuerpo^M

hackle
hackle^F
Nackenfeder^F
penne^F
pelillo^M

SPORTS AND GAMES

casting
pêche^F **au lancer**^{M}
Casting^N
pesca^F **al lancio**^{M}
pesca^F **de lanzado**^{M}

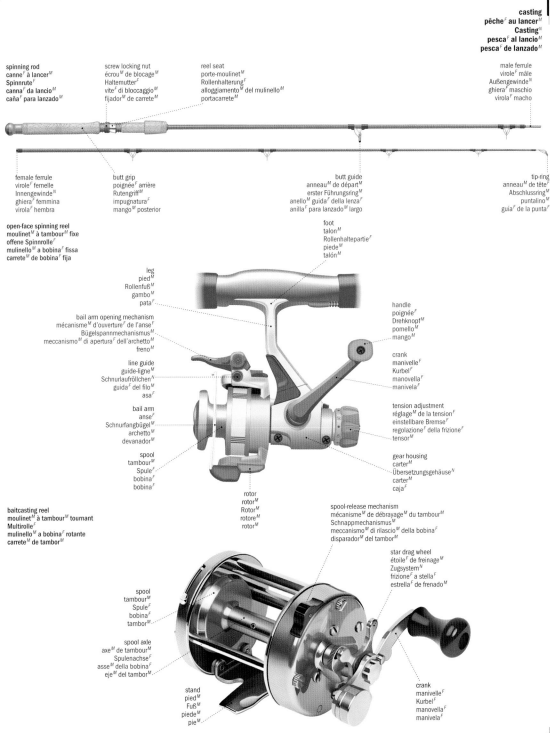

spinning rod
canne^F à lancer^M
Spinnrute^F
canna^F da lancio^M
caña^F para lanzado^M

screw locking nut
écrou^M de blocage^M
Haltemutter^F
vite^F di bloccaggio^M
fijador^M de carrete^M

reel seat
porte-moulinet^M
Rollenhalterung^F
alloggiamento^M del mulinello^M
portacarrete^M

male ferrule
virole^F mâle
Außengewinde^N
ghiera^F maschio
virola^F macho

female ferrule
virole^F femelle
Innengewinde^N
ghiera^F femmina
virola^F hembra

butt grip
poignée^F arrière
Rutengriff^M
impugnatura^F
mango^M posterior

butt guide
anneau^M de départ^M
erster Führungsring^M
anello^M guida^F della lenza^M
anilla^F para lanzado^M largo

tip-ring
anneau^M de tête^F
Abschlussring^M
puntalino^M
guía^F de la punta^F

open-face spinning reel
moulinet^M à tambour^M fixe
offene Spinnrolle^F
mulinello^M a bobina^F fissa
carrete^M de bobina^F fija

foot
talon^M
Rollenhaltepartie^F
piede^M
talón^M

leg
pied^M
Rollenfuß^M
gambo^M
pata^F

handle
poignée^F
Drehknopf^M
pomello^M
mango^M

bail arm opening mechanism
mécanisme^M d'ouverture^F de l'anse^F
Bügelspannmechanismus^M
meccanismo^M di apertura^F dell'archetto^M
freno^M

crank
manivelle^F
Kurbel^F
manovella^F
manivela^F

line guide
guide-ligne^M
Schnurlaufröllchen^N
guida^F del filo^M
asa^F

tension adjustment
réglage^M de la tension^F
einstellbare Bremse^F
regolazione^F della frizione^F
tensor^M

bail arm
anse^F
Schnurfangbügel^M
archetto^M
devanador^M

spool
tambour^M
Spule^F
bobina^F
bobina^F

gear housing
carter^M
Übersetzungsgehäuse^N
carter^M
caja^F

rotor
rotor^M
Rotor^M
rotore^M
rotor^M

spool-release mechanism
mécanisme^M de débrayage^M du tambour^M
Schnappmechanismus^M
meccanismo^M di rilascio^M della bobina^F
disparador^M del tambor^M

baitcasting reel
moulinet^M à tambour^M tournant
Multirolle^F
mulinello^M a bobina^F rotante
carrete^M de tambor^M

star drag wheel
étoile^F de freinage^M
Zugsystem^N
frizione^F a stella^F
estrella^F de frenado^M

spool
tambour^M
Spule^F
bobina^F
tambor^M

spool axle
axe^M de tambour^M
Spulenachse^F
asse^M della bobina^F
eje^M del tambor^M

stand
pied^M
Fuß^M
piede^M
pie^M

crank
manivelle^F
Kurbel^F
manovella^F
manivela^F

SPORTS AND GAMES

fishing

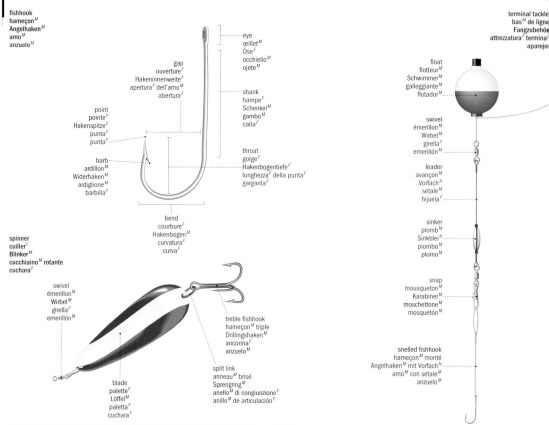

fishhook
hameçon[M]
Angelhaken[M]
amo[M]
anzuelo[M]

gap
ouverture[F]
Hakeninnenweite[F]
apertura[F] dell'amo[M]
abertura[F]

point
pointe[F]
Hakenspitze[F]
punta[F]
punta[F]

barb
ardillon[M]
Widerhaken[M]
ardiglione[M]
barbilla[F]

eye
œillet[M]
Öse[F]
occhiello[M]
ojete[M]

shank
hampe[F]
Schenkel[M]
gambo[M]
caña[F]

throat
gorge[F]
Hakenbogentiefe[F]
lunghezza[F] della punta[F]
garganta[F]

bend
courbure[F]
Hakenbogen[M]
curvatura[F]
curva[F]

terminal tackle
bas[M] de ligne
Fangzubehör
attrezzatura[F] terminale
aparejo

float
flotteur[M]
Schwimmer[M]
galleggiante[M]
flotador[M]

swivel
émerillon[M]
Wirbel[M]
girella[F]
emerillón[M]

leader
avançon[M]
Vorfach[N]
setale[M]
hijuela[F]

sinker
plomb[M]
Sinkblei[N]
piombo[M]
plomo[M]

snap
mousqueton[M]
Karabiner[M]
moschettone[M]
mosquetón[M]

snelled fishhook
hameçon[M] monté
Angelhaken[M] mit Vorfach[N]
amo[M] con setale[M]
anzuelo[M]

spinner
cuiller[F]
Blinker[M]
cucchiaino[M] rotante
cuchara[F]

swivel
émerillon[M]
Wirbel[M]
girella[F]
emerillón[M]

treble fishhook
hameçon[M] triple
Drillingshaken[M]
ancorina[F]
anzuelo[M]

split link
anneau[M] brisé
Sprengring[M]
anello[M] di congiunzione[F]
anillo[M] de articulación[F]

blade
palette[F]
Löffel[M]
paletta[F]
cuchara[F]

clothing and accessories
vêtements[M] et accessoires[M]
Kleidung[F] und Zubehör[N]
abbigliamento[M] e accessori[M]
ropa[F] y accesorios[M]

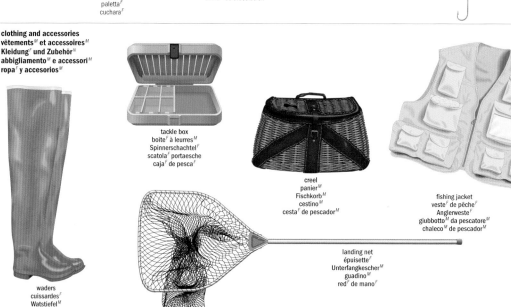

tackle box
boite[F] à leurres[M]
Spinnerschachtel[F]
scatola[F] portaesche
caja[F] de pesca[F]

creel
panier[M]
Fischkorb[M]
cestino[M]
cesta[F] de pescador[M]

fishing jacket
veste[F] de pêche[F]
Anglerweste[F]
giubbotto[M] da pescatore[M]
chaleco[M] de pescador[M]

waders
cuissardes[F]
Watstiefel[M]
stivaloni[M] impermeabili
botas[F] altas

landing net
épuisette[F]
Unterfangkescher[M]
guadino[M]
red[F] de mano[F]

English Index

A

a 298
A-line dress 252
abalone 157
abdomen 67, 68, 70, 71, 78, 92, 94
abdominal aorta 102, 107
abdominal cavity 111, 112
abdominal rectus 96
abdominal segment 67
above ground swimming pool 184
aboveground pipeline 404
absorbed solar radiation 46
absorber, shock 351
absorbing plate 410
absorption by clouds 46
absorption by Earth surface 46
absorption of water and mineral salts 54
absorption, carbon dioxide 54
abutment 284, 344
abyssal hill 33
abyssal plain 33
Abyssinian 87
acanthus leaf 200
acceleration lane 343
accelerator pedal 354
accent mark 299
access door 423
access gallery 407
access road 343, 388
access server 335
access window 333
accessories 356, 372
accessories, clothing and 538
accessory shoe 314
accidentals 299
accordion 296
accordion bag 276
accordion pleat 253
account identification 443
accumulator 357
Ace 468
achene 59, 60
acid rain 47, 48
acid snow 48
acidification, lake 48
acorn squash 129
acoustic ceiling 293
acoustic guitar 302
acoustic meatus 115, 116
acrobatic skate 527
acromion 99
acroterion 279
action buttons 471
action of wind 45
actor 290
actors' entrance 278
actors' seats 290
actress 291
actuator arm 333
acute angle 428
Adam's apple 92
adapter, plug 271

adapter, power 336
adaptor, mating 11
add in memory 337
add key 337
addition 427
additive colour synthesis 418
adductor muscle, anterior 73
adductor muscle, posterior 73
Aden, Gulf of 19, 20
adhesive disc 75
adhesive tape 461
adipose tissue 113, 114
adjustable buckle 527
adjustable catch 511
adjustable channel 222
adjustable clamp 206
adjustable frame 226
adjustable lamp 206
adjustable spanner 223
adjustable strap 260
adjustable thermostat 179
adjustable waist tab 244
adjuster 466
adjusting band 324
adjusting ring 236
adjusting screw 222
adjustment slide 246
administration 445
adobe house 288
adrenal gland 107
Adriatic Sea 18
adventitious roots 52
advertisement 313
advertisements, classified 313
advertising panel 378
advertising poster 380
adzuki bean 131
Aegean Sea 18
aerial 326, 327, 349
aerial ladder truck 455
aerial terminals 322
aerial, dish 321
aerial, home 316
aerial, telescopic 325
aerial, transceiving parabolic 316
aerocyst 51
aerodynamic brake 412
affluent 32
Afghanistan 452
Africa 14, 20, 34, 451
African Plate 27
Afro pick 268
aft shroud 7
afterbay 406, 407
aftershave 271
agar-agar 123
agency, travel 436
agitator 212
agricultural pollution 47
aileron 392
air bag 354
air bag restraint system 354
air bubbles 339

air compression unit 376
air concentrator 270
air conditioner 361
air conditioner compressor 360
air conditioning system 46
air cushion 262
air filter 235, 350
air hole 312
air horn 364
air inlet 367
air inlet control 192
air intake 362, 383, 395
air intake for engine cooling 525
air intake, engine 362
air mattress 530
air pollutants 47
air pollution 47
air pre-cleaner filter 398
air relief valve 385
air scoop 523
air shaft 278
air space 79
air temperature 39
air transport 388
air vent 214
air, cold 41
air, rising warm 43
air, subsiding cold 43
air, warm 41
air-inlet grille 270
air-outlet grille 270
air-pressure pump 461
air-supply tube 454
aircraft weather station 38
aircraft, business 394
aircraft, cargo 394
aircraft, examples of 394
aircraft, light 394
aircraft, movements of 395
airliner 37
airport 25, 388, 430
aisle 120, 285
ajowan 139
ala 117
alarm/charge indicator light 337
Alaska, Gulf of 16
Albania 450
albatross 80
albumen 79
alcohol bulb 424
alcohol column 424
Aleutian Islands 16
Aleutian Trench 34
alfalfa 130
alga 51
alga, brown 51
alga, green 51
alga, red 51
alga, structure of 51
algae, examples of 51
Algeria 451
alkaline manganese-zinc cell 417
alkekengi 132

all-season tyre 358
all-terrain bicycle 373
all-terrain vehicle 347
alley 490, 495
alligator 77
allspice 138
alluvial deposits 32
almond 57, 133
alphabetical keypad 338
alphanumeric keyboard 346, 442, 443
alphanumeric keypad 327, 330
alpine ski trail 512
alpine skier 510
alpine skiing 510
alpine snowboard 513
Alps 18
altar cross 446
altar, high 446
altar, secondary 446
altarpiece 446
alternate 330
alternate: level 3 select 330
alternating-current power cord 336
alternative key 330
alternator 350, 360, 413
altitude clamp 8, 9
altitude fine adjustment 8, 9
altitude scale 37
alto clef 298
altocumulus 42
altostratus 42
alula 78
aluminium foil 162
aluminium recycling container 49
alveolar bone 101
amaranth 143
Amazon River 17
amber light 434
amble 83
ambulance 460, 462
ambulatory 285
ambulatory care unit 465
America, Central 16
America, North 16, 34
America, South 17, 34
American bacon 156
American corn bread 145
American football 484
American football player 486
American mustard 140
American plug 198
Americas 448
Amery Ice Shelf 15
ammunition pouch 456
amoeba 66
amorphous solid 414
amount of substance, measurement of 426
ampere 426
amphibians 75
amphibians, examples of 75
amphibious firefighting aircraft 394
amphitheatre, Roman 281

ampli-tuner 325
ampli-tuner: back view 322
ampli-tuner: front view 322
amplitude 418
ampoule 467
ampulla of fallopian tube 113
anaesthesia room 464
anal cleft 93
anal fin 74
anal proleg 67
analogue camcorder: back view 320
analogue camcorder: front view 320
analogue watch 424
analytical balance 423
anatomy 96
anatomy of a bivalve shell 73
anatomy of a lobster 71
anchor 473
anchor pin 357
anchor point 70
anchorage block 344
anchovy 159
anconeus 97
Andes Cordillera 17
andirons 193
Andorra 449
andouillette 156
anemometer 413
angle, acute 428
angle, obtuse 428
angle, re-entrant 428
angle, right 428
angles, examples of 428
Angola 452
Anik 317
animal cell 66
animal dung 48
animal kingdom 66
anise 142
ankle 92, 94
ankle boot 241
ankle guard 476
ankle sock 247, 257
ankle-strap 241
ankle/wrist weight 500
annual ring 63
annular eclipse 4
anorak 263
ant 69
Antarctic Circle 15, 21, 22
Antarctic Peninsula 15
Antarctic Plate 27
Antarctica 14, 15
antefix 279
antelope 84
antenna 7, 67, 68, 71, 369, 392, 395, 457, 487
antenna cable, high-frequency 394
antenna, radio 525
antennule 71
anterior adductor muscle 73
anterior chamber 119
anterior end 73

ASTRONOMY > 2-13; EARTH > 14-49; PLANT KINGDOM >50-65; ANIMAL KINGDOM > 66-91; HUMAN BEING > 92-119; FOOD AND KITCHEN > 120-181; HOUSE > 182-215;
DO-IT-YOURSELF AND GARDENING > 216-237; CLOTHING > 238-263; PERSONAL ADORNMENT AND ARTICLES > 264-277; ARTS AND ARCHITECTURE > 278-311; COMMUNICATIONS AND
OFFICE AUTOMATION > 312-341; TRANSPORT AND MACHINERY > 342-401; ENERGY > 402-413; SCIENCE > 414-429; SOCIETY > 430-467; SPORTS AND GAMES > 468-538

539

ENGLISH INDEX

anterior fontanelle 100
anterior horn 109
anterior nasal spine 100
anterior notch 115
anterior root 110
anterior tibial 96
anterior tibial artery 102
anterior view 92, 94, 96, 98
anther 56
anti-friction pad 511
anti-reflection coating 410
anti-slip foot 219
anti-torque tail rotor 395
anti-vibration handle 235
anticline 403
anticollision light 392
anticyclone 39
Antigua and Barbuda 449
antihelix 115
antilock braking system (ABS) 357
antiseptic 461
antitragus 115
anus 71, 73, 106, 111, 112
anvil 425
aorta 104, 105
aortic valve 104
apartment block 512
apartment building 433
aperture 73
aperture door 7
apex 72, 73, 101, 118
apical foramen 101
apocrine sweat gland 114
apothecium 50
Appalachian Mountains 16
apple 133
apple corer 173
apple, section of 58
application launch buttons 337
application, fertilizer 47
appoggiatura 299
appointment book 338
approach ramp 344
approach runs 496
apricot 132
apron 200, 201, 202, 369, 388, 498
apse 285
apsidiole 284, 285
aquatic bird 79
aquatic sports 516
aqueous humour 119
aquifer, confined 402
Arabian Peninsula 19
Arabian Sea 19
arachnids, examples of 70
arachnids, insects and 67
arachnoid 109
Aral Sea 19
arame 123
arc 428
arc, island 33
arcade 281, 284
arcades 447
arch of aorta 102, 103, 104
arch of foot artery 102
archboard 340
archipelago 24
architecture 278
architecture, elements of 286
architrave 279
Arctic 14
Arctic Circle 21, 22
Arctic Ocean 14
area, floor exercise 496
area, high pressure 43
area, industrial 431
area, low pressure 43
area, parking 430, 445
area, receiving 120
area, reception 462, 465
area, ski 512
area, stretcher 462
area, waiting 442
area, water-tank 394
arena 281, 472
Arenberg parquet 190
areola 113
Argentina 448
Ariel 3
ark 447
arm 83, 91, 93, 95, 200, 206, 236, 297, 400, 421, 467
arm cylinder 400
arm guard 486
arm lock 499
arm slit 251

arm stump 200
arm, crossing 362
arm, remote-control 11
arm, suspension 351
armchair 200, 444
armchairs, examples of 200
Armenia 452
armhole 247
armless chair 444
armoire 202
armpit 92, 94
armrest 205, 352, 353, 467
armstand 518
arpeggio 299
arrays, photovoltaic 11
arrector pili muscle 114
arrival, ski lift 512
arrow rest 535
art director 290
arteries 102
artery, dorsal abdominal 71
artery, ventral 71
artery, ventral 71
artichoke 127
article 313
articles, miscellaneous 341
articulated bus 363
articulated joint 363
artificial fly 536
artificial lake 32
artificial satellite 37
artist, make-up 290
arts and architecture 278
arts, performing 294
asafœtida 139
ascending aorta 103
ascending colon 106
ascending passage 278
ash layer 28
Asia 14, 19, 34, 452
Asian noodles 147
Asian pear 137
asparagus 125
asphalt 405
asphalt still 405
aspirin 461
ass 84
assistant camera operator, first 290
assistant camera operator, second 290
assistant coach 489, 507
assistant director 291
assistant property man 291
assistant referee 509
assistants, counsels' 440
association football 480
asteroid belt 3
asthenosphere 26
astigmatism 419
astrakhan cap 238
astronautics 10
astronomical observation 7
astronomical observatory 7
astronomical observatory, cross section of an 7
astronomical unit 3
astronomical units 2
astronomy 2
asymmetrical bars 496, 497
Atacama Desert 17
Atlantic cod 161
Atlantic Ocean 14, 15, 18, 20
Atlantic salmon 161
atlas 99
atlas moth 69
Atlas Mountains 20
atmosphere 44, 48
atoll 35
atom 414
atoms 414
atrium 280
attaché case 274
attack line 487
attack zone 487
attacker, left 487
attacker, middle 487
attacker, right 487
attitude control thrusters 12
attraction 416
aubergine 128
audience 440
audio input/output jack 337
audio jack 329
audiometric examination room 465
auditory ossicles 116
auricle 116

auricle, ear 115
auriculars 78
Australia 14, 34, 453
Australian-Indian Plate 27
Austria 450
authorized landfill site 47
auto answer indicator 328
auto reverse button 326
autoclave 464
automatic dialling index 327
automatic electronic timer 517
automatic filter coffee maker 181
automatic sliding door 286
automatic teller machine 442, 443
automatically-controlled door 390
autotrophs 45
autumn 38
autumn squash 129
autumnal equinox 38
auxiliary handle 228
auxiliary tank 365
avenue 25, 433
avocado 128
awl 531
awning channel 361
axe 234
Axel 509
axial rib 73
axillary artery 102
axillary bud 53
axillary nerve 108
axillary vein 102
axis 99
axle 527
axle shaft 351
axle, spool 537
axon 110
axon hillock 110
Azerbaijan 452
azimuth clamp 8, 9
azimuth fine adjustment 8, 9
Aztec temple 283

B

b 298
baboon 91
baby doll 256
babygro 260
back 78, 83, 86, 93, 95, 115, 167, 169, 201, 205, 226, 244, 467
back boundary line 494
back brush 267
back judge 485
back line 515
back of a glove 243
back panel 210, 213
back pocket 246
back ribs 152
back suspension 522
back zone 487
back, middle 487
back, right 481, 487
backboard 489
backboard support 489
backcourt 491
backdrop 292
backgammon 469
backguard 212
backhoe 399
backhoe controls 399
backhoe loader 399
backpack 532
backplate 357
backrest 369, 523
backspace 331
backspace key 331
backstay 509
backstop 474, 489
backstroke 517
backstroke turn indicator 517
backward 518
backward bucket 399, 400
bacon, American 156
bacon, Canadian 156
badge 456
badge, identification 456
badger 88
badminton 494
badminton racket 494
Baffin Island 16
bag compartment 209
bag well 505
bag, air 354
bag, freezer 162
bag, mesh 162

bag, tea 148
bagel 144
baggage check-in counter 390
baggage claim area 390
baggage compartment 362
bagpipes 296
bags, carrier 121
Bahamas 448
Bahrain 452
Baikal, Lake 19
bail 479
bail arm 537
bail arm opening mechanism 537
bailey 282
baitcasting reel 537
baize 502
bakery 121
bakery/patisserie 437
baking sheet 172
baking utensils 172
balaclava 239, 524
balalaika 297
balance beam 496, 497
balance control 322
balancer 303
balcony 189, 447
balcony window 189
baling 49
Balkan Peninsula 18
ball 312, 332
ball bearing 413
ball boy 490
ball mount 356
ball peen 220
ball sports 474
ball, hitch 356
ball-cock supply valve 196
ball-peen hammer 220
baller, melon 173
balloon, sounding 38
ballpoint pen 312
ballroom 387
balm, lemon 142
balsamic vinegar 141
Baltic Sea 18
baluster 191
balustrade 283
bamboo shoot 125
banana 136
band ring 264
band select button 322
band, spiral cloud 43
band, wrist 500
Bangladesh 453
bangle 264
banister 188, 189, 191
banjo 296
bank 182, 342, 432, 437, 442, 469
bank note 469
banknote: back 441
banknote: front 441
banner 313
banquette 201
baptismal font 446
bar 273, 293, 309, 432, 436, 438, 469, 500, 501
bar counter 438
bar line 298
bar nose 235
bar stool 201, 438
bar, glazing 186
bar, horizontal 496
bar, push 286
barb 538
Barbados 449
barbell 500, 501
barber comb 268
barbican 282
Barents Sea 18
bark 63
barley 61, 143
barley: spike 61
barmaid 438
barn 122
barometric pressure 39
barometric tendency 39
barrel 269, 270, 312, 471, 534
barrel vault 281
barrier 205, 434
barrier barricade tape 457
barrier beach 35
barrier, tyre 524
barrow 396
bars, asymmetrical 496
bars, parallel 497
bartizan 282

basaltic layer 26
base 54, 179, 180, 192, 206, 227, 229, 269, 283, 318, 332, 342, 412, 421, 422, 454, 473, 534
base cabinet 164
base course 342
base line 533
base of splat 200
base plate 227, 511, 533
base, padded 489
baseball 474, 476
baseball, cross section of 477
baseline 491
basement 182
basement window 183
basic source of food 45
basil 142
basilic vein 102
basket 178, 211, 489, 510
basket weave pattern 190
basket, frying 171
basket, steamer 175
basket, waste 341
basketball 488
basketball player 488
basmati rice 147
bass 160
bass bridge 304
bass clarinet 295
bass clef 298
bass drum 295, 308
bass guitar 303
bass keyboard 296
bass pickup 303
bass register 296
Bass Strait 15
bass tone control 303, 322, 325
bass, sea 160
bassoon 306
bassoons 295
baster 173
bat 476, 477, 478
bat, softball 477
bath 189, 194, 195
bath and shower 439
bath and shower mixer 194
bath brush 267
bath platform 195
bath sheet 267
bath towel 267
bath, bubble 267
bathrobe 256
bathroom 189, 195, 439, 464
bathroom scale 423
bathroom skylight 189
baton 472
baton holder 456
baton, expandable 456
batsman 479
batten 292, 519, 520
batten pocket 519, 520
batter 475, 476
batter skin 297
batter's helmet 476
battery 221, 350, 359, 411, 416
battery box 365
battery case 359
battery cover 359
battery pack 228
battery pack, rechargeable 320
battery warning light 355
batting glove 476
battlement 282
baulk 502
baulk line 502
baulk line spot 502
bay 5, 24, 142
bay filler panel 329
Bay of Bengal 19
bay, cargo 12
Bay, Hudson 16
bayonet cap 199
beach 35
beach, barrier 35
bead 358
beaker, measuring 171
beam 283, 288, 422
beam balance 422
beam bridge 344
beam, balance 496
beam, laser 420
bean bag chair 201
bean thread cellophane noodles 147
bean, adzuki 131
bean, black 131
bean, lablab 130

ASTRONOMY > 2–13;   EARTH > 14–49;   PLANT KINGDOM >50–65;   ANIMAL KINGDOM > 66–91;   HUMAN BEING > 92–119;   FOOD AND KITCHEN > 120–181;   HOUSE > 182–2
DO-IT-YOURSELF AND GARDENING > 216–237;   CLOTHING > 238–263;   PERSONAL ADORNMENT AND ARTICLES > 264–277;   ARTS AND ARCHITECTURE > 278–311;   COMMUNICATIONS AN
OFFICE AUTOMATION > 312–341;   TRANSPORT AND MACHINERY > 342–401;   ENERGY > 402–413;   SCIENCE > 414–429;   SOCIETY > 430–467;   SPORTS AND GAMES > 468–538

bean, Lima 131
bean, mung 131
bean, pinto 131
bean, roman 131
bean, scarlet runner 131
bean, wax 131
beans 131
beans, dolichos 130
beans, green coffee 148
beans, yard-long 130
bear, black 89
bear, polar 89
beater 176
beater ejector 176
Beaufort Sea 16
beaver 82
becquerel 426
bed 183, 204, 342
bed and mattress 530
bed chamber 280
bed lamp 206
bed linen 204
bed, double 439
bed, gravel 524
bed, hospital 464
bed, single 439
bed, sofa 204
bedrock 27, 54
bedroom 189, 528
bedside lamp 439, 464
bedside table 439, 464
beech 64
beechnut 133
beef, cuts of 152
beef, diced 152
beef, minced 152
beehive 122
beer and wine 120
beer glass 165
beetroot 129
beginners' slope 512
begonia 56
Belarus 450
belfry 284
Belgium 449
Belize 448
bell 306, 307
bell bottoms 254
bell brace 306
bell tower 285, 446
bellows 296
bellows strap 296
belly 83
belongs to 427
below-stage 292
belt 225, 246, 248, 499
belt drive 383
belt loader 402
belt loop 246, 248, 531
belt, conveyor 49
belt, duty 456
belt, fan 350
belt, Kuiper 2
belt, safety 525
belt, tool 225
belt, waist 205, 532
beltclip 327
bench 201, 379, 437, 501
bench seat 353
bench, defence counsel's 440
bench, judges' 440
bench, prosecution counsel's 440
bench, substitutes' 481
bend 273, 538
Bengal, Bay of 19
Benin 451
beret 239
bergamot 134
bergère 200
bergschrund 30
Bering Sea 14
Bering Strait 16
Bermuda shorts 254
Bernard, Saint 86
berries 132
berry, juniper 138
bevel 460
bevel square 225
beverage can 163
beverage dispenser 463
Bhutan 453
bib 260, 261
bib necklace 264
biceps of arm 96

biceps of thigh 97
biconcave lens 419
biconvex lens 419
bicycle 370
bicycle parking 445
bicycle, accessories 372
bicycle, all-terrain 373
bicycle, city 373
bicycle, Dutch 373
bicycle, parts of a 370
bicycle, road 373
bicycle, touring 373
bicycles, examples of 373
bidet 195
Bight, Great Australian 15
bike carrier 356
bike, BMX 373
bike, quad 369
biking, mountain 522
bikini 259
bilberry 132
bill 78
billhook 234
billiard cue 503
billiard spot 502
billiards 502
bills, examples of 79
bimah 447
bin, compost 231
bin, recycling 49
binding 238, 513, 514
binding, comb 340
binding, safety 510
binocular microscope 421
biology 426
biosphere, structure of 44
biparous cyme 57
birch 64
bird 78
bird of prey 79
bird's eye chilli 139
bird's nest fern 52
bird, morphology of 78
birds 79
birds, examples of 80
biscuit cutters 172
Bishop 470
bison 84
bit 221, 403
bit, screwdriver 228
bit, spade 228
bit, twist 228
bits and drills, examples of 228
bitt 385
bitter melon 128
bivalve shell 73
bivalve shell, anatomy of 73
bivalve shell, morphology of 73
Black 470
black 418
black ball 503
black bean 131
black bear 89
black bread 144
black clamp 356
black gram 131
black mustard 138
black pepper 138
black pollock 161
black pudding 156
black radish 129
black salsify 129
Black Sea 14, 18, 19
black square 470
black stone 470
black tea 148
black-eyed pea 130
blackberry 132
blackboard 444
blackcurrant 132
blade 52, 55, 167, 169, 177, 180, 216, 219, 221, 226, 227, 229, 235, 270, 271, 398, 401, 412, 413, 493, 506, 509, 538
blade close stop 270
blade dispenser 271
blade lift cylinder 398, 401
blade lift fan 383
blade locking bolt 227
blade rotation cylinder 401
blade shifting mechanism 401
blade tilting lock 227
blade tilting mechanism 227
blade, cutting 341
blade, dance 509
blade, free-skating 509

blade, rudder 384
blank 468
blanket 204
blanket sleepsuit 261
blastodisc 79
blazer 254
blender 176
blender, pastry 172
blending attachment 176
blind spot mirror 362, 363
blinking lights 362
block 215, 305, 473
block, apartment 512
block, clamping 425
blocking glove 507
blood circulation 102
blood factor negative 426
blood factor positive 426
blood pressure monitor 461
blood vessel 104, 114
blood, composition of 104
blood, deoxygenated 104
blood, oxygenated 104
blouses, examples of 255
blow pipe 296
blowhole 90
blowtorch 218
blue 418
blue ball 503
blue beam 318
blue line 507
blue mussel 157
Blue, Danish 151
blue-veined cheeses 151
blueberry 132
bluefish 160
blusher brush 266
BMX bike 373
boa 77
boar, wild 84
board 470, 519
board game 469
board, bulletin 444
board, cutting 169
board, diving 184
board, game 469
board, memorial 447
boarding step 395
boarding walkway 389
boards 506
boat, centreboard 521
boat, keel 521
boater 238
boats and ships, examples of 382
bobble hat 239
bodies, celestial 2
body 118, 180, 208, 228, 255, 258, 303, 305, 306, 348, 361, 420, 523, 536
body care 267
body flap 13
body of fornix 109
body of nail 114
body side moulding 349
body temperature control unit 10
body tube 421
body, collection 365
body, packer 364
body, tanker 364
bodywork, examples of 347
bogie tank wagon 377
bole 63
bolero 254
boletus, edible 123
Bolivia 448
bolster 167, 169, 204
bolt 222, 223, 224
bolts 223
bomb, volcanic 28
bond, chemical 414
bone, frontal 100
bone, nasal 100
bone, occipital 100
bone, parietal 100
bone, sphenoid 100
bone, temporal 100
bone, zygomatic 100
bongos 309
boning knife 169
bonnet 348, 364
bony fish 74
bony fishes 159
book ends 341
bookcase 444
bookshop 436
boom 364, 399, 400, 520

boom cylinder 399, 400
boom operator 291
boom vang 520
booster parachute 12
booster seat 205
booster, brake 350, 357
booster, solid rocket 12
boot 241, 349, 509, 514, 525, 527
boot, flexible 513
boot, football 480
boot, hard 513
boot, hiking 242
boot, inner 527
boot, ski-jumping 513
bootee 240
booth 438
booth, coupon 443
booth, information 437
booth, photo 437
booth, projection 294
booth, ticket collecting 378
booth, undressing 465
borage 142
border 182, 293
borders 292
boreal forest 44
born 426
Bosnia-Herzegovina 450
Bothnia, Gulf of 18
Botswana 452
bottle 267, 532
bottle opener 170, 531
bottle, glass 163
bottom cap 417
bottom cushion 502
bottom deck 404
bottom deckboard 396
bottom face 510
bottom line 517
bottom pocket 502
bottom rail 185, 202
bottom stair 191
bottom-fold document case 274
boulevard 25, 433
bow 238, 301, 387, 519, 520
bow door 383
bow loading door 386
bow saw 533
bow thruster 387
bow tie 245
bow, compound 535
bow-winged grasshopper 69
bowl 167, 177, 180
bowl with serving spout 177
bowler 238, 479
bowling 436
bowling crease 479
bowstring 535
box 192, 293
box bag 276
box office 294
box, cheese 163
box, drink 163
box, jury 440
box, mitre 226
box, night deposit 443
box, safe deposit 443
box, sound 297
box, tool 225
box, top 369
boxer 498
boxer shorts 247
boxing 498
boxing gloves 498
boxing trunks 498
bra 259
brace 187, 219
brace clip 246
bracelets 264
braces 246
brachial 96
brachial artery 102
brachial plexus 108
brachioradialis 96, 97
bracket 283
bracket base 202
bracket, mounting 535
bract 60
brain 71
brains 154
brake 467, 501, 522
brake booster 350, 357
brake cable 371
brake caliper 366
brake fluid reservoir 357

brake handle 523
brake hose 357
brake lever 371
brake lever and shifter 522
brake light 352
brake lining 357
brake pad 357
brake pedal 350, 354, 357, 511
brake pressure modulator 357
brake shoe 357
brake van 377
brake, disc 350, 357, 525
brakes 357
braking circuit 350, 357
braking system 351
branch 62, 63, 65, 125, 194, 416, 460
branch clip 460
branches 63
branching, examples of 197
brandy glass 165
brass family 295
brassiere cup 259
brattice 282
brazier 283
Brazil 448
Brazil nut 133
bread 144
bread guide 178
bread knife 169
bread maker 179
bread, multigrain 145
bread, white 145
break 331
breaker 33
bream, sea 159
breast 78, 92, 94, 113
breast dart 248
breast pocket 245, 248
breast welt pocket 244
breaststroke 517
breech 306
breech guard 306
breechblock 534
breeds, dog 86
brick carton 163
brick-bond woodstrip flooring 190
bricklayer's hammer 216
bridge 25, 273, 297, 301, 302, 303, 420, 503
bridge assembly 303
bridge of nose 117
bridging 187
Brie 151
briefcase 274
briefs 247, 259
brightness control 329
brim 238, 239
bristle 271, 272
bristles 219
broad beans 130
broad ligament of uterus 113
broad welt side pocket 248, 251
broadleaved trees, examples of 64
broccoli 127
broccoli raab 127
brochure rack 442
broken line 342, 343
bronchus, lobe 105
bronchus, main 105
brook 32
brook charr 161
broom 193, 215
brow brush and lash comb 266
brown alga 51
brown ball 503
brown rice 147
brown sugar 149
browser 334
Brunei Darussalam 453
brush 61, 209, 215, 272
brush, back 267
brush, bath 267
brush, central 365
brush, curling 515
brush, lateral 365
Brussels sprouts 126
bubble 367
bubble bath 267
bubbles, air 339
bucket 215, 399
bucket cylinder 399, 400
bucket hinge pin 399
bucket lever 399
bucket seat: front view 353
bucket seat: side view 353
buckle 246, 248, 276, 353, 511

ASTRONOMY > 2-13; EARTH > 14-49; PLANT KINGDOM > 50-65; ANIMAL KINGDOM > 66-91; HUMAN BEING > 92-119; FOOD AND KITCHEN > 120-181; HOUSE > 182-215;
DO-IT-YOURSELF AND GARDENING > 216-237; CLOTHING > 238-263; PERSONAL ADORNMENT AND ARTICLES > 264-277; ARTS AND ARCHITECTURE > 278-311; COMMUNICATIONS AND
OFFICE AUTOMATION > 312-341; TRANSPORT AND MACHINERY > 342-401; ENERGY > 402-413; SCIENCE > 414-429; SOCIETY > 430-467; SPORTS AND GAMES > 468-538

541

buckle, tightening 532
buckwheat 61, 143
buckwheat: raceme 61
bud 54
bud, flower 53
bud, taste 118
bud, terminal 53
buffalo 84
buffer 287
buffer tank 404
buffers 375
buffet 438
bug, shield 69
bugle 307
building, apartment 433
building, office 432
bulb 125, 199, 217, 385, 416
bulb dibber 231
bulb vegetables 124
bulb, section of 54
bulbil 54
bulbocavernous muscle 111
Bulgaria 450
bulge 6
bulk carrier 382
bulk terminal 381
bull's-eye 471
bulldog 86
bulldozer 398
bullet 534
bulletin board 444
bumblebee 69
bump 487
bumper 209, 364, 369
bumper moulding 348
bumper, rear 369
bun tin 172
bunch 522
bunch of grapes 62
bunch, leading 522
bundle 125
bunk 361
bunker oil 405
bunker silo 122
bunker, sand 504
buoy weather station 38
burdock 129
bureau 203
burgundy glass 165
burial 49
Burkina Faso 451
burner 174, 210, 529
burner control knobs 210
burner frame 529
burner ring 174
Burundi 451
bus 362, 435
bus shelter 434
bus station 432
bus stop 434
bus, articulated 363
bus, city 362
bus, double-decker 363
bus, school 362
busbar 407
bush 230
bushing 406, 407
business aircraft 394
business counter 443
business district 430, 432
business transactions 335
butt 492, 494, 503, 536
butt cap 536
butt end 506
butt grip 537
butt guide 537
butt plate 534
butt section 536
butt-strap 273
butte 36
butter 150
butter compartment 211
butter cup 163
butter curler 169
butter dish 166
butter knife 168
butterfly 67
butterfly stroke 517
butterfly, morphology of 67
butterhead lettuce 126
buttermilk 150
buttock 93, 95, 111, 112
button 199, 245, 250, 296
button facing 245, 250
button loop 246
button strap 261

button, band select 322
button, call 287
button, cancel 333
button, CD/DVD-ROM eject 329
button, control 332
button, dial/action 337
button, display release 336
button, edit search 320
button, eject 315, 471
button, end search 320
button, erase 315
button, exit 337
button, floppy disk eject 329
button, image review 315
button, index/enlarge 315
button, indicators display 320
button, input select 322
button, lock-on 227, 229
button, memory 322
button, menu 315, 327
button, multi-image jump 315
button, paper feed 333, 443
button, power 318, 329, 333, 336
button, power and backlight 337
button, power zoom 320
button, preset tuning 322
button, read 327
button, reset 329, 471
button, select 327
button, settings display 315
button, test 454
button, title display 320
button, touch pad 336
button, voice recorder 337
button-through smock 255
buttondown collar 245
buttonhole 248
buttons, action 471
buttons, application launch 337
buttons, directional 471
buttons, image adjustment 320
buttons, programmable 332
buttons, special effects 320
buttons, tuning 322
buttress 284
by-pass taxiway 388

c

c 298
cab 398, 399, 400, 401
cabbage, red 126
cabbage, savoy 126
cabin 386, 395
cabinet 211, 212, 213, 318
cabinet, base 164
cabinet, wall 164
cable 228, 332, 356, 364, 535
cable distributor 316
cable guard 535
cable line 335
cable sleeve 228
cable, electrical 354
cable, spark plug 350
cable, steel 535
cable, sync 337
cables, jumper 356
cabriole chair 200
cabriole leg 200
caecum 106
cafeteria 445
cafetière with plunger 181
cage 281
caiman 77
cajun spice seasoning 139
cake mascara 266
cake tin 172
calcaneus 99
calculator 274
calculator, scientific 337
calculator/cheque book holder 274
calendar pad 338
calf 84, 93, 95
California, Gulf of 16
caliper 357
caliper, vernier 425
call button 287
call button, pedestrian 434
Callisto 2
calls indicator 328
calyx 56, 59, 60, 107
cambium 63
Cambodia 453
camel 85
Camembert 151

camera 290, 525
camera body 314
camera operator 290
camera, digital 315
camera, motorcycle-mounted 522
Cameroon 451
camisole 258
camp bed 530
camper 361
camping 528
camping equipment 531
camshaft 360
can, beverage 163
can, food 163
Canada 448
Canadian bacon 156
Canadian elk 84
canal lock 381
canary melon 135
cancel button 333
Cancer, Tropic of 20
candela 426
candle 446
candy, rock 149
cane pen 312
canine 101
canister, dust 229
canisters 162
canned goods 121
cannelloni 146
cannon 83
canopy 273, 286, 361, 394, 401, 528
cantaloupe 135
canteen 532
cantilever bridge 344
cantilever span 344
canvas 498
canvas divider 528
Canyon, Grand 16
cap 52, 126, 191, 199, 238, 312, 412,
    456, 467, 516
cap iron 229
cap nut 223
cap, bottom 417
cap, distributor 350
cap, lever 229
cap, screw 163
cap, top 417
capacitor, ceramic 417
capacitor, plastic film 417
capacitors, electrolytic 417
cape 24, 251
Cape Horn 17
Cape of Good Hope 20
Cape Verde Islands 451
capillary blood vessel 114
capillary tube 424
capital 23
capitals lock 330
capitals lock key 330
capitulum 57
capon 155
capped tee 193
Capricorn, Tropic of 20
capsule 51, 467
captain's quarters 387
caption 313
capture 470
car 347, 521
car ceiling 287
car coat 251
car cover 356
car dealer 433
car deck 386
car floor 287
car guide rail 287
car park 375, 381, 390
car safety 287
car systems 351
car systems: main parts 350
car wash 346
car, following 522
car, formula 1 525
car, formula 3000 524
car, formula Indy 524
car, lift 287
car, Micro Compact 347
car, police 457
car, rally 524
car, trailer 380
carafe 165
carambola 137
carapace 71, 76
caravan 361
caraway 138
carbon dioxide absorption 54

carbon rod (cathode) 417
carbon-zinc cell 417
carburettor 366
card 469
card games 468
card number 441, 443
card reader 321
card reader slot 346, 442, 443
card, Chance 469
card, Community chest 469
card, compass 23
card, credit 441
card, debit 443
cardamom 138
cardiac stomach 71
cardigan 250, 255
cardinal 80
cardoon 125
care, body 267
care, health and beauty 121
care, lawn 237
caretaker's cupboard 443
cargo aircraft 394
cargo bay 12
cargo bay door 13
cargo dispatch 391
cargo hold 393
cargo rack, rear 369
cargo reception 391
Caribbean Islands 448
Caribbean Plate 27
Caribbean Sea 14, 16
carina 74
carnation 56
carnivores 45
carnivorous mammals 86
carnivorous mammals, examples of 88
carom billiards 502
carp 160
Carpathian Mountains 18
Carpentaria, Gulf of 15
carpenter's hammer 220
carpentry: drilling tools 228
carpentry: gripping and tightening tools
    222
carpentry: measuring and marking tools
    225
carpentry: miscellaneous material 225
carpentry: nailing tools 220
carpentry: sawing tools 226
carpentry: screwing tools 221
carpentry: shaping tools 229
carpet and floor brush 209
carpet, pile 190
carriage 396
carrier 369, 370
carrier bags 121
carrier, bike 356
carrier, bulk 382
carrier, child 372
carrot 129
carrying handle 326
cartilaginous fish 74
cartilaginous fishes 158
cartography 21
carton 163
carton, brick 163
carton, egg 162
carton, small 163
cartoon 313
cartridge 216, 312, 459
cartridge (rifle) 534
cartridge (shotgun) 534
cartwheel hat 239
carving fork 169
carving knife 169
casaba melon 135
case 225, 265, 304, 424, 534
case fan 329
case, handcuff 456
case, lens 272
casement 186
casement window 287
casement window opening inwards 287
cash dispenser 437, 442
cash readout 346
cash register 121
cash supply 443
cashew 133
cashier 121
casing 186, 237
casing, steel 417
Caspian Sea 14, 19
cassava 124
Cassegrain focus 7
cassette 326, 333

cassette compartment 319, 320
cassette drive 333
cassette eject button 319
cassette holder 323
cassette player 326
cassette player controls 326
cassette tape deck 323
cassette, video 319
castanets 295, 309
caster 205, 209, 308
castes 68
casting 537
Castle 470
castle 282
casual shoe 241
cat 87
cat breeds 87
cat's head 87
catalytic converter 351
catalytic reforming plant 405
catamaran 521
catch 273, 536
catcher 474, 475, 476
catcher's glove 476
catching glove 507
catering foods 121
caterpillar 67
cathedral 284
cathedral, plan 285
catwalk 292
caudal fin 74, 90
cauliflower 127
caulking gun 216
cave 31, 35
cayenne 139
CD/DVD player 471
CD/DVD-ROM drive 329, 336
CD/DVD-ROM eject button 329
cedar of Lebanon 65
ceiling 193
ceiling collar 193
ceiling fitting 206
ceiling joist 187
ceiling, acoustic 293
ceiling, car 287
celeriac 129
celery 125
celestial bodies 2
cell 67, 281
cell body 110
cell membrane 50, 66
cell wall 50
cell, alkaline manganese-zinc 417
cell, carbon-zinc 417
cell, convective 43
cell, red blood 104
cell, white blood 104
cellar, wine 438
cello 301
cellos 295
cells 416, 440
cells, dry 417
Celsius scale 424
Celsius temperature, measurement of 426
Celsius, degree 426
celtuce 126
cement screed 190
cementum 101
cemetery 25, 433
censer 446
cent 440
Central African Republic 451
Central America 14, 16
central brush 365
central column 412
central focusing wheel 420
central incisor 101
central midfielder 481
central nave 447
central nervous system 109
central pumping station 404
central reservation 343, 434
central stile 185
centre 293, 428, 470, 485, 489, 507
centre back vent 244
centre circle 481, 488
centre console 354
centre electrode 359
centre face-off circle 507
centre field 475
centre fielder 474
centre flag 480
centre half 481
centre Keelson 385
centre lanes 343
centre line 484, 488, 493, 494, 507, 515

ASTRONOMY > 2-13;   EARTH > 14-49;   PLANT KINGDOM >50-65;   ANIMAL KINGDOM > 66-91;   HUMAN BEING > 92-119;   FOOD AND KITCHEN > 120-181;   HOUSE > 182-215;
DO-IT-YOURSELF AND GARDENING > 216-237;   CLOTHING > 238-263;   PERSONAL ADORNMENT AND ARTICLES > 264-277;   ARTS AND ARCHITECTURE > 278-311;   COMMUNICATIONS AN
OFFICE AUTOMATION > 312-341;   TRANSPORT AND MACHINERY > 342-401;   ENERGY > 402-413;   SCIENCE > 414-429;   SOCIETY > 430-467;   SPORTS AND GAMES > 468-538

ENGLISH INDEX

centre line judge 490
centre loudspeaker 321
centre mark 490
centre pocket 502
centre post 202
centre service line 491
centre span 344
centre spot 481, 502
centre strap 491
centre, city 431, 432
centre, convention 433
centre, day-care 437
centre, exhibition 430
centre, shopping 431, 436
centreboard 520
centreboard boat 521
centrifuge module 11
centring control 329
centring point 228
centriole 66
cephalic vein 102
cephalothorax 70, 71
ceramic capacitor 417
cereal products 144
cereals 61, 143
cerebellum 109
cerebro-spinal fluid 110
cerebropleural ganglion 73
cerebrum 109
cervical vertebra 99
cervix of uterus 112
Chac-Mool 283
Chad 451
Chad, Lake 20
chain 372
chain brake 235
chain guide 372
chain of dunes 36
chain of neurons 110
chain reaction 415
chain stay 370
chain wheel 522
chain wheel A 372
chain wheel B 372
chain, food 45
chainsaw 235
chainsaw chain 235
chair lift 512
chair lift departure 512
chair, armless 444
chair, high 205
chair, patient's 464
chairs, examples of 201
chaise longue 200
chalaza 79
chalice 446
chalk 503
chalk line 225
chamber, cold storage 120, 121
chamber, king's 278
chamber, magma 402
chamber, queen's 278
chamber, relieving 278
chamber, underground 278
chameleon 77
chamois leather 265
chamomile 148
champagne flute 165
champagne glass 165
Chance card 469
chandelier 207
change sign key 337
changing room 444
changing table 205
changing table 205
channel scan buttons 319
channel selector controls 319
Channel, English 18
Channel, Mozambique 20
chanter 296
chanterelle 123
Chantilly parquet 190
chapel 282
charge 534
charge indicator 271
charger 228
charging light 271
charging socket 271
Charleston cymbal 308
charlotte mould 172
charm bracelet 264
Charon 3
charr, brook 161
chart room 382
chat room 335
chayote 129

checkout 121
checkouts 121
cheek 83, 86, 94, 220, 536
cheese box 163
cheese counter 121
cheese knife 168
cheese, Chèvre 150
cheese, cottage 150
cheese, cream 150
cheeses, blue-veined 151
cheeses, fresh 150
cheeses, goat's-milk 150
cheeses, pressed 151
cheeses, soft 151
cheetah 89
chemical bond 414
chemical treatment 405
chemise 282
chemistry 414
cheque book 274
cheque book cover 275
cheque, traveller's 441
cheques 441
cherimoya 136
cherry 132
chervil 142
chess 470
chess notation 470
chessboard 470
chest 83
chest expander 500
chest freezer 211
chest protector 476, 486
chesterfield 200
chestnut 133
chestnut, water 124
chevet 285
Chèvre cheese 150
chicane 524
chick peas 130
chicken 155
chicory 127
chief timekeeper 516
chiffonier 203
child carrier 372
child seat 356
child's skull 100
child's tricycle 373
children's clothing 261
children's furniture 205
Chile 448
chilli 128
chilli powder 139
chilli, bird's eye 139
chilli, jalapeño 139
chillis, crushed 139
chillis, dried 139
chimney 183, 193
chimney connection 192
chimney pot 183
chimpanzee 91
chin 78, 94
chin protector 367
chin rest 301
chin strap 486, 522
China 453
chinois 171
chip cover 227
chipmunk 82
chipolata sausage 156
chive 124
chloroplast 50
chocolate 148
chocolate, dark 148
chocolate, milk 148
chocolate, white 148
choir 284, 285
choir organ manual 305
choker 264
chop 152, 153
chop, loin 153
chord 299
choroid 119
Christmas tree 404
chromatin 66
chromosphere 4
chrysalis 67
chuck 221, 228
chuck key 228
chuck, keyless 228
chukka 240
church 433, 446
chutney, mango 141
cicada 69
cider vinegar 141

cilia 66
ciliary body 119
ciliate 55
cilium 66
cinema 294, 386, 432, 436
cinnamon 138
Circle, Antarctic 15, 22
circle, parts of 428
circuit 524
circuit board, printed 417
circuit breaker 407
circuit vent 194
circuit, braking 350, 357
circuit, integrated 417
circuit, printed 417
circular body 296
circular saw 227
circular saw blade 227
circulation diagram 103
circumference 428
circumvallate papilla 118
cirque 5
cirrocumulus 42
cirrostratus 42
cirrus 42
cistern 195
cistern ball 196
cistern lid 196
citron 134
citrus fruits 134
city 23, 430
city bicycle 373
city bus 362
city centre 431, 432
clam 157
clam cleat 521
clam, hard-shell 157
clamp 198, 226, 269
clamp binder 339
clamp lever 269
clamp spotlight 206
clamp, black 356
clamp, pipe 224
clamp, red 356
clamping block 425
clamping screw 224
clamping screws 425
clapperboard 291
clapskate 508
clarinet 306
clarinets 295
clasp 274, 275
classic blouse 255
classified advertisements 313
classroom 444, 445
classroom for students with learning
   disabilities 444
clavicle 98
claw 71, 76, 78, 82, 220
claw hammer 220
clay 492
clean and jerk 500
clean utility room 462
cleaner height adjustment knob 209
cleaner, dry 437
cleaning brush 271
cleaning eye 197
cleaning tools 209
clear key 337
clear space 487
clear-entry key 337
cleat 520, 521
cleated shoe 486
cleaver 169
clefs 298
cleg 69
clerks' desk 440
clerks' office 440
clew 519
cliff 5, 29, 35
cliff, shore 35
climate control 354
climates of the world 40
climates, cold temperate 40
climates, dry 40
climates, warm temperate 40
climbing plant 230
clinical thermometer 424
clinical thermometers 461
clip 512, 535
clip earrings 264
clipboard 340
clipless pedal 522
clippers 269
clitoris 112
cloakroom 188, 443

cloakroom, customers' 438
cloakroom, staff 438, 465
cloche 239
clock 444
clock operator 488
clock radio 325
clock timer 178, 210
clog 242
closeness setting 271
clothing 238
clothing and accessories 538
clothing guard 467
clothing shop 436
clothing, children's 261
clothing, newborn children's 260
cloud 37, 41
cloud of volcanic ash 28
cloud, funnel 43
cloud, Oort 2
cloud, wall 43
clouds 42
clouds with vertical development 42
cloudwater 48
clove 138
cloverleaf 342, 343
club 468
club chair 200
clubhouse 504
clump of flowers 230
cluster, globular 6
clutch 350
clutch housing 368
clutch lever 366, 368
clutch pedal 354
coach 362, 489, 507
coach's box 474
coach, assistant 489, 507
coaches 509
coal storage yard 402
coal-fired thermal power station 402
coarse adjustment knob 421
coarse salt 141
coastal features 35
coat dress 252
coats 248, 251
cob 61
cobra 77
coccyx 98
cochlea 116
cochlear nerve 116
cockchafer 69
cockle 157
cockleshell 200
cockpit 520, 525
cocktail cabinet 203
cocktail glass 165
cocktail lounge 439
cocoa 148
coconut 133
Cocos Plate 27
cod, Atlantic 161
code, time 291
coeliac trunk 103, 107
coffee 148
coffee and infusions 148
coffee beans, roasted 148
coffee makers 181
coffee mill 180
coffee mug 166
coffee pot 531
coffee shop 432, 437
coffee spoon 168
coil spring 351
coin purse 275
coin: obverse 441
coin: reverse 441
cola nut 133
colander 171
cold air 41
cold coolant 408
cold storage chamber 120, 121
cold store 381
cold temperate climates 40
cold-water circuit 194
cold-water riser 194
cold-water supply 196, 197
collar 53, 244, 245, 248, 262, 271, 501
collar point 245
collar stiffener 245
collar, torque adjustment 228
collards 126
collateral 110
collection body 365
collection truck 364
collection, separate 49
collector, electron 417

collet 229
collie 86
Colombia 448
colour selection filter 318
colour shifting ink 441
colour supplement 313
colour synthesis 418
colour synthesis, additive 418
colour synthesis, subtractive 418
colour television camera 10
colour, hair 267
columella 73
columella fold 73
column 31, 207, 279, 313
column of mercury 424
column, steering 350
coma 6
comb binding 340
combat sports 498
combination lock 274
combination pliers 217
combination spanner 223
combinations 247
combs 268
combustion chamber 360
combustion space 192
comet 6
commandments, ten 447
commercial area 435
commercial concern 335
commercial zone 431
commissure of lips of mouth 116
common carotid artery 102
common coastal features 35
common extensor of fingers 97
common frog 75
common hair cap moss 51
common iliac artery 102, 107
common iliac vein 107
common nail 220
common periwinkle 157
common peroneal nerve 108
common plaice 161
common polypody 52
common toad 75
communicating ramus 110
communication by telephone 327
communication module 316
communication protocol 334
communication set 380
communication tunnel 13
communications 312
communications and office automation
   312
communications volume controls 10
communion rail 446
Community chest card 469
commuter train 375
Comoros 452
comouter, on-board 354
compact 266
compact disc 326
compact disc player 323, 325, 326
compact disc player controls 326
compact disc player, portable 325
compact disc recorder 325
compact disc rewritable recorder 333
compact memory card 315
compact video cassette adapter 320
compacting 49
compartment 203, 286
compartment, bag 209
compartment, baggage 362
compartment, cassette 320
compartment, engine 362
compartment, glove 354
compass bridge 382, 386, 387
compass card 23, 533
compass meridian line 533
compass saw 226
competition, road cycling 522
competitive course 517
complex dune 36
complex, sports 431
complexus 97
compluvium 280
composition of the blood 104
compost bin 231
compound bow 535
compound eye 67, 68
compound leaves 55
compressed-air cylinder 454
compression coupling 197
compression strap, front 532
compression strap, side 532
computer 444

ASTRONOMY > 2-13;   EARTH > 14-49;   PLANT KINGDOM > 50-65;   ANIMAL KINGDOM > 66-91;   HUMAN BEING > 92-119;   FOOD AND KITCHEN > 120-181;   HOUSE > 182-215;
DO-IT-YOURSELF AND GARDENING > 216-237;   CLOTHING > 238-263;   PERSONAL ADORNMENT AND ARTICLES > 264-277;   ARTS AND ARCHITECTURE > 278-311;   COMMUNICATIONS AND
OFFICE AUTOMATION > 312-341;   TRANSPORT AND MACHINERY > 342-401;   ENERGY > 402-413;   SCIENCE > 414-429;   SOCIETY > 430-467;   SPORTS AND GAMES > 468-538

543

computer programs 457
computer science room 444
computer screen 10
computer, dashboard 457
computer, desktop 334
computer, laptop 336
concave lens 419
concave primary mirror 9
concern, commercial 335
concertina file 340
concertina-type folding door 286
concha 115
conchiglie 146
concrete mixer truck 365
condensation 45, 414
condensation of steam into water 408
condenser 402, 421
condenser adjustment knob 421
condenser height adjustment 421
condiments 140
conditioner, hair 267
condor 80
conduction 415
conductor's podium 295
conduit, fuel 351
cone 65, 119, 429
conference room 442
confessionals 446
configuration of the continents 14
confined aquifer 402
confining bed, lower 402
confining bed, upper 402
confirmation key 443
confluent 32
Congo 451
Congo River 20
conic projection 22
conical washer 196
conifer 65
coniferous forest 44
conifers, examples of 65
conjunctiva 119
connecting cable 324
connecting gallery 345
connecting rod 360
connection 470
connection cable 332
connection pin 417
connection point 198
connection, network 198
connective tissue 114
console, game 471
constriction 424
consumer 317
contact 470
contact devices 198
contact lens, disposable 272
contact lens, hard 272
contact lens, soft 272
contact lenses 272
contact lever 207
container 176, 231, 383
container hold 383
container ship 381, 382
container terminal 381, 430
container truck 377
container, aluminium recycling 49
container, glass recycling 49
container, paper recycling 49
container, refuse 215
container, recycling 49
container-loading bridge 381
containers, recycling 49
containment building 408, 409
contest area 499
contestant 499
continent 33
continental crust 26
continental margin 33
continental rise 33
continental shelf 33
continental slope 33
continents, configuration 14
continuity person 291
continuous beam 344
contrabassoons 295
contractile vacuole 66
contrast control 329
control 330
control button 332
control deck 383
control key 330
control keys 328
control lobe 210, 212
control knobs, burner 210
control monitors, director's 290

control panel 178, 179, 210, 212, 213, 214, 455
control room 293, 406
control stick 395
control tower 388
control unit, electronic 357
control valve 529
control wheel 455
control, bass tone 325
control, cruise 354
control, remote 321
control, sound field 322
control, temperature 211
control, treble tone 325
control, tuning 325
control, volume 303, 325, 329
control: group select 330
controller 471
controller ports 471
controller, lightbar 457
controls, videotape operation 320
controls, winch 364
conurbation 430
convection 415
convection current 415
convection zone 4
convective cell 43
convenience food 121
convenience outlet 217
convention centre 433
conventional door 286
convergent plate boundaries 27
converging lenses 419
convertible 347
convex lens 419
conveyor 402
conveyor belt 49, 390
Cook Strait 15
cook's knife 169
cooked ham 156
cooker hood 164
cooker ring 210
cooker, gas 210
cooking dishes 179
cooking plate 179
cooking set 531
cooking surface 179
cooking utensils 174
cool tip 269
coolant 408
coolant inlet 410
coolant outlet 410
coolant, cold 408
coolant, hot 408
cooler 532
cooling 405
cooling cylinder 420
cooling fan 322, 350, 358, 360
cooling system 351
cooling tower 402
cooling vent 336
Coon, Maine 87
coping 526
coping saw 226
cor anglais 306
Coral Sea 15
coral snake 77
corbeille 293
corbel 282
corbel piece 192
cord, power 177, 227, 229, 269, 322
cord, spinal 109
cord, ventral nerve 71
cordate 55
Cordillera, Andes 17
cordless drill-driver 228
cordless mouse 332
cordless screwdriver 221
core 4, 58, 534
corer, apple 173
coriander 142
Corinthian column, engaged 281
Corinthian pilaster 281
cork 118
cork ball 477
cork tip 495
corkscrew 531
corn 143
corn oil 149
corn salad 127
corn syrup 149
corn: cob 61
cornea 119, 419
corner 498
corner arc 481
corner cupboard 203

corner flag 481
corner pad 498
corner stool 498
corner stud 187
corner tower 282
cornerpiece 277
cornet 295, 307
cornflour 144
comice 183, 185, 202, 279
corolla 56
corona 4
corona radiata 112
coronal suture 100
coronet 83
corpus callosum 109
corpus cavernosum 111
cors anglais 295
corselette 258
corset 259
cortex 107
corymb 57
cos lettuce 126
cosmetic tray 277
Costa Rica 448
costal shield 76
costume 290
cot 205
cottage cheese 150
cottage loaf 145
cotton applicators 461
cotton wool ball 461
cotyledon 53
coudé focus 7
cougar 88
cough syrup 467
coulis, tomato 140
coulomb 426
Coulommiers 151
counter 262, 443
counter reset button 323
counter, bar 438
counter, business 443
counter, cheese 121
counter, fresh meat 120
counterjib 397
counterjib ballast 397
countersunk head 221
counterweight 8, 287, 345, 397, 400, 401
counterweight guide rail 287
country 23, 431
coupé 347
coupler-tilt tablet 305
coupling 377
coupling guide device 376
coupon booth 443
courgette 128
course 504
course, golf 430
court 241, 440, 487, 488, 490, 494
courthouse 432
courtroom 440
courtyard 447
couscous 144
couscous kettle 175
cover 180, 198, 315, 454, 477, 505, 533
cover, car 356
cover, chip 227
cover, cylinder head 350
cover, front 333
cover, sliding 327
coverage, sky 39
coveralls 513
covered parapet walk 282
covering 493
cow 84
Cowper's gland 111
cowshed 122
Coyolxauhqui stone 283
crab 158
crab pulley 397
crab spider 70
cradle 8, 9
cradle, docking 337
cranberry 132
crane runway 397
cranes 397
cranial nerves 108
crank 170, 224, 372, 537
crank handle 225
crank, landing gear 365
crankshaft 360
crash helmet 367, 524
crash sensor, primary 354

crate, small 162
crate, small open 162
crater 5, 28
crater ray 5
cravat 245
crawl stroke 517
crayfish 158
cream 150
cream cheese 150
cream jug 166
cream, sour 150
cream, whipping 150
crease 246
credit card 441
credit card wallet 274
credit line 313
creel 538
creep 31
crenate 55
crepidoma 279
crescendo pedal 305
crescentic dune 36
cress, garden 127
crest 29, 33, 418, 477
crest of spillway 406
crevasse 30
crevice tool 209
crew neck 260
crew neck sweater 250, 255
crew quarters 382
crew return vehicle 11
cribriform plate of ethmoid 117
cricket 478
cricket ball 478
cricket player: batsman 478
cricket shoe 478
crime prevention 456
crimping 534
Croatia 450
crockery 166
crocodile 77
crocus 56
croissant 144
crook 306
crook key 306
crookneck squash 129
crosne 124
cross brace 467
cross head 221
cross rail 201
cross section of a baseball 477
cross section of a hydroelectric power plant 407
cross section of a molar 101
cross section of a reflecting telescope 9
cross section of a refracting telescope 8
cross section of a road 342
cross section of a street 434
cross section of an astronomical observatory 7
cross, altar 446
cross-country bicycle and cyclist 522
cross-country ski 514
cross-country ski trail 512
cross-country skier 514
cross-country skiing 514
cross-headed tip 221
cross-tip screwdriver 531
crossbar 297, 370
crosshead 396
crossing 284, 285
crossing arm 362
crossover 375
crossover cargo deck line 385
crossover mirror 362
crosspiece 202, 466
crosstree 520
crotch 247
crotch piece 255
crotchet 299
crotchet rest 299
Crottin de Chavignol 150
croup 83
crowbar 220
crown 63, 78, 101, 238, 239, 302, 308, 424
crown block 403
crucifix 446
crude oil 405
crude-oil pipeline 404
cruise control 354
cruiseliner 386
crus of helix 115
crushed chillis 139
crusher 49, 402
crust, continental 26

crust, oceanic 26
crustaceans 71, 158
crustose lichen 50
crystal button 207
crystal drop 207
crystallization 414
Cuba 448
cube 429
cucumber 128
cucumber, seedless 128
cue ball 502, 503
cuff 240, 245
culottes 253
cultivated mushroom 123
cultural organization 335
cumin 138
cumulonimbus 42
cumulus 42
cup 163, 531, 532, 534
cup gasket 459
cup, butter 163
cup, milk/cream 163
cupboard 164
cupboard, caretaker's 443
cupboard, janitor's 439
cupule 60
curler 515
curling 515
curling brush 515
curling iron 269
curling stone 515
curly endive 127
curly kale 126
currant tomato 128
currency name 441
current event scoreboard 497
current, convection 415
curry 138
cursor down 331
cursor left 331
cursor movement keys 331
cursor right 331
cursor up 331
curtain wall 282
curtain, iron 292
curtain, privacy 464
curtain, stage 292
curved jaw 222
customer service 443
customer's supply 198
customers' cloakroom 438
customers' entrance 438
customers' toilets 438
customs control 391
customs house 381
cut nail 220
cut-throat razor 271
cuticle nippers 265
cuticle pusher 265
cuticle scissors 265
cuticle trimmer 265
cutlery 167
cutlery basket 214
cutlery set 531
cuts of beef 152
cuts of lamb 153
cuts of pork 153
cuts of veal 152
cutter link 235
cutting blade 176, 180, 341
cutting board 169
cutting edge 167, 169, 270, 398, 399, 400
cutting head 341
cutting, key 437
cuttlefish 157
cyan 418
cycle lock 372
cycle, hydrologic 45
cycling 522
cycling helmet 372
cyclone 43
cyclone, tropical 43
cylinder 429
cylinder head cover 350
cylinder vacuum cleaner 209
cylinder, cooling 420
cylinder, elevating 364
cylinder, master 357
cylinder, reflecting 420
cylinder, ruby 420
cylindrical projection 22
cymbal 308
cymbals 295, 309
Cyprus 450
cytopharynx 66

ASTRONOMY > 2-13;   EARTH > 14-49;   PLANT KINGDOM > 50-65;   ANIMAL KINGDOM > 66-91;   HUMAN BEING > 92-119;   FOOD AND KITCHEN > 120-181;   HOUSE > 182-215;
DO-IT-YOURSELF AND GARDENING > 216-237;   CLOTHING > 238-263;   PERSONAL ADORNMENT AND ARTICLES > 264-277;   ARTS AND ARCHITECTURE > 278-311;   COMMUNICATIONS AN
OFFICE AUTOMATION > 312-341;   TRANSPORT AND MACHINERY > 342-401;   ENERGY > 402-413;   SCIENCE > 414-429;   SOCIETY > 430-467;   SPORTS AND GAMES > 468-538

cytoplasm 50, 66, 112
cytoproct 66
cytostome 66
Czech Republic 450

D

d 298
d quark 414
daffodil 56
daggerboard 519
daggerboard well 519
daikon 129
dairy 122
dairy compartment 211
dairy products 120, 150
dairy products receiving area 120
dalmatian 86
dam 406
dance blade 509
dandelion 127
Dane, Great 86
danger area 499
Danish Blue 151
Danish rye bread 145
Danube River 18
dark chocolate 148
dart 471
dartboard 471
dashboard 354
dashboard computer 457
dashboard equipment 457
data display 319, 328
data panel 314
data processing 38
data storage devices 333
database 335
date 132, 441
date display/recording button 320
date stamp 338
date, expiry 441
David, star of 447
davit 384
day-care centre 437
dead ball line 482
dead bolt 186
deadly poisonous mushroom 52
dealer, car 433
debit card 443
debris 43
decagon, regular 429
decanter 165
deceleration lane 343
deciduous forest 44
decimal key 337
deck 313, 344
deck, dual cassette 325
deck, sun 385
deck, upper 363
declination setting scale 8, 9
décolleté bra 259
decomposers 45
decorative articles shop 437
decorative braid 260
decoy 535
decrease, voltage 402
dedicated line 334
deed, title 469
deep fryer 178
deep peroneal nerve 108
deep-sea floor 26
defects, vision 419
defence counsel's bench 440
deferent duct 111
deflector 236, 237
deforestation 47
defrost drain 211
degree 428
degree Celsius 426
degrees Celsius 424
degrees Fahrenheit 424
Deimos 2
delegates, technical 509
delete 331
delete key 331
delicatessen 120, 156
delicious lactarius 123
delivery 479
delivery entrance 435
delta 32, 35
delta distributary 32
delta wing 394
deltoid 96
demisemiquaver 299
demisemiquaver rest 299
demitasse 166

Democratic People's Republic of Korea 453
Democratic Republic of Congo 451
dendrite 110
Denmark 450
denomination 441
dental alveolus 101
dental care 272
dental floss 272
dental floss holder 272
dentin 101
deodorant 267
department store 437
departure lounge 391
departure time indicator 374
departure, chair lift 512
departure, gondola 512
depolarizing mix 417
deposit slot 442
deposits, alluvial 32
depression 39
depth adjustment 229
depth of focus 27
depth-of-cut adjustment knob 229
depth-of-field preview button 314
derailleur 522
dermis 114
derrick 382, 385, 403, 404
derrick mast 385
descending aorta 103
descending colon 106
descending passage 278
desert 36, 40, 44
Desert, Atacama 17
Desert, Gobi 19
Desert, Great Sandy 15
Desert, Great Victoria 15
Desert, Kalahari 20
Desert, Namib 20
Desert, Sahara 20
designer, production 290
desk 439
desk lamp 206
desk lamp, halogen 206
desk tray 338
desk, clerks' 440
desk, front 439
desk, information 442, 463, 512
desk, reception 442
desk, student's 444
desk, teacher's 444
desktop computer 334
dessert fork 168
dessert knife 168
dessert spoon 168
destination 374
destroying angel 52
detachable control 179
detachable palm rest 330
detector, motion 286
detector, smoke 454
detergent dispenser 214
device, locking 535
device, projection 365
device, towing 364
devices, contact 198
dew 41
diable 175
diagonal buttress 284
diagonal move 470
diagonal step 514
dial 422, 424
dial, near/far 320
dial/action button 337
diameter 428
diamond 468
diamond interchange 342
diamond point 202
diaphragm 105, 324
dibber 231
dice and dominoes 468
dice cup 469
diced beef 152
diced lamb 153
diced veal 152
die 469
died 426
diesel engine compartment 399, 400, 401
diesel engine shed 375
diesel lift engine 383
diesel motor compartment 398
diesel oil 405
diesel propulsion engine 383
diesel-electric locomotive 377

differential 351
difficult slope 512
diffuser 290
diffuser pin 236
digestive gland 71, 73
digestive system 106
digging fork 233
digit 75, 82
digit, prehensile 91
digital audio player, portable 325
digital camera 315
digital display 423, 461
digital nerve 108
digital pulp 114
digital reflex camera: camera back 315
digital thermometer 461
digital versatile disc (DVD) 318
digital watch 424
Dijon mustard 140
dill 142
dimmer switch 198
dimple 505
dinette 164
dining room 188, 280, 386, 438, 439
dinner fork 168
dinner knife 168
dinner plate 166
diode 411
Dione 3
dip switch 368
dipped beam headlight 352
dipper arm 399
dipper arm cylinder 399
dipping/indicator stalk 354
direct home reception 316
direct-current power cord 336
direction of electron flow 416, 417
direction of Mecca 447
directional buttons 471
director 291
director of photography 291
director's chair 200
director's control monitors 290
director's office 443
director's seat 291
director, art 290
director, race 522
directory 334
disc 357, 501
disc brake 350, 357, 366, 525
disc brake, hydraulic 522
disc compartment 323
disc compartment control 323
disc drive 310
disc tray 318
disc, sanding 229
discharge outlet 184
discharge tube 199
discs 177
discus 472
discus and hammer 473
dish 179, 321
dish aerial 321
dish, soufflé 172
dishes, cooking 179
dishwasher 164, 214
disk 6, 333
diskette, floppy disk 333
dispenser, beverage 463
dispenser, cash 437, 442
dispenser, ice cube 164
displacement 418
display 318, 322, 325, 327, 336, 337, 338, 346, 423, 442, 443
display cabinet 203
display case, refrigerated 438
display panel 320
display preparation area 120
display release button 336
display setting 327
display, end aisle 121
display, frequency 325
display, liquid crystal 315, 320
display, radar 457
disposable camera 315
disposable contact lens 272
disposable gas cylinder 218
disposable nappy 260
disposable razor 271
dissemination of information 335
distal phalanx 114
distributary, delta 32
distribution board 198
distribution by aerial cable network 316
distribution by submarine cable 317

distribution by underground cable network 317
distributor 360
distributor cap 350
distributor service loop 198
district 25
district, business 430, 432
district, residential 431
ditali 146
ditch 342
divergent plate boundaries 27
diverging lenses 419
diversion tunnel 406
divide key 337
divider 274, 277
dividers 339
diving 518
diving apparatus 518
diving board 184
diving tower 518
diving well 184
division 427
djembe 297
Djibouti 451
Dnieper River 18
do-it-yourself 216
do-it-yourself and gardening 216
do-it-yourself shop 436
dock 381
dock, prisoner's 440
dock, unloading 437, 439
docking cradle 337
doctor, junior 464
document folder 339
document receiving 328
document-to-be-sent position 328
dodecagon, regular 429
does not belong to 427
dog 86, 535
dog breeds 86
dog, morphology of 86
dogfish, larger spotted 158
dolichos beans 130
dolina 31
dollar 440
dolly 297
dolly tracks 290
dolphin 90
dolphin, morphology of 90
dome 177
dome shutter 7
dome tent 529
domestic appliances 176, 208
domestic appliances, miscellaneous 180
domestic pollution 47
Dominica 449
Dominican Republic 449
dominoes, dice and 468
dominos 468
door 178, 202, 210, 213, 287, 349, 352, 361, 392, 439, 447, 528, 529
door grip 352
door handle 185, 186, 349
door lock 349
door open warning light 355
door panel 202
door pillar 349
door pocket 352
door shelf 211
door stop 211
door switch 213
door, cargo bay 13
door, entrance 362, 363
door, fire 286
door, lift 363
door, patio 164
door, screen 361
door, strip 286
door, two-leaf 362
doors, entrance 294
doors, examples of 286
Doric column, engaged 281
dormer window 182
dorsal abdominal artery 71
dorsal fin 90
dorsalis pedis artery 102
dorsum of nose 117
dorsum of tongue 118
double bass 301
double basses 295
double bed 439
double boiler 175
double flat 299

double plate 187
double reed 306
double ring 471
double room 439
double seat 380
double sharp 299
double sink 194
double slash 334
double-blank 468
double-breasted buttoning 248
double-breasted jacket 244
double-decker bus 363
double-edged razor 271
double-edged razor blade 271
double-leaf bascule bridge 345
double-six 468
double-twist auger bit 228
doubles service court 495
doubles sideline 490, 495
doublet 468
doubling die 469
doubly toothed 55
dough hook 176
dough, filo 145
dousing water tank 408
dovetail 420
down tube 371
downhill 511
downhill bicycle and cyclist 522
downhill/Super G ski 510
downpipe 182
drag 536
drag wheel, star 537
dragonfly 69
drain 197
drain hose 212, 214
drain valve 404
drain, defrost 211
drain, main 184
drainage circuit 194
draining spoon 173
Drake Passage 15, 17
draught 470
draught arm 400
draught tube 400, 407
draughtboard 470
draughts 470
draw hoe 233
draw tube 421
drawbridge 282
drawer 164, 202, 203, 205, 210
drawing pins 341
drawstring 249, 275
drawstring bag 275
drawstring hood 261
dredger 172
dress circle 293
dress, A-line 252
dresser 291
dresser, set 291
dresses, examples of 252
dressing room 290, 293
dressing room, private 290
dressing table 203
dried chillis 139
drill collar 403
drill pipe 403
drill ship 382
drill, masonry 228
drill, twist 228
drill-driver, cordless 228
drilling drawworks 403
drilling rig 403
drink box 163
drinks 120
drip bowl 210
drip moulding 349
drip tray 181
dripping pan 174, 179
drive belt 212
drive chain 370
drive shaft 383, 395
drive shaft, longitudinal 351
drive wheel 180
drive, CD/DVD-ROM 329, 336
drive, floppy disk 329
driver 524
driver seat 369
driver's cab 376, 377
driveway 183
driving glove 243
driving propeller 383
driving wheels 401
dromedary 85
drone 68
drone 296

droop nose 394
drop earrings 264
drop shot 491
drop waist dress 252
drop-leaf 202
drum 170, 212, 213, 357
drum, rotating 27
drum, talking 297
drumhead 308
drumlin 29
drums 308
drumstick 297
drupelet 59
dry cells 417
dry cleaner 437
dry climates 40
dry dock 381
dry fruits 60, 133
dry gallery 31
dual cassette deck 325
dual seat 367
dual swivel mirror 269
dual-in-line package 417
duck 81, 155
duck egg 155
duct, exhaust air 345
duct, fresh-air 345
duffle bag 276
duffle coat 249
dugout 474
dulse 123
dumbbell 500
dune 35
dunes, examples of 36
dung, animal 48
dungarees 254
dungarees with crossover back straps 261
duo 300
duodenum 106
dura mater 109, 110
durian 137
dust canister 229
dust receiver 208
dust tail 6
dusting brush 209
dustpan 215
Dutch bicycle 373
Dutch oven 175
duty belt 456
duty-free shop 391
DVD player 318
DVD recorder 333
dyke 28
dynamo 370

E

e 298
e-commerce 335
eagle 81
ear 92, 201
ear drum 116
ear flap 238
ear loaf 144
ear protection 458
ear studs 264
ear, auricle 115
ear, structure of 116
ear, wood 123
earlobe 115
earphone 324
earphone jack 329
earphones 325
earpiece 273, 460
earplugs 458
earrings 264
Earth 2, 3, 4, 5, 14
Earth coordinate system 21
earth foundation 342
earth station, satellite 335
earth terminal 198
earth wire 198
Earth's atmosphere, profile 37
Earth's crust 26, 27
Earth's crust, section 26
Earth's orbit 4, 5
Earth, structure 26
earthflow 31
earthing pin 198
earthquake 27
East 23
East China Sea 19
East Pacific Rise 34
East-Northeast 23
East-Southeast 23

Eastern hemisphere 21
Eastern meridian 22
eau de parfum 267
eau de toilette 267
eave 283
eccrine sweat gland 114
eclipses, types 4, 5
economy and finance 441
Ecuador 448
edge 441, 509, 510, 533
edging 230
edible boletus 123
edit search button 320
editorial 313
education 444
educational institution 335, 433
eel 159
effect, greenhouse 46
effluent 32
effusive volcano 28
egg 79, 112
egg beater 172
egg carton 162
egg noodles 147
egg poacher 175
egg slicer 173
egg timer 171
egg tray 211
egg, duck 155
egg, goose 155
egg, hen 155
egg, ostrich 155
egg, pheasant 155
egg, quail 155
eggs 155
Egypt 451
Egyptian reed pen 312
eiderdown 204
ejaculatory duct 111
eject button 315, 323, 471
ejector nozzle, variable 394
El Salvador 448
elastic 204
elastic loop 528
elastic strainer 529
elastic support bandage 461
elastic waistband 249
elastic webbing 246
elasticized leg opening 247
elbow 83, 86, 93, 95
elbow pad 486, 526, 527
elbows 146
electric charge, measurement of 426
electric cooker 210
electric current, measurement of 426
electric drill 228
electric fan motor 358
electric golf cart 505
electric guitar 303
electric knife 177
electric motor 235, 237
electric razor 271
electric resistance, measurement of 426
electric steamer 179
electric toothbrush 272
electric tumble dryer 213
electrical box 198
electrical cable 354
electrical circuit, parallel 416
electrical connection 365
electrical system 351
electricity 198
electricity cable 434
electricity meter 198
electricity tools 217
electricity transmission 408
electrolytic capacitors 417
electrolytic separator 417
electromagnetic spectrum 418
electron 414
electron beam 318
electron collector 417
electron flow, direction of 416, 417
electron gun 318
electronic ballast 199
electronic control unit 357
electronic drum pad 311
electronic instruments 310
electronic payment terminal 121, 443
electronic piano 311
electronic scale 423
electronic timer, automatic 517
electronic viewfinder 320
electronics 417

electronics shop 436
element, surface 210
elements of a house 185
elements of architecture 286
elephant 85
elevating cylinder 364, 397, 455
elevation 182
elevation adjustment 420
elevation zones and vegetation 44
elevator 393, 400
elevon 13
elk 85
email 335
email key 330
email software 334
embankment 342
emblem, team's 506
emergency 462
emergency brake 380
emergency physician's office 462
emergency station 345
emergency switch 368
emergency truck 345
emery boards 265
emission, nitric acid 48
emission, nitrogen oxide 48
emission, polluting gas 47
emission, sulphur dioxide 48
emission, sulphuric acid 48
Emmenthal 151
empty set 427
emptying hose 212
enamel 101
enclosure 122, 286
end 331
end aisle display 121
end button 301
end cap 409
end joist 187
end key 327, 331
end line 484, 487, 489, 493
end moraine 30
end piece 111
end plate 409
end search button 320
end stop 226, 521
end zone 484
end-piece 273
endocardium 104
endocarp 57, 58
endoplasmic reticulum 50, 66
endpiece 273
energy 402
energy integration to transmission network
413
energy release 415
energy saving bulb 199, 411
energy, heat 46
energy, measurement of 426
energy, solar 54
energy, thermal 402
engaged Corinthian column 281
engaged Doric column 281
engaged Ionic column 281
engagement ring 264
engine 366, 403
engine air intake 362
engine block 360
engine compartment 362, 396, 401
engine housing 235
engine mounting pylon 393
engine room 384, 386
engine, main 13
engine, outboard 385
engine, petrol 351
engineer, sound 291
engines, fire 455
English billiards 503
English Channel 18
English mustard 140
English stick 466
enhanced greenhouse effect 46
enoki mushroom 123
entablature 185, 279
enter key 331
enterprise 335
entire 55
entrance door 362, 363
entrance doors 294
entrance hall 188
entrance turnstile 378
entrance, actors' 278
entrance, customers' 438
entrance, main 445, 465
entrance, public 278

entrance, pyramid 278
entrance, staff 438, 445
entry 396
envelope, padded 339
environment 44
environment, natural 504
epaulet 248
epicalyx 59
epicentre 27
epicondyle 99
epidermis 114
epididymis 111
epidural space 110
epiglottis 105, 118
epitrochlea 99
equals key 337
Equator 22
equator 17, 20, 21, 43
Equatorial Guinea 451
equipment 472
equipment compartment 376
equipment storage room 444
equipment, dashboard 457
equipment, household 215
equipment, miscellaneous 231
equipment, sound recording 291
erase button 315, 328
eraser 341
erecting lenses 420
Eritrea 451
escalator 294, 378, 435
escape 330
escape key 330
escarole 126
escutcheon 73, 186, 197
escutcheon plate 198
espadrille 242
espresso coffee maker 181
espresso machine 181
estate car 347
Estonia 450
estuary 24, 35
eternal light 447
Ethernet port 336
Ethiopia 451
Eurasia 14
Eurasian Plate 27
euro 440
Europa 2
Europe 14, 18, 34, 449
European experiment module 11
European outlet 198
European plug 198
European robin 80
European Union flag 441
Eustachian tube 116, 117
Eutelsat 316
euthynteria 279
evacuation route 345
evaporated milk 150
evaporation 45, 414
evening glove 243
event platform 496
events, technical 511
ex-voto 446
examination and treatment room 463
examination room 465
examination, psychiatric 462
examples of aircraft 394
examples of algae 51
examples of amphibians 75
examples of angles 428
examples of arachnids 70
examples of armchairs 200
examples of bicycles 373
examples of bills 79
examples of birds 80
examples of bits and drills 228
examples of blouses 255
examples of boats and ships 382
examples of bodywork 347
examples of branching 57
examples of broadleaved trees 64
examples of carnivorous mammals 88
examples of chairs 201
examples of conifers 65
examples of currency abbreviations 440
examples of doors 285
examples of dresses 252
examples of dunes 36
examples of feet 79
examples of ferns 52
examples of flowers 56
examples of forks 168
examples of freight wagons 377
examples of heads 221

examples of holds 499
examples of insects 69
examples of instrumental groups 300
examples of interchanges 342
examples of jumps 509
examples of kitchen knives 169
examples of knives 168
examples of lagomorphs 82
examples of leaves 65
examples of lichens 50
examples of marine mammals 90
examples of mosses 51
examples of motorcycles 369
examples of nails 220
examples of pleats 253
examples of primates 91
examples of reptiles 77
examples of rodents 82
examples of shorelines 35
examples of skirts 253
examples of skis 510
examples of sleeping bags 530
examples of spectacles 273
examples of spoons 168
examples of tables 202
examples of tents 528
examples of tips 221
examples of trousers 254
examples of trucks 364
examples of tyres 358
examples of ungulate mammals 84
examples of volcanoes 28
examples of windows 287
exercise cycle 501
exercise wear 263
exhalation valve 459
exhaust air duct 345
exhaust manifold 350, 360
exhaust pipe 395
exhaust pipe stack 398
exhaust stack 364, 401
exhaust system 351
exhaust valve 360
exhibition centre 430
exit 343
exit button 337
exit taxiway 391
exit turnstile 378
exocarp 57, 58, 59
exosphere 37
expandable baton 456
expandable file pouch 274
expander 310
expansion bolt 221
expansion chamber 424
expert slope 512
expiry date 441
explosive volcano 28
exposure adjustment knob 314
exposure mode 314
extending table 202
extension 202
extension ladder 219
extension tube 209
exterior dome shell 7
exterior door 185
exterior of a house 182
exterior pocket 274, 276
exterior sign 378
external auditory meatus 100
external ear 116
external floppy disk drive 333
external fuel tank 12
external jugular vein 102
external nose 117
external oblique 96, 97
external socket 361
external tooth lock washer 222
extinguisher, fire 457
extractor hood 210
eye 43, 70, 71, 72, 76, 90, 94, 119,
220, 538
eye drops, lubricant 272
eye make-up 266
eye protection 458
eye ring 78
eye wall 43
eyeball 75, 119
eyebrow pencil 266
eyebrow stripe 78
eyebrow tweezers 265
eyecup 320
eyelash 119
eyelash curler 266
eyelashes 87
eyelet 240, 263, 275, 509

ASTRONOMY > 2-13;   EARTH > 14-49;   PLANT KINGDOM >50-65;   ANIMAL KINGDOM > 66-91;   HUMAN BEING > 92-119;   FOOD AND KITCHEN > 120-181;   HOUSE > 182-215;
DO-IT-YOURSELF AND GARDENING > 216-237;   CLOTHING > 238-263;   PERSONAL ADORNMENT AND ARTICLES > 264-277;   ARTS AND ARCHITECTURE > 278-311;   COMMUNICATIONS AND
OFFICE AUTOMATION > 312-341;   TRANSPORT AND MACHINERY > 342-401;   ENERGY > 402-413;   SCIENCE > 414-429;   SOCIETY > 430-467;   SPORTS AND GAMES > 468-538

ENGLISH INDEX

eyelet tab 240
eyelet, strap 315
eyelid 76
eyepiece 8, 9, 320, 420, 421
eyepiece holder 8
eyeshadow 266
eyestalk 72

F

f 298
fabric guide 208
façade 285
face 91, 92, 220, 493, 505
face flannel 267
face mask 478, 486, 507
face-off circle 506
face-off spot 506
facepiece 459
faceplate 186
factorial 427
factory 430
faculae 4
Fahrenheit scale 424
fairing 366, 523
fairings, side 525
fairlead 521
fairway 504
falcon 81
Falkland Islands 17
fall front 203
fallopian tube 112
fallopian tubes 113
fallow land 122
false rib 99
false tuck 260
family tent 528
family waiting room 462
fan 213
fan belt 350, 360
fan brush 266
fan housing 270
fan trellis 230
fan, case 329
fan, cooling 322, 350
fan, power supply 329
fang 70, 76
fantail 412
farmhouse 122
farmhouse loaf 145
farming, intensive 46, 48
farmstead 122
farmyard 122
fascia, front 348
fast data entry control 310
fast forward 319
fast forward key 319
fast-food restaurants 437
fast-forward button 323, 326, 328
fastener binder 339
fats and oils 149
fault 27
fax machine 328
feather crown 495
feathered shuttlecock 495
feed tube 177, 180
feeder lane 343
feedhorn 321
feet, examples of 79
feijoa 137
female 426
female cone 65
female ferrule 536, 537
female genital organs 112
femoral artery 102
femoral nerve 108
femoral vein 102
femur 98
fence 122, 182, 226
fence, outfield 475
fennec 88
fennel 125
fenugreek 138
fern 52
fern, bird's nest 52
fern, fiddlehead 125
fern, structure of 52
fern, tree 52
ferns, examples of 52
ferrule 219, 503
ferrule, female 537
ferrule, male 537
ferry boat 386
ferryboat 381
fertilization, soil 47

fertilizer application 47
fetlock 83
fetlock joint 83
fettucine 146
fibres 215
fibula 98
fiddlehead 52
fiddlehead fern 125
field 474, 479, 482
field lens 420
field lens adjustment 421
field line 416
field magnetic 416
field mouse 82
field, geothermal 402
field, paddy 47
field, track and 472
fielder's glove 477
fielders 479
fifth 298
fifth wheel 364
fifty 427
fig 137
figure skate 509
figure skating 509
Fiji 453
Fiji Islands 15
filament 56, 199
Filchner Ice Shelf 15
file 229, 334, 531
file format 334
file guides 340
file, nail 265
filiform papilla 118
filing box 340
filler cap 237, 358, 364
filler hole 208
filler neck 351
filler pipe 196
fillet roast 152
filleting knife 169
filling inlet 404
film advance mode 314
film rewind knob 314
film speed 314
film titles and schedules 294
film, heat-sealed 163
film, plastic 162
filo dough 145
filter 178, 181, 184, 210
filter cover 459
filter holder 181
filter, air 350
filtration, intrusive 47
fin, anal 74
fin, caudal 74, 90
fin, dorsal 90
fin, first dorsal 74
fin, pectoral 74, 90
fin, pelvic 74
fin, second dorsal 74
final drive 398
finance, economy and 441
financial services 442
finch 80
finderscope 8, 9
fine adjustment knob 421
fine adjustment wheel 425
fine data entry control 310
fine guidance system 7
finely threaded screw 425
finger 114, 477
finger button 307
finger flange 460
finger tip 339
fingerboard 296, 301, 303
fingerless mitt 243
fingernail 115
finial 283
finish line 473
finish wall 516
finishing nail 220
Finland 450
fir 65
fir needles 65
fire door 286
fire engines 455
fire extinguisher 457
fire hose 454
fire hydrant 434, 454
fire irons 193
fire prevention 454
fire station 433
fire, forest 47
fire-fighting material 454
firebrick 192

firebrick back 192
firefighter 454
firefighting aircraft, amphibious 394
fireplace 188, 192
fireplace screen 193
FireWire port 336
firing, wood 192
first aid equipment 460
first aid kit 457, 461
first aid manual 461
first assistant camera operator 290
first base 474
first baseman 474
first dorsal fin 74
first floor 182, 189
first leaves 53
first molar 101
first premolar 101
first quarter 5
first row 482
first space 489
first valve slide 307
first violins 295
first voltage increase 413
first-class cabin 392
fish dish 166
fish fork 168
fish kettle 174
fish knife 168
fish scaler 531
fish, bony 74
fish, cartilaginous 74
fishes 74
fishes, bony 159
fishes, cartilaginous 158
fishhook 536, 538
fishing 536
fishing jacket 538
fishnet stocking 257
fission of uranium fuel 408
fission products (radioactive nuclei) 415
fission, nuclear 415
fissionable nucleus 415
fissure, oblique 105
fitness equipment 500
fitted sheet 204
fitting 455
five 427
five hundred 427
five spice powder 139
fixed base 224
fixed bridges 344
fixed distance marking 391
fixed jaw 223, 224, 425
fjords 35
flag 482
flag pole, removable 504
flag, European Union 441
flageolet 131
flags 448
flagstone 230
flame 415
flame spreader 218
flame-resistant driving suit 524
flamingo 81
flank 78, 83
flank forward 482
flanking tower 282
flannel, face 267
flap 244, 275
flap pocket 244, 248
flap, self-sealing 339
flap, top 532
flare 4
flare nut spanner 223
flare, road 457
flash tube 420
flashing 193
flashlight 456
flask, vacuum 532
flat 299, 526
flat mirror 7
flat sheet 204
flat tip 221
flat truck 377
flat washer 222
flat-back brush 268
flat-plate solar collector 410
flea 69
flesh 57, 58, 59
fleshy fruit: berry fruit 59
fleshy fruit: citrus fruit 58
fleshy leaf 54
fleshy pome fruit 58
fleshy stone fruit 57

flews 86
flex 208, 209, 217, 235, 237, 270, 271
flex sleeve 218, 229
flex support 208
flexible boot 513
flexible hose 209
flexible skirt 383
flexible tube 460
flies 292
flight 471
flight bag 276
flight deck 12, 392, 395
flight information board 391
flight of stairs 191
flights 518
flint 218
flip 509
flip-flop 242
float 394, 538
float ball 196
float seaplane 394
floating crane 381
floating head 271
floating rib 98
floating roof 404
floating-roof tank 404
floodplain 32
floor 193, 412
floor brush 209
floor coverings, textile 190
floor drain 194
floor exercise area 496
floor joist 187
floor mat 356
floor mats 496
floor, car 287
floor, mezzanine 182
floor, ocean 33
floorboard 369
flooring strip 190
floppy disk drive 329
floppy disk drive, external 333
floppy disk eject button 329
florist 437
floss, dental 272
flour and semolina 144
flour, oat 144
flour, plain 144
flour, unbleached 144
flour, whole wheat 144
flow tube 410
flower 53, 56
flower bed 230
flower bud 53
flower, structure 56
flowering 62
flowers, examples of 56
flue 305
flue pipe 305
fluff trap 213
fluid, cerebro-spinal 110
fluorescent tube 199
flush 468
flush handle 196
flute 228
fluted land 228
flutes 295
fly 69, 246, 247, 260
fly agaric 52
fly front closing 251, 261
fly half 482
fly line 536
fly reel 536
fly rod 536
fly, tsetse 69
flyfishing 536
flying buttress 284, 285
flyover 343, 344
flysheet 528, 529
flywheel 360, 501
FM mode select button 322
foam 33
foam gun 385
foam pad 530
foam, shaving 271
focus 27, 419
focus mode selector 314
focus selector 320
focus, Cassegrain 7
focus, coudé 7
focusing knob 8, 9
focusing ring 420
fodder corn 122
fog 41
fog lamp 352

fog light 364
foie gras 156
foil stip, hologram 441
foil, aluminium 162
folder 340
folding chair 201
folding door 286
folding grill 533
folding nail file 265
folding ramp 386
folding shovel 532
foliage 63
foliate papilla 118
foliose lichen 50
follicle 60
following car 522
fondue fork 168
fondue pot 174
fondue set 174
fongiform papilla 118
font, baptismal 446
font, holy water 446
fontanelle, anterior 100
fontanelle, mastoid 100
fontanelle, posterior 100
fontanelle, sphenoidal 100
food 120
food and kitchen 120
food can 163
food chain 45
food mill 170
food processor 177
food store 439
food tray 162
food vacuole 66
food, convenience 121
foods, catering 121
foods, frozen 121
foot 72, 73, 91, 92, 93, 94, 95, 202, 247, 260, 302, 305, 308, 519, 536, 537
foot fault judge 491
foot hole 305
foot plate 501
foot protection 459
foot strap 519
football 480, 486
football boot 480
football, American 484
footballer 480
footboard 204, 523
footbridge 282, 375, 379
footing 187
footless tights 263
footlights 293
footrest 205, 224, 467
footstool 164, 201
footstrap 254, 501
for cooking 178
for correspondence 338
for cutting 177
for filing 339
for juicing 177
for measuring 171
for mixing and blending 176
for opening 170
for time use 338
foramen caecum 118
force, measurement of 426
fore-and-aft passage 385
forearm 86, 93, 95, 534
forearm crutch 466
forearm pad 486
forearm support 466
forecast, meteorological 38
forecastle 383, 387
forecourt 346, 491
forehead 78, 92
foreleg 67, 68
forelimb 75
forelock 83
foremast 385
forest 29
forest fire 47
forest, boreal 44
forest, coniferous 44
forest, deciduous 44
forest, mixed 44
forest, temporal 44
forest, tropical 44
forest, tropical rain 44
forestay 520
forewing 67
fork 8, 167, 371, 396, 522, 525, 531
fork arm 396
fork, front 522

ASTRONOMY > 2-13;   EARTH > 14-49;   PLANT KINGDOM > 50-65;   ANIMAL KINGDOM > 66-91;   HUMAN BEING > 92-119;   FOOD AND KITCHEN > 120-181;   HOUSE > 182-215;
DO-IT-YOURSELF AND GARDENING > 216-237;   CLOTHING > 238-263;   PERSONAL ADORNMENT AND ARTICLES > 264-277;   ARTS AND ARCHITECTURE > 278-311;   COMMUNICATIONS AND
OFFICE AUTOMATION > 312-341;   TRANSPORT AND MACHINERY > 342-401;   ENERGY > 402-413;   SCIENCE > 414-429;   SOCIETY > 430-467;   SPORTS AND GAMES > 468-538

547

ENGLISH INDEX

forked tongue 76
forklift truck 396
forks, examples of 168
format, file 334
formeret 284
forming food vacuole 66
formula 1 car 525
formula 3000 car 524
formula Indy car 524
fortified wall 447
forward 518
fossil energy, geothermy and 402
fossil fuel 46, 48
foul line 474
foul line post 475
foundation 187
foundation of tower 344
foundation slip 258
fountain for ritual ablutions 447
fountain pen 312
four-blade beater 176
four-door saloon 347
four-four time 298
four-of-a-kind 468
four-way lug wrench 356
four-way selector 315
fourchette 243
fourth 298
fovea 119
fowl, guinea 81, 154
fox 88
foyers 293
fraction 427
fractionating tower 405
frame 192, 202, 204, 219, 224, 226,
274, 277, 297, 309, 367, 396, 400,
401, 410, 411, 412, 425, 460, 476,
492, 494, 522, 527, 528
frame stile 202
France 449
frankfurter 156
free guard zone 515
free margin 114
free throw line 489
free-skating blade 509
freehold flats 289
freestyle snowboard 513
freewheel 372
freezer 164, 438
freezer bag 162
freezer compartment 211
freezer door 211
freezer, chest 211
freezer, reach-in 120
freezing 414
freezing rain 41
freight wagon 375
freight wagons, examples of 377
French bread 144
French horn 307
French horns 295
French loaf 144
frequency display 325
frequency, measurement of 426
fresco 280
fresh cheeses 150
fresh meat counter 120
fresh-air duct 345
fret 302, 303
friction strip 218
frieze 202, 279
frilly nylon tights 260
frilly pants 260
frog 75, 249, 301
frog, common 75
frog, morphology of 75
frog, Northern leopard 75
frog, wood 75
frog-adjustment screw 229
frond 52
front 244, 245
front apron 245
front axle 401
front beam 422
front brake 371
front brake lever 368
front compression strap 532
front cover 333
front derailleur 370, 372
front desk 439
front fascia 348
front foil 387
front footrest 367, 368
front fork 522
front fork, telescopic 369
front indicator 366, 368

front lamp 371
front leg 201
front lights 352
front mudguard 366
front page 313
front picture 313
front pipe 350
front pocket 275
front rigid section 363
front shock absorber 369
front sight 534
front tip 208
front top pocket 246
front view 478
front wheel 401, 467
front-end loader 399
frontal 96, 446
frontal bone 98, 100
frontal sinus 117
frontier 23
frontwall 365
frozen food storage 121
frozen foods 121
fruit branch 62
fruit tree 122
fruit vegetables 128
fruit, fleshy pome 58
fruit, fleshy stone 57
fruit, fleshy: berry fruit 59
fruit, fleshy: citrus fruit 58
fruit, passion 136
fruiting 62
fruits 57, 132
fruits and vegetables 120
fruits, citrus 134
fruits, dry 60, 133
fruits, pome 133
fruits, stone 132
fruticose lichen 50
frying basket 171
frying pan 175, 531
fuel 408
fuel bundle 409
fuel conduit 351
fuel gauge 355
fuel injector 360
fuel oil 405
fuel pellet 409
fuel rod 409
fuel supply system 351
fuel tank 235, 351, 364, 366, 369, 377,
395
fuel tank flap 349
fuel, fossil 46, 48
fulcrum 518
full back 482
full face mask 454
full house 468
full moon 5
full-face helmet 525
fullback 485
fumarole 28
function display 310
function keys 328, 330, 423
function keys, programmable 443
function selectors 327
fungicide 47
funiculus 59, 60
funnel 171, 318, 382, 386
funnel cloud 43
fur 82, 91
furniture, children's 205
furniture, house 200
furrow 118
fuse 198, 411
fuselage 393
fusilli 146
futon 204

G

g 298
G-clamp 224
gable 182, 285
gable stud 187
gable vent 182
gabletop 163
Gabon 451
gaffer 291
Gai-lohn 127
gaits, horse 83
galaxy 6
gall-bladder 106
gallery 285, 412
gallery, connecting 345
Gallery, Grand 278

galley 392
gallop 83
galosh 240
Gambia 451
game 154, 492
game board 469
game console 471
game of darts 471
game, board 469
game, online 471
game/MIDI port 329
games 468
games area 386
games, sports and 468
gamma rays 418
ganglion, cerebropleural 73
ganglion, spiral 109
gantry crane 406, 407
Ganymede 2
gap 538
garage 182
garage door, sectional 286
garage door, up-and-over 286
garam masala 139
garden 280
garden arch 230
garden cress 127
garden hose 236
garden line 231
garden path 182
garden shears 234
garden sorrel 127
garden spider 70
gardening 230
gardening gloves 232
garlic 124
garlic press 170
garter snake 77
gas 403, 405, 414
gas container 529
gas cooker 210
gas cylinder, medical 464
gas main 434
gas, greenhouse 46
gasket 214
gaskin 83
gastrocnemius 96, 97
gate 381, 407
gate-leg 202
gate-leg table 202
gather 255
gather skirt 253
gauntlet 243
gauze roller bandage 461
gear cable 372
gear housing 537
gear lever 350, 369, 371, 372
gear, landing 361, 365
gearbox 350
gearchange lever 354
gearchange pedal 367, 368
gelatin capsule 467
general view 186
generator 402
generator unit 407
generator, steam 402
Genoa salami 156
geographical map 444
geography 14
geology 26
geometrical shapes 428
geometry 428
Georgia 452
geothermal field 402
geothermy and fossil energy 402
germ 61
German mustard 140
German rye bread 145
German salami 156
German shepherd 86
Germany 450
germination 53
geyser 28
Ghana 451
ghee 150
gherkin 128
giant slalom 511
gibbon 91
Gibraltar, Strait of 18
gift shop 436
gill 52
gill openings 74
gills 73
ginger 139
ginkgo nut 133

giraffe 85
girder 187
girdle 259
glacial cirque 30
glacial lake 32
glacier 30, 32, 44
glacier tongue 30
gland, digestive 71, 73
gland, green 71
gland, salivary 118
glans penis 111
glass 410, 411
glass bottle 163
glass case 423
glass cover 211
glass protector 506
glass recycling container 49
glass roof 188, 374, 435
glass slide 421
glass sorting 49
glass, magnifying 421
glass-fronted display cabinet 203
glassware 165
glazed frost 41
glazing bar 186
gliding phase 514
global warming 46
globe 444, 529
globular cluster 6
glottis 76
glove 10, 478, 498, 506, 508, 513, 514,
522, 525
glove compartment 354
glove finger 243
glove storage 464
glove, back of 243
glove, blocking 507
glove, catching 507
glove, latex 460
glove, massage 267
glove, palm of 243
glove, softball 477
gloves 243
gloves, gardening 232
gloves, goalkeeper's 480
gloves, men's 243
gloves, women's 243
glucose 54
glue 190
glue stick 341
gluteal nerve 108
gluteus maximus 97
gnocchi 146
gnomon 424
go 469, 470
goal 480, 482, 485, 507
goal area 480
goal crease 507
goal judge 506
goal lights 507
goal line 482, 484, 506
goalkeeper 481, 506, 507
goalkeeper's gloves 480
goalkeeper's pad 507
goalkeeper's skate 507
goalkeeper's stick 507
goalpost 485
goat 84
goat's milk 150
goat's-milk cheeses 150
goatfish 159
Gobi Desert 19
goggles 218, 513, 522
goggles, protective 522, 525
goggles, swimming 516
golf 504
golf bag 505
golf ball 505
golf course 430
golf glove 505
golf shoes 505
golf trolley 505
Golgi apparatus 50, 66
gonad 73
gondola 121, 512
gondola departure 512
gong 295, 309
Good Hope, Cape of 20
goods station 375
goods, canned 121
goose 81, 155
goose egg 155
goose-neck 191
gooseberry 132
gooseneck 400

gored skirt 253
gorge 31, 32
Gorgonzola 151
gorilla 91
gorilla, morphology of 91
Gothic cathedral 284
gour 31
gourd, wax 128
government organization 335
governor tension sheave 287
governor, speed 287
grab handle 361, 364, 455
gracile 97
grader 401
graduated dial 533
graduated scale 422, 423
grain of wheat, section 61
grain terminal 381
gram, black 131
Grand Canyon 16
Grand Gallery 278
granitic layer 26
granivorous bird 79
granulated sugar 149
granulation 4
grape 62, 132
grape, section of 59
grapefruit 134
grapefruit knife 169
grass 492
grassbox 237
grasshopper, bow-winged 69
grassland 44
grate 210
grater 170
grater, nutmeg 170
grater, rotary cheese 170
grating, utensils for 170
gravel bed 524
gravy boat 166
gray matter 109
grease well 179
greases 405
great adductor 97
Great Australian Bight 15
Great Barrier Reef 15
Great Dane 86
Great Dividing Range 15
great green bush-cricket 69
great horned owl 81
Great Lakes 16
great organ manual 305
Great Sandy Desert 15
great saphenous vein 102
Great Victoria Desert 15
greater alar cartilage 117
greater covert 78
greater pectoral 96
greater trochanter 99
Greece 449
Greek bread 144
Greek temple 279
Greek temple, plan 279
Greek theatre 278
green 418, 504
green alga 51
green ball 503
green beam 318
green bean 131
green cabbage 126
green coffee beans 148
green gland 71
green light 434
green onion 124
green peas 130
green pepper 138
green russula 123
green sweet pepper 128
green tea 148
green walnut 60
greenhouse 122
greenhouse effect 46
greenhouse effect, enhanced 46
greenhouse effect, natural 46
greenhouse gas 46
greenhouse gas concentration 46
Greenland 16
Greenland Sea 14
Grenada 449
grey matter 110
grid 318
grid system 22
grid, lighting 291
grid, starting 524
griddle 179

grike 31
grill, indoor electric 179
grille 279, 296, 348
grille, security 442
grinding, utensils for 170
grip 290, 500, 505, 535
grip handle 226
grip tape 526
grip, key 290
groin 92, 94
groove 169, 359, 510
ground 404
ground floor 182, 188
ground moraine 30
ground pepper 139
ground terminal 322
ground, teeing 504
groundhog 82
growth line 72, 73
Gruyère 151
guard 169, 217, 489
guard rail 211, 526
guard, ankle 476
guard, cable 535
guard, leg 476
guard, point 489
guard, shin 513
guard, tooth 486
guard, wrist 527
guardhouse 282
guardrail 384
Guatemala 448
guava 137
guide bar 235
guide handle 229
guide rail, car 287
guide rail, counterweight 287
guide ring 536
guide, tape 341
guiding tower 345
Guinea 451
guinea fowl 81, 154
guinea pig 82
Guinea, Gulf of 20
Guinea-Bissau 451
guitar, bass 303
gulf 24
Gulf of Aden 19, 20
Gulf of Alaska 16
Gulf of Bothnia 18
Gulf of California 16
Gulf of Carpentaria 15
Gulf of Guinea 20
Gulf of Mexico 16
Gulf of Oman 19
Gulf of Panama 17
Gulf, Persian 19
gum 101, 116
gum massager 272
gumshield 498
gun 216
gun flap 248
gun, heat 219
gurnard 159
gusset 274, 276
gusset pocket 255
Gutenberg discontinuity 26
gutter 182
guy line 528
guy wire 412
Guyana 448
guyot 33
gymnasium 386, 444
gymnasium office 444
gymnast's name 497
gymnastics 496
gynaecological examination room 463
gyratory system 342

H

hack 515
hackle 536
hacksaw 226
haddock 161
hair 93, 95, 114, 301
hair bulb 114
hair clip 268
hair colour 267
hair conditioner 267
hair follicle 114
hair grip 268
hair roller 268
hair roller pin 268
hair shaft 114

hair slide 268
hair stylist 290
hairbrushes 268
haircutting scissors 270
hairdresser 436
hairdressing 268
hairpin 268
hairs, root 53
Haiti 448
half handle 169
half-glasses 273
half-mask respirator 459
half-slip 258
half-volley 490
halfway line 481, 483
halibut 161
hall 188, 386, 439
hall, entrance 188
hall, town 432
halo 6
halogen desk lamp 206
ham knife 169
ham, cooked 156
ham, smoked 153
hammer 304, 472, 534
hammer loop 225
hammer rail 304
hamster 82
hand 91, 93, 95, 115
hand blender 176
hand fork 232
hand grip 536
hand mitre saw 226
hand mixer 176
hand post 297
hand protector 235, 525
hand rest 332
hand tools 232
hand vacuum cleaner 208
hand warmer pocket 251
hand, 1/10 second 424
hand-warmer pocket 249
handbags 275
handbrake 350
handbrake lever 354
handcuff case 456
handgrip 366, 369, 466
handgrips 500
handicap spot 470
handle 167, 170, 176, 177, 178, 179,
    180, 192, 204, 208, 209, 210, 211,
    215, 216, 217, 219, 220, 221, 222,
    223, 224, 225, 226, 227, 229, 231,
    235, 236, 237, 269, 270, 271, 272,
    273, 274, 275, 276, 277, 301, 325,
    341, 356, 467, 477, 478, 492, 493,
    494, 510, 515, 531, 536, 537
handle, crank 225
handle, insulated 179
handle, twist 332
handlebar 501, 523
handlebar stem 371
handlebar, raised 522
handlebars 371, 523
handling 396
handrail 191, 287, 363, 380, 385
handsaw 226
handset 327
handset flex 327
hang-up ring 270
hanger bracket 467
hanger loop 250
hanging basket 230
hanging cupboard 203
hanging glacier 30
hanging pendant 206
hanging stile 185, 186, 202
hank 521
hapteron 51
harbour 381
hard boot 513
hard contact lens 272
hard disk drive 333
hard disk drive, removable 333
hard disk, removable 333
hard hat 458
hard palate 116, 117
hard surface (cement) 492
hard-shell clam 157
hare 82, 154
harissa 141
harmonica 296
harp 302
harps 295
hasp 277
hastate 55

hat switch 332
hatband 238
hatch 13
hatch, side 12
hatchback 347
hatchet 454, 533
hawk 216
hawse pipe 383, 387
hayloft 122
hazard, water 504
hazelnut 133
hazelnut, section 60
head 6, 67, 72, 78, 93, 95, 103, 111,
    125, 220, 221, 223, 229, 271, 272,
    301, 302, 303, 309, 492, 494, 505,
    536
head cover 505
head harness 459
head linesman 485
head nurse's office 463
head of femur 99
head of frame 186
head of humerus 99
head protection 458
head teacher's office 445
head, bird 78
head, cutting 341
head, snare 297
headband 324, 326, 458, 459
headbay 406
headboard 204, 205
headgear 238, 498
headgear, men's 238
headgear, unisex 239
headgear, women's 239
heading 313
headland 35
headlight 348, 364, 366, 368, 376, 377,
    523
headline 313
headphone jack 310, 311, 322, 326
headphone plug 326
headphones 324, 326
headrest 353
heads, examples of 221
health 460
health and beauty care 121
health organization 335
hearing 115
heart 71, 73, 104, 105, 154, 468
heartwood 63
heat deflecting disc 199
heat energy 46
heat gun 219
heat loss 46
heat production 408
heat ready indicator 269
heat selector switch 270
heat shield 12
heat transfer 415
heat-sealed film 163
heater 529
heating 192
heating duct 213
heating element 213, 214, 218
heating grille 380
heating oil 405
heating/air conditioning equipment 386
heavy machinery 398
heavy petroleum 405
heavy rainfall 43
heavy-duty boot 240
hedge 183, 230
hedge trimmer 235
heel 93, 95, 169, 226, 229, 240, 247,
    262, 301, 302, 477, 506, 509
heel grip 240
heel loop 467
heel rest 176, 208
heel stop 527
heel-piece 511
heelplate 514
height adjustment 501
height adjustment scale 227
helicopter 395
helix 115, 429
helmet 10, 454, 478, 486, 506, 508,
    510, 513, 522, 525, 526, 527
helmet ring 10
helmet, crash 524
helmet, full-face 525
hemidemisemiquaver 299
hemidemisemiquaver rest 299
hemisphere 429
hemispheres 21
hemlath 412

hen 81
hen egg 155
hen house 122
hendecagon, regular 429
hepatic vein 103
heptagon, regular 429
herbal teas 148
herbicide 47
herbivores 45
herbs 142
heron 80
herring 159
herringbone parquet 190
herringbone pattern 190
hertz 426
Hertzian wave transmission 316
heterotrophs 45
hex nut 359
hexagon 429
hexagon nut 223
hexagon, regular 429
hidden pocket 274
high altar 446
high card 468
high chair 205
high clouds 42
high jump 473
high pressure area 43
high wing 394
high-back dungarees 260
high-frequency antenna cable 394
high-rise block 289
high-speed exit taxiway 388
high-speed shaft 413
high-speed train 376
high-tension electricity transmission 402,
    413
highland 5, 40
highland climates 40
hijiki 123
hiking boot 242
hill 29
Himalayas 19
hind leg 67, 68
hind limb 75
hind toe 78, 79
hind wing 67
hinge 178, 185, 186, 202, 214, 274,
    277, 352, 420, 511
hinge pin 400
hip 93, 95
hip pad 486
hippopotamus 85
hitch ball 356
hitch pin 304
hitting area 477
hob 164, 210
hob edge 210
hock 83, 86, 153
hock glass 165
hoe 233
hoe-fork 233
hog line 515
hoisin sauce 140
hoisting block 397
hoisting rope 219, 287, 397
holdall 276
holder's name 441
holder's signature 441
holder, baton 456
holder, dental floss 272
holder, filter 181
holder, paper-clip 341
holding 499
holding area marking 390
hole 504
hollow barrel 460
hologram foil strip 441
holster 456
holy water font 446
home 331
home aerial 316
home key 331
home plate 475
home theatre 321
home user 335
home-plate umpire 475
homogenized milk 150
Honduras 448
honey 149
honeybee 68
honeydew melon 135
hood 192, 209, 249, 260, 508
hood, cooker 164
hooded sweat shirt 262
hooded towelling robe 260
hoof 83

hook 186, 217, 225, 364, 397, 423,
    460, 502, 509
hooker 482
hoop earrings 264
hopper, loading 364
horizontal bar 496, 497
horizontal control 329
horizontal ground movement 27
horizontal move 470
horizontal pivoting window 287
horizontal seismograph 27
horizontal-axis wind turbine 413
horn 354, 368, 377
horn, anterior 109
Horn, Cape 17
horn, posterior 109
horned melon 136
hornet 69
horny beak 76
hors d'oeuvre dish 166
horse 83, 85
horse, gaits 83
horse, morphology of 83
horse, pommel 496
horse, vaulting 496, 497
horseradish 129
horseshoe mount 7
hose 209, 257, 454
hose connector 236
hose nozzle 236
hose trolley 236
hospital 433, 462
hospital bed 464
hospital trolley 460
hot coolant 408
hot-air outlet 192
hot-shoe contact 314
hot-water circuit 194
hot-water heater 194
hot-water riser 194
hot-water supply 197
hotel 432, 439, 469, 512
hotel reservation desk 390
hotel room 439
hound, smooth 158
hour angle gear 7
house 182, 293, 469, 515
house dress 252
house furniture 200
house, adobe 288
house, elements of 185
house, exterior 182
house, one-storey 289
house, pilot 385
house, structure 188
house, two-storey 289
houseboat 385
household equipment 215
household products 120
household waste 47, 48
housing 199, 218, 228, 229, 271
hovercraft 383
hub 70, 341, 371, 413, 467
Hubble space telescope 7, 37
Hudson Bay 16
Huitzilopochtli, Temple of 283
hull 60, 520, 523
human being 92
human body 92
human denture 101
humerus 99
humid continental - hot summer 40
humid continental - warm summer 40
humid subtropical 40
hummingbird 80
hummus 140
Hungary 450
hunting 534
hunting cap 238
hurricane 43
hurricane lamp 532
husbandry, intensive 46, 47
husk 60, 61
hydrant intake 455
hydrant, fire 454
hydraulic disc brake 522
hydraulic jack 361
hydraulic resistance 501
hydraulic shovel 400
hydraulic system 396
hydroelectric complex 406
hydroelectricity 406
hydrofoil boat 387
hydrologic cycle 45
hydrometer 359
hydrosphere 44

ASTRONOMY > 2-13;   EARTH > 14-49;   PLANT KINGDOM >50-65;   ANIMAL KINGDOM > 66-91;   HUMAN BEING > 92-119;   FOOD AND KITCHEN > 120-181;   HOUSE > 182-215;
DO-IT-YOURSELF AND GARDENING > 216-237;   CLOTHING > 238-263;   PERSONAL ADORNMENT AND ARTICLES > 264-277;   ARTS AND ARCHITECTURE > 278-311;   COMMUNICATIONS AND
OFFICE AUTOMATION > 312-341;   TRANSPORT AND MACHINERY > 342-401;   ENERGY > 402-413;   SCIENCE > 414-429;   SOCIETY > 430-467;   SPORTS AND GAMES > 468-538

549

hyena 88
hyperlinks 334
hyperopia 419
hypha 52
hyssop 142

I

Iapetus 3
Iberian Peninsula 18
ice 45
ice cream container 180
ice cream maker 180
ice cream scoop 173
ice cube dispenser 164
ice cube tray 211
ice dispenser 346
ice hockey 506
ice hockey player 506
ice rink 512
Ice Shelf, Amery 15
Ice Shelf, Filchner 15
Ice Shelf, Ross 15
ice-breaker 384
iceberg lettuce 126
Iceland 18, 450
icing syringe 172
identification badge 456
identification, account 443
identity bracelet 264
identity tag 277
idler wheel 523
igloo 288
igloo tent 529
igneous rocks 26
ignition key 237
ignition lead 360
ignition switch 354, 368
iguana 77
ileum 106
iliohypogastric nerve 108
ilioinguinal nerve 108
ilium 98
illuminated mirror 269
image adjustment buttons 320
image review button 315
impervious rock 403
impluvium 280
impulse sprinkler 236
in goal 483
in-flight communications 317
inbound line 484
incandescent light bulb 199
incident neutron 415
incineration 49
incisors 101
incoming message cassette 328
increase, voltage 402
incus 116
Index 539
index 313
index finger 115
index/enlarge button 315
India 453
Indian chapati bread 145
Indian naan bread 145
Indian Ocean 14, 15, 19, 20
indicator 352
indicator light 454
indicator lights 331
indicator, position 287
indicator telltale 355, 368
indicator, water level 179
indicators 318, 323
indicators display button 320
Indonesia 19, 453
indoor electric grill 179
industrial 431
industrial communications 317
industrial pollution 47
industrial waste 47, 48
industry 335
inert gas 199
inferior cymbal 308
inferior dental arch 116
inferior mesenteric artery 107
inferior nasal concha 117
inferior rectus muscle 119
inferior vena cava 102, 103, 104, 107
infield 474
infiltration 45
infinity 427
inflated carrying tyre 380
inflated guiding tyre 380
inflator 530
inflator-deflator 530

inflorescent vegetables 127
information booth 437
information counter 390
information desk 442, 463, 512
information, dissemination of 335
infrared port 336, 337
infrared radiation 46, 418
infraspinatus 97
infundibulum of fallopian tube 113
infusions, coffee and 148
inhalation valve 459
inhaler, metered dose 467
initials of issuing bank 441
injection well 402
ink 312
ink, colour shifting 441
inkjet printer 333
inlaid parquet 190
inlet manifold 360
inlet valve 360
inline skating 527
inner boot 511, 527
inner circle 515
inner core 26
inner door shell 352
inner lip 73
inner planets 3
inner string 191
inner table 469
inner tent 528, 529
inner toe 78
inorganic matter 45
input devices 330
input lights 322
input select button 322
input selector 322
input tray 333
input wire 199
input/output video jacks 322
insectivorous bird 79
insects and arachnids 67
insects, examples of 69
insert 331
insert key 331
inside linebacker 484
inside-leg snap-fastening 260, 261
insignia, rank 456
inspection light 217
instant-read thermometer 171
instep 92
institution, educational 335, 433
instructions, operating 346
instrument cluster 366, 368
instrument panel 355
insulated blade 217
insulated handle 179, 217
insulating material 190, 214
insulation 410
insulator 359
insurance services 442
intake, air 362
integral 427
integrated circuit 417
integrated circuit, packaged 417
Intelsat 317
intensive care unit 464
intensive farming 46
intensive farming 48
intensive husbandry 46, 47
interchange 431
interchanges, examples of 342
intercostal nerve 108
interior dome shell 7
interior door handle 352
interior door lock button 352
interior pocket 277
intermediate booster station 404
intermediate slope 512
intermodal car 377
internal boundary 23
internal ear 116
internal filum terminale 109
internal iliac artery 102, 103, 107
internal iliac vein 103
internal jugular vein 102
internal modem port 329, 336
internal tooth lock washer 222
international space station 11
international system of units 426
Internet 334
Internet keys 330
Internet service provider 335
Internet user 334
Internet uses 335
intermode 53
interrupted projection 22

intersection 427
intertragic notch 115
intervals 298
interventricular septum 104
interview 313
interview rooms 440
intestine 71, 73, 103
intravenous stand 464
intrusive filtration 47
intrusive rocks 26
inverted pleat 253
inward 518
Io 2
ion tail 6
Ionic column, engaged 281
Iran 452
Iraq 452
Ireland 449
iris 119
Irish moss 123
Irish Sea 18
Irish soda bread 145
iron 505
iron curtain 292
iron, straightening 269
is approximately equal to 427
is contained in 427
is equal to 427
is equal to or greater than 427
is equal to or less than 427
is equivalent to 427
is greater than 427
is identical with 427
is less than 427
is not equal to 427
is not identical with 427
is not parallel to 428
is parallel to 428
isba 288
ischium 99
island 24, 164, 343
island arc 33
Island, Baffin 16
Island, Newfoundland 16
Islands, Aleutian 16
Islands, Falkland 17
Islands, Fiji 15
islet, rocky 35
isobar 39
isolation room 462
isoseismal line 27
Israel 452
isthmus 24
isthmus of fallopian tube 113
isthmus of fauces 116
Isthmus of Panama 16
Italy 450
items, news 313
Ivory Coast 451

J

jaboticaba 137
Jack 468
jack 356, 397, 400, 455
jack plug 324
jack, audio 329
jack, audio input/output 337
jack, earphone 329
jack, stabilizer 361
jacket 251, 417, 499, 534
jackets 244
jackfruit 136
jaguar 89
jail 469
jalapeño chilli 139
jalousie 186
Jamaica 448
jamb 185, 192
janitor's cupboard 439
Japan 19, 453
Japan Trench 34
Japan, Sea of 19
Japanese experiment module 11
Japanese persimmon 137
Jarlsberg 151
Java Trench 34
javelin 472, 473
jaw 217, 221, 224, 228, 265
jaw, fixed 425
jaw, sliding 425
jaws 224, 535
jay 80
jazz band 300
jeans 254
jejunum 106

jerboa 82
jerk, clean and 500
jersey 483, 522
Jerusalem artichoke 124
jet fuel 405
jet tip 272
jet, supersonic 37, 394
jets, water 518
Jew's harp 297
jewellery 264
jewellery shop 436
Jewish challah 145
jib 397, 520
jib tie 397
jibsheet 520
jicama 124
jigsaw 227
jingle 309
jockey rollers 372
jogging pants 262
John dory 161
joint 312, 355, 503, 536
joint filler 216
joint, articulated 363
joist 190
Joker 468
Jordan 452
joule 426
joystick 332
joysticks 471
judge 498, 499
judge, centre line 490
judge, line 496
judge, side 485
judges 496, 497, 509, 518
judges' bench 440
judges' office 440
judges, turning 517
judo 499
judogi 499
jug 181
jug, measuring 171
juice extractor 180
juice sac 58
jujube 137
jumper cables 356
jumper, ski 513
jumping ski 513
jumping, ski 513
jumps, examples of 509
jumpsuit 254, 261
junior doctor 464
juniper berry 138
Jupiter 2
jurors' room 440
jury box 440
justice 440

K

Kalahari Desert 20
kale, ornamental 126
kale, sea 126
Kamchatka Peninsula 19
Kazakhstan 452
keel boat 521
keep 282
keeper ring 536
kelly 403
kelvin 426
Kenya 451
kerb 434, 524
Kermadec-Tonga Trench 34
kernel 61
kerosene 405
ketchup 141
kettle 29, 180
kettledrum 308
key 296, 304, 306
key case 275
key cutting 437
key finger button 306
key grip 290
key guard 306
key lever 306
key lock 274
key signature 299
key, alternative 330
key, backspace 331
key, capitals lock 330
key, confirmation 443
key, delete 331
key, email 330
key, end 327, 331

key, enter 331
key, escape 330
key, home 331
key, insert 331
key, numeric lock 331
key, page down 331
key, page up 331
key, pause/break 331
key, power 327
key, print screen/system request 331
key, scrolling lock 331
key, selection 327
key, start 330
key, tabulation 330
key, talk 327
keybed 304
keyboard 304, 310, 336
keyboard and pictograms 330
keyboard instruments 304
keyboard port 329
keyboard, alphanumeric 346, 442, 443
keyless chuck 228
keypad, alphabetical 338
keypad, alphanumeric 327, 330
keypad, numeric 338
keys 311
keys, function 330
keys, Internet 330
keys, operation 442, 443
keystone 284
kick pleat 253
kick, skating 514
kicker 313
kickstand 367, 369
kidney 73, 103, 154
kidney bean, red 131
kielbasa sausage 156
killer whale 90
kilogram 426
kilt 253
kimono 256
King 468, 470
king's chamber 278
King's side 470
kingfisher 80
kingpin 365
kiosk 346, 379
Kiribati 453
kit, first aid 457
kit, tool 372
kit, waxing 514
kitchen 162, 164, 188, 280, 439, 445
kitchen knife 169
kitchen knives, examples of 169
kitchen scale 171
kitchen shears 173
kitchen timer 171
kitchen towel 215
kitchen utensils 169
kitchen, food and 120
kitchen-diner 188
kiwi 136
knee 83, 86, 92, 94
knee pad 476, 486, 526, 527
knee sock 257
knee wrap 500
knee-length sock 247
knickerbockers 254
knife 167, 531, 533
knife pleat 246, 253
knife, electric 177
Knight 470
knives, examples of 168
knob 202, 229, 477
knob handle 227
knob, coarse adjustment 421
knob, fine adjustment 421
knob, steam control 181
knobby tyre 369
knurled bolt 219
kohlrabi 125
Kola Peninsula 18
kombu 123
kora 297
Korean Peninsula 19
Kuiper belt 2
kumquat 134
Kuril Trench 34
Kuwait 452
Kyrgyzstan 452

ASTRONOMY > 2-13;   EARTH > 14-49;   PLANT KINGDOM >50-65;   ANIMAL KINGDOM > 66-91;   HUMAN BEING > 92-119;   FOOD AND KITCHEN > 120-181;   HOUSE > 182-215;
DO-IT-YOURSELF AND GARDENING > 216-237;   CLOTHING > 238-263;   PERSONAL ADORNMENT AND ARTICLES > 264-277;   ARTS AND ARCHITECTURE > 278-311;   COMMUNICATIONS AND
OFFICE AUTOMATION > 312-341;   TRANSPORT AND MACHINERY > 342-401;   ENERGY > 402-413;   SCIENCE > 414-429;   SOCIETY > 430-467;   SPORTS AND GAMES > 468-538

ENGLISH INDEX

L

label maker 340
labial palp 67
labium majus 112, 113
labium minus 112, 113
lablab bean 130
laboratory 7
laboratory air lock 13
laboratory, pathology 465
laboratory, U.S. 11
laccolith 28
lace 477, 498, 509
lace-up 240
lachrymal canal 119
lachrymal caruncle 119
lachrymal gland 119
lactiferous duct 113
ladder 184, 288, 361, 401, 404
ladder pipe nozzle 455
ladders 219
ladies' toilet 294, 439
ladle 173
Ladoga, Lake 18
Lady chapel 284, 285
ladybird 69
lagomorphs, examples of 82
lagomorphs, rodents and 82
lagoon 35
lake 5, 24, 29, 32
lake acidification 48
Lake Chad 20
Lake Baikal 19
Lake Eyre North 15
Lake Ladoga 18
Lake Malawi 20
Lake Tanganyika 20
Lake Titicaca 17
Lake Victoria 20
lake, artificial 32
lake, glacial 32
lake, oxbow 32
lake, tectonic 32
lake, volcanic 32
lakes 32
Lakes, Great 16
lamb, cuts of 153
lamb, diced 153
lamb, leg 153
lamb, minced 153
lambdoid suture 100
lamina 51
lamp 421
lamp, bedside 439, 464
lamp, sanctuary 446
lamp, signal 179
lampholder 199
lamprey 159
lanceolate 55
land 228
land pollution 47
land station 38
landfill 431
landfill site, authorized 47
landing 189, 191
landing area 472
landing gear 361, 365
landing gear crank 365
landing light 395
landing net 538
landing window 395
landslides 31
lane 433, 472, 516
lane line 473
lane rope 517
lane timekeeper 516
lane, pit 524
lantern 230, 529
Laos 453
lap belt 353
lapel 244
laptop computer 336
laptop computer: front view 336
laptop computer: rear view 336
larch 65
lard 149
larding needle 173
large blade 531
large intestine 106
large wheel 467
large-screen television set 321
larger spotted dogfish 158
larynx 105
lasagne 146
laser beam 420

laser, pulsed ruby 420
last quarter 5
latch 178, 214, 277
latch bolt 186
latch, mitre 226
lateral bar 501
lateral brush 365
lateral condyle of femur 99
lateral cutaneous femoral nerve 108
lateral incisor 101
lateral line 74, 515
lateral moraine 30
lateral semicircular canal 116
lateral view of skull 100
lateral-adjustment lever 229
latex glove 460
latex glove case 456
latissimus dorsi 97
latrines 287
Latvia 450
laundry 439
laundry room 188
lava flow 28
lava layer 28
lawn 183, 230
lawn aerator 237
lawn care 237
lawn edger 233
lawn rake 237
layer, ozone 37
layers, waste 47
leaching 48
lead 313, 326, 515
lead pencil 312
leader 538
leading bunch 522
leading edge 393
leading motorcycle 522
leaf 51, 53, 54, 55, 125
leaf axil 55
leaf lettuce 126
leaf margins 55
leaf node 53
leaf vegetables 126
leaf, fleshy 54
leaf, scale 54
leaf, structure of 55
leakproof cap 529
leather end 246
leather goods 274
leather goods shop 436
leather sheath 533
leather skin 478
leather, chamois 265
leaves, examples of 65
leaves, first 53
Lebanon 452
Lebanon, cedar of 65
lectern 446
ledger board 187
ledger line 298
leech 519
leek 124
left atrium 103, 104
left attacker 487
left back 481, 487
left centre 482
left channel 324
left cornerback 484
left defence 506
left defensive end 484
left defensive tackle 484
left field 475
left fielder 474
left forward 489
left guard 485
left kidney 107
left lung 103, 105
left midfielder 481
left pulmonary vein 104
left safety 484
left service court 491
left side 272
left tackle 485
left ventricle 103, 104
left wing 482, 507
left-luggage office 374
leg 76, 91, 93, 95, 202, 204, 205, 231, 247, 308, 493, 537
leg curl bar 501
leg extension bar 501
leg guard 476
leg of lamb 153
leg, walking 70
leg-warmer 263
leghold trap 535

legumes 130
leisure, outdoor 528
lemon 134
lemon balm 142
lemon squeezer 170, 177
lemur 91
length, measurement of 426
lengthways bulkhead 384
lens 119, 273, 314, 332, 419
lens accessories 314
lens cap 314
lens case 272
lens hood 8, 314
lens release button 314
lens system 420
lens, concave 419
lens, convex 419
lens, macro 314
lens, toric 419
lens, zoom 320
lenses 314, 419
lenses, contact 272
lentils 130
leopard 89
leotard 263
Lesotho 452
lesser covert 78
letter opener 339
letter scale 339
letters to editor 313
lettuce, butterhead 126
lettuce, iceberg 126
lettuce, leaf 126
lettuce, sea 123
leucoplast 50
level crossing 375
level, reception 439
level, sea 37
levelling foot 212, 213, 214
levelling screw 423
lever 178, 197, 222, 265, 534
lever cap 229
lever corkscrew 170
lever nutcracker-tap 197
lever, gear 350, 369
lever, locking 224
Liberia 451
libero 487
library 433, 444
Libya 451
lichen 50
lichen, crustose 50
lichen, foliose 50
lichen, fruticose 50
lichen, structure of 50
lichens, examples of 50
lid 174, 177, 178, 179, 180, 181, 210, 211, 212, 215, 225, 417
Liechtenstein 450
lierne 284
life buoy 387
life raft 383
life support system 10
life support system controls 10
lifeboat 382, 386
lifebuoy 457
lift 281, 287, 435, 439
lift arm 399
lift bridge 345
lift car 287
lift chain 196
lift door 363
lift span 345
lift, chair 512
lift, wheelchair 363
lift-arm cylinder 399
lift-fan air inlet 383
lifting chain 396
lifting hook 403
ligament 73
ligature 306
light 7, 8, 9, 380
light aircraft 394
light bar 455
light ray 419
light shield 7
light, amber 434
light, eternal 447
light, green 434
light, indicator 454
light, paper feed 333
light, power 333
light, print cartridge 333
light, reading 457
light, red 434
light, underwater 184

light, visible 418
lightbar 457
lightbar controller 457
lighthouse 381
lighting 199, 269
lighting cable 361
lighting grid 291
lighting technician 291
lighting, safety 457
lightning 41
lightning conductor 183, 407
lightning rod 413
lights 206
lights, blinking 362
lights, goal 507
lights, indicator 331
lights, input 322
lights, pedestrian 434
lights, sound mode 322
lights, traffic 434
lily 56
lily of the valley 56
Lima bean 131
limb 63, 535
limb top 421
lime 134
limit switch 287
limpet 157
linden 148
line 225, 298, 443
line guide 537
line judge 485, 496
line map 378
line of scrimmage 485
line, 10 m 482
line, 15 m 483
line, 22 m 482
line, 5 m 483
line, back 515
line, broken 342, 343
line, cable 335
line, chalk 225
line, credit 313
line, dedicated 334
line, field 416
line, hog 515
line, neutral 416
line, solid 342
line, starting 524
line, submarine 334
line, tee 515
line, telephone 334
linear 55
linen chest 203
linen room 439
lines of latitude 22
lines of longitude 22
linesman 481, 487, 490, 494, 507
lingerie shop 436
lingual tonsil 118
lining 240, 244, 245, 262, 274, 509
lint filter 212
lintel 185, 187, 192, 285
lion 89
lip 83, 87
lip make-up 266
lipbrush 266
lipid droplet 50
lipliner 266
lipstick 266
liqueur glass 165
liquid 414, 415
liquid crystal display 315, 320
liquid eyeliner 266
liquid foundation 266
liquid mascara 266
liquid-crystal display 424
liquid/gas separator 359
listen button 328
lists 282
litchi; lychee 137
literary supplement 313
lithosphere 26, 44
Lithuania 450
litter, plant 54
little finger 115
little finger hook 307
liver 103, 106, 154
lizard 77
lizard, monitor 77
llama 84
loader, belt 402
loading bridge 381
loading dock 435

loading door 192
loading hopper 364
loaf pan 179
loan services 442
lob 491
lobate 55
lobate toe 79
lobby 390, 435, 439, 440, 442
lobe 79
lobe bronchus 105
lobe, lower 105
lobe, upper 105
lobster 71, 158
lobster, anatomy of 71
lobster, morphology of 71
local station 316
location 182
location of the statue 279
lock 185, 186, 202, 211, 275, 277, 352
lock dial 332
lock forward 482
lock nut 425
lock rail 185
luck, capitals 330
lock, numeric 331
lock-on button 227, 229
lockers, students' 445
locket 264
locking button 208
locking device 209, 219, 535
locking lever 224
locking ring 221
locknut 197
locomotive 376
loculus 58
lodge, main 512
lodge, mountain 512
lodge, skiers' 512
lodge, summit 512
lodging 512
log carrier 193
log chute 406
loin 83, 93, 95
loin chop 153
long adductor 96
long extensor of toes 96
long johns 247
long jump and triple jump 472
long palmar 96
long peroneal 96
long radial extensor of wrist 97
long residue 405
long service line 494
long track 508
long-range jet airliner 392
longan 136
longitudinal drive shaft 351
longitudinal dunes 36
loop 245, 343
loop, hammer 225
loop, strap 532
loop, toe 509
loose head prop 482
loose powder 266
loose powder brush 266
lopping shears 234
lore 78
loss, heat 46
loudspeaker 324, 325, 455
loudspeaker system select buttons 322
loudspeaker terminals 322
loudspeaker, centre 321
loudspeaker, main 321
loudspeaker, surround 321
lounge 386, 439
lounge, cocktail 439
lounge, nurses' 465
lounge, staff 443, 463
louse 69
louvre-board 285
louvred window 287
lovage 142
love seat 439
low clouds 42
low fuel warning light 355
low pressure area 43
low-speed shaft 413
low-tension distribution line 198
lower blade guard 227
lower bowl 181
lower confining bed 402
lower eyelid 75, 87, 119
lower guard retracting lever 227
lower lateral lobe 62
lower lateral sinus 62
lower limb 103

ASTRONOMY > 2-13;   EARTH > 14-49;   PLANT KINGDOM >50-65;   ANIMAL KINGDOM > 66-91;   HUMAN BEING > 92-119;   FOOD AND KITCHEN > 120-181;   HOUSE > 182-215;
DO-IT-YOURSELF AND GARDENING > 216-237;   CLOTHING > 238-263;   PERSONAL ADORNMENT AND ARTICLES > 264-277;   ARTS AND ARCHITECTURE > 278-311;   COMMUNICATIONS AND
OFFICE AUTOMATION > 312-341;   TRANSPORT AND MACHINERY > 342-401;   ENERGY > 402-413;   SCIENCE > 414-429;   SOCIETY > 430-467;   SPORTS AND GAMES > 468-538

551

lower lip 116, 305
lower lobe 105
lower mandible 78
lower mantle 26
lower radiator hose 358
lower shell 511
lubricant eye drops 272
lubricants plant 405
lubricating oils 405
Luer-Lock tip 460
luff 519
lug 308
luggage 276
luggage compartment 376, 395
luggage elastic 277
luggage lockers 374
luggage rack 361, 369, 523
luggage racks 383
luggage trolley 277, 374
lumbar pad 486
lumbar plexus 108
lumbar vertebra 99, 110
luminous intensity, measurement of 426
lunar eclipse 5
lunar features 5
lungs 105
lunula 114, 115
lunule 73
lupine 130
Lutz 509
Luxembourg 449
lynx 88
lyre 297
lysosome 66

M

macadamia nut 133
macaque 91
macaw 80
Macedonia 450
machicolation 282
machine hall 406, 407
machine, automatic teller 442, 443
machine, espresso 181
machine, snow-grooming 512
machinery shed 122
machinery, transport and 342
Mackenzie River 16
mackerel 159
macro lens 314
macronucleus 66
macula 119
Madagascar 20, 452
magazine 313
magenta 418
magma 28, 33
magma chamber 28, 402
magnesium powder 497
magnet 341, 416
magnetic compass 533
magnetic damping system 422
magnetic field 318, 416
magnetic gasket 211
magnetic lid holder 180
magnetic needle 533
magnetic separation 49
magnetic strip 441
magnetic tape 319
magnetism 416
magnifier 531
magnifying glass 421
magnifying glass and microscopes 421
main beam headlight 352
main beam indicator light 355
main beam warning light 368
main bronchus 105
main circuit vent 194
main cleanout 194
main deck 385
main drain 184, 194
main engine 13
main entrance 188, 435, 445, 465
main junction box 198
main landing gear 393
main line 375
main lodge 512
main loudspeaker 321
main road 343
main rooms 188
main scale 425
main scope tube 420
main sewer 434
main stand 367
main switch 198
main transformer 376

main tube 8, 9
main vent 28
main waiting room 465
Maine Coon 87
mainsail 520
mainsheet 520
maintenance hangar 389
maître d'hôtel 438
major inner reaping throw 499
major motions 470
major outer reaping throw 499
make-up 266
make-up artist 290
maker, bread 179
malanga 129
malar region 78
Malawi 452
Malawi, Lake 20
Malaysia 453
Maldives 453
male 426
male cone 65
male ferrule 536, 537
male genital organs 111
male grounding pin 198
male urethra 111
Mali 451
mallet 220, 308
mallets 309
malleus 116
malt vinegar 141
Malta 450
mammals, carnivorous 86
mammals, marine 90
mammals, primate 91
mammals, ungulate 83
mammary gland 113
man 92
man, property 291
mandarin 134
mandible 67, 74, 98, 100
mandolin 297
mandoline 170
mandown alarm 454
mane 83
manganese mix (cathode) 417
mangetout 130
mango 137
mango chutney 141
mangosteen 136
manhole 404, 434
manicure 265
manicure set 265
manned manœuvring unit 10
manœuvring engine 13
mantid 69
mantle 72, 73, 192
mantlepiece 192
manual release 511
manual revolving door 286
manual sorting 49
manuals 305
Manx 87
map projections 22
map, geographical 444
map, weather 38
maple 64
maple syrup 149
maquis 44
margarine 149
margin 55
marginal shield 76
Mariana Trench 34
Marie Byrd Land 15
marinade spices 139
marine 40
marine diesel 405
marine mammals 90
marine mammals, examples of 90
maritime communications 317
maritime transport 381
marker 312
marker, position 303
marmoset 91
marrow 128, 154
Mars 2, 3
Marshall Islands 453
marten 88
marten, stone 88
mascara brush 266
mask 476
mask, face 478
mason's trowel 216
masonry drill 228
masonry nail 220
masonry tools 216

mass 27
mass, measurement of 426
massage glove 267
masseter 96
massif 24
mast 281, 396, 519, 520
mast foot 519
mast operating lever 396
mast sleeve 519
masthead 313, 519
masthead light 383
mastoid fontanelle 100
mastoid process 100
mat 499
mat, floor 356
mater, dura 109
mater, pia 109
material handling 396
material, fire-fighting 454
material, sealing 417
mathematics 427
matinee-length necklace 264
mating adaptor 11
mats, floor 496
matter 414
matter, grey 109
matter, inorganic 45
matter, states of 414
matter, white 109
mattress 204, 205, 460
mattress cover 204
Mauritania 451
Mauritius 452
maxilla 74, 98, 100, 117
maxillary bone 101
meadow 122
mean position 418
meander 32
measurement of amount of substance 426
measurement of Celsius temperature 426
measurement of electric charge 426
measurement of electric current 426
measurement of electric potential difference 426
measurement of electric resistance 426
measurement of energy 426
measurement of force 426
measurement of frequency 426
measurement of length 425, 426
measurement of luminous intensity 426
measurement of mass 426
measurement of power 426
measurement of pressure 426
measurement of radioactivity 426
measurement of temperature 424
measurement of thermodynamic temperature 426
measurement of thickness 425
measurement of time 424
measurement of weight 422
measuring beaker 171
measuring cups 171
measuring devices 424
measuring jug 171
measuring spoons 171
measuring, utensils 171
meat 152
meat counter, self-service 120
meat keeper 211
meat thermometer 171
meatus, external auditory 100
mechanical mouse 332
mechanical stage 421
mechanical stage control 421
mechanism, spool-release 537
medial condyle of femur 99
medial moraine 30
median lingual sulcus 118
median nerve 108
medical equipment storage room 465
medical gas cylinder 464
medical records 465
medical team 499
Mediterranean Sea 14, 18, 20
Mediterranean subtropical 40
medium format SLR (6 x 6) 315
medium-tension distribution line 198
medlar 133
medulla 107
medulla oblongata 109
medullary ray 63
meeting room 439, 442, 445
Meissner's corpuscle 114

Melanesia 15
melody strings 296
melon baller 173
melon, bitter 128
melon, canary 135
melon, casaba 135
melon, honeydew 135
melon, horned 136
melon, Ogen 135
melons 135
melting 414
meltwater 30
membrane, plasma 66
memo pad 338
memorial board 447
memory button 322, 327
memory cancel 337
memory card slots 471
memory card, compact 315
memory key 323
memory recall 337
men 469, 470
men's bag 276
men's clothing 244
men's gloves 243
men's headgear 238
men's shoes 240
men's toilet 294, 439
meninges 109
menorah 447
menu button 315, 327
Mercury 2, 3
mercury bulb 424
mercury thermometer 461
merguez sausage 156
méridienne 200
mesa 36
mesh 205, 493
mesh bag 162
mesh strainer 171
mesocarp 57, 58, 59
mesopause 37
mesosphere 37
metal arm 236
metal counterhoop 308
metal frame 304
metal rod 309
metal sorting 49
metal structure 374
metallic contact grid 410
metamorphic rocks 26
meteorological forecast 38
meteorology 37
meteorology, station model 39
metered dose inhaler 467
methylated spirits 405
metre 426
Mexico 448
Mexico, Gulf of 16
mezzanine 378
mezzanine floor 182, 189
mezzanine stairs 189
Micro Compact Car 347
microfilament 66
micrometer caliper 425
Micronesia 453
micronucleus 66
microphone 320, 327, 328, 332, 337, 456
microphones 457
microscope 421
microscopes, magnifying glass and 421
microtubule 66
microwave oven 164, 178
microwave relay station 334
microwaves 418
Mid-Atlantic Ridge 34
mid-calf length sock 247
Mid-Indian Ridge 34
mid-ocean ridge 33
middle attacker 487
middle back 487
middle clouds 42
middle covert 78
middle ear 116
middle finger 115
middle leg 67, 68
middle linebacker 484
middle lobe 105
middle nasal concha 117
middle panel 185
middle phalanx 114
middle piece 111
middle primary covert 78
middle sole 262
middle toe 78

midfielder, central 481
midfielder, left 481
midfielder, right 481
midrange pickup 303
midrange speaker 324
midrib 51, 55, 60
midriff band 259
Mihrab 447
Mihrab dome 447
mileometer 355
military communications 317
milk 150
milk chocolate 148
milk, evaporated 150
milk, goat's 150
milk, homogenized 150
milk, powdered 150
milk/cream cup 163
Milky Way 6
Milky Way (seen from above) 6
Milky Way (side view) 6
mill, food 170
millet 61, 143
millet: spike 61
Mimas 3
minaret 447
Minbar 447
minced beef 152
minced lamb 153
minced pork 153
minced veal 152
mincer 170
mini briefs 247
mini stereo sound system 325
minibus 347, 363
minim 299
minim rest 299
mink 88
minor sciatic nerve 108
minor surgery 462
mint 142
minute 428
minute hand 424
Miranda 3
mirror 195, 277, 366, 368, 369, 421, 439, 523
mirror, blind spot 362, 363
mirror, concave primary 9
mirror, crossover 362
mirror, outside 362
mirror, partially reflecting 420
mirror, secondary 7, 9
mirror, totally reflecting 420
mirror, West Coast 363
miscellaneous articles 341
miscellaneous domestic appliances 180
miscellaneous equipment 231
miscellaneous utensils 173
Mississippi River 16
mist 41
mitochondrion 50, 66
mitral valve 104
mitre box 226
mitre latch 226
mitre scale 226
mitten 243
mix, depolarizing 417
mix, water-steam 402
mixed forest 44
mixing bowl 176
mixing bowls 172
moat 282
mobile remote servicer 11
mobile telephone 327
mobile unit 316
mobile X-ray unit 462
moccasin 242
mock pocket 251
mode selectors 326
modem 334
modem, cable 335
moderator 408
modulation wheel 310
module, European experiment 11
module, Japanese experiment 11
module, Russian 11
module, U.S. habitation 11
Mohorovicic discontinuity 26
moistener 339
molar, cross section 101
molars 101
molasses 149
Moldova 450
mole 426
mole wrench 222

molecule 414
molluscs 72, 157
Monaco 450
money and modes of payment 441
Mongolia 453
mongoose 88
monitor lizard 77
monkfish 160
mono-hulls 521
Monopoly® 469
mons pubis 112
monument 25
Moon 2, 4, 5
Moon's orbit 4, 5
Moon, phases 5
moons 2
mooring winch 385
mop 215
moped 369
moraine, end 30
moraine, terminal 30
mordent 299
morel 123
Morocco 451
morphology of a bird 78
morphology of a bivalve shell 73
morphology of a butterfly 67
morphology of a dog 86
morphology of a dolphin 90
morphology of a frog 75
morphology of a gorilla 91
morphology of a honeybee: worker 68
morphology of a horse 83
morphology of a lobster 71
morphology of a perch 74
morphology of a rat 82
morphology of a shark 74
morphology of a snail 72
morphology of a spider 70
morphology of a turtle 76
morphology of a univalve shell 73
morphology of a venomous snake: head
   76
morphology of an octopus 72
mortadella 156
mortar 170
mosaic 280
mosque 447
mosquito 69
moss 51
moss, common hair cap 51
moss, Irish 123
moss, structure of 51
mosses, examples of 51
moth, atlas 69
motion detector 286
motocross and supercross motorcycle 525
motor 212, 213, 214, 227, 229, 237
motor bogie 376
motor car 380
motor end plate 110
motor neuron 110
motor racing 524
motor root 109, 110
motor scooter 369
motor sports 524
motor unit 176, 177, 180, 208, 272, 376
motor vehicle pollution 47
motor yacht 385
motto 441
motorcycle 366
motorcycle, leading 522
motorcycle, off-road 369
motorcycle, touring 369
motorcycle-mounted camera 522
motorcycle: view from above 368
motorcycles, examples of 369
motorcycling 525
motorway 25, 343, 431
motorway number 25
mould, charlotte 172
moulding, bumper 348
mount, ball 356
mountain 29
mountain biking 522
mountain lodge 512
mountain range 5, 24, 26
mountain slope 29
mountain torrent 29
Mountains, Appalachian 16
Mountains, Atlas 20
Mountains, Carpathian 18
Mountains, Rocky 16
Mountains, Transantarctic 15
Mountains, Ural 18

mounting bracket 535
mounting plate 199
mouse pad 332
mouse port 329
mouse, cordless 332
mouse, field 82
mouse, mechanical 332
mouse, optical 332
mouse, wheel 332
mouth 71, 72, 73, 75, 90, 94, 116, 305
mouthparts 68
mouthpiece 306, 307, 311, 467
mouthpiece receiver 307
mouthpipe 307
mouthwash 272
movable bridges 344
movable jaw 223, 224
movable maxillary 76
movable stands 444
movement, horizontal ground 27
movement, vertical ground 27
movements of aircraft 395
Mozambique 452
Mozambique Channel 20
mozzarella 150
Mt Everest 37
mud flap 349, 364, 365
mud hut 288
mud injection hose 403
mud pit 403
mud pump 403
mudflow 31
mudguard 370
muff 276
muffler felt 304
mule 84, 242
mullet 160
multi-hulls 521
multi-image jump button 315
multi-purpose solution 272
multigrain bread 145
multipack 163
multiple exposure mode 314
multiple light fitting 207
multiplication 427
multiply key 337
multipurpose tool 217
mummy 530
mung bean 131
Munster 151
muscle fibre 110
muscles 96
museum 433
mushroom 52
mushroom, enoki 123
mushroom, structure 52
mushrooms 123
music 296
music rest 305, 311
music room 444
musical instrument digital interface (MIDI)
   cable 311
musical notation 298
muskmelon 135
muslin 117
mustard, American 140
mustard, black 138
mustard, Dijon 140
mustard, English 140
mustard, German 140
mustard, powdered 140
mustard, white 138
mustard, wholegrain 140
mute 307
muzzle 83, 86, 87, 534
Myanmar 453
mycelium 52
myelin sheath 110
myocardium 104
myopia 419

N

nacelle 413
nacelle cross-section 413
nail 220
nail bed 114
nail cleaner 265
nail clippers 265
nail file 265
nail groove 531
nail matrix 114
nail scissors 265
nail set 220
nail shaper 265
nail varnish 265

nail whitener pencil 265
nail, common 220
nail, cut 220
nail, finishing 220
nail, masonry 220
nail, spiral 220
nails, examples of 220
naked strangle 499
name, currency 441
name, domain 334
name, gymnast's 497
name, holder's 441
nameplate 313
names, tropical cyclone 43
Namib Desert 20
Namibia 452
naos 279
nape 78, 93, 95
nappy 260
nappy, disposable 260
naris 117
nasal bone 100, 117
nasal cavity 105
nasal fossae 117
nasopharynx 117
national broadcasting network 316
national park 25
nationality 497
natural 299
natural arch 35
natural environment 504
natural greenhouse effect 46
natural sponge 267
Nauru 453
nautical sports 516
nave 285
navel 92, 94
navigation light 383, 393
Nazca Plate 27
Neapolitan coffee maker 181
near/far dial 320
neck 76, 83, 93, 94, 95, 101, 111, 167,
   297, 301, 302, 303, 318
neck end 245
neck of femur 99
neck pad 486
neck strap 458
neck support 525
neck, filler 351
neckhole 247
necklaces 264
neckroll 204
necktie 245
nectarine 132
needle 36, 460
needle hub 460
needle, larding 173
needle, trussing 173
needle-nose pliers 217
negative contact 410, 411
negative meniscus 419
negative plate 359
negative plate strap 359
negative region 410
negative terminal 359, 416, 417
negligee 256
neon lamp 217
Nepal 453
Neptune 2, 3
nerve 114
nerve fibre 114
nerve termination 114
nerve, olfactory 117
nerve, spinal 109
nervous system 108
nest of tables 202
net 487, 489, 491, 493, 495
net band 491
net judge 491
net support 493
Netherlands 449
nettle 127
network connection 198
network port 329
neurons 110
neutral conductor 198
neutral indicator 368
neutral line 416
neutral zone 484, 507
neutron 414
neutron, incident 415
névé 30
New Caledonia 15
new crescent 5
new moon 5
new shekel 440

New Zealand 15, 453
newborn children's clothing 260
newel post 191
Newfoundland Island 16
news items 313
newsagent's shop 437
newspaper 313
newt 75
newton 426
nib 312
Nicaragua 448
niche, safety 345
nictitating membrane 87
Niger 451
Niger River 20
Nigeria 451
night deposit box 443
nightgown 256
nightingale 80
nightshot switch 320
nightwear 256
Nile 20
nimbostratus 42
nipple 92, 94, 113
nitric acid emission 48
nitrogen oxide emission 48
no. 8 forward 482
nocking point 535
node 416
node of Ranvier 110
non-biodegradable pollutants 47
non-breaking space 330
non-reusable residue waste 49
nonagon, regular 429
noodles, Asian 147
noodles, bean thread cellophane 147
noodles, egg 147
noodles, rice 147
noodles, soba 147
noodles, somen 147
noodles, udon 147
nori 123
normal sight 419
North 23
North America 14, 16, 34
North American Plate 27
North Pole 21
north pole 416
North Sea 14, 18
North-Northeast 23
North-Northwest 23
Northeast 23
Northern hemisphere 21
Northern leopard frog 75
Northwest 23
Norway 450
Norwegian Sea 18
nose 82, 83, 94, 117, 392, 526, 534
nose landing gear 392
nose leather 87
nose of the quarter 240, 262
nose pad 273
nose, droop 394
nosepiece, revolving 421
nosing 191
nostril 74, 75, 76, 78, 83
notch 244, 422, 473, 503
notched double-edged thinning scissors
   270
notched edge 270
notched lapel 248
notched single-edged thinning scissors
   270
note presenter 442
note values 299
note, bank 469
noticeboard 341
nozzle 12, 216, 219, 236
nozzle cleaners 218
nozzle, steam 181
nubby tyre 525
nuclear energy 408
nuclear fission 415
nuclear membrane 50, 66
nuclear reactor 409
nuclear waste 48
nuclear whorl 72
nucleolus 50, 66, 112
nucleus 6, 50, 66, 110, 112, 414
nucleus splitting 415
nucleus, fissionable 415
number 473
number key 328, 337
number plate 525
number plate light 352
number, card 441, 443

number, player's 488, 506
number, pump 346
number, room 439
number, serial 441
numbering stamp 338
numerals, Roman 427
numeric keyboard 423
numeric keypad 331, 338
numeric lock 331
numeric lock key 331
numeric pager 327
nurse 464
nursery 205
nurses' lounge 465
nurses' station (ambulatory emergency)
   463
nurses' station (major emergency) 462
nut 222, 223, 301, 302, 303
nut, cola 133
nut, ginkgo 133
nut, hexagon 223
nut, macadamia 133
nutcracker 170
nutmeg 138
nutmeg grater 170
nuts 223
nylon line 237

O

oak 64
oar 501
oasis 32, 36
oat flour 144
oats 61, 143
oats: panicle 61
Oberon 3
obituary 313
object 419
object balls 502
objective 421
objective lens 8, 420
oblique fissure 105
oboe 306
oboes 295
observation deck 391
observation post 7
observation room 462, 465
observation window 7
observation, astronomical 7
observatory 7
obturator nerve 108
obtuse angle 428
occipital 97
occipital bone 99, 100
ocean 5, 24, 45
ocean floor 33
ocean trenches and ridges 34
ocean weather station 38
Ocean, Atlantic 15, 18, 20
Ocean, Indian 15, 19, 20
Ocean, Pacific 14, 15, 19
Oceania 14, 15
Oceania and Polynesia 453
oceanic crust 26
oche 471
octagon, regular 429
octahedron, regular 429
octave 298
octave mechanism 306
octopus 72, 157
octopus, morphology of 72
odd pinnate 55
oesophagus 105, 106
off-road motorcycle 369
offal 154
office 346, 374, 438, 439
office automation 329
office building 381, 432, 435
office tower 435
office, clerks' 440
office, emergency physician's 462
office, gymnasium 444
office, head nurse's 463
office, head teacher's 445
office, judges' 440
office, post 433, 437
office, proctors' 445
office, professional training 442
office, school secretary's 445
office, social worker's 463
officer, director's 443
officer, police 456
official signature 441

ASTRONOMY > 2-13;   EARTH > 14-49;   PLANT KINGDOM >50-65;   ANIMAL KINGDOM > 66-91;   HUMAN BEING > 92-119;   FOOD AND KITCHEN > 120-181;   HOUSE > 182-215;
DO-IT-YOURSELF AND GARDENING > 216-237;   CLOTHING > 238-263;   PERSONAL ADORNMENT AND ARTICLES > 264-277;   ARTS AND ARCHITECTURE > 278-311;   COMMUNICATIONS AND
OFFICE AUTOMATION > 312-341;   TRANSPORT AND MACHINERY > 342-401;   ENERGY > 402-413;   SCIENCE > 414-429;   SOCIETY > 430-467;   SPORTS AND GAMES > 468-538

553

ENGLISH INDEX

official, penalty bench 507
officials' bench 507
offshore well 404
Ogen melon 135
ohm 426
oil 403
oil drain plug 360
oil pollution 48
oil pressure warning indicator 368
oil spill 48
oil tank 235
oil terminal 381
oil warning light 355
oil, corn 149
oil, olive 149
oil, peanut 149
oil, sesame 149
oil, sunflower-seed 149
oils, fats and 149
okapi 84
okra 128
old crescent 5
olecranon 99
olfactory bulb 117
olfactory mucosa 117
olfactory nerve 117
olfactory tract 117
olive 128
olive oil 149
Oman 452
Oman, Gulf of 19
on-board computer 354
on-deck circle 474
on-off button 180
on-off indicator 269
on-off switch 177, 181, 206, 208, 209,
  218, 269, 270, 271, 272
on/off 326
on/off light 327
on/off switch 209, 314
on/off/volume 326
on/play button 328
one 427
one hundred 427
one pair 468
one thousand 427
one way head 221
one-arm shoulder throw 499
one-bar shoe 241
one-person tent 529
one-storey house 289
onion, green 124
onion, red 124
onion, white 124
online game 335
oolong tea 148
Oort cloud 2
open strings 296
open-air terrace 387
open-ended spanner 223
open-face spinning reel 537
open-plan coach 376
opening 243
opening, utensils 170
openings, gill 74
opera 432
opera glasses 273
opera-length necklace 264
operating instructions 346
operating panel 287
operating suite 464
operating table 464
operating theatre 464, 465
operation keys 442, 443
operator's cab 397
operator's cab 397
operator, boom 291
operator, camera 290
operculum 74
ophthalmology and ENT room 463
opisthodomos 279
opposable thumb 91
opposite prompt side 293
optic chiasm 109
optic nerve 119
optical mouse 332
optical scanner 121
optical sensor 332
optical sorting 49
optician 437
oral cavity 105, 106
oral irrigator 272
orange 134

orange, section of 58
orangutan 91
orbicularis oculi 96
orbiculate 55
orbit, Earth's 4, 5
orbital-action selector 227
orbiter 12, 13
orchard 122
orchestra 278
orchestra pit 292
orchid 56
order 285
ordinary die 468
oregano 142
organ 305
organ console 305
organization, cultural 335
organization, government 335
organization, health 335
organizer, personal 338
organs, sense 114
Orinoco River 17
ornamental kale 126
ornamental tree 122, 182, 230
ornaments 299
ortho-stick 466
oscillating sprinkler 236
ostrich 81
ostrich egg 155
other signs 299
otter, river 88
ottoman 201
outboard engine 385
outdoor leisure 528
outer circle 515
outer core 26
outer lip 73
outer planets 2
outer ring 441
outer string 191
outer table 469
outer toe 78
outfield fence 475
outgoing announcement cassette 328
outlet, discharge 184
outlet, European 198
outlet, oxygen 464
outlet, switched 322
output devices 333
output jack 303
output tray 333
output, S-Video 336
outside counter 240
outside linebacker 484
outside mirror 348, 362
outside mirror control 352
outside ticket pocket 244
outsole 240, 263
outwash plain 30
ovary 56, 112, 113
ovate 55
oven 164, 210
oven control knob 210
oven thermometer 171
oven, microwave 164
overall standings scoreboard 496
overbed table 464
overcoat 248, 251
overflow 194, 195
overflow pipe 196
overflow protection switch 214
overhead frame 401
overhead guard 396
overhead wires 376
overshirt 255
overtaking lane 343
overtaking zone 472
ovule 56
owl, great horned 81
ox 85
oxbow 32
oxbow lake 32
oxford shoe 240
oxygen outlet 464
oxygen pressure actuator 10
oxygen, release of 54
oxygenated blood 104
oyster 157
oyster fork 168
oyster knife 169
oyster mushroom 123
ozone layer 37

P

Pacific Ocean 14, 15, 19
Pacific Plate 27
Pacific salmon 161
Pacific-Antarctic Ridge 34
Pacinian corpuscle 114
pack, battery 228
package 163
package, dual-in-line 417
packaged integrated circuit 417
packaging 162
packaging products 120
packer 121
packer body 364
pad 478
pad arm 273
pad plate 273
pad, elbow 526, 527
pad, forearm 486
pad, knee 526, 527
pad, mouse 332
pad, neck 486
pad, sanding 229
pad, scouring 215
pad, touch 336
padded base 489
padded envelope 339
padded upright 489
paddy field 47
page down 331
page down key 331
page up 331
page up key 331
page, front 313
pager, numeric 327
pagoda 283
paint roller 219
paintbrush 219
painting upkeep 219
pair 509
pak-choi 126
Pakistan 452
palatine tonsil 118
palatoglossal arch 116
Palau 453
paling fence 230
pallet truck 396
palm 115, 243, 477
palm grove 36
palm of a glove 243
palm rest, detachable 330
palm tree 64
palmate 55
palmette 200
palp 73
pan 422, 423, 535
pan hook 422
pan, dripping 174, 179
pan, loaf 179
Panama 448
panama 238
Panama, Gulf of 17
Panama, Isthmus of 16
pancake pan 175
pancetta 156
pancreas 106
pane 186
panel 185, 246, 259
panel, bay filler 329
panel, control 179, 210
panel, display 320
panel, operating 287
pannier bag 372
panoramic window 435
panpipe 297
pantograph 376
pantry 188
panty corselette 258
panty girdle 259
papaya 137
paper clips 341
paper collection unit 49
paper fasteners 341
paper feed button 333, 443
paper feed light 333
paper guide 328
paper punch 340
paper recycling container 49
paper shredder 341
paper, parchment 162
paper, waxed 162
paper-clip holder 341
paper/paperboard separation 49
paper/paperboard sorting 49
papers, rice 147

papilla 114, 119
papilla, circumvallate 118
papilla, filiform 118
papilla, foliate 118
papilla, fongiform 118
papillary muscle 104
paprika 139
Papua New Guinea 15, 453
par 5 hole 504
parabolic dune 36
paraffin 405
paraffins 405
Paraguay 448
parallel 22
parallel bars 496, 497
parallel electrical circuit 416
parallel port 329
parallelepiped 429
parallelogram 429
paramecium 66
Paraná River 17
parapet 344
parapet walk 282
parboiled rice 147
parcel tape dispenser 341
parcels office 374
parchment paper 162
parfum, eau de 267
parietal bone 99, 100
parietal pleura 105
paring knife 169
paripinnate 55
park 25, 433
parka 249
parking 435, 504, 512
parking area 389, 430, 445
parking, bicycle 445
Parmesan 151
parsley 142
parsnip 129
parterre 293
partial eclipse 4, 5
partially reflecting mirror 420
partition 60, 457
partlow chart 365
partridge 80
parts 200, 201, 204
parts of a bicycle 370
parts of a circle 428
parts of a shoe 240
parts of spectacles 273
pascal 426
pass 29
passage, ascending 278
passage, descending 278
Passage, Drake 15, 17
passage, fore-and-aft 385
passbook update slot 442
passenger cabin 383, 386, 387, 393
passenger car 376, 380
passenger platform 374
passenger seat 369
passenger station 374, 375
passenger terminal 381, 389, 390
passenger train 374
passenger transfer vehicle 391
passion fruit 136
passport case 275
passport control 391
pasta 146
pasta maker 170
paste, tomato 140
pastern 83
pastry bag and nozzles 172
pastry blender 172
pastry brush 172
pastry cutting wheel 172
pasture 122
Patagonia 17
patch pocket 244, 249, 260
patella 98
patera 200
path 230, 504
path, garden 182
pathology laboratory 465
patient 464
patient room 464
patient's chair 464
patio 182, 230
patio door 164, 188
patisserie/bakery 437
patrol and first-aid station 512
pattypan squash 129
pause 299, 331
pause button 323
pause/break key 331

pause/still 319
pause/still key 319
pavement 183, 434
pavilion 432
Pawn 470
pay phone 294, 437, 438, 463
payment terminal, electronic 443
PC card slot 336
PDA 337
pe-tsai 126
pea 60
pea jacket 251
pea, black-eyed 130
peach 132
peach, section of 57
peacock 81
peak 29, 238, 239, 458
peak level meter 323
peaked lapel 244
peanut 130
peanut oil 149
pear 133
pear, Asian 137
pear, prickly 137
pear-shaped body 297
peas 130
peas, split 130
pecan nut 133
peccary 84
pectoral deck 501
pectoral fin 74, 90
pedal 302, 308, 370, 372, 473, 501,
  522
pedal key 305
pedal keyboard 305
pedal pushers 254
pedal rod 304
pedal spindle 372
pedal with wide platform 522
pedal, brake 350, 357
pedal, clipless 522
pedestal 302
pedestrian call button 434
pedestrian crossing 434
pedestrian lights 434
pedicel 59, 62
pediment 279
pedipalp 70
peduncle 56, 57, 58, 59, 62
peel 58
peeler 169
peg 202, 224, 301, 302, 528, 529
peg box 301
peg loop 528, 529
peg, tuning 303
pelerine 251
pelican 80
pellets 534
peltate 55
pelvic fin 74
pen 27
pen holder 274
penalty arc 480
penalty area 480
penalty area marking 480
penalty bench 507
penalty bench official 507
penalty spot 480
pencil 312
pencil point tip 218
pencil sharpener 341
pendant 264
penguin 80
penholder grip 493
peninsula 24
Peninsula, Antarctic 15
Peninsula, Arabian 19
Peninsula, Balkan 18
Peninsula, Iberian 18
Peninsula, Kamchatka 19
Peninsula, Kola 19
Peninsula, Korean 19
Peninsula, Scandinavian 18
Peninsula, Yucatan 16
penis 92, 111
penne 146
penstock 406, 407
pentagon, regular 429
penumbra 4, 5
pepino 137
pepper spray 456
pepper, black 138
pepper, green 138
pepper, ground 139
pepper, pink 138
pepper, white 138

pepperoni 156
pepperpot 166
percent 427
percent key 337
perch 160
perch, morphology of 74
perch, pike 160
perching bird 79
percolator 181
percussion instruments 295, 308
perforated toe cap 240
perforation 243
performance tyre 358
performing arts 294
perfume shop 436
pergola 230
pericardium 105
pericarp 60
periodontal ligament 101
peripheral 431
peripheral nervous system 108
peristome 66
peristyle 279, 280
peritoneum 111, 112
peroxide 461
peroxisome 66
perpendicular 428
perpetual snows 29
Persian 87
Persian Gulf 19
person, continuity 291
personal adornment 264
personal adornment and articles 264
personal articles 271
personal communications 317
personal computer 329
personal identification number (PIN) pad
443
personal organizer 338
personal radio cassette player 326
personal watercraft 523
Peru 448
Peru-Chile Trench 34
peso 440
pesticide 47, 48
pestle 170
pet food and supplies 121
pet shop 436
petal 56
petiolar sinus 62
petiole 52, 55
petrochemical industry 405
petrochemicals 405
petrol 405
petrol engine 351, 360
petrol pump 346
petrol pump hose 346
petrol tank cap 368
petroleum 405
petroleum trap 403
pew 446
pharmaceutical forms of medication 467
pharmacy 436, 462, 465
pharynx 105, 106
phase conductor 198
phase, gliding 514
phase, pushing 514
phases of the Moon 5
pheasant 81, 154
pheasant egg 155
Philippine Plate 27
Philippine Trench 34
Philippines 19, 453
philtrum 117
phloem 63
Phobos 2
phone, pay 437, 438, 463
phosphorescent coating 199
photo booth 437
photographer 436
photographer, still 291
photography 314
photography, director of 291
photon 420
photoreceptors 119
photosphere 4
photosynthesis 54
photovoltaic arrays 11
physical map 24
physician 464, 498
physics: electricity and magnetism 416
physics: optics 418
pi 428
pia mater 109
piano 295
piccolo 295, 306

pick 233
pickguard 303
pickling onion 124
pickup selector 303
pickup truck 347
pickups 303
picture tube 318
picture, front 313
pie tin 172
pier 285, 344
pierce lever 180
pig 84
pig, guinea 82
pigeon 81, 154
pigsty 122
pika 82
pike 160
pike perch 160
pike pole 454
pike position 518
pilaster, Corinthian 281
pile 190
pile carpet 190
pile dwelling 288
pillar 27, 283, 284, 302
pillbox hat 239
pillion footrest 367, 368
pillow 204
pillow cover 204
pillowcase 204
pilot house 385
pilot light 178, 180, 181, 208, 210, 214
pin 198, 199, 454
pin base 199
pin block 304
pin, connection 417
pin, male grounding 198
pinafore 252
pinch 199
pine needles 65
pine nut 133
pine seed 65
pineal body 109
pineapple 136
pink ball 503
pink pepper 138
pinna 52, 82
pinnacle 282, 284, 285
pinnatifid 55
pinto bean 131
pip 58, 59, 468
pipe 224
pipe clamp 224
pipe section 193
pipe wrench 216
pipeline 404
pistachio nut 133
pistil 56
pistol 456
pistol grip 534
pistol grip handle 218, 228
pistol nozzle 236
pistol, starting 472
piston 357, 360
piston lever 216
piston release 216
piston ring 360
piston skirt 360
pit 76
pit lane 524
pit, orchestra 292
pitch 395, 475, 479
pitch wheel 310
pitcher 474, 475
pitcher's mound 475
pitcher's plate 475
pitchfork comb 268
pith 63
Pitot tube 525
pits 524
pitta bread 145
pituitary gland 109
pivot 217, 270, 271, 533
pivot cab 400
pivot spindle 355
placing judge 516
plaice, common 161
plain 24, 32
plain flour 144
plan 279, 285
plan reading, elevation 182
plane 229
plane projection 22
plane surfaces 428
planets 2
planets, inner 3

planets, outer 2
planisphere 14
plano-concave lens 419
plano-convex lens 419
plant 53
plant cell 50
plant kingdom 50
plant litter 54
plant, sorting 49
plant, structure 53
plantain 136
plantar 97
plantar interosseous 96
plasma 104
plasma membrane 66
plasmodesma 50
plaster dressing 461
plaster room 463
plastic arts room 444
plastic case 534
plastic film 162
plastic film capacitor 417
plastics sorting 49
plastron 76
plate 118, 269, 531
plate boundaries, convergent 27
plate boundaries, divergent 27
plate boundaries, transform 27
plate grid 359
Plate, African 27
Plate, Antarctic 27
Plate, Australian-Indian 27
Plate, Caribbean 27
Plate, Cocos 27
plate, cooking 179
Plate, Eurasian 27
Plate, Nazca 27
Plate, North American 27
plate, number 525
Plate, Pacific 27
Plate, Philippine 27
plate, protective 525
Plate, Scotia 27
Plate, South American 27
plateau 24, 29
platelet 104
plates, tectonic 27
platform 219, 363, 379, 390, 423, 516,
526
platform edge 374, 379
platform entrance 374
platform ladder 219
platform number 374
platform shelter 375
platform, 10 m 518
platform, 3 m 518
platform, 5 m 518
platform, 7,5 m 518
platform, event 496
play 319
play button 323, 326
play key 319
play/pause 323
player positions 474, 481, 482, 489
player's number 486, 488, 506
player's stick 506
player, basketball 488
player, CD/DVD 471
player, compact disc 325
player, DVD 318
player, rugby 485
players 492
players' bench 485, 487, 506
players' position 482
playground 445
playing area 471
playing field 480
playing field for American football 484
playing surface 493
playing surfaces 492
pleasure garden 230
pleats, examples of 253
plectrum 297
pleura, parietal 105
pleura, visceral 105
pleural cavity 105
plexus of nerves 101
pliers 222
plimsoll 242
plug 228
plug adapter 198, 271
plug, power 337
plug, power cable 329
plug, sealing 417
plum 132
plum sauce 141

plumber's snake 216
plumbing 194
plumbing system 194
plumbing tools 216
plumbing wrench 216
plunger 216, 460
plus or minus 427
Pluto 2, 3
pneumatic armlet 461
pocket 225, 274, 502, 505
pocket calculator 337
pocket handkerchief 244
podium 283, 435, 444
podium and basements 435
point 167, 169, 301, 312, 469, 471, 538
point guard 489
point of interest 25
point, anchor 70
point, nocking 535
pointed tab end 245
pointer 422, 423
points 375, 492
poisonous mushroom 52
poker 193
poker die 468
Poland 450
polar axis 7
polar bear 89
polar climates 40
polar ice cap 40
polar lights 37
polar tundra 40
polarizing filter 314
Polaroid® Land camera 315
pole 321, 490
pole grip 514
pole position 524
pole shaft 514
pole vault 472
Pole, North 21
pole, north 416
Pole, South 15, 21
pole, south 416
police car 457
police officer 456
police station 433
political map 23
politics 448
pollen basket 68
pollock, black 161
pollutants, air 47
pollutants, non-biodegradable 47
polluting gas emission 47
pollution, agricultural 47
pollution, air 47
pollution, domestic 47
pollution, industrial 47
pollution, land 47
pollution, motor vehicle 47
pollution, oil 48
pollution, water 48
polo dress 252
polo neck 514
polo shirt 250, 255, 492
polo-neck sweater 250
polygons 429
polypody, common 52
pome fruits 133
pomegranate 136
pomelo 134
pommel horse 496
poncho 251
pond 230, 504
pons Varolii 109
Pont-l'Évêque 151
poodle 86
pool 184, 502
popping crease 479
poppy 56
poppy seeds 139
popular terms 58, 59
porch 183, 285, 447
porch dome 447
porcupine 82
pore 50, 60, 114
pork, cuts of 153
pork, minced 153
Porro prism 420
port 431
port glass 165
port hand 387
port, Ethernet 336
port, FireWire 336
port, game/MIDI 329
port, infrared 336, 337

port, internal modem 329, 336
port, keyboard 329
port, mouse 329
port, network 329
port, parallel 329
port, power adapter 336
port, serial 329
port, USB 329, 336
port, video 329, 336
portable CD radio cassette recorder 326
portable compact disc player 325
portable digital audio player 325
portable fire extinguisher 454
portable radio 325
portable shower head 195
portable sound systems 325
portal 285
portal vein 103
porthole 386
portrait 441
ports, controller 471
Portugal 449
position indicator 287
position light 376, 395
position marker 302, 303
position, mean 418
position, pole 524
positions, player 474, 481, 489
positive contact 410, 411
positive meniscus 419
positive plate 359
positive plate strap 359
positive region 410
positive terminal 359, 416, 417
positive/negative junction 410
post 412, 487, 495
post binder 339
post lantern 207
post mill 412
post office 433, 437
post, foul line 475
post, hand 297
post, observation 7
poster 294
posterior adductor muscle 73
posterior chamber 119
posterior end 73
posterior fontanelle 100
posterior horn 109
posterior root 110
posterior rugae 95
posterior semicircular canal 116
posterior view 93, 95, 97, 99, 113
postern 282
posting surface 341
potato 124
potato masher 173
potato, sweet 124
pothole 31
pouch 162, 531
pouch of Douglas 112
pouch, ammunition 456
poultry 155
poultry shears 173
pound 440
pouring spout 215
powder blusher 266
powder puff 266
powder, chilli 139
powder, five spice 139
powder, magnesium 497
powdered milk 150
powdered mustard 140
powdered sugar 149
power adapter 336
power adapter port 336
power and backlight button 337
power button 318, 319, 322, 323, 329,
333, 336
power cable plug 329
power cord 177, 227, 229, 269, 322
power cord, alternating-current 336
power cord, direct-current 336
power indicator 329
power key 327
power light 333
power mower 237
power plant 406
power plug 337
power socket 326
power source 416
power supply fan 329
power switch 311, 315, 329
power train 372
power zoom button 320
power, measurement of 426

ASTRONOMY > 2-13;   EARTH > 14-49;   PLANT KINGDOM >50-65;   ANIMAL KINGDOM > 66-91;   HUMAN BEING > 92-119;   FOOD AND KITCHEN > 120-181;   HOUSE > 182-215;
DO-IT-YOURSELF AND GARDENING > 216-237;   CLOTHING > 238-263;   PERSONAL ADORNMENT AND ARTICLES > 264-277;   ARTS AND ARCHITECTURE > 278-311;   COMMUNICATIONS AND
OFFICE AUTOMATION > 312-341;   TRANSPORT AND MACHINERY > 342-401;   ENERGY > 402-413;   SCIENCE > 414-429;   SOCIETY > 430-467;   SPORTS AND GAMES > 468-538

555

power-on button 328
power-on light 328
power-on/paper-detect light 443
power/functions switch 320
practice green 504
prairie 24
prawn 158
prayer hall 447
precipitation 45
precipitation area 39
precipitations 41
precipitations, winter 41
precision and accuracy sports 502
prehensile digit 91
premaxilla 74
premolars 101
prepuce 111
present state of weather 39
presenter, note 442
presenter, slip 346
preset buttons 319
preset tuning button 322
press bar 501
pressed cheeses 151
pressed powder 266
pressure bar 304
pressure change 39
pressure control 272
pressure control valve 461
pressure cooker 174
pressure demand regulator 454
pressure gauge 461
pressure modulator, brake 357
pressure regulator 174, 529
pressure tube 409
pressure, measurement of 426
pressurized refuge 345
prevailing wind 43
prevention, crime 456
previous sets 492
price per gallon/litre 346
prickly pear 137
prickly sphagnum 51
primaries 78
primary consumers 45
primary covert 78
primary crash sensor 354
primary mirror 7
primary root 53
primate mammals 91
primates, examples of 91
prime focus 7
prime focus observing capsule 7
prime meridian 22
primer 534
princess dress 252
princess seaming 258
print cartridge light 333
print screen 331
print screen/system request key 331
printed circuit 417
printed circuit board 417
printer, inkjet 333
printing calculator 337
printout 423
prism binoculars 420
prisoner's dock 440
privacy curtain 464
private broadcasting network 316
private dressing room 290
probe socket 178
proboscis 67
procedure checklist 10
process, mastoid 100
process, styloid 100
processing, data 38
proctors' office 445
producer 291
product code 423
production designer 290
production of electricity by generator 408
production of electricity from geothermal energy 402
production of electricity from nuclear energy 408
production of electricity from thermal energy 402
production of electricity from wind energy 413
production platform 404
production well 402
products, cereal 144
products, dairy 120, 150
products, household 120
products, packaging 120
professional training office 442

profile of the Earth's atmosphere 37
profile, soil 54
program selector 213, 214, 310, 314
programmable buttons 332
programmable function keys 443
programs, computer 457
projection booth 294
projection device 365
projection room 294
projection screen 294
projector 294
proleg 67
promenade deck 386
prominence 4
prompt side 293
pronaos 279
propagation 418
propane gas cylinder 361
propane or butane appliances 529
propellant 534
propeller 384, 386, 387
propeller duct 383
propeller shaft 387
propeller, rear 384
propeller, stem 384
propeller, three-blade 394
propeller, two-blade 394
propelling pencil 312
property line 182
property man 291
property man, assistant 291
propulsion module 316
proscenium 292
prosciutto 156
prospecting, surface 403
prostate 111
protect tab 333
protection layer 10
protection, rub 525
protective casing 237
protective cup 486, 507
protective equipment 486
protective goggles 522, 525
protective plate 525
protective suit 525
protective surround 471
protective window 318
protector, glass 506
protector, hand 525
protocol, communication 334
proton 414
protoneuron 110
province 23
pruning and cutting tools 234
pruning saw 234
pseudopod 66
psychiatric examination 462
psychiatric observation room 462
pubis 92, 94
public building 25
public entrance 278
public garden 435
puck 507
pudding, black 156
Puerto Rico Trench 34
pull star 277
pull, ring 163
pulley 219, 360
pulling ring 460
pulmonary artery 102, 105
pulmonary trunk 104
pulmonary valve 104
pulmonary vein 102
pulp 58, 101
pulp chamber 101
pulpit 446, 447
pulsed ruby laser 420
pulverizer 402
pump 184, 212, 214, 241, 529
pump and motor assembly 357
pump nozzle 346
pump number 346
pump room 384
pump sprayer 236
pumper 455
pumping station 404
pumpkin 129
punch hole 240, 246, 263
punchbag 498
punchball 498
pupil 87, 119
pure alcohol 461
purfling 301, 302
purse 275
purslane 127

push bar 286
push button 176, 214
push buttons 327
push frame 398
push rim 467
push-button 312
push-up bra 259
push-up stand 501
pusher 170, 177, 180
pushing phase 514
putter 505
pygal shield 76
pyjamas 256
pyloric stomach 71
pyramid 278, 429
pyramid entrance 278
pyramid spot 502
Pyrenees 18
python 77

Q

Qatar 452
Qibla wall 447
quad bike 369
quadrant 428
quadrilateral 429
quadruped stick 466
quail 81, 154
quail egg 155
quarter 240, 262
quarter window 349
quarter-deck 386
quarterback 485
quartet 300
quaver 299
quaver rest 299
quay 381, 430
quay ramp 381
quayside crane 381
quayside railway 381
Queen 468, 470
queen 68
Queen Maud Land 15
queen's chamber 278
Queen's side 470
queen, honeybee 68
quiche tin 172
quick ticket system 294
quill 312
quill brush 268
quince 133
quinoa 143
quintet 300

R

raab, broccoli 127
rabbi's seat 447
rabbit 82, 154
raccoon 88
race director 522
raceme 57
racing suit 508, 525
racing, motor 524
racing, road 522
rack 174, 178, 210, 214, 473, 503
rack, brochure 442
rack, luggage 369
rack, ski 356
racket sports 493
Raclette 151
raclette with grill 179
radar 382, 383, 386, 387
radar display 457
radar mast 384
radar transceiver 457
radar, weather 38
radial nerve 108
radial thread 70
radiation 415
radiation zone 4
radiation, absorbed solar 46
radiation, infrared 46, 418
radiation, reflected solar 46
radiation, solar 45, 46, 410
radiation, ultraviolet 418
radiator 350, 358
radiator core 358
radiator grille 364
radiator panel 13
radiators 11
radicchio 126
radicle 53, 63
radio 457
radio antenna 382, 384, 386, 387, 525

radio section 326
radio waves 418
radio, clock 325
radio, portable 325
radioactivity, measurement of 426
radish 129
radish, black 129
radius 98, 428
rafter 187
raglan 251
raglan sleeve 248, 251, 261
rail 202, 502
rail shuttle service 390
rail transport 374
rail, communion 446
rail, guard 526
rail, top 205
railing 189
railway 375
railway station 25, 375, 430, 432
railway track 432
rain 41
rain cap 193
rain hat 239
rain, acid 47, 48
rain, freezing 41
rainbow 41
raincoat 248
rainfall, heavy 43
raining, utensils for 171
raised handlebar 522
raised head 221
rake 233
rake comb 268
rally car 524
rambutan 137
ramekin 166
ramp 279, 281, 526
rampart 282
random orbit sander 229
Range, Great Dividing 15
rangefinder camera 315
rank insignia 456
ras el hanout 139
raspberry 132
raspberry, section 59
rat 82
rat, morphology of 82
ratchet 221
ratchet knob 425
ratchet ring spanner 223
ratchet socket wrench 223
rattlesnake 77
raven 80
ravioli 146
ray, crater 5
ray, light 419
rays, gamma 418
razor clam 157
re-entrant angle 428
reach-in freezer 120
reaction, chain 415
reactor 408
reactor building 409
reactor vessel 409
read button 327
read/write head 333
reader, card 321
reading light 457
reading mirror 10
rear apron 245
rear beam 422
rear brake 370
rear brake pedal 368
rear bumper 369, 523
rear cargo rack 369
rear derailleur 370, 372
rear foil 387
rear indicator 367, 368
rear leg 201
rear light 352, 367, 368, 370
rear lights 352
rear propeller 384
rear rigid section 363
rear seat 353
rear sight 534
rear step 455
rearview mirror 354
receipt, transaction 443
receiver 321, 327, 490, 495
receiver volume control 327
receiver, wide 485
receiving area 120
receptacle 51, 56, 59
reception area 462, 465
reception desk 442

reception hall 447
reception level 439
receptors, taste 118
rechargeable battery pack 320
recharging base 208
recliner 201
reclining back 460
record 319
record announcement button 328
record button 319, 323
record muting button 323
record shop 436
recorder, DVD 333
recording level control 323
recording start/stop button 320
recording, seismographic 403
records, medical 465
recovery room 464
rectangle 429
rectangular 530
rectum 106, 111, 112
rectus femoris 96
recycling 49
recycling bin 49
recycling containers 49
Red 469
red 418
red alga 51
red ball 502, 503
red balls 503
red beam 318
red blood cell 104
red cabbage 126
red clamp 356
red kidney bean 131
red light 434
red onion 124
Red Sea 14, 19, 20
red sweet pepper 128
red whortleberry 132
red-kneed tarantula 70
redcurrant 132
redfish 161
reed 306
reed pipe 305
Reef, Great Barrier 15
reel 236, 319
reel crank 236
reel seat 536, 537
reel, baitcasting 537
referee 481, 483, 485, 487, 488, 498, 499, 507, 509, 516, 518
referee, assistant 509
refill 312
refill pipe 196
refinery 404, 431
refinery products 405
reflected solar radiation 46
reflecting cylinder 420
reflecting telescope 9
reflecting telescope, cross section 9
reflector 217, 365, 370, 523
refracting telescope 8
refracting telescope, cross section 8
refrigerated display case 438
refrigerated semitrailer 365
refrigeration unit 365
refrigerator 164, 211, 438
refrigerator compartment 211
refrigerator van 377
refrigerators 438
refuge, pressurized 345
refuse container 215
regions, vegetation 44
register, cash 121
regular decagon 429
regular dodecagon 429
regular hendecagon 429
regular heptagon 429
regular hexagon 429
regular nonagon 429
regular octagon 429
regular octahedron 429
regular pentagon 429
reindeer 84
reinforced edging 277
reinforced toe 459
relay station 316
relay station, microwave 334
release lever 222
release of oxygen 54
release, energy 415
relieving chamber 278
religion 446
remote control 319, 321
remote control sensor 318, 323

ASTRONOMY > 2-13;   EARTH > 14-49;   PLANT KINGDOM >50-65;   ANIMAL KINGDOM > 66-91;   HUMAN BEING > 92-119;   FOOD AND KITCHEN > 120-181;   HOUSE > 182-215;
DO-IT-YOURSELF AND GARDENING > 216-237;   CLOTHING > 238-263;   PERSONAL ADORNMENT AND ARTICLES > 264-277;   ARTS AND ARCHITECTURE > 278-311;   COMMUNICATIONS AND
OFFICE AUTOMATION > 312-341;   TRANSPORT AND MACHINERY > 342-401;   ENERGY > 402-413;   SCIENCE > 414-429;   SOCIETY > 430-467;   SPORTS AND GAMES > 468-538

ENGLISH INDEX

remote control terminal 314, 315
remote manipulator system 11, 12
remote-control arm 11
removable flag pole 504
removable hard disk 333
removable hard disk drive 333
removable-bottomed tin 172
renal artery 102, 107
renal hilus 107
renal papilla 107
renal pelvis 107
renal vein 102, 107
reniform 55
repair shop 346
repeat keys 323
repeat mark 298
repeater 317
reprography 442
reptiles 76
reptiles, examples of 77
Republic of Korea 453
repulsion 416
reservoir 181, 406, 407
reservoir, brake fluid 357
reset button 319, 329, 424, 471
reset key 328
residential district 431
resistance adjustment 501
resistors 417
resonator 305, 309, 324
resort, ski 512
respirator 459
respiratory system 105
respiratory system protection 459
rest area 25
rest area, vehicle 345
rest values 299
rest, arrow 535
rest, hand 332
restaurant 386, 432, 435, 436, 438
restaurant car 376
restaurant review 313
restaurants, fast-food 437
restricted area 489
restricting circle 488
results, table of 518
resurgence 31
resuscitation room 462
retaining strap 277
reticle 420
retina 119, 419
retractable handle 274
retractable step 361
return 331
return crease 479
return spring 357
reverse 518
reversing light 352
reversing switch 221, 228
review, restaurant 313
revolving door, manual 286
revolving nosepiece 421
revolving sprinkler 236
rewind 319
rewind button 319, 323, 326, 328
Rhea 3
rhinoceros 85
rhizoid 51
rhizome 52
rhombus 429
rhubarb 125
rhythm selector 311
rias 35
rib 125, 273, 301, 302, 401, 458
rib pad 486
rib roast 152
ribbing 250, 261, 536
ribosome 50, 66
ribs 98
ribs, back 152
rice 61, 143, 147
rice noodles 147
rice papers 147
rice vermicelli 147
rice vinegar 141
rice, basmati 147
rice, brown 147
rice, parboiled 147
rice, white 147
rice, wild 143
rice: panicle 61
ridge 29
ridge tent 529
Ridge, Mid-Atlantic 34
Ridge, Mid-Indian 34

Ridge, Pacific-Antarctic 34
Ridge, Southeast Indian 34
Ridge, Southwest Indian 34
riding coat 251
riegel 30
rifle (rifled bore) 534
rigatoni 146
right angle 428
right ascension setting scale 8, 9
right atrium 103, 104
right attacker 487
right back 481, 487
right centre 482
right channel 324
right cornerback 484
right defence 506
right defensive end 484
right defensive tackle 484
right field 475
right fielder 474
right forward 489
right guard 485
right kidney 107
right lung 103, 105
right midfielder 481
right pulmonary vein 104
right safety 484
right service court 491
right side 272
right tackle 485
right ventricle 103, 104
right wing 482, 507
rigid section, front 363
rigid section, rear 363
rigid tube 209
rillettes 156
rim 273, 366, 371, 489
rim soup bowl 166
rime 41
rinceau 200
rind 58
ring 52, 273, 307, 423, 424, 498
ring binder 339
ring motorway 25
ring post 498
ring pull 163
ring road 25
ring spanner 223
ring step 498
ring, 25 471
ring, outer 441
ring, tuning 297
ringhandle 270
ringing volume control 327
rings 264, 496, 497
ringside 498
rink 506, 509
rink corner 506
rink, ice 512
rinse-aid dispenser 214
rip fence 227
ripeness 62
ripening 62
ripper 398
ripper cylinder 398
ripper shank 398
ripper tip tooth 398
rise 191
Rise, East Pacific 34
riser 191
rising main 194
rising warm air 43
river 24, 25, 32
river otter 88
River, Amazon 17
River, Congo 20
River, Danube 18
River, Dnieper 18
River, Mackenzie 16
River, Mississippi 16
River, Niger 20
River, Orinoco 17
River, Paraná 17
River, Saint Lawrence 16
River, Senegal 20
River, Vistula 18
River, Volga 18
rivet 169, 222
road 25, 430
road bicycle 373
road communications 317
road cycling competition 522
road flare 457
road map 25
road number 25
road racing 522

road system 342
road transport 342, 381
road tunnel 345
road, cross section 342
road-racing bicycle and cyclist 522
roadway 342, 345, 434
roast 152, 153
roast, fillet 152
roast, rib 152
roasted coffee beans 148
roasting pans 174
Roberval's balance 422
robin, European 80
rock basin 30
rock candy 149
rock garden 230
rocker arm 360
rocket 127
rocking chair 200, 201
rockslide 31
rocky desert 36
rocky islet 35
Rocky Mountains 16
rod 119
rodent 82
rodents and lagomorphs 82
rodents, examples of 82
roll 395
roll structure 525
roller 268, 332
roller frame 219
roller hockey skate 527
roller shade 356
roller skate 527
roller sleeve 219
roller speed skate 527
rolling pin 172
Roman amphitheatre 281
roman bean 131
Roman house 280
Roman metal pen 312
Roman numerals 427
Romania 450
Romano 151
rompers 260, 261
roof 183, 193, 283, 349, 361
roof pole 529
roof timber 279
roof vent 194, 361
room number 439
room, anaethesia 464
room, audiometric examination 465
room, changing 444
room, clean utility 462
room, computer science 444
room, conference 442
room, control 293
room, dining 438, 439
room, double 439
room, equipment storage 444
room, examination 465
room, examination and treatment 463
room, gynaecological examination 463
room, hotel 439
room, isolation 462
room, jurors' 440
room, linen 439
room, meeting 439, 442, 445
room, music 444
room, observation 462, 465
room, ophthalmology and ENT 463
room, patient 464
room, plaster 463
room, plastic arts 444
room, projection 294
room, psychiatric observation 462
room, recovery 464
room, resuscitation 462
room, science 444
room, scrub 464
room, single 439
room, soiled utility 462, 464
room, specimen collection 465
room, sterilization 464, 465
room, students' 445
room, supply 464
room, teachers' 445
room, technical 345
room, treatment 465
room, triage 463
room, waiting 463
rooms, interview 440
rooms, main 188
rooster 81
root 54, 101, 118, 167
root canal 101

root cap 53
root hairs 53
root of nail 114
root rib 392
root system 53, 62
root vegetables 129
root, motor 109
root, primary 53
root, secondary 53
root-hair zone 63
roots, adventitious 52
rope 264, 498
rope, false start 516
rope, tension 297
Roquefort 151
rorqual 90
rose 56, 186, 236, 302
rose window 285
rosemary 142
Ross Ice Shelf 15
rotary cheese grater 170
rotary file 338
rotary system 403
rotary table 403
rotating dome 7
rotating drum 27
rotating light 455
rotini 146
rotor 412, 537
rotor blade 395
rotor head 395
rotor hub 395
rotunda 435
rough 504
round brush 268
round head 221
round pronator 96
roundabout 25
route sign 362, 363
route, evacuation 345
router 229, 334
row 272, 293
row, first 482
row, second 482
row, third 482
rowing machine 501
royal agaric 123
royal flush 468
rub protection 525
rubber boot 454
rubber bulb 460
rubber ferrule 466
rubber gasket 197
rubber stamp 338
rubber stopper 219
ruby cylinder 420
ruching 260
ruck 483
rudder 13, 383, 384, 386, 393, 520
rudder blade 384
Ruffini's corpuscle 114
ruffled skirt 253
rug 190
rugby 482
rugby ball 483
rugby player 483
rugby shoes 483
rule 313
ruler 425, 531
rump 78
run 191
run-up 473
runabout 385
rung 219
runner 469
running shoe 262, 473
running shorts 263
runs, approach 496
runway 390
runway centre line markings 390
runway designation marking 390
runway side stripe markings 390
runway threshold markings 391
runway touchdown zone marking 391
rupee 440
Russian black bread 145
Russian Federation 450
Russian module 11
Rwanda 451
rye 61, 143
rye crispbread 145
rye: spike 61
Ryukyu Trench 34

S

S-Video output 336
sacral plexus 108
sacristy 446
sacrum 98, 99
saddle 370
saddle pillar 370
saddlebag 369
safari jacket 255
safe 443
safe deposit box 443
safety 454
safety area 499
safety belt 525
safety binding 510, 511
safety boot 459
safety cage 473
safety earmuffs 458
safety glasses 458
safety goggles 458
safety handle 237
safety lighting 457
safety line 379
safety niche 345
safety rail 219, 377
safety scissors 217
safety tether 10
safety thermostat 213
safety valve 174, 408
saffron 138
sagittal section 111, 112
Sahara Desert 20
sail 412, 519
sail cloth 412
sail panel 520
sailbar 412
sailboard 519
sailing 520
sailing boat 520
sailor tunic 255
Saint Bernard 86
Saint Kitts and Nevis 449
Saint Lawrence River 16
Saint Lucia 449
Saint Vincent and the Grenadines 449
salad bowl 166
salad crisper 211
salad dish 166
salad fork 168
salad plate 166
salad spinner 171
salamander 75
salami, Genoa 156
salami, German 156
Salchow 509
salivary gland 118
salivary glands 106
salmon, Atlantic 161
salmon, Pacific 161
salsify 129
salt lake 36
salt, coarse 141
salt, sea 141
salt, table 141
saltcellar 166
sambal oelek 141
Samoa 453
sampler 310
San Marino 450
sanctuary lamp 446
sand bunker 504
sand island 35
sand shoe 365
sandal 242
sandbank 33
sandbox 377
sander, random orbit 229
sanding disc 229
sanding pad 229
sandpaper 229
sandy desert 36
Sao Tome and Principe 451
saphenous nerve 108
sapodilla 137
sapwood 63
sardine 159
sarong 253
sartorius 96
sash frame 186
sash window 287
satchel bag 275
satellite 316
satellite broadcasting 316

ENGLISH INDEX

ASTRONOMY > 2-13;   EARTH > 14-49;   PLANT KINGDOM >50-65;   ANIMAL KINGDOM > 66-91;   HUMAN BEING > 92-119;   FOOD AND KITCHEN > 120-181;   HOUSE > 182-215;
DO-IT-YOURSELF AND GARDENING > 216-237;   CLOTHING > 238-263;   PERSONAL ADORNMENT AND ARTICLES > 264-277;   ARTS AND ARCHITECTURE > 278-311;   COMMUNICATIONS AND
OFFICE AUTOMATION > 312-341;   TRANSPORT AND MACHINERY > 342-401;   ENERGY > 402-413;   SCIENCE > 414-429;   SOCIETY > 430-467;   SPORTS AND GAMES > 468-538

557

satellite earth station 335
satellite terminal 389
satellite, telecommunication 335
satellite, weather 38
Saturn 2, 3
sauce, hoisin 140
sauce, plum 141
sauce, soy 140
sauce, Tabasco 140
sauce, Worcestershire 140
saucepan 175, 531
saucepan, small 175
Saudi Arabia 452
sausage, chipolata 156
sausage, kielbasa 156
sausage, merguez 156
sausage, Toulouse 156
sauté pan 175
savanna 44
savory 142
savoy cabbage 126
saw, compass 226
saw, coping 226
saw, hand mitre 226
saxhorn 307
saxophone 306
scale 74, 76, 79, 225, 298, 424, 425,
   460, 533
scale leaf 54
scale, main 425
scale, mitre 226
scale, vernier 425
scalelike leaves of the cypress 65
scallop 157
scampi 158
scan 323
Scandinavian crispbread 145
Scandinavian Peninsula 18
scanner, optical 121
scapula 98, 99
scapular 78
scarlet runner bean 131
scatter cushion 204
scene 278
scenic route 25
schedule, television programme 313
schnauzer 86
school 444
school bus 362
school secretary's office 445
school, ski 512
sciatic nerve 108
science 414
science room 444
scientific calculator 337
scientific instruments 7, 13
scientific symbols 426
scientific terms 58, 59
scissors 461, 531
sclera 119
sconce 207
scooter, motor 369
score 497
scoreboard 471, 472, 492, 497, 499
scoreboard, current event 497
scoreboard, overall standings 496
scorer 487, 488
scorers and timekeepers 499
scorpion 70
Scotia Plate 27
scouring pad 215
scraper 219, 400, 514
screen 271, 318, 407, 439, 479
screen door 361
screen print 260, 261
screen window 528
screen, fireplace 193
screen, print 331
screen, projection 294
screen, touch 337
screw 221, 301
screw cap 163, 199
screw earrings 264
screw locking nut 536, 537
screw, clamping 224
screw, lock 332
screw, tension adjustment 341
screw-in studs 480
screwdriver 221, 531
screwdriver bit 228
screwdriver, cordless 221
screws, clamping 425
scrimmage: defence 484
scrimmage: offence 485
scroll 301
scroll case 407

scroll foot 200
scroll wheel 327, 332
scrolling 331
scrolling lock key 331
scrolls, Torah 447
scrotum 92, 111
scrub room 464
scrum half 482
scuff rib 358
scuffle hoe 233
scuttle panel 348
sea 5, 24, 32
sea bass 160
sea bream 159
sea kale 126
sea lettuce 123
sea level 26, 33, 37
sea lion 90
sea salt 141
Sea of Japan 19
Sea, Adriatic 18
Sea, Aegean 18
Sea, Arabian 19
Sea, Aral 19
Sea, Baltic 18
Sea, Barents 18
Sea, Beaufort 16
Sea, Black 18, 19
Sea, Caribbean 16
Sea, Caspian 19
Sea, Coral 15
Sea, East China 19
Sea, Irish 18
Sea, Mediterranean 18, 20
Sea, North 18
Sea, Norwegian 18
Sea, Red 19, 20
Sea, South China 19
Sea, Tasman 15
Sea, Weddell 15
sea-level pressure 39
seafood 121
seal 90
sealing material 417
sealing plug 417
sealing ring 404
seam 243, 478
seam pocket 251
seaming 244
seamount 33
seaplane, float 394
search 335
seasoning, cajun spice 139
seasons of the year 38
seat 195, 196, 200, 201, 205, 294, 353,
   369, 467, 501, 523
seat adjuster lever 353
seat back 353
seat back adjustment knob 353
seat belt 353
seat cover 196
seat stay 370
seat tube 370
seat, booster 205
seat, child 356
seat, director's 291
seat, driver 369
seat, love 439
seat, passenger 369
seat, rabbi's 447
seat-belt warning light 355
seats 201, 293
seats, actors' 290
seaweed 123
sebaceous gland 114
secateurs 234
second 298, 428, 498, 515
second assistant camera operator 290
second base 474
second baseman 474
second dorsal fin 74
second hand 424
second molar 101
second premolar 101
second row 482
second space 489
second valve slide 307
second violins 295
second voltage increase 413
second-level domain 334
secondaries 78
secondary altar 446
secondary consumers 45
secondary mirror 7, 9
secondary road 25
secondary root 53

secondary waiting room 465
secretariat 443
section 313
section of a bulb 54
section of a capsule: poppy 60
section of a follicle: star anise 60
section of a grape 59
section of a hazelnut 60
section of a legume: pea 60
section of a peach 57
section of a raspberry 59
section of a silique: mustard 60
section of a strawberry 59
section of a walnut 60
section of an apple 58
section of an orange 58
section of the Earth's crust 26
section, vertical 526
sectional garage door 286
sector 428
security check 391
security grille 442
security guard's workstation 463
security thread 441
security trigger 235
security vestibule 440
sedimentary rocks 26
seed 53, 57, 58, 59, 60
seed coat 57, 61
seeder 231
seeding and planting tools 231
seedless cucumber 128
seeds, poppy 139
segment 58
segment score number 471
seismic wave 27
seismogram 27
seismograph, vertical 27
seismographic recording 403
seismographs 27
select button 327
selection key 327
selective sorting of waste 49
selector, focus 320
selector, four-way 315
selector, orbital-action 227
selector, sound mode 322
selector, speed 176
self-adhesive labels 340
self-contained breathing apparatus 454
self-inflating mattress 530
self-sealing flap 339
self-service meat counter 120
self-timer indicator 314
semaphore signal 375
semi-circle 488
semi-detached houses 289
semi-mummy 530
semibreve 299
semibreve rest 299
semicircle 428
semimembranosus 97
seminal vesicle 111
semiquaver 299
semiquaver rest 299
semitendinosus 97
semolina 144
semolina, flour and 144
Senegal 451
Senegal River 20
sense organs 114
sensitive root 109
sensor probe 178
sensor wiring circuit 357
sensor, optical 332
sensor, safing 354
sensor, wheel speed 357
sensory impulse 110
sensory neuron 110
sensory receptor 110
sensory root 110
sent document recovery 328
sepal 56, 58, 59
septic tank 48
septum 60, 117
septum pellucidum 109
sequencer 310
sequencer control 310
serac 30
serial number 441

serial port 329
serrate 55
serve 487, 490
server 334, 335, 491, 494
server, access 335
service area 25, 389
service bay 346
service judge 490, 494
service line 491
service module 316
service provider, Internet 335
service road 388
service room 447
service station 346, 433
service table 438
service zones 495
service, customer 443
servicer, mobile remote 11
services, financial 442
services, insurance 442
services, loan 442
services, social 465
serving dish 166
serving trolley 202
sesame oil 149
set 291, 492
set dresser 291
set of bells 309
set of utensils 173
set, nail 220
set, socket 223
set, television 439, 444
set-in sleeve 245
sets, previous 492
setsquare 225
setting indicator 511
settings display button 315
seventh 298
sewer 434
sewn-in groundsheet 528, 529
sextet 300
Seychelles 452
shackle 521
shad 160
shade 206
shade, roller 356
shadow 424
shaft 245, 471, 492, 494, 503, 505, 506
shaft, air 278
shaft, axle 351
shake-hands grip 493
shallot 124, 305
shallow root 63
sham 204
shampoo 267
shank 152, 153, 220, 221, 228, 270,
   538
shank protector 398
shaped handle 269
shapes, geometrical 428
shapka 238
shark, morphology of 74
sharp 299
sharpening steel 169
sharpening stone 169
shaving 271
shaving brush 271
shaving foam 271
shaving mug 271
shears, kitchen 173
sheath 55, 533
sheath dress 252
sheath of Schwann 110
sheath skirt 253
sheathing 187
shed 182, 230
sheep 84
sheep shelter 122
sheepskin jacket 249
sheet 515
sheet lead 521
sheet, baking 172
sheet, bath 267
shekel, new 440
shelf 203, 210, 211, 219
shelf channel 211
shell 60, 72, 73, 79, 277, 308, 404
shell membrane 79
shell, bivalve 73
shell, univalve 73
shell, upper 527
shelter 345
shepherd, German 86
shield bug 69
shift key 330
shift: level 2 select 330

shiitake 123
shin guard 480, 513
ship's side 385
shirt 245, 260, 473, 488
shirt, polo 250
shirt, team 486
shirttail 245, 255
shirtwaist dress 252
shock absorber 351, 523
shock absorber, front 369
shock wave 403
shoe 488, 522, 524
shoe shop 437
shoe, parts 240
shoelace 240, 262
shoes 240
shoes, golf 505
shoes, men's 240
shoes, rugby 483
shoes, unisex 242
shoes, women's 241
shoot 53, 63
shoot, bamboo 125
shooting stage 290
shooting star 37
shop 280, 432
shop, clothing 436
shop, coffee 432, 437
shop, decorative articles 437
shop, do-it-yourself 436
shop, electronics 436
shop, gift 436
shop, jewellery 436
shop, leather goods 436
shop, lingerie 436
shop, newsagent's 437
shop, perfume 436
shop, pet 436
shop, record 436
shop, shoe 437
shop, sporting goods 437
shop, tobacconist's 436
shopping bag 276
shopping centre 431, 436
shopping street 432
shopping trolleys 121
shore 33
shore cliff 35
shorelines, examples of 35
short extensor of toes 96
short glove 243
short palmar 96
short peroneal 97
short radial extensor of wrist 97
short service line 495
short sock 257
short track 508
short track skate 508
shortening 149
shorts 254, 261, 313, 473, 480, 483,
   488, 500, 522
shorts, running 263
shortstop 474
shot 472
shot put 472
shot, drop 491
shotgun (smooth-bore) 534
shoulder 83, 86, 92, 94, 223, 302, 342,
   492, 536
shoulder bag 276
shoulder bag with zip 276
shoulder belt 353
shoulder blade 93, 95
shoulder bolt 223
shoulder pad 486
shoulder strap 259, 276, 456, 505, 532
shovel 193, 233, 510, 514
shower 189, 464
shower cubicle 195
shower head 195, 197
shower hose 195, 197
shower, bath and 439
shredder, paper 341
shredding 49
shroud 520
shunt 416
shutoff valve 196, 197
shutter 186, 333
shutter release button 314
shutting stile 185
shuttlecock, feathered 495
shuttlecock, synthetic 495
Siamese 87
sickle 234
side 167, 293
side back vent 244

ASTRONOMY > 2-13;   EARTH > 14-49;   PLANT KINGDOM >50-65;   ANIMAL KINGDOM > 66-91;   HUMAN BEING > 92-119;   FOOD AND KITCHEN > 120-181;   HOUSE > 182-215;
DO-IT-YOURSELF AND GARDENING > 216-237;   CLOTHING > 238-263;   PERSONAL ADORNMENT AND ARTICLES > 264-277;   ARTS AND ARCHITECTURE > 278-311;   COMMUNICATIONS AND
OFFICE AUTOMATION > 312-341;   TRANSPORT AND MACHINERY > 342-401;   ENERGY > 402-413;   SCIENCE > 414-429;   SOCIETY > 430-467;   SPORTS AND GAMES > 468-538

ENGLISH INDEX

side chair 201
side chapel 284
side compression strap 532
side door 380
side electrode 359
side fairings 525
side footboard 377
side handrail 380
side hatch 12
side judge 485
side lane 343
side line 493
side marker light 352, 364, 365
side mirror 269
side panel 248
side plate 166
side rail 219, 365
side span 344
side vent 28, 361
side view 478
side wall 517
side, left 272
side, right 272
sideboard 203
sidelinc 484, 487, 488
sidepiece 273
sideshoot 53
sidewall 358, 365
siding 375
Sierra Leone 451
sieve 171
sifter 172
sight 119, 533, 535
sight, normal 419
sighting line 533
sighting mirror 533
sigmoid colon 106
sign, route 362, 363
signal box 375
signal gantry 375
signal lamp 179
signature, holder's 441
signature, official 441
signet ring 264
silencer 351, 367, 368, 369
silk 61
sill 28
sill of frame 186
sill plate 187
sill rail 187
silos 381
simple eye 67
simple leaves 55
simple organisms and echinoderms 66
Singapore 453
single bed 439
single reed 306
single room 439
single seat 380
single-breasted jacket 244
single-burner camp stove 529
single-leaf bascule bridge 345
single-lens reflex (SLR) camera: front view
314
singles service court 495
singles sideline 491, 495
singlet 500
sink 164, 197, 439, 464
sink with waste disposal unit 197
sink, surgeon's 465
sinker 538
siphon 72
siphonal canal 73
siren 455
sistrum 309
site plan 183
sitting room 188
sixth 298
skate 158, 506
skate, acrobatic 527
skate, goalkeeper's 507
skate, ice hockey 527
skate, roller speed 527
skate, short track 508
skateboard 526
skateboarder 526
skateboarding 526
skater 527
skater: long track 508
skater: short track 508
skates, speed 508
skating kick 514
skating step 514
skating, figure 509
skating, inline 527
skating, speed 508

skeg 519
skeleton 98
skerry 35
ski 510, 523
ski area 512
ski boot 510, 511
ski glove 510
ski goggles 510
ski hat 514
ski jumper 513
ski jumping 513
ski lift arrival 512
ski pants 254
ski pole 510, 514
ski rack 356
ski resort 512
ski school 512
ski stop 511
ski suit 510, 514
ski tip 514
ski trail, alpine 512
ski trail, cross-country 512
ski, downhill/Super G 510
ski, jumping 513
ski, slalom 510
ski, slalom G 510
ski-jumping boot 513
ski-jumping suit 513
skid 395
skiers' lodge 512
skimmer 173, 184
skin 57, 58, 59, 110, 114
skin surface 114
skins, won ton 147
skip 400, 515
skipping-rope 500
skirt 251, 492
skirt finger 383
skirting board 191
skirts, examples of 253
skis, examples of 510
skull 92
skull, child's 100
skull, lateral view of 100
skullcap 238
skunk 88
sky coverage 39
skylight 183
skylight, bathroom 189
skylight, stairwell 189
slalom G ski 510
slalom ski 510
slalom, giant 511
slalom, special 511
slalom, super giant 511
slash, double 334
slat 205
sled 236
sleeper-cab 364
sleeping bags, examples of 530
sleeping car 376
sleepsuit 261
sleet 41
sleeve 244, 395, 501
sleeve strap 248
sleeve strap loop 248
sleigh bells 309
slice 173
slide 214
slide, glass 421
sliding cover 327
sliding door 195, 286
sliding door, automatic 286
sliding folding window 287
sliding jaw 425
sliding rail 353, 521
sliding seat 501
sliding weight 422
sliding window 287
slingback shoe 241
slip 258
slip joint 222
slip joint pliers 222
slip presenter 346
slip, stage 421
slip-on 242
slip-on pyjamas 261
slip-stitched seam 245
slipover 250
sliproad 343
slope 342
slope, beginners' 512
slope, difficult 512
slope, expert 512
slope, intermediate 512
sloping comice 279

slot 167, 178, 221, 274
slot, card reader 346, 442, 443
slot, deposit 442
slot, passbook update 442
slot, PC card 336
slot, transaction record 442
slots, memory card 471
Slovakia 450
Slovenia 450
slow lane 343
slow-burning stove 192
slow-motion 319
small blade 531
small carton 163
small crate 162
small drawstring bag 276
small hand cultivator 232
small intestine 106
small open crate 162
small saucepan 175
smash 491
smell and taste 116
smelt 159
smock 255
smog 47
smoke baffle 192
smoke detector 454
smoked ham 153
smooth hound 158
snacks' sale counter 294
snail 72, 157
snail dish 173
snail tongs 173
snail, morphology of 72
snake 76
snake, coral 77
snake, garter 77
snap 538
snap fastener 243, 249, 274
snap shackle 521
snap-fastening front 261
snap-fastening tab 249
snap-fastening waist 260
snare 308, 535
snare drum 295, 308
snare head 297, 308
snare strainer 308
snatch 500
snelled fishhook 538
snooker 503
snout 74, 75
snow 41
snow brush with scraper 356
snow guard 523
snow, acid 48
snow-grooming machine 512
snowblower 365
snowboard 513
snowboard, alpine 513
snowboard, freestyle 513
snowboarder 513
snowboarding 513
snowmobile 523
snowsuit 261
snuggle suit 260
soap dish 195
soap, toilet 267
soba noodles 147
social services 465
social worker's office 463
society 430
sock 257, 480, 486, 492
socket head 221
socket set 223
socket tester 217
socket-contact 198
socks 247, 483
sofa 200
sofa bed 204
soft cheeses 151
soft contact lens 272
soft palate 116, 117
soft pedal 304, 311
soft ray 74
soft shell clam 157
soft-drink dispenser 346
softball 477
softball bat 477
softball glove 477
software, email 334
soil 48
soil and waste stack 194
soil fertilization 47
soil profile 54
soiled utility room 462, 464
solar array 316

solar cell 337, 410, 411
solar eclipse 4
solar energy 54, 410
solar panel 7
solar radiation 45, 46, 410, 411
solar reflectors 316
solar shield 10
solar system 2
solar-cell panel 411
solar-cell system 411
solder 218
soldering and welding tools 218
soldering gun 218
soldering iron 218
sole 161, 229, 247, 509, 511
soleplate 208
soleus 96
solid 414, 415
solid body 303
solid centre auger bit 228
solid line 342
solid rocket booster 12
solid, amorphous 414
solids 429
solitaire ring 264
Solomon Islands 453
solution, multi-purpose 272
solvent extraction unit 405
Somalia 451
somen noodles 147
sorghum 61
sorghum: panicle 61
sorting plant 49
sorting, glass 49
sorting, manual 49
sorting, metal 49
sorting, optical 49
sorting, paper/paperboard 49
sorting, plastics 49
sorus 52
sostenuto pedal 304
sou'wester 239
soufflé dish 172
sound box 297, 302
sound engineer 291
sound field control 322
sound hole 301
sound mode lights 322
sound mode selector 322
sound receiver 460
sound recording equipment 291
sound system 354
soundboard 296, 297, 301, 302, 304
soundbox 302
sounding balloon 38
soup bowl 166
soup spoon 168
soup tureen 166
sour cream 150
source, power 416
South 23
South Africa 452
South America 14, 17, 34
South American Plate 27
South China Sea 14, 19
South Pole 15, 21
south pole 416
South-Southeast 23
South-Southwest 23
Southeast 23
Southeast Indian Ridge 34
Southern hemisphere 21
Southwest 23
Southwest Indian Ridge 34
soy sauce 140
soybean sprouts 131
soybeans 131
space 298, 330, 469
space bar 330
space probe 37
space shuttle 12, 37
space shuttle at takeoff 12
space, epidural 110
space, non-breaking 330
spacelab 13
spacer 409, 467
spacesuit 10
spade 233, 468
spade bit 228
spadix 57
spaghetti 146
spaghetti squash 129
spaghetti tongs 173
spaghettini 146
Spain 449
spar 392

spare tyre 361
spareribs 153
spark plug 359, 360
spark plug body 359
spark plug cable 350
spark plug gap 359
spark plug seat 359
sparking plug 237
sparrow 80
spatula 173
spatulate 55
speaker 294, 320, 326, 327, 328, 336,
518
speaker cover 324
spear 125
special effects buttons 320
special effects selection dial 320
special slalom 511
specification plate 228
specimen collection centre waiting room
465
specimen collection room 465
spectacles 273
spectacles case 275
spectacles, examples of 273
spectrum, electromagnetic 418
speed control 176
speed governor 287
speed grand prix motorcycle and rider 525
speed selector 176, 177
speed selector switch 227, 228, 270
speed skates 508
speed skating 508
speed-increasing gearbox 413
speedometer 355, 368, 501
spelt wheat 143
spencer 254
spent fuel storage bay 409
sperm whale 90
spermatozoon 111
sphagnum, prickly 51
sphenoid bone 100
sphenoidal fontanelle 100
sphenoidal sinus 117
sphere 429
sphincter muscle of anus 106
spices 138
spices, marinade 139
spicules 4
spider 70
spider web 70
spider, crab 70
spider, garden 70
spider, morphology of 70
spider, water 70
spike 57, 473
spike file 341
spiked shoe 476
spill, oil 48
spillway 406
spillway chute 406
spillway gate 406
spinach 127
spinach tagliatelle 146
spinal column 98, 109
spinal cord 109, 110
spinal cord, structure of 109
spinal ganglion 109, 110
spinal nerve 109, 110
spindle 177, 201, 425
spine of scapula 99
spine, anterior nasal 100
spinner 538
spinneret 70
spinning rod 537
spinous process 110
spiny lobster 158
spiny ray 74
spiracle 67
spiral 221
spiral arm 6
spiral beater 176
spiral binder 340
spiral cloud band 43
spiral nail 220
spiral rib 73
spiral screwdriver 221
spiral thread 70
spire 285
spirit level 225
spirulina 123
spit 35
splat 200
splay 285
spleen 103
splenius muscle of head 97

ASTRONOMY > 2-13;   EARTH > 14-49;   PLANT KINGDOM >50-65;   ANIMAL KINGDOM > 66-91;   HUMAN BEING > 92-119;   FOOD AND KITCHEN > 120-181;   HOUSE > 182-215;
DO-IT-YOURSELF AND GARDENING > 216-237;   CLOTHING > 238-263;   PERSONAL ADORNMENT AND ARTICLES > 264-277;   ARTS AND ARCHITECTURE > 278-311;   COMMUNICATIONS AND
OFFICE AUTOMATION > 312-341;   TRANSPORT AND MACHINERY > 342-401;   ENERGY > 402-413;   SCIENCE > 414-429;   SOCIETY > 430-467;   SPORTS AND GAMES > 468-538;

splints 461
split link 538
split peas 130
splitting, nucleus 415
spoiler 366, 392
sponge-tipped applicator 266
sponson 523
spool 536, 537
spool axle 537
spool-release mechanism 537
spoon 167, 531
spoon, tasting 173
spoons, examples of 168
spores 52
sporting goods shop 437
sports and games 468
sports car 347
sports complex 431
sports on wheels 526
sports, ball 474
sports, motor 524
sports, precision and accuracy 502
sports, racket 493
sports, strength 500
sportswear 262
spot 207
spotlight 290, 455
spotlights 293
spout 180, 181
spout assembly 197
spout, pouring 215
spray 208
spray arm 214
spray button 208
spray control 208
spray nozzle 236
spray, pepper 456
sprayer 236
spread collar 245
spreader 273
spring 27, 32, 38, 206, 212, 222, 312, 535
spring balance 423
spring binder 339
spring onion 124
spring toggle 221
spring washer 222
spring, coil 351
springboard 496
springboard, 1 m 518
springboard, 3 m 518
sprinkler hose 236
sprinklers 408
sprocket 523
sprouts, soybean 131
spruce 65
sprung base 204
spur 29, 228, 308
squamous suture 100
square 429
square move 470
square root key 337
square root of 427
square trowel 216
square-headed tip 221
squash, acorn 129
squash, crookneck 129
squash, pattypan 129
squash, spaghetti 129
squash, straightneck 129
squid 157
squirrel 82
Sri Lanka 453
stabilizer 467
stabilizer fin 386
stabilizer jack 361
stack 35, 402
stacking chairs 201
stadium 431
staff 298
staff cloakroom 438, 465
staff entrance 438, 445
staff lounge 443, 463
stage 278, 292, 293, 421
stage clip 421
stage curtain 292, 293
stage, shooting 290
stage-house 292
stained glass 285
stained-glass window 446
stair 293, 294
stairs 188, 191, 283, 345, 378, 404, 439
stairways 283
stairwell 189

stairwell skylight 189
stake 230, 231
stalactite 31
stalagmite 31
stalk 51, 57, 58, 59, 125
stalk vegetables 125
stamen 56, 58
stamp pad 338
stanchion 509
stand 27, 174, 176, 206, 269, 277, 308, 537
stand, intravenous 464
stand, witness 440
standard lamp 206
standard poker hands 468
stands, movable 444
stapes 116
staple remover 341
stapler 341
staples 341
star diagonal 8
star drag wheel 537
star of David 447
starboard hand 387
starch 61
starch granule 50
starling 80
start button 424
start key 328, 330
start line 473
start switch 213
starter 237, 516
starter button 368
starter handle 235
starting block 516
starting grid 524
starting grip (backstroke) 516
starting line 524
starting line, 1,500 m 473
starting line, 10,000 m and 4 x 400 m relay 473
starting line, 100 m and 100 m hurdles 472
starting line, 110 m hurdles 472
starting line, 200 m 472
starting line, 400 m, 400 m hurdles, 4 x 100 m relay 473
starting line, 5,000 m 472
starting line, 800 m 473
starting pistol 472
starting positions 518
state 23
states of matter 414
station circle 39
station concourse 374
station entrance 378
station model 39
station name 378
station platform 375
station, bus 432
station, emergency 345
station, fire 433
station, international space 11
station, land 38
station, police 433
station, railway 430, 432
station, relay 316
station, service 433
station, underground railway 432
stationery 337
statue 446
steak 152
steak knife 168
steam 402
steam control knob 181
steam generator 402
steam iron 208
steam nozzle 181
steam pressure drives turbine 408
steamer 175
steamer basket 175
steamer, electric 179
steel 259
steel cable 535
steel casing 417
steel pen 312
steelyard 422
steeplechase 472
steering column 350
steering cylinder 400
steering system 351
steering tube 371
steering wheel 350, 354, 385, 525
stem 51, 52, 53, 54, 181, 199, 384, 424
stem bulb 387
stem propeller 384

stem, underground 54
step 191, 219, 364
step chair 201
step groove 191
step stool 219
step, diagonal 514
step, skating 514
stepladder 219
stepladders 219
steppe 40
stepper 501
steps 184, 188, 412
steps to ripeness 62
stereo control 326
stereo sound system 322
stereo sound system, mini 325
sterile dressing 461
sterilization room 464, 465
stern 386, 519
sternal artery 71
sternocleidomastoid 96
sternum 98
stethoscope 460
stick 273, 301
sticks 309
stifle 83
stigma 56, 60
stile 201
stile groove of sash 186
stile tongue of sash 186
still camera, 35 mm 10
still cameras 315
still photographer 291
still water level 33
Stilton 151
sting 68
stipule 55
stirrup sock 476
stitch 240
stitches 477
stitching 243, 262
stock 296, 412, 534
stock pot 175
stockade 282
stocking 257, 259, 506
stomach 73, 103, 106
stomach throw 499
stomach, cardiac 71
stomach, pyloric 71
stone 57
stone deflector 376, 377
stone for sacrifice 283
stone fruits 132
stone marten 88
stone steps 183
stone, Coyolxauhqui 283
stone, sharpening 169
stoner 173
stool, bar 438
stop 86, 319
stop button 235, 323, 328, 424
stop key 319
stop knob 305
stop, end 226
stop, tail 224
stop/clear key 323
stopcock 194
stopper 267, 532
stopwatch 424
storage compartment 361, 364, 455
storage door 211
storage furniture 202
storage room, medical equipment 465
storage tank 405
storage, frozen food 121
storage, glove 464
store, department 437
store, food 439
storeroom 438, 444
stork 80
storm collar 193
stormy sky 41
straight 468
straight flush 468
straight jaw 222
straight position 518
straight skirt 253
straight-up ribbed top 247
straightening iron 269
straightneck squash 129
strainer 174, 177, 180
strainer body 197
strainer coupling 197
strainer, mesh 171
straining, utensils for 171
strait 24

Strait of Gibraltar 18
Strait, Bass 15
Strait, Bering 16
Strait, Cook 15
Strait, Torres 15
strap 265, 424, 477, 500
strap eyelet 315
strap loop 532
strap system 303
strap, chin 522
strap, shoulder 456, 532
strapless brassiere 259
stratocumulus 42
stratopause 37
stratosphere 37
stratum basale 114
stratum corneum 114
stratum granulosum 114
stratum lucidum 114
stratum spinosum 114
stratus 42
straw 163
straw hut 288
strawberry 132
strawberry, section 59
street 25, 433, 435
street light 434
street sweeper 365
street, shopping 432
strength sports 500
stretch-limousine 347
stretcher 202, 460
stretcher area 462
strider, water 69
striker 218, 481
string 301, 302
stringed instruments 301
stringer 396
stringing 492, 494
strings 297, 304
strip 286
strip door 286
strip, magnetic 441
strip, tackless 190
stroke judge 516
strokes 490
structure 186
structure of a fern 52
structure of a flower 56
structure of a house 188
structure of a leaf 55
structure of a lichen 50
structure of a moss 51
structure of a mushroom 52
structure of a plant 53
structure of a tree 63
structure of an alga 51
structure of the biosphere 44
structure of the ear 116
structure of the Earth 26
structure of the spinal cord 109
structure of the Sun 4
structure, roll 525
structure, truss 11
strut 187, 308, 387, 412
strut, wing 394
stud 187, 263, 357, 478
studded tyre 358
student 444
student's desk 444
students' lockers 445
students' room 445
study 189
stump 63, 479
sturgeon 158
style 56, 57, 58, 59, 60
stylist, hair 290
stylobate 279
styloid process 100
stylus 312, 337
subarctic 40
subbase 342
subclavian artery 102
subclavian vein 102
subcutaneous tissue 114
subduction 27
subfloor 187, 190
subgrade 342
subhead 313
sublimation 414
submarine canyon 33
submarine line 334
submarine pipeline 404
subsiding cold air 43
subsoil 54
substitutes' bench 481

substructure 403
subterranean stream 31
subtract from memory 337
subtract key 337
subtraction 427
subtractive colour synthesis 418
suburb 431
suburban commuter railway 375
suburbs 25
subway 375
subwoofers 321
sucker 62, 72
suction hose 455
Sudan 451
sudoriferous duct 114
sugar 149
sugar bowl 166
sugar thermometer 171
sugar, brown 149
sugar, granulated 149
sugar, powdered 149
suit 251
suit carrier 277
suit, protective 525
suit, racing 508, 525
suit, ski-jumping 513
suitcase 277
suite, operating 464
sulcus terminalis 118
sulphur dioxide emission 48
sulphuric acid emission 48
sum 427
sumac 139
summer 38
summer solstice 38
summit 29, 512
summit lodge 512
sump 360
sump gasket 360
Sun 2, 4, 5, 38
sun deck 385
sun roof 349
sun visor 354, 356, 361
Sun, structure 4
sundae spoon 168
sundeck 387
sundial 424
sundress 252
sunflower 56
sunflower-seed oil 149
sunglasses 273
sunken swimming pool 184
sunspot 4
super giant slalom 511
supercooling 414
superficial peroneal nerve 108
superior cymbal 308
superior dental arch 116
superior mesenteric artery 102, 107
superior mesenteric vein 102
superior nasal concha 117
superior rectus muscle 119
superior semicircular canal 116
superior vena cava 102, 103, 104
supermarket 120, 433, 437
supersonic jet 37, 394
supplement, colour 313
supplement, literary 313
supply pipe 197
supply point 198
supply room 464
supply, cash 443
support 9, 199, 201, 375
support, backboard 489
support, neck 525
sural nerve 108
surface course 342
surface element 210
surface insulation 12
surface of the water 518
surface prospecting 403
surface runoff 45
surface water drain 434
surface, cooking 179
surface, hard (cement) 492
surface, posting 341
surface, synthetic 492
surface, working 224
surface-piercing foils 387
surfaces, plane 428
surfaces, playing 492
surgeon's sink 465
surgery, minor 462
Suriname 448
surround loudspeaker 321

ASTRONOMY > 2-13;   EARTH > 14-49;   PLANT KINGDOM >50-65;   ANIMAL KINGDOM > 66-91;   HUMAN BEING > 92-119;   FOOD AND KITCHEN > 120-181;   HOUSE > 182-215;
DO-IT-YOURSELF AND GARDENING > 216-237;   CLOTHING > 238-263;   PERSONAL ADORNMENT AND ARTICLES > 264-277;   ARTS AND ARCHITECTURE > 278-311;   COMMUNICATIONS AND
OFFICE AUTOMATION > 312-341;   TRANSPORT AND MACHINERY > 342-401;   ENERGY > 402-413;   SCIENCE > 414-429;   SOCIETY > 430-467;   SPORTS AND GAMES > 468-538

suspended span 344
suspender 259, 344
suspender belt 259
suspension 380
suspension arm 212, 351
suspension band 458
suspension bogie 376
suspension bridge 344
suspension cable 344
suspension file 340
suspension strut 367
suspension system 351
suspension, back 522
suspensory ligament 119
sustaining pedal 304, 311
suture 60, 73
suture, coronal 100
suture, lambdoid 100
suture, squamous 100
swallow 80
swallow hole 31
Swaziland 452
sweat shirt 262
sweater, crew neck 255
sweaters 250, 254
swede 129
Sweden 450
sweeper, street 365
sweeping hip throw 499
sweet pepper, green 128
sweet pepper, red 128
sweet pepper, yellow 128
sweet potato 124
sweetbreads 154
sweetcorn 61
swell organ manual 305
swell pedals 305
swift 80
swimming 516
swimming goggles 516
swimming pool 386, 517
swimming pool, above ground 184
swimming pool, sunken 184
swimming trunks 263
swimsuit 263, 516
swing bridge 344
Swiss army knife 531
Swiss chard 125
switch 198, 211, 219, 229, 416
switch lock 228
switch, hat 332
switch, limit 287
switch, nightshot 320
switch, on-off 177, 181
switch, on/off 209
switch, power 315
switch, power/functions 320
switch, reversing 221, 228
switch, speed selector 227, 228
switch, trigger 227, 228, 229
switched outlet 322
Switzerland 450
swivel 403, 535, 538
swivel base 224
swivel flex 269
swivel head 224
swivel lock 224
swivel wall lamp 207
swordfish 159
symbols 468
symbols, scientific 426
sympathetic ganglion 109
symphony orchestra 295
symphysis pubis 111, 112
synagogue 447
synapse 110
sync cable 337
synthesis, colour 418
synthesizer 310
synthetic shuttlecock 495
synthetic sponge 266
synthetic surface 492
Syria 452
syringe 460
syringe for irrigation 460
syrup, corn 149
syrup, cough 467
syrup, maple 149
system buttons 310
system of units, international 426
system, air conditioning 46
system, braking 351
system, cooling 351
system, electrical 351
system, fuel supply 351
system, remote manipulator 11, 12

system, solar 2
system, steering 351
system, strap 303
system, suspension 351
system, transmission 351
systems, car 351

T

T-bar 512
T-shirt dress 261
T-strap shoe 241
tab 248, 274, 340
Tabasco™ sauce 140
tabernacle 446
table 202, 493, 502
table lamp 206
table mixer 176
table of results 518
table salt 141
table tennis 493
table tennis ball 493
table tennis bat 493
table, bedside 439, 464
table, changing 205
table, operating 464
table, overhead 464
table, service 438
table, water 48
tables, examples of 202
tablespoon 168
tablet 467
tablinum 280
tabloid 313
tabulation key 330
tabulation left 330
tabulation right 330
tachometer 355, 368
tack 220, 519
tackle box 538
tackless strip 190
tag 240, 262
tagliatelle, spinach 146
tahini 140
tail 71, 76, 82, 83, 86, 90, 111, 393,
510, 514, 526, 536
tail assembly 393
tail boom 395
tail comb 268
tail feather 78
tail fin 393, 395
tail of helix 115
tail pipe 351
tail pipe 351
tail pole 412
tail skid 395
tail stop 224
tail, ion 6
tailback 485
tailored collar 251
tailpiece 297, 301
tailplane 393, 395
tailrace 407
Tajikistan 452
tajine 174
talk key 327
talking drum 297
tall tumbler 165
talon 79
talus 99
tamarillo 136
tamarin 91
tamarind paste 140
tambourine 309
tamper 181
tandem 373
tang 167, 169, 216
Tanganyika, Lake 20
tank 13, 385, 454
tank farm 404
tank hatch cover 385
tank, fuel 351, 366, 369
tank, septic 48
tank, water 181
tanker 364, 381, 384
tanker body 364
Tanzania 451
tap 195
tape 225
tape counter 323
tape dispenser 341
tape guide 341
tape lock 225
tape measure 225
tape recorder select button 322
tape selector 323

tape, grip 526
tape, magnetic 319
tape, Teflon 216
tape, white 487
taproot 63
tarantula, red-kneed 70
taro 124
tarragon 142
tarsus 78
Tasman Sea 15
Tasmania 15
taste bud 118
taste receptors 118
tasting spoon 173
taxiway 388
taxiway line 389
tea 148
tea bag 148
tea cup 166
tea infuser 173
tea, black 148
tea, green 148
tea, oolong 148
teacher 444
teacher's desk 444
teachers' room 445
team shirt 476, 480, 486
team's emblem 506
team, medical 499
teapot 166
tear-off calendar 338
teas, herbal 148
teaser comb 268
teaspoon 168
technical delegates 509
technical events 511
technical room 345
technical specifications 358
technical terms 57
technician, lighting 291
techniques 487
tectonic lake 32
tectonic plates 27
teddy 258
tee 505, 515
tee line 515
teeing ground 504
teeth 101
Teflon tape 216
telecommunication antenna 386, 387
telecommunication satellite 335
telecommunication satellites 316
telecommunications by satellite 317
telephone 327, 439
telephone answering machine 328
telephone cable 434
telephone index 338
telephone line 334
telephone list 327
telephone network 317
telephone, communication 327
telephoto lens 314
teleport 317
telescope 7
telescope base 7
telescope, Hubble space 37
telescopic aerial 325
telescopic boom 397, 455
telescopic corridor 389
telescopic fork 366
telescopic front fork 369
telescopic leg 460
telescopic sight 420, 534
television 318
television programme schedule 313
television set 318, 439, 444
television set, large-screen 321
telltale 520
telson 71
temperate forest 44
temperature control 178, 208, 211
temperature gauge 355
temperature of dew point 39
temperature scale 37
temperature selector 178, 212, 213
temperature sensor 358
temple 92
Temple of Huitzilopochtli 283
Temple of Tlaloc 283
temple, Aztec 283
tempo control 311
temporal bone 98, 100
ten 427
ten commandments 447
tendril 62
tennis 490

tennis ball 492
tennis player 492
tennis racket 492
tennis shoe 492
tenor drum 308
tension adjuster 528
tension adjustment 537
tension adjustment screw 341
tension rod 308
tension rope 297
tension screw 308
tension spring 355, 500
tensor of fascia lata 96
tent, trailer 361
tentacle 72
tents, examples of 528
tepee 288
teres major 97
teres minor 97
terminal 198, 210, 404
terminal arborization 110
terminal box 411
terminal bronchiole 105
terminal bud 53
terminal filament 109
terminal lobe 62
terminal moraine 30
terminal tackles 538
terminal, container 430
terminal, electronic payment 121
terminal, ground 322
terminal, negative 416, 417
terminal, positive 416, 417
terminal, remote control 315
terminals, aerial 322
terminals, loudspeaker 322
terminals, video and digital 315
termite 69
terraced houses 289
terrine 174
tertial 78
tertiary consumers 45
test button 454
test-lamp 217
tester screwdriver 217
testicle 111
testis 71
Tethys 3
textile floor coverings 190
Thailand 453
thallus 50, 51
theatre 292, 432, 433
theatre, Greek 278
theatre, home 321
theatre, operating 464, 465
thermal energy 402
thermodynamic temperature,
measurement of 426
thermometer 404, 424
thermometer, instant-read 171
thermometer, oven 171
thermometer, sugar 171
thermopause 37
thermosphere 37
thermostat 178
thermostat control 211
thermostat, adjustable 179
thigh 78, 83, 86, 93, 95, 111, 112
thigh pad 486
thigh stocking 257
thigh-boot 241
thimble 425
thinning razor 269
third 298
third base 474
third baseman 474
third finger 115
third row 482
third valve slide 307
thoracic legs 71
thoracic vertebra (12) 99
thorax 67, 68, 92, 94
thread 221
thread, radial 70
thread, security 441
thread, spiral 70
thread, support 70
threaded rod 223
three-blade propeller 394
three-four time 298
three-of-a-kind 468
three-pin socket 198
three-quarter coat 248
three-tier car carrier 377
threshold 185
throat 78, 224, 492, 538

throat protector 476
throttle 237
throttle cable 237
throttle control 235, 332
throwing circle 472, 473
thrust device 312
thrust tube 312
thruster 10
thrusters, attitude control 12
thumb 115, 243, 477
thumb hook 307
thumb piston 305
thumb rest 306, 460
thumb, opposable 91
thumbscrew 223
thyme 142
tibia 98
tibial nerve 108
tick 70
ticket collecting booth 378
ticket collector 294, 374
ticket counter 390
tie 273, 299
tie beam 187
tier 281
tierceron 284
Tierra del Fuego 17
tiers 278
tiger 89
tight end 485
tight head prop 482
tightening buckle 532
tights 257
tile 12, 279, 280, 283
tiller 520
tilt-back head 176
timber 280
timber frame 187
time code 291
time display/recording button 320
time signatures 298
timekeeper 488, 498, 509
timekeepers, scorers and 499
timer 178, 179, 501
timer socket 210
timetable 374
timing belt 360
timpani 295
tin opener 170, 180, 531
tine 167
tip 55, 125, 167, 216, 218, 220, 221,
227, 246, 273, 487, 503, 510, 536
tip of nose 117
tip protector 460
tip section 536
tip, finger 339
tip-ring 536, 537
tipper body 401
tipper truck 401
tips, examples of 221
tissue holder 195
Titan 3
Titania 3
Titicaca, Lake 17
title deed 469
title display button 320
Tlaloc, Temple of 283
toad, common 75
toaster 178
tobacconist's shop 436
toe 79, 86, 92, 94, 226, 229, 247
toe binding 514
toe clip 370, 372
toe guard 459, 476
toe loop 509
toe pick 509
toe piston 305
toe-piece 511
toe-strap 242
toenail scissors 265
toepiece 514
toggle 249
toggle bolt 221
Togo 451
toilet 188, 189, 194, 195, 196, 439,
440, 443, 445, 464
toilet bag 276
toilet bowl 196
toilet soap 267
toilet, ladies' 294, 439
toilet, men's 294, 439
toilets 437, 463, 465
toilets, customers' 438
toilette, eau de 267
token 469
tom-tom 308

ASTRONOMY > 2-13;   EARTH > 14-49;   PLANT KINGDOM >50-65;   ANIMAL KINGDOM > 66-91;   HUMAN BEING > 92-119;   FOOD AND KITCHEN > 120-181;   HOUSE > 182-215;
DO-IT-YOURSELF AND GARDENING > 216-237;   CLOTHING > 238-263;   PERSONAL ADORNMENT AND ARTICLES > 264-277;   ARTS AND ARCHITECTURE > 278-311;   COMMUNICATIONS AND
OFFICE AUTOMATION > 312-341;   TRANSPORT AND MACHINERY > 342-401;   ENERGY > 402-413;   SCIENCE > 414-429;   SOCIETY > 430-467;   SPORTS AND GAMES > 468-538

561

tomatillo 128
tomato 128
tomato coulis 140
tomato paste 140
tomato, currant 128
tombolo 35
tone control 303
tone control, bass 303
tone control, treble 303
Tonga 453
tongs 173, 193
tongue 106, 116, 117, 154, 240, 246, 262, 297, 305, 509, 511
tongue sheath 76
tongue, dorsum 118
tonsil 116
tool belt 225
tool box 225
tool holder 229
tool kit 372
tool shelf 219
tool storage area 209
tool tether 10
tools 209
tools for loosening earth 233
tools, electricity 217
tools, hand 232
tools, masonry 216
tools, plumbing 216
tools, pruning and cutting 234
tools, seeding and planting 231
tools, soldering and welding 218
tools, watering 236
tooth 74, 76, 226, 227, 235, 270, 398, 400
tooth guard 486
toothbrush 272
toothbrush shaft 272
toothbrush well 272
toothed jaw 222
toothpaste 272
top 63, 202, 219
top box 369
top cap 417
top cushion 502
top deck 404
top deckboard 396
top flap 532
top hat 238
top ladder 455
top lift 240
top of dam 406
top pocket 502
top rail 185, 201, 202, 205
top rail of sash 186
top stitched pleat 253
top stitching 246, 260
top-level domain 334
topping 536
topsoil 54
toque 239
Torah scrolls 447
toric lens 419
tornado 43
tornado and waterspout 43
torque adjustment collar 228
torque converter 212
Torres Strait 15
tortellini 146
tortilla 145
torus 429
total 423
total eclipse 4, 5
totally reflecting mirror 420
tote bag 276
toucan 80
touch 114
touch judge 483
touch pad 336
touch pad button 336
touch screen 337
touchline 481, 483
Toulouse sausage 156
touring bicycle 373
touring motorcycle 369
touring tyre 358
tow bar 361
tow safety chain 361
tow truck 364
towel rail 195
towel, bath 267
towel, kitchen 215
tower 284, 344, 412, 413
tower case: back view 329
tower case: front view 329
tower control room 388

tower crane 397
tower ladder 455
tower mast 397
tower mill 412
tower silo 122
tower, bell 446
tower, cooling 402
tower, transmitting 316
towing device 364
towing hitch 361
town hall 432
town houses 289
toyshop 436
tracery 285
trachea 105
track 374, 378, 398, 431, 472, 523, 524
track and field 472
track frame 207
track idler 398
track lighting 207
track number 323
track roller frame 398
track search keys 323
track, long 508
track, railway 432
track, short 508
tracklaying tractor 398
tracks, dolly 290
tractor engine compartment 400
tractor unit 364
traditional dwellings 288
traditional musical instruments 296
traffic lane 343
traffic lights 434
tragus 115
trail-view mirror 364
trailer car 380
trailer caravan 361
trailer tent 361
trailing edge 392
trailing edge flap 392
train direction sign 379
train indicator 374
trainer 489, 498
training set 261
training suit 262
training wall 406
transaction receipt 443
transaction record slot 442
transactions, business 335
Transantarctic Mountains 15
transceiver, radar 457
transceiving dish 316
transceiving parabolic aerial 316
transept 285
transept spire 284
transfer of heat to water 408
transfer ticket dispensing machine 379
transfer, heat 415
transform plate boundaries 27
transformer 207, 407
transit shed 381
transmission 212
transmission dish 316
transmission system 351
transmission to consumers 402, 413
transmitter 327
transmitting tower 316
transparent pockets 274
transpiration 45
transport and machinery 342
transverse bulkhead 384
transverse colon 106
transverse dunes 36
transverse process 110
transverse flute 306
trap 194, 196, 197, 292
trap coupling 197
trap, leghold 535
trap, petroleum 403
trapdoor 281
trapezius 96, 97
trapezoid 429
travel agency 436
travel bag 276
traveller 520, 521
traveller's cheque 441
travelling block 403
travelling crab 397
travelling crane 407
traverse arch 284
trawler 384
tray 205, 219, 225, 277
tray, disc 318
tray, drip 181
tray, food 162

tray, input 333
tray, output 333
tread 191
tread design 358
treatment room 465
treble bridge 304
treble clef 298
treble fishhook 538
treble keyboard 296
treble pickup 303
treble register 296
treble ring 471
treble tone control 303, 322, 325
tree 63
tree fern 52
tree frog 75
tree pruner 234
tree, ornamental 182
tree, palm 64
tree, structure 63
tree, trunk 63
trees 504
trefoil 285
trench 33
trench coat 248
Trench, Aleutian 34
Trench, Japan 34
Trench, Java 34
Trench, Kermadec-Tonga 34
Trench, Kuril 34
Trench, Mariana 34
Trench, Peru-Chile 34
Trench, Philippine 34
Trench, Puerto Rico 34
Trench, Ryukyu 34
triage room 463
triangle 295, 309, 429
triangular bandage 461
triangular body 297
triangular fossa 115
triceps bar 501
triceps of arm 97
tricuspid valve 104
tricycle, child's 373
trifoliate 55
trigger 235, 332, 454, 534
trigger guard 534
trigger switch 227, 228, 229
trilby 238, 239
trill 299
trim 299
trim panel 352
trim ring 210
trimaran 521
trimmer 237, 271
Trinidad and Tobago 449
trio 300
trip lever 196
trip mileometer 355
tripe 154
tripod 8
tripod accessories shelf 8
tripod stand 308
triticale 143
Triton 3
trolleys, shopping 121
trombone 307
trombones 295
Tropic of Cancer 20, 21, 22
Tropic of Capricorn 20, 21, 22
tropical climates 40
tropical cyclone 43
tropical cyclone names 43
tropical forest 44
tropical fruits 136
tropical rain forest 40, 44
tropical wet-and-dry (savanna) 40
tropopause 37, 46
troposphere 37
trot 83
trough 33, 39, 418
trousers 246, 263, 476, 486, 499, 506, 525
trousers, examples of 254
trout 161
trowel 232
truck 526, 527
truck crane 397
truck, collection 364
truck, concrete mixer 365
truck, emergency 345
truck, tow 364
trucking 364
trucks, examples of 364
truffle 123
trumpet 307

trumpet interchange 342
trumpets 295
trunk 52, 62, 63, 75, 93, 95, 277
trunk, cross section 63
trunks, boxing 498
truss structure 11
trussing needle 173
tsetse fly 69
tub 212, 214, 230
tub rim 212
tuba 295, 307
tube 163, 199, 461
tube retention clip 199
tube, draw 421
tube, flash 420
tube, Pitot 525
tube, watering 365
tuber vegetables 124
tubular bells 295, 309
tubular element 210
tubular heater 405
tuck position 518
tug 384
tulip 56
tuna 160
tundra 44
tungsten-halogen bulb 199
tunic 255
tunic dress 252
tuning buttons 322
tuning control 325, 326
tuning controls 318
tuning gauge 308
tuning knob 326
tuning peg 302, 303
tuning pin 304
tuning ring 297
tuning slide 307
tuning wire 305
Tunisia 451
tunnel 378
tunnel, road 345
turban 239
turbine 402
turbine shaft turns generator 408
turbo-alternator unit 402
turbojet engine 393
turbot 161
Turkey 452
turkey 81, 155
Turkmenistan 452
turmeric 138
turn 299
turn-up 246
turnbuckle 498, 521
turning judges 517
turning wall 517
turnip 129
turnouts 454
turntable 176, 344, 400, 401
turntable mounting 455
turret 282
turret cap 420
turtle 76
turtle, morphology of 76
Tuvalu 453
TV mode 319
TV power button 319
TV/video button 319
tweeter 324
tweezers 461
twig 63
twin-set 255
twist 228
twist bar 500
twist bit 228
twist drill 228
twist grip throttle 368
twist handle 332
two pairs 468
two-blade propeller 394
two-burner camp stove 529
two-leaf door 362
two-person tent 528
two-seater settee 200
two-storey house 289
two-two time 298
two-way collar 248
tympanum 75, 279, 285
type of air mass 39
type of fuel 346
type of high cloud 39
type of low cloud 39
type of middle cloud 39
types of eclipses 4, 5
types of golf club 505

types of grip 493
types of inflorescence 57
types of move 470
types of passenger coach 376
types of stroke 517
typhoon 43
tyre 349, 358, 364, 371, 522, 525
tyre barrier 524
tyre inflator 346
tyre pump 370
tyre valve 371
tyre, all-season 358
tyre, knobby 369
tyre, nubby 525
tyre, performance 358
tyre, spare 361
tyre, studded 358
tyre, touring 358
tyre, winter 358
tyres, examples of 358

U

u quark 414
U.S. habitation module 11
U.S. laboratory 11
udon noodles 147
Uganda 451
Ukraine 450
ulna 98
ulnar extensor of wrist 97
ulnar flexor of wrist 96, 97
ulnar nerve 108
ultraviolet radiation 418
umbel 57
umbo 73
umbra 4, 5
umbrella 273
umbrella pine 65
umbrella stand 273
Umbriel 3
umpire 479, 485, 487, 490, 495, 515
unbleached flour 144
under tail covert 78
underarm briefcase 275
underarm crutch 466
underarm rest 466
undergarment 524
underground 281, 435
underground chamber 278
underground flow 45
underground map 379, 380
underground railway 378
underground railway station 432
underground station 378
underground stem 54
underground train 378, 380
underlay 190
underpass 344
undershirt 476
underwater light 184
underwear 247, 258
underwiring 259
undressing booth 465
ungulate mammals 83
ungulate mammals, examples of 84
unicellulars 66
uniform 456
union 427
uniparous cyme 57
unisex headgear 239
unisex shoes 242
unison 298
unit price 423
unit, ambulatory care 465
unit, glass collection 49
unit, intensive care 464
unit, paper collection 49
unit, turbo-alternator 402
United Arab Emirates 452
United Kingdom of Great Britain and Northern Ireland 449
United States of America 448
univalve shell 73
univalve shell, morphology of 73
university 432
unleavened bread 145
unloading dock 437, 439
up-and-over garage door 286
uphaul 519
upholstery nozzle 209
upkeep, painting 219
upper 511
upper blade guard 227
upper bowl 181
upper confining bed 402

upper cuff 511
upper deck 363, 392
upper edge 493
upper eyelid 75, 87, 119
upper lateral lobe 62
upper lateral sinus 62
upper limb 103
upper lip 116, 305
upper lobe 105
upper mandible 78
upper mantle 26
upper shell 511, 527
upper strap 511
upper tail covert 78
upperworks 521
upright 184, 466
upright piano 304
upright vacuum cleaner 209
upright, padded 489
upstage 292, 293
Ural Mountains 18
Uranus 2, 3
urban map 25
ureter 107
urethra 107, 112
urinary bladder 107, 111, 112
urinary meatus 111
urinary system 107
URL 334
URL (uniform resource locator) 334
uropod 71
Uruguay 448
USB port 329, 336
used syringe box 457
user, home 335
user, Internet 334
uses, Internet 335
usual terms 57
utensils, set 173
uterovesical pouch 112
uterus 112, 113
uvula 116, 117
Uzbekistan 452

V

V-neck 244, 250
V-neck cardigan 250
vacuole 50, 66
vacuole, contractile 66
vacuole, food 66
vacuole, forming food 66
vacuum cleaner, upright 209
vacuum coffee maker 181
vacuum diaphragm 360
vacuum distillation 405
vacuum flask 532
vagina 112, 113
valance 204
valley 29, 32
valve 60, 73, 307
valve casing 307
valve cover 360
valve seat 196
valve spring 360
vamp 240, 263
van 365
vanilla extract 140
vanity cabinet 195
vanity case 277
vanity mirror 354
Vanuatu 453
vapour 415
variable ejector nozzle 394
varnish, nail 265
vastus lateralis 96, 97
vastus medialis 96
Vatican City State 450
vault 284, 443
vault, barrel 281
vaulting horse 496, 497
VCR controls 319
VCR mode 319
VCR power button 319
veal, cuts of 152
veal, diced 152
veal, minced 152
vegetable brush 173
vegetable dish 166
vegetable garden 122, 182
vegetable sponge 267
vegetables 124
vegetables, fruits and 120
vegetation and biosphere 44
vegetation regions 44

vehicle rest area 345
vehicle, crew return 11
veil 536
vein 55
veins 102
velarium 281
Velcro® closure 260
velvet-band choker 264
Venezuela 448
venom canal 76
venom gland 76
venom-conducting tube 76
vent 354
vent brush 268
vent door 365
vent, cooling 336
ventilated rib 534
ventilating circuit 194
ventilating grille 209
ventilator 380
ventral artery 71
ventral nerve cord 71
Venus 2, 3
verbena 148
vermicelli, rice 147
vermiform appendix 106
vernal equinox 38
vernier 422, 425
vernier caliper 425
vernier scale 425
Versailles parquet 190
vertebra, cervical 99
vertebra, lumbar 99
vertebral body 110
vertebral shield 71
vertical control 329
vertical ground movement 27
vertical move 470
vertical pivoting window 287
vertical pupil 76
vertical section 526
vertical seismograph 27
vertical side band 487
vertical-axis wind turbine 412
vessel, blood 104
vest 247, 261, 263
vestibular nerve 116
vestibule 116, 280
vestibule, security 440
vibrating mudscreen 403
vibrato arm 303
vibrissa 82
vice 224
vice-skip 515
Victoria, Lake 20
video and digital terminals 315
video cassette 319
video entertainment system 471
video monitor 329
video port 329, 336
videocassette recorder 319
videotape operation controls 320
Vietnam 453
view camera 315
view, anterior 92, 94
view, front 478
view, posterior 93, 95
view, side 478
viewfinder 315
viewfinder, electronic 320
village 430, 512
vine leaf 62, 126
vine shoot 62
vine stock 62
vinegar, balsamic 141
vinegar, cider 141
vinegar, malt 141
vinegar, rice 141
vinegar, wine 141
vinyl grip sole 261
viola 301
violas 295
violet 56
violin 301
violin family 295, 301
viper 77
visceral ganglion 73
visceral pleura 105
visible light 418
vision 419
vision defects 419
visor 367, 459, 506, 525
visor hinge 367
visor, sun 356
Vistula River 18
visual display 471

vitelline membrane 79
vitreous body 119
vocal cord 105
voice edit buttons 310
voice recorder button 337
voice selector 311
volcanic bomb 28
volcanic island 33
volcanic lake 32
volcano 26, 28
volcano during eruption 28
volcano, effusive 28
volcano, explosive 28
volcanoes, examples of 28
Volga River 18
volley 490
volleyball 487
volt 426
voltage decrease 402, 413
voltage increase 402, 408
volume control 303, 310, 311, 319, 322,
    325, 326, 328, 329
volume readout 346
volute 200
volva 52
vulture 80
vulva 94, 113

W

wad 534
waders 538
wadi 36
wading bird 79
waffle iron 178
wagon tent 528
waist 93, 95, 240, 301
waist belt 205, 532
waistband 246, 247, 249
waistband extension 246
waistcoat 244, 255
waistcoats and jackets 254
waiter, wine 438
waiting area 442
waiting room 463
waiting room, family 462
waiting room, main 465
waiting room, secondary 465
wakame 123
walk 83
walk-in wardrobe 189
walkie-talkie 456
walking aids 466
walking frame 466
walking leg 67, 70
walking stick 273, 466
walkway 436
wall 5, 58, 184, 528
wall cabinet 164
wall cloud 43
wall lantern 207
wall light 207
wall tent 528
wall, eye 43
wall, inuch 516
wallet 275, 337
wallet section 274
walnut 64, 133
walnut, section 60
waning gibbous 5
wardrobe 189, 203, 439
wardrobe, walk-in 189
warehouse 430
warm air 41
warm temperate climates 40
warm-air baffle 192
warming plate 181
warming, global 46
warning lights 355
warning plate 228
warning track 475
wasabi 141
wash tower 214
washbasin 194, 195
washer 417
washer nozzle 348
washers 222
washing machine 194, 212
wasp-waisted corset 259
Wassily chair 200
waste basket 341
waste disposal unit 197
waste layers 47
waste pipe 194, 196
waste water 48
waste, household 47, 48

waste, industrial 47, 48
waste, non-reusable residue 49
waste, nuclear 48
waste, selective sorting of 49
water 402
water and mineral salts, absorption of 54
water bottle 371
water bottle clip 371
water cannon 455
water carrier 532
water chestnut 124
water cools used steam 408
water goblet 165
water hazard 504
water hose 214
water intake 407
water is pumped back into steam
    generator 408
water jets 518
water jug 166
water key 307
water level 181
water level indicator 179
water main 434
water meter 194
water pollution 48
water pressure gauge 455
water pump pliers 222
water service pipe 194
water spider 70
water strider 69
water table 31, 48
water tank 181, 272
water turns into steam 408
water, waste 48
water-level selector 212
water-level tube 208
water-steam mix 402
water-tank area 394
watercourse 32, 48
watercraft, personal 523
watercress 127
waterfall 31, 32
watering can 236
watering tools 236
watering tube 365
watermark 441
watermelon 135
waterproof pants 260
waterspout 43
watt 426
wave 33, 418
wave base 33
wave clip 268
wave height 33
wave length 33
wave, shock 403
wavelength 418
waves, radio 418
wax 514
wax bean 131
wax gourd 128
wax seal 196
waxed paper 162
waxing gibbous 5
waxing kit 514
Way, Milky 6
Way, Milky (seen from above) 6
Way, Milky (side view) 6
weasel 88
weather map 38, 39
weather radar 38, 392
weather satellite 38
weather station, aircraft 38
weather station, buoy 38
weather station, ocean 38
weatherboard 185, 186
web 75, 79, 477
web frame 385
web, spider 70
webbed foot 75
webbed toe 79
Webcam 332
Weddell Sea 15
wedding ring 264
wedge 305
wedge lever 229
weeder 232
weeding hoe 233
weekend case 277
weeping willow 64
weighing platform 423
weight 422, 423, 500
weight trainer 501
weightlifting 500
weightlifting belt 500

weightlifting shoe 500
weights 501
well, diving 184
well, injection 402
well, production 402
welt 240, 244
welt pocket 244, 250
West 23
West Coast mirror 363
West Indies 16
West-Northwest 23
West-Southwest 23
Western hemisphere 21
Western meridian 22
whale 90
whale, killer 90
whale, sperm 90
wheat 61, 143
wheat, grain 61
wheat, spelt 143
wheat: spike 61
wheel 231, 277, 364, 522, 525, 526,
    527, 535
wheel cylinder 357
wheel mouse 332
wheel speed sensor 357
wheel tractor 399
wheel trim 349
wheel, chain 522
wheel, fine adjustment 425
wheel, scroll 327, 332
wheel, steering 350, 385, 525
wheelbarrow 231
wheelchair 467
wheelchair lift 363
wheelhouse 384
wheels, sports on 526
whelk 157
whipping cream 150
whisk 172
whiskers 87
whisky tumbler 165
whistle 180
White 469, 470
white 418
white blood cell 104
white bread 145
white cabbage 126
white chocolate 148
white cue ball 503
white matter 109, 110
white mustard 138
white onion 124
white pepper 138
white rice 147
white spot ball 502, 503
white square 470
white stone 470
white tape 487, 493, 495
white wine glass 165
white-tailed deer 84
whiting 161
whole wheat flour 144
wholegrain mustard 140
wholemeal bread 145
whorl 72, 73
whortleberry, red 132
wicket 479
wicketkeeper 479
wide receiver 485
wide-angle lens 314
wigwam 288
wild boar 84
wild rice 143
Wilkes Land 15
willow 478
willow, weeping 64
winch 287, 364, 521
winch controls 364
wind 47, 48
wind deflector 364
wind direction 39
wind direction and speed 39
wind energy 412
wind indicator 520
wind instruments 306
wind speed 39
wind synthesizer controller 311
wind turbines and electricity production
    412
wind vane 413
wind, prevailing 43
windbag 296
windcheater 249
winding adjustment 420
windmill 412

ASTRONOMY > 2-13; EARTH > 14-49; PLANT KINGDOM >50-65; ANIMAL KINGDOM > 66-91; HUMAN BEING > 92-119; FOOD AND KITCHEN > 120-181; HOUSE > 182-215;
DO-IT-YOURSELF AND GARDENING > 216-237; CLOTHING > 238-263; PERSONAL ADORNMENT AND ARTICLES > 264-277; ARTS AND ARCHITECTURE > 278-311; COMMUNICATIONS AND
OFFICE AUTOMATION > 312-341; TRANSPORT AND MACHINERY > 342-401; ENERGY > 402-413; SCIENCE > 414-429; SOCIETY > 430-467; SPORTS AND GAMES > 468-538

563

ENGLISH INDEX

window 178, 179, 186, 189, 210, 274, 349, 352, 361, 380, 392, 519
window awning 528
window tab 340
window winder handle 352
window, balcony 189
window, dormer 182
window, stained-glass 446
windows, examples of 287
windscreeen 385
windscreen 348, 364, 366, 369, 392, 523
windscreen wiper 348, 355
windscreen wiper blade 355
windshaft 412
wine cellar 438
wine vinegar 141
wine waiter 438
wine waiter corkscrew 170
wine, beer and 120
wing 13, 68, 78, 286, 348, 364, 393, 525, 536
wing covert 78
wing nut 223
wing pallet 396
wing rib 392
wing slat 393
wing strut 394
wing vein 67
wing, bird 78
wing, high 394

winglet 393, 394
wings 292
winter 38
winter precipitations 41
winter solstice 38
winter sports 515
winter tyre 358
wiper arm 355
wiper blade rubber 355
wiper control 354
wire 417, 501
wire beater 176
wire brush 309
wire cutter 217
wire frame 529
wire nut 217
wire stripper 217
wiring circuit, sensor 357
wisdom tooth 101
wishbone boom 519
withers 83, 86
witness stand 440
wok 174
wok set 174
wolf 88
woman 94
women's clothing 251
women's gloves 243
women's headgear 239
women's shoes 241
won ton skins 147

wood 505
wood chisel 229
wood ear 123
wood firing 192
wood flooring 190
wood flooring on cement screed 190
wood flooring on wooden base 190
wood flooring types 190
wood frog 75
wood storage space 192
woodpecker 80
woods 25
woodstrip flooring 190
woodwind family 295
woofer 324
Worcestershire sauce 140
work bench and vice 224
work surface 164
worker 68
worker, honeybee 68
working surface 224
workstation, security guard's 463
worm 365
wrap, knee 500
wrapover dress 252
wrapover skirt 253
wrapover top 255
wrench, four-way lug 356
wrench, ratchet socket 223
wrenches 216, 223
wrist 86, 93, 95, 115

wrist band 500
wrist guard 527
wrist strap 510, 514
wrist-length glove 243
wristband 486, 492
writing brush 312
writing case 275
writing instruments 312

X

X-ray unit, mobile 462
X-rays 418
xylophone 295, 309

Y

Y-tube 460
yacht, motor 385
yak 85
yard 430
yard line 484
yard, coal storage 402
yard-long bean 130
yarn ball 477
yaw 395
yellow 418
yellow ball 503
yellow onion 124
yellow sweet pepper 128
yellowjacket 69

Yemen 452
yen 440
yogurt 150
yoke 245, 249, 255
yoke skirt 253
yolk 79
Yucatan Peninsula 16
Yugoslavia 450
yurt 288

Z

Zambia 452
zebra 84
zester 169
Zimbabwe 452
zinc can (anode) 417
zinc-electrolyte mix (anode) 417
zip 261, 265, 277, 528
zip fastener 249
zither 296
zona pellucida 112
zone, commercial 431
zone, free guard 515
zone, overtaking 472
zones, service 495
zoom lens 314, 320
zygomatic bone 98, 100

ASTRONOMY > 2-13;   EARTH > 14-49;   PLANT KINGDOM >50-65;   ANIMAL KINGDOM > 66-91;   HUMAN BEING > 92-119;   FOOD AND KITCHEN > 120-181;   HOUSE > 182-215
DO-IT-YOURSELF AND GARDENING > 216-237;   CLOTHING > 238-263;   PERSONAL ADORNMENT AND ARTICLES > 264-277;   ARTS AND ARCHITECTURE > 278-311;   COMMUNICATIONS AND
OFFICE AUTOMATION > 312-341;   TRANSPORT AND MACHINERY > 342-401;   ENERGY > 402-413;   SCIENCE > 414-429;   SOCIETY > 430-467;   SPORTS AND GAMES > 468-538

Index français

A

abaissement de la tension 402, 413
abat-jour 206
abat-son 285
abats 154
abattant 195, 196, 202, 203
abdomen 67, 68, 70, 71, 78
abeille 68
abeille : ouvrière, morphologie 68
abri 345, 375
abri des joueurs 474
abribus 434
abricot 132
abside 285
absidiole 284, 285
absorption d'eau 54
absorption de dioxide de carbone 54
absorption de sels minéraux 54
absorption par le sol 46
absorption par les nuages 46
abyssin 87
accastillage 521
accent 299
accès au réservoir à essence 349
accès aux quais 374
accessoires 209, 356, 372
accessoires au butane 529
accessoires au propane 529
accessoires de foyer 193
accessoires de l'objectif 314
accessoires, automobile 356
accessoires, pêche 538
accessoiriste 291
accord 299
accordéon 296
accotement 342
accottoir 200
accoudoir 205, 467
accouplement électrique 365
accroche-mouche 536
accueil 442
accumulateur 357
acidification des lacs 48
acromion 99
acrotère 279
acteur 290
action du vent 45
actrice 291
adaptateur de cassette vidéo compacte
320
adaptateur de courant 336
adaptateur de fiche 198, 271
addition 337, 427
addition en mémoire 337
administration 445
adresse URL 334
adresse URL (localisateur universel de
ressources) 334
aérateur à gazon 237
aérateur de toit 361
aérateur latéral 361

aérocyste 51
aérofrein 412
aérogare 390
aérogare de passagers 389
aérogare satellite 389
aéroglisseur 383
aéroport 25, 388, 430
affichage 337
affichage de l'heure de départ 374
affichage des données 319
affichage des fonctions 310
affichage des stations 325
affichage numérique 423, 461
affichage radar 457
affiche 294
affiche publicitaire 380
afficheur 318, 322, 325, 327, 423
afficheur prix 346
afficheur totaliseur 346
afficheur volume 346
affluent 32
Afghanistan 452
Afrique 14, 20, 34, 451
Afrique du Sud 452
agar-agar 123
agence de voyages 436
agenda 338
agent de police 456
agglomération 430
agitateur 212
agneau haché 153
agrafe 312
agrafes 341
agrafeuse 341
agriculture intensive 46, 48
agrumes 134
aide de caisse 121
aide-arbitre 488
aide-mémoire des procédures 10
aides à la marche 466
aigle 81
aiguillage 375
aiguille 35, 36, 422, 460
aiguille à brider 173
aiguille à piquer 173
aiguille aimantée 533
aiguille des dixièmes de seconde 424
aiguille des minutes 424
aiguilles de nettoyage 218
aiguilles de pin 65
aiguilles de sapin 65
aiguillon 68
ail 124
aile 13, 68, 78, 348, 364, 393, 412, 536
aile antérieure 67
aile arrière 387
aile avant 387
aile Dame 470
aile de quartier 240, 262
aile droite 482
aile du nez 117
aile gauche 482

aile haute 394
aile postérieure 67
aile Roi 470
aile, oiseau 78
aileron 392, 519, 525
ailes en V 387
ailette 213, 393, 394
ailette à ressort 221
ailier défensif droit 484
ailier défensif gauche 484
ailier droit 482, 489, 507
ailier gauche 482, 489, 507
ailier rapproché 485
aimant 341, 416
aimant de retenue 180
aine 92, 94
air chaud 41
air chaud ascendant 43
air froid 41
air froid subsident 43
aire d'accueil 462, 465
aire d'attente 442
aire de jeu 471
aire de jeux 386
aire de manœuvre 388
aire de préparation de l'étalage 120
aire de ravitaillement 346
aire de réception 120
aire de réception des produits laitiers 120
aire de repos 25
aire de service 25, 389
aire de stationnement 389
aire de trafic 388
airelle 132
aisselle 92, 94
ajowan 139
akène 59, 60
Albanie 450
albatros 80
albumen 79
albumen farineux 61
alcool à 90° 461
Algérie 451
algue 51
algue brune 51
algue rouge 51
algue verte 51
algue, structure 51
algues 123
alimentation 120
alimentation solaire 337
alimentation sur secteur 326
aliments congelés 121
aliments prêts-à-servir 121
alkékenge 132
allée 120, 230, 504
allée de jardin 182
Allemagne 450
alliance 264
alligator 77
allumeur 350, 360
allures, cheval 83

alluvions 32
alose 160
Alpes 18
altérations 299
alternateur 350, 360, 402, 413
alternative 330
alternative : sélection du niveau 3 330
alto 301
alto-cumulus 42
alto-stratus 42
altos 295
alule 78
alvéole 198, 505
alvéole de plaque 359
alvéole dentaire 101
amande 57, 133
amanite vireuse 52
amarante 143
amas globulaire 6
Amazone 17
amble 83
ambulance 460, 462
Amérique centrale 14, 16
Amérique du Nord 14, 16, 34
Amérique du Sud 14, 17, 34
Amériques 448
ameublement de la maison 200
amibe 66
amidon, grain 50
amorce 534
amorti 491
amortisseur 270, 287, 351, 523
amortisseur arrière 367
amortisseur avant 369
amortisseur magnétique 422
ampère 426
amphibiens 75
amphithéâtre romain 281
ampli-syntoniseur 325
ampli-syntoniseur : vue arrière 322
ampli-syntoniseur : vue avant 322
amplitude 418
ampoule 199, 416, 467
ampoule de la trompe utérine 113
amygdale 116
amygdale linguale 118
amygdale palatine 118
ananas 136
anatomie 96
anatomie du coquillage bivalve 73
anatomie du homard 71
anche 305, 306
anche double 306
anche simple 306
anchois 159
anconé 97
Andorre 449
andouillette 156
âne 84
anémomètre 413
aneth 142
angle aigu 428

angle droit 428
angle obtus 428
angle rentrant 428
Angola 452
anguille 159
Anik 317
animalerie 436
anis 142
anneau 52, 210, 270, 271, 423, 424,
489, 536
anneau brisé 538
anneau d'étanchéité en cire 196
anneau de départ 537
anneau de retenue 460
anneau de suspension 270
anneau de tête 537
anneau de traction 460
anneau oculaire 78
anneaux 264, 496, 497
annonce publicitaire 313
annonceur 518
annulaire 115
anode 417
anorak 263
anse 215, 236, 537
Antarctique 14, 15
antéfixe 279
antenne 7, 67, 68, 71, 326, 327, 349,
369, 392, 395, 457, 487
antenne d'émission 316
antenne d'émission/réception 316
antenne de télécommunication 386, 387
antenne domestique 316
antenne parabolique 321
antenne parabolique d'émission/réception
316
antenne radio 382, 384, 386, 387, 525
antenne télescopique 325
antennule 71
anthélix 115
anthère 56
anticlinal 403
anticyclone 39
Antigua-et-Barbuda 449
Antilles 14, 448
antilope 84
antiseptique 461
antitragus 115
anus 71, 73, 106, 111, 112
aorte 104, 105
aorte abdominale 102, 107
aorte ascendante 103
aorte descendante 103
apex 72, 73, 101, 118
apophyse épineuse 110
apophyse mastoïde 100
apophyse styloïde 100
apophyse transverse 110
apothécie 50
Appalaches 16
appareil à télémètre couplé 315

ASTRONOMIE > 2-13;   TERRE > 14-49;   RÈGNE VÉGÉTAL > 50-65;   RÈGNE ANIMAL > 66-91;   ÊTRE HUMAIN > 92-119;   ALIMENTATION ET CUISINE > 120-181;   MAISON > 182-215;   BRICO-
AGE ET JARDINAGE > 216-237;   VÊTEMENTS > 238-263;   PARURE ET OBJETS PERSONNELS > 264-277;   ARTS ET ARCHITECTURE > 278-311;   COMMUNICATIONS ET BUREAUTIQUE > 312-341;
RANSPORT ET MACHINERIE > 342-401;   ÉNERGIES > 402-413;   SCIENCE > 414-429;   SOCIÉTÉ > 430-467;   SPORTS ET JEUX > 468-538

565

appareil à visée reflex mono-objectif : vue avant 314
appareil à visée reflex numérique : dos 315
appareil de forage 403
appareil de Golgi 50, 66
appareil de prise de son et d'enregistrement 291
appareil de protection respiratoire 454
appareil de radiographie mobile 462
appareil digestif 106
appareil jetable 315
appareil numérique 315
appareil photographique 35 mm 10
appareil reflex 6 X 6 mono-objectif 315
appareil respiratoire 105
appareil urinaire 107
appareils de conditionnement physique 500
appareils de mesure 424
appareils de son portatifs 325
appareils électroménagers 176, 208
appareils électroménagers divers 180
appareils photographiques 315
appareils scientifiques 7
appartement du commandant 387
appartements en copropriété 289
appartenance 427
appeau 535
appendice vermiculaire 106
applicateur-mousse 266
applique 207
applique du robinet 197
applique orientable 207
appoggiature 299
approvisionnement en numéraire 443
appui de fenêtre 187
appui-bras 352, 353
appui-flèche 535
appui-pied 515
appui-pieds 224
appui-tête 353
après-rasage 271
aquifère captif 402
ara 80
Arabie saoudite 452
arachnides 67
arachnoïde 109
araignée 70
araignée, morphologie 70
araignée-crabe 70
aramé 123
arbitre 479, 481, 483, 485, 488, 490, 495, 498, 499, 507, 509, 515
arbitre adjoint 509
arbitre en chef 475, 485
arborisation terminale 110
arbre 63, 177, 412
arbre à cames 360
arbre cannelé 355
arbre d'ornement 122, 230
arbre d'ornement 182
arbre de l'hélice 387
arbre de Noël 404
arbre de roue 351
arbre de transmission 383
arbre de transmission longitudinal 351
arbre fruitier 122
arbre lent 413
arbre moteur 395
arbre rapide 413
arbre, structure 63
arbres 504
arbres feuillus, exemples 64
arbuste 230
arc 428
arc à poulies 535
arc de cercle 480
arc de l'aorte 102, 103, 104
arc diagonal 284
arc formeret 284
arc insulaire 33
arc-boutant 284, 285
arc-doubleau 284
arc-en-ciel 41
arcade 281, 284
arcade dentaire inférieure 116
arcade dentaire supérieure 116
arceau 230, 458, 519
arche 447
arche naturelle 35
archet 301
archipel 24
architecture 278
architrave 279

archives médicales 465
Arctique 14
ardillon 246, 538
arène 281
aréole 113
arête 29, 526
arête supérieure 493
Argentine 448
argyronète 70
Ariel 3
armature 219, 259, 277, 528
armature de la clé 299
armoire 202
armoire inférieure 164
armoire réfrigérée 120
armoire supérieure 164
armoire-penderie 203
arpège 299
arraché 500
arrache-clou 220
arrangements des parquets 190
arrêt 319, 323, 328
arrêt d'autobus 434
arrêt-court 474
arrêt/effacement de mémoire 323
arrière 482, 489, 518
arrière centre 487
arrière court 491
arrière droit 481, 487
arrière gauche 481, 487
arrivée des remontées mécaniques 512
arrondie 55
arrondissement 25
arroseur canon 236
arroseur oscillant 236
arroseur rotatif 236
arrosoir 236
arsenal stérile 464
artère abdominale dorsale 71
artère arquée 102
artère axillaire 102
artère brachiale 102
artère carotide primitive 102
artère dorsale du pied 102
artère fémorale 102
artère iliaque 103
artère iliaque commune 102, 107
artère iliaque interne 102, 107
artère mésentérique inférieure 107
artère mésentérique supérieure 102, 107
artère pulmonaire 102, 104, 105
artère rénale 102, 107
artère sous-clavière 102
artère sternale 102
artère tibiale antérieure 102
artère ventrale 71
artères 102
artichaut 127
article 313
articles de bureau 337
articles de maroquinerie 274
articles divers, bureau 341
articles ménagers 215
articulation 355, 536
articulation de la pelleteuse 399
arts 278
arts de la scène 294
As 468
asa-fœtida 139
ascenseur 281, 287, 435, 439
ascot 245
Asie 14, 19, 34, 452
asperge 125
asphalte 405
aspirateur 407
aspirateur à main 208
aspirateur-balai 209
aspirateur-traineau 209
aspirine 461
assaisonnement au chili 139
assiette à dessert 166
assiette à salade 166
assiette creuse 166
assiette plate 166, 531
assistance 440
assistant-accessoiriste 291
assistant-réalisateur 291
assistants des avocats 440
astéroïdes, ceinture 3
asthénosphère 26
astigmatisme 419
astragale 99
astronautique 10
astronomie 2

atelier de mécanique 346
atelier diesel 375
athlète : bloc de départ 473
athlétisme 472
Atlas 20
atlas 69, 99
atmosphère 44, 48
atmosphère terrestre, coupe 37
atoll 35
atome 414
atomes 414
âtre 192
atrium 280
attache 273, 308, 535
attache d'accordage 297
attache de pavillon 306
attache de sécurité 10
attache du tube 199
attache pour outils 10
attaches parisiennes 341
attaquant central 487
attaquant de pointe 481
attaquant de soutien 481
attaquant droit 487
attaquant gauche 487
attaque 485
attelles 461
attraction 416
aubergine 128
aubier 63
augmentation de l'effet de serre 46
auriculaire 115
aurore polaire 37
Australie 14, 34, 453
autel secondaire 446
auto-caravane 361
auto-inversion 326
autobus 362, 435
autobus à impériale 363
autobus articulé 363
autobus scolaire 362
autocar 362
autoclave 464
autocuiseur 174
automne 38
automobile 347
automobile, organes des systèmes 350
autoroute 25, 343, 431
autoroute de ceinture 25
autotrophes 45
autres signes 299
Autriche 450
autruche 80
auvent 348, 361, 401, 528
auvent de fenêtre 528
avance rapide 319, 323, 326, 328
avançon 538
avant 518
avant court 491
avant droit 482
avant gauche 482
avant-bras 86, 93, 95
avant-champ 474
avant-scène 292
avant-toit 283
aven 31
avenue 25, 433
avertisseur 354, 368, 377
avertisseur de détresse 454
avertisseur pneumatique 364
avion d'affaires 394
avion de ligne 37
avion de ligne supersonique 394
avion léger 394
avion long-courrier 392
avion supersonique 37
avion, mouvements 395
avion-cargo 394
avion-citerne amphibie 394
avions, exemples 394
avocat 128
avoine 61, 143
avoine : panicule 61
axe central 491
axe de tambour 537
axe du pédalier 372
axe horaire 7
axel 509
axis 99
axone 110
Azerbaïdjan 452
azimut 9

B

babeurre 150
babines 86
bâbord 387
babouin 91
bac 219
bac à boue 403
bac à compost 231
bac à glaçons 211
bac à légumes 211
bac à plante 230
bac à viande 211
bac d'alimentation 333
bac de ramassage 237
bac de recyclage 49
bac de sortie 333
bac ramasse-jus 179
bâche spirale 407
bacon américain 156
bacon canadien 156
badminton 494
bagage à main 276
bagages 276
bagel 144
bague 307
bague de blocage 221, 425
bague de correction dioptrique 420
bague de fiançailles 264
bague de réglage 236
bague de réglage du couple de serrage 228
bague de serrage 306
bagues 264
baguette 243, 301
baguette de flanc 349
baguette épi 144
baguette parisienne 144
baguettes 309
Bahamas 448
Bahreïn 452
baie 5, 24, 59
baie d'Hudson 16
baie de genièvre 138
baies 132
baignoire 189, 194, 195, 439
bain moussant 267
bain-marie 175
baladeur 326
baladeur numérique 325
baladeur pour disque compact 325
baladeuse 217
balai 193, 215
balai à feuilles 237
balai à franges 215
balai à neige à grattoir 356
balai d'essuie-glace 355
balai métallique 309
balalaïka 297
balance à fléau 422
balance de cuisine 171
balance de précision 423
balance de Roberval 422
balance électronique 423
balance romaine 422
balancier 236
balancier d'extension 501
balancier de traction 501
balayeuse 365
balcon 189, 293, 447
balconnet 211
baleine 90, 259, 273
baleine de col 245
ballast électronique 199
balle 534
balle de baseball 476
balle de baseball, coupe 477
balle de cricket 478
balle de fil 477
balle de golf 505
balle de liège 477
balle de softball 477
balle de tennis 492
balle de tennis de table 493
ballerine 241
ballon 181
ballon de basket 488
ballon de boxe 498
ballon de football 480, 486
ballon de rugby 483
ballon de volleyball 487
ballon-sonde 38
balluchon 276
balustrade 283
banane 136

banane plantain 136
banc 201, 379, 437, 446
banc de musculation 501
banc de sable 33
banc des accusés 440
banc des avocats de l'accusation 440
banc des avocats de la défense 440
banc des joueurs 485, 487, 506
banc des juges 440
banc des officiels 507
banc des pénalités 507
banc des remplaçants 481
banc du jury 440
bandage triangulaire 461
bande 502, 506
bande antidérapante 526
bande blanche 487
bande d'ancrage 190
bande de gaze 461
bande de filet 491
bande de tissu élastique 461
bande élastique 246
bande magnétique 319, 441
bande métallisée holographique 441
bande nuageuse spirale 43
bande transporteuse 49
bande ventilée 534
bande verticale de côté 487
bandoulière 276
Bangladesh 453
banjo 296
banlieue 25, 431
banque 432, 437, 442, 469
banque de données 335
banquette 195, 201, 353
banquette arrière 353
banquise d'Amery 15
banquise de Filchner 15
banquise de Ross 15
bar 203, 293, 386, 432, 436, 438
bar commun 160
bar-salon 439
barbacane 282
Barbade 449
barbe 61
barboteuse 261
barbotin 398
bardane 129
barmaid 438
barmaid 438
barquette 162
barrage 406
barre 273, 500, 501, 520
barre à dorsaux 501
barre à pectoraux 501
barre à triceps 501
barre blindée 407
barre d'écoute 520, 521
barre d'espacement 330, 467
barre de flèche 520
barre de maintien 363
barre de mesure 298
barre de poussée 286
barre de pression 304
barre de repos des marteaux 304
barre de reprise 298
barre de retenue 211
barre des témoins 440
barre fixe 496, 497
barreau 191, 201, 205, 479
barres asymétriques 496, 497
barres parallèles 496, 497
barrette 268
barrette négative 359
barrette positive 359
barrière 205, 434
barrière de pneus 524
bas 257, 259, 506
bas de ligne 538
bas résille 257
bas-cuissarde 257
base 7, 118, 269, 370, 454, 533
base de dormant 186
base de la vague 33
baseball 474
baseball, lancer 475
baseball, position des joueurs 474
basilaire 435
basilic 142
basketball 488
basque 259
bassin 230, 381, 517
bassin de compétition 517
bassin de radoub 381
bassinet 107
basson 306
bassons 295

INDEX FRANCAIS

ASTRONOMIE > 2-13;   TERRE > 14-49;   RÈGNE VÉGÉTAL > 50-65;   RÈGNE ANIMAL > 66-91;   ÊTRE HUMAIN > 92-119;   ALIMENTATION ET CUISINE > 120-181;   MAISON > 182-215;   BRIC
LAGE ET JARDINAGE > 216-237;   VÊTEMENTS > 238-263;   PARURE ET OBJETS PERSONNELS > 264-277;   ARTS ET ARCHITECTURE > 278-311;   COMMUNICATIONS ET BUREAUTIQUE > 312-34
TRANSPORT ET MACHINERIE > 342-401;   ÉNERGIES > 402-413;   SCIENCE > 414-429;   SOCIÉTÉ > 430-467;   SPORTS ET JEUX > 468-538

bateaux et embarcations, exemples 382
bâti 202
bâti du brûleur 529
bâtiment administratif 381
bâtiment du réacteur 409
bâton 476, 477, 514
bâton de ski 510
bâton de softball 477
bâtonnet 119
bâtonnet de colle 341
bâtons de golf, types 505
battant 186, 309
batte 478
batterie 221, 228, 308, 416
batterie d'accumulateurs 359, 411
batterie d'accumulateurs 350
batterie de cuisine 174
batterie rechargeable 320
batteur 478, 479
batteur à main 176
batteur à œufs 172
batteur sur socle 176
baudrier 353
bavette 260, 261
bavette garde-boue 349, 364, 365
bavette garde-neige 523
bavoir 260
bavolet 248
bec 78, 167, 197, 216, 306, 311
bec corné 76
bec de bord d'attaque 393
bec fixe 425
bec mobile 425
bec verseur 180, 181, 215
bec-de-cane 186
bécarre 299
bêche 233
becquerel 426
bégonia 56
Bélarus 450
Belgique 449
Belize 448
bémol 299
Bénin 451
bénitier 446
benne 400
benne à ordures 364
benne basculante 401
benne tasseuse 364
béquet 366
béquille de l'inclinaison 227
béquille centrale 367
béquille d'appoint 361
béquille d'appui 361
béquille d'avant-bras 466
béquille latérale 367, 369
béret 239
bergamote 134
berge 342
berger allemand 86
bergère 200
bergerie 122
berline 347
berlingot 163
bermuda 254
bette à carde 125
betterave 129
beurre 150
beurrier 166
Bhoutan 453
biais 260
bibliothèque 433, 444
biceps brachial 96
biceps crural 97
bicyclette 370
bicyclette de course 373
bicyclette de tourisme 373
bicyclette de ville 373
bicyclette hollandaise 373
bicyclette, accessoires 372
bicyclettes, exemples 373
bidet 195
bidon 371
bidon à eau 532
bief d'amont 406
bief d'aval 406, 407
bielle 360
bière 120
bifteck 152
bigorneau 157
bigoudi 268
bijouterie 264, 436

billard 502
billard anglais 503
billard français 502
billard pool 502
bille 312, 332
bille blanche 503
bille blanche mouchetée 503
bille bleue 503
bille brune 503
bille de choc 502, 503
bille de visée blanche 502
bille jaune 503
bille noire 503
bille rose 503
bille rouge 502, 503
bille verte 503
billes numérotées 502
billes rouges 503
billet de banque 441, 469
billetterie 294, 390
billetterie express 294
bimah 447
binette 233
biologic 426
biosphère 44
biosphère, structure 44
biseau 305, 460
bison 84
bitte 385
blaireau 88, 271
blanc 418, 468
blanche 299
Blancs 469, 470
blazer 254
blé 61, 143
blé : épi 61
bleu 418
bleu danois 151
bloc 473
bloc convertisseur 321
bloc d'arrêt 229
bloc de culasse 534
bloc de départ 473
bloc de pression 425
bloc opératoire 464
bloc pneumatique 376
bloc-cylindres 360
bloc-éphéméride 338
bloc-essieu 526, 527
bloc-moteur 176, 177, 180, 208, 272, 376
bloc-notes 338
blocage de l'inclinaison 227
blocage de l'interrupteur 228
blocage du pivot 224
bloquer droit 485
bloquer gauche 485
blouson court 249
blouson long 249
blousons 248
boa 77
bob 239
bobine 319
bocal 306
body 255, 258
bogie moteur 376
bogie porteur 376
bois 25, 505
bois de cœur 63
bois, famille 295
boisseau d'embouchure 307
boissons 120
boîte à courrier 338
boîte à fromage 163
boîte à gants 354
boîte à leurres 538
boîte à onglets 226
boîte à outils 225
boîte à œufs 162
boîte à poussière 229
boîte d'encastrement 198
boîte d'engrenage multiplicateur 413
boîte de conserve 163
boîte de vitesses 350
boîte électrique 411
boîte en zinc (anode) 417
boîte pour seringues usagées 457
boîte-classeur 340
boîtes alimentaires 162
boîtier 199, 218, 225, 228, 229, 271, 314, 424
boîtier à double rangée de connexions 417
boîtier de batterie 359, 365
boîtier du moteur 271
boîtier du ventilateur 270

boîtier tour : vue arrière 329
boîtier tour : vue avant 329
bol 166, 176, 177
bol à raser 271
bol à salade 166
bol verseur 177
boléro 254
Bolivie 448
bols à mélanger 172
bols de cuisson 179
bombe volcanique 28
bôme 520
bonbon 240
bonde 197
bonde de fond 184
bongo 309
bonnet 259, 514, 516
bonnet à pompon 239
bord 55, 238, 239
bord antérieur 73
bord d'attaque 393
bord d'une feuille 55
bord de fuite 392
bord externe 73
bord interne 73
bord libre 114
bord postérieur 73
bord tranchant 398
bord-côte 247, 250, 261
bordure 182, 205, 519, 524
bordure d'allée 230
bordure de quai 374, 379
bordure de trottoir 434
borne 198, 210, 359
borne d'incendie 434
borne d'incendie 454
borne de gonflage 346
borne de mise à la terre 322
borne négative 359, 416, 417
borne positive 359, 416, 417
bornes de raccordement des antennes 322
bornes de raccordement des enceintes 322
Bosnie-Herzégovine 450
Botswana 452
botte 125, 241, 525
botte de caoutchouc 454
botte rigide 513
botte souple 513
bottillon 240
bottine 241
bouche 71, 72, 73, 75, 90, 94, 116, 305, 534
bouche d'air 354
boucherie 120
bouchon 176, 267, 409, 460, 532
bouchon antifuite 529
bouchon de dégorgement 197
bouchon de remplissage 237, 358
bouchon de scellement 417
bouchon de vidange 194, 211
bouchon de vidange d'huile 360
bouchon du réservoir 364, 368
boucle 246, 276, 343, 353, 511
boucle de ceinture 248
boucle de piquet 528, 529
boucle de réglage 527, 532
boucle piquée 509
boucles d'oreille 264
boucles d'oreille à pince 264
boucles d'oreille à tige 264
boucles d'oreille à vis 264
bouclier 235, 507
bouclier arrière 7
bouclier thermique 12
boudin 156
bouée de sauvetage 387, 457
bougie 237
bougie d'allumage 359, 360
bouilloire 180
boulangerie 121
boulangerie-pâtisserie 437
boule à thé 173
boule d'attelage 356
bouleau 64
bouledogue 86
boulet 83
boulevard 25, 433
boulevard périphérique 25
boulon 220, 223, 224
boulon à ailettes 221
boulon à épaulement 223
boulon à gaine d'expansion 221
boulons 223
bourdalou 238

bourdon 69, 296
bourgeon 54
bourgeon axillaire 53
bourgeon gustatif 118
bourgeon terminal 53
bourrache 142
bourre 534
bourrelet 358
bourse à monnaie 275
boussole magnétique 533
bout 167, 536
bout du nez 83
bout fleuri 240
bouteille 532
bouteille à gaz médical 464
bouteille d'air comprimé 454
bouteille en verre 163
bouteille isolante 532
bouteur 398
boutique 280
boutique hors taxe 391
bouton 199, 202, 245, 250, 296, 301
bouton à friction 425
bouton alimentation papier 333
bouton champignon 332
bouton d'alimentation papier 443
bouton d'appel 287
bouton d'appel pour piétons 434
bouton d'arrêt 235
bouton d'éjection 323
bouton d'éjection 315
bouton d'éjection de la disquette 329
bouton d'éjection du CD/DVD-ROM 329
bouton d'enregistreur vocal 337
bouton d'essai 454
bouton de blocage 225, 229
bouton de clé 306
bouton de combinaisons 305
bouton de commande 210
bouton de contrôle 332
bouton de démarrage 329, 336
bouton de démarrage et de rétroéclairage 337
bouton de démarreur 368
bouton de déverrouillage de l'écran 336
bouton de mise au point 8, 9
bouton de mise en circuit 328
bouton de piston 307
bouton de registre 305
bouton de réinitialisation 329, 471
bouton de remise à zéro 323
bouton de sortie 337
bouton de vaporisation 208
bouton de verrouillage 352
bouton de verrouillage de l'interrupteur 227
bouton du pavé tactile 336
bouton fixe-courroie 303
bouton floral 53
bouton marche/arrêt 180, 333
bouton moleté 219
bouton-guide 425
bouton-poussoir 176, 214, 312
bouton-pression 245, 249
boutonnage sous patte 251
boutonnière 246, 248
boutons de lancement d'applications 337
boutons de réglage 318
boutons programmables 332
bowling 436
box 438
boxe 498
boxeur 498
bœuf 85
bœuf haché 152
bracelet 424, 486
bracelet lesté 500
bracelet tubulaire 264
bracelets 264
brachial antérieur 96
bractée 60
braguette 246, 247, 260
brancard 231, 400, 460
branche 125, 222, 270, 273, 416, 460, 535
branche à fruits 62
branche d'embouchure 307
branche maîtresse 63
branchement au réseau 198
branchement de l'abonné 198
branchement du distributeur 198
branchement pluvial 434
branchement, exemples 197
branchies 73
brandebourg 249

bras 83, 91, 93, 95, 206, 236, 399, 400, 412, 467
bras d'éloignement 362
bras d'essuie-glace 355
bras de delta 32
bras de fourche 28, 396
bras de levage 399
bras de plaquette 273
bras de suspension 212, 351
bras du longeron 398
bras gicleur 214
bras mort 32
bras spiral 6
brasero 283
brassard 486
brassard pneumatique 461
brasse 517
brassière 260
break 347
brelan 468
Brésil 448
brèche 282
bretelle 259, 343, 375, 388, 532
bretelle boutonnée 261
bretelle de raccordement 343
bretelle réglable 260
bretelles 246
brèves 313
bricolage 216
bride 265
bride de fixation 8, 9
bride de suspension 250
brie 151
brique 163
brique réfractaire 192
briquet 218
briquette 163
brise-glace 384
brise-jet 236
broche 198, 199
broche de connexion 417
brochet 160
brocoli 127
brocoli italien 127
brodequin de randonnée 242
brodequin de sécurité 459
brodequin de travail 240
bronche lobaire 105
bronche principale 105
bronchiole terminale 105
brosse 61, 209, 215, 272
brosse à dents 272
brosse à épousseter 209
brosse à légumes 173
brosse à mascara 266
brosse à planchers 209
brosse anglaise 268
brosse centrale 365
brosse de curling 515
brosse de nettoyage 271
brosse latérale 365
brosse pneumatique 268
brosse pour le bain 267
brosse pour le dos 267
brosse ronde 268
brosse-araignée 268
brosse-peigne pour cils et sourcils 266
brosses à cheveux 268
brou 60
brouette 231
brouillard 41
broyeur 49, 197, 402
brûleur 210, 529
brûleur bec plat 218
brûleur flamme crayon 218
brume 41
Brunéi Darussalam 453
buanderie 188, 439
buccin 157
bûcher 192
bûchette 249
buffet 203, 438
buffet-vaisselier 203
buffle 84
buisson 43
bulbe 6, 114, 125
bulbe d'étrave 385, 387
bulbe olfactif 117
bulbe rachidien 109
bulbe, coupe 54
Bulgarie 450
bulles d'air 339
bureau 188, 438, 439
bureau d'élève 444
bureau de formation professionnelle 442
bureau de l'enseignant 444

ASTRONOMIE > 2-13;   TERRE > 14-49;   RÈGNE VÉGÉTAL > 50-65;   RÈGNE ANIMAL > 66-91;   ÊTRE HUMAIN > 92-119;   ALIMENTATION ET CUISINE > 120-181;   MAISON > 182-215;   BRICO-
LAGE ET JARDINAGE > 216-237;   VÊTEMENTS > 238-263;   PARURE ET OBJETS PERSONNELS > 264-277;   ARTS ET ARCHITECTURE > 278-311;   COMMUNICATIONS ET BUREAUTIQUE > 312-341;
TRANSPORT ET MACHINERIE > 342-401;   ÉNERGIES > 402-413;   SCIENCE > 414-429;   SOCIÉTÉ > 430-467;   SPORTS ET JEUX > 468-538

567

bureau de l'infirmière en chef 463
bureau de l'urgentiste 462
bureau de poste 433, 437
bureau de réservation de chambres d'hôtel 390
bureau des douanes 381
bureau des greffiers 440
bureau des surveillants 445
bureau du directeur 443, 445
bureau du gymnase 444
bureau du travailleur social 463
bureautique 329
Burkina Faso 451
Burundi 451
buse 216, 219, 236, 270, 272
buse de refoulement 184
buse vapeur 181
bustier 259
but 480, 482, 485, 489, 507
butée 511, 514, 521
butée 226
butée de porte 211
butée talonnière 467
butoir 375
butte 36

C

caban 251
cabas 276
cabine 386, 395, 398, 399, 400, 401
cabine d'ascenseur 287
cabine de commande 397
cabine de conduite 376, 377
cabine de déshabillage 465
cabine de douche 195
cabine de pilotage 383, 385
cabine de première classe 392
cabine de projection 294
cabine des passagers 383, 386, 387
cabine touriste 393
cabinet des juges 440
câble 228, 332, 356, 364, 501, 535
câble d'accélération 237
câble d'acier 535
câble de bougie 350, 360
câble de commande 372
câble de frein 371
câble de l'antenne haute fréquence 394
câble de levage 287, 397
câble de raccordement 324
câble de synchronisation 337
câble électrique 354, 434
câble porteur 344
câble pour interface numérique d'instruments de musique (MIDI) 311
câble téléphonique 434
câbles de démarrage 356
câblodistributeur 316
cabriolet 200, 347
cacahuète 130
cacao 148
cachalot 90
cache-cœur 255
cache-oreilles abattant 238
cæcum 106
cadenas 372
cadran 422, 424, 533
cadran solaire 424
cadre 204, 274, 277, 297, 367, 412, 460, 492, 494, 502, 522
cadre métallique 304
cadreur 290
café 148, 432, 437
café et infusions 148
café torréfié, grains 148
café verts, grains 148
cafétéria 445
cafetière 531
cafetière à infusion 181
cafetière à piston 181
cafetière espresso 181
cafetière filtre 181
cafetière napolitaine 181
cafetières 181
cage 281, 473
cage d'escalier 189
cage de scène 292
cage vitrée 423
cageot 162
cagoule 239, 524, 530
cahier 313
caïeu 54
caille 81, 154
caïman 77
caisse 121, 231, 303, 304

caisse bombée 297
caisse circulaire 296
caisse claire 295, 308
caisse de batterie électronique 311
caisse de résonance 296, 297, 302
caisse enregistreuse 121
caisse roulante 308
caisse triangulaire 297
caisses 121
cassette 162
caissière 121
caisson 192
caisson de portière 352
calame 312
calandre 348, 364, 409
calcanéum 99
calculatrice à imprimante 337
calculatrice scientifique 337
calculette 274, 337
cale 224
cale à conteneurs 383
cale-pied 370, 372, 501
caleçon 247
caleçon long 247
calendrier-mémorandum 338
calice 56, 59, 60, 107, 446
calicule 59
Callisto 2
calmar 157
caloporteur 408
caloporteur chaud 408
caloporteur refroidi 408
calot 238
calotte 78, 238, 239, 412
calotte glaciaire 40
cambium 63
Cambodge 453
cambre 273
cambrure 240
caméléon 77
camembert 151
caméra 290, 525
caméra de télévision couleur 10
Cameroun 451
caméscope analogique 320
camion porteur fourgon 365
camion-benne 401
camion-citerne 364
camion-toupie 365
camionnage 364
camionnette 347
camions d'incendie 455
camions, exemples 364
camomille 148
campagne 431
camping 528
Canada 451
canadienne 249
canal à venin 76
canal de fuite 407
canal de projection 365
canal déférent 111
canal droit 324
canal du Mozambique 20
canal éjaculateur 111
canal gauche 324
canal lacrymal 119
canal radiculaire 101
canal semi-circulaire antérieur 116
canal semi-circulaire externe 116
canal semi-circulaire postérieur 116
canal siphonal 73
canal sudoripare 114
canalisation 357
canalisation d'arrosage 365
canalisation de branchement 194
canapé 200
canapé capitonné 200
canapé convertible 204
canard 81, 155
candela 426
caniche 86
canine 101
canne 273
canne à lancer 537
canne à mouche 536
canne avec poignée orthopédique 466
canne avec quadripode 466
canne en C 466
canne en T 466
canneberge 132
cannelle 138
cannelloni 146
cannelure 359
cannette 163
canon 83, 534

canon à électrons 318
canon à mousse 385
canot pneumatique de sauvetage 383
canotier 238
cantaloup 135
cantonnière 277
canyon sous-marin 33
cap 24
cap de Bonne-Espérance 20
cap Horn 17
Cap-Vert 451
cape 251
cape de bain 260
capeline 239
capitaine 515
capitale 23
capitule 57
capot 208, 209, 333, 348, 364, 417, 523
capsule 51
capsule à membrane 360
capsule à vis 163
capsule, coupe 60
capteur de télécommande 318, 323
capteur de vitesse de roue 357
capteur optique 332
capteur solaire plan 410
capture 470
capuche 260
capuchon 249, 312, 467, 505, 508
capuchon coulissé 261
capuchon d'objectif 314
capuchon de connexion 217
capuchon de protection 420
caquelon 174
car de reportage 316
carabine (canon rayé) 534
caraco 258
carafe 165
carafon 165
carambole 137
carapace 71
caravane 361
caravane flottante 385
caravane pliante 361
caravane tractée 361
carburant diesel 405
carburateur 366
carburéacteur 405
cardamome 138
carde 125
cardigan 250, 255
cardinal 81
cardon 125
carénage 366
carénage avant 348
carène 74
caricature 313
carillon tubulaire 295, 309
carlingue centrale 385
carnivores 45
caroncule lacrymale 119
carotte 129
Carpates 18
carpe 160
carré 509, 510
carré 429, 468
carreau 186, 468
carrefour giratoire 342
carrosserie 212, 213, 348
carrosseries, exemples 347
carte 469
carte Caisse de communauté 469
carte Chance 469
carte de circuit imprimé 417
carte de crédit 441
carte de débit 443
carte de ligne 378
carte de mémoire 315
carte de réseau 379, 337
carte géographique 444
carte isolée 468
carte météorologique 38, 39
carte physique 24
carte politique 23
carte routière 25
carter 237, 360, 537
carter d'embrayage 368
carter de sécurité 237
cartes 468
cartes, symboles 468
cartilage de l'aile du nez 117
cartilage de la cloison 117
cartographie 21
carton 51
cartouche 216, 312, 459

cartouche (carabine) 534
cartouche (fusil) 534
cartouche jetable 218
carvi 138
casaque 255
case 288, 469
case blanche 470
case noire 470
caserne de pompiers 433
casier 203
casier à beurre 211
casier laitier 211
casiers des élèves 445
casque 10, 454, 478, 486, 498, 506, 508, 510, 513, 522, 524, 525, 526, 527
casque antibruit 458
casque d'écoute 324, 326
casque de frappeur 476
casque de protection 367, 372
casque de sécurité 458
casque intégral 525
casquette 235, 456
casquette norvégienne 238
casse-noix 170
Cassegrain, foyer 7
casserole 175
cassette 326, 333
cassette annonce 328
cassette messages 328
cassette vidéo 319
cassette vidéo compacte, adaptateur 320
cassis 132
cassonade 149
castagnettes 295, 309
castes 68
castor 82
catadioptre 370, 523
catamaran 521
caténaire 376
cathédrale 284
cathédrale gothique 284
cathédrale, plan 285
cathode 417
causeuse 200, 439
Cavalier 470
cave à vins 438
cavité abdominale 111, 112
cavité buccale 105, 106
cavité nasale 105
cavité pleurale 105
cédrat 134
cèdre du Liban 65
ceinture 200, 201, 202, 225, 246, 248, 499, 532
ceinture d'astéroïdes 3
ceinture d'haltérophilie 500
ceinture de Kuiper 2
ceinture de sécurité 353, 525
ceinture élastique 247, 249
ceinture montée 246, 249
ceinture porte-outils 225
ceinture ventrale 205
ceinturon de service 456
céleri 125
céleri-rave 129
cellule 67, 281
cellule animale 66
cellule convective 43
cellule végétale 50
cellules 440
cément 101
cent 427, 440
centrale 66
centrale hydroélectrique, coupe 407
centrale thermique au charbon 402
centre 293, 428, 470, 481, 482, 485, 507, 515
centre arrière 485
centre commercial 431, 436
centre de tri 49
centre droit 482
centre gauche 482
centre-ville 431, 432
centrifugeuse 11, 180
centriole 66
cep de vigne 62
cèpe 123
céphalothorax 70, 71
cercle 273
cercle central 481, 488, 507
cercle d'ascension droite 8, 9
cercle d'attente 474
cercle de déclinaison 8, 9
cercle de la station 39
cercle de lancer 472, 473

cercle de mise au jeu 506
cercle de serrage 308
cercle extérieur 515
cercle intérieur 515
cercle polaire antarctique 15, 21, 22
cercle polaire arctique 21, 22
cercle porte-lame 401
cercle restrictif 488
céréales 61, 143
cerf de Virginie 84
cerf du Canada 84
cerfeuil 142
cerise 132
cerne annuel 63
cerneau 60
cerques 536
cerveau 71, 109
cervelet 109
cervelle 154
Chac-Mool 283
chaîne 370, 372
chaîne alimentaire 45
chaîne coupante 235
chaîne de levage 396
chaîne de montagnes 5, 24, 26
chaîne de neurones 110
chaîne de sûreté 361
chaîne nerveuse ventrale 71
chaîne stéréo 322
chaînette de levage 196
chaire 446
chaise 201, 444
chaise berçante 201
chaise haute 205
chaise longue 201
chaise pliante 201
chaise-escabeau 201
chaises empilables 201
chaises, exemples 201
chalaze 79
chalet de montagne 512
chalet du sommet 512
chalet principal 512
chaloupe de sauvetage 382, 386
chalumeau 296
chalutier 384
chambranle 185, 186
chambre 189, 528
chambre à air 79
chambre antérieure 119
chambre d'expansion 424
chambre d'hôpital 464
chambre d'isolement 462
chambre d'observation 462, 465
chambre d'observation psychiatrique 462
chambre de combustion 192, 360
chambre de décharge 278
chambre de la reine 278
chambre des pompes 384
chambre double 439
chambre du roi 278
chambre forte 443
chambre froide 120, 121
chambre photographique 315
chambre postérieure 119
chambre principale, plafond cathédrale 189
chambre principale, toit cathédrale 189
chambre pulpaire 101
chambre simple 439
chambre souterraine 278
chambres d'hôtel 439
chameau 85
champ centre 475
champ droit 475
champ gauche 475
champ géothermique 402
champ magnétique 318, 416
champignon 52
champignon de couche 123
champignon mortel 52
champignon vénéneux 52
champignon, structure 52
champignons 123
chanfrein 83
changement de piste 323
chanterelle commune 123
chape 190
chapeau 52, 313
chapeau de feutre 238, 239
chapeau de ventilation 194
chapelle 282
chapelle axiale 284, 285
chapelle latérale 284
chapiteau 302
chapon 155

ASTRONOMIE > 2-13; TERRE > 14-49; RÈGNE VÉGÉTAL > 50-65; RÈGNE ANIMAL > 66-91; ÊTRE HUMAIN > 92-119; ALIMENTATION ET CUISINE > 120-181; MAISON > 182-215; BRICOLAGE ET JARDINAGE > 216-237; VÊTEMENTS > 238-263; PARURE ET OBJETS PERSONNELS > 264-277; ARTS ET ARCHITECTURE > 278-311; COMMUNICATIONS ET BUREAUTIQUE > 312-341; TRANSPORT ET MACHINERIE > 342-401; ÉNERGIES > 402-413; SCIENCE > 414-429; SOCIÉTÉ > 430-467; SPORTS ET JEUX > 468-538

hapska 238
harcuterie 156
harge électrique, mesure 426
hargeur 228
hargeuse frontale 399
hargeuse-pelleteuse 399
hariot 290, 397, 421, 505, 521
hariot à bagages 374
hariot élévateur 396
hariots 121
harles IX 241
hamière 178, 214, 274, 277, 352, 420, 511
hamière de la visière 367
haron 3
harpente 187, 279, 280
hasse 534
hasse-clou 220
hasse-neige à soufflerie 365
hasse-pierres 376, 377
hâssis 308, 309, 396, 400, 401
hasuble 252
hat 87
hat de l'île de Man 87
hat, tête 87
hâtaigne d'eau 124
hâteau fort 282
hats, races 87
hauffage 192
hauffage au bois 192
hauffe-eau 194
hauferette 529
haumard 521
haussée 342, 345, 434
haussette 247, 257, 480, 486, 492
haussette-étrier 476
haussettes 247
haussettes hautes 483
hausson intérieur 511, 527
haussure 478, 488, 509, 514, 522, 524, 527
haussure à crampons 476, 483, 486
haussure d'haltérophilie 500
haussure de football 480
haussure de piste 473
haussure de saut à ski 513
haussure de ski 510, 511
haussure de sport 262
haussure de tennis 492
haussure, parties 240
haussures 240
haussures d'homme 240
haussures de femme 241
haussures de golf 505
haussures unisexes 242
hayote 129
hef décorateur 290
hef électricien 291
hef machiniste 290
hef opérateur du son 291
hemin 504
hemin d'évacuation 345
hemin de fer 25
hemin de fer métropolitain 378
hemin de ronde 282
hemin de ronde couvert 282
hemin de roulement 397
heminée 28, 183, 188, 193, 382, 402
heminée à foyer ouvert 192
heminée antisue 386
heminée d'échappement 364, 401
hemise 245, 340, 534
hemise du donjon 282
hemise en acier 417
hemisier classique 255
henê 64
henets 193
henille 67, 398, 523
hèque de voyage 441
hèques 441
hercheur 8, 9
hérimole 136
heval 83, 85
heval d'arçons 496
heval d'arçons 496
heval sautoir 496, 497
heval, morphologie 83
hevalet 297, 301, 302, 303
hevalet des aigus 304
hevalet des basses 304
hevalière 264
hevelu 63
hevet 285
heveux 93, 95

cheville 92, 94, 202, 301, 302
cheville d'accord 304
chevillier 301
chèvre 84
chèvre frais 150
chevron 187
chiasma optique 109
chicane 524
chicorée de Trévise 126
chicorée frisée 127
chien 86, 534, 535
chien, morphologie 86
chiens, races 86
chiffonnier 203
chiffres romains 427
Chili 448
chimie 414
chimpanzé 91
Chine 453
chinois 171
chipolata 156
chirurgie mineure 462
chloroplaste 50
chocolat 148
chocolat au lait 148
chocolat blanc 148
chocolat noir 148
chope à bière 165
chope à café 166
chorizo 156
choroïde 119
chou cavalier 126
chou de Milan 126
chou frisé 126
chou laitue 126
chou marin 126
chou pommé blanc 126
chou pommé rouge 126
chou pommé vert 126
chou-fleur 127
chou-rave 125
choux de Bruxelles 126
chœur 284, 285
chromatine 66
chromosphère 4
chronique 313
chronomètre 424
chronomètre électronique automatique 517
chronométreur 488, 498, 509
chronométreur de couloir 516
chronométreur des trente secondes 488
chronométreur en chef 516
chronométreurs 499
chrysalide 67
chukka 240
chute 31, 519
chute d'eau 32
chutney à la mangue 141
Chypre 450
cible 471
ciboule 124
ciboulette 124
ciel d'orage 41
cierge 446
cigale 69
cigogne 80
cil 66, 119
cilié 55
cils 87
cime 63
cimetière 25, 433
cimier moulin 7
cinéma 294, 386, 432, 436
cinq 427
cinq cents 427
cinquante 427
cinq-épices chinois 139
cintres 292
circonférence 428
circuit capteurs 357
circuit d'eau chaude 194
circuit d'eau froide 194
circuit d'évacuation 194
circuit de freinage 350, 357
circuit de photopiles 411
circuit de plomberie 194
circuit de ventilation 194
circuit électrique en parallèle 416
circuit imprimé 417
circuit intégré 417
circuit intégré en boîtier 417
circuit, course automobile 524
circulation sanguine 102
circulation sanguine, schéma 103
cirque 5

cirque glaciaire 30
cirro-cumulus 42
cirro-stratus 42
cirrus 42
cisaille à haies 234
cisaille à volaille 173
ciseau à bois 229
ciseaux 461, 531
ciseaux à cuticules 265
ciseaux à effiler 270
ciseaux à ongles 265
ciseaux de coiffeur 270
ciseaux de cuisine 173
ciseaux de pédicure 265
ciseaux de sûreté 265
ciseaux sculpteurs 270
citerne 364, 385
cithare 296
citron 134
citron vert 134
citrouille 129
civière 460
clairon 307
clapet 196, 327
claque 240, 263
claquette 291
clarinette 306
clarinette basse 295
clarinettes 295
classeur 339
classeur à soufflets 274
clavardage 335
clavicule 98
clavier 304, 310, 327, 330, 336
clavier accompagnement 296
clavier alphanumérique 327, 346, 442, 443
clavier chant 296
clavier d'identification personnelle 443
clavier de grand orgue 305
clavier de positif 305
clavier de récit 305
clavier numérique 423
claviers manuels 305
clayette 211
clé 306
clé à douille à cliquet 223
clé à fourches 223
clé à molette 223
clé à tuyau 216
clé coudée à tuyau 216
clé d'ut 298
clé de bocal 306
clé de bras 499
clé de contact 237
clé de fa 298
clé de mandrin 228
clé de sol 298
clé de voûte 284
clé en croix 356
clé mixte 223
clé polygonale 223
clé polygonale à cliquet 223
clé polygonale à têtes fendues 223
clés 216, 223, 298, 311
client 317
climatiseur 361
climats arides 40
climats de montagne 40
climats du monde 40
climats polaires 40
climats tempérés chauds 40
climats tempérés froids 40
climats tropicaux 40
cliquet 221
clitoris 112
cloche 239
clocher 285, 446
clocheton 282, 284, 285
clochettes 309
cloison 58, 117, 457, 469, 528
cloison longitudinale 384
cloison transversale 384
clôture 122, 182
clôture du champ extérieur 475
clôture en lattis 230
clou 220
clou à maçonnerie 220
clou à tête homme 220
clou à tige spiralée 220
clou commun 220
clou coupé 220
clou de girofle 138
clous, exemples 220
cobra 77
coccinelle 69

coccyx 98
cochlée 116
cochon d'Inde 82
cockpit 520
code des produits 423
code temporel 291
coffre 203, 349, 369, 410, 411
coffre à bagages 361
coffre d'appareillage 376
coffre de rangement 364, 455
coffre-fort 443
coffret 318
coffret de branchement 198
coffret de sûreté 443
coiffe 53, 536
coiffeur 290
coiffeuse 195, 203
coiffure 238, 268
coiffures d'homme 238
coiffures de femme 239
coiffures unisexes 239
coin 305, 498
coin de patinoire 506
coin-repas 164, 188
coing 133
col 29, 244, 245, 248, 262, 318
col de l'utérus 112
col du fémur 99
col italien 245
col pointes boutonnées 245
col roulé 250, 514
col tailleur 245
col transformable 248
col-de-cygne 191, 400
colibri 80
collant 257
collant fantaisie 260
collant sans pieds 263
collatéral 285
collatérale 110
colle 190
collecte sélective 49
collecteur d'appareil 194
collecteur d'échappement 350, 360
collecteur d'électrons 417
collecteur d'évacuation 194
collecteur de graisse 179
collecteur principal 194
collet 53, 101, 167, 193, 535
collet de l'axone 110
colley 86
collier 174, 511
collier coupe-feu 193
collier de perles, longueur matinée 264
collier de serrage 501
collier de serrage du casque 10
collier de soirée 264
collier-de-chien 264
colliers 264
colline 29
colline abyssale 33
collybie à pied velouté 123
Colombie 448
côlon ascendant 106
côlon descendant 106
côlon pelvien 106
côlon transverse 106
colonne 31, 279, 302, 313, 380
colonne corinthienne engagée 281
colonne d'alcool 424
colonne de collecte du papier 49
colonne de collecte du verre 49
colonne de direction 350
colonne de mercure 424
colonne de ventilation 194
colonne de ventilation principale 194
colonne dorique engagée 281
colonne ionique engagée 281
colonne montante d'eau chaude 194
colonne montante d'eau froide 194
colonne vertébrale 98, 109
colorant capillaire 267
columelle 73
coma 6
combattant 499
combinaison 247, 261, 513, 525
combinaison de course 508
combinaison de nuit 261
combinaison de protection 525
combinaison de saut à ski 513
combinaison de ski 510, 514
combinaison résistante au feu 524
combinaison-jupon 258
combinaison-pantalon 258
combinaisons au poker 468
combiné 258, 327

combiné 2 dans 1 268
combiné bucco-dentaire 272
combiné-culotte 258
combustible 408
combustible fossile 46, 48
comète 6
commande amovible 179
commande d'accélération 235
commande d'arrêt 319
commande d'avance rapide 319
commande d'éjection de la cassette 319
commande d'enregistrement 319
commande d'essuie-glace 354
commande de chauffage 354
commande de dossier 353
commande de lecture 319
commande de rebobinage 319
commande de remise à zéro 319
commande de température 211
commande de vitesse 176
commande de volume 328
commande de volume de la sonnerie 327
commande de volume du récepteur 327
commande du chariot 421
commande du rétroviseur 352
commande électrique du zoom 320
commande mémoire 327
commandes de la bande vidéo 320
commandes de préréglage 319
commandes du magnétoscope 319
commandes du treuil 364
commerce électronique 335
commissure labiale 116
communication par téléphone 327
communications 312
communications aériennes 317
communications individuelles 317
communications industrielles 317
communications maritimes 317
communications militaires 317
communications routières 317
commutateur alimentation/fonctions 320
commutateur d'alimentation 315
commutateur d'allumage 354, 368
commutateur de prise de vues nocturne 320
commutateur marche/arrêt 314
Comores 452
compactage 49
compartiment 286
compartiment bagages 376
compartiment d'accessoires 209
compartiment de réservoirs d'eau 394
compartiment de sac 209
compartiment des voitures 386
compartiment moteur 362
compartiment voyageurs 376
compartiment-couchette 364
compétition de cyclisme sur route 522
complexe hydroélectrique 406
complexe sportif 431
compluvium 280
composition du sang 104
compresse stérilisée 461
compresseur du climatiseur 360
comprimé 467
compte-tours 355
compteur 194, 323
compteur d'électricité 198
compteur kilométrique 355
comptoir d'enregistrement 390
comptoir de renseignements 390, 442, 463
comptoir de vente de friandises 294
comptoir des fromages 121
comptoir des viandes libre-service 120
comptoir du bar 438
concentration des gaz à effet de serre 46
concentré de tomate 140
concessionnaire d'automobiles 433
conchiglie 146
concombre 128
concombre sans pépins 128
condensateur à film plastique 417
condensateur céramique 417
condensateurs électrolytiques 417
condensation 45, 414
condensation de la vapeur 408
condenseur 402, 414
condiments 140
conditionnement d'air 386
condor 80
conducteur d'alimentation 198
conducteur de mise à la terre 198
conducteur dérivé 416
conducteur neutre 198

conduction 415
conduit auditif 116
conduit auditif externe 100
conduit d'aération 278
conduit d'essence 351
conduit de chauffage 213
conduit de la glande 76
conduit de raccordement 192
conduit lactifère 113
conduite à la terre 404
conduite d'alimentation 194
conduite d'eau 214
conduite d'eau chaude 197
conduite d'eau froide 197
conduite d'eau potable 434
conduite de gaz 434
conduite forcée 406, 407
conduite principale 196
condyle externe 99
condyle interne 99
cône 65, 119, 318, 429
cône adventif 28
cône d'ombre 4, 5
cône de pénombre 4, 5
cône femelle 65
cône mâle 65
confessionnal 446
configuration des continents 14
configuration du littoral 35
confluent 32
congélateur 164, 211, 438
congélateur coffre 211
Congo 20, 451
conifère 65
conifères, exemples 65
conjonctive 119
connexion 470
conque 115
conserves 121
consigne automatique 374
console 283, 302
console centrale 354
console d'accotoir 200
console d'orgue 305
console de jeu 471
consommateurs primaires 45
consommateurs secondaires 45
consommateurs tertiaires 45
contact 470
contact de terre 198
contact électrique 314
contact négatif 410, 411
contact positif 410, 411
conteneur 383
conteneur à boîtes métalliques 49
conteneur à papier 49
conteneur à verre 49
conteneurs de collecte sélective 49
continent 5, 33
continental humide, à été chaud 40
continental humide, à été frais 40
continents, configuration 14
contre-fer 229
contre-flèche 397
contrebasse 301
contrebasses 295
contrebassons 295
contrefort 29, 262, 284
contremarche 191
contrepoids 8, 287, 345, 397, 400, 401
contrevent 186
contrôle 330
contrôle : sélection de groupe 330
contrôle de la stéréophonie 326
contrôle de la température du corps 10
contrôle de la vapeur 208
contrôle de sécurité 391
contrôle de tonalité des aigus 303, 322, 325
contrôle de tonalité des graves 303, 322, 325
contrôle des passeports 391
contrôle douanier 391
contrôle du champ sonore 322
contrôle du plateau 323
contrôle du séquenceur 310
contrôle du volume 310
contrôles de l'équipement de survie 10
contrôles du lecteur de cassette 326
contrôles du lecteur de disque compact 326
contrôleur 374
contrôleur à vent de synthétiseur 311
convection 415
convertisseur catalytique 351
convertisseur de couple 212

convoyeur 402
coordonnées terrestres 21
copropriété 512
coq 81
coque 60, 157, 277, 361, 367, 520, 523
coque inférieure 511
coque spiralée 73
coquelicot 56
coquillage bivalve 73
coquillage bivalve, anatomie 73
coquillage bivalve, morphologie 73
coquillage univalve 73
coquillage univalve, morphologie 73
coquille 72, 73, 79, 200, 486, 507
coquille Saint-Jacques 157
coquilleur à beurre 169
cor anglais 306
cor d'harmonie 307
corbeau 80, 192, 282
corbeille 293
corbeille à papier 341
corbeille à pollen 68
corbeille suspendue 230
corde 301, 302, 498, 535
corde à sauter 500
corde de couloir 517
corde de faux départ 516
corde de tension 297
corde de tirage 219
corde vocale 105
cordeau 225, 231
cordeau à tracer 225
cordée 512
cordes 297, 304
cordes d'accompagnement 296
cordes de mélodie 296
cordes de timbre 308
cordier 297, 301
Cordillère australienne 15
cordillère des Andes 17
cordon 208, 209, 217, 235, 237, 326
cordon coulissant 249
cordon d'alimentation 270, 271
cordon d'alimentation 177, 227, 229, 269, 322
cordon d'alimentation en courant continu 336
cordon d'alimentation pivotant 269
cordon d'alimentation secteur 336
cordon de combiné 327
cordon de dunes 36
cordon littoral 35
coriandre 142
corne antérieure 109
corne de feu 455
corne de guidage de l'attelage 376
corne postérieure 109
cornée 119, 419
cornemuse 296
cornet à dés 469
cornet à pistons 295, 307
cornet inférieur 117
cornet moyen 117
cornet supérieur 117
corniche 183, 185, 202, 279
cornichon 128
corolle 56
corona radiata 112
corps 118, 180, 228, 270, 305, 306, 312, 421, 425, 471, 536
corps calleux 109
corps caverneux 111
corps célestes 2
corps cellulaire 110
corps ciliaire 119
corps de garde 282
corps de l'ongle 114
corps de piston 307
corps de pompe 460
corps du fornix 109
corps humain 92
corps vertébral 110
corps vitré 119
corpuscule de Meissner 114
corpuscule de Pacini 114
corpuscule de Ruffini 114
correction d'exposition 314
cors anglais 295
cors d'harmonie 295
corsaire 254
corset 259
corymbe 57
cosse 60
Costa Rica 448
costume 290
côte 33, 152, 153, 536

côté 293
côte axiale 73
côte cour 293
Côte d'Ivoire 451
côte flottante (2) 98
côté jardin 293
côte spiralée 73
côtelette 153
côtes 98
côtes levées de dos 152
côtes, exemples 35
coton hydrophile 461
coton-tige 461
cotret 412
cottage 150
cotylédon 53
cou 76, 93, 94, 95, 111
cou-de-pied 92
couche 260
couche antireflet 410
couche arable 54
couche basale 114
couche claire 114
couche cornée 114
couche d'ozone 37
couche de cendres 28
couche de laves 28
couche de Malpighi 114
couche de surface 342
couche fluorescente 199
couche granuleuse 114
couche imperméable 403
couche-culotte 260
couches de déchets 47
coude 83, 86, 93, 95, 273
coudes 146
coudière 486, 527
coulant 273
coulée de boue 31
coulée de lave 28
couleur 468
couleurs, synthèse 418
couleuvre rayée 77
coulis de tomate 140
coulisse 246
coulisse d'accord 307
coulisse du deuxième piston 307
coulisse du premier piston 307
coulisse du troisième piston 307
coulisses 292
couloir 472, 490, 495, 516
couloir ascendant 278
couloir de sécurité 440
couloir descendant 278
coulomb 426
coulommiers 151
coup de patin 514
coupé 347
coupe à mousseux 165
coupe d'un bulbe 54
coupe d'un follicule : anis étoilé 60
coupe d'un grain de blé 61
coupe d'un observatoire astronomique 7
coupe d'un raisin 59
coupe d'un télescope 9
coupe d'une capsule : pavot 60
coupe d'une centrale hydroélectrique 407
coupe d'une fraise 59
coupe d'une framboise 59
coupe d'une gousse : pois 60
coupe d'une lunette astronomique 8
coupe d'une molaire 101
coupe d'une noisette 60
coupe d'une noix 60
coupe d'une orange 58
coupe d'une pêche 57
coupe d'une pomme 58
coupe d'une route 342
coupe d'une rue 434
coupe d'une silique : moutarde 60
coupe de l'atmosphère terrestre 37
coupe de la croûte terrestre 26
coupe de la nacelle 413
coupe sagittale 111, 112
coupe transversale du tronc 63
coupe-bordures 233
coupe-circuit d'urgence 368
coupe-cuticules 265
coupe-fil 217
coupe-ongles 265
coupe-œuf 173
coupe-papier 339
coupelle 207
coupelle d'étanchéité 459
couperet 169
couple 509

coupole du mihrab 447
coupole du porche 447
coupole rotative 7
coups 490
cour 122, 282, 447
cour de récréation 445
courant de convection 415
courant électrique, mesure 426
courant, adaptateur 336
courbure 538
courge 128
courge à cou droit 129
courge à cou tors 129
courge spaghetti 129
courgeron 129
courgette 128
couronne 4, 83, 101, 286, 308, 424, 441
couronne d'orientation 400
couronnement 191
courrier des lecteurs 313
courrier électronique 335
courroie d'entraînement 212
courroie de distribution 360
courroie de tige 511
courroie de transmission 383
courroie de ventilateur 350, 360
cours d'eau 32, 48
course automobile 524
coursier d'évacuateur 406
court 490
court de service droit 491
court de service gauche 491
court péronier latéral 97
courte piste 508
courtine 282
couscous 144
couscoussier 175
coussin arrière 502
coussin carré 204
coussin d'air 262
coussin de rembourrage 498
coussin de tête 502
coussinet en mousse 458
couteau 157, 167, 176, 177, 180, 531, 533
couteau à beurre 168
couteau à bifteck 168
couteau à découper 169
couteau à désosser 169
couteau à dessert 168
couteau à filets de sole 169
couteau à fromage 168
couteau à huîtres 169
couteau à jambon 169
couteau à pain 169
couteau à pamplemousse 169
couteau à poisson 168
couteau à zester 169
couteau d'office 169
couteau de chef 169
couteau de cuisine 169
couteau de table 168
couteau électrique 177
couteau suisse 531
couteaux de cuisine, exemples 169
couteaux, exemples 168
couture 477, 478
couture d'assemblage 243
couture médiane 245
couturier 96
couvercle 174, 177, 178, 179, 180, 181, 196, 198, 211, 212, 215, 225, 315, 454, 533
couvercle de batterie 359
couvercle de culasse 350, 360
couvercle de propreté 210
couvercle de réservoir 196
couvercle inférieur 417
couvercle supérieur 417
couverts 167
couverture 204
couvre-filtre 459
couvre-oreiller 204
Cowper, glande 111
cœur 58, 71, 73, 104, 105, 154, 192, 468, 492
crabe 158
cracker de seigle 145
cracker scandinave 145
craie 503
crampon 263, 478
crampon de fermeture 277
crampons interchangeables 480
cran 234, 246, 422, 473, 536
cran de réglage 222, 511
crâne 92

crâne d'enfant 100
crâne, vue latérale 100
crapaud commun 75
cratère 5
cravate 245
crawl 517
crayon 312, 409
crayon à sourcils 266
crayon blanchisseur d'ongles 265
crayon contour des lèvres 266
crayon en plomb 312
crédit photographique 313
crémaillère 178, 211, 473
crème 150
crème aigre 150
crème épaisse 150
crémier 166
crénelé 55
crépis 279
cresson alénois 127
cresson de fontaine 127
crête 29, 33, 406, 418
creux 33, 167, 418
creux barométrique 39
crevasse 30
crevette 158
cric 356
cricket 478
crinière 83
criquet mélodieux 69
cristallin 119, 419
cristallisation 414
cristaux liquides 424
critique gastronomique 313
Croatie 450
croche 299
crochet 70, 73, 186, 217, 225, 364, 397, 423, 460, 502, 509
crochet à venin 76
crochet de levage 403
crochet de petit doigt 307
crochet de pouce 307
crochet du plateau 422
crochet pétrisseur 176
crocodile 77
crocus 56
croisée 284
croisée du transept 285
croisillon 467
croissant 5, 144
croix d'autel 446
croix de Saint-André 187
crosne 124
crosse 52, 302, 466, 534
crosse de fougère 125
crosse de gardien de but 507
crosse de joueur 506
crottin de Chavignol 150
croupe 83
croupion 78
croûte basaltique 26
croûte continentale 26
croûte de cuir 246
croûte granitique 26
croûte océanique 26
croûte terrestre 26, 27
croûte terrestre, coupe 26
crucifix 446
crustacés 71, 158
Cuba 448
cube 429
cubes d'agneau 153
cubes de bœuf 152
cubes de veau 152
cubiculum 280
cubital antérieur 96, 97
cubital postérieur 97
cubitus 98
cuiller 167, 531, 538
cuiller à café 168
cuiller à dessert 168
cuiller à égoutter 173
cuiller à glace 173
cuiller à goûter 173
cuiller à soda 168
cuiller à soupe 168
cuiller à thé 168
cuiller de table 168
cuiller parisienne 173
cuilleron 167
cuillers doseuses 171
cuillers, exemples 168
cuisine 120, 162, 164, 188, 280, 439, 445
cuisinière à gaz 210
cuisinière électrique 210

ASTRONOMIE > 2-13;   TERRE > 14-49;   RÈGNE VÉGÉTAL > 50-65;   RÈGNE ANIMAL > 66-91;   ÊTRE HUMAIN > 92-119;   ALIMENTATION ET CUISINE > 120-181;   MAISON > 182-215;   BRICO
LAGE ET JARDINAGE > 216-237;   VÊTEMENTS > 238-263;   PARURE ET OBJETS PERSONNELS > 264-277;   ARTS ET ARCHITECTURE > 278-311;   COMMUNICATIONS ET BUREAUTIQUE > 312-341;
TRANSPORT ET MACHINERIE > 342-401;   ÉNERGIES > 402-413;   SCIENCE > 414-429;   SOCIÉTÉ > 430-467;   SPORTS ET JEUX > 468-538

INDEX FRANÇAIS

cuissard 486, 522
cuissarde 241
cuissardes 538
cuisse 83, 86, 93, 95, 111, 112
cuit-vapeur 175
cuit-vapeur électrique 179
cuivres, famille 295
cul-de-sac de Douglas 112
cul-de-sac dural 109
cul-de-sac vésico-utérin 112
culasse 306
culbuteur 360
culée 284, 344
culot 199, 318, 359, 534
culot à baïonnette 199
culot à broches 199
culot à vis 199
culotte 259, 500, 506
culotte à ruchés 260
cumin 138
cumulo-nimbus 42
cumulus 42
cupule 60
curcuma 138
cure-ongles 265
curiosité 25
curieuse 515
curling 515
curry 138
curseur 422
curseur vers la droite 331
curseur vers la gauche 331
curseur vers le bas 331
curseur vers le haut 331
cuve 211, 212, 214
cuvette 196, 210, 302
cuvette ramasse-gouttes 181
cyan 418
cycle de l'eau 45
cycle des saisons 38
cyclisme 522
cyclisme sur route 522
cyclomoteur 369
cyclone 43
cyclone tropical 43
cylindre 429
cylindre de roue 357
cylindre de rubis 420
cylindre enregistreur 27
cylindre réflecteur 420
cymbale charleston 308
cymbale inférieure 308
cymbale supérieure 308
cymbale suspendue 308
cymbales 295, 309
cymbalette 309
cyme bipare 57
cyme unipare 57
cytopharynx 66
cytoplasme 50, 66, 112
cytoprocte 66
cytostome 66

D

dalle 230
dalmatien 86
Dame 468, 470
dames 469
dameuse 512
damier 470
Danemark 450
danois 86
Danube 18
date d'expiration 441
datte 132
dauphin 90
dauphin, morphologie 90
dé 469
dé à poker 468
dé doubleur 469
dé régulier 468
déambulateur 466
déambulatoire 285
débarbouillette 267
débardeur 250, 261, 263
débit de tabac 436
début 331
décagone régulier 429
décapeuse 400
décapsuleur 170, 531
décharge 431
déchets industriels 47
déchets nucléaires 48
déchiquetage 49

déclencheur 314
déclivité du terrain 182
décomposeurs 45
décor 291
décorateur 291
découpe 244
découpe princesse 258
découpes d'agneau 153
découpes de bœuf 152
découpes de porc 153
découpes de veau 152
défauts de la vision 419
défense 484
défenseur droit 506
défenseur gauche 506
défilement 331
déflecteur 236, 237, 364
déflecteur d'air chaud 192
déflecteur de chaleur 199
déflecteur de copeaux 227
déflecteur de fumée 192
défonceuse 229, 398
déforestation 47
dégagement d'air des citernes 385
dégagement du piston 216
dégrafeuse 341
degré 428
degré Celsius 426
Deimos 2
déjections animales 48
délégués techniques 509
delta 32, 35
deltoïde 96
démarrage manuel 237
déméloir 268
demeure seigneuriale 282
demi d'ouverture 482
demi de coin droit 484
demi de coin gauche 484
demi de mêlée 482
demi de sûreté droit 484
demi de sûreté gauche 484
demi offensif 485
demi-cercle 428, 488
demi-court de service en double 495
demi-court de service en simple 495
demi-lune 273
demi-manche 169
demi-membraneux 97
demi-pause 299
demi-soupir 299
demi-tendineux 97
demi-volée 490
dendrite 110
dénominations des cyclones tropicaux 43
dénoyauteur 173
dent 74, 76, 167, 226, 227, 235, 270, 398, 400, 503, 509
dent de défonceuse 398
dent de godet 399
dent de sagesse 101
denté 55
dentifrice 272
dents 101
denture humaine 101
dénude-fil 217
déodorant 267
dépanneuse 364
départ 469
départ des 400 m (course, haies, relais) 473
départ des télécabines 512
départ des télésièges 512
départ du 10 000 m et du relais 4 x 400 m 473
départ du 100 m (course et haies) 472
départ du 110 m haies 472
départ du 1500 m 473
départ du 200 m 472
départ du 5000 m 472
départ du 800 m 473
déplacement 418
déplacement des électrons, sens 416, 417
déplacement diagonal 470
déplacement en équerre 470
déplacement horizontal 470
déplacement vertical 470
déplacements, échecs 470
déporteur 392
dépression 39
dérailleur 372
dérailleur arrière 370, 372
dérailleur avant 370, 372
derby 240
dérive 393, 395, 519, 520

dérive aérienne 383
dériveur 520, 521
derme 114
dernier croissant 5
dernier quartier 5
dés 468
descente 511
descente de gouttière 182
désert 36, 40, 44
désert d'Atacama 17
désert de Gobi 19
désert de pierres 36
désert de sable 36
désert du Kalahari 20
désert du Namib 20
désert du Sahara 20
déshabillé 256
desserte 202
dessous 292
destination 374
destructeur de documents 341
détecteur d'impact primaire 354
détecteur de mouvement 286
détecteur de fumée 454
détecteur de sécurité 354
détente 534
détroit 24
détroit de Bass 15
détroit de Béring 16
détroit de Cook 15
détroit de Drake 15, 17
détroit de Gibraltar 18
détroit de Torres 15
deuxième but 474
deuxième espace 489
deuxième joueuse 515
deuxième ligne 482
deuxième molaire 101
deuxième prémolaire 101
deuxième radial externe 97
deuxième but 474
devant 244, 245
devant d'autel 446
déverrouillage de l'objectif 314
déversement d'hydrocarbures 48
dévidoir 236
dévidoir de ruban adhésif 341
dévidoir pistolet 341
dévidoir sur roues 236
devise 441
diable 175, 396
diamètre 428
diaphragme 105
dièse 299
diesel-navire 405
différence de potentiel électrique, mesure 426
différentiel 351
diffuseur 290
diffusion d'information 335
dinde 155
dindon 81
diode 411
Dioné 3
directeur artistique 290
directeur de course 522
directeur de la photographie 291
direction de La Mecque 447
direction du vent 39
direction et force du vent 39
discontinuité de Gutenberg 26
discontinuité de Mohorovicic 26
disjoncteur 407
dispositif anti-bascule 467
dispositif antidébordement 214
dispositif de blocage 219
dispositif de fermeture 535
dispositif de poussée 312
dispositif de remorquage 364
dispositifs de contact 198
disposition des informations d'une station 39
disquaire 436
disque 6, 333, 357, 472, 501
disque abrasif 229
disque compact 326
disque de papier-diagramme 365
disque dur amovible 333
disque numérique polyvalent (DVD) 318
disques 177
disquette 333
distillation sous vide 405
distributeur d'essence 346
distributeur de billets 437, 442
distributeur de boissons 346, 463
distributeur de correspondances 379

distributeur de détergent 214
distributeur de glaçons 164, 346
distributeur de lames 271
distributeur de produit de rinçage 214
distributeur de trombones 341
distribution de la végétation 44
ditali 146
division 337, 427
division du noyau 415
division territoriale 23
divisions cartographiques 22
dix 427
Dix commandements 447
djembé 297
Djibouti 451
Dniepr 18
do 298
dodécagone régulier 429
doigt 75, 79, 82, 114, 243, 477
doigt de juge 383
doigt externe 78
doigt interne 78
doigt lobé 79
doigt médian 78
doigt palmé 75, 79
doigt postérieur 78
doigt préhensile 91
doigtier 339
doline 31
dolique à œil noir 130
dolique asperge 130
dolique d'Égypte 130
doliques 130
dollar 440
domaine de premier niveau 334
domaine de second niveau 334
domaine skiable 512
Dominique 449
domino d'accouplement 305
dominos 468
donjon 282
dorade 159
dormant 186, 202
dormeuse-couverture 261
dors-bien 260
dorsale du Pacifique Est 34
dorsale médio-atlantique 34
dorsale médio-indienne 34
dorsale médio-océanique 33
dorsale Pacifique-Antarctique 34
dorsale Sud-Est-indienne 34
dorsale Sud-Ouest-indienne 34
dorsales océaniques 34
dos 78, 83, 86, 93, 95, 115, 167, 169, 226, 244
dos d'un gant 243
dos de la langue 118
dos du nez 117
dossard 473
dosseret 210, 212, 213
dossier 201, 205, 353, 369, 467, 523
dossier inclinable 460
dossier suspendu 340
dossière 76
double 468
double barre oblique 334
double bémol 299
double boutonnage 248
double croche 299
double dièse 299
double paire 468
double platine cassette 325
double toit 528, 529
double-blanc 468
double-six 468
doublement denté 55
doublure 240, 244, 245, 262, 274, 509
douche 189, 439, 464
douchette 195, 197
Douglas, cul-de-sac 112
douille 534
douille de lampe 199
douille de plastique 534
douilles, jeu 223
douve 282
dragonne 277, 510, 514
drap 204
drap de bain 267
drap-housse 204
drapeau 482
drapeau amovible 504
drapeau de centre 480
drapeau de coin 481
drapeau de l'Union Européenne 441
drapeaux 448
droit antérieur de la cuisse 96

droit interne 97
dromadaire 85
drumlin 29
drupéole 59
duffle-coat 249
dune 35
dune complexe 36
dune en croissant 36
dune parabolique 36
dunes longitudinales 36
dunes transversales 36
dunes, exemples 36
duo 300
duodénum 106
dure-mère 109, 110
durian 137
durite de radiateur 358
dyke 28
dynamo 370

E

eau 402
eau de fonte 30
eau de parfum 267
eau de toilette 267
eau dentifrice 272
eau des nuages 48
eau oxygénée 461
eaux usées 48
éboulement 31
ébrancheur 234
ébrasement 285
écaille 54, 74, 76, 79
écailles de cyprès 65
écailleur 531
écartement des électrodes 359
échalote 124
échancrure 301
échancrure de la conque 115
échangeur 431
échangeur en losange 342
échangeur en trèfle 342, 343
échangeur en trompette 342
échangeurs, exemples 342
échantillonneur 310
échappement 330
écharpe 187
échauguette 282
échecs 470
échecs, mouvements 470
échelle 184, 288, 361, 401, 404, 533
échelle Celsius 424
échelle coulissante 219
échelle d'onglet 226
échelle de profondeur 227
échelle de tête 455
échelle des altitudes 37
échelle des températures 37
échelle Fahrenheit 424
échelle graduée 422, 423
échelles 219
échelon 219
échenilloir-élagueur 234
échinodermes 66
échiquier 470
éclair 41
éclairage 199, 269, 380
éclairage de sécurité 457
éclairage/clignotant 354
éclipse annulaire 4
éclipse de Lune 5
éclipse de Soleil 4
éclipse partielle 4, 5
éclipse totale 4, 5
éclipses de Lune, types 5
éclipses de Soleil, types 4
éclisse 301, 302
écluse 381
école 444
école de ski 512
économie 441
écorce 58, 63
écoulement souterrain 45
écoute 328
écoute de foc 520
écoute de grand-voile 520
écouteur 324
écouteurs 325
écoutille 13
écoutille d'accès 12
écran 318, 329, 336, 338, 346, 439, 442, 443, 471, 479
écran à cristaux liquides 315, 320
écran d'affichage 339
écran de contrôle 314

ASTRONOMIE > 2-13; TERRE > 14-49; RÈGNE VÉGÉTAL > 50-65; RÈGNE ANIMAL > 66-91; ÊTRE HUMAIN > 92-119; ALIMENTATION ET CUISINE > 120-181; MAISON > 182-215; BRICO-LAGE ET JARDINAGE > 216-237; VÊTEMENTS > 238-263; PARURE ET OBJETS PERSONNELS > 264-277; ARTS ET ARCHITECTURE > 278-311; COMMUNICATIONS ET BUREAUTIQUE > 312-341; TRANSPORT ET MACHINERIE > 342-401; ÉNERGIES > 402-413; SCIENCE > 414-429; SOCIÉTÉ > 430-467; SPORTS ET JEUX > 468-538

571

INDEX FRANÇAIS

écran de l'ordinateur 10
écran de projection 294
écran de protection 474
écran protecteur 7
écran tactile 337
écrevisse 158
écritoire 275
écriture, instruments 312
écrou 222, 223
écrou à collet 197
écrou à oreilles 223
écrou borgne 223
écrou de blocage 536, 537
écrou de bonde 197
écrou de fixation 197
écrou de la lame 227
écrou de montage 535
écrou du porte-outil 229
écrou hexagonal 223, 359
écrous 223
écubier 383, 387
écueil 35
écume 33
écumoire 173
écureuil 82
écusson 73, 186, 477
édicule 378
édifice à bureaux 432, 435
édifice public 25
éditorial 313
édredon 204
éducation 444
effacement 328
effacement arrière : effacement 331
effacement de mémoire 337
effacement partiel 337
effacement total 337
effet de serre 46
effet de serre naturel 46
effigie 441
effluent 32
égal ou plus grand que 427
égal ou plus petit que 427
égale 427
égale à peu près 427
églefin 161
église 433, 446
égout 32
égout collecteur 434
Égypte 451
éjecteur de fouets 176
El Salvador 448
élan 85
élastique 204
électricien 291
électricité 198
électricité : outils 217
électrode centrale 359
électrode de masse 359
électron 414
électronique 417
élément chauffant 213, 214, 218
élément tubulaire 210
éléments d'architecture 286
éléments de la maison 185
éléphant 85
élevage intensif 46, 47
élévateur 400
élévateur pour fauteuils roulants 363
élévation 182
élévation de la tension 402, 408, 413
élève 444
élevon 13
émail 101
emballage 162
embase 473, 511
embase de plat de dos 200
emblème d'équipe 506
embouchure 307
embout 219, 221, 506, 536
embout auriculaire 460
embout buccal 307
embout de baleine 273
embout de caoutchouc 466
embout de protection 459
embout de vissage 228
embout isolant 269
embout Luer Lock 460
embrasse 466
embrayage 350
émerillon 535, 538
émetteur-récepteur radar 457
Émirats arabes unis 452
émission d'acide nitrique 48
émission d'acide sulfurique 48
émission d'oxyde d'azote 48

émission de dioxyde de soufre 48
émission de gaz polluants 47
émissole 158
emmanchure 247
emmarchement 191
emmenthal 151
empennage 393, 471, 495
empiècement 245, 249, 255
emplacement 182
emplacement de la statue 279
emporte-pièces 172
en équilibre 518
en-but 483
encadrement 192
enceinte acoustique 324, 325
enceinte ambiophonique 321
enceinte centrale 321
enceinte de confinement 408, 409
enceinte principale 321
enceintes d'extrêmes graves 321
encensoir 446
enclos 122
enclume 116
encoignure 203
encolure 83, 247
encolure en V 244, 250
encolure ras-de-cou 260
encre 312
encre à couleur changeante 441
endive 127
endocarde 104
endocarpe 57, 58
énergie calorifique 46
énergie éolienne 412, 413
énergie fossile 402
énergie géothermique 402
énergie nucléaire 408
énergie solaire 54, 410
énergie thermique 402
énergie, mesure 426
énergies 402
enfouissement 49
engrenage horaire 7
enjoliveur 349
ennéagone régulier 429
enregistrement 319, 323, 328
enregistrement des bagages 374
enregistrement sismographique 403
enseignant 444
enseigne directionnelle 379
enseigne extérieure 378
ensemble du chevalet 303
ensemble vide 427
entablement 185, 279
entier 55
entonnoir 72, 171, 177, 180
entraînement de la turbine par la vapeur 408
entraînement du rotor de l'alternateur 408
entraîneur 489, 498, 507
entraîneur adjoint 489, 507
entraîneurs 509
entre-nœud 53
entredent 167
entrée 343, 396
entrée d'air 395
entrée d'air du ventilateur 383
entrée de courant 199
entrée de garage 183
entrée de la pyramide 278
entrée des clients 438
entrée des marchandises 435
entrée des originaux 328
entrée du caloporteur 410
entrée du personnel 438, 445
entrée du public 278
entrée principale 188, 435, 445, 465
entrées des acteurs 278
entrejambe 202, 247
entrejambe pressionné 260, 261
entreposage des produits congelés 121
entrepôt 430
entrepôt frigorifique 381
entreprise 335
entreprise de distribution/vente 393
entretoise 219, 396, 412
enveloppe 477, 478, 505
enveloppe extérieure 7
enveloppe intérieure 7
enveloppe matelassée 339
environnement 44
environnement naturel 504
éolienne à axe horizontal 413
éolienne à axe vertical 412
éoliennes et production d'électricité 412
épaisseur, mesure 425

épandage d'engrais 47
épaule 83, 86, 92, 94, 492, 536
épaulé-jeté 500
épaulement 169, 223
épaulière 486
épeautre 143
épeire 70
éperlan 159
éperon 308
épi 57, 61
épi, blé 61
épi, maïs 61
épi, millet 61
épi, orge 61
épi, seigle 61
épicarpe 57, 58, 59
épicéa 65
épicentre 27
épicerie fine 120
épices 138
épices à marinade 139
épicondyle 99
épiderme 114
épididyme 111
épiglotte 105, 118
épinard 127
épine de l'omoplate 99
épine nasale antérieure 100
épingle à bigoudi 268
épingle à cheveux 268
épiphyse 104
épitrochlée 99
éplucheur 169
éponge à récurer 215
éponge de mer 267
éponge synthétique 266
éponge végétale 267
épreuves, ski alpin 511
épuisette 538
Équateur 448
équateur 17, 20, 21, 22, 43
équerre 225
équilibrage des haut-parleurs 322
équinoxe d'automne 38
équinoxe de printemps 38
équipe au champ 479
équipe médicale 499
équipement 472
équipement de survie 10
équipement de survie, contrôles 10
équipement divers 231
équipement du tableau de bord 457
équivaut à 427
érable 64
éruption 4
Érythrée 451
escabeau 219
escabeaux 219
escalier 184, 188, 191, 283, 293, 294, 345, 378, 404, 412, 439, 498
escalier de la mezzanine 189
escalier mécanique 294, 378, 435
escaliers 283
escargot 72, 157
escargot, morphologie 72
escarpin 241
escarpin-sandale 241
espace 330
espace épidural 110
espace insécable 330
espaceur de câbles 535
espadon 159
espadrille 242
Espagne 449
esquimau 261
essence 405
essence lourde 405
essieu 527
essieu avant 401
essoreuse à salade 171
essuie-glace 348, 355
Est 23
est identique à 427
Est Nord-Est 23
Est Sud-Est 23
estomac 73, 103, 106
estomac cardiaque 71
estomac pylorique 71
Estonie 450
estrade 283, 444
estragon 142
estuaire 24, 35
sturgeon 158
étable 122
établi étau 224
établissement d'enseignement 335

établissement scolaire 433
étage 182, 189, 412
étai avant 520
étamine 56, 58
étang 504
étapes de maturation 62
État 23
État de la cité du Vatican 450
état présent du temps 39
états de la matière 414
États fédérés de Micronésie 453
États-Unis d'Amérique 448
étau 224
été 38
Éthiopie 451
étiquette 423
étiquettes autocollantes 340
étoile de David 447
étoile de freinage 537
étoile filante 37
étourneau 80
étranglement 424, 499
étrave 384, 520
être humain 92
étrésillon 187
étrier 116, 198, 357, 366
étui 265, 337, 531
étui à lentilles 272
étui à lunettes 275
étui à menottes 456
étui à munitions 456
étui à pistolet 456
étui de cuir 533
étui pour gants de latex 456
Eurasie 14
euro 440
Europe 2, 14, 18, 34, 449
Eutelsat 316
euthynterie 279
évacuateur 406
évaporation 45
évent 90, 312
évent de pignon 182
évier 164, 197
évier double 194
évier-broyeur 197
évolution de la pression 39
Ex-République yougoslave de Macédoine 450
ex-voto 446
examen psychiatrique 462
exemples d'algues 51
exemples d'amphibiens 75
exemples d'angles 428
exemples d'arachnides 70
exemples d'arbres feuillus 64
exemples d'avions 394
exemples d'échangeurs 342
exemples d'insectes 69
exemples d'oiseaux 80
exemples d'unités monétaires 440
exemples de bateaux et d'embarcations 382
exemples de becs 79
exemples de bicyclettes 373
exemples de branchement 197
exemples de camions 364
exemples de carrosseries 347
exemples de chaises 201
exemples de clous 220
exemples de conifères 65
exemples de corsages 255
exemples de côtes 35
exemples de couteaux 168
exemples de couteaux de cuisine 169
exemples de cuillers 168
exemples de dunes 36
exemples de fauteuils 200
exemples de fenêtres 287
exemples de feuilles 65
exemples de fleurs 56
exemples de fougères 52
exemples de fourchettes 168
exemples de groupes instrumentaux 300
exemples de jupes 253
exemples de lichens 50
exemples de lunettes 273
exemples de mammifères carnivores 86
exemples de mammifères lagomorphes 82
exemples de mammifères marins 90
exemples de mammifères ongulés 84
exemples de mammifères primates 91
exemples de mammifères rongeurs 82
exemples de mèches et de forets 228
exemples de motos 369
exemples de mousses 51

exemples de pantalons 254
exemples de pattes 79
exemples de plis 253
exemples de pneus 358
exemples de pointes 221
exemples de portes 286
exemples de prises 499
exemples de reptiles 77
exemples de robes 252
exemples de sacs de couchage 530
exemples de sauts 509
exemples de skis 510
exemples de tables 202
exemples de tentes 528
exemples de têtes 221
exemples de volcans 28
exemples de wagons 377
exosphère 37
expandeur 310
expédition du fret 391
extenseur 500
extenseur commun des doigts 97
extenseur commun des orteils 96
extérieur d'une maison 182
extincteur 454, 457
extrait de vanille 140
eye-liner liquide 266

F

fa 298
façade 285
face 91, 167, 493, 505
face antérieure 92, 94, 96
face postérieure 93, 95, 97
facteur rhésus négatif 426
facteur rhésus positif 426
factorielle 427
facules 4
faille 27
faine 133
faisan 81, 154
faisceau bleu 318
faisceau d'électrons 318
faisceau laser 420
faisceau rouge 318
faisceau vert 318
faîtage 187
faîteau 283
faîtout 175, 531
faits divers 313
falaise 5, 29, 35
falaise côtière 35
Fallope, trompe 112
famille des bois 295
famille des cuivres 295
famille du violon 295, 301
fanon 83
fard à joues en poudre 266
farine d'avoine 144
farine de blé complet 144
farine de maïs 144
farine et semoule 144
farine non blanchie 144
farine tout usage 144
fart 514
faucille 234
faucon 81
fausse côte (3) 99
fausse oronge 52
fausse poche 251
fausse-équerre 225
fauteuil 200, 293, 294, 444
fauteuil à bascule 200
fauteuil club 200
fauteuil de repos 464
fauteuil du réalisateur 291
fauteuil metteur en scène 200
fauteuil roulant 467
fauteuil Wassily 200
fauteuil-sac 201
fauteuils des acteurs 290
fauteuils, exemples 200
faux bourdon 68
Fédération de Russie 450
feijoa 137
femelle 426
femme 94
fémur 98
fenêtre 186, 189, 243, 361, 380, 519
fenêtre à guillotine 287
fenêtre à jalousies 287
fenêtre à l'anglaise 287
fenêtre à la française 287
fenêtre basculante 287
fenêtre coulissante 287

ASTRONOMIE > 2-13; TERRE > 14-49; RÈGNE VÉGÉTAL > 50-65; RÈGNE ANIMAL > 66-91; ÊTRE HUMAIN > 92-119; ALIMENTATION ET CUISINE > 120-181; MAISON > 182-215; BRIC●
LAGE ET JARDINAGE > 216-237; VÊTEMENTS > 238-263; PARURE ET OBJETS PERSONNELS > 264-277; ARTS ET ARCHITECTURE > 278-311; COMMUNICATIONS ET BUREAUTIQUE > 312-34
TRANSPORT ET MACHINERIE > 342-401; ÉNERGIES > 402-413; SCIENCE > 414-429; SOCIÉTÉ > 430-467; SPORTS ET JEUX > 468-538

fenêtre de lecture 333
fenêtre de sous-sol 183
fenêtre en accordéon 287
fenêtre moustiquaire 528
fenêtre panoramique 435
fenêtre pivotante 287
fenêtres, exemples 287
fenil 122
fennec 88
fenouil 125
fente 178, 221, 274
fente de dépôt 442
fente de mise à jour du livret bancaire 442
fente de relevé d'opération 442
fente du lecteur de carte 346, 442, 443
fente latérale 244
fente médiane 244
fente pour carte PC 336
fentes branchiales 74
fentes d'aération 336
fenugrec 138
fer 229, 505
fer à friser 269
fer à souder 218
fer à vapeur 208
fer droit 505
ferme 122
fermeture à glissière 249, 261, 265, 277, 528
fermeture du soufflet 296
fermeture sous patte 261
fermeture Velcro® 260
fermoir 274, 275
ferret 240, 262, 273
ferrure 277
ferrure d'attelage 356
fertilisation des sols 47
fesse 93, 95, 111, 112
fettucine 146
feu antibrouillard 352, 364
feu anticollision 392
feu arrière 367, 368, 370
feu clignotant 352
feu clignotant arrière 367, 368
feu clignotant avant 366, 368
feu de circulation 434
feu de croisement 352
feu de freinage 352
feu de gabarit 364, 365
feu de navigation 383, 393
feu de plaque 352
feu de position 352, 376, 395
feu de recul 352
feu de route 352
feu de tête de mât 383
feu jaune 434
feu pour piétons 434
feu rouge 434
feu rouge arrière 352
feu vert 434
feuillage 63
feuille 51, 53, 54, 55, 61, 125
feuille d'acanthe 200
feuille de vigne 62, 126
feuille, bord 55
feuille, structure 55
feuilles composées 55
feuilles simples 55
feuilles, exemples 65
feuillets 274
feuillets intercalaires 339
feutre d'étouffoir 304
feux arrière 352
feux avant 352
feux intermittents 362
fèves 130
fibre musculaire 110
fibre nerveuse 114
fibres 215
fibres musculaires 110
fiche 228
fiche américaine 198
fiche d'alimentation 337
fiche européenne 198
fiche pour jack 324
fiche, adaptateur 198, 271
fichier 334
fichier rotatif 338
Fidji 453
figue 137
figue de Barbarie 137
fil 417
fil d'attache 70
fil de nylon 237
fil de sécurité 441
fil dentaire 272
filament 199

file d'attente 443
filet 56, 205, 221, 301, 302, 313, 487, 489, 491, 493, 495
filet de bœuf 152
filière 70
filigrane 441
filoir d'écoute 521
filtre 178, 184, 210
filtre à air 235, 350, 398
filtre à charpie 212, 213
filtre de polarisation 314
filtre terminal 109
filum terminal 109
fin 331
finance 441
fines herbes 142
Finlande 450
fission de l'uranium 408
fission nucléaire 415
fixation 473, 513, 514
fixation à butée avant 514
fixation de sécurité 510, 511
fjords 35
flacon 267
flageolet 131
flamant 81
flamme 415
flanc 78, 83, 358
fléau 422
fléau arrière 422
fléau avant 422
flèche 285, 397, 399, 400, 469, 503
flèche de transept 284
flèche littorale 35
flèche télescopique 397, 455
fléchette 471
flétan 161
fleur 53, 56
fleur, structure 56
fleuriste 437
fleurs, exemples 56
fleuve 24, 25, 32
flexible 195, 197
flexible d'injection de boue 403
flexible de distribution 346
flip 509
floraison 62
flotteur 196, 394, 519, 538
flûte à champagne 165
flûte de Pan 297
flûte traversière 306
flûtes 295
foc 520
foie 103, 106, 154
foie gras 156
follicule 60, 114
follicule, coupe 60
fonctions système 310
fond 526
fond d'yeux 167
fond de l'océan 26
fond de l'océan 33
fond de protection 471
fond de robe 258
fond de teint liquide 266
fond de tour 405
fondation de pylône 344
fondation inférieure 342
fondation supérieure 342
fongicide 47
fontaine des ablutions 447
fontanelle antérieure 100
fontanelle mastoïdienne 100
fontanelle postérieure 100
fontanelle sphénoïdale 100
fonts baptismaux 446
football 480
football américain 484
football américain, protection 486
footballeur 480, 486
foramen apical 101
foramen cæcum 118
force du vent 39
force, mesure 426
forêt 29
forêt boréale 44
forêt de conifères 44
forêt de feuillus 44
foret de maçonnerie 228
foret hélicoïdal 228
forêt mixte 44
forêt tempérée 44
forêt tropicale 44
forêt tropicale humide 44
format du fichier 334
formation de jazz 300
formes géométriques 428

formes pharmaceutiques des médicaments 467
forte pluie 43
fossé 342
fosse à plonger 184
fosse abyssale 33
fosse d'orchestre 292
fosse de Java 34
fosse de Porto Rico 34
fosse de sable 504
fosse des Aléoutiennes 34
fosse des Kouriles 34
fosse des Mariannes 34
fosse des Philippines 34
fosse des Ryukyu 34
fosse des Tonga-Kermadec 34
fosse du Japon 34
fosse Pérou-Chili 34
fosse septique 48
fosses nasales 117
fosses océaniques 34
fossette 76
fossette de l'anthélix 115
Fou 470
fouet 172, 176
fouet à fil 176
fouet en spirale 176
fouet quatre pales 176
fouets 176
fougère 52
fougère arborescente 52
fougère nid d'oiseau 52
fougère, structure 52
fouine 88
four 164, 210
four à micro-ondes 164, 178
four tubulaire 405
fourche 8, 371, 522, 525
fourche à bêcher 233
fourche à fleurs 232
fourche avant 522
fourche télescopique 369
fourche télescopique hydraulique 366
fourches 396
fourchette 167, 243, 531
fourchette à découper 169
fourchette à dessert 168
fourchette à fondue 168
fourchette à huîtres 168
fourchette à poisson 168
fourchette à salade 168
fourchette de table 168
fourchettes, exemples 168
fourgon-pompe 455
fourgonnette 347
fourmi 69
fourmi 69
fournisseur de services Internet 335
fourreau 519
fourreau de la langue 76
fovéa 119
foyer 27, 419
foyer Cassegrain 7
foyer coudé 7
foyer des élèves 445
foyer primaire 7
foyer, accessoires 193
foyers 293
fraction 427
fraise 132
fraise, coupe 59
framboise 132
framboise, coupe 59
France 449
frappeur 475, 476
frein 501, 511, 522, 536
frein à disque 350, 357, 366, 525
frein à main 350
frein à tambour 357
frein arrière 370
frein avant 370
frein d'urgence 380
frein de chaîne 235
frein de talon 527
frein hydraulique à disque 522
freins 357
frelon 69
fréquence, mesure 426
fresque 280
frette 302, 303
frise 185, 202, 279, 293
frises 292
friteuse 178
fromage à tartiner 150
fromages à pâte molle 151
fromages à pâte persillée 151
fromages à pâte pressée 151

fromages de chèvre 150
fromages frais 150
fronce 255
fronde 51, 52
front 78, 92
frontal 96, 98, 100
frontière 23
fronton 279
frottoir 218
fruit charnu 59
fruit charnu : agrume 58
fruit charnu à noyau 57
fruit charnu à pépins 58
fruit de la Passion 136
fruits 57, 120, 132
fruits à noyau 132
fruits à pépins 133
fruits secs 60, 133
fruits tropicaux 136
fumerolle 28
funicule 59, 60
furet de dégorgement 216
fuseau 254
fusée à propergol solide 12
fusée éclairante 457
fuselage 393
fusible 198, 411
fusil 169
fusil (canon lisse) 534
fusilli 146
fusion 414
fût 63, 207, 221, 308, 471, 534
futon 204

G

gâble 285
Gabon 451
gâchette 235, 332, 454
gâchette de sécurité 235
gaffe 454
Gai Ion 321
gaine 55, 259, 417, 533
gaine d'air frais 345
gaine d'air vicié 345
gaine de myéline 110
gaine de Schwann 110
gaine-culotte 259
galaxie 6
galerie 285, 412
galerie de dérivation 406
galerie de liaison 345
galerie de visite 407
galerie marchande 435
galerie sèche 31
galet 332
galets tendeurs 372
galettes de riz 147
galon 238
galon d'ornement 260
galop 83
Gambie 451
gamme 298
ganache 298
ganglion cérébropleural 73
ganglion du tronc sympathique 109
ganglion spinal 109, 110
ganglion viscéral 73
ganse 531
gant 10, 477, 478, 498, 506, 508, 513, 514, 522, 525
gant à crispin 243
gant court 243
gant de conduite 243
gant de crin 267
gant de frappeur 476
gant de golf 505
gant de receveur 476
gant de ski 510
gant de softball 477
gant de toilette 267
gant en latex 460
gant long 243
gant saxe 243
gants 243
gants d'homme 243
gants de boxe 498
gants de femme 243
gants de gardien de but 480
gants de jardinage 232
Ganymède 2
garage 182, 345
garam masala 139
garant 240
garde de clé 306
garde de culasse 306

garde droit 485
garde gauche 485
garde-boue 370
garde-boue arrière 369
garde-boue avant 366
garde-corps 219, 344, 377
garde-fou 189
garde-manger 164, 188
garde-robe 189
gardien de but 481, 506, 507
gardien de guichet 479
gare 25, 375, 430, 432
gare de marchandises 375
gare de triage 430
gare de voyageurs 374, 375
gare maritime 381
gare routière 432
garniture 277
garniture de frein 357
garrot 83, 86
gaufrier-gril 178
gaz 403, 405, 414
gaz à effet de serre 46
gaz inerte 199
gazole 405
gazon 230, 492
geai 80
gélule 467
gencive 101, 116
générateur de vapeur 402
genou 83, 86, 92, 94
genouillère 476, 486, 500, 526, 527
géographie 14
géologie 26
géométrie 428
Géorgie 452
géothermie 402
gerboise 82
germe 61, 79
germes de soja 131
germination 53
geyser 28
Ghana 451
ghee 150
gibbeuse croissante 5
gibbeuse décroissante 5
gibbon 91
gibier 154
gicleur de lave-glace 348
gicleurs 408
gigot 153
gilet 244, 255
gilet de laine 250
gingembre 139
girafe 85
giron 191
girouette 413, 520
gisement de pétrole 403
givre 41
glace 45, 349, 352
glace de custode 349
glacier 30, 32, 44
glacier suspendu 30
glacière 532
glacis précontinental 33
gland 111
glande à venin 76
glande de Cowper 111
glande digestive 71, 73
glande lacrymale 119
glande mammaire 113
glande salivaire 106
glande sébacée 114
glande sudoripare apocrine 114
glande sudoripare eccrine 114
glande surrénale 107
glandes salivaires 106
glissement de terrain 31
glissière 214
glissière d'ajustement 324
glissière d'auvent 361
glissière de fixation 420
glissoir 240
globe 529
globe oculaire 75, 119
globe terrestre 444
globule blanc 104
globule rouge 104
glotte 76
glucose 54
gnocchi 146
go 470
godet 399
godet à poussière 208
godet de beurre 163
godet de lait/crème 163

godet rétro 399, 400
golf 504
golfe 24
golfe d'Aden 19, 20
golfe d'Alaska 16
golfe d'Oman 19
golfe de Botnie 18
golfe de Californie 16
golfe de Carpentarie 15
golfe de Guinée 20
golfe de Panama 17
golfe du Bengale 19
golfe du Mexique 16
golfe Persique 19
Golgi 50, 66
gombo 128
gomme 341
gonade 73
gond 185, 202
gondole 121
gonfleur 530
gonfleur-dégonfleur 530
gong 295, 309
gorge 31, 32, 78, 224, 538
gorgonzola 151
gorille 91
gorille, morphologie 91
gouffre 31
goujon 357
goujure 228
goulot de remplissage 351
goupille 454
gour 31
gourde 532
gourmand 62
gourmette 264
gourmette d'identité 264
gousse, coupe 60
gousset de latte 519, 520
goût 116
gouttelette lipidique 50
gouttes ophtalmiques lubrifiantes 272
gouttière 182, 207, 349
gouvernail 13, 384, 386, 412, 520
gouverne de direction 393
gouverne de profondeur 393
goyave 137
gradateur 198
gradins 278, 281
gradins mobiles 444
graduation 225, 424, 425, 460, 533
graduation de la règle 425
graduation du vernier 425
grain 61
grain d'amidon 50
grain de blé, coupe 61
graine 53, 57, 58, 59, 60
graine de soja 131
graines de pavot 139
grains de café torréfiés 148
grains de café verts 148
graisses 405
grand adducteur 97
Grand Canyon 16
grand complexus 97
Grand Désert de Sable 15
Grand Désert Victoria 15
grand dorsal 97
grand droit de l'abdomen 96
grand duc d'Amérique 81
grand fauchage extérieur 499
grand fauchage intérieur 499
grand fessier 97
grand oblique de l'abdomen 96, 97
grand palmaire 96
grand pectoral 96
grand rond 97
grand trochanter 99
grand-voile 520
Grande Baie australienne 15
grande échelle 455
grande galerie 278
grande lame 531
grande lèvre 112, 113
grande roussette 158
grande sauterelle verte 69
grande sus-alaire 78
grande ville 23
grandes lignes 375
Grands Lacs 16
grange 122
granulation 4
grappe 33
grappe de combustible 409
grappe de raisin 62
grappe, sarrasin 61

grasset 83
gratte-ongles 265
grattoir 219
graveur de disque compact 325
graveur de disque compact réinscriptible
    333
graveur de DVD 333
grébiche 274
Grèce 450
grelots 309
Grenade 449
grenade 136
grenouille 75
grenouille des bois 75
grenouille léopard 75
grenouille rousse 75
grenouille, morphologie 75
grenouillère 260
grésil 41
griffe 71, 76, 82
griffe à fleurs 232
griffe porte-accessoires 314
gril barbecue 179
gril électrique 179
gril pliant 533
grillage de protection 217
grille 174, 210, 271, 279, 296, 318,
    358, 407, 476
grille d'aération 214, 380
grille d'aspiration 270
grille d'éclairage 291
grille d'entrée d'air 367
grille d'extrémité 409
grille de chauffage 380
grille de départ 524
grille de sécurité 442
grille de sortie d'air 270
grille de ventilation 209
grille des programmes de télévision 313
grille métallique conductrice 410
grille stabilisatrice 529
grille-pain 178
Groenland 16
grondin 159
gros intestin 106
gros sel 141
groseille à grappes 132
groseille à maquereau 132
grosse caisse 295, 308
grotte 31, 35
groupe électropompe 357
groupe frigorifique 365
groupe turbo-alternateur 402, 407
groupes instrumentaux, exemples 300
grue à flèche 381
grue à tour 397
grue sur ponton 381
grue sur porteur 397
grues 397
gruppetto 299
gruyère 151
Guatemala 448
guépard 89
guêpe 69
guêpière 259
guichet 443, 479
guichet automatique bancaire 442, 443
guichet commercial 443
guichet de nuit 443
guichet de vente des billets 378
guide 178, 226, 333
guide des températures 208
guide parallèle 227
guide-bande 341
guide-chaîne 235, 372
guide-ligne 537
guide-papier 328
guides de classement 340
guidon 237, 371, 507, 523, 534
guidon surélevé 522
guimbarde 297
guindant 519
guindeau 384
Guinée 451
Guinée équatoriale 451
Guinée-Bissau 451
guitare acoustique 302
guitare basse 303
guitare électrique 303
Gutenberg, discontinuité 26
Guyana 448
guyot 33
gymnase 386, 444
gymnastique 496
gyrophare 455

H

habilleur 290
habitacle 12, 525
habitation 122
hache 234, 454
hachette 533
hachoir 170
hackle 536
haie 183, 230
Haïti 448
halebas 520
hall 435, 439
hall d'entrée 188
hall public 390
halo 6
halte-garderie 437
haltère court 500
haltère long 500, 501
haltérophilie 500
hameçon 536, 538
hameçon monté 538
hameçon triple 538
hampe 538
hamster 82
hanche 93, 95
hanche ailée 499
hangar 122, 389
hangar de transit 381
hanneton 69
haptère 51
hareng 159
haricot adzuki 131
haricot d'Espagne 131
haricot de Lima 131
haricot jaune 131
haricot mungo 131
haricot mungo à grain noir 131
haricot noir 131
haricot pinto 131
haricot romain 131
haricot rouge 131
haricot vert 131
haricots 131
harissa 141
harmonica 296
harpe 302
harpes 295
hastée 55
hauban 370, 394, 412, 520, 528
hausse 301, 534
haut-de-forme 238
haut-parleur 294, 320, 326, 327, 328,
    336, 455
haut-parleur d'aigus 324
haut-parleur de graves 324
haut-parleur de médiums 324
hautbois 295, 306
hauteur de la vague 33
hauteur de marche 191
hébergement 512
hélice 384, 386, 387, 429
hélice arrière 384
hélice bipale 394
hélice d'étrave 384
hélice de propulsion 383
hélice tripale 394
hélicoptère 395
hélix 115
hémisphère 429
hémisphère austral 21
hémisphère boréal 21
hémisphère occidental 21
hémisphère oriental 21
hémisphères 21
hendécagone régulier 429
heptagone régulier 429
herbe longue 504
herbicide 47
herbivores 45
héron 80
herse 292
hertz 426
hétérotrophes 45
hêtre 64
hexagone régulier 429
hijiki 123
hile du rein 107
Himalaya 19
hippopotame 85
hirondelle 80
hiver 38
hockey sur glace 506
hockeyeur 506
homard 71, 158
homard, anatomie 71

homard, morphologie 71
home cinéma 321
homme 92
Honduras 448
Hongrie 450
hôpital 433, 462
horloge programmatrice 178, 210
hors-bord 385
hôtel 432, 439, 469, 512
hôtel de ville 432
hotte 164, 192, 210
houppette 266
houppier 63
housse à vêtements 277
housse d'oreiller 204
housse pour automobile 356
houe 233
hoummos 140
huile d'arachide 149
huile d'olive 149
huile de maïs 149
huile de sésame 149
huile de tournesol 149
huiles 149
huiles lubrifiantes 405
huitième de soupir 299
huître creuse du Pacifique 157
huître plate 157
huîtrier 119
Hubble, télescope spatial 7, 37
hublot 178, 179, 210, 386, 392
hublot d'atterrissage 395
hublot d'observation 13
huméro-stylo-radial 96
humérus 98
humeur aqueuse 119
hutte 288
hydravion à flotteurs 394
hydroélectricité 406
hydromètre 359
hydroptère 387
hydrosphère 44
hyène 88
hygiène dentaire 272
hyperliens 334
hypermétropie 419
hyphe 52
hypoderme 114
hypophyse 109
hysope 142

I

identification du compte 443
igloo 288
igname 124
iguane 77
île 24
île de sable 35
île de Terre-Neuve 16
île volcanique 33
iléon 106
îles Aléoutiennes 16
îles Falkland 17
îles Fidji 15
îles Marshall 453
îles Salomon 453
îlot 164, 343
îlot rocheux 35
immeuble résidentiel 433
immobilisation 499
imparipennée 55
impériale 363
imperméable 248
impluvium 280
impression de l'écran 331
imprimante à jet d'encre 333
incendie de forêt 47
incinération 49
incisive centrale 101
incisive latérale 101
incisives 101
inclinaison de la semelle 227
inclusion 427
indicateur de charge 271
indicateur de ligne 362, 363
indicateur de microsillon 323
indicateur de niveau 515
indicateur de niveau d'eau 179
indicateur de niveau du carburant 355
indicateur de position 287
indicateur de réglage 511
indicateur de température 355

indicateur de vitesse 355, 368, 501
Indonésie 19, 453
industrie 335
infiltration 45, 47
infini 427
infirmière 464
inflorescence, modes 57
influx nerveux 110
infrastructure 342
inhalateur doseur 467
initiales de la banque émettrice 441
injecteur 360
insectes 67
insectes, exemples 69
insertion 331
insigne 456
insigne d'identité 456
insigne de grade 456
instruments à clavier 304
instruments à cordes 301
instruments à percussion 295, 308
instruments à vent 306
instruments d'écriture 312
instruments de bord 355
instruments électroniques 310
instruments scientifiques 13
instruments traditionnels 296
intégrale 427
intégration de l'électricité au réseau de
    transport 413
Intelsat 317
intensité lumineuse, mesure 426
interligne 298
internaute 334
Internet 334
interosseux 96
interrupteur 177, 181, 198, 206, 208,
    209, 211, 218, 219, 269, 270,
    271, 272, 327, 329, 416
interrupteur à gâchette 227, 228, 229
interrupteur d'accord 323
interrupteur d'alimentation 311, 318,
    319, 322, 323
interrupteur d'alimentation 318
interrupteur d'éclairage 269
interrupteur de démarrage 213
interrupteur de fin de course 287
interrupteur de la porte 213
interrupteur du magnétoscope 319
interrupteur du téléviseur 319
interrupteur principal 198
interruption 331
intersection 427
intertitre 313
intervalles 298
interview 313
intestin 71, 73, 103
intestin grêle 106
inverseur de marche 221, 228
inverseur de signe 337
inverseur route-croisement 368
Io 2
Iran 452
Iraq 452
iris 119
Irlande 449
isba 288
ischion 99
Islande 18, 450
isobare 39
isolant 190, 214, 410
isolateur 359
isoloir 443
Israël 452
isthme 24
isthme de la trompe utérine 113
isthme de Panama 16
isthme du gosier 116
Italie 450
ivoire 101

J

jaboticaba 137
jachère 122
jack de sortie 303
jacquet 469
jaguar 89
Jamahiriya arabe libyenne 451
Jamaïque 448
jambage 197
jambe 83, 91, 93, 95, 247
jambe élastique 247
jambier antérieur 96
jambière 263, 476, 478
jambière de gardien de but 507

ASTRONOMIE > 2-13;   TERRE > 14-49;   RÈGNE VÉGÉTAL > 50-65;   RÈGNE ANIMAL > 66-91;   ÊTRE HUMAIN > 92-119;   ALIMENTATION ET CUISINE > 120-181;   MAISON > 182-215;   BRICO-
LAGE ET JARDINAGE > 216-237;   VÊTEMENTS > 238-263;   PARURE ET OBJETS PERSONNELS > 264-277;   ARTS ET ARCHITECTURE > 278-311;   COMMUNICATIONS ET BUREAUTIQUE > 312-341;
TRANSPORT ET MACHINERIE > 342-401;   ÉNERGIES > 402-413;   SCIENCE > 414-429;   SOCIÉTÉ > 430-467;   SPORTS ET JEUX > 468-538

jambon cuit 156
jambon fumé 153
jan extérieur 469
jan intérieur 469
jante 366, 371
Japet 3
Japon 19, 453
jaque 136
jardin 280
jardin d'agrément 230
jardin potager 122, 182
jardin public 435
jardinage 216, 230
jarlsberg 151
jarret 83, 86, 152, 153
jarretelle 259
jaune 79, 418
javelot 472
jazz, formation 300
jean 254
jéjunum 106
jet d'eau 185, 186
jet dentaire 272
jets d'eau 518
jeu 492
jeu d'ustensiles 173
jeu de brides 459
jeu de dames 470
jeu de douilles 223
jeu de fléchettes 471
jeu de petits outils 232
jeux 468
jeux de plateau 469
jeux en ligne 335
jicama 124
joint 214, 312
joint à coulisse 222
joint d'étanchéité 197, 404
joint de bougie 359
joint de carter 360
joint magnétique 211
Joker 468
jonc 264
jonction positif/négatif 410
jonquille 56
Jordanie 452
joue 86, 94, 220, 536
joueur de basketball 488
joueur de cricket : batteur 478
joueurs 492
joueuse de tennis 492
joule 426
journal 313
judo 499
judogi 499
juge 498, 499
juge arbitre 516, 518
juge de but 506
juge de champ arrière 485
juge de classement 516
juge de départ 516
juge de faute de pied 491
juge de filet 491
juge de ligne 487, 490, 494, 496, 507
juge de ligne en chef 485
juge de ligne médiane 490
juge de mêlée 485
juge de nage 516
juge de service 490, 494
juge de touche 481, 483, 485
juges 496, 497, 509, 518
juges de virages 517
jugulaire 486
jujube 137
jumeau 96, 97
jumelles à prismes 420
juge 251
jupe à empiècement 253
jupe à lés 253
jupe à volants étagés 253
jupe de masque 459
jupe de piston 360
jupe droite 253
jupe fourreau 253
jupe froncée 253
jupe portefeuille 253
jupe souple 383
jupe-culotte 253
jupes, exemples 253
jupette 492
jupon 258
Jupiter 2
justaucorps 263
justice 440

K

kaki 137
Kazakhstan 452
kelvin 426
Kenya 451
kérosène 405
ketchup 141
kettle 29
kilogramme 426
kilt 253
kimono 256
kiosque 346, 379
Kirghizistan 452
Kiribati 453
kiwi 136
knicker 254
kombu 123
kora 297
Koweït 452
Kuiper, ceinture 2
kumquat 134

L

la 298
laboratoire 7
laboratoire américain 11
laboratoire de pathologie 465
laboratoire européen 11
laboratoire japonais 11
laboratoire spatial 13
lac 5, 24, 29, 32
lac artificiel 32
lac Baïkal 19
lac d'origine glaciaire 32
lac d'origine tectonique 32
lac d'origine volcanique 32
lac en croissant 32
lac Eyre Nord 15
lac Ladoga 18
lac Malawi 20
lac salé 36
lac Tanganyika 20
lac Tchad 20
lac Titicaca 17
lac Victoria 20
laccolite 28
lacet 240, 262, 395, 477, 498, 509
lacet de serrage 275
lacs 32
lactaire délicieux 123
lagomorphes 82
lagon 35
lagune 35
lait 150
lait concentré 150
lait de chèvre 150
lait en poudre 150
lait homogénéisé 150
laiterie 122
laitue asperge 126
laitue de mer 123
laitue frisée 126
laitue iceberg 126
laitue pommée 126
laize 520
lama 84
lambourde 187
lame 167, 169, 177, 190, 198, 216, 219, 221, 226, 227, 235, 279, 291, 297, 309, 341, 355, 398, 401, 506, 509
lame à double tranchant 271
lame criblée de l'ethmoïde 117
lame de coupe 180
lame de danse sur glace 509
lame de scie circulaire 227
lame dentée 270
lame droite 270
lame isolée 217
lame porte-objet 421
lame pour programme libre 509
lame racleuse 400
lamelle 52, 190
lampadaire 206
lampe 217, 421
lampe à économie d'énergie 199, 411
lampe à halogène 199
lampe à incandescence 199
lampe à souder 218
lampe au néon 217
lampe d'architecte 206
lampe de bureau 206
lampe de bureau halogène 206

lampe de chevet 439, 464
lampe de lecture 457
lampe de sanctuaire 446
lampe de table 206
lampe liseuse 206
lampe-tempête 532
lampe-torche 456
lampes témoins 318, 355
lamproie 159
lance à eau 455
lance d'arrosage 236
lance-canon 455
lancéolée 55
lancer 475, 479
lancer disque 473
lancer du javelot 473
lancer du poids 472
lancer marteau 473
lanceur 474, 475, 479
langouste 158
langoustine 158
langue 106, 116, 117, 154
langue bifide 76
langue glaciaire 30
langue, dos 118
languette 240, 262, 305, 509, 511
lanière 286, 500
lanterne 230, 529
lanterne de pied 207
lanterne murale 207
lanterneau 183
lanterneau de la cage d'escalier 189
lanterneau de la salle de bains 189
lapiaz 31
lapin 82, 154
lard 149
larynx 105
lasagne 146
laser à rubis pulsé 420
latitude 8, 9, 22
latrines 280
latte 412, 519, 520
laurier 142
lavabo 194, 195, 439, 464
lavabo du chirurgien 465
lave-auto 346
lave-linge 194, 212
lave-vaisselle 164, 214
lèchefrite 174
lecteur CD/DVD 471
lecteur de carte 321
lecteur de cassette 326, 333
lecteur de CD/DVD-ROM 329, 336
lecteur de disque compact 323, 325, 326
lecteur de disque dur 333
lecteur de disque dur amovible 333
lecteur de disquette 310, 329
lecteur de disquette externe 333
lecteur de DVD vidéo 318
lecteur optique 121
lecture 319, 323, 326
lecture rapide 323
lecture/pause 323
légende 313
légumes 120, 124
légumes bulbes 124
légumes-feuilles 126
légumes fleurs 127
légumes fruits 128
légumes racines 129
légumes tiges 125
légumes tubercules 124
légumier 166
légumineuses 130
lémurien 91
lentille biconcave 419
lentille biconvexe 419
lentille concave 419
lentille convexe 419
lentille cylindrique 419
lentille de champ 420
lentille jetable 272
lentille objectif 8, 420
lentille plan-concave 419
lentille plan-convexe 419
lentille rigide 272
lentille souple 272
lentilles 130, 419
lentilles convergentes 419
lentilles de contact 272
lentilles de redressement 420
lentilles divergentes 419
léopard 89
Lesotho 452
lessivage du sol 48
lest 397

Lettonie 450
leucoplaste 50
lève-fil 208
levier 197, 222, 265, 269, 534
levier coudé 399
levier d'embrayage 366, 368
levier de blocage 224
levier de clé 306
levier de déclenchement 196
levier de dégagement 222
levier de frein à main 354
levier de frein avant 368
levier de manœuvre du mât 396
levier de perçage 180
levier de réglage latéral 229
levier de serrage 224
levier de vibrato 303
levier de vitesse 354
levier de vitesses 350
levier du bloc 229
levier du piston 216
levier du protège-lame inférieur 227
levier plat 220
lèvre 83, 87, 228
lèvre inférieure 116, 305
lèvre supérieure 116, 305
lézard 77
liaison 299
liaison chimique 414
Liban 452
libellule 69
liber 63
libération d'énergie 415
Liberia 451
libero 481, 487
librairie 436
lice 282
lichen 50
lichen crustacé 50
lichen foliacé 50
lichen fruticuleux 50
lichen, structure 50
lichens, exemples 50
Liechtenstein 450
liège 514
lierne 284
lieu noir 161
lièvre 82, 154
ligament 73
ligament alvéolo-dentaire 101
ligament large de l'utérus 113
ligament suspenseur 119
ligne 298
ligne arrière 515
ligne bleue 507
ligne câblée 335
ligne centrale 493, 507
ligne continue 342
ligne d'arrivée 473
ligne d'attaque 487
ligne de balayage 515
ligne de ballon mort 482
ligne de but 482, 484, 506
ligne de cadre 502
ligne de centre 484, 515
ligne de côté 487
ligne de couloir 473
ligne de croissance 72, 73
ligne de départ 473, 524
ligne de distribution à basse tension 198
ligne de distribution à moyenne tension 198
ligne de double 490, 495
ligne de fond 484, 487, 489, 491, 493, 494, 517
ligne de force 416
ligne de jeu 471, 474, 515
ligne de lancer franc 489
ligne de mêlée 485
ligne de retrait 479
ligne de sécurité 379
ligne de service 490, 494
ligne de service court 495
ligne de service long 494
ligne de simple 491, 495
ligne de surface de réparation 480
ligne de suture 73
ligne de touche 481, 483, 484, 488
ligne de visée 533
ligne dédiée 334
ligne des 10 m 482
ligne des 15 m 483
ligne des 22 m 482
ligne des 5 m 483
ligne des verges 484
ligne discontinue 342, 343

ligne isosiste 27
ligne latérale 74, 493, 515
ligne médiane 481, 483, 488, 494
ligne médiane de service 491
ligne méridienne 533
ligne neutre 416
ligne sous-marine 334
ligne supplémentaire 298
ligne téléphonique 334
limbe 52, 55
lime 229, 265, 531
lime à ongles 265
limes-émeri 265
limite de retour 479
limite du batteur 479
limite du terrain 182
limiteur de surchauffe 213
limon à crémaillère 191
limon à la française 191
limousine 347
linéaire 55
lingerie 439
linteau 185, 187, 192, 285
lion 89
liquette 255
liquide 414, 415
liquide céphalo-rachidien 110
lis 56
lisse d'assise 187
listel 228
lit 204, 361, 530
lit à barreaux 205
lit à deux places 439
lit à une place 439
lit d'hôpital 464
lit de camp pliant 530
lit de l'ongle 114
lit pliant 205
litchi 137
literie 204
lithosphère 26, 44
litière 54
littoral, configuration 35
Lituanie 450
livèche 142
livre 440
livrée 479
lob 491
lobe 79, 115
lobé 55
lobe du nez 117
lobe inférieur 105
lobe latéral inférieur 62
lobe latéral supérieur 62
lobe moyen 105
lobe supérieur 105
lobe terminal 62
local d'entreposage du matériel 444
local d'entretien 439, 443, 444
local technique 345
locaux administratifs 374
locaux de l'équipage 382
locaux de service 447
locomotive diesel-électrique 377
loge 58, 293
loge d'artiste 293
loge privée 293
logement de cassette 323
logement de la cassette 319, 320
logement droit 272
logement du plateau 323
logement gauche 272
logiciel de courrier électronique 334
lointain 292, 293
loisirs de plein air 528
long péronier latéral 96
long supinateur 97
longane 136
longeron 365, 392
longeron de chenille 398
longitude 22
longue piste 508
longueur d'onde 418
longueur de la vague 33
longueur, mesure 425, 426
loquet 178, 214
lorgnette 273
lorum 78
losange 429
louche 173
loup 88
loupe 421, 531
loupe et microscopes 421
loutre de rivière 88
lucarne 182
Luer Lock, embout 460

ASTRONOMIE > 2-13; TERRE > 14-49; RÈGNE VÉGÉTAL > 50-65; RÈGNE ANIMAL > 66-91; ÊTRE HUMAIN > 92-119; ALIMENTATION ET CUISINE > 120-181; MAISON > 182-215; BRICO-LAGE ET JARDINAGE > 216-237; VÊTEMENTS > 238-263; PARURE ET OBJETS PERSONNELS > 264-277; ARTS ET ARCHITECTURE > 278-311; COMMUNICATIONS ET BUREAUTIQUE > 312-341; TRANSPORT ET MACHINERIE > 342-401; ÉNERGIES > 402-413; SCIENCE > 414-429; SOCIÉTÉ > 430-467; SPORTS ET JEUX > 468-538

575

INDEX FRANÇAIS

luette 116, 117
lumière 7, 8, 9, 305
lumière perpétuelle 447
lumière visible 418
lumières de but 507
luminaires 206
Lune 2, 4, 5
Lune, éclipse 5
Lune, phases 5
Lune, relief 5
lunette astronomique 8
lunette astronomique, coupe 8
lunette de visée 420, 534
lunettes 218, 273, 513, 522
lunettes de nage 516
lunettes de protection 458, 522, 525
lunettes de sécurité 458
lunettes de ski 510
lunettes de soleil 273
lunettes, exemples 273
lunettes, parties 273
lunule 73, 114, 115
lupin 130
lustre 207
lutrin 446
lutz 509
Luxembourg 449
luzerne 130
lynx 88
lyre 297
lysosome 66

M

macaque 91
mâche 127
mâchicoulis 282
machine à espresso 181
machine à faire les pâtes 170
machinerie 342
machinerie lourde 398
machiniste 290
mâchoire 217, 224
mâchoire dentée 222
mâchoire droite 222
mâchoire fixe 223
mâchoire incurvée 222
mâchoire mobile 223
mâchoires 224, 535
Mackenzie 16
maçonnerie : outils 216
macronucleus 66
Madagascar 20, 452
magasin 432
magasin à rayons 437
magasin d'articles de sport 437
magasin d'électronique 436
magasin de bricolage 436
magasin de cadeaux 436
magasin de chaussures 437
magasin de décoration 437
magasin de jouets 436
magasin de lingerie 436
magasin de prêt-à-porter 436
magazine 313
magenta 418
magma 28, 33
magnésie 497
magnétisme 416
magnétoscope 319
mail 436
maille 493
maillet 220
mailloche 297, 308
mailloches 309
maillon-gouge 235
maillot 473, 483, 488, 522
maillot d'équipe 476, 486
maillot d'équipe 480
maillot de bain 263, 516
maillot de corps 247, 476, 500
main 91, 93, 95, 115
main courante 191, 287, 385, 467
main pleine 468
Maine coon 87
maïs 61, 143
maïs : épi 61
maïs fourrager 122
maison 182, 469, 515
maison à étage 289
maison de plain-pied 289
maison en adobe 288
maison jumelée 289
maison romaine 280
maison sur pilotis 288
maison, ameublement 200

maison, charpente 187
maison, éléments 185
maison, extérieur 182
maison, principales pièces 188
maison, structure 188
maisons de ville 289
maisons en rangée 289
maisons traditionnelles 288
maître d'hôtel 438
maître-autel 446
maître-cylindre 357
majeur 115
majuscule : sélection du niveau 2 330
malaire 98, 100
Malaisie 453
malanga 129
Malawi 452
Maldives 453
mâle 426
Mali 451
malle 277
mallette de toilette 277
mallette porte-documents 274
Malpighi, couche 114
Malte 450
mamelon 92, 94, 113
mammifères carnivores 86
mammifères carnivores, exemples 88
mammifères lagomorphes, exemples 82
mammifères marins 90
mammifères marins, exemples 90
mammifères ongulés 83
mammifères ongulés, exemples 84
mammifères primates 91
mammifères primates, exemples 91
mammifères rongeurs 82
Manche 18
manche 167, 215, 216, 217, 219, 220,
   221, 223, 244, 271, 272, 273, 297,
   301, 302, 303, 477, 478, 492, 493,
   494, 503, 505, 506
manche à balai 332, 395
manche isolant 217
manche isolé 459
manche montée 245
manche raglan 248, 251, 261
manche rotatif 332
manches à balai 471
manches précédentes 492
manchette 313, 487
manchon 219, 276, 395, 501
manchon de câble 228
manchon du cordon 218, 229
manchon refroidisseur 420
manchot 80
mandarine 134
mandibule 67, 74, 78
mandoline 170, 297
mandrin 221, 228
mandrin autoserrant 228
manette 178
manette d'admission d'air 192
manette de chasse d'eau 196
manette de contact 207
manette de dérailleur 371, 372, 522
manette de glissement 353
manette de jeu 471
manette des gaz 332
manette du frein 523
manette vapeur 181
mangoustan 136
mangouste 88
mangue 137
manille 521
manioc 124
manivelle 170, 224, 236, 365, 372,
   537
manivelle d'enroulement 225
manivelle de lève-glace 352
manomètre 455, 461
manomètre d'accord 308
manœuvre de la pelleteuse 399
mante religieuse 69
manteau 72, 73, 192, 251
manteau inférieur 26
manteau supérieur 26
manteaux 248, 251
manucure 265
manuel de premiers soins 461
manutention 396
maquereau 159
maquillage 266
maquillage des lèvres 266
maquillage des yeux 266
maquilleuse 290
maquis 44

marbre 475
marchand de journaux 437
marche 191, 219
marche de départ 191
marche/arrêt 326
marche/arrêt/volume 326
marchepied 219, 364, 395, 523
marchepied arrière 455
marchepied escamotable 361
marchepied latéral 377
margarine 149
marge continentale 33
margose 128
marinière 255
maritime, transport 381
marmite 175
marmotte 82
Maroc 451
maroquinerie 436
marque centrale 490
marque d'aire de prise de contact 391
marque d'axe de piste 390
marque de distance constante 391
marque de point d'attente 390
marques d'identification 390
marques de circulation 389
marques de seuil de piste 391
marques latérales de piste 390
marqueur 312, 487, 488
marqueurs 499
marron 133
Mars 2, 3
marteau 116, 304, 472
marteau à panne ronde 220
marteau de charpentier 220
marteau de maçon 216
marteau de menuisier 220
martin-pêcheur 80
martinet 80
martre 88
mascara en pain 266
mascara liquide 266
masque 476, 478, 486, 507
masque bucco-nasal 459
masque complet 454
masque de sélection des couleurs 318
masque respiratoire 459
masse 27
masse, mesure 422, 426
masse-tige 403
masséter 96
massif 183
massif d'ancrage des câbles 344
massif de fleurs 230
massif de fondation 403
massif montagneux 24
mât 281, 321, 396, 519, 520
mât avant 385
mât de charge 385
mât de toit 529
mât radar 384
matelas 204, 205, 460, 530
matelas autogonflant 530
matelas mousse 530
matelas pneumatique 530
mâtereau 385
matériau de scellement 417
matériel de camping 531
matériel de lutte contre les incendies 454
matériel de secours 460
mathématiques 427
matière 414
matière inorganique 45
matières grasses 149
matraque télescopique 456
matrice de l'ongle 114
maturation, vigne 62
maturité 62
Maurice 452
Mauritanie 451
maxillaire 74, 117
maxillaire basculant 79
maxillaire inférieur 98, 100
maxillaire supérieur 98, 100, 100
mazout domestique 405
mazout léger 405
mazout lourd 405
méandre 32
méat de l'urètre 111
mécanique d'accordage 303
mécanique d'accordage 303
mécanisme en octave 306
mécanisme d'ouverture de l'anse 532
mécanisme de débrayage du tambour 537
mécanisme de déplacement de la lame
   401

mécanisme de propulsion 372
mèche 301
mèche à centre plat 228
mèche hélicoïdale 228
mèche hélicoïdale à âme centrale 228
mèche hélicoïdale à double torsade 228
médaillon 264
médecin 464, 498
médiator 297
médicaments, formes 467
méditerranéen 40
Meissner, corpuscule 114
Mélanésie 15
mélange au manganèse (cathode) 417
mélange d'épices cajun 139
mélange de zinc et d'électrolyte (anode)
   417
mélange dépolarisant 417
mélange eau-vapeur 402
mélangeur 176
mélangeur à main 176
mélangeur à pâtisserie 172
mélangeur bain-douche 194
mélasse 149
mêlée : attaque 485
mêlée : défense 484
mêlée spontanée 483
mélèze 65
mélisse 142
melon 238
melon à cornes 136
melon brodé 135
melon Casaba 135
melon d'Espagne 135
melon d'hiver chinois 128
melon d'Ogen 135
melon miel 135
melons 135
membrane 324
membrane cellulaire 66
membrane coquillière 79
membrane cytoplasmique 50
membrane du tympan 116
membrane médiane 60
membrane nucléaire 50, 66
membrane pellucide 112
membrane plasmique 66
membrane squelettique 50
membrane vitelline 79
membre inférieur 103
membre supérieur 103
meneur de jeu 489
méninges 109
ménisque convergent 419
ménisque divergent 419
menora 447
menthe 142
menton 78, 94
mentonnière 301, 367, 522
menuiserie : instruments de traçage et de
   mesure 225
menuiserie : matériel divers 225
menuiserie : outils pour clouer 220
menuiserie : outils pour façonner 229
menuiserie : outils pour percer 228
menuiserie : outils pour scier 226
menuiserie : outils pour serrer 222
menuiserie : outils pour visser 221
mer 5, 24, 32
mer Adriatique 18
mer Baltique 18
mer Caspienne 14, 19
mer d'Aral 19
mer d'Irlande 18
mer d'Oman 19
mer de Barents 18
mer de Beaufort 16
mer de Béring 14
mer de Chine méridionale 14, 19
mer de Chine orientale 19
mer de Corail 15
mer de Norvège 18
mer de Tasman 15
mer de Weddell 15
mer des Antilles 14, 16
mer du Groenland 14
mer du Japon 19
mer du Nord 14, 18
mer Égée 18
mer Méditerranée 14, 18, 20
mer Noire 14, 18, 19
mer Rouge 14, 19, 20
Mercure 2, 3
merguez 156
méridien de Greenwich 22
méridien est 22

méridien ouest 22
méridienne 200
merlan 161
mesa 36
mésocarpe 57, 58, 59
mésopause 37
mésosphère 37
mesure à deux temps 298
mesure à quatre temps 298
mesure à trois temps 298
mesure de l'énergie 426
mesure de l'épaisseur 425
mesure de l'intensité lumineuse 426
mesure de la charge électrique 426
mesure de la différence de potentiel
   électrique 426
mesure de la force 426
mesure de la fréquence 426
mesure de la longueur 425, 426
mesure de la masse 422, 426
mesure de la pression 426
mesure de la puissance 426
mesure de la quantité de matière 426
mesure de la radioactivité 426
mesure de la résistance électrique 426
mesure de la température 424
mesure de la température Celsius 426
mesure de la température
   thermodynamique 426
mesure du courant électrique 426
mesure du temps 424
mesure, appareils 424
mesures 171, 298
météorologie 37
mètre 426
mètre à ruban 225
métro 435
meubles d'enfants 205
meubles de rangement 202
Mexique 448
mezzanine 182, 189, 378
mi 298
mi-bas 247, 257
mi-chaussette 247, 257
micro 303
micro de fréquences aiguës 303
micro de fréquences graves 303
micro de fréquences moyennes 303
micro-ondes 418
micro-ordinateur 329
microfilament 66
micromètre palmer 425
micronucleus 66
microphone 320, 327, 328, 332, 337,
   456
microphones 457
microscope 421
microscope binoculaire 421
microtubule 66
miel 149
mihrab 447
milieu défensif 481
milieu offensif droit 481
milieu offensif gauche 481
mille 427
millésime 441
millet 61, 143
millet : épi 61
Mimas 3
minaret 447
minbar 447
minibus 363
minichaîne stéréo 325
minislip 247
minute 428
minuterie 178, 179
minuteur 171, 501
Miranda 3
mire 533, 535
miroir 195, 277, 421, 439, 533
miroir à réflexion partielle 420
miroir à réflexion totale 420
miroir concave 7
miroir de courtoisie 354
miroir de lecture 10
miroir de traversée avant 362
miroir double pivotant 269
miroir latéral 269
miroir lumineux 269
miroir plan rétractable 7
miroir primaire 7
miroir primaire concave 9
miroir secondaire 7, 9
mise en balles 49
mise en marche 328
Mississippi 16

mitaine 243, 507
mitigeur d'évier 197
mitochondrie 50, 66
mitre 167, 169, 193
mitron 183
mocassin 242
mode d'emploi 346
mode d'entraînement du film 314
mode d'exposition 314
mode de mise au point 314
mode magnétoscope 319
mode télévision 319
modem 334
modem-câble 335
modérateur 408
modes d'inflorescence 57
modification fine des variables 310
modification rapide des variables 310
modulateur de pression de freinage 357
modulation de la hauteur du son 310
modulation du timbre du son 310
module d'habitation américain 11
module de commande électronique 357
module de communication 316
module de photopiles 411
module de propulsion 316
module de service 316
module russe 11
moelle 63, 154
moelle épinière 109, 110
moelle épinière, structure 109
Mohorovicic, discontinuité 26
moineau 80
molaire, coupe 101
molaires 101
mole 426
molécule 414
molette 223
molette d'ajustage 425
molette d'entraînement 180
molette de mise au point 420
molette de réglage de la saillie 229
molette de réglage près/loin 320
molette de sélection des effets spéciaux 320
mollet 93, 95
mollusques 72, 157
Monaco 450
Mongolie 453
moniteurs de contrôle du réalisateur 290
monnaie et modes de paiement 441
monocoques 521
Monopoly® 469
mont de Vénus 112
montagne 29
montagnes Rocheuses 16
montant 184, 187, 201, 219, 297, 466, 509
montant de bâti 202
montant de ferrage 185, 202
montant de la serrure 185
montant de rive 186
montant embrevé 186
montant latéral 349
montant mouton 186
montant rembourré 489
monticule 475
montre à affichage analogique 424
montre à affichage numérique 424
monts Oural 18
monts Transantarctiques 15
monture 215, 224, 226, 296
monture en fer à cheval 7
monture réglable 226
monument 25
moquette 190
moraillon 277
moraine de fond 30
moraine frontale 30
moraine latérale 30
moraine médiane 30
moraine terminale 30
mordant 299
morille 123
morphologie de l'abeille : ouvrière 68
morphologie de l'araignée 70
morphologie de l'escargot 72
morphologie de l'oiseau 78
morphologie de la grenouille 75
morphologie de la perche 74
morphologie de la pieuvre 72
morphologie de la tortue 76
morphologie du cheval 83
morphologie du chien 86
morphologie du coquillage bivalve 73
morphologie du coquillage univalve 73

morphologie du dauphin 90
morphologie du gorille 91
morphologie du homard 71
morphologie du papillon 67
morphologie du rat 82
morphologie du requin 74
morphologie du serpent venimeux : tête 76
mors 221, 228, 265
mors fixe 224
mors mobile 224
mort 426
mortadelle 156
mortier 170
morue de l'Atlantique 161
mosaïque 280
mosquée 447
moteur 212, 213, 214, 227, 229, 237, 366, 396, 401, 403
moteur à essence 351, 360
moteur de manœuvre 13
moteur diesel 398, 399, 400, 401
moteur diesel de propulsion 383
moteur diesel de sustentation 383
moteur électrique 235, 237, 358
moteur hors-bord 385
moteur principal 13
motif 260, 261
moto 366
moto : vue en plongée 368
moto de Grand Prix et pilote 525
moto de motocross et supercross 525
moto de tête 522
moto de tourisme 369
moto tout-terrain 369
moto-caméra 522
motocyclisme 525
motoneige 523
motrice 376, 380
mouche 69, 502
mouche artificielle 536
mouche centrale 502
mouche de ligne de cadre 502
mouche supérieure 502
mouche tsé-tsé 69
mouffette 88
moufle 243
moufle fixe 403
moufle mobile 403
mouflon 84
mouilleur 339
moule 157
moule à charlotte 172
moule à fond amovible 172
moule à gâteau 172
moule à muffins 172
moule à pain 179
moule à quiche 172
moule à soufflé 172
moule à tarte 172
moulin à café 180
moulin à légumes 170
moulin à vent 412
moulin pivot 412
moulin tour 412
moulinet à mouche 536
moulinet à tambour fixe 537
moulinet à tambour tournant 537
moulure de pare-chocs 348
mousqueton 521, 538
mousqueton à ressort 521
mousse 51
mousse à raser 271
mousse d'Irlande 123
mousse, structure 51
mousseline 171
moustaches 87
moustique 69
moutarde à l'ancienne 140
moutarde allemande 140
moutarde américaine 140
moutarde anglaise 140
moutarde blanche 138
moutarde de Dijon 140
moutarde en poudre 140
moutarde noire 138
mouton 84
mouvement horizontal du sol 27
mouvement vertical du sol 27
mouvements de l'avion 395
mouvements de terrain 31
moyen adducteur 96
moyenne sus-alaire 78
moyenne tectrice primaire 78
moyeu 341, 371, 413, 467
moyeu rotor 395

Mozambique 452
mozzarella 150
Mt Everest 37
muguet 56
mule 242
mulet 84, 160
mulot 82
multicoques 521
multiplication 337, 427
munster 151
muqueuse olfactive 117
mur 184, 528
mur bajoyer 406
mur d'arrivée 516
mur de fondation 187
mur de l'œil 43
mur de la qibla 447
mur de nuages 43
mur de virage 517
mur fortifié 447
mur latéral 517
muraille 385
mûre 132
muscle adducteur antérieur 73
muscle adducteur postérieur 73
muscle arrecteur 114
muscle bulbo-caverneux 111
muscle droit inférieur 119
muscle droit supérieur 119
muscle papillaire 104
muscles 96
museau 74, 75, 86, 87
musée 433
musique 296
Myanmar 453
mycélium 52
mye 157
mygale du Mexique 70
myocarde 104
myopie 419
myrtille 132
myrtille d'Amérique 132

N

n'égale pas 427
n'est pas identique à 427
nacelle 413
nacelle d'observation 7
nacelle, coupe 413
nage sur le dos 517
nageoire anale 74
nageoire caudale 71, 74, 90
nageoire dorsale 71, 90
nageoire pectorale 74, 90
nageoire pelvienne 74
nages, types 517
naissance 426
Namibie 452
naos 279
nappe phréatique 31, 48
narine 74, 75, 76, 78, 117
nasal 100
naseau 83
natation 516
nationalité 497
Nauru 453
navet 124
navette ferroviaire 390
navette spatiale 12, 37
navette spatiale au décollage 12
navigateur 334
navire de forage 382
navire porte-conteneurs 381, 382
nébulosité 39
nécrologie 313
nectarine 132
nef 285
nef centrale 447
nèfle du Japon 133
neige 41
neiges acides 48
neiges éternelles 29
Népal 453
néphridie 71
Neptune 2, 3
nerf 114
nerf circonflexe 108
nerf cochléaire 116
nerf crural 108
nerf cubital 108
nerf digital 108
nerf fémoro-cutané 108
nerf fessier 108
nerf grand abdomino-génital 108
nerf grand sciatique 108

nerf intercostal 108
nerf médian 108
nerf musculo-cutané 108
nerf obturateur 108
nerf olfactif 117
nerf optique 119
nerf petit abdomino-génital 108
nerf petit sciatique 108
nerf rachidien 109, 110
nerf radial 108
nerf saphène externe 108
nerf saphène interne 108
nerf sciatique poplité externe 108
nerf sciatique poplité interne 108
nerf tibial antérieur 108
nerf vestibulaire 116
nerfs crâniens 108
nervure 401, 458
nervure d'aile 392
nervure d'emplanture 392
nervure médiane 51
nervure principale 55, 60
nervure secondaire 55
neurone moteur 110
neurone sensoriel 110
neurones 110
neutron 414
neutron incident 415
névé 30
newton 426
nez 82, 94, 229, 392, 526
nez basculant 394
nez du guide 235
nez, parties externes 117
nez-de-marche 191
Nicaragua 448
niche de sécurité 345
nid d'ange 260
Niger 20, 451
Nigeria 451
Nil 20
nimbo-stratus 42
niveau à bulle 225
niveau d'eau 181
niveau d'équilibre 33
niveau de la mer 26, 33, 37
niveau de la réception 439
niveleuse 401
noir 418
noire 299
Noirs 470
noisette 133
noisette, coupe 60
noix 133
noix de cajou 133
noix de coco 133
noix de cola 133
noix de ginkgo 133
noix de macadamia 133
noix de muscade 138
noix de pécan 133
noix du Brésil 133
noix, coupe 60
nom de domaine 334
nom de la monnaie 441
nom de la station 378
nom du gymnaste 497
nom du titulaire 441
nombril 92, 94
non-appartenance 427
non-parallèle 428
Nord 23
Nord Est 23
Nord Nord-Est 23
Nord Nord-Ouest 23
Nord Ouest 23
nori 123
Norvège 450
notation algébrique 470
notation musicale 298
note 497
nouaison 62
nouilles asiatiques 147
nouilles aux œufs 147
nouilles de haricots mungo 147
nouilles de riz 147
nouilles soba 147
nouilles somen 147
nouilles udon 147
nouvelle Lune 5
Nouvelle-Calédonie 15
Nouvelle-Zélande 15, 453
noyau 4, 6, 50, 57, 66, 110, 112, 305, 414, 534
noyau externe 26
noyau fissile 415

noyau galactique 6
noyau interne 26
noyer 64
nœud 53, 416
nœud d'arrimage de l'orbiteur 11
nœud de Ranvier 110
nœud papillon 245
nœud plat 238
nu-pied 242
nuage 37, 41
nuage de cendres 28
nuage de Oort 2
nuage en entonnoir 43
nuages 42
nuages à développement vertical 42
nuages de basse altitude 42
nuages de haute altitude 42
nuages de moyenne altitude 42
nucléole 50, 66, 112
nuisette 256
numéro d'autoroute 25
numéro de carte 441, 443
numéro de chambre 439
numéro de la piste 323
numéro de la pompe 346
numéro de quai 374
numéro de route 25
numéro de série 441
numéro du joueur 486, 488, 506
numéroteur 338
nuque 78, 93, 95

O

oasis 32, 36
Obéron 3
objectif 314, 332, 421
objectif grand-angulaire 314
objectif macro 314
objectif zoom 314, 320
objectif, accessoires 314
objectifs 314
objet 419
objets personnels 264, 271
observation astronomique 7
observatoire 7
observatoire astronomique 7
observatoire astronomique, coupe 7
obstacle d'eau 504
obstacle d'eau 504
obturateur de baie 329
occipital 97, 99, 100
océan 5, 24, 45
océan Arctique 14
océan Atlantique 14, 15, 18, 20
océan Indien 14, 15, 19, 20
océan Pacifique 14, 15, 19
océan, dorsale 33
Océanie 14, 15, 453
océanique 40
octaèdre régulier 429
octave 298
octogone régulier 429
oculaire 8, 9, 320, 420, 421, 459
oculaire coudé 8
odorat 116
œil 43, 70, 71, 72, 76, 90, 94, 119, 220
œil composé 67, 68
œil simple 67
œillet 56, 240, 263, 275, 509, 538
œillet d'attache 315
œilleton 320
œsophage 105, 106
œuf 79
œuf d'autruche 155
œuf d'oie 155
œuf de caille 155
œuf de cane 155
œuf de faisane 155
œuf de poule 155
œufrier 211
œufs 155
office 392
ohm 426
oie 81, 155
oignon à mariner 124
oignon blanc 124
oignon jaune 124
oignon rouge 124
oignon vert 124
oiseau 78
oiseau aquatique 79
oiseau de proie 79
oiseau échassier 79
oiseau granivore 79
oiseau insectivore 79

ASTRONOMIE > 2-13;   TERRE > 14-49;   RÈGNE VÉGÉTAL > 50-65;   RÈGNE ANIMAL > 66-91;   ÊTRE HUMAIN > 92-119;   ALIMENTATION ET CUISINE > 120-181;   MAISON > 182-215;   BRICOLAGE ET JARDINAGE > 216-237;   VÊTEMENTS > 238-263;   PARURE ET OBJETS PERSONNELS > 264-277;   ARTS ET ARCHITECTURE > 278-311;   COMMUNICATIONS ET BUREAUTIQUE > 312-341;   TRANSPORT ET MACHINERIE > 342-401;   ÉNERGIES > 402-413;   SCIENCE > 414-429;   SOCIÉTÉ > 430-467;   SPORTS ET JEUX > 468-538

oiseau percheur 79
oiseau, morphologie 78
oiseaux 78
oiseaux, exemples 80
okapi 84
olécrâne 99
oléoduc 404
oléoduc sous-marin 404
oléoduc surélevé 404
olive 128
ombelle 57
ombilic 30
omble de fontaine 161
ombre 424
ombre à paupières 266
omoplate 93, 95, 98, 99
onde 418
onde de choc 403
onde sismique 27
ondes radio 418
ongle 78, 115
onglet 163, 340, 531
onglet à fenêtre 340
Oort, nuage 2
opéra 432
opercule 74
opercule thermoscellé 163
opisthodome 279
opticien 437
optique 418
orang-outan 91
orange 134
orange, coupe 58
orbiculaire des paupières 96
orbite lunaire 4, 5
orbite terrestre 4, 5
orbiteur 12, 13
orchestre 278
orchestre symphonique 295
orchidée 56
ordinateur 444
ordinateur de bord 354, 457
ordinateur de bureau 334
ordinateur de poche 337
ordinateur portable 336
ordinateur portable : vue arrière 336
ordinateur portable : vue avant 336
ordures ménagères 47, 48
oreille 92, 201
oreille externe 116
oreille interne 116
oreille moyenne 116
oreille, pavillon 115
oreille, structure 116
oreille-de-Judas 123
oreiller 204
oreillette droite 103, 104
oreillette gauche 103, 104
Orénoque 17
organes des sens 114
organes génitaux féminins 112
organes génitaux masculins 111
organisation gouvernementale 335
organiseur 338
organisme culturel 335
organisme de santé 335
organismes simples 66
orge 61, 143
orge : épi 61
orgue 305
orifice d'alimentation 455
orifice de remplissage 208
orifice du conduit auditif 115
orifice du pied 305
origan 142
ormeau 157
ornements 299
oronge vraie 123
orque 90
orteil 86, 92, 94
ortie 127
os alvéolaire 101
os iliaque 98
os maxillaire 101
os propre du nez 117
oseille 127
osselets 116
otarie 90
oued 36
Ouest 23
Ouest Nord-Ouest 23
Ouest Sud-Ouest 23
Ouganda 451
ouïe 115, 301
ouïe, protection 458

ouistiti 91
ouragan 43
ours 313
ours noir 89
ours polaire 89
outils pour arroser 236
outils pour couper 234
outils pour remuer la terre 233
outils pour scier 226
outils pour semer et planter 231
outils pour serrer 222
outils pour visser 221
outils, électricité 217
outils, plomberie 216
ouverture 73, 538
ouvre-boîtes 170, 180, 531
ouvrière 68
ouvrière, abeille 68
Ouzbékistan 452
ovaire 56, 112, 113
ovoïde 55
ovule 56, 112

P
Pacini, corpuscule 114
pack 163
page précédente 331
page suivante 331
pagode 283
paiement électronique, terminal 443
paille 163
pain 144
pain azyme 145
pain blanc 145
pain chapati indien 145
pain complet 145
pain de campagne 145
pain de maïs américain 145
pain de mie 145
pain de seigle allemand 145
pain de seigle danois 145
pain de seigle noir 144
pain grec 144
pain irlandais 145
pain multicéréales 145
pain naan indien 145
pain noir russe 145
pain parisien 144
pain pita 145
pain tchallah juif 145
paire 468
pak-choï 126
Pakistan 452
palais de justice 432
palais des congrès 433
Palaos 453
pale 412, 413
pale de rotor 395
palet 507
palette 248, 251
palette 493, 535, 538
palette à ailes 396
palier 189, 191
palissade 282
palmée 55
palmeraie 36
palmette 200
palmier 64
palmure 75, 79
palonnier 400
palourde 157
palpe 73
palpe labial 67
pampille 207
pamplemousse 134
pan 245, 248, 255
pan arrière 245
pan avant 245
panais 129
Panama 448
panama 238
pancetta 156
pancréas 106
panicule, avoine 61
panicule, sorgho 61
panier 178, 181, 211, 214, 477, 489,
538
panier à couverts 214
panier à friture 171
panier cuit-vapeur 175
panier de lavage 212
panne 218
panne ronde 220
panneau 185, 489

panneau de citerne 385
panneau de commande 328, 455
panneau de distribution 198
panneau de fonctions 328
panneau de garniture 352
panneau de l'écran 320
panneau de protection latéral 467
panneau de refroidissement 13
panneau de séparation 277
panneau de vantail 202
panneau indicateur 374
panneau publicitaire 378
panneau solaire 7, 316
panneaux solaires 11
pansement adhésif 461
pantalon 246, 263, 476, 486, 499, 525
pantalon molleton 262
pantalon pattes d'éléphant 254
pantalons, exemples 254
pantographe 376
paon 81
papaye 137
papier aluminium 162
papier de verre 229
papier paraffiné 162
papier sulfurisé 162
papille 114, 119
papille caliciforme 118
papille filiforme 118
papille foliée 118
papille fongiforme 118
papille rénale 107
papillon 67, 517
papillon, morphologie 67
Papouasie-Nouvelle-Guinée 15, 453
paprika 139
paquebot 386
paquet 163
parachute 12
parachute de cabine 287
paraffines 405
parafoudre 407
Paraguay 448
parallèle 22, 428
parallélépipède 429
parallélogramme 429
paramécie 66
Paraná 17
parapet 282
parapharmacie et cosmétiques 121
parapluie 273
parasoleil 314
paratonnerre 183, 413
parc 25, 433
parc à charbon 402
parc à échelles 455
parc à vélos 445
parc de stationnement 390, 430, 445,
512
parc de stockage 404
parc de stockage terminal 404
parc des expositions 430
parc national 25
parcours 504
parcours pittoresque 25
pardessus 248
pare-brise 348, 364, 366, 369, 385, 392,
523
pare-chocs 209, 364, 369
pare-chocs arrière 523
pare-feu 193
pare-soleil 8, 354, 356, 361
paréo 253
parfumerie 436
pariétal 99, 100
paripennée 55
parka 249
parking 375, 381
parmesan 151
paroi avant 365
paroi latérale 365
parquet 190
parquet à bâtons rompus 190
parquet à coupe de pierre 190
parquet à coupe perdue 190
parquet Chantilly 190
parquet d'Arenberg 190
parquet en chevrons 190
parquet en vannerie 190
parquet mosaïque 190
parquet sur chape de ciment 190
parquet sur ossature de bois 190
parquet Versailles 190
parquets, arrangements 190
parterre 293
parties 200, 201, 204

parties d'un cercle 428
parties d'une bicyclette 370
parties d'une chaussure 240
parties des lunettes 273
parties externes du nez 117
parure 264
pas 83
pas alternatif 514
pas de patineur 514
pascal 426
passage à niveau 375
passage inférieur 344
passage pour piétons 434
passage souterrain 375
passage supérieur 343, 344
passant 245, 246, 248
passavant 385
passe à billes 406
passe-bras 251
passe-sangle 532
passerelle 282, 292, 375, 379
passerelle de navigation 382, 386, 387
passerelle télescopique 389
passoire 171, 177, 180
passoire fine 171
pastèque 135
pastille de combustible 409
Patagonie 17
patate 124
pâte de tamarin 140
pâte phyllo 145
patelle 157
patère 207
pâtes alimentaires 146
pâtes won-ton 147
patient 464
patin 395, 506
patin à roues alignées 527
patin acrobatique 527
patin antidérapant 219
patin clap 508
patin d'appui 409
patin d'espacement 409
patin de courte piste 508
patin de figure 509
patin de gardien de but 507
patin de hockey 527
patin de vitesse 527
patinage artistique 509
patinage de vitesse 508
patineur : courte piste 508
patineur : longue piste 508
patineur d'eau 69
patineuse 527
patinoire 506, 509, 512
patins de course 508
pâtisson 129
patte 76, 244, 246, 248, 274, 477
patte à boutons-pression 249
patte ambulatoire 70
patte anale 67
patte antérieure 67, 68, 75
patte autocollante 339
patte boutonnée 246
patte capucin 245
patte d'entrejambe 255
patte d'épaule 248
patte d'épaule 456
patte de boutonnage 245
patte de serrage 248
patte locomotrice 70
patte médiane 67, 68
patte polo 250
patte postérieure 67, 68, 75
patte ventouse 67
pattes thoraciques 71
pattes, exemples 79
pâturage 122
paturon 83
paume 115, 243, 477
paume d'un gant 243
paumelle 186
paupière 76
paupière inférieure 75, 87, 119
paupière interne 87
paupière supérieure 75, 87, 119
pause 299, 323, 331
pause/arrêt sur l'image 319
pavé alphabétique 338
pavé alphanumérique 330
pavé numérique 331, 338
pavé tactile 336
pavillon 82, 116, 305, 306, 307, 349,
432, 460, 504
pavillon de la trompe utérine 113
pavillon des skieurs 512

pavillon, oreille 115
pavot, graines 139
pays 23
Pays-Bas 449
paysage végétal selon l'altitude 44
pe-tsaï 126
peau 57, 58, 59, 110, 114, 309
peau de batterie 297, 308
peau de chamois 265
peau de timbre 297, 308
pécari 84
pêche 132, 536
pêche à la mouche 536
pêche au lancer 537
pêche, coupe 57
pédale 302, 308, 370, 372, 501, 522
pédale automatique 522
pédale avec cale élargie 522
pédale crescendo 305
pédale d'accélérateur 354
pédale de chaussage 511
pédale de combinaisons 305
pédale de débrayage 354
pédale de déchaussage 511
pédale de frein 350, 354, 357
pédale de frein arrière 368
pédale de sourdine 304
pédale douce 304, 311
pédale forte 304, 311
pédales d'expression 305
pédalier 305
pédicelle 51, 59, 62
pédieux 96
pédipalpe 70
pédoncule 56, 57, 58, 59, 62
peigne à crêper 268
peigne à tige 268
peigne afro 268
peigne de coiffeur 268
peignes 268
peignoir 256
peinture d'entretien 219
pelage 82, 91
pèlerine 251
pélican 80
pelle 173, 193, 233
pelle à poussière 215
pelle hydraulique 400
pelle-pioche pliante 532
pelleteuse 399
pellicule plastique 162
peloton 522
peloton de tête 522
pelouse 183
peltée 55
pendants d'oreille 264
pendeloque 207
pendentif 264
penderie 189, 203, 439
pendule 444
pêne demi-tour 186
pêne dormant 186
péninsule 24
péninsule Antarctique 15
péninsule d'Arabie 19
péninsule des Balkans 18
péninsule du Yucatan 16
péninsule Ibérique 18
péninsule Scandinave 18
pénis 92
penne 146
pennée 55
pennon 520
pentagone régulier 429
pente difficile 512
pente expert 512
pente facile 512
pente intermédiaire 512
pépin 58, 59
pepino 137
pepperoni 156
perceuse électrique 228
perceuse-visseuse sans fil 228
perche 160
perche truitée 160
perchiste 291
percolateur 181
perdrix 80
perforation 240, 243, 263
perforatrice 340
pergola 230
péricarde 105
péricarpe 60
périphérique 431
périphériques d'entrée 330
périphériques de sortie 333

périphériques de stockage 333
péristome 66
péristyle 279, 280
péritoine 111, 112
péroné 98
Pérou 448
peroxysome 66
perpendiculaire 428
perron 183, 188
persan 87
persienne 186
persil 142
perte de chaleur 46
pèse-lettres 339
pèse-personne 423
peso 440
peson 423
pesticide 47, 48
pétale 56
pétiole 52, 55
petit bois 186
petit montant 185
petit palmaire 96
petit rond 97
petite lèvre 112, 113
petite sus-alaire 78
petite valise 277
petites annonces 313
petits outils, jeu 232
petits pois 130
pétoncle 157
pétrole 403
pétrole brut 405
pétrolier 381, 384
peuplier 64
phalange distale 114
phalange médiane 114
phare 348, 364, 366, 368, 377, 381, 523
phare central 376
phare d'atterrissage 395
pharmacie 436, 462, 465
pharynx 105, 106
phase de glisse 514
phase de poussée 514
phases de la Lune 5
Philippines 19, 453
Phobos 2
phoque 90
photographe 436
photographe de plateau 291
photographie 314
photographie à la une 313
photomaton® 437
photon 420
photopile 410, 411
photorécepteurs 119
photosphère 4
photosynthèse 54
physique : électricité 416
physique : magnétisme 416
physique : optique 418
pi 428
piano 295
piano droit 304
piano électronique 311
pic 29, 80
piccolo 295, 306
pichet 166, 180
pictogrammes 330
pie-mère 109
pièce : avers 441
pièce : revers 441
pièce de jonction 455
pièce intermédiaire 111
pièce terminale 111
pièces 470
pièces buccales 68
pied 52, 72, 73, 91, 92, 93, 94, 95, 125, 199, 202, 204, 205, 206, 231, 247, 260, 302, 305, 308, 421, 493, 536, 537
pied à coulisse à vernier 425
pied à perfusion 464
pied arrière 201
pied avant 201
pied cambré 200
pied de lit 204
pied de mât 519
pied de nivellement 212, 213, 214
pied télescopique 460
pied-mélangeur 176
piédroit 285
pieds, protection 459
piège à patte à mâchoires 535

pierre 218
pierre à affûter 169
pierre blanche 470
pierre de Coyolxauhqui 283
pierre de curling 515
pierre noire 470
pierre sacrificielle 283
piètement 201, 219
pieuvre 72, 157
pieuvre, morphologie 72
pigeon 81, 154
pignon 65, 133, 163, 182
pika 82
pilastre 191
pilastre corinthien 281
pile 344
pile alcaline manganèse-zinc 417
pile carbone-zinc 417
piles 416
piles sèches 417
pilier 27, 283, 284
pilier droit 482
pilier du voile 116
pilier gauche 482
pilon 170, 173
pilote 524
piment 128
piment de Cayenne 139
piment de la Jamaïque 138
piment Jalapeño 139
piment oiseau 139
piments broyés 139
piments séchés 139
pin parasol 65
pinacle 284
pince 71, 173, 193, 246, 269
pince à boucles de cheveux 268
pince à cheveux 268
pince à cuticules 265
pince à défriser 269
pince à échardes 461
pince à épiler 265
pince à escargots 173
pince à étiqueter 340
pince à joint coulissant 222
pince à long bec 217
pince à spaghettis 173
pince d'électricien 217
pince de ceinture 327
pince de mise en plis 268
pince de taille 248
pince multiprise 222
pince noire 356
pince rouge 356
pince universelle 217
pince-étau 222
pinceau 219, 312
pinceau à lèvres 266
pinceau à pâtisserie 172
pinceau éventail 266
pinceau pour fard à joues 266
pinceau pour poudre libre 266
pincement 199
pinces 222
pinnule 52
pinson 80
pintade 81, 154
pioche 233
Pion 470
pion 469
pique 468
pique-notes 341
piquet 479, 528, 529
piscine 184, 386
piscine de stockage du combustible irradié 409
piscine enterrée 184
piscine hors sol 184
pissenlit 127
pistache 133
piste 390, 472, 515, 524
piste d'avertissement 475
piste d'élan 473
piste de ski alpin 512
piste de ski de fond 512
pistes d'élan 496
pistil 56
pistolet 216, 456
pistolet à calfeutrer 216
pistolet à souder 218
pistolet arrosoir 236
pistolet d'arrosage 236
pistolet de départ 472
pistolet de distribution 346
piston 307, 357, 360, 460
piston à décorer 172

piton sous-marin 33
pivot 217, 270, 271, 412, 489, 518, 533
pivot d'attelage 365
plafond 193
plafond acoustique 293
plafond cathédrale 189
plafond de cabine 287
plafonnier 206
plage 35
plage arrière 386
plage avant 383, 387
plaine 24, 32
plaine abyssale 33
plaine d'inondation 32
plaine fluvio-glaciaire 30
plan 279, 285
plan à langer 205
plan de travail 164
plan du terrain 183
plan urbain 25
plan, élévation 182
planche 501
planche à découper 169
planche à roulettes 526
planche à voile 519
plancher 193, 369
plancher de cabine 287
plancher inférieur 396
plancher supérieur 396
planchette à arches 340
planchette à pince 340
planchiste 526
planètes 2
planètes externes 2
planètes internes 3
planisphère 14
plantaire grêle 97
plante 53
plante grimpante 230
plante, structure 53
plantoir 231
plantoir à bulbes 231
plaque 178, 269
plaque à pâtisserie 172
plaque absorbante 410
plaque africaine 27
plaque antarctique 27
plaque antifriction 511
plaque chauffante 181
plaque costale 76
plaque d'instructions 228
plaque de commutateur 198
plaque de couche 534
plaque de protection 303, 525
plaque des Caraïbes 27
plaque des îles Cocos 27
plaque du lanceur 475
plaque eurasiatique 27
plaque indo-australienne 27
plaque marginale 76
plaque motrice 110
plaque Nazca 27
plaque négative 359
plaque nord-américaine 27
plaque pacifique 27
plaque philippine 27
plaque positive 359
plaque Scotia 27
plaque signalétique 228
plaque sud-américaine 27
plaque supra-caudale 76
plaque tournante 344
plaque vertébrale 76
plaque-numéro 525
plaques convergentes 27
plaques divergentes 27
plaques tectoniques 27
plaques transformantes 27
plaquette 104, 273, 357
plaqueur droit 484
plaqueur gauche 484
plasma 104
plasmodesme 50
plastron 76, 259, 476, 486
plat 478
plat à escargots 173
plat à poisson 166
plat de dos 200
plat ovale 166
plate-bande 230
plate-forme 179, 363, 423, 516, 526
plate-forme de 10 m 518
plate-forme de 3 m 518
plate-forme de 5 m 518
plate-forme de 7,5 m 518

plate-forme de production 404
plateau 24, 29, 54, 202, 205, 219, 224, 225, 277, 278, 422, 423, 470, 522
plateau A 372
plateau B 372
plateau continental 33
plateau de chargement 318
plateau de clavier 304
plateau de frein 357
plateau de jeu 469
plateau de ponçage 229
plateau de tournage 290
plateau pour accessoires 8
plateau tournant 176
platine 421, 527
platine cassette 323
plats à rôtir 174
pleine Lune 5
pleurote en forme d'huître 123
plèvre pariétale 105
plèvre viscérale 105
plexus brachial 108
plexus lombaire 108
plexus sacré 108
pli 246
pli creux 253
pli d'aisance 253
pli de la columelle 73
pli plat 246, 253
pli surpiqué 253
plie commune 161
plinthe 191
plis, exemples 253
plissé accordéon 253
plomb 538
plomberie 194
plomberie : outils 216
plomberie, circuit 194
plombs 534
plongeoir 518
plongeon 518
plot de départ 516
pluie 41
pluie verglaçante 41
pluies acides 47, 48
plume 27, 312
plume creuse de roseau 312
plume d'oie 312
plume métallique 312
plume métallique romaine 312
plus grand que 427
plus ou moins 427
plus petit que 427
Pluton 2, 3
pneu 349, 358, 364, 371, 522, 525
pneu à crampons 358, 369, 525
pneu autoroutier 358
pneu d'hiver 358
pneu de performance 358
pneu toutes saisons 358
pneumatique de guidage 380
pneumatique porteur 380
pneus, exemples 358
poche 225, 502, 505
poche à douilles 172
poche à rabat 248
poche américaine 274
poche cavalière 246
poche centrale 502
poche extérieure 274, 276
poche frontale 275
poche gilet 244
poche inférieure 277
poche intérieure 277
poche intérieure isolante 260
poche passepoilée 250
poche plaquée 244, 249, 260
poche poitrine 245, 248
poche prise dans une couture 251
poche raglan 248, 251
poche repose-bras 249, 251
poche secrète 274
poche supérieure 502
poche tiroir 244
poche-revolver 246
poche-ticket 244
pochette 244, 274
pochette d'homme 276
pochette d'information 339
pochette de classement 340
pocheuse 175
podium des épreuves 496
poêle à combustion lente 192
poêle à crêpes 175
poêle à frire 175, 531

poêlon 175, 179
poids 422, 423, 472, 500, 501
poignée 170, 176, 177, 178, 179, 180, 192, 204, 208, 209, 210, 211, 215, 219, 221, 225, 226, 227, 229, 235, 269, 270, 273, 274, 275, 276, 277, 301, 325, 326, 341, 349, 366, 369, 380, 466, 492, 494, 500, 505, 510, 514, 515, 534, 535, 536, 537
poignée antivibrations 235
poignée arrière 537
poignée auxiliaire 228
poignée d'appui 501
poignée de conduite 467
poignée de départ (dos) 516
poignée de frein 371, 467, 522
poignée de guidage 229
poignée de maintien 352
poignée de porte 185
poignée de sécurité 237
poignée des gaz 368
poignée du démarreur 235
poignée intérieure 352
poignée isolante 179
poignée montoir 361, 364, 455
poignée profilée 269
poignée rentrante 274
poignée-pistolet 218, 228
poignées à ressort 500
poignet 86, 93, 95, 115, 245
poignet de force 500
poil 114, 272
poils absorbants 53
poinçon 531
point 468
point d'alimentation 198
point d'amure 519
point d'articulation 400
point d'attache 55
point d'attache 70
point d'écoute 519
point d'encochage 535
point d'information 437
point d'orgue 299
point de handicap 470
point de mise au jeu 506
point de raccordement 198
point de réparation 480
point fixe 357
point indicateur de température 269
pointage de l'épreuve en cours 497
pointe 35, 55, 125, 167, 169, 220, 221, 226, 227, 246, 247, 301, 312, 471, 473, 510, 534, 538
pointe avant 208
pointe carrée 221
pointe cruciforme 221
pointe d'attache 304
pointe de centrage 228
pointe de col 245
pointe de dent 398
pointe de diamant 202
pointe de ski 514
pointe plate 221
pointes, exemples 221
pointeur 533
points 492
poire 133
poire à jus 173
poire de gonflage 461
poireau 124
pois 60, 130
pois cassés 130
pois chiches 130
pois mange-tout 130
poisson cartilagineux 74
poisson osseux 74
poissonnerie 121
poissonnière 174
poissons 74
poissons cartilagineux 158
poissons osseux 159
poitrail 83
poitrine 78
poivre blanc 138
poivre moulu 139
poivre noir 138
poivre rose 138
poivre vert 138
poivrière 166
poivron jaune 128
poivron rouge 128
poivron vert 128
Polaroid® 315
pôle Nord 21, 416
pole position 524

ASTRONOMIE > 2-13; TERRE > 14-49; RÈGNE VÉGÉTAL > 50-65; RÈGNE ANIMAL > 66-91; ÊTRE HUMAIN > 92-119; ALIMENTATION ET CUISINE > 120-181; MAISON > 182-215; BRICO-
LAGE ET JARDINAGE > 216-237; VÊTEMENTS > 238-263; PARURE ET OBJETS PERSONNELS > 264-277; ARTS ET ARCHITECTURE > 278-311; COMMUNICATIONS ET BUREAUTIQUE > 312-341;
TRANSPORT ET MACHINERIE > 342-401; ÉNERGIES > 402-413; SCIENCE > 414-429; SOCIÉTÉ > 430-467; SPORTS ET JEUX > 468-538

579

INDEX FRANÇAIS

pôle Sud 15, 21, 416
polissoir d'ongles 265
politique 448
polluants atmosphériques 47
polluants non biodégradables 47
pollution agricole 47
pollution automobile 47
pollution de l'air 47
pollution de l'eau 48
pollution domestique 47
pollution du sol 47
pollution industrielle 47
pollution par le pétrole 48
polo 250, 255, 492
polochon 204
Pologne 450
polygones 429
Polynésie 453
polypode commun 52
polytric commun 51
pomelo 134
pomme 133, 236
pomme d'Adam 92
pomme de douche 195
pomme de terre 124
pomme poire 137
pomme, coupe 58
pommeau 229, 477
pompe 184, 212, 214, 370, 529
pompe à boue 403
pompier 454
ponceuse excentrique 229
poncho 251
pont 25, 273, 420
pont à poutre 344
pont bain de soleil 387
pont basculant à double volée 345
pont basculant à simple volée 345
pont cantilever 344
pont de Varole 109
pont inférieur 404
pont levant 345
pont principal 385
pont roulant 407
pont supérieur 392, 404
pont suspendu à câble porteur 344
pont tournant 344
pont-l'évêque 151
pont-levis 282
pont-promenade 386
pontet 534
ponton 525
ponts fixes 344
ponts mobiles 344
popote 531
porc 84
porc haché 153
porc-épic 82
porche 183, 285, 447
porcherie 122
pore 50, 60
pore sudoripare 114
porque 385
Porro, prisme 420
port 431
port clavier 329
port Ethernet 336
port FireWire 336
port infrarouge 336, 337
port jeux/MIDI 329
port maritime 381
port modem interne 329, 336
port parallèle 329
port pour adaptateur de courant 336
port réseau 329
port série 329
port souris 329
port USB 329, 336
port vidéo 329, 336
portail 285
porte 178, 210, 211, 213, 287, 361,
  381, 392, 423, 439, 447, 528, 529
porte à deux vantaux 362
porte à lanières 286
porte à tambour manuelle 286
porte accordéon 286
porte automatique 390
porte avant 383, 386
porte classique 286
porte coulissante 195, 286
porte coulissante automatique 286
coupe-feu 286
porte d'entrée 362, 363
porte de garage basculante 286
porte de garage sectionnelle 286

porte de l'élévateur 363
porte de la soute 13
porte étagère 211
porte extérieure 185
porte latérale 380
porte moustiquaire 361
porte pliante 286
porte-adresse 277
porte-bagages 277, 361, 369, 370
porte-bagages arrière 369
porte-bidon 371
porte-bûches 193
porte-cartes 274
porte-chéquier 274, 275
porte-clés 275
porte-coupures 275
porte-documents à soufflet 274
porte-documents plat 275
porte-fenêtre 164, 188, 189
porte-fil dentaire 272
porte-filtre 181
porte-foyer 192
porte-jarretelles 259
porte-marteau 225
porte-matraque 456
porte-mine 312
porte-monnaie 275
porte-moulinet 536, 537
porte-outil 229
porte-parapluies 273
porte-passeport 275
porte-rouleau 195
porte-sac 505
porte-savon 195
porte-serviettes 195
porte-skis 356
porte-stylo 274
porte-tube 421
porte-vélos 356
portée 298
portefeuille 275
portes d'entrée 294
portes, exemples 286
portière 361, 363
portique 381, 397, 406, 407, 447
portique de chargement de conteneurs
  381
portique de signalisation 375
ports pour carte mémoire 471
ports pour manette 471
Portugal 449
position carpée 518
position d'équilibre 418
position des joueurs 474, 481, 482, 489
position droite 518
position groupée 518
positions de départ, plongeon 518
poste d'aiguillage 375
poste d'observation 7
poste de communication 380
poste de l'agent de sécurité 463
poste de patrouille 512
poste de pilotage 392, 395
poste de police 433
poste de secours 345, 512
poste des infirmières (urgence
  ambulatoire) 463
poste des infirmières (urgence majeure)
  462
poste téléphonique 327
postillon 469
pot 163
pot d'échappement 351, 367, 368
pot d'échappement 369
poteau 187, 487, 490, 495
poteau cornier 187
poteau de but 485
poteau de ligne de jeu 475
poteau du ring 498
potence 371, 421, 467
poterne 282
potiron 129
pou 69
poubelle 215
pouce 79, 115, 243, 477
pouce opposable 91
poudre 534
poudre libre 266
poudre pressée 266
poudrier 266
pouf 201
poulailler 122
poule 81
poulet 155
poulie 219, 360, 535
poulie de chariot 397

poulie de tension du régulateur 287
poumon droit 103, 105
poumon gauche 103, 105
poumons 105
poupe 386, 519
pour broyer et râper 170
pour couper 177
pour cuire 178
pour l'emploi du temps 338
pour la correspondance 338
pour la pâtisserie 172
pour le classement 339
pour mélanger et battre 176
pour mesurer 171
pour ouvrir 170
pour passer et égoutter 171
pour presser 177
pourcentage 337, 427
pourpier 127
pousse 256
pousse de bambou 125
poussoir 170, 177, 180, 460
poussoir d'arrêt 424
poussoir de mise en marche 424
poussoir de remise à zéro 424
poutre 187, 283, 288, 496
poutre cantilever 344
poutre continue 344
poutre d'équilibre 497
poutre de levage 364
poutre de queue 395
poutre suspendue 344
poutre-châssis 401
prairie 157
prairie 24, 122
prairie tempérée 44
praticable pour exercices au sol 496
précipitation 45
précipitations 41
précipitations hivernales 41
prémaxillaire 74
premier arbitre 487
premier assistant-cadreur 290
premier but 474
premier croissant 5
premier quartier 5
premier radial externe 97
premier-but 474
première jouteuse 515
première ligne 482
première molaire 101
première prémolaire 101
premières feuilles 53
premiers violons 295
prémolaires 101
préposé au banc des pénalités 507
préposé au contrôle des billets 294
prépuce 111
près du ring 498
présentoir de brochures 442
présentoir réfrigéré 438
présent terrestre 403
pression à la taille 260
pression au niveau de la mer 39
pression barométrique 39
pression devant 261
pression, mesure 426
prétoire 440
prévention de la criminalité 456
prévention des incendies 454
prévisions météorologiques 38
principales pièces d'une maison 188
principaux organes des systèmes
  automobiles 350
printemps 38
prise audio 329
prise casque 310, 311, 322, 326
prise chronométrée 210
prise classique 493
prise d'air 383, 523
prise d'air 362
prise d'air de refroidissement du moteur
  525
prise d'air du moteur 362
prise d'alimentation 329
prise d'eau 407
prise d'entrée/sortie audio 337
prise d'oxygène 464

prise de charge 271
prise de courant 198, 217
prise de courant commutée 322
prise de courant européenne 198
prise de la sonde thermique 178
prise de télécommande 314, 315
prise électrique 361
prise porte-plume 493
prise pour écouteurs 329
prises d'entrée/de sortie audio/vidéo 322
prises vidéo et numérique 315
prises, exemples 499
prisme de Porro 420
prison 469
prix à l'unité 423
prix à payer 423
procédé 503
producteur 291
production d'électricité par énergie
  éolienne 413
production d'électricité par énergie
  géothermique 402
production d'électricité par énergie
  nucléaire 408
production d'électricité par énergie
  thermique 402
production d'électricité par l'alternateur
  408
production de chaleur 408
produits céréaliers 144
produits d'emballage 120
produits d'entretien 120
produits de fission (noyaux radioactifs)
  415
produits de la raffinerie 405
produits de traiteur 121
produits laitiers 120, 150
produits pétrochimiques 405
produits pour animaux familiers 121
profil du sol 54
profondeur du foyer 27
programmateur 212, 213, 214
programmation des voix 310
programmes informatiques 457
projecteur 290, 294, 371, 376
projecteur orientable 455
projecteur sous-marin 184
projecteurs 293
projection conique 22
projection cylindrique 22
projection d'épaule par un côté 499
projection en cercle 499
projection horizontale 22
projection interrompue 22
projections cartographiques 22
pronaos 279
propagation 418
propulseur 10
propulseur d'étrave 387
propulseurs de commande d'orientation
  12
prosciutto 156
prospection terrestre 403
prostate 111
protecteur d'avant-bras 486
protecteur d'embout 460
protecteur lombaire 486
protection d'usure 525
protection de l'ouïe 458
protection de la tête 458
protection des pieds 459
protection des voies respiratoires 459
protection des yeux 458
protège-cheville 476
protège-côtes 486
protège-cou 486
protège-coude 526
protège-dents 486, 498
protège-gorge 476
protège-hanche 486
protège-lame inférieur 227
protège-lame supérieur 227
protège-main 525
protège-matelas 204
protège-orteils 459, 460
protège-poignet 527
protège-tibia 480, 513
protège-tympan 458
protocole de communication 334
proton 414
protoneurone sensitif 110
protubérance 4
proue 387, 519
province 23
prune 132
pseudopode 66

pubis 92, 94
puce 69
puisard 194
puissance, mesure 426
puits 278
puits d'injection 402
puits de dérive 519
puits de production 402
puits sous-marin 404
pulls 250, 254
pulpe 57, 58, 59, 101, 114
pulvérisateur 236, 402
puma 88
punaise rayée 69
punaises 341
pupille 87, 119
pupille verticale 76
pupitre 305, 311
pupitre du chef d'orchestre 295
pyjama 256
pylône 344, 375
pylône du moteur 393
pyramide 278, 429
Pyrénées 18
python 77

Q

Qatar 452
quad 369
quadrant 428
quadrilatère 429
quadruple croche 299
quai 375, 379, 381, 390, 430
quai d'embarquement 389
quai de chargement 435
quai de déchargement 437, 439
quai de gare 374
quantité de matière, mesure 426
quark d 414
quark u 414
quart de soupir 299
quart-arrière 485
quarte 298
quartier 5, 58, 240, 262
quartier des affaires 430, 432
quatuor 300
queue 57, 58, 59, 76, 82, 83, 86, 90,
  111, 228, 393, 412, 526, 531
queue de billard 503
queue de l'hélix 115
queue de poussières 6
queue ionique 6
quesot 199
quillard 521
quinoa 143
quinte 298, 468
quinte royale 468
quintette 300

R

rabat 244, 275, 532
rabot 229
raccord à compression 197
raccord de robinet 236
raccord de signalisation 361
raccord de tuyau 236
races de chats 87
races de chiens 86
racine 54, 101
racine antérieure 110
racine carrée 337
racine carrée de 427
racine de l'hélix 115
racine de l'ongle 114
racine du nez 117
racine motrice 109, 110
racine pivotante 63
racine postérieure 110
racine principale 53
racine secondaire 53
racine sensitive 109, 110
racine traçante 63
racines adventives 52
raclette 151
raclette-gril 179
racloir 514
radar 382, 383, 386, 387
radar météorologique 38, 392
radiateur 350, 358
radiateurs 11
radicelle 53, 63
radicule 57
radio 326, 457
radio portable 325

ASTRONOMIE > 2-13; TERRE > 14-49; RÈGNE VÉGÉTAL > 50-65; RÈGNE ANIMAL > 66-91; ÊTRE HUMAIN > 92-119; ALIMENTATION ET CUISINE > 120-181; MAISON > 182-215; BRICO-
LAGE ET JARDINAGE > 216-237; VÊTEMENTS > 238-263; PARURE ET OBJETS PERSONNELS > 264-277; ARTS ET ARCHITECTURE > 278-311; COMMUNICATIONS ET BUREAUTIQUE > 312-341;
TRANSPORT ET MACHINERIE > 342-401; ÉNERGIES > 402-413; SCIENCE > 414-429; SOCIÉTÉ > 430-467; SPORTS ET JEUX > 468-538

radio-réveil 325
radioactivité, mesure 426
radiocassette laser 326
radis 129
radis noir 129
radis oriental 129
radius 98
raffinerie 404, 431
raglan 251
raie 158
raie des fesses 93, 95
raie sourcilière 78
raifort 129
rail d'éclairage 207
rail de glissement 353, 521
rail-guide de contrepoids 287
rail-guide de la cabine 287
rails de travelling 290
rainette 75
rainure 169, 510
raisin 62, 132
raisin, coupe 59
ralenti 319
rallonge 202, 209
ramasseur 490
rambarde 384, 526
rambutan 137
rame 501
rame de métro 378, 380
rameau 53, 62, 63, 65
rameau communicant 110
ramequin 166
rameur 501
ramille 63
rampant 279
rampe 188, 189, 191, 279, 281, 293
rampe d'accès 344, 386
rampe d'éclairage 207
rampe de quai 381
rampe de signalisation 455, 457
rampe, planche à roulettes 526
ramure 63
rang 272
rangée 293
rangement pour les gants 464
râpe 170
râpe à fromage cylindrique 170
râpe à muscade 170
rappel de mémoire 337
raquette de badminton 494
raquette de tennis 492
raquette de tennis de table 493
ras-de-cou 250, 255, 264
ras-el-hanout 139
rasage 271
rasette 305
rasoir à double tranchant 271
rasoir à manche 271
rasoir effileur 269
rasoir électrique 271
rasoir jetable 271
rat 82
rat, morphologie 82
rate 103
râteau 233, 503
ratissoire 233
raton laveur 88
ravier 166
ravioli 146
rayon 70, 273, 371, 428
rayon épineux 74
rayon lumineux 419
rayon médullaire 63
rayon mou 74
rayonnement 415
rayonnement infrarouge 46, 418
rayonnement solaire 45, 46, 410, 411
rayonnement solaire absorbé 46
rayonnement solaire réfléchi 46
rayonnement ultraviolet 418
rayons gamma 418
rayons X 418
ré 298
réacteur 408
réacteur nucléaire 409
réaction en chaîne 415
réalisateur 291
rebobinage 314, 319, 323, 326, 328
rebord 210
rebord de cuve 212
rebras 243
récamier 200
réceptacle 51, 56, 59
réceptacle à déchets 365
réceptacle de brosses 272
récepteur 327

récepteur de son 460
récepteur sensoriel 110
récepteurs du goût 118
réception 439
réception des messages 328
réception directe 316
réception du fret 391
receveur 474, 475, 476, 490, 495
receveur éloigné 485
recharge 312
réchaud 174
réchaud à deux feux 529
réchaud à un feu 529
réchauffement de la planète 46
recherche 335
recherche des canaux 319
récif de la Grande Barrière 15
récipient 176
recourbe-cils 266
rectangle 429
rectangle des instructeurs 474
rectangulaire 530
rectrice 78
rectum 106, 111, 112
recyclage 49
redingote 251
réflecteur 217, 321, 365
réflecteurs solaires 316
réformeur catalytique 405
réfrigérateur 164, 211, 438
réfrigérateurs 438
refroidissement 405
refroidissement de la vapeur par l'eau 408
regard de visite 434
régie 293
région auriculaire 78
région malaire 78
région négative 410
région positive 410
registre des aigus 296
registre des basses 296
réglage 466
réglage de centrage 329
réglage de hausse 420
réglage de l'afficheur 327
réglage de l'angle 229
réglage de la balance 303
réglage de la hauteur 501
réglage de la luminosité 329
réglage de la pression 277
réglage de la pression d'oxygène 10
réglage de la résistance 501
réglage de la tension 537
réglage de la tonalité 303
réglage de niveau d'enregistrement 323
réglage de profondeur 229
réglage de tempo 311
réglage des températures 208
réglage du contraste 329
réglage du diaphragme 421
réglage du four 210
réglage du volume 303, 311, 319, 322, 325, 326, 329
réglage du volume des communications 10
réglage en hauteur du condenseur 421
réglage horizontal 329
réglage latéral 420
réglage micrométrique (azimut) 9
réglage micrométrique (azimuth) 8
réglage micrométrique (latitude) 8, 9
réglage vertical 329
règle 425
règle graduée 425, 531
règne animal 66
règne végétal 50
régulateur de pression 174, 529
régulateur de vitesse 287, 354
rehausseur 205
rein 73, 103
rein droit 107
rein gauche 107
reine 68
reine, abeille 68
reins 83, 93, 95
rejet 63
rejet d'oxygène 54
rejets industriels 47, 48
relevé de transaction 443
relief lunaire 5
religion 446
reliure à anneaux plastiques 340
reliure à glissière 339
reliure à pince 339
reliure à ressort 339
reliure à vis 339

reliure spirale 340
rémige primaire 78
rémige secondaire 78
rémige tertiaire 78
remise 182, 230
remorque 380
remorqueur 384
rempart 5, 282
remplage 285
remplissage 404
renard 88
renfort de nuque 525
réniforme 55
renne 84
renseignements 512
renversé 518
repère de ligne de marche 533
repère de niveau d'eau 208
repère de touche 302, 303
repère de virage de dos 517
répertoire 334
répertoire téléphonique 327, 338
répéteur 317
répondeur téléphonique 328
repose-main 332
repose-pied 467
repose-pied du passager 367, 368
repose-pied du pilote 367, 368
repose-pieds 205
repose-poignets détachable 330
repousse-chair 265
reproduction de clés 437
reprographie 442
reptation 31
reptiles 76
République arabe syrienne 452
République centrafricaine 451
République de Corée 453
République de Moldova 450
République démocratique du Congo 451
République démocratique populaire lao 453
République dominicaine 449
République populaire démocratique de Corée 453
République tchèque 450
République-Unie de Tanzanie 451
répulsion 416
requin, morphologie 74
réseau d'oléoducs 404
réseau national 316
réseau nerveux 101
réseau privé 316
réseau téléphonique 317
réserve d'eau 272
réserves alimentaires 439
réservoir 13, 181, 406, 407, 454, 529
réservoir à carburant 364, 377, 395
réservoir à essence 351, 366, 369
réservoir à toit flottant 404
réservoir auxiliaire 365
réservoir d'alcool 424
réservoir d'arrosage 408
réservoir d'eau 181
réservoir d'essence 235
réservoir d'huile 235
réservoir de brut 405
réservoir de chasse d'eau 195
réservoir de liquide de frein 357
réservoir de mercure 424
réservoir externe 12
réservoir magmatique 28, 402
réservoir propane 361
réservoir tampon 404
résidente 464
résidus non recyclables 49
résistance électrique, mesure 426
résistance hydraulique 501
résistances 417
résonateur 324
ressort 27, 206, 222, 312, 535
ressort athlétique 500
ressort de rappel 357
ressort de soupape 360
ressort de suspension 212
ressort de tension 355, 500
ressort hélicoïdal 351
restaurant 386, 432, 435, 436, 438
restauration rapide 437
résurgence 31
retable 446
réticule 420
réticulum endoplasmique 50, 66
rétine 119, 419
retour 331

retour de l'eau au générateur de vapeur 408
retourné 518
rétroviseur 354, 363, 364, 366, 368, 369, 523
rétroviseur extérieur 348, 362
rétroviseur grand-angle 362, 363
réunion 427
réverbère 434
revers 240, 244, 246
revers à cran aigu 244
revers cranté 248
revêtement 187, 493
revêtement de sécurité 10
revêtement synthétique 492
revêtement thermique 12
revêtements de sol textiles 190
revitalisant capillaire 267
rez-de-chaussée 182, 188
Rhéa 3
rhino-pharynx 117
rhinocéros 85
rhizoïde 51
rhizome 52
rhodyménie palmé 123
rhubarbe 125
rias 35
ribosome 50, 66
richelieu 240
ricotta 150
rideau de fer 292
rideau de scène 292, 293
rideau séparateur 464
ridoir 521
rigatoni 146
rillettes 156
rimaye 30
rinceau 200
ring 498
ris 154
riz 61, 143, 147
riz : panicule 61
riz basmati 147
riz blanc 147
riz complet 147
riz étuvé 147
riz sauvage 143
rizière 47
robe 404
robe bain-de-soleil 252
robe chemisier 252
robe de maison 252
robe enveloppe 252
robe fourreau 252
robe princesse 252
robe taille basse 252
robe tee-shirt 252
robe trapèze 252
robe tunique 252
robe-manteau 252
robe-polo 252
Roberval, balance 422
robes, exemples 252
robinet 195
robinet d'arrêt 196, 197
robinet d'arrêt général 194
robinet de réglage de débit 454
robinet de vidange 404
robinet flotteur à clapet 196
robinet relais 529
robinets 210
robot boulanger 179
robot de cuisine 177
roc 27
rocaille 230
roche mère 54
roches d'intrusion 26
roches ignées 26
roches métamorphiques 26
roches sédimentaires 26
rognons 154
Roi 468, 470
romaine 126
romano 151
romarin 142
rond pronateur 96
rond-point 25
ronde 299
rondelle 417, 510
rondelle à denture extérieure 222
rondelle à denture intérieure 222
rondelle à ressort 222
rondelle conique 196

rondelle plate 222
rondelles 222
rongeur 82
roquefort 151
roquette 127
rorqual 90
rosace 302
rose 56, 285
rose des vents 23
rosée 41
rosette 186
rossignol 80
rôti 152, 153
rôti de côtes 152
rotini 146
rotonde 435
rotor 412, 537
rotor anticouple 395
rotule 98, 224
roue 231, 364, 467, 522, 525, 527
roue avant 401
roue de secours 361
roue de support 523
roue dentée 523
roue folle 398
roue libre 372
roue pivotante 467
roues motrices 401
rouge 418
rouge à lèvres 266
rouge-gorge 80
Rouges 469
rouget barbet 159
rouleau 219, 268
rouleau à pâtisserie 172
rouleaux de la Torah 447
roulement à billes 413
roulette 205, 209, 277, 308, 526
roulette de commande 337
roulette de défilement 327, 332
roulette de pâtissier 172
roulis 395
Roumanie 450
roupie 440
route 25, 343, 430
route d'accès 388
route secondaire 25
route, coupe 342
routeur 334
Royaume-Uni de Grande-Bretagne et d'Irlande du Nord 449
ruban 225
ruban blanc 493, 495
ruban de bouclage 457
ruban de Téflon 216
ruban de tissu adhésif 461
ruche 122
ruché 260
rue 25, 433, 435
rue commerçante 432
rue, coupe 434
ruelle 433
Ruffini, corpuscule 114
rugby 482
rugbyman 483
ruisseau 32
ruissellement 45
russule verdoyante 123
rutabaga 129
Rwanda 451

S

sablier 171
sablière 377
sablière double 187
sabot 83, 224, 365, 473
sabot de protection 398
sac 296
sac à bandoulière 276
sac à dos 532
sac à provisions 276
sac accordéon 276
sac besace 276
sac boîte 276
sac cartable 276
sac de congélation 162
sac de golf 505
sac de sable 498
sac fourre-tout 276
sac gonflable 354
sac marin 276
sac polochon 276
sac seau 275
sac-filet 162
sachet 162

ASTRONOMIE > 2-13;   TERRE > 14-49;   RÈGNE VÉGÉTAL > 50-65;   RÈGNE ANIMAL > 66-91;   ÊTRE HUMAIN > 92-119;   ALIMENTATION ET CUISINE > 120-181;   MAISON > 182-215;   BRICO-
LAGE ET JARDINAGE > 216-237;   VÊTEMENTS > 238-263;   PARURE ET OBJETS PERSONNELS > 264-277;   ARTS ET ARCHITECTURE > 278-311;   COMMUNICATIONS ET BUREAUTIQUE > 312-341;
TRANSPORT ET MACHINERIE > 342-401;   ÉNERGIES > 402-413;   SCIENCE > 414-429;   SOCIÉTÉ > 430-467;   SPORTS ET JEUX > 468-538

581

INDEX FRANÇAIS

sacoche 369, 372
sacristie 446
sacrum 98, 99
sacs à main 275
sacs à provisions 121
sacs de couchage, exemples 530
safran 138, 384
saharienne 255
saindoux 149
saint-bernard 86
Saint-Kitts-et-Nevis 449
Saint-Laurent 16
Saint-Marin 450
saint-pierre 161
Saint-Vincent-et-les Grenadines 449
Sainte-Lucie 449
saisons, cycle 38
saladier 166
salamandre 75
salami allemand 156
salami de Gênes 156
salchow 509
salière 166
salle 293
salle à manger 188, 386, 438
salle d'anesthésie 464
salle d'arts plastiques 444
salle d'attente 463
salle d'attente des familles 462
salle d'attente du centre de prélèvements 465
salle d'attente principale 465
salle d'attente secondaire 465
salle d'embarquement 391
salle d'entreposage 438
salle d'examen 465
salle d'examen audiométrique 465
salle d'examen et de soins 463
salle d'examen gynécologique 463
salle d'habillage 290
salle d'informatique 444
salle d'opération 464, 465
salle d'ophtalmologie et d'oto-rhino-laryngologie 463
salle de bains 189, 195, 439, 464
salle de bal 387
salle de classe 444, 445
salle de classe pour élèves en difficultés d'apprentissage 444
salle de commande 406
salle de conférences 442
salle de contrôle des machines 384
salle de musique 444
salle de plâtre 463
salle de prélèvements 465
salle de préparation chirurgicale 464
salle de prière 447
salle de projection 294
salle de rangement du matériel médical 465
salle de réanimation 462
salle de réception 447
salle de repos des infirmiers 465
salle de restaurant 439
salle de réunion 439, 442, 445
salle de réveil 464
salle de sciences 444
salle de séjour 188
salle de soins 465
salle de spectacle 292, 432
salle de stérilisation 464, 465
salle de stockage du matériel souillé 462, 464
salle de stockage du matériel stérile 462
salle de triage 463
salle des cartes 382
salle des enseignants 445
salle des jurés 440
salle des machines 386, 406, 407
salle des pas perdus 374
salles d'entrevue 440
salomé 241
salon 188, 386
salon d'attente 439
salon de coiffure 436
salon des employés 443
salon du personnel 463
salopette 254
salopette à bretelles croisées 261
salopette à dos montant 260
salsifis 129
sambal oelek 141
Samoa 453
sandale 241
sandalette 242
Sandow® 528, 529

sandre 160
sang désoxygéné 104
sang oxygéné 104
sang, composition 104
sangle 353, 491, 501, 505
sangle d'amortissement 458
sangle de compression 532
sangle de fermeture 532
sangle de nuque 458
sangle élastique 277
sangle serre-vêtements 277
sanglier 84
santé 460
São Tomé-et-Príncipe 451
sapin 65
sapotille 137
sarcloir 233
sardine 159
sarment 62
sarrasin 61, 143
sarrasin : grappe 61
sarriette 142
sas 286
sas du laboratoire 13
sas pressurisé 345
satellite 316
satellite artificiel 37
satellite de télécommunications 335
satellite météorologique 38
satellites 2
satellites de télécommunications 316
Saturne 2, 3
sauce aux prunes 141
sauce hoisin 140
sauce soja 140
sauce Tabasco® 140
sauce Worcestershire 140
saucière 166
saucisse de Francfort 156
saucisse de Toulouse 156
saucisson kielbasa 156
sauge 142
saule pleureur 64
saumon de l'Atlantique 161
saumon du Pacifique 161
saupoudreuse 172
saut à la perche 472
saut à ski 513
saut en hauteur 473
saut en longueur 472
sauterelle 402
sauteur 513
sauteuse 175
sautoir 264
sautoir, longueur opéra 264
sauts, exemples 509
savane 40, 44
savon de toilette 267
saxhorn 307
saxophone 306
scaphandre spatial 10
scapulaire 78
scarole 126
scellement, matériau 417
scène 278, 292, 293
schéma de la circulation 103
schnauzer 86
Schwann, gaine 110
scie à chantourner 226
scie à guichet 226
scie à onglet manuelle 226
scie circulaire 227
scie d'élagage 234
scie de camping 533
scie égoïne 226
scie sauteuse 227
science 414
scion 536
scissure oblique 105
sclérotique 119
scooter 369
scooter de mer 523
score doublé 471
score triplé 471
scorpion 70
scorsonère 129
scripte 291
scrotum 92, 111
sculptures 358
seau 215
seau isotherme 180
sébaste 161
sécateur 234
sèche-cheveux 270
sèche-linge électrique 213

second arbitre 487
second assistant-cadreur 290
seconde 298, 428
secondeur extérieur droit 484
secondeur extérieur gauche 484
secondeur intérieur 484
seconds violons 295
secrétaire 203
secrétariat 443, 445
secteur 428
secteur des civières 462
section articulée 363
section de conduit 193
sécurité 454
segment 357, 360
segment abdominal 67
seiche 157
seigle 61, 143
seigle : épi 61
sein 92, 94, 113
séisme 27
seizième de soupir 299
séjour 528
sel fin 141
sel marin 141
sélecteur d'entrée 322
sélecteur d'inclinaison de la lame 227
sélecteur de bandes 323
sélecteur de coupe 271
sélecteur de fonctions 314
sélecteur de hauteur 209
sélecteur de micro 303
sélecteur de mise au point 320
sélecteur de mode 326
sélecteur de mode sonore 322
sélecteur de niveau d'eau 212
sélecteur de programme 310
sélecteur de régime 237
sélecteur de rythme 311
sélecteur de stations 325, 326
sélecteur de température 178, 212, 213, 270
sélecteur de vitesse 176, 177, 227, 270
sélecteur de vitesse de rotation 228
sélecteur de vitesses 367, 368, 369
sélecteur de voix 311
sélecteur quadridirectionnel 315
sélecteur télé/vidéo 319
sélecteurs de fonctions 327
sélection des canaux 319
selle 369, 370, 501, 523
selle biplace 367
selle conducteur 369
selle passager 369
sellette d'attelage 364
semelle 187, 208, 227, 229, 247, 509, 510, 511
semelle antidérapante 261
semelle d'usure 240, 263
semelle intercalaire 262
semelle pivotante 224
semence 220
semi-rectangulaire 530
semi-remorque frigorifique 365
semoir à main 231
semoule 144
Sénégal 20, 451
sens de déplacement des électrons 416, 417
sensibilité du film 314
sépale 56, 58, 59
séparateur 359, 384, 402, 417
séparateur électrolytique 417
séparateur liquide/gaz 359
séparation magnétique 49
séparation papier/carton 49
séparation-classeur 274
septième 298
septum interventriculaire 104
septum lucidum 109
séquence 468
séquenceur 310
sérac 30
serfouette 233
seringue 460
seringue pour lavage de cavités 460
serpe 234
serpent 76
serpent à sonnette 77
serpent corail 77
serpent venimeux, morphologie 76
serpentin 210
serre 79, 122
serre-joint 224, 226
serre-joint à tuyau 224
serre-livres 341

serre-poignet 492
serre-tête 324, 326, 459
serrure 185, 186, 202, 211, 275, 277, 349, 352
serrure à clé 274
serrure à combinaison 274
sertissage 534
serveur 334, 335, 491, 494
serveur d'accès 335
service 487, 490
service à fondue 174
service à la clientèle 443
service de colis 374
services d'assurance 442
services de crédit 442
services financiers 442
services sociaux 465
serviette 274
serviette de toilette 267
servofrein 350, 357
seuil 185
seuil de l'évacuateur 406
sextuor 300
Seychelles 452
shampooing 267
shekel 440
shiitake 123
short 254, 261, 473, 480, 483, 488
short boxeur 263
short de boxe 498
si 298
siamois 87
siège 196, 200, 201, 205, 353, 467
siège coulissant 501
siège de sécurité pour enfant 356
siège de vélo pour enfant 372
siège double 380
siège du rabbin 447
siège simple 380
siège-baquet : vue de face 353
siège-baquet : vue de profil 353
sièges 201
Sierra Leone 451
sifflet 180
signal de voie 375
signature du titulaire 441
signature officielle 441
silique, coupe 60
sill 28
sillet 301, 302, 303
sillon 118
sillon antérieur 115
sillon médian 118
sillon naso-labial 117
sillon terminal 118
silo-couloir 122
silo-tour 122
silos 381
simulateur d'escalier 501
Singapour 453
sinus frontal 117
sinus latéral inférieur 62
sinus latéral supérieur 62
sinus pétiolaire 62
sinus sphénoïdal 117
siphon 194, 196, 197
sirop antitussif 467
sirop d'érable 149
sirop de maïs 149
sismogramme 27
sismographe horizontal 27
sismographe vertical 27
sismographes 27
sistre 309
site d'enfouissement 47
sixte 298
ski 510, 523
ski alpin 510
ski de descente/super-G 510
ski de fond 514
ski de grand slalom 510
ski de saut 513
ski de slalom 510
skieur alpin 510
skieur de fond 514
skimmer 184
skis, exemples 510
slalom géant 511
slalom spécial 511
slip 247, 259
slip de bain 263
Slovaquie 450
Slovénie 450
smash 491
smog 47

snooker 503
société 430
socle 27, 176, 179, 180, 192, 206, 332, 412, 422
socle fixe 224
socle rembourré 489
socle-chargeur 208
socque 242
socquette 257
softball 477
soie 167, 169, 216, 271, 536
soies 219
soigneur 489, 498
soins de la pelouse 237
soins du corps 267
soja, germes 131
soja, graine 131
sol 48, 298
sol naturel 342
solarium 385
sole 161
soléaire 96
Soleil 2, 4, 5, 38
Soleil, éclipse 4
Soleil, structure 4
solide 414, 415
solide amorphe 414
solidification 414
solin 193
solitaire 264
solive 190
solive de plafond 187
solive de plancher 187
solive de rive 187
solstice d'été 38
solstice d'hiver 38
solution multifonctions 272
Somalie 451
sommaire 313
sommation 427
sommelier 438
sommet 29, 512
sommier 304
sommier tapissier 204
sonde spatiale 37
sonde thermique 178
sorbetière 180
sore 52
sorgho 61
sorgho : panicule 61
sortie 343
sortie d'air chaud 192
sortie de piste 391
sortie de piste à grande vitesse 388
sortie des billets 442
sortie des originaux 328
sortie des tickets 346
sortie du caloporteur 410
sortie S-Video 336
soubassement 202, 283
souche 63
soudage : outils 218
Soudan 451
soudure 218
soufflet 274, 276, 296
soupape 174
soupape d'admission 360
soupape d'échappement 360
soupape d'évacuation 307, 461
soupape de sûreté 408
soupape expiratoire 459
soupape inspiratoire 459
soupière 166
soupir 299
source 32
source alimentaire fondamentale 45
source de courant 416
sourcils 87
sourdine 307
souris à roulette 332
souris mécanique 332
souris optique 332
souris sans fil 332
sous-couche 190
sous-épineux 97
sous-fondation 342
sous-pied 254
sous-plancher 187, 190
sous-sol 54, 182, 281, 435
sous-titre 313
sous-vêtement 524
sous-vêtements 247, 258
soustraction 337, 427
soustraction en mémoire 337
soute 12, 393
soute à bagages 362, 383, 395

ASTRONOMIE > 2-13; TERRE > 14-49; RÈGNE VÉGÉTAL > 50-65; RÈGNE ANIMAL > 66-91; ÊTRE HUMAIN > 92-119; ALIMENTATION ET CUISINE > 120-181; MAISON > 182-215; BRICO-LAGE ET JARDINAGE > 216-237; VÊTEMENTS > 238-263; PARURE ET OBJETS PERSONNELS > 264-277; ARTS ET ARCHITECTURE > 278-311; COMMUNICATIONS ET BUREAUTIQUE > 312-341; TRANSPORT ET MACHINERIE > 342-401; ÉNERGIES > 402-413; SCIENCE > 414-429; SOCIÉTÉ > 430-467; SPORTS ET JEUX > 468-538

soutien-gorge 259
soutien-gorge balconnet 259
soutien-gorge corbeille 259
spadice 57
spaghetti 146
spaghettini 146
spatule 173, 510, 514
spatulée 55
spécifications techniques 358
spectre électromagnétique 418
spencer 254
spermatozoïde 111
sphaigne squarreuse 51
sphénoïde 100
sphère 429
sphincter anal 106
spicule 4
spirale 70, 221
spirale carrée 70
spiruline 123
splénius de la tête 97
spores 52
sports 468
sports à roulettes 526
sports aquatiques 516
sports d'hiver 515
sports de balle 474
sports de ballon 474
sports de combat 498
sports de force 500
sports de précision 502
sports de raquette 493
sports gymniques 496
sports motorisés 524
sports nautiques 516
spot 207
spot à pince 206
squelette 98
Sri Lanka 453
stabilisateur 393, 395, 397, 400, 455, 523
stabilisateur de roulis 386
stade 431, 472
stalactite 31
stalagmite 31
stands 524
station d'accueil 337
station de métro 378, 432
station de pompage 404
station de pompage intermédiaire 404
station de pompage principale 404
station de ski 512
station locale 316
station météorologique d'aéronef 38
station météorologique océanique 38
station météorologique sur bouée 38
station météorologique, disposition des informations 39
station spatiale internationale 11
station terrestre 38
station terrestre de télécommunications 335
station-relais 316
station-relais à micro-ondes 334
station-service 346, 433
stationnement 435, 504
statue 446
steeple 472
steppe 40
sterno-cléido-mastoïdien 96
sternum 98
stéthoscope 460
stigmate 56, 60, 67
stilton 151
stimulateur de gencives 272
stipule 55
stop 86
stoppeur 481
store à enroulement automatique 356
strato-cumulus 42
stratopause 37
stratosphère 37
stratus 42
structure 186, 342
structure antitonneau 525
structure d'un arbre 63
structure d'un champignon 52
structure d'un lichen 50
structure d'une algue 51
structure d'une feuille 55
structure d'une fleur 56
structure d'une fougère 52
structure d'une maison 188
structure d'une mousse 51
structure d'une plante 53
structure de l'oreille 116

structure de la biosphère 44
structure de la moelle épinière 109
structure de la Terre 26
structure du Soleil 4
structure en treillis 11
structure métallique 374
style 56, 57, 58, 59, 60, 424
stylet 312, 337
stylo-bille 312
stylo-plume 312
stylobate 279
subarctique 40
subduction 27
sublimation 414
substance blanche 109, 110
substance corticale 107
substance grise 109, 110
substance médullaire 107
substratum imperméable 402
subtropical humide 40
suceur à tapis et planchers 209
suceur plat 209
suceur triangulaire à tissus 209
sucre 149
sucre candi 149
sucre glace 149
sucre granulé 149
sucrier 166
Sud 23
Sud Est 23
Sud Ouest 23
Sud Sud-Est 23
Sud Sud-Ouest 23
Suède 450
Suisse 450
sumac 139
super-géant 511
supermarché 120, 433, 437
supplément en couleurs 313
supplément littéraire 313
support 174, 199, 269, 308, 493
support à bagages 523
support de fixation 9, 206
support de main 297
support de panneau 489
support de plaquette 273
support de pouce 306
suppression 331
surf acrobatique 513
surf alpin 513
surf des neiges 513
surface d'affichage 341
surface de but 480
surface de coin 481
surface de combat 499
surface de cuisson 179
surface de frappe 477
surface de jeu 493
surface de l'eau 518
surface de la glace 515
surface de réparation 480
surface de sécurité 499
surface dure (ciment) 492
surface verticale 526
surfaces 428
surfaces de jeu 492
surfeur 513
surfusion 414
surimpression 314
Suriname 448
suroît 239
surpiqûre 240, 246, 260, 262
surtitre 313
survêtement 262
suspension 206, 380
suspension arrière 522
suspente 344
suture 60
suture coronale 100
suture lambdoïde 100
suture squameuse 100
Swaziland 452
sweat-shirt 262
sweat-shirt à capuche 262
symboles scientifiques usuels 426
symboles, cartes 468
symphyse pubienne 111, 112
synagogue 447
synapse 110
synthèse additive 418
synthèse des couleurs 418
synthèse soustractive 418
synthétiseur 310
système audio 354
système d'alimentation en essence 351

système d'échappement 351
système de climatisation 46
système de contrôle de la rampe de signalisation 457
système de direction 351
système de freinage 351
système de freinage antiblocage 357
système de jeux vidéo 471
système de lentilles 420
système de pointage fin 7
système de refroidissement 351
système de retenue à sacs gonflables 354
système de suspension 351
système de transmission 351
système de verrouillage 209
système électrique 351
système hydraulique 396
système international d'unités 426
système nerveux 108
système nerveux central 109
système nerveux périphérique 108
système racinaire 53, 62
système rotary 403
système routier 342
système solaire 2
systèmes automobiles 351

T

T.G.V. 376
tabernacle 446
table 202, 493, 502
table à abattants 202
table à langer 205
table à rallonges 202
table d'harmonie 301, 302, 304
table d'opération 464
table de chevet 439, 464
table de communion 446
table de cuisson 164, 210
table de lecture 447
table de lit 464
table de rotation 403
table de service 438
table des greffiers 440
table des résultats 518
tableau 444
tableau d'affichage 341, 444, 492, 499
tableau d'affichage des vols 391
tableau de bord 354, 366, 368
tableau de classement général 496
tableau de commande 178, 179, 210, 212, 213, 214
tableau de manœuvre 287
tableau de pointage 497
tableau des scores 471
tableau du souvenir 447
tableau horaire 374
tableau indicateur 472
tables gigognes 202
tables, exemples 202
tablette 192, 203, 219
tablette de verre 211
tablette porte-outil 219
tablier 344, 369, 396, 498
tablier-blouse 255
tablinum 280
tabloïd 313
tabouret 164, 201, 498
tabouret de bar 201, 438
tabouret-escabeau 219
tabulation à droite 330
tabulation à gauche 330
tache 4
tache jaune 119
tachymètre 368
Tadjikistan 452
tagliatelle aux épinards 146
tahini 140
taie d'oreiller 204
taille 93, 95
taille-bordures 237
taille-crayon 341
taille-haies 235
tailleur 251
tajine 174
talkie-walkie 456
taloche 216
talon 93, 95, 169, 226, 229, 240, 247, 262, 273, 301, 302, 358, 477, 492, 494, 503, 506, 509, 510, 514, 536, 537
talon d'appui 176, 208
talonnette de dessus 240
talonneur 482
talonnière 511, 514

talus 342
talus continental 33
tam-tam 308
tamarillo 136
tamarin 91
tambour 170, 213, 357, 425, 536, 537
tambour d'aisselle 297
tambour de basque 309
tamia 82
tamis 171, 492, 494
tamis à farine 172
tamis vibrant 403
tampon encreur 338
tandem 255, 373
tangage 395
taon 69
tapis 190, 498, 499, 502
tapis de plancher 356
tapis de réception 496
tapis de sol cousu 528, 529
tapis de souris 332
tapis roulant 390
taquet 520, 521
taquet coinceur 521
taquet de verrouillage 333
taro 124
tarse 78
Tasmanie 15
tasse 531, 532
tasse à café 166
tasse à mesurer 171
tasse à thé 166
tassergal 160
Tchad 451
té 505
té de base 193
techniques 487
tectrice primaire 78
tectrice sous-caudale 78
tectrice sus-alaire 78
tectrice sus-caudale 78
teddy 258
tégument 61
tégument de la graine 57
téléavertisseur numérique 327
télécabine 512
télécommande 319, 321
télécommunications par satellite 317
télécopieur 328
télédiffusion par satellite 316
télémanipulateur 11, 12
téléobjectif 314
téléphone 439
téléphone portable 327
téléphone public 294, 437, 438, 463
téléport 317
télescope 7, 9
télescope spatial Hubble 7, 37
télescope, coupe 9
télésiège 512
téléski biplace 512
téléviseur 318, 439, 444
téléviseur grand écran 321
télévision 318
telson 71
témoin 472
témoin d'alimentation 329
témoin d'ouverture de porte 355
témoin de bas niveau de carburant 355
témoin de ceinture de sécurité 355
témoin de charge 355
témoin de clignotants 355, 368
témoin de niveau d'huile 355
témoin de phare 368
témoin de position neutre 368
témoin de pression d'huile 368
témoin des feux de route 355
témoin du retardateur 314
témoin lumineux 454
tempe 92
température Celsius, mesure 426
température de l'air 39
température du point de rosée 39
température thermodynamique, mesure 426
température, mesure 424
temple aztèque 283
temple de Huitzilopochtli 283
temple de Tlaloc 283
temple grec 279
temple grec, plan 279
temporal 98, 100
temps, mesure 424
tendance barométrique 39
tendeur 528

tendeur de timbre 308
tennis 242, 490
tennis de table 493
tenon 273
tenseur du fascia lata 96
tensiomètre 461
tentacule 72
tentacule oculaire 72
tentacule tactile 72
tente canadienne 529
tente deux places 528
tente dôme 529
tente familiale 528
tente grange 528
tente igloo 529
tente individuelle 529
tente intérieure 528, 529
tente rectangulaire 528
tentes, exemples 528
tenue d'exercice 261, 262
tenue d'intervention 454
termes familiers 57, 58, 59
termes techniques 57, 58, 59
terminaison nerveuse 114
terminal à céréales 381
terminal à conteneurs 381, 430
terminal de paiement électronique 121, 443
terminal de vrac 381
terminal numérique 321
terminal pétrolier 381
termite 69
terrain 474, 479, 480, 482, 487, 488, 494
terrain de football américain 484
terrain de golf 430
terrasse 182, 230, 391
terrasse extérieure 387
terrassement 342
Terre 2, 3, 4, 5, 14
terre battue 492
Terre de Baffin 16
Terre de Feu 17
Terre de la Reine-Maud 15
Terre de Wilkes 15
Terre Marie-Byrd 15
Terre, structure 26
terre-plein 434
terre-plein central 343
terrine 174
tertre de départ 504
testicule 111
testicules 71
tête 6, 67, 72, 78, 87, 93, 95, 103, 111, 220, 221, 223, 229, 271, 272, 301, 302, 303, 492, 494, 503, 505, 536
tête à sens unique 221
tête basculante 176
tête bombée 221
tête creuse 221
tête cruciforme 221
tête d'attelage 361, 377
tête d'injection 403
tête de coupe 341
tête de dormant 186
tête de frappe 220
tête de gondole 121
tête de l'humérus 99
tête de lecture/écriture 333
tête de lit 204, 205
tête de mât 519
tête de rotor 395
tête de scion 536
tête du fémur 99
tête du vérin de levage 396
tête en liège 495
tête flottante 271
tête plate 221
tête ronde 221
tête, oiseau 78
tête, protection 458
têtes, exemples 221
Téthys 3
têtière 186
Thaïlande 453
thalle 50, 51
thé 148
thé en sachet 148
thé noir 148
thé oolong 148
thé vert 148
théâtre 433
théâtre grec 278
théière 166
thermocontact 358
thermomètre 404, 424

ASTRONOMIE > 2-13;   TERRE > 14-49;   RÈGNE VÉGÉTAL > 50-65;   RÈGNE ANIMAL > 66-91;   ÊTRE HUMAIN > 92-119;   ALIMENTATION ET CUISINE > 120-181;   MAISON > 182-215;   BRICO-
LAGE ET JARDINAGE > 216-237;   VÊTEMENTS > 238-263;   PARURE ET OBJETS PERSONNELS > 264-277;   ARTS ET ARCHITECTURE > 278-311;   COMMUNICATIONS ET BUREAUTIQUE > 312-341;
TRANSPORT ET MACHINERIE > 342-401;   ÉNERGIES > 402-413;   SCIENCE > 414-429;   SOCIÉTÉ > 430-467;   SPORTS ET JEUX > 468-538

583

thermomètre à mercure 461
thermomètre à mesure instantanée 171
thermomètre à sucre 171
thermomètre à viande 171
thermomètre de four 171
thermomètre médical 424
thermomètre numérique 461
thermomètres médicaux 461
thermopause 37
thermosphère 37
thermostat 178, 211
thermostat réglable 179
thon 160
thorax 67, 68, 92, 94
thym 142
tibia 78, 98
tierce 298
tierceron 284
tige 51, 53, 54, 125, 181, 220, 221, 272, 424, 509, 511, 514
tige carrée d'entraînement 403
tige de carbone (cathode) 417
tige de forage 403
tige de selle 370
tige du poil 114
tige filetée 223
tigre 89
tilleul 148
timbale 308
timbales 295
timbre caoutchouc 338
timbre dateur 338
timon 361
timonerie 384
tipi 288
tique 70
tirant 308, 397
tirant de réglage 244
tirant des cordes 498
tire-bouchon 531
tire-bouchon à levier 170
tire-bouchon de sommelier 170
tire-joint 216
tire-racine 232
tire-veille 519
tiroir 164, 202, 203, 205, 210
tisanes 148
tisonnier 193
tissu adipeux 113, 114
tissu conjonctif 114
Titan 3
Titania 3
titre 313
titre de propriété 469
titre du journal 313
titres et horaires des films 294
Togo 451
toile 273
toile d'araignée 70
toile de fond 292
toilettes femmes 294
toilettes hommes 294
toit 183, 193, 283, 361
toit cathédrale 189
toit de protection 396
toit flottant 404
toit imperméable 402
toit ouvrant 349
tomate 128
tomate en grappe 128
tomatille 128
tombolo 35
tondeuse 269, 271
tondeuse à moteur 237
tong 242
Tonga 453
topinambour 124
toque 239
torchon 215
tore 429
tornade 43
tornade marine 43
torrent 29
torsade 228
tortellini 146
tortilla 145
tortue 76
tortue, morphologie 76
totalisateur journalier 355
toucan 80
touche 296, 301, 303, 304, 487
touche alternative 330
touche d'affichage de titre 320
touche d'affichage des indicateurs 320
touche d'affichage des réglages 315
touche d'annulation 333

touche d'appel 327
touche d'arrêt du défilement 331
touche d'échappement 330
touche d'effacement 331
touche d'effacement 315
touche d'éjection 471
touche d'enregistrement 320
touche d'impression de l'écran/d'appel système 331
touche d'index/agrandissement 315
touche d'insertion 331
touche de composition automatique 328
touche de confirmation 443
touche de contrôle 330
touche de correction 328
touche de courriel 330
touche de décimale 337
touche de démarrage 330
touche de fin d'appel 327
touche de l'heure 320
touche de la date 320
touche de lecture 327
touche de menu 327
touche de modulation 322
touche de pause/d'interruption 331
touche de pédalier 305
touche de présélection 322
touche de raccord d'enregistrement 320
touche de résultat 337
touche de retour 331
touche de saut d'images 315
touche de sélection 327
touche de sélection d'entrée 322
touche de sélection des menus 315
touche de sélection du magnétophone 322
touche de sélection du mode FM 322
touche de suppression 331
touche de tabulation 330
touche de verrouillage des majuscules 330
touche de verrouillage numérique 331
touche de visualisation des images 315
touche début 331
touche fin 331
touche fixe 425
touche majuscule 330
touche numérique 322, 323
touche mobile 425
touche numérique 337
touche page précédente 331
touche page suivante 331
toucher 114
touches d'action 471
touches d'effets spéciaux 320
touches d'opérations 442, 443
touches de déplacement du curseur 331
touches de fonction 330
touches de fonctions 423
touches de fonctions programmables 443
touches de réglage de l'image 320
touches de répétition 323
touches de sélection des enceintes 322
touches de sélection des stations 322
touches directionnelles 471
touches Internet 330
toundra 40, 44
toupet 83
toupie 177
Tour 470
tour 284, 397, 412, 413
tour à bureaux 435
tour d'angle 282
tour d'émission 316
tour d'habitation 289
tour de contrôle 388
tour de coquille 72
tour de cou 245
tour de flanquement 282
tour de forage 382, 403, 404
tour de fractionnement 405
tour de guidage 345
tour de refroidissement 402
tour de spire 73
tour de tête 458
tour du plongeoir 518
tournesol 56
tournevis 221, 531
tournevis à spirale 221
tournevis cruciforme 531
tournevis sans fil 221
tourniquet d'accès 378

tourniquet de sortie 378
trachée 105
traçoir 228
tracteur 399
tracteur à chenilles 398
tracteur routier 364
tracteur-remorqueur 400
tractus olfactif 117
tragus 115
train 374
train à grande vitesse 376
train d'atterrissage avant 392
train d'atterrissage principal 393
train de banlieue 375
traîneau 236
traînée lumineuse 5
trait de mise au jeu 484
traitement chimique 405
traitement des données 38
tranchant 167, 169, 270
tranche 441
transactions financières 335
transbordeur 381, 386, 391
transept 285
transfert de la chaleur 415
transformateur 207, 407
transformateur principal 376
transformation de l'eau en vapeur 408
transmission 212
transmission de la chaleur à l'eau 408
transmission hertzienne 316
transmission par câble aérien 316
transmission par câble sous-marin 317
transmission par câble souterrain 317
transpalette manuelle 396
transpiration 45
transplantoir 232
transport 342
transport aérien 388
transport de l'électricité 408
transport de l'électricité à haute tension 402, 413
transport ferroviaire 374
transport maritime 381
transport routier 342, 381
transport vers les usagers 402, 413
trapèze 96, 97, 429
trappe 281, 292
travée centrale 344
travée latérale 344
travée levante 345
travers 153
traverse 202, 297, 466
traverse de chargement 385
traverse inférieure 185, 202
traverse intermédiaire 185
traverse médiane 201
traverse supérieure 185, 201, 202
traverse supérieure d'ouvrant 186
traversée de transformateur 406, 407
traversin 204
trèfle 285, 468
treillis 230, 324
trémie de chargement 364
tremplin 184, 496
tremplin de 1 m 518
tremplin de 3 m 518
trench 248
trépan 403
trépied 8, 308
trépointe 240
tréteau 202
treuil 287, 364
treuil d'amarrage 385
treuil de forage 403
treuil de levage 397
tri des métaux 49
tri du papier/carton 49
tri du plastique 49
tri du verre 49
tri manuel 49
tri optique 49
tri sélectif des déchets 49
triangle 295, 309, 429, 503
tribord 387
tribunal 440
tribune 313
triceps brachial 97
triclinium 280
tricycle d'enfant 373
trifoliée 55
trille 299
trimaran 521
tringle de pédale 304
tringle de tension 308
Trinité-et-Tobago 449

trio 300
tripes 154
triple croche 299
triple saut 472
triticale 143
Triton 3
triton 75
trois-portes 347
troisième but 474
troisième ligne 482
troisième but 474
trombe marine 43
trombone 307
trombones 295, 341
trompe 67
trompe d'Eustache 116, 117
trompe de Fallope 112
trompe utérine, ampoule 113
trompes de Fallope 113
trompette 307
trompettes 295
tronc 52, 62, 63, 75, 93, 95
tronc cœliaque 103, 107
tronc, coupe transversale 63
tronçon rigide arrière 363
tronçon rigide avant 363
tronçonneuse 235
trop-plein 194, 195, 196
tropical humide 40
tropical humide et sec (savane) 40
tropique du Cancer 20, 21, 22
tropique du Capricorne 20, 21, 22
tropopause 37, 46
troposphère 37
trot 83
trotteur 241
trotteuse 424
trottoir 183, 434
trou 504
trou d'homme 404
trou de normale 5 504
trousse de dépannage 372
trousse de fartage 514
trousse de manucure 265
trousse de secours 457, 461
trousse de toilette 276
truelle de maçon 216
truelle de plâtrier 216
truffe 87, 123
truite 161
trumeau 285
tuba 295, 307
tube 8, 9, 163, 199, 269, 420, 461
tube à éclairs 420
tube capillaire 424
tube d'alimentation 197
tube d'alimentation en air 454
tube de circulation 410
tube de direction 371
tube de force 409
tube de Pitot 525
tube de poussée 312
tube de remplissage de la cuvette 196
tube de remplissage du réservoir 196
tube de résonance 309
tube de selle 370
tube droit 209
tube en Y 460
tube fluorescent 199
tube horizontal 370
tube oblique 371
tube porte-oculaire 8, 421
tube-image 318
tubulure d'admission 360
tuile 12, 279, 280, 283
tulipe 56, 181
tunique 54, 255
Tunisie 451
tunnel 378
tunnel de communication 13
tunnel routier 345
turban 239
turbine 402
turboréacteur 393
turbot 161
turion 125
Turkménistan 452
Turquie 452
tuteur 230, 231
Tuvalu 453
tuyau 224, 454
tuyau à anche 305
tuyau à bouche 305
tuyau arrière 351
tuyau d'arrosage 236

tuyau d'aspiration 455
tuyau d'échappement 350, 351, 398
tuyau d'évacuation 194, 197, 212
tuyau d'insufflation 296
tuyau de chute 194, 196
tuyau de refoulement 454
tuyau de vidange 212, 214
tuyau flexible 209
tuyau perforé 236
tuyère 12, 383, 395
tuyère à section variable 394
tympan 75, 279, 285
type de carburant 346
type de la masse d'air 39
type de nuage bas 39
type de nuage élevé 39
type de nuage moyen 39
types d'éclipses 4, 5
types de bâtons de golf 505
types de déplacements 470
types de nages 517
types de prises 493
types de voitures 376
typhon 43

U

Ukraine 450
Umbriel 3
un 427
une 313
unicellulaires 66
uniforme 456
unisson 298
unité astronomique 2, 3
unité d'extraction par solvant 405
unité de soins ambulatoires 465
unité de soins intensifs 464
unité mobile d'entretien télécommandée 11
unités monétaires, exemples 440
université 432
Uranus 2, 3
uretère 107
urètre 107, 112
urètre pénien 111
urgence ambulatoire 463
urgence majeure 462
urgences 462
uropode 71
Uruguay 448
usager domestique 335
usine 430
usine à asphalte 405
usine des lubrifiants 405
usine pétrochimique 405
ustensiles de campeur 531
ustensiles de cuisine 169
ustensiles divers 173
ustensiles, jeu 173
utérus 112, 113
utilisations d'Internet 335

V

vache 84
vacuole 50, 66
vacuole contractile 66
vacuole digestive 66
vacuole digestive en formation 66
vagin 112, 113
vague 33
vague déferlante 33
vaisseau capillaire 114
vaisseau sanguin 104, 114
vaisselle 166
Valet 468
valet 421
valeur 441
valeur des notes 299
valeur des segments 471
valeur des silences 299
valise 277
vallée 29, 32
valve 60, 73, 371
valvule aortique 104
valvule mitrale 104
valvule pulmonaire 104
valvule tricuspide 104
vanne 406, 407
vantail 202, 286
Vanuatu 453
vapeur 402, 415
vaporisateur 208, 236
vaporisateur de poivre 456
vaporisation 414

ASTRONOMIE > 2-13; TERRE > 14-49; RÈGNE VÉGÉTAL > 50-65; RÈGNE ANIMAL > 66-91; ÊTRE HUMAIN > 92-119; ALIMENTATION ET CUISINE > 120-181; MAISON > 182-215; BRICOLAGE ET JARDINAGE > 216-237; VÊTEMENTS > 238-263; PARURE ET OBJETS PERSONNELS > 264-277; ARTS ET ARCHITECTURE > 278-311; COMMUNICATIONS ET BUREAUTIQUE > 312-341; TRANSPORT ET MACHINERIE > 342-401; ÉNERGIES > 402-413; SCIENCE > 414-429; SOCIÉTÉ > 430-467; SPORTS ET JEUX > 468-538

INDEX FRANCAIS

varan 77
Varole, pont 109
vaste externe du membre inférieur 96, 97
vaste interne du membre inférieur 96
vautour 80
veau 84
veau haché 152
végétation 44
végétation, distribution 44
véhicule de sauvetage 11
véhicule de secours 345
véhicule spatial autonome 10
véhicule tout-terrain 347
veine axillaire 102
veine basilique 102
veine cave inférieure 102, 103, 104, 107
veine cave supérieure 102, 103, 104
veine céphalique 102
veine fémorale 102
veine iliaque 103
veine iliaque commune 107
veine jugulaire externe 102
veine jugulaire interne 102
veine mésentérique supérieure 102
veine porte 103
veine pulmonaire 102
veine pulmonaire droite 104
veine pulmonaire gauche 104
veine rénale 102, 107
veine saphène interne 102
veine sous-clavière 102
veine sus-hépatique 103
veines 102
velarium 281
vélo cross 373
vélo d'exercice 501
vélo de course et cycliste 522
vélo de cross-country et cycliste 522
vélo de descente et cycliste 522
vélo de montagne 522
vélo tout-terrain (VTT) 373
velours 190
Venezuela 448
vent 47, 48
vent dominant 43
ventilateur 213, 322, 350, 358, 360
ventilateur de sustentation 383
ventilateur du bloc d'alimentation 329
ventilateur du boîtier 329
ventouse 72, 75, 216
ventre 83, 92, 94
ventricule droit 103, 104
ventricule gauche 103, 104
Vénus 2, 3
véraison 62
verge 111
verger 122
verglas 41
vérificateur de circuit 217
vérificateur de prise de courant 217
vérificateur de tension 217
vérification de la profondeur de champ
    314
vérin 364
vérin d'orientation de la lame 401
vérin de défonceuse 398
vérin de direction 400
vérin de dressage 397, 455
vérin de la flèche 399, 400

vérin de levage de la lame 398, 401
vérin du bras 399, 400
vérin du bras de levage 399
vérin du godet 399, 400
vérin du godet rétro 399
vérin hydraulique 361
vermicelles de riz 147
vernier 422, 425
vernis à ongles 265
verre 273
verre à bordeaux 165
verre à bourgogne 165
verre à cocktail 165
verre à cognac 165
verre à eau 165
verre à gin 165
verre à liqueur 165
verre à mesurer 171
verre à porto 165
verre à vin blanc 165
verre à vin d'Alsace 165
verre à whisky 165
verres 165
verrière 188, 374, 394, 435
verrou 30, 332
verrou d'onglet 226
verrouillage 208
verrouillage des majuscules 330
verrouillage numérique 331
versant 29
verseuse 181
vert 418, 504
vert d'entraînement 504
vertèbre cervicale (7) 99
vertèbre dorsale (12) 99
vertèbre lombaire 110
vertèbre lombaire (5) 99
verveine 148
vésicule biliaire 106
vésicule séminale 111
vessie 107, 111, 112
veste 251, 499
veste de pêche 538
veste droite 244
vestes 254
vestiaire 188, 443, 444
vestiaire des clients 438
vestiaire du personnel 438, 465
veston croisé 244
veston et veste 244
vêtements 238
vêtements d'enfant 261
vêtements d'exercice 263
vêtements d'homme 244
vêtements de femme 251
vêtements de nouveau-né 260
vêtements de nuit 256
vêtements, pêche 538
viande 152
vibrisse 82
vice-capitaine 515
vide-poches 352
vide-pomme 173
Viet Nam 453
vigie 388
vigne 62
vilebrequin 360
village 430, 512

ville 430
vin 120
vinaigre balsamique 141
vinaigre de cidre 141
vinaigre de malt 141
vinaigre de riz 141
vinaigre de vin 141
violette 56
violon 301
violon, famille 295, 301
violoncelle 301
violoncelles 295
vipère 77
virole 219, 503
virole femelle 536, 537
virole mâle 536, 537
vis 221, 301
vis calante 423
vis de blocage 425
vis de blocage (azimut) 8
vis de blocage (azimuth) 9
vis de blocage (latitude) 8, 9
vis de réglage 222
vis de réglage de tension 341
vis de réglage du condenseur 421
vis de serrage 224
vis de tension 308
vis macrométrique 421
vis micrométrique 421, 425
vis sans fin 365
visage 92
viseur 315
viseur électronique 320
visière 238, 239, 367, 458, 506, 525
visière antisolaire 10
vision 419
vision normale 419
vision, défauts 419
vison 88
Vistule 18
vitrage 410
vitrail 285, 446
vitre 411
vitre de protection 506
vitre protectrice 318
vitrine 203
voie 378
voie d'accélération 343
voie de banlieue 375
voie de circulation 343, 388
voie de décélération 343
voie de dépassement 343
voie de service 375, 388
voie des stands 524
voie ferrée 374, 431, 432
voie ferrée bord à quai 381
Voie lactée 6
voie latérale 343
voie pour véhicules lents 343
voies de circulation 343
voies respiratoires, protection 459
voile 412, 519, 520, 536
voile du palais 116, 117
voilure delta 394
voiture 380
voiture classique 376
voiture de formule 1 525
voiture de formule 3000 524
voiture de formule Indy 524

voiture de police 457
voiture de rallye 524
voiture micro-compacte 347
voiture restaurant 376
voiture sport 347
voiture suiveuse 522
voiture-lit 376
voitures, types 376
voiturette de golf électrique 505
volaille 155
volant 204, 350, 354, 360, 385, 525
volant d'inertie 501
volant de manœuvre 455
volant de plumes 495
volant synthétique 495
volcan 26, 28
volcan effusif 28
volcan en éruption 28
volcan explosif 28
volcans, exemples 28
volée 191, 490
volet 13, 333
volet d'air 365
volet de bord de fuite 392
volet mobile 7
volet transparent 274
Volga 18
volleyball 487
vols, plongeon 518
volt 426
voltigeur de centre 474
voltigeur droit 474
voltigeur gauche 474
volumes 429
volute 200, 301
volve 52
voussure 285
voûte 284
voûte du palais 116, 117
voûte en berceau 281
voyant cartouche d'impression 333
voyant chargement du papier 333
voyant d'alarme/de mise en charge 337
voyant d'alimentation 333
voyant de charge 271
voyant de mise en circuit 327, 328
voyant de mise sous tension/détection du
    papier 443
voyant de réception de messages 328
voyant de réponse automatique 328
voyant lumineux 178, 179, 180, 181,
    208, 210, 214, 269
voyants 331
voyants d'entrée 322
voyants d'indication du mode sonore 322
voyants de contrôle 323
vraquier 382
vrille 62
vue 119
vue antérieure 98
vue d'ensemble 186
vue de face 478
vue de profil 478
vue postérieure 99, 113
vulve 94, 113

W

w.-c. 188, 189, 194, 195, 196, 437, 438,
    439, 440, 443, 445, 463, 464, 465
w.-c. femmes 439
w.-c. hommes 439
wagon 375
wagon à bestiaux 377
wagon de queue 377
wagon intermodal 377
wagon plat 377
wagon porte-automobiles 377
wagon porte-conteneurs 377
wagon réfrigérant 377
wagon-citerne 377
wagons, exemples 377
wakamé 123
wasabi 141
watt 426
webcaméra 332
wigwam 288
winch 521
wishbone 519
wok 174

X

xylophone 295, 309

Y

yacht à moteur 385
yack 85
yaourt 150
Yémen 452
yen 440
yeux, protection 458
Yougoslavie 450
yourte 288

Z

Zambie 452
zèbre 84
zeste 58, 60
Zimbabwe 452
zone commerciale 431
zone d'attaque 487
zone de basse pression 43
zone de but 484, 507
zone de chute 472
zone de convection 4
zone de danger 499
zone de défense 487
zone de garde protégée 515
zone de haute pression 43
zone de passage du témoin 472
zone de précipitation 39
zone de radiation 4
zone de retrait des bagages 390
zone industrielle 431
zone libre 487
zone neutre 484, 507
zone réservée 489
zone résidentielle 431
zones de service 495

ASTRONOMIE > 2-13; TERRE > 14-49; RÈGNE VÉGÉTAL > 50-65; RÈGNE ANIMAL > 66-91; ÊTRE HUMAIN > 92-119; ALIMENTATION ET CUISINE > 120-181; MAISON > 182-215; BRICO-
LAGE ET JARDINAGE > 216-237; VÊTEMENTS > 238-263; PARURE ET OBJETS PERSONNELS > 264-277; ARTS ET ARCHITECTURE > 278-311; COMMUNICATIONS ET BUREAUTIQUE > 312-341;
TRANSPORT ET MACHINERIE > 342-401; ÉNERGIES > 402-413; SCIENCE > 414-429; SOCIÉTÉ > 430-467; SPORTS ET JEUX > 468-538

585

Deutsches Register

1-Meter-Brett 518
10-m-Linie 482
10-Meter-Turm 518
100-m- und 100-m-Hürdenlauf, Start 472
10000-m- und 4-x-400-m-Lauf, Start 473
110-m-Hürdenlauf, Start 472
15-m-Linie 483
1500-m-Lauf, Start 473
200-m-Lauf, Start 472
22-m-Linie 482
3-Meter-Brett 518
3-Meter-Turm 518
35mm-Fotoapparat 10
400-m-, 400-m-Hürden-, 4-x-100-m-Lauf, Start 473
4x4-Geländemotorrad 369
5-Meter-Linie 483
5000-m-Lauf, Start 472
7,5-Meter-Turm 518
800-m-Lauf, Start 473

A

A 298
Aal 159
Abblendlicht 352
Abblendschalter 368
Abbruch 330
Abbruchtaste 333, 337
Abdeckscheibe 417
Abdeckung 210, 315, 324, 454
Abdomenarterie 71
Abendhandschuh, langer 243
Abessinierkatze 87
Abfahrt, Seilbahn 512
Abfahrt, Sessellift 512
Abfahrtslauf 511
Abfahrtsski 510
Abfahrtzeiten 374
Abfall, radioaktiver 48
Abfalleimer 215
abfallendes Revers 248
Abflugwartehalle 391
Abfluss 32, 194
Abfluss, oberirdischer 45
Abfluss, unterirdischer 45
Abflusskreislauf 194
Abflusssieb 197
Abflußrohr 197
Abgabe von Sauerstoff 54
Abgasleitung 395
abgesenkte Nase 394
abgesteppte Falte 253
Abhalter 372
Abisolierzange 217
Abklingbecken 409
Ablage 219, 339
Ablassventil 404
Ablauf, Boden 184
Ablaufrohr 196
Ablaufschlauch 212, 214
Abluftleitung 345

abnehmbare Handballenauflage 330
abnehmender Mond 5
Abreißkalender 338
Abrollbahn 391
Absatz 240, 262, 509
Absatzoberflecken 240
Absatzplatte 514
Absatzstopper 527
Absatzteil 511
Abscheider 384
Abschlagplatz 504
Abschlagsbereich 504
Abschleppkran 364
Abschleppwagen 364
Abschluss, oberer 205
Abschlusskappe 536
Abschlusskappe, obere 417
Abschlusskappe, untere 417
Abschlussplatte 409
Abschlussring 536, 537
Abseihkelle 173
Abseihlöffel 173
absinkende kalte Luft 43
Absorber 410
absorbierte Sonneneinstrahlung 46
Absorption der Erdoberfläche 46
Absperrarm 362
Absperrband 457
Absperrventil 194, 196, 197
Abspieltaste 319
Abstandstück 467
absteigende Aorta 103
absteigender Dickdarm 106
absteigender Gang 278
Abstellfläche 345
Abstellplatz 389
Abstellrost 211
Abstoßsäge 509
Abstoßung 416
Abteilklammer 268
Abteilung 121
Abtropfen 171
Abwasser 48
Abwasserkanal 434
Abwehrhandschuh 507
Abwehrspieler, mittlerer 487
Abwehrspieler, rechter 487
Abweiser 524
Abzeichen 456
abziehbarer Temperaturregler 179
Abziehklinge 514
Abzug 454, 534
Abzugbügel 534
Abzweig 416
Abzweigleitung 194
Achse 72, 526, 527
Achselarterie 102
Achselhöhle 92, 94
Achselknospe 53
Achselkrücke 466
Achselnerv 108
Achselstütze 466
Achselvene 102

Achswelle 351
Achteck, regelmäßiges 429
Achtelnote 299
Achtelpause 299
Adamsapfel 92
Adapter 198, 271, 336
Adapterschnittstelle 336
Addition 427
Additionstaste 337
additive Farbmischung 418
Aden, Golf 19, 20
Aderhaut 119
Adler 81
Adria 18
aerodynamische Bremse 412
Afghanistan 452
Afrika 14, 20, 34, 451
Afrikanische Platte 27
After 71, 73, 106, 111, 112
Afterflosse 74
Afterfurche 93
Afterschließmuskel 106
Ägäis 18
Agar-Agar 123
Aggregatzustände 414
Ägypten 451
Ahle 531
Ahorn 64
Ahornsirup 149
Ährchen 61
Ähre 57, 61
Ährenbrot 144
Ährenrispe 61
Airbag 354
Airbag-Rückhaltesystem 354
Ajowan 139
Akanthusblatt 200
Akkord 299
Akkordeon 296
Akku 228, 320
Akku-Bohrschrauber 228
Akku-Mini-Staubsauger 208
Akkumulator 357
Akromion 99
Akroterion 279
Aktenbox 340
Aktenkoffer 274
Aktenmappe 340
Aktenordner 339
Aktentasche 274, 275
Aktenvernichter 341
Aktionstasten 471
Akustikdecke 293
akustische Gitarre 302
Alarm, Kontrollleuchte 337
Alaska, Golf 16
Albanien 450
Albatros 80
Aleuten 16
Aleutengraben 34
Alge 51
Alge, Aufbau 51
Algen, Beispiele 51

Algerien 451
alkalische Zink-Mangan-Zelle 417
Alkoholkolben 424
Alkoholsäule 424
Allee 25
Alligator 77
Alluvion 32
Alpen 18
alphabetische Tastatur 338
alphanumerische Tastatur 327, 330, 346, 442, 443
Alpin-Skipiste 512
Alpinboard 513
alpiner Skiläufer 510
alpines Skilaufen 510
Alse 160
Alt-Taste 330
Altaluminium-Sammelbehälter 49
Altarbild 446
Altarkreuz 446
Altarm 32
Alternative 330
Altglas-Container 49
Altglas-Sammelbehälter 49
Altokumulus 42
Altostratus 42
Altpapier-Container 49
Altpapier-Sammelbehälter 49
Altschlüssel 298
Aluminiumfolie 162
Alveolarknochen 101
Amarant 143
Amazonas 17
Amboss 116, 534
ambulante Unfallstation 463
Ameise 69
American Football 484
Amerika 448
Amerika, Vereinigte Staaten 448
amerikanischer Bacon 156
amerikanischer Senf 140
amerikanisches Labor 11
amerikanisches Maisbrot 145
amerikanisches Wohnmodul 11
Amery-Eisschelf 15
Amöbe 66
amorpher Festkörper 414
Ampel 230
Ampere 426
Amphibien 75
Amphibien, Beispiele 75
Amphibien-Löschflugzeug 394
Amphitheater, römisches 281
Amplitude 418
Amplituner: Rückansicht 322
Ampulle 467
amtliche Unterschrift 441
An Aus-Kontrolllampe 327
Analfuß 67
Analog-Camcorder: Rückansicht 320
Analog-Camcorder: Vorderansicht 320
Analoguhr 424
Ananas 136

Ananasguave 137
Anästhesieraum 464
Anatomie 96
Anatomie einer zweischaligen Muschel 73
Anatomie eines Hummers 71
Anden 17
andere Zeichen 299
Andorra 449
Anemometer 413
angehobener Lenkerbügel 522
Angehörige, Warteraum 462
Angel 167, 169, 216
Angelhaken 536, 538
Angelhaken mit Vorfach 538
Angelwurzel 169
Anglerweste 538
Angola 452
Angriff 485
Angriffslinie 487
Angriffszone 487
Anhänger 264
Anhängerkupplung 356, 361
Anik 317
Anis 142
Anker 473
Ankerbolzen 357
Ankerklüse 383, 387
Anklagebank 440
Ankleideraum 189, 290
Ankleideraum, privater 290
Anlage 182
Anlage, elektrische 351
Anlagen, unterirdische 281
Anlasser 237
Anlaufbahn 496
Anlaufhülse 229
Anlaufstrecke 473
annähernd gleich 427
Anode 417
Anorak 263
anorganische Substanzen 45
Anrufbeantworter 328
Ansagekassette 328
Ansatz 223
Ansatzrohr 209
Ansauggitter 270
Anschlag 226, 425, 521
Anschlagfläche 341
Anschlagrahmen 202
Anschluss 210
Anschluss für Zündkabel 359
Anschlussbuchse 303
Anschlussbuchsen für Video- und Digitalübertragung 315
Anschlüsse, Beispiele 197
Anschlusskabel 227, 324
Anschlusskasten 411
Anschlussklemme 198
Anschlussleitung 194
Anschlussstelle 431
Anschlussstellen, Beispiele 342
Anschlussstifte 417
Anschreiber 487, 488

ASTRONOMIE > 2-25;   ERDE > 26-71;   PFLANZENREICH >72-89;   TIERREICH > 90-143;   MENSCH > 144-177;   NAHRUNGSMITTEL UND KÜCHE > 178-241;   HAUS > 242-295;
HEIMWERKEN UND GARTENARBEIT > 296-333;   KLEIDUNG > 334-371;   PERSÖNLICHE AUSSTATTUNG > 372-391;   KUNST UND ARCHITEKTUR > 392-465;   KOMMUNIKATION UND BÜROTECHNIK > 466-535;
TRANSPORT UND FAHRZEUGE > 536-643;   ENERGIE > 644-677;   WISSENSCHAFT > 678-705;   GESELLSCHAFT > 706-785;   SPORT UND SPIELE > 786-920

587

Ansicht 182
Anspielkreis 506
Anspielpunkt 506
Anstoßlinie 502
Anstoßpunkt 481, 502
Anstoßraum 502
Anstreichen 219
Antarktis 14, 15
Antarktische Halbinsel 15
Antarktische Platte 27
Antenne 7, 67, 68, 71, 326, 327, 349, 369, 392, 395, 457, 487
Antenne für die Linienzugbeeinflussung 376
Antennenbuchsen 322
Antennula 71
Antependium 446
anthropogener Treibhauseffekt 46
Anti-Reflex-Beschichtung 410
Antiblockiersystem (ABS) 357
Antigua und Barbuda 449
Antiklinale 403
Antilope 84
Antiseptikum 461
antiseptische Flüssigkeit 461
Antriebsmodul 316
Antriebsrad 398, 523
Antriebsräder 401
Antriebsriemen 360
Antriebssystem 351
Antriebswelle 177
Antriebswerk 403
Antrittspfosten 191
Antrittsstufe 191
Anwendungsstarttasten 337
Anzeige 313, 337, 346, 422, 423
Anzeige "Sicherheitsgurte anlegen" 355
Anzeigen 323
Anzeigeskala 423
Anzeigetafel 472, 492, 497, 499, 518
Anzeigetafel für das Gesamtergebnis 496
Anzeigetafel für die Einzeldisziplin 497
Anzeigetaste 320
Anziehung 416
Anzünder 218
Aorta 104, 105
Aorta, absteigende 103
Aorta, aufsteigende 103
Aortenbogen 102, 103, 104
Aortenklappe 104
Apex 72, 73
Apfel 133
Apfel im Querschnitt 58
Apfelessig 141
Apfelfrucht, fleischige 58
Apfelfrüchte 133
apokrine Schweißdrüse 114
Apotheke 436
Appalachen 16
Appartements 512
Aprikose 132
Äquator 17, 20, 21, 22, 43
Äquatorialguinea 451
äquivalent 427
Ara 80
Arabische Halbinsel 19
Arabisches Meer 19
Arachnoidea 109
Aralsee 19
Arame 123
Arbeiterin 68
Arbeitsbrett 219
Arbeitskittel 255
Arbeitsleuchte 206
Arbeitsplatte 164, 224
Arbeitsstiefel 240
Arbeitszimmer 189
Archipel 24
Architektur 278
Architekturelemente 286
Architrav 279
Archivolte 285
Arena 281
Arenberg-Parkett 190
Argentinien 448
Ariel 3
Arkade 281, 284
Arkaden 447
Arktis 14
Arm 83, 91, 93, 95, 206, 467
Armaturenbrett 354
Armaturenbrettausrüstung 457
Armausschnitt 247
Armband 264
Armbänder 264
Armbeuger 96

Armdecken, große 78
Armdecken, kleine 78
Armdecken, mittlere 78
Ärmel 244
Ärmel, eingesetzter 245
Ärmelkanal 18
Ärmellasche 248
ärmelloses Sporthemd 500
Ärmelschlitz 245
Armenien 452
Armgeflecht 108
Armhebel 499
Armlehne 200, 205
Armlehnstuhl 200
Armreif 264
Armschutz 486
Armschützer 486
Armschwingen 78
Armstrecker, dreiköpfiger 97
Armstrecker, zweiköpfiger 96
Armstuhl 444
Armstühle, Beispiele 200
Armstütze 200, 352, 353, 467
Arpeggio 299
Arretierhebel 224, 229
Arretierknopf 229
Art der hohen Wolken 39
Art der mittelhohen Wolken 39
Art der tiefen Wolken 39
Arten von Blütenständen 57
Arten von Golfschläger 505
Arterien 102
Artikel 313
Artischocke 127
Arzneimittel-Darreichungsformen 467
Arzt 498
Ärzteteam 499
Asche, vulkanische 28
Aschenbahn 472
Ascheschicht 28
Aserbeidschan 452
asiatische Birne 137
asiatische Eiernudeln 147
asiatische Teigwaren 147
Asien 14, 19, 34, 452
Asphalt 405
Asphalt-Destillationsanlage 405
Aspirin 461
Ass 468
Assistenzarzt 464
Assistenzschiedsrichter 509
Assistenztrainer 507
Ast 63, 65
Äste 63
Asteroidengürtel 3
Asthenosphäre 26
Astigmatismus 419
Astronomie 2
astronomische Einheit 2, 3
Astschere 234
Asukibohne 131
Atacama-Wüste 17
Atemluftzufuhrschlauch 454
Atemschutz 459
Atemschutzmaske, leichte 459
Atemschutzsystem, geschlossenes 454
Äthiopien 451
Athletin 473
Atlantik 14
atlantischer Kabeljau 161
atlantischer Lachs 161
Atlantischer Ozean 15, 18, 20
Atlas 99
Atlasgebirge 20
Atlasspinner 69
Atmosphäre 44, 48
Atoll 35
Atom 414
Atome 414
Atomkern 414
Atrium 280
Aubergine 128
Audio-Ausgänge 337
Audio-Eingänge 337
Audiobuchse 329
Audiometrie- Untersuchungsraum 465
Aufbau 361
Aufbau der Biosphäre 44
Aufbau der Sonne 4
Aufbau des Ohres 116
Aufbau des Rückenmarks 109
Aufbau einer Alge 51
Aufbau einer Blume 56
Aufbau einer Flechte 50
Aufbau einer Pflanze 53
Aufbau eines Baumes 63

Aufbau eines Blatts 55
Aufbau eines Farns 52
Aufbau eines Mooses 51
Aufbau eines Pilzes 52
Aufbauspieler, linker 489
Aufbauspieler, rechter 489
Aufbewahrungsmöbel 202
aufblasbare Manschette 461
Aufdruck 260
Aufenthaltsraum 439
Auffahrt 343, 344
Auffangschale 181
Auffangschüssel 210
Aufgeber 494
aufgesetzte Tasche 244, 249, 260
aufgewirbelter Staub 43
Aufhängeband 119
Aufhängeöse 270
Aufhänger 250
Aufhängung 308, 351
Aufladen, Kontrollleuchte 337
Auflage 204
Auflagehumus 54
Auflaufförmchen 166
Auflösungszeichen 299
Aufnahme 462, 465
Aufnahme von Kohlendioxid 54
Aufnahme von Wasser und Mineralstoffen 54
Aufnahme-Starttaste 320
Aufnahme-Stopptaste 320
Aufnahme-Taste 323
Aufnahme-Ziffer 291
Aufnahmebühne 290
Aufnahmetaste 319
Aufprallsensor 354
Aufreißer 398
Aufreißerspitze 398
Aufreißerzylinder 398
Aufsatz 174
Aufsatzstück 296
Aufschäumdüse 181
Aufschlag 246, 487, 490
Aufschläger 491
Aufschlagfeld für das Doppelspiel 495
Aufschlagfeld für das Einzelspiel 495
Aufschlagfelder 495
Aufschlaglinie 491
Aufschlaglinienrichter 490
Aufschlagrichter 490, 494
Aufschnitt 305
Aufsetzzonenmarkierungen 391
Aufsteckbürste 272
Aufsteckdüse 272
aufsteigende Aorta 103
aufsteigende warme Luft 43
aufsteigender Dickdarm 106
aufsteigender Gang 278
Aufstellpunkt 502
Aufwachraum 464
Aufzeichnung, seismologische 403
Aufzeichnungskassette 328
Aufzeichnungstaste 328
Aufziehbrett 216
Aufzug 281, 287, 435, 439
Aufzugseil 397
Augapfel 75, 119
Auge 43, 70, 71, 72, 76, 90, 94, 119, 220, 270, 468
Augen-Make-up 266
Augenbehandlungsraum 463
Augenbrauenpinzette 265
Augenbrauenstift 266
Augengläser, Beispiele 273
Augenkammer, hintere 119
Augenkammer, vordere 119
Augenlid 76
Augenlid, oberes 75, 87
Augenlid, unteres 75, 87
Augenmuskel, unterer gerader 119
Augenring 78
Augenringmuskel 96
Augenschutz 458
Augenstreif 78
Augenträger 72
Augenwand 43
Ausatmungsventil 459
Ausbeinmesser 169
Ausbreitung, Fortpflanzung 418
Ausbruchstätigkeit, Vulkan 28
Ausdehnungskammer 424
ausfahrbarer Baum 397
ausfahrbarer Leiterbaum 455
Ausfahrt 343
Ausfahrtspur 343
Ausführungsgang, Schweißdrüse 114

Ausgabebank, Kürzel 441
Ausgabegeräte 333
Ausgangssperre 378
Ausgangstür, zweiflügelige 362
Ausgleichsbecken 406, 407
Ausguss 215
Ausgussreiniger 216
Ausklapparretierung 219
ausklappbare Stützvorrichtung 365
Auslassventil 360, 461
Auslauf 122
Auslaufgarnitur 197
Auslaufrohr 407
Ausleger 397, 399, 400
Auslegerbrücke 344
Auslegerseil 397
Auslegerzylinder 399, 400
Auslenkungsrichtung 418
Auslinie 482
Auslöser 314
Auspressen 177
Auspuffanlage 351
Auspuffendrohr 351
Auspuffkrümmer 350, 360
Auspuffrohr 364, 367, 368, 369, 398, 401
Auspuffrohr, hinteres 351
Auspuffrohr, vorderes 350
Ausrichtschraube 423
Ausschalter 235, 327
Ausschnitt, halsnaher 250, 255, 260
Ausstatter 290
Ausstattung, persönliche 264
Ausstechformen 172
Aussteuerung, manuelle 323
Auster 157
Austerngabel 168
Austernmesser 169
Austernseitling 123
Australien 14, 34, 453
Australische Kordilleren 15
Austrittskante 392
auswärts 518
Auswaschung 48
Auswechselbank 481
Auswurf-Taste 323
Auswurftaste 176, 315, 471
Auswurftaste für das 323
ausziehbare Fluggastbrücke 389
ausziehbarer Griff 274
Ausziehbein 202
Ausziehleiter 219
Ausziehtisch 202
Auszug 202, 210
Außenangreifer, linker 487
Außenangreifer, rechter 487
Außenansicht eines Hauses 182
Außenbordmotor 385
Außenbrett 469
Außendreiviertel links 482
Außendreiviertel rechts 482
Außenfeldspieler, linker 474
Außenfeldspieler, mittlerer 474
Außenfeldspieler, rechter 474
Außengewinde 537
außengezahnte Fächerscheibe 222
Außenkelch 59
Außenkreis 515
Außenlippe 73
Außenring 441
Außenrohr, druckfestes 409
Außenschicht 477
Außenspiegel 362, 363
Außenstechküsse 536
Außenstürmer links 482
Außenstürmer rechts 482
Außentank 12
Außentasche 274, 276
äußere Drosselvene 102
äußere Kappe 240
äußere Kuppelhülle 7
äußere Merkmale einer einschaligen Muschel 73
äußere Merkmale einer Giftschlange: Kopf 76
äußere Merkmale einer Honigbiene: Arbeiterin 68
äußere Merkmale einer Ratte 82
äußere Merkmale einer Schildkröte 76
äußere Merkmale einer Schnecke 72
äußere Merkmale einer Spinne 70
äußere Merkmale einer zweischaligen Muschel 73
äußere Merkmale eines Delphins 90
äußere Merkmale eines Flußbarschs 74
äußere Merkmale eines Froschs 75

äußere Merkmale eines Gorillas 91
äußere Merkmale eines Hais 74
äußere Merkmale eines Hummers 71
äußere Merkmale eines Hundes 86
äußere Merkmale eines Pferdes 83
äußere Merkmale eines Schmetterlings 67
äußere Merkmale eines Tintenfischs 72
äußere Merkmale eines Vogels 78
äußere Nase 117
äußere Oberschenkelkondyle 99
äußere Planeten 2
äußerer Bull 471
äußerer Gehörgang 100
äußerer Hausflur 280
äußerer Kern 26
äußerer Linebacker 484
äußerer Ohrmuschelrand 115
äußerer Schenkelmuskel 96, 97
äußerer Schneidezahn 101
äußerer schräger Bauchmuskel 96, 97
äußeres Ohr 116
Auto 347
Autobahn 25, 343, 431
Autobahnnummer 25
Autocoat 251
Autofocus-Umschalter 314
Autohandschuh 243
Autohaus 433
Autoklav 464
Automat für Umsteigekarten 379
automatische Schiebetür 286
automatische Tür 390
automatischer Bankschalter 442, 443
automatischer Zeitmesser 517
Autoplane 356
Autorennen 524
Autoreverse-Taste 326
Autotransportwagen 377
autotrophe Organismen 45
Autowaschanlage 346
Avocado 128
Axel 509
Axialrippe 73
Axon 110
Axt 234
Azimutalprojektion 22
Azimutfeineinstellung 8, 9
Azimutfesteller 9
Azimutfeststeller 9
aztekischer Tempel 283

B

B 299
Baby-Doll 256
Babybekleidung 260
Bach 32
Bachsaibling 161
Back 383, 387
Backblech 172
Backbordseite 387
Backe 86, 273
Backe, bewegliche 223, 224
Backe, feste 223, 224
Backen 217, 221, 224, 228, 511
Backenhörnchen 82
Backenzahn im Längsschnitt 101
Backenzahn, erster 101
Backenzahn, erster vorderer 101
Backenzahn, zweiter 101
Backenzahn, zweiter vorderer 101
Backenzähne 101
Backenzähne, vordere 101
Bäckerei 437
Backfett 149
Backform 179
Backgammon 469
Backgerät 172
Backline 515
Backofen 164, 210
Backofenfolie 162
Backofenschalter 210
Backofenthermometer 171
Backofentür 210
Backrost 210
Backsteinhaus 288
Backwaren 121
Bacon, amerikanischer 156
Bacon, kanadischer 156
Bad 189, 439, 464
Badeanzug 263
Badebürste 267
Badehose 263, 516
Badekappe 516
Badeleiter 184
Bademantel 256

ASTRONOMIE > 2-25; ERDE > 26-71; PFLANZENREICH >72-89; TIERREICH > 90-143; MENSCH > 144-177; NAHRUNGSMITTEL UND KÜCHE > 178-241; HAUS > 242-295; HEIMWERKEN UND GARTENARBEIT > 296-333; KLEIDUNG > 334-371; PERSÖNLICHE AUSSTATTUNG > 372-391; KUNST UND ARCHITEKTUR > 392-465; KOMMUNIKATION UND BÜROTECHNIK > 466-535; TRANSPORT UND FAHRZEUGE > 536-643; ENERGIE > 644-677; WISSENSCHAFT > 678-705; GESELLSCHAFT > 706-785; SPORT UND SPIELE > 786-920

Badetuch 267
Badetuch mit Kapuze 260
Badewanne 189, 194, 195, 439
Badezimmer-Oberlicht 189
Badminton 494
Badmintonplatz 494
Badmintonschläger 494
Baffinland 16
baggern 487
Baggerstiel 400
Baggerstielzylinder 400
Baguette 144
Bahamas 448
Bahn 220, 472, 515, 516
Bahnende 517
Bahnenplissee 253
Bahnenrock 253
Bahnhof 25, 374, 375, 430, 432
Bahnhofshalle 374
Bahnmarkierung 473
Bahnsei 517
Bahnsteig 374, 375, 379, 390
Bahnsteigkante 374, 379
Bahnsteigüberdachung 375
Bahnübergang 375
Bahnzeitnehmer 516
Bahrain 452
Baikalsee 19
Bajonettfassung 199
Balalaika 297
Balanceregler 322
Balg 296
Balg, Schnitt 60
Balgenverschluss 296
Balkanhalbinsel 18
Balken 109, 279, 280, 283, 288, 422
Balken, hinterer 422
Balken, vorderer 422
Balkenbrücke 344
Balkenwaage 422
Balkon 189
Balkontür 189
Ballerinaschuh 241
Ballfangzaun 474
Balljunge 490
Ballonsonde 38
Ballsportarten 474
Ballungsgebiet 430
Balsamessig 141
Balustrade 283
Bambussprosse 125
Banane 136
Bande 506
Bandführung 341
Bandring 264
Bandsortenschalter 323
Bandsperre 225
Bandwahltaste 322
Bangladesch 453
Banjo 296
Bank 201, 432, 437, 442, 469, 501
Bankett 342
Banknote: Rückseite 441
Banknote: Vorderseite 441
Bankschalter, automatischer 442, 443
Bar 293, 432, 438, 469
Barbados 449
Barbakane 282
Bardame 438
Barentssee 18
Bargeldbestückung 443
Barhocker 201, 438
Baronstange 302
Barren 496, 497
Barriereriff, Großes 15
Barsch 160
Bart 61
Bartregion 78
Basalschicht 114
Basaltschicht 26
Baseball 474, 476
Baseball im Querschnitt 477
Basilikum 142
Basis 318, 473
Basis der Rückenlehne 200
Baskenmütze 239
Basketball 488
Basketballspiel 488
Basketballspieler 488
Basmatireis 147
Bass-Straße 15
Bass-Tonabnehmer 303
Bassgitarre 303
Bassklarinette 295
Bassregister 296
Bassregler 322, 325

Bassschlüssel 298
Basssteg 304
Basstastatur 296
Basstrommel 295, 308
Bast 63
Batterie 221, 350, 359, 411, 416
Batterie-Schraubendreher 221
Batteriegehäuse 359
Batteriekasten 365
Batterieladekontrollleuchte 355
Bauch 78, 83, 92, 94
Bauchaorta 102, 107
Baucharterie 71
Bauchfell 111, 112
Bauchflosse 74
Bauchfuß 67
Bauchhöhle 111, 112
Bauchmuskel, äußerer Schräger 96
Bauchmuskel, äußerer schräger 97
Bauchmuskel, gerader 96
Bauchpanzer 76
Bauchspeck 156
Bauchspeicheldrüse 106
Bauer 470
Bauernbrot 145
Bauernhof 122
Baum 63, 520
Baum, Aufbau 63
Baum, ausfahrbarer 397
Bäume 504
Baumfarn 52
Baumschere 234
Baumstamm im Querschnitt 63
Baumstütze 231
Baumtomate 136
Baumvogel 79
Bauchmuskel 97
Bautischlerei 220, 221, 222, 225, 226, 228, 229
Beaufortsee 16
Becher 163, 166, 532
Becken 184, 295, 308, 309
Becken, oberes 308
Becken, unteres 308
Beckengurt 353
Becquerel 426
Bedienblende 178
Bedienkonsole 455
Bedienleiste 210, 212, 213, 214
Bedientasten 318
Bedienungsanleitung 346
Bedienungsfeld 179
Bedienungstafel 287
Bedienungstasten 328
Beere 59
Beeren 132
Beet 183
Beete, rote 129
befestigte Umfassungsmauer 447
Befestigungshebel 207
Befestigungsschiene 420
Befeuchter 339
begehbarer Kleiderschrank 189
Begonie 54
begrenzte Zone 489
Begrenzungsleuchte 352
Behaarung 82, 91
Behälter 176, 180
Behälter für gebrauchte Spritzen 457
Behälter mit Gießer 177
Behandlung, chemische 405
Behandlungsraum 463, 465
Beichtstuhl 446
Beifahrer-Fußraste 368
Beifahrerfußraste 367
Beil 454, 533
Beilage, farbige 313
Bein 76, 91, 93, 95, 202, 247, 308, 403
Beinausschnitt, elastischer 247
Beincurler 501
Beininnenseite 260, 261
Beinpolster 507
Beinschutz 476
Beinstreckerzug 501
Beispiele für Algen 51
Beispiele für Amphibien 75
Beispiele für Anschlussstellen 342
Beispiele für Armstühle 200
Beispiele für Augengläser 273
Beispiele für Bits und Bohrer 228
Beispiele für Blumen 56
Beispiele für Blusen und Hemden 255
Beispiele für Boote und Schiffe 382
Beispiele für Falten 253

Beispiele für Farne 52
Beispiele für Fenster 287
Beispiele für Flechten 50
Beispiele für Flugzeuge 394
Beispiele für Gabeln 168
Beispiele für Güterwagen 377
Beispiele für Hasentiere 82
Beispiele für Hosen 254
Beispiele für Huftiere 84
Beispiele für Insekten 69
Beispiele für Instrumentalgruppierungen 300
Beispiele für Karosserien 347
Beispiele für Kleider 252
Beispiele für Küchenmesser 169
Beispiele für Lastkraftwagen 364
Beispiele für Laubhölzer 64
Beispiele für Löffel 168
Beispiele für Meeressäugetiere 90
Beispiele für Messer 168
Beispiele für Moose 51
Beispiele für Motorräder 369
Beispiele für Nadelblätter 65
Beispiele für Nadelhölzer 65
Beispiele für Nägel 220
Beispiele für Nagetiere 82
Beispiele für Primaten 91
Beispiele für Raubtiere 88
Beispiele für Reptilien 77
Beispiele für Röcke 253
Beispiele für Schlafsäcke 530
Beispiele für Skier 510
Beispiele für Spinnentiere 70
Beispiele für Sprünge 509
Beispiele für Stühle 201
Beispiele für Tische 202
Beispiele für Türen 286
Beispiele für Vogelfüße 79
Beispiele für Vogelschnäbel 79
Beispiele für Währungsabkürzungen 440
Beispiele für Winkel 428
Beispiele für Zelte 528
Beitrag, redaktioneller 313
Beiwagen 380
Bekleidungsgeschäft 436
Belegausgabe 346
Beleuchterbrücke 292
beleuchteter Spiegel 269
Beleuchtung 199, 269
Beleuchtungsgitter 291
Beleuchtungsschiene 207
Belgien 449
Belichtungseinstellung 314
Belichtungskorrekturknopf 314
Belichtungsmesser 314
Belize 448
Belüftungsfenster 182
Belüftungsschlitz 214
bemannte Manövriereinheit 10
Bengalen, Golf 19
Benin 451
Benzin 405
Benzinmotor 351
Benzintankverschluss 368
Beobachtung des Weltraums 7
Beobachtungsposten 7
Beobachtungsraum 462, 465
Beobachtungsraum, psychiatrischer 462
Bereitschaftsanzeige 269, 328
Berg 29
Bergamotte 134
Bergère 200
Bergfried 282
Berghang 29
Berghütte 512
Bergkette 5
Bergschrund 30
Bergwacht 512
Beringsee 14
Beringstraße 16
Berme 342
Bermudashorts 254
Bernhardiner 86
Berührung 470
Besatzungsunterkünfte 382
Beschichtung 493
Beschläge 521
Beschleunigungsspur 343
Besen 193, 215
Besitzkarte 469
Bespannung 492, 494, 502
Besprechungszimmer 440
Besteckkorb 214
Bestückung 227
Besuchertreppe 391
Betriebsanzeigen 318

Betriebseinstellung 326
Betriebsraum 447
Betriebsschalter 337
Bett 204, 361
Bett mit Matratze 530
Betttuch 204
Bettwäsche 204
Beutel 162
Beutelfach 209
Beutelklammern 341
Beuteltasche 275
Beuteltasche, kleine 276
Beweger 212
bewegliche Backe 223, 224
bewegliche Brücken 344
bewegliche Tribünen 444
beweglicher Oberkiefer 76
Bewegungen eines Flugzeugs 395
Bewegungsmelder 286
Bezeichnungen tropischer Wirbelstürme 43
Bezugsstoff 273
BH 259
Bhutan 453
Biber 82
Bibliothek 433, 444
Bidet 195
Bienenstock 122
Bier 120
Bierkrug 165
bikonkave Linse 419
bikonvexe Linse 419
Bildanzeige 315
Bildeinstelltasten 320
Bildröhre 318
Bildschirm 318, 329
Bildschirminhalt drucken 331
Bildschirmverriegelung 336
Bildung 444
Bildungseinrichtung 335, 433
Bildunterschrift 313
Bildvorlauf 315
Billard 502
Billardqueue 503
Billardtisch 502
Billettasche 244
Bimah 447
Binde, elastische 461
Bindebogen 299
Bindegewebe 114
Bindehaut 119
Bindeteil 245
Bindung 513
Bindung, chemische 414
Binokularmikroskop 421
Binsenstängel 132
Bioabfallbehälter 49
Biologie 426
biologisch nicht abbaubare Schadstoffe 47
Biosphäre 44
Biosphäre, Aufbau 44
Birke 64
Birne 133
Birne, asiatische 137
birnenförmiger Korpus 297
Birnenmelone 137
Bison 84
Bit 221
Bits und Bohrer, Beispiele 228
Bittermelone 128
Bitterschokolade 148
Blank 468
Blase 51
Blasebalg 530
Blasebalgtasche 255
Blasinstrumente 306
Blaspfeife 296
Blassynthesizer 311
Blatt 53, 54, 55, 125, 216, 219, 226, 227, 270, 493, 506
Blatt, Aufbau 55
Blatt, Säge 226, 227
Blattachsel 55
Blattader 55
Blattansatz 55
Blättchen 51
Blätter, einfache 55
Blätter, zusammengesetzte 55
Blätterpapille 118
Blätterteig 145
Blattgemüse 126
Blattgrund 53
Blattrand 55
Blattscheide 55
Blattschraube 306
Blattspindel 52

Blattstiel 55
Blattstieleinschnitt 62
Blau 418
blaue Linie 507
blaue Luzerne 130
blauer Ball 503
Blaufisch 160
Blaulicht 455
Blaustrahl 318
Blazer 251, 254
Blechbläser 295
Blechverkleidung 192
Bleikopf 305
Bleistift 312
Bleistiftspitzer 341
Blende 210, 212, 213, 277
Blendenöffnung 7
Blendrahmen 186
Blendrahmen oben 186
Blinddarm 106
blinde Tasche 251
blinder Fleck 119
Blinker 538
Blinkerhebel 354
Blinkerkontrollleuchte 368
Blinkleuchte 352, 366, 367, 368
Blinklichter 362
Blinklichtkontrolle 355
Blitz 41
Blitzableiter 183, 407, 413
Blitzkontakt 314
Blitzröhre 420
Block 473
Block, numerischer 331
Blockdeckel 359
Blouson 249
Blume, Aufbau 56
Blumen, Beispiele 56
Blumenbeet 230
Blumenkohl 127
Blumenkrone 56
Blumenladen 437
Blumenrabatte 230
Bluse, klassische 255
Blusen und Hemden, Beispiele 255
Blut, sauerstoffarmes 104
Blut, sauerstoffreiches 104
Blutbestandteile 104
Blutdruckmessgerät 461
Blüte 53, 56, 62
Blütenblatt 56
Blütenboden 56, 59
Blütengemüse 127
Blütenkelch 56
Blütenknospe 52
Blütenständen, Arten 57
Blütenstandskiel 54
Blütenstiel 56, 62
Blutgefäß 104, 114
Blutkörperchen, rotes 104
Blutkörperchen, weißes 104
Blutkreislauf 102
Blutkreislauf, Schema 103
Blutplasma 104
Blutwurst 156
BMX-Rad, Mountainbike 373
Boa 77
Böckchen 308
Bockkran 406, 407
Bockmühle 412
Bocksfuß 200
Bockshornkleesamen 138
Boden 48, 180, 534
Boden, gewachsener 342
Bodenablauf 184, 194
Bodenbalken 187
Bodenbeläge, textile 190
Bodenbewegung, horizontale 27
Bodenbewegung, vertikale 27
Bodenbewegungen 31
Bodendiele 190
Bodendüngung 47
Bodendüse 209
Bodenkriechen 31
Bodenlinie 517
Bodenplättchen 302
Bodenplatte 308, 533
Bodenprofil 54
Bodenstaubsauger 209
Bodenturmfläche 496
Bodenverschmutzung 47
Bodyshirt 255
Bodysuit 258
Bogen 301, 306, 428
Bogenansatz 301
Bogenarm 535

ASTRONOMIE > 2-25;   ERDE > 26-71;   PFLANZENREICH > 72-89;   TIERREICH > 90-143;   MENSCH > 144-177;   NAHRUNGSMITTEL UND KÜCHE > 178-241;   HAUS > 242-295;
HEIMWERKEN UND GARTENARBEIT > 296-333;   KLEIDUNG > 334-371;   PERSÖNLICHE AUSSTATTUNG > 372-391;   KUNST UND ARCHITEKTUR > 392-465;   KOMMUNIKATION UND BÜROTECHNIK > 466-535;
TRANSPORT UND FAHRZEUGE > 536-643;   ENERGIE > 644-677;   WISSENSCHAFT > 678-705;   GESELLSCHAFT > 706-785;   SPORT UND SPIELE > 786-920

589

Bogenfeld 285
Bogengang, äußerer knöcherner 116
Bogengang, hinterer knöcherner 116
Bogengang, oberer knöcherner 116
Bogenminute 428
Bogensäge 533
Bogenschutz 306
Bogensekunde 428
Bohne, Flageolet 131
Bohne, grüne 131
Bohne, römische 131
Bohne, schwarzäugige 130
Bohne, schwarze 131
Bohnen 130, 131
Bohnenkraut 142
Bohranlage 403
Bohrer 221, 228
Bohrfutter 221, 228
Bohrfutterschlüssel 228
Bohrgestänge 403
Bohrkopf 403
Bohrkörper 228
Bohrkragen 403
Bohrmaschine, elektrische 228
Bohrschiff 382
Bohrturm 403, 404
Bohrwerkzeuge 228
Bolero 254
Bolivien 448
Bolzen 222, 224, 270, 271
Bombe, vulkanische 28
Bongos 309
Boot 240
Boote und Schiffe, Beispiele 382
Bordcomputer 354, 457
Bordeauxglas 165
Bordküche 392
Bordstein 434
Bordunpfeife 296
borealer Wald 44
Boretsch 142
Borke 63
Borste 271, 272
Borsten 215, 219
Böschung 182
Böschung im Auftrag 342
Bosnien und Herzegowina 450
Botswana 452
Bottich 214
Bottichrand 212
Bottnischer Meerbusen 18
Boulevard 25, 433
Boulevardblatt 313
Bowlingbahn 436
Box 272
Box für die Aufsteckbürsten 272
Boxen 498, 524
Boxengasse 524
Boxer 498
Boxerhose 498
Boxershorts 247
Boxhandschuhe 498
Boxtasche 276
Brachacker 122
Brandbekämpfung 454
Brandbekämpfungsmaterial 454
Brandungspfeiler 35
Brandungstor 35
Brasilien 448
Braten 153
Bratenthermometer, digitales 171
Bratentopf, flacher 175
Bräter 174
Bratpfanne 175, 531
Bratsche 301
Bratschen 295
Bratwurst 156
Brauchdampf 408
Brauenbürstchen 266
Braunalge 51
brauner Ball 503
brauner Zucker 149
Braunreis 147
Brause 236
Brausegarnitur 194
Brausekopf 195, 197
Brauseschlauch 195, 197
Brecher 33
Breiapfel 137
Breitbild-Fernseher 321
Breitengrade 22
Breitenkreis 22
breiter Rückenmuskel 97
breites Mutterband 113
Breitfußgeschoss 435

Bremsanlage 351
Bremsbacke 357
Bremsbelag 357
Bremse 69, 467, 501, 522, 525, 536
Bremsen 357
Bremsflüssigkeitsbehälter 357
Bremsgriff 371, 522
Bremshebel 523
Bremskraftregler 357
Bremskraftverstärker 350, 357
Bremskreis 357
Bremsleitung 350
Bremsleuchte 352
Bremspedal 350, 354, 357, 368
Bremssattel 357, 366
Bremsscheibe 357
Bremsschlauch 357
Bremsträger 357
Bremstrommel 357
Bremswagen 377
Bremszug 371
Bremszylinder 357
Brenner 174, 210, 529
Brennholzstauraum 192
Brennpunkt 419
Brennraum 192
Brennsockel 529
Brennspiritus 405
Brennstab 409
Brennstabbündel 409
Brennstoff 408
Brennstoff, fossiler 48
Brennstofftablette 409
Brett 519
Brett, schwarzes 444
Brettspiel 469
Brie 151
Brieföffner 339
Brieftasche 275
Briefwaage 339
Brille 273, 513, 522
Brille, Teile 273
Brillenetui 275
Broccoli 127
Brombeere 132
Brot 144
Brotbackautomat 179
Brothalter 178
Brotmesser 169
Browser 334
Bruch 427
Brücke 25, 109, 273, 420
Brücken, bewegliche 344
Brücken, starre 344
Brückenlift 381
Brunei 453
Brunnen für rituelle Waschungen 447
Brunnenkresse 127
Brust 78, 83, 92, 94, 113
Brustbein 98
Brustbeine 71
Brustdrüse 113
Brustflosse 74, 90
Brustkorb 92, 94
Brustleistentasche 244
Brustmuskel, großer 96
Brustschutz 476, 486
Brustschwimmen 517
Brusttasche 245, 248
Brüstungsriegel 187
Brustwarze 92, 94, 113
Brustwirbel 99
Brutzwiebel 54
Bube 468
Buche 64
Buchecker 133
Bücherregal 444
Bücherstütze 341
Buchhandlung 436
Buchsenhalter 198
Büchsenöffner 170
Bucht 5, 24
Bucht, Große Australische 15
Buchweizen 61, 143
Buckelwal 90
Büfett 203
Büffel 84
Buffet 438
Bug 384, 387, 392, 519, 520
Bügel 226, 273, 301, 324, 535
Bügel, verstellbarer 273
Bügelanschlag 273
Bügelende 273
Bügelfalte 246
Bügelhebel 534
Bügelheck 208

Bügelhorn 307
Bügelrundung 273
Bügelsäge 226
Bügelsohle 208
Bügelspannmechanismus 537
Bugfahrwerk 392
Bugladeklappe 386
Bugpropeller 384
Bugstrahler 387
Bugtür 383
Bugwulst 385, 387
Bühne 278, 292, 293
Bühnenhaus 278, 292
Bühnenhintergrund 292
Bulbospongiosus 111
Bulgarien 450
Bull's eye 471
Bullauge 386
Bulldogge 86
Bund 125, 249, 302, 303
Bund mit Druckknöpfen 260
Bund, elastischer 249
Bündchen 247
Bundesstaat 23
Bundmarkierung 303
Bundverlängerung 246
Bunker 504
Bunkeröl 405
Burg 282
Bürgersteig 434
Burggraben 282
Burghof 282
Burkina Faso 451
Büro 374, 438, 439
Büro der Oberschwester 463
Büro der Schulaufsicht 445
Büro des diensthabenden Arztes 462
Büro des Direktors 443
Büro des Richters 440
Büro des Schulleiters 445
Bürogebäude 381, 432, 435
Büroklammerhalter 341
Büroklammern 341
Bürotechnik 312, 329
Büroturm 435
Bürste 209, 215, 272
Bürstenkörper 215
Burundi 451
Bürzel 78
Bus 362, 435
Busbahnhof 432
Bushaltestelle 434
Büstenhalter, trägerloser 259
Büstenschale 259
Butter 150
Butterdose 163, 166
Butterfach 211
Buttermesser 168
Buttermilch 150
Butterroller 169
Button-Down-Kragen 245

C

C 298
Cabanjacke 251
Café 432, 437
Cafeteria 445
Cajun-Gewürzmischung 139
Callisto 2
Camcorder 320
Camembert 151
Camisol 125
Camping 528
Campingausrüstung 531
Candela 426
Cannelloni 146
Cañon, unterseeischer 33
Cape 251
Caprihose 254
Carapax 71
Cardigan 255
Carina 74
Carpentariagolf 15
Casabamelone 135
Cashewkern 133
Cassegrain-Fokus 7
Casting 537
Cayennepfeffer 139
CD 326
CD DVD-Auswurftaste 329
CD DVD-Laufwerk 329, 336
CD-Einschub 471
CD-Fach 323
CD-Rekorder 325

CD-Spieler 323, 325, 326
CD-Spieler, tragbarer 325
CD-Tasten 326
Celli 295
Cello 301
Celsius-Temperatur, Maßeinheit 426
Celsiusskala 424
Cent 440
Centerlautsprecher 321
Centre 485
Cephalica 102
Cephalothorax 70
Chac-Mool 283
Chaiselongue 200
Chamäleon 77
Chamilly-Parkett 190
Charlestonmaschine 308
Charlottenform 172
Charon 3
Chatroom 335
Chayote 129
Check-in-Schalter 390
Checkliste 10
Chef-Kameramann 291
Chefmaschinist 290
Chemie 414
chemische Behandlung 405
chemische Bindung 414
chemische Reinigung 437
Chesterfieldsofa 200
Chicorée 127
Chiffonière 203
Chile 448
Chili, Jalapeño 139
Chilipulver 139
Chilis, getrocknete 139
Chilis, zerstoßene 139
China 453
China-Broccoli 127
Chinakohl 126
chinesische Dattel 137
Chirimoya 136
Chirurgen-Waschraum 465
Chirurgie, kleine 462
Chloroplast 50
Chokerkette 264
Chor 284, 285
Chorhaupt 285
Chorizo-Wurst 156
Chorlampe 446
Chorscheitelkapelle 284, 285
Chorumgang 285
Chromatin 66
Chromosphäre 4
Chutney 141
Climber 501
Clip 312
Cliphalterung 199
Clubsessel 200
Coach-Box 474
Cockpit 13, 392, 520, 525
Cocktailbar 203, 439
Cocktailglas 165
Cocos-Platte 27
Collie 86
Compluvium 280
Computer 444
Computerbildschirm 10
Computerprogramme 457
Computerraum 444
Conchiglie 146
Container 383
Containerbrücke 381
Containerflachwagen 377
Containerlaschsystem 383
Containerschiff 381, 382
Containerterminal 381, 430
Controller 471
Controller-Schnittstellen 471
Cookstraße 15
Costa Rica 448
Costalschild 76
Coudé-Fokus 7
Coulomb 426
Coulommiers 151
Coupé 347
Couscous 144
Couscoustopf 175
Cowper-Drüse 111
Coyolxauhqui-Stein 283
Crêpe-Pfanne 175
Cricket 478
Cricketball 478
Cricketschuh 478
Cricketspieler 478
Crochetwinkel 244

Croissant 144
Crottin de Chavignol 150
Cubiculum 280
Curling 515
Curlingbesen 515
Curlingstein 515
Curry 138
Curryklemme 521
Cursor an Zeilenanfang 331
Cursor an Zeilenende 331
Cursor nach links 331
Cursor nach oben 331
Cursor nach rechts 331
Cursor nach unten 331

D

D 298
Dach 183, 193, 283, 349, 361
Dachfenster 183
Dachkranz, vorkragender 283
Dachluke 361
Dachrinne 182
Dachs 88
Dachziegel 283
Dalmatiner 86
Dame 468, 470
Damenflanke 470
Damenhandschuhe 243
Damenkleidung 251
Damenkopfbedeckungen 239
Damenschuhe 241
Damentoilette 294, 439
Damm 406
Dammkrone 406
Dampf 402, 408, 415
Dampfbügeleisen 208
Dampfdruck 408
Dampfdüse 208
Dämpfeinsatz 175
Dämpfer 307
Dampferzeuger 402
Dampfgenerator 408
Dampfkochtopf 175
Dampfregler 181
Dampfstärkeregler 208
Dämpfung, magnetische 422
Dänemark 450
Dänische Dogge 86
dänisches Roggenbrot 145
Danish Blue 151
Darm 71, 73, 103
Darmbein 98
Darreichungsformen, Arzneimittel 467
darstellende Künste 294
Dartscheibe 471
Dartspiel 471
Datei 334
Dateiformat 334
Dateiauswertung 38
Datenbank 335
Datendisplay 328
Dateneingabe, Feinregler 310
Dateneingabe, Grobregler 310
Dattel 132
Dattel, chinesische 137
Datumaufnahmetaste 320
Datumeinblendetaste 320
Datumstempel 338
Dauerbrand 192
Daumen 115, 243, 477
Daumen, opponierbarer 91
Daumenauflage 306
Daumenfittich 78
Daumenring 307
Daumenteil 460
Daunendecke 204
Davidstern 447
Deckblatt 60
Decke 193, 204, 342
Deckel 174, 177, 178, 179, 180, 181, 211, 212, 215, 225, 533
Deckelhalter, magnetischer 180
Deckelknopf 176
Deckeltasche 532
Deckenbalken 187, 190
Deckendurchführung 193
Deckenleuchte 206
Deckfeder 78
Deckleiste 186
Deimos 2
Deklinationsachse 8, 9
Dekorateur 291
Dekorationsgeschäft 437
Delegierte, technische 509
Delle 505

Delphin 90
Delphin, äußere Merkmale 90
Delta 32, 35
Delta-Arm 32
Deltaflügel 394
Deltamuskel 96
Dendrit 110
Denkmal 25
Deodorant 267
Depolarisationsgemisch 417
Derrickkran 382
Dessertgabel 168
Dessertlöffel 168
Dessertmesser 168
Deutscher Schäferhund 86
deutscher Senf 140
Deutsches Register 539
deutsches Roggenbrot 145
Deutschland 450
diagonaler Schlittschuhschritt 514
diagonaler Zug 470
Dichtemesser 359
dichtes Windelhöschen 260
Dichtring 404
Dichtung, magnetische 211
Dichtungsring 214
Dichtverschluss 529
Dickdarm 106
Dickdarm, absteigender 106
Dickdarm, aufsteigender 106
Dickdarm, quer verlaufender 106
dicke Bohnen 130
Dickemessung 425
Diele 188, 190
Diensteingang 445
Dienstgradabzeichen 456
Dienstgürtel 456
diensthabender Arzt, Büro 462
dieselelektrische Lokomotive 377
Dieselkraftstoff 405
Dieselmotor 383
Dieselmotorraum 398, 399, 400, 401
Dieseltriebwerk 383
Differenzial 351
Digitalanzeige 423, 461
digitale Spiegelreflexkamera: Rückansicht 315
digitales Bratenthermometer 171
Digitalkamera 315
Digitalthermometer 461
Digitaluhr 424
Digitus 82
Dijon-Senf 140
Dill 142
Dimmerschalter 198
Dinkel 143
Diode 314, 411
Dione 3
Direktor, Büro 443
Dirigent(in) 295
Dirigentenpult 295
Dirndl-BH 259
Diskantregister 296
Diskantsteg 304
Diskanttastatur 296
Diskette 333
Disketten-Auswurftaste 329
Diskettenlaufwerk 310, 329
Diskettenlaufwerk, externes 333
Diskus 472
Diskus- und Hammerwerfen 473
Display 314, 318, 319, 322, 325, 327, 336, 338, 442, 443
Display-Panel 320
Displayeinstellung 327
Distanzstück 409
Disziplinen 511
divergierende Plattengrenzen 27
Division 427
Divisionstaste 337
Djembe 297
Djnepr 18
Dock 381
Docking-Station 337
Dogge, Dänische 86
Dokumente 328
Dokumentenablage 338
Dokumentenmappe 339
Dolde 57
Doldenrispe 61
Doldentraube 57
Doline 31
Dollar 440
Dolly 290
Dollyschienen 290

Dom 284
Dom, gotischer 284
Dom, Grundriss 285
Domain zweiten Grades 334
Domain, Toplevel 334
Domainname 334
Dominica 449
Dominikanische Republik 449
Dominosteine 468
Donau 18
Doppel-B 299
Doppel-Kassettendeck 325
Doppelbett 439
Doppelblank 468
Doppelblatt 306
Doppeldeckerbus 363
Doppelhaus 289
Doppelklappbrücke 345
Doppelkreuz 299
Doppelmaulschlüssel 223
Doppelriegel 187
Doppelringschlüssel 223
Doppelringschlüssel, offener 223
Doppelschlag 299
Doppelschrägstrich 334
Doppelsitz 380
Doppelspiel 490
Doppelspüle 194
Doppelstockschub 514
doppelt gesägt 55
Doppelzimmer 439
Dopplerwürfel 469
Dorf 430, 512
dorische Halbsäule 281
Dorn 246
Dornablage 341
Dornfortsatz 110
Dose 163
Dose, Konserven 163
Dosenöffner 163, 180, 531
Dosier-Aerosol 467
Dotterhaut 79
Double 471
Douglasscher Raum 112
Down-Quark 414
Downhillrad 522
Draht 417, 501
Drahtbesen 176
Drahtbürste 268
Drahtschneider 217
Drahtschneidezange 217
Drakestraße 15, 17
Drehbohrverfahren 403
Drehbrücke 344
Drehdüse 236
Drehflügel nach außen 287
Drehflügel nach innen 287
Drehflügeltür 286
Drehgehäuse 286
Drehgeschwindigkeitssensor, Räder 357
Drehgestell 376
Drehgestellflachwagen 377
Drehgriff 332
Drehjustierung 420
Drehkartei 338
Drehknopf 536, 537
Drehkranz 344, 400
Drehkuppel 7
Drehleiterfahrzeug 455
Drehmoment-Einstellring 228
Drehmomentwandler 252
Drehscheibe 176, 455
Drehspiegel 269
Drehtisch 403
Drehtür 286
Drehwalze 27
Drehzahlmesser 355, 368
Drehzahlschalter 228
Drehzapfen 217
Dreieck 429, 503
Dreieckfenster 349
dreieckiger Korpus 297
Dreiecksgruppe 115
Dreiecktuch 461
dreiflügeliger Propeller 394
Dreifußständer 308
dreiköpfiger Armstrecker 97
Dreipass 285
dreipolige Steckdose 198
dreipoliger, amerikanischer Stecker 198
Dreirad 373
Dreisprung 472
dreitürige Kombilimousine 347
Dreiviertellange Jacke 248
Dreivierteltakt 298
dreizählig 55

Dressiernadel 173
Drilling 468
Drillingshaken 538
Drillschraubenzieher 221
Drittbelegung 330
dritte Reihe 482
dritte Zehe 78
dritter Malspieler 474
dritter Ventilzug 307
drittes Mal 474
Drohne 68
Dromedar 85
Drosselvene, äußere 102
Drosselvene, innere 102
Druck, Maßeinheit 426
Druckbleistift 312
Drücker 307
Drückerbügel 216
druckfestes Außenrohr 409
Druckkammer 345
Druckknopf 243, 249, 305, 312
Druckknopfleiste 249, 261
Druckknopfleiste an der Beininnenseite 260, 261
Druckluft 346
Druckluftflasche 454
Druckmechanik 312
Druckmessgerät 461
Druckmotiv 261
Druckregler 272, 454
Druckrohr 312
Druckschalter 227, 228, 229, 235
Drückstange 501
Drucksteg 304
Drucktaste 176, 214
Drucktendenz 39
Druckverschluss 274
Druckverstärkerpumpanlage 404
Druckwelle 403
Druckzahnrädchen 180
Drumlin 29
Dschibuti 451
Dual-in-line-Gehäuse 417
Dudelsack 296
Duffelcoat 249
Dulse 123
Düne 35
Düne, komplexe 36
Dünenformen 36
Dünenzug 36
Dung 48
Düngemitteln, Einsatz 47
dunkles Roggenbrot 144
Dünndarm 106
Dunst 41
Dunstabzugshaube 164, 210
Dunstrohrabzug 194
Duo 300
Durchflussrohr 410
Durchführung 406, 407
durchgehende Linie 342
Durchgrifftasche 251
Durchlaufträger 344
Durchmesser 428
Durchschnitt, Erdatmosphäre 37
durchsichtiger Reiter 340
Durchziehschnur 249
Durianfrucht 137
Dusche 189, 439, 464
Duschkabine 195
Düse 12, 216, 219, 236
Düsenflugzeugbenzin 405
Düsenreiniger 218
Duty-free-Shop 391
DVD 318
DVD-Einschub 471
DVD-Lade 318
DVD-Rekorder 333
DVD-Spieler 318
Dynamo 370

E

E 298
E-Commerce 335
E-Mail-Software 334
E-Mail-Taste 330
Eau de parfum 267
Eau de toilette 267
Ebene 24
ebene Flächen 428
ebener Spiegel 7
Echinodermen 66
echte Teilmenge von 427
echter Reizker 123
Eckballfahne 481

Eckbogen 481
Ecke 498, 506
Eckhocker 498
Eckpfosten 187
Eckpolster 498
Eckschrank 201
Eckstück 277
Eckturm 282
Eckzahn 101
Ecuador 449
Edelgas 199
Edelpilzkäse 151
Editier-Such-Taste 320
Effiliermesser 269
Effilierschere, einseitig gezahnte 270
Effilierschere, zweiseitig gezahnte 270
effusiver Vulkan 28
Ehering 264
Ehrensessel, steinerner 447
Ei 79
Eiche 64
Eichel 111
Eichelhäher 80
Eichelkürbis 129
Eichhörnchen 82
Eidechse 77
Eier 155
Eier, Karton 162
Eierfach 211
Eierkarton 162
Eiernudeln, asiatische 147
Eierschneider 173
Eierstock 112, 113
Eieruhr 171
eiförmig 55
Eigelb 79
Eigentumswohnungen 289
Eileiter 112, 113
Eileiterampulle 113
Eileiterenge 113
Eileitertrichter 113
Eimer 215
Eimer, Abfall 215
ein Pärchen 468
Ein- und Ausschalter 177, 180, 181
Ein/Ausschalter 206, 208, 209, 218, 314, 318, 329, 333, 336
Ein/Aus 326
Ein/Aus/Lautstärke 326
einarmiger Schulterwurf 499
Einatmungsventil 459
Einbauwaschtisch 195
Einbuchtung, vordere 115
einfache Blätter 55
einfache Falte 246, 253
einfache Organismen 66
Einfahröffnung 396
Einfahrt 343
Einfassband 238
Einfassung 230, 240
Einfassung, seitliche 192
einflammiger Gasbrenner 529
Einfügen 331
Einfügetaste 331
Einfülllöffnung 208
Einfüllschacht 177, 180
Einfüllstutzen 237, 351, 404
Eingabe 331
Eingabe-Löschtaste 337
Eingabegerät für persönliche Identifikationsnummer (PIN) 443
Eingabegerät 330
Eingabetaste 331, 443
Eingang 278, 378, 447, 528, 529
Eingangshalle 188, 390, 435
Eingangsschalter 322
Eingangssperre 378
Eingangstüren 294
eingebautes Schwimmbecken 184
eingehängte Spannweite 344
eingenähter Boden 528, 529
eingerollter junger Wedel 52
eingeschlossenes Grundwasser 402
eingesetzter Ärmel 245
Eingeweideganglion 73
eingliedrige Trugdolde 57
Einhand-Mischbatterie 197
Einhand-Rohrzange 216
Einheit, mobile 316
Einheitensystem, internationales 426
Einkaufsstraße 432
Einkaufstasche 276
Einkaufstasche, große 276
Einkaufstüten 121
Einkaufswagen 121

Einkaufszentrum 431, 436
Einlage 225, 301, 302
Einlassventil 360
Einlegegurke 128
Einmachthermometer 171
Einpackhilfe 121
Einpersonenzelt 529
Einreiher 244
Einreißhaken 454
Einrumpfboote 521
Eins 427
Einsatz 277
Einsatz für Imbusschrauben 221
Einsatz für Kreuzschlitzschrauben 221
Einsatz für Schlitzschrauben 221
Einsatz von Düngemitteln 47
Einsätze 179
Einsatzkleidung 454
einschalige Muschel 73
einschalige Muschel, äußere Merkmale 73
Einschalter 213
Einschalttaste 328
Einschnitt, oberer seitlicher 62
Einschnitt, unterer seitlicher 62
einseitig gezahnte Effilierschere 270
Einspangenschuh 241
Einspeisung in das Leitungsnetz 413
Einspritzdüse 360
Einstechhebel 180
Einstecktuch 244
Einstiegegriff 380
Einstiegestation, radiale 389
Einstiegetreppe 395
Einstellanzeige 511
einstellbare Bremse 537
Einstellkerbe 511
Einstellrad 353
Einstellspanner 527
Einstellung 324
Einstellung der Deklinationsachse 8, 9
Einstellung der Rektaszensionsachse 8, 9
Einstellung, horizontale 329
Einstellung, Pendelhub 227
Einstellung, vertikale 329
Einstellungsanzeige 315
Einstiegsloch 31
Einstiegsluke 13, 404
Einstiegstür 362, 363, 380
einstöckiges Haus 289
einteilige Klappbrücke 345
Einteilung 274
Eintrittskarte 393
Eintrittskartenautomat 294
einwärts 518
Einwärtsdreher, runder 96
Einweg-Brennstoffflasche 218
Einwegkamera 315
Einwegkontaktlinse 272
Einwegrasierer 271
Einzahlungsschlitz 442
Einzelbett 439
Einzeldisziplin, Anzeigetafel 497
Einzeller 66
Einzelsitz 380
Einzelspiel 491
Einzelzimmer 439
Eipochierer 175
Eis 45
Eisautomat 346
Eisbär 89
Eisbehälter 180
Eisbein 153
Eisbergsalat 126
Eisbrecher 384
Eisenbahn 25
Eisenbahnstrecke 431
Eisenschläger 505
Eisenträger 374
eiserner Vorhang 292
Eisfläche 506, 509, 515
Eishockey 506
Eishockeyschläger 506
Eishockeyspieler 506
Eiskappe 49
Eiskratzer 356
Eiskunstlauf 509
Eiskunstlaufkufe 509
Eiskunstlaufstiefel 509
Eislaufplatz 512
Eismaschine 180
Eisportionierer 173
Eisschelf, Amery 15
Eisschnelllauf 508
Eisschnelllauf-Schlittschuhe 508
Eisschnellläuferin 508
Eisschnellläufer: Kurzstrecke 508

ASTRONOMIE > 2-25;   ERDE > 26-71;   PFLANZENREICH >72-89;   TIERREICH > 90-143;   MENSCH > 144-177;   NAHRUNGSMITTEL UND KÜCHE > 178-241;   HAUS > 242-295;
HEIMWERKEN UND GARTENARBEIT > 296-333;   KLEIDUNG > 334-371;   PERSÖNLICHE AUSSTATTUNG > 372-391;   KUNST UND ARCHITEKTUR > 392-465;   KOMMUNIKATION UND BÜROTECHNIK > 466-535;
TRANSPORT UND FAHRZEUGE > 536-643;   ENERGIE > 644-677;   WISSENSCHAFT > 678-705;   GESELLSCHAFT > 706-785;   SPORT UND SPIELE > 786-920

Eisschnellläufer: Langstrecke 508
Eistanzkufe 509
Eisvogel 80
Eiswürfelschale 211
Eiswürfelspender 164
Eiweiß 79
Eizelle 112
Ejakulationsgang 111
ekkrine Schweißdrüse 114
El Salvador 448
elastische Binde 461
elastische Schürze 383
elastischer Beinausschnitt 247
elastischer Bund 249
elastischer Fingerhut 339
Elch 85
Elefant 85
elektrische Anlage 351
elektrische Bohrmaschine 228
elektrische Gitarre 303
elektrische Heckenschere 235
elektrische Schiebetür 363
elektrische Steuereinheit 357
elektrische Stichsäge 227
elektrische Stromstärke, Maßeinheit 426
elektrische Zahnbürste 272
elektrischer Bund 249
elektrischer Golfwagen 505
elektrischer Schnellkocher 179
Elektrischer Tischgrill 179
elektrischer Widerstand, Maßeinheit 426
elektrisches Potential, Maßeinheit 426
Elektrizität 198
Elektrizität aus Wasserkraft 406
Elektrizität und Magnetismus 416
Elektrizitätserzeugung 412
Elektrizitätserzeugung aus geothermischer Energie 402
Elektrizitätserzeugung aus Kernenergie 408
Elektrizitätserzeugung aus Wärmeenergie 402
Elektrizitätserzeugung aus Windenergie 413
Elektrizitätserzeugung durch den Generator 408
Elektrizitätsmenge, Maßeinheit 426
Elektroherd 210
Elektroinstallateurwerkzeuge 217
Elektrokabel 354
Elektrolytkondensatoren 417
Elektrolytseparator 417
elektromagnetisches Spektrum 418
Elektromesser 177
Elektromotor 235, 237, 358
Elektron 414
Elektronenflussrichtung 416, 417
Elektronenkanone 318
Elektronenkollektor 417
Elektronenstrahl 318
Elektronik 417
Elektronikgeschäft 436
elektronische Instrumente 310
elektronische Post 335
elektronische Waage 423
elektronischer Sucher 320
elektronisches Piano 311
elektronisches Schlagpolster 311
elektronisches Vorschaltgerät 199
elektronisches Zahlungsterminal 121, 443
Elektropumpe 357
Elektrorasierer 271
Element 427
Element von 427
Elfeck, regelmäßiges 429
Elfenbeinküste 451
Elfmeterpunkt 480
Ellbogen 83, 86, 93, 95
Ellbogenfortsatz 99
Ellbogenpolster 486
Ellbogenschützer 526, 527
Elle 98
Ellennerv 108
Ellenseite, Handbeuger 96, 97
Ellenseite, Handstrecker 97
Elsasglas 165
Embryonalgewinde 73
Emission schädlicher Gase 47
Emission von Salpetersäure 48
Emission von Schwefeldioxid 48
Emission von Schwefelsäure 48
Emission von Stickoxiden 48
Emmentaler 151
Empfang 439, 442
Empfang von Dokumenten 328
Empfangsantenne 316
Empfangsebene 439

Empfangshalle 439, 447
Empfangsteil 326
End-Suchtaste 320
Endanschlag 226
Endbande 502
Ende 510, 514
Ende, hinteres 73, 226, 229
Ende, vorderes 73
Ende-Taste 327
Endfaden 109
Endivie, krause 127
Endknospe 53
Endlagerung 49
Endlappen 62
Endlinie 484, 487, 489, 493
Endlosperlenkette 264
Endmoräne 30
Endokarp 57, 58
endoplasmatisches Retikulum 50, 66
Endplatte, motorische 110
Endschalter 287
Endstück 111, 409, 503, 526
Endteil 245
Endverzweigung 110
Endzone 484
Energie 402
Energie, fossile 402
Energie, geothermische 402
Energie, Maßeinheit 426
Energiefreisetzung 415
Energiesparlampe 199, 411
englischer Senf 140
englischer Stock 466
englisches Weißbrot 145
Englischhorn 306
Englischhörner 295
Enoki 123
Ente 81, 155
Entenei 155
Entklammerer 341
Entkleidungsraum 465
Entladerampe 437, 439
Entladungsröhre 199
Entlastungsraum 278
Entleerungsschlauch 212
Entlüftungskreis 194
Entlüftungskreislauf 194
Entlüftungsventil 385
Entnahmeraum 465
Entnahmeraum, Wartebereich 465
Entriegelungstaste 208
Entsafter 180
Entsteiner 173
Entwaldung 47
Entwässerungsrinne 342
Epiduralraum 110
Epizentrum 27
Erbse 60
Erbsen 130
Erbsen, gespaltene 130
Erbsen, grüne 130
Erdatmosphäre im Querschnitt 37
Erdaufbau 26
Erdaufschüttung 342
Erdbahn 4, 5
Erdbeben 27
Erdbeere 132
Erdbeere im Querschnitt 59
Erdbewegung, Geräte 233
Erde 2, 3, 4, 5, 14
Erdaufbau 26
Erdfunkstelle 335
Erdgas 403
Erdgeschoß 182, 188
Erdkröte, gemeine 75
Erdkruste 26, 27
Erdkruste im Querschnitt 26
Erdkugel, Koordinatensystem 21
Erdleitung 198
Erdnuss 130
Erdnussöl 149
Erdoberfläche 14
Erdoberfläche, Absorption 46
Erdöl 403, 405
Erdöleruptionskreuz 404
Erdölterminal 404
Erdölvorkommen 403
Erdrutsch 31
Erdsatellit, künstlicher 37
Erdung 404
Erdungsklemme 198
Erdungsstift 198
Ereigniskarte 469
Eritrea 451
Erstarren 414
erste Holzlage 187

erste Laubblätter 53
erste Reihe 482
erste Rückenflosse 74
erste Spannungserhöhung 413
erste Violinen 295
Erste-Hilfe-Anleitung 461
Erste-Hilfe-Kasten 457, 461
erster Backenzahn 101
erster Führungsring 537
erster Kamera-Assistent 290
erster Malspieler 474
erster Rang 293
erster Raum 489
erster Schiedsrichter 485, 487
erster Stock 182, 189
erster Ventilzug 307
erster vorderer Backenzahn 101
erstes Mal 474
Eruptivgesteine 26
Erwärmung, globale 46
Erweiterungskartei 340
Erythrozyt 104
Escapetaste 330
Esel 84
Eskariol 126
Espadrille 242
Espresso-Maschine 181
Espressomaschine 181
Essbesteck 531
Essecke 164
Essig 141
Esskastanie 133
Esslöffel 168
Esstablett 205
Esszimmer 188
Estragon 142
Estland 450
Ethernet-Schnittstelle 336
Etui 265, 337
Etui für Taschenrechner und Scheckheft 274
Etuirock 253
Eurasiatische Platte 27
Eurasien 14
Euro 440
Europa 2, 14, 18, 34, 449
Europäische Union, Flagge 441
europäisches Experimentiermodul 11
Eutelsat 316
Euthynterie 279
Evakuierungskapsel 11
ewiger Schnee 29
Ewiges Licht 447
Exokarp 57, 58, 59
Exosphäre 37
Expander 310, 500
Experimentiermodul, europäisches 11
Experimentiermodul, japanisches 11
Expertenpiste 512
explosiver Vulkan 28
externes Diskettenlaufwerk 333
externes Festplattenlaufwerk 333
Extrakt, Vanille 140
Exzenterschleifer 229
Eyeliner, flüssiger 266
Eyesee 15

F

F 298
Fabrik 430
Facettenauge 67, 68
Fach 203, 274
Fach für Molkereiprodukte 211
Facharzt 464
Fächerpinsel 266
Fächerscheibe, außengezahnte 222
Fächerscheibe, innengezahnte 222
Fackeln 4
fadenförmige Papille 118
Fadenkreuz 420
Fagott 306
Fagotte 295
Fahne 482
Fahrbahn 342, 344, 345, 434
fahrbares Röntgengerät 462
Fähre 386
Fahrenheitskala 424
Fahrer 522
Fahrersitz 369
Fahrgastanlage 381
Fahrkartenkontrolleur 374
Fahrkartenschalter 378
Fahrkorb 287
Fahrkorb-Fangvorrichtung 287
Fahrkorb-Führungsschiene 287

Fahrkorbboden 287
Fahrkorbdecke 287
Fahrkran 397
Fahrmotor 376
Fahrplan 374
Fahrrad 370
Fahrrad, Teile 370
Fahrräder, Beispiele 373
Fahrradhelm 372
Fahrradständer 445
Fahrradträger 356
Fahrtrage 460
Fahrtreppe 294
Fahrtrichtungsanzeige 379
Fahrzeuge 342
Fairway 504
Fakultät 427
Falke 81
Falkland-Inseln 17
Falle 186
Fallleitung 406, 407
Fallschirm für die Feststoffrakete 12
Fallstrang 194
Falltür 291
Falltür, abgesteppte 253
Falte, einfache 253
Falten, Beispiele 253
Faltfenster 287
Faltgrill 533
Falttür 286
Faltverschluss 534
Falz 186
Familie der Blechbläser 295
Familie der Holzblasinstrumente 295
Familienzelt 528
Fanfare 364
Fangen 470
Fänger 474, 475, 476
Fanghandschuh 476, 507
Fangvorrichtung, Fahrkorb 287
Fangzubehör 538
Farbabbrennervorsatz 218
Farben 468
Farbfernsehkamera 10
Farbfilter 318
Farbmasse 312
Farbmischung 418
Farbmischung, additive 418
Farbmischung, subtraktive 418
Farbroller 219
Farn 52
Farn, Aufbau 52
Farne, Beispiele 52
Farnspitze 125
Fasan 81, 154
Fasanenei 155
Fase 228
Faserwurzel 53, 63
Fassade 285
Fastfood-Restaurant 437
Faulbecken 48
Fausthandschuh 498
Fäustling 243
Feder 37, 206, 212, 222, 273, 312, 535
Federball 495
Federball, Kunststoff 495
Federflügel 221
Federkiel 312
Federkranz 495
Federring 222
Federstange 500
Federung 380
Federwaage 423
Fehlstartleine 516
Feige 137
Feile 531
feine Salami 156
Feinkost 120
Feinmahlanlage 402
Feinnachführungssystem 7
Feinregler für Dateneingabe 310
Feintrieb 421
Feld 469, 479
Feld, geothermisches 402
Feld, magnetisches 318, 416
Feldbett 530
Feldflasche 532
Feldlinie 416
Feldlinse 420
Feldlinseneinstellung 421
Feldmaus 82
Feldsalat 127
Feldspieler 479
Feldstärkeregler 322

Felge 366, 371
Felgenbremse, hintere 370
Felgenbremse, vordere 371
Fell 309
Fellmütze 238
Felsen 5
Felsenbecken 30
Felseninselchen 35
Felssäule 35
Fenchel 125
Fenster 186, 189, 352, 361, 380, 392, 519
Fenster, Beispiele 287
Fensterbrett 186
Fensterheber 352
Fensterladen 186
Fensterüberdachung 528
Fernbedienung 319, 321
Fernbedienungssensor 323
ferngesteuertes Servicemodul 11
Fernlicht 352
Fernlichtanzeige 355
Fernlichthebel 354
Fernlichtkontrollleuchte 368
Fernmeldeantenne 386
Fernmeldesatelliten 316
Fernmeldeturm 316
Fernsehapparat 318
Fernsehen 318
Fernsehgerät 439, 444
Fernsehprogramm 313
Fernsteuerungsanschlussbuchse 315
Ferse 93, 95, 247
Fersenautomatik 511
Fersenbein 99
Fersenhalter 240
Fersenrand 262
Fersenriemen 241
Fersenstütze 467
Fertiggerichte 121
Fessel 83
Festabstandmarkierung 391
feste Backe 223, 224
fester Sockel 224
Festkörper 414, 415
Festkörper, amorpher 414
Festplatte, herausnehmbare 333
Festplattenlaufwerk 333
Festplattenlaufwerk, externes 333
feststehender Messsschnabel 425
Feststellknopf 227, 228
Feststellring 221
Feststellschraube 341, 425
Feststellschraube für das Blatt 227
Feststellschraube für Schrägstellung 227
Feststellschrauben 425
Feststellspitze 308
Feststelltaste, Scrollen 331
Feststoff-Booster 12
Feststoffrakete, Fallschirm 12
Fett-Tröpfchen 50
Fettauffangschale 179
Fette 149, 405
Fettgewebe 113, 114
Fettgießer 173
Fettpfanne 174, 179
Fettuccine 146
feucht-kontinental - heißer Sommer 40
feucht-kontinental - warmer Sommer 40
feuchte Subtropen 40
Feuerbecken 283
Feuerbock 193
Feuerbohne 131
feuerfester Rennanzug 524
Feuerland 17
Feuerlöscher 457
Feuerschutzhelm 454
Feuerschutztür 286
Feuerstätte 192
Feuerstein 218
Feuertaste 332
Feuerwache 433
Feuerwehrmann 454
Feuerzange 193
Fiale 282, 284
Fichte 65
Fidschi 453
Fidschiinseln 15
Fieberthermometer 424, 461
Fieder 52
fiederteilig 55
Filchner-Schelfeis 15
Filiermesser 169
Filigrangewinde 425
Filmempfindlichkeit 314
Filmkamera 290
ASTRONOMIE > 2-25;   ERDE > 26-71;   PFLANZENREICH >72-89;   TIERREICH > 90-143;   MENSCH > 144-177;   NAHRUNGSMITTEL UND KÜCHE > 178-241;   HAUS > 242-295;
HEIMWERKEN UND GARTENARBEIT > 296-333;   KLEIDUNG > 334-371;   PERSÖNLICHE AUSSTATTUNG > 372-391;   KUNST UND ARCHITEKTUR > 392-465;   KOMMUNIKATION UND BÜROTECHNIK > 466-535;
TRANSPORT UND FAHRZEUGE > 536-643;   ENERGIE > 644-677;   WISSENSCHAFT > 678-705;   GESELLSCHAFT > 706-785;   SPORT UND SPIELE > 786-920

Filmset 291
Filmtitel 294
Filmtransporteinstellung 314
Filter 178, 184, 210
Filterabdeckung 459
Filterhalter 181
filum terminale 109
Filzhut 238, 239
Finanzabteilung 442
Finanzwesen 441
Finger 75, 114, 243, 477
Finger, kleiner 115
Fingerbeere 114
Fingerendglied 114
Fingerhut, elastischer 339
fingerloser Spitzenhandschuh 243
Fingermittelglied 114
Fingernagel 115
Fingernerv 108
Fingerrand 460
Fingerstrecker, gemeinsamer 97
Fink 80
Finnland 450
Finsternis, partielle 4, 5
Finsternis, ringförmige 4
Finsternis, totale 4, 5
Finsternisarten 4, 5
FireWire-Schnittstelle 336
Firmenkundenschalter 443
Firn 30
Firstpfette 187
Fisch 121
Fische 74
Fischgabel 168
Fischgrätmuster 190
Fischgrätparkett 190
Fischkochtopf 174
Fischkorb 538
Fischmesser 168
Fischplatte 166
Fischschupper 531
Fitnessgeräte 500
Fjordküste 35
flache Frisierbürste 268
flache Kuchenform 172
Flächen, ebene 428
flacher Bratentopf 175
flacher Teller 166
Flachfeile 229
Flachfräsbohrer 228
Flachland 32
Flachsilo 122
Flachstück 532
Flachwurzel 63
Flageolet-Bohne 131
Flagge der Europäischen Union 441
Flagge, umsetzbare 504
Flaggen 448
Flamingo 81
Flamme 415
Flanke 78, 83
Flare 4
Flasche 267, 532
Flasche, Glas 163
Flaschenöffner 170, 531
Flechte 50
Flechte, Aufbau 50
Flechten, Beispiele 50
Fleck, blinder 119
Fleck, gelber 119
Fleisch 152
Fleisch- und Wurstfach 211
Fleisch-Selbstbedienungstheke 120
Fleischpresse 45
fleischige Apfelfrucht 58
fleischige Frucht 58, 59
fleischige Steinfrucht 57
Fleischtheke 120
Fleischthermometer 171
Fleischwolf 170
flexibler Schlauch 209
Fliege 69, 245
Fliegenfenster 528
Fliegenfischen 536
Fliegengittertür 361
Fliegenpilz 52
Fliegenrolle 536
Fliegenrute 536
Fliegenschnur 536
Flip 509
Floh 69
Flosse 394
Flossenstrahl 74
Flügel 68, 78, 186, 286, 295, 412, 525, 536

Flügelader 67
Flügelmutter 223
Flügelrahmen 186
Flügelstrebe 394
Flügeltasche 246
Flügelwurzel 392
Fluggastbrücke 389
Fluggastbrücke, ausziehbare 389
Flughafen 25, 388, 430
Fluginformationsanzeige 391
Flugtasche 276
Flugzeug, Bewegungen 395
Flugzeuge, Beispiele 394
Flugzeugwartungshalle 389
Flunder 161
Flusensieb 212
Flush 468
Fluss 24, 25, 32
Flussbarsch 160
flüssige Grundierung 266
flüssiger Eyeliner 266
flüssiges Mascara 266
Flüssigkeit 414, 415
Flüssigkeit, antiseptische 461
Flüssigkeits-Gasscheider 359
Flüssigkristallanzeige 315, 320
Flusskrebs 158
Flusslandschaft 32
Flussmündung 24, 35
Flußbarsch, äußere Merkmale 74
Fly-Half 482
Fock 520
Fokussiersteuerung 320
Folie 163
Folie, Aluminium 162
Fön 270
Fondue-Set 174
Fonduegabel 168
Fonduetopf 174
Föngehäuse 270
Fontanelle, hintere 100
Football 486
Football, American 484
Footballspieler 486
Foramen caecum 118
Förderanlage 402
Förderband 49, 390
Förderplattform 404
Förderwagen 374
Forelle 161
Formel 1 525
Formel 3000 524
Formel Indy 524
Formel-1-Auto 525
Formel-3000-Auto 524
Formel-Indy-Auto 524
Formen, geometrische 428
Formwerkzeuge 229
Fortbildungsbüro 442
Fortpedal 304, 311
fossiler Brennstoff 46, 48
Fotoapparate 315
Fotograf 436
Fotografie 314
Fotokopiergerät 442
Foullinie 474
Foullinienpfosten 475
Foyers 293
Frachtempfang 391
Frachtflugzeug 394
Frachtraum 393
Frachtschiff 382
Frachtversand 391
Fraktionierturm 405
Frankfurter Würstchen 156
Frankreich 449
französisches Weißbrot 144
Frau 94
Free Guard Zone 515
Freestyleboard 513
frei endende Rippe 98
freie Rippe 99
freier Nagelrand 114
Freilauf 372
freilaufender Sitz 501
Freileitungen, Verteilung 316
Freilufterrasse 387
Freiraum 487
Freisaiten 296
freistehendes Schwimmbecken 184
Freiwange 191
Freiwurflinie 489
Freizeit in der Natur 528
Frequenz, Maßeinheit 426
Frequenzanzeige 325
Frequenzwähler 325

Fresko 280
Friedhof 25, 433
Fries 202, 279
Frischhaltefolie 162
Frischkäse 150
Friseesalat 126
Friseur 290, 436
Frisierbürste, flache 268
Fritteuse 178
Frittierkorb 171, 178
Frontabdeckung 333
Frontblech 369
Frontscheibe 210
Frontscheinwerfer 352
Frontstoßdämpfer 369
Frontstoßfänger 348
Frosch 75, 301
Frosch, äußere Merkmale 75
Fruchtbecher 60
Fruchtbildung 62
Fruchtblatt 60
Früchte 57
Fruchtfleisch 58
Fruchtfleisch 57, 58, 59
Fruchtgemüse 128
Fruchtholz 62
Fruchtkapsel 60
Fruchtknoten 56
Fruchtknotenfach 58
Fruchtkörper 50
Fruchtwand 58, 60
Frühling 38
Frühlingsäquinoktium 38
Frühlingszwiebel 124
Fuchs 88
Fuchsschwanz 226
Fugendüse 209
Fugenkelle 216
Führerhaus 401
Führerkabine 397, 398, 399, 400, 401
Führerraum 395
Führerstand 376, 377
Führungsgriff 227, 229
Führungsgruppe 522
Führungsmotorrad 522
Führungsrille 510
Führungsring 536
Führungsschiene 353
Führungsschiene, Fahrkorb 287
Führungsständer 396
Führungsturm 345
Full House 468
Fullback 482, 485
Füllfederhalter 312
Füllmengenanzeige 346
Füllrohr 196
Fülltür 192
Füllung 185
Fumarole 28
Fundament 187
Fundamentstreifen 187
Fünf 427
Fünf-Kräuter-Gewürz 139
Fünfeck, regelmäßiges 429
Fünfhundert 427
Fünfzig 427
Fungizid 47
Funkantenne 382, 384, 386, 387, 394, 525
Funkenstrecke 359
Funkgerät 457
Funkmaus 332
Funkmeldeempfänger 454
Funktionsanzeige 310
Funktionsdisplay 310
Funktionsschalter 320
Funktionstasten 328, 330, 423, 442, 443
Funktionstasten, programmierbare 443
Funktionswahltaste 327
Funkübertragungssystem 10
Furche 118
Fusilli 146
Fusselfilter 213
Fuß 62, 73, 91, 92, 93, 94, 95, 202, 204, 206, 229, 236, 247, 260, 302, 305, 332, 421, 519, 537
Fuß, geschwungener 200
Fuß, Handgelenksgewicht 500
Fußball 480
Fußballschuh 480
Fußballspieler 480
Fußboden 193
Fußbohrung 305
Fußende 204
Fußgängerampel 434
Fußgängerbrücke 375, 379

Fußgängerknopf 434
Fußgängerüberweg 434
Fußgelenk 86
Fußgestell 201
Fußgewölbearterie 102
Fußholz 185
Fußnagelschere 265
Fußplatte 227
Fußraste, vordere 367, 368
Fußraummatte 356
Fußriemen 501
Fußrückenarterie 102
Fußschlaufe 519
Fußschutz 459
Fußstütze 205, 224, 369, 467, 473, 501
Fußtritt 305
Fußweg 436
Futter 240, 244, 245, 262, 274, 509
Futtergetreide 122

G

G 298
Gabel 8, 167, 396, 525, 531
Gabelarm 396
Gabelbaum 519
Gabeln, Beispiele 168
Gabelstapler 396
Gabun 451
Galaxie 6
Galerie 285, 292, 412, 447
Galerie, Große 278
Gallenblase 106
Galopp 83
Gambia 451
Gammastrahlen 418
Ganasche 83
Gang 28, 120, 278
Gang, absteigender 278
Gang, aufsteigender 278
Gangarten 83
Ganglion, symphatisches 109
Gans 81, 155
Gänseei 155
Ganymed 2
ganze Note 299
ganze Pause 299
Ganzjahresreifen 358
ganzrandig 55
Garage 182
Garam Masala 139
Garderobe 188, 293, 443
Garderobier 290
Garnball 477
Garnele 158
Garnierspritze 172
Garten 280
Garten-Sauerampfer 127
Gartenarbeit 216, 230
Gartenhandschuhe 232
Gartenkresse 127
Gartenkürbis 128
Gartenschlauch 236
Gartenspritze 236
Gartenteich 230
Gartenweg 182, 230
Gas 405, 414
Gasbehälter 396
Gasflasche, medizinische 464
Gashebel 235, 368
Gasherd 210
Gasleitung 434
Gasmaske 459
Gasöl 405
Gaspedal 354
Gasstromregulierung 529
Gästeeingang 438
Gästegarderobe 438
Gästehnerhals 112
Gästetoiletten 438
Gaststätte 436
Gaszug 237
Gaumen, harter 116, 117
Gaumen, weicher 116, 117
Gaumenbogen, vorderer 116
Gaumenmandel 118
Gebäk 185, 279
Gebärmutter 112, 113
Gebärmutterhals 112
Gebäude, öffentliches 25
Gebel 185, 279
Gebirge, Transantarktisches 15
Gebirgsbach 24
Gebirgskette 24, 26
Gebirgsmassiv 24

Gebiss, menschliches 101
Gebläse 213
geboren 426
gebräuchliche Bezeichnungen 57, 58, 59
gebrauchte Spritzen, Behälter 457
gebrauchtes Material, Lagerraum 462, 464
gebuchtet 55
gedeckter Wehrgang 282
Gedenktafel 447
Gedränge 483, 484, 485
Gedrängehalbspieler 482
gedruckte Schaltung 417
Gefahrenbereich 499
Gefängnis 469
Geflügel 155
Geflügelschere 173
Gefrierbeutel 162
gefrierender Regen 41
Gefrierfach 211
Gefrierschrank 120, 164, 438
Gefriertruhe 211
Gegenauslegen 397
Gegenauslegerballast 397
Gegengewicht 8, 287, 345, 397, 400, 401
Gegengewichtsführung 287
Gegenleiste 115
Gegenlichtblende 314
Gegensprechanlage 380
gegenwärtige Wetterlage 39
Gehäuse 72, 180, 199, 208, 212, 213, 218, 225, 228, 229, 237, 271, 304, 318, 424
Gehäuse, hinteres 7
Gehäusedach 286
Gehäuselüfter 329
Gehfalte 253
Gehgestell 466
Gehhilfen 466
Gehirn 71
Gehirn-Rückenmark-Flüssigkeit 110
Gehkrücke 466
Gehörgang 115, 116
Gehörgang, äußerer 100
Gehörknöchelchen 116
Gehörschutz 458
Gehrmaß 226
Gehrungssäge 226
Gehrungsschneidlade 226
Gehweg 183
Geier 80
Geigenfamilie 295
gekerbt 55
gekerbtes Scherenblatt 270
gekochter Schinken 156
Gekröse 154
gekrümmte Greifbacke 222
Geländefahrzeug 524
Geländemotorrad 369
Geländemotorrad, 4x4 369
Geländer 188, 189, 191, 344, 526
Geländerstab 191
Geländewagen 347
Gelatinekapsel 467
Gelb 418
gelbe Zucchini 129
gelber Ball 503
gelber Fleck 119
gelber Paprika 128
gelbes Licht 434
Geld 441
Geldausgabeautomat 437, 442
Geldbeutel 275
Geldbeutel für Münzen 275
Geldscheinausgabe 442
Geldscheinfach 274
Gelenk 240, 355, 363, 400, 511
Gelenkbus 363
Gelenkhöcker 99
Gelenkschäkel 521
gemahlener Pfeffer 139
gemäßigter Wald 44
gemeine Erdkröte 75
gemeiner Tüpfelfarn 52
gemeines Widertonmoos 51
gemeinsame Hüftarterie 102, 107
gemeinsame Hüftvene 107
gemeinsamer Fingerstrecker 97
gemeinsamer Wadenbeinnerv 108
Gemeinschaftskarte 469
Gemüse 120, 124
Gemüsebürste 173
Gemüsegarten 122, 182
Gemüseterrine 166
Gemüsezwiebel 124

ASTRONOMIE > 2-25;   ERDE > 26-71;   PFLANZENREICH >72-89;   TIERREICH > 90-143;   MENSCH > 144-177;   NAHRUNGSMITTEL UND KÜCHE > 178-241;   HAUS > 242-295;
HEIMWERKEN UND GARTENARBEIT > 296-333;   KLEIDUNG > 334-371;   PERSÖNLICHE AUSSTATTUNG > 372-391;   KUNST UND ARCHITEKTUR > 392-465;   KOMMUNIKATION UND BÜROTECHNIK > 466-535;
TRANSPORT UND FAHRZEUGE > 536-643;   ENERGIE > 644-677;   WISSENSCHAFT > 678-705;   GESELLSCHAFT > 706-785;   SPORT UND SPIELE > 786-920

Generator 402, 408, 413
Generator, Elektrizitätserzeugung 408
Generatoreinheit 407
Genicklasche 458
Geographie 14
Geologie 26
Geometrie 428
geometrische Formen 428
Georgien 452
geothermische Energie,
  Elektrizitätserzeugung 402
geothermisches Feld 402
Gepäck 276
Gepäckanhänger 277
Gepäckaufbewahrung 374
Gepäckausgabe 390
Gepäckcontainer 383
Gepäckraum 362, 376, 395
Gepäckroller 277
Gepäckschließfächer 374
Gepäckschnur 277
Gepäckträger 361, 369, 370, 523
Gepard 89
gepolsterte Korbstütze 489
gepolsterter Sockel 489
gerade Greifbacke 222
gerader Bauchmuskel 96
gerader Rock 253
gerader Schenkelmuskel 96
gerades Rippenbündchen 247
Geradseite 385
Geräte 472
Geräte zur Erdbewegung 233
Geräte, verschiedene 231
Geräteanschluss 271
Gerätefach 376
Geräteraum 444
Geräteschuppen 122
Geräteturnanlage 496
Geräteturnen 496
geräumige Tasche 276
Gericht 440
Gerichtsgebäude 432
Gerichtskanzlei 440
Gerichtssaal 440
Gerichtsschreiber, Tisch 440
geröstete Kaffeebohnen 148
Gerste 61, 143
Geruchssinn 116
Geruchsverschluss 194, 196, 197
gesägt 55
Gesamtansicht 186
Gesamtergebnis, Anzeigetafel 496
Gesäß 93, 95, 111, 112
Gesäßmuskel, großer 97
Gesäßnerv 108
Gesäßspalte 95
Gesäßtasche 246
Geschäft 432
Geschäftsbeleg 443
Geschäftsviertel 430, 432
geschaltete Steckdose 322
Geschenkwarenladen 436
Geschirr 166
Geschirrspüler 164
Geschirrspülmaschine 214
Geschirrtuch 215
Geschlechtsorgane, männliche 111
Geschlechtsorgane, weibliche 112
geschlossene Traube 57
geschlossener Gesichtsschutz 454
geschlossenes Atemschutzsystem 454
Geschmacksknospe 118
Geschmacksrezeptoren 118
Geschmackssinn 116
geschnittener Nagel 220
geschütztes Leerzeichen 330
Geschwindigkeitsregelung 176, 177
Geschwindigkeitsregler 237, 287
Geschwindigkeitswähler 176
Geschworenenbank 440
Geschworenenraum 440
geschwungener Fuß 200
Gesellschaft 430
Gesicht 91, 92
Gesichtsmaske 478, 486
Gesichtsschutz 506
Gesichtsschutz, geschlossener 454
Gesichtsschutzmaske 507
Gesichtsstück 459
Gesims 183, 185
gespaltene Erbsen 130
gespaltene Zunge 76
gespreizter Kragen 245
Gestänge 55
gestanztes Loch 240, 246, 263

Gestein, undurchlässiges 403
Gestell 205, 219, 273, 460
gestorben 64
Gesundheit 460
Gesundheitsorganisation 335
Getränke 120
Getränkeautomat 346, 463
Getränkedose 163
Getränkekarton 163
Getränkekarton, kleiner 163
Getreide 61, 143
Getreideprodukte 144
Getreidesee 32
Getreidesilo 381
getrennte Sammlung 49
Getriebe 212, 350
getrocknete Chilis 139
gewachsener Boden 342
Gewände 285
Gewebe-Einstellskala 208
Geweih (gezogener Lauf) 534
Gewerbegebiet 431
Gewicht 422, 423, 500
Gewichte 501
Gewichtheben 500
Gewichthebergürtel 500
Gewichtheberschuh 500
gewimpert 55
Gewinde 221, 503
Gewindegang 228
Gewindeschaft 223
Gewitterwolken 43
gewöhnlicher Nagel 220
gewöhnlicher Würfel 468
Gewölbe 284
Gewölbekörper 109
gewölbter Zentralbereich 6
Gewürz, Fünf-Kräuter 139
Gewürze 138
Gewürzmischung, Cajun 139
Gewürznelke 138
Geysir 28
gezahnte Greifbacke 222
Ghana 451
Ghee 150
Gibbon 91
Gibraltar, Straße 18
Giebel 163, 182
Giebeldach 189
Giebeldecke 189
Giebeldreieck 279
Giebelständer 187
Gierbewegung 395
Gießbrause 236
Gießgerät 236
Gießkanne 236
Gießpistole 236
Gift-Leitfurche 76
Giftdrüse 76
Giftkanal 76
Giftklaue 70
Giftpilz 52
Giftschlange, äußere Merkmale 76
Giftzahn 76
Gingkonuss 133
Gipfel 29, 512
Gipfel, Hütte 512
Gipfelhütte 512
Gipsbinden 461
Gipsraum 463
Giraffe 85
Gitarre, akustische 302
Gitarre, elektrische 303
Gitter 279, 296, 318
Gitterbett 205
Gittereinsatz 174
Glanzschicht 114
Glas 273, 529
Glas, Sortierung 49
Glasabdeckung 410, 411
Glasdach 188, 435
Gläser 165
Glasflasche 163
Glasgehäuse 423
Glaskolben, oberer 181
Glaskolben, unterer 181
Glaskörper 119
Glasmalerei 285
Glasnudeln 147
Glasplatte 211
Glasscheibe 419
Glasüberdachung 374
gleich 427
gleich oder größer als 427
gleich oder kleiner als 427
Gleichgewichtslage 418
Gleichstrom-Netzkabel 336

Gleichtaste 337
Gleis 374, 378, 432
Gleiskette 398
Gleiskettenschlepper 398
Gleiskreuzung 375
Gleisnummer 374
Gleitfuge 222
Gleitphase 514
Gleitschuh 227
Gleitschutz 511
Gletscher 30, 32, 44
Gletschersee 32
Gletscherspalte 30
Gletscherzunge 30
Gliedmaßen, obere 103
Gliedmaßen, untere 103
Glimmlampe 217
globale Erwärmung 46
Globus 444
Glockenband 309
Glockendichtung 196
Glockenstube 284, 285
Glockenturm 285, 446
Glottis 76
Glühbirne 217
Glühfaden 199
Glühlampe 199, 416
Glukose 54
Gnocchi 146
Gnomon 424
Go 470
Goldbrasse 159
Golf 24
Golf von Aden 19, 20
Golf von Alaska 16
Golf von Bengalen 19
Golf von Guinea 20
Golf von Kalifornien 16
Golf von Mexiko 16
Golf von Oman 19
Golf von Panama 17
Golf, Persischer 19
Golfball 505
Golfhandschuh 505
Golfplatz 430, 504
Golfschuhe 505
Golfspiel 504
Golftasche 505
Golfwagen 505
Golgi-Apparat 50, 66
Gonade 73
Gong 295, 309
Gorgonzola 151
Gorilla 91
Gorilla, äußere Merkmale 91
gotischer Dom 284
Gottesanbeterin 69
Graben, Kermadec-Tonga 34
Graben, Peru-Chile 34
Graben, Puerto-Rico 34
Grabgabel 233
Grabkammer der Königin 278
Grabkammer des Königs 278
Grabschaufel 233
Grad 428
Grad Celsius 424, 426
Grad Fahrenheit 424
Gradeinteilung 533
Gradnetz 22
Granatapfel 136
Grand Canyon 16
Grand-Prix-Rennmaschine 525
Granitschicht 26
Granne 61
Granulation 4
Grapefruit 134
Grapefruitmesser 169
Graphitstift 312
Grasfang 237
grasgrüner Täubling 123
Grasland 44
Grat 29
graue Substanz 109, 110
Grauwal 90
Greif- und Spannwerkzeuge 222
Greifbacke, gekrümmte 222
Greifbacke, gerade 222
Greiffinger 91
Grenada 449
Griechenland 450
griechischer Tempel 279
griechischer Tempel, Grundriss 279
griechisches Brot 144
griechisches Theater 278
Grieß 144

Griff 167, 170, 176, 177, 178, 179, 180,
  192, 204, 208, 210, 211, 215, 216,
  217, 219, 222, 223, 225, 226, 227,
  229, 231, 235, 236, 237, 269, 270,
  271, 272, 273, 274, 275, 276, 277,
  301, 341, 466, 477, 478, 492, 493,
  494, 500, 505, 510, 515, 531, 535,
  536
Griff, ausziehbarer 274
Griff, isolierter 217
Griff, wärmeisolierter 179
Griff, zusätzlicher 228
Griff- und Wurfbeispiele 499
Griffband 526
Griffbrett 296, 301, 303
Griffel 56, 57, 58, 60
Griffelfortsatz 100
Griffhebel für S-Bogen 306
Griffkamm 268
Grifftechniken 493
Griffteil 503
Grill, Raclette 179
Grillfläche 179
Grillplatte 179
Grillrost 210
Gripzange 222
grobe Salami 156
Grobeinstellung 421
grobes Salz 141
Grobregler für Dateneingabe 310
Grobtrieb 421
Grönland 16
Grönlandsee 14
groß gefleckter Katzenhai 158
große Armdecken 78
Große Australische Bucht 15
Große Außensichel 499
große Einkaufstasche 276
Große Galerie 278
große Handdecken 78
Große Innensichel 499
große Klinge 531
große Nackenrolle 204
große Rosenvene 102
große Schamlippe 112, 113
Große Sandwüste 15
Große Seen 16
Große Victoriawüste 15
größer als 427
großer Brustmuskel 96
großer Gesäßmuskel 97
großer Nasenflügelknorpel 117
großer Oberschenkelanzieher 97
großer Rundmuskel 97
Großes Barriereriff 15
großes Kettenblatt 372
Großformatkamera 315
Großhirn 109
Großrad 467
Großraumwagen 376
Großschot 520
Großschriftfeststellung 330
Großschriftfeststellungstaste 330
Großschriftumschaltung 330
Großsegel 520
Grubenorgan 76
Grün 418, 504
Grünalge 51
Grünanlage 435
Grundgestein 27
Grundierung, flüssige 266
Grundlinie 491
Grundlinienrichter 491
Grundmoräne 30
Grundplatte 511
Grundriss 279, 285
Grundstücksgrenze 182
Grundwasser, eingeschlossenes 402
Grundwasserspiegel 31, 48
grüne Bohne 131
grüne Erbsen 130
grüne Tagliatelle 146
grüner Ball 503
grüner Paprika 128
grüner Pfeffer 138
grüner Tee 148
grünes Licht 434
Grünkohl 126
Grünstrahl 318
Gruppenwahl 330
Gruyèrekäse 151
Guatemala 448
Guave 137
Guinea 451
Guinea, Golf 20
Guinea-Bissau 451

Gummiband 204, 246
Gummihöschen 260
Gummikappe 466
Gummipfropfen 460
Gummiring 197
Gummischlauch 460
Gummispannring 528, 529
Gummistiefel 454
Gummistöpsel 219
Gurke 128
Gurt 205
Gurtbefestigung 303
Gurtbogen 284
Gürtel 244, 248, 499
Gürtelband 246
Gürtelclip 327
Gürtelschlaufe 246, 248, 531
Gürtelschnalle 246
Gürtelspitze 246
Gurtschließe 353
Gusseker 282
Gutenberg-Diskontinuität 26
Güterbahnhof 375, 430
Güterwagen 375
Güterwagen, Beispiele 377
Guyana 448
Guyot 33
gynäkologischer Untersuchungsraum 463

H

H 298
Haar 93, 95, 114, 301
Haaraufrichter 114
Haarbalg 114
Haarbürsten 268
Haarclip 268
Haarfärbemittel 267
Haarglätter 269
Haarklemme 268
Haarliftkamm 268
Haarpflege 268
Haarschaft 114
Haarschneidekamm 268
Haarschneider 269
Haarschneidescheren 270
Haarspange 268
Haarspülung 267
Haarstecker 268
Haarzwiebel 114
Hachse 152, 153
Hack 515
Hafen 381, 431
Hafenbahn 381
Hafenfähre 381
Hafenzollamt 381
Hafer 61, 143
Hafermehl 144
Haferwurz 129
Haftgurtband 260
Haftorgan 51
Haftscheibe 75
Hagelschnur 79
Hahn 81, 534
Hai, äußere Merkmale 74
Haiti 448
Haken 217, 225, 364, 397, 423, 460,
  502
Hakenbogen 538
Hakenbogentiefe 538
Hakenhalteöse 536
Hakeninnenweite 538
Hakenspitze 538
Hakenverriegelung 186
Hakler 482
Halbbrille 273
halbe Note 299
halbe Pause 299
halbes Heft 169
Halbinsel 24
Halbinsel, Antarktische 15
Halbinsel, Arabische 19
Halbinsel, Iberische 18
Halbinsel, Kamtschatka 19
Halbinsel, Kola 18
Halbinsel, Skandinavische 18
Halbinsel, Yucatan 16
Halbkreis 428, 488
Halbkugel 429
Halbmond (erstes Viertel) 5
Halbmond (letztes Viertel) 5
Halbmumienschlafsack 530
Halbsäule, dorische 281
Halbsäule, ionische 281
Halbsäule, korinthische 281
Halbschale 259

ASTRONOMIE > 2-25;   ERDE > 26-71;   PFLANZENREICH >72-89;   TIERREICH > 90-143;   MENSCH > 144-177;   NAHRUNGSMITTEL UND KÜCHE > 178-241;   HAUS > 242-295
HEIMWERKEN UND GARTENARBEIT > 296-333;   KLEIDUNG > 334-371;   PERSÖNLICHE AUSSTATTUNG > 372-391;   KUNST UND ARCHITEKTUR > 392-465;   KOMMUNIKATION UND BÜROTECHNIK > 466-535;
TRANSPORT UND FAHRZEUGE > 536-643;   ENERGIE > 644-677;   WISSENSCHAFT > 678-705;   GESELLSCHAFT > 706-785;   SPORT UND SPIELE > 786-920

Halbschatten 4, 5
Halbsehnenmuskel 97
Halbspieler 474
Halbstiefel 240
Halbvolleyball 490
Halfter 456
Halm 270
Halo 6
Halogen-Tischleuchte 206
Hals 53, 76, 83, 93, 94, 95, 101, 111, 167, 297, 301, 302, 303, 318, 492, 519
Halsausschnitt 247
Halskette in Matineelänge 264
Halskette in Opernlänge 264
Halskette, mehrreihige 264
Halsketten 264
halsnaher Ausschnitt 260
Halsschlagader 102
Halsschutz 476
Halstalje 520
Halsumklammerung 499
Halswirbel 99
Haltebügel 467
Haltegriff 361, 363, 455
Haltegriffe 499
Haltemutter 536, 537
Halteplatte 514
Halter 199
Halterung 9, 371, 423
Haltestange 364
Hammer 116, 220, 236, 304, 472
Hammer mit runder Bahn 220
Hammerhalter 225
Hammerleiste 304
Hamster 82
Hand 91, 93, 95, 115
Hand-Funksprechgerät 456
Hand-Gehrungssäge 226
Handauflage 332
Handballenauflage, abnehmbare 330
Handbeuger der Ellenseite 96, 97
Handblasebalg 461
Handbramse 195
Handbremse 350
Handbremshebel 354
Handdecken, große 78
Handdecken, mittlere 78
Handelsunternehmen 335
Handfeuerlöscher 454
Handfläche 115, 477
handförmig 55
Handgabel 232
Handgelenk 93, 95, 115
Handgelenkpolster 486
Handgelenksbandage 500
Handgelenkschützer 527
Handgriff 229, 286, 297
Handhabung 396
Handheld-Computer 337
Handkreissäge 227
Handkultivator 233
Handkurbel 225
Handlampe 217
Handlauf 191, 287
Handlöser 511
Handmuskeltrainer 500
Handrührgerät 176
Handschellentasche 456
Handschlaufe 510, 514
Handschuh 10, 477, 478, 506, 508, 513, 514, 522, 525
Handschuh-Außenseite 243
Handschuh-Innenseite 243
Handschuhe 243
Handschuhfach 354
Handschuhspender 464
Handschutz 235, 525
Handschwingen 78
Handstand 518
Handstange 380
Handstaubsauger 209
Handstrecker der Ellenseite 97
Handstrecker, kurzer 97
Handstrecker, langer 97
Handtaschen 275
Handtuch 267
Handtuchhalter 195
Handwaage 422
Handwerkzeuge 232
Handwurzel 477
Handy 327
Hängebrücke 344
Hängegletscher 30
Hängeleuchte 206

Hängemappe 340
Hänger 344
Hantel 500, 501
Hantelstange 501
Hardboots 513
Harfe 302
Harfen 295
Harissasoße 141
Harmonikatür 286
Harnapparat 107
Harnblase 107, 111, 112
Harnleiter 107
Harnröhre 107, 111, 112
Harnröhrengang 111
harte Kontaktlinse 272
harte Rückenmarkshaut 109, 110
harter Gaumen 116, 117
Hartkäse 151
Hartkäse 154
Hartplatz (Zement) 492
Hase 82, 154
Haselnuss 133
Haselnuss, Längsschnitt 60
Hasentiere 82
Hasentiere, Beispiele 82
Hat-Switch 332
Haube 209
Hauptanschluss 198
Hauptapsis 285
Hauptbronchus 105
Hauptdeck 385
Haupteingang 188, 435, 445, 465
Hauptentlüftungssteigrohr 194
Hauptfahrwerk 393
Hauptfeld 522
Hauptgleis 375
Hauptlautsprecher 321
Hauptlinienrichter 485
Hauptmaßstab 425
Haupträume 188
Hauptschalter 198, 315, 320
Hauptschiedsrichter 475
Hauptschlot 28
Hauptschwert 519
Hauptschwerteinzug 519
Hauptspiegel 7, 9
Hauptspielzüge 470
Hauptspuren 343
Hauptstadt 23
Hauptständer 367
Hauptstiel 62
Haupttransformator 376
Haupttriebwerk 13
Hauptunterkunft 512
Hauptvorhang 292, 293
Hauptwarteraum 465
Hauptwurzel 53
Hauptzeitnehmer 516
Hauptzylinder 357
Haus 182, 469, 515
Haus, einstöckiges 289
Haus, Teile 185
Haus, zweistöckiges 289
Hausanschluss 198
Hausantenne 316
Hausboot 385
Hauseinrichtung 200
Häuserformen in der Stadt 289
Hausflur, äußerer 280
Haushaltsartikel 120
Haushaltsgegenstände 215
Haushaltsgeräte 176, 208
Haushaltsgeräte, verschiedene 180
Haushaltsmehl 144
Hauskleid 252
Hausmeisterraum 443
Hausmüll 47, 48
Haustür 185
Hauszelt 529
Haut 57, 59, 110, 114
Hautnerv, seitlicher 108
Hautoberfläche 114
Hebel 18, 197, 222, 265, 368
Hebel für den Klemmbügel 269
Hebel-Korkenzieher 170
Hebeleisen 220
Hebeleiste der unteren Schutzhaube 227
Heber 400
Hebestück 403
Hebewerk 403
Hecht 160
Hechtsprungstellung 518
Heck 176, 386, 393, 519
Hecke 183, 230
Heckenschere 234
Heckleuchten 352
Heckpropeller 384

Heckrotor 395
Hecksporn 395
Heft 221
Heft, halbes 169
Hefter 339, 341
Heftklammern 341
Heftpflaster 461
Heidelbeere 132
Heilbutt 161
Heimkino 321
Heimtierbedarf 121
Heimwerken 216
Heimwerkerladen 436
Heißluftaustritt 192
Heißluftpistole 219
heißversiegelte Folie 163
Heizelement 213, 214, 218
Heizöl 405
Heizspirale 210
Heizstrahler 529
Heizung 192, 386
Heizungsgitter 380
Helix 429
Helixende 115
Helligkeitsregelung 10
Helligkeitsregler 329
Helm 10, 476, 478, 508, 513, 522, 524, 525, 526, 527
Helmbohne 130
Hemd 245, 473
Hemdblusenkleid 252
Hemdchen 260
Hemdhose 247
Hemisphäre, nördliche 21
Hemisphäre, östliche 21
Hemisphäre, südliche 21
Hemisphäre, westliche 21
Hemisphären 21
Henkel 215
heranwachsende Nahrungsvakuole 66
herausklappbare Schreibplatte 203
herausnehmbare Festplatte 333
Herbizid 47
Herbst 38
Herbstäquinoktium 38
Herd 27
Herdkante 210
Herdtiefe 27
Hering 159, 528, 529
Heringskönig 161
Heringsschlaufe 528, 529
Herrenhalbschuh 240
Herrenhandschuhe 243
Herrenkleidung 244
Herrenkopfbedeckungen 238
Herrenring 264
Herrenschuhe 240
Herrentasche 276
Herrentoilette 294, 439
Hertz 426
Heruntertransformation der Spannung 402, 413
Herz 71, 73, 104, 105, 154, 468, 492
Herzbeutel 105
Herzförmig 55
Herzkammer, linke 103, 104
Herzkammer, rechte 103, 104
Herzmuschel 157
Herzmuskel 104
Herzwandschicht 104
heterotrophe Organismen 45
Heuboden 122
HiFi-System 325
Hijiki 123
Hilfe 121
Hilfslinie 298
Hilfsschwert 519
Himalaja 19
Himbeere 132
Himbeere im Querschnitt 59
Himmel, stürmischer 41
Himmelsbedeckung 39
Himmelskörper 2
Hinterbein 67, 68, 75, 201
Hinterbühne 293
hintere Augenkammer 119
hintere Felgenbremse 370
hintere Fontanelle 100
hintere Klappe 3
hintere Nervenwurzel 109, 110
hintere Schaufel 399
hintere Seitenfontanelle 100

hinterer Balken 422
hinterer knöcherner Bogengang 116
hinterer Kotflügel 369
hinterer Schließmuskel 73
hinterer Stoßdämpfer 367
hinterer Streben 370
hinterer Tragflügel 387
hinterer Umwerfer 370, 372
hinteres Auspuffrohr 351
hinteres Gehäuse 7
hinteres Trittbrett 455
Hinterflügel 67
Hintergrundbeleuchtung 337
Hinterhauptbein 100
Hinterhauptmuskel 97
Hinterhauptsbein 99, 100
Hinterhorn 109
Hinterkappe 262
Hinterleib 67, 68, 70, 71
Hinterleibssegment 67
Hinterpartie 536
Hinterzehe 78, 79
Hippe 234
Hirn 154
Hirnanhangdrüse 109
Hirnnerven 108
Hirse 61, 143
Hitzeschild 12
Hobel 229
Hobeleisen 229
Hobeleisen-Stellschraube 229
Hobelschar 401
Hobelzahn 235
Hochaltar 446
Hochdruckgebiet 39, 43
Hochebene 29
Hochgebirge 40
Hochgeschwindigkeitszug 376
Hochland 5
Hochlandklimate 40
Hochschrank 164
Hochsilo 122
Hochspannungsleitung 402, 413
Hochsprung 473
höchste Karte 468
Hochstuhl 205
Hochtöner 324
Hochtransformation der Spannung 402, 408
Hochwasserentlastungswehr 406
Hochwasserentlastungswehr, Verschluss 406
Hocker 164, 201
Hockey 471
Hockeyskate 527
Hoden 71, 111
Hodensack 92, 111
Hof 122
Hogline 515
hohe Rippe 152
hohe Wolken 42
Höhen-Tonabnehmer 303
Höheneinstellung 420
Höhenfeineinstellung 8, 9
Höhenfeststeller 8, 9
Höhenflosse 393, 395
Höhenlagen, Vegetationsbild 44
Höhenregler 303, 322, 325
Höhenruder 393
Höhenskala 37
Höhenverstellskala 227
Höhenverstellung 209, 501
Höhle 31, 35
Höhlenraum, trocken liegender 31
Hohlhandmuskel, kurzer 96
Hohlhandmuskel, langer 96
Hohlvene, obere 102, 103, 104
Hohlvene, untere 102, 103, 104, 107
Hoisinsoße 140
Hollandrad 373
Holm 219, 392, 466
Hologramm, metallisiertes 441
Holzbeheizung 192
Holzhammer 220
Holzkiste 162
Holzleibung 186
Holzohr 123
Holzschläger 505
Holzträger 193
Holzunterbau 190
homogenisierte Milch 150
Honduras 448

Honig 149
Honigbiene 68
Honigbiene, äußere Merkmale 68
Honigmelone 135
Höraufsatz 460
Hörer 327
horizontale Bodenbewegung 27
horizontale Einstellung 329
horizontaler Zug 470
horizontales Schiebefenster 287
Horizontalseismograph 27
Hörmuschel 327
Horn 455, 519
Hörnchennudeln 146
Hörnerv 116
Hornhaut 119, 419
Hornisse 69
Hornschicht 114
Hornschnabel 76
Hornschuppe 79
Hors-d'Oeuvre-Schale 166
Hose 83, 246, 263, 476, 480, 486, 499, 500, 506, 525
Hose, kurze 261, 483, 488
Hosen, Beispiele 254
Hosenbluse 255
Hosenbund 246
Hosenrock 253
Hosenschlitz 246
Hosenträger 246
Hotel 432, 439, 469, 512
Hotelreservierungsschalter 390
Hotelzimmer 439
Hubarm 399
Hubarmzylinder 399
Hubble-Weltraumteleskop 7, 37
Hubbrücke 345
Hubgebläse 383
Hubkette 396
Hubschrauber 395
Hubwinde 397
Hubzahlvorwahl 227
Hubzylinder 364, 397, 455
Hudson Bay 16
Huf 83
Hufeisenmontierung 7
Hüft-Becken-Nerv 108
Hüft-Leisten-Nerv 108
Hüftarterie, gemeinsame 102, 107
Hüftarterie, innere 102, 103, 107
Hüfte 93, 95
Hüftgurt 532
Huftiere 83
Huftiere, Beispiele 84
Hüftlochnerv 108
Hüftpolster 486
Hüftvene, gemeinsame 107
Hüftvene, innere 103
Hüftwurf 499
Hügel 29
Huhn 81, 155
Hühnerei 155
Hühnerstall 122
Huitzilopochtli-Tempel 283
Hülle 60, 505, 531
Hüllen, Wan-tan 147
Hülse 61, 534
Hülse, Schnitt 60
Hülsenfrüchte 130
Humeruskopf 99
Hummel 69
Hummer 71, 158
Hummer, Anatomie 71
Hummer, äußere Merkmale 71
Hummus 140
Hund 86
Hund, äußere Merkmale 86
Hunderassen 86
Hundert 427
Hundshai 158
Hupe 354, 368
Hürdenlauf 472
Hurrikan 43
Hustensirup 467
Hut 52
Hutband 238
Hutmutter 223
Hüttenkäse 150
Hyäne 88
Hydrant 434
Hydranntenanschluss 455
Hydraulik 396
Hydraulik-Heber 361
Hydraulik-Hochlöffelbagger 400
hydraulische Scheibenbremse 522
hydraulischer Widerstand 501

Hydrosphäre 44
Hyperlinks 334

I

Iapetus 3
Iberische Halbinsel 18
identisch 427
Identitätsband 264
Idiotenhügel 512
Iglu 288
Igluzelt 529
Ileum 106
Imbussschrauben 221
Impluvium 280
Impressum 313
Impulslaser, Rubin 420
Impulsregner 236
Inbound-Linie 484
Incisura intertragica 115
Indexanzeigeregler 315
Indien 453
Indisch-Antarktischer Rücken 34
Indisch-Australische Platte 27
Indischer Ozean 14, 15, 19, 20
indisches Fladenbrot 145
indisches Naanbrot 145
Indonesien 19, 453
Industrie 335
Industrie, petrochemische 405
Industrieabfälle 47, 48
Industriegebiet 431
industrielle Telekommunikation 317
industrielle Verschmutzung 47
Infiltration 45, 47
Informationsschalter 390, 442, 463, 512
Informationsstand 437
Informationsverbreitung 335
Infrarotschnittstelle 336, 337
Infrarotstrahlung 46, 418
Infusionsständer 464
Ingwer 139
Inhaber, Name 441
Inhaber, Unterschrift 441
Inhalt 313
Injektionsbohrung 402
Inlineskating 527
Innenbeleuchtung 380
Innenbrett 469
Innenfeld 474
Innenfläche 243
Innengewinde 537
innengezahnte Fächerscheibe 222
Innenhof 447
Innenkreis 515
Innenlippe 73
Innenohr 116
Innenohrvorhof 116
Innenstadt 431, 432
Innensteckhülse 536
Innenstiefel 511, 527
Innentasche 277
Innentür 211
Innenverteidiger 481
Innenzelt 528, 529
innere Drosselvene 102
innere Hüftarterie 102, 103, 107
innere Hüftvene 103
innere Kuppelhülle 7
innere Oberschenkelkondyle 99
innere Planeten 3
Innereien 154
innerer Kern 26
innerer Oberarmgelenkhöcker 99
innerer Schenkelmuskel 96
Insekten 67
Insekten, Beispiele 69
Insektenfresser 79
Insel 24, 343
Inselkette 33
Instrumentalgruppierungen, Beispiele 300
Instrumente 7, 523
Instrumente, elektronische 310
Instrumente, wissenschaftliche 13
Instrumententafel 355, 366, 368
Integral 427
integrierter Helm 525
integrierte Schaltung 417
integrierte Schaltung mit Gehäuse 417
Intelsat 317
intensive Kultur 46, 47
intensive Landwirtschaft 46, 48
Intensivstation 464
Interlobärspalt, schräger 105
internationale Raumstation 11
internationales Einheitensystem 426

interne Modemschnittstelle 329, 336
Internet 334
Internet-Nutzer 334
Internet-Nutzung 335
Internet-Provider 335
Internet-Tasten 330
Intervalle 298
Interview 313
Intrusivgesteine 26
Io 2
Ionenschweif, Plasmaschweif 6
ionische Halbsäule 281
Irak 452
Iran 452
Iris 119
Irisch Moos 123
Irische See 18
irisches Brot 145
Irland 449
Isba 288
Ischiasnerv 108
Ischiasnerv, kleiner 108
Island 18, 450
Isobare 39
Isolator 359
Isoliermaterial 214
Isolierraum 462
Isolierstoff 190
isolierte Klinge 217
isolierter Griff 217
Isolierung 410
Isoseiste 27
Israel 452
ist annähernd gleich 427
ist äquivalent mit 427
ist gleich 427
ist gleich oder größer als 427
ist gleich oder kleiner als 427
ist größer als 427
ist identisch mit 427
ist kleiner als 427
ist nicht identisch mit 427
ist nicht parallel zu 428
ist parallel zu 428
ist senkrecht zu 428
ist ungleich 427
Italien 451

J

Jaboticaba 137
Jacke 251, 499
Jacke, dreiviertellange 248
Jacken 248, 251, 254
Jackett 244
Jackfrucht 136
Jagdkappe 238
Jagen 534
Jaguar 89
Jahresring 63
Jahreszahl 441
Jahreszeiten 38
Jakobsmuschel 157
Jalapeño-Chili 139
Jalousie 186
Jalousiefenster 287
Jalousieschwellter 305
Jamaika 448
Jamaikapfeffer 138
Japan 19, 453
Japangraben 34
japanischer Rettich 129
japanisches Experimentiermodul 11
Japanisches Meer 19
Jarlsberg 151
Javagraben 34
Jazzband 300
Jazzbesen 309
Jeans 254
Jemen 452
Jetski 523
Jicama 124
Jocharm 297
Jochbein 98, 100
Jochweite 344
Joggingschuh 262
Joghurt 150
Johannisbeere 132
Johannisbeere, schwarze 132
Joker 468
Jolle 521
Jordanien 452
Joule 426
Joystick 332
Joysticks 471
jüdisches Weißbrot 145

Judo 499
Judogi 499
Judokämpfer Wettkampfteilnehmer 499
Jugoslawien 450
Jupiter 2
Jurte 288
Justierring 271
Justiz 417
Juweliergeschäft 436

K

Kabel 209, 217, 228, 235, 237, 326,
    332, 356, 364, 535
Kabel der Schnittstelle für digitale
    Musikinstrumente (MIDI) 311
Kabel, Anschluss 227
Kabeljau, atlantischer 161
Kabelleitung 335
Kabelmantel 218, 229
Kabelmodem 335
Kabelmuffe 228
Kabelschutz 535
Kabeltülle 217
Kabelverstärkung 208
Kabelverteiler 316
Kabine 386, 443
Kabriolett 347
Kachel 12
Kaffee 148
Kaffee-Filterkanne 181
Kaffeebohnen, geröstete 148
Kaffeekanne 531
Kaffeelöffel 168
Kaffeemaschine 181
Kaffeemaschinen 181
Kaffeemühle 180
Kaffeepresser 181
Käfig 281
Kai 381
Kaianlage 430
Kaiman 77
Kairampe 381
Kaiserling 123
Kakao 148
Kaki 137
Kaktusfeige 137
Kalahari 20
Kalb 84
Kalbfleisch 152
Kalbfleischwürfel 152
Kalbshackfleisch 152
Kaldaune 154
Kalifornien, Golf 16
Kalmar 157
kalte Luft 41
kaltes Kühlmittel 408
kaltgemäßigte Klimate 40
Kaltwasserkreislauf 194
Kaltwassersteigleitung 194
Kaltwasserzulauf 196, 197
Kambium 63
Kambodscha 453
Kamel 85
Kamera 525
Kamera-Assistent, erster 290
Kamera-Assistent, zweiter 290
Kameragehäuse 314
Kameramann 290
Kamerun 451
Kamille 148
Kamin 188, 192, 193
Kaminabdeckung 193
Kaminabdichtung 193
Kaminanschluss 192
Kaminaufsatz 183
Kaminbesteck 193
Kamineinfassung 192, 193
Kamingitter 193
Kaminsims 192
Kamm 29
Kämme 268
Kammer, unterirdische 278
Kammerseptum 104
Kammerwasser 119
Kammmuschel 157
Kampfbereich 499
Kampfrichter 496, 497, 498, 499, 509
Kampfsportarten 498
Kamtschatka-Halbinsel 19
Kanada 448
kanadischer Bacon 156
Kanal, linker 324
Kanal, rechter 324
Kanaleinstiegsschacht 434
Kanalisation 194

Kanalschleuse 381
Kanalsuchtasten 319
Kanalwahltasten für Lautsprecher 322
Kanapee 200
kanarische Melone 135
Kandiszucker 149
Kaninchen 82, 154
Kanne 181
Kante 533
Kantenschiene 526
Kantenstecher 233
Kanüle 460
Kanülenansatz 460
Kanzel 446, 447
Kap 24
Kap der Guten Hoffnung 20
Kap Horn 17
Kap Verde 451
Kapaun 155
Kapelle 282
Kapillargefäß 114
Kapillarröhrchen 424
Käppchen 208
Kappe 198, 312, 494
Kappe, äußere 240
Kapsel 51, 467
Kapsel, Schnitt 60
Kapuze 249, 260, 508
Kapuze mit Zugband 261
Kapuzenmuskel 96, 97
Kapuzenmütze 239
Kar 5, 30
Karabiner 538
Karabinerhaken 521
Karaffe 165
Karaffe, kleine 165
Karambolagebillard 502
Kardamom 138
Kardinal 80
Kardone 125
Karibik 14, 16
Karibische Inseln 448
Karibische Platte 27
Karikatur 313
Karo 468
Karosserie 348, 361
Karosserien, Beispiele 347
Karotte 129
Karpaten 18
Karpfen 160
Karte 469
Karte, politische 23
Karteiregister 340
Kartendarstellungen 22
Kartenkontrolleur 294
Kartenlesegerät 442, 443
Kartenleser 321
Kartenleserschlitz 346
Kartennummer 441, 443
Kartenraum 382
Kartenschacht, PC 336
Kartenspiele 468
Kartoffel 124
Kartoffelstampfer 173
Kartographie 21
Karton 163
Kartusche 216, 459
Kartuschenpistole 216
Kasachstan 452
Käsemesser 168
Käsereibe 170
Käsescharchtel 163
Käsetheke 121
Kaspisches Meer 14, 19
Kasse 121, 294, 346
Kassen 121
Kassette 326, 333
Kassettenauswurfschalter 319
Kassettendeck 323, 325
Kassettendecktasten 326
Kassettenfach 323
Kassettenlaufwerk 333
Kassettenrekorder-Wahltaste 322
Kassettenschacht 319
Kassettenteil 326
Kassiererin 121
Kastagnetten 295, 309
Kasten 68
Katalysator 351
katalytische Umwandlungsanlage 405
Katamaran 521
Katar 452
Kathode 417
Katze 87
Katze, Kopf 87
Katzenhai, groß gefleckter 158

Katzenrassen 87
Kaufhaus 437
Kaumuskel 96
Kegel 177, 429
Kegelprojektion 22
Kehldeckel 105, 118
Kehle 78, 305
Kehlkopf 105
Kehrschaufel 215
Keil 243, 274, 276, 305
Keilbein 100
Keilbeinhöhle 117
Keilhebel 229
Keilriemen 212, 350, 360
Keim 61
Keimblatt, verwelkendes 53
Keimscheibe 79
Keimung 53
Keimwurzel 53
Kelch 59, 60, 468
Kelchblatt 56, 59
Keller 182
Kellerfalte 253
Kellerfenster 183
Kellnerbesteck 170
Kelvin 426
Kenia 451
Kennzeichnung 358
Keramikkondensator 417
Kerbe 422, 503
Kerbel 142
Kermadec-Tonga-Graben 34
Kern 6, 57, 58, 59, 61, 305, 534
Kern, äußerer 26
Kern, innerer 26
Kern, spaltbarer 415
Kernenergie 408
Kernenergie, Elektrizitätserzeugung 408
Kerngehäuse 58
Kerngehäuseausstecher 173
Kernholz 63
Kernkörperchen 50, 112
kernlose Salatgurke 128
Kernmembran 50, 66
Kernreaktor 409
Kernschatten 4, 5
Kernspalte 305
Kernspaltung 415
Kernspaltung des Uranbrennstoffs 408
Kerosin 405
Kerze 446
Kessel 29, 308
Kesselpauke 308
Kesselwagen 377
Ketchup 141
Kette 196, 370, 372, 523
Kettenblatt, großes 372
Kettenblatt, kleines 372
Kettenblattumwerfer 370, 372
Kettenbremse 235
Kettenführung 372
Kettenlaufwerkrahmen 398
Kettenrad 522
Kettenreaktion 415
Kettensäge 235
Kettenstrebe 370
Keule 86
Kibla 447
Kichererbsen 130
Kidneybohne, rote 131
Kiefernnadeln 65
Kieferschutz 486
Kiefertaster 70
Kielbasa-Wurst 156
Kielboot 521
Kiemen 73
Kiemendeckel 74
Kiemenspalten 74
Kiesbett 524
Kilogramm 426
Kilometerzähler 355
Kimme 524
Kimono 256
Kinderbekleidung 261
Kinderbetreuung 437
Kindermöbel 205
Kindersessel 205
Kindersitz 356, 372
Kinn 78, 94
Kinnriemen 486
Kinnschutz 367, 522
Kinnstütze 301
Kino 294, 386, 432, 436
Kinoleinwand 294
Kinosaal 2
Kiosk 346, 379

ASTRONOMIE > 2-25; ERDE > 26-71; PFLANZENREICH >72-89; TIERREICH > 90-143; MENSCH > 144-177; NAHRUNGSMITTEL UND KÜCHE > 178-241; HAUS > 242-295
HEIMWERKEN UND GARTENARBEIT > 296-333; KLEIDUNG > 334-371; PERSÖNLICHE AUSSTATTUNG > 372-391; KUNST UND ARCHITEKTUR > 392-465; KOMMUNIKATION UND BÜROTECHNIK > 466-535
TRANSPORT UND FAHRZEUGE > 536-643; ENERGIE > 644-677; WISSENSCHAFT > 678-705; GESELLSCHAFT > 706-785; SPORT UND SPIELE > 786-920

Kippermulde 401
Kipphebel 467
Kirche 433, 446
Kirchenbank 446
Kirchenfenster 446
Kirgisistan 452
Kiribati 453
Kirsche 132
Kirschtomate 128
Kissen, kleines 204
Kiste 162
Kittelbluse 255
Kiwano 136
Kiwi 136
Klaffmuschel 157
Klampe 520, 521
Klangfarbenregler 303
Klangfell 297
Klangwahlanzeige 322
Klangwahlschalter 322
klappbare Laderampe 386
klappbare Nagelfeile 265
Klappbrücke, einteilige 345
Klappe 73, 202, 229, 244, 291, 306
Klappe, hintere 13
Klappendrücker 306
Klappenschutz 306
Klappenstiel 306
Klappentasche 244, 248
Klapperschlange 77
Klappschlittschuh 508
Klappspaten 532
Klappstufe 361
Klappstuhl 201
Klapptisch 202
Klarinette 306
Klarinetten 295
Klarsichtfenster 274
Klarsichthüllen 274
Klarsichtscheibe 523
Klarspülmittelbehälter 214
Klassenzimmer 444, 445
Klassenzimmer für Schüler mit
    Lernschwierigkeiten 444
klassische Bluse 255
Klaue 71, 82, 220
Klaviaturboden 304
Klavier 304
Klebeband 190
Klebebandabroller 341
Klebefilmspender 341
Klebestift 341
Klebstoff 190
Kleeblatt 342, 343
Kleid in Trapez-Form 252
Kleid mit angesetztem Schoß 252
Kleid, mit angesetztem Schoß 252
Kleider, Beispiele 252
Kleidersack 277
Kleiderschrank 189, 202, 203, 439
Kleiderschutz 467
Kleidung 238, 538
Kleidung, feuer- und wasserfeste 454
Kleinanzeigen 313
Kleinbus 363
kleine Armdecken 78
kleine Beuteltasche 276
kleine Chirurgie 462
kleine Karaffe 165
kleine Klinge 531
kleine Schamlippe 112, 113
kleine Trommel 295, 308
kleiner Finger 115
kleiner Getränkekarton 163
kleiner Ischiasnerv 108
kleiner Lehnstuhl 200
kleiner Rundmuskel 97
kleiner Teller 166
kleines Tentakel 72
kleines Kettenblatt 372
kleines Kissen 204
Kleinhirn 109
Kleinwagen 347
Klemmbacke 265
Klemmbrett 340
Klemmbügel 269
Klemmbügel, Hebel 269
Klemme, rote 356
Klemme, schwarze 356
Klemme, verstellbare 206
Klemmhefter 339
Klemmspot 206
Klemmverschraubung 197

Klemmvorrichtung 425
Klemmnerwerkzeuge 216
Klettenwurzel 129
Kletterpflanze 230
Klickpedal 522
Kliff, Klippe 35
Klimaanlage 46, 361, 386
Klimate der Welt 40
Klimate, kaltgemäßigte 40
Klimate, tropische 40
Klimate, warmgemäßigte 40
Klinge 167, 169, 177, 221, 271
Klinge, isolierte 217
Klinge, zweischneidige 271
Klingenarten 221
Klingendose 271
Klingenstopper 270
Klips 246, 264
Klistierspritze 460
Klitoris 112
Klosettbecken 196
Klosettdeckel 196
Klubhaus 504
Knarre 223, 536
Knauf 201, 202, 477, 492, 506
Knebel 224
Knebelbolzen 221
Knebelverschluss 249
Kneten 178
Knethaken 176
Knickschutztülle 269
Knie 83, 86, 92, 94
Kniebandage 500
Kniebundhose 254
Kniepolster 486
Kniescheibe 83, 98
Knieschützer 476, 525, 526, 527
Kniestrumpf 247, 257
Knoblauch 124
Knoblauchpresse 170
Knöchel 92, 94
knöchelhohe Stiefelette 241
Knöchelschutz 476
Knöchelsocke 247
Knochenfisch 74
Knochenfische 159
Knolle 125
Knollenblätterpilz 52
Knollengemüse 124
Knollensellerie 129
Knollenziest 124
Knopf 199, 227, 245, 250, 296
Knopfflasche 246
Knopfleiste 245, 250
Knopfleiste, verdeckte 251, 261
Knopfloch 248
Knorpelfisch 74
Knorpelfische 158
Knorrenmuskel 97
Knospe 54
Knoten 416
Knurrhahn 159
Kobra 77
Kochen 178
Kochfeld 179
Kochgeräte 174
Kochgeschirr 531
Kochmesser 169
Kochmulde 164, 210
Kochplatte 210
Kochtopf 531
Koffer 277
Kofferradio 325
Kofferraum 349
Kognakschwenker 165
Kohl 126
Kohle-Zink-Zelle 417
Kohlekraftwerk 402
Kohlendioxid, Aufnahme 54
Kohlenhalde 402
Kohlenschaufel 193
Kohlestab (Kathode) 417
Kohlrabi 125
Kohlrübe 129
Kokosnuss 133
Kola-Halbinsel 18
Kolanuss 133
Kolben 57, 61, 199, 357, 360
Kolbenhals 534
Kolbenring 360
Kolbenschaft 360
Kolibri 81
Kolk 31
Kollaterale 110
Kollegmappe 274
Kollegmappe mit Griff 274

Koller 248
Kolumbien 448
Koma 6
Kombi 347
Kombi-Pflegelösung 272
Kombimaske 233
Kombilimousine, dreitürige 347
Kombipumpe 530
Kombizange 217, 222
Kombu 123
Komet 6
Kommandobrücke 383
Kommataste 337
Kommode 203
Kommunikation 312
Kommunikationsmodul 316
Kommunikationsprotokoll 334
Kommunionbank 446
Komoren 452
Kompaktkopfer 266
Kompaktspeisesystem 321
Kompassrose 533
komplexe Düne 36
Kompositbogen 535
Kompostkiste 231
Kompressionsgurt, seitlicher 532
Kompressor für Klimaanlage 360
Kondensation 45
Kondensationskammer 402
Kondensieren 414
Kondensmilch 150
Kondensor 402, 421
Kondensoreinstellung 421
Kondensorhöhenverstellung 421
Konditorei 437
Kondor 80
Konferenzraum 442, 445
Kongo 20, 451
Kongresszentrum 433
König 468, 470
König, Grabkammer 278
Königin 68
Königin, Grabkammer 278
Königin-Maud-Land 15
königliche Vene 102
Königsbaum 412
Königsflanke 470
konkave Linse 419
konkavkonvexe Linse 419
Konserven 121
Konservendose 163
Konsole 283
Konstruktion 186
Konstruktion eines Hauses 188
Konsument 317
Kontaktelemente 198
Kontaktlinse, harte 272
Kontaktlinse, weiche 272
Kontaktlinsen 272
Kontaktlinsenbehälter 272
Kontermutter 197
Kontinent 33
kontinentale Kruste 26
Kontinentalfuß 33
Kontinentalhang 33
Kontinentalrand 33
Kontinentalschelf 33
Kontinente, Lage 14
Kontoidentifikation 443
Kontrabass 301
Kontrabasse 295
Kontrafagott 295
Kontrastregler 329
Kontrolllampe 269
Kontrollleuchte 178, 179, 180, 181, 208,
    210, 214, 443, 454
Kontrollleuchte Netzspannung 443
Kontrollleuchte Papiereinzug 333
Kontrollleuchte, Tintenpatrone 333
Kontrollleuchten 331
Kontrollleuchten für Tonsignalquellen 322
Kontrollmonitore, Regie 290
Kontrollraum 388
Kontrolltower 388
Konvektion 415
Konvektionsströmung 415
Konvektionszelle 43
Konvektionszone 4
konvergierende Plattengrenzen 27
konvexe Linse 419
konvexkonkave Linse 419
Koordinatensystem der Erdkugel 21
Kopf 6, 67, 72, 78, 93, 95, 103, 111,
    220, 221, 223, 229, 271, 272, 301,
    303, 492, 494, 505, 536
Kopf der Katze 87

Kopfarten 221
Kopfband 458, 459
Kopfbedeckungen 238, 239
Kopfbruststück 71
Kopfbügel 326
Kopfende 204
Kopfganglion 73
Kopfhörer 324, 325, 326
Kopfhöreranschlussbuchse 310, 311, 329
Kopfhörerbuchse 322, 326
Kopfhörerstecker 326
Kopfkissen 204
Kopfkissenbezug 204
Kopfkissenschonbezug 204
Kopfnicker 96
Kopfregal 121
Kopfriegel 185
Kopfriemen 459
Kopfsalat 126
Kopfschutz 458, 498
Kopfstütze 353
Kopfteil 191, 205, 238, 239
Kopfwurf 470
Koppel-Kipptaste 305
Koppelungsmodul 11
Koppen 207
Kora 297
Korallenmeer 15
Korallennatter 77
Korb 211, 214, 489
Korbanlage 489
Korbbrett 489
Korbbretthalter 489
Körbchen 57
Korbring 489
Korbstütze, gepolsterte 489
Kordilleren, Australische 15
Korea 19
Koriander 142
korinthische Halbsäule 281
korinthischer Pilaster 281
Kork 514
Korkball 477
Korkenzieher 531
Korkspitze 495
Korn 534
Körner 220
Körnerfresser 79
Körnerschicht 114
Kornett 295, 307
Korona 4
Körper 118, 305, 429, 536
Körper, menschlicher 92
Körperchen, Ruffinisches 114
Körperchen, Vater-Pacinisches 114
Körperpflege 121, 264
Körpertemperaturregelung 10
Korpus 303, 306
Korpus, birnenförmiger 297
Korpus, dreieckiger 297
Korpus, massiver 303
Korpus, runder 296
Korrespondenz 338
Korselett 258
Korsett 259
Kosakenmütze 238
Kosmetikeinsatz 277
Kosmetikkoffer 277
Kostüm 251, 290
Köte 83
Kotelett 152, 153
Kötengelenk 83
Kotflügel 348, 364
Kotflügel, hinterer 369
Krabbe 158
Krabbenspinne 70
Kraft, Maßeinheit 426
Kraftfahrzeuganlagen 351
Kraftfahrzeuge: Hauptbauteile 350
Kraftsport 500
Kraftstoffanlage 351
Kraftstoffanzeige 355
Kraftstoffleitung 351
Kraftstoffreserveanzeige 355
Kraftstofftank 235, 351, 364, 366, 369,
    377
Kraftübertragung 372
Kragen 244, 245, 248, 302, 303
Kragen, gespreizter 245
Kragenspitze 245
Kragenstäbchen 245
Kragstein 192, 282
Kragträger 344
Krake 157
Kralle 76, 78, 79, 232
Kranbahn 397

Käne 397
Kranführerkabine 397
Krankenakten 465
Krankenhaus 433, 462
Krankenhausbett 464
Krankenschwester 464
Krankentisch 464
Krankentrage 460
Krankenzimmer 464
Kranzgesims 279
Kranznaht 100
Kranzprofil 202
Krater 5, 28
Kraterstrahlen 5
Kraterwall 5
Kraulen 517
krause Endivie 127
Kräuselfalte 255
Kräuselrock 253
Kräuter 142
Kräutertees 148
Krawatte 245
Krawattenschal 245
Krebs, Wendekreis 20, 21, 22
Krebse 71
Krebstier 158
Kreditabteilung 442
Kreditkarte 441
Kreditkartenetui 274
Kreditkartenfach 274
Kreide 503
Kreis, Teile 428
Kreisregner 236
Kreissägeblatt 227
Kreisverkehr 25
Krempe 238, 239
Kreolen 264
Krepis 279
Kreuz 299, 468
Kreuzaussteifung 187
Kreuzbein 98, 99
Kreuzblume 283
Kreuzgeflecht 108
Kreuzhacke 233
Kreuzkopf 396
Kreuzkümmel 138
Kreuzmuster-Teppichmuschel 157
Kreuzrippe 284
Kreuzschlitzschrauben 221
Kreuzschlitzschraubenzieher 531
Kreuzschlüssel 356
Kreuztisch 421
Kreuztischeinstellung 421
Kriechstrombarriere 359
Kringel 144
Kristallisation 414
Kristalltropfen 207
Kristallzucker 149
Kroatien 450
Krokodil 77
Krokus 56
Krone 63, 83, 101, 167, 169, 302, 424
Kronenabschnitt der Pulpahöhle 101
Kronleuchter 207
Krummhalskürbis 129
Krümmling 191
Kruppe 83
Kruste, kontinentale 26
Kruste, ozeanische 26
Krustenflechte 50
Kruzifix 446
Kuba 448
Kübel 230
Küche 120, 162, 164, 188, 280, 439,
    445
Küchenbeil 169
Küchenform 172
Kuchenform, flache 172
Kücheninsel 164
Küchenmaschine 177
Küchenmesser 169
Küchenmesser, Beispiele 169
Kuchenpinsel 172
Küchenrad 172
Küchenreibe 170
Küchenschere 173
Küchenset 173
Küchenuhr 171
Küchenutensilien 169
Küchenwaage 171
Kufe 395, 506, 509, 523
Kugel 312, 332, 429, 472, 534
Kugel-Sternhaufen 6
Kugelhalterung 332
Kugellager 413
Kugelmaus 332

ASTRONOMIE > 2-25;   ERDE > 26-71;   PFLANZENREICH >72-89;   TIERREICH > 90-143;   MENSCH > 144-177;   NAHRUNGSMITTEL UND KÜCHE > 178-241;   HAUS > 242-295;
HEIMWERKEN UND GARTENARBEIT > 296-333;   KLEIDUNG > 334-371;   PERSÖNLICHE AUSSTATTUNG > 372-391;   KUNST UND ARCHITEKTUR > 392-465;   KOMMUNIKATION UND BÜROTECHNIK > 466-535;
TRANSPORT UND FAHRZEUGE > 536-643;   ENERGIE > 644-677;   WISSENSCHAFT > 678-705;   GESELLSCHAFT > 706-785;   SPORT UND SPIELE > 786-920

597

Kugelschreiber 312
Kugelstoßen 472
Kuh 84
Kühlabteilung 120, 121
Kühlaggregat 365
Kühlbox 532
Kühler 350, 358
Kühleranlage 351
Kühleranschluss, unterer 358
Kühlerblock 358
Kühlergrill 348, 364
Kühlerhaube 364
Kühlerverschlussdeckel 358
Kühlfach 211
Kühlhaus 381
Kühlmittel 408
Kühlmittel, erwärmtes 408
Kühlmittel, kaltes 408
Kühlmittelauslass 410
Kühlmitteleinlass 410
Kühlraum 121
Kühlsattelschlepper 365
Kühlschrank 164, 211, 438
Kühlschränke 438
Kühlturm 402
Kühlung 405
Kühlvitrine 438
Kühlwagen 377
Kühlwassertank 408
Kühlzylinder 420
Kuhstall 122
Kuiper-Gürtel 2
Kulissen 292
Kultbild, Standort 279
Kultur, intensive 46, 47
Kulturbeutel 276
Kulturorganisation 335
Kümmel 138
Kumquat 134
Kumulonimbus 42
Kumulus 42
Kundenbetreuung 443
Kunst 278
Künste, darstellende 294
Kunstfliege 536
künstlerischer Leiter 290
künstlicher Erdsatellit 37
künstlicher See 32
Kunstraum 444
Kunstschwamm 266
Kunstspringen 518
Kunststoff, Sortierung 49
Kunststoff-Federball 495
Kunststoffboden 492
Kunststoffkondensator 417
kunststoffummantelter Stoßfänger 348
Kunstturnen 496
Kuppe 503
Kuppel 394
Kuppel des Mihrab 447
Kuppelhülle, äußere 7
Kuppelhülle, innere 7
Kuppelspaltabdeckung 7
Kuppelzelt 529
Kuppenring 503
Kupplung 350
Kupplungsbügel 377
Kupplungsgehäuse 368
Kupplungshebel 366, 368
Kupplungspedal 354
Kurbel 170, 224, 236, 356, 372, 537
Kurbel der Stützvorrichtung 365
Kurbelwelle 360
Kürbis 129
Kurilengraben 34
Kurkuma 138
Kurs 524
Kursbuchtafeln 374
Kurtine 282
kurze Hose 261, 483, 488, 522
Kürzel der Ausgabebank 441
kurzer Hohlhandmuskel 96
kurzer Wadenbeinmuskel 97
kurzer Zehenstrecker 96
Kurzhandschuh 243
Kurzmeldungen 313
Kurzsichtigkeit 419
Kurzsocke 257
Kurzstrecke 508
Kurzstreckenschlittschuh 508
Küste 33
Küstenformen 35
Küstenformen, typische 35
Kuttelwurst 156
Kuwait 452

L

Labor 7
Labor, amerikanisches 11
Labor, pathologisches 465
Lachs, atlantischer 161
Lachs, pazifischer 161
Lackieren 219
Lade-Anschlussbuchse 208
Ladeanzeige 271
Ladebagger 402
Ladebaum 384, 385
Ladegerät 228
Ladekontrolllampe 271
Lademast 385
Laden 280
Ladenpassage 435
Laderampe 435
Laderampe, klappbare 386
Ladevorrichtung 364
Ladogasee 18
Ladung 534
Laffe 167
Lage der Kontinente 14
Lageplan 183
Lagergang 28
Lagerhaus 430
Lagerholz 187
Lagerraster 409
Lagerraum 438
Lagerraum für gebrauchtes Material 462, 464
Lagerraum für medizinische Geräte 465
Lagerraum für Sterilgut 462, 464
Lagertank 405
Lagune 35
Lakkolith 28
Lama 84
Lambdanaht 100
Lamelle 52
Lammfelljacke 249
Lammfleisch 153
Lammfleischwürfel 153
Lammhackfleisch 153
Lampe 421, 529
Lampen 206
Lampenfassung 199
Lampenreihe 207
Land 23, 431
Landebereich 472
Landefenster 395
Landeklappe 392
Landenge 24
Landenge von Panama 16
Landescheinwerfer 395
Landkarte 444
landschaftlich schöne Strecke 25
Landspitze 35
Landwirtschaft, intensive 46, 48
landwirtschaftliche Verschmutzung 47
Landzunge 35
lange Unterhose 247
Länge, Maßeinheit 426
Längengrade 22
Längenmessung 425
Längenverstellung 466
langer Abendhandschuh 243
langer Hohlhandmuskel 96
langer Oberschenkelanzieher 96
langer Wadenbeinmuskel 96
langer Zehenstrecker 96
Langhaarschneider 271
Langhandschuh 243
Langlauf-Rattenfallbindung 514
Langläufer 514
Langlaufloipe 512
Langlaufski 514
langsam drehende Welle 413
Längsdünen 36
Längslenkerachse 351
Längsschnitt durch ein Weizenkorn 61
Längsschnitt durch eine Haselnuss 60
Längsschnitt durch eine Walnuss 60
Längsschnitt, Backenzahn 101
Längsschott 384
Langstrecke 508
Langstrecken-Düsenflugzeug 392
Languste 158
Langustine 158
lanzettförmig 55
Laos 453
Lappen 79
Lappen, oberer seitlicher 62
Lappen, unterer seitlicher 62
Lappenbronchus 105
Laptop 336

Laptop: Rückansicht 336
Laptop: Vorderansicht 336
Lärche 65
Lasagne 146
Lasche 249, 274
Lasche, selbstklebende 339
Laserstrahl 420
Lastenfortbewegung 396
Lastkraftfahrzeuge 364
Lastkraftwagen, Beispiele 364
Laterne 230
Latexhandschuh 460
Latissimuszug 501
Latrinen 280
Latte 519
Lattentasche 520
Lattenzaun 230
Lätzchen 260, 261
Latzhose 254
Latzhose mit gekreuzten Rückenträgern 261
Latzhose mit hohem Rückenteil 260
Laub 63
Laubblatt 54
Laubblätter, erste 53
Laubflechte 50
Laubfrosch 75
Laubheuschrecke 69
Laubhölzer, Beispiele 64
Laubsäge 226
Laubwald 44
Laubwerk 200
Lauch 124
Lauf 78
Laufbein 67, 70
Laufbrett 377
Laufbrücke 385
Läufer 469, 470
Laufgewicht 422
Laufkatze 397
Laufkatzenrolle 397
Laufkran 407
Laufrad, pneubreiftes 380
Laufrolle 205, 332
Laufschiene 534
Laufschuh 473
Laufsohle 240, 263, 510
Laugenbottich 212
Laus 69
Lautsprecher 294, 320, 321, 325, 326, 327, 328, 336, 455
Lautsprecher, Kanalwahltasten 322
Lautsprecherbox 324
Lautsprecherbuchsen 322
Lautstärkeregler 10, 303, 310, 311, 319, 322, 325, 326, 328, 329
Lautstärkeregler für den Hörer 327
Lautstärkeregler für den Rufton 327
Lavaschicht 28
Lavastrom 28
LCD-Anzeige 424
Lead 515
Lebenserhaltungssystem 10
Lebenserhaltungssystem, Steuerung 10
Leber 103, 106, 154
Lebervene 103
LED-Pegelanzeige 323
Lederhaut 114, 119, 478
Lederschutz 533
Lederstrippe 246
Lederwaren 274
Lederwarengeschäft 436
Leerdarm 106
leere Menge 427
Leerlaufanzeige 368
Leertaste 330
Leerzeichen 330
Leerzeichen, geschütztes 330
Left-Wing 482
Lefzen 86
Leggins 263
Leguan 77
Legwarmer 263
Lehmhütte 288
Lehnstuhl, kleiner 200
Lehrer/Lehrerin 444
Lehrerpult 444
Lehrerzimmer 445
Leichtathletik 472
leichte Atemschutzmaske 459
leichtes Sonnenkleid 252
Leichtflugzeug 394
Leinwand 439
Leiste 92, 94
Leistentasche 244
Leistung, Maßeinheit 426

Leiter 184, 288, 361, 401, 404
Leiter, künstlerischer 290
Leiterbaum, ausfahrbarer 455
Leitern 219
Leiterplatte 417
Leiterstrahlrohr 455
Leitöse 521
Leitrad, pneubreiftes 380
Leitspruch 441
Leitungsnetz, Einspeisung 413
Leitwerk 393, 406
Leitwerksträger 395
Lemure 91
Lende 83, 93, 95
Lendengeflecht 108
Lendenpolster 486
Lendenwirbel 99, 110
Lenkanlage 351
Lenker 523
Lenkerbügel, angehobener 522
Lenkergriff 366, 369
Lenkkopf 371
Lenkrad 350, 354, 385, 525
Lenkrolle 209
Lenksäule 350
Lenkstange 501
Lenkzylinder 402
Leopard 89
Leopardfrosch 75
Leselampe 457, 464
Leseleuchte 206
Leserbriefe 313
Lesetaste 327
Lesotho 452
Lettland 450
Leuchtanzeige 329
Leuchtrakete 457
Leuchtstoffröhre 199
Leuchtturm 381
Leukoplast 50
Leukozyt 104
Libanon 452
Libanonzeder 65
Libelle 69
Liberia 451
Libero 487
Libyen 451
Licht 7, 8, 9
Licht, Ewiges 447
Licht, gelbes 434
Licht, grünes 434
Licht, rotes 434
Licht, sichtbares 418
Lichtleiste 469
Lichtleistensteuerung 457
Lichtmaschine 350, 360
Lichtrezeptoren 119
Lichtschutzschirm 7
Lichtstärke, Maßeinheit 426
Lichtstrahl 419
Lichttechniker 291
Lidschatten 266
Liebstöckel 142
Liechtenstein 450
Lieferanteneinfahrt 435
Liegestuhl 201
Likörglas 165
Lilie 56
Limabohne 131
Limette 134
Limonadenlöffel 168
Limousine, viertürige 347
Linde 148
Lineal 425, 531
linealisch 55
Linie, durchgehende 342
Linie, neutrale 416
Linie, unterbrochene 342, 343
Linienanzeige 362, 363
Linienbus 362
Linienrichter 481, 485, 487, 490, 494, 496, 507
Liniensystem 298
linke Herzkammer 103, 104
linke Lunge 103, 105
linke Lungenvene 104
linke Niere 107
linke Seite 272
linker Abwehrspieler 487
linker Angriffsspieler 489
linker Aufbauspieler 489
linker Außenangreifer 487
linker Außenfeldspieler 474
linker Centre 482
linker Corner Back 484
linker Defensive End 484

linker Defensive Tackle 484
linker Guard 485
linker Kanal 324
linker Mittelfeldspieler 481
linker Safety 484
linker Stürmer 507
linker Tackle 485
linker Verteidiger 481, 506
linker Vorfoor 103, 104
linkes Aufschlagfeld 491
linkes Feld 475
links 293
Linse 119, 419
Linse, bikonkave 419
Linse, bikonvexe 419
Linse, konkave 419
Linse, konkavkonvexe 419
Linse, konvexe 419
Linse, konvexkonkave 419
Linse, plankonkave 419
Linse, plankonvexe 419
Linsen 130, 419
Linsenfernrohr 8
Linsenfernrohr im Querschnitt 8
Linsenkopf mit Schlitz 221
Linsensystem 420
Lippe 83, 87, 521
Lippen-Make-up 266
Lippenkonturenstift 266
Lippenpfeife 305
Lippenpinsel 266
Lippenstift 266
Lippentaster 67, 73
Litauen 450
Litchi 137
Literaturbeilage 313
Lithosphäre 26, 44
Litze 273
Lob 491
Loch 504
Loch, gestanztes 240, 246
Loch, Par-5 504
Lochbillard 503
Locher 340
Lockennadel 268
Lockenstab 269
Lockente 535
Lockenwickler 268
Löffel 167, 400, 531, 538
Löffel, Beispiele 168
Löffelstiel 399
Löffelstielzylinder 399
Loge 293
Lokale Station 316
Lokomotive 376
Lokomotive, dieselelektrische 377
Lokschuppen 375
Longanfrucht 136
Longdrinkglas 165
Lorbeer 142
Löschen 331
löschender Rückschritt 331
Löschfahrzeuge 455
Löschflugzeug 394
Löschmittelbehälter 454
Löschtaste 315, 323, 328, 331, 337
loser Puder 266
Löshebel 222
Lötkolben 218
Lötlampe 218
Lötpistole 218
Lötspitze 218
Lötwerkzeuge 218
Lötzinn 218
Lounge 386
Löwe 89
Löwenzahn 127
Luchs 88
Luer-Lock-Spitze 460
Luffaschwamm 267
Luft, absinkende kalte 43
Luft, aufsteigende warme 43
Luft, kalte 41
Luft, warme 41
Luftansaugrohr 383
Luftaustrittsöffnung 270
Luftaustrittsschlitz 209
Luftdruck 39
Luftdruck in Meereshöhe 39
Luftdruckänderung 39
Luftdüse 354
Lufteinlass 361, 362, 367, 383, 523
Lufteinlauf 395
Lüfter 322, 336, 350, 358, 360
Luftfahrt 317
Luftfilter 235, 350, 398

Luftkammer 79
Luftkissenfahrzeug 383
Luftklappe 365
Luftkompressor 376
Luftloch 312
Luftmasse 39
Luftmatratze 530
Luftmatratze, selbstaufblasbare 530
Luftpolster 262, 339
Luftpolsterumschlag 339
Luftpropeller 383
Luftpumpe 370
Luftröhre 105
Luftschacht 278
Luftschadstoffe 47
Luftschleuse 13
Luftstromrichtdüse 270
Luftstromschalter 270
Lufttemperatur 39
Lüftung 380
Luftverkehr 388
Luftverschmutzung 47
Luftwege 105
Luftzufuhr 525
Luftzufuhrregler 192
Lunge, linke 103, 105
Lunge, rechte 103, 105
Lungen 105
Lungenarterie 102, 105
Lungenarterienstamm 104
Lungenfell 105
Lungenmittellappen 105
Lungenoberlappen 105
Lungenunterlappen 105
Lungenvene 102
Lungenvene, linke 104
Lungenvene, rechte 104
Lunula 73
Lupe 421, 531
Lupine 130
Lutz 509
Luxemburg 449
Luzerne, blaue 130
Lyra 297
Lysosom 66

M

Mäander 32
Macadamianuss 133
Macchie 44
Mackenzie 16
Madagaskar 20, 452
Magen 73, 103, 106
Magenmund 71
Magenpförtner 71
Magenstütze 259
Magenta 418
Magma 28, 33
Magmakammer 28, 402
Magnesia 497
Magnet 341, 416
Magnetband 319
magnetische Dämpfung 422
magnetische Dichtung 211
magnetische Trennung 49
magnetischer Deckelhalter 180
magnetisches Feld 318, 416
Magnetismus 416
Magnetkompass 533
Magnetnadel 533
Magnetstreifen 441
Mähne 83
Maiglöckchen 56
Maikäfer 69
Maine Coon 87
Mais 61, 143
Maismehl 144
Maisöl 149
Maissirup 149
Makak 91
Make-up 266
Makrele 159
Makronukleus 66
Makroobjektiv 314
Mal 479
Mal, drittes 474
Mal, zweites 474
Malawi 452
Malawisee 20
Malaysia 453
Malediven 453
Malerpinsel 219
Mali 451
Malspieler, dritter 474
Malspieler, erster 474

Malspieler, zweiter 474
Malta 450
Malzessig 141
Mandarine 134
Mandel 116, 133
Mandoline 297
Manganmischung (Kathode) 417
Mango 137
Mangochutney 141
Mangold 125
Mangostane 136
Maniküre 265
Maniok 124
Mann 92
männlich 426
männliche Blütenstände 65
männliche Geschlechtsorgane 111
Mannschaftsabzeichen 506
Mannschaftstrikot 476, 480, 486
Mannschaftszelt 528
Manövriereinheit, bemannte 10
Mansardenfenster 182
Manschette 245, 501
Manschette, aufblasbare 461
Mantel 72, 73, 248, 251, 417, 534
Mäntel 248, 251
Mantel, oberer 26
Mantel, unterer 26
Mantelblech 404
Mantelkleid 252
Mantelmauer 282
Manual für das Hauptwerk 305
Manual für das Oberwerk 305
Manual für das Rückpositiv 305
Manuale 305
manuelle Aussteuerung 323
Manxkatze 87
Marcato-Zeichen 299
Marder 88
Margarine 149
Marginalschild 76
Marianengraben 34
Marie-Byrd-Land 15
Marienkäfer 69
Marine-Dieselkraftstoff 405
Mariniergewürze 139
maritim 40
Mark 63, 107, 140, 154
Mark, verlängertes 109
Marker 312
Markierschnur 225
Markierungslinie 533
Markscheide 110
Markstrahlen 63
Marokko 451
Mars 2, 3
Marshallinseln 453
Mascara, flüssiges 266
Mascarabürstchen 266
Mascarastein 266
Maschen 493
Maschinenhalle 406, 407
Maschinenraum 384, 386
Maschinist 290
Maske 476
Maskenbildner 290
Maskendichtung 459
Massagebürste 267
Massagehandschuh 267
Massagespitze 272
Masse 27
Masse, Maßeinheit 426
Masseelektrode 359
Massekontakt 322
Massengut-Terminal 381
massiver Korpus 303
Mast 519, 520
Mastdarm 106, 111, 112
Masthalterung 321
Mastlager 519
Mastspitze 519
Maststeuerhebel 396
Masttasche 519
Maß 171
Maßband 225
Maßeinheit der Celsius-Temperatur 426
Maßeinheit der elektrischen Ladung 426
Maßeinheit der elektrischen Spannung 426
Maßeinheit der elektrischen Stromstärke 426
Maßeinheit der Energie 426
Maßeinheit der Frequenz 426
Maßeinheit der Kraft 426
Maßeinheit der Länge 426
Maßeinheit der Leistung 426

Maßeinheit der Lichtstärke 426
Maßeinheit der Masse 426
Maßeinheit der Radioaktivität 426
Maßeinheit der Stoffmenge 426
Maßeinheit der thermodynamischen
    Temperatur 426
Maßeinheit des Drucks 426
Maßeinheit des elektrischen Widerstands
    426
Maßwerk 285
Matchbeutel 276
Materialraum 444
Materie 414
Mathematik 426
Matratze 204, 205
Matratzenauflage 204
Matrosenbluse 255
Matte 498, 499
Matten 499
Mauernagel 220
Mauersegler 80
Mauerturm 282
Mauertürmchen 282
Maul 74, 83, 90
Maul-Ringschlüssel 223
Maultier 84
Maultrommel 297
Maurerhammer 216
Maurerkelle 216
Maurerwerkzeuge 216
Mauretanien 451
Mauritius 452
Maus, mechanische 332
Maus, optische 332
Mauspad 332
Mausschnittstelle 329
mechanische Maus 332
Medaillon 264
mediane Zungenfurche 118
Medikamentenraum 462, 465
mediterrane Subtropen 40
medizinische Gasflasche 464
medizinische Geräte, Lagerraum 465
Meer 24
Meer, Arabisches 19
Meer, Japanisches 19
Meer, Kaspisches 19
Meer, Ostchinesisches 19
Meer, Rotes 19, 20
Meer, Schwarzes 18, 19
Meer, Südchinesisches 19
Meeräsche 160
Meerbarbe, rote 159
Meerbusen, Bottnischer 18
Meerenge 24
Meeresalgen 123
Meeresboden 33
Meeressäugetiere 90
Meeressäugetiere, Beispiele 90
Meeresspiegel 26, 33, 37
Meerkohl 126
Meerneunauge 159
Meerohr 157
Meerrettich 129
Meersalat 123
Meersalz 141
Meerschweinchen 82
Mehl 144
Mehl, ungebleichtes 144
Mehlsieb 171, 172
Mehrkombrot 145
mehrreihige Halskette 264
Mehrrumpfboote 521
Mehrzweckzeug 217
Meissnersches Tast-Körperchen 114
Melanesien 15
Melasse 149
Melodiepfeife 296
Melodiesaiten 296
Melone 238
Melone, kanarische 135
Melonen 135
Melonenlöffel 173
Membran 324
Mengenschnitt 427
Mengenvereinigung 427
Menora 447
Mensch 92
menschlicher Körper 92
menschliches Gebiss 101
Menügabel 168
Menümesser 168
Menütaste 315, 327
Merguez-Wurst 156

Meridian, östlicher 22
Meridian, westlicher 22
Meridianlinie 533
Merkur 2, 3
Mesenterialarterie, obere 102, 107
Mesenterialarterie, untere 107
Mesenterialvene, obere 102
Mesokarp 57, 58, 59
Mesopause 37
Mesosphäre 37
Mess- und Markierinstrumente 225
Messband 225
Messbecher 171
Messbügel 425
Messen 171
Messer 167, 180, 235, 341, 531, 533
Messer, Beispiele 168
Messermuschel 157
Messerschutz 176
Messezentrum 430
Messingkörper 197
Messinstrumente 424
Messlöffel 171
Messschnabel, feststehender 425
Messschnabel, verschiebbarer 425
Messspindel 425
Messtrommel 425
Metall, Sortierung 49
Metallaufsatz 529
Metallfeder, römische 312
metallische Tinte 441
metallisiertes Hologramm 441
Metallkontaktgitter 410
Metallrahmen 304
Metallspannreifen 308
Metallwinkel 225
metamorphe Gesteine 26
Meteorologie 37
Meter 426
Mexikanische Rotknievogelspinne 70
Mexiko 448
Mexiko, Golf 16
Middle Linebacker 484
MIDI (Schnittstelle für digitale
    Musikinstrumente), Kabel 311
MIDI-Schnittstelle 329
Mieder 259
Miederhose 259
Miesmuschel 157
Mihrab 447
Mikrofilament 66
Mikrofon 320, 327, 328, 332, 337, 456,
    457
Mikromesien 453
Mikronukleus 66
Mikroskop 421
Mikroskope 421
Mikrotubulus 66
Mikrowellen 418
Mikrowellen-Relaisstation 334
Mikrowellengerät 178
Mikrowellenherd 164
Milch 150
Milch, homogenisierte 150
Milchbecher 163
Milchgang 113
Milchkammer 122
Milchkännchen 166
Milchprodukte 120, 150
Milchprodukte, Wareneingang 120
Milchpulver 150
Milchschokolade 148
Milchstraße 6
Milchstraße (Ansicht von oben) 6
Milchstraße (Seitenansicht) 6
militärische Telekommunikation 317
Milz 103
Mimas 3
Minarett 447
Minbar 447
Mine 312
Mini-HiFi-System 325
Minibus 347
Minislip 247
Minusbereich 410
Minusglas 419
Minuskontakt 410, 411
Minusplatte 359
Minuspol 359, 417
Minuspolbrücke 317
Minutenzeiger 424
Minze 142
Miranda 3
Mischwald 44
Mischwasserkanal 434

Mispel 133
Mississippi 16
Mitarbeiter der Rechtsanwälte 440
Mithörtaste 328
Mitnehmerrippe 213
Mitnehmerstange 403
Mitochondrium 50, 66
Mitralklappe 104
Mitte 293
Mittelamerika 14, 16
Mittelangreifer 487
Mittelarmnerv 108
Mittelatlantischer Rücken 34
Mittelbein 67, 68
Mitteldarmdrüse 71, 73
Mittelelektrode 359
Mittelfahne 480
Mittelfeld 475
Mittelfeldspieler, linker 481
Mittelfeldspieler, rechter 481
Mittelfeldspieler, zentraler 481
Mittelfinger 115
Mittelformatkamera SLR (6 x 6) 315
Mittelfuß 83
mittelhohe Wolken 42
Mittelkielschwein 385
Mittelkonsole 354
Mittelkreis 481, 488
Mittellage-Tonabnehmer 303
Mittellinie 481, 483, 484, 488, 493, 494,
    507, 515
Mittelmeer 14, 18, 20
Mittelmoräne 30
Mittelohr 116
Mittelpaneele 185
Mittelpunkt 428, 470, 502
Mittelrippe 51, 55, 60
Mittelsäule 207, 349, 412
Mittelschiff 285, 447
mittelschwere Piste 512
Mittelspannungsleitung 198
Mittelspur 343
Mittelsteg 519
Mittelstreifen 343, 434, 491
Mittelstück 111
Mitteltasche 502
Mitteltöner 324
Mittelwagen 376, 380
Mittelzeichen 490
mittlere Armdecken 78
mittlere Aufschlaglinie 491
mittlere Handdecken 78
mittlere Nasenmuschel 117
mittlerer Abwehrspieler 487
mittlerer Angriffsspieler 489
mittlerer Anspielpunkt 507
mittlerer Außenfeldspieler 474
mittlerer Linebacker 484
mittlerer Schneidezahn 101
Mixen 176
Mixer 176
mobile Einheit 316
Modem 334
Modemschnittstelle, interne 329, 336
Moderator 408
Moderatorfilz 304
Moderatorpedal 304
Modul, russisches 11
Modulationsrad 310
Mofa 369
Mohn 56, 60
Mohnsamen 139
Mohorovicic-Diskontinuität 26
Mohrenhirse 61
Mokassin 242
Mokkatasse 166
Mol 426
Molch 75
Moldawien 450
Molekül 414
Mollusken 157
Monaco 450
Mond 2, 4, 5
Mond, Oberflächenformationen 5
Mondbahn 4, 5
Monde 2
Mondfinsternis 5
Mondphasen 5
Mondsichel (abnehmender Mond) 5
Mondsichel (zunehmender Mond) 5
Mongolei 453
Monitor 471
Monopoly® 469
Moos 51
Moos, Aufbau 51
Moose, Beispiele 51

Mop 215
Morchel 123
Mordent 299
Mörser 170
Mortadella 156
Mosaik 280
Mosaikparkett 190
Mosambik 452
Moschee 447
Moskito 69
Motocross-Motorrad 525
Motor 212, 213, 214, 227, 229, 237, 366, 403
Motorblock 176, 177, 180, 208, 272, 360
Motorboot 385
Motorgehäuse 235
Motorhaube 348
motorische Endplatte 110
motorisches Neuron 110
Motorjacht 385
Motorkühlung 525
Motorlufteinlass 362
Motorrad 366
Motorrad, Touring 369
Motorrad: Draufsicht 368
Motorräder, Beispiele 369
Motorradfahrer 525
Motorradkamera 522
Motorradsport 525
Motorrasenmäher 237
Motorraum 362, 396, 400, 401
Motorroller 369
Motorsport 524
Mount Everest 37
Mountain Bike 373
Mountainbike 522
Mozambique, Straße 20
Mozzarella 150
MP3-Spieler 325
Muffe 395
Muffinform 172
Mufflon 84
Mufftasche 249, 251, 276
Mulde 231
Muldenkipper 401
Müllabfuhrwagen 364
Mülldeponie 47, 431
Müllschichten 47
Müllschlucker 197
Mülltrennung 49
Mullverband 461
Multipack 163
Multiplikation 427
Multiplikationstaste 337
Multirolle 537
Multitrainer 501
Mumienschlafsack 530
Mund 71, 72, 75, 94, 116
Munddusche 272
Mundharmonika 296
Mundhöhle 105, 106
Mundöffnung 73
Mundrohr 307
Mundschutz 498
Mundspeicheldrüse 106
Mundstück 306, 307, 311, 467
Mundstückaufnahme 307
Mündung 73, 534
Mundwasser 272
Mundwerkzeuge 68
Mundwinkel 116
Mungo 88
Mungobohne 131
Mungobohne, schwarze 131
Munster 151
Münze: Rückseite 441
Münze: Vorderseite 441
Münzfernsprecher 294, 437, 438, 463
Muschel 200
Muschel, einschalige 73
Muschel, zweischalige 73
Museum 433
Musik 296
Musikinstrumente, traditionelle 296
Musiknotation 298
Musikraum 444
Muskatnuss 138
Muskatnussreibe 170
Muskel, oberer gerader 119
Muskelfaser 110
Muskeln 96
Musselin 171
Mutter 222, 223
Mutterband, breites 113
Muttergestein 54

Muttern 223
Mütze 456
Mützenschirm 238, 239
Myanmar 453
Myzel 52

N

Nabe 70, 341, 371, 413, 467
Nabel 92, 94
Nabelschwein 84
Nabelstrang 59, 60
Nachfüllmine 312
Nachfüllrohr 196
Nachläufer, steifer 363
Nachrichten 313
Nachrichtenanzeige 328
Nachrichtensatellit 317
Nachsortierung von Hand 49
nächste Seite 331
Nachtaufnahmeschalter 320
Nachthemd 256
Nachtigall 80
Nachtigall-Grashüpfer 69
Nachtschalter 443
Nachttisch 439, 464
Nachttischlampe 439
Nachtwäsche 256
Nacken 78, 93, 95
Nackenfeder 536
Nackenrolle 204
Nackenrolle, große 204
Nackenschutz 486
Nadel 36
Nadelbaum 65
Nadelblätter, Beispiele 65
Nadelhölzer, Beispiele 65
Nadelwald 44
Nagel 220
Nägel, Beispiele 220
Nagel, geschnittener 220
Nagel, gewöhnlicher 220
Nagelbett 114
Nagelbettepitel 114
Nagelfeile 265
Nagelfeile, klappbare 265
Nagelhalbmond 114, 115
Nagelhautentferner 265
Nagelhautschaber 265
Nagelhautschere 265
Nagelhautschieber 265
Nagelknipser 265
Nagelkörper 114
Nagellack 265
Nagelnecessaire 265
Nagelrand, freier 114
Nagelreiniger 265
Nagelschere 265
Nagelweißstift 265
Nagelwerkzeuge 220
Nagelwurzel 114
Nagelzange 265
Nagelzieher 531
Nagetier 82
Nagetiere 82
Nagetiere, Beispiele 82
Nahrungskette 45
Nahrungsmittel 120
Nahrungsmittelquelle, primäre 45
Nahrungsvakuole 66
Nahrungsvakuole, heranwachsende 66
Naht 60, 73, 240, 243, 262
Nähte 477
Nahttasche 251
Nahverkehrszug 375
Name der Station 378
Name des Inhabers 441
Name des Turners/der Turnerin 497
Namensschild 456
Namib 20
Namibia 452
Naos 279
Napfschnecke 157
Narbe 56, 60
Narzisse 56
Nase 74, 82, 83, 94, 526
Nase, abgesenkte 394
Nase, äußere 117
Nasen-Bartschere 265
Nasenbein 100, 117
Nasenflügel 117
Nasenflügelknorpel, großer 117
Nasenhöhle 105, 117
Nasenloch 75, 76, 78, 117
Nasenmuschel, mittlere 117
Nasenmuschel, obere 117

Nasenmuschel, untere 117
Nasenöffnung 74
Nasenrachenraum 117
Nasenrücken 117
Nasenspiegel 87
Nasenspitze 117
Nasenstachel 100
Nasenwurzel 117
Nashorn 85
Nationalität 497
Nationalpark 25
Natur, Freizeit 528
naturbelassene Umgebung 504
natürlicher Treibhauseffekt 46
Naturschwamm 267
Nauru 453
Nazca-Platte 27
Neapolitanische Tropfkanne 181
Nebel 41
Nebelleuchte 352
Nebelscheinwerfer 364
Nebenaltar 446
Nebengleis 375
Nebenhoden 111
Nebenniere 107
Nebenschluss 416
Nebenstraße 25
negativer Pol 416
Negligé 256
Nehrung 35
Nektarine 132
Nelke 56
Nepal 453
Nephridium 71
Neptun 2, 3
Nerv 114
Nervenendung 114
Nervenfaser 114
Nervengeflecht 101
Nervenimpuls 110
Nervenstrang, ventraler 71
Nervensystem 108
Nervensystem, peripheres 108
Nervensystem, zentrales 108
Nervenwurzel, hintere 109, 110
Nervenwurzel, vordere 109, 110
Nerz 88
Nessel 127
Nestfarn 52
Netz 162, 205, 477, 487, 489, 491, 493, 495
Netzanschluss 326
Netzanschlussbuchse 329
Netzband 491
Netzhalter 493
Netzhaut 119, 419
Netzhautgrube 119
Netzkabel 177, 208, 229, 269, 270, 271, 322
Netzkabel, Gleichstrom 336
Netzkabel, Wechselstrom 336
Netzkante 487
Netzkontrollampe 328
Netzkontrollleuchte 333
Netzplan 378
Netzrichter 491
Netzschalter 311, 318, 319, 322, 323, 328, 329
Netzstecker 337
Netzstrumpf 257
Netzteilfilter 329
Netzwerkschnittstelle 329
neuer Schekel 440
Neufundland 14
Neukaledonien 15
Neumond 5
Neuneck, regelmäßiges 429
Neuron, motorisches 110
Neuron, peripher-sensorisches 110
Neuron, sensibles 110
Neuronenkette 110
neutrale Linie 416
neutrale Zone 484, 507
Neutron 414
Neutron, einfallendes 415
Newton 426
Nicaragua 448
nicht Element von 427
nicht identisch 427
nicht wärmeleitende Spitze 269
nicht wieder verwertbarer Restmüll 49
Nickbewegung 395
Nickhaut 87
Niederlande 449
Niederschlag 45

Niederschläge 41
Niederschlagsgebiet 39
Niederspannungsleitung 198
Niere 73, 103, 154
Niere, linke 107
Niere, rechte 107
Nierenbecken 107
nierenförmig 55
Nierenhilus 107
Nierenkelch 107
Nierenpapille 107
Nierenvene 102, 107
Nierenarterie 102, 107
Niete 169, 222
Niger 20, 451
Nigeria 451
Nil 20
Nilpferd 85
Nimbostratus 42
Nivellierfuß 212, 213, 214
Nockenwelle 360
Nockpunkt 535
Nonius 425
Nord 23
Nord-Korea 453
Nord-Nordost 23
Nord-Nordwest 23
Nordamerika 14, 16, 34
Nordamerikanische Platte 27
nördliche Halbkugel 21
nördliche Hemisphäre 21
nördlicher Polarkreis 21, 22
Nordmeer 18
Nordost 23
Nordpol 21, 416
Nordpolarmeer 14
Nordsee 14, 18
Nordwest 23
Nori 123
normale Pokerblätter 468
Normalsichtigkeit 419
Norwegen 450
Notation 470
Notbremse 380
Note 497
Note, ganze 299
Note, halbe 299
Notenablage 305, 311
Notenlinie 298
Notenschlüssel 298
Notenwerte 299
Notfallausrüstung 460
Notizblock 338
Notrufnische 345
Notschalter 368
Nudelholz 172
Nudelmaschine 170
Nukleolus 66
Nullleiter 198
Nullmeridian 22
numerische Tastatur 338
numerischer Block 331
numerisches Tastenfeld 331, 423
Nummer-8-Forward 482
Nummerierstempel 338
Nummernschildbeleuchtung 352
Nummerntasten 328
Nussknacker 170
Nüster 83
Nut 191
Nutzer, Internet 334
Nutzer, privater 335
Nutzlastraum 12
Nutzlastraum, Tür 13
Nylonschnur 237

O

Oase 32, 36
oben liegender Rahmen 401
Oberarmarterie 102
Oberarmgelenkhöcker, innerer 99
Oberarmknochen 98
Oberarmspeichenmuskel 96, 97
Oberbeleuchter 291
Oberboden 54
Oberdeck 363, 392, 404
obere Abschlusskappe 417
obere Gliedmaßen 103
obere Hohlvene 102, 103, 104
obere Manschette 511
obere Mesenterialarterie 102, 107
obere Mesenterialvene 102
obere Nasenmuschel 117
obere Querleiste 202
obere Schale 511

obere Schutzhaube 227
obere Sohlschicht 402
obere Sprosse 201
obere Tasche 502
obere Tragschicht 342
obere Vertäfelung 396
obere Zahnreihe 116
oberer Abschluss 205
oberer gerader Muskel 119
oberer Glaskolben 181
oberer knöcherner Bogengang 116
oberer Mantel 26
oberer seitlicher Einschnitt 62
oberer seitlicher Lappen 62
oberes Augenlid 75, 87
oberes Becken 308
oberes Verschlussband 511
Oberfläche 493
Oberflächenerkundung 403
Oberflächenformationen des Mondes 5
Oberflächenisolierung 12
oberflächlich Wadenbeinnerv 108
Oberfräse 229
Oberhaut 114
oberirdischer Abfluss 45
Oberkante 493
Oberkellner 438
Oberkiefer 74, 98, 117
Oberkiefer, beweglicher 76
Oberkiefer, vorderer 74
Oberkieferknochen 100, 101
Oberleiter 455
Oberleitung 376
Oberlicht, Badezimmer 189
Oberlicht, Treppenhaus 189
Oberlid 119
Oberlippe 116, 305
Oberlippennerve 117
Obermaschinerie 292
Oberon 3
Oberpartie 536
Oberrohr 370
Oberschale 367, 527
Oberschenkel 93, 95, 186
Oberschenkelanzieher, großer 97
Oberschenkelanzieher, langer 96
Oberschenkelarterie 102
Oberschenkelbereich 112
Oberschenkelknochen 98
Oberschenkelkopf 99
Oberschenkelnerv 108
Oberschenkelpolster 486
Oberschenkelregion 111
Oberschenkelvene 102
Oberschiedsrichter 509
Oberschnabel 78
Oberschrank 164
Oberschwanzdecken 78
Oberschwester, Büro 463
Oberwasser 406
Objekt 419
Objektiv 8, 314, 332, 420, 421
Objektivauswurf 314
Objektive 314
Objektivrevolver 421
Objektivschutzdeckel 314
Objektivzubehör 314
Objektklammer 421
Objekttisch 421
Oboe 306
Oboen 295
Obst 120, 132
Obst- und Gemüseschale 211
Obstbaum 122
Obstgarten 122
Ochse 85
Ofen 192
offene Spinnrolle 537
offener Doppelringschlüssel 223
öffentliches Gebäude 25
öffentliches Übertragungsnetz 316
Offizielenbank 507
Offizierskabine 387
Öffnen 170
Öffner, Dosen 163
Öffnung 243
Ogenmelone 135
Ohm 426
Ohr 92
Ohr, Aufbau 116
Ohr, äußeres 116
Ohrdecken 78
Ohrenschützer 238, 458
Ohrgehänge 264
Ohrläppchen 115
Ohrmuschel 82, 115, 116, 324

ASTRONOMIE > 2-25;   ERDE > 26-71;   PFLANZENREICH >72-89;   TIERREICH > 90-143;   MENSCH > 144-177;   NAHRUNGSMITTEL UND KÜCHE > 178-241;   HAUS > 242-29
HEIMWERKEN UND GARTENARBEIT > 296-333;   KLEIDUNG > 334-371;   PERSÖNLICHE AUSSTATTUNG > 372-391;   KUNST UND ARCHITEKTUR > 392-465;   KOMMUNIKATION UND BÜROTECHNIK > 466-53
TRANSPORT UND FAHRZEUGE > 536-643;   ENERGIE > 644-677;   WISSENSCHAFT > 678-705;   GESELLSCHAFT > 706-785;   SPORT UND SPIELE > 786-920

Ohrmuschelhöcker 115
Ohrmuschelhöhlung 115
Ohrmuschelrand, äußerer 115
Ohrmuschelwindung 115
Ohrringe 264
Ohrringe mit Schraubverschluss 264
Ohrstecker 264
Ohrstöpsel 458, 460
Ohrtrompete 116, 117
Okapi 84
Okraschote 128
Oktaeder, regelmäßiges 429
Oktave 298
Oktavmechanik 306
Okular 8, 9, 420, 421
Okularhalterung 8
Okulartubus 421
Ölablassschraube 360
Ölausfluss 48
Öldruckkontrollleuchte 368
Öldruckwarnleuchte 355
Öle 149
Olive 128
Olivenöl 149
Öllöschbrücke 381
Ölsumpf 235
Ölverschmutzung 48
Ölwanne 360
Ölwannendichtung 360
Oman 452
Oman, Golf 19
On-Deck-Circle 474
Online-Spiel 335
Oolong-Tee 148
Oortsche Wolke 2
Operationsabteilung 464
Operationssaal 464, 465
Operationstisch 464
Opernglas 273
Opernhaus 432
Opferstein 283
Opisthodomos 279
opponierbarer Daumen 91
Optik 418
Optiker 437
optische Maus 332
optische Sortierung 49
optischer Sensor 332
Orang-Utan 91
Orange 134
Orange im Querschnitt 58
Orbiter 12
Orchester 278
Orchestergraben 292
Orchidee 56
Ordner, Verzeichnis 334
Organismen, autotrophe 45
Organismen, heterotrophe 45
Organizer 338
Orgel 305
Orgelspieltisch 305
Orientierungseinlage 302, 303
Origano 142
Originaleinzug 328
Originalrückführung 328
Orinoko 17
orthopädischer Stock 466
Öse 263, 275, 535, 538
Öse für Tragriemen 315
Ost 23
Ost-Nordost 23
Ost-Südost 23
Ostchinesisches Meer 19
Österreich 450
östliche Hemisphäre 21
Östlicher Indischer Rücken 34
östlicher Meridian 22
Ostpazifischer Rücken 34
Ostsee 18
Ottomotor 360
Outfieldzaun 475
Overall 254, 261
Overknee-Strumpf 257
Ozean 5, 24, 45
Ozean, Atlantischer 15, 18, 20
Ozean, Indischer 15, 19, 20
Ozean, Pazifischer 15, 19
Ozeanien 14, 15, 453
Ozeanische Gräben 34
ozeanische Kruste 26
Ozeanischer Rücken 34
ozeanischer Rücken 33
Ozonschicht 37

P

Paar 509
paarig gefiedert 55
Packlage 342
Packriemen 277
Packung 163
Pager 327
Pagode 283
Pak-Choi 126
Paketannahme 374
Pakistan 452
Palau 453
Palette 173
Palettenhubwagen 396
Palisade 282
Palme 64
Palmenhain 36
Palmette 200
Pampelmuse 134
Panama 448
Panama, Golf 17
Panama, Landenge 16
Panamahut 238
Panflöte 297
Panoramafenster 435
Pantoffel 242
Pantolette 242
Panty-Korselett 258
Papaya 137
Papier/Pappe, Sortierung 49
Papierausgabe 333
Papiereinzug, Kontrollleuchte 333
Papiereinzugstaste 443
Papiereinzugtaste 333
Papierführung 328
Papierkassette 333
Papierkorb 341
Papillarmuskel 104
Papille 114
Papille, fadenförmige 118
Pappel 64
Paprika 139
Paprika, gelber 128
Paprika, grüner 128
Paprika, roter 128
Papua-Neuguinea 15, 453
Par-5-Loch 504
Parabeldüne 36
Parabolantenne 316, 321
Paraffine 405
Paraguay 448
parallel 428
Parallelanschlag 227
Parallelepiped 429
Parallelogramm 429
Parallelschaltung 416
Parallelschnittstelle 329
Paramecium 66
Paraná 17
Paranuss 133
Parboiled Reis 147
Parfümerie 436
Park 25, 433
Parka 249
Parkdeck 435
Parkettboden 190
Parkettmuster 190
Parkplatz 375, 381, 390, 430, 445, 504, 512
Parmesan 151
Parterre 293
partielle Finsternis 4, 5
Partlow-Schreiber 365
Pascal 426
Pasch 468
Paspel 260
Paspeltasche 250
Pass 29
Passagierdampfer 386
Passagierkabine 383, 386, 387
Passagierraum 393, 395
Passagierraum 1. Klasse 392
Passagierterminal 391
Passagiertransferfahrzeug 391
Passbildautomat 437
Passiergerät 170
Passiersieb 171
Passierte Tomaten 140
Passionsfrucht 136
Passkontrolle 391
Paste 141
Pastinake 129
Paßgang 83
Patagonien 17
Patent-Strickbündchen 250
Patera 200
pathologisches Labor 465
Patient 464
Patientenstuhl 464
Patisson 129
Patisson-Kürbis 129
Patrone (Gewehr) 534
Patrone (Schrotflinte) 534
Patronentasche 456
Patte 244
Pattentasche, schräge 248, 251
Pauken 295
Pause 299, 331
Pause, ganze 299
Pause, halbe 299
Pause-Taste 323
Pausenraum 445
Pausenzeichen 299
Pausetaste 319
Pavian 91
Pavillon 432
Pazifik 14
Pazifische Platte 27
pazifischer Lachs 161
Pazifischer Ozean 15, 19
PC 329
PC-Kartenschacht 336
Pecannuss 133
Pechnase 282
Pecorino Romano 151
Pedal 302, 308, 370, 372, 501, 522
Pedalhaken 370, 372
Pedalklaviatur 305
Pedalstange 304
Pedaltaste 305
Peildeck 382, 386, 387
Peilstableuchte 364, 365
Pelerine 251
Pelikan 80
Pendelaufhängung 27
Pendelhub-Einstellung 227
Pendelzug 390
Penholdergriff 493
Penis 92, 111
Penne 146
Pepperoniwurst 156
perforierte Vorderkappe 240
Perforierung 243
Pergola 230
peripher-sensorisches Neuron 110
peripheres Nervensystem 108
Peristom 66
Peristyl 279, 280
Perlhuhn 81, 154
Perlzwiebel 124
Peroxyd 461
Peroxysom 66
Perserkatze 87
Persischer Golf 19
Personalcomputer 329
Personaleingang 438
Personalgarderobe 438
Personalraum 443, 463
Personalumkleideraum 465
Personenbahnhof 375
Personenwaage 423
Personenzüge 376
Persönliche Artikel 271
persönliche Ausstattung 264
persönliche Identifikationsnummer (PIN),
   Eingabegerät 443
Peru 448
Peru-Chile-Graben 34
Peso 440
Pestizid 47, 48
Petersilie 142
Petrochemikalien 405
petrochemische Industrie 405
Petroleum 405
Pfahlbau 288
Pfahlwurzel 63
Pfännchen 179
Pfanne 175
Pfannenwender 173
Pfau 81
Pfeffer, gemahlener 139
Pfeffer, grüner 138
Pfeffer, rosa 138
Pfeffer, schwarzer 138
Pfeffer, weißer 138
Pfefferschote 128
Pfefferspray 456
Pfefferstreuer 166
Pfeife 181
Pfeifhase 82
Pfeilanlagepunkt 535
Pfeiler 281, 283, 284, 285, 344, 375
Pfeilerfundament 344
Pfeilförmig 55
Pferd 83, 85
Pferd, äußere Merkmale 83
Pfifferling 123
Pfirsich 132
Pfirsich im Querschnitt 57
Pflanze 53
Pflanze, Aufbau 53
Pflanzenfresser 45
Pflanzenreich 50
Pflanzenzelle 50
Pflanzholz 231
Pflanzkelle 232
Pflanzlochstecher 231
Pflanzschnur 231
Pflanzwerkzeuge 231
Pflasterstein 230
Pflaume 132
Pflaumensoße 141
Pflegelösung 272
Pfortader 103
Pfosten 187, 487, 490, 495
Pfropf 534
Pfund 440
Phase 198
Philippinen 19, 453
Philippinen-Platte 27
Philippinengraben 34
Phobos 2
Phosphorschicht 199
Photon 420
Photosphäre 4
Photosynthese 54
Physalis 132
Physik 416, 418
Physiotherapeut 489
physische Karte 24
Pi 428
Pia Mater 109
Piano, elektronisches 311
Pianopedal 304, 311
Pickup 347
Pik 468
Pikkoloflöte 295, 306
Piktogramme 330
Pilaster, korinthischer 281
Pillbox 239
Pilz 52
Pilz, Aufbau 52
Pilz, tödlich giftiger 52
Pilze 123
Pilzfaden 52
Pilzpapille 118
Pinguin 80
Pinie 65
Pinienkern 65, 133
Pinne 520, 533
Pinnwand 341
Pinseläffchen 91
Pintobohne 131
Pinzette 461
Pipeline 404
Pipeline, überirdische 404
Pistazie 133
Piste, Anfänger 512
Piste, Experte 512
Piste, mittelschwere 512
Piste, schwere 512
Pisten-Mittellinienmarkierungen 390
Pistenbezeichnungsmarkierung 390
Pistenrandmarkierungen 390
Pistenraupe 512
Pistole 216, 456
Pistolengriff 218, 228, 534
Pitot-Rohr 525
Pittabrot 145
Plakat 294
Planeten 2
Planeten, äußere 2
Planeten, innere 3
Planierraupe 398
Planierschaufel 398
Planierschild 398
plankonkave Linse 419
plankonvexe Linse 419
Plantainbanane 136
Planum 342
Plasmabrücke 50
Plasmamembran 66
Plastikhülse 534
Plateau, Hochebene 24
Platte 178, 269, 309, 333
Platte, Afrikanische 27
Platte, Antarktische 27
Platte, Cocos 27
Platte, Eurasiatische 27
Platte, Indisch-Australische 27
Platte, Karibische 27
Platte, Nazca 27
Platte, Nordamerikanische 27
Platte, Pazifische 27
Platte, Philippinen 27
Platte, Scotia 27
Platte, Südamerikanische 27
Platten, tektonische 27
Plattengitter 359
Plattengrenzen, divergierende 27
Plattengrenzen, konvergierende 27
Plattenstift 304
Plattform 219, 363, 516, 526
Plattformpedal 522
Plattsehnenmuskel 97
Platzierungsrichter 516
Play-Taste 323
Plektron 297
Pleuelstange 360
Pleurahöhle 105
plus oder minus 427
Plusbereich 410
Plusglas 419
Pluskontakt 410, 411
Plusplatte 359
Pluspol 359, 417
Pluspolbrücke 359
Pluto 2, 3
PN-Übergang 410
pneubereiftes Laufrad 380
pneubereiftes Leitrad 380
Podest 7, 191, 195, 219
Podium 283, 444
Pokerwürfel 468
Pol, negativer 416
Pol, positiver 416
Polachse 7
Polarisationsfilter 314
Polarklimate 40
Polarkreis, nördlicher 21
Polarkreis, südlicher 15, 22
Polarlicht 37
Polartundra 40
Polen 450
Poleposition 524
Poliklinik 465
Politik 448
politische Karte 23
Polizeibeamter 456
Polizeifahrzeug 457
Polizeirevier 433
Pollenkörbchen 68
Poller 385
Polohemd 255, 492
Polokleid 252
Poloshirt 250
Polster 478
Polsterauflage 460
Polsterdüse 209
Polynesien 453
Poncho 251
Pont-l'Évêque 151
Pool 502
Pore 50, 60, 114
Porro-Prisma 420
Portal 285, 447
Portalkuppel 447
Portierszimmer 439
Porträt 441
Portugal 449
Portulak 127
Portweinglas 165
Posaune 307
Posaunen 295
Positionsleuchte 376
Positionslicht 383, 393, 395
positiver Pol 416
Post, elektronische 335
Postamt 433, 437
Poterne 282
Pottwal 90
Präger 340
Prärie 24
Präzisionssport 502
Präzisionswaage 423
Preis pro Einheit 423
Preis pro Liter/Gallone 346
Preiselbeere 132
Prellbock 375
Pressfilterkanne 181
Presshebel 170, 216
primäre Nahrungsmittelquelle 45
Primärfokus 7

Primärfokuskabine 7
Primärkonsumenten 45
Primärspiegel 7
Primärwurzel 53
Primaten 91
Primaten, Beispiele 91
Prime 298
Prinzesskleid 252
Prinzessnaht 258
Prismenfernglas 420
pritschen 487
private Telekommunikation 317
privater Ankleideraum 290
privater Nutzer 335
privates Rundfunknetz 316
Privatflugzeug 394
Probierlöffel 173
Produktionsbohrung 402
Produzent 291
Profil 358
programmierbare Funktionstasten 443
programmierbare Tasten 332
Programmiertasten 319
Programmwähler 212, 213, 214
Programmwahlschalter 310
Programmwählscheibe 314
Programmwahltasten 319
Projektor 294
Promenadendeck 386
Pronaos 279
Propan- oder Butangas-Geräte 529
Propanflasche 361
Propeller, dreiflügeliger 394
Propeller, zweiflügeliger 394
Propellerummantelung 383
Prospektständer 442
Prospektzug 292
Prostata 111
Proton 414
Protuberanz 4
Provider, Internet 335
Provinz 23
Provinzgrenze 23
Prozent 427
Prozenttaste 337
Prüflampe 217
Pseudopodium 66
psychiatrischer Beobachtungsraum 462
psychiatrischer Untersuchungsraum 462
Publikumseingang 278
Puck 507
Pudel 86
Pudelmütze 239
Puder, loser 266
Puderdose 266
Puderkissen 266
Puderpinsel 266
Puderrouge 266
Puderzucker 149
Puerto-Rico-Graben 34
Puff 201
Puffer 287
Puffertank 404
Pullman Limousine 347
Pullover 250, 255
Pullunder 250
Pulmonalklappe 104
Pulpa 101
Pulpahöhle, Kronenabschnitt 101
pulsierende Vakuole 66
Pult 446
Pulver 140
Puma 88
Pumpe 184, 212, 214, 529
Pumpenraum 384
Pumplöschfahrzeug 455
Pumps 241
Pumpstation 404
Pumpstation, zentrale 404
Punchingball 498
Punktauge 67
Punktbrenner 218
Punkte 492
Punktetabelle 471
Pupille 87, 119
Pupille, senkrechte 76
Puppe 67
Pushup-Griff 501
Puter 155
Putter 505
Putzkelle 216
Putzschwamm 215
Pygalschild 76
Pylon 344
Pylon zur Aufhängung des Triebwerks 393
Pyramide 278, 429

Pyrenäen 18
Python 77

Q

Quadrant 428
Quadrat 429
Quadratwurzel 427
Quadratwurzel aus 427
Quadratwurzeltaste 337
Quark 414
Quarte 298
Quarterback 485
Quarterdeck 386
Quartett 300
Quartier 240, 262
Quecksilberkolben 424
Quecksilbersäule 424
Quecksilberthermometer 461
Quelle 32
Quellenangabe 313
Quellwolken 42
quer verlaufender Dickdarm 106
Querdünen 36
Querfeldeinrad 522
Querflöte 306
Querflöten 295
Querfortsatz 110
Querholz 201, 479
Querjoch 297
Querleiste 202
Querleiste, obere 202
Querleiste, untere 202
Querriegel 185
Querrippe 152
Querruder 13, 392
Querschiff 285
Querschnitt durch eine Sternwarte 7
Querschnitt, Apfel 58
Querschnitt, Baseball 477
Querschnitt, Baumstamm 63
Querschnitt, Erdbeere 59
Querschnitt, Erdkruste 26
Querschnitt, Himbeere 59
Querschnitt, Linsenfernrohr 8
Querschnitt, Orange 58
Querschnitt, Pfirsich 57
Querschnitt, Rotorgondel 413
Querschnitt, Spiegelteleskop 9
Querschnitt, Straße 342, 434
Querschnitt, Wasserkraftwerk 407
Querschnitt, Weintraube 59
Querschnitt, Zwiebel 54
Querschott 384
Querstraße, Allee 433
Querstrebe 467
Querstück 202, 466
Quetschfuß 199
Quetschverschraubung 197
Quicheform 172
Quinte 298
Quintett 300
Quitte 133
Quittungsausgabe 442

R

Rabatte 182
Rabe 80
Rachen 105, 106
Rachenenge 116
Raclette 151
Raclette-Grill 179
Rad 231, 364, 522, 525
Rad-Schneeschläger 172
Radar 382, 383, 386, 387
Radaranlage 457
Radaranlagendisplay 457
Radarmast 384
Radbefestigungsbolzen 357
Rädelung 223
Räder-Drehgeschwindigkeitssensor 357
Radgabel 522
radiale Einsteigestation 389
Radialkapelle 284, 285
Radiator 11
Radiatoren 13
Radicchio 126
Radiergummi 341
Radieschen 129
Radio 315
Radio-Kassettengerät 354
Radio-Wellen 316
radioaktive Kerne 415
radioaktiver Abfall 48
Radioaktivität, Maßeinheit 426
Radiorecorder mit CD-Spieler 326

Radiowellen 418
Radius 428
Radkappe 349
Radlader 399
Radsport 522
Radtraktor 399
Raffinerie 404, 431
Raffinerieerzeugnisse 405
Raglanärmel 248, 251, 261
Raglanmantel 251
Rahmen 187, 192, 202, 204, 224, 240,
    274, 277, 297, 309, 367, 396, 400,
    401, 410, 411, 412, 492, 494, 502,
    522
Rahmen, oben liegender 401
Rahmenleiste 202
Rahmenspant 385
Rambutan 137
Rampe 279, 281, 343, 526
Rampenlicht 293
Rand 273, 441
Rändelbolzen 219
Rang, erster 293
Ränge 278, 281
Ranviersche Schnürringe 110
Ras-El-Hanout 139
Rasen 183, 230, 492
Rasenbesen 237
Rasenpflege 237
Rasentrimmer 237
Rasierer, zweischneidiger 271
Rasiermesser 271
Rasierpinsel 271
Rasierschaum 271
Rasierwasser 271
Raste 473
Rasterleiste 271
Rasthebel 235
Rastplatz 25
Raststätte 25
Raststütze 369
Rasur 271
Rathaus 432
Ratsche 221
Ratschenringschlüssel 223
Ratte 82
Ratte, äußere Merkmale 82
Rau 50
Raubtiere 86
Raubtiere, Beispiele 88
Raubvogel 79
Räucherschinken 153
Rauchklappe 192
Rauchmantel 192
Rauchmelder 454
Rauke 127
Raum, Douglasscher 112
Raum, Douglasscher, vorderer 112
Raumanzug 10
Raumfähre 12, 13, 37
Raumfähre beim Start 12
Raumfahrt 10
Raumlaboratorium 13
Raumsonde 37
Raumstation, internationale 11
Raumteiler 528
Raupe 67
Raupenschere mit Teleskopstiel 234
Raureif 41
Raute 342
Rautenspitze 202
Ravioli 146
Reaktor 408
Reaktorgebäude 409
Reaktorkessel 409
Reanimationsraum 462
Rebe 62
Rebhuhn 80
Rebstock 62
Receiver 321, 325
Receiver: Vorderansicht 322
Rechen 233, 407
rechte Herzkammer 103, 104
rechte Lunge 103, 105
rechte Lungenvene 104
rechte Niere 107
rechte Seite 272
rechte Spur 343
Rechteck 429
Rechteckschlafsack 530
rechter Abwehrspieler 487
rechter Angriffsspieler 489
rechter Aufbauspieler 489
rechter Außenangreifer 487
rechter Außenfeldspieler 474
rechter Centre 482

rechter Corner Back 484
rechter Defensive End 484
rechter Defensive Tackle 484
rechter Guard 485
rechter Kanal 324
rechter Mittelfeldspieler 481
rechter Stürmer 507
rechter Tackle 485
rechter Verteidiger 481, 506
rechter Vorhof 103, 104
rechter Winkel 428
rechtes Aufschlagfeld 491
rechtes Feld 475
rechts 293
Rechtsanwälte, Mitarbeiter 440
Reck 496, 497
Recycling 49
redaktioneller Beitrag 313
Redaktionsteil 313
Redingote 251
reflektierte Sonneneinstrahlung 46
Reflektor 217, 321
Regal 121
regelbarer Thermostat 179
regelmäßiges Achteck 429
regelmäßiges Elfeck 429
regelmäßiges Fünfeck 429
regelmäßiges Neuneck 429
regelmäßiges Oktaeder 429
regelmäßiges Sechseck 429
regelmäßiges Siebeneck 429
regelmäßiges Zehneck 429
regelmäßiges Zwölfeck 429
Regelschalter 210
Regen 41
Regen, gefrierender 41
Regen, saurer 47, 48
Regenbogen 41
Regenfälle, heftige 43
Regenhut 239
Regenleiste 349
Regenmantel 248
Regenrohr 182
Regenwald, tropischer 40, 44
Regenwasserabfluss 434
Regie-Kontrollmonitore 290
Regieassistent 291
Regieraum 293
Regierungsorganisation 335
Regiestuhl 200, 291
Regisseur 291
Register 539
Registerzug 305
Registratoren 499
Registriereinlagen 499
Registrierkasse 121
Registriertrommel 27
Regler 178
Reglerspanngewicht 287
Reglerventil 529
Regnerschlauch 236
Reh 84
Reibe 170
Reibefläche 218
Reif 41
Reife, Stufen 62
Reifen 349, 358, 364, 371, 522, 525
Reifenarten 358
Reifenflanke 358
Reifenstapel 524
Reifeprozess 62
Reihe 272, 293
Reihe, dritte 482
Reihe, erste 482
Reihe, zweite 482
Reihenhaus 289
Reiher 80
Reinigung, chemische 437
Reinigungsbürste 271
Reinigungsmittelbehälter 214
Reinigungsöffnung 194, 197
Reinigungswelle 216
Reis 61, 143, 147
Reis, weißer 147
Reisebett mit Wickelauflage 205
Reisebüro 436
Reisebus 362
Reisessig 141
Reisetasche 276
Reisezug 374
Reisfadennudeln 147
Reisfeld 47
Reismelde 143
Reisnudeln 147
Reispapier 147

Reißen 500
Reißnägel 341
Reißschenkelschutz 398
Reißverschluss 249, 261, 265, 277, 528
Reiter 340
Reiter, durchsichtiger 340
Rektaszensionsachse 8, 9
Relaisstation 316
Relaisstation, Mikrowellen 334
Relaisstelle 317
Religion 446
Reling 384, 385
Rennanzug 508, 525
Rennanzug, feuerfester 524
Rennbügel 371
Rennfahrer 524
Rennleiter 522
Rennrad 373
Rentier 84
Reparaturwerkstatt 346
Reportage 313
Reptilien 76
Reptilien, Beispiele 77
Republik Kongo 451
Requisiteur 291
Requisiteurassistent 291
Reserverad 361
Resettaste 329, 471
Resonanzboden 304
Resonanzdecke 296, 297, 301, 302
Resonanzfell 308
Resonanzkasten 302
Resonanzkörper 297, 302
Resonanzröhren 309
Ressourcenzugriff, vereinheitlichter 334
Restaurant 386, 432, 435, 436, 438
Restaurantkritik 313
Restmüll, nicht wieder verwertbarer 49
Retikulum, endoplasmatisches 50, 66
Rettich 129
Rettich, japanischer 129
Rettungsboot 382, 386
Rettungsfloß 383
Rettungsring 387, 457
Rettungsschacht 345
Rettungsstation 345
Rettungswagen 345, 460, 462
Revers 244
Revers, abfallendes 248
Revers, steigendes 244
Revisionsöffnung 193
Rewritable-Rekorder 333
Rezeptakel 51
Rezeptor, sensorischer 110
Rhabarber 125
Rhea 3
Rhesusfaktor negativ 426
Rhesusfaktor positiv 426
Rhizoid 51
Rhizom 52
Rhombus 429
Rhythmuswahlschalter 311
Riasküste 35
Ribosom 50, 66
Richter, Büro 440
Richtertisch 440
Richtung Mekka 447
Richtungstasten 331, 471
Ricotta 150
Riechbahn 117
Riechkolben 117
Riechnerv 117
Riechschleimhaut 117
Riegel 30, 178, 186, 214, 248, 277
Riemen 225, 477, 500
Riemenantrieb 383
Riemenmuskel 97
Riemenscheibe 360
Riemenschlaufe 532
Riesenkohl 126
Riesenslalom 511
Riesenslalomski 510
Riffküste 35
Rigatoni 146
Right-Wing 482
Rillettes 156
Rinde 107
Rinderfilet 152
Rinderhackfleisch 152
Rindfleisch 152
Rindfleischwürfel 152
Ring 52, 271, 307, 424, 498
Ringablage 340
Ringbuch 339
Ringbuchkalender 338
Ringe 264, 496, 497

ASTRONOMIE > 2-25;   ERDE > 26-71;   PFLANZENREICH >72-89;   TIERREICH > 90-143;   MENSCH > 144-177;   NAHRUNGSMITTEL UND KÜCHE > 178-241;   HAUS > 242-29
HEIMWERKEN UND GARTENARBEIT > 296-333;   KLEIDUNG > 334-371;   PERSÖNLICHE AUSSTATTUNG > 372-391;   KUNST UND ARCHITEKTUR > 392-465;   KOMMUNIKATION UND BÜROTECHNIK > 466-53
TRANSPORT UND FAHRZEUGE > 536-643;   ENERGIE > 644-677;   WISSENSCHAFT > 678-705;   GESELLSCHAFT > 706-785;   SPORT UND SPIELE > 786-920

DEUTSCHES REGISTER

Ringelnatter 77
Ringfinger 115
ringförmige Finsternis 4
Ringpfosten 498
Ringstufe 498
Ringumgebung 498
Ringumrandung 498
Ringverschluss 10
Rippe 125
Rippe, frei endende 98
Rippe, freie 99
Rippe, hohe 152
Rippen 98
Rippenbündchen 261
Rippenbündchen, gerades 247
Rippenfell 105
Rippenpolster 486
Rispe 61
Roberval-Waage 422
Roboterarm 11, 12
Robotersystem 11
Rochen 158
Rock 251, 492
Rock, gerader 253
Röcke, Beispiele 253
Rocky Mountains 16
Rodehacke 233
Roggen 61, 143
Roggenknäckebrot 145
roher Schinken 156
Rohkaffee 148
Rohöl 405
Rohölpipeline 404
Rohr 224, 534
Rohrbatch 193
Rohrblatt 306
Röhre 181, 424
Röhrenfassung 199
Röhrenglocken 295, 309
Röhrenkessel 405
Rohrfeder 523
Rohrschraubstock 224
Rohrstück 460
Rohrzangen 216
Rollbahn 388
Rollbahnmarkierung 389
Rollbewegung 395
Rollbraten 152
Rolle 277, 308, 526, 527, 535
Rollenfuß 536, 537
Rollenhaltepartie 537
Rollenhalterung 536, 537
Rollgabelschlüssel 223
Rollkragen 514
Rollkragenpullover 250
Rollring 196
Rollschuh 527
Rollschweller 305
Rollsport 526
Rollstuhl 467
Rollstuhllift 363
Rolltreppe 378, 435
Romagna-Salat 126
Römerpantolette 242
Römertopf 175
römische Bohne 131
römische Metallfeder 312
römische Ziffern 427
römisches Amphitheater 281
römisches Wohnhaus 280
Röntgengerät, fahrbares 462
Röntgenstrahlen 418
Roquefort 151
rosa Ball 503
rosa Pfeffer 138
Rose 56
Rosenkohl 126
Rosennerv 108
Rosenvene, große 102
Rosette 186, 285
Rosmarin 142
Ross-Schelfeis 15
Rösselsprung 470
Rost 210
Rot 418, 469
Rotalge 51
Rotbarsch 161
rote Bälle 503
rote Beete 129
rote Heidelbeere 132
rote Kidneybohne 131
rote Klemme 356
rote Meerbarbe 159
roter Zwiebel 124
roter Ball 503
roter Paprika 128

roter Stoßball 502
rotes Licht 434
Rotes Meer 14, 19, 20
Rotini 146
Rotkehlchen 80
Rotknievogelspinne, Mexikanische 70
Rotkohl 126
Rotor 412, 537
Rotorblatt 395, 412, 413
Rotorgondel im Querschnitt 413
Rotorkopf 395
Rotornabe 395
Rotstrahl 318
Rotunde 435
Rotweinglas 165
Rougepinsel 266
Router 334
Royal Flush 468
Ruanda 451
Rübe 129
Rübenhacke 233
Rübenspross 127
Rubin-Impulslaser 420
Rubinzylinder 420
Rückansicht 97, 99, 113
Rückbank 353
Rücken 78, 83, 86, 93, 95, 167, 169,
    226, 228, 244
Rücken, Indisch-Antarktischer 34
Rücken, Mittelatlantischer 34
Rücken, Östlicher Indischer 34
Rücken, Ostpazifischer 34
Rücken, ozeanischer 33
Rücken, Westlicher Indischer 34
Rücken, Zentralindischer 34
Rückenansicht 93, 95
Rückenflosse 90
Rückenflosse, erste 74
Rückenflosse, zweite 74
Rückenlehne 200, 201, 205, 353, 369,
    467, 523
Rückenlehne, Basis 200
Rückenmark 109, 110
Rückenmark, Aufbau 109
Rückenmarkshaut 109
Rückenmarkshaut, harte 109, 110
Rückenmarksnerv 109, 110
Rückenmittelschlitz 244
Rückenmuskel, breiter 97
Rückenpanzer 76
Rückenschlitz, seitlicher 244
Rückenschutz 525
Rückenschwimmen 517
Rückenschwimmen, Startgriffe 516
Rückenspange 244
Rückenteil 260
Rückenteil, verstellbares 460
Rückenträger, gekreuzt 261
Rückenverstärkung 509
Rückfahrscheinwerfer 352
Rückfeld 491
Rückfeldschiedsrichter 485
Rückgrat 536
Rückhaltesystem, Airbag 354
Rückholfeder 357
Rücklagenstütze 511
Rücklauf 323
Rücklauf-Taste 323
Rücklauftaste 326, 328
Rücklicht 370
Rucksack 532
Rückschläger 490, 495
Rückschlaghinderer 534
Rückschritt, löschender 331
Rückspiegel 354, 366, 523
Rücksprungpalette 396
Rückspulknopf 314
Rückspultaste 319
Rückstellknopf 424
Rückstelltaste 319, 323, 328
Rückstoßtriebwerk, vorderes 12
Rückstrahler 365, 370, 523
rückwärtige Begrenzungslinie 494
rückwärts 518
Rückwurflinie 479
Ruder 13, 383, 384, 386, 501, 520
Ruderblatt 384
Rudergerät 501
Ruderhaus 384
Ruffinisches Körperchen 114
Rufnummernregister 327
Rufnummernregister für automatische
    Wahl 327
Ruftaste 287, 327
Rugby 482
Rugbyball 483

Rugbyschuhe 483
Rugbyspieler 483
Rührbesen 176
Rührschüssel 176
Rührschüsseln 172
Rumänien 450
Rumpf 75, 93, 95, 393, 471, 520, 523
rund 55
Rundbürste 268
runde Bahn 522
runder Einwärtsdreher 96
runder Korpus 296
Rundfunknetz, privates 316
Rundkopf mit Schlitz 221
Rundmuskel, großer 97
Rundmuskel, kleiner 97
Rupie 440
Rüschen 260
Rüschenhöschen 260
Rüschenstrumpfhose 260
Rüssel 67
russischer Pumpenkuchel 145
russisches Modul 11
Russland 450
Rutengriff 537
Rutenschwellkörper 111
rutschfester Fuß 219
Ryukyugraben 34

S

S-Bahn-Strecke 375
S-Bogen 306
S-Bogen, Griffhebel 306
S-Video-Ausgang 336
Saal 386
Sackkarren 396
Safarijacke 255
Safran 138
Saftrinne 169
Sägeblatt 226, 227
Sägekette 235
Sägewerkzeuge 226
Sagittalschnitt 111, 112
Sahara 20
Sahne 150
Sahne, saure 150
Sahnebecher 163
Saint Kitts und Nevis 449
Saint Vincent und die Grenadinen 449
Saite 301, 302
Saiten 297
Saitenaufhängung 303
Saitenbezug 304
Saitenhalter 301
Saitenhalterung 297
Saiteninstrumente 301
Säkelle 231
Sakristei 446
Salamander 75
Salami, feine 156
Salami, grobe 156
Salatgabel 168
Salatgurke, kernlose 128
Salatschale 166
Salatschleuder 171
Salatschüssel 166
Salatteller 166
Salbei 142
Salchow 509
Saling 520
Salomoninseln 453
Salpetersäure, Emission 48
Saltostellung 518
Salz, grobes 141
Salzsee 20
Salzstreuer 166
Sambal Oelek 141
Sambia 452
Samen 53, 57, 58, 59, 60
Samenanlage 501
Samenbläschen 111
Samenleiter 111
Samenmantel 57
Samenschale 61
Sammelbehälter 345
Sammellinsen 419
Sammelscheine 407
Sammlung, getrennte 49
Samoa 453
Sampler 310
Samtkropfband 264
San Marino 450
Sand 492
Sandale 242
Sandale mit Zehenriemchen 242

Sandalette 241
Sandbank 33
Sandblattfeilen 265
Sandinsel 35
Sandkasten 377
Sandsack 498
Sandwüste 36
Sandwüste, Große 15
Sanitärinstallation 194, 195, 197
Sanitärinstallationssystem 194
Sankt-Lorenz-Strom 16
São Tomé und Principe 451
Sardelle 159
Sardine 159
Sarong 253
Satellit 316
Satelliten-Direktempfang 316
Satellitenübertragungstechnik 316
Sattel 245, 249, 255, 301, 302, 303,
    370
Sattelkupplung 364
Sattelrock 253
Sattelschlepper 364
Sattelstütze 370
Satteltasche 372
Saturn 2, 3
Satz 492
Sätze, vorherige 492
Satztische 202
Sauciere 166
Saudi-Arabien 452
Sauerstoff, Abgabe 54
Sauerstoffanschluss 464
sauerstoffarmes Blut 104
Sauerstoffdruck-Stelleinrichtung 10
sauerstoffreiches Blut 104
Saugarm 400
Saugbürste 209
Saugnapf 72
Saugrohr 209, 360, 400, 407, 455
Saugzubehör 209
Säule 31, 279
Saum 478
Saumlatte 412
saure Sahne 150
saurer Regen 47, 48
saurer Schnee 48
Savanne 40, 44
Säwerkzeuge 231
Saxhorn 307
Saxophon 306
Scanner 121
Schaber 219
Schach 470
Schachbrett 470
Schachfiguren 470
Schachtel, Käse 163
Schädel 92, 100
Schädel eines Kleinkindes 100
Schädel, Seitenansicht 100
schädliche Gase, Emission 47
Schadstoffe, biologisch nicht abbaubare
    47
Schaf 84
Schäferhund, Deutscher 86
Schafstall 122
Schaft 220, 221, 228, 471, 492, 494,
    503, 505, 506
Schaftstiefel 241
Schäftung 534
Schäkel 521
Schale 58, 60, 73, 79, 162, 277
Schalenhaut 79
Schalenschuh 527
Schalensitz: Seitenansicht 353
Schalensitz: Vorderansicht 353
Schäler 169
Schallbecher 305
Schallbecherstütze 306
Schallbrett 285
Schalldämpfer 351
Schalloch 301
Schallplattenladen 436
Schallrose 302
Schälmesser 169
Schalotte 124
Schalter 198, 210, 211, 219, 227, 229,
    269, 270, 271, 272, 416, 443
Schalter für Belüftung 354
Schalter für Heizung 354
Schalterabdeckplatte 198
Schalthebel 350, 354, 369, 371, 372,
    522
Schaltpedal 367, 368
Schaltuhr 210

Schaltung, integrierte 417
Schaltzug 372
Scham 94, 113
Schambein 92, 94
Schamhügel 112
Schamlippe, große 112, 113
Schamlippe, kleine 112, 113
Schamotteplatte 192
Schamottestein 192
Schardrehkranz 401
Schardrehzylinder 401
Scharfeinstellung 8, 9
Schärfentiefenknopf 314
Scharfstellrad, zentrales 420
Scharfstellring 420
Scharhubzylinder 401
Scharnier 178, 185, 186, 202, 214, 274,
    277, 352, 367, 402
Scharverstellvorrichtung 401
Scharwachturm 282
Schatten 424
Schaufel 399, 510, 514
Schaufel, hintere 399
Schaufelarm 399
Schaufelbolzengelenk 399
Schaufellader 399
Schaufelzahn 400
Schaufelzylinder 399, 400
Schaukelstuhl 200, 201
Schaum 33
Schaumanzeiger 385
Schaumbad 267
Schaumgummimatratze 530
Schaumgummipolsterung 458
Schauspieler 290
Schauspielereingang 278
Schauspielerin 291
Schauspielerstühle 290
Scheckheft 274
Scheckhülle 275
Scheckkarte 443
Schecks 441
Scheibe 6, 186, 501
Scheiben 177
Scheibenbremse 350, 357, 366, 525
Scheibenbremse, hydraulische 522
Scheibenhantel 500
Scheibenwaschdüse 348
Scheibenwischer 348, 355
Scheibenwischerhebel 354
Scheide 52, 112, 113, 533
Scheide, Schwannsche 110
Scheider 359
Scheidewand 58, 60, 117
Scheidewandknorpel 117
Scheinwerfer 290, 293, 348, 364, 366,
    368, 371, 376, 377, 455, 523
Scheitel 78
Scheitelbein 99, 100
Scheitelrippe 284
Schekel, neuer 440
Schelfeis, Filchner 15
Schelfeis, Ross 15
Schelle 309
Schellen 309
Schellfisch 161
Schema des Blutkreislaufs 103
Schenkel 78, 83, 538
Schenkelbein 99
Schenkelbindenspanner 96
Schenkelhals 99
Schenkelmuskel, äußerer 96, 97
Schenkelmuskel, gerader 96
Schenkelmuskel, innerer 96
Schenkelmuskel, zweiköpfiger 97
Schere 71, 461, 531
Scherenblatt, gekerbtes 270
Scherenleuchte 207
Scherenstromabnehmer 376
Scherkopf 271
Scherkopfhalter 271
Scheuerleiste 358
Scheune 122
Schiebedach 349
Schiebefenster, horizontales 287
Schiebefenster, vertikales 287
Schiebegriff 467
Schiebeleiter 455
Schiebeöffnung 423
Schieber 273, 425
Schieberad 407
Schiebetür 195, 286
Schiebetür, automatische 286
Schiebetür, elektrische 363
Schieblehre, Messschieber 425

ASTRONOMIE > 2-25;   ERDE > 26-71;   PFLANZENREICH >72-89;   TIERREICH > 90-143;   MENSCH > 144-177;   NAHRUNGSMITTEL UND KÜCHE > 178-241;   HAUS > 242-295;
HEIMWERKEN UND GARTENARBEIT > 296-333;   KLEIDUNG > 334-371;   PERSÖNLICHE AUSSTATTUNG > 372-391;   KUNST UND ARCHITEKTUR > 392-465;   KOMMUNIKATION UND BÜROTECHNIK > 466-535;
TRANSPORT UND FAHRZEUGE > 536-643;   ENERGIE > 644-677;   WISSENSCHAFT > 678-705;   GESELLSCHAFT > 706-785;   SPORT UND SPIELE > 786-920

Schiedsrichter 479, 481, 483, 488, 490, 495, 498, 499, 507, 515, 516, 518
Schienbein 98
Schienbeinarterie, vordere 102
Schienbeinmuskel, vorderer 96
Schienbeinnerv 108
Schienbeinschützer 480, 513
Schiene 207, 214, 473, 527
Schienen 461
Schienenräumer 376, 377
Schienenverkehr 374
Schifffahrt 381
Schiffsbodenverband 190
Schiffsschraube 384
Schiitakepilz 123
Schikane 524
Schild 169, 458
Schildbogen 284
Schildchen 73
schildförmig 55
Schildhubzylinder 398
Schildkröte 76
Schildkröte, äußere Merkmale 76
Schildwanze 69
Schimpanse 91
Schinken, gekochter 156
Schinken, roher 156
Schinkenmesser 169
Schirm 206, 273, 479
Schirmfeder 78
Schirmmütze 238
Schirmständer 273
Schlafanzug 256, 261
Schlafanzug in Schlupfform 261
Schlafanzug, zweiteilig 260
Schlafcouch 204
Schläfe 92
Schläfenbein 98, 100
Schlafkabine 364
Schlafraum 528
Schlafsäcke, Beispiele 530
Schlafwagen 376
Schlafzimmer 189
Schlafzimmer, großes 189
Schlagbereich 477
Schläge 490
Schläger 476, 477
Schlägerabdeckung 505
Schlagfläche 505
Schlaghandschuh 476
Schlagholz 478
Schlaghose 254
Schlaginstrumente 295, 308
Schlagmal 475
Schlagmallinie 479
Schlagmann 475, 476, 478, 479
Schlagpolster, elektronisches 311
Schlagsahne 150
Schlagschutz 303
Schlagstockhalter 456
Schlagzeile 313
Schlammfluss 31
Schlammgrube 403
Schlammpumpe 403
Schlammpumpenschlauch 403
Schlange 76
Schlangenbohrer mit doppeltem Gewindegang 228
Schlankmuskel 97
Schlauch 209, 454, 461
Schlauch, flexibler 209
Schlauchdüse 236
Schlauchkleid 252
Schlauchkupplung 236
Schlauchleitung 454
Schlauchwagen 236
Schlaufe 245, 265, 343
Schlegel 308, 309
Schleier 536
Schleifblatt 229
Schleife 238
Schleifpapier 229
Schleifteller 229
Schlepper 384
Schlepplift 512
Schleppvorrichtung 364
Schleuder 365
Schließe 532
Schließfach 443
Schließfrucht 60
Schließmuskel, hinterer 73
Schließmuskel, vorderer 73
Schlinge 535
Schlitten 521
Schlittschuh 506
Schlittschuhe, Eisschnelllauf 508

Schlittschuhschritt 514
Schlittschuhschritt, diagonaler 514
Schlitz 167, 178, 221, 247, 260
Schlitzschrauben 221
Schloss 186, 202, 211, 275, 277, 372
Schlossbrett 185
Schloßband 73
Schlucht 31, 32
Schluckloch 31
Schlupfform 261
Schlüssel 223
Schlüsselbein 98
Schlüsselbeinarterie 102
Schlüsselbeinvene 102
Schlüsseldienst 437
Schlüsseletui 275
Schlüsselschild 186
Schlüsselschloss 277
Schlussleuchte 352, 367, 368
Schlussstein 284
Schmelz 101
Schmelzen 414
Schmelzwasser 30
Schmetterball 491
Schmetterling 67
Schmetterling, äußere Merkmale 67
Schmetterlingsstil 517
Schmiermittelraffinerie 405
Schmieröle 405
Schmorpfanne 175
Schmuck 264
Schmuck und Schönheitspflege 264
Schmutzfänger 349, 364, 365
Schnabel 78
Schnalle 248, 276
Schnappmechanismus 537
Schnappschloss 274
Schnappverschluss 275
Schnarrsaite 308
Schnarrsaitenspanner 308
Schnauze 75, 86, 87
Schnauzer 86
Schnecke 72, 116, 157, 301, 365
Schnecke, äußere Merkmale 72
Schneckenbohrer 228
Schneckenpfännchen 173
Schneckenzange 173
Schnee 41
Schnee, ewiger 29
Schnee, saurer 48
Schneeanzug 261
Schneebesen 172
Schneefeger 356
Schneefräse 365
Schneemobil 523
Schneeregen 41
Schneesack 260
Schneidbrett 169
Schneide 167, 169, 221, 270, 509
Schneiden 177
Schneiderkragen 251
Schneidermuskel 96
Schneidezahn, äußerer 101
Schneidezahn, mittlerer 101
Schneidezähne 101
Schneidkante 398, 399, 400
Schneidklinge 180
Schneidkopf 341
Schneidlade, Gehrung 226
Schneidmesser 176, 177
Schneidwerkzeuge 234
schnell drehende Welle 413
Schnellablaufbahn 388
Schnellhefter 339
Schnellkocher, elektrischer 179
Schnellkochtopf 174
Schnellspannbohrfutter 228
Schnellstraße 343
Schnellvorlauf-Taste 323
Schnellvorlauftaste 326
Schnittfläche 235
Schnittlauch 124
Schnittstelle, Ethernet 336
Schnittstelle, FireWire 336
Schnittstelle, serielle 329
Schnittstelle, USB 329, 336
Schnittstellen, Controller 471
Schnitzel 152
Schnur 225, 327
Schnürband 477
Schnurfangbügel 537
Schnürhaken 509
Schnurlaufröllchen 537
Schnürloch 240
Schnürlochteil 240
Schnüröse 509

Schnurrhaare 87
Schnurringe, Ranviersche 110
Schnürschuh 240
Schnürsenkel 240, 262, 498, 509
Schnürsenkelende 240, 262
Schokolade 148
Schokolade, weiße 148
Scholle 161
Schollenmuskel 96
Schöpflöffel 173
Schöpfteil 167
Schornstein 183, 382, 386, 402
Schössling 53, 63
Schoß 245, 255
Schote 60
Schote, Schnitt 60
Schottenrock 253
Schotterfläche 30
Schräge 460
schräge Pattentasche 248, 251
schräger Interlobarspalt 105
Schräggeison 279
Schrägmaß 225
Schrägstellungsvorrichtung 227
Schrankteil 203
Schrapper 400
Schratten 31
Schraube 221, 301, 384, 386, 387
Schrauben 223
Schraubenbolzen 223
Schraubenbolzen mit Ansatz 223
Schraubendreher 221
Schraubenfeder 351
Schraubenwelle 383, 387
Schraubenzieher 221, 531
Schrauberbit 228
Schraubfassung 199
Schraubstock 224
Schraubstollen 480
Schraubverschluss 163
Schraubwerkzeuge 221
Schreib Lesekopf 333
Schreiber 27
Schreibgeräte 312
Schreibmappe 275
Schreibpinsel 312
Schreibplatte, herausklappbare 203
Schreibschutz 333
Schreibspitze 27
Schreibtisch 439
Schreibtischleuchte 206
Schreibwaren 337
Schritt 83, 247, 255
Schrot 534
Schrotflinte (glatter Lauf) 534
Schubdüse 10
Schubkarre 231
Schubkasten 205
Schubkontrolle 332
Schublade 164, 202, 203
Schubphase 514
Schubrahmen 398
Schuh 240, 488, 522, 524
Schuh mit Stoßplatten 486
Schuhe 240
Schuhgeschäft 437
Schukosockdose 198
Schukostecker 198
Schulaufsicht, Büro 445
Schulbank 444
Schulbus 362
Schule 444
Schüler mit Lernschwierigkeiten, Klassenzimmer 444
Schüler/Schülerin 444
Schülerspinde 445
Schulhof 445
Schulleiter, Büro 445
Schulter 83, 86, 92, 94, 302, 536
Schulterblatt 93, 95, 98, 99
Schulterblattgräte 99
Schulterbolzen 248, 456
Schultergurt 353, 505, 532
Schulterklappe 248, 456
Schulterpolster 486
Schulterriemen 276
Schultertasche 276
Schuppe 74, 76
Schuppen 182, 230
Schuppenblatt 54
Schuppennaht 100
Schürfkübel 400
Schürhaken 193
Schürze, elastische 383
Schürzenfinger 383
Schüssel 177

Schüttelsieb 403
Schutz 227
Schutzanzug 525
Schutzausrüstung 486
Schutzbezug 204
Schutzblech 370, 523
Schutzblech, vorderes 366
Schutzbrille 218, 458, 522, 525
Schutzdach 396
Schutzdeckel 329
Schützer, Schienbein 513
Schutzgehäuse 237
Schutzgeländer 377
Schutzgitter 205, 217, 442
Schutzglas 318
Schutzhaube, obere 227
Schutzhaube, untere 227
Schutzhelm 367, 458, 486, 506
Schutzkäfig 473
Schutzkappe 420, 460, 467
Schutzkontaktstiegel 198
Schutzmaske 458
Schutzplatte 525
Schutzraum 345
Schutzring 210
Schutzschicht 10
Schutzumrandung 471
Schutzwand 506
schwacher Punkt 470
Schwadenblech 237
Schwalbe 80
Schwamm 215
Schwammstäbchen 266
Schwanenhals 400
Schwannsche Scheide 110
Schwanz 71, 76, 82, 83, 86, 90, 111, 536
Schwanzfächer 71
Schwanzfeder 78
Schwanzflosse 74, 90
Schwarz 418, 470
schwarzäugige Bohne 130
Schwarzbär 89
schwarze Bohne 131
schwarze Johannisbeere 132
schwarze Klemme 356
schwarze Mungobohne 131
schwarze Senfkörner 138
schwarzer Ball 503
schwarzer Pfeffer 138
schwarzer Stein 470
schwarzer Tee 148
schwarzes Brett 444
schwarzes Feld 470
Schwarzes Meer 14, 18, 19
Schwarzrettich 129
Schwarzwurzel 129
Schwebebalken 496, 497
Schweden 450
Schwefeldioxid, Emission 48
Schwefelsäure, Emission 48
Schwein 84
Schweinefleisch 153
Schweinehackfleisch 153
Schweinespeck 149
Schweinestall 122
Schweißband 492
Schweißdrüse, apokrine 114
Schweißdrüse, Ausführungsgang 114
Schweißdrüse, ekkrine 114
Schweißwerkzeuge 218
Schweiz 450
schweizer Offiziersmesser 531
Schwelle 185
Schwellenmarkierungen 391
Schwenkarm 176
Schwenkbrückenstand 400
Schwenkkopf 224
Schwenksockel 224
Schwenkverschluss 224
schwere Piste 512
Schwerfahrzeugen, Transport 377
Schwerkraftmodul 11
Schwermaschinen 398
Schweröl 405
Schwert 235, 520
Schwertfisch 159
Schwertwal 90
Schwesternstation 462, 463
Schwesternzimmer 465
Schwimmbecken 184, 516
Schwimmbecken, eingebautes 184
Schwimmbrille 516
Schwimmdach 404
Schwimmdachtank 404

Schwimmen 516
Schwimmer 196, 538
Schwimmerventil 196
Schwimmfuß 75
Schwimmhaut 75, 79
Schwimmhautzeh 79
Schwimmkörper 394
Schwimmkran 381
Schwimmlappenzeh 79
Schwingflügel 287
Schwinggaragentor 286
Schwinghebel 360
schwingungsdämpfender Bügelgriff 235
Schwingungsdämpfer 212
Schwungrad 360, 501
Scotia-Platte 27
Scrimmage-Linie 485
Scriptgirl 391
Scrollen 331
Scrollen-Feststelltaste 331
Scrollrad 327, 332
Sechseck, regelmäßiges 429
Sechserpack 468
Sechskantmutter 223, 359
Sechzehntelnote 299
Sechzehntelpause 299
Second 515
Sedimentgesteine 26
See 5, 24, 29, 32
See, Irische 18
See, künstlicher 32
See, tektonisches 32
See, vulkanischer 32
Seebarsch 160
Seehund 90
Seelachs 161
Seelöwe 90
Seen 32
Seen, Größe 16
Seenversauerung 48
Seeotter 89
Seeteufel 160
Segel 519
Segelboot 520
Segelkleid 520
Segellatte 519, 520
Segelsport 520
Segelstange 412
Segeltasche 519
Segeltuchbespannung 412
Segmentpunktzahl 471
Sehen 419
Sehenswürdigkeit 25
Sehfehler 419
Sehne 535
Sehnerv 119
Sehnervenkreuzung 109
Seifenbecher 211
Seifenschale 195
Seiher 171
Seil 219, 498
Seilbahn 512
Seilbahnabfahrt 512
Seilverspannung 498
Seilzug 219
seismische Welle 27
Seismogramm 27
Seismographen 27
seismologische Aufzeichnung 403
Seite 167, 293
Seite, linke 272
Seite, nächste 331
Seite, rechte 272
Seite, vorherige 331
Seitenansicht 478
Seitenansicht eines Schädels 100
Seitenauslinie 491
Seitenband, vertikales 487
Seitenfach 352
Seitenfenster 349
Seitenflosse 393, 395
Seitenfontanelle, hintere 100
Seitenfontanelle, vordere 100
Seitengriff 352
Seitenkapelle 284
Seitenkästen 525
Seitenkoffer 369
Seitenlinie 74, 483, 484, 487, 488, 491, 515
Seitenlinie für das Doppelspiel 490, 495
Seitenlinie für das Einzelspiel 491, 495
Seitenluke 12
Seitenmoräne 30
Seitenöffnung 344
Seitenrad 412
Seitenrichter 483

ASTRONOMIE > 2-25;   ERDE > 26-71;   PFLANZENREICH >72-89;   TIERREICH > 90-143;   MENSCH > 144-177;   NAHRUNGSMITTEL UND KÜCHE > 178-241;   HAUS > 242-295;
HEIMWERKEN UND GARTENARBEIT > 296-333;   KLEIDUNG > 334-371;   PERSÖNLICHE AUSSTATTUNG > 372-391;   KUNST UND ARCHITEKTUR > 392-465;   KOMMUNIKATION UND BÜROTECHNIK > 466-535;
TRANSPORT UND FAHRZEUGE > 536-643;   ENERGIE > 644-677;   WISSENSCHAFT > 678-705;   GESELLSCHAFT > 706-785;   SPORT UND SPIELE > 786-920

DEUTSCHES REGISTER

Seitenruder 393
Seitenschiff 285
Seitenschlot 28
Seitenspiegel 269, 348, 364, 368
Seitenspiegelverstellhebel 352
Seitenständer 367
Seitensteg 273
Seitenstück 201
Seitentasche 505
Seitenteil 248
Seitenverkleidung 349
Seitenverstellhebel 229
Seitenwand 365, 517
Seitenwurzel 53
seitliche Einfassung 192
seitlicher Hautnerv des Oberschenkels 108
seitlicher knöcherner Bogengang 116
seitlicher Kompressionsgurt 532
seitlicher Rückenschlitz 244
Seitpferd 496
Sekretär 203
Sekretariat 443, 445
Sektionalgaragentor 286
Sektkelch 165
Sektor 428
Sektschale 165
Sekundant 498
Sekundärkonsumenten 45
Sekundärspiegel 7, 9
Sekunde 298
Sekundenzeiger 424
selbstaufblasbare Luftmatratze 530
Selbstauslöser 314
Selbstauslöser-Lichtsignal 314
Selbstbedienungstheke 120
Selbstklebeetiketten 340
selbstklebende Lasche 339
Sendeantenne 316
Sendereinstellung 326
Sendersuchlauftasten 322
Sendung mit Radio-Wellen 316
Senegal 20, 451
Senf 60, 140
Senf, amerikanischer 140
Senf, deutscher 140
Senf, englischer 140
Senfkörner 140
Senfkörner, schwarze 138
Senfkörner, weiße 138
Senfpulver 140
Senkkopf mit Imbus 221
Senkkopf mit Kreuzschlitz 221
Senkkopf mit Schlitz 221
senkrechte Pupille 76
sensibles Neuron 110
Sensor 178
Sensor für Fernbedienung 318
Sensor, optischer 332
Sensorhülse 178
sensorischer Rezeptor 110
Sensorkreis 357
Sepalum 58
Separator 417
Septime 298
Septum pellucidum 109
Sequencer 310
Sequenzregler 310
Serac 30
serielle Schnittstelle 329
Seriennummer 441
Server 334, 335
Service-Bereich 346
Servicemodul, ferngesteuertes 11
Servierplatte 166
Serviertisch 438
Servierwagen 202
Sesamöl 149
Sessellift 512
Sesselliftabfahrt 512
Setzholz 202
Setzstufe 191
Sexte 298
Sextett 300
Seychellen 452
Shake-Hands-Griff 493
Shampoo 267
Shorts 254, 263
Siamkatze 87
Sichel 234
Sicheldüne 36
Sicherheit 454
Sicherheitsbereich 499
Sicherheitsbindung 510, 511
Sicherheitsdienst 463
Sicherheitsfaden 441

Sicherheitsgriff 237
Sicherheitsgurt 353, 525
Sicherheitshinweisschild 228
Sicherheitsholm 219
Sicherheitshülle 408, 409
Sicherheitskarte 361
Sicherheitskontrolle 391
Sicherheitsleiste 211
Sicherheitsleuchte 457
Sicherheitsnaht 440
Sicherheitsriemen 10
Sicherheitsschuh 459
Sicherheitssensor 354
Sicherheitsspiegel 202
Sicherheitsstreifen 379
Sicherheitsthermostat 213
Sicherheitsventil 174, 408
Sicherung 198, 411
Sicherungsautomat 407
Sicherungsknopf 352
Sicherungskopf 221
Sicherungsstift 454
sichtbares Licht 418
Sichtfenster 13, 178, 179, 210
Sichtlinie 533
Sieb 177, 180
Siebbeinplatte 117
Sieben 171
Siebeneck, regelmäßiges 429
Sierra Leone 451
Sigmoid 106
Signal 375
Signalbrücke 375
Signalhorn 377
Signalleiste 455
Silberbesteck 167
Silos 381
Simbabwe 452
Sinfonieorchester 295
Singapur 453
Sinkblei 538
Sinnesorgane 114, 115, 119
Sinushaar 82
Siphonalkanal 73
Sistrum 309
Sitz 195, 196, 200, 201, 205, 353, 369,
467, 501, 523
Sitzbank 201, 353, 367, 379, 523
Sitzbein 99
Sitzmöbel 201
Sitzplatz 294
Sitzplätze 293
Sitzrohr 370
Sitzsack 201
Sitzungsraum 442
Sitzungssaal 439
Sitzverstellung 353
Skala 225, 422, 424, 425, 460, 533
Skandinavische Halbinsel 18
skandinavisches Knäckebrot 145
Skateboard 526
Skateboarder 526
Skateboarding 526
Skaterin 527
Skelett 98
Skelettbürste 268
Ski 510
Skianzug 510, 513, 514
Skibremse 511
Skibrille 510, 513
Skier, Beispiele 510
Skigebiet 512
Skihandschuhe 510
Skihütte 512
Skikanglauf 514
Skiliftankunft 512
Skimmer 184
Skimütze 514
Skip 515
Skipiste 512
Skipisten 512
Skischule 512
Skispitze 514
Skispringen 513
Skispringer 513
Skisprunganzug 513
Skisprungschuh 513
Skistiefel 510, 511, 514
Skistock 510, 514
Skiträger 356
Skorpion 70
Slalomski 510
Slingpumps 241
Slip 247, 259
Slipper 242
Slowakische Republik 450

Slowenien 450
SLR-Kamera 314
Smog 47
Snackbar 294
Snooker 503
Snowboard 513
Snowboarden 513
Snowboarder 513
Sobanudeln 147
Söckchen 257
Socke 257, 486, 492
Sockel 192, 199, 206, 269, 283, 302,
412, 422
Sockel, fester 224
Sockel, gepolsterter 489
Sockelgeschoß 477
Sockelleiste 191
Sockelprofil 202
Socken 247, 480
Sofa 200
Sofa, zweisitziges 439
Soffitte 293
Soffitten 292
Sofortbildkamera 315
Softball 477
Softballhandschuh 477
Softballschläger 477
Softboots 513
Software, E-Mail 334
Sohle 229, 247, 509, 511
Sohlenspanner 97
Sohlschicht, obere 402
Sohlschicht, untere 402
Sojabohnen 131
Sojasoße 140
Sojasprossen 131
Solarreflektoren 316
Solarzelle 337, 410, 411
Solarzellengenerator 11
Solarzellensystem 411
Solitärring 264
Solvent-Extraktionsanlage 405
Somalia 451
Somennudeln 147
Sommer 38
Sommersonnenwende 38
Sonne 2, 4, 5, 38
Sonne, Aufbau 4
Sonnenblende 8, 354, 361
Sonnenblume 56
Sonnenblumenöl 149
Sonnenbrille 273
Sonnendeck 385, 387
Sonneneinstrahlung 46
Sonneneinstrahlung, absorbierte 46
Sonneneinstrahlung, reflektierte 46
Sonnenenergie 54, 410
Sonnenfinsternis 4
Sonnenfleck 4
Sonnenkleid, leichtes 252
Sonnenrollo 356
Sonnenschutz, Windschutzscheiben 356
Sonnenschutzblende 320
Sonnenschutzschicht 10
Sonnensegel 7
Sonnenstrahlen 45
Sonnenstrahlung 410, 411
Sonnensystem 2
Sonnenuhr 424
Sonnenzellenauslöser 316
Sonnenzellenkollektor 411
Sortieranlage 49
Sortierung von Glas 49
Sortierung von Kunststoff 49
Sortierung von Metall 49
Sortierung von Papier/Pappe 49
Sortierung, optische 49
Sorus 52
Soufflérom 172
Sozialarbeiterbüro 463
Sozialdiensträume 465
Soziussitz 369
Spaghetti 146
Spaghettikürbis 129
Spaghettini 146
Spaghettizange 173
Spalier 230
Spalierbogen 230
Spalt 58
spaltbarer Kern 415
Spalte 313
Spaltprodukte (radioaktive Kerne) 415
Späneschutz 227
Spangang 228
Spange 248
Spanien 449

Spann 92
Spannbetttuch 204
Spanner 528
Spanner, Werkstück 226
Spannfeder 500
Spanngriff 224
Spannkabel 412
Spannpratze 224
Spannrad 398
Spannschnur 297
Spannschraube 224, 229, 308
Spannungserhöhung, erste 413
Spannungserhöhung, zweite 413
Spannungsprüfer 217
Spannungsstift 198
Spannweite 224
Spannweite, eingehängte 344
Sparbuchnachtrag 442
Spareribs/Schälrippchen 153
Spargel 125
Spargelbohne 130
Spargelsalat 126
Sparren 187
sparriges Torfmoos 51
spatelförmig 55
Spaten 233
Spazierstock 273, 466
Specht 80
Speedskate 527
Speer 472
Speerwurf 473
Speiche 70, 98, 371
Speicheldrüse 118
Speichernerv 108
Speichenseite, Handstrecker 97
Speicheradditionstaste 337
Speicheranzeigetaste 337
Speichergeräte 333
Speicherkarte 315
Speicherkartenschächte 471
Speicherkraftwerk 406
Speicherlöschtaste 337
Speichersubtraktionstaste 337
Speichertaste 322, 323, 327
Speisekammer 188
Speiseröhre 105, 106
Speisesaal 386, 438, 439
Speisewagen 376
Spektrum, elektromagnetisches 418
Spenzer 254
Sperling 80
Spermium 111
Sperrdrehknopf 425
Sperre 434
Sperrengeschoss 378
Spezialflachwagen 377
Spezialitäten 156
Spezialslalom 511
Spicknadel 173
Spiegel 10, 195, 277, 354, 369, 421,
439, 533
Spiegel, beleuchteter 269
Spiegel, ebener 7
Spiegel, teilreflektierender 420
Spiegel, vollreflektierender 420
Spiegelreflexkamera, digitale 315
Spiegelreflexkamera, einäugige 314
Spiegelteleskop 9
Spiegelteleskop im Querschnitt 9
Spiegelzylinder 420
Spiel 492
Spielanzug 261
Spielball 502, 503
Spielbereich 471
Spielbrett 469, 470
Spiele 468
Spiele mit Schlägern 493
Spielekonsole 471
Spieler 492
Spielerbank 474, 485, 487, 506
Spielerinnen 492
Spielernummer 486, 488, 506
Spielerpositionen 474, 481, 482, 489
Spielerschnittstelle 471
Spielfeld 469, 474, 479, 480, 482, 487,
488
Spielfeld für American Football 484
Spielfeldbeläge 492
Spielfigur 469
Spielfläche 493
Spielgeld 469
Spielstein 470
Spielwarengeschäft 436
Spike 473
Spikereifen 358
Spikulen 4

Spinalganglion 109, 110
Spinat 127
Spindel 73
Spindelfalte 73
Spinne 70
Spinne, äußere Merkmale 70
Spinnentiere 67
Spinnentiere, Beispiele 70
Spinnenschachtel 538
Spinnrute 537
Spinnwarze 70
Spiralarm 6
Spiralbindung 536
Spiralbohrer 228
Spirale 228
spiralförmiges Wolkenband 43
Spiralheftung 340
Spiralkneter 176
Spiralnagel 220
Spiralringbuch 340
Spiralskulptur 73
Spiralspindel 127
Spirulina 123
Spitze 29, 55, 101, 125, 167, 169, 208,
216, 220, 221, 226, 247, 273, 301,
312, 471, 510, 534, 536
Spitze, nicht wärmeleitend 269
Spitzenhandschuhe, fingerloser 243
spitzer Winkel 428
Spitzsieb 171
Spitzzange 217
Splintholz 63
Spoiler 366
Sporen 52
Sport 468
Sportanlagen 431
Sportartikelgeschäft 437
Sportfischerei 536
Sporthalle 386
Sporthose 473
Sportkleidung 262, 263
Sportplatz 386
Sportreifen 358
Sportset 261
Sportwagen 347
Spot 207
Sprachaufnahmetaste 337
Sprecher 518
Sprechmuschel 327
Sprechtrommel 297
Spreite 51, 52, 55
Spreizdübel 221
Sprengring 538
Springeinrichtungen 518
Springer 470
Springform 172
Springseil 500
Sprinkler 408
Spritzbeutel 172
Spritze 460
Spritzenkolben 460
Spritzenkörper 460
Spritzloch 90
Spross 54
Sprosse 185, 186, 205, 219
Sprosse, obere 201
Sprossenarretierung 219
Sprossengemüse 125
sprossbürtige Wurzeln 52
Sprüharm 214
Sprühflasche 236
Sprühknopf 267
Sprungbein 99
Sprungbrett 184, 496
Sprünge, Beispiele 509
Sprungfederrahmen 204
Sprungfiguren 518
Sprunggelenk 83, 86
Sprungpferd 496, 497
Sprungrichter 518
Sprungski 513
Sprungturm 518
Spülarm 196
Spule 319, 536, 537
Spüle 164, 197
Spulenachse 537
Spülhebel 196
Spülkasten 195
Spülkastendeckel 196
Spülkopf 403
Spur, rechte 343
Sri Lanka 453
St. Lucia 449
Staatsanwaltschaft, Tisch 440
Staatsgrenze 23

Stab 199, 230, 259, 479
Stäbchen 119
Stabhochsprung 472
Stabilisator 523
Stabilisierungsflosse 386
Stabkranz 112
Stablampe 456
Stabmixer 176
Stabparkett 190
Stachel 68
Stachelbeere 132
Stachelschwein 82
Stachelzellenschicht 114
Stadion 431, 472
Stadtplan 25
Stadtrad 373
Stadtteil 25
Staffelstab 472
Staffelübergabebereich 472
Stahldraht 535
Stahlkante 510
Stahlkappe 459
Stahlmantel 417
Stahlschreibfeder 312
Stahlstab 309
Stalagmit 31
Stalaktit 31
Stamm 52, 62, 63
Stämmchen 51
Ständer 174, 176, 269, 277, 308
Standfotograf 291
Standhahn-Mutternschlüssel 216
Standleitung 334
Standleuchte 206
Standort des Kultbildes 279
Standortanzeiger 287
Standsockel 27
Standtom 308
Stange 125, 273, 301, 501
Stangensellerie 125
Stapelstühle 201
Star 80
Stärke 61
Stärkekörnchen 50
starre Brücken 344
Start 469
Start 100-m- und 100-m-Hürdenlauf 472
Start 10000-m- und 4-x-400-m-Lauf 473
Start 110-m-Hürdenlauf 472
Start 1500-m-Lauf 473
Start 200-m-Lauf 472
Start 400-m-, 400-m-Hürden-, 4-x-100-m-
    Lauf 473
Start 5000-m-Lauf 472
Start 800-m-Lauf 473
Start- und Landebahn 390
Start/Pause 323
Startaufstellung 524
Startblock 473, 516
Starter 516
Startergriff 235
Startgriffe (Rückenschwimmen) 516
Starthilfekabel 356
Startknopf 424
Startlinie 473, 524
Startmenütaste 330
Startnummer 473, 525
Startpistole 472
Startpositionen 518
Starttaste 328
Stationskreis 39
Stationsmodell 39
Stativ 8, 421
Stativablage 8
Statue 446
Staub, aufgewirbelter 43
Staubbehälter 208, 229
Staubbeutel 56
Staubblatt 56, 58
Staubfaden 56
Staubschweif 6
Staufach 455
Staumoräne 30
Stauraum 361, 364
Stausee 406, 407
Steak 152
Steakmesser 168
Steckbuchse 198
Steckdose 361
Steckdose, dreipolige 198
Steckdose, geschaltete 322
Steckdosenprüfer 217
Stecker 228, 324
Stecker, dreipoliger, amerikanischer 198
Steckschlüsselsatz 223

Steg 201, 254, 273, 282, 297, 301, 302,
    303, 503
Steghose 254
Stegplättchen 273
Stegspangenschuh 241
Stegstütze 273
Stehleiter 219
Stehleitern 219
steifer Nachläufer 363
steifes Vorderteil 363
Steigbügel 116
steigendes Revers 244
Steigleitung 194
Steigung 191
Steigungseinstellung 395
Steilhang 29
Steilküste 35
Steilwandzelt 528
Stein 57
Steinbock, Wendekreis 20, 21, 22
Steinbohrer 228
Steinbutt 161
Steine 469
steinerner Ehrensessel 447
Steinfrucht, fleischige 57
Steinfrüchtchen 59
Steinfrüchte 132
Steingarten 230
Steinmarder 88
Steinpilz 123
Steinschlag 31
Steinwüste 36
Steißbein 98
Stellmutter 535
Stellring 236
Stellschraube 224, 308
Stellwerk 375
Stemmeisen 229
Stempel 56, 338
Stempelkissen 338
Stengel 53
Stengelgemüse 125
Stengelgliederd 53
Steppe 40
Stereotaste 326
sterile Wundauflage 461
Sterilgut, Lagerraum 462, 464
Sterilisationsraum 464, 465
Sternalarterie 71
Sternanis 60
Sternfrucht 137
Sternschnuppe 37
Sternwarte 7
Sternwarte, Querschnitt 7
Stert 412
Stethoskop 460
Steuerbordseite 387
Steuereinheit, elektrische 357
Steuerfeder 471
Steuerhaus 385
Steuerknüppel 395
Steuertaste 332
Steuertriebwerk 13
Steuerung 330
Steuerung des Lebenserhaltungssystems
    10
Steuerungstaste 330
Steuerzentrale 406
Stichsäge 226
Stichsäge, elektrische 227
Stickoxiden, Emission 48
Stiefel 241, 305, 509, 525, 527
Stiefelette, knöchelhohe 241
Stiel 51, 52, 54, 57, 58, 59, 125, 167,
    215, 220, 503
Stielgrund 125
Stielkamm 268
Stielkasserolle 175
Stift 198, 199, 337
Stifthalter 274
Stiftsockel 199
Stigma 67
Stillwasserspiegel 33
Stilton 151
Stilus 312
Stimmanzeiger 308
Stimmband 105
Stimmeinrichtung 308
Stimmenwahlschalter 310, 311
Stimmkrücke 305
Stimmnagel 304
Stimmring 297
Stimmstock 304
Stimmwirbel 302, 303
Stimmzug 307
Stinktier 88

Stint 159
Stirn 78, 92, 96, 229
Stirnbalken 187
Stirnbande 502
Stirnbein 98, 100
Stirnfontanelle 100
Stirnhöhle 117
Stirnschopf 83
Stirnwand 365, 401
Stirnziegel 279
Stock 219, 273
Stock, orthopädischer 466
Stock, vierfüßiger 466
Stöcke 309
Stockgriff 514
Stockschaft 514
Stockteller 510
Stoffmenge, Maßeinheit 426
Stollen 263, 478
Stollenreihen 369, 525
Stollenschuh 476
Stop 86
Stopfen 267
Stopfer 177, 180
Stopfleber 156
Stopp-Taste 323
Stoppball 491
Stopptaste 319, 323, 328
Stoppknopf 424
Stoppuhr 424
Stör 158
Storch 80
Störklappe 392
Stoßdämpfer 351, 523
Stoßdämpfer hinten 522
Stoßdämpfer, hinterer 367
Stößel 170
Stoßen 500
Stoßfänger 364, 369
Stoßfänger, kunststoffummantelter 348
Stoßleiste 209
Stoßstange 523
Strafbank 507
Strafbankbetreuer 507
Straffergurt, vorderer 532
Strafraum 480
Strafraumbogen 480
Strafraumlinie 480
Strahlenkörper 119
Strahler 184
Strahlstörer 236
Strahlung 415
Strahlung, ultraviolette 418
Strahlungszone 4
Strähnenkamm 268
Straight Flush 468
Strampelhöschen 260
Strand 35
Strandschnecke 157
Strang 519
Straße 25, 430, 433, 435, 468
Straße im Querschnitt 342, 434
Straße von Gibraltar 18
Straße von Mozambique 20
Straße, Bass 15
Straßenbau 342
Straßengüterverkehr 381
Straßenhobel 401
Straßenkarte 25
Straßenkehrmaschine 365
Straßenlaterne 207, 434
Straßennummer 25
Straßenradrennen 522
Straßenradsport 522
Straßenrennrad 522
Straßenschuh 241
Straßentunnel 345
Straßenverkehr 317, 342
Stratokumulus 42
Stratopause 37
Stratosphäre 37
Stratus 42
Strauch 230
Strauchflechte 50
Strauß 81
Straußenei 155
Strebe 187, 308
Strebebogen 284, 285
Streben, hinterer 370
Strebepfeiler 284
Strecke 524
Strecke, landschaftlich schöne 25
Streichkäse 150
Streifen 286
Streifenvorhang 286
Streuer 172

Streuscheibe 290
Strickjacke 250
Strickjacke mit V-Ausschnitt 250
Strohhalm 163
Strohhut 238
Strohhütte 288
Stromanschluss 365
Stromanschlusskabel 361
Stromanschlusspunkt 198
Stromfortleitung 408
Stromleitung an die Verbraucher 413
Stromleitung zu den Verbrauchern 402
Stromquelle 416
Stromversorgungskabel 434
Stromzähler 198
Strumpf 257, 259
Strümpfe 257
Strumpfhalter 259
Strumpfhaltergürtel 259
Strumpfhose 257
Stufe 191, 219
Stufen 184, 283
Stufen der Reife 62
Stufenbarren 496, 497
Stufenrock 253
Stuhl 201, 444
Stühle, Beispiele 201
Stulp 186
Stulpe 243
Stulpen 483
Stulpenhandschuh 243
Stummaufnahme-Taste 323
Stummel 536
Stumpf 63
stumpfer Winkel 428
Stundenwinkelantrieb 7
Stuntskate 527
Stürmer 481
stürmischer Himmel 41
Sturmlampe 532
Sturmspitze 507
Sturz 185, 187, 192
Sturzhelm 510, 513
Stützarm 397
Stützausleger 455
Stütze 184, 231, 361, 387
Stutzen 476, 506
Stützfuß 361, 365
Stützpunkt 518
Stützvorrichtung, ausklappbare 365
Stützvorrichtung, Kurbel 365
Stylobat 279
Stylus 59
subarktisch 40
Subduktionszone 27
Sublimation 414
Substanz, graue 109, 110
Substanz, weiße 109, 110
Substanzen, anorganische 45
Substraktion 427
Substraktionstaste 337
subtraktive Farbmischung 418
Subtropen, feuchte 40
Subtropen, mediterrane 40
Subwoofer 321
Sucharm 333
Suche 335
Sucher 320
Sucher, elektronischer 320
Sucherkamera 315
Sucherokular 315
Suchfernrohr 8, 9
Süd 23
Süd-Korea 453
Süd-Südost 23
Süd-Südwest 23
Südafrika 452
Südamerika 14, 17, 34
Südamerikanische Platte 27
Sudan 451
Südchinesisches Meer 14, 19
Südfrüchte 136
südliche Halbkugel 21
südliche Hemisphäre 21
südlicher Polarkreis 15, 21, 22
Südost 23
Südpol 15, 21, 416
Südwest 23
Südwester 239
Sulcus terminalis 118
Sumach 139
Summe 423, 427
Super-G 511
Supercross-Motorrad 525
Supermarkt 120, 433, 437
Superriesenslalom 511

Superriesenslalom-Ski 510
Suppenlöffel 168
Suppenschale 166
Suppenteller 166
Suppenterrine 166
Suppentopf 175
Surfbrett 519
Surinam 448
Surround-Lautsprecher 321
Suspensorium 486, 507
Süßkartoffel 124
Swasiland 452
Sweatshirt 262
Sweatshirt mit Kapuze 262
Swimmingpool 386
Symbole, wissenschaftliche 426
symphatisches Ganglion 109
Symphyse 111, 112
Synagoge 447
Synapse 110
Synchronisationskabel 337
Synthesizer 310
Syrien 452
Systemschalter 310

T

T-Shirt Kleid 261
Tabakwarengeschäft 436
Tabasco™-Soße 140
Tabernakel 446
Tablette 467
Tablinum 280
Tabulator nach links 330
Tabulator nach rechts 330
Tabulatortaste 330
Tachometer 355, 368, 501
Tadschikistan 452
Tafel 444
Tafelberg 36
Tafelsalz 141
Tageskilometerzähler 355
Tagliatelle, grüne 146
Tahinisoße 140
Taifun 43
Tailback 485
Taille 93, 95
Taillenabnäher 248
Tajine 174
Taktarten 298
Taktstrich 298
Tal 29, 32
Talgdrüse 114
Tamarin 91
Tamarindenmark 140
Tamburin 309
Tandem 373
Tanganjikasee 20
Tank 13, 364, 385
Tankanlage 404
Tankdeckel 349, 364
Tanker 381, 384
Tanklukendeckel 385
Tankstelle 346, 433
Tankwagen 364
Tanne 65
Tannennadeln 65
Tansania 451
Tanzsaal 387
Taro 124
Tasche 225, 274, 502
Tasche für Latexhandschuhe 456
Tasche, aufgesetzte 244, 249, 260
Tasche, blinde 251
Tasche, geräumige 276
Taschenrechner 274, 337
Taschenrechner, wissenschaftlicher 337
Taschenträger 505
Tasmanien 15
Tasmansee 15
Tasse 166, 531
Tast-Körperchen, Meissnersches 114
Tastatur 304, 310, 330, 336
Tastatur, alphabetische 338
Tastatur, alphanumerische 327, 330, 346,
    442, 443
Tastatur, numerische 338
Tastaturschnittstelle 329
Tastaturschutz, verschiebbarer 327
Taste 296, 304
Taste Cursor an Zeilenanfang 331
Taste Druck 331
Taste Ende 331
Taste löschender Rückschritt 331
Taste nächste Seite 331
Taste numerischer Block 331

ASTRONOMIE > 2-25;   ERDE > 26-71;   PFLANZENREICH >72-89;   TIERREICH > 90-143;   MENSCH > 144-177;   NAHRUNGSMITTEL UND KÜCHE > 178-241;   HAUS > 242-295;
HEIMWERKEN UND GARTENARBEIT > 296-333;   KLEIDUNG > 334-371;   PERSÖNLICHE AUSSTATTUNG > 372-391;   KUNST UND ARCHITEKTUR > 392-465;   KOMMUNIKATION UND BÜROTECHNIK > 466-535;
TRANSPORT UND FAHRZEUGE > 536-643;   ENERGIE > 644-677;   WISSENSCHAFT > 678-705;   GESELLSCHAFT > 706-785;   SPORT UND SPIELE > 786-920

Taste Pause 331
Taste Systemabfrage 331
Taste Unterbrechung 331
Taste vorherige Seite 331
Tasten 311, 327
Tasten, programmierbare 332
Tastenfeld, numerisches 331, 423
Tasteninstrumente 304
Tau 41
Taube 81, 154
Täubling, grasgrüner 123
Taufbecken 446
Taupunkttemperatur 39
Tausend 427
Tauwasserablauf 211
Techniken 487
technische Delegierte 509
Teddy 258
Tee 148, 505, 515
Tee, grüner 148
Tee, Oolong 148
Tee, schwarzer 148
Tee-Ei 173
Teebeutel 148
Teekanne 166
Teeline 515
Teelöffel 168
Teflonband 216
Teich 504
Teigmischer 172
Teigwaren 146
Teigwaren, asiatische 147
Teile 200, 201, 204
Teile der Brille 273
Teile des Schuhs 240
Teile eines Fahrrads 370
Teile eines Hauses 185
Teile eines Kreises 428
teilgetauchter Tragflügel 387
Teilmenge, echte 427
teilreflektierender Spiegel 420
Teilungsnaht 244
tektonische Platten 27
tektonischer See 32
Telefaxgerät 328
Telefon 439
Telefonapparat 327
Telefonieren 327
Telefonkabel 434
Telefonleitung 334
Telefonnetz 317
Telefonnummernverzeichnis 338
Telekommunikation 317
Telekommunikation für die Schifffahrt 317
Telekommunikation, industrielle 317
Telekommunikation, militärische 317
Telekommunikation, private 317
Telekommunikation, Schifffahrt 317
Telekommunikationsantenne 387
Telekommunikationssatellit 335
Teleobjektiv 314
Teleport 317
Teleskop 7
Teleskopantenne 325
Teleskopgabel 366, 369
Teleskopschlagstock 456
Teleskoptragbein 460
Teller 207, 531, 535
Teller, flacher 166
Teller, kleiner 166
Tellerbürste 365
Tellereisen 535
Telson 71
Tempel, aztekischer 283
Tempel, griechischer 279
Tempel, Huitzilopochtli 283
Tempel, Tlaloc 283
Temperaturanzeige 355
Temperaturfühler 358
Temperaturmessung 424
Temperaturregler 178, 208, 211
Temperaturregler, abziehbarer 179
Temperaturschalter 270
Temperaturskala 37
Temperaturwähler 178, 212, 213
Tempomat 354
Temporegler 311
Tennis 490
Tennisball 492
Tennisplatz 490
Tennisschläger 492
Tennisschuh 242, 492
Tennisspielerin 492
Tentakel 72
Tentakel, kleiner 72
Teppich 190

Teppichboden 190
Teppichmuschel, Kreuzmuster 157
Terminalochiole 105
Terminkalender 338
Terminplanung 338
Termite 69
Terrasse 182, 230
Terrassentür 188
Terrine 174
Tertiärkonsumenten 45
Terz 298
Testknopf 454
Teufelsdreck 139
textile Bodenbeläge 190
Thailand 453
Thallus 50, 51
Theater 292, 432, 433
Theater, griechisches 278
Theke 438
thermodynamische Temperatur, Maßeinheit 426
Thermometer 404, 424
Thermopause 37
Thermoschutzhaube 524
Thermosflasche 532
Thermosphäre 37
Thermostat 178
Thermostat, regelbarer 179
Thetys 3
Third 515
Thoiarollen 447
Thoraschrein 447
Thorax 67, 68
Thrombozyt 104
Thunfisch 160
Thymian 142
Ticketschalter 390
Tiefdruckgebiet 39, 43
tiefe Wolken 42
Tiefeneinstellung 229
Tiefenregler 303
tiefer Wadenbeinnerv 108
Tiefkühlprodukte 121
Tieflöffel 399
Tieflöffelsteuerung 399
Tiefsee-Ebene 33
Tiefseeberg 33
Tiefseeboden 26
Tiefseegraben 33
Tiefseehügel 33
Tiefseekabel 334
Tiefseekabel, Verteilung 317
Tieftöner 324
Tierceron 284
Tierhandlung 436
tierische Zelle 66
Tierreich 66
Tiger 89
Tight End 485
Timer 501
Tinte, metallische 441
Tintenfisch 72, 157
Tintenfisch, äußere Merkmale 72
Tintenpatronen-Kontrollleuchte 333
Tintenraum 312
Tintenstrahldrucker 333
Tipi 288
Tisch 202, 438
Tisch der Staatsanwaltschaft 440
Tisch der Verteidigung 440
Tisch des Gerichtsschreibers 440
Tischcomputer 334
Tische, Beispiele 202
Tischklammer 421
Tischleuchte 206
Tischleuchte, Halogen 206
Tischplatte 202
Tischrechner mit Druckerteil 337
Tischrührgerät 176
Tischtennis 493
Tischtennisball 493
Tischtennisplatte 493
Tischtennisschläger 493
Titan 3
Titania 3
Titeleinblendetaste 320
Titelnummer 323
Titelseite 313
Titelsuchtasten 323
Titelzeile 313
Titicacaesee 17
TL-Triebwerk 393
Tlaloc-Tempel 283
Toaster 178
Todesanzeigen 313

tödlich giftiger Pilz 52
Toeloop 509
Togo 451
Toilette 194, 195, 196, 445
Toiletten 437, 440, 443, 463, 465
Toilettenpapierhalter 195
Toilettenseife 267
Tomate 128
Tomatenmark 140
Tomatillo 128
Tomtom 308
Tonabnehmer 303
Tonabnehmer-Wahlschalter 303
Tonabnehmerregler 303
Tonartvorzeichen 299
Tonassistent 291
Tonaufnahmegeräte 291
Tonga 453
Tonhöhenrad 310
Tonleiter 298
Tonmeister 291
Tonnengewölbe 281
Tonsignalquellen, Kontrollleuchten 322
Tonsignalquellen-Wahltaster 322
Tonwiedergabesystem 322
Tonwiedergabesysteme, tragbare 325
Topcase 369
Topfhut 239
Topinambur 124
Toplevel-Domain 334
Topplicht 383
Toprückstand 405
Toque 239
Tor 381, 480, 482, 485, 507
Torbereich 483
Torfmoos, sparriges 51
Torhüter 479
Torlampen 507
Torlinie 482, 484, 506
Tornado 43
Torpfosten 485
Torraum 480, 507
Torresstraße 15
Torrichter 506
Torselett 259
Tortellini 146
Tortilla 145
Torus 429
Torwart 481, 506, 507
Torwarthandschuhe 480
Torwartschläger 507
Torwartschlittschuh 507
totale Finsternis 4, 5
Touchpad 336
Touchpad-Taste 336
Touchscreen 337
Toulouser Wurst 156
Toupierkamm 268
Tourenrad 373
Touring-Motorrad 369
Touringreifen 358
Towergehäuse: Rückansicht 329
Towergehäuse: Vorderansicht 329
Trab 83
traditionelle Musikinstrumente 296
traditionelle Wohnhäuser 288
tragbare Tonwiedergabesysteme 325
tragbarer CD-Spieler 325
Trageband 458
Tragebügel 325, 326
Tragegriff 209
Tragen-Abstellraum 462
Träger 187, 259, 396, 509
Träger mit Knopf 261
Träger, verstellbarer 260
Trägerhemd 247, 263
Trägerhormchen 261
trägerloser Büstenhalter 259
Trägerrock 252
Trägerstruktur 11
Tragfaden 70
Tragflügel 13, 393, 394
Tragflügel, hinterer 387
Tragflügel, teilgetauchter 387
Tragflügel, vorderer 387
Tragflügelschiff 387
Tragkabel 344
Tragriemen, Öse 315
Tragschicht, obere 342
Tragschicht, untere 342
Tragseil 287
Tragus 115
Trainer 489, 498, 507, 509
Trainerassistent 489
Trainingsanzug 262
Trainingshose 262

Tranchiergabel 169
Tranchiermesser 169
Tränendrüse 119
Tränengang 119
Tränenwarze 119
Transantarktisches Gebirge 15
Transformator 207, 407
Transformstörungen 27
Transitlagerschuppen 381
Transpiration 45
Transport 342
Transporter 365
Transportmischer 365
Traube, geschlossene 57
Traubenhenkel 62
Trauerweide 64
Traveller 520, 521
Travellerscheck 441
Traverse 202
Trawler 384
Treble 471
Treibhaus 122
Treibhauseffekt 46
Treibhauseffekt, anthropogener 46
Treibhauseffekt, natürlicher 46
Treibhausgas 46
Treibhausgaskonzentration 46
Treibladung 534
Treibscheibe 287
Treibstoffart 346
Treibstofftank 395
Trenchcoat 248
Trennklappe 277
Trennlinie 313
Trennvorhang 464
Trennwand 457
Treppe 188, 189, 191, 283, 293, 294, 345, 378, 412, 439
Treppenabsatz 189
Treppenaufgang 404
Treppenhaus 189
Treppenhaus-Oberlicht 189
Treppenlauf 191
Treppenstufe 191
Treppenvorbau 183
Tresor 443
Tresorraum 443
Tretlager 372
Triageraum 463
Triangel 295, 309
Tribünen, bewegliche 444
Trichter 72, 171, 306, 307, 318
Trickeffekttasten 320
Trickeffektwähler 320
Trieb 62
Triebdrehgestell 376
Triebwagen 380
Triebwerk 393
Trift 406
Triklinium 280
Trikot 263, 483, 488, 522
Trikuspidalklappe 104
Triller 299
Trimaran 521
Trinidad und Tobago 449
Trinkflasche 371
Trinkpackung 163
Trinkwasserleitung 434
Trio 300
Triticale 143
Triton 3
Tritt 219
Trittbrett 523
Trittbrett, hinteres 455
Tritthocker 201, 219
Trittleiter 219
Trittplatte 55
Trittstufe 191, 364
Trizepszug 507
trocken liegender Höhlenraum 31
Trockendock 381
Trockenelemente 417
Trockenfrüchte 60, 133
Trockenklimate 40
Trog 39
Trommel 170, 212, 213, 236
Trommel, kleine 295, 308
Trommelbremse 357
Trommelfell 75, 116, 297, 308
Trommeln 308
Trommelschlegel 297
Trompete 307, 342
Trompeten 295
Tropenwald 44
Tropfen für trockene Augen 272
tropisch feucht und trocken 40

tropische Klimate 40
tropische Wirbelstürme, Bezeichnungen 43
tropischer Regenwald 40, 44
tropischer Wirbelsturm 43
Tropopause 37, 46
Troposphäre 37
Trüffel 123
Trugdolde, eingliedrige 57
Trugdolde, zweigliedrige 57
Truhe 203
Truhenkörper 211
Truncus coeliacus 103, 107
Truthahn 81
Tschad 451
Tschadsee 20
Tschechische Republik 450
Tsetsefliege 69
Tuba 295, 307
Tube 163
Tubus 8, 9, 420, 421
Tubusträger 421
Tuch, Geschirr 215
Tukan 80
Tülle 180, 181
Tüllen 172
Tulpe 56
Tundra 44
Tunesien 451
Tunika 255
Tunikakleid 252
Tunnel 378
Tüpfelfarn, gemeiner 52
Tür 178, 202, 211, 213, 287, 349, 361, 392, 439
Tür zum Nutzlastraum 13
Tür, automatische 390
Turban 239
Turbine 402, 408
Turbinengenerator 402
Turbinenwelle 408
Türen, Beispiele 286
Türfach 211
Türfüllung 202
Türgriff 186, 349
Türinnenverschalung 352
Türkei 452
Turkmenistan 452
Türknopf 185
Turm 284, 412, 413, 470
Turmkran 397
Turmmast 397
Turmrollen 403
Turmspitze 285
Turmwindmühle 412
Turners/Turnerin, Name 497
Turnhalle 444
Turnhallenbüro 444
Türöffnungshebel 352
Türpfosten 185
Türschloss 185, 213, 349, 352
Türstopper 211
Türsturz 285
Türverkleidung 352
Türzapfen 185
Tuvalu 453
TV-Einstellung 319
TV-Netzschalter 319
TV/Video-Taste 319
Twinset 255
Tympanon 279
Typenschild 228
typische Küstenformen 35

U

U-Bahn 378, 435
U-Bahn-Netzplan 379, 380
U-Bahn-Schild 378
U-Bahn-Station 378, 432
U-Bahn-Zug 378, 380
Überbau 345
Überdach 528, 529
Überdruckventil 174
Überfallrinne 406
Überfallschloss 277
Überflurhydrant 454
Überführung 343, 344
Überholrollbahn 388
Überholspur 343
überirdische Pipeline 404
Überlauf 184, 194, 195, 196
Überlaufkrone 406
Überlaufschutz 214
Überrollschutz 528
Überschallflugzeug 37, 394
Überschlag 275

Überschwemmungsebene 32
Überseekoffer 277
Übersetzungsgehäuse 537
Übersetzungsgetriebe 413
Überstand 191
überstumpfer Winkel 428
Übertragungsarten, öffentliches 316
Überwachungsraum 345
Überwurfmutter 197
Überziehschuh 240
Übungsgrün 504
Udonnudeln 147
Uganda 451
Uhr 444
Uhrband 424
Uhrenmeister 488
Uhrenradio 325
Uhu 81
Ukraine 450
UKW-Wahltaste 322
ultraviolette Strahlung 418
Umbriel 3
Umfang 428
Umgebung, naturbelassene 504
Umgehungsstraße 25, 431
Umhängetasche mit Dehnfalte 276
Umhängetasche mit Reißverschluss 276
Umkehrlinsen 420
Umkleideraum 444
Umladeabschnitt 385
Umlaufkammer 407
Umleitungskanal 406
Umlenkstern 235
Umschalter 221, 228
Umschalttasten 330
umsetzbare Flagge 504
Umwandlungsanlage, katalytische 405
Umwelt 44
Umwerfer 522
Umwerfer, hinterer 370, 372
undurchlässiges Gestein 403
unendlich 427
Unfallstation 462
Ungarn 450
ungebleichtes Mehl 144
ungesäuertes Brot 145
ungleich 427
Uniform 456
Unisex-Kopfbedeckungen 239
Unisex-Schuhe 242
Universität 432
Unkrautstecher 232
unpaarig gefiedert 55
unregelmäßiges Trapez 429
Unterarm 86, 93, 95
Unterarmmappe 275
Unterarmstütze 466
Unterbau 403
Unterboden 54, 187, 190
Unterbrechung 331
unterbrochene Linie 342, 343
Unterbruststäbchen 259
Unterbühne 292
Unterdeck 404
untere Abschlusskappe 417
untere Gliedmaßen 103
untere Hohlvene 102, 103, 104, 107
untere Mesenterialarterie 107
untere Nasenmuschel 117
untere Querleiste 202
untere Schale 511
untere Schutzhaube 227
untere Sohlschicht 402
untere Tasche 502
untere Tragschicht 342
untere Vertäfelung 396
untere Zahnreihe 116
unterer gerader Augenmuskel 119
unterer Glaskolben 181
unterer Kühleranschluss 358
unterer Mantel 26
unterer seitlicher Einschnitt 62
unterer seitlicher Lappen 62
unteres Augenlid 75, 87
unteres Becken 308
Unterfach 274
Unterfangkescher 538
Unterführung 344, 375
Untergeschoss 435
Untergrätenmuskel 97
Untergrund 342
Unterhautbindegewebe 114
Unterhemd 476
Unterhose, lange 247
unterirdische Anlagen 281

unterirdische Kammer 278
unterirdischer Abfluss 45
unterirdisches Gerinne 31
unterirdisches Kabelnetz, Verteilung 317
Unterkante 506
Unterkiefer 67, 74, 98
Unterkieferknochen 100
Unterkleid 258
Unterkühlen 414
Unterkunft 512
Unterkünfte 512
Unterlage 190
Unterlegscheibe 222
Unterlegscheiben 222
Unterlid 119
Unterlippe 116, 305
Unternehmen 335
Unterrock 258
Unterrohr 371
Untersattel 301
unterschiedliche Vogeltypen 80
Unterschnabel 78
Unterschrank 164
Unterschrift des Inhabers 441
Unterschrift, amtliche 441
Unterschwanzdecken 78
unterseeischer Cañon 33
Unterstock 273
Untersuchungsraum 463, 465
Untersuchungsraum, Audiometrie 465
Untersuchungsraum, gynäkologischer 463
Untersuchungsraum, psychiatrischer 462
Unterteil 179, 356, 454
Untertitel 313
Unterwäsche 247, 258, 524
Unterwäschegeschäft 436
Unterwasser-Strahler 184
Unterwasserbohrung 404
Unterwasserpipeline 404
Up-Quark 414
Ural 18
Uranbrennstoff, Kernspaltung 408
Uranus 2, 3
URL-Adresse 334
Ursprungskegel 110
Uruguay 448
USB-Schnittstelle 329, 336
Usbekistan 452
Utensilien, verschiedene 173

V

V-Ausschnitt 244, 250
Vakuole 50, 66
Vakuole, pulsierende 66
Vakuum-Kaffeemaschine 181
Vakuumdestillation 405
Vanille-Extrakt 140
Vanuatu 453
Vater-Pacinisches Körperchen 114
Vatikanstadt 450
VCR-Einstellung 319
VCR-Netzschalter 319
VCR-Tasten 319
Vegetation 44
Vegetationsbild nach Höhenlagen 44
Vegetationspunkt 53
Vegetationszonen 44
Veilchen 56
Velarium 281
Velours 190
Vene, königliche 102
Venen 102
Venezuela 448
Ventil 196, 307, 371
Ventilbüchse 307
Ventilfeder 360
Ventilsitz 196
Ventilzug, dritter 307
Ventilzug, erster 307
Ventilzug, zweiter 307
ventraler Nervenstrang 71
Venus 2, 3
Venusmuschel 157
Verandatür 164
Verankerung 344
Verankerungspunkt 70
Verbene 148
Verbindung 312, 470
Verbindungsast 110
Verbindungsclip 460
Verbindungsgang 345
Verbindungskabel 332
Verbindungspunkt 198
Verbindungsstutzen 455
Verbindungstunnel 13

Verbraucher, Stromleitung 402, 413
Verbrechensbekämpfung, vorbeugende 456
Verbrennung 49
Verbrennungsraum 360
Verdampfen 414
Verdauungsapparat 106
verdeckte Knopfleiste 251
Verdichter 364
Verdichtung 49
Verdunstung 45
Vereinigte Arabische Emirate 452
Vereinigte Staaten von Amerika 448
Vereinigtes Königreich von Großbritannien und Nordirland 449
Verengung 424
Verfallsdatum 441
Verfolgerauto 522
Vergaser 366
Verhol-Winde 385
Verkehrsampel 434
Verkehrsflugzeug 37
Verkleidung 187, 366
Verklicker 520
verlängertes Mark 109
Verlobungsring 264
Verpackung 49
Verpackungen 162
Verpackungsmaterial 120
Verpackungsraum 120
Versailles-Parkett 190
verschiebbarer Messschnabel 425
verschiebbarer Tastaturschutz 327
verschiedene Geräte 231
verschiedene Haushaltsgeräte 180
verschiedene Schwimmstile 517
verschiedene Utensilien 173
Verschiedenes 341
verschiedenes Zubehör 225
Verschlagwagen 377
Verschluss 163, 209, 226, 261, 333, 511, 532, 535
Verschluss des Hochwasserentlastungswehrs 406
Verschlussdeckel 417
Verschlussmaterial 417
Verschlussstopfen 417
Verschlussstück 534
Verschmutzung 47
Verschmutzung durch Autoabgase 47
Verschmutzung durch Haushalte 47
Verschmutzung, industrielle 47
Verschmutzung, landwirtschaftliche 47
Versenkmagel 220
Versenkpodium 292
Versetzungszeichen 299
Versicherungsabteilung 442
Versorgungsbereich 389
Versorgungsmodul 316
Versorgungsstraße 388
Verstärkungsrippe 401
Verstärkungsschwelle 458
Versteifungsrippe 392
verstellbare Klemme 206
verstellbarer Bügel 226
verstellbarer Träger 260
verstellbares Rückenteil 460
Verstelldüse 394
Versteller 246
Verstellnut 222
Verstellung 222
Verstrebung 412
Vertäfelung, obere 396
Vertäfelung, untere 396
Vertebralschild 76
Verteidiger, rechter 481
Verteidigung 484
Verteidigungszone 487
Verteiler 342
Verteilerkasten 198
Verteilerschleife 198
Verteilung über Freileitungen 316
Verteilung über Tiefseekabel 317
Verteilung über unterirdisches Kabelnetz 317
Vertikale 526
vertikale Bodenbewegung 27
vertikale Einstellung 329
vertikaler Zug 470
vertikales Schiebefenster 287
vertikales Seitenband 487
Vertikalseismograph 27
Vertikutierer 237
Verwaltung 445
verwelkendes Keimblatt 53
Verwerfung 27

Verziehnaht 245
Verzierungen 299
Vestibulamerv 116
Vibratohebel 303
Victoriasee 20
Victoriawüste, Große 15
Video- und Digitalübertragung, Anschlussbuchsen 315
Video-Ausgänge 322
Video-Eingänge 322
Videobandsteuerungen 320
Videokassette 319
Videokassettenadapter 320
Videokassettenschacht 320
Videorecorder 319
Videoschnittstelle 329, 336
Videospielsystem 471
Vielecke 429
Viereck 429
Viereckregner 237
vierfüßiger Stock 466
Vierling 468
vierte Zehe 78
Viertelnote 299
Viertelpause 299
Vierundsechzigstelnote 299
Vierundsechzigstelpause 299
Vierung 284, 285
Vierungsturm 284
Vierviertteltakt 299
Vierwegeregler 315
Vietnam 453
Vinyl-Laufsohle 261
Violine 301
Violinen, erste 295
Violinen, zweite 295
Violinfamilie 301
Violinschlüssel 298
Viper 77
Visier 367, 459, 525, 533, 535
Visiergestell 476
Vitrine 203
Vitrinenschrank 203
Vizeskip 515
Vogel 78
Vögel 78
Vogel, äußere Merkmale 78
Vogelaugenchili 139
Vogelfüße, Beispiele 79
Vogelschnäbel, Beispiele 79
Vogeltypen, unterschiedliche 80
Volant 204
Vollachsel-Unterkleid 258
Volleyball 487, 490
Volleyballspiel 487
Vollkornbrot 145
Vollkornmehl 144
Vollmond 5
vollreflektierender Spiegel 420
Vollreife 62
Volt 426
Volute 200
Vorbau 183, 371
vorbeugende Verbrechensbekämpfung 456
Vorbühne 292
Vordach 361, 528
Vordachrille 361
Vorderachse 401
Vorderansicht 92, 94, 96, 98, 478
Vorderbein 67, 68, 75, 201
Vorderblatt 240, 263
Vorderbremse 368
vordere Aufschlaglinie 495
vordere Augenkammer 119
vordere Backenzähne 101
vordere Druckknopfleiste 261
vordere Einbuchtung 115
vordere Felgenbremse 371
vordere Fußraste 367, 368
vordere Nervenwurzel 109, 110
vordere Schienbeinarterie 102
vordere Seitenfontanelle 100
vorderer Balken 422
vorderer Douglasscher Raum 112
vorderer Gaumenbogen 116
vorderer Oberkiefer 74
vorderer Schienbeinmuskel 96
vorderer Schultermuskel 73
vorderer Strafferguart 532
vorderer Tragflügel 387
vorderes Ende 73
vorderes Rückstoßtriebwerk 12
vorderes Schutzblech 366

Vorderfeld 491
Vorderflügel 67
Vordergabel 371
Vorderhorn 109
Vorderkappe, perforierte 240
Vordermast 385
Vorderrad 401, 467
Vorderschaft 534
Vorderseite 244, 245
Vorderteil 240, 245, 262
Vorderteil, steifes 363
Vorfach 538
Vorfeld 388
Vorflügel 393
Vorführraum 294
Vorführzeiten 294
Vorfußbindung 514
Vorhalle 439, 440, 442
Vorhang, eiserner 292
Vorhaut 111
vorherige Sätze 492
vorherige Seite 331
vorherrschender Wind 43
Vorhof 346
Vorhof, linker 103, 104
Vorhof, rechter 103, 104
Vorkommen 403
vorkragender Dachkranz 283
Vorlauf 323
Vorlauftaste 328
Vorliek 519
Vororte 25
Vorratsdosen 162
Vorratsschrank 439
Vorschaltgerät, elektronisches 199
Vorschlag 299
Vorschneider 228
Vorschot 520
Vorsprung 29
Vorspultaste 319
Vorstadt 431
Vorstag 520
Vortasche 275
Vortitel 313
Vorwahlsender-Wahltaste 322
vorwärts 518
Vorzeichentaste 337
Vulkan 26, 28
Vulkan mit Ausbruchstätigkeit 28
Vulkan, effusiver 28
Vulkan, explosiver 28
vulkanische Asche 28
vulkanische Bombe 28
vulkanische Insel 33
vulkanischer See 32
Vulkantypen 28

W

Waage, elektronische 423
Waagschale 422, 423
Waagschalenhaken 422
Wache 282
Wacholderbeere 138
Wachs 514
Wachsausrüstung 514
Wachsbohne 131
Wachskürbis 128
Wachspapier 162
Wachtel 81, 154
Wachtleis 155
Wade 93, 95
Wadenbein 98
Wadenbeinmuskel, kurzer 97
Wadenbeinmuskel, langer 96
Wadenbeinnerv, gemeinsamer 108
Wadenbeinnerv, oberflächlicher 108
Wadenbeinnerv, tiefer 108
Wadennerv 108
Wadenstrumpf 247
Wadi 36
Waffeleisen 178
Wagen 121, 521, 527
Wagenanzug 261
Wagendeck 386
Wagenheber 356
Wagenradhut 239
Wagentür 332
Wagentypen 376
Wahlrad 337
Wahltaste 327
Währungsangabe 441
Wakame 123
Wal 90
Wald 25, 29
Wald, borealer 44
ASTRONOMIE > 2-25; ERDE > 26-71; PFLANZENREICH >72-89; TIERREICH > 90-143; MENSCH > 144-177; NAHRUNGSMITTEL UND KÜCHE > 178-241; HAUS > 242-295;
HEIMWERKEN UND GARTENARBEIT > 296-333; KLEIDUNG > 334-371; PERSÖNLICHE AUSSTATTUNG > 372-391; KUNST UND ARCHITEKTUR > 392-465; KOMMUNIKATION UND BÜROTECHNIK > 466-535;
TRANSPORT UND FAHRZEUGE > 536-643; ENERGIE > 644-677; WISSENSCHAFT > 678-705; GESELLSCHAFT > 706-785; SPORT UND SPIELE > 786-920

Wald, gemäßigter 44
Waldbrand 47
Waldfrosch 75
Waldhorn 307
Waldmurmeltier 82
Walkman® mit Radioteil 326
Wallpapille 118
Wallpapillen 118
Walnuss 64, 133
Walnuss, Längsschnitt 60
Walze 219
Walzenbefestigung 219
Walzenbürste 365
Wan-tan-Teigblätter 147
Wand 184
Wand-Untergurt 365
Wanderschuh 242
Wandlaterne 207
Wandleuchte 207
Wandwange 191
Wange 94, 220, 536
Wanne 219
Wannengarnitur 194
Want 521
Wantenspanner 521
Wantenverklicker 520
Wapitihirsch 84
Wappen 477
Waran 77
Warencode 423
Wareneingang 120
Wareneingang für Milchprodukte 120
Warengeschäfte 335
warme Luft 41
Wärmeabgabe an Wasser 408
Wärmedeflektorscheibe 199
Wärmeenergie 46, 402
Wärmeenergie, Elektrizitätserzeugung 402
Wärmeerzeugung 408
wärmeisolierter Griff 179
Wärmeleitung 415
Wärmeübertragung 415
Wärmeverlust 46
warmgemäßigte Klimate 40
Warmhalteplatte 181
Warmluftklappe 192
Warmluftzufuhr 213
Warmwasserbereiter 194
Warmwasserkreislauf 194
Warmwassersteigleitung 194
Warmwasserzulauf 197
Warnblinklicht 392
Warnleuchte "Tür offen" 355
Warnleuchten 355
Wartebereich 442
Wartebereich für den Entnahmeraum 465
Wartebereichmarkierung 390
Wartehäuschen 434
Warteraum 463
Warteraum für Angehörige 462
Warteraum, zweiter 465
Warteschlange 443
Wartungskasten 198
Warzenfortsatz 100
Warzenhof 113
Wasabipaste 141
Waschbär 88
Waschbecken 194, 195, 464
Wäschekammer 439
Wascharm 214
Wäscherei 439
Wäschetrockner 213
Waschhandschuh 267
Waschküche 188
Waschlappen 267
Waschmaschine 194, 212
Waschraum 464
Waschtisch 439
Wasser 402, 408
Wasser verdampft 408
Wasser, Wärmeabgabe an 408
Wasser-Dampf-Gemisch 402
Wasserbadtopf 175
Wasserbehälter 181, 272
Wasserdruckanzeiger 455
Wassereinlass 407
Wasserfall 31, 32
Wasserflugzeug 394
Wasserfrosch 75
Wasserglas 165
Wasserhahn 195, 455
Wasserhindernis 504
Wasserhose 43
Wasserkanister 532
Wasserkanone 455

Wasserkessel 180
Wasserklappe 307
Wasserkraftwerk 406
Wasserkraftwerk im Querschnitt 407
Wasserkreislauf 45
Wasserkrug 166
Wasserlauf 48
Wasserläufer 69
Wassermelone 135
Wassermuss 124
Wasseroberfläche 518
Wasserpumpen-Zange 222
Wasserschlauch 214
Wasserspinne 70
Wassersport 516
Wassersprühdüse 365
Wasserstand 181
Wasserstandsanzeige 208
Wasserstandsanzeiger 179
Wasserstandsregler 212
Wasserstrahl 518
Wassertank 181, 394
Wasserverschmutzung 48
Wasservogel 79
Wasserwaage 225
Wasserzähler 194
Wasserzeichen 441
Wassily-Stuhl 200
Watstiefel 538
Watt 426
Wattestäbchen 461
Wattetupfer 461
Watvogel 79
WC 188, 189, 439, 464
Webcam 332
Wechselanlage für die Rücklage 517
Wechselstrom-Netzkabel 336
Weddellmeer 15
Wedel 52
Wedel, eingerollter junger 52
Weg 504
Wehrgang 282
Wehrgang, gedeckter 282
Wehrmauer 282
weiblich 426
weibliche Blütenstände 65
weibliche Geschlechtsorgane 112
Weiche 375
weiche Kontaktlinse 272
weicher Gaumen 116, 117
Weichkäse 151
Weichsel 18
Weichtiere 72
Weideland 122
Weidenholz 478
Weihgabe 446
Weihrauchkessel 446
Weihwasserbecken 446
Wein 120
Weinblatt 62, 126
Weinessig 141
Weinkeller 438
Weinkellner, Sommelier 438
Weinranke 62
Weintraube 62, 132
Weintraube im Querschnitt 59
Weisheitszahn 101
Weiß 418, 469, 470
Weißbrot 145
weiße Schokolade 148
weiße Senfkörner 138
weiße Substanz 109, 110
weiße Zwiebel 124
weißer Pfeffer 138
weißer Punktball 502, 503
weißer Reis 147
weißer Spielball 503
weißer Stein 470
weißes Band 493, 495
weißes Feld 470
Weißfisch 161
Weißkohl 126
Weißrussland 450
Weißweinglas 165
Weitsichtigkeit 419
Weitsprung 472
Weitwinkelobjektiv 314
Weitwinkelspiegel 362, 363
Weizen 61, 143
Weizenkorn, Längsschnitt 61
Welle 33, 412, 418
Welle, langsam drehende 413
Welle, schnell drehende 413
Wellenbasis 33
Wellenberg 418

Wellenhöhe 33
Wellenkamm 33
Wellenlänge 33, 418
Wellental 33, 418
Wellhornschnecke 157
Weltraum, Beobachtung 7
Weltraumteleskop, Hubble 37
Wendeflügel 287
Wendekampfrichter 517
Wendekragen 248
Wendekreis des Krebses 20, 21, 22
Wendekreis des Steinbocks 20, 21, 22
Wendewand 517
Werbetafel 378, 380
Werfer 474, 475, 479
Werftkran 381
Werkbank 224
Werkstückspanner 226
Werkzeugfutter 229
Werkzeuggürtel 225
Werkzeughalter 10
Werkzeugkasten 225
Werkzeugsatz 372
Wertangabe 441
Wertstoff-Sammelbehälter 49
Wespe 69
West 23
West-Nordwest 23
West-Südwest 23
Weste 244, 255
Westen 254
Westindien 16
westliche Hemisphäre 21
Westlicher Indischer Rücken 34
westlicher Meridian 22
Wetterboje 38
Wetterflugzeug 38
Wetterkarte 38, 39
Wetterlage, gegenwärtige 39
Wetterradar 38, 392
Wettersatellit 38
Wetterschenkel 185, 186
Wetterschiff 38
Wetterstation 38
Wettervorhersage 38
Wettkampfbecken 517
Wetzstahl 169
Wetzstein 169
Whiskyglas 165
Wickelauflage 205
Wickelbluse 255
Wickelkleid 252
Wickelkommode 205
Wickelrock 253
Wickler 268
Wicklung 536
Wide Receiver 485
Widerhaken 538
Widerlager 284, 344
Widerrist 83, 86
Widerstand 417
Widerstandseinstellung 501
Widertonmoos, gemeines 51
Wiederaustritt 31
Wiedergabetaste 319, 326, 328
Wiederholungstasten 323
Wiederholungszeichen 298
Wiege 8, 9
Wiegeetikett 423
Wiegefläche 423
Wiegen 422
Wiese 122
Wiesel 88
Wigwam 288
Wild 154
Wildleder 265
Wildreis 143
Wildschwein 84
Wilkesland 15
Wimper 66, 119
Wimpern 285
Wimpern 87
Wimpernkämmchen 266
Wimpernzange 266
Wind 47, 48
Wind, vorherrschender 43
Wind, Wirkung 45
Windabweiser 364
Winde 364
Windel 260
Windelhöschen, dichtes 260
Windenergie 412
Windenergie, Elektrizitätserzeugung 413
Windensteuerung 364
Windfahne 413
Windgeschwindigkeit 39

Windjacke 249
Windkraftwerk mit horizontaler Achse 413
Windkraftwerk mit vertikaler Achse 412
Windkraftwerke 412
Windlaufquerteil 348
Windmühle 412
Windmühlenhaube 412
Windrichtung 39
Windrose 23
Windrute 412
Windsack 296
Windschutzscheibe 348, 364, 366, 369, 385, 392
Windschutzscheiben-Sonnenschutz 356
Windung 72, 73
Winglet 393
Winkel, Beispiele 428
Winkel, rechter 428
Winkel, spitzer 428
Winkel, stumpfer 428
Winkel, überstumpfer 428
Winsch 521
Winter 38
Winterniederschläge 41
Winterreifen 358
Wintersonnenwende 38
Wintersport 515
Wipfel 63
Wirbel 73, 301, 302, 538
Wirbelkasten 301
Wirbelkörper 110
Wirbelsäule 98, 109
Wirbelschäkel 535
Wirbelscheibe 355
Wirbelschraube 303
Wirbelsturm 43
Wirbelsturm, tropischer 43
Wirkung des Windes 45
Wirsing 126
Wirtschaft 441
Wischblatt 355
Wischerachse 355
Wischerarm 355
Wischgummi 355
Wissenschaft 414
wissenschaftliche Bezeichnungen 57, 58, 59
wissenschaftliche Instrumente 13
wissenschaftliche Symbole 426
wissenschaftlicher Taschenrechner 337
Wissenschaftsraum 444
Wochenendkoffer 277
Wohnblock 289, 433
Wohngebiet 431
Wohnhaus 122
Wohnhaus, römisches 280
Wohnhäuser, traditionelle 288
Wohnküche 188
Wohnmobil 361
Wohnmodul, amerikanisches 11
Wohnraum 528
Wohnwagen 361
Wohnzimmer 188
Wok 174
Wok-Set 174
Wolf 88
Wolfram-Halogenlampe 199
Wolga 18
Wolke 37, 41
Wolke, Oortsche 2
Wolken 42
Wolken, hohe 39, 42
Wolken, mittelhohe 39, 42
Wolken, tiefe 39, 42
Wolkenabsorption 46
Wolkenband, spiralförmiges 43
Wolkentrichter 43
Wolkenwasser 48
Worcestershire-Soße 140
Wulst 358
Wundauflage, sterile 461
Wurf 475, 479
Würfel 429, 468, 469
Würfelbecher 469
Würfelmusterparkett 190
Wurfhügel 475
Wurfkreis 472, 473
Wurflinie 479
Wurfmal 475
Wurfpfeil 471
Wurmfortsatz 106
Wurst, Chorizo 156
Wurst, Kielbasa 156
Wurst, Merguez 156
Wurst, Toulouser 156
Würstchen, Frankfurter 156
Wurzel 54, 101, 167

Wurzelgemüse 129
Wurzelhaare 53
Wurzelhaarzone 63
Wurzelhaube 53
Wurzelhaut 101
Wurzelkanal 101
Wurzeln, sproßbürtige 52
Wurzelspitzenöffnung 101
Wurzelsystem 53, 62
Würzen 140
Wüste 36, 40, 44
Wüste Gobi 19
Wüste, Atacama 17
Wüstenfuchs 88
Wüstenspringmaus 82

X

Xylophon 295, 309

Y

Y-Schlauch 460
Yak 85
Yardlinie 484
Yen 440
Ysop 142
Yucatan-Halbinsel 16

Z

Zahlenschloss 274
Zahlungsbetragsanzeige 346
Zahlungsmodalitäten 441
Zahlungsterminal, elektronisches 121, 443
Zählwerk 323
Zahn 74, 76, 226, 227, 270, 398
Zahnbein 101
Zahnbürste 272
Zahnbürste, elektrische 272
Zähne 101
Zahnfach 101
Zahnfleisch 101, 116
Zahnpasta 272
Zahnpflege 272
Zahnreihe, obere 116
Zahnreihe, untere 116
Zahnseide 272
Zahnseidenhalter 272
Zander 160
Zange 173
Zangen 222
Zäpfchen 116, 117
Zapfen 65, 119, 202
Zapfhahn 346
Zapfsäule 346
Zapfsäulennummer 346
Zapfschlauch 346
Zarge 200, 201, 202, 301, 302
Zaun 122, 182
Zebra 84
Zecke 70
Zeh 86, 92, 94
Zehe 79
Zehe, dritte 78
Zehe, vierte 78
Zehe, zweite 78
Zehenriemchen 242
Zehenschützer 459, 476
Zehenstrecker, kurzer 96
Zehenstrecker, langer 96
Zehn 427
Zehn Gebote 447
Zehneck, regelmäßiges 429
Zehntelsekundenzeiger 424
Zeichen 299
Zeigefinger 115
Zeiger 422, 423
Zeitaufnahmetaste 320
Zeiteinblendetaste 320
Zeitlupe 319
Zeitmesser, automatischer 517
Zeitmessung 424
Zeitnehmer 488, 498, 499, 509
Zeitschalter 178
Zeitschaltuhr 179
Zeitschrift 313
Zeitschriftenladen 437
Zeituhr 178
Zeitung 313
Zeitungskopf 313
Zeitungsname 313
Zellafter 66
Zelle 67, 281, 286, 413

ASTRONOMIE > 2-25; ERDE > 26-71; PFLANZENREICH >72-89; TIERREICH > 90-143; MENSCH > 144-177; NAHRUNGSMITTEL UND KÜCHE > 178-241; HAUS > 242-295;
HEIMWERKEN UND GARTENARBEIT > 296-333; KLEIDUNG > 334-371; PERSÖNLICHE AUSSTATTUNG > 372-391; KUNST UND ARCHITEKTUR > 392-465; KOMMUNIKATION UND BÜROTECHNIK > 466-535;
TRANSPORT UND FAHRZEUGE > 536-643; ENERGIE > 644-677; WISSENSCHAFT > 678-705; GESELLSCHAFT > 706-785; SPORT UND SPIELE > 786-920

609

Zelle, tierische 66
Zellen 416, 440
Zellkern 50, 66, 110, 112
Zellkörper 110
Zellwand 50
Zelte, Beispiele 528
Zeltspannleine 528
Zeltstange 529
Zeltwagen 361
Zeltwand 528
Zement 101
Zement, Hartplatz 492
Zementestrich 190
Zenitprisma 8
Zentralafrikanische Republik 451
Zentralbereich 4
Zentralbereich, gewölbter 6
zentrale Pumpstation 404
zentraler Mittelfeldspieler 481
zentrales Scharfstellrad 420
Zentralindischer Rücken 34
Zentralnervensystem 109
Zentriereinstellung 329
Zentrierspitze 228
Zentriol 66
Zerkleinerer 49
Zerkleinern 170
Zerkleinerung 49
Zerkleinerungswerk 402
zerlappte Projektion 22
Zerreiben 170
zersetzende Organismen 45
Zerstäuberstift 236
zerstoßene Chilis 139
Zerstreuungslinsen 419
Zeugenberg 36
Zeugenstand 440
Ziege 84
Ziegel 279, 280
Ziegenfrischkäse 150
Ziegenkäse 150
Ziegenmilch 150
Ziehbügel 460
Ziehhacke 233
Ziehharmonikafach 274
Ziel 516

Zielbahnhof 374
Zielbälle 502
Zielfernrohr 420, 534
Ziellinie 473
Zier-Steppnaht 246, 260
Zierbaum 122, 182, 230
Zierborte 260
Ziergarten 230
Zierkohl 126
Ziernaht 243
Zifferblatt 424
Ziffern, römische 427
Zifferntaste 337
Zikade 69
Zimmermannshammer 220
Zimmernummer 439
Zimtstangen 138
Zink-Elektrolytmischung (Anode) 417
Zink-Mangan-Zelle, alkalische 417
Zinke 167
Zinkzylinder (Anode) 417
Zinnenkranz 282
Zirbeldrüse 109
Zirrokumulus 42
Zirrostratus 42
Zirrus 42
Zither 296
Zitronatzitrone 134
Zitrone 134
Zitronenmelisse 142
Zitronenpresse 170
Zitronenschaber 169
Zitrusfrucht 58
Zitrusfrüchte 134
Zitruspresse 177
Zollkontrolle 391
Zona pellucida 112
Zoomer 320
Zoomobjektiv 314, 320
Zoomregler 315
Zoomwippe 320
Zubehör 209, 356, 372, 538
Zubehörfach 209
Zubehörschuh 314
Zubringer 431
Zucchini 128

Zucchini, gelbe 129
Zuchtchampignon 123
Zucker 149
Zucker, brauner 149
Zuckerdose 166
Zuckererbsen 130
Zuckermelone 135
Zufahrtsstraße 388
Zufahrtsweg 183
Zufluss 32
Zugang 407
Zugang zum Gleis 374
Zugangsserver 335
Zugarten 470
Zugbrücke 282
Zügel 78
Zugentlastungsklemme 198
Zugfeder 355
Zugrichter 516
Zugriemen 277
Zugriffsöffnung 333
Zugsattelzapfen 365
Zugschnur 275
Zugsystem 537
Zulauf 197
Zuleitungsdraht 199
Zuluftleitung 345
Zündhütchen 534
Zündkabel 360
Zündkabel, Anschluss 359
Zündkerze 237, 359, 360
Zündkerzendichtring 359
Zündkerzengehäuse 359
Zündkerzenkabel 350
Zündschalter 368
Zündschloss 354
Zündschlüssel 237
Zündverstellers 360
Zündverteiler 350, 360
zunehmender Mond 5
Zunge 106, 116, 117, 154, 240, 262, 297, 305, 509, 511
Zunge, gespaltene 76
Zungenmandel 118
Zungenpfeife 305
Zungenrücken 118

Zungenscheide 76
Zungenspitze 118
Zungenwurzel 118
Zusammenfassung 313
Zusammenfluss 32
zusammengesetzte Blätter 55
zusätzlicher Griff 228
Zusatzsteckdose 217
Zusatzstecker 210
Zusatztank 365
Zuschauer 440
Zuschauergrenze 475
Zuschauerraum 293
Zuwachsstreifen 72, 73
Zwecke 220
zwei Pärchen 468
zweiflammiger Gasbrenner 529
zweiflügelige Ausgangstür 362
zweiflügeliger Propeller 394
Zweig 53, 63
zweigliedrige Trugdolde 57
Zweihalbetakt 298
zweiköpfiger Armstrecker 96
zweiköpfiger Schenkelmuskel 97
Zweipersonenzelt 528
Zweireiher 244
zweireihig 248
zweischalige Muschel 73
zweischalige Muschel, Anatomie 73
zweischalige Muschel, äußere Merkmale 73
zweischneidige Klinge 271
zweischneidiger Rasierer 271
zweiseitig gezahnte Effilierschere 270
Zweisitzer 200
zweisitziges Sofa 439
zweistöckiges Haus 289
Zweitbelegung 330
zweite Reihe 482
zweite Rückenflosse 74
zweite Spannungserhöhung 413
zweite Violinen 295
zweite Zehe 78
Zweite-Reihe-Stürmer links 482
Zweite-Reihe-Stürmer rechts 482
zweiteiliger Schlafanzug 260

zweiter Backenzahn 101
zweiter Halswirbel 99
zweiter Kamera-Assistent 290
zweiter Malspieler 474
zweiter Raum 489
zweiter Schiedsrichter 485, 487
zweiter Ventilzug 307
zweiter vorderer Backenzahn 101
zweiter Warteraum 465
zweites Mal 474
Zweiunddreißigstelnote 299
Zweiunddreißigstelpause 299
Zwerchfell 105
Zwiebel im Querschnitt 54
Zwiebel, rote 124
Zwiebel, weiße 124
Zwiebelgemüse 124
Zwillingswadenmuskel 96, 97
Zwinge 224
Zwinger 282
Zwischengeschoß 182, 189
Zwischenknochenmuskel 96
Zwischenrad 523
Zwischenraum 298
Zwischenrippennerv 108
Zwischensohle 262
Zwischentitel 313
Zwölfeck, regelmäßiges 429
Zwölffingerdarm 106
Zyan 418
Zylinder 238, 269, 270, 429
Zylinderglas 419
Zylinderkopfabdeckung 350
Zylinderkopfdeckel 360
Zylinderprojektion 22
Zypern 450
Zypressennadeln 65
Zytopharynx 66
Zytoplasma 50, 66, 112
Zytoplasmamembran 50, 66
Zytostom 66

ASTRONOMIE > 2-25;   ERDE > 26-71;   PFLANZENREICH >72-89;   TIERREICH > 90-143;   MENSCH > 144-177;   NAHRUNGSMITTEL UND KÜCHE > 178-241;   HAUS > 242-295;
HEIMWERKEN UND GARTENARBEIT > 296-333;   KLEIDUNG > 334-371;   PERSÖNLICHE AUSSTATTUNG > 372-391;   KUNST UND ARCHITEKTUR > 392-465;   KOMMUNIKATION UND BÜROTECHNIK > 466-535;
TRANSPORT UND FAHRZEUGE > 536-643;   ENERGIE > 644-677;   WISSENSCHAFT > 678-705;   GESELLSCHAFT > 706-785;   SPORT UND SPIELE > 786-920

Indice dei nomi Italiani

A

abat-son 285
abbaino 182
abbellimenti 299
abbigliamento 238, 538
abbigliamento da ginnastica 263
abbigliamento femminile 251
abbigliamento maschile 244
abbigliamento sportivo 262
abbigliamento, negozio di 436
abbottonatura a doppiopetto 248
abbottonatura a polo 250
abbottonatura a pressione 260
abbottonatura anteriore a pressione 261
abbottonatura della cintura 246
abete 65
abete, aghi d' 65
abissino 87
abitacolo 525
abitazioni urbane 289
abiti, esempi di 252
abito a polo 252
abito a T-shirt 261
abito a trapezio 252
abito a tunica 252
abito a vestaglia 252
abito a vita bassa 252
abito da casa 252
ABS, sistema frenante antibloccaggio 357
abside 285
acagiù, noce di 133
acanto, foglia di 200
accappatoio 256
acceleratore, manopola dell' 368
acceleratore, pedale dell' 354
accelerazione, cavo di 237
accelerazione, grilletto di 235
accensione, blocchetto di 354
accensione, candela di 237
accensione, chiave dell' 237
accensione, interruttore di 336
accensione, pulsante di 213
accensione/spegnimento, spia luminosa di 327
accento 299
accesso, pista di 388
accesso, portello di 385
accesso, strada di 388
accessori 209, 356, 372, 538
accessori a propano o butano 529
accessori dell'obiettivo 314
accessori di bellezza 264
accessori di pulitura 209
accessori per la sciolinatura 514
accessori personali 264
accessori, espulsore degli 176
accessori, scomparto degli 209
accessori, slitta per gli 314
accetta 234, 533
accettazione 462, 465
acchito 502
acchito centrale 502

acchito della linea di battuta 502
acchito superiore 502
acciaio, corpo d' 417
acciaiolo 169
acciarino 218
accidenti 299
acciuga 159
accompagnamento, corde per l' 296
acconciatura, articoli per 268
accoppiamento, adattatore di 11
accordatura, anello d' 297
accordo 299
accordo, asta d' 305
accumulatore 357
acero 64
acero, sciroppo d' 149
aceto balsamico 141
aceto di malto 141
aceto di mele 141
aceto di riso 141
aceto di vino 141
acetosa 127
achenio 59, 60
acidificazione dei laghi 48
acido nitrico, emissione di 48
acido solforico, emissione di 48
acino 62
acino, sezione di un 59
acqua 402, 408
acqua calda, colonna montante dell' 194
acqua calda, rete di distribuzione dell' 194
acqua di disgelo 30
acqua fredda, colonna montante dell' 194
acqua fredda, rete di distribuzione dell' 194
acqua ossigenata 461
acqua, attacco del tubo di alimentazione dell' 214
acqua, bicchiere da 165
acqua, bottiglia dell' 371
acqua, chiave dell' 307
acqua, contatore dell' 194
acqua, corso d' 32, 48
acqua, getti d' 518
acqua, inquinamento dell' 48
acqua, livello dell' 181
acqua, serbatoio dell' 181, 272
acqua, superficie dell' 518
acquasantiera 446
acquascooter 523
acque reflue 48
acquifero artesiano 402
acromion 99
acroterio 279
acuti, ponticello degli 304
acuti, registro degli 296
acuti, tastiera degli 296
Adamo, pomo d' 92
adattatore 198, 271
adattatore di accoppiamento 11
adattatore per oculare 320
adattatore per videocassette compatte 320

addebito, carta di 443
addetto ai 24 secondi 488
addetto al controllo biglietti 294
addetto alla panca dei punti 507
addizione 427
addome 67, 68, 70, 71, 78, 92, 94
adduttore lungo 96
Aden, Golfo di 19, 20
Adriatico, Mar 18
aerazione, canale di 278
aerazione, comando dell' 354
aerazione, griglia di 182
aereo da ricognizione meteorologica 38
aereo di linea 37
aerocisti 51
aeroplani, esempi di 394
aeroplano anfibio antincendio 394
aeroplano da carico 394
aeroplano leggero 394
aeroplano privato 394
aeroplano, movimenti di un 395
aeroporto 25, 388, 430
affari, quartiere degli 430, 432
affettauova 173
affettaverdure 170
affissione, superficie di 341
affluente 32
affresco 280
Afghanistan 452
Africa 14, 20, 34, 451
agar-agar 123
agarico delizioso 123
agenda 338
agente di polizia 456
agente di sicurezza, postazione dell' 463
aggancio, pulsante di 227
aggetto, manopola di regolazione dell' 229
aghi d'abete 65
aghi di pino 65
aglio 124
agnello, tagli di 153
ago 460
ago magnetico 533
ago per legare 173
agricoltura intensiva 46, 48
agrippina 200
agrume 58
agrumi 134
air bag 354
air bag, sistema di ritenuta degli 354
airone 80
aiuola 183, 230
aiutante 121
aiuto attrezzista 291
aiuto regista 291
ajowan 139
ala 13, 68, 78, 117, 393, 536
ala a delta 394
ala alta 394
ala anteriore 67
ala destra 482, 489, 507

ala poppiera 387
ala posteriore 67
ala prodiera 387
ala semiimmersa 387
ala sinistra 482, 489, 507
alamaro 249
alano 86
alari 193
Alaska, Golfo dell' 16
Albania 450
albatros 80
albergo 432, 439, 469, 512
albergo, camera d' 439
alberi 504
albero 63, 412, 519, 520
albero a bassa velocità 413
albero a camme 360
albero a gomiti 360
albero ad alta velocità 413
albero da frutto 122
albero del derrick 385
albero dell'elica 387
albero della vite 62
albero delle pedivelle 372
albero di Natale 404
albero di trasmissione 383
albero di trasmissione longitudinale 351
albero motore 395
albero ornamentale 122, 230
albero prodiero 385
albero, struttura di un 63
albicocca 132
albume 79
alburno 63
alce 85
alchechengi 132
alcol puro 461
alcool, bulbo d' 424
alcool, colonna d' 424
alesatore per la pulizia degli ugelli 218
aletta 244, 275, 393, 394, 460
aletta a molla 221
aletta del parafango 364
aletta parasole 354
aletta staccata 248
aletta, tasca applicata con 245
aletta, tasca interna con 244, 248, 249, 251
aletta, tasca profilata con 244, 248
aletta, taschino con 244
aletta, taschino tagliato con 244
alette 471
alettone 392, 525
alettone parafango 365
Aleutine, Isole 16
alfiere 470
alga 51
alga bruna 51
alga rossa 51
alga verde 51

alga, struttura di un' 51
Algeria 451
alghe, esempi di 51
alimentatore 336
alimentatore, ventola dell' 329
alimentazione dell'acqua, tubo di 214
alimentazione dell'aria, tubo di 454
alimentazione, cavo di 177, 229
alimentazione, cavo di 227, 269, 270, 322
alimentazione, cordone dell' 271
alimentazione, presa di 326, 329
alimentazione, pulsante di 318
alimentazione, sistema di 351
alimentazione, spia luminosa di 328
alimentazione, spina di 337
alimentazione, tubo di 197
alimenti e prodotti per animali 121
alimenti, latta per 163
alimenti, rete per 162
alimenti, vaschetta per 162
aliscafo 387
all'indietro 518
allacciamento alla rete 198
allacciamento, esempi di 197
allacciamento, punto di 198
allacciatura con bottoni a pressione 249
allarme, dispositivo di 454
allenatore 489, 498, 507
allenatore, zona dell' 474
allenatori 509
allevamento intensivo 46, 47
alligatore 77
alloggi 512
alloggi dell'equipaggio 382
alloggiamento 199, 286, 337
alloggiamento del bocchino 307
alloggiamento del mulinello 536, 537
alloggiamento del ventilatore 270
alloggio del comandante 387
alloro 142
alone 6
alosa 160
Alpi 18
alta pressione, area di 43
altare maggiore 446
altare secondario 446
altare, croce dell' 446
altare, pala dell' 446
alte frequenze, pick-up per 303
alternato 330
alternato: selezione di livello 3 330
alternatore 350, 360, 402, 408, 413
altezza dell'onda 33
altezza, indice di regolazione dell' 227
altezza, regolazione micrometrica dell' 8, 9
alti, regolatore degli 322
altitudine 44
altitudini, scala delle 37
altocumulo 42
altoparlante 320, 326, 327, 328, 336, 380, 455
altoparlanti, bilanciamento degli 322

ASTRONOMIA > 2-25; TERRA > 26-71; REGNO VEGETALE >72-89; REGNO ANIMALE > 90-143; ESSERE UMANO > 144-177; GENERI ALIMENTARI E CUCINA > 178-241; CASA > 242-295;
FAI DA TE E GIARDINAGGIO > 296-333; ABBIGLIAMENTO > 334-371; ACCESSORI E ARTICOLI PERSONALI > 372-391; ARTE E ARCHITETTURA > 392-465; COMUNICAZIONI E BUROTICA > 466-535;
TRASPORTI E VEICOLI > 536-643; ENERGIA > 644-677; SCIENZA > 678-705; SOCIETÀ > 706-785; SPORT E GIOCHI > 786-920

611

INDICE DEI NOMI ITALIANI

altopiano 5, 24, 29
altostrato 42
altri segni 299
alula 78
alveolo della presa 198
alveolo dentario 101
alzata 191, 210, 212, 213
alzatore destro 487
amanita muscaria 52
amanita virosa 52
amaranto 143
Amazzoni, Rio delle 17
ambiente 44
ambiente naturale 504
ambio 83
ambulanza 460, 462
ameba 66
America Centrale 14, 16
America Meridionale 14, 17, 34
America Settentrionale 14, 16, 34
America, Stati Uniti d' 448
Americhe 448
Amery, Banchisa di 15
amido 61
ammasso globulare 6
amministrazione 445
ammiraglia 522
ammortizzatore 287, 351, 523
ammortizzatore anteriore 369
ammortizzatore posteriore 367
amo 536, 538
amo con setale 538
amo, apertura dell' 538
ampere 426
ampiezza 418
ampolla della tuba di Falloppio 113
ananas 136
anatomia 96
anatomia di un astice 71
anatomia di una conchiglia bivalve 73
anatomia patologica, laboratorio di 465
anatra 81, 155
anatra, uovo di 155
ancia 305, 306
ancia doppia 306
ancia semplice 306
ancia, canna ad 305
anconeo 97
ancora a scatto 221
ancoraggio 473
ancorina 538
andature 83
Ande, Cordigliera delle 17
Andorra 449
anelli 264, 496, 497
anelli addominali 536
anello 52, 270, 307, 423, 424, 489
anello a fascia 264
anello a strappo 163
anello centrale esterno da 25 punti 471
anello con sigillo 264
anello d'accordatura 297
anello dei doppi 471
anello dei tripli 471
anello di attacco 535
anello di bloccaggio 332
anello di chiusura 210
anello di congiunzione 538
anello di fidanzamento 264
anello di regolazione 236
anello di regolazione della coppia di
serraggio 228
anello di regolazione diottrica 420
anello di sospensione 270
anello di traino 460
anello esterno 515
anello fermadisco 501
anello fermamulinello 536
anello guida della lenza 536, 537
anello interno 515
anello oculare 78
anello, orecchini ad 264
anemometro 413
anestesia, stanza per l' 464
aneto 142
anfibi 75
anfibi, esempi di 75
anfiteatro romano 281
anfora, gonna ad 253
Angola 452
angolare 277
angoli, esempi di 428
angoli, lenzuolo con 204
angoliera 203
angolo 481, 498
angolo acuto 428

angolo concavo 428
angolo della pista 506
angolo di elevazione, regolazione dell' 420
angolo ottuso 428
angolo retto 428
anguilla 159
anice 142
anice stellato 60
anidride carbonica, assorbimento di 54
anidride solforosa, emissione di 48
Anik 317
anima 305
anima, canna ad 305
animali, negozio di 436
animelle 154
annaffiatoio 236
anno 441
anno, stagioni dell' 38
annodatura 245
ano 71, 73, 106, 111, 112
anodo 417
anta, pannello dell' 202
Antartide 14, 15
antefissa 279
antelice 115
antenna 7, 67, 68, 71, 326, 327, 349,
369, 392, 395, 457, 487
antenna ad alta frequenza, cavo dell' 394
antenna di captazione 321
antenna di casa 316
antenna di trasmissione/ricezione 316
antenna emittente 316
antenna parabolica 321
antenna parabolica ricetrasmittente 316
antenna per telecomunicazioni 386, 387
antenna radio 382, 384, 386, 387, 525
antenna telescopica 325
antenne, terminali di collegamento delle
322
antennula 71
antera 56
antiallagamento, dispositivo 214
anticlinale 403
anticollisione, luce 392
Antigua e Barbuda 449
Antille, Isole delle 448
antilope 84
antipastiera 166
antisettico 461
antitrago 115
antivibrazione, impugnatura con sistema
235
anulare 115
aorta 104, 105
aorta addominale 102, 107
aorta ascendente 103
aorta discendente 103
aorta, arco dell' 102, 104
ape 68
ape operaia 68
ape operaia, morfologia di un' 68
ape regina 68
apertura 73, 224, 243, 247
apertura dell'amo 538
apertura per le braccia 251
apice 55, 72, 73, 101, 118
apoteocio 50
apparato del Golgi 50, 66
apparato digerente 106
apparato radicale 53, 62
apparato respiratorio 105
apparato urinario 107
apparecchio telefonico 327
appartamenti 512
appartiene a 427
appendice vermiforme 106
applicatore a spugnetta 266
appoggiamano 466
appoggiapiedi 224, 369, 467, 501
appoggiapiedi del guidatore 367, 368
appoggiapiedi del passeggero 367, 368
appoggiatura 299
appoggio del mignolo 307
appoggio del pollice 306, 307
appoggio del polpaccio 511
appoggio, barra d' 219
appoggio, filo d' 70
appoggio, piano di 396
appoggio, piastra d' 229
appoggio, punto d' 75
approssimativamente uguale a 427
apribottiglie 170, 531
apriscatole 170, 180, 531
aptero 51
aquila 81
Arabia Saudita 452

Arabico, Mare 19
arachide 130
arachidi, olio di 149
aracnidi 67
aracnide 109
aragosta 158
Aral, Lago di 19
arame 123
arancia 134
arancia, sezione di un' 58
arbitro 479, 481, 483, 488, 495, 498,
499, 507, 516, 518
arbitro capo 475
arborizzazione terminale 110
arca 447
arcata 281, 284
arcata dentale inferiore 116
arcata dentale superiore 116
archetto 301, 425, 460, 537
archetto, meccanismo di apertura dell'
537
archi, famiglia degli 295, 301
architettura 278
architrave 185, 192, 279, 285
archiviazione 339
archivio delle cartelle cliniche 465
archivio, scatola per 340
archivolto 285
arcipelago 24
arco 428
arco aortico 102, 103, 104
arco composto 535
arco diagonale 284
arco insulare 33
arco longitudinale 284
arco naturale 35
arco palatoglosso 116
arco rampante 284, 285
arco trasversale 284
arcobaleno 41
ardiglione 246, 538
area commerciale 435
area d'attesa 442
area dei tre secondi 489
area di alta pressione 43
area di atterraggio 472
area di bassa pressione 43
area di combattimento 499
area di gioco 386, 471
area di meta 483, 484
area di parcheggio 389
area di porta 480, 507
area di precipitazione 39
area di rifornimento 346
area di rigore 480
area di servizio 25, 389
area di sicurezza 499
area di sosta 25
area di sosta dei veicoli 345
area per il ritiro dei bagagli 390
arena 281
areola 113
argani di perforazione 403
argano 287
Argentina 448
argine 342
aria calda 41
aria calda ascendente 43
aria calda, deflettore dell' 192
aria calda, uscita dell' 192
aria compressa, bombola di 454
aria fredda 41
aria fredda discendente 43
aria, compressore dell' 376
aria, filtro dell' 235, 398
aria, inquinamento dell' 47
aria, presa d' 367, 383, 395
aria, temperatura dell' 39
aria, tipo di massa d' 39
Ariele 3
aringa 159
armadietti degli studenti 445
armadio 202, 213, 439
armadio appendiabiti 203
armadio frigorifero 438
armatura di chiave 299
armatura protettiva del tronco 486
Armenia 452
armonica a bocca 296
arnia 122
aromatiche, piante 142
arpa 302
arpe 295
arpeggio 299
arredamento per la casa 200

arresto, blocco d' 229
arresto, pulsante di 229, 424
arresto, tasto di 319, 323, 328
arresto/cancellazione, tasto di 323
arricciaburro 169
arricciacapelli 269
arricciatura 255
arridatoio 521
arrivo della sciovia 512
arrivo, parete di 516
arrosto 153
arrotolato 152
arte 278
arteria addominale dorsale 71
arteria ascellare 102
arteria brachiale 102
arteria carotide comune 102
arteria dell'arco del piede 102
arteria dorsale del piede 102
arteria femorale 102
arteria iliaca comune 102, 107
arteria iliaca interna 102, 103, 107
arteria mesenterica inferiore 107
arteria mesenterica superiore 102, 107
arteria polmonare 102, 104, 105
arteria renale 102, 107
arteria sternale 71
arteria succlavia 102
arteria tibiale anteriore 102
arteria ventrale 71
arterie 102
arti plastiche, aula di 444
arti sceniche 294
arti toracici 71
articolazione 355
articolazione del nodello 83
articoli da regalo, negozio di 436
articoli di cancelleria 337
articoli di pelletteria 274
articoli per acconciatura 268
articoli personali 264, 271
articoli sportivi, negozio di 437
articoli vari 341
articolo 313
articolo di spalla 313
Artide 14
artiglio 79, 82
arto anteriore 75
arto inferiore 103
arto locomotore 70
arto locomotore 67
arto posteriore 75
arto superiore 103
ascella 92, 94
ascella fogliare 55
ascensione retta, cerchio graduato dell' 8,
9
ascensore 287, 435, 439
ascensore, cabina dell' 287
asciugacapelli 270
asciugamano 267
asciugamano da bagno 267
asciugatrice 213
Asia 14, 19, 34, 452
asino 84
asola 246, 531
asola per il picchetto 528, 529
asparago 125
aspirapolvere 209
aspirapolvere verticale 209
aspirazione, tubo di 455
aspirina® 461
assafetida 139
assale 527
assale anteriore 401
asse della bobina 537
asse di trasmissione del motore 177
asse orizzontale, regolazione micrometrica
dell' 9
asse polare 7
assegni 441
assegni libretto degli 274
assistente sociale, ufficio dell' 463
assistenti degli avvocati 440
asso 468
assone 110
assorbimento attraverso la superficie
terrestre 46
assorbimento attraverso le nuvole 46
assorbimento d'acqua e sali minerali 54
assorbimento di anidride carbonica 54
asta 199, 424, 503, 505, 506, 514, 534
asta d'accordo 305
asta del meccanismo a scatto 312
asta di perforazione 403
asta di sostegno 380

asta mobile 425
asta motrice quadra 403
astata 55
astenosfera 26
asteroidi, fascia degli 3
astice 71, 158
astice, anatomia di un 71
astice, morfologia di un 71
astigmatismo 419
astragalo 99
astronautica 10
astronomia 2
astuccio 265
astuccio delle manette 456
astuccio per i guanti di lattice 456
astuccio per occhiali 275
Atacama, Deserto di 17
atlante 99
Atlante, Monti dell' 20
Atlantico, merluzzo dell' 161
Atlantico, Oceano 14, 15, 18, 20
Atlantico, salmone dell' 161
atleta 473
atletica leggera 472
atmosfera 44, 48
atmosfera terrestre, profilo dell' 37
atollo 35
atomi 414
atomizzatore 236
atomo 414
atrio 280, 374, 435, 439, 440, 442
atrio destro 103, 104
atrio sinistro 103, 104
attaccante 481
attaccante centrale 487
attaccante destro 485
attaccante sinistro 485, 487
attacco 199, 273, 485, 513, 514, 526
attacco a baionetta 199
attacco a spina 199
attacco a vite 199
attacco del manubrio 371
attacco del tubo di alimentazione
dell'acqua 236
attacco del tubo di scarico 192
attacco della campana 306
attacco di sicurezza 10, 510, 511
attacco per attrezzi 10
attacco, leva di apertura dell' 511
atterraggio, faro di 395
atterraggio, finestrino di 395
attesa, area d' 442
attizzatoio 193
attore 290
attori, ingresso degli 278
attori, sedie degli 290
attrazione 416
attrezzatura 472
attrezzatura elettrica 217
attrezzatura terminale 538
attrezzatura varia 231
attrezzatura, ripostiglio per l' 444
attrezzature da campeggio 531
attrezzi da muratore 216
attrezzi di brasatura 218
attrezzi di saldatura 218
attrezzi di serraggio 222
attrezzi domestici 215
attrezzi ginnici 500
attrezzi idraulici 216
attrezzi per annaffiare 236
attrezzi per chiodare 220
attrezzi per piccoli lavori di giardinaggio
232
attrezzi per potare e tagliare 234
attrezzi per sagomare 229
attrezzi per seminare e piantare 231
attrezzi per smuovere la terra 233
attrezzi per trapanare 228
attrezzi, cassetta degli 225
attrezzi, kit di 372
attrezzistica 473
attrezzo multiuso 501
attrice 291
audio, sistema di registrazione 291
augnatura manuale, sega per 226
augnatura, cassetta ad 226
aula 444, 445
aula di arti plastiche 444
aula di informatica 444
aula di musica 444
aula di scienze 444
aula di trucha 440
aula per studenti con difficoltà
d'apprendimento 444
aumento di tensione 402, 408

ASTRONOMIA > 2-25;   TERRA > 26-71;   REGNO VEGETALE >72-89;   REGNO ANIMALE > 90-143;   ESSERE UMANO > 144-177;   GENERI ALIMENTARI E CUCINA > 178-241;   CASA > 242-295;
FAI DA TE E GIARDINAGGIO > 296-333;   ABBIGLIAMENTO > 334-371;   ACCESSORI E ARTICOLI PERSONALI > 372-391;   ARTE E ARCHITETTURA > 392-465;   COMUNICAZIONI E BUROTICA > 466-535;
TRASPORTI E VEICOLI > 536-643;   ENERGIA > 644-677;   SCIENZA > 678-705;   SOCIETÀ > 706-785;   SPORT E GIOCHI > 786-920.

INDICE DEI NOMI ITALIANI

auricolare 325
aurora polare 37
Australia 14, 34, 453
Austria 450
auto da formula 1 525
auto da formula 3000 524
auto da formula Indy 524
auto da rally 524
auto-reverse, tasto dell' 326
autobotte 364
autobus 362, 435
autobus a due piani 363
autobus articolato 363
autobus urbano 362
autobus, fermata dell' 434
autobus, stazione degli 432
autocaravan 361
autocarro a cassone ribaltabile 401
autoclave 464
autogrù 364, 397
autoguida, cabina dell' 397
autolavaggio 346
automobile 347
automobilismo 524
automotrice 376
autopompa 455
autoradio 354
autoreggente, calza 257
autorespiratore 454
autoscala 455
autoscatto, spia luminosa dell' 314
autostrada 25, 343, 431
autostrada, numero di 25
autotrofi, organismi 45
autoveicoli industriali 364
autovetture, ponte per le 386
autunno 38
autunno, equinozio d' 38
avambraccio 86, 93, 95
avambraccio, protezione per l' 486
avanti 482
avanzamento della carta, tasto di 443
avanzamento rapido, tasto di 319, 323, 326, 328
avena 61, 143
avena, farina di 144
avena: pannocchia 61
avenue 25, 433
aviogetto a lungo raggio 392
aviorimessa 389
avocado 128
avvertenza, targhetta delle 228
avviamento, manovella di 235
avviamento, motorino d' 237
avvio, tasto di 328
avvisatore acustico 377
avvisatore acustico a tromba 364
avvocati dell'accusa, banco degli 440
avvocati, assistenti degli 440
avvolgimento, manovella d' 225
avvoltoio 80
axel 509
Azerbaigian 452
azienda 335
azienda commerciale 335
azione del vento 45
azzeramento, pulsante di 424
azzeramento, tasto di 319

B

babbuino 91
baby-doll 256
bacca 59
bacca di ginepro 138
baccello 60
bacche 132
bacchetta 301
bacchetta di metallo 309
bacchette 309
bacheca 341, 444
bacinella raccogligocce 210
bacinella raccogligrasso 179
bacino 381, 406, 407
bacino a monte 406
bacino a valle 406, 407
bacino di carenaggio 381
bacino, porta del 381
backgammon 469
backspace 331
bacon americano 156
bacon canadese 156
badile 233
badile pieghevole 532
Baffin, Isola di 16
bagagli 276

bagagli, deposito 374
bagagli, scompartimento 376
bagagliai 383
bagagliaio 362, 393, 395
bagaglio a mano 276
bagher 487
bagno degli uomini 294
bagno delle donne 294
bagno, costume da 263
bagno, lucernaio del 189
bagno, slip da 263
bagno, stanza da 439
bagno, vasca da 195
bagnomaria, pentola per cucinare a 175
bagnoschiuma 267
baguette 144
Bahama 448
Bahrein 452
baia 5, 24
Baia di Hudson 16
Baikal, Lago 19
baionetta, attacco a 199
baita di montagna 512
balalaica 297
balaustra 188, 189, 283
balaustra della comunione 446
balaustre 506
balaustro 191
balconata 447
balconcino, reggiseno a 259
balcone 189, 412
balena 90
balenottera 90
ballatoi 292
ballerina 241
ballerino 160
ballo, sala da 387
balsamo per capelli 267
Baltico, Mar 18
balze, gonna a 253
bambini, vestiti per 261
bambino, cranio di 100
banana 136
banana plantain 136
banca 432, 437, 442, 469
banca di emissione, iniziali della 441
banchina 381
banchina di scarico delle merci 437, 439
banchina laterale 342
Banchisa di Amery 15
Banchisa di Filchner 15
Banchisa di Ross 15
banco 444
banco degli avvocati dell'accusa 440
banco degli avvocati difensori 440
banco dei formaggi 121
banco dei giudici 440
banco dei testimoni 440
banco dell'imputato 440
banco della carne fresca 120
banco della carne self-service 120
banco della giuria 440
banco della reception 442
banco delle informazioni 390, 437, 442, 463
banco di registrazione 390
banco di sabbia 33
banco per la prenotazione degli hotel 390
bancomat, sportello 437, 442
bancone del bar 438
banconota 469
banconota: dritto 441
banconota: rovescio 441
banconote, emissione di 442
banconote, scomparto per 274
banda 286
banda magnetica 441
banda nuvolosa a spirale 43
banda olografica 441
banda, tasto di selezione della 322
bande verticali, porta a 286
bandella di rinforzo 277
banderuola 413
bandiera dell'Unione Europea 441
bandiera rimovibile 504
bandiere 448
bandierina 482
bandierina centrale 480
bandierina del calcio d'angolo 481
Bangladesh 453
banjo 296
bar 293, 432, 436, 438
bar, bancone del 438
bar, mobile 203
bar, sgabello da 438
barattoli 162

barba 61
barba, pennello da 271
barbabietola 129
barbacane 282
Barbados 449
barbaforte 129
barbetta 61
barbone 86
barca a chiglia 521
barca a vela 520
barcana 36
barche, esempi di 382
bardana 129
barelle, deposito delle 462
Barents, Mar di 18
barista 438
barra 412, 469
barra collettrice 407
barra d'appoggio 219
barra dei martelletti 304
barra del timone 520
barra di comando 395
barra di partenza 516
barra di pressione 304
barra di traino 361
barra distanziatrice 362
barra per i dorsali 501
barra per i pettorali 501
barra per i tricipiti 501
barra spaziatrice 330
barretta 273
barretta di combustibile 409
barriera 434
barriera di pneumatici 524
basamento 27, 227, 283, 435, 498
basamento del telescopio 7
basamento imbottito 489
baschina, gonna con 253
basco 239
base 164, 174, 176, 179, 180, 192, 197, 206, 229, 269, 277, 296, 308, 332, 412, 421, 422, 454, 473
base del bulbo 54
base del tergale 200
base dell'intelaiatura 186
base di sostegno 202
base fissa 224
base girevole 224
base, piastra di 27, 227
baseball 474
basilico 142
Bass, Stretto di 15
bassa pressione, area di 43
bassa tensione, linea di distribuzione a 198
basse frequenze, pick-up per 303
bassi, bottoniera dei 296
bassi, ponticello dei 304
bassi, registro dei 296
bassi, regolatore dei 322
basso, chiave di 298
bastoncello 119
bastoncino di carbone (catodo) 417
bastone 273, 507
bastone con manico anatomico 466
bastone da passeggio 273, 466
bastone del giocatore 506
bastone estendibile 456
bastone inglese 466
bastone, pomolo del 506
battagliola 384
battente 286
batteria 221, 228, 308, 350, 359, 411, 416
batteria elettronica 311
batteria ricaricabile 320
batteria, contenitore della 359
battistrada, scultura del 358
battitoio 297, 308
battitore 475, 476, 478, 479, 491, 494
battuta, zona di 477
baule 277
bauletto 369
bavaglino 260
Beaufort, Mar di 16
beauty-case 277
beccatello 282
beccheggio 395
becchi lunghi, pinza a 217
becchi, esempi di 79
becco 78
becco corneo 76
beccuccio 180, 181, 215, 268
beccuccio spruzzatore 272
beccuccio, vaschetta con 177
becquerel 426

begonia 56
Belgio 449
Belize 448
bemolle 299
benda elastica 461
Bengala, Golfo del 19
benna retro 400
benzina 405
benzina avio 405
benzina leggera 405
benzina pesante 405
bequadro 299
bergamotto 134
bergère 200
Bering, Mar di 14
Bering, Stretto di 16
berlina 347
bermuda 254
berretto 238, 456, 514
berretto con pompon 239
berretto da cacciatore 238
berretto impermeabile 239
bersaglio 471
bertesca 282
bestiame, carro 377
betoniera 365
betulla 64
Bhutan 453
biancheria da letto 204
biancheria da notte 256
biancheria intima 247, 258
biancheria intima, negozio di 436
biancheria, loale per la 439
bianchi 470
bianco 418, 469
bibita, bicchiere da 165
bibita, cucchiaio da 165
bibite 120
bibite, distributore di 463
biblioteca 433, 444
bicchiere 176, 532
bicchiere da acqua 165
bicchiere da bibita 165
bicchiere da Bordeaux 165
bicchiere da Borgogna 165
bicchiere da brandy 165
bicchiere da porto 165
bicchiere da vino alsaziano 165
bicchiere da vino bianco 165
bicchierino da liquore 165
bicicletta 370
bicicletta da corsa 373, 522
bicicletta da cross-country 522
bicicletta da downhill 522
bicicletta da turismo 373
bicicletta olandese 373
bicicletta, componenti di una 370
biciclette, esempi di 373
biciclette, parcheggio per le 445
bicipite brachiale 96
bicipite femorale 97
bicipiti femorali, rullo per i 501
bidè 195
bidello, ufficio del 445
bidone carrellato per il riciclaggio del vetro 49
bidone carrellato per il riciclaggio dell'alluminio 49
bidone carrellato per il riciclaggio della carta 49
bidone dei rifiuti 207
biella 360
Bielorussia 450
bietola da coste 125
bietta 301
biglia battente 502, 503
biglia battente dell'avversario 502, 503
biglia bianca battente 503
biglia blu 503
biglia gialla 503
biglia marrone 503
biglia nera 503
biglia rosa 503
biglia rossa 502, 503
biglia verde 503
biglie da colpire 502
biglie rosse 503
biglietteria 294, 390
biglietteria automatica 294
biglietti, distributore automatico di 379
biglietti, vendita dei 378
bigodino 268
bilancia 292
bilancia a molla 423
bilancia a sospensione inferiore 422

bilancia da analisi 423
bilancia da cucina 171
bilancia di precisione 422
bilancia elettronica 423
bilancia pesapersone 423
bilanciamento 303
bilanciamento degli altoparlanti 322
bilanciere 360, 500, 501
bilanciere, placchetta a 305
biliardo 502
biliardo inglese 503
biliardo per carambola 502
bimah 447
binari del carrello 290
binario 207, 374, 378, 431
binario di raccordo 375
binario ferroviario 432
binario morto 375
binario, faretto da 207
binario, numero del 374
bindella ventilata 534
binocolo da teatro 273
binocolo prismatico 420
biologia 426
biosfera 44
biosfera, struttura della 44
birra 120
birra, boccale da 165
biscroma 299
biscroma, pausa di 299
bisonte 84
bistecca 152
bistecca, coltello da 168
bitta 385
bitume 405
blastodisco 79
blazer 254
bloc-notes 338
bloccaggio della base 224
bloccaggio, dispositivo di 209
bloccaggio, ghiera di 221
bloccaggio, leva di 224
bloccaggio, pulsante di 208
bloccaggio, viti di 425
blocchetto 308
blocchetto di accensione 354
blocchetto di avviamento 368
blocco 305, 473
blocco d'arresto 229
blocco del ponticello 303
blocco della culatta 534
blocco delle maiuscole 330
blocco di ancoraggio dei cavi 344
blocco di chiusura 425
blocco di partenza 473, 516
blocco motore 176, 177, 180, 208, 272
blocco numerico 331
blocco operatorio 464
blocco, dispositivo di 219, 226
blu 418
boa 77
boa di ricognizione meteorologica 38
bobina 319, 536, 537
bobina, asse della 537
bobina, meccanismo di rilascio della 537
bocca 71, 72, 73, 75, 90, 94, 116, 220, 305, 534
bocca di carico 208
bocca di erogazione 197
boccaglio 467
boccale da birra 165
boccaporto 13
bocchetta 177, 180
bocchetta 186
bocchetta del serbatoio 237
bocchetta di ventilazione 354
bocchetta per fessure 209
bocchetta per tappezzeria 209
bocchette 172
bocchettone di riempimento 351
bocchino 306, 307, 311
body 255, 258, 263
bolero 254
Bolivia 448
bolla, livella a 225
bolle d'aria 339
bollitore 180
boma 519, 520
bomba vulcanica 28
bombetta 238
bombo 69
bombola 454, 529
bombola del gas 218
bombola di aria compressa 454
bombola di gas medicale 464
bombola di gas propano 361

ASTRONOMIA > 2-25; TERRA > 26-71; REGNO VEGETALE > 72-89; REGNO ANIMALE > 90-143; ESSERE UMANO > 144-177; GENERI ALIMENTARI E CUCINA > 178-241; CASA > 242-295;
FAI DA TE E GIARDINAGGIO > 296-333; ABBIGLIAMENTO > 334-371; ACCESSORI E ARTICOLI PERSONALI > 372-391; ARTE E ARCHITETTURA > 392-465; COMUNICAZIONI E BUROTICA > 466-535;
TRASPORTI E VEICOLI > 536-643; ENERGIA > 644-677; SCIENZA > 678-705; SOCIETÀ > 706-785; SPORT E GIOCHI > 786-920

613

bongos 309
booster, paracadute del 12
bordame 519
Bordeaux, bicchiere da 165
bordo 205
bordo a coste 250, 261
bordo del piano di cottura 210
bordo della scarpetta 511
bordo di attacco 393
bordo di rifinitura 277
bordo di uscita 392
bordo elastico 247
bordo superiore 493
bordone 296
bordoniera 308
bordura 182, 230
Borgogna, bicchiere da 165
borra 534
borraccia 532
borragine 142
borsa a manicotto 276
borsa a soffietto 274
borsa a telaio rigido 276
borsa a tracolla 276
borsa da postino 276
borsa da viaggio 276
borsa della spesa 276
borsa laterale 369
borse 275
borsellino 275
borsello 276
borsone da viaggio 276
boschi, rana dei 75
bosco 25
Bosnia ed Erzegovina 450
bossolo 534
bossolo di plastica 534
Botnia, Golfo di 18
botola 281, 292
Botswana 452
bottega 280
bottiglia 267, 532
bottiglia da tavola 165
bottiglia dell'acqua 371
bottiglia di vetro 163
bottone 199, 245, 250, 296, 301
bottone a pressione 243, 249
bottone della tracolla 303
bottoniera dei bassi 296
boulevard 25, 433
bowling 436
box 524
box doccia 195
boxer 247
bozzello 397, 521
braccia, apertura per le 251
bracciale con ciondoli 264
bracciale con piastrina 264
bracciale pneumatico 461
bracciale tubolare 264
bracciali 264
braccio 83, 91, 93, 95, 206, 236, 270, 297, 333, 395, 397, 412, 421, 467
braccio del tergicristallo 355
braccio del tremolo 303
braccio della forca 396
braccio della pala caricatrice 399
braccio della sospensione 351
braccio della spirale 6
braccio di posizionamento 400
braccio di scavo 400
braccio di sollevamento 364, 399, 400
braccio di sospensione 212, 467
braccio distanziatore 219
braccio manipolatore telecomandato 12
braccio metallico 236
braccio spruzzante 214
braccio telecomandato 11
braccio telescopico 397, 455
braccio, tirante del 397
bracciolo 200, 205, 352, 353, 467
bracciolo, sostegno del 200
brachiale 96
brachioradiale 96, 97
braciere 283
braciola 152, 153
branca 222
branchie 73
branda 530
brandina smontabile 530
brandy, bicchiere da 165
brano, numero del 323
brano, tasti di ricerca del 323
branzino 160
Brasile 448
Brasile, noce del 133

brattea 60
bretella abbottonabile 261
bretella di raccordo 343
bretella di uscita 391
bretella di uscita della pista ad alta velocità 388
bretella regolabile 260
bretelle 246
bricco del latte 166
brick 163
brick a tappo 163
bricolage, negozio di 436
brie 151
brillamento 4
brillante, serbatoio per il 214
brina 41
broccolo 127
brochure, espositore di 442
brodo, cucchiaio da 168
bronchiolo terminale 105
bronco lobare 105
bronco principale 105
browser 334
bruciatore 210, 529
bruciatore a corona 174
bruciatore, telaio del 529
bruco 67
Brunei 453
Bruxelles, cavolini di 126
buca 502, 504
buca centrale 502
buca inferiore 502
buca par 5 504
buca superiore 502
buccia 57, 58, 59
buccino 157
bue 85
bufalo 84
buffet 438
bugna 519
bulbillo 54
bulbo 125, 199, 385, 387
bulbo d'alcool 424
bulbo del pelo 114
bulbo di mercurio 424
bulbo olfattivo 117
bulbo, base del 54
bulbo, fusto del 54
bulbo, sezione di un 54
Bulgaria 450
bulldog 86
bulldozer 398
bulletta 220
bullone 222, 223, 224, 357
bullone a espansione 221
bullone di spallamento 223
bullone zigrinato 219
bulloni 223
bunker di sabbia 504
Buona Speranza, Capo di 20
Burkina Faso 451
burotica 312
burotica e forniture per l'ufficio 329
burriera 166
burro 150
burro, coltello da 168
burro, scomparto per il 211
Burundi 451
bussola magnetica 533
bussole, set di 223
bussolotto 469
busta imbottita 339
busta portadocumenti 275
bustina 238
bustina di tè 148
bustine trasparenti 274
button-down, collo 245

C

C, morsetto a 224
cabina 386, 398, 399, 400, 401, 443
cabina del gruista 397
cabina del gruista 397
cabina dell'ascensore 287
cabina dell'autogruista 397
cabina della torre di controllo 388
cabina di classe turistica 393
cabina di guida 376, 377
cabina di manovra 375
cabina di osservazione del fuoco primario 7
cabina di pilotaggio 12, 385, 392, 395
cabina di prima classe 392
cabina di proiezione 294
cabina di regia 293

cabina passeggeri 395
cabina, guida della 287
cabina, pavimento della 287
cabina, soffitto della 287
cabriolet 200
cacao 148
caccia 534
cacciapietre 376, 377
cacciavite 221, 531
cacciavite automatico 221
cacciavite con batteria incorporata 221
cacciavite con punta a croce 531
cachi 137
caditoia 282
caduta di poppa 519
caduta di prua 519
caffè 148, 432, 437, 445
caffè, chicchi tostati di 148
caffè, chicchi verdi di 148
caffè, cucchiaino da 168
caffè, macchine da 181
caffè, tazza alta da 166
caffè, tazzina da 166
caffettiera 531
caffettiera a filtro 181
caffettiera a infusione 181
caffettiera a pistone 181
caffettiera napoletana 181
caffettiera per espresso 181
caimano 77
calabrone 69
calamaro 157
calamita 341
calamo vegetale 312
calaza 79
calcagno 99, 247
calcagno, rinforzo esterno del 240
calcagno, rinforzo interno del 240
calciatore 480
calcio 480, 503, 534
calciolo 534
calcolatrice 274
calcolatrice da tavolo 337
calcolatrice scientifica 337
calcolatrice tascabile 337
caldaia 308
calendario a fogli staccabili 338
calendario da tavolo 338
calibro a corsoio con nonio 425
calice 56, 59, 60, 107, 446
calice da cocktail 165
calice gustativo 118
calicetto 59
California, Golfo di 16
Callisto 2
calore 408
calore, dispersione di 46
calore, produzione di 408
calore, trasferimento di 415
calotta 208, 209, 238, 239, 367, 412
calotta della torretta 420
calotta di sicurezza 237
calotta filtrante 459
calotta polare, della 40
calza 257, 259
calza a rete 257
calza autoreggente 257
calza con reggicalze 476
calza dell'albero 519
calze 247, 257
calzerotto 247, 257
calzettone 257, 480, 486, 506
calzettoni 483
calzino 257, 492
calzino corto 247
calzino lungo 247
camaleonte 77
cambio 63
cambio, cavo del 372
cambio, leva del 350, 354, 371, 372
cambio, pedale del 367, 368, 369
cambio, scatola del 350
Cambogia 453
Camciatca, Penisola di 19
camembert 151
camera a spirale 407
camera anteriore 119
camera blindata 443
camera d'albergo 439
camera d'aria 79
camera da letto 189, 528
camera da letto principale 189
camera del re 278
camera della regina 278
camera di espansione 424

camera di scarico 278
camera di scoppio 360
camera doppia 439
camera magmatica 38, 402
camera matrimoniale 439
camera posteriore 119
camera pressurizzata 345
camera pulpare 101
camera sotterranea 278
camera, numero della 439
cameraman 290
camerino 290, 293
camerino privato 290
Camerun 451
camicetta classica 255
camicetta incrociata 255
camicette, esempi di 255
camicia 245
camicia da notte 256
camicia, collo a 245
camicia, lembo della 245
camicione 255
camiciotto 255
caminiera 192
camino 183, 188, 192, 193
camino principale 28
camino, ferri per il 193
camion, esempi di 364
cammello 85
cammino di ronda 282
cammino di ronda coperto 282
camomilla 148
camoscio, pelle di 265
campagna 431
campana 306, 307
campana per la raccolta del vetro 49
campana per la raccolta della carta 49
campana, attacco della 306
campane tubolari 295, 309
campanelle 309
campanile 446
campata centrale 344
campata laterale 344
campeggio 528
campeggio, attrezzature da 531
campi solcati 31
campionatore 310
campo 474, 479, 482, 484, 487, 488, 490, 494, 506, 515
campo da golf 430
campo di allenamento 504
campo di gioco 480, 515
campo di servizio del doppio 495
campo di servizio del singolo 495
campo geotermico 402
campo magnetico 318, 416
Canada 448
canale del sifone 73
Canale della Manica 18
canale della radice 101
canale deltizio 32
canale destro 324
canale di aerazione 278
Canale di Drake 15, 17
Canale di Mozambico 20
canale di scarico 407
canale lacrimale 119
canale per le acque meteoriche 434
canale semicircolare laterale 116
canale semicircolare posteriore 116
canale semicircolare superiore 116
canale sinistro 324
canale velenifero 76
canale, chiusa di un 381
canali, tasti di selezione dei 319
cancellazione 331
cancellazione, pulsante di 315
cancellazione, tasto di 328
cancelleria, articoli di 337
cancellieri, scrivania dei 440
cancellieri, ufficio dei 440
cancello 202
Cancro, Tropico del 20, 21, 22
candela 359, 360, 426, 446
candela di accensione 237
candela, cavo della 350, 360
cane 86, 534, 535
cane, morfologia di un 86
canestro 489
canino 101
canna 370, 534
canna ad ancia 305
canna ad anima 305
canna da lancio 537
canna da mosca 536
canna della melodia 296

canna di imboccatura 307
canna, zucchero di 149
cannella 138
cannello 296
cannelloni 146
cannocchiale 8
cannocchiale cercatore 8, 9
cannocchiale di mira 420
cannolicchio 157
cannoncino 245
cannone 83
cannone elettronico 318
cannotto reggisella 370
cannuccia 163
canottiera 247, 261, 263, 500
cantalupo 135
cantarello 123
cantina dei vini 438
canyon sottomarino 33
capanna di fango 288
capanna di paglia 288
capannoni delle merci in transito 381
capasanta 157
capelli 93, 95
capelli, pinza per 268
capelli, spazzole per 268
capezzale 204
capezzolo 92, 94, 113
capitale 23
capitano 515
capo 24, 67, 72, 78
Capo di Buona Speranza 20
Capo Horn 17
Capo Verde 451
capocroce 285
capodoglio 90
capolino 57
capomacchinista 290
caposala, ufficio del 463
caposquadra 291
capotasto 301, 302, 303
cappa 164, 192, 210
cappella 282
cappella assiale 284, 285
cappella laterale 284
cappella radiale 284, 285
cappelletto 247
cappello 52, 191, 286, 313
cappello a falda larga 239
cappello da marinaio 239
cappello di feltro 238, 239
cappello terminale 409
cappio 510, 514
cappone 155
cappotti, esempi di 248, 251
cappotto 248, 251
cappotto alla raglan 251
cappotto con pellegrina 251
cappuccio 249, 260, 312, 467, 508
cappuccio con cordoncino 261
cappuccio di protezione 460
cappuccio, felpa con 262
capra 84
capra, formaggi di 150
capra, latte di 150
Capricorno, Tropico del 20, 21, 22
capsula 51, 467
capsula a depressione 360
capsula di gelatina 467
capsula di risonanza 460
capsula ermetica 529
capsula, sezione di una 60
captazione, antenna di 376
caraffa 165, 166, 181
carambola 137
carapace 71, 76
caratteristiche della costa 35
caratteristiche della Luna 5
carbone, deposito di 402
carburante, condotto del 351
carburante, serbatoio del 235, 351, 366, 369, 377
carburante, serbatoio per il 364
carburante, tipo di 346
carburatore 366
carcassa 228, 229
carciofo 127
cardamomo 138
cardigan 250, 255
cardigan con scollo a V 250
cardinale 80
cardine 352
cardio 157
cardo 125
carena 74
carenaggio, bacino di 381

ASTRONOMIA > 2-25;   TERRA > 26-71;   REGNO VEGETALE > 72-89;   REGNO ANIMALE > 90-143;   ESSERE UMANO > 144-177;   GENERI ALIMENTARI E CUCINA > 178-241;   CASA > 242-295;
FAI DA TE E GIARDINAGGIO > 296-333;   ABBIGLIAMENTO > 334-371;   ACCESSORI E ARTICOLI PERSONALI > 372-391;   ARTE E ARCHITETTURA > 392-465;   COMUNICAZIONI E BUROTICA > 466-535;
TRASPORTI E VEICOLI > 536-643;   ENERGIA > 644-677;   SCIENZA > 678-705;   SOCIETÀ > 706-785;   SPORT E GIOCHI > 786-920

carenatura 366, 523
carenatura laterale 525
Caribico, Mar 14, 16
carica di lancio 534
carica elettrica, unità di misura della 426
carica, indicatore di 271
caricabatteria 228
caricabasso 520
caricatore di lamette 271
carico, aeroplano da 394
carico, bocca di 208
carico, piano di 396
carico, piattaforma di 423
carico, tubo di 196
cariosside 61
carne 152
carne, cassetto per la 211
carnivori 45
Caronte 3
carota 129
carpa 160
Carpentaria, Golfo di 15
carpenteria 220, 221, 222, 225, 226, 228, 229
carpo, flessore ulnare del 96, 97
carré 249, 255
carreggiata 343
carrelli 121
carrello 236, 290, 376, 396, 397, 505, 521, 527
carrello a forca per pallette di carico 396
carrello anteriore 376, 392
carrello avvolgitubo 236
carrello elevatore 396
carrello portabagagli 277, 374
carrello portavivande 202
carrello principale 393
carrello tenda 361
carrello, binari del 290
carri merci, esempi di 377
carriola 231
carro bestiame 377
carro bisarca 377
carro cisterna 377
carro frigorifero 377
carro merci 375
carro pianale 377
carro pianale portacontainer 377
carrozza passeggeri 380
carrozzeria 348, 361, 523
carrozzerie, esempi di 347
carrucola del carrello 397
carta 469
carta cerata 162
carta da forno 162
carta dei continenti 14
carta del tempo 38, 39
carta della rete metropolitana 379, 380
carta delle probabilità 469
carta di addebito 443
carta di credito 441
carta fisica 24
carta geografica 444
carta più alta 468
carta politica 23
carta stradale 25
carta vetrata 229
carta, guida della 328
carta, numero della 441, 443
carta, pulsante di alimentazione della 333
carta, spia di alimentazione della 333
carte di credito, portafoglio per 274
carte di credito, scomparto per 274
carte, lettore di 442, 443
cartella 275
cartella con linguetta 339
cartella con pressino 339
cartella per documenti 339
cartella sospesa 340
cartelletta 340
cartellino di identificazione 456
cartello indicatore delle stazioni della linea 378
cartello pubblicitario 378, 380
carter 537
cartilagine alare maggiore 117
cartilagine del setto nasale 117
cartoccio 61
cartografia 21
cartone 163
cartone piccolo 163
cartuccia 216, 312
cartuccia per fucile a canna liscia 534
cartuccia per fucile a canna rigata 534

cartuccia, spia della 333
cartucciera 456
caruncola lacrimale 119
carvi 138
casa 182, 469, 515
casa a due piani 289
casa a un piano 289
casa colonica 122
casa galleggiante 385
casa in mattoni cotti 288
casa, abito da 252
casa, arredamento per la 200
casa, elementi della 185
casa, esterno di una 182
casa, struttura di una 188
casacca 255
casalinghi 120
casatorre 289
cascata 31, 32
caschetto 498
casco 10, 476, 478, 486, 506, 508, 510, 513, 522, 524, 526, 527
casco di protezione 367, 372
casco integrale 525
casco per cross 525
case a schiera 289
case tradizionali 288
casella 469
casella bianca 470
casella nera 470
caserma dei vigili del fuoco 433
Caspio, Mar 14, 16
cassa 121, 218, 271, 303, 304, 424
cassa acustica 294, 324, 325
cassa acustica centrale 321
cassa acustica principale 321
cassa acustica surround 321
cassa armonica circolare 296
cassa armonica eretta 297
cassa armonica triangolare 297
cassa chiara 295, 308
cassa di risonanza 297, 302
cassa piena 303
cassa portabatteria 365
cassa, registratore di 121
cassaforte 443
cassapanca 203
casse 121
casse acustiche, tasti di selezione delle 322
casse acustiche, terminali di collegamento delle 322
cassero poppiero 386
casseruola 175
cassetta 162, 326, 333
cassetta ad augnatura 226
cassetta aperta 162
cassetta degli attrezzi 225
cassetta dei messaggi in entrata 328
cassetta del messaggio registrato 328
cassetta di pronto soccorso 457, 461
cassetta di sicurezza 443
cassetta filtro 181
cassetta, coperchio della 196
cassetta, vano 319
cassetta, vano della 323
cassette di deposito per bagagli 374
cassettiera 203
cassetto 164, 202, 203, 205, 210
cassiera 121
cassone 231, 400
cassone ribaltabile, autocarro a 401
cassone di compattazione 364
cassone di raccolta dei rifiuti 365
cassone per legna da ardere 192
cassone ribaltabile 401
castagna 133
castagna d'acqua 124
caste 68
castello 282, 383
castello di prua 387
castello motore 393
castoro 82
catamarano 521
catarifrangente 365, 370, 523
catena 370, 372
catena alimentare 45
catena di dune 36
catena di neuroni 110
catena di sicurezza 361
catena di sollevamento 396
catena montuosa 5, 24, 26
catena trinciante 235

catena, freno della 235
catena, guida della 235, 372
catodo 417
cattedra 444
cattedrale 284
cattedrale gotica 284
cattedrale, pianta della 285
cattura 470
cavalcavia 343, 344
cavalletta 69
cavalletta verde 69
cavalletto centrale 367
cavalletto laterale 367, 369
cavallo 83, 85, 247, 255, 470
cavallo con maniglie 496
cavallo per volteggi 496, 497
cavallo, morfologia di un 83
cavatappi 531
cavatappi a leva 170
cavatappi da cameriere 170
cavatorsoli 173
cavea 278, 281
cavetto di acciaio 535
cavi di accoppiamento 356
cavi, blocco di ancoraggio dei 344
cavia 82
cavicchiera 301
cavicchio 301, 302, 303
caviglia 92, 94, 302, 304
cavigliera 304, 500
cavità addominale 111, 112
cavità nasale 105
cavità orale 105, 106
cavità pleurica 105
cavo 228, 326, 332, 356, 364, 418, 501, 535
cavo d'alimentazione 177, 229
cavo del cambio 372
cavo del freno 371
cavo dell'antenna ad alta frequenza 394
cavo dell'elettricità 434
cavo della candela 350, 360
cavo di accelerazione 237
cavo di alimentazione 227, 269, 270, 322
cavo di alimentazione a corrente alternata 336
cavo di alimentazione a corrente continua 336
cavo di collegamento 324
cavo di interfaccia digitale per strumenti musicali (MIDI) 311
cavo di messa a terra 198
cavo di raccordo per luci di segnalazione 361
cavo di sincronizzazione 337
cavo di sollevamento 397
cavo di sospensione 344
cavo elettrico 354
cavo telefonico 434
cavo, manicotto del 228
cavolfiore 127
cavolini di Bruxelles 126
cavolo bianco 126
cavolo marittimo 126
cavolo ornamentale 126
cavolo rapa 125
cavolo riccio 126
cavolo rosso 126
cavolo verza 126
cavolo verzotto 126
cazzuola da muratore 216
ceci 130
cedro 134
cedro del Libano 65
cefalo 160
cefalotorace 70, 71
cella 67, 281
cella frigorifera 120, 121
cella solare 337, 410, 411
celle 440
celle solari, pannello di 411
celle solari, sistema a 411
cellula animale 50
cellula convettiva 43
cellula del succo 58
cellula vegetale 50
cellula, membrana della 50, 66
cellula, parete della 50
Celsius, gradi 424
Celsius, grado 426
Celsius, scala 424
cemento 101
cemento, sottofondo di 190
ceneri vulcaniche, nube di 28
ceneri, strato di 28

cent 440
centina 392
centina di radice alare 392
cento 427
Centrafricana, Repubblica 451
centrale 485
centrale elettrica 406
centrale idroelettrica, sezione trasversale di una 407
centrale termoelettrica a carbone 402
centratura, regolatore di 329
centrifuga 180, 212
centrifuga scolainsalata 171
centriolo 66
centro 293, 428, 470, 471, 515
centro commerciale 431, 436
centro della città 431, 432
centro della ragnatela 70
centro di alta pressione 39
centro di bassa pressione 39
centro prelievi, sala d'attesa del 465
centroattacco 507
centrocampista centrale 481
centrocampista di destra 481
centrocampista di sinistra 481
ceppo 63
ceramica, condensatore di 417
cercafase 217
cercapersone 327
cerchia annuale 63
cerchio 366, 371
cerchio centrale 488
cerchio del battitore successivo 474
cerchio di centrocampo 481, 488, 507
cerchio di ingaggio 506
cerchio di serraggio 308
cerchio di stazione 39
cerchio graduato dell'ascensione retta 8, 9
cerchio graduato della declinazione 8, 9
cerchio, parti di un 428
cerchione 349
cereali 61, 143
cerfoglio 142
cerimolia 136
cerniera 73, 178, 185, 186, 202, 214, 420
cerniera della visiera 367
cerniera lampo 265, 277, 528
cerniera regolabile 222
cerotto 461
cerotto adesivo 461
cervella 154
cervelletto 109
cervello 71, 109
cervo dalla coda bianca 84
cesoie 234
cesoie da giardino 234
cespo 125
cespuglio 230
cestella 68
cestello 177, 178, 180, 211, 212, 214
cestello di refrigerazione 180
cestello per friggere 171
cestello per la cottura a vapore 175
cestello per le posate 214
cestino 341, 538
cetriolino 128
cetriolo 128
cetriolo senza semi 128
Chac-Mool 283
chanel, scarpa 241
charleston 308
charlotte, stampo per 172
châssis: dorso 329
châssis: vista frontale 329
chat room 335
chayote 129
chela 71
chelicero 70
chemisier 252
cherosene 405
Chesterfield, divano 200
chiamata automatica, tasti di 327
chiamata, pulsante di 287
chiamata, tasto di 327
chiambrana 186
chiasma ottico 109
chiave 306
chiave a bussola a cricchetto 223
chiave a croce 356
chiave a forchetta doppia 223
chiave a rullino 223
chiave combinata 223
chiave del chiver 306
chiave del mandrino 228
chiave dell'accensione 237

chiave dell'acqua 307
chiave di basso 298
chiave di contralto 298
chiave di violino 298
chiave di volta 284
chiave poligonale a cricco 223
chiave poligonale doppia 223
chiave poligonale doppia ad anello aperto 223
chiave regolabile da lavandino 216
chiave, leva della 306
chiave, serratura a 274
chiavi 216, 223, 298, 311
chiavi di tensione 308
chiavi, negozio per la riproduzione delle 437
chiavi, protezione delle 306
chiavistello a scatto 186
chiavistello senza scatto 186
chicchi di caffè tostati 148
chicchi di caffè verdi 148
chicco di grano, sezione di un 61
chiesa 433, 446
chimica 414
chinois 171
chiocciola 72, 157
chiocciola per nastro adesivo 341
chiocciola, morfologia di una 72
chiocciole, molle per 173
chiocciole, tegamino per 173
chiodi, esempi di 220
chiodo 220, 473
chiodo a spirale 220
chiodo comune 220
chiodo da muratore 220
chiodo di finitura 220
chiodo di garofano 138
chiodo troncato 220
chioma 6, 63
chiosco 346
chirurgia minore, sala per operazioni di 462
chirurgo, lavandino del 465
chitarra acustica 302
chitarra basso 303
chitarra elettrica 303
chiusa di un canale 381
chiusura 274, 275
chiusura a occhiello 277
chiusura a scatto 178, 214
chiusura in rilievo 163
chiusura, anello di 210
chiusura, blocco di 425
chiusura, cordoncino di 275
chiusura, dispositivo di 535
chiusura, valvola di 196
chiver 306
chiver, chiave del 306
chorizo 156
chutney al mango 141
Ciad 451
Ciad, Lago 20
ciak 291
ciambella 144
ciano 418
cibi pronti 121
cicala 69
ciccioli 156
ciclismo 522
ciclismo su strada 522
ciclismo su strada, gara di 522
ciclista 522
ciclo idrologico 45
ciclomotore 369
ciclone 43
ciclone tropicale 43
cicloni tropicali, denominazione dei 43
cicogna 80
cieco 106
cieletti 292
cieletto 293
cielo tempestoso 41
cielo, copertura del 39
ciglia 66, 119
ciglio 66, 119
Cile 448
ciliato 55
ciliegia 132
cilindretto 357
cilindro 238, 429, 460
cilindro del braccio di scavo 400
cilindro del braccio di sollevamento 399, 400
cilindro della pala caricatrice 399, 400

ASTRONOMIA > 2-25; TERRA > 26-71; REGNO VEGETALE >72-89; REGNO ANIMALE > 90-143; ESSERE UMANO > 144-177; GENERI ALIMENTARI E CUCINA > 178-241; CASA > 242-295;
FAI DA TE E GIARDINAGGIO > 296-333; ABBIGLIAMENTO > 334-371; ACCESSORI E ARTICOLI PERSONALI > 372-391; ARTE E ARCHITETTURA > 392-465; COMUNICAZIONI E BUROTICA > 466-535;
TRASPORTI E VEICOLI > 536-643; ENERGIA > 644-677; SCIENZA > 678-705; SOCIETÀ > 706-785; SPORT E GIOCHI > 786-920

615

cilindro dello scarificatore 398
cilindro di raffreddamento 420
cilindro di riflessione 420
cilindro di rotazione della lama 401
cilindro di rubino 420
cilindro di sollevamento 364, 397, 399, 455
cilindro di sollevamento della lama 398, 401
cilindro direzionale 400
cilindro principale 357
cima 29, 63, 219
cima bipara 57
cima di recupero 519
cima unipara 57
cimasa 202
cime di rapa 127
cimice rigata 69
ciminiera 402
cimino 536
cimitero 25, 433
Cina 453
cinema 294, 386, 432, 436
cinescopio 318
Cinese Meridionale, Mar 14, 19
Cinese Orientale, Mar 19
cinghia del mantice 296
cinghia del ventilatore 360
cinghia della ventola 350
cinghia di compressione frontale 532
cinghia di compressione laterale 532
cinghia di distribuzione 360
cinghia di trasmissione 212
cinghia per i piedi 519
cinghiale 84
cinghietta posteriore di regolazione 458
cingolo 398, 523
cinquanta 427
cinque 427
cinque spezie, miscela di 139
cinquecento 427
cinta muraria 282
cintura 225, 246, 248, 499
cintura a vita 532
cintura di sollevamento pesi 500
cintura di Kuiper 2
cintura di ritenuta 205
cintura di servizio 456
cintura di sicurezza 353, 525
cintura portautensili 225
cintura ventrale 353
cintura, abbottonatura della 246
cintura, gancio della 327
cintura, passante della 248
cinturino 273, 424, 477, 500
cinturino a T, scarpa con 241
cinturino della manica 248
cinturino regolabile 244
cinturino, scarpa con 241
cioccolato 148
cioccolato al latte 148
cioccolato bianco 148
cioccolato fondente 148
ciondoli, bracciale con 264
ciotola 176
ciotole per mescolare 172
cipolla 236
cipolla bianca 124
cipolla d'inverno 124
cipolla di Spagna 124
cipolla rossa 124
cipolla verde 124
cipollina 124
cipresso, foglie squamiformi del 65
cipria compatta 266
cipria in polvere 266
cipria in polvere, pennello da 266
cipria, piumino da 266
Cipro 450
circo 5
circo glaciale 30
circolazione del sangue 102
circolazione, schema della 103
circolo 504
Circolo Polare Antartico 15, 21, 22
Circolo Polare Artico 21, 22
circonferenza 428
circonvallazione 25
circuito 524
circuito di distribuzione 198
circuito elettrico dei sensori 357
circuito elettrico parallelo 416
circuito frenante 350, 357
circuito integrato 417
circuito integrato inscatolato 417
circuito stampato 417

circuito stampato, scheda del 417
cirro 42
cirrocumulo 42
cirrostrato 42
cisterna 364, 385
cisterna, carro 377
cisterna, nave 384
cistifellea 106
citofaringe 66
citopigio 66
citoplasma 50, 66, 112
citostoma 66
città 23, 430
Città del Vaticano 450
città, centro della 431, 432
città, pianta di 25
city bike 373
ciuffo 83
clacson 354, 368
clarinetti 295
clarinetto 306
clarinetto basso 295
classifica generale, tabellone della 496
classificatore a soffietto 340
clavicola 98
clessidra per uova alla coque 171
climatizzazione, sistema di 46
climi aridi 40
climi dei mondo 40
climi di montagna 40
climi polari 40
climi temperati caldi 40
climi temperati freddi 40
climi tropicali 40
clip, orecchini a 264
clitoride 112
cloche 239
cloroplasto 50
cobra 77
coccige 98
coccinella 69
cocco, noce di 133
coccodrillo 77
cocktail, calice da 165
coclea 116
cocomero 135
Cocos, placca delle 27
coda 71, 76, 82, 83, 86, 90, 111, 393, 510, 514, 526, 536
coda dell'elice 115
coda di polvere 6
coda ionica 6
coda, pattino di 395
coda, trave di 395
codetta 299
codice del prodotto 423
codice temporale 290
codolo 167, 169, 216, 228, 471
codrione 78
cofano anteriore 348, 364
cofano posteriore 349
coincide con 427
cola, noce di 133
colapasta 171
colata di fango 31
colata lavica 28
colbacco 238
colibrì 80
colino 171
colla in stick 341
collana 264
collana a cinque giri 264
collana lunga 264
collana lunga alla vita 264
collane 264
collant 257
collante 190
collare 193, 229, 273
collare del solaio 193
collare di chiusura del casco 10
collare tagliafuoco 193
collarino di velluto 264
collegamenti ipertestuali 334
collegamento elettrico 365
collegamento, cavo di 324
colletto 53, 101, 245, 271
colletto, punta del 245
collettore di alimentazione 360
collettore di elettroni 417
collettore di scarico 194, 350, 360
collettore principale 194
collettore solare piatto 410
collibia 123
collie 86
collina 29
collina abissale 33

collo 76, 83, 93, 94, 95, 111, 167, 240, 244, 248, 262, 318, 492
collo a camicia 245
collo a uomo 251
collo alto 514
collo button-down 245
collo d'oca 191, 400
collo del femore 99
collo del piede 92
collo dell'utero 112
collo, sostegno per il 525
colloquio, sale di 440
collutorio 272
Colombia 448
colon ascendente 106
colon discendente 106
colon sigmoideo 106
colon trasverso 106
colonna 31, 207, 279, 302, 313
colonna centrale 412
colonna d'alcool 424
colonna di frazionamento 405
colonna di mercurio 424
colonna di ventilazione 194
colonna montante dell'acqua calda 194
colonna montante dell'acqua fredda 194
colonna principale di scarico 194
colonna principale di ventilazione 194
colonna vertebrale 98, 109
colore 468
colori, sintesi dei 418
colpi 490
colpo di pattino 514
coltelli da cucina, esempi di 169
coltelli, esempi di 168
coltello 167, 176, 531, 533
coltello da bistecca 168
coltello da burro 168
coltello da cucina 169
coltello da dessert 168
coltello da formaggio 168
coltello da ostriche 169
coltello da pane 169
coltello da pesce 168
coltello da pompelmo 169
coltello da prosciutto 169
coltello da tavola 168
coltello elettrico 177
coltello miscelatore 176
coltello per affettare 169
coltello per disossare 169
coltivatore 233
columella 73
columella, piega della 73
comandi del retroescavatore 399
comandi del VCR 319
comandi del verricello 364
comandi della videocassetta 320
comandi di sintonia 318
comando a distanza, presa per il 314, 315
comando del tavolino traslatore 421
comando del tergicristallo 354
comando del tiraggio 192
comando dello zoom elettrico 320
comando, ponte di 382, 383, 386, 387
comando, quadro di 178, 179, 210, 212, 213, 214
combinazione 274
combinazione, serratura a 274
combinazioni del poker 468
combustibile 408
combustibile esaurito, vasca di deposito del 409
combustibile fossile 46, 48
combustibile per motori diesel 405
combustibile per motori diesel marini 405
combustibile, barretta di 409
combustibile, pastiglia di 409
combustione lenta, stufa a 192
cometa 6
comignolo 183
commessura labiale 86, 116
commutatore delle luci 368
comò 203
comodino 439, 464
comodino, lampada da 439
Comore 452
compact disc 326
compattatore 364
compattazione 49
compensazione dell'esposizione, pulsante di 314
complesso scolastico 433
complesso sportivo 431
completo da ginnastica 261

compluvio 280
componenti di una bicicletta 370
composizione del sangue 104
composta, contenitore della 231
compressore del climatizzatore 360
compressore dell'aria 376
computer 444
computer da tavolo 334
computer di bordo 354, 457
computer portatile 336
computer portatile: dorso 336
computer portatile: vista frontale 336
computer tascabile 337
computer, programmi del 457
comunicazione via telefono 327
comunicazione, modulo di 316
comunicazione, tunnel di 13
comunicazioni 312
comunicazioni aeree 317
comunicazioni industriali 317
comunicazioni marittime 317
comunicazioni militari 317
comunicazioni private 317
comunicazioni stradali 317
comunione, balaustra della 446
conca 115
conca di concrezione 31
conca nasale inferiore 117
conca nasale media 117
conca nasale superiore 117
concentrato di pomodoro 140
concentrazione di gas serra 46
concessionaria di automobili 433
conchiglia 72, 73, 200
conchiglia bivalve 73
conchiglia bivalve, anatomia di una 73
conchiglia bivalve, morfologia di una 73
conchiglia di protezione 486, 507
conchiglia univalve 73
conchiglia univalve, morfologia di una 73
conchiglie 146
concime organico 48
condensatore 402, 421
condensatore a pellicola plastica 417
condensatore di ceramica 417
condensatore, manopola di regolazione del 421
condensatori elettrolitici 417
condensazione 45, 414
condilo laterale del femore 99
condilo mediale del femore 99
condimenti 140
condimento alle spezie cajun 139
condizionatore 361
condominio 433
condor 80
condotta dell'acquedotto 434
condotta fognaria 434
condotta fognaria principale 434
condotta forzata 406, 407
condotto 278
condotto del carburante 351
condotto dello scarico dell'aria 345
condotto dell'aria pulita 345
condotto di alimentazione 194
condotto di riscaldamento 213
conduttore di fase 198
conduttore di messa a terra 404
conduttore neutro 198
conduttura del gas 434
conduttura dell'acqua calda 197
conduttura dell'acqua fredda 197
conduzione 415
conferma, tasto di 443
confessionale 446
confezionamento, prodotti per 120
confezione in cartone per uova 162
confezione multipla 163
confezioni 162
confezioni farmaceutiche di medicinali 467
confine di proprietà 182
confine internazionale 23
confine interno 23
confluente 32
congelatore 164, 438
congelatore orizzontale 211
congelatore, porta del 211
congelatore, scomparto di 211
congiuntiva 119
Congo 451
Congo, Fiume 20
Congo, Repubblica Democratica del 451
congressi, palazzo dei 433
conifera 65
conifere, esempi di 65

conifere, foresta di 44
coniglio 82, 154
connessione, spinotto di 417
cono 65, 119, 429, 460
cono avventizio 28
cono d'ombra 4, 5
cono di emergenza 110
cono di penombra 4, 5
cono di spremitura 177
cono femminile 65
cono maschile 65
console 471
console centrale 354
console dell'organo 305
consumatori primari 45
consumatori secondari 45
consumatori terziari 45
contachilometri parziale 355
contachilometri totale 355
contagiri 355, 368
container 383
containers, deposito per 430
contaminuti 171, 178, 179, 210
contanti, rifornimento di 443
contatore 323
contatore dell'acqua 194
contatore elettrico 198
contatore, tasto di azzeramento del 323
contatto 470
contatto caldo 314
contatto negativo 410, 411
contatto positivo 410, 411
contatto, dispositivi di 198
contatto, leva di 207
contenitore della batteria 359
contenitore della composta 231
contenitore delle siringhe usate 457
contenitore in calcestruzzo 408, 409
contenitore per filo interdentale 272
contenitore per il riciclaggio 49
contenitore termico 532
contenitori per la raccolta differenziata 49
contenuto in 427
continentale umido - estate calda 40
continentale umido - estate torrida 40
continente 33
continenti, carta dei 14
conto, tasti di identificazione del 443
contorno 441
contrabbassi 295
contrabbasso 301
contrafforte 284
contralto, chiave di 298
contrappeso 8, 287, 345, 397, 400, 401
contrappeso, guida del 287
contrassegno per la virata a dorso 517
contrasto, regolatore di 329
contratto 469
controbraccio 397
controfagotti 295
controferro 229
controllo 330
controllo biglietti, addetto al 294
controllo dei passaporti 391
controllo del campo audio 322
controllo del sequencer 310
controllo del tempo 311
controllo del volume 310, 311
controllo dell'accelerazione 332
controllo della velocità di crociera 354
controllo di sicurezza 391
controllo fine dei dati 310
controllo veloce dei dati 310
controllo: selezione di gruppo 330
controllore 374
controporta attrezzata 211
controporta, scomparto della 211
contropunta 425
controstecca 273
controtelaio 186
controvento 187
courbazione 430
convertitore 321
convertitore catalitico 351
convertitore di coppia 212
convezione 415
convezione, corrente di 415
convogliatore 402
Cook, Stretto di 15
coordinate terrestri, sistema di 21
coperchio 174, 177, 178, 179, 180, 181, 198, 210, 211, 212, 215, 225, 303, 315, 333, 359, 417, 454, 533
coperchio del sedile 196
coperchio della cassetta 196
coperchio delle punterie 350, 360

coperchio di protezione dell'obiettivo 314
coperchio inferiore 417
coperchio protettivo 333
coperchio scorrevole 327
coperchio superiore 417
coperta 204
copertura 273, 505, 536
copertura boccaporto della cisterna 385
copertura del cielo 39
copiglia 454
coppa da spumante 165
coppa del reggiseno 259
coppa dell'olio 235, 360
coppa dell'olio, guarnizione della 360
coppa inferiore 181
coppa superiore 181
coppetta 207
coppetta per l'insalata 166
coppetta per latte/panna 163
coppia 468, 509
coppia di serraggio, anello di regolazione della 228
coppia, convertitore di 212
copricapi 238
copricapi femminili 239
copricapi maschili 238
copricapi unisex 239
copricerniera 273
coprifiltro 459
copriguanciale 204
coprilegno 505
coprimaterasso 204
copripunta 273
copritrice primaria 78
copritrice primaria media 78
copritrice secondaria mediana 78
Coralli, Mar dei 15
corda 301, 302, 498, 500, 535
corda di tensione 297
corda vocale 105
cordata 55
corde 297, 304
corde per l'accompagnamento 296
corde per la melodia 296
corde, strumenti a 301
cordiera 297, 301, 308
Cordigliera delle Ande 17
cordolo 434, 524
cordoncino 219
cordoncino di chiusura 275
cordoncino, cappuccio con 261
cordone 208, 209, 217, 235, 237
cordone del microfono 327
cordone dell'alimentazione 271
cordone litorale 35
cordone nervoso ventrale 71
cordone, manicotto del 218, 229
cordone, supporto del 208
Corea, Repubblica Democratica Popolare di 453
Corea, Repubblica di 453
coriandolo 142
corimbo 57
comamusa 296
cornea 119, 419
cornetta 295, 307
comi 295
comi inglesi 295
cornice 185, 202, 279
cornice inclinata 279
comicione 183
corno 307
corno anteriore 109
corno inglese 306
corno posteriore 109
coro 284, 285
coroide 119
corolla 56
corona 4, 83, 101, 302, 308, 344, 424, 441
corona di penne 495
corona radiata 112
coronamento 406
corpi celesti 2
corpo 118, 180, 228, 270, 305, 306, 312, 420, 536
corpo calloso 109
corpo cavernoso 111
corpo cellulare 110
corpo ciliare 119
corpo cilindrico 471
corpo d'acciaio 417
corpo del fornice 109
corpo dell'unghia 114
corpo della macchina fotografica 314

corpo della valvola 307
corpo di guardia 282
corpo isolante 359
corpo libero, pedana per il 496
corpo stradale 342
corpo umano 92
corpo vertebrale 110
corpo vitreo 119
corpo, cura del 267
corpuscolo di Meissner 114
corpuscolo di Pacini 114
corpuscolo di Ruffini 114
corrente di convezione 415
corrente di fondazione 187
corrente elettrica, unità di misura della 426
corrente orizzontale 187
corrente, doppio 187
corrente, presa di 217
corrente, presa temporizzata di 210
corrente, regolatore di 199
corrente, sorgente di 416
corridoio 490, 495
corridoio di discesa 278
corridoio di salita 278
corridoio di sicurezza 440
corridoio telescopico 389
corrimano 191, 287, 363, 385
corrimano di spinta 460
corrispondenza 338
corsa, bicicletta da 373
corsa, direttore della 522
corsa, scarpa da 262
corsetto 259
corsia 120, 434, 472, 516
corsia dei box 524
corsia di accelerazione 343
corsia di decelerazione 343
corsia di entrata 343
corsia di marcia normale 343
corsia di sorpasso 343
corsia di traffico lento 343
corsia di uscita 343
corsia laterale 343
corso d'acqua 32, 48
corso d'acqua sotterraneo 31
corteccia 63
cortile 122, 282, 445, 447
cortina 282
corvo 80
coscia 83, 86, 93, 95, 111, 112
costa 33, 125, 167, 169
costa a rias 35
costa assiale 73
Costa d'Avorio 451
Costa Rica 448
costa spirale 73
costa, caratteristiche della 35
costate 152
coste, bordo a 250, 261
costine 152
costole 98
costole false 99
costole fluttuanti 98
costolette 153
costolone dorsale 284
costolone intermedio 284
costruttore, targhetta del 228
costume 290
costume da bagno 263, 516
costumista 290
cotiledone 53
cotone idrofilo 461
cottage cheese 150
cotton fioc® 461
cottura a vapore, cestello per la 175
cottura, piano di 164, 179, 210
cottura, piastra di 179
cottura, piatti di 179
coulisse 249
coulomb 426
coulommiers 151
coupé 347
Cowper, ghiandola di 111
Coyolxauhqui, pietra di 283
cranio 92
cranio di bambino 100
cranio, vista laterale del 100
cratere 5, 28
cratere, scia luminosa del 5
cravatta 245
credenza 203
credenza con vetrina 203
credito, carta di 441
cremagliera 473
crenato 55

crepaccio 30
crepaccio terminale 30
crêpe, padella per 175
crepidine 279
crescione 127
crescione d'orto 127
cresta 29, 33, 418
cric 356
cricchetto 221
cricco, chiave poligonale a 223
criceto 82
cricket 478
crimine, prevenzione del 456
crinale 29
crine 301
criniera 83
crisalide 67
cristalleria 165
cristallino 119, 419
cristallizzazione 414
cristallo di sicurezza 318
cristallo, goccia di 207
Croazia 450
croce dell'altare 446
croce di sant'Andrea 187
croce, punta a 221
croce, testa a 221
crocetta 520
crociera 284, 285
crocifisso 446
croco 56
croissant 144
croma 299
croma, pausa di 299
cromatina 66
cromosfera 4
cronometrista 488, 498, 509
cronometrista capo 516
cronometrista di corsia 516
cronometrista 499
cronometro 424
cronometro elettronico automatico 517
crosne 124
cross, motocicletta da 369
crosta continentale 26
crosta oceanica 26
crosta terrestre 26, 27
crosta terrestre, sezione della 26
crostacei 71, 158
crostata, stampo per 172
crottin de chavignol 150
cruchello di segale, pane 145
cruscotto 366, 368
cruscotto, equipaggiamento del 457
Cuba 448
cubetti di ghiaccio, vaschetta per 211
cubia 383, 387
cubicolo 280
cubo 429
cuccetta 364
cucchiai dosatori 171
cucchiai, esempi di 168
cucchiaino da caffè 168
cucchiaino da tè 168
cucchiaino rotante 538
cucchiaio 167, 531
cucchiaio da assaggio 173
cucchiaio da bibita 168
cucchiaio da brodo 168
cucchiaio da dessert 168
cucchiaio da tavola 168
cucchiaio forato 173
cucina 120, 162, 164, 188, 280, 439, 445
cucina a gas 210
cucina di bordo 392
cucina elettrica 210
cucina, bilancia da 171
cucina, coltello da 169
cucina, forbici da 173
cucina, robot da 177
cucina, strofinaccio da 215
cucina, utensili da 169
cucinare 178
cucitrice 341
cucitura 243, 244, 477, 478
cucitura a princesse 258
cucitura a sottopunto 245
cucitura, tasca inserita nella 251
cuffia 324, 326, 516
cuffia, presa per 310, 311, 326
cuffia, spinotto della 326
cuffie di sicurezza 458
culatta, blocco della 534
cumino 138
cumulo 42

cumulonembo 42
cuneo 224, 305
cuoio 478, 503
cuore 71, 73, 104, 105, 154
cuore del legno 63
cuori 468
cupola 60
cupola rotante 7
cupola sul mihrab 447
cupola sul porticato 447
cupola, portellone della 7
cupola, volta esterna della 7
cupola, volta interna della 7
cura del corpo 267
cura del prato 237
cura intensiva, unità di 464
curcuma 138
curling 515
curling, pietra da 515
curling, scopa da 515
curry 138
cursore 246
cursore a destra 331
cursore a sinistra 331
cursore in alto 331
cursore in basso 331
curva 306
curva, rinforzo della 306
curvatura 273, 538
cuscinetti antirumore 458
cuscinetto a sfere 413
cuscinetto ad aria 262
cuscino 204
cuscino a rullo 204
cuscus 144
cuscus, pentola per 175
custodia 337
custodia a pareti di vetro 423
cute 110, 114
cute, superficie della 114
cuticole, forbicine per 265
cuticole, tronchesina per 265
cyclette 501

D

dadi 223, 468
dado 222, 223, 469
dado cieco 223
dado comune 468
dado da poker 468
dado del raddoppio 469
dado di fissaggio 197
dado di serraggio 197
dado esagonale 223, 359
dalmata 86
dama 470
Danimarca 450
danish blue 151
Danubio, Fiume 18
danza, lama per 509
data base 335
data di scadenza 441
datario 424
dati tecnici 358
dati, controllo fine dei 310
dati, controllo veloce dei 310
dati, elaborazione dei 38
dattero 132
davanti 244, 245
David, stella di 447
deambulatore 466
deambulatorio 285
deasfaltizzazione, impianto di 405
decagono regolare 429
decimi di secondo, lancetta dei 424
declinazione, cerchio graduato della 8, 9
décolleté, reggiseno 259
décolleté, scarpa 241
decompositori, organismi 45
decoratore scenico 291
decorazione a trifoglio 285
deflettore 236, 237
deflettore dell'aria calda 192
deflusso superficiale 45
deforestazione 47
degenza postoperatoria, stanza di 464
degenza, stanza di 464
Deimos 2
delfino 90
delfino, morfologia di un 90
delimitazione, nastro di 457
della calotta polare 40
della tundra polare 40

delta 32, 35
deltoide 96
demi-volée 490
denaro 441
dendrite 110
denominazione dei cicloni tropicali 43
densimetro 359
dentato 55
dentatura nell'uomo 101
dente 74, 76, 226, 227, 235, 244, 270, 398, 400, 503
dente del giudizio 101
dente dello scarificatore 398
dente di leone 127
dente velenifero 76
denti 101
denti, spazzolino da 272
denti, spazzolino elettrico da 272
dentifricio 272
dentina 101
deodorante 267
depositi alluvionali 32
deposito bagagli 374
deposito dei cereali 381
deposito dei containers 381
deposito del materiale medico 465
deposito del materiale sporco 464
deposito del materiale sterile 464
deposito del petrolio 381
deposito delle barelle 462
deposito delle rinfuse 381
deposito di carbone 402
deposito per containers 430
deposito, fessura per il 442
deragliatore 522
deragliatore anteriore 370, 372
deragliatore posteriore 370, 372
deriva 393, 395, 520, 521
deriva a scomparsa 519
derivazione 416
derma 114
derrick 382, 385
derrick, albero del 385
desertico 40
deserto 36, 44
Deserto dei Gobi 19
Deserto del Kalahari 20
Deserto del Namib 20
Deserto del Sahara 20
Deserto di Atacama 17
deserto roccioso 36
deserto sabbioso 36
deserto, volpe del 88
designer di produzione 290
desquamatore 531
dessert, coltello da 168
dessert, cucchiaio da 168
dessert, forchetta da 168
destinazione 374
detersivo, vaschetta per il 214
detriti 43
di montagna 40
diaframma 105, 324
diagramma di carico 365
diamante 474
diamante, punta di 202
diametro 428
dicco 28
didascalia 313
dieci 427
dieci comandamenti 447
diesis 299
dietro 244
difensore ala destra 484
difensore ala sinistra 484
difensore centrale 481
difensore destro 487, 506
difensore esterno destro 481
difensore sinistro 487, 506
difensori 479
difesa 484
difetti della vista 419
differenziale 351
diffusione di informazioni 335
diffusore 290
diffusore della fiamma 218
diga 406
digiuno 106
diminuzione di tensione 402, 413
dinamo 370
diodo 411
Dione 3
directory 334
direttore artistico 290
direttore d'orchestra, podio di 295

ASTRONOMIA > 2-25; TERRA > 26-71; REGNO VEGETALE >72-89; REGNO ANIMALE > 90-143; ESSERE UMANO > 144-177; GENERI ALIMENTARI E CUCINA > 178-241; CASA > 242-295;
FAI DA TE E GIARDINAGGIO > 296-333; ABBIGLIAMENTO > 334-371; ACCESSORI E ARTICOLI PERSONALI > 372-391; ARTE E ARCHITETTURA > 392-465; COMUNICAZIONI E BUROTICA > 466-535;
TRASPORTI E VEICOLI > 536-643; ENERGIA > 644-677; SCIENZA > 678-705; SOCIETÀ > 706-785; SPORT E GIOCHI > 786-920

617

INDICE DEI NOMI ITALIANI

direttore della corsa 522
direttore della fotografia 291
direttore, ufficio del 443
direzione del flusso di elettroni 416, 417
direzione del vento 39
direzione della Mecca 447
direzione e forza del vento 39
discarica 431
discarica autorizzata 47
discesa libera 511
discesa, corridoio di 278
dischetto 507
dischetto del rigore 480
dischetto di centrocampo 481
dischi 177
dischi, negozio di 436
disco 6, 321, 333, 357, 472, 501
disco abrasivo 229
disco abrasivo, supporto del 229
disco adesivo 75
disco deflettore del calore 199
disco del freno 366
disco versatile digitale (DVD) 318
disco, freno a 525
disco, vano del 323
discontinuità di Gutenberg 26
discontinuità di Mohorovicic 26
disegno stampato 260, 261
disgelo, acqua di 30
disinnesto del pistone 216
dispensa 164, 188, 439
dispersione di calore 46
display 314, 318, 319, 322, 325, 327,
   328, 336, 337, 338, 346, 423, 442,
   443
display a cristalli liquidi 315, 320
display del radar 457
display delle frequenze 325
display delle funzioni 310
display digitale 423, 461
display, pannello del 320
display, pulsante di apertura del 336
display, regolatore del 327
dispositivi di contatto 198
dispositivi di entrata 330
dispositivi di memorizzazione dei dati 333
dispositivi di uscita 333
dispositivo antiallagamento 214
dispositivo di agganciamento 372
dispositivo di bloccaggio 209
dispositivo di blocco 219, 226
dispositivo di blocco dell'inclinazione della
   lama 227
dispositivo di blocco dell'interruttore 228
dispositivo di chiusura 535
dispositivo di espulsione del cestello 178
dispositivo di fissaggio del tubo 199
dispositivo di regolazione 511, 527
dispositivo di rimorchio 364
dispositivo di smorzamento magnetico
   422
disposizione 182
distanza tra le puntine 359
distanziatore 467, 535
distillazione sotto vuoto 405
distintivo 456
distributore automatico di biglietti 379
distributore del ghiaccio 346
distributore di bibite 346, 463
distributore di ghiaccio in cubetti 164
distributore via cavo 316
distribuzione del fertilizzante 47
distribuzione della vegetazione 44
distribuzione, quadro di 198
distruggidocumenti 341
ditale in gomma 339
ditali 146
dito 75, 79, 82, 86, 114, 477
dito del guanto 243
dito del piede 92, 94
dito esterno 78
dito interno 78
dito lobato 79
dito medio 78
dito palmato 79
dito posteriore 78, 79
dito prensile 91
divanetto 201
divani 200
divano 200
divano a due posti 200, 439
divano Chesterfield 200
divano posteriore 353
divano-letto 204
diverso da 427

divisa da incendio 454
divisione 427
divison 339
divisori alfabetici per schedario 340
divisori dentata 55
divisorio 427
divisorio di tela 528
djembé 297
do 298
doccetta 197
doccia 189, 195, 439, 464
doccia a telefono 195
doccia orale 272
doccia, box 195
dodecagono regolare 429
dogana 381, 391
dolcevita, maglione 250
dolci, miscelatore per 172
dolci, pennello per 172
dolci, stampini per 172
dolci, utensili per 172
dolichi 130
dolina 31
dollaro 440
Dominica 449
Dominicana, Repubblica 449
dominio di livello superiore 334
dominio di secondo livello 334
dominio, nome del 334
domino 468
dondolo, sedia a 200, 201
donna 94, 468
donna, scarpe da 241
donnola 88
dopobarba 271
doppia coppia 468
doppia piastra di registrazione 325
doppiamente dentato 55
doppio bemolle 299
doppio corrente 187
doppio diesis 299
doppio lavello 194
doppio slash 334
doppio-sei 468
doppio-zero 468
doppione 468
doppiopetto, abbottonatura a 248
doppiopetto, giacca a 244
Dorsale Medio-Atlantica 34
Dorsale Medio-Indiana 34
Dorsale medio-oceanica 33
Dorsale Pacifico-Antartica 34
Dorsale Pacifico-Orientale 34
Dorsale Sud Occidentale Indiana 34
Dorsale Sud Orientale Indiana 34
dorsali oceaniche 34
dorsali, barra per i 501
dorso 78, 83, 86, 115, 167, 215, 226,
   516, 517
dorso del guanto 243
dorso del naso 117
dorso della lingua 118
dotto deferente 111
dotto eiaculatore 111
dotto galattoforo 113
dotto sudoriparo 114
dotto velenifero 76
Douglas, Canale di 112
dragoncello 142
Drake, Canale di 15, 17
drenaggio, tubo di 212, 214
drenaggio, valvola di 211
dritta 387
drive per cassette 333
dromedario 85
drumlin 29
drupa 57
drupe 132
drupeola 59
due metà, tempo di 298
dulse 123
duna 35
duna complessa 36
duna parabolica 36
dune longitudinali 36
dune trasversali 36
dune, catena di 36
dune, esempi di 36
duo 300
duodeno 106
dura madre 109, 110
durian 137
duty free 391

E

e-commerce 335
eau de toilette 267
echinodermi 66
eclissi anulare 5
eclissi di Luna 5
eclissi di Sole 4
eclissi parziale 4, 5
eclissi totale 4, 5
economia 441
Ecuador 448
edicola 379, 437
edificio del reattore 409
edificio per uffici 432, 435
edificio pubblico 25
editing del suono, tasti per l' 310
editoriale 313
effetti speciali, rotella di selezione degli
   320
effetti speciali, tasti degli 320
effetto serra 46
effetto serra naturale 46
effetto serra, incremento dell' 46
effigie 441
Egeo, Mare 18
Egitto 451
eglefino 161
El Salvador 448
elaborazione dei dati 38
elastici stringitesta 459
elastico 204, 247, 528, 529
elastico ferma abiti 277
elastico regolabile per il capo 459
elefante 85
elementi architettonici 286
elementi della casa 185
elemento della canna fumaria 193
elemento di combustibile 409
elemento riscaldante 213, 214, 218
elettricità 198, 408, 413
elettrodo centrale 359
elettrodo di massa 359
elettrodo negativo 359
elettrodo positivo 359
elettrodomestici 176, 208
elettrodomestici vari 180
elettrone 414
elettroni, collettore di 417
elettroni, direzione del flusso di 416, 417
elettronica 417
elettronica, negozio di 436
elevatore 281, 400
elevatore a nastro 402
elevatore per sedie a rotelle 363
elevone 13
elica 228, 384, 386, 387, 429
elica bipala 394
elica di propulsione 383
elica di prua 384
elica posteriore 384
elica tripala 394
elica, albero dell' 387
elica, mantello d' 383
elice 115
elice, coda dell' 115
elice, radice dell' 115
eliche 146
elicottero 395
elmetto 458
elmo 454
emergenza, freno di 380
Emirati Arabi Uniti 452
emisferi 21
emisfero meridionale 21
emisfero occidentale 21
emisfero orientale 21
emisfero settentrionale 21
emissario 32
emissione dello scontrino 346
emissione di acido nitrico 48
emissione di acido solforico 48
emissione di anidride solforosa 48
emissione di banconote 442
emissione di gas inquinanti 47
emissione di ossido d'azoto 48
emittenti, tasti di ricerca 319
emmental 151
endecagono regolare 429
endocardio 104
endocarpo 57, 58
energia 402
energia eolica 412
energia eolica, produzione di elettricità da
   413
energia fossile 402

energia geotermica 402
energia geotermica, produzione di
   elettricità da 402
energia nucleare 408
energia nucleare, produzione di elettricità
   da 408
energia solare 54, 410
energia termica 46, 402
energia termica, produzione di elettricità
   da 402
energia, rilascio di 415
energia, unità di misura dell' 426
enneagono regolare 429
enti sanitari 335
entrata principale 188
epeira 70
epicarpo 58
epicentro 27
epicondilo 99
epidermide 114
epididimo 111
epifisi 109
epiglottide 105, 118
epistrofeo 99
epitroclea 99
Equatore 17, 20, 21, 22, 43
equilibratore orizzontale 395
equilibrio, posizione d' 418
equinozio d'autunno 38
equinozio di primavera 38
equipaggiamento del cruscotto 457
equipaggiamento protettivo 486
equipaggio, alloggi dell' 382
equivalente a 427
erba 492
erba cipollina 124
erba medica 130
erbicida 47
erbivori 45
Eritrea 451
erogatore del tubo della scala 455
erogazione, bocca di 197
eruzione, vulcano in 28
esagono regolare 429
esame audiometrico, stanza per l' 465
esame psichiatrico, stanza per 462
escape 330
escavatore idraulico 400
esempi di abiti 252
esempi di aeroplani 394
esempi di alghe 51
esempi di anfibi 75
esempi di angoli 428
esempi di aracnidi 70
esempi di becchi 79
esempi di biciclette 373
esempi di camicette 255
esempi di camion 364
esempi di carri merci 377
esempi di carrozzerie 347
esempi di chiodi 220
esempi di coltelli 168
esempi di coltelli da cucina 169
esempi di conifere 65
esempi di cucchiai 168
esempi di dune 36
esempi di felci 52
esempi di finestre 287
esempi di fiori 56
esempi di foglie 65
esempi di forchette 168
esempi di giacche e pullover 254
esempi di gonne 253
esempi di gruppi strumentali 300
esempi di insetti 69
esempi di lagomorfi 82
esempi di latifoglie 64
esempi di licheni 50
esempi di linee di costa 35
esempi di mammiferi carnivori 88
esempi di mammiferi marini 90
esempi di mammiferi ungulati 84
esempi di mecchie e punte da trapano
   228
esempi di motociclette e ciclomotore 369
esempi di muschi 51
esempi di occhiali 273
esempi di pantaloni 254
esempi di pieghe 253
esempi di pneumatici 358
esempi di porte 286
esempi di prese 499
esempi di primati 91
esempi di raccordo 342
esempi di rettili 77
esempi di roditori 82

esempi di sacchi a pelo 530
esempi di salti 509
esempi di sci 510
esempi di sedie 201
esempi di simboli e valute 440
esempi di tavoli 202
esempi di tende 528
esempi di uccelli 80
esempi di vulcani 28
esempi di zampe 79
esocarpo 57, 58, 59
esofago 105, 106
esosfera 37
espadrille 242
espansione fissa 425
espansione mobile 425
espansione, bullone a 221
espansione, camera di 424
espositore di brochure 442
espositore di fine corsia 121
espressione, pedali d' 305
espulsione del cestello, dispositivo di 178
espulsione, pulsante di 315
espulsione, tasto di 319, 323
espulsore degli accessori 176
essere umano 92
Est 23
Est Nord-Est 23
Est Sud-Est 23
estate 38
estate, solstizio d' 38
estensore 500
estensore breve delle dita 96
estensore comune delle dita 97
estensore lungo delle dita 96
estensore radiale breve del carpo 97
estensore radiale lungo del carpo 97
estensore ulnare del carpo 97
esterno centro (giocatore) 474
esterno centro (posizione) 475
esterno destro 474
esterno destro (posizione) 475
esterno di una casa 182
esterno sinistro 474
esterno sinistro (posizione) 475
estintore 457
estintore portatile 454
estirpatore 232
Estonia 450
estratto conto, fessura di aggiornamento
   dell' 442
estratto di vaniglia 140
estrazione dell'aria, tubo di 199
estremità del braccio 421
estremità della guida 235
estremo 482
estremo di destra 484
estremo di sinistra 484
estuario 24, 35
eterotrofi, organismi 45
etichetta portaindirizzo 277
etichettatrice 340
etichette autoadesive 340
Etiopia 451
ettagono regolare 429
Eurasia 14
euro 440
Europa 2, 14, 18, 34, 449
Eustachio, tuba di 116, 117
Eutelsat 316
euthynteria 279
evacuazione, percorso di 345
evaporazione 45, 414
evidenziatore 312
ex voto 446
expander 310
eye-liner 266
Eyre, Lago 15

F

fa 298
faccetta 228
faccia 92, 493, 505
facciata scanalata 228
facciata 285
facole 4
faggio 64
faggiola 133
fagiano 81, 154
fagiano, uovo di 155
fagioli 131
fagioli mungo, spaghetti di 147
fagiolino 131
fagiolino giallo 131
fagiolo adzuki 131
INDICE DEI NOMI ITALIANI

ASTRONOMIA > 2-25;   TERRA > 26-71;   REGNO VEGETALE >72-89;   REGNO ANIMALE > 90-143;   ESSERE UMANO > 144-177;   GENERI ALIMENTARI E CUCINA > 178-241;   CASA > 242-295;
FAI DA TE E GIARDINAGGIO > 296-333;   ABBIGLIAMENTO > 334-371;   ACCESSORI E ARTICOLI PERSONALI > 372-391;   ARTE E ARCHITETTURA > 392-465;   COMUNICAZIONI E BUROTICA > 466-535;
TRASPORTI E VEICOLI > 536-643;   ENERGIA > 644-677;   SCIENZA > 678-705;   SOCIETÀ > 706-785;   SPORT E GIOCHI > 786-920

fagiolo asparagio 130
fagiolo borlotto 131
fagiolo cannellino 131
fagiolo dall'occhio nero 130
fagiolo di Lima 131
fagiolo di Spagna 131
fagiolo egiziano 130
fagiolo mungo 131
fagiolo mungo nero 131
fagiolo nero 131
fagiolo pinto 131
fagiolo romano 131
faglia 27
fagotti 295
fagotto 306
Fahrenheit, gradi 424
Fahrenheit, scala 424
fai da te 216
faina 88
fairway 504
falange, seconda 114
falange, terza 114
falcetto 234
falco 81
falda 248
falda freatica 48
falda larga, cappello a 239
falesia 29, 35
falesia costiera 35
Falkland, Isole 17
Falloppio, tuba di 112
Falloppio, tube di 113
falsa partenza, fune di 516
falsa zampa 67
falsa zampa anale 67
falsabraca 282
falso puntone 187
famiglia degli archi 295, 301
famiglia degli ottoni 295
famiglia dei legni 295
familiari, sala d'attesa dei 462
fanale 377
fanale anteriore 371, 376
fanale di testa 376
fanale di testa dell'albero 383
fanale posteriore 367, 368, 370
fango, colata di 31
fante 468
faraglione 35
faraona 81, 154
fard in polvere 266
fard, pennello da 266
faretto a pinza 206
faretto da binario 207
faretto orientabile 207
farfalla 67, 517
farfalla, morfologia di una 67
farina 144
farina di avena 144
farina di mais 144
farina integrale 144
farina non trattata 144
farina semplice 144
faringe 105, 106
farmacia 436, 462, 465
faro 381
faro di atterraggio 395
faro fendinebbia 352, 364
faro subacqueo 184
farro 143
fascetta 265
fascia 301, 302, 360
fascia degli asteroidi 3
fascia di chiusura 511
fascia di cuoio 246
fascia di regolazione 324
fascia elastica 249
fascia di sospensione 458
fascia lata, tensore della 96
fascia laterale 349
fascia protettiva della fronte 459
fascia reggibraccio 461
fascia sopracigliare 78
fascia stringitesta 458
fasciatoio 205
fascio blu 318
fascio elettronico 318
fascio rosso 318
fascio verde 318
fascione anteriore 348
fase di scivolamento 514
fase di spinta 514
fase, conduttore di 198
fasi della Luna 5
fast food 437
ast food 437
attore Rh negativo 426

fattore Rh positivo 426
fattoria 122
fattoriale 427
fauci, istmo delle 116
fave 130
fazzoletto da taschino 244
fede nuziale 264
federa 204
Federazione Russa 450
fegato 103, 106, 154
feijoa 137
felce 52
felce arborea 52
felce, struttura di una 52
felci, esempi di 52
felpa 262
felpa con cappuccio 262
feltro, cappello di 238, 239
femminella 62
femminile 426
femore 98
femore, collo del 99
femore, condilo laterale del 99
fcmore, condilo mediale del 99
femore, testa del 99
fendinebbia, faro 352, 364
fenicottero 81
feritoia 178
fermacampioni 341
fermacapelli 268
fermagli 341
fermaglio 246, 312
fermapiedi 370, 372, 501
fermaporta 211
fermata dell'autobus 434
fermo a molla 273
fermo del nastro 225
fermo della lama 270
fermo di testa 521
ferodo 357
ferretto 259
ferri per il camino 193
ferro 229, 505
ferro da stiro a vapore 208
ferrovia 25
fertilizzante, distribuzione del 47
fertilizzazione del suolo 47
ferzo 520
fessura 93, 95, 167, 274, 305
fessura di aggiornamento dell'estratto
  conto 442
fessura di registrazione della transazione
  442
fessura per il deposito 442
fessura per la scheda PC 336
fessure branchiali 74
fessure, bocchetta per 209
fettuccine 146
fiala 467
fiamma 415
fiancata 467
fianco 78, 83, 93, 95, 358
fianco esterno 191
fianco interno 191
fiato, strumenti a 306
fibbia 246, 248, 276, 353
fibbia di regolazione 532
fibra muscolare 110
fibra nervosa 114
fico 137
fico d'India 137
fidanzamento, anello di 264
fienile 122
fieno greco 138
Figi 453
Figi, Isole 15
fila 272, 293
filamento 56, 199
Filchner, Banchisa di 15
file 334
file, formato del 334
filettatura 301, 302
filetto 221, 313
filetto 152
filiera 70
filigrana 441
Filippine 19, 453
Filippine, Fossa delle 34
filo 167, 169, 225, 417
filo conduttore 199
filo d'appoggio 70
filo da giardino 231
filo della lama 270
filo di nylon 237
filo di sicurezza 441
filo di tracciamento 225

filo interdentale 272
filo interdentale, contenitore per 272
filo per saldatura 218
filo radiale 70
filo spirale 70
filone francese 144
filone strato 28
filtrare 171
filtro 117, 178, 184, 210, 459
filtro dell'aria 235, 350, 398
filtro dello scarico 197
filtro per il tè 173
filtro per lanugine 212, 213
filtro polarizzatore 314
filtro, cassetta 181
filtro, macchina da caffè a 181
filum terminale esterno 109
filum terminale interno 109
finanza 441
fine 331
fine chiamata, tasto di 327
fine corsa, interruttore di 287
fine, tasto di ricerca della 320
finecorsa 226
finestra 186, 189, 477, 519
finestra a battenti 287
finestra a battenti con apertura all'interno
  287
finestra a bilico orizzontale 287
finestra a bilico verticale 287
finestra a gelosia 287
finestra a ghigliottina 287
finestra a libro 287
finestra del seminterrato 183
finestra di accesso 333
finestra di controllo 178, 179, 210
finestra panoramica 435
finestra scorrevole 287
finestra zanzariera 528
finestra, traversa inferiore di 187
finestra, traversa superiore di 187
finestre, esempi di 287
finestrino 349, 352, 361, 380, 392
finestrino di atterraggio 395
finestrino di osservazione 13
finitura, chiodo di 220
Finlandia 450
finocchio 125
finta 251, 261
fiocco 238, 520
fioraio 437
fiordi 35
fiore 53, 56
fiore del pinnacolo 283
fiore, struttura di un 56
fiori 468
fiori, esempi di 56
fiori, macchia di 230
fioritura 62
fiosso 240
firma del titolare 441
firma ufficiale 441
fisarmonica 296
fischio 180
fisica: elettricità e magnetismo 416
fisica: ottica 418
fissaggio del tubo, dispositivo di 199
fissione dell'uranio 408
fissione nucleare 415
fiume 24, 25, 32
Fiume Congo 20
Fiume Danubio 18
Fiume Dnepr 18
Fiume Mackenzie 16
Fiume Mississippi 16
Fiume Niger 20
Fiume Orinoco 17
Fiume Paranà 17
Fiume San Lorenzo 16
Fiume Senegal 20
Fiume Vistola 18
Fiume Volga 18
flacone 467
flap 392
flash, tubo a 420
flauti 295
flauto di Pan 297
flauto traverso 306
flessometro 225
flessore ulnare del carpo 96, 97
flettante 535
flip 509
floema 63
floppy disk 333
fluido vettore caldo 408
fluido vettore freddo 408

fluido vettore, ingresso del 410
fluido vettore, uscita del 410
flusso sotterraneo 45
flûte 165
Fobos 2
foca 90
focolare 192
fodera 240, 244, 245, 262, 274, 509
fodera del guanciale 204
fodero 531, 533
fodero di pelle 533
foglia 51, 53, 54, 55, 125
foglia carnosa 54
foglia di acanto 200
foglia, struttura di una 55
fogliame 63
foglie composte 55
foglie semplici 55
foglie squamiformi del cipresso 65
foglie, esempi di 65
fogliolina arrotolata 52
foie-gras 156
follicolo 60
follicolo pilifero 114
follicolo, sezione di un 60
fondale 292
fondale oceanico 33
fondazione 342
fondazione del pilone 344
fondazione naturale 342
fondazione, corrente di 187
fondazione, muro di 187
fondello 318, 492, 494, 534
fondello metallico 534
fondina 456
fondista 514
fondo 528, 529
fondo abissale 26
fondo dell'onda 33
fondo protettivo 471
fondo refrattario 192
fondo, pista da 512
fondocampo 491
fondotinta fluido 266
fonduta, forchetta da 168
fonduta, servizio da 174
fonduta, tegame per 174
fonendoscopio 460
fontana per le abluzioni 447
fontanella anteriore 100
fontanella mastoidea 100
fontanella posteriore 100
fontanella sfenoidale 100
fonte alimentare primaria 45
fonte battesimale 446
fonte del servizio 313
football americano 484
forame cieco 118
forbice sfoltitrice a doppia lama dentellata
  270
forbice sfoltitrice a lama singola dentellata
  270
forbici 461, 531
forbici da cucina 173
forbici da parrucchiere 270
forbici di sicurezza 265
forbici per unghie dei piedi 265
forbici tagliasiepi 234
forbicine per cuticole 265
forbicine per unghie 265
forca 396
forca, braccio della 396
forcella 8, 371, 522, 525
forcella anteriore 522
forcella inferiore 370
forcella superiore 370
forcella telescopica anteriore 366, 369
forchetta 167, 531
forchetta da dessert 168
forchetta da fonduta 168
forchetta da insalata 168
forchetta da ostriche 168
forchetta da pesce 168
forchetta da tavola 168
forchette, esempi di 168
forchettone 169
forcina 268
forcone 233
foresta 29
foresta boreale 44
foresta di caducifoglie 44
foresta di conifere 44
foresta mista 44
foresta pluviale tropicale 44
foresta temperata 44
foresta tropicale 44

foreste, incendio delle 47
formaggi a pasta dura 151
formaggi a pasta molle 151
formaggi di capra 150
formaggi erborinati 151
formaggi freschi 150
formaggio cremoso 150
formaggio fresco di capra 150
formaggio, coltello da 168
formato del file 334
formazione professionale, ufficio di 442
forme geometriche 428
formica 69
formina da forno 166
formula 1, auto da 525
formula 3000, auto da 524
formula Indy, auto da 524
fornellino 174
fornello da campo a due fuochi 529
fornello da campo con un bruciatore 529
fornice, corpo del 109
fornitore del servizio Internet 335
forno 164, 210
forno a microonde 164, 178
forno tubolare 405
forno, manopola del 210
forno, teglia da 172
foro 240, 243, 246, 263
foro apicale 101
foro del piede 305
foro di risonanza 301
forti precipitazioni 43
forza del vento 39
forza, linea di 416
forza, unità di misura della 426
foschia 41
Fossa del Giappone 34
Fossa delle Aleutine 34
Fossa delle Curili 34
Fossa delle Filippine 34
Fossa delle Marianne 34
Fossa delle Ryukyu 34
Fossa di Giava 34
Fossa di Kermadec-Tonga 34
Fossa di Puerto Rico 34
fossa oceanica 33
Fossa Perù-Cile 34
fossa settica 48
fossa triangolare 115
fossato 282, 342
fosse nasali 117
fosse oceaniche 34
fossetta 76, 505
foto in prima pagina 313
fotocamera 35 mm 10
fotocopiatrice 442
fotografia 314
fotografia, direttore della 291
fotografo 436
fotografo di scena 291
fotone 420
fotorecettori 119
fotosfera 4
fototessere, macchina per 437
fovea 119
foyer 293
fragola 132
fragola, sezione di una 59
frana 31
francesina 241
Francia 449
Francoforte, salsiccia di 156
frangente 33
frangia, scopa a 215
frangizolle 237
frantumatore 402
frantumatrice 49
frattazzo 216
frazione 427
freccetta 471
freccette 471
freccia di orientamento 533
freestyle, snowboard per 513
fregio 279
freni 357
freno 467, 501, 511, 522
freno a disco 350, 357, 525
freno a disco idraulico 522
freno a disco, pinza del 366
freno a mano 350
freno a mano, leva del 354
freno a tamburo 357
freno a tampone 527
freno aerodinamico 412
freno anteriore 371
ASTRONOMIA > 2-25; TERRA > 26-71; REGNO VEGETALE >72-89; REGNO ANIMALE > 90-143; ESSERE UMANO > 144-177; GENERI ALIMENTARI E CUCINA > 178-241; CASA > 242-295;
AI DA TE E GIARDINAGGIO > 296-333; ABBIGLIAMENTO > 334-371; ACCESSORI E ARTICOLI PERSONALI > 372-391; ARTE E ARCHITETTURA > 392-465; COMUNICAZIONI E BUROTICA > 466-535;
RASPORTI E VEICOLI > 536-643; ENERGIA > 644-677; SCIENZA > 678-705; SOCIETÀ > 706-785; SPORT E GIOCHI > 786-920

619

INDICE DEI NOMI ITALIANI

freno anteriore, leva del 368
freno della catena 235
freno di emergenza 380
freno posteriore 370
freno posteriore, pedale del 368
freno, cavo del 371
freno, disco del 366
freno, leva del 371, 523
freno, pedale del 350, 354, 357
freno, tubazione del 357
frequenza, unità di misura della 426
frequenze, display delle 325
fresatrice verticale 229
friggitrice 178
frigo portatile 532
frigoriferi 438
frigorifero 164, 211, 438
frigorifero, scomparto del 211
fringuello 80
frizione 350, 536
frizione a stella 537
frizione, leva della 366, 368
frizione, pedale della 354
frizione, regolazione della 537
frizione, scatola della 368
fronda 52
fronda arrotolata 125
frontale 96, 191
fronte 78, 92
frontone 279
frullare 176
frullatore 176
frullatore a immersione 176
frullatore elettrico a mano 176
frullino 172
frumento 143
frusta 172, 176
frusta a quattro bracci 176
frusta a spirale 176
frusta ad anello 176
fruste 176
frutta 120
frutteto 122
frutti 57, 132
frutti secchi 60, 133
frutti tropicali 136
fruttificazione 62
frutto carnoso 58, 59
frutto carnoso: mela 58
frutto del jack 136
frutto, albero da 122
fucile a canna liscia 534
fucile a canna rigata 534
fuco 68
fuga, via di 524
fulcro 518
full 468
fulmine 41
fumaiolo 382, 386
fumarola 28
fumo, deflettore del 192
fumo, rivelatore di 454
fune di corsia 517
fune di falsa partenza 516
fune di sollevamento 219, 287
funghi 123
fungicida 47
fungo 52
fungo coltivato 123
fungo velenoso 52
fungo velenoso e mortale 52
fungo, struttura di un 52
funicolo 59, 60
funivia, partenza della 512
funzionamento automatico, indicatore del
328
funzionamento, pannello di 287
funzione, selettori di 327
funzione, tasti 328, 423, 442
funzioni, display delle 310
fuoco 27, 419
fuoco Cassegrain 7
fuoco coudé 7
fuoco primario 7
fuoco primario, cabina di osservazione del
7
fuoco, profondità di 27
Fuoco, Terra del 17
fuoristrada 347
fuoriuscita di idrocarburi 48
furgone 365
fuseau 254
fusibile 198, 411
fusilli 146
fusione 414

fusoliera 393
fusto 53, 125, 273, 492, 493, 494
fusto del bulbo 54
futon 204

G

gabbia 281, 308
gabbia del palcoscenico 292
gabbia di protezione 217, 473
gabbia, lampada portatile a 217
Gabon 451
Gai-lohn 127
galassia 6
galleggiante 196, 394, 538
galleggiante, valvola del 196
galleria 285, 345, 378
galleria di collegamento 345
galleria di derivazione 406
galleria di ispezione 407
galleria secca 31
galleria, prima 293
galleria, seconda 293
galletta di segale 145
galletta scandinava 145
gallette di riso 147
galletto 223
gallina 81
gallina, uovo di 155
gallo 81
galloccia 520, 521
galoppo 83
galoscia 240
gamba 83, 91, 93, 95, 202, 204, 205,
247, 493
gamba a capriolo 200
gamba anteriore 201
gamba posteriore 201
gamba telescopica 460
gambale 478, 511, 527
gambaletto 257
gamberetto 158
gambero di acqua dolce 158
Gambia 451
gambo 51, 52, 181, 220, 221, 537, 538
gambo a innesto dello spazzolino 272
gambo filettato 223
ganasce 224, 535
ganascia 217, 224, 265, 357
ganascia curva 222
ganascia dentata 222
ganascia diritta 222
ganascia fissa 223, 224
ganascia mobile 223, 224
ganci di fissaggio 501
gancio 186, 217, 225, 364, 397, 423,
460, 502, 509, 511
gancio del manganello 456
gancio del piatto 422
gancio della cintura 327
gancio di chiusura 277
gancio di sollevamento 403
gancio di traino 361
gancio per l'impasto 176
ganglio cerebropleurale 73
ganglio simpatico 109
ganglio spinale 109, 110
ganglio viscerale 73
Ganimede 2
gara di ciclismo su strada 522
gara, numero di 525
garage 182
garage, porta basculante del 286
garage, porta sezionale del 286
garam masala 139
garbatta 282
garofano 56
garofano, chiodo di 138
garrese 83, 86
garretto 83, 86
garza sterile 461
gas 403, 405, 414
gas di scarico delle automobili,
inquinamento da 47
gas inerte 199
gas inquinanti, emissione di 47
gas serra 46
gas serra, concentrazione di 46
gas, manopola di regolazione del 529
gasolio 405
gastrocnemio 96, 97
gastronomia 156
gatti, razze di 87
gatto 87
gatto del Maine 87
gatto dell'isola di Man 87

gatto delle nevi 512, 523
gatto, testa di 87
gattone 285
gattuccio 226
gattuccio stellato 158
gelatiera 180
gelato, porzionatore per 173
gelone 123
gemma 54
gemma apicale 53
gemma ascellare 53
gemma fiorale 53
gemma terminale 53
generatore 408
generatore di vapore 402
generatore, gruppo del 407
generi alimentari 120
gengiva 101, 116
genitali femminili, organi 112
genitali maschili, organi 111
Genova, salame di 156
geografia 14
geologia 26
geometria 428
Georgia 452
gerboa 82
Germania 450
germe 61
germinazione 53
germogli di soia 131
germoglio 53
germoglio di bambù 125
gessetto 503
gestione del tempo 338
getti d'acqua 518
geyser 28
Ghana 451
ghepardo 89
gheriglio 60
ghettina con ruches 260
ghi 150
ghiacciaio 30, 32, 44
ghiaccio 45
ghiandaia 80
ghiandola di Cowper 111
ghiandola digestiva 71, 73
ghiandola lacrimale 119
ghiandola mammaria 113
ghiandola salivare 118
ghiandola sebacea 114
ghiandola sudoripara apocrina 114
ghiandola sudoripara eccrina 114
ghiandola surrenale 107
ghiandola veleningena 76
ghiandole salivari 106
ghiera 219
ghiera di bloccaggio 221, 425
ghiera di tenuta 197
ghiera femmina 536, 537
ghiera maschio 536, 537
giacca 251, 499
giacca a doppiopetto 244
giacca a un petto 244
giacca a vento 249
giacca alla marinara 251
giacche 244
giacche e pullover, esempi di 254
giacche, esempi di 251
giaccone 251
giacconi, esempi di 248
giaguaro 89
giallo 418
Giamaica 448
Giapeto 3
Giappone 19, 453
Giappone, Fossa del 34
Giappone, Mar del 19
giardinaggio 216, 230
giardinaggio, guanti da 232
giardiniere, sega da 234
giardino 230, 280
giardino pubblico 435
giardino roccioso 230
giardino, filo da 231
giarrettiera 259
Giava, Fossa di 34
giavellotto 472
gibbone 91
Gibilterra, Stretto di 18
Gibuti 451
giglio 56
giglio di mare 158
ginco, noce di 133
ginepro, bacca di 138
ginnasta, nome del 497
ginnastica 496

ginnastica, abbigliamento da 263
ginnastica, completo da 261
ginocchiera 476, 486, 500, 526, 527
ginocchio 83, 86, 92, 94
giocatore 483, 486, 488, 506, 515
giocatore, bastone del 506
giocatore, numero del 486, 488, 506
giocatore: battitore 478
giocatori 492
giocatori, panchina dei 474, 485
giocatori, posizioni dei 474, 481, 482,
489
giocattoli, negozio di 436
giochi 468
giochi con la racchetta 493
giochi da tavola 469
giochi di carte 468
gioco 492
gioco del volano 494
gioco online 335
gioco, area di 386
giogo 422
giogo anteriore 422
giogo di supporto 8, 9
giogo posteriore 422
gioielleria 436
gioielli 264
Giordania 452
giornale 313
giornale, nome del 313
Giove 2
giraffa 85
giraffista 291
girasole 56
giratubi 216
girella 535, 538
girello 503
giro 72
giro della spira 73
giro embrionale 73
girocollo 260, 264
girocollo, maglia 255
girocollo, maglione 250
giubbotto da pescatore 538
giudice 498, 499
giudice di arrivo 516
giudice di campo 485
giudice di linea 483, 485, 487, 490, 494,
496, 507, 515
giudice di linea centrale 490
giudice di porta 506
giudice di rete 491
giudice di sedia 490
giudice di servizio 490, 494
giudice di stile 516
giudice laterale 485
giudici 496, 497, 509, 518
giudici di virata 517
giudici, banco dei 440
giudici, ufficio dei 440
giudizio, dente del 101
giuggiola 137
giunto 503, 536
giunto a compressione 197
giunto scorrevole 222
giunto scorrevole, pinza a 222
giunzione a linguetta del telaio 186
giunzione positivo-negativa 410
giunzione scanalata del telaio 186
giurati, stanza dei 440
giuria, banco della 440
giustizia 440
giustizia, palazzo di 432
Glaciale Artico, Mar 14
glande 111
globo di vetro 529
globo oculare 75, 119
globulo bianco 104
globulo rosso 104
glottide 105
glucosio 54
gnocchi 146
gnomone 424
go 470
Gobi, Deserto del 19
gocce oftalmiche lubrificanti 272
goccia di cristallo 207
gocciolatoio 185, 186, 349
gola 31, 32, 78, 305
golf 504
golf, campo da 430
golf, vettura da 505
golfo 24
Golfo del Bengala 19
Golfo del Messico 16

Golfo dell'Alaska 16
Golfo di Aden 19, 20
Golfo di Botnia 18
Golfo di California 16
Golfo di Carpentaria 15
Golfo di Guinea 20
Golfo di Oman 19
Golfo di Panama 17
golfo mistico 292
Golfo Persico 19
Golgi, apparato del 50, 66
gombo 128
gomiti 146
gomitiera 526, 527
gomito 83, 86, 93, 95
gomma 341
gomma di tenuta del grembiule 383
gomma, guarnizione di 197
gomma, piedino di 219
gommino 460
gonade 73
gonfiatore 530
gonfiatore a soffietto 530
gong 295, 309
gonna 251
gonna a balze 253
gonna a portafoglio 253
gonna a teli 253
gonna ad anfora 253
gonna arricciata 253
gonna con baschina 253
gonna diritta 253
gonna pantalone 253
gonne, esempi di 253
gonnellino 492
gorgonzola 151
gorilla 91
gorilla, morfologia di un 91
gracile 97
gradi 456
gradi Celsius 424
gradi Fahrenheit 424
gradino 191, 219, 364
gradino di accesso 395
gradino posteriore 455
gradino rientrabile 361
gradino, larghezza del 191
gradino, lunghezza del 191
grado 428
grado Celsius 426
gramigna crestata 126
Gran Deserto Sabbioso 15
Gran Deserto Vittoria 15
gran dorsale 97
granaio 122
grancassa 295, 308
granchio 158, 220
Grand Canyon 16
grande adduttore 97
Grandi Laghi 16
Grande Baia Australiana 15
Grande Barriera Corallina 15
Grande Catena Divisoria 15
grande complesso 97
grande copritrice secondaria 78
grande falciata esterna 499
grande falciata interna 499
grande galleria 278
grande gluteo 97
grande labbro 112, 113
grande pettorale 96
grande rotondo 97
grande safena 102
grande trocantere 99
grandi magazzini 437
grano 61
grano saraceno 61, 143
grano, chicco di 61
grano: spiga 61
granturismo 347
granulazione 4
granulo d'amido 50
granulo lipidico 50
grappolo d'uva 62
grassella 83
grassi 149
grassi lubrificanti 405
grasso alimentare 149
grattugia 170
grattugia per noce moscata 170
grattugiaformaggio 170
grattugiare 170
Grecia 450
green 504
grembiule 383
grembiule, gomma di tenuta del 383

Grenada 449
griffa 221, 228
griglia 174, 210, 271, 318, 324, 358, 359, 407, 529
griglia dei ripiani 211
griglia del radiatore 364
griglia del riscaldamento 380
griglia di aerazione 182, 380
griglia di contatto metallica 410
griglia di illuminazione 291
griglia di partenza 524
griglia di sicurezza 442
griglia di uscita dell'aria 270
griglia di ventilazione 209
griglia elettrica 178
griglia elettrica per interni 179
griglia per casco 476
griglia per raclette 179
griglia terminale 409
grill pieghevole 533
grilletto 235, 332, 454, 534
grilletto di accelerazione 235
grilletto di sicurezza 235
grillo 521
Groenlandia 16
Groenlandia, Mar di 14
gronda 283
grondaia 182
groppa 83
grotta 31, 35
groviera 151
gru 384, 397
gru a ponte 407
gru a portale 381, 406, 407
gru a torre 397
gru mobile a braccio 381
gru su pontone 381
gruccia 466
gruista, cabina del 397
gruppetto 299
gruppi strumentali, esempi di 300
gruppo 470, 522
gruppo del generatore 407
gruppo del turbo-alternatore 402
gruppo dell'elettropompa 357
gruppo delle sospensioni 351
gruppo dello sterzo 351
gruppo di testa 522
gruppo frigorifero 365
guadino 538
guaiava 137
guaina 55
guaina della lingua 76
guaina di Schwann 110
guaina mielinica 110
guancia 83, 86, 94, 220, 536
guanciale 204
guanciale, fodera del 204
guanti 243
guanti da donna 243
guanti da giardinaggio 232
guanti da uomo 243
guanti di lattice, astuccio per i 456
guanto 10, 476, 477, 478, 505, 506, 508, 510, 513, 514, 522, 525
guanto alla scuderia 243
guanto corto 243
guanto da guida 243
guanto da presa 507
guanto da respinta 507
guanto da sera 243
guanto del difensore 477
guanto di crine 267
guanto di lattice 460
guanto lungo 243
guanto, dito del 243
guanto, dorso del 243
guanto, palmo del 243
guantone 498
guantoni 498
guardalinee 481, 485
guardaroba 188, 203, 443
guardaroba dei clienti 438
guardaroba del personale 438
guardia 169, 489
guardia destra 485
guardia giurata, stanzino della 443
guardia sinistra 485
guardolo 240
guardrail 526
guarnizione 214, 260, 404
guarnizione conica 196
guarnizione della coppa dell'olio 360
guarnizione di gomma 197
guarnizione magnetica 211

Guatemala 448
guepière 259
gufo reale 81
guglia 36, 284, 285
guida 214, 396
guida del contrappeso 287
guida del filo 537
guida del nastro 341
guida della cabina 287
guida della carta 328
guida della catena 235, 372
guida di appoggio 226
guida di scorrimento 521
guida fine, sistema di 7
guida parallela 227
guida per il pane 178
guida, cabina di 376
guida, leva di manovra della 396
guida, ruota di 380
Guinea 451
Guinea Bissau 451
Guinea Equatoriale 451
Guinea, Golfo di 20
guscio 60, 79, 277
gusto 116
Gutenberg, discontinuità di 26
Guyana 448
guyot 33

H

Haiti 448
hall 196
handicap, punto di 470
hard disk estraibile 333
harissa 141
hat switch 332
hertz 426
hijiki 123
Himalaya 19
hockey su ghiaccio 506
home 331
home theatre 321
Honduras 448
Horn, Capo 17
hovercraft 383
Hubble, telescopio spaziale 7
Hudson, Baia di 16
Huitzilopochtli, tempio di 283
hummus 140
humus 54

I

identificazione, cartellino di 456
idrante a colonna 454
idrante antincendio 434
idrante, presa dell' 455
idraulica 194, 197
idrocarburi, fuoriuscita di 48
idroelettricità 406
idrosfera 44
idrovolante a due galleggianti 394
iena 88
ifa 52
igiene orale 272
igloo 288
iguana 77
ileo 98, 106
illuminazione 199
illuminazione, griglia di 291
ilo renale 107
imballaggio 49
imbarco, passerella di 389
imbardata 395
imboccatura, canna di 307
imbottitura dell'angolo 498
imbuto 171, 318
immagine, raddrizzatori di 420
immagine, tasti di regolazione dell' 320
immagini, pulsante per il salto di 315
immagini, pulsante di visualizzazione delle 315
immersione, frullatore a 176
impalcato 344
imparipennata 55
impastatrice 176, 179
impasto, gancio per l' 176
impennaggio verticale 393
impermeabile 248
impianto di climatizzazione 386
impianto di deasfaltizzazione 405
impianto di estrazione con solventi 405

impianto di produzione dei lubrificanti 405
impianto di raffreddamento 351
impianto di reforming catalitico 405
impianto di smistamento 49
impianto di trivellazione 403
impianto elettrico 351
impianto frenante 351
impianto hi-fi di riproduzione del suono 322
impianto idraulico 194
impianto idroelettrico 406
impieghi di Internet 335
impluvio 280
importo da pagare 346
imposta 186
impostazioni, pulsante di visualizzazione delle 315
impugnatura 170, 176, 177, 178, 180, 208, 217, 221, 226, 227, 229, 235, 237, 269, 271, 272, 301, 466, 467, 477, 478, 500, 501, 505, 510, 514, 515, 535, 536, 537
impugnatura a penna 493
impugnatura a pistola 218, 228, 534
impugnatura a stretta di mano 493
impugnatura con sistema antivibrazione 235
impugnatura di sicurezza 237
impugnatura laterale 228
impugnatura rotante 332
impugnatura sagomata 269
impugnature, tipi di 493
impulsi, irrigatore a 236
impulso sensoriale 110
impuntura 240, 243, 246, 260, 262
imputato, banco dell' 440
in avanti 518
inalatore dosimetrico 467
incamiciatura 534
incandescenza, lampadina a 199
incasso, scatola da 198
incavo 167
incendi, prevenzione degli 454
incendio delle foreste 47
incenerimento 49
incernieramento, perno di 400
inchiostro 312
inchiostro a colori cangianti 441
incisivi 101
incisivo centrale 101
incisivo laterale 101
incisura anteriore 115
incisura intertragica 115
incocco, punto di 535
incordatura 492, 494
incremento dell'effetto serra 46
incudine 116
India 453
Indiano, Oceano 14, 15, 19, 20
indicatore del funzionamento automatico 328
indicatore del livello d'acqua 179
indicatore del livello dell'acqua 208
indicatore del livello di carburante 355
indicatore del piano 287
indicatore della pressione dell'acqua 455
indicatore della regolazione 511
indicatore della temperatura del liquido di raffreddamento 355
indicatore delle telefonate 328
indicatore di carica 271
indicatore di destinazione 379
indicatore di direzione 352
indicatore di direzione, comando del' 354
indicatore di linea 362, 363
indicatore di temperatura 269
indicatore generale degli orari 374
indicatori 323
indicatori, tasto di visualizzazione degli 320
indicazione del valore 441
indicazioni di tempo 298
indice 115, 313, 422, 423
indice dei nomi Italiani 539
indice di regolazione dell'altezza 227
indice, pulsante per l' 315
Indie Occidentali 16
indivia riccia 127
Indonesia 19, 453
industria 351
industria petrolchimica 405
infermeria 464
infermieri, postazione degli 462, 463

inferriata 279
infiltrazione 45, 47
infilzacarte 341
infinito 427
infiorescenze, tipi di 57
inforcamento, tasca di 396
informatica, aula di 444
informazioni, banco delle 390, 437, 442, 463
informazioni, diffusione di 335
infradito 242
infraspinato 97
infundibolo della tuba di Falloppio 113
infusi 148
ingaggio, cerchio di 506
ingaggio, punto di 506
ingegnere del suono 291
inghiottitoio 31
ingranaggio di trascinamento 180
ingranaggio per il moto orario 7
ingrandimento, pulsante per l' 315
ingressi uscite audio/video 322
ingresso 188
ingresso al marciapiede 374
ingresso alla piramide 278
ingresso degli attori 278
ingresso dei clienti 438
ingresso del fluido vettore 410
ingresso del personale 438, 445
ingresso del pubblico 278
ingresso dell'alimentazione dell'utente 198
ingresso della stazione 378
ingresso delle merci 435
ingresso principale 435, 445, 465
ingresso, porte di 294
ingresso, selettore di 322
ingresso/uscita audio 337
inguine 92, 94
iniettore 534
iniziali della banca di emissione 441
innesco 534
innesto della sonda 178
inquinamento agricolo 47
inquinamento da gas di scarico delle automobili 47
inquinamento del suolo 47
inquinamento dell'acqua 48
inquinamento dell'aria 47
inquinamento domestico 47
inquinamento industriale 47
inquinamento petrolifero 48
inquinanti atmosferici 47
inquinanti non biodegradabili 47
insalata belga 127
insalata riccia 126
insalata, coppetta per l' 166
insalata, forchetta da 168
insalatiera 166
insegna esterna 378
insegnante 444
inserimento 331
inserimento dei documenti da trasmettere, punto di 328
inserto 313
inserzione pubblicitaria 313
insetti 67
insetti, esempi di 69
insieme vuoto 427
integrale 427
integrazione di energia alla rete di trasmissione 413
intelaiatura 192, 528
intelaiatura, base dell' 186
intelaiatura, parte superiore dell' 186
Intelsat 317
intensità luminosa, unità di misura dell' 426
interbase 474
interiora 154
Internet 334
interno gamba con abbottonatura a pressione 260, 261
internodo 53
interosseo plantare 96
interramento 49
interruttore 176, 177, 180, 181, 198, 206, 208, 209, 211, 218, 219, 229, 269, 270, 271, 272, 311, 327, 416
interruttore a grilletto 227, 228, 229
interruttore automatico 407
interruttore del portello 213

interruttore di accensione 314, 315, 318, 320, 322, 323, 326, 329, 333, 336
interruttore di accensione del VCR 319
interruttore di accensione della TV 319
interruttore di accensione e del volume 326
interruttore di avviamento 368
interruttore di emergenza 368
interruttore di fine corsa 368
interruttore generale 319
interruttore principale 198
interruttore, dispositivo di blocco dell' 228
interruttore, placca dell' 198
interruzione 331
intersezione 427
intersuola 262
intervalli 298
intervista 313
intestino 71, 73, 103
intestino crasso 106
intestino tenue 106
intonazione, rotella di 310
inverno 38
inverno, solstizio d' 38
invertitore 221, 228
invio 331
invito, scalino d' 191
involucro 192, 225
involucro di zinco (anodo) 417
Io 2
ipermetropia 419
ipersostentatore 13
ipersostentatore sul bordo di attacco 393
ipofisi 109
ippoglosso 161
ippopotamo 85
Iran 452
Iraq 452
iride 119
Irlanda 449
Irlanda, Mar d' 18
irrigatore a impulsi 236
irrigatore oscillante 236
irrigatore rotativo a pioggia 236
isba 288
ischio 99
Islanda 18, 450
isobara 39
isola 24, 164, 343
Isola di Baffin 16
isola di Man, gatto dell' 87
Isola di Terranova 16
isola vulcanica 33
isolamento, stanza di 462
isolamento, tappo di 417
isolante 410
isolante termico 12
Isole Aleutine 16
Isole delle Antille 448
Isole Falkland 17
Isole Figi 15
Isole Marshall 453
Isole Salomone 453
isolotto roccioso 35
isolotto sabbioso 35
ispezione, tappo di 197
Israele 452
issopo 142
istituzioni educative 335
istmo 24
istmo della tuba di Falloppio 113
istmo delle fauci 116
Istmo di Panama 16
istruzione 444
istruzioni per l'uso 346
Italia 450
Iugoslavia 450
iurta 288

J

jaboticaba 137
jarlsberg 151
jazz-band 300
jeans 254
jet supersonico 37, 394
jicama 124
jolly 468
joule 426
joystick 332, 471
judo 499
judogi 499

ASTRONOMIA > 2-25; TERRA > 26-71; REGNO VEGETALE >72-89; REGNO ANIMALE > 90-143; ESSERE UMANO > 144-177; GENERI ALIMENTARI E CUCINA > 178-241; CASA > 242-295;
FAI DA TE E GIARDINAGGIO > 296-333; ABBIGLIAMENTO > 334-371; ACCESSORI E ARTICOLI PERSONALI > 372-391; ARTE E ARCHITETTURA > 392-465; COMUNICAZIONI E BUROTICA > 466-535;
TRASPORTI E VEICOLI > 536-643; ENERGIA > 644-677; SCIENZA > 678-705; SOCIETÀ > 706-785; SPORT E GIOCHI > 786-920

621

INDICE DEI NOMI ITALIANI

K

k-way 263
Kalahari, Deserto del 20
Kazakistan 452
kelvin 426
Kenya 451
Kermadec-Tonga, Fossa di 34
ketchup 141
kilogrammo 426
kilt 253
kimono 256
Kirghizistan 452
Kiribati 453
kit di attrezzi 372
kiwano 136
kiwi 136
Kola, Penisola di 18
kombu 123
kora 297
Kuiper, cintura di 2
kumquat 134
Kuwait 452

L

la 298
labbra, pennellino per 266
labbra, trucco per le 266
labbro 83, 87
labbro esterno 73
labbro inferiore 116, 305
labbro interno 73
labbro superiore 116, 305
laboratorio 7
laboratorio americano 11
laboratorio di anatomia patologica 465
laboratorio spaziale 13
laccio 262, 535
laccio di pelle 246
laccolite 28
Ladoga, Lago 18
laghetto 230
laghi 32
laghi, acidificazione dei 48
lago 5, 24, 29, 32
lago artificiale 32
Lago Baikal 19
Lago Ciad 20
Lago di Aral 19
lago di meandro abbandonato 32
Lago Eyre 15
lago glaciale 32
Lago Ladoga 18
Lago Malawi 20
lago salato 36
Lago Tanganica 20
lago tettonico 32
Lago Titicaca 17
Lago Vittoria 20
lago vulcanico 32
lagomorfi 82
lagomorfi, esempi di 82
laguna 35
lama 84, 167, 169, 177, 180, 216, 219, 221, 226, 227, 235, 270, 271, 341, 398, 401, 506, 509
lama dentellata 270
lama di sega circolare 227
lama dritta 270
lama isolata 217
lama per danza 509
lama per pattinaggio libero 509
lama piccola 531
lama, cilindro di rotazione della 401
lama, cilindro di sollevamento della 398, 401
lama, dispositivo di blocco dell'inclinazione della 227
lama, fermo della 270
lama, filo della 270
lama, meccanismo di spostamento della 401
lama, regolatore dell'inclinazione della 227
lama, vite di blocco della 227
lamella 52
lametta a due tagli 271
lamette, caricatore di 271
lamina 1, 52, 55, 509, 510
lamina assorbente 410
lamina cribrosa dell'etmoide 117
lampada 421
lampada a braccio regolabile 206
lampada a petrolio 532

lampada a risparmio energetico 411
lampada a sospensione 206
lampada a stelo 206
lampada al neon 217
lampada alogena al tungsteno 199
lampada alogena da tavolo 206
lampada da comodino 439
lampada da lettura 206
lampada da notte 464
lampada da parete 207
lampada da parete con braccio estensibile 207
lampada da tavolo 206
lampada del presbiterio 446
lampada per saldare 218
lampada portatile a gabbia 217
lampada provacircuiti 217
lampadaoro 207
lampade in serie 207
lampadina 217, 416
lampadina a incandescenza 199
lampadina a risparmio di energia 199
lampeggiante 455, 457
lampeggiante, sistema di controllo del 457
lampeggiatore anteriore 366, 368
lampeggiatore posteriore 367, 368
lampione 207, 230, 434
lampione da parete 207
lampone 132
lampone, sezione di un 59
lampreda 159
lanceolata 55
lancetta dei decimi di secondo 424
lancetta dei minuti 424
lancetta dei secondi 424
lancia 236
lancia antincendio 455
lancia antincendio schiumogena 385
lanciatore 474, 475, 479
lancio 475, 479
lancio del disco 473
lancio del giavellotto 473
lancio del martello 473
lancio del peso 472
lanterna 529
lanugine, filtro per 212, 213
Laos 453
lapide commemorativa 447
lardatoio 173
lardo 149
larghezza del gradino 191
larice 65
laringe 105
lasagne 146
laser a rubino pulsato 420
lastra di vetro 211
lastrico, pietra da 230
latifoglie, esempi di 64
latitudine 22
lato 167, 293, 498
lato del re 470
lato della regina 470
lato destro 272
lato di destra 293
lato di sinistra 293
lato sinistro 272
latrine 280
latta per alimenti 163
latte 150
latte di capra 150
latte evaporato 150
latte in polvere 150
latte omogeneizzato 150
latte, bricco del 166
latteria 122
latticello 150
latticini 120
latticini, scomparto per i 211
lattina 163
lattuga asparago 126
lattuga cappuccina 126
lattuga iceberg 126
lattuga marina 123
lattuga romana 126
lava, strato di 28
lavabo 194
lavaggio, torre di 214
lavagna 444
lavallière 245
lavanderia 188, 439
lavanderia a secco 437
lavandino 195, 439, 464
lavandino del chirurgo 465
lavaparabrezza, ugello del 348
lavastoviglie 164, 214

lavatrice 194, 212
lavello 164, 197
lavello con tritarifiuti 197
lavello, doppio 194
lavoro, piano di 164, 224
leccarda 174, 179
LED indicatore del livello di picco 323
legabagagli elastico 277
legame chimico 414
legamento 73
legamento largo dell'utero 113
legamento periodontale 101
legamento sospensore 119
legatura 299, 306
leggio 305, 311, 446
legna da ardere, cassone per 192
legni, famiglia dei 295
legno 505
legume, sezione di un 60
legumi 130
legumiera 166
lembo 255
lembo anteriore 245
lembo della camicia 245
lembo posteriore 245
lemure 91
lente 273, 531
lente a contatto monouso 272
lente a contatto morbida 272
lente a contatto rigida 272
lente biconcava 419
lente biconvessa 419
lente concava 419
lente convessa 419
lente di campo 420
lente di ingrandimento 421
lente obiettivo 420
lente piano-concava 419
lente piano-convessa 419
lente torica 419
lenti 419
lenti a contatto 272
lenti convergenti 419
lenti divergenti 419
lenti, sistema di 420
lenticchie 130
lenza 536
lenzuolo 204
lenzuolo con angoli 204
leone 89
leone marino 90
leopardo 89
lepre 82, 154
lepre fischiante 82
lesena corinzia 281
lesena dorica 281
lesena ionica 281
Lesotho 452
lettere al direttore 313
lettiga 460
lettino 460
lettino a sponde 205
lettino pieghevole con fasciatoio 205
letto 204, 361
letto d'ospedale 464
letto matrimoniale 439
letto singolo 439
letto ungueale 114
letto, biancheria da 204
letto, vagone 376
Lettonia 450
lettore audio digitale portatile 325
lettore CD 329, 336
lettore CD portatile 325
lettore CD/DVD 471
lettore di carte 346, 442, 443
lettore di compact disc 323, 325, 326
lettore di compact disc, tasti del 326
lettore di schede 321
lettore DVD 318
lettore DVD-ROM 329, 336
lettura, luce di 457
lettura, specchio di 10
lettura, tasto di 327
leucoplasto 50
leva 178, 197, 222, 265, 534
leva del cambio 350, 354, 371, 372, 522
leva del freno 371, 522, 523
leva del freno a mano 354
leva del freno anteriore 368
leva del pedale 304
leva del pistone 216
leva della chiave 304
leva della frizione 366, 368
leva della pinza 269
leva di apertura dell'attacco 511

leva di bloccaggio 224
leva di bloccaggio dell'altezza 8, 9
leva di bloccaggio dell'asse orizzontale 8, 9
leva di contatto 207
leva di manovra della guida 396
leva di regolazione laterale 229
leva di sbloccaggio 222
leva di scatto 196
leva di scorrimento 353
leva di serraggio 224, 229
leva per togliere il paralama inferiore 227
levapunti 341
levetta 170
levetta dello sciacquone 196
Libano 452
libellula 69
Liberia 451
libero 481, 487
Libia 451
libreria 436, 444
libretto degli assegni 274
libretto, scala a 219
lichene 50
lichene crostoso 50
lichene fogliaceo 50
lichene fruticoso 50
lichene, struttura di un 50
licheni, esempi di 50
Liechtenstein 450
lima 229, 531
limetta 134, 265
limetta di cartoncino vetrato 265
limetta pieghevole 265
limite del campo 475
limone 134
limousine 347
lince 88
linea 298
linea aerea di alimentazione 376
linea blu di zona 507
linea cablata 335
linea centrale 493, 494
linea centrale di servizio 491
linea continua 342
linea d'acchito 502
linea dedicata 334
linea del 10 metri 482
linea dei 15 metri 483
linea dei 22 metri 482
linea dei 5 metri 483
linea del battitore 479
linea del bersaglio 515
linea del traguardo 473
linea dell'area di rigore 480
linea della corsia 473
linea della fila di attesa 443
linea delle yards 484
linea di accrescimento 72, 73
linea di attacco 487
linea di centro 515
linea di centrocampo 484, 488, 507
linea di demarcazione 479
linea di direzione 533
linea di distribuzione a bassa tensione 198
linea di distribuzione a media tensione 198
linea di fallo 515
linea di fondo 484, 487, 489, 491, 493, 494, 515, 517
linea di forza 416
linea di fuoricampo 474
linea di fuoricampo, palo della 475
linea di lancio 471
linea di messa in gioco 484
linea di meta 482, 484
linea di metà campo 481, 483
linea di mira, regolazione della 420
linea di mischia 485
linea di pallone morto 482
linea di partenza 473, 524
linea di partenza degli 800 metri piani 473
linea di partenza dei 100 metri piani e dei 100 metri ostacoli 472
linea di partenza dei 10000 metri piani e della staffetta 4 x 400 m 473
linea di partenza dei 110 metri ostacoli 472
linea di partenza dei 1500 metri piani 473
linea di partenza dei 200 metri piani 472
linea di partenza dei 400 metri piani, dei 400 metri ostacoli 473
linea di partenza dei 5000 metri piani 472

linea di partenza della staffetta 4 x 100 metri 473
linea di porta 506
linea di puntamento 533
linea di rimando 479
linea di rullaggio 389
linea di servizio 491
linea di servizio corto 495
linea di servizio lungo 494
linea di sicurezza 379
linea di tiro libero 489
linea di uscita laterale 483
linea ferroviaria locale 375
linea ferroviaria principale 375
linea isosismica 27
linea laterale 74, 481, 484, 487, 488, 493, 515
linea laterale del doppio 490, 495
linea laterale del singolo 491, 495
linea meridiana 533
linea neutra 416
linea sottomarina 334
linea telefonica 334
linea tratteggiata 342, 343
linea, aereo di 37
linea, giudice di 490, 494, 496
lineare 55
linebacker centrale 484
linebacker esterno 484
linebacker interno 484
linee di costa, esempi di 35
lingua 106, 116, 117, 154
lingua biforcuta 76
lingua di cervo 62
lingua di terra 35
lingua glaciale 30
lingua, dorso della 118
lingua, guaina della 76
linguella 243
linguetta 240, 248, 262, 274, 297, 340, 509
linguetta con finestra 340
linguetta di protezione 333
linguettone 15
liquido 414, 415
liquido cefalorachidiano 110
liquido dei freni, serbatoio del 357
liquore, bicchierino da 165
lira 297
liscio 55
lisciviazione 48
lisosoma 66
lista di controllo delle procedure 10
lista serratura 304
listarella 211
listello 412
listello rompitratta 186
litchi 137
litosfera 26, 44
litri erogati 346
littorina 157
Lituania 450
livella a bolla 225
livellatrice 401
livello base del moto ondoso 33
livello del mare 26, 33, 37
livello dell'acqua 181
livello dell'acqua, indicatore del 208
livello dell'acqua, selettore del 212
livello di carburante, indicatore del 355
livello di mare calmo 33
livello superiore, dominio di 334
livello, vite di 423
lizza 282
lobato 55
lobo 79, 115
lobo inferiore 105
lobo laterale inferiore 62
lobo laterale superiore 62
lobo medio 105
lobo superiore 105
lobo terminale 62
locale delle pompe 384
locale per la biancheria 439
locale tecnico 345
locomotiva diesel-elettrica 377
loculo 58
lombo 83, 93, 95
longan 136
longherone 392
longherone laterale 365
longitudine 22
lontra comune 88
lonza 153
loop di punta 509
lottatore 499

ASTRONOMIA > 2-25;   TERRA > 26-71;   REGNO VEGETALE >72-89;   REGNO ANIMALE > 90-143;   ESSERE UMANO > 144-177;   GENERI ALIMENTARI E CUCINA > 178-241;   CASA > 242-295;
FAI DA TE E GIARDINAGGIO > 296-333;   ABBIGLIAMENTO > 334-371;   ACCESSORI E ARTICOLI PERSONALI > 372-391;   ARTE E ARCHITETTURA > 392-465;   COMUNICAZIONI E BUROTICA > 466-535;
TRASPORTI E VEICOLI > 536-643;   ENERGIA > 644-677;   SCIENZA > 678-705;   SOCIETÀ > 706-785;   SPORT E GIOCHI > 786-920

lubrificanti, impianto di produzione dei 405
lucchetto 372
luccio 160
luce 7, 8, 9, 269, 380
luce anticollisione 392
luce della targa 352
luce di arresto 352
luce di ingombro laterale 352, 364, 365
luce di lettura 457
luce di navigazione 383, 393, 395
luce di posizione 352, 376
luce di posizione posteriore 352
luce di retromarcia 352
luce di sicurezza 457
luce gialla 434
luce perpetua 447
luce rossa 434
luce rotante 455
luce verde 434
luce visibile 418
lucernario 183
lucernario del bagno 189
lucernario della tromba delle scale 189
lucertola 77
luci 206
luci abbaglianti, spia delle 368
luci anteriori 352
luci dei goal 507
luci delle sorgenti 322
luci intermittenti 362
luci pedonali 434
luci posteriori 352
luci, commutatore delle 368
luci, tecnico delle 291
lucidaunghie 265
lucioperca 160
luminosità, regolatore di 329
Luna 2, 4, 5
Luna calante 5
Luna crescente 5
Luna gibbosa calante 5
Luna gibbosa crescente 5
Luna nuova 5
Luna piena 5
Luna, caratteristiche della 5
Luna, eclissi di 5
Luna, orbita della 4, 5
Luna, fasi della 5
lunetta 240, 480, 488
lunghezza d'onda 418
lunghezza del gradino 191
lunghezza dell'onda 33
lunghezza della punta 538
lunghezza, misura della 425
lunghezza, unità di misura della 426
lunotto laterale 349
lunula 73, 114, 115
lupino 130
lupo 88
Lussemburgo 449
lutz 509

M

macaco 91
macadamia, noce di 133
macao 80
macchia 44
macchia di fiori 230
macchia solare 4
macchina da caffè a filtro 181
macchina della polizia 457
macchina fotografica a lastre 315
macchina fotografica autofocus 315
macchina fotografica digitale 315
macchina fotografica reflex (6x6) 315
macchina fotografica reflex digitale: dorso 315
macchina fotografica reflex monoculare: vista frontale 314
macchina fotografica usa e getta 315
macchina fotografica, corpo della 314
macchina per espresso 181
macchina per fare la pasta 170
macchina per fototessere 437
macchine da caffè 181
macchine fotografiche 315
macchine pesanti 398
macchine, sala 384, 386
macchinetta 269
macchinista 290
Macedonia 450
macinacaffè 180
macinare 170
macinato 152, 153
Mackenzie, Fiume di 16
macronucleo 66
macula 119
Madagascar 20, 452
magazzino 430, 438, 444
magazzino dei surgelati 121
magazzino frigorifero 381
magenta 418
maggese 122
maggiolino 69
maggiore di 427
maggiore o uguale a 427
maglia 483, 488, 493, 522
maglia della squadra 476, 480, 486
maglia dentata 235
maglia girocollo 255
maglietta 473
maglietta alla marinara 255
maglietta intima 260
maglione dolcevita 250
maglione girocollo 250
maglioni 250
magma 28, 33
magnesia, polvere di 497
magnete 416
magnete fermacoperchio 180
magnetismo 416
maiale 84
maiale, tagli di 153
mais 61, 143
mais foraggero 122
mais, farina di 144
mais, motore di 13
mais, olio di 149
mais, pane americano di 145
mais, sciroppo di 149
mais: pannocchia 61
maitre 438
maiuscola 330
malanga 129
Malawi 452
Malawi, Lago 20
Malaysia 453
Maldive 453
Mali, Repubblica del 451
mallo 60
Malta 450
malto, aceto di 141
mammiferi carnivori 86
mammiferi carnivori, esempi di 88
mammiferi marini 90
mammiferi marini, esempi di 90
mammiferi ungulati 83
mammiferi ungulati, esempi di 84
mandarino 134
mandibola 67, 74, 98, 100
mandibola inferiore 78
mandibola superiore 78
mandolino 297
mandorla 57, 133
mandrino 228
mandrino autoserrante 228
mandrino, chiave del 228
manette, astuccio delle 456
manganello, gancio del 456
mango 137
mangostano 136
mangusta 88
manica 244
manica a giro 245
manica alla raglan 248, 251, 261
Manica, Canale della 18
manichetta antincendio 454
manico 167, 215, 216, 219, 220, 223, 236, 270, 271, 272, 273, 274, 275, 276, 277, 297, 301, 302, 303, 341, 492, 493, 494, 531
manico a scomparsa 274
manico isolato 217
manicotto del cavo 228
manicotto del cordone 218, 229
manicotto di attacco dello scalpello 403
manicotto inferiore del radiatore 358
manicotto, borsa a 276
manicure 265
manicure, set per 265
manifesto 294
maniglia 178, 179, 185, 186, 204, 209, 210, 211, 225, 277, 325, 326, 349, 361, 455
maniglia di salita 364
maniglia di spinta 286
maniglia di traino 276
maniglia fissa 352
maniglia interna 352
maniglia isolata 179
maniglia laterale 380
maniglie, cavallo con 496
manioca 124
manipolazione a distanza, sistema di 11
mannaia 169
mano 91, 93, 95, 115
mano, scudo di protezione della 235
manometro 461
manopola 192, 210, 243, 267, 366, 369
manopola alzacristalli 352
manopola del forno 210
manopola del volume 325, 326
manopola dell'acceleratore 368
manopola della messa a fuoco 8, 9
manopola della sintonia 326
manopola di controllo 471
manopola di regolazione del condensatore 421
manopola di regolazione del gas 529
manopola di regolazione dell'aggetto 229
manopola di regolazione dell'altezza 209
manopola di regolazione dello schienale 353
manopola di scorrimento 327
manopola di sintonizzazione 325
manopole di comando dei bruciatori 210
manovella 224, 236, 356, 537
manovella d'avvolgimento 225
manovella del supporto 365
manovella di avviamento 235
manovra, motore di 13
mansardato, piano 189
mantella 251
mantello 72, 73
mantello d'elica 383
mantello del pistone 360
mantello inferiore 26
mantello superiore 26
mantice a soffietto 296
mantide religiosa 69
manto di usura 342
manuale del grand'organo 305
manuale dell'organo espressivo 305
manuale dell'organo positivo 305
manuale di pronto soccorso 461
manuale, pistoncino del 305
manuali 305
manubrio 371, 500, 501, 523
manubrio rialzato 522
manubrio, attacco del 371
manzo, tagli di 152
mappamondo 444
Mar Adriatico 18
Mar Baltico 18
Mar Caribico 14, 16
Mar Caspio 14, 19
Mar Cinese Meridionale 14, 19
Mar Cinese Orientale 19
Mar d'Irlanda 18
Mar dei Coralli 15
Mar del Giappone 19
Mar di Barents 18
Mar di Beaufort 16
Mar di Bering 14
Mar di Groenlandia 14
Mar di Norvegia 18
Mar Glaciale Artico 14
Mar Mediterraneo 14, 18, 20
Mar Nero 14, 18, 19
Mar Rosso 14, 19, 20
maracuja 136
marciapiede 183, 375, 379, 390, 434
marciapiede dei viaggiatori 374
marciapiede, ingresso al 374
marciapiede, margine del 379
mare 5, 24, 32
mare calmo, livello di 33
Mare del Nord 14, 18
Mare di Tasmania 15
Mare di Weddell 15
Mare Egeo 18
mare, livello del 26, 33, 37
mare, orecchia di 157
mare, passera di 161
mare, pressione a livello del 39
mare, tartufo di 157
margarina 149
margine 55
margine anteriore 73
margine continentale 33
margine del marciapiede 379
margine fogliare 55
margine libero 114
margine posteriore 73
Marie Byrd, Terra di 15
marinaio, sacca da 276
marino 40
marmitta 29, 351
marmotta 82
Marocco 451
Marte 2, 3
martelletti, barra dei 304
martelletto 304
martello 116, 472
martello a penna tonda 220
martello da carpentiere 220
martello da falegname 220
martello da muratore 216
martin pescatore 80
martinetto idraulico 361
martora 88
mascara compatto 266
mascara liquido 266
mascara, spazzolino per 266
mascella 74, 98, 100, 117
mascellare mobile 76
maschera 454, 476, 478, 486, 507
maschera a pieno facciale bifiltro 459
maschera forata 318
mascherina 296, 348, 459
mascherina perforata 240
maschile 426
maschio 282
maschio della messa a terra 198
massa 27
massa d'aria, tipo di 39
massa, unità di misura della 426
massaggiatore 489
massetere 96
massetto 187
massiccio montuoso 24
mastice di tenuta 196
matematica 427
materassi 459
materassino 205, 460, 530
materassino autogonfiante 530
materassino isolante 530
materassino pneumatico 530
materasso 204, 205
materia 414
materia inorganica 45
materia, stati della 414
materiale antincendio 454
materiale isolante 190, 214, 417
materiale medico, deposito del 465
materiale pulito, ripostiglio del 462
materiale sporco, deposito del 464
materiale sporco, ripostiglio del 462
materiale sterile, deposito del 464
materiale vario 225
materiali metallici, smistamento dei 49
materiali, movimentazione dei 396
matita 312
matita per sopracciglia 266
matita sbiancante per unghie 265
matite per il contorno delle labbra 266
matrice ungueale 114
matterello 172
mattone refrattario 192
maturazione 62
maturazione, stadi di 62
maturità 62
Mauritania 451
Maurizio 452
mazza 308, 476, 477, 478
mazze 309
mazze, tipi di 505
mazzo 125
mazzuolo 220, 297
meandro 32
meandro abbandonato 32
meandro abbandonato, lago di 32
meato auricolare 115, 116
meato uditivo esterno 100
meato urinario 111
Mecca, direzione della 447
meccanismo a scatto 312
meccanismo antiritorno 536
meccanismo dell'ottava 306
meccanismo di apertura dell'archetto 537
meccanismo di rilascio della bobina 537
meccanismo di spostamento della lama 401
mecchia 228
mecchia a doppia elica 228
mecchia a lancia 228
mecchia a tortiglione 228
mecchia elicoidale 228
mecchie e punte da trapano, esempi di 228
medaglione 264
media tensione, linea di distribuzione a 198
mediano di apertura 482
mediano di mischia 482
medicinali, confezioni farmaceutiche di 467
medico 464, 498
medico di guardia, ufficio del 462
medico interno 464
medie frequenze, pick-up per 303
medio 115
Mediterraneo, Mar 14, 18, 20
Meissner, corpuscolo di 114
mela 133
mela cotogna 133
mela, sezione di una 58
Melanesia 15
melanzana 128
melassa 149
mele, aceto di 141
melissa 142
melodia, canna della 296
melodia, corde per la 296
melograno 136
melone amaro 128
melone giallo canario 135
melone invernale 129, 135
melone mieloso 135
melone Ōgen 135
melone retato 135
meloni 135
membrana 309
membrana cellulare 50, 66
membrana del timpano 116
membrana interdigitale 75, 79
membrana nittitante 87
membrana nucleare 50, 66
membrana plasmatica 66
membrana testacea 79
membrana vitellina 79
memorizzazione dei dati, dispositivi di 333
memorizzazione, tasto di 322, 323, 327
meningi 109
menisco convergente 419
menisco divergente 419
menorah 447
mensola 192, 283, 302
mensola portaccessori 8
mensola portautensili 219
mensolone 192
menta 142
mento 78, 94
mento, protezione del 367
mentoniera 301
menu, pulsante del 315
menu, tasto di 327
merci, banchina di scarico delle 437, 439
merci, ingresso delle 435
merci, scalo 375, 430
Mercurio 2, 3
mercurio, bulbo di 424
mercurio, colonna di 424
merguez 156
meridiana 424
meridiano fondamentale 22
meridiano occidentale 22
meridiano orientale 22
méridienne 200
merlano 161
merlano nero 161
merluzzo dell'Atlantico 161
mesa 36
mesocarpo 57, 58, 59
mesopausa 37
mesosfera 37
messa a fuoco, manopola della 8, 9
messa a fuoco, selettore della 314, 320
messa a terra, maschio della 198
messa a terra, terminale della 322
Messico 448
Messico, Golfo del 16
mestolo 173
meta, area di 484
meta, linea di 484
metallo, bacchetta di 309
meteorologia 37
metodi di pagamento 441
metro 426
metropolitana 378, 380, 435
metropolitana, stazione della 378, 432
metropolitana, treno della 378
mezza sfera di sughero 495
mezzanino 378
mezzi occhiali 273
mezzo di pronto intervento 345
mezzo manico 169

mezzoguanto 243
mi 298
micelio 52
microfilamento 66
microfoni 457
microfono 320, 327, 328, 332, 337, 456
micrometro a vite 425
Micronesia 453
micronucleo 66
microonde 418
microonde, forno a 178
microscopi 421
microscopio 421
microscopio binoculare 421
microtelefono 327
microtelefono, cordone del 327
microtubulo 66
microvettura compatta 347
MIDI (cavo di interfaccia digitale per
    strumenti musicali) 311
midollo 63, 154
midollo allungato 109
midollo spinale 109, 110
midollo spinale, struttura del 109
midrange 324
miele 149
migale del Messico 70
miglio 61, 143
miglio: spiga 61
mignolo 115
mihrab 447
mihrab, cupola sul 447
mille 427
milza 103
Mimas 3
minareto 447
minbar 447
mini impianto hi-fi 325
miniaspiratutto 208
minibus 363
minima 299
minima, pausa di 299
minore di 427
minore o uguale a 427
minuti, lancetta dei 424
miocardio 104
miopia 419
mira, cannocchiale di 420
Miranda 3
mirino 315, 534, 535
mirino a cannocchiale 534
mirino elettronico 320
mirtillo 132
mirtillo palustre 132
mirtillo rosso 132
miscela di cinque spezie 139
miscela di manganese (catodo) 417
miscela di sostanze depolarizzanti 417
miscela di zinco ed elettroliti (anodo) 417
miscelare 176
miscelatore 197
miscelatore per dolci 172
miscelatore vasca/doccia 194
mischia 484, 485
mischia spontanea 483
mischia, linea di 485
Mississippi, Fiume 16
misura del peso 422
misura del tempo 424
misura della lunghezza 425
misura della temperatura 424
misura dello spessore 425
misurini 171
mitilo 157
mitocondrio 50, 66
mitra 193
mobile 318
mobile bar 203
mobile portaccessori 195
mobili contenitori 202
mobili per bambini 205
mocassino 242
mocassino classico 242
modalità FM, tasto di selezione della 322
modanatura 348
modellatore aperto 258
modellatore sgambato 258
modello di stazione 39
modem 334
modem cablato 335
moderatore 408
modo di esposizione, tasto per il 314
modo TV 319
modo VCR 319
modo, selettori di 326
modulatore della pressione dei freni 357

modulazione, rotella di 310
moduli fotovoltaici 11
modulo abitativo americano 11
modulo centrifugo 11
modulo di comunicazione 316
modulo di propulsione 316
modulo di servizio 316
modulo di sperimentazione europeo 11
modulo di sperimentazione giapponese 11
modulo russo 11
moffetta 88
Mohorovicic, discontinuità di 26
molare, sezione trasversale di un 101
molari 101
Moldavia 450
mole 426
molecola 414
molla 27, 206, 212, 222, 312, 460, 535
molla della valvola 360
molla di richiamo 357
molla di tensione 355, 500
molla sturatrice per scarichi 216
molla, aletta a 221
molle 173, 193
molle a forbice 500
molle per chiocciole 173
molle per spaghetti 173
molle, rete a 204
molletta 268
molletta fermavetrino 421
molluschi 72, 157
molo 430
moltiplica, ruota della 522
moltiplicatore 413
moltiplicazione 427
Monaco, Principato di 450
mondo, climi del 40
moneta: diritto 441
moneta: rovescio 441
Mongolia 453
monitor 329
monitor della pressione sanguigna 461
monitor di controllo del regista 290
monoblocco 360
Monopoli® 469
monoscafi 521
monovolume 347
montaggio, tasto di 320
montagna 29
montagna sottomarina 33
montagna, climi di 40
Montagne Rocciose 16
montante 184, 186, 187, 219, 281, 349
montante centrale 185, 202
montante d'angolo 187
montante del telaio 202
montante del timpano 187
montante dell'ala 394
montante della ferratura 185
montante della serratura 185
montante imbottito 489
montante verticale 201, 202
montatura 273
montatura a ferro di cavallo 7
monte di lancio 475
monte di Venere 112
Monte Everest 37
montgomery 249
Monti Appalachi 16
Monti Carpazi 18
Monti dell'Atlante 20
Monti Transantartici 15
Monti Urali 18
montone 249
monumento 25
moquette 190
mora 132
mordente 299
morena di fondo 30
morena frontale 30
morena laterale 30
morena mediana 30
morena terminale 30
morfologia di un astice 71
morfologia di un cane 86
morfologia di un cavallo 83
morfologia di un delfino 90
morfologia di un gorilla 91
morfologia di un persico 74
morfologia di un polpo 72
morfologia di un ragno 70
morfologia di un ratto 82
morfologia di un serpente velenoso: testa
    76
morfologia di un uccello 78
morfologia di un'ape: operaia 68

morfologia di una chiocciola 72
morfologia di una conchiglia bivalve 73
morfologia di una conchiglia univalve 73
morfologia di una farfalla 67
morfologia di una rana 75
morfologia di una tartaruga 76
morfologia di uno squalo 74
morsa 224
morsa serratubi 224
morsettiera 411
morsetto 198, 221, 226
morsetto a C 224
morsetto nero 356
morsetto regolabile 206
morsetto rosso 356
morsetto terminale a spina 359
mortadella 156
mortaio 170
morte 426
mosaico 280
mosca 69
mosca artificiale 536
mosca tse-tse 69
moschea 447
moschettiera, stivale alla 241
moschettone 521, 538
mosse principali 470
moto da Gran premio 525
moto ondoso, livello base del 33
motocicletta 366
motocicletta con telecamera 522
motocicletta da cross 369
motocicletta da motocross 525
motocicletta da supercross 525
motocicletta da turismo 369
motocicletta di testa 522
motocicletta: vista dall'alto 368
motociclette e ciclomotore, esempi di 369
motociclismo 525
motociclista 525
motofalciatrice 237
motore 212, 213, 214, 227, 229, 237,
    366, 403
motore a benzina 351, 360
motore di manovra 13
motore di traino, vano del 400
motore diesel del ventilatore di
    sostentamento 383
motore diesel di propulsione 383
motore diesel, vano del 398, 399, 400,
    401
motore elettrico 235, 237, 358
motore fuoribordo 385
motore principale 13
motore, asse di trasmissione del 177
motore, blocco 176, 177, 180, 208
motore, rivestimento del 235
motore, vano 396
motore, vano del 401
motore, yacht a 385
motori diesel marini, combustibile per 405
motori diesel, combustibile per 405
motorino d'avviamento 237
motoscafo da diporto 385
motosega 235
motrice 364, 380
motto 441
mountain bike 373, 522
mountain bike da cross 373
mouse a rotella 332
mouse meccanico 332
mouse ottico 332
mouse senza fili 332
mouse, tappetino del 332
movimentazione 396
movimentazione dei materiali 396
movimenti del terreno 31
movimenti di un aeroplano 395
movimento a L 470
movimento diagonale 470
movimento orizzontale 470
movimento orizzontale del suolo 27
movimento verticale 470
movimento verticale del suolo 27
movimento, rilevatore di 286
Mozambico 452
Mozambico, Canale di 20
mozzarella 150
mozzo 341, 371, 413, 467
mozzo del rotore 395
mucca 84
mucosa olfattiva 117
muffa 123
muffola 321
muflone 84
mughetto 56
mulinello 536

mulinello a bobina fissa 537
mulinello a bobina rotante 537
mulinello, alloggiamento del 536, 537
mulino a pilastro 412
mulino a torre 412
mulino a vento 412
mulo 84
multiscafi 521
mummia 530
municipio 432
munster 151
mura fortificate 447
murata 385
muro di fondazione 187
muro di fondo 292, 293
muro di sponda 406
muschi, esempi di 51
muschio 51
muschio d'Irlanda 123
muschio, struttura di un 51
muscoli 96
muscolo adduttore anteriore 73
muscolo adduttore posteriore 73
muscolo bulbocavernoso 111
muscolo erettore del pelo 114
muscolo papillare 104
muscolo retto inferiore 119
muscolo retto superiore 119
museo 433
musica 296
musica, aula di 444
muso 75, 83, 86, 87, 91, 392
muso abbassabile 394
mussolina 171
mutande 247
mutandina 259
mutandina con ruches 260
mutandina elastica 259
mutandina impermeabile 260
mutandoni 247
muting 323
Myanmar 453

N

n. 8 avanti 482
nacchere 295, 309
Namib, Deserto del 20
Namibia 452
naos 279
narice 74, 75, 76, 78, 83, 117
nascita 426
nasello 273
nashi 137
naso 82, 83, 94
naso esterno 117
naso, dorso del 117
naso, punta del 117
naso, radice del 117
nasofaringe 117
nastratrice 341
nastro 225, 238, 491
nastro adesivo, chiocciola per 341
nastro bianco 487, 493, 495
nastro centrale 491
nastro di delimitazione 457
nastro di teflon 216
nastro frenante 212
nastro magnetico 319
nastro trasportatore 49, 390
nastro verticale laterale 487
nastro, fermo del 225
nastro, selettore del 323
natica 93, 95, 111, 112
Nauru 453
navata centrale 285, 447
navata laterale 285
nave cisterna 384
nave da ricognizione meteorologica 38
nave per il trasporto delle merci 382
nave portacontainer 381, 382
nave traghetto 386
navetta per il trasbordo dei passeggeri
    391
navetta spaziale 12, 37
navetta spaziale al decollo 12
navi, esempi di 382
navicella 413
navicella, sezione trasversale di una 413
navigazione, luce di 383, 393
navone 129
Nazca, placca di 27
nazionalità 497
nebbia 41
nebulizzatore 236
necrologia 313

nefridio 71
negozio 432
negozio di abbigliamento 436
negozio di animali 436
negozio di articoli da regalo 436
negozio di articoli sportivi 437
negozio di biancheria intima 436
negozio di bricolage 436
negozio di dischi 436
negozio di elettronica 436
negozio di giocattoli 436
negozio di oggettistica 437
negozio di scarpe 437
negozio per la riproduzione delle chiavi
    437
nembostrato 42
neon, lampada al 217
neonati, vestiti per 260
Nepal 453
neri 470
nero 418
Nero, Mar 14, 18, 19
nervatura 55, 401, 458
nervatura alare 67
nervatura centrale 51, 55, 60
nervi cranici 108
nervo 114
nervo ascellare 108
nervo cocleare 116
nervo cutaneo laterale della coscia 108
nervo cutaneo posteriore della coscia 108
nervo digitale 108
nervo femorale 108
nervo gluteo 108
nervo ileoinguinale 108
nervo ileoipogastrico 108
nervo intercostale 108
nervo ischiatico 108
nervo mediano 108
nervo olfattivo 117
nervo ottico 119
nervo otturatorio 108
nervo peroniero comune 108
nervo peroniero profondo 108
nervo peroniero superficiale 108
nervo radiale 108
nervo safeno esterno 108
nervo safeno interno 108
nervo spinale 109, 110
nervo tibiale 108
nervo ulnare 108
nervo vestibolare 116
nervoso centrale, sistema 109
nervoso periferico, sistema 108
nervoso, sistema 108
nespola del Giappone 133
nettarina 132
Nettuno 2, 3
neurone motorio 110
neurone sensoriale 110
neuroni, catena di 110
neutrone 414
neutrone incidente 415
nevato 30
neve 41
neve acida 48
nevi perenni 29
nevischio 41
newton 426
Nicaragua 448
nicchia di sicurezza 345
Niger 451
Niger, Fiume 20
Nigeria 451
Nilo 20
nocciola 133
nocciola, sezione di una 60
nocciolo 57
noce 64, 133
noce del Brasile 133
noce di acagiù 133
noce di cocco 133
noce di cola 133
noce di ginco 133
noce di macadamia 133
noce di pecan 133
noce moscata 138
noce, sezione di una 60
nodello 83
nodo 53, 167, 169, 416
nodo di Ranvier 110
nome del dominio 334
nome del ginnasta 497
nome del giornale 313
nome del titolare 441
nome della stazione 378

ASTRONOMIA > 2-25;   TERRA > 26-71;   REGNO VEGETALE >72-89;   REGNO ANIMALE > 90-143;   ESSERE UMANO > 144-177;   GENERI ALIMENTARI E CUCINA > 178-241;   CASA > 242-295
FAI DA TE E GIARDINAGGIO > 296-333;   ABBIGLIAMENTO > 334-371;   ACCESSORI E ARTICOLI PERSONALI > 372-391;   ARTE E ARCHITETTURA > 392-465;   COMUNICAZIONI E BUROTICA > 466-535
TRASPORTI E VEICOLI > 536-643;   ENERGIA > 644-677;   SCIENZA > 678-705;   SOCIETÀ > 706-785;   SPORT E GIOCHI > 786-920

nome della valuta 441
non appartiene a 427
non coincide con 427
non parallelo a 428
nonio 422, 425
nonio, scala graduata del 425
Nord 23
Nord Nord-Est 23
Nord Nord-Ovest 23
Nord, Mare del 14, 18
Nord-Est 23
Nord-Ovest 23
nori 123
Norvegia 450
Norvegia, Mar di 18
notazione degli scacchi 470
notazione musicale 298
note, valori di durata delle 299
notizie 313
notizie in breve 313
notte, camicia da 256
nottolino a scatto 425
nube 41
nube a proboscide 43
nube alta, tipo di 39
nube bassa, tipo di 39
nube di ceneri vulcaniche 28
nube di Oort 2
nube media, tipo di 39
nubi 42
nubi a sviluppo verticale 42
nubi alte 42
nubi basse 42
nubi medie 42
nuca 78, 93, 95
nuclei radioattivi 415
nucleo 4, 6, 50, 66, 110, 112, 414, 534
nucleo esterno 26
nucleo fissile 415
nucleo interno 26
nucleo, membrana del 50
nucleo, scissione del 415
nucleolo 50, 66, 112
numeratore 338
numeri romani 427
numero 473
numero del binario 374
numero del brano 323
numero del giocatore 486, 488, 506
numero della camera 439
numero della carta 441, 443
numero della pompa 346
numero di autostrada 25
numero di gara 525
numero di serie 441
numero di strada 25
nuoto 516
nuoto, stili di 517
Nuova Caledonia 15
Nuova Zelanda 15, 453
nuovo shekel 440
nuvola 37
nuvole, assorbimento attaverso le 46
nuvole, parete di 43

O

oasi 32, 36
Oberon 3
obiettivi 314
obiettivo 8, 314, 332, 421
obiettivo grandangolare 314
obiettivo macro 314
obiettivo zoom 314
obiettivo, accessori dell' 314
obiettivo, coperchio di protezione dell' 314
obiettivo, lente 420
obiettivo, pulsante di sblocco dell' 314
obliquo esterno dell'addome 96, 97
oblò 386
oboe 306
oboi 295
oca 81, 155
oca, uovo di 155
occhi, trucco per gli 266
occhiali 273, 510, 513, 522
occhiali da sole 273
occhiali di protezione 518
occhiali di protezione con ripari laterali 458
occhiali di protezione panoramici 458
occhiali protettivi 522, 525
occhiali, astuccio per 275
occhiali, esempi di 273
occhiali, mezzi 273
occhiali, parti degli 273

occhialini da nuoto 516
occhiello 240, 248, 263, 275, 313, 509, 538
occhiello per la tracolla 315
occhio 43, 70, 71, 72, 76, 90, 94, 119, 220, 312
occhio composto 67, 68
occhio semplice 67
occhio, orbicolare dell' 96
occhio, parete dell' 43
occhione di traino 356
occipitale 97
Oceania 14, 15, 453
oceano 5, 24, 45
Oceano Atlantico 14, 15, 18, 20
Oceano Indiano 14, 15, 19, 20
Oceano Pacifico 14, 15, 19
oculare 8, 9, 320, 420, 421
offerta, prodotti in 121
officina di riparazione dei locomotori diesel 375
officina meccanica 346
oftalmologia, sala di 463
oggetto 419
ohm 426
okapi 84
olecrano 99
oleodotti, rete di 404
oleodotto 404
oleodotto di superficie 404
oleodotto sottomarino 404
olfatto 116
oli 149
olii lubrificanti 405
olio combustibile leggero 405
olio combustibile per stufe 405
olio combustibile pesante 405
olio d'oliva 149
olio di arachidi 149
olio di mais 149
olio di semi di girasole 149
olio di sesamo 149
olio, tappo di scarico dell' 360
oliva 128
oliva auricolare 460
oliva, olio d' 149
olivetta 249
Oman 452
Oman, Golfo di 19
ombelico 30, 92, 94
ombra 424
ombrella 57
ombrello 273
ombretto 266
omero 98
omero, testa dell' 99
onda 33, 418
onda d'urto 403
onda sismica 27
onda, altezza dell' 33
onda, fondo dell' 33
onda, lunghezza d' 418
onda, lunghezza dell' 33
onde hertziane, trasmissione a 316
onde radio 418
Oort, nube di 2
Opera 432
opera morta 521
opercolo 74
opilione 77
opistodomo 279
ora, tasto di visualizzazione dell' 320
orangotango 91
orari 374
orari dei film 294
orari, tabellone degli 374
orata 159
orbicolare 55
orbicolare dell'occhio 96
orbita della Luna 4, 5
orbita della Terra 4, 5
orbiter 12, 13
orca 90
orchestra 278
orchestra sinfonica 295
orchidea 56
ordinata rinforzata 385
orecchia di mare 157
orecchie, tappi per le 458
orecchini 264
orecchini a clip 264
orecchini a perno 264
orecchini a vite 264
orecchini ad anello 264
orecchini pendenti 264
orecchio 92

orecchio di Giuda 123
orecchio esterno 116
orecchio interno 116
orecchio medio 116
orecchio, struttura dell' 116
organi di senso 114, 115, 119
organi di trasmissione 372
organi genitali femminili 112
organi genitali maschili 111
organismi autotrofi 45
organismi decompositori 45
organismi eterotrofi 45
organismi semplici 66
organizer 338
organizzazione culturale 335
organizzazione governativa 335
organo 305
organo di raccordo 364
origano 142
Orinoco, Fiume 17
orlatura a stella 534
orlo 238
orlo della vasca 212
ormeggio, verricello di 385
orologio 444
orologio analogico 424
orologio contaminuti 178
orologio digitale 424
orso bruno 89
orso polare 89
ortaggi 124
ortaggi da bulbo 124
ortaggi da foglia 126
ortaggi da frutto 128
ortaggi da fusto 125
ortaggi da infiorescenza 127
ortaggi da radice 129
ortaggi da tubero 124
ortica 127
orto 122, 182
orzo 61, 143
orzo: spiga 61
ospedale 433, 462
ospite 267
osservatorio 7
osservatorio astronomico 7
osservatorio astronomico, sezione trasversale di un 7
osservazione astronomica 7
osservazione psichiatrica, stanza per 462
osservazione, finestrino di 13
osservazione, punto di 7
osservazione, stanza di 462, 465
ossicini dell'udito 116
ossido d'azoto, emissione di 48
ossigeno, presa dell' 464
ossigeno, produzione di 54
ossigeno, regolazione della pressione dell' 10
osso alveolare 101
osso frontale 98, 100
osso mascellare 101
osso nasale 100, 117
osso occipitale 99, 100
osso parietale 99, 100
osso sfenoide 100
osso temporale 98, 100
osso zigomatico 98, 100
ossobuco 152
ostacolo d'acqua 504
ostrica 157
ostriche, coltello da 169
ostriche, forchetta da 168
otorinolaringoiatria, sala di 463
ottaedro regolare 429
ottagono regolare 429
ottava 298
ottava, meccanismo dell' 306
ottavino 295, 306
ottico 437
ottoni, famiglia degli 295
otturatore 329
ovaia 112, 113
ovario 56
ovata 55
Ovest 23
Ovest Nord-Ovest 23
Ovest Sud-Ovest 23
ovile 122
ovolo buono 123
ovulo 56, 112
oxford, scarpa 240
ozono, strato di 37

P

pacchetto 163
Pacifico, Oceano 14, 15, 19
Pacifico, placca del 27
Pacifico, salmone del 161
Pacini, corpuscolo di 114
padella 531
padella doppia 175
padella per crêpe 175
padella per friggere 175
padella per rosolare 175
padiglione 116, 305, 432
padiglione auricolare 82, 115
paese 23, 430
Paesi Bassi 449
pagamento elettronico, terminale per il 121
pagina precedente 331
pagina successiva 331
pagliaccetto 258, 261
paglietta 238
pagnottella inglese 145
pagoda 283
pak-choi 126
Pakistan 452
pala 213, 412, 413, 478, 506
pala ausiliaria 412
pala caricatrice anteriore 399
pala caricatrice posteriore 399
pala caricatrice, braccio della 399
pala caricatrice, cilindro della 399
pala del rotore 395
pala del timone 384
pala dell'altare 446
palafitta 288
palanchino 220
palato duro 116, 117
palato molle 116, 117
Palau 453
palazzo dei congressi 433
palazzo di giustizia 432
palazzo in condominio 289
palazzo residenziale 282
palchetto 293
palcoscenico 278, 292, 293
palcoscenico, gabbia del 292
palestra 386, 444
palestra, ufficio della 444
paletta 167, 173, 193, 215, 302, 303, 538
paletta di carico ad alette 396
paletta riempipiunti 216
palette di carico, carrello a forca per 396
paletto 498
paliotto 446
palizzata 230, 282
palla 476, 477, 478, 492, 505
palla di filo 477
palla di sughero 477
palla ovale 483, 486
palla, sezione di una 477
pallacanestro 488
pallavolo 487
palleggio 487
pallina 493
pallini 534
pallone 480, 487, 488
pallone sonda 38
pallonetto 491
pallottola 534
palma 64
palmare breve 96
palmare lungo 96
palmata 55
palmeto 36
palmetta 200
palmo 115, 243
palmo del guanto 243
palo 321, 485, 487, 490, 495
palo della linea di fuoricampo 475
palo frontale 529
palombo liscio 158
palpebra 76
palpebra inferiore 75, 87, 119
palpebra superiore 75, 87, 119
palpo 73
palpo labiale 67
pampino 62, 126
Panama 448
panama 238
Panama, Golfo di 17
Panama, Istmo di 16
panca 446, 502
panca degli ufficiali di gara 507
panca dei puniti 507

panca dei puniti, addetto alla 507
pancetta 156
panchina 201, 379, 437, 481
panchina dei giocatori 474, 485, 487, 506
panciera 259
pancreas 106
pane 144
pane azzimo 145
pane bianco 145
pane chapati indiano 145
pane di mais americano 145
pane di segale danese 145
pane e burro, piattino per 166
pane ebraico 145
pane greco 144
pane integrale 145
pane irlandese 145
pane multicereali 145
pane naan indiano 145
pane nero di segale 144
pane pita 145
pane, coltello da 169
pane, guida per il 178
pane, stampo per 179
panetteria 121, 437
panna 150
panna acida 150
panna da montare 150
pannello 185, 259, 352
pannello del display 320
pannello dell'anta 202
pannello di celle solari 411
pannello di comando 455
pannello di copertura 348
pannello di funzionamento 287
pannello di mezzo 185
pannello di protezione 369
pannello divisorio 274, 277
pannello solare 7, 316
panno 502
pannocchia 61
pannolino 260
pannolino usa e getta 260
pantacollant 263
pantaloncini 261, 473, 480, 483, 488, 498, 500, 522
pantaloncini da corsa 263
pantaloni 246, 263, 476, 486, 499, 506, 525
pantaloni a zampa di elefante 254
pantaloni alla pescatora 254
pantaloni alla zuava 254
pantaloni felpati 262
pantaloni, esempi di 254
pantografo 376
papaia 137
papalina 238
papavero 56, 60
papavero, semi di 139
papilla 114
papilla caliciforme 118
papilla circonvallata 118
papilla filiforme 118
papilla foliata 118
papilla fungiforme 118
papilla ottica 119
papilla renale 107
papillon 245
paprika 139
Papua Nuova Guinea 453
Papuasia-Nuova Guinea 15
parabraccia 486
parabrezza 348, 364, 366, 369, 385, 392, 394, 523
paracadute 287
paracadute del booster 12
paracoccige 486
paracollo 486
paracosce 486
paracostole 486
paradenti 486, 498
parafango 348, 349, 364, 370
parafango anteriore 366
paraffine 405
parafianchi 486
parafulmine 183, 407, 413
parafuoco 193
paragambe 507
paragola 476
paragomito 486
paragrilletto 534
Paraguay 448
paralama inferiore 227
paralama inferiore, leva per togliere il 227

ASTRONOMIA > 2-25; TERRA > 26-71; REGNO VEGETALE >72-89; REGNO ANIMALE > 90-143; ESSERE UMANO > 144-177; GENERI ALIMENTARI E CUCINA > 178-241; CASA > 242-295; FAI DA TE E GIARDINAGGIO > 296-333; ABBIGLIAMENTO > 334-371; ACCESSORI E ARTICOLI PERSONALI > 372-391; ARTE E ARCHITETTURA > 392-465; COMUNICAZIONI E BUROTICA > 466-535; TRASPORTI E VEICOLI > 536-643; ENERGIA > 644-677; SCIENZA > 678-705; SOCIETÀ > 706-785; SPORT E GIOCHI > 786-920

625

INDICE DEI NOMI ITALIANI

paralama superiore 227
parallele 496, 497
parallele asimmetriche 496, 497
parallelepipedo 429
parallelo 22
parallelo a 428
parallelogramma 429
paraluce 8, 314
paralume 206
paramano 525
paramecio 66
paramezzale centrale 385
Paranà, Fiume 17
paraneve 523
pararorecchi 238
parapetto 191, 282, 344, 377
parapetto, pilastro del 191
parapunta 476
parasole 356
parasole, aletta 354
paraspalle 486
parastinchi 476, 480, 513
paratia longitudinale 384
paratia trasversale 384
paratoia 407
paratoia dello sfioratore 406
paratrucioli 227
paraurti 364, 369
paraurti posteriore 369, 523
parcheggio 375, 381, 390, 430, 435,
     445, 504, 512
parcheggio per le biciclette 445
parco 25, 433
parco nazionale 25
parete 5, 58, 184, 528
parete anteriore 365
parete cellulare 50
parete dell'occhio 43
parete della qibla 447
parete di arrivo 516
parete di virata 517
parete inferiore 404
parete laterale 365, 404, 517
parete superiore 404
parete, lampada da 207
parete, lampione da 207
pareti di vetro, custodia a 423
paripennata 55
parka 249
parmigiano 151
parquet 190
parquet a listelli 190
parquet a listoni 190
parquet a mosaico 190
parquet a spina di pesce 190
parquet a tessitura di vimini 190
parquet Arenberg 190
parquet Chantilly 190
parquet su sottofondo di cemento 190
parquet su struttura lignea 190
parquet Versailles 190
parquet, tipi di 190
parrucchiere 290, 436
parrucchiere, forbici da 270
parte anteriore del quartiere 240, 262
parte inferiore del tronco 63
parte intermedia 111
parte inferiore dell'intelaiatura 186
parte terminale 111
partenza della funivia 512
partenza della seggiovia 512
partenza, griglia di 524
partenza, piazzola di 504
partenza, pulsante di 424
parti 200, 201, 204
parti boccali 68
parti degli occhiali 273
parti di un cerchio 428
parti di una scarpa 240
pascal 426
pascolo 122
passacavo 521
passacinghia 532
passaggio a livello 375
passaggio a soffietto 363
passaggio pedonale 434, 436
passamontagna 239
passante 245, 246, 250
passante del cinturino 248
passante della cintura 248
passascotte 521
passata di pomodoro 140
passavanti 385
passaverdure 170
passeggeri, carrozza 380

passeggeri, sala 383, 386, 387
passeggeri, terminal satellite dei 389
passeggeri, treno 374
passeggiata, ponte di 386
passera di mare 161
passerella 282, 292, 379
passerella di imbarco 389
passerotto 80
passo 29, 83
passo alternato 514
passo d'uomo 404
passo pattinato 514
pasta 146
pasta di tamarindo 140
pasta sfoglia 145
pasta won ton 147
pasta, macchina per fare la 170
pasticceria 437
pastiglia 357, 467
pastiglia di combustibile 409
pastinaca 129
pastoia 83
pastore tedesco 86
Patagonia 17
patata 124
patata americana 124
patella 157
patera 200
patio 182, 230
patio, porta del 188
patta 246, 260
patta di chiusura 532
pattinaggio artistico 509
pattinaggio di velocità 508
pattinaggio in linea 527
pattinaggio libero, lama per 509
pattinatore 508, 527
pattini per velocità 508
pattino 395, 506
pattino a rotelle 527
pattino acrobatico 527
pattino ad incastro 508
pattino da hockey 527
pattino da short track 508
pattino da velocità 527
pattino del portiere 507
pattino di coda 395
pattino distanziatore 509
pattino per pattinaggio artistico 509
pattino, colpo di 514
pausa 331
pausa di biscroma 299
pausa di croma 299
pausa di minima 299
pausa di semibiscroma 299
pausa di semibreve 299
pausa di semicroma 299
pausa di semiminima 299
pausa, tasto di 323
pause, valori di durata delle 299
pavimenti, spazzola per 209
pavimento 193
pavimento della cabina 287
pavimento, rivestimenti in tessuto per 190
pavone 81
paziente 464
pe-tsai 126
pecari 84
pecora 84
pecorino romano 151
pedale 302, 305, 308, 370, 372, 473,
     501, 522
pedale ad ampio appoggio 522
pedale del cambio 367, 368, 369
pedale del crescendo 305
pedale del freno 350, 354, 357, 511
pedale del freno posteriore 368
pedale del piano 304, 311
pedale dell'acceleratore 354
pedale della frizione 354
pedale della sordina 304
pedale di risonanza 304, 311
pedale di sollevamento 467
pedale senza fermapiedi 522
pedale, leva del 304
pedale, pistoncino del 305
pedali d'espressione 305
pedaliera 305
pedana 423, 496, 523
pedana di lancio 472, 473
pedana elastica 496
pedana per il corpo libero 496
pedane di rincorsa 496
pedata 191
pediera 204
pedine 469

pedipalpo 70
pedivella 372
pedivelle albero delle 372
pedone 470
pedula 242
peduncolo 52, 56, 57, 58, 59, 62
peli radicali 53
pelle armonica 297
pelle di camoscio 265
pelle, laccio de 246
pellegrina 251
pelletteria 436
pelletteria, articoli di 274
pellicano 80
pelliccia 82, 91
pellicola d'alluminio 162
pellicola plastica, condensatore a 417
pellicola sigillata a caldo 163
pellicola trasparente 162
pellicola, pulsante di riavvolgimento della
     314
pellicola, tasto per l'avanzamento della
     314
pellicola, tasto per la sensibilità della 314
pelo 114
pelo, muscolo erettore del 114
peltata 55
pelvi renale 107
pendenti 264
pene 92, 111
penisola 24
Penisola Antartica 15
Penisola Arabica 19
Penisola Balcanica 18
Penisola Coreana 19
Penisola dello Yucatan 16
Penisola di Camciatca 19
Penisola di Kola 18
Penisola Iberica 18
Penisola Scandinava 18
penna a sfera 312
penna con pennino metallico 312
penna copritrice 78
penna copritrice inferiore della coda 78
penna copritrice superiore della coda 78
penna d'oca 312
penna stilografica 312
penna timoniera 78
penna tonda 220
pennatifida 55
penne 146, 536
pennellino per labbra 266
pennello 219
pennello a ventaglio 266
pennello da barba 271
pennello da cipria in polvere 266
pennello da fard 266
pennello per dolci 172
pennello per scrivere 312
pennello, spazzola a 209
pennino 27, 312
pensile 164
pensilina 375, 434
pentagono regolare 429
pentagramma 298
pentola 175
pentola a pressione 174
pentola a vapore 175
pentola a vapore elettrica 179
pentola per cucinare a bagnomaria 175
pentola per cuscus 175
pepaiola 166
pepe bianco 138
pepe della Giamaica 138
pepe di Cayenna 139
pepe macinato 139
pepe nero 138
pepe rosa 138
pepe verde 138
peperoncini secchi 139
peperoncino 128, 139
peperoncino in polvere 139
peperoncino rosso 139
peperoncino tritato 139
peperoncino, spray ai 456
peperone giallo 128
peperone rosso 128
peperone verde 128
pepino 137
per aprire 170
per misurare 171
pera 133
percento 427
percorso 504
percorso di evacuazione 345
percussione, strumenti a 295, 308

peretta per ingrassare 173
perforatore 340
pergola 230
pergola, bordo del 210
pericardio 105
pericarpo 60
peristilio 279, 280
peristoma 66
peritoneo 111, 112
perlina di cristallo 207
pernice 80
perno 217, 270, 271, 533, 535
perno di agganciamento 365
perno di ancoraggio 357
perno di incernieramento 400
perno di incernieramento della pala
     caricatrice 399
perno oscillante 355
perno, orecchini a 264
perone 98
peroneo breve 97
peroneo lungo 96
perossisoma 66
perpendicolare 428
persiana 186
persiano 87
persico 160
persico trota 160
Persico, Golfo 19
persico, morfologia di un 74
personal computer 329
personale, ingresso del 445
personale, stanza del 463
Perù 448
Perù-Cile, Fossa 34
pesalettere 339
pesca 132, 536
pesca a mosca 536
pesca al lancio 537
pesca, sezione di una 57
pescatora, pantaloni alla 254
pesce 121
pesce cappone 159
pesce cartilagineo 74
pesce osseo 74
pesce rospo 160
pesce San Pietro 161
pesce spada 159
pesce, coltello da 168
pesce, forchetta da 168
pesce, piatto per il 166
peschereccio 384
pesci 74
pesci cartilaginei 158
pesci ossei 159
pesciera 174
pesi 501
peso 422, 423, 440, 472, 500
peso, misura del 422
pestello 170
pesticida 47, 48
petalo 56
petroliera 381
petrolio 403
petrolio greggio 405
pettine 157
pettine a coda 268
pettine a forchetta 268
pettine afro 268
pettine da barbiere 268
pettine per cotonare 268
pettine rado 268
pettini 268
pettinino per ciglia e spazzolino per
     sopracciglia 266
pettirosso 80
petto 78, 83
pettorali, barra per i 501
pettorali, piastra per i 501
pettorina 260, 261
pettorina di protezione 476
pezzi 470
pi greco 428
pia madre 109
pialla 229
piana da dilavamento glaciale 30
piana inondabile 32
pianella 242
pianerottolo 189, 191
pianeti 2
pianeti esterni 2
pianeti interni 3
piano 202, 412, 526
piano a scomparti 225
piano della reception 439
piano di appoggio 396
piano di caricamento 435

piano di carico 396
piano di cottura 164, 179, 210
piano di cottura, bordo del 210
piano di lavoro 164, 224
piano di lavoro a morsa 224
piano elettronico 311
piano mansardato 182, 189
piano stradale 342
piano superiore 363
piano, indicatore del 287
piano, pedale del 304, 311
piano, primo 182, 189
pianoforte 295
pianoforte verticale 304
pianta 53, 183
pianta del tempio greco 279
pianta della cattedrale 285
pianta di città 25
pianta ornamentale 182
pianta rampicante 230
pianta, struttura di una 53
piantabulbi 231
piantatoio 231
piante aromatiche 142
pianterreno 182, 188
piantone del volante 350
pianura 24, 32
pianura abissale 33
piastra 178, 208, 269, 309
piastra costale 76
piastra d'appoggio 229
piastra di base 27, 227, 511, 533
piastra di cottura 179
piastra di protezione 525
piastra di registrazione 323
piastra di supporto 199
piastra elettrica 179, 210
piastra marginale 76
piastra negativa 359
piastra neurale 76
piastra per i pettorali 501
piastra portaforche 396
piastra positiva 359
piastra riscaldante 181
piastra sopracaudale 76
piastra stiracapelli 269
piastrella 12
piastrina 104, 186
piastrina, bracciale con 264
piastrone 76
piattaforma 219, 363, 516, 526
piattaforma continentale 33
piattaforma della vasca 195
piattaforma di 10 metri 518
piattaforma di 3 metri 518
piattaforma di 5 metri 518
piattaforma di 7,5 metri 518
piattaforma di carico 423
piattaforma di produzione 404
piattaforma girevole 176, 455
piattaforma, scala con 219
piatti 295, 309
piatti di cottura 179
piattino per pane e burro 166
piatto 179, 308, 422, 423, 531
piatto da portata 166
piatto del lanciatore 475
piatto della casa-base 475
piatto fondo 166
piatto frutta / insalata 166
piatto inferiore 308
piatto per il pesce 166
piatto piano 166
piatto portaceppi 357
piatto superiore 308
piatto, gancio del 422
piazzale 388
piazzola di partenza 504
picche 468
picchetto 528, 529
picchetto, asola per il 528, 529
picchio 80
picchio 29
piccione 81, 154
picco 29
piccola copritrice secondaria 78
piccola forca a mano 232
piccoli annunci 313
piccolo labbro 112, 113
piccolo rotondo 97
piccolo tegame 175
piccone 233
piccozza 454
picea 65
pick-up 303

ASTRONOMIA > 2-25;   TERRA > 26-71;   REGNO VEGETALE >72-89;   REGNO ANIMALE > 90-143;   ESSERE UMANO > 144-177;   GENERI ALIMENTARI E CUCINA > 178-241;   CASA > 242-29
FAI DA TE E GIARDINAGGIO > 296-333;   ABBIGLIAMENTO > 334-371;   ACCESSORI E ARTICOLI PERSONALI > 372-391;   ARTE E ARCHITETTURA > 392-465;   COMUNICAZIONI E BUROTICA > 466-53
TRASPORTI E VEICOLI > 536-643;   ENERGIA > 644-677;   SCIENZA > 678-705;   SOCIETÀ > 706-785;   SPORT E GIOCHI > 786-920

INDICE DEI NOMI ITALIANI

pick-up per alte frequenze 303
pick-up per basse frequenze 303
pick-up per medie frequenze 303
pick-up, selettore dei 303
pickup 347
pidocchio 69
piede 72, 73, 91, 92, 93, 94, 95, 202, 231, 247, 260, 302, 305, 536, 537
piede a voluta 200
piede d'albero 519
piede di appoggio 365
piede palmato 75
piede, dito del 92, 94
piede, foro del 305
piedino 153, 308
piedino di gomma 219
piedino regolabile 212, 213, 214
piedino snodato antiscivolo 219
piedritto 285
piega 246
piega a coltello 253
piega della columella 73
piega impunturata 253
piega invertita 253
piega piatta 246
piega sovrapposta 253
piegaciglia 266
pieghe, esempi di 253
pietra affilacoltelli 169
pietra bianca 470
pietra da curling 515
pietra da lastrico 230
pietra di Coyolxauhqui 283
pietra focaia 218
pietra nera 470
pietra sacrificale 283
pigiama 256, 261
pigiamino 261
pigiamino a due pezzi 260
pigiatore 170
pila 344
pila a carbone-zinco 417
pila alcalina a manganese-zinco 417
pilastro 27, 283, 284, 412
pilastro corinzio 281
pilastro del parapetto 191
pile 416
pile a secco 417
pilone 344, 375
pilone destro 482
pilone sinistro 482
piloriza 53
pilota 524
pilotaggio, cabina di 12, 385, 392, 395
pinguino 80
pinna 519
pinna anale 74
pinna caudale 74, 90
pinna dorsale 90
pinna pelvica 74
pinna pettorale 74, 90
pinna stabilizzatrice 386
pinnacolo 282, 284
pinnacolo, fiore del 283
pinnula 52
pino domestico 65
pino, aghi di 65
pinolo 65, 133
pinza 269, 357
pinza a becchi lunghi 217
pinza a giunto scorrevole 222
pinza a scatto 222
pinza del freno a disco 366
pinza multiuso 217
pinza per capelli 268
pinza regolabile 222
pinza universale 217
pinza, faretto a 206
pinze 222
pinzette 461
pinzette per sopracciglia 265
piogge acide 47, 48
pioggia 41
pioggia congelantesi 41
pioggia, irrigatore rotativo a 236
piolo 219, 479
piombo 538
pioppo 64
piramide 278, 429
piramide, ingresso alla 278
Pirenei 18
piscina 184, 386
piscina fuori terra 184
piscina interrata 184
piscina olimpionica 517
piselli 130

piselli mangiatutto 130
piselli secchi spaccati 130
pisello 60
pista 390, 472, 524
pista a difficoltà elevata 512
pista a difficoltà intermedia 512
pista da fondo 512
pista di accesso 388
pista di pattinaggio 509, 512
pista di rincorsa 473
pista di rullaggio 388
pista lunga 508
pista per esperti 512
pista per principianti 512
pista per sci alpino 512
pistacchio 133
piste da sci 512
pistillo 56
pistola 216, 456
pistola dello starter 472
pistola di erogazione 346
pistola per sverniciatura 219
pistola turapori 216
pistola, impugnatura a 218, 228
pistola, polverizzatore a 236
pistola, saldatore a 218
pistoncino 357
pistoncino del manuale 305
pistoncino del pedale 305
pistone 307, 360
pistone, disinnesto del 216
pistone, leva del 216
pitone 77
Pitot, tubo di 525
pittogrammi 330
più o meno 427
piumino da cipria 266
pivot 489
placca africana 27
placca antartica 27
placca antifrizione 511
placca caribica 27
placca del Pacifico 27
placca dell'interruttore 198
placca delle Cocos 27
placca di Nazca 27
placca di Scozia 27
placca euroasiatica 27
placca filippina 27
placca indoaustraliana 27
placca motrice 110
placca nordamericana 27
placca sudamericana 27
placcatore destro 484
placcatore sinistro 484
placche convergenti 27
placche divergenti 27
placche tettoniche 27
placche trasformi 27
placchetta a bilanciere 305
placchetta del portanasello 273
plafoniera 206
plancia 354
planisfero 14
plantare 97
plasma 104
plasmodesma 50
plastica, smistamento della 49
platea 293
playmaker 489
plesso brachiale 108
plesso dentale 101
plesso lombare 108
plesso sacrale 108
plettro 297
pleura parietale 105
pleura viscerale 105
plissé 253
Plutone 2, 3
pluviale 182
pneumatici, barriera di 524
pneumatici, esempi di 358
pneumatico 349, 358, 364, 371, 522, 525
pneumatico chiodato 358
pneumatico granturismo 358
pneumatico invernale 358
pneumatico per tutte le stagioni 358
pneumatico scolpito 369, 525
pneumatico sportivo 358
podio 283, 444
podio del direttore d'orchestra 295
poggiafreccia 535
poggiamano 227, 297, 332
poggiamano amovibile 330
poggiapiedi 205

poggiatesta 353
poker 468
poker, combinazioni del 468
polacchina 241
Polaroid 315
pole position 524
poliambulatorio 465
poligoni 429
Polinesia 453
polipodio comune 52
politica 448
politrico comune 51
polizia, agente di 456
polizia, macchina della 457
polizia, stazione di 433
pollaio 122
pollice 115, 243, 477
pollice opponibile 91
pollice, appoggio del 307
pollo 155
pollone 63
polmone destro 103, 105
polmone sinistro 103, 105
polmoni 105
polo 250, 255, 492
polo negativo 359, 416, 417
Polo Nord 21
polo nord 416
polo positivo 359, 416, 417
Polo Sud 15, 21
polo sud 416
polo, abito a 252
Polonia 450
polpa 57, 58, 59, 101
polpaccio 93, 95
polpastrello 114
polpo 72, 157
polpo, morfologia di un 72
polsiera 500, 527
polsino 245, 486, 492, 500
polso 86, 93, 95, 115
poltrona 200
poltrona da salotto 200
poltrona sacco 201
poltrona Wassily 200
poltroncina del paziente 464
poltroncina per bambini 205
poltrone 200
polvere di magnesia 497
polverizzatore 402
polverizzatore a pistola 236
pomello 202, 536, 537
pomello della sicura 352
pomello in gomma 536
pomelo 134
pomi 133
pomo 201, 477
pomo d'Adamo 92
pomodorini a grappolo 128
pomodoro 128
pomodoro, passata di 140
pomolo 229
pomolo del bastone 506
pompa 184, 212, 214, 370, 529
pompa della benzina 346
pompa di circolazione del fango 403
pompa per gli pneumatici 346
pompa, numero della 346
pompa, tubo della 346
pompe, locale delle 384
pompelmo 134
pompelmo, coltello da 169
pompetta ad aria 461
pompieri, carri dei 455
poncho 251
pont-l'évêque 151
ponte 25, 420
ponte a cantilever 344
ponte a travata 344
ponte di caricamento per containers 381
ponte di comando 382, 383, 386, 387
ponte di coperta 385
ponte di passeggiata 386
ponte di Varolio 109
ponte girevole 344
ponte levatoio 282
ponte luce 293
ponte pedonale 375
ponte per le autovetture 386
ponte ribaltabile a due ali 345
ponte ribaltabile a un'ala 345
ponte segnali 375
ponte sollevabile 345
ponte sospeso 344
ponte superiore 392
ponti fissi 344

ponti mobili 344
ponticello 273, 297, 301, 302, 303
ponticello degli acuti 304
ponticello dei bassi 304
ponticello, blocco del 303
pool 502
poppa 386, 519
porcellana 127
porcile 122
porcino 123
porcospino 82
poro 50, 60
poro sudoriparo 114
porro 124
Porro, prisma di 420
porta 202, 287, 361, 380, 439, 447, 479, 480, 482, 485, 507, 528, 529
porta a bande verticali 286
porta a due battenti 362
porta a fisarmonica 286
porta a infrarossi 336, 337
porta a libro 286
porta a un battente 286
porta a zanzariera 361
porta anticendio 286
porta automatica 390
porta basculante del garage 286
porta del bacino 381
porta del congelatore 211
porta del laboratorio a tenuta stagna 13
porta del modem interno 329, 336
porta del mouse 329
porta del patio 188
porta dell'elevatore 363
porta della tastiera 329
porta di entrata 362, 363
porta di prua 383
porta di rete 329
porta di rete telefonica 317
porta esterna 185
porta Ethernet 336
porta FireWire 336
porta giochi 329
porta girevole manuale 286
porta MIDI 329
porta parallela 329
porta per l'alimentatore 336
porta scorrevole 195, 286
porta scorrevole automatica 286
porta seriale 329
porta sezionale del garage 286
porta USB 329, 336
porta video 329, 336
porta, area di 507
porta-finestra 164, 189
portabagagli 361, 523
portabatteria, cassa 365
portabici 356
portabiti 277
portablocco 275, 340
portablocco, tavoletta 340
portabottiglia 371
portacalcolatrice 274
portacarte a soffietto 274
portaceppi 193
portachiavi 275
portacipria 266
portafermagli 341
portafiltro 181
portafoglio 275
portafoglio per carte di credito 274
portaindirizzo, etichetta 277
portalampada 199
portale 285
portalenti 272
portamartello 225
portamine 312
portamonete 275
portanasello 273
portanasello, placchetta del 273
portaobiettivi a revolver 421
portaoculare 8
portaoggetti 421
portaombrelli 273
portapacchi 369, 370
portapacchi posteriore 369
portapassaporto 275
portapenne 274
portarotolo 195
portasacca 505
portasapone 195
portasci 356
portasegni 274, 275
portata, piatto di 166
portatabulati 339

portatrucchi 277
portautensili 229
porte d'ingresso 294
porte di controllo 471
porte per le memory card 471
porte, esempi di 286
portello 213, 392
portello di apertura 7
portello, interruttore del 213
portellone della cupola 7
portellone dello scomparto di carico 13
portellone laterale 12
portellone prodiero di carico 386
porticato 447
portico 183, 285
portico coperto 447
portiera 349, 352
portiera, telaio interno della 352
portiere 479, 481, 506, 507
portiere, pattino del 507
portiere, stanzino del 439
porto 431
porto marittimo 381
porto, bicchiere da 165
Portogallo 449
porzionatore per gelato 173
posate 531
posate, cestello per le 214
posateria 167
posizionamento, braccio di 400
posizionamento, tubo di 400
posizione carpiata 518
posizione d'equilibrio 418
posizione della statua 279
posizione raggruppata 518
posizione tesa 518
posizione, luce di 376
posizione, tasto di 302, 303
posizioni dei giocatori 474, 481, 482, 489
posizioni di partenza 518
posta elettronica 335
posta elettronica, software di 334
postazione degli infermieri (pronto soccorso ambulatoriale) 463
postazione degli infermieri (pronto soccorso principale) 462
postazione dell'agente di sicurezza 463
posti a sedere 205
posti, divano a due 200
postierla 282
postino, borsa da 276
posto a sedere 294
potenza elettrica, unità di misura della 426
potenziale elettrico, unità di misura della differenza di 426
pouf 201
pozzetto 520
pozzetto d'ispezione 434
pozzo 31
pozzo di iniezione 402
pozzo di produzione 402
pozzo off-shore 404
prateria 24, 44
prato 122, 183, 230
prato, cura del 237
precipitazione 45
precipitazione, area di 39
precipitazioni 41
precipitazioni invernali 41
precipitazioni, forti 43
prelievi, sala dei 465
premascellare 74
premolari 101
prendisole 252
preparazione chirurgica, stanza per la 464
prepuzio 111
presa a croce 499
presa a terra 499
presa d'acqua 407
presa d'aria 362, 365, 367, 383, 395, 523
presa d'aria del motore 362
presa d'aria del ventilatore di sostentamento 383
presa d'aria laterale 361
presa d'aria per il raffreddamento del motore 525
presa d'aria posteriore 270
presa d'aria sul tetto 361
presa d'uscita 303
presa dell'idrante 455
presa dell'ossigeno 464
presa di alimentazione 326, 329

presa di corrente 217, 361
presa di corrente commutata 322
presa di corrente temporizzata 210
presa di ricarica 271
presa europea 198
presa per cuffia 310, 311, 322, 326
presa per cuffie 329
presa per il comando a distanza 314, 315
presa per ricarica 208
presa per spina americana 198
presa, alveolo della 198
presa, tester di 217
presbiterio, lampada del 446
prese digitali 315
prese video 315
prese, esempi di 499
preside, ufficio del 445
presidente di giuria 509
presidente di giuria, assistente del 509
pressacaffè 181
pressatore 177, 180
pressione a livello del mare 39
pressione alta, centro di 39
pressione atmosferica 39
pressione bassa, centro di 39
pressione dei freni, modulatore della 357
pressione sanguigna, monitor della 461
pressione, bottone a 249
pressione, pentola a 174
pressione, regolatore della 272
pressione, regolatore di 174
pressione, unità di misura della 426
pressione, variazione di 39
prevenzione degli incendi 454
prevenzione del crimine 456
previsioni meteorologiche 38
prezzemolo 142
prezzo per litro/gallone 346
prezzo unitario 423
prigione 469
prima base 474
prima base (posizione) 474
prima galleria 293
prima linea 482
prima maglia 476
prima pagina 313
prima pagina, foto in 313
prima pinna dorsale 74
primati 91
primati, esempi di 91
primavera 38
primavera, equinozio di 38
prime foglie 53
primi violini 295
primo 428
primo arbitro 485, 487
primo assistente cameraman 290
primo aumento di tensione 413
primo giocatore al lancio 515
primo molare 101
primo piano 182, 189
primo premolare 101
primo quarto 5
primo spazio 489
princesse 252
princesse, cucitura a 258
Principato di Monaco 450
prisma astronomico 8
prisma di Porro 420
proboscide 67
processo mastoideo 100
processo spinoso 110
processo stiloideo 100
processo trasverso 110
procione 88
prodotti caseari 150
prodotti cerealicoli 144
prodotti di fissione 415
prodotti di raffinazione 405
prodotti in offerta 121
prodotti per confezionamento 120
prodotti petrolchimici 405
prodotto, codice del 423
produttore 291
produzione di calore 408
produzione di elettricità 412
produzione di elettricità da alternatore 408
produzione di elettricità da energia eolica
    413
produzione di elettricità da energia
    geotermica 402
produzione di elettricità da energia
    nucleare 408
produzione di elettricità da energia termica
    402

produzione di ossigeno 54
produzione, designer di 290
produzione, segretaria di 291
profilo del suolo 54
profilo dell'atmosfera terrestre 37
profilo dello spacco 245
profilo sbieco 260
profondità del fuoco 27
profondità di campo, pulsante di controllo
    della 314
profondità, regolatore di 229
profumeria 436
profumeria e igiene personale 121
profumo 267
programma, selettore di 310
programmatore 212, 213, 214
programmazione, tasti di 319
programmi del computer 457
programmi televisivi 313
proiettore 290, 294, 348, 364, 366, 368,
    523
proiettore abbagliante e anabbagliante
    352
proiettore orientabile 455
proiettori 293
proiettori, comando dei 354
proiezione cilindrica 22
proiezione conica 22
proiezione di spalla a braccio 499
proiezione interrotta 22
proiezione piana 22
proiezione, cabina di 294
proiezione, sala di 294
proiezione, schermo di 294
proiezioni cartografiche 22
prolunga 202
prolunga, tubo rigido di 209
promontorio 35
pronao 279
pronatore rotondo 96
pronto intervento, mezzo di 345
pronto soccorso 462, 512
pronto soccorso, cassetta di 457, 461
pronto soccorso, manuale di 461
pronto soccorso, stazione di 345
pronto soccorso, strumenti per il 460
propagazione 418
proprietà, confine di 182
propulsione, modulo di 316
propulsore 10
propulsore di prua 387
propulsori per il controllo direzionale 12
proscenio 292
prosciutto 156
prosciutto affumicato 153
prosciutto cotto 156
prosciutto, coltello da 169
prospetto 182
prospezione terrestre 403
prostata 111
proteggicavo 217
protezione antisfregamento 525
protezione antiurto 209
protezione del dente 398
protezione del mento 367
protezione delle chiavi 306
protezione per gli occhi 458
protezione per i piedi 459
protezione per l'avambraccio 486
protezione per la testa 458
protezione per le orecchie 458
protezione per le vie respiratorie 459
protezione posteriore 7
protezione, gabbia di 217
protezione, occhiali di 218
protezione, piastra di 525
protezione, schermo di 474
protocollo di comunicazione 334
protone 414
protoneurone 110
protuberanza 4
prova in corso, tabellone della 497
prova, pulsante di 454
provacircuiti, lampada 217
provincia 23
prua 384, 387, 519, 520
prua, castello di 387
prua, elica di 384
prua, porta di 383
prua, propulsore di 387
prugna 132
prugne, salsa di 141
pseudopodio 66
pubblico 440
pubblico, ingresso del 278
pube 92, 94

pugilato 498
pugile 498
pulce 69
puleggia 219, 360, 535
puleggia di tensione del regolatore 287
pulisci unghie 265
pulitura, accessori di 209
pullman 362
pulpito 446, 447
pulsante 214, 312
pulsante del menu 315
pulsante del registratore vocale 337
pulsante del touch pad 336
pulsante del vaporizzatore 208
pulsante di accensione 213, 328
pulsante di aggancio 227
pulsante di alimentazione 318, 337
pulsante di alimentazione della carta 333
pulsante di annullamento 333
pulsante di apertura del display 336
pulsante di arresto 229, 235, 424
pulsante di azzeramento 424
pulsante di bloccaggio 208
pulsante di cancellazione 315
pulsante di chiamata 287
pulsante di chiamata pedonale 434
pulsante di compensazione
    dell'esposizione 314
pulsante di controllo 332
pulsante di controllo della profondità di
    campo 314
pulsante di controluce 337
pulsante di espulsione 315, 471
pulsante di espulsione del CD 329
pulsante di espulsione del DVD-ROM 329
pulsante di espulsione del floppy disk 329
pulsante di partenza 424
pulsante di prova 454
pulsante di reset 329, 471
pulsante di riavvolgimento della pellicola
    314
pulsante di sblocco dell'obiettivo 314
pulsante di scatto 314
pulsante di uscita 327
pulsante di visualizzazione delle immagini
    315
pulsante di visualizzazione delle
    impostazioni 315
pulsante per il salto di immagini 315
pulsanti di avvio delle applicazioni 337
pulsanti di azione 471
pulsanti direzionali 471
pulsanti programmabili 332
puma 88
Pumpernickel russo 145
punching ball 498
pungiglione 68
punta 125, 167, 169, 208, 216, 218,
    220, 221, 226, 227, 229, 246, 301,
    312, 460, 469, 471, 510, 514, 526,
    534, 536, 538
punta a croce 221
punta a testa quadra 221
punta da muro 228
punta del colletto 245
punta del naso 117
punta dello sci 514
punta dentellata 509
punta di centratura 228
punta di diamante 202
punta elicoidale 228
punta fredda 269
punta Luer-Lock 460
punta per piastra 304
punta piana 221
punta, lunghezza della 538
puntale 221, 240, 262, 466, 511
puntale di protezione 459
puntale rinforzato 459
puntalino 536, 537
punte, tipi di 221
punteggio 497
punterie, coperchio delle 350, 360
punteruolo 531
punti 492
punti metallici 341
puntine da disegno 341
puntine, distanza tra le 359
punto 468
punto coronato 299
punto d'appoggio 70
punto di alimentazione 198
punto di allacciamento 198
punto di handicap 470
punto di incocco 535
punto di raggio 506

punto di inserimento dei documenti da
    trasmettere 328
punto di interesse 25
punto di mura 519
punto di osservazione 7
puntone 412
pupilla 87, 119
pupilla verticale 76
putter 505

Qatar 452
qibla, parete della 447
quadrante 422, 424, 428
quadrante a cristalli liquidi 424
quadrante graduato 533
quadrato 429, 498
quadri 468
quadricipiti, rullo per i 501
quadrilatero 429
quadripode 456
quadro degli strumenti di controllo 355
quadro delle temperature 208
quadro di comando 178, 179, 210, 212,
    213, 214
quadro di distribuzione 198
quaglia 81, 154
quaglia, uovo di 155
quantità di sostanza, unità di misura della
    426
quarantottore 277
quark d 414
quark u 414
quarta 298
quarterback 485
quartetto 300
quartiere 25, 240, 262
quartiere degli affari 430, 432
quartiere fieristico 430
quartiere residenziale 431
quartiere, parte anteriore del 240, 262
quattro quarti, tempo di 298
quercia 64
quinoa 143
quinta 298
quinte 292
quintetto 300

Qatar 452

rabarbaro 125
rabbino, seggio di 447
raccattapalle 490
racchetta 492, 493, 494, 510, 514
racchetta, giochi con la 493
raccoglierba 237
raccogligocce, bacinella 210
raccoglipolvere 229
raccoglitore a molla 339
raccoglitore ad anelli 339
raccolta del vetro, campana per la 49
raccolta della carta, campana per la 49
raccolta differenziata 49
raccolta differenziata, contenitori per la 49
raccolta, vaschetta di 181
raccordo 312, 455
raccordo a losanga 342
raccordo a quadrifoglio 342, 343
raccordo a rotatoria 342
raccordo a T 193
raccordo a tromba 342
raccordo a Y 460
raccordo, esempi di 342
racemo 57, 200
rachide 62
raclette 179
raclette, griglia per 179
radar 382, 383, 386, 387
radar meteorologico 38, 392
radar, albero del 384
radar, display dei 457
raddrizzatori di immagine 420
radiatore 13, 350, 358
radiatore, griglia del 364
radiatore, manicotto inferiore del 358
radiatori 11
radiazione 415
radiazione infrarossa 46, 418
radiazione solare 45, 46, 410, 411
radiazione solare assorbita 46
radiazione solare riflessa 46
radiazione ultravioletta 418
radicchio 126
radice 54, 101, 118, 167

radice a fittone 63
radice anteriore 110
radice del naso 117
radice dell'elice 115
radice dell'unghia 114
radice filettata 359
radice laterale 53
radice motoria 109, 110
radice posteriore 110
radice principale 53
radice quadrata di 427
radice secondaria 53
radice sensoriale 109, 110
radice superficiale 63
radichetta 53, 63
radici avventizie 52
radio 98, 457
radio portatile 325
radio, antenna 384, 525
radioattività, unità di misura della 426
radioregistratore con compact disc 326
radiosveglia 325
radiotelefono portatile 456
rafano giapponese 129
raffinazione, prodotti di 405
raffineria 404, 431
raffreddamento 405
raffreddamento del motore, presa d'aria
    per il 525
raffreddamento, cilindro di 420
raganella 75
raggi gamma 418
raggi X 418
raggio 371, 428
raggio laser 420
raggio luminoso 419
raggio midollare 63
raggio molle 74
raggio spinoso 74
ragnatela 70
ragnatela, centro della 70
ragno 70
ragno acquatico 70
ragno, morfologia di un 70
ragno-granchio 70
ralla di rotazione 400, 401
rallentatore, riproduzione al 319
rally, auto da 524
rambutan 137
rami 63
ramificazione collaterale 110
ramo 62, 63, 65, 416
ramo comunicante 110
ramo con frutti 62
ramo primario 63
ramo secondario 63
ramoscello 53
rampa 279, 341, 343, 344, 526
rampa ad anello 343
rampa di accesso 386
rampa di scale 191
rampicante, pianta 230
rampone 454
rana 75, 517
rana comune 75
rana dei boschi 75
rana leopardo 75
rana, morfologia di una 75
randa 520
Ranvier, nodo di 110
rapa 129
ras el hanout 139
rasatura 271
raschietto 219
raschietto metallico 514
rasoio a mano libera 271
rasoio di sicurezza 271
rasoio elettrico 271
rasoio sfoltitore 269
rasoio usa e getta 271
rastrello 233
rastrello scopa 237
ratto 82
ratto, morfologia di un 82
ravanello 129
ravanello nero 129
ravioli 146
razza 158
razze canine 86
razze di gatti 87
razzo a propellente solido 12
razzo illuminante 457
re 298, 468, 470
re, camera del 278
re, sala del 470
Rea 3

ASTRONOMIA > 2-25; TERRA > 26-71; REGNO VEGETALE > 72-89; REGNO ANIMALE > 90-143; ESSERE UMANO > 144-177; GENERI ALIMENTARI E CUCINA > 178-241; CASA > 242-295;
FAI DA TE E GIARDINAGGIO > 296-333; ABBIGLIAMENTO > 334-371; ACCESSORI E ARTICOLI PERSONALI > 372-391; ARTE E ARCHITETTURA > 392-465; COMUNICAZIONI E BUROTICA > 466-535;
TRASPORTI E VEICOLI > 536-643; ENERGIA > 644-677; SCIENZA > 678-705; SOCIETÀ > 706-785; SPORT E GIOCHI > 786-920.

reattore 408
reattore nucleare 409
reattore, recipiente del 409
reazione a catena 415
rebbio 167
recensione gastronomica 313
reception 439
reception, banco della 442
reception, piano della 439
recettore sensoriale 110
recettori gustativi 118
recinto 122
recinzione 122, 475
recipiente del reattore 409
recipiente graduato 171
redine 78
redingote 251
referenti tecnici 509
refill 312
reforming catalitico, impianto di 405
refrattario, mattone 192
refrigerante 408
refrigerazione, cestello di 180
reggicalze 259
reggicoperchio 274, 277
reggilibri 341
reggiseno 259
reggiseno a balconcino 259
reggiseno a bustino 259
reggiseno décolleté 259
reggiseno, coppa del 259
reggiseno, sottoveste con 258
regia, cabina di 293
regina 470
Regina Maud, Terra della 15
regina, camera della 278
regina, lato della 470
regione auricolare 78
regione malare 78
regione pilifera 63
regista 291
regista, monitor di controllo del 290
regista, sedia da 200
regista, sedia del 291
registratore di cassa 121
registratore di compact disc 325
registratore di compact disc riscrivibili 333
registratore DVD 333
registratore, tasto di selezione del 322
registrazione notturna, selettore di 320
registrazione sismografica 403
registrazione, banco di 390
registrazione, tasto di 319, 323
registrazione, tasto di avvio/arresto 320
registro degli acuti 296
registro dei bassi 296
registro, tasto di 305
regno animale 66
Regno Unito di Gran Bretagna e Irlanda del Nord 449
regno vegetale 50
regolatore 466
regolatore degli alti 322
regolatore dei bassi 322
regolatore dei toni alti 325
regolatore dei toni bassi 325
regolatore del display 327
regolatore del getto di vapore 208
regolatore del tirante 528
regolatore del volume 328
regolatore del volume di ricezione 327
regolatore dell'altezza 228
regolatore dell'inclinazione della lama 227
regolatore della pressione 272
regolatore della velocità 237
regolatore delle testine 271
regolatore dello sforzo 501
regolatore di centratura 329
regolatore di contrasto 329
regolatore di corrente 199
regolatore di luminosità 329, 529
regolatore di pressione 174
regolatore di profondità 229
regolatore di velocità 176, 287
regolatore di volume 322
regolatore staccabile 179
regolatore, puleggia di tensione del 287
regolazione dei toni 303
regolazione dei toni alti 303
regolazione dei toni bassi 303
regolazione del diaframma 421
regolazione del livello sonoro delle comunicazioni 10
regolazione del sistema di sopravvivenza 10
regolazione del vapore 181

regolazione del volume 303
regolazione dell'altezza, manopola di 209
regolazione dell'angolo di elevazione 420
regolazione della frizione 537
regolazione della linea di mira 420
regolazione della pressione dell'ossigeno 10
regolazione della temperatura corporea 10
regolazione dello specchietto retrovisore esterno 352
regolazione in altezza del condensatore 421
regolazione laterale, leva di 229
regolazione micrometrica dell'altezza 8, 9
regolazione micrometrica dell'asse orizzontale 8, 9
regolazione orizzontale 329
regolazione verticale 329
regolazione, anello di 236
regolazione, dispositivo di 511
regolazione, indicatore della 511
regolazione, vite di 222, 229
religione 446
remigante primaria 78
remigante secondaria 78
remigante terziaria 78
remo 501
rene 73, 103
rene destro 107
rene sinistro 107
reniforme 55
renna 84
reostato 198
replo 60
reptazione 31
Repubblica Ceca 450
Repubblica Centrafricana 451
Repubblica del Mali 451
Repubblica Democratica del Congo 451
Repubblica Democratica Popolare di Corea 453
Repubblica di Corea 453
Repubblica di San Marino 450
Repubblica Dominicana 449
Repubblica Sudafricana 452
repulsione 416
reset, tasto di 328
residuo lungo 405
resistenza elettrica, unità di misura della 426
resistenza idraulica 501
resistenza 417
respingente 375
respiratorio, apparato 105
rete 487, 491, 493, 495
rete a molle 204
rete di distribuzione dell'acqua calda 194
rete di distribuzione dell'acqua fredda 194
rete di oleodotti 404
rete di scarico 194
rete di trasmissione, integrazione di energia alla 413
rete di ventilazione 194
rete per alimenti 162
rete stabilizzante 199
rete telefonica 317
rete trasmittente nazionale 316
rete trasmittente privata 316
rete, supporto della 493
reticolato geografico 22
reticolo 420
reticolo endoplasmatico 50, 66
retina 119, 205, 419, 489
retroescavatore 399
retroescavatore, comandi del 399
rettangolare 530
rettangolo 429
rettangolo destro di servizio 491
rettangolo di battuta 502
rettangolo sinistro di servizio 491
rettili 76
rettili, esempi di 77
retto 106, 111, 112
retto dell'addome 96
retto della coscia 96
revers 244, 248
revers a punta 244
revolver, caricatore 421
rialzo continentale 33
rianimazione, sala di 462
riavvolgimento, tasto di 319, 323, 326, 328
ribalta 202, 203
ribes 132
ribes nero 132
ribosoma 50, 66

ricarica, presa di 271
ricarica, presa per 208
riccio 301
ricerca 335
ricerca rapida, tasti di 323
ricetrasmettitore radar 457
ricettacolo 51, 56, 59
ricevimento merci 391
ricevitore 321, 327, 474, 475, 476, 490, 495
ricevitore auricolare 324
ricevitore esterno 485
ricevuta della transazione 443
ricezione privata diretta 316
richiamo 535
riciclaggio 49
riciclaggio del vetro, bidone carrellato per il 49
riciclaggio dell'alluminio, bidone carrellato per il 49
riciclaggio della carta, bidone carrellato per il 49
riciclaggio, contenitore per il 49
ricognizione meteorologica, aereo da 38
ricognizione meteorologica, boa di 38
ricognizione meteorologica, nave da 38
ricotta 150
riduttore 270
riempimento, tubo di 196
rifiuti domestici 47, 48
rifiuti industriali 47, 48
rifiuti non riciclabili 49
rifiuti nucleari 48
rifiuti, bidone dei 215
rifiuti, smistamento selettivo dei 49
rifiuti, strati di 47
riflessione parziale, specchio a 420
riflessione totale, specchio a 420
riflessione, cilindro di 420
riflettore 217
riflettori solari 316
rifornimento di contanti 443
rifugio 345
rifugio in vetta 512
rifugio principale 512
rigatoni 146
righello 425, 531
righello, scala graduata del 425
rigonfiamento 6
rilascio di energia 415
rilegatura con spirale 340
rilevatore di fumo 454
rilevatore di movimento 286
rimessa 122, 182, 230
rimorchi 361
rimorchi, carro pianale per il trasporto di 377
rimorchiatore 384
rimorchio 380
rimorchio, dispositivo di 364
rinario 87
rincorsa, pedane di 496
rinforzo a crociera 467
rinforzo del calcagno 262
rinforzo della curva 306
rinforzo esterno del calcagno 240
rinforzo interno del calcagno 240
rinforzo per serratura 185
rinforzo posteriore 509
rinforzo, bandella di 277
rinfuse, deposito delle 381
ringhiera 189
rinoceronte 85
Rio delle Amazzoni 17
ripetitore 317
ripetizione, tasti di 323
ripiani, griglia dei 211
ripiano 203, 211, 219
riposiglio per il materiale pulito 462
riposiglio per il materiale sporco 462
riposiglio per l'attrezzatura 444
ripresa 248
riprese, set delle 290
riproduttore a cassette 326
riproduttore a cassette, tasti di 326
riproduttori portatili 325
riproduzione al rallentatore 319
riproduzione, tasto di 319, 323, 326
riproduzione/pausa, tasto di 323
riquadro 274
risaia 47
riscaldamento 192
riscaldamento a legna 192
riscaldamento, comando del 354
riscaldamento, condotto di 213
riscaldamento, griglia del 380

riso 61, 143, 147
riso basmati 147
riso bianco 147
riso integrale 147
riso nero selvatico 143
riso parboiled 147
riso, aceto di 141
riso, gallette di 147
riso, spaghetti di 147
riso, vermicelli di 147
riso: pannocchia 61
risonanza, cassa di 297, 302
risonatore 309, 324
risorgiva 31
risparmio di energia, lampadina a 199
ristorante 386, 432, 435, 436, 438
ristorante, vagone 376
ristoro per sciatori 512
risultati, tabella dei 518
risvolto 246
ritmo, selettore del 311
ritornata 518
ritornello 298
rivestimenti in tessuto per pavimento 190
rivestimento 187, 417, 493
rivestimento antiriflettente 410
rivestimento del motore 235
rivestimento esterno 477
rivestimento fluorescente 199
rivetto 169, 222
rivista 313
rizoide 51
rizoma 52
robe-manteau 252
robot da cucina 177
rocce ignee 26
rocce intrusive 26
rocce metamorfiche 26
rocce sedimentarie 26
roccia impermeabile 403
roccia in posto 54
roditore 82
roditori 82
roditori, esempi di 82
rogone 154
rollio 395
Romania 450
romano 422
rombo 161, 429
rompigetto, vite 236
rompighiaccio 384
roncola 234
rondella 417
rondella di tenuta 359
rondine 80
rondone 80
roquefort 151
rosa 56, 302
rosa dei venti 23, 533
rosetta 186
rosetta a dentatura esterna 222
rosetta a dentatura interna 222
rosetta elastica 222
rosetta piatta 222
rosette 222
rosmarino 142
rosone 285
rospo comune 75
Ross, Banchisa di 15
rossetto 266
rosso 418, 469
Rosso, Mar 14, 19, 20
rostro 74
rotaia del carrello di scotta 520, 521
rotaia di scorrimento 353, 397
rotatoria 25
rotazione, sistema a 403
rotella 510, 527
rotella centrale di messa a fuoco 420
rotella del volume 329
rotella di comando 337
rotella di intonazione 310
rotella di modulazione 310
rotella di regolazione 325
rotella di selezione degli effetti speciali 320
rotella orientabile 308
rotella regolatrice vicino/lontano 320
rotella tagliapasta 172
rotellina di scorrimento 332
rotoli della Torah 447
rotolo di benda garzata 461
rotonda 25
rotore 412, 537
rotore anticoppia 395
rotore, mozzo del 395

rotore, pala del 395
rotore, pilone del 395
rotore, testa del 395
rotula 98
rough 504
roulotte 361
router 334
rovesciata 518
rovesciata all'indietro 499
Ruanda 451
rubinetto 195
rubinetto di arresto 197
rubinetto di regolazione della pressione 454
rubinetto generale 194
rubino pulsato, laser a 420
rubino, cilindro di 420
rubrica telefonica 327, 338
ruches 260
ruches, ghettina con 260
rucola 127
Ruffini, corpuscolo di 114
rugby 482
rugiada 41
rugiada, temperatura di 39
rullaggio, linea di 389
rullaggio, pista di 388
rulli dei cingoli, telaio dei 398
rullini tenditori 372
rullino 223, 332
rullo 219, 268, 269
rullo per i bicipiti femorali 501
rullo per i quadricipiti 501
rullo, cuscino a 204
rullo, supporto del 219
runner 469
ruota 231, 277, 364, 522, 525, 526, 527
ruota anteriore 401
ruota della moltiplica 522
ruota dentata A 372
ruota dentata B 372
ruota dentata motrice 523
ruota di guida 380
ruota di scorta 361
ruota di spinta 467
ruota folle 523
ruota girevole 205
ruota libera 372
ruota motrice 398
ruota orientabile 209
ruota piena o gonfiabile 467
ruota pivotante 467
ruota portante 380
ruota tendicingolo 398
ruote motrici 401
rupia 440
ruscello 32
ruspa 400

S

sabbiera 377
sacca 505
sacca a tracolla 276
sacca da marinaio 276
saccatura 39
sacchetti 121
sacchetto 162
sacchetto per freezer 162
sacchetto, scomparto del 209
sacchi a pelo, esempi di 530
sacco 296, 477, 498
sacco, poltrona 201
sacrestia 446
sacro 98, 99
Sahara, Deserto del 20
sahariana 255
Saint Kitts e Nevis 449
Saint Lucia 449
Saint Vincent e Grenadine 449
sala 293, 386
sala d'attesa 463
sala d'attesa dei familiari 462
sala d'attesa del centro prelievi 465
sala d'attesa principale 465
sala d'attesa secondaria 465
sala da bagno 464
sala da ballo 387
sala da pranzo 188, 386, 438, 439
sala degli infermieri 465
sala dei prelievi 465
sala del personale 443
sala della preghiera 447
sala di controllo 406
sala di imbarco 391
sala di ingresso 188, 447

ASTRONOMIA > 2-25; TERRA > 26-71; REGNO VEGETALE >72-89; REGNO ANIMALE > 90-143; ESSERE UMANO > 144-177; GENERI ALIMENTARI E CUCINA > 178-241; CASA > 242-295;
FAI DA TE E GIARDINAGGIO > 296-333; ABBIGLIAMENTO > 334-371; ACCESSORI E ARTICOLI PERSONALI > 372-391; ARTE E ARCHITETTURA > 392-465; COMUNICAZIONI E BUROTICA > 466-535;
TRASPORTI E VEICOLI > 536-643; ENERGIA > 644-677; SCIENZA > 678-705; SOCIETÀ > 706-785; SPORT E GIOCHI > 786-920

629

INDICE DEI NOMI ITALIANI

sala di proiezione 294
sala di rianimazione 462
sala di servizio 447
sala di sterilizzazione 465
sala gessi 463
sala macchine 384, 386, 406, 407
sala nautica 382
sala operatoria 464, 465
sala passeggeri 383, 386, 387
sala per conferenze 442
sala per i cocktail 439
sala per operazioni di chirurgia minore
    462
sala per riunioni 439, 442, 445
salamandra 75
salame di Genova 156
salame di Tolosa 156
salame tedesco 156
salchow 509
saldatore a pistola 218
saldatore elettrico 218
saldatura, filo per 218
sale di colloquio 440
sale fino 141
sale grosso 141
sale marino 141
salice piangente 64
saliera 166
salita, corridoio di 278
salmerino di fontana 161
salmone del Pacifico 161
salmone dell'Atlantico 161
salmone rosso 161
salone 386, 390
salopette 254, 260
salopette a tutina 260
salopette con bretelle incrociate 261
salotto 188, 439
salotto, poltrona da 200
salsa di prugne 141
salsa di soia 140
salsa hoisin 140
salsa tabasco 140
salsa Worcestershire 140
salsefica 129
salsiccia alle cipolle 156
salsiccia di Francoforte 156
salsiccia di trippa 156
salsiccia kielbasa 156
salsiccia piccante 156
salsiera 166
saltatore 513
salti, esempi di 509
salto con gli sci 513
salto con l'asta 472
salto in alto 473
salto in lungo 472
salto triplo 472
salute 460
salvagente 387, 457
salvatacchi 240
salvataggio, scialuppa di 382, 386
salvataggio, zattera di 383
salvia 142
sambal oelek 141
Samoa 453
San Lorenzo, Fiume 16
San Marino, Repubblica di 450
sanbernardo 86
sandalo 241, 242
sandalo indiano 242
sangue deossigenato 104
sangue ossigenato 104
sangue, circolazione del 102
sangue, composizione del 104
sanguinaccio 156
santoreggia 142
São Tomé e Príncipe 451
sapone da barba, tazza per 271
saponetta 267
sapotiglia 137
saracco 226
sarchiello 233
sarchiello a mano 232
sarchio 233
sardina 159
sarong 253
sartia 520
sartorio 96
sassofono 306
satellite 316
satellite artificiale 37
satellite meteorologico 38
satellite per le telecomunicazioni 335
satelliti 2
satelliti per telecomunicazioni 316

Saturno 2, 3
savana 40, 44
saxhorn 307
sbadacchio 187
sbarra 205, 501
sbarra orizzontale 496, 497
sbarra pieghevole 500
sbuccialimoni 169
sbucciatore 169
scacchi 470
scacchi, notazione degli 470
scacchiera 470
scacciapensieri 297
scadenza, data di 441
scaffale 121
scafo 511, 520, 523
scaglia 74
scala 188, 225, 288, 293, 294, 298,
    361, 412, 468
scala a libretto 219
scala aerea 455
scala Celsius 424
scala con piattaforma 219
scala delle altitudini 37
scala delle temperature 37
scala di accesso al piano mansardato 189
scala estensibile 219
scala esterna 183
scala Fahrenheit 424
scala graduata 226, 422, 423, 424, 425,
    460, 533
scala graduata del nonio 425
scala graduata del righello 425
scala mobile 294, 378, 435
scala reale 468
scala reale massima 468
scala sgabello 219
scaldabagno 194
scaldamuscoli 263
scale 191, 219, 283, 345, 378, 404,
    439
scale a libretto 219
scale, rampa di 191
scale, tromba delle 189
scaletta 184, 401, 498
scaletta laterale 377
scalfo 247
scalinata 283
scalini 184
scalino d'invito 191
scalo ferroviario 381
scalo merci 375, 430
scalogno 124
scalpello 403
scalpello da falegname 229
scalpello dello scarificatore 398
scambio 375
scampo 158
scanalatura 169, 228, 359, 510
scanner ottico 121
scapo 114
scapola 93, 95, 98, 99
scapola, spina della 99
scapolare 78
scappamento 351
scappamento, tubo di 367, 368, 369
scaricatore 184
scarichi, molla sturatrice per 216
scarico 184, 194
scarico, camera di 278
scarico, colonna principale di 194
scarico, rete di 194
scarico, tappo di 194
scarico, tubo di 194, 196, 212, 395, 398,
    401
scarificatore 398
scarificatore, cilindro dello 398
scarificatore, dente dello 398
scarificatore, scalpello dello 398
scarola 126
scarpa 473, 478, 480, 483, 488, 500,
    509, 522, 524, 527
scarpa a collo alto 240
scarpa chanel 241
scarpa con cinturino 241
scarpa con cinturino a T 241
scarpa con tacchetti 476, 486
scarpa da corsa 262
scarpa da tennis 242, 492
scarpa décolleté 241
scarpa oxford 240
scarpa stringata 240
scarpa, parti di una 240
scarpata 5, 182, 342
scarpata continentale 33

scarpe 240, 505
scarpe da donna 241
scarpe da uomo 240
scarpe unisex 242
scarpe, negozio di 437
scarpetta interna 511, 527
scarpetta, bordo della 511
scarponcino 240
scarponcino di sicurezza 459
scarpone 240, 510, 511, 513, 514
scarpone morbido 513
scarpone rigido 513
scassa di deriva 519
scatola a doppia linea di connessione 417
scatola di incasso 198
scatola degli ingranaggi del moltiplicatore
    413
scatola del cambio 350
scatola della frizione 368
scatola di servizio 198
scatola per archivio 340
scatola per formaggio 163
scatola portaesche 538
scatola portaprisma 421
scatolame 121
scatto, ancora a 221
scatto, chiavistello a 186
scatto, chiavistello senza 186
scatto, chiusura a 178, 214
scatto, pulsante di 314
scavamelone 173
scavo, braccio di 400
scena 278
scena, fotografo di 291
scheda del circuito stampato 417
scheda di memoria 315
scheda PC, fessura per la 336
schedario rotativo 338
schedario, divisori alfabetici per 340
scheletro 98
schema della circolazione 103
schermo 7, 318, 439, 479
schermo del computer 10
schermo di proiezione 294
schermo di protezione 474
schiaccianoci 170
schiacciapatate 173
schiacciata 491
schiena 93, 95
schienale 201, 205, 353, 369, 467, 523
schienale reclinabile 460
schienale, manopola di regolazione dello
    353
schiniere 476
schiuma 33
schiuma da barba 271
schiumaiola 173
schizzetto 460
schnauzer 86
Schwann, guaina di 110
sci 510, 523
sci alpino 510
sci alpino, pista per 512
sci alpino, snowboard per 513
sci da discesa libera 510
sci da fondo 514
sci da salto 513
sci da slalom 510
sci da slalom gigante 510
sci da supergigante 510
sci, esempi di 510
sci, piste da 512
sci, scuola di 512
sci, tuta da 261
scia luminosa del cratere 5
scia, punta dello 514
sciacquone 195
sciacquone, levetta dello 196
scialuppa di salvataggio 382, 386
sciatore 510
scienza 414
scienze, aula di 444
scimpanzé 91
sciolina 514
sciolinatura, accessori per la 514
sciovia 512
sciovia, arrivo della 512
sciroppo d'acero 149
sciroppo di mais 149
scissione del nucleo 415
scissura obliqua 105
scivolamento, fase di 514
scivolo della banchina 381
scivolo dello sfioratore 406
scivolo per tronchi d'albero 406
sclera 119

scocca 237, 361
scodella 166
scoglio 35
scoiattolo 82
scolainsalata, centrifuga 171
scolare 171
scollo 247
scollo a V 244, 250
scolpitura del battistrada 358
scompartimento bagagli 376
scomparto 203
scomparto degli accessori 209
scomparto del congelatore 211
scomparto del frigorifero 211
scomparto del sacchetto 209
scomparto della controporta 211
scomparto della strumentazione 376
scomparto di carico 12
scomparto di carico, portellone dello 13
scomparto per banconote 274
scomparto per carte di credito 274
scomparto per i guanti 464
scomparto per i latticini 211
scomparto per il burro 211
scomparto per le uova 211
scomparto portadocumenti 274
scontrino 423
scooter 369
scopa 193, 215
scopa a frangia 215
scopa da curling 515
scopa, rastrello 237
scorpione 70
scorrimento 331
scorrimento, manopola di 327
scorza 58
scorzetta 58
scorzonera 129
scossalina 193
scotta del fiocco 520
scotta della randa 520
scotta, rotaia del carrello di 520, 521
Scozia, placca di 27
scrivania 439
scrivania dei cancellieri 440
scroto 92, 111
scudo di protezione della mano 235
scudo termico 12
scuola 444
scuola di sci 512
scuolabus 362
scutello 73
secchiello con cordoncino 275
secchiello piccolo con cordoncino 276
secchio 215
seconda 298
seconda base 474
seconda base (posizione) 474
seconda falange 114
seconda galleria 293
seconda linea 482
seconda linea destra 482
seconda linea sinistra 482
seconda pinna dorsale 74
secondi violini 295
secondi, lancetta dei 424
secondo 428, 498
secondo allenatore 507
secondo arbitro 485, 487
secondo assistente cameraman 290
secondo aumento di tensione 413
secondo giocatore al lancio 515
secondo livello, dominio di 334
secondo molare 101
secondo premolare 101
secondo spazio 489
secrétaire 203
sedano 125
sedano di monte 142
sedano rapa 129
sede della valvola di tenuta 196
sedia 201
sedia a dondolo 200, 201
sedia a rotelle 467
sedia a sdraio 201
sedia con braccioli 444
sedia da regista 200
sedia del regista 291
sedia pieghevole 201
sedia scala 201
sedia senza braccioli 444
sedie degli attori 290
sedie impilabili 201
sedie, esempi di 201
sedile 195, 196, 200, 201, 205
sedile doppio 380

sedile scorrevole 501
sedile singolo 380
sedile: vista anteriore 353
sedile: vista laterale 353
sedili 201
seduta 353, 467
seduta del divano posteriore 353
sega a mano 533
sega circolare 227
sega circolare, lama di 227
sega da giardiniere 234
sega per augnatura manuale 226
segale 61, 143
segale, galletta di 145
segale, pane danese di 145
segale, pane nero di 144
segale, pane tedesco di 145
segale: spiga 61
seggio del rabbino 447
seggiolino per bambini 356, 372
seggiolone 205
seggiovia 512
seggiovia, partenza della 512
seghetto 226
seghetto alternativo 227
seghetto da traforo 226
segmento addominale 67
segnalatore di pericolo 454
segnale dell'area di attesa 390
segnale di distanza fissa 391
segnale di identificazione della pista 390
segnale di zona di contatto 391
segnali dell'asse della pista 390
segnali della soglia della pista 391
segnali laterali 390
segnalino 469
segnapunti 487, 488, 499
segnavento 520
segno centrale 490
segreteria di produzione 291
segreteria, ufficio della 443
segreteria scolastica, ufficio della 445
segreteria telefonica 328
selettore dei pick-up 303
selettore dei programmi 314
selettore del livello dell'acqua 212
selettore del livello di registrazione 323
selettore del movimento orbitale 227
selettore del nastro 323
selettore del ritmo 311
selettore del timbro 311
selettore della messa a fuoco 314, 320
selettore della modalità audio 322
selettore della temperatura 178, 270
selettore della velocità 270
selettore di ingresso 322
selettore di programma 310
selettore di registrazione notturna 320
selettore di velocità 176, 177, 227, 228
selettore quadridirezionale 315
selettore stereo/mono 326
selettori di funzione 327
selettori di modo 326
selezione, tasto di 320, 327
sella 369, 370, 501, 523
sella biposto 367
sella del guidatore 369
sella del passeggero 369
selvaggina 154
semaforo 375, 434
seme 53, 57, 58, 59, 60
semi di girasole, olio di 149
semi di papavero 139
semi di soia 131
semi-mummia 530
semiasse 351
semibiscroma 299
semibiscroma, pausa di 299
semibreve 299
semibreve, pausa di 299
semicerchio 428
semicroma 299
semicroma, pausa di 299
semimembranoso 97
semiminima 299
semiminima, pausa di 299
seminatoio a mano 231
seminterrato 182
seminterrato, finestra del 183
semirimorchio frigorifero 365
semisfera 429
semitendinoso 97
semolino 144
senape americana 140
senape bianca 138
senape di Digione 140

ASTRONOMIA > 2-25; TERRA > 26-71; REGNO VEGETALE >72-89; REGNO ANIMALE > 90-143; ESSERE UMANO > 144-177; GENERI ALIMENTARI E CUCINA > 178-241; CASA > 242-295;
FAI DA TE E GIARDINAGGIO > 296-333; ABBIGLIAMENTO > 334-371; ACCESSORI E ARTICOLI PERSONALI > 372-391; ARTE E ARCHITETTURA > 392-465; COMUNICAZIONI E BUROTICA > 466-535;
TRASPORTI E VEICOLI > 536-643; ENERGIA > 644-677; SCIENZA > 678-705; SOCIETÀ > 706-785; SPORT E GIOCHI > 786-920

senape in granuli 140
senape in polvere 140
senape inglese 140
senape nera 60, 138
senape tedesca 140
Senegal 451
Senegal, Fiume 20
seno 92, 94, 113
seno frontale 117
seno laterale inferiore 62
seno laterale superiore 62
seno peziolato 62
seno sfenoidale 117
sensore del telecomando 318, 323
sensore di collisione principale 354
sensore di sicurezza 354
sensore di temperatura 358
sensore di velocità delle ruote 357
sensore ottico 332
sepalo 56, 58, 59
separatore 359, 384, 402, 417
separatore elettrolitico 417
separatore liquido/gas 359
separazione del cartone 49
separazione della carta 49
separazione magnetica 49
séparé 438
seppia 157
sequencer 310
sequencer, controllo del 310
seracco 30
serbatoi di stoccaggio 404
serbatoio 13, 181
serbatoio a tetto galleggiante 404
serbatoio ausiliario 365
serbatoio del carburante 235, 351, 366,
    369, 377, 395
serbatoio del liquido dei freni 357
serbatoio dell'acqua 181, 272
serbatoio dell'acqua di raffreddamento
    408
serbatoio dell'acqua, vano del 394
serbatoio di stoccaggio 405
serbatoio di stoccaggio temporaneo 404
serbatoio esterno del combustibile 12
serbatoio per il brillantante 214
serbatoio per il carburante 364
serbatoio, bocchetta del 237
serbatoio, sportello del 349
serbatoio, tappo del 364, 368
serie, lampade in 207
serie, numero di 441
serpente 76
serpente a sonagli 77
serpente corallo 77
serpente giarrettiera 77
serpente velenoso: testa, morfologia di un
    76
serpentina 210
serra 122
serraggio, leva di 224, 229
serraggio, vite di 224
serratura 185, 186, 202, 211, 275, 277,
    349, 352
serratura a chiave 274
serratura a combinazione 274
server 334, 335
server d'accesso 335
servizi assicurativi 442
servizi di credito 442
servizi finanziari 442
servizi sociali 465
servizio 487, 490
servizio corto, linea di 495
servizio da fonduta 174
servizio da wok 174
servizio del doppio, campo di 495
servizio del singolo, campo di 495
servizio di assistenza ai clienti 443
servizio di babysitteraggio 437
servizio di navetta 390
servizio Internet, fornitore del 335
servizio lungo, linea di 494
servizio manutenzione 346
servizio mobile a distanza, unità di 11
servizio pacchi 374
servizio, cintura di 456
servizio, fonte del 313
servizio, giudice di 490, 494
servizio, linea centrale di 491
servizio, linea di 491
servizio, modulo di 316
servizio, stazione di 433
servizio, tavolo di 438
servizio, zona di 491
servizio, zone di 495

servofreno 350, 357
sesamo, olio di 149
sesta 298
sestetto 300
set 291, 492
set delle riprese 290
set di bussole 223
set di utensili 173
set per cucinare 531
set per manicure 265
set precedenti 492
setaccio 171, 172
setale 538
setola 271, 272
setole 215, 219
settima 298
setto 60, 117
setto interventricolare 104
setto nasale, cartilagine del 117
setto pellucido 109
settore 428
Seychelles 452
sezione della crosta terrestre 26
sezione di un acino 59
sezione di un bulbo 54
sezione di un cannocchiale 8
sezione di un lampone 59
sezione di un telescopio 9
sezione di un'arancia 58
sezione di una fragola 59
sezione di una mela 58
sezione di una nocciola 60
sezione di una noce 60
sezione di una palla 477
sezione di una pesca 57
sezione rigida anteriore 363
sezione rigida posteriore 363
sezione sagittale 111, 112
sezione trasversale di un molare 101
sezione trasversale di un osservatorio
    astronomico 7
sezione trasversale di un tronco 63
sezione trasversale di una centrale
    idroelettrica 407
sezione trasversale di una navicella 413
sezione trasversale di una strada 342,
    434
sezione variabile, ugello a 394
sfagno pungente 51
sfera 312, 332, 429
sfera, penna a 312
sfera, supporto della 356
sfiatatoio 90, 214
sfiato 194
sfiato, valvola di 385
sfintere anale 106
sfioratore 406
sfioratore, paratoia dello 406
sfioratore, scivolo dello 406
sfioratore, soglia dello 406
sgabello 164, 201, 498
sgabello alto 201
sgabello da bar 438
sgambatura elasticizzata 247
sgombro 159
shampoo 267
shekel, nuovo 440
shiitake 123
short track 508
shorts 254
si 298
siamese 87
sicurezza 84
sicurezza, cassetta di 443
sicurezza, cintura di 525
sicurezza, corridoio di 440
sicurezza, griglia di 442
sicurezza, grilletto di 235
sicurezza, impugnatura di 237
sicurezza, linea di 379
sicurezza, luce di 457
sicurezza, termostato di 213
sicurezza, valvola di 174
siepe 183, 230, 472
Sierra Leone 451
sifone 72, 194, 196, 197
siliqua, sezione di una 60
silo orizzontale 122
silo verticale 122
silos 381
simboli 468
simboli scientifici 426
simbolo della squadra 506
sinagoga 447
sinapsi 110
sinfisi pubica 111, 112

Singapore 453
sinistra 387
sintesi additiva 418
sintesi dei colori 418
sintesi sottrattiva 418
sintetizzatore 310
sintetizzatore a fiato 311
sintoamplificatore 325
sintoamplificatore: dorso 322
sintoamplificatore: vista frontale 322
sintonia, comandi di 318
sintonia, manopola della 326
sintonia, tasti di selezione della 322
sintonia, tasto di preselezione della 322
sintonizzatore 326
sintonizzazione, manopola di 325
sipario 292, 293
sipario tagliafuoco 292
Siria 452
siringa 460
siringa per decorazioni 172
siringhe usate, contenitore delle 457
sismografi 27
sismografo orizzontale 27
sismografo verticale 2 /
sismogramma 27
sistema a celle solari 411
sistema a rotazione 403
sistema di alimentazione 351
sistema di climatizzazione 46
sistema di controllo del lampeggiante 457
sistema di coordinate terrestri 21
sistema di guida fine 7
sistema di lenti 420
sistema di manipolazione a distanza 11
sistema di registrazione audio 291
sistema di ritenuta degli air bag 354
sistema di sopravvivenza 10
sistema di trasmissione 351
sistema idraulico 396
sistema internazionale di unità di misura
    426
sistema nervoso 108
sistema nervoso centrale 109
sistema nervoso periferico 108
sistema solare 2
sistema stradale 342
sistema, tasti di 310
sistemi dell'automobile 351
sistemi dell'automobile: componenti
    principali 350
sistro 309
skateboard 526
skater 526
skimmer 184
slalom gigante 511
slalom speciale 511
slalom supergigante 511
slancio 500
slip 247, 259
slip da bagno 263
slitta 236
slitta di fissaggio 420
slitta per accessori 314
Slovacchia 450
Slovenia 450
smalto 101
smalto per unghie 265
smerigliatrice eccentrica 229
sminuzzamento 49
smistamento dei materiali metallici 49
smistamento del cartone 49
smistamento del vetro 49
smistamento della carta 49
smistamento della plastica 49
smistamento manuale 49
smistamento ottico 49
smistamento selettivo dei rifiuti 49
smog 47
smorzamento magnetico, dispositivo di
    422
smorzata 491
smottamento 31
snack bar 294
snocciolatore 173
snodo 511
snooker 503
snowboard 513
snowboard di cemento 190
snowboard per freestyle 513
snowboard per sci alpino 513
snowboardista 513
sobborghi 25
società 430
soffietto 274, 276
soffietto, borsa a 274
soffietto, mantice a 296

soffietto, portacarte a 274
soffietto, tasca applicata a 255
soffitto a due spioventi 189
soffitto acustico 293
soffitto della cabina 287
soffitto, travetto del 187
software di posta elettronica 334
soggiorno 188
soglia 185
soglia dello sfioratore 406
soglia glaciale 30
sogliola 161
soia, germogli di 131
soia, salsa di 140
soia, semi di 131
sol 298
solaio 193
solaio, collare del 193
solarium 385, 387
solco 118
solco mediano 118
solco terminale 118
Sole 2, 4, 5, 38
Sole, eclissi di 4
sole, occhiali da 273
Sole, struttura del 4
soleo 96
soletta 247
soletta antiscivolo 261
solidi 429
solidificazione 414
solido 414, 415
solido amorfo 414
solitario 264
sollevacuticole 265
sollevamento pesi 500
sollevamento, braccio di 399, 400
sollevamento, catena di 396
sollevamento, cavo di 397
sollevamento, cilindro di 397, 455
sollevamento, fune di 287
solstizio d'estate 38
solstizio d'inverno 38
soluzione multiuso 272
solventi, impianto di estrazione con 405
Somalia 451
sommatoria 427
sommelier 438
sonagli 309
sonda spaziale 37
sonda, inchino della 178
sopracciglia, matita per 266
sopracciglia, pinzette per 265
soprafusione 414
soprasponda 502
soprastruttura 342
sopravveste a grembiule 255
sopravvivenza, regolazione del sistema di
    10
sopravvivenza, sistema di 10
sordina 304, 307
sordina, pedale della 304
sorgente 32
sorgente di corrente 416
sorgenti, luci delle 322
sorgenti, tasto di selezione delle 322
sorgo 61
sorgo: pannocchia 61
soro 52
sospensione 351, 380
sospensione posteriore 522
sospensione, braccio di 212
sospensione, lampada a 206
sospensioni, gruppo delle 351
sostanza bianca 109, 110
sostanza corticale 107
sostanza grigia 109, 110
sostanza midollare 107
sostegno 201, 509
sostegno del bracciolo 200
sostegno dell'ala 387
sostegno per il collo 525
sostegno, base di 202
sotterraneo 281, 435
sottocasco 524
sottofondo 187, 190
sottofondo di cemento 190
sottofondo di cemento, parquet su 190
sottogola 486, 522
sottogonna 258
sottopalco 292
sottopassaggio 375
sottopunto, cucitura a 245
sottostruttura 403
sottosuolo 54

sottotitolo 313
sottotuta 524
sottoveste 258
sottoveste con reggiseno 258
sottovia 344
sottrazione 427
spacco centrale 244
spacco laterale 244
spadice 57
spaghetti 146
spaghetti all'uovo 147
spaghetti asiatici 147
spaghetti di fagioli mungo 147
spaghetti di riso 147
spaghetti soba 147
spaghetti somen 147
spaghetti udon 147
spaghetti, molle per 173
spaghettini 146
Spagna 449
spalla 83, 86, 92, 94, 284, 302, 344,
    492, 536
spallaccio 532
spallamento 223
spalliera 230
spalliera ad arco 230
spallina 248, 259, 456
spartitraffico 343, 434
sparviero 216
spatola 173, 510, 514
spatola metallica 355
spatolata 55
spaziatore 409
spazio 298, 330
spazio epidurale 110
spazio unificatore 330
spazzaneve a turbina 365
spazzata d'anca 499
spazzatrice 365
spazzola 173, 209, 215, 272
spazzola a dorso piatto 268
spazzola a pennello 209
spazzola antistatica 268
spazzola da bagno 267
spazzola da neve con raschietto 356
spazzola di gomma 355
spazzola metallica 309
spazzola per la schiena 267
spazzola per pavimenti 209
spazzola per tappeti e pavimenti 209
spazzola ragno 268
spazzola rotante centrale 365
spazzola rotante laterale 365
spazzola rotonda 268
spazzole per capelli 268
spazzolino da denti 272
spazzolino da denti elettrico 272
spazzolino di pulizia 271
spazzolino per mascara 266
spazzolino, gambo a innesto dello 272
speaker 518
specchietto 523
specchietto anteriore di accostamento
    362
specchietto di cortesia 354
specchietto per il punto cieco 362, 363
specchietto retrovisore 354, 363, 366,
    368, 369
specchietto retrovisore esterno 348, 362,
    364
specchio 195, 271, 421, 439
specchio a riflessione parziale 420
specchio a riflessione totale 420
specchio di lettura 10
specchio di puntamento 533
specchio doppio girevole 269
specchio laterale 269
specchio luminoso 269
specchio piano 7
specchio primario 7
specchio primario concavo 9
specchio secondario 7, 9
specialità 511
specialità gastronomiche 120
spedizione merci 391
spelafili 217
spelucchino 169
spencer 254
sperlano 159
spermatozoo 111
sperone 29
spesa, borsa della 276
spessore 224
spessore, misura dello 425
spettro elettromagnetico 418
spezie 138

spezie cajun, condimento alle 139
spezie marinate 139
spezzatino 152, 153
spia 269
spia cinture di sicurezza non allacciate 355
spia dei proiettori abbaglianti 355
spia dell'indicatore di direzione 355, 368
spia della batteria 355
spia della cartuccia 333
spia della posizione di folle 368
spia della pressione dell'olio 355, 368
spia della riserva di carburante 355
spia delle luci abbaglianti 368
spia di accensione 443
spia di alimentazione 329, 333
spia di alimentazione della carta 333
spia di allarme 337
spia di messa in carica 337
spia di rilevamento della carta 443
spia luminosa 178, 179, 180, 181, 208, 210, 214, 454
spia luminosa dell'autoscatto 314
spia luminosa di accensione/spegnimento 327
spia luminosa di alimentazione 328
spia luminosa di carica 271
spia porte aperte 355
spiaggia 35
spicchio 58
spicole 4
spider 347
spie 355
spie della modalità audio 322
spie luminose 318, 331
spiga 57, 144
spillone 268
spina 228
spina americana, presa per 198
spina americana 198
spina della scapola 99
spina di alimentazione 337
spina europea 198
spina nasale anteriore 100
spinacio 127
spingicuticole 265
spingistantuffo 460
spinotto 198, 199, 324
spinotto della cuffia 326
spinotto di connessione 417
spinotto di messa a terra 198
spinta, fase di 514
spinta, maniglia di 286
spinta, telaio di 398
spinterogeno 350, 360
spirale 221
spirale, braccio della 6
spirulina 123
splenio 97
spogliatoio 444, 465
spogliatoio del personale 465
spoiler 364, 366, 392
spolverino 172
sponda inferiore 502
sponda protettiva 205
sponda superiore 502
spore 52
sporgenza 191
sport 468
sport a motore 524
sport acquatici 516
sport con la palla 474
sport di combattimento 498
sport di forza 500
sport di precisione 502
sport invernali 515
sport nautici 516
sport su rotelle 526
sporta 276
sportello 178, 210, 423, 443
sportello automatico 442, 443
sportello bancomat 437, 442
sportello commerciale 443
sportello del serbatoio 349
sportello di carico 192
sportello notturno 443
spostamento 418
spray al peperoncino 456
spremere 177
spremiaglio 170
spremiagrumi 170
spremiagrumi elettrici 177
spremitura, cono di 177
sprone 245
spruzzatore 236
spruzzatori 408

spugna abrasiva 215
spugna naturale 267
spugna sintetica 266
spugna vegetale 267
spugnetta 339
spugnetta, applicatore a 266
spugnola 123
spumante, coppa da 165
squadra 225
squadra falsa 225
squadra, simbolo della 506
squalo, morfologia di uno 74
squama 76, 79
Sri Lanka 453
stabilimento industriale 430
stabilizzatore 393, 397, 400, 455, 523
stacconata 182
stadera 122
stadi di maturazione 62
stadio 431, 472
staff medico 499
staffa 116, 254
staffa di lancio 515
staggio 219
stagioni dell'anno 38
stagno 504
stalagmite 31
stalattite 31
stalla 122
stame 56, 58
stampa 331
stampante a getto di inchiostro 333
stampella canadese 466
stampini per dolci 172
stampo per charlotte 172
stampo per crostata 172
stampo per pane 179
stanga 231
stanghetta 273, 298
stantuffo 460
stanza da bagno 188, 189, 195, 439
stanza degli insegnanti 445
stanza degli studenti 445
stanza dei giurati 440
stanza del personale 463
stanza del triage 463
stanza di degenza 464
stanza di degenza postoperatoria 464
stanza di isolamento 462
stanza di osservazione 462, 465
stanza di sterilizzazione 464
stanza per esame psichiatrico 462
stanza per l'anestesia 464
stanza per l'esame audiometrico 465
stanza per la preparazione chirurgica 464
stanza per le terapie 465
stanza per le visite mediche 465
stanza per osservazione psichiatrica 462
stanza per visite ginecologiche 463
stanze principali 188
stanzino del portiere 439
stanzino della guardia giurata 443
starter 516
starter, pistola dello 472
stati della materia 414
Stati Uniti d'America 448
station wagon 347
stato 23
stato presente del tempo 39
statua 446
statua, posizione della 279
stazione degli autobus 432
stazione dei viaggiatori 374, 375, 381
stazione della metropolitana 378, 432
stazione di pattugliamento 512
stazione di polizia 433
stazione di pompaggio 404
stazione di pompaggio intermedia 404
stazione di pompaggio principale 404
stazione di pronto soccorso 345
stazione di servizio 346, 433
stazione di superficie 38
stazione di trasformazione 406, 407
stazione ferroviaria 25, 375, 430, 432
stazione locale 316
stazione ripetitrice 316
stazione ripetitrice a microonde 334
stazione sciistica 512
stazione spaziale internazionale 11
stazione terminale 404
stazione terrestre per le telecomunicazioni 335
stazione, cerchio di 39
stazione, ingresso della 378
stazione, modello di 39
stazione, nome della 378

stecca 259, 273, 503, 519, 520
stecche 461
stella cadente 37
stella di David 447
stelo 51, 54, 221
stelo, lampada a 206
stemma 477
stepper 501
steppico 40
stereo/mono, selettore 326
sterilizzazione, sala di 465
sterilizzazione, stanza di 464
sterlina 440
sterno 98
sternocleidomastoideo 96
sterzo, gruppo dello 351
stigma 56, 60, 67
stile libero o crawl 517
stili di nuoto 517
stilo 56, 57, 58, 59, 60, 312, 337
stilo di canna 312
stilo di piombo 312
stilo metallico romano 312
stilobate 279
stilton 151
stimolatore gengivale 272
stinco 153
stipite 185, 192
stipola 55
stiva per i containers 383
stivale 241, 305, 525
stivale alla moschettiera 241
stivale di gomma 454
stivaloni impermeabili 538
stoccaggio temporaneo, serbatoio di 404
stoccaggio, serbatoi di 404
stoccaggio, serbatoio di 405
stomaco 73, 103, 106
stomaco cardiaco 71
stomaco pilorico 71
stop 86
stopper 481
storione 158
stornello 80
strada 25, 345, 430, 435
strada di accesso 388
strada di servizio 388
strada panoramica 25
strada secondaria 25
strada, numero di 25
strada, sezione trasversale di una 342
stradina 504
strallo 412
strallo di prua 520
strappo 500
strati di rifiuti 47
strato 42
strato basale 114
strato basaltico 26
strato corneo 114
strato di base 342
strato di ceneri 28
strato di collegamento 342
strato di lava 28
strato di ozono 37
strato granitico 26
strato granulare 114
strato impermeabile 190
strato inferiore confinante 402
strato lucido 114
strato protettivo 10
strato spinoso 114
strato superficiale del suolo 54
strato superiore confinante 402
stratocumulo 42
stratopausa 37
stratosfera 37
strega 503
stretto 24
Stretto di Bass 15
Stretto di Bering 16
Stretto di Cook 15
Stretto di Gibilterra 18
Stretto di Torres 15
stringa 240, 477, 498, 509
striscia antiabrasiva 358
striscia di gioco 479
striscia di sfregamento 218
striscia di sicurezza 374
strofinaccio da cucina 215
strombatura 285
strozzascotte 521
strozzatura 301, 424
strumentazione scientifica 13
strumenti a corde 301
strumenti a fiato 306

strumenti a percussione 295, 308
strumenti a tastiera 304
strumenti di misura 424
strumenti di misurazione e tracciamento 225
strumenti elettronici 310
strumenti musicali tradizionali 296
strumenti per il pronto soccorso 460
strumenti scientifici 7
strumenti scrittori 312
struttura 186, 187
struttura del midollo spinale 109
struttura del Sole 4
struttura dell'orecchio 116
struttura della biosfera 44
struttura della Terra 26
struttura di un albero 63
struttura di un fiore 56
struttura di un fungo 52
struttura di un lichene 50
struttura di un muschio 51
struttura di un'alga 51
struttura di una casa 188
struttura di una felce 52
struttura di una foglia 55
struttura di una pianta 53
struttura esterna 211, 212
struttura lignea, parquet su 190
struttura metallica 374
struttura protettiva 525
strutture per i tuffi 518
struzzo 81
struzzo, uovo di 155
studente 444
studenti, armadietti degli 445
studenti, stanza degli 445
studio 189
stufa a combustione lenta 192
stufa a gas 529
stufe, olio combustibile per 405
sturalavandini 216
sub woofer 321
subartico 40
subduzione 27
sublimazione 414
subtropicale mediterraneo 40
subtropicale umido 40
suburbio 431
Sud 23
Sud Sud-Est 23
Sud Sud-Ovest 23
Sud-Est 23
Sud-Ovest 23
Sudafricana, Repubblica 452
Sudan 451
sufflè, tegamino per 172
sughero 514
sumac 139
suola 240, 263, 509, 510, 511
suolo 48
suolo, fertilizzazione del 47
suolo, inquinamento del 47
suolo, movimento orizzontale del 27
suolo, movimento verticale del 27
suolo, profilo del 54
suolo, strato superficiale del 54
suoneria, regolatore della 327
suono, ingegnere del 291
superfici 428
superfici di gioco 492
superficie antiscivolo 526
superficie dell'acqua 518
superficie della cute 114
superficie di affissione 341
superficie di gioco 493
superficie dura (cemento) 492
superficie sintetica 492
superficie terrestre, assorbimento attraverso la 46
superficie verticale 526
superficie, stazione di 38
supermercato 120, 433, 437
superstrada 343
supplemento a colori 313
supplemento letterario 313
supporti per camminare 466
supporto 9, 199, 269, 308
supporto anteriore retrattile 361
supporto del cordone 208
supporto del disco abrasivo 229
supporto del rullo 219
supporto del tabellone 489
supporto della rete 493
supporto della sfera 356
supporto elastico 324, 326, 458

supporto per il braccio 466
supporto per il tallone 467
supporto retrattile 365
supporto sottoascellare 466
supporto stabilizzatore 361
supporto, piastra di 199
supporto, telaio di 401
surgelati 121
surgelati, magazzino dei 121
Suriname 448
surriscaldamento globale 46
sutura 60, 73
sutura coronale 100
sutura coronaria 100
sutura lambdoidea 100
sutura squamosa 100
sverniciatura, pistola per 219
svettatoio 234
Svezia 450
svincolo 431
Svizzera 450
Swaziland 452

T

tabaccheria 436
tabasco, salsa 140
tabella dei risultati 518
tabellone 489
tabellone degli arrivi e delle partenze 391
tabellone degli orari 374
tabellone della classifica generale 496
tabellone della prova in corso 497
tabellone segnapunti 471, 472, 492, 497, 499
tabellone, supporto del 489
tabernacolo 446
tablino 280
tabloid 313
tabulazione a destra 330
tabulazione a sinistra 330
tacca 422, 473
tacca di mira 534
tacchetti intercambiabili 480
tacchetto 263, 478
tacchino 81, 155
tacco 240, 509, 536
tachimetro 355, 368, 501
tafano 69
Tagikistan 452
tagli di agnello 153
tagli di maiale 153
tagli di manzo 152
tagli di vitello 152
taglia fissa 403
taglia mobile 403
tagliabasette 271
tagliabiscotti 172
tagliabordi 233, 237
tagliacarte 339
tagliacuticole 265
tagliafili 217
tagliare 177
tagliasiepi 235
tagliasiepi, forbici 234
tagliatelle verdi 146
tagliente 180, 228, 398, 399, 400
tagliere 169
taglio 221
taglio addizionale 298
tagliola 535
tahini 140
Tailandia 453
tailback 485
tailleur 251
tajina 174
tallo 50, 51
tallonatore 482
tallone 93, 95, 169, 226, 229, 262, 301, 302, 358, 477, 506
tallone d'appoggio 176
tallone di appoggio 208
talloniera 511, 514
tamarillo 136
tamarindo, pasta di 140
tamarino 91
tamburello 309
tamburo 170, 213, 357, 425
tamburo parlante 297
tamburo rotante 27
tamburo tenore 308
tamia 82
tampone 338
tandem 373
Tanganica, Lago 20
tangenziale 25, 431

ASTRONOMIA > 2-25; TERRA > 26-71; REGNO VEGETALE >72-89; REGNO ANIMALE > 90-143; ESSERE UMANO > 144-177; GENERI ALIMENTARI E CUCINA > 178-241; CASA > 242-295;
FAI DA TE E GIARDINAGGIO > 296-333; ABBIGLIAMENTO > 334-371; ACCESSORI E ARTICOLI PERSONALI > 372-391; ARTE E ARCHITETTURA > 392-465; COMUNICAZIONI E BUROTICA > 466-535;
TRASPORTI E VEICOLI > 536-643; ENERGIA > 644-677; SCIENZA > 678-705; SOCIETÀ > 706-785; SPORT E GIOCHI > 786-920

Tanzania 451
tappeti e pavimenti, spazzola per 209
tappetino 356
tappetino del mouse 332
tappeto 190, 498, 499
tappezzeria, bocchetta per 209
tappi per le orecchie 458
tappo 176, 267, 358, 532
tappo a vite 163
tappo del serbatoio 364, 368
tappo di isolamento 417
tappo di ispezione 197
tappo di scarico 194
tappo di scarico dell'olio 360
targhetta del costruttore 228
targhetta delle avvertenze 228
taro 124
tarso 78
tartaruga 76
tartaruga, morfologia di una 76
tartufo 123
tartufo di mare 157
tasca 172, 225, 274, 505
tasca anteriore 246
tasca applicata 244, 249, 260
tasca applicata a soffietto 255
tasca applicata con aletta 245
tasca della stecca 519
tasca di Douglas 112
tasca di inforcamento 396
tasca esterna 274, 276
tasca finta 251
tasca frontale 275
tasca inserita nella cucitura 251
tasca interna 277
tasca interna con aletta 244, 248, 249, 251
tasca nascosta 274
tasca per la stecca 520
tasca portaoggetti 352
tasca posteriore 246
tasca profilata 250
tasca profilata con aletta 244, 248
tasca tagliata in verticale 251
tasca vescicouterina 112
taschino 248
taschino con aletta 244
taschino tagliato con aletta 244
taschino, fazzoletto da 244
Tasmania 15
Tasmania, Mare di 15
tassello 202
tasso 88
tasti degli effetti speciali 320
tasti del cursore 331
tasti del lettore di compact disc 326
tasti del riproduttore a cassette 326
tasti di chiamata automatica 327
tasti di comando 328
tasti di identificazione del conto 443
tasti di programmazione 319
tasti di regolazione del volume 319
tasti di regolazione dell'immagine 320
tasti di ricerca del brano 323
tasti di ricerca delle emittenti 319
tasti di ricerca emittenti 319
tasti di ricerca rapida 323
tasti di ripetizione 323
tasti di selezione dei canali 319
tasti di selezione della sintonia 322
tasti di selezione delle casse acustiche 322
tasti di sistema 310
tasti funzione 328, 330, 423, 442, 443
tasti funzione programmabili 443
tasti Internet 330
tasti per l'editing del suono 310
tastiera 296, 301, 303, 304, 310, 327, 330, 336
tastiera alfanumerica 330, 346, 442, 443
tastiera degli acuti 296
tastiera numerica 328
tastiera, strumenti a 304
tastierina per il codice di identificazione personale (PIN) 443
tastierino alfabetico 338
tastierino alfanumerico 327
tastierino numerico 331, 338, 423
tasto 296, 304, 306
tasto Alt 330
tasto Avvio 330
tasto backspace 331
tasto Control 330
tasto del menu 327
tasto dell'auto-reverse 326
tasto delle maiuscole 330

tasto di addizione 337
tasto di arresto 319, 323, 328
tasto di arresto e di scorrimento 331
tasto di arresto/cancellazione 328
tasto di ascolto diretto 328
tasto di avanzamento della carta 443
tasto di avanzamento rapido 319, 323, 326, 328
tasto di avvio 328
tasto di avvio registrazione 320
tasto di azzeramento 319, 337
tasto di azzeramento del contatore 323
tasto di azzeramento ultimo dato 337
tasto di blocco delle maiuscole 330
tasto di blocco numerico 331
tasto di cambio segno 337
tasto di cancellazione 328, 331
tasto di cancellazione della memoria 337
tasto di chiamata 327
tasto di conferma 443
tasto di divisione 337
tasto di espulsione 319, 323
tasto di fine chiamata 327
tasto di lettura 327
tasto di memorizzazione 322, 323, 327
tasto di moltiplicazione 337
tasto di pagina giù 331
tasto di pagina su 331
tasto di pausa 323
tasto di pausa/fermo immagine 319
tasto di percentuale 337
tasto di posizione 302, 303
tasto di preselezione della sintonia 322
tasto di punto decimale 337
tasto di radice quadrata 337
tasto di registrazione 319, 323
tasto di registrazione del messaggio 328
tasto di registrazione e di visualizzazione dell'ora 320
tasto di registrazione e di visualizzazione della data 320
tasto di registro 305
tasto di reset 328
tasto di riascolto dei messaggi 328
tasto di riavvolgimento 319, 323, 326, 328
tasto di ricerca della fine 320
tasto di richiamo della memoria 337
tasto di riproduzione 319, 323, 326
tasto di riproduzione/pausa 323
tasto di selezione 327
tasto di selezione del registratore 323
tasto di selezione della banda 322
tasto di selezione della modalità FM 322
tasto di selezione delle sorgenti 322
tasto di somma in memoria 337
tasto di sottrazione 337
tasto di sottrazione in memoria 337
tasto di tabulazione 330
tasto di uguale 337
tasto di visualizzazione degli indicatori 320
tasto di visualizzazione dei titoli 320
tasto email 330
tasto Esc 330
tasto Fine 331
tasto Home 331
tasto Ins 331
tasto Invio 331
tasto numerico 337
tasto pausa 331
tasto per il modo di esposizione 314
tasto per l'avanzamento della pellicola 314
tasto per la sensibilità della pellicola 314
tasto per le esposizioni multiple 314
tasto stampa 331
tasto TV/video 319

tavola 469, 519
tavola armonica 296, 297, 301, 302, 304
tavola di rotazione 403
tavola esterna 469
tavola interna 469
tavola, coltello da 168
tavola, cucchiaio da 168
tavola, forchetta da 168
tavola, vasellame da 166
tavoletta 190
tavoletta portablocco 340
tavoli, esempi di 202
tavolini sovrapponibili 202
tavolino da letto 464
tavolino traslatore 421
tavolino traslatore, comando del 421
tavolo 202, 493, 502
tavolo a cancello 202
tavolo allungabile 202

tavolo di servizio 438
tavolo operatorio 464
tavolo, lampada da 206
tazza 531
tazza alta da caffè 166
tazza da tè 166
tazza graduata 171
tazza per sapone da barba 271
tazzina da caffè 166
tè 148
tè nero 148
tè oolong 148
tè verde 148
tè, bustina di 148
tè, cucchiaino da 168
tè, filtro per il 173
tè, tazza da 166
teatro 292, 432, 433
teatro greco 278
teatro, binocolo da 273
tecniche 487
tecnico delle luci 291
tee 505
tegame 175, 531
tegame per fonduta 174
tegame per uova in camicia 175
tegamino per chiocciole 173
tegamino per soufflé 172
teglia con fondo staccabile 172
teglia da forno 172
teglia per torta 172
teglie da forno 174
tegola 279, 280, 283
tegumento del seme 57
tegumento seminale 61
teiera 166
tela 412
telaio 186, 200, 201, 202, 204, 224, 226, 274, 277, 297, 309, 367, 396, 400, 401, 410, 411, 412, 466, 492, 494, 522, 527
telaio dei rulli del cingoli 398
telaio del bruciatore 529
telaio di spinta 398
telaio di supporto 401
telaio interno della portiera 352
telaio metallico 304
telaio per tenda esterna 361
telaio regolabile 226
telaio rigido, borsa a 276
telaio, giunzione a linguetta del 186
telaio, giunzione scanalata del 186
telaio, montante del 202
telaio, traverso superiore del 186
telecamera 290, 525
telecamera a colori 10
telecomando 319, 321
telecomando, sensore del 318, 323
telecomunicazioni via satellite 317
telecomunicazioni, satelliti per 316
telefax 328
telefono 439
telefono cellulare 327
telefono pubblico 294, 437, 438, 463
teleobiettivo 314
telescopio 7, 9
telescopio spaziale Hubble 7, 37
telescopio, basamento del 7
telescopio, sezione di un 9
televisione 318, 439, 444
televisore 318
televisore a grande schermo 321
teli, gonna a 253
telo di spugna con cappuccio 260
telo esterno 528, 529
telone proteggiauto 356
telson 71
temperamatite 341
temperatura Celsius, unità di misura della 426
temperatura corporea, regolazione della 10
temperatura del liquido di raffreddamento, indicatore della 355
temperatura dell'aria 39
temperatura di rugiada 39
temperatura termodinamica, unità di misura della 426
temperatura, indicatore di 269
temperatura, misura della 424
temperatura, selettore della 178
temperature, scala delle 37
temperino multiuso 531
tempia 92
tempio azteco 283
tempio di Huitzilopochtli 283

tempio di Tlaloc 283
tempio greco 279
tempio greco, pianta del 279
tempo di due metà 298
tempo di quattro quarti 298
tempo di tre quarti 298
tempo, barca del 38, 39
tempo, controllo del 311
tempo, indicazioni di 298
tempo, misura del 424
tempo, stato presente del 39
tenda a cupola 529
tenda a due posti 528
tenda a igloo 529
tenda a un posto 529
tenda canadese 529
tenda coprifinestra 528
tenda da campo 528
tenda da cucina 528
tenda di tipo familiare 528
tenda interna 528, 529
tende, esempi di 528
tendenza barometrica 39
tendicollo 245
tendina divisoria 464
tendina parasole avvolgibile 356
tennis 490
tennis da tavolo 493
tennis, scarpa da 242
tennista 492
tensione, aumento di 402, 408
tensione, chiavi di 308
tensione, corda di 297
tensione, diminuzione di 402, 413
tensione, primo aumento di 413
tensione, secondo aumento di 413
tensore della fascia lata 96
tentacolo 72
tentacolo oculare 72
tenuta, mastice di 196
tenuta, valvola di 196
tepee 288
terapie, stanza per le 463, 465
tergale 200
tergale, base del 200
tergicristallo 348, 355
tergicristallo, comando del 354
terminal dei passeggeri 389, 390
terminal satellite dei passeggeri 389
terminale 198, 210, 273
terminale della messa a terra 322
terminale di messa a terra 198
terminale di pagamento elettronico 443
terminale di scarico 351
terminale per il pagamento elettronico 121
terminali di collegamento delle antenne 322
terminali di collegamento delle casse acustiche 322
terminazione nervosa 114
termini comuni 57, 58, 59
termini tecnici 57, 58, 59
termite 69
termometri clinici 461
termometro 404, 424
termometro a lettura istantanea 171
termometro a mercurio 461
termometro clinico 424
termometro del forno 171
termometro digitale 461
termometro per carne 171
termometro per zucchero 171
termopausa 37
termosfera 37
termosonda 178
termostato 178, 208, 211, 212, 213
termostato di sicurezza 213
termostato regolabile 179
terna 399
Terra 2, 3, 4, 5, 14
terra battuta 492
Terra del Fuoco 17
Terra della Regina Maud 15
Terra di Marie Byrd 15
Terra di Wilkes 15
terra, lingua di 35
Terra, orbita della 4, 5
terra, presa di messa a 198
Terra, struttura della 26
terra, terminale di messa a 198
Terranova, Isola di 16
terrapieno 342
terrazza 39
terrazza scoperta 387

terremoto 27
terrina 174
terza 298
terza base 474
terza base (posizione) 474
terza falange 114
terza linea 482
terzino 481, 485
terzino di destra 484
terzino di sinistra 484
tesa 238, 239
tessuto adiposo 113, 114
tessuto connettivo 114
tessuto elastico 246
tessuto sottocutaneo 114
testa 6, 93, 95, 103, 111, 220, 221, 223, 229, 272, 492, 494, 503, 505, 536
testa a croce 221
testa bombata 221
testa concava 221
testa d'albero 519
testa del femore 99
testa del martinetto elevatore 396
testa del rotore 395
testa dell'omero 99
testa di gatto 87
testa di iniezione del fango 403
testa di taglio 341
testa non svitabile 221
testa orientabile 224
testa piatta 221
testa quadra, punta a 221
testa ribaltabile 176
testa tonda 221
testata 313
testatina 313
teste, tipi di 221
tester di presa 217
testicoli 71
testicolo 111
testiera 204, 205
testimone 36, 472
testimone, zona del passaggio del 472
testimoni, banco dei 440
testina 271, 301
testina di lettura/scrittura 333
testina rotante 271
Teti 3
tetto 183, 193, 283, 349, 361, 401
tetto a due spioventi 189
tetto a vetro 188
tetto di vetro 435
tetto galleggiante 404
tettoia 528
tettoia vetrata 374
tettuccio 361
tettuccio apribile 349
tettuccio di protezione 396
thermos 532
tibia 78, 98
tibiale anteriore 96
tifone 43
tight end 485
tiglio 148
tigre 89
timbro di gomma 338
timbro, selettore del 311
timer 501
timo 142
timone 13, 383, 384, 386, 412, 520
timone di direzione 393
timone di profondità 393
timone, barra del 520
timone, pala del 384
timoneria 384
timpani 295
timpano 75, 182, 279, 285, 308
timpano, montante del 187
tinello 188
tintura per capelli 267
tipi di eclissi 4, 5
tipi di impugnature 493
tipi di inforescenze 57
tipi di mazze 505
tipi di movimenti 470
tipi di parquet 190
tipi di punte 221
tipi di teste 221
tipi di vagoni passeggeri 376
tipo di carburante 346
tipo di nube alta 39
tipo di nube bassa 39
tipo di nube media 39
tirante 196, 308, 344, 528
tirante a vite 308, 498

ASTRONOMIA > 2-25; TERRA > 26-71; REGNO VEGETALE >72-89; REGNO ANIMALE > 90-143; ESSERE UMANO > 144-177; GENERI ALIMENTARI E CUCINA > 178-241; CASA > 242-295;
FAI DA TE E GIARDINAGGIO > 296-333; ABBIGLIAMENTO > 334-371; ACCESSORI E ARTICOLI PERSONALI > 372-391; ARTE E ARCHITETTURA > 392-465; COMUNICAZIONI E BUROTICA > 466-535;
TRASPORTI E VEICOLI > 536-643; ENERGIA > 644-677; SCIENZA > 678-705; SOCIETÀ > 706-785; SPORT E GIOCHI > 786-920

633

INDICE DEI NOMI ITALIANI

tirante del braccio 397
tirante della cordiera 308
tirante, regolatore del 528
tisane 148
Titania 3
Titano 3
Titicaca, Lago 17
titolare, firma del 441
titolare, nome del 441
titoli dei film 294
titoli, tasto di visualizzazione del 320
titolo 313
titolo a caratteri cubitali 313
Tlaloc, tempio di 283
tocco 239
Togo 451
toilette 437, 440, 443, 445, 463, 465
toilette degli uomini 439
toilette delle donne 439
toilette per i clienti 438
Tolosa, salame di 156
tom tom 308
tomaia 240, 263
tomatillo 128
tombolo 35
Tonga 453
toni alti, regolatore dei 325
toni alti, regolazione dei 303
toni bassi, regolatore dei 325
toni bassi, regolazione dei 303
toni, regolazione dei 303
tonno 160
tonsilla 116
tonsilla linguale 118
tonsilla palatina 118
top 258
topinambur 124
topo campagnolo 82
toque 239
torace 67, 68, 92, 94
Torah, rotoli della 447
torcia 456
tornado 43
tornelli di entrata 378
tornelli di uscita 378
toro 429
torre 284, 412, 413, 470
torre a traliccio 397
torre angolare 282
torre campanaria 285
torre di controllo 388
torre di controllo, cabina della 388
torre di fiancheggiamento 282
torre di guida 345
torre di lavaggio 214
torre di perforazione 403, 404
torre di raffreddamento 402
torre per i tuffi 518
torre per uffici 435
torre trasmittente 316
torrente montano 29
Torres, Stretto di 15
torretta 282, 284, 285, 400
torretta, calotta della 420
torsolo 58
torta, teglia per 172
tortellini 146
tortiera 172
tortilla 145
tostapane 178
totale 423
touch pad 336
touch pad, pulsante del 336
touch screen 337
trabeazione 185, 279
tracciamento, filo di 225
trachea 105
tracolla 276, 505
tracolla, borsa a 276
tracolla, bottone della 303
traforo 285
traghetto 381
trago 115
traguardo 533
tralcio 62
traliccio, torre a 397
tramoggia di caricamento 364
trampoliere, uccello 79
trampolino 184
trampolino di 1 metro 518
trampolino di 3 metri 518
transatlantico 386
transazione, fessura di registrazione della 442
transazione, ricevuta della 443
transazioni commerciali 335

transetto 285
trapano elettrico 228
trapano senza fili 228
trapezio 96, 97, 429
trapezio, abito a 252
trapiantatoio 232
trappola petrolifera 403
trapunta 204
trascinamento, ingranaggio di 180
trasferimento di calore 415
trasformatore 207, 407
trasformatore principale 376
trasmissione 212
trasmissione a cinghia 383
trasmissione a onde hertziane 316
trasmissione agli utenti 402, 413
trasmissione dell'elettricità 408
trasmissione di elettricità ad alta tensione 402, 413
trasmissione via cavo aereo 317
trasmissione via cavo sotterraneo 317
trasmissione via cavo sottomarino 317
trasmissione via satellite 316
trasmissione, albero di 383
trasmissione, cinghia di 212
trasmissione, organi di 372
trasmissione, sistema di 351
traspirazione 45
trasporti 342
trasporto aereo 388
trasporto marittimo 381
trasporto su rotaia 374
trasporto su strada 342, 381
trattamento chimico 405
tratto olfattivo 117
trattore cingolato 398
trattore gommato 399
travata a cantilever 344
travata appoggiata 344
travata continua 344
travata sollevabile 345
travatura reticolare 11
trave 187, 283, 288
trave di coda 395
trave di colmo 187
trave di equilibrio 496, 497
trave in legno 279, 280
traveller's cheque 441
traversa 185, 201, 202, 297, 479
traversa del cancello 202
traversa inferiore 202
traversa inferiore di finestra 187
traversa mediana 201
traversa orizzontale 188
traversa superiore 201, 202
traversa superiore di finestra 187
traversina 302, 303
traverso superiore del telaio 186
travetto 190
travetto del soffitto 187
travetto del solaio 187
travetto di testata 187
trazione integrale 4x4, veicolo a 369
tre quarti, tempo di 298
tremolo, braccio del 303
trench 248
treno ad alta velocità 376
treno della metropolitana 378
treno locale 375
treno passeggeri 374
treppiede 8, 308
trequarti 248
trequarti centrodestro 482
trequarti centrosinistro 482
triage, stanze del 463
triangolo 295, 309, 429, 503
triangolo divisorio 259
tribunale 440
tribunale, aula di 440
tribune mobili 444
triciclo 373
tricipite brachiale 97
tricipiti, barra per i 501
triclinio 280
trifogliata 55
triglia 159
trillo 299
trimarano 521
trinciante 169
trinciapollo 173
Trinidad e Tobago 449
trio 300
trippa 154
trippa, salsiccia di 156
tris 468
tritacarne 170

tritarifiuti 197
triticale 143
Tritone 3
tritone 75
trivellazione, impianto di 403
tromba 307, 455
tromba delle scale 189
tromba marina 43
tromba militare 307
trombe 295
trombone 56, 307
tromboni 295
tronchesina per cuticole 265
tronchesina per unghie 265
tronco 52, 62, 63, 75, 93, 95
tronco celiaco 103, 107
tronco di testa della scala 455
tronco, armatura protettiva del 486
tronco, parte inferiore del 63
tronco, sezione trasversale di un 63
tropicale della foresta pluviale 40
tropicale umido e secco (savana) 40
Tropico del Cancro 20, 21, 22
Tropico del Capricorno 20, 21, 22
tropopausa 37, 46
troposfera 37
troppopieno 194, 195
troppopieno, tubo del 196
trota 161
trotto 83
trousse 276
truccatore 290
trucco 266
trucco per gli occhi 266
trucco per il viso 266
trucco per le labbra 266
trumeau 285
tuba 295, 307
tuba di Eustachio 116, 117
tuba di Falloppio 112
tuba di Falloppio, ampolla della 113
tuba di Falloppio, infundibolo della 113
tuba di Falloppio, istmo della 113
tubazione del freno 357
tubazione di allacciamento 194
tubazione di riempimento 404
tube di Falloppio 113
tubetto 163
tubino 252
tubo 199, 224, 461
tubo a flash 420
tubo annaffiatore 365
tubo aspirante 407
tubo capillare 424
tubo del troppopieno 196
tubo dell'acqua fredda 196
tubo della pompa 346
tubo della prima valvola 307
tubo della scala, erogatore del 455
tubo della seconda valvola 307
tubo della terza valvola 307
tubo di accordo 307
tubo di alimentazione 197
tubo di alimentazione dell'acqua 214
tubo di alimentazione dell'aria 454
tubo di aspirazione 455
tubo di carico 196
tubo di circolazione 410
tubo di drenaggio 212, 214
tubo di estrazione dell'aria 199
tubo di getto laterale 365
tubo di iniezione del fango 403
tubo di Pitot 525
tubo di posizionamento 400
tubo di riempimento 196
tubo di scappamento 351, 364, 367, 368, 369
tubo di scarico 194, 196, 197, 212, 350, 395, 398, 401
tubo di scarico, attacco del 192
tubo di sterzo 371
tubo flessibile 195, 197, 209, 236, 454, 460
tubo fluorescente 199
tubo in pressione 409
tubo metallico 526
tubo obliquo 371
tubo per irrigazione 236
tubo portaoculare 421
tubo principale 8, 9
tubo rigido 209
tubo rigido di prolunga 209
tubo telescopico principale 420
tubo verticale 370
tubolatura di carico trasversale 385
tucano 80

tuffi 518
tuffi, strutture per i 518
tuffi, torre per i 518
tulipano 56
tumbler 165
tundra 44
tundra polare, della 40
tungsteno, lampada alogena al 199
tunica 54
tunica, abito a 252
Tunisia 451
tunnel di comunicazione 13
tuorlo 79
turapori, pistola 216
turbante 239
turbina 402, 408
turbina ad asse verticale 412
turbina eolica ad asse orizzontale 413
turbina, albero della 408
turbine eoliche 412
turbo-alternatore, gruppo del 402
turboreattore 393
Turchia 452
turibolo 446
turione 125
turismo, bicicletta da 373
Turkmenistan 452
tuta 254, 261, 508, 510, 513, 514
tuta da competizione 525
tuta da sci 261
tuta ignifuga 524
tuta protettiva 525
tuta spaziale 10
tuta sportiva 262
tutina a sacco 260
tutore 230, 231
Tuvalu 453
TV/video, tasto 319
tweeter 324
twin-set 255

U

uadi 36
uccelli 78
uccelli, esempi di 80
uccello 78
uccello acquatico 79
uccello granivoro 79
uccello insettivoro 79
uccello passeriforme 79
uccello predatore 79
uccello trampoliere 79
uccello, morfologia di un 78
Ucraina 450
uffici 346, 374, 381
uffici, edificio per 432, 435
uffici, torre per 435
ufficio 438, 439
ufficio dei cancellieri 440
ufficio dei giudici 440
ufficio del bidello 445
ufficio del capolsala 463
ufficio del direttore 443
ufficio del medico di guardia 462
ufficio del preside 445
ufficio dell'assistente sociale 463
ufficio della palestra 444
ufficio della segretaria 443
ufficio della segreteria scolastica 445
ufficio delle informazioni 512
ufficio di formazione professionale 442
ufficio postale 433, 437
Uganda 451
ugello 12, 216, 218, 219, 236
ugello a sezione variabile 394
ugello del lavaparabrezza 348
ugello vaporizzatore 181
ugola 116, 117
uguale a 427
uistiti 91
ulna 98
ultimo quarto 5
umbone 73
Umbriel 3
umidità contenuta nelle nuvole 48
umor acqueo 119
Ungheria 450
unghia 71, 76, 78, 115
unghia per apertura 531
unghia, corpo dell' 114
unghie dei piedi, forbici per 265
unghie, forbicine per 265
unghie, matita sbiancante per 265
unghie, tronchesina per 265
unicellulari 66

uniforme 456
unione 427
Unione Europea, bandiera dell' 441
unisono 298
unità a disco 310
unità astronomica 3
unità astronomiche 2
unità di controllo elettronico 357
unità di cura intensiva 464
unità di misura dell'energia 426
unità di misura dell'intensità luminosa 426
unità di misura della carica elettrica 426
unità di misura della corrente elettrica 426
unità di misura della differenza di potenziale elettrico 426
unità di misura della forza 426
unità di misura della frequenza 426
unità di misura della lunghezza 426
unità di misura della massa 426
unità di misura della potenza elettrica 426
unità di misura della pressione 426
unità di misura della quantità di sostanza 426
unità di misura della radioattività 426
unità di misura della resistenza elettrica 426
unità di misura della temperatura Celsius 426
unità di misura della temperatura termodinamica 426
unità di misura, sistema internazionale di 426
unità di servizio mobile a distanza 11
unità floppy disk 329
unità floppy disk esterna 333
unità hard disk 333
unità hard disk estraibile 333
unità individuale di propulsione e manovra 10
unità mobile 316
unità motrice 376
unità radiologica mobile 462
università 432
uno 427
uomo 92
uomo, collo e 251
uomo, scarpe da 240
uova 155
uova alla coque, clessidra per 171
uova in camicia, tegame per 175
uova, confezione in cartone per 162
uova, scomparto per le 211
uovo 79
uovo di anatra 155
uovo di fagiano 155
uovo di gallina 155
uovo di oca 155
uovo di quaglia 155
uovo di struzzo 155
uragano 43
Urano 2, 3
uretere 107
uretra 107, 111, 112
urinario, apparato 107
URL 334
URL (localizzatore universale di risorse) 334
uropodio 71
Uruguay 448
uscita del fluido vettore 410
uscita dell'aria calda 192
uscita S-Video 336
uscita, bordo di 392
usignolo 80
utensili da cucina 169
utensili per avvitare 221
utensili per cucinare 174
utensili per dolci 172
utensili per segare 226
utensili vari 173
utensili, set di 173
utente 317
utente di Internet 334
utente privato 335
utente, ingresso dell'alimentazione dell' 198
utero 112, 113
utero, collo dell' 112
utero, legamento largo dell' 113
uva 132
uva, grappolo d' 62
uvaspina 132
Uzbekistan 452

V

vacuolo 50, 66
vacuolo digerente 66
vacuolo digerente in formazione 66
vacuolo pulsante 66
vagina 112, 113
vagone di coda del personale viaggiante 377
vagone intermodale 377
vagone letto 376
vagone ristorante 376
vagone viaggiatori 376
vagoni passeggeri, tipi di 376
valerianella 127
valigia 277
valle 29, 32
valore del segmento 471
valore, indicazione del 441
valori di durata delle note 299
valori di durata delle pause 299
valuta 60, 73
valute, esempi di simboli di 440
valva 60, 73
valvola 307, 371
valvola aortica 104
valvola del galleggiante 196
valvola di aspirazione 360
valvola di chiusura 196
valvola di drenaggio 211
valvola di espirazione 459
valvola di inspirazione 459
valvola di regolazione della pressione 461
valvola di scarico 360
valvola di sfiato 385
valvola di sicurezza 174, 408
valvola di spurgo 404
valvola di tenuta 196
valvola di tenuta, sede della 196
valvola mitrale 104
valvola polmonare 104
valvola tricuspide 104
valvola, corpo della 307
valvola, molla della 360
Vanessa atalanta 69
vanga 233
vaniglia, estratto di 140
vano 286
vano cassetta 319
vano del disco 323
vano del motore 401
vano del motore di traino 400
vano del motore diesel 398, 399, 400, 401
vano del serbatoio dell'acqua 394
vano della cassetta 323
vano della videocassetta 320
vano motore 362, 396
vano portamateriale 455
vano portaoggetti 354, 364
vano portaspazzolini 272
vano portattrezzi 361
vano raccoglipolvere 208
Vanuatu 453
vapore 402, 408, 415
vapore, ferro da stiro a 208
vapore, generatore di 402
vapore, pentola a 175
vapore, regolatore del getto di 208
vapore, regolazione del 181
vaporizzatore 208
varano 77
variante 524
variazione di pressione 39
Varolio, ponte di 109
vasca 212, 214, 517
vasca da bagno 189, 194, 195, 439
vasca del fango 403
vasca di deposito del combustibile esaurito 409
vasca per immersione 184
vasca, orlo della 212
vasca, piattaforma della 195
vasca/doccia, miscelatore 194
vaschetta 219
vaschetta con beccuccio 177
vaschetta di raccolta 181
vaschetta filtrante 177, 180
vaschetta per alimenti 162

vaschetta per burro 163
vaschetta per cubetti di ghiaccio 211
vaschetta per il detersivo 214
vaschetta portacorrispondenza 338
vasellame da tavola 166
vasetto 163
vaso 196, 230
vaso capillare 114
vaso sanguigno 104, 114
vaso sospeso 230
vassoio 205, 277
vassoio dei documenti ricevuti 328
vassoio dei documenti trasmessi 328
vassoio di alimentazione 333
vassoio di uscita 333
vassoio portadischi 318
vasto laterale 96, 97
vasto mediale 96
Vaticano, Città del 450
VCR, comandi del 319
vedretta 30
vegetazione 44
vegetazione, distribuzione della 44
veicoli 342
veicolo a trazione integrale 4x4 369
veicolo d'emergenza per l'equipaggio 11
vela 519, 520
velario 281
velcro® 260
velluto, collarino di 264
velo 536
velocità di crociera, controllo della 354
velocità, regolatore di 176, 287
velocità, selettore di 176, 177, 227, 228
vena ascellare 102
vena basilica 102
vena cava inferiore 102, 103, 104, 107
vena cava superiore 102, 103, 104
vena cefalica 102
vena epatica 103
vena femorale 102
vena giugulare esterna 102
vena giugulare interna 102
vena iliaca comune 107
vena iliaca interna 103
vena mesenterica superiore 102
vena polmonare 102
vena polmonare destra 104
vena polmonare sinistra 104
vena porta 103
vena renale 102, 107
vena succlavia 102
vendita dei biglietti 378
vene 102
Venere 2, 3
Venere, monte di 112
Venezuela 448
venti, rosa dei 23
ventilatore 213, 358, 360
ventilatore di sostentamento 383
ventilatore, alloggiamento del 270
ventilazione, colonna principale di 194
ventilazione, griglia di 209
ventilazione, rete di 194
ventiquattrore 274
vento 47, 48
vento predominante 43
vento, azione del 45
vento, direzione del 39
vento, direzione e forza del 39
vento, forza del 39
vento, giacca a 249
ventola 322
ventola dell'alimentatore 329
ventola dello châssis 329
ventola di raffreddamento 336, 350
ventola, cinghia della 350
ventosa 72
ventre 83
ventricolo destro 103, 104
ventricolo sinistro 103, 104
verbena 148
verde 418
verdone 123
verdura 120, 173
verdura, cassetto per la 211
vermicelli di riso 147
verniciatura: manutenzione 219

verricello 364
verricello di ormeggio 385
verricello, comandi del 364
versante 29
vertebra lombare 110
vertebre cervicali 99
vertebre dorsali 99
vertebre lombari 99
verticale sulle braccia 518
vertice 78
vescica 111, 112
vescica urinaria 107
vescichetta seminale 111
vespa 69
vestaglia 256
vestaglia, abito a 252
vestibolo 116, 280
vestiti per bambini 261
vestiti per neonati 260
vetrata 446
vetrina 203
vetrinette refrigerate apribili 120
vetrino 421
vetro 186, 410, 411
vetro colorato 285
vetro di protezione 506
vetro, lastra di 211
vetro, smistamento del 49
vetro, tetto a 188
vetrone 41
vetta 512
vettura a tre porte 347
vettura da golf 505
via 25, 433, 469
via commerciale 432
via di fuga 524
Via Lattea 6
Via Lattea (vista dall'alto) 6
Via Lattea (vista laterale) 6
viaggi, agenzia di 436
viaggiatori, marciapiede dei 374
viaggiatori, stazione dei 374, 375, 381
viaggiatori, vagone 376
viaggio, borsa da 276
viaggio, borsone da 276
vialetto 230
vialetto del giardino 182
vialetto di accesso 183
vibrissa 82
vibrisse 87
vibrovaglio per la depurazione del fango 403
viceallenatore 489
vicecapitano 515
vicolo 433
video 471
videocamera portatile: dorso 320
videocamera portatile: vista frontale 320
videocassetta 319
videocassetta, comandi della 320
videocassetta, vano della 320
videocassette compatte, adattatore per 320
videogioco 471
videoregistratore 319
Vietnam 453
vigile del fuoco 454
vigili del fuoco, caserma dei 433
vignetta 313
villaggio 512
villetta bifamiliare 289
vinacciolo 59
vini, cantina dei 438
vino 120
vino alsaziano, bicchiere da 165
vino bianco, bicchiere da 165
vino, aceto di 141
viola 56, 301
viole 295
violino 301
violino, chiave di 298
violoncelli 295
violoncello 301
vipera 77
virata a dorso, contrassegno per la 517
virata, giudici di 517
virata, parete di 517
visiera 238, 239, 367, 458, 506, 525
visiera antisolare 10

visiera parasole 361
visione di insieme 186
visite ginecologiche, stanza per 463
visite mediche, stanza per le 463, 465
viso, trucco per il 266
visone 88
visore 459
vista 419
vista anteriore 92, 94, 96, 98
vista frontale 478
vista laterale 478
vista laterale del cranio 100
vista normale 419
vista posteriore 93, 95, 97, 99, 113
vista, difetti della 419
Vistola, Fiume 18
vita 93, 95
vita bassa, abito a 252
vite 62, 221, 301
vite di bloccaggio 536, 537
vite di blocco della lama 227
vite di fissaggio 535
vite di livello 423
vite di regolazione 222, 229
vite di regolazione della tensione 341
vite di serraggio 224
vite macrometrica 421
vite micrometrica 421, 425
vite rompigetto 236
vite senza fine 365
vite, albero della 62
vite, attacco a 199
vite, orecchini a 264
vitello 84
vitello, tagli di 152
viti di bloccaggio 425
viticcio 62
Vittoria, Lago 20
volano 360, 501
volano a penne naturali 495
volano sintetico 495
volano, gioco del 494
volant 204
volante 350, 354, 385, 525
volante di direzione 455
volante, piantone di 350
volatili 155
volée 490
Volga, Fiume 18
voli 518
volpe 88
volpe del deserto 88
volt 426
volta 284
volta a botte 281
volta esterna della cupola 7
volta interna della cupola 7
volteggi, cavallo per 496, 497
volume di ricezione, regolatore del 327
volume, controllo del 310, 311
volume, manopola del 325, 326
volume, regolatore del 327, 328
volume, regolazione del 303
volume, rotella del 329
volume, tasti di regolazione del 319
voluta 200
voluta, piede a 200
volva 52
vongola 157
vongola molle 157
vulcani, esempi di 28
vulcano 26, 28
vulcano esplosivo 28
vulcano in eruzione 28
vulva 94, 113

W

wakame 123
walkman 326
wapiti 84
wasabi 141
Wassily, poltrona 200
water 189, 194, 195, 196, 439, 464
watt 426
webcam 332

Weddell, Mare di 15
wigwam 288
Wilkes, Terra di 15
winch 521
windsurf 519
wok 174
wok, servizio da 174
woofer 324

X

xilofono 295, 309

Y

yacht a motore 385
yak 85
yards, linea delle 484
Yemen 452
yen 440
yogurt 150
Yucatan, Penisola dello 16

Z

zafferano 138
zaino 372, 532
Zambia 452
zampa 76
zampa anteriore 67, 68
zampa di elefante, pantaloni a 254
zampa mediana 67, 68
zampa posteriore 67, 68
zampe, esempi di 79
zanzara 69
zappa 233
zappetta tridente 233
zattera di salvataggio 383
zavorra 397
zebra 84
zecca 70
zenzero 139
zero 468
Zimbabwe 452
zither 296
zoccolo 83, 185, 191, 242, 302
zona abitabile 528
zona commerciale 431
zona convettiva 4
zona di passaggio del testimone 472
zona dell'allenatore 474
zona di attacco 487
zona di battuta 477
zona di difesa 487
zona di pericolo 499
zona di preparazione dei prodotti 120
zona di ricevimento dei latticini 120
zona di ricevimento delle merci 120
zona di servizio 491
zona industriale 431
zona libera 487
zona negativa 410
zona neutra 484, 507
zona pellucida 112
zona positiva 410
zona pranzo 164
zona protetta 515
zona radiativa 4
zone di servizio 495
zoom 320
zoom, comando elettrico dello 320
zucca 129
zucca a collo allungato 129
zucca bianca 128
zucca di Napoli 128
zucca pasticcina 129
zucca spaghetti 129
zucca torta 129
zuccheriera 166
zucchero 149
zucchero a velo 149
zucchero candito 149
zucchero di canna 149
zucchero in grani 149
zucchetta 129
zucchina 128
zuppiera 166

ASTRONOMIA > 2-25;   TERRA > 26-71;   REGNO VEGETALE >72-89;   REGNO ANIMALE > 90-143;   ESSERE UMANO > 144-177;   GENERI ALIMENTARI E CUCINA > 178-241;   CASA > 242-295;
FAI DA TE E GIARDINAGGIO > 296-333;   ABBIGLIAMENTO > 334-371;   ACCESSORI E ARTICOLI PERSONALI > 372-391;   ARTE E ARCHITETTURA > 392-465;   COMUNICAZIONI E BUROTICA > 466-535;
TRASPORTI E VEICOLI > 536-643;   ENERGIA > 644-677;   SCIENZA > 678-705;   SOCIETÀ > 706-785;   SPORT E GIOCHI > 786-920

635

INDICE DEI NOMI ITALIANI

Indice español

A

abdomen 67, 68, 70, 71, 78, 92, 94
abdomen, oblicuo mayor 96, 97
abdomen, recto 96
abedul 64
abeja 68
abeja trabajadora, morfología 68
abejorro 69
abertura 538
abertura con tirilla 245
abertura para el brazo 251
abertura trasera central 244
abertura trasera lateral 244
aberturas branquiales 74
aberturas para los nudillos 243
abeto 65
abisinio 87
abocinamiento 285
abono compuesto, cajón 231
abrazadera 8, 9, 198, 277, 521
abrebotellas 170, 531
abrecartas 339
abrelatas 170, 180, 531
abreviaciones de monedas, ejemplos 440
abrigo 248, 251
abrigo con esclavina 251
abrigo de tres cuartos 248
abrigo raglán 251
abrigo redingote 251
abrigos 248, 251
ábside 285
absorción de agua y sales minerales 54
absorción por el suelo 46
absorción por las nubes 46
acampada 528
acantilado 29, 35
acceso a los andenes 374
accesorios 209, 356, 372, 538
accesorios de golf 504
accesorios para el objetivo 314
accesorios personales 264
accesorios, cajetín 209
accesorios, objetivos 314
accidentales 299
acción del viento 45
accionador de presión del oxígeno 10
acedera 127
aceite de cacahuete 149
aceite de girasol 149
aceite de maíz 149
aceite de oliva 149
aceite de sésamo 149
aceites 149
aceites lubricantes 405
aceituna 128
acelerador 235, 368
acelga 125
acento 299
acera 183, 434
achicoria de Treviso 126
acicular 55
acidificación de los lagos 48

acondicionador 267
acoplamiento de pedal 305
acorazonada 55
acorde 299
acordeón 296
acromion 99
acrotera 279
actor 290
actores, entrada 278
actriz 291
acuífero confinado 402
acumulador 357, 411
adaptador 271
adaptador de acoplamiento 11
adaptador de cinta de vídeo compacto 320
adaptador de corriente 336
adaptador de enchufes 198
adarve 282
adarve cubierto 282
Adén, golfo 19, 20
adición en la memoria 337
administración 445
adobes, casa 288
adormidera, semillas 139
adornos 299
Adriático, mar 18
aduana 381, 391
aductor del muslo 96
aductor mayor 97
aerocisto 51
aerodeslizador (hovercraft) 383
aeropuerto 25, 388, 430
aerosol de pimienta 456
afeitado 271
afeitado, loción 271
Afganistán 452
afilador 169
afinación 308
afinador 305
afluente 32
África 14, 20, 34, 451
agar-agar 123
agarrador 467
agencia de viajes 436
agenda 275, 338
agenda electrónica 338
agenda telefónica 327, 338
agente de policía 456
agitador de aspas 212
agricultura intensiva 46, 48
agu bendita, pila 446
agua 402
agua de colonia 267
agua de deshielo 30
agua de nubes 48
agua de perfume 267
agua, castaña 124
agua, corriente 32
agua, depósito 181
agua, sales minerales, absorción 54
aguacate 127
aguanieve 41

aguas residuales 48
aguaturma 124
aguijón 68
águila 81
aguja 36, 285, 460
aguja de cambio 375
aguja de coser 173
aguja de décimas de segundo 424
aguja del transepto 284
aguja imantada 533
aguja picadora 173
agujas del abeto 65
agujas del pino 65
agujero apical 101
agujero ciego 118
airbag 354
airbag, sistema de restricción 354
aire acondicionado 361
aire cálido ascendente 43
aire caliente 41
aire frío 41
aire frío subsidente 43
aire libre, ocio 528
aislador 359
aislante 214, 410
aislante de cera 196
ajedrea 142
ajedrez 470
ajo 124
ajoWan 139
ajustador de la bota 511
ajuste de altura 501
ajuste de elevación 420
ajuste de la altura del condensador 421
ajuste de la lente de campo 421
ajuste de profundidad 229
ajuste de resistencia 501
ajuste de tonos agudos 303
ajuste de tonos bajos 303
ajuste del display 327
ajuste fino de la altura 8, 9
ajuste fino del acimut 8, 9
ajuste lateral 420
ala 13, 68, 78, 238, 239, 275, 393, 536
ala alta 394
ala cerrado 485
ala de la nariz 87
ala de popa 387
ala defensivo derecho 484
ala defensivo izquierdo 484
ala del cuarto 240, 262
ala delantera 67
ala delta 394
ala derecho 482
ala izquierdo 482
ala trasera 67
alamar 249
álamo 64
alas, tarima 396
Alaska, golfo 16
albahaca 142
Albania 450
albañilería 216

albaricoque 132
albatros 80
albornoz 256
albúmina 79
albura 63
alcachofa 127
alcachofa de la ducha 195
alcantarilla 434
alcantarilla principal 434
alcaravea 138
alce 85
alcohol puro 461
aldabilla 277
Alemania 450
alerce 65
alero 279, 283
alero derecho 489
alero izquierdo 489
alerón 13, 392, 525
aleta 213, 393, 394, 395
aleta abdominal 74
aleta anal 74
aleta caudal 74, 90
aleta de fuselaje 13
aleta de la nariz 117
aleta de penetración superficial 387
aleta de proa 387
aleta del borde de fuga 392
aleta dorsal 90
aleta estabilizadora 386
aleta hipersustentadora 393
aleta pectoral 74, 90
aleta pélvica 74
Aleutianas, fosa 34
Aleutianas, islas 16
alfalfa 130
alféizar 186, 187
alfil 470
alfiler 268
alfombra 190
alfombrilla 356
alfombrilla de ratón 332
alga 51
alga parda 51
alga roja 51
alga verde 51
alga, estructura 51
algas 123
algas, ejemplos 51
algodón hidrófilo 461
alheña 142
alianza 264
alicates 222
alicates de electricista 217
alicates de presión 222
alicates de punta 217
alicates para cutículas 265
alicates pico de loro 222
aligátor 77
alimentación, cordón 177, 269
alimentación, fuente 416
alimentador 321
alimentos para animales 121

alimentos selectos 120
alitán 158
aliviadero 406
alma 305
almacén 444
almacén de congelados 121
almacén de material estéril 462
almacén de material sucio 462
almacén material sucio 464
almacenamiento de información, unidades 333
almeja 157
almena 282
almendra 57, 133
almidón 61
almidón, glóbulo 50
almirez 170
almohada 204
alojamiento de la casete 323
alojamiento de la cinta 320
alojamiento para el disco 323
alojamiento para la cinta 319
alojamientos 512
alpargata 242
Alpes 18
alquequenje 132
alta montaña, climas 40
alta presión, área 43
alta velocidad, tren 376
altar lateral 446
altar mayor 446
altar, cruz 446
altavoces extremos de graves 321
altavoz 294, 320, 324, 325, 326, 328, 336, 455, 518
altavoz central 321
altavoz de comunicación 380
altavoz de frecuencias de graves 324
altavoz de frecuenciasde medias 324
altavoz defrecuencias altas 324
altavoz principal 321
altavoz surround 321
alternado: selección de nivel 3 330
alternador 350, 360, 413
alternativa 330
altitud 44
alto de caña 511
altocúmulos 42
altostratos 42
altramuz 130
altura de la ola 33
altura del peldaño 191
alubias 131
álula 78
alumno 444
alumno, pupitre 444
alveolo 198
alvéolo dental 101
alza 301, 534
alzado 182, 212
amanita virosa 52
amapola 56, 60
amaranto 143

ASTRONOMÍA > 2-25;   TIERRA > 26-71;   REINO VEGETAL > 72-89;   REINO ANIMAL > 90-143;   SER HUMANO > 144-177;   PRODUCTOS ALIMENTARIOS Y DE COCINA > 178-241;   CASA > 242-295;
BRICOLAJE Y JARDINERÍA > 296-333;   VESTIDO > 334-371;   ACCESORIOS Y ARTÍCULOS PERSONALES > 372-391;   ARTE Y ARQUITECTURA > 392-465;   COMUNICACIONES Y AUTOMATIZACIÓN DE
OFICINA > 466-535;   TRANSPORTE Y VEHÍCULOS > 536-643;   ENERGÍA > 644-677;   CIENCIA > 678-705;   SOCIEDAD > 706-785;   DEPORTES Y JUEGOS > 786-920

637

amarillo 418
amarra 385
amarre 521
amarre anterior retráctil 361
amasadora 179
Amazonas, río 17
ambiente 44
ambiente natural 504
ambulancia 460, 462
ambulatorio 465
ameba 66
América Central 14, 16
América del Norte 14, 16, 34
América del Sur 14, 17, 34
americana 254
americano, clavija de tipo 198
Américas 448
Amery, Plataforma de Hielo 15
amígdala 116
amígdala lingual 118
amígdala palatina 118
amortiguador 287, 351, 367, 523
amortiguador de fieltro 304
amortiguador delantero 369
amperio 426
ampliación del voltaje 408
amplificador 310
amplificador /sintonizador : vista frontal 322
amplificador /sintonizador : vista posterior 322
amplificador-sintonizador 325
amplitud 418
ampolla 199, 467
ampolla de la trompa uterina 113
ampolla de vidrio 199
anacardo 133
anaquel 203, 211
anatomía 96
anatomía de un árbol 63
anatomía de un bogavante 71
anatomía de un hongo 52
anatomía de una concha bivalva 73
anatomía de una planta 53
anclaje 344
ancóneo 97
andador 466
andaduras 83
andén 375, 379, 390
andén de pasajeros 374
Andes, cordillera 17
andouillette 156
anemómetro 413
anfibios 75
anfibios, ejemplos 75
anfiteatro romano 281
Angola 452
anguila 159
ángulo agudo 428
ángulo entrante 428
ángulo horario 7
ángulo obtuso 428
ángulo recto 428
ángulos, ejemplos 428
Anik 317
anilla 423, 424
anilla de sujeción 536
anilla guía 536
anilla para colgar 270
anilla para lanzado largo 537
anillas 496, 497
anillas para flexiones 501
anillo 52, 271, 273, 307
anillo de ajuste 221, 306
anillo de articulación 538
anillo de compromiso 264
anillo de crecimiento 63
anillo de enfoque 420
anillo de reglaje del par de apriete 228
anillo de unión del casco 10
anillo graduado de ascensión recta 8, 9
anillo graduado de declinación 9
anillo ocular 78
anillo sellador 404
anillos 264
anillos de sonido 297
anís 142
anís estrellado 60
anjova 160
ano 71, 73, 106, 111, 112
ánodo 417
anorak 263
anotador 487, 488
anotadores 499
Antártica 14, 15
Antártica, península 15
antebrazo 86, 93, 95

antefija 279
antehélix 115
antena 7, 67, 68, 71, 326, 327, 349, 369, 392, 395, 457, 487
antena de alta frecuencia, cable 394
antena de emisión 316
antena de emisión /recepción 316
antena de radio 382, 384, 386, 387, 525
antena de telecomunicaciones 386, 387
antena doméstica 316
antena parabólica 321
antena parabólica de recepción 316
antena parabólica de transmisión 316
antena telescópica 325
anténula 71
anteojo buscador 8, 9
antera 56
anticiclón 39
anticlinal 403
Antigua y Barbuda 449
Antillas 16
antílope 84
antiséptico 461
antitrago 115
anuario 203
anulación de la memoria 337
anuncio 313
anuncios por palabras 313
anuncios, tablero 341
anzuelo 536, 538
aorta 104, 105
aorta abdominal 102, 107
aorta ascendente 103
aorta descendente 103
aorta, cayado 102, 103, 104
aovada 55
Apalaches, montes 16
aparador 203
aparador con vitrina 203
aparato de Golgi 50, 66
aparato de respiración autónomo 454
aparato digestivo 106
aparato respiratorio 105
aparato urinario 107
aparatos de ejercicios 500
aparatos de medición 424
aparatos electrodomésticos 176, 208
aparcamiento 390, 435, 445, 504, 512
aparcamiento de bicicletas 445
aparejo 538
apartado 438
apartamentos 512
apéndice vermiforme 106
apéndices bucales 68
apéndices torácicos 71
apertura terminal 73
ápice 72, 73, 101, 118
apio 125
apio nabo 129
aplicador de esponja 266
aplicadores de algodón 461
aplique 207
apófisis espinosa 110
apófisis estiloides 100
apófisis mastoides 100
apófisis trasversa 110
apotecio 50
apoya-flecha 535
apoyador 484
apoyador exterior 484
apoyador interior 484
apoyatura 299
apoyo del macillo 304
apoyo del pulgar 460
apoyo para el mentón 301
apoyo, punto 70
aquenio 59, 60
Arabia Saudí 452
Arabia, península 19
Arábigo, mar 19
arácnidos 67
arácnidos, ejemplos 70
aracnoides 109
Aral, mar 19
arame 123
araña 70, 207
araña cangrejo 70
araña de agua 70
araña, morfología 70
araña, tela 70
arándano 132
arándano agrio 132
arándano negro 132
arándano rojo 132
arandela 207, 210, 417, 510
arandela de presión 222
arandela de presión de dientes externos 222

arandela de presión de dientes internos 222
arandela plana 222
arandelas 222
árbitro 479, 481, 483, 485, 488, 495, 498, 507, 515, 516
árbitro de base meta 475
árbitro de la defensa 485
árbol 63
árbol de la hélice 387
árbol de levas 360
árbol de Navidad 404
árbol de transmisión 395
árbol de transmisión longitudinal 351
árbol frutal 122
árbol ornamental 122, 182, 230
árbol, anatomía 63
árboles 504
árboles latifoliados, ejemplos 64
arborización terminal 110
arbotante 284, 285
arbusto 230
arca 447
arcada 281, 284
arce 64
arce, jarabe 149
archipiélago 24
archivador colgante 340
archivador de fuelle 340
archivar 339
archivo 334
archivo médico 465
archivo, formato 334
arco 301, 428
arco compuesto 535
arco dentario inferior 116
arco dentario superior 116
arco formero 284
arco insular 33
arco iris 41
arco natural 35
arco tensor 308
arcón congelador 211
ardilla 82
ardilla listada 82
área de alta presión 43
área de baja presión 43
área de caída 472
área de competición 496
área de descanso 25
área de estacionamiento 430
área de juego 471, 515
área de peligro 499
área de penalti 480
área de servicio 25
área pequeña 480
arena 281
arenera 377
arenque 159
aréola 113
Argelia 451
Argentina 448
argolla para tirar 460
armadura 299, 528
armario 164, 202, 439
armario alto 164
armario bajo 164
armario del lavabo 195
armazón 187, 192, 202, 204, 207, 208, 212, 213, 219, 229, 277, 309, 412
armazón de empuje 398
armazón de la máscara 476
armazón de madera 279
armazón de metal 304
armazón del quemador 529
Armenia 452
armónica 296
aro 273, 489
arpa 302
arpas 295
arpegio 299
arquitectura 279
arquitrabe 279
arquivoltas 285
arranque 500
Arrecifes, Gran Barrera 15
arrendajo 80
arriate 182, 230
arroyo 32
arroz 61, 143, 147
arroz basmati 147
arroz blanco 147
arroz integral 147
arroz silvestre 143
arroz vaporizado 147
arroz, fideos 147

arroz, galletas 147
arroz, vermicelli 147
arroz: panícula 61
arrozal 47
arte 278
arteria arcuata 102
arteria axilar 102
arteria braquial 102
arteria carótida primitiva 102
arteria dorsal del pie 102
arteria dorsoabdominal 71
arteria esternal 71
arteria femoral 102
arteria ilíaca común 102, 107
arteria ilíaca interna 102, 103, 107
arteria mesentérica inferior 107
arteria mesentérica superior 102, 107
arteria pulmonar 102, 104, 105
arteria renal 102, 107
arteria subclavia 102
arteria tibial anterior 102
arteria ventral 71
arterias principales 102
artes escénicas 294
Ártico 14
Ártico, océano Glacial 14
articulación 355, 503, 536
artículo 313
artículos de escritorio 337
artículos de limpieza 120, 215
artículos de marroquinería 274
artículos para animales 121
artículos personales 264, 271
artículos varios 341
as 468
asa 176, 177, 178, 179, 180, 204, 209, 210, 215, 225, 226, 227, 229, 236, 274, 275, 276, 277, 326, 537
asa aislante 179
asa extensible 274
asado 152
asado de cerdo 153
asadores 174
asafétida 139
ascensor 287, 435, 439
ascensor, cabina 287
aseo 188, 440, 443
aseo de caballeros 439
aseo de señoras 439
aseos 437, 445, 463, 465
aseos de caballeros 294
aseos de señoras 294
aseos para los clientes 438
asfalto 405
Asia 14, 19, 34, 452
asidero 352, 361, 364, 455
asidero : (espalda) 516
asidero lateral 380
asidero vertical 380
asidero, espalda 516
asiento 195, 196, 200, 201, 205, 342, 353, 369, 467, 501, 523
asiento : vista frontal 353
asiento : vista lateral 353
asiento de corredera 501
asiento del rabino 447
asiento del tapón 196
asiento del teclado 304
asiento doble 380
asiento individual 380
asiento trasero 353
asientos 201
asistente de presidente del jurado 509
asistentes de los abogados 440
asno 84
aspa 412, 413
aspirador 209
aspirador manual 208
aspirina 461
asta 471
astada 55
astigmatismo 419
astil 422
astil, balanza 422
astrágalo 99
astronáutica 10
astronomía 2
Atacama, desierto 17
atención al cliente 443
aterrizaje, pista 390
atizador 193
Atlántico medio, dorsal 34
Atlántico, océano 14, 15, 18, 20
atlas 99
Atlas, cordillera 20
atleta : taco de salida 473
atletismo 472

atmósfera 44, 48
atmósfera terrestre, corte 37
atolón 35
átomo 414
átomos 414
atracción 416
atrecista 291
atril 305, 311, 446
atrio 280
atún 160
audiencia 440
audio player portátil digital 325
aula 445
aula de artes plásticas 444
aula de ciencias 444
aula de informática 444
aula de música 444
aula para alumnos con dificultad de aprendizaje 444
aumento de la tensión 402
aumento del efecto invernadero 46
aurícula derecha 103, 104
aurícula izquierda 103, 104
auricular 324, 327, 460
auriculares 78, 324, 325, 326
aurora polar 37
Australia 14, 34, 453
Austria 450
autobomba tanque 455
autobús 362, 435
autobús articulado 363
autobús escolar 362
autobús urbano 362
autobuses, estación 432
autocar 362
autocar de dos pisos 363
autocaravana 361
autoclave 464
autoescalera 455
automatización de la oficina 329
automóvil 347
automóvil urbanita 347
automóviles : componentes principales 350
automóviles, contaminación 47
autopista 25, 343, 431
autótrofos 45
auxiliares ortopédicos para caminar 466
avance rápido 319
ave 78
ave acuática 79
ave de rapiña 79
ave granívora 79
ave insectívora 79
ave zancuda 79
avellana 133
avellana, corte 60
avena 61, 143
avena : panícula 61
avena, harina 144
avenida 25, 433
aves 78
aves acuáticas 79
aves de corral 155
aves de rapiña 79
aves paseriformes 79
avestruz 81
avión de carga 394
avión de línea 37
avión ligero 394
avión particular 394
avión supersónico 394
avión turborreactor de pasajeros 392
avión, movimientos 395
aviones, ejemplos 394
avisador de alarma 454
avispa 69
avispón 69
axel 509
axila 92, 94
axiómetro 520
axis 99
axón 110
ayudante 121, 498
ayudante del atrecista 291
ayudante del director 291
ayuntamiento 432
azada 233
azada de doble filo 233
azadón 233
azafrán 138
Azerbaiyán 452
azúcar 149
azúcar candi 149
azúcar glas 149
azúcar granulado 149
azúcar moreno 149

azúcar, termómetro 171
azucarero 166
azucena 56
azuela 233
azul 418
azul danés 151

B

babero 260
babilla 83
babor 387
babuino 91
bacalao del Atlántico 161
backgammon 469
bacón americano 156
bacón canadiense 156
bádminton 494
Baffin, bahía 16
baguette 144
Bahamas 448
bahía 5, 24
bahía de Baffin 16
bahía de Bengala 19
bahía de Hudson 16
Bahrein 452
Baikal, lago 19
bailarina 241
baile, cuchilla 509
bajada de aguas 182
bajante 196
bajo 303
bala 534
balalaika 297
balancín 360
balanza de astil 422
balanza de precisión 423
balanza de Roberval 422
balanza para cartas 339
balaustrada 283
balaustre 191
Balcanes, península 18
balcón 189, 293, 447
baldosa 230
ballena 90, 245
balón de baloncesto 488
balón de fútbol 480
balón de fútbol americano 486
balón de rugby 483
baloncesto 488
balsa salvavidas 383
Báltico, mar 18
bambalina 292
bambú, brote 125
banana 136
banco 201, 379, 432, 437, 442, 446,
    469, 501
banco de arena 33
banco de trabajo 224
banco emisor, iniciales 441
banda 481, 484, 487, 488, 495
banda acolchada 526
banda antiadherente 526
banda blanca 487
banda de ajuste 324, 326
banda de goma 502
banda de jazz 300
banda de la cabecera 502
banda de suspensión 458
banda de ventilación 534
banda elástica 246
banda frontal 348
banda holográfica metalizada 441
banda lateral de la red 487
banda lateral protectora 365
banda magnética 441
banda nubosa en espiral 43
banda protectora 358
bandeja 179, 205, 225, 277
bandeja de alimentación 333
bandeja de correspondencia 338
bandeja de pastelería 172
bandeja de pintura 219
bandeja de salida 333
bandeja de vidrio 211
bandeja del disco 318
bandeja para cosméticos 277
bandeja para cubitos de hielo 211
bandeja para herramientas 219
bandeja para los entremeses 166
bandera 482
bandera de la Unión Europea 441
banderas 448
banderín de línea de centro 480
banderín de saque de esquina 481
banderín móvil 504

bandolera 276
bañera 189, 194, 195, 439, 520
Bangladesh 453
banjo 296
baño 439, 464
banqueta 201
banquillo 481, 498
banquillo de jugadores 474, 485, 487
banquillo de los acusados 440
banquillo de los jugadores 506
banquillo de los penaltis 507
banquillo del entrenador 474
banquisa de Ross 15
baqueta 297
baquetas 309
bar 293, 294, 432, 436, 438
bar, barra 438
bar, taburete 438
baraja 468
baranda 502
barandilla 188, 189, 191, 219, 377,
    384, 526
barbacana 282
Barbados 449
barbecho 122
barbilla 538
barco perforador 382
bardana 129
Barents, mar 18
barján 36
barqueta 162
barra 35, 237, 273, 309, 370, 469, 500,
    501
barra antivibración 235
barra colectora 407
barra con pesas 500
barra de arrastre 400
barra de combustible 409
barra de compás 298
barra de dirección 350
barra de equilibrio 496, 497
barra de escotas 521
barra de extensión de piernas 501
barra de flexión de piernas 501
barra de pan 144
barra de remolque 361
barra de repetición 298
barra de torsión 500
barra de tríceps 501
barra del bar 438
barra distanciadora 362
barra espaciadora 330
barra fija 496, 497
barra sujetadora 188
barras paralelas 496, 497
barras paralelas asimétricas 496, 497
barredora 365
barrena 403
barrena de muro 228
barrera 205
barrera de contención 524
barrote 205
basamento 283
báscula de baño 423
báscula de cocina 171
báscula electrónica 423
báscula romana 422
base 125, 179, 180, 206, 227, 229,
    269, 318, 332, 412, 421, 422, 454,
    489
base con protecciones 489
base de cemento 190
base de cemento, parqué sobre 190
base de datos 335
base de la ola 33
base de lanzamiento 475
base del bulbo 54
base del hogar 192
base del respaldo 200
base del telescopio 7
base del tronco 63
base del tubo 199
base exterior 469
base fija 224
base giratoria 224
base impermeable 190
base interior 469
base líquida 266
base meta 475
Bass, estrecho 15
bastidor 224, 226, 274, 277, 367, 410,
    411, 492, 494, 522, 527
bastidor de los rodillos 398
bastidores 292
bastón 273
bastón cuadrangular 466

bastón de esquí 510, 514
bastón del portero 507
bastón inglés 466
bastón ortopédico 466
bastón para caminar 466
bastoncillo 119
bastones 273, 505
basura, cubo 215
bata 256
batata 124
bate 476, 477, 478
bate de softball 477
bateador 475, 476, 478, 479
batería 221, 228, 308, 350, 359, 416
batería electrónica 311
batidor 172
batidor mecánico 172
batidora de mano 176
batidora de mesa 176
batidora de pie 176
batidora de vaso 176
batiente 186
batir 176
baúl 203, 277
bayas 132
bayas de enebro 138
bayeta de cocina 215
bayeta, cocina 215
bazo 103
Beaufort, estrecho 16
bebé, ropa 260
bebidas 120
becquerel 426
becuadro 299
begonia 56
béisbol 474, 476
belfo 83
belfos 86
Bélgica 449
Belice 448
bemol 299
Bengala, bahía 19
Benin 451
berberecho 157
berenjena 128
bergamota 134
Bering, estrecho 16
Bering, mar 14
berlina 347
bermudas 254
berro 127
berros de jardín 127
berza 126
besuguera 174
biblioteca 433, 444
biceps braquial 96
biceps femoral 97
bicicleta 370
bicicleta BMX 373
bicicleta de carreras 522
bicicleta de carretera 373
bicicleta de ciudad 373
bicicleta de cross 522
bicicleta de descenso 522
bicicleta de turismo 373
bicicleta estática 501
bicicleta holandesa 373
bicicleta todo terreno 373
bicicleta, partes 370
bicicletas, ejemplos 373
bidé 195
biela 360
Bielorrusia 450
bígaro 157
bigotes 87
billar 502
billar francés 502
billar inglés 503
billete : verso 441
billete, recto 441
billete, verso 441
billete: recto 441
billetera 274, 275
billetero 275
billetes de banco 469
billetes, emisión 442
bimah 447
biología 426
biosfera 44
biosfera, estructura 44
bisagra 178, 185, 186, 202, 214, 274,
    277, 352, 420
bisel 460
bisonte 84
bistec 152
bita 385

bizna 60
blanca 299, 468, 469
blanca doble 468
blancas 470
blanco 418, 471
blastodisco 79
bloque 305
bloque de apartamentos 289, 433, 512
bloque de cierre de la recámara 534
bloque de cierre de recámara 534
bloque de cirugía 464
bloque de contención 409
bloque del motor 360
bloqueo 425
bloqueo corrimiento 331
bloqueo eje 526
bloqueo mayúsculas 330
bloqueo numérico 331
bloqueo, tornillos 425
blusas, ejemplos 255
blusón 255
blusón con tirilla 255
boa 77
bobina 319, 536, 537
boca 71, 72, 73, 75, 90, 94, 116, 220,
    224, 305, 534
boca de acceso 404
boca de aspiración de aire 383
boca de llenado 351
boca de riego 434, 454
boca del depósito 237
boca para la manguera 236
bocina neumática 364
bodega 438
bodega de carga 12
bodega de contenedores 383
bodega de equipaje 393, 395
body 255, 258, 263
bogavante 71, 158
bogavante, anatomía 71
bogavante, morfología 71
bogie 527
bogie del motor 376
boina 239
bol 177
bol mezclador 176
bol para ensalada 166
bola 220
bola amarilla 503
bola azul 503
bola blanca 502, 503
bola de corcho 477
bola de hilo 477
bola de rodamiento 312
bola marrón 503
bola negra 503
bola pinta 502, 503
bola roja 502, 503
bola rosa 503
bola verde 503
bolas numeradas 502
bolas rojas 503
bolera 436
bolero 254
bolero con botones 254
boles para batir 172
boleto comestible 123
bolígrafo 312
Bolivia 448
bolsa 162
bolsa de cuero 337
bolsa de golf 505
bolsa de lona 276
bolsa de malla 162
bolsa para congelados 162
bolsa, cajetín 209
bolsas 121
bolsillo 225, 250, 274, 502, 505
bolsillo con cartera 244, 248
bolsillo de fuelle 255
bolsillo de ojal 244, 249, 251
bolsillo de parche 244, 249, 260
bolsillo de ribete 244
bolsillo de ribete ancho 248, 251
bolsillo del cambio 244
bolsillo delantero 246, 274
bolsillo disimulado 251
bolsillo exterior 275, 276
bolsillo lateral 352
bolsillo secreto 274
bolsillo simulado 251
bolsillo superior 245, 248
bolsillo trasero 246
bolsita de té 148
bolso clásico 275
bolso de bandolera 276
bolso de fuelle 276

bolso de hombre 276
bolso de la compra 276
bolso de vestir 276
bolso de viaje 276
bolso interior 277
bolso manguito 276
bolso saco 276
bolso tipo cubo 275
bolsos 275
bomba 184, 212, 214, 529
bomba de aire 370
bomba para lodos 403
bomba volcánica 28
bombachos 254
bombardino 307
bombero 454
bombilla 217, 416
bombilla de bajo consumo 199
bombilla de bayoneta 199
bombilla de rosca 199
bombilla incandescente 199
bombo 295, 308
bombona de aire comprimido 454
bombona de gas 529
bombona de gas desechable 218
bombona de gas médico 464
bongos 309
boniato 124
boquerón 159
boquilla 196, 216, 219, 236, 306, 307,
    311, 406, 407, 467
boquilla de llenado 208
boquilla de vertido 184
boquilla para concentrar la llama 218
boquilla para expandir la llama 218
boquilla para suelos y alfombras 209
boquilla para tapicería 209
boquilla pulverizadora 236
boquilla rinconera 209
borde 55, 205, 210, 526
borde 526
borde de ataque 393
borde de fuga 392
borde de la cuba 212
borde de la punta 228
borde del andén 374, 379
borde del lomo 228
borde, hoja 55
bordes, podadora 237
bordillo 230, 434
borla 266
borne 359
borne negativo 359, 416
borne positivo 359, 417
borraja 142
borrar 331
Bosnia-Herzegovina 450
bosque 29
bosque de coníferas 44
bosque de hoja caduca 44
bosque mixto 44
bosque templado 44
bosque tropical 44
bosque tropical húmedo 44
bosques 25
Bostuana 452
bota 241, 506, 509, 510, 514, 525, 527
bota blanda 513
bota de fútbol 480
bota de medio muslo 241
bota de montaña 242
bota de salto de esquí 513
bota de seguridad 459
bota de trabajo 240
bota externa 511, 527
bota rígida 513
botador 220
botalón 520
botas altas 538
botas de caucho 454
botas de tacos de rugby 483
botas para esquiar 511
botavara 519, 520
bote salvavidas 382, 386
botella 267, 371
botella de vidrio 163
botella del termo 532
botella, vidrio 163
botes herméticos 162
botín 240, 241
botín interior 511, 527
botiquín 465
botiquín de primeros auxilios 461
botiquín de urgencias 457
Botnia, golfo 19
botón 199, 245, 250, 296, 301
botón de acoplamiento 305

botón de ajuste a cero del contador 323
botón de ajuste fino 421
botón de ajuste grueso 421
botón de alimentación del papel 333, 443
botón de apagado 235
botón de avance rápido 319, 323, 328
botón de avance/parada 333
botón de bloqueo 225, 227
botón de bloqueo de la pantalla 336
botón de cancelación 315
botón de cierre 208
botón de compensación de la exposición 314
botón de control 332
botón de control del alojamiento del disco 323
botón de control remoto 315
botón de desbloqueo del objetivo 314
botón de encendido 318, 322, 328
botón de encendido del touch pad 336
botón de encendido TV 319
botón de encendido VCR 319
botón de enclavamiento 229
botón de enfoque 8, 9
botón de ensayo 454
botón de expulsión 315, 319, 323, 471
botón de expulsión de CD/DVD-ROM 329
botón de expulsión de disquete 329
botón de funcionamiento 326
botón de grabación 319, 328
botón de grabación silenciosa 323
botón de grabador vocal 337
botón de índice /ampliación 315
botón de inicio 337
botón de inicio de grabación 323
botón de inicio de marcha 424
botón de inicio del contador 424
botón de la bandolera 303
botón de la llave 306
botón de la memoria 323
botón de lectura 327
botón de llamada para peatones 434
botón de madera 249
botón de mando 210
botón de memoria 327
botón de montaje 320
botón de nivel de grabación 323
botón de parada 424
botón de pausa 323
botón de presión 243, 249, 260, 312
botón de previsionado de profundidad de campo 314
botón de rebobinado 319, 323, 326, 328
botón de rebobinado automático 326
botón de rebobinado de la película 314
botón de rebobinado rápido 326
botón de registro 305
botón de reiniciación 326
botón de reproducción 319, 323, 328
botón de reset 471
botón de retroiluminación 337
botón de salida 337
botón de salto de imágenes 315
botón de selección 320, 327
botón de selección del menú 315
botón de seta 332
botón de sintonización 326
botón de stop 319, 323, 328
botón de velocidades 370
botón de visualización de ajustes 315
botón de visualización de imágenes 315
botón del contador a cero 319
botón del horno 210
botón del menú 327
botón del seguro 352
botón del vaporizador 208
botón del zoom eléctrico 320
botón grabación fecha 320
botón grabación hora 320
botón para borrar 328
botón para buscar las pistas 323
botón para parar y borrar 323
botón TV video 319
botón visualización fecha 320
botón visualización hora 320
botonadura cruzada 248
botonera de cabina 287
botones de acción 471
botones de ajuste 319
botones de ajuste de imagen 320
botones de búsqueda de canales 319
botones de dirección 471
botones de efectos especiales 320

botones de lanzamiento de las aplicaciones 337
botones de presión de la pierna 261
botones de presión delanteros 261
botones para búsqueda de canales 319
botones para editar la voz 310
botones programables 332
bóveda 284
bóveda de cañón 281
bóveda del salpicadero 348
bóveda palatina 116, 117
boxeador 498
boxeo 498
boxes 524
bráctea 60
braga 259
braga de volantes 260
bragueta 246, 247, 260
branquias 73
braquial anterior 96
brasero 283
Brasil 448
braza 517
brazalete de identificación 264
brazalete neumático 461
brazalete tubular 264
brazaletes 264
brazo 83, 91, 93, 95, 200, 206, 231, 236, 243, 270, 297, 355, 400, 421, 467
brazo actuador 333
brazo de arrastre 400
brazo de elevación 364
brazo de la horquilla 396
brazo de la plaqueta 273
brazo de la sierra 235
brazo de presión 224
brazo de suspensión 212, 351
brazo del cucharón 399
brazo delantero 422
brazo elevador 399
brazo espiral 6
brazo metálico 236
brazo muerto 32
brazo por control remoto 11
brazo telescópico 397
brazo trasero 422
brazos 205
brécol 127
brécol chino 127
brick 163
brick pequeño 163
bricolaje 216
brie 151
broca 221
broca de atornillado 228
broca de pala 228
broca helicoidal 228
broca helicoidal central 228
broca salomónica de canal angosto 228
brocas, barrenas, ejemplos 228
brocha 61, 219, 266
brocha aplicadora de colorete 266
brocha de afeitar 271
brocha en forma de abanico 266
broche 274, 275
broche automático 274
bronquio lobular 105
bronquio principal 105
bronquiolo terminal 105
brote 53
brote de bambú 125
brotes de soja 131
brújula magnética 533
Brunei 453
buccino 157
Buena Esperanza, cabo 20
buey 85
búfalo 84
bufete 203
buffet 438
búho real 81
buitre 80
buje 395
bujía 237, 359, 360
bujías, cable 350
bulbillo 54
bulbo 6, 125, 385, 387
bulbo olfatorio 117
bulbo piloso 114
bulbo raquídeo 109
bulbo, base 54
bulbo, corte 54
bulbos 124
buldog 86
bulevar 25, 433
Bulgaria 450

bulldozer 398
buque de carga 382
buque portacontenedores 381
buque trasatlántico 386
burbujas de aire 339
Burkina Faso 451
burra 503
Burundi 451
buscapersonas 327
búsqueda 335
butaca 200, 294
butacas 293
butacas, ejemplos 200
Bután 453
buzo 254
buzón de depósito nocturno 443

C

caballa 159
caballete 187
caballete central 367
caballete lateral 367
caballete portapoleas 403
caballo 83, 85, 470
caballo con arcos 496
caballo con aros 496
caballo, morfología 83
cabeceo 395
cabecera 204, 205, 285, 313
cabellera 6
cabello, tinte 267
cabestrante 364
cabeza 6, 67, 72, 78, 87, 93, 95, 103, 111, 169, 220, 221, 223, 229, 271, 301, 302, 303, 492, 494, 503, 505, 536
cabeza cortadora 341
cabeza de empalme 377
cabeza de inyección 403
cabeza de lectura /escritura 333
cabeza de mástil 519
cabeza del fémur 99
cabeza del gato elevador 396
cabeza del húmero 99
cabeza hexagonal 272
cabeza móvil 176
cabeza; tipos 221
cabezal 167, 187, 204
cabezal flotante 271
cabezuela 57
cabina 395, 398, 399, 400, 401, 443
cabina armario 189
cabina de clase turista 393
cabina de control 293, 397
cabina de la ducha 195
cabina de la torre de control 388
cabina de mando 12, 383, 392, 395, 397
cabina de pasajeros 386, 387
cabina de pilotaje 385
cabina de primera clase 392
cabina de proyección 294
cabina del ascensor 287
cabina del maquinista 376, 377
cabina en el foco primario 7
cabina giratoria 400
cabina para desvestirse 465
cabina para dormir 364
cabina, botonera 287
cabina, guía 287
cabina, suelo 287
cabina, techo 287
cabio alto 185
cabio bajo 185
cable 217, 228, 235, 237, 326, 332, 356, 364, 501, 535
cable de acero 535
cable de alimentación 227, 269, 270, 271, 322
cable de alumbrado 361
cable de bujía 360
cable de conexión 324, 332
cable de elevación 397
cable de interfaz digital para instrumentos musicales (MIDI) 311
cable de la antena de alta frecuencia 394
cable de las bujías 350
cable de sincronización 337
cable de tracción 287
cable del acelerador 237
cable del auricular 327
cable del cambio 372
cable del freno 371
cable distribuidor 316
cable eléctrico 354, 434
cable portante 344

cables de baja tensión 198
cables de conexión 198
cables de emergencia 198
cables de suministro 198
cables de tensión mediana 198
cabo 24, 296, 536
cabo de Buena Esperanza 20
cabo de Hornos 17
cabo de soporte 70
Cabo Verde, islas(f) de 451
cabra 84
cabra, quesos 150
cabrio 187
cacahuete 130
cacahuete, aceite 149
cacao 148
cacerola 175
cacerola para baño de María 175
cacerola para fondue 174
cacerola refractaria 175
cachalote 90
cadena 235, 372, 522
cadena alimentaria 45
cadena de dunas 36
cadena de elevación 396
cadena de neuronas 110
cadena de seguridad 361
cadena de transmisión 370
cadena, reacción 415
cadena, sierra 235
cadena, transmisión 372
cadenita del tapón 196
cadera 93, 95
café 148
café expres, máquina 181
café, granos torrefactos 148
café, granos verdes 148
cafetera 181, 531
cafetera de émbolo 181
cafetera de filtro automática 181
cafetera de infusión 181
cafetera italiana 181
cafetera napolitana 181
cafeteras 181
cafetería 432, 437, 445
caída de popa 519
caída de proa 519
caída de tensión 402
caimán 77
caja 121, 162, 218, 225, 231, 237, 271, 303, 304, 314, 318, 537
caja abierta 162
caja archivo 340
caja basculante 401
caja circular 296
caja clara 295, 308
caja colectora de polvo 229
caja de cambios 350
caja de caracol 407
caja de cinc (ánodo) 417
caja de conexiones 198
caja de doble fila de conexiones 417
caja de herramientas 225
caja de ingletes 226
caja de jeringuillas usadas 457
caja de la batería 359
caja de pesca 538
caja de resonancia 296, 297, 302
caja de seguridad 443
caja de servicio 198
caja de terminales 411
caja del acumulador 365
caja del motor 235
caja del ventilador 270
caja fuerte 443
caja mediа pera 297
caja orza de quilla 519
caja para la ceniza 192
caja para queso 163
caja registradora 121
caja triangular 297
caja, queso 163
cajas 121
cajas de cartón para huevos 162
cajas de cartón, huevos 162
cajera 121
cajero automático 437, 442, 443
cajetín de accesorios 209
cajetín portabolsa 209
cajón 164, 202, 203, 205
cajón calientaplatos 210
cajón de abono compuesto 231
cajón de basura 365
cajón para carnes 211
calabacín 128
calabaza bonetera 129
calabaza bonetera amarilla 129

calabaza común 129
calabaza de China 128
calabaza de cuello largo 129
calabaza de cuello retorcido 129
calabaza romana 129
calamar 157
cálamo egipcio 312
calandra 348, 364
calandria 409
calapié 372
calcáneo 99
calcetín 257, 480, 492
calcetín a media pantorrilla 247
calcetín con tirante 476
calcetín corto 247
calcetín largo 257
calcetín largo ejecutivo 247
calcetines 247, 506
calcetines altos 483
calculadora 274
calculadora científica 337
calculadora con impresora 337
calculadora de bolsillo 337
calderón 299
calefacción 192
calefacción de leña 192
calendario de sobremesa 338
calentador 529
calentador de agua 194
calentador de pierna 263
calibrador 357
calibre de ajuste de profundidad de corte 229
cálculo 59
California, golfo 16
caliptra 53
Calisto 2
cáliz 56, 59, 60, 107, 446
calle 25, 433, 435, 472, 516
calle comercial 432
callejón 433
calor, transmisión 415
calzada 342, 434
calzado 240
calzado unisex 242
calzapié 370
calzoncillos 247
calzoncillos largos 247
cama 204
cama de hospital 464
cama doble 439
cama individual 439
cama, coche 376
camaleón 77
cámara 290, 525
cámara acorazada 443
cámara anterior 119
cámara de aire 79, 262
cámara de combustión 360
cámara de descarga 278
cámara de expansión 424
cámara de fuelle 315
cámara de la reina 278
cámara de magma 28
cámara de televisión en color 10
cámara del rey 278
cámara del timón 384
cámara desechable 315
cámara digital 315
cámara frigorífica 120
cámara frigorífica 121, 381
cámara lenta 319
cámara magmática 402
cámara Polaroid Land 315
cámara posterior 119
cámara pulpar 101
cámara reflex de formato medio SLR (6x6) 315
cámara réflex digital: vista posterior 315
cámara réflex monocular: vista frontal 314
cámara rígida de 35 mm 10
cámara subterránea 278
cámara web 332
cámaras fijas 315
camarera 438
camarote 386
camarote del capitán 387
camarotes de la tripulación 382
camas y colchonetas 530
cambiador 205
cambio de marchas delantero 370, 372
cambio de marchas trasero 370, 372
cambio de presión 39
cambio de velocidades 522
cambium 63
Camboya 453
cambrillón 262

ASTRONOMÍA > 2-25;   TIERRA > 26-71;   REINO VEGETAL >72-89;   REINO ANIMAL > 90-143;   SER HUMANO > 144-177;   PRODUCTOS ALIMENTARIOS Y DE COCINA > 178-241;   CASA > 242-295;
BRICOLAJE Y JARDINERÍA > 296-333;   VESTIDO > 334-371;   ACCESORIOS Y ARTÍCULOS PERSONALES > 372-391;   ARTE Y ARQUITECTURA > 392-465;   COMUNICACIONES Y AUTOMATIZACIÓN DE
OFICINA > 466-535;   TRANSPORTE Y VEHÍCULOS > 536-643;   ENERGÍA > 644-677;   CIENCIA > 678-705;   SOCIEDAD > 706-785;   DEPORTES Y JUEGOS > 786-920

INDICE ESPAÑOL

camello 85
camembert 151
camerino 290, 293
camerino privado 290
Camerún 451
camilla 460
camino de evacuación 345
camión cisterna 364
camión tractor 364
camiones 364
camiones de bomberos 455
camiones, ejemplos 364
camioneta 347, 365
camisa 245, 255, 282
camisa de pistón 360
camisa marinera 255
camisera clásica 255
camiseta 247, 260, 261, 263, 473, 476, 483, 488
camiseta de cuerpo entero 261
camiseta del equipo 480, 486
camiseta interior 476
camiseta sin mangas 500
camisola 258
camisón 256
campana 192, 210
campana de cocina 164
campanario 285, 446
campanas tubulares 295, 309
campanillas 309
campo 431, 474, 479, 480
campo de golf 430, 504
campo de juego 482
campo de juego de fútbol americano 484
campo geotérmico 402
campo magnético 318, 416
campo, línea 416
caña 83, 305, 312, 534, 538
caña del timón 520
caña para lanzado 537
caña para mosca 536
caña simple 306
Canadá 448
canal 228
canal de ajuste 222
canal de descarga 407
canal de la Mancha 18
canal de Mozambique 20
canal del aliviadero 406
canal del sifón 73
canal del veneno 76
canal derecho 324
canal izquierdo 324
canal lacrimal 119
canalón 182
canasta 477, 489
canastilla 178
Cáncer, trópico 20, 21, 22
cancha 487, 488, 490, 494
cancha de fondo 491
candado para bicicleta 372
candela 426
candelabro de siete braz 447
canela 138
canelones 146
cañería 194
cañería del desagüe 194
cañerías 194
canesú 245, 255, 258
cangrejo de mar 158
cangrejo de río 158
caniche 86
caño 305
cañón 471, 534
cañón de electrones 318
cañón expulsor de espuma 385
cañón lanza agua 455
cañón submarino 33
canotier 238
cantidad de materia, unidad de medida 426
cantimplora 532
canto 226, 441, 509, 510
cantonera 534
capa 251
capa basáltica 26
capa de ozono 37
capa de rodadura 342
capa granítica 26
capa protectora 10
capa superficial del suelo 54
capa superior impermeable 402
caparazón 71
capas de residuos 47
capazo 276
caperuza 193
caperuza de la chimenea 183

capilla 282
capilla axial 284, 285
capilla lateral 284
capilla radial 284, 285
capital 23
capitán 515
capó 348, 364, 523
capón 155
Capricornio, trópico 20, 21, 22
cápsula 51, 60, 467
cápsula de gelatina 467
captura 470
capucha 249
capucha con cordón 261
capuchón 260, 314, 460, 467, 508
capuchón de bastones 505
capuchón de plástico 217
capuchón de protección 420
capullo 53
caqui 134
cara 91, 92, 167, 493, 505
caracol 72
caracol terrestre 157
caracol, morfología 72
carambola 137
caramillo 296
caravana 361
caravana plegable 361
carbonero 161
carburador 366
cárcel 469
cardamomo 138
cardenal 80
cardo 125
carena 74
carenado 366
careta 459
carga 312
carga de perdigones 534
carga del reactor nuclear 409
carga eléctrica, unidad de medida 426
carga y descarga 439
carga, muelle 437
cargador 208, 228
cargadora, retroexcavadora 399
cargadora-retroexcavadora 399
carguero portacontenedores 382
Caribe, islas del 448
Caribe, mar 14, 16
Caribe, placa 27
caricatura 313
carlota, molde 172
carne 152
carne de cordero troceada 153
carne de temera troceada 152
carne de vacuno troceada 152
carne picada 152
carne picada de cerdo 153
carne picada de cordero 153
carne picada de vacuno 152
carnívoros 45
Carón 3
carpa 160
Cárpatos, montes 18
Carpentaria, golfo 15
carpeta con guardas 339
carpeta de archivo 340
carpeta de argollas 339
carpeta de broches 339
carpeta de costilla de resorte 339
carpeta de espiral 340
carpeta de tornillos 339
carpintería 225
carpintería 220, 221, 222, 225, 226, 228, 229
carreras de coches 524
carrete 236
carrete de bobina fija 537
carrete de tambor 537
carrete giratorio 537
carretera 25, 343, 345, 430
carretera de acceso 388
carretera secundaria 25, 431
carretera, sección transversal 342
carretera, túnel 345
carreteras, mapa 25
carreteras, sistema 342
carretilla 231, 396
carretilla elevadora de horquilla 396
carretilla para manguera 236
carril de aceleración 343
carril de adelantamiento 343
carril de desaceleración 343

carril de enlace 375
carril de tránsito 343
carril de tránsito lento 343
carriles 343
carrillo 536
carrito de golf 505
carrito del supermercado 121
carrito portamaletas 277
carro 521
carro de golf eléctrico 505
carro portaequipaje 374
carrocería 348, 361, 523
carrocerías, ejemplos 347
carta 469
carta Caja de Comunidad 469
carta de la Suerte 469
cartas al editor 313
cartas altas 468
cartel 294
cartel comercial 380
cartelera 294
cárter 228, 360
cárter del embrague 368
cartera 274, 372
cartera de fondo plegable 274
cartera portadocumentos 275
cartílago alar mayor 117
cartílago nasal del tabique 117
cartilla, puesta al día 442
cartografía 21
cartón 163
cartón pequeño 163
cartuchera 456
cartucho 216, 459
cartucho de escopeta 534
cartucho de rifle 534
carúncula lacrimal 119
casa 182, 469, 515
casa club 504
casa de adobes 288
casa de dos plantas 289
casa de una planta 289
casa flotante 385
casa romana 280
casa, elementos 185
casa, estructura 188
casa, exterior 182
casaca 255
casas adosadas 289
casas pareadas 289
cascabel 309
cascabeles 309
cascada 32
cascanueces 170
cáscara 60, 61
cascarón 79
casco 10, 83, 367, 404, 454, 478, 486, 498, 506, 508, 510, 513, 520, 522, 523, 524, 525, 526, 527
casco de seguridad 458
casco del bateador 476
casco integral 367, 525
casco protector 372
cascos de seguridad 458
casete 326, 333
casete con saludo 328
casete para grabar los mensajes 328
casi igual a 427
casilla 469
casillero 203
Caspio, mar 14, 19
casquete 412
casquete del distribuidor 360
casquillo 199, 503, 534
castaña 133
castaña de agua 124
castañuelas 295, 309
castas 68
castillo 282
castillo de proa 383, 387
castor 82
catamarán 521
catedral 284
catedral gótica 284
catedral, plano 285
cátodo 417
catre desmontable 530
cauda helícis 115
cávea 278, 281
cavidad abdominal 111, 112
cavidad bucal 105, 106
cavidad nasal 76, 105
cavidad pleural 105
cayado de la aorta 102, 103, 104
caza 154, 534
cazadora 249
cazo 173

cazuela 531
cazuela vaporera 175
cebada 61, 143
cebada : espiga 61
cebolla amarilla 124
cebolla blanca 124
cebolla roja 124
cebolla tierna 124
cebolleta 124
cebollino 124
cebra 84
cedro del Líbano 65
cefalotórax 70, 71
ceja 304
cejilla 301, 302, 303
celda 67, 281
celdas 440
celdilla 58
celosía veneciana 186
célula animal 66
célula convectiva 43
célula de Schwann 110
célula solar 337, 410, 411
célula vegetal 50
cementerio 25, 433
cemento 101
centavo 440
centeno 61, 143
centeno : espiga 61
central 485
central eléctrica 406
central hidroeléctrica, sección transversal 407
central térmica de carbón 402
centriolo 66
centro 293, 428, 470, 507
centro ciudad 431, 432
centro comercial 431, 436
centro de negocios 430, 432
centro del campo 481
centro derecho 482
centro educativo 433
centro izquierdo 482
cepa de vid 62
cepillo 209, 215, 229, 272
cepillo aplicador de rímel 266
cepillo con base de goma 268
cepillo de baño 267
cepillo de curling 515
cepillo de dientes 272
cepillo de dientes eléctrico 272
cepillo de espalda 267
cepillo de esqueleto 268
cepillo de púas 268
cepillo para cejas y pestañas 266
cepillo para suelos 209
cepillo para verduras 173
cepillo redondo 268
cepillo-plumero 209
cepillos 268
cepo 535
cera 514
cerámica, condensador 417
cerca 122
cercado 122
cerda 272
cerdas 215, 219, 271
cerdo 84
cerdo, asado 153
cerdo, carne picada 153
cerdo, cortes 153
cereales 61, 143, 144
cerebelo 109
cerebro 71, 109
cereza 132
cerradura 185, 186, 202, 274, 277, 349, 352
cerradura de combinación 274
cerrajería 186, 437
cerveza 120
cerviz 78
césped 183, 230
cesta de freír 171
cesta de pescador 538
cestillo 68
cesto 211, 214
cesto de cocción al vapor 175
cesto para cubiertos 214
cesto para verdura 211
Chac-Mool 283
Chad 451
Chad, lago 20
chalaza 79
chaleco 244, 255
chaleco de pescador 538
chaleco de punto 250
chalecos 244

chalecos , jerseys y chaquetas 254
chalecos, jerseys, chaquetas 254
chalote 124
champiñón 123
champú 267
chancleta 242
chancleta playera 242
chanclo de goma 240
chapa 186
chapka 238
chaqueta 251
chaqueta cruzada 244, 255
chaqueta de punto 250, 255
chaqueta recta 244
chaquetas 244
chaquetón 251
chaquetón de tres cuartos 251
chaquetón marinero 251
chaquetones 251
charcutería 156
chamela lateral 367
chasis 396, 400, 401, 460
chasis delantero 401
chateo 335
chayote 129
cheque de viaje 441
chequera con calculadora 274
cheques 441
chesterfield 200
chicana 524
chifonier 203
Chile 448
chile 128
chile jalapeño 139
chimenea 183, 188, 192, 193, 382, 386, 402
chimenea de expulsión 365
chimenea lateral 28
chimenea principal 28
chimenea, conexión 192
chimenea, utensilios 193
chimpancé 91
China 453
China Meridional, mar 14, 19
China Oriental, mar 19
chinche de campo 69
chinchetas 341
chino 171, 524
Chipre 450
chirimoya 136
chirivía 129
chistera 238
chocolate 148
chocolate amargo 148
chocolate blanco 148
chocolate con leche 148
chorizo 156
chorro de agua 518
choza 288
choza indígena 288
chuleta 152, 153
chuletón 152
chutney de mango 141
chutney, mango 141
cian 418
ciclismo 522
ciclismo de montaña 522
ciclismo por carretera 522
ciclismo por carretera, competición 522
ciclista 522
ciclo hidrológico 45
ciclomotor 369
ciclón 43
ciclón tropical 43
ciclones tropicales, denominación 43
cidra cayote 129
ciego 106
cielo turbulento 41
cien 427
ciencia 414
ciere, tapa 417
cierre 211, 273, 275, 528
cierre en relieve 163
ciervo 84
ciervo de Virginia 84
cigala 158
cigarra 69
cigüeña 80
cigüeñal 360
cilantro 142
ciliada 55
cilindro 429, 460
cilindro de dirección 400
cilindro de elevación de la hoja 401
cilindro de elevación del zanco 398
cilindro de freno 357
cilindro de orientación de la pala 401

ASTRONOMÍA > 2-25; TIERRA > 26-71; REINO VEGETAL >72-89; REINO ANIMAL > 90-143; SER HUMANO > 144-177; PRODUCTOS ALIMENTARIOS Y DE COCINA > 178-241; CASA > 242-295;
BRICOLAJE Y JARDINERÍA > 296-333; VESTIDO > 334-371; ACCESORIOS Y ARTÍCULOS PERSONALES > 372-391; ARTE Y ARQUITECTURA > 392-465; COMUNICACIONES Y AUTOMATIZACIÓN DE
OFICINA > 466-535; TRANSPORTE Y VEHÍCULOS > 536-643; ENERGÍA > 644-677; CIENCIA > 678-705; SOCIEDAD > 706-785; DEPORTES Y JUEGOS > 786-920

641

ÍNDICE ESPAÑOL

cilindro del brazo 400
cilindro del brazo elevador 399
cilindro del cucharón 399, 400
cilindro del elevador 399, 400
cilindro del elevador de la pala 398
cilindro elevador 364, 397, 455
cilindro maestro 357
cilio 66
cima 29, 63, 512
cima bípara 57
cima unípara 57
cimiento del pilón 344
cinco 427
cinco especias chinas 139
cincuenta 427
cine 294, 432, 436
cinta 225, 238, 458, 459, 493, 495
cinta adhesiva 190
cinta cargadora 402
cinta central 491
cinta de acordonamiento 457
cinta de la red 491
cinta de teflón 216
cinta magnética 319
cinta métrica 225
cinta transportadora 49, 390, 402
cintura 93, 95
cinturón 246, 248, 499, 500, 532
cinturón de asteroides 3
cinturón de herramientas 225
cinturón de hombros 353
cinturón de Kuiper 2
cinturón de seguridad 205, 353, 525
cinturón de servicio 456
cinturón subabdominal 353
circo 5
circo glaciar 30
circuito 524
circuito de agua caliente 194
circuito de agua fría 194
circuito de desagüe 194
circuito de frenado 350, 357
circuito de ventilación 194
circuito eléctrico de los captadores 357
circuito eléctrico en paralelo 416
circuito impreso 417
circuito impreso, placa 417
circuito integrado 417
circulación sanguínea 102
circular 176
círculo 25 471
Círculo Antártico 15, 21, 22
círculo central 481, 488, 515
círculo de espera 474
círculo de la estación 39
círculo de lanzamiento 472, 473
círculo de reanudación del juego 506
círculo de saque inicial 507
círculo doble 471
círculo exterior 515
círculo graduado de declinación 8
Círculo polar Ártico 21, 22
círculo triple 471
círculo, partes 428
circunferencia 428
circunvalación 25
cirrocúmulos 42
cirros 42
cirrostratos 42
ciruela 132
cirugía menor 462
cisterna 364
cisterna del inodoro 195
cisura oblicua 105
citara 297
citofaringe 66
citoplasma 50, 66, 112
citoprocto 66
citostoma 66
cítricos 134
ciudad 23, 430
Ciudad del Vaticano 450
cizallas para setos 234
claqueta 291
clarín 307
clarinete 306
clarinete bajo 295
clarinetes 295
clase 444
clasificación de plásticos 49
clasificación general, marcador 496
clasificador de fuelle 274
clave 284
clave de do 298
clave de fa 298
clave de sol 298
clavel 56

claves 298
clavícula 98
clavija 301, 302, 304, 324, 454
clavija de acorde 303
clavija de afinación 303
clavija de alimentación 337
clavija de conexión 417
clavija de tensión 308
clavija de tipo americano 198
clavija europea 198
clavijero 301, 304
clavo 138, 220
clavo cortado 220
clavo de albañil 220
clavo helicoidal 220
clavo sin cabeza 220
clavos, ejemplos 220
claxon 368
claxón 354
clientes, entrada 438
clientes, guardarropa 438
climas áridos 40
climas de montaña 40
climas polares 40
climas templados cálidos 40
climas templados fríos 40
climas tropicales 40
climatizador automático 354
clip 341
clip de ajuste 199
clips, distribuidor 341
clítoris 112
cloroplasto 50
cobaya 82
cobertera inferior de la cola 78
cobertera superior de la cola 78
coberteras 78
coberteras mayores 78
coberteras medias 78
coberteras menores 78
coberteras primarias 78
coberteras primarias medias 78
cobertizo 122, 182, 230
cobertizo para ovejas 122
cobra 77
cocción al vapor, cesto 175
cocción, placa 179
cocción, platos 179
cóccix 98
coche cama 376
coche de fórmula 1 525
coche de fórmula 3000 524
coche de Indy 524
coche de policía 457
coche de rally 524
coche de tracción 380
coche del equipo 522
coche familiar 347
cocina 162, 164, 188, 280, 439, 445
cocina de a bordo 392
cocina de campo 529
cocina de gas 210
cocina eléctrica 210
cocina, tijeras 173
cocina, utensilios 169, 174
cocinar 178
cóclea 116
coco 133
cocodrilo 77
Cocos, placa 27
codera 486, 526, 527
código del producto 423
codillo 83, 86, 153
codo 86, 93, 95, 273
codorniz 81, 154
cofre 369
cojín 204
cojín para sellos 338
cojinete de bolas 413
cojinete móvil 519
col 126
col china 126
col lombarda 126
col marina 126
col ornamental 126
col rizada 126
col rizada de otoño 126
col verde 126
cola 71, 76, 82, 83, 86, 90, 111, 190, 393, 510, 514, 526, 536
cola de ion 6
cola de polvo 6
colada de lava 28
colador 177, 180, 197
colador fino 171
coladores 171

colchón 205, 460
colchón de muelles 204
colchoneta aislante 530
colchoneta de aire 530
colchoneta de espuma 530
colchoneta de recepción 496
colector de admisión 360
colector de electrones 417
colector de escape 350, 360
colector de grasa 179
colector principal 434
colector solar plano 410
colegio 444
coles de Bruselas 126
colgador de intravenosos 464
colgante 207
colibrí 80
coliflor 127
colina 29
colina abisal 33
colina de salida 504
colinabo 125
collar 219
collar cortafuego 193
collar de 5 vueltas , peto 264
collar de perforación 403
collar de una vuelta , matinée 264
collar de una vuelta , ópera 264
collares 264
collarín 193, 223, 229, 501
colleja 127
collie 86
colmena 122
colmillo 76, 101
Colombia 448
colon ascendente 106
colon descendente 106
colon sigmoideo 106
colon transverso 106
colonia, agua de 267
color 468
colores aditivos síntesis 418
colores sustractivos, síntesis 418
colores, síntesis 418
colorete en polvo 266
columela 73
columna 31, 207, 279, 302, 313
columna central 412
columna corintia adosada 281
columna de alcohol 424
columna de mercurio 424
columna dórica adosada 281
columna fraccionadora 405
columna jónica adosada 281
columna vertebral 98, 109
colutorio 272
comadreja 88
combinación 258
combinación con sujetador 258
combustible 408
combustible fósil 46, 48
combustible para aviones 405
combustible para calderas 405
combustible para calefacción 405
comedor 188, 386, 438, 439
comedor, vagón 376
comercio electrónico 335
cometa 6
comino 138
comisaría de policía 433
comisura labial 116
cómoda 203
comodín 468
Comoras 452
compactadora 364
compartimento para almacenamiento 361
compartimento para equipaje 376
compartimento para los equipos 376
compartimiento 286
compartimiento de almacenamiento 455
compartimiento de pasajeros 383
compartimiento del depósito del agua 394
compartimiento motor 362
compartimiento para lácteos 211
compartimiento para mantequilla 211
compás 298
competición de ciclismo por carretera 522
complejo hidroeléctrico 406
complejo mayor 97
compluvio 280
composición de la sangre 104
compresa de gasa 461
compresión 49
compresor de aire 376
compresor del aire acondicionado 360
compuerta 381, 407
compuerta del aliviadero 406

comulgatorio 446
comunicación por teléfono 327
comunicación vía satélite 316
comunicaciones 312
comunicaciones aéreas 317
comunicaciones industriales 317
comunicaciones marítimas 317
comunicaciones militares 317
comunicaciones particulares 317
comunicaciones terrestres 317
concentrado de tomate 140
concentrado, tomate 140
concentrador de aire 270
concesionariode automóviles 433
concha 72, 73, 115, 200, 308
concha bivalva 73
concha bivalva, anatomía 73
concha bivalva, morfología 73
concha univalva 73
concha univalva, morfología 73
conchitas 146
condensación 45, 414
condensador 402, 421
condensador de cerámica 417
condensador de película plástica 417
condensadores electrolíticos 417
cóndilo externo 99
cóndilo interno 99
condimento de especias cajún 139
condimentos 140
cóndor 80
conducción 415
conducción forzado 407
conducto de aire caliente 213
conducto de aire fresco 345
conducto de aire viciado 345
conducto de ventilación 278
conducto deferente 111
conducto del veneno 76
conducto eyaculador 111
conducto galactóforo 113
conducto principal del gas 434
conducto radicular 101
conducto semicircular lateral 116
conducto semicircular posterior 116
conducto semicircular superior 116
conducto sudorífero 114
conductor de fase 198
conductor neutral 198
conector 455
conector de alimentación del adaptador 336
conector de altavoces 322
conector de puesta a tierra 322
conector de salida 303
conector de tierra macho 198
conector de tierra, macho 198
conector del desagüe 194
conectores de antenas 322
conejo 82, 154
conexión 198, 470
conexión a la red 198
conexión de la chimenea 192
conexión de tierra 198
conexión eléctrica a tierra 404
conexión, clavija 417
conexión, galería 345
conexiones 365
conexiones, ejemplos 197
confesionarios 446
configuración de los continentes 14
configuración del litoral 35
confirmación, tecla 443
confluente 32
congelador 164, 438
congelador incorporado 211
congelados 121
Congo 451
Congo, río 20
congresos, palacio 433
conífera 65
coníferas, ejemplos 65
conjuntiva 119
conjunto deportivo 261
conjunto vario 427
conjuntos instrumentales, ejemplos 300
conmutador de alimentación 315
conmutador de corriente 322
conmutador de grabación nocturna 320
conmutador de intensidad 198
cono 119, 318, 429
cono de penumbra 4, 5
cono de sombra 4, 5
cono femenino 65
cono masculino 65
conservas 121
consigna 374

consola 302, 305
consola central 354
consola de juego 471
consultorio 463, 465
consultorio ginecológico 463
consumidor 317
consumidores primarios 45
consumidores secundarios 45
consumidores terciarios 45
contacto 198, 199, 470
contacto central 314
contacto de conexión a tierra 198
contacto negativo 410, 411
contacto positivo 410, 411
contacto, dispositivos 198
contador 323
contador de agua 194
contador eléctrico 198
contaminación agrícola 47
contaminación de automóviles 47
contaminación de petróleo 48
contaminación del agua 48
contaminación del aire 47
contaminación del suelo 47
contaminación doméstica 47
contaminación industrial 47
contaminantes del aire 47
contaminantes no biodegradables 47
contenedor 383, 400
contenedor de reciclado de aluminio 49
contenedor de reciclado de papel 49
contenedor de reciclado de vidrio 49
contenedor de recogida de papel 49
contenedor de recogida de vidrio 49
contenedores de reciclaje 49
contenedores, terminal 430
contera 277, 536
contera de caucho 466
contestador automático 328
continente 5, 33
continente húmedo 40
continentes, configuración 14
contorno del cuello 245
contrabajo 301
contrabajos 295
contrafagots 295
contrafuerte 262, 284, 344, 509, 511
contrafuerte del talón 240
contrahoja 229
contrahuella 191
contrapeso 8, 287, 345, 397, 400, 401
contrapeso, guía 287
contrapiso 187, 190
contrapluma 397
contraquilla 385
contratuerca 197
contraventana 186
control 330
control : selección de grupo 330
control de agudos 322
control de balance 322
control de brillo 329
control de centrado 329
control de contraste 329
control de entrada de información fina 310
control de entrada de información rápida 310
control de graves 322
control de la entrada de aire 192
control de la plataforma corrediza 421
control de pasaportes 391
control de presión 272
control de secuencias 310
control de seguridad 391
control de sintonización 326
control de temperatura 267
control de tonos de bajos 325
control de tonos de graves 325
control de velocidad 237, 332
control de volumen 303, 310, 311, 319, 326, 329
control de volumen del auricular 327
control de volumen del timbre 327
control del campo audio 322
control del espejo retrovisor exterior 352
control del sonido 303
control del tiempo 311
control del vaporizador 208
control del volumen 303, 322, 328
control estéreo 326
control horizontal 329
control remoto, unidad móvil de servicio 11
control vertical 329
controlador de entradas 294
controlador de viento del sintetizador 311

ASTRONOMÍA > 2-25;   TIERRA > 26-71;   REINO VEGETAL >72-89;   REINO ANIMAL > 90-143;   SER HUMANO > 144-177;   PRODUCTOS ALIMENTARIOS Y DE COCINA > 178-241;   CASA > 242-295;
BRICOLAJE Y JARDINERÍA > 296-333;   VESTIDO > 334-371;   ACCESORIOS Y ARTÍCULOS PERSONALES > 372-391;   ARTE Y ARQUITECTURA > 392-465;   COMUNICACIONES Y AUTOMATIZACIÓN DE
OFICINA > 466-535;   TRANSPORTE Y VEHÍCULOS > 536-643;   ENERGÍA > 644-677;   CIENCIA > 678-705;   SOCIEDAD > 706-785;   DEPORTES Y JUEGOS > 786-920

controles de la pletina 326
controles de sintonización 318
controles de volumen de comunicaciones 10
controles del lector de discos compactos 326
controles del sistema de soporte vital 10
controles VCR 319
conurbación 430
convección 415
convención, corriente 415
conversión del agua en vapor 408
convertidor catalítico 351
convertidor de tensión 212
Cook, estrecho 15
coordenadas terrestres, sistema 21
copa 63, 163, 238, 239, 259
copa de agua 165
copa de champaña 165
copa de cóctel 165
copa de flauta 165
copa para brandy 165
copa para licores 165
copa para oporto 165
copa para vino blanco 165
copa para vino de Alsacia 165
copa para vino de Borgoña 165
copa para vino de Burdeos 165
copete 83, 536
coquilla 486, 507
coquina 157
Coral, mar 15
corazón 58, 71, 73, 104, 105, 154, 468
corbata 245
corbata inglesa 245
corchea 299
corcheras 517
corchete 509
corcho 495, 514
cordaje 492, 494
cordal 297, 301
cordero, carne picada 153
cordero, carne troceada 153
cordero, cortes 153
cordero, pierna 153
cordillera 5, 24, 26
cordillera de los Andes 17
cordillera del Atlas 20
cordón 208, 209, 225, 240, 249, 262, 275, 477, 509
cordón de alimentación 177, 229, 269
cordón de alimentación de corriente alterna 336
cordón de alimentación de corriente continua 336
cordón de alimentación, corriente continua 336
cordón de trazar 225
cordón litoral 35
cordón nervioso ventral 71
cordoncillo 441
cordones 498
Corea, península 19
corimbo 57
córnea 119, 419
córner 481
corneta inferior 117
corneta medio 117
corneta superior 117
cornetín 295, 307
comisa 183, 185, 202, 279
como francés 295, 307
como inglés 306
comos ingleses 295
coro 284, 285
coroides 119
corola 56
corona 4, 83, 101, 302, 308, 424
corona externa de la cadena 372
corona interna de la cadena 372
corona radiata 112
corona rotatoria 401
corpúsculo de Meissner 114
corpúsculo de Pacini 114
corpúsculo de Ruffini 114
corral 122
corral, aves 155
correa 265, 277, 424, 500, 505, 519
correa de ajuste 511
correa de barbilla 486
correa de cierre 532
correa de compresión 532
correa de distribución 360
correa de la manga 248
correa de retención 277
correa de seguridad 10
correa de transmisión 383

correa del tambor 212
correa del ventilador 350, 360
correa elástico 277
correa para el cuello 458
correa para herramientas 10
correa para la mano 510, 514
correas 459
corredera de afinamiento 307
corredera de ajuste 246
corredor 412
corredor de poder 485
correo electrónico 335
correo electrónico, programa 334
correos 433
correos, oficina 437
correspondencia 338
corriente de agua 32, 48
corriente de convección 415
corriente eléctrica, unidad de medida 426
corriente subterránea 31
corrimiento 31
corsé de cintura de avispa 259
cortacésped con motor 237
cortacutículas 265
cortador de alambre 217
cortador de huevos duros 173
cortapastas 172
cortapatillas 271
cortar 177
cortasetas eléctrico 235
cortauñas 265
corte de la atmósfera terrestre 37
corte de la corteza terrestre 26
corte de la pelota de béisbol 477
corte de un bulbo 54
corte de un grano de trigo 61
corte de un melocotón 57
corte de una avellana 60
corte de una frambuesa 59
corte de una fresa 59
corte de una manzana 58
corte de una naranja 58
corte de una nuez 60
corte de una uva 59
corte prensa 252
corte transversal de un molar 101
corte transversal de un tronco 63
cortes de cerdo 153
cortes de cordero 153
cortes de ternera 152
cortes de vacuno 152
corteza 58, 63
corteza continental 26
corteza cortical 107
corteza oceánica 26
corteza terrestre 26, 27
corteza terrestre, corte 26
cortina 200
cortina de enrollamiento automático 356
cortina separadora 464
corvejón 83, 86
costa 33
Costa de Marfil 451
Costa Rica 448
costado 358
costas, ejemplos 35
costilla 536
costilla axial 73
costilla de encastre 392
costilla espiral 73
costilla falsa 99
costilla flotante 98
costillar 152, 153
costillas 98
costura 240, 243, 244, 477, 478
costura de corte princesa 258
costura invisible 245
cotiledón 53
cotillo 229
coulommiers 151
Cowper, glándula 111
cráneo 92
cráneo de un niño 100
cráneo, vista lateral 100
cráter 5, 28
cráter, estela luminosa 5
cremallera 249, 261, 265, 277, 473
cremallera de fijación 420
crepidoma 279
cresta 29, 33, 418
cresta de la presa 406
cresta del aliviadero 406
cricket 478
criminalidad, prevención 456
crin 83, 301
crisálida 67
cristal 410, 411

cristal de protección 506
cristalería 165
cristalino 119
cristalización 414
Croacia 450
croco 56
crol 517
cromatina 66
cromosfera 4
cronometrador 488, 498, 509
cronometrador de calle 516
cronometradores 499
cronómetro 424
cronómetro electrónico automático 517
crosne 124
Crottin de Chavignol 150
cruasán 144
crucero 284, 285
cruces de carreteras, ejemplos 342
cruceta 520
crucifijo 446
crudo, oleoducto 404
crus hélix 115
crustáceos 71, 158
cruz 83, 86
cruz del altar 446
cuaderna 385, 401
cuadrado 429
cuadrante 424, 428
cuadrilátero 429, 498
cuadro 183, 502
cuadro de bateo 477
cuadro de saque 491
cuadro de saque derecho 491
cuadro de saque izquierdo 491
cuadro de servicio de dobles 495
cuadro de servicio de individuales 495
cuadro de temperaturas 208
cuarta 298
cuarteto 300
cuartilla 83
cuarto 240, 262
cuarto creciente 5
cuarto de baño 189, 195
cuarto de estar 528
cuarto de la limpieza 443
cuarto menguante 5
Cuba 448
cuba 211, 212
cuba de lavado 214
cubertería 167, 531
cubeta colectora de gotas 181
cubeta congeladora 180
cubeta de alcohol 424
cubeta de mercurio 424
cubículo 280
cubierta 180, 386
cubierta de popa 386
cubierta de seguridad 237
cubierta de sol 385
cubierta de tejas 279
cubierta exterior de la cúpula 7
cubierta inferior 404
cubierta interior de la cúpula 7
cubierta para automóviles 386
cubierta principal 385
cubierta protectora 401
cubierta superior 387, 392, 404
cubierta térmica 12
cubilete 469
cubital anterior 96, 97
cubital posterior 97
cúbito 98
cubitos de hielo, bandeja 211
cubo 215, 341, 413, 429, 467
cubo de basura 215
cubo de basura reciclable 49
cubo del rotor 395
cuchara 167, 531, 538
cuchara de degustación 173
cuchara de helado 168
cuchara de mesa 168
cuchara de postre 168
cuchara de sopa 168
cuchara de té 168
cuchara para servir helado 173
cucharas dosificadoras 171
cucharas, ejemplos 168
cucharita de café 168
cucharón 399
cucharón hacia atrás 400
cucharón trasero 399
cuchilla 176, 177, 180, 226, 235, 270, 341, 506
cuchilla de baile 509
cuchilla de corte 398, 400
cuchilla de patinaje artístico 509

cuchilla del cucharón 399
cuchilla para delimitar el césped 233
cuchilla, mecanismo de desplazamiento 401
cuchillas para batir 176
cuchillo 167, 531, 533
cuchillo de carne 168
cuchillo de carnicero 169
cuchillo de cocina 169
cuchillo de mantequilla 168
cuchillo de mesa 168
cuchillo de pan 169
cuchillo de pelar 169
cuchillo de pescado 168
cuchillo de postre 168
cuchillo de queso 168
cuchillo de trinchar 169
cuchillo eléctrico 177
cuchillo filetero 169
cuchillo para deshuesar 169
cuchillo para jamón 169
cuchillo para ostras 169
cuchillo para pomelos 169
cuchillos de cocina, ejemplos 169
cuchillos, ejemplos 168
cuello 53, 76, 83, 93, 94, 95, 101, 111, 167, 244, 245, 247, 248, 318
cuello con botones 245
cuello de cisne 191
cuello de doble vista 248
cuello de ganso 400
cuello de pico 250
cuello del fémur 99
cuello del útero 112
cuello en V 244
cuello hechura sastre 251
cuello italiano 245
cuello redondo 260
cuello redondo, jersey 255
cuenca oceánica 33
cuenco 167
cuenco de queso blando 166
cuentakilómetros 355
cuentalitros 346
cuerda 231, 301, 302, 498, 500, 535
cuerda de elevación 219
cuerda de salida falsa 516
cuerda de tensión 297
cuerda vocal 105
cuerda, instrumentos 301
cuerdas 297, 304, 308
cuerdas de acompañamiento 296
cuerdas melódicas 296
cuerno anterior 109
cuerno posterior 109
cuero 246
cuerpo 180, 228, 306, 425, 536
cuerpo calloso 109
cuerpo cavernoso 111
cuerpo celular 110
cuerpo ciliar 119
cuerpo de guardia 282
cuerpo de la uña 114
cuerpo del fórnix 109
cuerpo humano 91
cuerpo metálico de la bujía 359
cuerpo sólido 303
cuerpo vertebral 110
cuerpo vítreo 119
cuerpos celestes 2
cuerpos de Nissl 110
cuerpos sólidos 429
cuervo 80
cueva 35
cuidado del césped 237
cuidado personal 267
culata 534
culata de los cilindros 360
culombio 426
culote 534
cultivador 233
cultivador de mano 232
cúmulo globular 6
cumulonimbos 42
cúmulos 42
cuna 205
cuña 305
cuna plegable 205
cuneta 342
cupé 347
cúpula 60
cúpula del Mihrab 447
cúpula del pórtico 447
cúpula giratoria 7
cúrcuma 138
curling 515
curry 138

cursor abajo 331
cursor arriba 331
cursor hacia la derecha 331
cursor hacia la izquierda 331
curva 343, 538
cuscús 144

dado 469
dado común 468
dado de póquer 468
dado doble 469
dados 468
dálmata 86
dama 469, 470
damas 470
damas, tablero 470
Danubio, río 18
dardo 471
dátil 132
datos, tratamiento 38
David, estrella 447
de aspas 176
de cuatro cuartos 298
de dos mitades 298
de gancho 176
de momia 530
de servicio 491
de tres cuartos 298
deambulatorio 285
decágono regular 429
decantador 165
decorador 291
decorador jefe de producción 290
dedalitos 146
dedil 339
dedo 75, 79, 82, 114, 243, 477
dedo anular 115
dedo de pata lobulada 79
dedo de pata palmípeda 79
dedo del corazón 115
dedo del pie 92, 94
dedo externo 78
dedo índice 115
dedo interno 78
dedo medio 78
dedo meñique 115
dedo palmeado 75
dedo posterior 78, 79
dedos del pie, extensor largo 96
dedos prensiles 91
dedos, extensor común 97
defectos de la visión 419
defensa central 481
defensa derecho 506
defensa izquierdo 506
deflector 236, 237
deflector de viento 364
deforestación 47
degustación, cuchara 173
Deimos 2
dejada 491
delantero 244, 245, 481
delantero derecho 482, 487
delantero izquierdo 482, 487
delantero medio 487
delantero número 8 482
delco 350
delegados técnicos 509
delfín 90
delfín, morfología 90
delineador 266
delineador de labios 266
delta 32, 35
deltoides 96
demarcación 471
dendrita 110
denominación de los ciclones tropicales 43
dentada 55
dentadura humana 101
dentífrico 272
dentina 101
deportes 468
deportes acuáticos 516
deportes de balón 474
deportes de combate 498
deportes de fuerza 500
deportes de invierno 515
deportes de motor 524
deportes de pelota 474
deportes de precisión 502
deportes de puntería 502
deportes de raqueta 493
deportes náuticos 516

ASTRONOMÍA > 2-25; TIERRA > 26-71; REINO VEGETAL >72-89; REINO ANIMAL > 90-143; SER HUMANO > 144-177; PRODUCTOS ALIMENTARIOS Y DE COCINA > 178-241; CASA > 242-295; BRICOLAJE Y JARDINERÍA > 296-333; VESTIDO > 334-371; ACCESORIOS Y ARTÍCULOS PERSONALES > 372-391; ARTE Y ARQUITECTURA > 392-465; COMUNICACIONES Y AUTOMATIZACIÓN DE OFICINA > 466-535; TRANSPORTE Y VEHÍCULOS > 536-643; ENERGÍA > 644-677; CIENCIA > 678-705; SOCIEDAD > 706-785; DEPORTES Y JUEGOS > 786-920

643

deportes sobre ruedas 526
deportivo 347
depósito de aceite 235
depósito de agua 181
depósito de carbón 402
depósito de combustible 377
depósito de contenedores 381
depósito de gasolina 351, 366, 369
depósito de gasolina, tapón 349
depósito de lodos 403
depósito de los utensilios 444
depósito de mercancía en tránsito 381
depósito de mercancías 430
depósito de polvo 208
depósito del agua 272
depósito del combustible 395
depósito del líquido de frenos 357
depósito esterilizado 464
depósito externo de combustible 12
depósito nocturno, buzón 443
depósitos aluviales 32
depresión 39
depresión barométrica 39
derecha del actor 293
derecha del espectador 293
deriva móvil 521
derivación 416
derivación de la toma de aire 194
dermis 114
derrubios 31
derrumbamiento 31
desagüe 194, 195
desagüe de fondo 184
desagüe principal 194
desatascador 216
descamador 531
descapotable 347
descarga, cámara 278
descenso 511
descomponedores 45
descorazonador 173
desenganchador 216
desenganchador manual 511
desértico 40
deshuesador 173
desierto 36, 44
desierto arenoso 36
desierto de Atacama 17
desierto de Gobi 19
desierto de Kalahari 20
desierto de Namibia 20
desierto del Sahara 20
desierto rocoso 36
desmenuzamiento 49
desnivel 182
desodorante 267
despacho 189, 439
despacho de la enfermera jefe 463
despacho del asistente social 463
despacho del bedel 445
despacho del director 443, 445
despacho del gimnasio 444
despacho del juez 440
despacho del secretario judicial 440
despegue, pista 390
despensa 188, 438, 439
desplantador 232
desplazamiento 331, 418
despojos 154
desprendimiento 31
desprendimientos de tierras 31
destellos, tubo 420
destilador para asfalto 405
destinos 374
destornillador 221, 531
destornillador de trinquete 221
destornillador en cruz 531
destornillador inalámbrico 221
desyerbador 232
detector de humo 454
detector de tensión 217
detritos 43
devanador 537
diadema 458
diafragma 105, 324
diafragma de vacío 360
diagrama de la circulación 103
diamante 468, 474
diámetro 428
diana 471
diapasón 301, 303
dibujo 260, 261
dibujo de la superficie de rodadura 358
diente 74, 76, 167, 226, 227, 235, 270, 398, 400, 523
diente de la desterronadora 398
diente de león 127

dientes 101, 509
dientes, cepillo 272
diésel 405
diésel para barcos 405
diez 427
diez mandamientos 447
diferencia de potencial eléctrico, unidad de medida 426
diferencial 351
difusión de información 335
difusor 290
digestivo, aparato 106
Dinamarca 450
dínamo 370
dinamómetro 423
dinero 441
dinero en efectivo, provisión 443
dintel 185, 192, 285
diodo 411
Dione 3
dióxido de carbono, absorción 54
dique 28, 381
dique seco 381
dirección de flujo de electrones 417
dirección de la Meca 447
dirección del flujo de los electrones 416
dirección del viento 39
dirección URL 334
director 291
director artístico 290
director de carrera 522
director de fotografía 291
director, monitor de control 290
directorio 334
disco 6, 177, 227, 333, 357, 472, 501, 507
disco abrasivo 229
disco compacto 326
disco compacto regrabable, grabador 333
disco compacto, lector 323
disco compacto, reproductor 325
disco de articulación 364
disco desviador de calor 199
disco duro extraíble 333
disco giratorio 176
disco versátil digital (DVD) 318
discontinuidad de Gutenberg 26
disminución de la tensión 413
disparador 236, 314, 454
disparador del tambor 537
display 322, 325, 327, 346, 443, 461
display de frecuencia 325
display de funciones 310
display de las funciones 310
disposición 182
dispositivo de amarre 365
dispositivo de bloqueo 219
dispositivo de cierre 535
dispositivo de protección 306
dispositivo de remolque 364
dispositivos de contacto 198
disquete 333
disquete externo, unidad 333
distribución de la vegetación 44
distribución, tablero 198
distribuidor de bebidas 463
distribuidor de clips 341
distribuidor de hojas de afeitar 271
distrito 25
divanes, ejemplos 200
división 427
divisores 339
divisorio 457
Dniéper, río 18
do(C) 298
doble barra oblicua 334
doble bemol 299
doble caña 306
doble dentada 55
doble filo, tijeras para entresacar 270
doble fuelle 296
doble pletina de casete 325
doble sostenido 299
doble techo 528
doble toldo 529
doblez hacia el interior 534
dodecágono regular 429
dólar 440
dolichos 130
Dominica 449
dominio 334
dominio de primer nivel 334
dominio de segundo nivel 334
dominio, nombre 334
dominó 468
dominós 468

dorada 159
dormitorio 189, 528
dormitorio principal 189
dorsal ancho 97
dorsal del Atlántico medio 34
dorsal del Índico sureste 34
dorsal del Índico suroeste 34
dorsal del Pacífico oriental 34
dorsal del Pacífico-Antártico 34
dorsal oceánica 33
dorso 115, 118
dorso de la nariz 117
dorso de un guante 243
dos doble 468
dos pares 468
dosificador 467
Douglas, saco 112
Drake, paso 15, 17
drenaje de aguas superficiales 434
dromedario 85
drumlin 29
drupa 57
drupas 132
drupéola 59
ducha 189, 439, 464
ducha de teléfono 195
ducha y bañera 194
ducha, bañera 194
dulse 123
duna 35
duna compleja 36
duna parabólica 36
dunas longitudinales 36
dunas transversales 36
dunas, ejemplos 36
dúo 300
duodeno 106
duramadre 109, 110
duramen 63
durión 137

E

eclipse anular 4
eclipse de Luna 5
eclipse parcial 4, 5
eclipse solar 4
eclipse total 4, 5
eclipses, tipos 4, 5
economía 441
Ecuador 22, 448
ecuador 17, 20, 21, 43
edificio de hormigón 408
edificio de oficinas 432, 435
edificio del reactor 409
edificio público 25
editorial 313
edredón 204
educación 444
efecto invernadero 46
efecto invernadero natural 46
efecto invernadero, aumento 46
efecto invernadero, concentración de gas 46
efecto invernadero, gas 46
efluente 32
Egeo, mar 18
Egipto 451
egfelino 161
eje 177, 271, 527
eje de alta velocidad 413
eje de baja velocidad 413
eje de la rueda 371
eje de las aspas 412
eje del cepillo 272
eje del pedal 372
eje del tambor 537
eje delantero 401
eje horizontal, turbina de viento 413
eje polar 7
eje propulsor 383
eje vertical, turbina de viento 412
ejemplos de abreviaciones de monedas 440
ejemplos de anfibios 75
ejemplos de arácnidos 70
ejemplos de aviones 394
ejemplos de barcos 382
ejemplos de bicicletas 373
ejemplos de blusas 255
ejemplos de brocas y barrenas 228
ejemplos de camiones 364
ejemplos de carrocerías 347
ejemplos de clavos 220
ejemplos de conexiones 197

ejemplos de coníferas 65
ejemplos de conjuntos instrumentales 300
ejemplos de costas 35
ejemplos de cucharas 168
ejemplos de cuchillos 168
ejemplos de cuchillos de cocina 169
ejemplos de dunas 36
ejemplos de embarcaciones 382
ejemplos de enlaces de carreteras 342
ejemplos de esquís 510
ejemplos de faldas 253
ejemplos de flores 56
ejemplos de gafas 273
ejemplos de helechos 52
ejemplos de hojas 65
ejemplos de insectos 69
ejemplos de lagomorfos 82
ejemplos de latifolios 65
ejemplos de líquenes 50
ejemplos de llaves 499
ejemplos de mamíferos carnívoros 88
ejemplos de mamíferos marinos 90
ejemplos de mamíferos ungulados 84
ejemplos de mesas 202
ejemplos de motocicletas 369
ejemplos de musgos 51
ejemplos de neumáticos 358
ejemplos de pájaros 80
ejemplos de pantalones 254
ejemplos de patas 79
ejemplos de picos 79
ejemplos de piruetas 509
ejemplos de primates 91
ejemplos de puertas 286
ejemplos de reptiles 77
ejemplos de roedores 82
ejemplos de sacos de dormir 530
ejemplos de sillas 201
ejemplos de tablas 253
ejemplos de tenedores 168
ejemplos de tiendas de campaña 528
ejemplos de vagones 377
ejemplos de ventanas 287
ejemplos de vestidos 252
ejemplos de volcanes 28
el agua enfría el vapor utilizado 408
el agua regresa al generador de vapor 408
el eje de la turbina hace girar el generador 408
El Salvador 448
el vapor se condensa en agua 408
elástico 204
electricidad 198, 217
electrodo central 359
electrodo de masa 359
electrodomésticos, aparatos 176, 208
electrodos 199
electrón 414
electrones, cañón 318
electrones, colectores 417
electrones, dirección de flujo 417
electrónica 417
elefante 85
elemento de combustible 409
elementos arquitectónicos 286
elementos de la casa 185
elevación continental 33
elevación de la cuadrícula, cilindro 401
elevador 281, 399, 400
elevador telescópico 455
embalaje 49
embalse 406, 407
embalse a monte 406
embalse de compensación 406, 407
embarque del telesilla 512
embarque teleférico 512
emblema 477
emblema del equipo 506
embocadura 306
embocadura del cable 208
émbolo 460
embrague 350
embudo 171
emergencia, estación 345
emergencia, vehículo 345
emerillón 538
emisión de billetes 442
emmenthal 151
empalizada 230, 282
empaquetadora 364
empate de la boquilla 307
empeine 92, 247
empella 240, 263
empleo del tiempo 338
empresa 335
empresas distribución /venta 335

empujador 170, 177, 180
empuñaderas 500
empuñadura 227, 229, 273, 341, 466, 477, 492, 494, 500, 505, 510, 534, 535, 536
en espiral 192
encañado 230
encendedor 218
encendido 237
encendido/apagado 326
encendido/apagado/volumen 326
enchufe 198, 210, 217, 228, 326
enchufe con control de tiempo 210
enchufe de tipo europeo 198
enchufe del termómetro 178
enchufe para auriculares 326
enchufe y selector desmontables 179
encía 101, 116
encimera 164, 210
encofrado metálico 417
encuadernación de anillas 340
endecágono regular 429
endivia 142
endocardio 104
endocarpio 57, 58
enebro, bayas 138
eneldo 142
energía 402
energía calorífica 46
energía eólica 412
energía eólica, producción de electricidad 413
energía fósil 402
energía geotérmica 402
energía nuclear 408
energía nuclear, producción de electricidad 408
energía solar 54, 410
energía térmica 402
energía, liberación 415
energía, unidad de medida 426
enfermera 464
enfoque 419
enfranque 240
enganche 353, 535
enganche de bola 356
enganche del remolque 361
engranaje de avance 180
engrasador 173
enlace de arcén 342
enlace de diamante 342
enlace de glorieta 342
enlace de trébol 342, 343
enlace químico 414
enlosado del jardín 182
enramada 230
enredadera 230
ensaladera 166
ensamble hembra 536
ensamble macho 536
entablado 187
entablamento 185, 279
entarimado 190, 498
entarimado sobre estructura de madera 190
entera 55
enterramiento 49
entrada 189, 343, 396, 439, 440, 442
entrada a boxes 524
entrada de actores 278
entrada de agua 407
entrada de aire 395, 523
entrada de clientes 438
entrada de corriente 199
entrada de la estación 378
entrada de la pirámide 278
entrada de público 278
entrada del garaje 183
entrada del personal 438, 445
entrada del refrigerante 410
entrada del suministro 198
entrada para mercancías 435
entrada principal 188, 435, 445, 465
entradas, taquilla 294
entradilla 313
entrecejo 86
entrediente 167
entrega de equipaje 390
entrenador 489, 498, 507
entrenador adjunto 489, 507
entrenadores 509
entrenudo 53
entrepaño 202, 219
entrepaño horizontal 185
entrepaño vertical 185
entrepierna 247, 255

ASTRONOMÍA > 2-25;   TIERRA > 26-71;   REINO VEGETAL >72-89;   REINO ANIMAL > 90-143;   SER HUMANO > 144-177;   PRODUCTOS ALIMENTARIOS Y DE COCINA > 178-241;   CASA > 242-295;
BRICOLAJE Y JARDINERÍA > 296-333;   VESTIDO > 334-371;   ACCESORIOS Y ARTÍCULOS PERSONALES > 372-391;   ARTE Y ARQUITECTURA > 392-465;   COMUNICACIONES Y AUTOMATIZACIÓN DE
OFICINA > 466-535;   TRANSPORTE Y VEHÍCULOS > 536-643;   ENERGÍA > 644-677;   CIENCIA > 678-705;   SOCIEDAD > 706-785;   DEPORTES Y JUEGOS > 786-920

entrepiso 378
entresuelo 182, 189
entrevista 313
envase 163
envases 162
envero 62
envión 500
epeira 70
eperlano 159
epicarpio 57, 58, 59
epicentro 27
epicóndilo 99
epidermis 114
epidídimo 111
epífisis 109
epiglotis 105, 118
epitróclea 99
equilibrador 303
equilibrio, posición 418
equinoccio de otoño 38
equinoccio de primavera 38
equinodermos 66
equipaje 276
equipamiento 472
equipamiento del salpicadero 457
equipamiento para acampar 531
equipamiento vario 231
equipo de alimentación, ventilador 329
equipo de alta fidelidad 322
equipo de climatización 386
equipo de grabación 291
equipo de primeros auxilios 460
equipo de protección 486
equipo de sonido 291
equipo electrobomba 357
equipo médico 499
equipo receptor 479
equipo turboalternador 402
equipos de gas 529
equivalente a 427
Eritrea 451
erupción 4
erupción, volcán 28
es paralelo a 428
escabel 201
escala 225, 298, 460, 533
escala Celsius 424
escala de altitud 37
escala de altura 227
escala de inclinación 227
escala de ingletes 226
escala de la regla 425
escala de temperaturas 37, 424
escala Fahrenheit 424
escala graduada 422, 423, 425
escala graduada de vernier 425
escalera 184, 191, 288, 404, 412, 468, 498, 501
escalera con boquilla telescópica 455
escalera de color 468
escalera de plataforma 219
escalera de tijera 219
escalera del entresuelo 189
escalera extensible 219
escalera mecánica 294, 378, 435
escalera real 468
escalera telescópica 455
escalera, hueco 189
escaleras 188, 293, 294, 345, 378, 439
escaleras de mano 219
escalerilla 361, 401, 404
escalerilla lateral 377
escalfador de huevos 175
escalinata 183, 283
escalón 364
escalón retráctil 361
escalones 184, 283
escama 74, 76, 79
escanda común 143
Escandinava, península 18
escáner óptico 121
escape 330
escápula 93, 95, 98, 99
escapulares 78
escaque blanco 470
escaque negro 470
escarabajo 69
escarcha 41
escarola 126
escarola rizada 127
escena, número 291
escenario 278, 292, 293
escisión del núcleo 415
esclavina 251
esclerótica 119
esclusa científica de aire 13
esclusa de canal 381

escoba 215
escoba central 365
escoba de nieve con rascador 356
escoba eléctrica 209
escoba lateral 365
escobén 383, 387
escobilla 193
escobilla limpiadora 271
escobilla metálica 309
Escocia, plancha 27
escollo 35
escolta 489
escopeta 534
escoplo 229
escorpión 70
escorrentía subterránea 45
escorrentía superficial 45
escorzonera 129
escota 520
escota foque 520
escota mayor 520
escotadura 301
escotadura intertrágica 115
escotera 521
escotero 520
escotilla 12, 13
escotilla del depósito 385
escritorio 203, 439
escritorio, artículos 337
escroto 92, 111
escuadra 225
escudilla 166
escudo 507
escudo solar 7
escuela de esquí 512
escurridera 173
escurridor 171
escurridores 171
escúter 369
esfagno 51
esfera 332, 422, 429
esfera de té 173
esfera graduada 533
esfínter anal 106
eslabón de corte 235
eslabón giratorio 535
eslalon especial 511
eslalon gigante 511
eslalon supergigante 511
Eslovaquia 450
Eslovenia 450
esmalte 101
esmalte de uñas 265
esófago 105, 106
espacio 298, 330
espacio epidural 110
espacio interior 211
espacio para almacenamiento 364
espacio para la chispa 359
espacio sin pausa 330
espada 468
espádice 57
espagueti 146
espalda 83, 93, 95, 244, 517
espaldar 76
espaldera 532
España 449
esparadrapo 461
esparavel 216
espárrago 125
espátula 173
espatulada 55
especias 138
especias para salmuera 139
especificaciones técnicas 358
espectro electromagnético 418
espejo 195, 277, 421, 439, 523, 533
espejo cóncavo primario 9
espejo de cercanías 362
espejo de cortesía 354
espejo de lectura 10
espejo de reflexión parcial 420
espejo de reflexión total 420
espejo doble giratorio 269
espejo lateral 269, 348, 364
espejo luminoso 269
espejo plano 7
espejo primario 7
espejo retrovisor 354, 363, 366, 369
espejo retrovisor exterior 362
espejo secundario 7, 9
espermatozoide 111
espesor, medición 425
espículas 4
espiga 57, 167, 169, 202, 216, 273, 357
espina escapular 99

espina nasal anterior 100
espinaca 127
espinacas, tallarines 146
espinillera 476, 480
espira 72
espiráculo 90
espiral 70, 73, 221
espiral central 70
espiral embrionaria 73
espirulina 123
esplenio 97
espoiler 366
espolón 83, 228, 308
espolvoreador 172
esponja natural 267
esponja sintética 266
esponja vegetal 267
esporas 52
espuma 33
espuma de afeitar 271
espumadera 173
esqueleto 98
esquí 510, 523
esquí alpino 510
esquí alpino, pista 512
esquí de descenso 510
esquí de eslalon 510
esquí de eslalon gigante 510
esquí de fondo 514
esquí supergigante 510
esquí, pista 512
esquí, salto 513
esquiador alpino 510
esquina 506
esquinero derecho 484
esquinero izquierdo 484
esquís, ejemplos 510
estabilizador 397, 523
estabilizador horizontal 395
establo 122
estaca 479
estación central de bombeo 404
estación de autobuses 432
estación de carga 375
estación de emergencia 345
estación de esquí 512
estación de ferrocarril 374, 375
estación de ferrocarriles 430, 432
estación de metro 378, 432
estación de servicio 346, 433
estación espacial internacional 11
estación local 316
estación meteorológica aeronaval 38
estación meteorológica oceánica 38
estación repetidora 316
estación repetidora de microondas 334
estación terrestre 38
estación terrestre de telecomunicaciones 335
estación, metro 378
estación, modelo 39
estacionamiento 375, 381
estadio 431, 472
estado 23
estado actual del tiempo 39
estados de la materia 414
Estados Unidos de América 448
estalactita 31
estalagmita 31
estambre 56, 58
estanco 436
estaño de soldar 218
estanque 230, 504
estaquilla 528, 529
estatua 446
estay de proa 520
Este 23
Este Noreste 23
Este Sudeste 23
estela luminosa del cráter 5
estepario 40
esternocleidomastoideo 96
esternón 98
estigma 56, 60, 67
estilo 56, 57, 58, 59, 60, 312, 424
estilóbato 279
estilos de natación 517
estimulador de encías 272
estípula 55
estómago 73, 103, 106
estómago cardiaco 71
estómago pilórico 71
Estonia 450
estornino 80
estrado 444
estrado de la acusación 440
estrado de los jueces 440

estrado de los secretarios judiciales 440
estrado de los testigos 440
estrado del abogado defensor 440
estrado del director 295
estragón 142
estrangulación 499
estrato basal 114
estrato córneo 114
estrato de cenizas 28
estrato de lava 28
estrato de Malpighi 114
estrato granuloso 114
estrato lúcido 114
estratocúmulos 42
estratopausa 37
estratos 42
estratosfera 37
estrechamiento 424
estrecho 24
estrecho de Bass 15
estrecho de Bering 16
estrecho de Cook 15
estrecho de Gibraltar 18
estrecho de Torres 15
estrella de David 447
estrella de frenado 537
estrella fugaz 37
estribación 29
estribera 367, 368
estribera del pasajero 367, 368
estribo 116, 284, 395, 523
estribor 387
estropajo con esponja 215
estropajo, esponja 215
estructura 186, 297
estructura de la biosfera 44
estructura de la médula espinal 109
estructura de la Tierra 26
estructura de madera, entarimado sobre 190
estructura de metal 374
estructura de un alga 51
estructura de un musgo 51
estructura de una casa 188
estructura de una hoja 55
estructura del ala 392
estructura del oído 116
estructura del Sol 4
estructura inferior 403
estructura interna 286
estructura protectora 525
estuario 24, 35
estuche 225, 265, 424
estuche de encerado 515
estuche de hilo dental 272
estuche de las esposas 456
estuche de manicura 265
estuche portalentes 272
estufa de leña a fuego lento 192
esturión 158
etapas de la maduración 62
Etiopía 451
etiqueta de identificación 277
etiquetas adhesivas 340
etmoides, lámina cribosa 117
Eurasia 14
euro 440
Europa 2, 14, 18, 34, 449
europeo, clavija de tipo 198
Eustaquio, trompa 116, 117
Eutelsat 316
euthynteria 279
evaporación 45, 414
Everest, monte 37
examen psiquiátrico 462
excavación vesicouterina 112
excavadora 399
excrementos de animales 48
exosfera 37
expedición de carga 391
expedidor de recibo 346
explosivo 534
expositor de final de pasillo 121
expositor de folletos 442
exprimidor 170, 177
exprimidor de cítricos 177
exprimir 177
extensión 202
extensión plegable 202
extensor 273
extensor común de los dedos 97
extensor largo de los dedos del pie 96
exterior 475
exterior de una casa 182
exterior derecho 475
exterior izquierdo 475
extintor 457

extintor portátil 454
extracto de vainilla 140
extracto, vainilla 140
extremo 273
extremo anterior 73
extremo del brazo 235
extremo derecho 507
extremo izquierdo 507
extremo libre 114
extremo posterior 73
exvoto 446
eyector de las varillas 176
Eyre, lago 15

F

fa(F) 298
fábrica 430
fachada 285
factor RH negativo 426
factor RH positivo 426
factorial 427
facturación de equipaje 390
fáculas 4
fagot 306
fagotes 295
fairway 504
faisán 81, 154
faja 259
faja braga 259
faja con liguero 259
faja con sostén 258
faja corsé 258
falangeta 114
falangina 114
falda 251, 492
falda acampanada 253
falda combinación 258
falda cruzada 253
falda de piezas 253
falda de tubo 253
falda de volantes 253
falda escocesa 253
falda fruncida 253
falda pantalón 253
falda recta 253
falda sarong 253
faldas, ejemplos 253
faldón 204, 255
faldón de la camisa 245
faldón delantero 245
faldón flexible 383
faldón trasero 245
falla 27
fallas transformantes 27
Falopio, istmo de la trompa 113
Falopio, pabellón de la trompa 113
Falopio, trompa 112, 113
falsa doblez 260
falsa escuadra 225
falsa oronja 52
falso almohadón 204
familia de instrumentos de madera 295
familia de los metales 295
familia de los violines 295, 301
farallón 35
faringe 105, 106
farmacia 436, 462, 465
faro 381
faro de carretera 457
faro de destello 455
faro delantero 348, 364, 366, 368, 376, 377, 523
faro reflector 455
farol 207, 230, 434
farola 207
faros delanteros 352
faros intermitentes 362
fascia lata, tensor 96
fase de deslizamiento 514
fase de impulsión 514
fase de impulso 514
fases de la Luna 5
fauces, istmo 116
fax 328
fecha 441
fecha de vencimiento 441
fechador 338
Federación Rusa 450
feijoa 137
femenino 426
femeninos, órganos genitales 112
fémur 98
fémur, cabeza 99
fémur, cuello 99
fenec 88

ASTRONOMÍA > 2-25;   TIERRA > 26-71;   REINO VEGETAL >72-89;   REINO ANIMAL > 90-143;   SER HUMANO > 144-177;   PRODUCTOS ALIMENTARIOS Y DE COCINA > 178-241;   CASA > 242-295;
BRICOLAJE Y JARDINERÍA > 296-333;   VESTIDO > 334-371;   ACCESORIOS Y ARTÍCULOS PERSONALES > 372-391;   ARTE Y ARQUITECTURA > 392-465;   COMUNICACIONES Y AUTOMATIZACIÓN DE
OFICINA > 466-535;   TRANSPORTE Y VEHÍCULOS > 536-643;   ENERGÍA > 644-677;   CIENCIA > 678-705;   SOCIEDAD > 706-785;   DEPORTES Y JUEGOS > 786-920

645

fenogreco 138
ferrocarril del muelle 381
ferrocarril, estación 374, 375
fertilización del suelo 47
fertilizante, esparcimiento 47
festoneada 55
fetuchinas 146
fiador 528
fiador elástico 528, 529
fibra muscular 110
fibra nerviosa 114
fíbula 98
ficha 469
fichero giratorio 338
fideos 146
fideos asiáticos 147
fideos de arroz 147
fideos de huevo 147
fideos de judías mungo 147
fideos de soba 147
fideos de somen 147
fideos de udon 147
fiel 422, 423
fijación 513
fijación de seguridad del esquí 511
fijación para el pie 514
fijaciones 510
fijador 514
fijador de carrete 537
Fiji 453
Fiji, islas 15
filamento 56, 199
Filchner,plataforma de hielo 15
filete 301, 302, 313
filigrana 441
Filipinas 19, 453
Filipinas, fosa 34
Filipinas, placa 27
filmación, plató 290
filo 167, 169, 270
filo simple, tijeras para entresacar 270
filón-capa 28
filtro 178, 181, 184, 210
filtro de aire 235, 398
filtro de pelusa 212, 213
filtro de polarización 314
filtro del aire 350
filtro selector del color 318
filum terminal 109
filum terminal interno 109
fin 331
final de carrera 226, 287
finanzas 441
Finlandia 450
fiordo 35
firma del titular 441
firma oficial 441
física : electricidad y magnetismo 416
física : óptica 418
fisión nuclear 415
flamenco 81
flanco 78
flauta travesera 306
flautas traverseras 295
flexo 206
flip 509
flor 53, 56
flor, estructura 56
floración 62
flores, ejemplos 56
floristería 437
florón 283
flotador 196, 394, 457, 538
flujo de los electrones, dirección 416
Fobos 2
foca 90
foco 207, 419
foco Cassegrain 7
foco coudé 7
foco primario 7
foco subacuático 184
focos 293
fogón 192
foie gras 156
foliador 338
folículo 60
folículo piloso 114
follaje 63, 200
fondista 514
fondo 292
fondo del escenario 293
fondo oceánico 33
fonendoscopio 460
fontanela anterior 100
fontanela esfenoidal 100
fontanela mastoidea 100

fontanela posterior 100
fontanería 194, 216
foque 520
formación profesional, oficina 442
formas de agarrar la paleta 493
formas farmacéuticas de medicamentos 467
formas geométricas 428
formato del archivo 334
fórmula 1, coche 525
fómix, cuerpo 109
forro 240, 244, 245, 262, 274, 477, 509
forro de cuero 478
forro de la lengua 76
fosa abisal 33
fosa de agua 504
fosa de almacenamiento de combustible agotado 409
fosa de Japón 34
fosa de Java 34
fosa de Kermadec-Tonga 34
fosa de Kuril 34
fosa de las Aleutianas 34
fosa de las Filipinas 34
fosa de las Marianas 34
fosa de Puerto Rico 34
fosa Ryukyu 34
fosa séptica 48
fosa triangular 115
fosas nasales 117
foso 282
foso de arena 504
foso de escenario 292
foso de orquesta 292
foto 313
fotocopiadora 442
fotografía 314
fotógrafo 436
fotógrafo de plató 291
fotomatón® 437
fotón 420
fotorreceptores 119
fotosfera 4
fotosíntesis 54
fóvea 119
foyer 293
fracción 427
frambuesa 132
frambuesa, corte 59
Francia 449
franja del faldón 383
frecuencia, unidad de medida 426
fregadero 164, 197
fregadero con triturador de basura 197
fregadero doble 194
fregona 215
freidora 178
freno 467, 501, 511, 522, 536, 537
freno aerodinámico 412
freno de disco 350, 357, 366, 525
freno de disco hidráulico 522
freno de emergencia 380
freno de la cadena 235
freno de mano 350, 354
freno de tambor 357
freno delantero 371
freno trasero 370, 527
frenos 357, 392
frente 78, 92
fresa 132
fresa, corte 59
fresadora 229
fresco 280
frigorífico 164, 211, 438
frigoríficos 438
frijol 131
friso 202, 279
fronda 52
frontal 96, 446
frontera interna 23
frontera internacional 23
frontón 279
frotador 218
fructificación 62
fruncido 255
fruta 120
fruta de jack 136
fruta de la pasión 136
frutas 132
frutas pomo 133
frutas secas 133
frutas tropicales 136
frutos 57
frutos secos 60
fuelle 274, 276
fuente 31
fuente básica de alimento 45

fuente de alimentación 416
fuente de servicio 313
fuente de servir 166
fuente de verdura 166
fuente para abluciones 447
fuente para pescado 166
fuertes lluvias 43
fuerza, unidad de medida 426
full 468
fulminante 534
fumarola 28
funcionamiento 319
funciones programables, teclas 443
funda 417, 531, 533
funda de almohada 204
funda de automóvil 356
funda de colchón 204
funda de cuero 533
funda de gafas 275
funda de guantes de látex 456
funda de la almohada 204
funda de mástil 519
funda del sable 519, 520
funguicida 47
funículo 59, 60
furgón de cola 377
fusa 299
fuselaje 393
fusible 198, 411
fusilli 146
fusión 414
fuste del bastón 514
fútbol 480
fútbol americano 484
futbolista 480
futón 204

G

gablete 285
Gabón 451
gafa 273
gafas 273, 522
gafas : partes 273
gafas de baño 516
gafas de esquí 510, 513
gafas de seguridad 458
gafas de sol 273
gafas protectoras 218, 458, 522
gafas, ejemplos 273
gaita 296
gajo 58
galaxia 6
galería 285
galería de acceso 407
galería de conexión 345
galería seca 31
galleta de centeno 145
galleta escandinava 145
galletas de arroz 147
gallina 81
gallinero 122
gallineta 161
gallo 81
galope 83
gamba 158
Gambia 451
ganadería intensiva 46, 47
gancho 217, 225, 364, 397, 423
gancho de arrastre 356
gancho de tracción 403, 460
gancho del meñique 307
gancho del pulgar 306, 307
gancho para el platillo 422
gancho para la porra 456
ganglio cerebropleural 73
ganglio espinal 109, 110
ganglio simpático 109
ganglio visceral 73
Ganimedes 2
garaje 182, 345
garaje, entrada 183
garaje, puerta basculante 286
garam masala 139
garbanzos 130
garduña 88
garganta 31, 32, 78, 492, 538
gargantilla 264
gargantilla de terciopelo 264
garita 87
garra 79, 82, 86
garrafa 165
garrapata 70
garrucha montacarga 397
garza 80
gas 403, 405, 414

gas de efecto invernadero 46
gas inerte 199
gasóleo 405
gasolina 405
gasolina pesada 405
gasolina, motor 360
gatillo 216, 235, 332, 534
gatillo de seguridad 235
gato 356, 455
gato doméstico 87
gato estabilizador 361
gato hidráulico 361
gatos, razas 87
géiser 28
gel de baño 267
gemelos 96, 97
gemelos de teatro 273
generador 402
generador de vapor 402
geografía 14
geología 26
geometría 428
Georgia 452
germen 61
germinación 53
Ghana 451
gibón 91
Gibraltar, estrecho 18
gimnasia 496
gimnasio 386, 444
girasol 56
girasol, aceite 149
glaciar 30, 32, 44
glaciar suspendido 30
glande 111
glándula de Cowper 111
glándula de veneno 76
glándula digestiva 71, 73
glándula lacrimal 119
glándula mamaria 113
glándula salival 118
glándula sebácea 114
glándula sudorípara apocrina 114
glándula sudorípara ecrina 114
glándula suprarrenal 107
glándulas salivales 106
globo 491, 529
globo ocular 75, 119
globo sonda 38
globo terráqueo 444
glóbulo blanco 104
glóbulo rojo 104
glotis 76
glucosa 54
glúteo mayor 97
go (sun-tse) 470
Gobi, desierto 19
gofrera 178
gol 485
golf 24
golfo de Adén 19, 20
golfo de Alaska 16
golfo de Botnia 18
golfo de California 16
golfo de Carpentaria 15
golfo de Guinea 20
golfo de México 16
golfo de Omán 19
golfo de Panamá 17
golfo Pérsico 19
Golgi, aparato 50, 66
golondrina 80
golpe de patín 514
golpes 490
goma 341
gombo 128
gónada 73
góndola 121, 413
góndola, sección transversal 413
gong 295, 309
gorgonzola 151
gorila 91
gorila, morfología 91
gorra 238, 456
gorra de cuartel 238
gorra noruega 238
gorrión 80
gorro 514
gorro de baño 516
gorro de marinero 239
gorro de punto con borla 239
gota 207
gotas oftalmológicas lubricantes 272
grabación 319
grabación nocturna, conmutador 320
grabador de disco compacto regrabable 333

gradas móviles 444
grado 428
grado Celsius 426
grados C 424
grados F 424
Gran Bahía australiana 15
Gran Cañón 16
Gran Cordillera divisoria 15
Gran Danés 86
Gran Desierto de Arena 15
Gran Desierto Victoria 15
Gran Galería 278
gran roncón 296
gran siega interior 499
Granada 449
granada 136
grandes almacenes 437
Grandes Lagos 16
grandes titulares 313
granero 122
granja 122
grano 61
grano de almidón 50
grano de trigo, corte 61
granos torrefactos de café 148
granos verdes de café 148
granulación 4
gránulo de lípido 50
grapadora 341
grapas 341
grasa para cocinar 149
grasa, glóbulo 50
grasas 149, 405
grasera 174, 179
gravilla 524
Grecia 450
green 504
green de entrenamiento 504
grieta 30
grifo 195
grifo de cocina de tres vías 197
grillete 521
grillete de resorte 521
grillo campestre 69
Groenlandia 16
Groenlandia, mar 14
grosella 132
grosella espinosa 132
grosella negra 132
grúa 385
grúa de caballete 406, 407
grúa de muelle 381
grúa de puente 407
grúa flotante 381
grúa móvil 397
grúa remolque 364
grúa torre 397
grúas 397
grupa 83
grupeto 299
grupo motor 376
grupo turboalternador 407
gruta 31
gruyère 151
guacamayo 80
guante 10, 478, 498, 506, 508, 513, 514, 522, 525
guante a la muñeca 243
guante corto 243
guante de bateo 476
guante de crin 267
guante de esquí 510
guante de golf 505
guante de recogida 477
guante de softball 477
guante del receptor 476
guante largo 243
guante para conducir 243
guante rígido 243
guante, dorso 243
guante, palmo 243
guantera 354
guantes 243
guantes de boxeo 498
guantes de hombre 243
guantes de jardinería 232
guantes de látex 460
guantes de mujer 243
guantes del portero 480
guantes protectores 525
guarda 169
guarda fija del disco 227
guarda móvil del disco 227
guardabarros 348, 349, 364, 365, 370
guardabarros delantero 366
guardamonte 534
guardanieve 523

ASTRONOMÍA > 2-25; TIERRA > 26-71; REINO VEGETAL >72-89; REINO ANIMAL > 90-143; SER HUMANO > 144-177; PRODUCTOS ALIMENTARIOS Y DE COCINA > 178-241; CASA > 242-295; BRICOLAJE Y JARDINERÍA > 296-333; VESTIDO > 334-371; ACCESORIOS Y ARTÍCULOS PERSONALES > 372-391; ARTE Y ARQUITECTURA > 392-465; COMUNICACIONES Y AUTOMATIZACIÓN DE OFICINA > 466-535; TRANSPORTE Y VEHÍCULOS > 536-643; ENERGÍA > 644-677; CIENCIA > 678-705; SOCIEDAD > 706-785; DEPORTES Y JUEGOS > 786-920

guardarropa 188, 189, 203, 443
guardarropa de los clientes 438
guardarropa del personal 438, 465
guardería 437
guardia derecho 485
guardia izquierdo 485
guarnición 201, 202, 277, 511
Guatemala 448
guayaba 137
guepardo 89
guía 226, 521
guía de cabina 287
guía de cinta 341
guía de corte 227
guía de enganche 376
guía de escotas 521
guía de la cadena 372
guía de la punta 536, 537
guía del contrapeso 287
guía del papel 328
guías de archivo 340
guiñada 395
guindilla 139
guindilla molida 139
guindilla seca 139
guindilla triturada 139
Guinea 451
Guinea Ecuatorial 451
Guinea, golfo 20
Guinea-Bissau 451
guisante 60
guisantes 130
guisantes mollares 130
guisantes partidos 130
guitarra clásica 302
guitarra eléctrica 303
gusto 116
Gutenberg, discontinuidad 26
Guyana 448
guyot 33

H

habas 130
habitación de observación 462
habitación de aislamiento 462
habitación de un paciente 464
habitación doble 439
habitación individual 439
habitaciones principales 188
habitáculo 525
hacha 234, 454, 533
hacha de cocinero 169
Haiti 448
halcón 81
halibut 161
hall de entrada 188
halo 6
haltera 501
halterofilia 500
hamada 36
hámster 82
hangar de mantenimiento 389
hapterio 51
harina 144
harina común 144
harina de avena 144
harina de maíz 144
harina integral 144
harina sin blanquear 144
harissa 141
hastial 182
haya 64
hayuco 133
haz azul 318
haz de electrones 318
haz rojo 318
haz verde 318
hebilla 246, 248, 276, 511
hebilla de ajuste 527
hebilla de regulación 532
heladera 180
helecho 52
helecho arbóreo 52
helecho canela 125
helecho nido de pájaro 52
helecho, estructura 52
helechos, ejemplos 52
hélice 384, 386, 387, 429
hélice de dos aspas 394
hélice de proa 384
hélice de tres aspas 394
hélice posterior 384
hélice propulsora 383
helicóptero 395

hélix 115
hemisferio 429
hemisferio Norte 21
hemisferio occidental 21
hemisferio oriental 21
hemisferio Sur 21
hemisferios 21
henil 122
heptágono regular 429
herbicida 47
herbívoros 45
hercio 426
herraje 277
herramientas 216, 217, 372
herramientas de perfilado 229
herramientas de soldadura 218
herramientas para apretar 222
herramientas para clavar 220
herramientas para cortar 234
herramientas para plantar 231
herramientas para regar 236
herramientas para remover la tierra 233
herramientas para segar 226
herramientas para sembrar 231
herramientas percutoras 228
herramientas, caja 225
herramientas, cinturón 225
herramientaspara atomillar 221
herrete 240, 262
hervidero 29
hervidor 180
heterótrofos 45
hexagonal 359
hexágono regular 429
hidroavión cisterna 394
hidroavión de flotadores 394
hidrocarburos, vertido 48
hidroelectricidad 406
hidróptero 387
hidrosfera 44
hielo 41, 45
hielos perpetuos 40
hielos, distribuidor 164
hiena 88
hierba 492
hierbabuena 142
hierbas aromáticas 142
hierro 505
hifa 52
hígado 103, 106, 154
higiene dental 272
higiene personal 121
higo 137
higo chumbo 137
hijiki 123
hijuela 538
hilera 272
hileras 70
hilio renal 107
hilo 417
hilo de nailon 237
hilo de seguridad 441
hilo dental 272
Himalaya 19
hinojo 125
hipermetropía 419
hipervínculos 334
hipocentro 27
hipófisis 109
hipopótamo 85
hisopo 142
hocico 74, 86, 87
hockey sobre hielo 506
hogar 192
hogar, muebles 200
hoja 51, 53, 54, 55, 61, 125, 167, 169,
    216, 219, 221, 226, 227, 229, 270,
    271, 286
hoja corta 531
hoja de acanto 200
hoja de afeitar 271
hoja de cuchilla 504
hoja de parra 126
hoja dentada 270
hoja flexible 54
hoja larga 531
hoja, estructura 55
hojaldre, pasta 145
hojas compuestas 55
hojas escamadas del ciprés 65
hojas simples 55
hojas, ejemplos 65
hojita enrollada 52
hombre 92
hombre, guantes 243
hombre, ropa de 244

hombre, sombreros 238
hombre, zapatos 240
hombrera 248, 302, 456, 486
hombrillo 249
hombro 92, 94, 492, 536
home theatre 321
Honduras 448
hongo 52
hongo mortal 52
hongo venenoso 52
hongo, anatomía 52
hongos 123
horario de la programación televisiva 313
horarios 374
horarios de las películas 294
horca 233
hormiga 69
hormigonera 365
hornear, utensilios para 172
hornillo 210, 529
horno 164, 210
horno microondas 164, 178
horno tubular 405
horno, termómetro 171
Hornos, cabo 17
horquilla 8, 243, 268, 371, 396, 522,
    525
horquilla de mano 232
horquilla de moño 268
horquilla frontal 522
horquilla telescópica 366, 369
horquilla trasera 370
horquilla, carretilla elevadora 396
hortalizas 125
hortalizas de fruto 128
hortalizas de tallos 125
hospedería para esquiadores 512
hospital 433, 462
hotel 432, 439, 469, 512
hotel, habitación 439
hoyo 31, 504
hoyo de par 5 504
hoyuelo 505
hoz 234
Hubble, telescopio espacial 7, 37
Hudson, bahía 16
hueco de la escalera 189
hueco del motor 396
huella 191
huerta 122
huerto 122, 182
huesillos auditivos 116
hueso 57
hueso alveolar 101
hueso cigomático 100
hueso esfenoides 100
hueso frontal 98, 100
hueso ilíaco 98
hueso maxilar 101
hueso nasal 100, 117
hueso occipital 100
hueso parietal 100
hueso temporal 98, 100
huevera 211
huevo 79
huevo de avestruz 155
huevo de codorniz 155
huevo de faisán 155
huevo de gallina 155
huevo de oca 155
huevo de pato 155
huevo, fideos 147
huevos 155
Huitzilopochtli, templo 283
humano, cuerpo 92
humero 98
húmero, cabeza 99
hummus 140
humor acuoso 119
humus 54
Hungría 450
huracán 43
husillo 425

I

Ibérica, península 18
idéntico a 427
identificación de cuenta 443
iglesia 433, 446
iglú 288
igual a 427
igual o mayor que 427
igual o menor que 427
iguana 77
ijar 83

íleon 106
iluminación 199, 269
iluminación de la placa de matrícula 352
imán 211, 341, 416
imaripinnada 55
impermeable 248
impermeables 248
impluvio 280
impresión pantalla 331
impresora de líneas 333
impresora, calculadora 337
impulso nervioso 110
impulso, irrigador 236
incendio forestal 47
incensario 446
incineración 49
incisivo central 101
incisivo lateral 101
incisivos 101
incisura angular 115
inclusión 427
India 453
indicador 340
indicador de ajuste 511
indicador de alimentación 333
indicador de carga del papel 333
indicador de encendido 329
indicador de hora de salida 374
indicador de línea 362, 363
indicador de llamadas 328
indicador de luz larga 368
indicador de nivel de gasolina 355
indicador de número de andén 374
indicador de posición 287
indicador de puesta en marcha de papel
    443
indicador de punto muerto 368
indicador de recarga 271
indicador de respuesta automática 328
indicador de temperatura 269, 355
indicador de tiempo 314
indicador de velocidad 314
indicador dedetección de papel 443
indicador del cartucho 333
indicador del importe total 346
indicador del intermitente 368
indicador del nivel del agua 179
indicador del precio por litro /galón 346
indicador digital 423
indicador luminoso 179, 423
indicador para viraje en nado de espalda
    517
indicador transparente 340
indicadores 318, 323
indicadores de entrada 322
indicadores del modo audio 322
Índice 539
Índice español 539
Índice medio, dorsal 34
Índice sureste, dorsal 34
Índico suroeste, dorsal 34
Índico, océano 14, 15, 19, 20
Indonesia 19, 453
industria 335
industria petroquímica 405
infiltración 45, 47
infinito 427
inflador 530
inflorescencias 127
inflorescencias, variedades 57
información 437, 442, 463
infraestructura 342
infraspinoso 97
infusiones 148
ingeniero de sonido 291
ingle 92, 94
húmero, cabeza 99
inhalador 467
inicio 331
inmovilización 499
inmovilización de brazo 499
inodoro 189, 194, 195, 196, 439, 464
insectos 67
insectos, ejemplos 69
insert 331
insertar 331
insignia 456
insignia de grado 456
institución educativa 335
instrucciones operativas 346
instrumentos científicos 7, 13
instrumentos de cuerda 301
instrumentos de madera, familia 295
instrumentos de percusión 295, 308
instrumentos de teclado 304
instrumentos de trazado y medición 225

instrumentos de viento 306
instrumentos del salpicadero 355
instrumentos electrónicos 310
instrumentos musicales tradicionales 296
instrumentos para escribir 312
integración de energía a la red de
    transporte 413
integral 427
Intelsat 317
intensidad luminosa, unidad de medida
    426
interior derecho 481
interior izquierdo 481
intermitente 352, 355
intermitente delantero 366, 368
intermitente trasero 367, 368
internauta 334
Internet 334
Internet, usos 335
interóseos del pie 96
interruptor 177, 180, 181, 198, 206,
    207, 208, 209, 211, 213, 218, 219,
    229, 269, 270, 271, 272, 311, 319,
    323, 327, 329, 416
interruptor alimentación 320
interruptor automático 407
interruptor de alimentación 318
interruptor de comunicación 336
interruptor de emergencia 368
interruptor de encendido 329, 354, 368
interruptor de encendido/apagado 314
interruptor de gatillo 227, 228, 229
interruptor de la puerta 213
interruptor de ráfagas 368
interruptor del limpiaparabrisas 354
interruptor funciones 320
interruptor on/off 209
interruptor principal 198
interruptor selector de velocidad 227
intersección 427
intertítulo 313
intervalos 298
intestino 71, 73, 103
intestino delgado 106
intestino grueso 106
invernadero 122
inversor 221, 228
invierno 38
inyector 360
Ío 2
Irán 452
Iraq 452
iris 119
Irish moss 123
Irlanda 449
Irlanda, mar 18
irrigador bucal 272
irrigador de impulso 236
irrigador giratorio 236
irrigador oscilante 236
isba 288
isla 24, 164, 343
isla de arena 35
isla de Terranova 16
isla volcánica 33
Islandia 18, 450
islas Aleutianas 16
islas de Cabo Verde 451
islas del Caribe 448
islas Fiji 15
islas Malvinas 17
Islas Marshall 453
Islas Salomón 453
islote rocoso 35
isobara 39
isosista 27
isquion 99
Israel 452
istmo 24
istmo de la trompa de Falopio 113
istmo de las fauces 116
istmo de Panamá 16
Italia 450

J

jabalí 84
jabalina 472
jabón de tocador 267
jabonera 195, 271
jaboticaba 137
jaguar 89
Jamaica 448
jamba 185, 192
jamón ahumado 153
jamón de York 156

ASTRONOMÍA > 2-25; TIERRA > 26-71; REINO VEGETAL >72-89; REINO ANIMAL > 90-143; SER HUMANO > 144-177; PRODUCTOS ALIMENTARIOS Y DE COCINA > 178-241; CASA > 242-295;
BRICOLAJE Y JARDINERÍA > 296-333; VESTIDO > 334-371; ACCESORIOS Y ARTÍCULOS PERSONALES > 372-391; ARTE Y ARQUITECTURA > 392-465; COMUNICACIONES Y AUTOMATIZACIÓN DE
OFICINA > 466-535; TRANSPORTE Y VEHÍCULOS > 536-643; ENERGÍA > 644-677; CIENCIA > 678-705; SOCIEDAD > 706-785; DEPORTES Y JUEGOS > 786-920

647

ÍNDICE ESPAÑOL

jamón serrano 156
Jápeto 3
Japón 19, 453
Japón, fosa 34
Japón, mar 19
jarabe de arce 149
jarabe de maíz 149
jarabe para la tos 467
jardín 230, 280
jardín de rocalla 230
jardín público 435
jardín, enlosado 182
jardinería 216, 230
jardinería, guantes 232
jarlsberg 151
jarra de agua 166
jarra de cerveza 165
jarra medidora 171
jarra para café 166
jarrita de leche 166
jaula 281
jaula de protección 473
Java, fosa 34
jefe de cronometradores 516
jefe de luminotecnia 291
jefe de vestuario 290
jengibre 139
jerbo 82
jeringa de decoración 172
jeringuilla de Luer-Lock 460
jeringuilla 460
jeringuilla de irrigación 460
jersey de cuello de cisne 514
jersey de cuello de tortuga 250
jersey de cuello redondo 250, 255
jerseys 250
jerseys combinados 255
jet supersónico 37
jícama 124
jirafa 85
jojoba 137
Jordania 452
jota 468
joyería 264, 436
joystick 332
joysticks 471
judía adzuki 131
judía amarilla 131
judía china larga 130
judía de Egipto 130
judía de Lima 131
judía mungo 131
judía mungo negra 131
judía negra 131
judía pinta 131
judía roja 131
judía roja 131
judía romana 131
judías de ojo 130
judías verdes 131
judo 499
judoji 499
judoka neutral 499
jueces 496, 497, 509, 518
jueces de virajes 517
juego 492
juego de casquillos 223
juego de dardos 471
juego de mesas 202
juego de pequeñas herramientas 232
juego de utensilios 173
juego en línea 335
juegos 468
juegos de mesa 469
juez 485, 498, 499
juez de brazado 516
juez de faltas de pie 491
juez de gol 506
juez de línea 481, 483, 485, 487, 490,
    494, 496, 507
juez de línea de saque 490
juez de llegada 516
juez de red 491
juez de salida 516
juez de servicio 490, 494
juez de silla 490
juez externo 485
juez-árbitro 518
jugador 469, 486, 506
jugador con el servicio 491
jugador de baloncesto 488
jugador de críquet 478
jugador de primera base 474
jugador de rugby 482
jugador de saque 494
jugador de segunda base 474
jugador de tercera base 474

jugador exterior central 474
jugador exterior derecho 474
jugador exterior izquierdo 474
jugador medio 474
jugadores 492
jugadores, posición 481, 482
juguetería 436
julio 426
junta 214, 359
junta cónica 196
junta de goma 197
junta del cárter 360
junta positivo/negativo 410
Júpiter 2
justicia 440
Justicia, Palacio 432

K

Kalahari, desierto 20
Kamchatka, península 19
Kazajistán 452
kelvin 426
Kenia 451
Kermadec-Tonga, fosa 34
ketchup 141
kilogramo 426
kimono 256, 499
kiosco 346, 379
Kirguizistán 452
Kiribati 453
kiwano 136
kiwi 136
Kola, península 18
kombu 123
kora 297
Kuiper, cinturón 2
Kuril, fosa 34
Kuwait 452

L

la hoja según su borde 55
la presión del vapor impulsa las turbinas
    408
la(A) 298
labio 83, 87
labio córneo 76
labio externo 73
labio inferior 116, 305
labio interno 73
labio mayor 112, 113
labio menor 112, 113
labio superior 116, 305
laboratorio 7
laboratorio americano 11
laboratorio espacial 13
laboratorio patológico 465
lacolito 28
ladera 29
ladillo 313
lado 293
lado de la reina 470
lado del rey 470
lado derecho 272
lado izquierdo 272
Ladoga, lago 18
ladrillo refractario 192
ladrillos refractarios 192
ladronera 282
lagarto 77
lago 5, 24, 29, 32
lago artificial 32
lago Baikal 19
lago Chad 20
Lago Eyre Norte 15
lago glaciar 32
lago Ladoga 18
lago Malaui 20
lago Tanganyika 20
lago tectónico 32
lago Titicaca 17
lago Victoria 20
lago volcánico 32
lagomorfos 82
lagomorfos, ejemplos 82
lagos 32
lagos, acidificación 48
laguna 35
laguna salada 36
lama 412
lámina 51
lámina cribosa del etmoides 117
lámina de contacto de positiva 359
lámina de contacto negativa 359
laminillas 52

lámpara 380, 421
lámpara de ahorro de energía 411
lámpara de cabecera 206, 439, 464
lámpara de despacho halógena 206
lámpara de escritorio 206
lámpara de lectura 457
lámpara de mesa 206
lámpara de neón 217
lámpara de petróleo 532
lámpara de pie 206
lámpara de pinza 206
lámpara de prueba de neón 217
lámpara de techo 206
lámpara del santuario 446
lámpara halógena 199
lámpara orientable de pared 207
lámparas 206
lámparas en serie 207
lamprea 159
lanceolada 55
lancha pequeña 385
langosta marina 158
lanzador 474, 475, 477
lanzamiento 475, 479
lanzamiento de jabalina 473
lanzamiento de martillo y disco 473
lanzamiento de peso 472
Laos 453
lapa 157
lapiaz 31
lápida conmemorativa 447
lápiz 312
lápiz adhesivo 341
lápiz blanco para uñas 265
lápiz de cejas 266
lápiz de grafito 312
larguerillo 396
larguero 186, 201, 219, 392, 412
larguero de la bisagra 202
larguero del marco 202
laringe 105
lasañas 146
láser de rubí pulsado 420
lata 163
lata de conserva 163
latas 162
lateral derecho 481
lateral izquierdo 481
laurel 142
lavabo 194, 195, 439, 464
lavabo de cirujano 465
lavado de automóviles 346
lavadora 194, 212
lavandería 188, 439
lavavajillas 164, 214
laya 233
lazo 238, 264, 535
leche 150
leche de cabra 150
leche en polvo 150
leche evaporada 150
leche homogeneizada 150
leche, suero 150
lecho oceánico 26
lecho ungular 114
lechuga de cogollo 126
lechuga de tallo 126
lechuga iceberg 126
lechuga marina 123
lechuga rizada 126
lechuga romana 126
lector CD/DVD 471
lector de casetes 326
lector de disco compacto 323, 325
lector de discos compactos 326
lector de tarjeta 321, 442, 443
lectura /pausa 323
lectura de tarjeta, ranura 346
legumbre 60
legumbres 130
lema 441
lémur 91
lencería 256, 436, 439
leñera 192
lengua 106, 116, 117, 118, 154
lengua bífida 76
lengua glaciar 30
lenguado 161
lengüeta 240, 248, 262, 274, 305, 306,
    509, 511
lengüeta de cuero 246
lengüeta de la caña 297
lengüeta protectora 333
lengüeta, tubo 305
lente 273, 419
lente cóncava 419

lente convexa 419
lente convexo-plana 419
lente de campo 420
lente tórica 419
lentejas 130
lentes 419
lentes bicóncavas 419
lentes biconvexas 419
lentes cóncavas 419
lentes cóncavo-planas 419
lentes convergentes 419
lentes convexas 419
lentes de contacto 272
lentes de contacto blandas 272
lentes de contacto desechables 272
lentes de contacto duras 272
lentes de imágen recta 420
lentes divergentes 419
león 89
leopardo 89
Lesoto 452
Letonia 450
letrinas 280
leucoplasto 50
Líbano 452
libélula 69
líber 63
liberación de energía 415
liberador del seguro 222
Liberia 451
libero 487
Libia 451
libra 440
librería 436, 444
libreta 338
lichi 137
licuadora 180
líder 515
liebre 82, 154
Liechtenstein 450
liga 259
ligadura 299
ligamento 73
ligamento alveolo-dentario 101
ligamento ancho del útero 113
ligamento suspensorio 119
liguero 259
lija 229
lijadora excéntrica 229
lima 134, 229, 531
lima de uñas 265
limbo 52
limitador de velocidad 287
limitador de velocidad, polea tensora 287
limón 134
limpiador 355
limpiador de boquillas 218
limpiador de uñas 265
limpiaparabrisas 348, 355
limpieza 215
limusina 347
lince 88
lindero 182
línea 298
línea azul 507
línea cableada 335
línea central 515
línea central de servicio 491
línea de «touche» 483
línea de 10 m 482
línea de 15 m 483
línea de 22 m 482
línea de 5 m 483
línea de área de penalti 480
línea de ataque 487
línea de banda 493, 515
línea de campo 416
línea de centro 481
línea de crecimiento 72, 73
línea de cuadro 502
línea de devolución 479
línea de dobles 490
línea de fondo 482, 484, 487, 489, 491,
    493, 494
línea de foul 474
línea de gol 484, 506
línea de juego 515
línea de la calle 473
línea de lanzamiento 479
línea de marca 482
línea de medio campo 483
línea de melé 485
línea de pista 389
línea de referencia 533
línea de retirada 479
línea de salida 273, 524
línea de salida 100 m 472

línea de salida 800 m 473
línea de salida de 1.500 m 473
línea de salida de 10.000 m 473
línea de salida de 100 m vallas 472
línea de salida de 110 m vallas 472
línea de salida de 200 m 472
línea de salida de 400 m 473
línea de salida de 400 m vallas, línea de
    relevos de 4x100 m 473
línea de salida de 5.000 m 473
línea de salida de relevos 4 x 400 m 473
línea de seguridad 379
línea de servicio 491
línea de servicio corto 495
línea de servicio largo 494
línea de tee 515
línea de tiro libre 489
línea de visión 533
línea del fondo de la piscina 517
línea divisoria central 493, 494
línea lateral 74, 343
línea lateral de dobles 495
línea lateral de individuales 491, 495
línea límite de inicio de jugada 484
línea media 484, 488, 507
línea meridiana 533
línea neutra 416
línea reservada 334
línea submarina 334
línea suplementaria 298
línea telefónica 334
línea trasera 515
línea yardas 484
líneas de latitud 22
líneas de longitud 22
linterna 456, 529
linterna movible 217
liquen 50
liquen custráceo 50
liquen foliáceo 50
liquen fruticuloso 50
liquen, estructura 50
líquenes, ejemplos 50
líquido 414, 415
líquido cerebroespinal 110
lira 297
lisosoma 66
lista de procedimientos 10
lista superciliar 78
listón 211
litera 361
litoral, configuración 35
litosfera 26, 44
Lituania 450
lixiviación 48
liza 282
llama 84, 415
llama perpetua 447
llana 216
llanta 366, 371
llanta neumática de tracción 380
llanta neumática guía 380
llanura 24, 32
llanura abisal 33
llave 306, 307
llave combinada 223
llave de apriete 224
llave de carraca 223
llave de embocadura 306
llave de estrella abierta 223
llave de estrella común 223
llave de estrella hexagonal 223
llave de fontanero 216
llave de paso 194, 196, 197
llave de tuercas española 223
llave del mandril 228
llave en cruz 356
llave inglesa 216, 223
llave para agua 307
llavero 275
llaves 216, 223
llegada 473
llegada del telesquí 512
lluvia 41
lluvia ácida 47, 48
lluvia helada 41
lobo 88
lobulada 55
lóbulo 79, 115, 117
lóbulo inferior 105
lóbulo lateral inferior 62
lóbulo lateral superior 62
lóbulo medio 105
lóbulo superior 105
lóbulo terminal 62
local técnico 345
loción para después del afeitado 271

ASTRONOMÍA > 2-25; TIERRA > 26-71; REINO VEGETAL >72-89; REINO ANIMAL > 90-143; SER HUMANO > 144-177; PRODUCTOS ALIMENTARIOS Y DE COCINA > 178-241; CASA > 242-295;
BRICOLAJE Y JARDINERÍA > 296-333; VESTIDO > 334-371; ACCESORIOS Y ARTÍCULOS PERSONALES > 372-391; ARTE Y ARQUITECTURA > 392-465; COMUNICACIONES Y AUTOMATIZACIÓN DE
OFICINA > 466-535; TRANSPORTE Y VEHÍCULOS > 536-643; ENERGÍA > 644-677; CIENCIA > 678-705; SOCIEDAD > 706-785; DEPORTES Y JUEGOS > 786-920

locomotora 376
locomotora diésel eléctrica 377
lóculo 58
lomo 78, 83, 86, 152, 167, 169, 215
lomo con canal 228
lona 412, 498
lona de separación 528
longan 136
longitud de la ola 33
longitud de onda 418
longitud, medición 425
longitud, unidad de medida 426
loop de puntera 509
loseta 12
lubina 160
lucernario 183
lucernario del baño 189
lucernario del hueco de la escalera 189
lucernas del campanario 285
luces de advertencia 355
luces de estado 331
luces de gol 507
luces de seguridad 457
luces traseras 352
lucio 160
lucioperca 160
luminotécnico 291
Luna 2, 4, 5
Luna creciente 5
Luna llena 5
Luna menguante 5
Luna nueva 5
Luna, eclipse 5
Luna, fases 5
luneta 293
lúnula 73, 114, 115
lupa 421, 531
lutz 509
Luxemburgo 449
luz 7, 8, 9
luz ámbar 434
luz anticolisión 392
luz antiniebla 352, 364
luz de advertencia de la gasolina 355
luz de advertencia de puerta abierta 355
luz de advertencia del aceite 355
luz de advertencia del alternador 355
luz de advertencia del cinturón de
    seguridad 355
luz de aterrizaje 395
luz de cruce 352
luz de encendido 271, 328
luz de encendido/apagado 327
luz de freno 352
luz de marcha atrás 352
luz de navegación 383, 393, 395
luz de posición 352, 376
luz de tope 383
luz delantera 371
luz indicadora de cargado 337
luz indicadora de la presión del aceite 368
luz indicadora de luz larga 355
luz larga 352
luz lateral 364, 365
luz piloto 269
luz roja 434
luz trasera 352, 367, 368, 370
luz verde 434
luz visible 418

M

macaco 91
macarrones 146
Macedonia 450
maceta 230
maceta colgante 230
macillo 304
macizo 24
macizo de flores 230
Mackenzie, río 16
macronúcleo 66
mácula lútea 119
Madagascar 20, 452
madera 505
madera, pisos de 190
maduración, etapas 62
madurez 62
magacín 313
magenta 418
magma 28, 33
magnetismo 416
Maine Coon 87
maitre 438
maíz 61, 143
maíz : mazorca 61

maíz forrajero 122
maíz, aceite 149
maíz, harina 144
maíz, jarabe 149
maíz, pelo 61
malanga 129
Malasia 453
Malaui 452
Malaui, lago 20
Maldivas 453
maleta 369
maleta clásica 277
maleta de fin de semana 277
maletero 349, 362
maletín 274, 276
maleza 504
malla 493, 522
mallas 263
mallas con volantes 260
Malpighi, estrato 114
Malta 450
Malvinas, islas 17
mamíferos acuáticos 90
mamíferos carnívoros 86
mamíferos carnívoros, ejemplos 88
mamíferos marinos 90
mamíferos marinos, ejemplos 90
mamíferos primates 91
mamíferos ungulados 83
mamíferos ungulados, ejemplos 84
mancha solar 4
Mancha, canal 18
mandarina 134
mandíbula 67, 74, 98, 100
mandíbula deslizante 425
mandíbula fija 425
mandíbula inferior 78
mandíbula superior 78
mandioca 124
mando 471
mando a distancia 319, 321
mandolina 170, 297
mandos de la videocinta 320
mandos de los quemadores 210
mandos del cabestrante 364
mandril 221, 228
manecilla de vapor 181
manejo de materiales 396
maneta del embrague 366, 368
maneta del freno delantero 368
manga 244, 492
manga raglán 248, 251, 261
manga empotrada 245
manga y boquillas 172
mangas anteriores 492
mango 137, 167, 169, 170, 208, 216,
    217, 218, 219, 220, 221, 222, 223,
    224, 226, 228, 235, 269, 270, 271,
    272, 301, 325, 478, 492, 493, 494,
    503, 505, 506, 515, 531, 537
mango aislado 217
mango aislante 217
mango auxiliar 228
mango posterior 537
mangosta 88
mangostán 136
manguera 195, 197, 236, 454
manguera de alimentación 214
manguera de aspiración 455
manguera de desagüe 212, 214
manguera de incendios 454
manguera de inyección de lodo 403
manguera de líquido para frenos 357
manguera de riego 236
manguera de servicio 346
manguera de vaciado 212
manguera del rebosadero 196
manguera, carretilla 236
manguito inferior del radiador 358
manicura 265
manicura, estuche 265
manilla 185, 186, 192, 211
manilla de la puerta 349
manillar 366, 369, 371, 501, 522, 523
maniobra de la excavadora 399
manipulación 396
manivela 170, 224, 356, 365, 372, 536,
    537
manivela de enrollado 225
manivela de la ventanilla 352
manivela del carrete 236
mano 91, 93, 95, 115, 170
manojo 125
manómetro 455, 461
manopla 243
manopla de baño 267
manos de póquer 468
manta 204

manteca de cerdo 149
mantenimiento 346
mantenimiento de pinturas 219
mantequera 166
mantequilla 150
mantequilla clarificada 150
mantis 69
manto 72, 73, 192
manto externo 26
manto freático 48
manto interno 26
manual de primeros auxilios 461
Manx 87
manzana 133
manzana, corte 58
manzanilla 148
mapa de carreteras 25
mapa de la ruta 378
mapa de ruta 380
mapa de rutas 379
mapa físico 24
mapa geográfico 444
mapa meteorológico 38, 39
mapa político 23
mapa urbano 25
mapache 88
maquillador 290
maquillaje 266
maquillaje facial 266
maquillaje labial 266
maquillaje para ojos 266
máquina 287
máquina de afeitar eléctrica 271
máquina de café exprés 181
máquina expendedora de bebidas 346
máquina expendedora de billetes 379
máquina para hacer pasta italiana 170
máquina pisanieve 512
maquinaria pesada 398
maquinilla de afeitar 271
maquinilla desechable 271
maquinilla para cortar el cabello 269
maquinista 290
maquinista jefe 290
maquis 44
mar 5, 24, 32
mar Adriático 18
mar Arábigo 19
mar Báltico 18
mar Caribe 14
mar Caspio 14, 19
mar de Aral 19
mar de Barents 18
mar de Beaufort 14
mar de Bering 14
mar de Caribe 16
mar de Coral 15
mar de Groenlandia 14
mar de Irlanda 18
mar de Japón 19
mar de la China Meridional 14, 19
mar de la China Oriental 19
mar de Noruega 18
mar de Tasmania 15
mar de Weddell 15
mar del Norte 14, 18
mar Egeo 18
mar Mediterráneo 14, 20
mar Negro 14, 18, 19
mar Rojo 14, 19, 20
marca central 490
marcador 312, 471, 472, 492, 497, 499
marcador automático 327
marcador de clasificación general 496
marcador de posición 302, 303
marcador del evento en curso 497
marco 186
marco ajustable 226
margarina 149
Marianas, fosa 34
Marie Byrd, Tierra 15
mariposa 67, 517
mariposa de resorte 221
mariposa, morfología 67
mariquita 69
marítimo 40
marmota 82
marquesina 434
marquesina del andén 375
marroquinería, artículos 274
Marruecos 451
marta 88
Marte 2, 3
martillo 116, 472
martillo de albañil 216
martillo de bola 220
martillo de carpintero 220

martillo de uña 220
martín pescador 80
más o menos 427
masa 27
masa de aire 39
masa inerte 27
masa, unidad de medida 426
máscara 454, 476, 478, 486
máscara antigás 459
máscara para el polvo 459
mascarilla 459
masculino 426
masculinos, órganos genitales 111
masetero 96
mástil 281, 297, 301, 302, 303, 321,
    396, 519, 520
matacán 282
matemáticas 427
materia 414
materia inorgánica 45
materia, estados 414
material aislante 190
material de cierre 417
material de lucha contra los incendios
    454
material impermeable 260
materiales varios 225
materiales, manejo 396
matraca 536
matriz ungular 114
Mauricio 452
Mauritania 451
maxilar 74, 100, 117
maxilar separable 76
maxilar superior 98
mayor que 427
mayúscula 330
maza 309
mazo 220
mazorca 61
meandro 32
meato auditivo 115, 116
meato auditivo externo 100
meato urinario 111
mecanismo de desplazamiento de la hoja
    401
mecanismo de empuje 312
mecanismo para las octavas 306
mecedora 200, 201
medallón 264
media 257, 486
media antideslizante 257
media de malla 257
media luna 273
media volea 490
mediana 343, 434
medias 257, 259
medicamentos, formas farmacéuticas 467
medición de la longitud 425
medición de la temperatura 424
medición del espesor 425
medición del peso 422
medición del tiempo 424
médico 464, 498
médico interno 464
medida instantánea, termómetro 171
medidor de agua 359
medidor de altos niveles de frecuencia
    323
medio centro 481
medio de apertura 482
medio de red 482
medio tubo 526
medir, utensilios 171
Mediterráneo, mar 14, 18, 20
médula 51, 107, 154
médula espinal 109, 110
médula espinal, estructura 109
Meissner, corpúsculo 114
mejilla 94
mejillón 157
Melanesia 15
melaza 149
melazas 149
melé espontánea 483
melé : 484, 485
melisa 142
melocotón 132
melocotón, corte 57
melón amarillo 135
melón cantalupo 135
melón de Ogen 135
melón de miel 135
melón escrito 135
melón invernal 135
melones 135
membrana 58, 75

membrana celular 50, 66
membrana de plasma 66
membrana del cascarón 79
membrana del tímpano 116
membrana interdigital 79
membrana nuclear 50, 66
membrana plásmica 66
membrana vitelina 79
membrillo 133
meninges 109
menisco convergente 419
menisco divergente 419
menor que 427
ménsula 192, 283
mentón 78, 94
mentonera 522
menudillo 83
Mercurio 2, 3
meridiana 200
meridiano occidental 22
meridiano oriental 22
meridiano principal 22
merlán 161
mesa 36, 164, 202, 493, 502
mesa arbitral 507
mesa de cama 464
mesa de hojas abatibles 202
mesa de servicio 438
mesa operatoria 464
mesa plegable 202
mesa rotatoria 403
mesas, ejemplos 202
meseta 24, 29
mesilla de cabecera 464
mesilla de noche 439
mesita de servicio 202
mesocarpio 57, 58, 59
mesopausa 37
mesosfera 37
metal, selección 49
metales, familia 295
meteorología 37
metro 378, 426, 435
México 448
México, golfo 16
mezcla de agua y vapor 402
mezcla de manganeso (cátodo) 417
mezcla de zinc y electrolito (ánodo) 417
mezclador de pastelería 172
mezclar 176
mezquita 447
mi(E) 298
micelio 52
microfilamento 66
micrófono 320, 327, 328, 332, 337, 456
micrófonos 457
micrómetro 425
Micronesia 453
micronúcleo 66
microondas 418
microscopio 421
microscopio binocular 421
microscopios 421
microtúbulo 66
miel 149
miembro inferior 103
miembro superior 103
migala 70
mihrab 447
mijo 61, 143
mijo : espiga 61
mil 427
Mimas 3
mimbar 447
minarete 447
mini-cadena estéreo 325
minibús 363
miniporción de leche /nata 163
miniporción, leche/nata 163
minutero 171, 179, 424
minuto 428
miocardio 104
miopía 419
mira 535
mira telescópica 534
mirador 391
Miranda 3
Mississippi, río 16
mitocondria 50
mitocondrio 66
mitón largo 243
mízcalo 123
mobiliario para el hogar 200
mocasín 242
mochila 532
modalidad de avance de la película 314
modalidad de exposición 314

ASTRONOMÍA > 2-25; TIERRA > 26-71; REINO VEGETAL >72-89; REINO ANIMAL > 90-143; SER HUMANO > 144-177; PRODUCTOS ALIMENTARIOS Y DE COCINA > 178-241; CASA > 242-295;
BRICOLAJE Y JARDINERÍA > 296-333; VESTIDO > 334-371; ACCESORIOS Y ARTÍCULOS PERSONALES > 372-391; ARTE Y ARQUITECTURA > 392-465; COMUNICACIONES Y AUTOMATIZACIÓN DE
OFICINA > 466-535; TRANSPORTE Y VEHÍCULOS > 536-643; ENERGÍA > 644-677; CIENCIA > 678-705; SOCIEDAD > 706-785; DEPORTES Y JUEGOS > 786-920

649

modalidad de exposición múltiple 314
modalidad TV 319
modalidad VCR 319
modelo de estación 39
módem 334
módem cableado 335
moderador 376, 408
modillón 282
modos de pago 441
modulador de presión de frenado 357
módulo centrifugo 11
módulo de células solares 411
módulo de comunicación 316
módulo de habitación americano 11
módulo de propulsión 316
módulo de servicio 316
módulo para experimentos europeo 11
módulo para experimentos japonés 11
módulo ruso 11
mofeta 88
Mohorovic, discontinuidad 26
molar, corte transversal 101
molares 101
Moldavia 450
molde acanalado 172
molde de carlota 172
molde de pan 179
molde de soufflé 172
molde para bizcocho 172
molde para magdalenas 172
molde para tartas 172
molde redondo con muelles 172
moldeador de cuticulas 265
moldes de pastas 172
moldura 358
moldura lateral 349
moldura superior 493
mole 426
molécula 414
moler 170
molinete 412
molinillo de café 180
molino de plataforma giratoria 412
molino de torre 412
molino de viento 412
mollejas 154
moluscos 72, 157
moneda : anverso 441
moneda, anverso 441
moneda, reverso 441
moneda: reverso 441
monedero 275
Mongolia 453
monitor de control del director 290
monitor de video 329
mono 261
mono de esqui con capucha 261
monocascos 521
monopatin 526
monopatin 526
Monopoly® 469
monovolumen 347
montacargas 397
montaña 29, 512
montañas Rocosas 16
montante 184, 187, 394, 466, 509
montante central 185, 186, 202, 349
montante de la bisagra 185
montante de la cerradura 185
montante embarillado 186
montante esquinero 187
montante quicial 186
monte de Venus 112
monte Everest 37
montes Apalaches 16
montes Cárpatos 18
montes marinos 33
montes Urales 18
montura en herradura 7
monumento 25
moqueta 190
moras 132
morcilla 156
morcillo 152
mordaza 217, 221, 222, 224, 226, 228,
   229, 265
mordaza curva 222
mordaza fija 223, 224
mordaza móvil 223, 224
mordaza recta 222
mordazas 224, 535
mordente 299
morfología de un bogavante 71
morfología de un caballo 83
morfología de un caracol 72
morfología de un delfín 90
morfología de un gorila 91

morfología de un pájaro 78
morfología de un perro 86
morfología de un pulpo 72
morfología de un tiburón 74
morfología de una abeja trabajadora 68
morfología de una araña 70
morfología de una concha bivalva 73
morfología de una concha univalva 73
morfología de una mariposa 67
morfología de una perca 74
morfología de una rana 75
morfología de una rata 82
morfología de una serpiente venenosa:
   cabeza 76
morfología de una tortuga 76
morilla 123
morillos 193
morral 276
morrena central 30
morrena de fondo 30
morrena frontal 30
morrena lateral 30
morrena terminal 30
morro 392
morro abatible 394
mortadela 156
mosaico 280
mosca 69, 502
mosca artificial 536
mosca central 502
mosca de la linea de cuadro 502
mosca superior 502
mosca tsetsé 69
mosquetón 521, 538
mosquito 69
mostaza 60
mostaza alemana 140
mostaza americana 140
mostaza blanca 138
mostaza de Dijon 140
mostaza en grano 140
mostaza en polvo 140
mostaza inglesa 140
mostaza negra 138
mostrador 390
mostrador de carne de autoservicio 120
mostrador de carne fresca 120
mostrador de quesos 121
mostrador frigorifico 438
mostrador, carne 120
mostrador, quesos 121
moto acuática 523
moto cámara 522
moto de cabeza 522
moto de carreras y motociclista 525
moto de motocross 525
moto nieve 523
moto, motociclista 525
motocicleta 366, 525
motocicleta : vista desde lo alto 368
motocicleta de turismo 369
motocicleta todo terreno 369
motocicletas, ejemplos 369
motor 176, 177, 180, 208, 212, 213,
   214, 227, 229, 237, 272, 366, 401,
   403
motor de arranque 237
motor de elevación diésel 383
motor de gasolina 351, 360
motor de propulsión diésel 383
motor del tractor 400
motor diesel 399, 400, 401
motor diésel 398
motor eléctrico 235, 237, 358
motor fueraborda 385
motor principal 13
motor, bogie 376
movimiento diagonal 470
movimiento en ángulo 470
movimiento horizontal 470
movimiento horizontal del suelo 27
movimiento vertical 470
movimiento vertical del suelo 27
movimientos de un avión 395
Mozambique 452
Mozambique, canal 20
mozzarella 150
mucosa olfatoria 117
mueble bar 203
muebles contenedores 202
muebles infantiles 205
muela del juicio 101
muelle 381, 430, 460, 535
muelle de carga 435, 437
muelle helicoidal 351
muelle para inflar y desinflar 530
muerte 426

muesca 244, 422, 503
muesca de apertura 531
muestreador 310
muflón 84
muguete 56
mujer 94
mujer, guantes 243
mujer, ropa 251
mujer, sombreros 239
mujer, zapatos 241
mújol 160
mula 84
muleta de antebrazo 466
muleta de sobaco 466
multicasco 521
multipack 163
multiplicación 427
multiplicador 413
muñeca 93, 95, 115
muñequera 486, 492, 500, 527
munster 151
muralla 282
muro 5, 184, 528
muro de cimentación 187
muro de encauzamiento 406
muro de la Qibla 447
muro de llegada 516
muro de nubes 43
muro del ojo 43
muro fortificado 447
músculo aductor anterior 73
músculo aductor posterior 73
músculo bulbocavernoso 111
músculo erector del pelo 114
músculo papilar 104
músculo recto inferior 119
músculo recto superior 119
músculos 96
muselina 171
museo 433
musgo 51
musgo, estructura 51
musgos, ejemplos 51
música 296
muslera 486
muslo 78, 83, 86, 93, 95, 111, 112
muslo, aductor 96
muslo, recto interno 97
musola 158
Myanmar 453

N

nabiza 127
nabo 129
nabo sueco 129
nacimiento 426
nacionalidad 497
nalga 93, 95, 111, 112
Namibia 452
Namibia, desierto 20
naos 279
naranja 134
naranja china 134
naranja, corte 58
narciso 56
narina 74, 75, 76, 78
nariz 82, 94, 117, 534
nariz, aleta 117
nariz, dorso 117
nariz, ventana 117
nasofaringe 117
nata 150
nata agria 150
nata de montar 150
natación 516
Nauru 453
navaja 157
navaja de barbero 271
navaja jardinera 234
navaja multiusos suiza 531
navaja para entresacar 269
nave 285
nave central 447
nave espacial 37
nave lateral 285
navegador 334
Nazca, placa 27
neblina 41
neceser 276, 277
necrológico 313
nectarina 132
nefridio 71
negra 299
negras 470
negro 418

muesca 244, 422, 503
Negro, mar 14, 18, 19
Nepal 453
Neptuno 2, 3
nervadura central 60
nervadura principal 55
nervadura secundaria 55
nervio 67, 114
nervio abdominogenital mayor 108
nervio abdominogenital menor 108
nervio auditivo 116
nervio central 51
nervio ciático mayor 108
nervio ciático menor 108
nervio ciático popliteo externo 108
nervio ciático popliteo interno 108
nervio circunflejo 108
nervio crural 108
nervio cubital 108
nervio diagonal 284
nervio digital 108
nervio espinal 109
nervio femorocutáneo 108
nervio glúteo 108
nervio intercostal 108
nervio mediano 108
nervio musculocutáneo de la pierna 108
nervio obturador 108
nervio olfatorio 117
nervio óptico 119
nervio radial 108
nervio raquideo 110
nervio safeno externo 108
nervio safeno interno 108
nervio secundario 284
nervio tibial anterior 108
nervio transversal 284
nervio vestibular 116
nervios craneales 108
nervioso, sistema 108
neumático 349, 358, 364, 371, 522, 525
neumático de invierno 358
neumático de rendimiento 358
neumático de tacos 358, 369, 525
neumático de todas las estaciones 358
neumático de turismo 358
neumáticos, ejemplos 358
neurona motora 110
neurona sensorial 110
neuronas, cadena 110
neutrón 414
neutrón incidente 415
nevera 346, 532
neviza 30
newton 426
Nicaragua 448
nicho de seguridad 345
niebla 41
nieve 41
nieve ácida 48
nieves perpetuas 29
Níger 451
Niger, rio 20
Nigeria 451
Nilo 20
nimbostratos 42
niño, cráneo 100
niños, ropa 261
Nissl, cuerpos 110
nivel de agua 181
nivel de aire 225
nivel de equilibrio del agua 33
nivel de la recepción 439
nivel del agua 208
nivel del mar 26, 33, 37
nivel del mar, presión barométrica 39
nivel el agua, indicador 179
nivel freático 31
nivelador 229
niveladora 401
no es idéntico a 427
no es igual a 427
no es paralelo a 428
no pertenece a 427
nódulo de Ranvier 110
nogal 64
nombre de la estación 378
nombre de la moneda 441
nombre del dominio 334
nombre del gimnasta 497
nombre del periódico 313
nombre del titular 441
nonágono regular 429
nonio 422
ñoquis 146
Nor Noroeste 23
Noreste 23

nori 123
Noroeste 23
Norte 23
Norte Noreste 23
Norte, mar 14, 18
Noruega 450
Noruega, mar 18
notación del ajedrez 470
notación musical 298
notas musicales, valores 299
noticias breves 313
nube 37, 41
nube alta, tipo 39
nube baja, tipo 39
nube de cenizas 28
nube de Oort 2
nube en forma de embudo 43
nube media, tipo 39
nubes 42
nubes altas 42
nubes bajas 42
nubes de desarrollo vertical 42
nubes medias 42
nubes, absorción 46
nuca 93, 95
núcleo 4, 6, 50, 66, 110, 112, 414, 534
núcleo externo 26
núcleo fisionable 415
núcleo interno 26
núcleo, escisión 415
nucléolo 50, 66, 112
núcleos radioactivos 415
nudo 53, 416
nudo viario 431
Nueva Caledonia 15
Nueva Zelanda 15, 453
nuevo shekel 440
nuez 92, 133
nuez de cola 133
nuez de ginkgo 133
nuez de macadamia 133
nuez del Brasil 133
nuez moscada 138
nuez moscada, rallador 170
nuez verde 60
nuez, corte 60
número de habitación 439
número de identificación personal (PIN),
   teclado 443
número de la autopista 25
número de la carretera 25
número de la escena 291
número de la tarjeta 441
número de pista 323
número de serie 441
número de tarjeta 443
número del jugador 488, 506
número del surtidor 346
número dorsal 473
números romanos 427
nutria de rio 88

O

oasis 32, 36
obenque 520
Oberón 3
obispillo 78
objetivo 8, 314, 332, 420, 421
objetivo gran angular 314
objetivo macro 314
objetivo zoom 314, 320
objetivos 314
objeto 419
oblicuo mayor del abdomen 96, 97
oboe 306
oboes 295
obra muerta 521
obrera 68
observación astronómica 7
observación, puesto 7
observatorio 7
observatorio astronómico 7
observatorio astronómico, sección
   transversal 7
obstáculo 470
obturador 333
obturador de la cúpula 7
oca 81, 155
occidental 493
occipital 97, 99
Oceania 14, 15, 453
océano 5, 24, 45
océano Atlántico 14, 15, 18, 20
océano Glacial Ártico 14
océano Índico 14, 15, 19, 20

ASTRONOMÍA > 2-25;   TIERRA > 26-71;   REINO VEGETAL >72-89;   REINO ANIMAL > 90-143;   SER HUMANO > 144-177;   PRODUCTOS ALIMENTARIOS Y DE COCINA > 178-241;   CASA > 242-295;
BRICOLAJE Y JARDINERÍA > 296-333;   VESTIDO > 334-371;   ACCESORIOS Y ARTÍCULOS PERSONALES > 372-391;   ARTE Y ARQUITECTURA > 392-465;   COMUNICACIONES Y AUTOMATIZACIÓN DE
OFICINA > 466-535;   TRANSPORTE Y VEHÍCULOS > 536-643;   ENERGÍA > 644-677;   CIENCIA > 678-705;   SOCIEDAD > 706-785;   DEPORTES Y JUEGOS > 786-920

océano Pacífico 14, 15, 19
ocelo 67
ocio al aire libre 528
octaedro regular 429
octágono regular 429
octava 298
ocular 8, 9, 320, 420, 421
ocular acodado 8
odómetro 355
Oeste 23
Oeste Noroeste 23
Oeste Suroeste 23
office 188
oficial del banco de los penaltis 507
oficina 346, 374, 438
oficina de correos 433, 437
oficina de formación profesional 442
oficina de reservas de hotel 390
oficina de urgencias 462
oficina del puerto 381
ofimática 312
oftalmología 463
ohm 426
ohmnio 426
oído 115, 301
oído interno 116
oído medio 116
oído, estructura 116
ojal 248, 275, 509
ojera 320
ojete 240, 246, 263, 538
ojete para la correa 315
ojo 43, 70, 71, 72, 76, 90, 94, 119, 220, 270
ojo compuesto 67, 68
ojo de buey 386
ojos, maquillaje 266
okapi 84
ola 33
olécran 99
oleoducto 404
oleoducto de superficie 404
oleoducto para crudo 404
oleoducto submarino 404
olfato 116
oliva, aceite 149
olla 175
olla a presión 174
olla para cuscús 175
Omán 452
Omán, golfo 19
ombligo 30, 92, 94
omoplato 93, 95, 98, 99
onda 418
onda de choque 403
onda sísmica 27
onda, longitud 418
ondas hertzianas, transmisión 316
ondas radio 418
Oort, nube 2
opera 432
operación rápida 323
operación, teclas 442, 443
operador de cámara 290
operador de jirafa 291
operador del reloj de 30 segundos 488
opérculo 74
opilión 69
opistodomo 279
óptica 437
orangután 91
orbicular 55
orbicular de los párpados 96
órbita lunar 4, 5
órbita terrestre 4, 5
orbitador 12, 13
orca 90
ordenador 444
ordenador portátil 336
ordenador de a bordo 354, 457
ordenador de bolsillo 337
ordenador personal 329
ordenador portátil: vista frontal 336
ordenador portátil: vista posterior 336
ordenador: vista frontal 336
ordenador: vista posterior 329
orégano 142
oreja 92, 116, 240
oreja de Judas 123
oreja de mar 157
oreja, pabellón 82
orejera 238
orellana 123
organismo cultural 335
organismo de salud 335
organismos simples 66
organización gubernamental 335

órgano 305
órganos genitales femeninos 112
órganos genitales masculinos 111
órganos sensoriales 114
orientación de la cuchilla, cilindro 401
oriental 493
orificio 312
orificio del pie 305
orificio nasal 83
Orinoco, río 17
orla decorativa 260
oronja 123
orquesta 278
orquesta sinfónica 295
orquídea 56
ortiga 127
oruga 67, 398
oruga de polilla 69
orza de popa 519
orza de quilla 519, 520
oscilación 395
oso negro 89
oso polar 89
osoto-gari (gran siega) exterior 499
ostra 157
otaria 90
otoño 38
otorrinolaringología 463
otros signos 299
ovario 56, 112, 113
oveja 84
óvulo 56, 112
oxígeno, producción 54

P

pabellón 306, 307, 432
pabellón auricular 115, 116
pabellón de la oreja 82
pabellón de la trompa de Falopio 113
pacana 133
paciente 464
Pacífico Oriental, dorsal 34
Pacífico, océano 14, 15, 19
Pacífico, Placa 27
Pacífico-Antártico, dorsal 34
Pacini, corpúsculo de 114
página adelante 331
página atrás 331
pago electrónico, terminal 443
pagoda 283
país 23
Países Bajos 449
pajarita 245
pájaro carpintero 80
pájaro, morfología 78
pájaros, ejemplos 80
pajita 163
pak-choi 126
Pakistán 452
pala 193, 233, 398, 401, 478, 493, 510, 535
pala de timón 384
pala del rotor 395
pala del stick 506
pala del timón 520
pala del ventilador de sustentación 383
pala hidráulica 400
pala plegable 532
palacio de congresos 433
Palacio de Justicia 432
paladar, velo 117
palafito 288
palanca 178, 197, 220, 265, 269, 306, 534
palanca de arranque 235
palanca de bloqueo 229
palanca de bloqueo de la altura 8, 9
palanca de bloqueo del acimut 8, 9
palanca de cambio 350
palanca de cambio de velocidades 354, 367, 368, 369
palanca de cierre 214
palanca de enclavamiento 224
palanca de la cisterna 196
palanca de la cuña 229
palanca de luces e intermitentes 354
palanca de mando 395
palanca de maniobra 396
palanca de perforación 180
palanca de regulación de altura 209
palanca de seguridad 237
palanca de vibración 303
palanca del cambio de velocidades 371, 372
palanca del cucharón 399

palanca del deslizador 353
palanca del freno 371, 522, 523
palanca del tapón 196
palanca estabilizadora 467
palanca retráctil de la guarda móvil 227
palanca rotativa 332
Palau 453
palco 293
palé con alas 396
paleta 152, 173, 493, 535
paleta de albañil 216
paleta de relleno 216
paletilla 86, 153
palillo 308
palma 115, 243, 477
palma de un guante 243
palmar 36
palmar mayor 96
palmar menor 96
palmeada 55
palmera 64
palmeta 200
palo 215
palo de la tienda 529
palo de proa 385
palo del jugador 506
palo del radar 384
paloma 81
palos 482
palpo 73
palpo labial 67
pamela 239
pan 144
pan ácimo 145
pan alemán de centeno 145
pan americano de maíz 145
pan blanco 145
pan campesino 145
pan danés de centeno 145
pan de centeno negro 144
pan de flor 145
pan de pita 145
pan espiga 144
pan griego 144
pan indio chapati 145
pan indio naan 145
pan integral 145
pan irlandés 145
pan judío hallah 145
pan multicereales 145
pan negro ruso 145
pan, molde 179
panadería 121, 437
pañal 260
pañal desechable 260
Panamá 448
panamá 238
Panamá, golfo 17
Panamá, istmo 16
panceta 156
páncreas 106
pandereta 309
panel de cierre 329
panel de control 212, 213, 214
panel de controles 314
panel de la puerta 352
panel de la vela 520
panel de mandos 178, 179, 210, 213
panel de publicidad 378
panel de separación 277
panel del display 320
panel frontal 365
panel lateral 365
panel protector 467
panel radiador 13
panel solar 7, 316
paneles fotovoltaicos 11
paño lateral 248
pantalla 193, 199, 206, 318, 336, 337, 338, 439, 442, 471, 479
pantalla de cristal líquido 315
pantalla de protección 474
pantalla de proyección 294
pantalla del ordenador 10
pantalla del radar 457
pantalla táctil 320
pantalla táctil 337
pantalla, tubo 318
pantalón 473, 476, 486, 499, 500, 506
pantalón corto 254, 261
pantalón de boxeo 263
pantalón de peto 260
pantalón peto 254
pantalones 246, 263, 480, 525
pantalones acampanados 254
pantalones cortos 483, 488
pantalones de boxeo 498

pantalones de chándal 262
pantalones de peto 261
pantalones de tubo 254
pantalones elásticos 522
pantalones, ejemplos 254
pantis 257
pantógrafo 376
pantorrilla 93, 95
pantufla 242
pañuelo de bolsillo 244
papaya 137
papel de aluminio 162
papel de celofán 162
papel encerado 162
papel para el horno 162
papelera 341
papila 114
papila circunvalada 118
papila filiforme 118
papila foliada 118
papila fungiforme 118
papila gustativa 118
papila óptica 119
papila renal 107
Papua Nueva Guinea 15, 453
paquete 163
parábola 321
parabrisas 348, 364, 366, 369, 385, 392, 394, 523
paracaídas 287
paracaídas auxiliar 12
parachoques 364, 369, 523
parachoques posterior 369
parada de autobús 434
parafinas 405
paraguas 273
Paraguay 448
paragüero 273
paralelepípedo 429
paralelo 22
paralelogramo 429
paramecio 66
Paraná, río 17
parapeto 344
pararrayos 183, 407, 413
parasol 8, 354, 356, 361
parche 309
parche inferior 308
parche superior 308
pared celular 50
pared de viraje 517
pared lateral 385, 517
pared transversal de contención 384
pareja 509
parietal 99
paripinnada 55
parka 249
parlante 327
parmesano 151
párpado 76
párpado inferior 75, 87, 119
párpado interno 87
párpado superior 75, 87, 119
párpados, orbicular 96
parque 25, 433
parqué 190
parqué alternado a la inglesa 190
parqué Arenberg 190
parqué Chantilly 190
parque de bomberos 433
parqué de cestería 190
parque de estacionamiento 389
parqué de mosaico 190
parqué en punta de Hungría 190
parqué espinapez 190
parque nacional 25
parqué sobre base de cemento 190
parqué sobrepuesto 190
parqué Versalles 190
parqué, tipos 190
parrilla 178, 210
parrilla de salida 524
parrilla eléctrica 179
parrilla estabilizadora 529
parrilla plegable 533
parte superior 219
parteluz 186, 285
partes 200, 201, 204
partes de un círculo 428
partes de un zapato 240
partes de una bicicleta 370
pasadizo ascendente 278
pasadizo descendente 278
pasador 186, 246, 268, 532
pasaje subterráneo 375
pasajeros, aire turborreactor 392
pasajeros, terminal 390

pasajeros, vagones 376
pasamano 363, 385
pasamanos 191, 287
pasamontañas 239, 524
pasapuré 173
pasapurés 170
pasarela 282, 292, 375
pasarela superior 379
pasarela telescópico 389
pascal 426
paseo 230
pasillo 120, 436
pasillo de dobles 490
pasillo de seguridad 440
paso 29, 83
paso a nivel 375
paso alternativo 514
paso de Drake 15, 17
paso de patinador 514
paso de peatones 434
paso de popa a proa 385
paso elevado 344
paso inferior 344
pasta 146
pasta de hojaldre 145
pasta won ton 147
pastelería 437
pastelería, bandeja 172
pastelería, mezclador 172
pastilla 467
pastilla de combustible 409
pastilla de fricción 357
pastor alemán 86
pata 76, 91, 199, 201, 202, 204, 205, 231, 308, 537
pata anal 67
pata curvada 200
pata de la mesa 493
pata de locomoción 70
pata delantera 67, 68, 75, 201
pata lobulada, dedo 79
pata media 67, 68
pata móvil 202
pata palmípeda, dedo 79
pata telescópica 460
pata torácica 67
pata trasera 67, 68, 75, 201
pata ventosa 67
Patagonia 17
patas, ejemplos 79
patata 124
pátera 200
patilla 273
patín de aterrizaje 395
patín de cola 395
patín de los accesorios 314
patín de pista corta 508
patín de pista larga 508
patín del portero 507
patín en línea 527
patín en línea de hockey 527
patín en línea, 527
patin para figuras 509
patinador 508, 527
patinaje acrobático 527
patinaje artístico 509
patinaje artístico, cuchilla 509
patinaje de velocidad 508
patinaje en línea 527
patinaje sobre hielo, pista 509
patinaje, pista 512
patines de carreras 508
patio 230, 445, 447
patio de armas 282
patio de butacas 293
patio de tanques 404
pato 81, 155
patrulla de primeros auxilios y puesto de socorro 512
pausa 331
pausa /imagen fija 319
pavimento 342
pavo 81, 155
pavo real 81
PC 334
peatones, semáforo 434
pécari 84
peces 74
peces cartilaginosos 158
peces óseos 159
pecho 83, 92
pechuga 78
pecíolo 52, 55
pecorino romano 151
pectoral 486, 501
pectoral mayor 96
pedal 302, 308, 370, 372, 501, 522

pedal automático 522
pedal crescendo 305
pedal de expresión 305
pedal de la sordina 304
pedal de los bajos 311
pedal de los frenos 354
pedal del acelerador 354
pedal del embrague 354
pedal del freno 350, 357
pedal del freno trasero 368
pedal fuerte 304, 311
pedal plano 522
pedal suave 304
pedalero 305
pedernal 218
pedestal 206, 302, 473
pedio 96
pedipalpo 70
pedúnculo 51, 56, 57, 58, 59, 62
peinado 268
peinazo 202
peinazo de la cerradura 185
peinazo inferior 201, 202
peinazo superior 201, 202
peine afro 268
peine combinado 268
peine de cardar 268
peine de iluminación 291
peine de mango 268
peine de peluquero 268
peine para desenredar 268
peine y cuchilla 271
peines 268
pelaje 82, 91
pelapatatas 169
peldaño 191, 219
peldaño de arranque 191
peldaño posterior 455
pelele 261
pelele de dos piezas 260
peletería 436
pelícano 80
película plástica, condensador 417
película termosoldada 163
pelillo 536
pelo 93, 95, 114, 190
pelo de maíz 61
pelos absorbentes 53
pelos radicales 53
pelota 493
pelota de béisbol, corte 477
pelota de cricket 478
pelota de golf 505
pelota de softball 477
pelota de tenis 492
pelotón 522
pelotón de cabeza 522
peltada 55
peluquería 436
peluquero 290
peluquero, tijeras 270
pelvis renal 107
penacho 78
penacho de plumas 495
pendiente 264
pendientes 264
pendientes de aro 264
pendientes de clip 264
pendientes de espiga 264
pendientes de tornillo 264
pene 92, 111
península 24
península Antártica 15
península de Arabia 19
península de Corea 19
península de Kamchatka 19
península de Kola 18
península de los Balcanes 18
península del Yucatán 16
península Escandinava 18
península Ibérica 18
pentágono regular 429
pentagrama 298
peón 470
pepinillo 128
pepino 128
pepino amargo 128
pepino dulce 137
pepino sin pepitas 128
pepita 58, 59
pepperoni 156
pera 133
pera asiática 137
pera de goma 460, 461
pera de maíz 498
perca 160
perca, morfología 74

percha 515
percoladora 181
percusión, instrumentos 295, 308
percutor 534
pérdida de calor 46
perdiz 80
perejil 142
perfil del suelo 54
perfil, suelo 54
perforación 263
perforación, torre 403
perforaciones 240, 243
perforadora 340
perfumería 121, 436
pérgola 230
pericardio 105
pericarpio 60
perifollo 142
perilla 227
periódico 313
periódico, nombre 313
peristilo 279, 280
peristoma 66
peritoneo 111, 112
pemo 222, 223, 224
pemo con collarín 223
pemo de articulación del cucharón 399
pemo de expansión 221
pemo de fijación 357
pemo de la bisagra 400
pemo difusor 236
pemo maestro 365
pemo para falso plafón 221
pemos 223
peroné 98
peroneo corto 97
peroneo largo 96
peróxido 461
peroxisoma 66
perpendicular 428
perro 86, 535
perro, morfología 86
perros, razas 86
persa 87
Pérsico, golfo 19
personal, entrada 438
personal, guardarropa 438
pertenece a 427
Perú 448
Perú-Chile, fosa 34
pesa 422
pesa corrediza 422
pesas 500, 501
pesas para muñecas y tobillos 500
pesca 536
pesca con monosca 536
pesca de lanzado 537
pescado 121
pescante 384, 397
peso 423, 440, 472
peso, medición 422
pespunte 243, 246, 260
pespunteada 253
pespunteado 262
pestaña 119, 251
pestaña de arrojo 460
pestañas 87
pesticida 47, 48
pestillo 186
pestillo de ingletes 226
pétalo 56
petición del sistema 331
petirrojo 80
peto 260, 261, 476, 486
petróleo 403, 405
petróleo crudo 405
petrolero 381, 384
pez cartilaginoso 74
pez de San Pedro 161
pez espada 159
pez óseo 74
pezón 92, 94, 113
pi 428
piamadre 109
piano 295
piano electrónico 311
piano vertical 304
pica 82, 454
picadora de carne 170
picardía 256
piccolo 295, 306
pícea 65
pichi 252
pichón 154
pickguard 303
pico 29, 78, 233
pico de rey 425

picos, ejemplos 79
pictogramas 330
pie 52, 72, 73, 91, 92, 93, 94, 95, 176,
    199, 260, 302, 305, 421, 536, 537
pie ajustable 212, 213, 214
pie de foto 313
pie de la cama 204
pie de voluta 200
pie derecho 187, 285
pie, arteria dorsal 102
pie, dedo 92, 94
pie, interóseos 96
piedra blanca 470
Piedra Coyolxauhqui 283
piedra de afilar 169
piedra de curling 515
piedra de sacrificio 283
piedra negra 470
piel 57, 58, 59, 110, 114, 297
piel armónica 297
piel de gamuza 265
pierna 83, 93, 95, 247
pierna de cordero 153
pierna elástica 247
pieza de talón 514
piezas 470
pijama 256, 261
pijama de una pieza 247
pila 416
pila alcalina de manganeso-zinc 417
pila bautismal 446
pila de agua bendita 446
pila de carbón-cinc 417
pila recargable 320
pilar 27, 283, 284, 344
pilar anterior del velo del paladar 116
pilar derecho 482
pilar izquierdo 482
pilas secas 417
pilastra corintia 281
pilón 344
pilón del turborreactor 393
pilón guía 345
piloto 178, 180, 181, 208, 210, 214,
    524
pimentero 166
pimentón, 139
pimienta blanca 138
pimienta de cayena 139
pimienta de Jamaica 138
pimienta molida 139
pimienta negra 138
pimienta rosa 138
pimienta verde 138
pimiento dulce amarillo 128
pimiento dulce rojo 128
pimiento dulce verde 128
piña 65, 136
pináculo 282, 284, 285
pinatifida 55
pincel 312
pincel de repostería 172
pincel para labios 266
pinchador 341
pingüino 80
pinna 52
pino piñonero 65
piñón 65, 133
piñón libre 372
pintada 81, 154
pintalabios 266
pinza 71, 246, 248, 269, 312
pinza de cinturón 327
pinza del freno 366
pinza negra 356
pinza para el cabello 268
pinza para rizar 268
pinza roja 356
pinza sujetamuestras 421
pinzas 173, 461
pinzas multiuso 217
pinzas para caracoles 173
pinzas para depilar cejas 265
pinzas para espagueti 173
pinzas pelacables 217
pinzas universales 222
pinzón 80
piojo 69
pirámide 278, 429
pirámide, entrad 278
pirata 254
Pirineos 18
piruetas, ejemplos 509
piscina 184, 386, 517
piscina elevada 184
piscina enterrada 184
piscina olímpica 517

piso 193, 412, 526
piso cosido 528, 529
piso superior 363
pisos de madera 190
pista 472, 504, 506, 524
pista corta 508
pista de enlace 388
pista de esquí alpino 512
pista de estacionamiento 388
pista de fondo 512
pista de patinaje 512
pista de patinaje sobre hielo 509
pista de rodaje 388
pista de salto 473
pista larga 508
pista para avanzados 512
pista para expertos 512
pista para intermedios 512
pista para principiantes 512
pistacho 133
pistas de carreras 496
pistas de esquí 512
pistilo 56
pistola 216, 456
pistola de calor 219
pistola de salida 472
pistola del surtidor 346
pistola para calafateo 216
pistola para soldar 218
pistola pulverizadora 236
pistolera 456
pistón 307, 357, 360
pitón 77
pitorro 181, 215
pivot 489
pivote 217, 270, 511, 533
pivote móvil 222
pizarra 444
placa 164, 197
placa africana 27
placa antártica 27
placa antifricción 511
placa base 511
placa calcárea 73
placa costal 76
placa de absorción 410
placa de advertencias 228
placa de circuito impreso 417
placa de cocción 179
placa de especificaciones 228
placa de freno 511
placa de identificación 456
placa de instalación 199
placa de número 525
placa del Pacífico 27
placa eléctrica 210
placa euroasiática 27
placa indoaustraliana 27
placa marginal 76
placa motora 110
placa negativa 359
placa norteamericana 27
placa positiva 359
placa protectora 525
placa sudamericana 27
placa supracaudal 76
placa térmica 181
placa terminal 409
placa vertebral 76
placas convergentes 27
placas divergentes 27
placas tectónicas 27
plafón 206
plancha 179, 208, 269
plancha de muelles 496
plancha de pelo 269
plancha de vapor 208
plancha eléctrica 179
plancha superior 178
planetas 2
planetas externos 2
planetas internos 3
planicie 24
planicie fluvio-glaciar 30
planisferio 14
plano de deriva 393
plano de la catedral 285
plano del templo griego 279
plano del terreno 183
plano horizontal 393
plano vertical 393
planta 53, 247
planta alta 182, 189
planta baja 182, 188
planta de bombeo 404
planta de lubricantes 405

planta de reforma catalítica 405
planta de separación selectiva 49
planta intermedia de refuerzo 404
planta, anatomía 53
plantador 231
plantador de bulbos 231
plantar delgado 97
plaqueta 104, 273
plasma 104
plasmodesmo 50
plástico transparente 274
plásticos transparentes 274
plásticos, clasificación 49
plastrón 76
plataforma 27, 219, 342, 363, 377, 396,
    423, 526
plataforma continental 33
plataforma de 10 m 518
plataforma de 3 m 518
plataforma de 5 m 518
plataforma de 7,5 m 518
plataforma de hielo de Amery 15
plataforma de hielo de Filchner 15
plataforma de lanzamiento 475
plataforma de producción 404
plataforma de salida 516
plataforma elevadora para silla de ruedas
    363
plataforma giratoria 455
plataforma giratoria, molino 412
plataforma inferior 396
plátano 136
platea 278
platija 161
platillo 422, 423
platillo high hat 308
platillo inferior 308
platillo superior 308
platillo suspendido 308
platillos 295, 309
platina 421
platina mecánica 421
platito para el pan 166
plato 531
plato de postre 166
plato de retroceso 357
plató de rodaje 290
plato giratorio 224, 400
plato lijador 229
plato llano 166
plato para caracoles 173
plato sopero 166
platos de cocción 179
playa 35
pletina 326
pletina de casete 323
pleura parietal 105
pleura visceral 105
plexo braquial 108
plexo lumbar 108
plexo nervioso 101
plexo sacro 108
pliegue anal 93, 95
pliegue de la columela 73
pliegues, ejemplos 253
plisada 253
plomo 538
pluma 27, 400
pluma de ave 312
pluma de caña 312
pluma estilográfica 312
pluma metálica 312
pluma metálica romana 312
plumas timoneras 78
Plutón 2, 3
pocilga 122
podadera 234
podadera de árboles 234
podadora de bordes 237
podio 283, 435
podio de salida 516
podio y sótanos 435
pole position 524
polea 219, 360, 535
polea del montacargas 397
polea tensora del limitador de velocidad
    287
poleas de tensión 372
polideportivo 431
polígono industrial 431
polígonos 429
Polinesia 453
polipasto 403
polipodio común 52
política 448
político 51
pollo 155

ASTRONOMÍA > 2-25;   TIERRA > 26-71;   REINO VEGETAL >72-89;   REINO ANIMAL > 90-143;   SER HUMANO > 144-177;   PRODUCTOS ALIMENTARIOS Y DE COCINA > 178-241;   CASA > 242-295;
BRICOLAJE Y JARDINERÍA > 296-333;   VESTIDO > 334-371;   ACCESORIOS Y ARTÍCULOS PERSONALES > 372-391;   ARTE Y ARQUITECTURA > 392-465;   COMUNICACIONES Y AUTOMATIZACIÓN DE
OFICINA > 466-535;   TRANSPORTE Y VEHÍCULOS > 536-643;   ENERGÍA > 644-677;   CIENCIA > 678-705;   SOCIEDAD > 706-785;   DEPORTES Y JUEGOS > 786-920

polo 250, 255, 492
polo negativo 417
polo Norte 21
polo norte 416
polo positivo 416
polo Sur 15, 21
polo sur 416
Polonia 450
polvera 266
polvo compacto 266
polvo de magnesio 497
polvos sueltos 266
pomelo 134
pomo 201, 202, 229, 506
pomo carnoso 58
pómulo 98
poncho 251
Pont-l'Éveque 151
pool 502
popa 386, 519
póquer 468
porcentaje 427
porche 183
poro 50, 60, 114
porra 456
porta martillo 225
porta pasaportes 275
porta-celo 341
porta-cinta adhesiva 341
porta-esquí 356
porta-filtro 181
portaagujas 460
portabicicletas 356
portabolsa 505
portabotellas 371
portacarrete 536, 537
portaequipajes 361, 369, 370, 383, 523
portaequipajes posterior 369
portahorquilla 396
portal 285
portalámparas 199
portaleños 193
portaminas 312
portamonedas 275
portante 83
portaobjetivo rotatorio 421
portaobjeto 421
portaobjetos 421
portaocular 8
portaplumas 274
portarrollos de papel higiénico 195
portatrajes 277
portatubo 421
portaviento 296
portería 439, 480, 507
portero 479, 481, 506, 507
portero del equipo receptor 479
pórtico 285, 447
Portugal 449
posición A - en plancha 518
posición B - hacer la carpa 518
posición C - cuerpo encogido 518
posición de equilibrio 418
posición de lanzamiento, transbordador espacial 12
posición de los jugadores 474, 481, 482
posición del documento a enviar 328
posiciones de los jugadores 489
posiciones de salto 518
poste 191, 375, 485, 487, 490, 495, 498
poste con protecciones 489
poste de foul 475
poste de la grúa 385
poste del asiento 370
potencia eléctrica, unidad de medida 426
poterna 282
potro 496, 497
pozo 278
pozo de inyección 402
pozo de producción 402
pozo marino 404
practicable para ejercicios de suelo 496
pradera 122
praderas 44
prado 122
precio total 423
precio unitario 423
precipitación 45
precipitaciones 41
precipitaciones invernales 41
precisión, balanza 423
precocinados 121
premaxilar 74

premolares 101
prensa en C 224
prensa-café 181
preparador 489
prepucio 111
presa 406
presidente de jurado 509
presilla 245, 246, 531
presilla de estaquilla 528, 529
presilla de la manga 248
presilla del cinturón 248
presión 501
presión barométrica 39
presión barométrica a nivel del mar 39
presión, unidad de medida 426
pretina 284, 249
pretina con botones de presión 260
pretina elástica 247, 249
prevención de incendios 454
prevención de la criminalidad 456
previsión meteorológica 38
primates, ejemplos 91
primavera 38
primer árbitro 487
primer aumento de la tensión 413
primer ayudante de cámara 290
primer espacio 489
primer jugador 515
primer molar 101
primer pistón móvil 307
primer premolar 101
primera aleta dorsal 74
primera base 474
primera línea 482
primera plana 313
primera plana, foto 313
primeras hojas 53
primeros auxilios, botiquín 460
primeros auxilios, puesto de socorro 512
primeros violines 295
Principado de Andorra 449
Principado de Mónaco 450
principales movimientos 470
prisma de Porro 420
prismáticos binoculares 420
proa 384, 387, 519, 520
probador de contactos con tierra 217
probóscide 67
producción de calor 408
producción de electricidad por energía eólica 413
producción de electricidad por energía geotérmica 402
producción de electricidad por energía nuclear 408
producción de electricidad por energía térmica 402
producción de electricidad por generador 408
producción de oxígeno 54
producción eléctrica 412
productor 291
productos alimenticios 120
productos de cocina 120
productos de fisión 415
productos del refinado 405
productos en oferta 121
productos lácteos 120, 150
productos para envasar 120
productos petroquímicos 405
productos, oferta 121
profesor 444
profesor, pupitre 444
profundidad del hipocentro 27
programa de correo electrónico 334
programación televisiva, horario 313
programador 212, 213, 214
programas informáticos 457
promontorio 35
pronador redondo 96
pronaos 279
propagación 418
proporción de nubes 39
propulsor 10, 12
propulsor de maniobras 13
propulsor de proa 387
propulsor sólido 12
propulsores de control de actitud 12
proscenio 292
prospección terrestre 403
próstata 111
protección para el sistema respiratorio 459
protección para la cabeza 458
protección para los oídos 458

protección para los ojos 458
protección para los pies 459
protector 210, 235, 248, 471, 478, 498
protector bucal 498
protector contra virutas 227
protector de antebrazo 486
protector de cuello 486
protector de espuma 458
protector de la barbilla 367
protector de la culata 306
protector de la garganta 476
protector de mano 525
protector del brazo 486
protector del zanco 398
protector dental 486
protector facial 507
protector lumbar 486
protector para las costillas 486
protector solar 10
protocolo de comunicación 334
protón 414
protoneurona 110
protuberancia 4
proveedor de servicios Internet 335
provincia 23
provisión de dinero en efectivo 443
provisión de guantes 464
proyección cilíndrica 22
proyección cónica 22
proyección en círculo 499
proyección interrumpida 22
proyección plana 22
proyección por encima del hombro con una mano 499
proyección primera de cadera 499
proyección, cabina 294
proyección, pantalla 294
proyección, sala 294
proyecciones cartográficas 22
proyector 290, 294, 376
proyectores 293
pruebas 511
pseudópodo 66
púa 297
pubis 92, 94
público, entrada 278
pueblo 430, 512
puente 25, 78, 273, 297, 301, 302, 303, 343, 381, 420
puente cantilever 344
puente colgante 344
puente de carga para contenedores 381
puente de ensamblaje 303
puente de la nariz 117
puente de los altos 304
puente de los bajos 304
puente de luces 455, 457
puente de luces, sistema de control 457
puente de mando 382, 386, 387
puente de señales 375
puente de Varolio 109
puente de viga 344
puente elevador 345
puente giratorio 344
puente levadizo 282
puente levadizo doble 345
puente levadizo sencillo 345
puentes fijos 344
puentes móviles 344
puerco espín 82
puerro 124
puerta 7, 178, 202, 210, 213, 287, 349, 352, 361, 392, 423, 439, 447, 479, 528, 529
puerta automática 390
puerta basculante de garaje 286
puerta convencional 286
puerta corredera 286
puerta corredera automática 286
puerta cortafuego 286
puerta de dos hojas 362
puerta de entrada 185, 362, 363
puerta de garaje seccional 286
puerta de la bodega de carga 13
puerta de la plataforma elevadora 363
puerta de librillo 286
puerta de proa 383, 386
puerta de tiras 286
puerta del congelador 211
puerta del fogón 192
puerta del refrigerador 211
puerta giratoria manual 286

puerta lateral 380
puerta mosquitera 361
puerta plegable 195, 286
puerta trasera 188
puerta ventana 164, 189
puertas de entrada 294
puertas, ejemplos 286
puerto 381, 431
puerto de Ethernet 336
puerto de infrarrojos 336
puerto de módem interno 329, 336
puerto de red 329
puerto de salida de S-video 336
puerto de salida de TV 336
puerto de video 329
puerto FireWire 336
puerto infrarrojos 337
puerto juego 329
puerto MIDI 329
puerto paralelo 329
puerto ratón 329
Puerto Rico, fosa 34
puerto serial 329
puerto teclado 329
puerto USB 329, 336
puertos para el mando 471
puertos para tarjeta de memoria 471
puesto de bombeo 346
puesto de enfermeras (ambulatorio de urgencias) 463
puesto de enfermeras (urgencias) 462
puesto de información 390
puesto de la guardia de seguridad 463
puesto de observación 7
puf 201
pujamen 519
pulga 69
pulgar 115, 243, 477
pulgar oponible 91
pulmón derecho 103, 105
pulmón izquierdo 103, 105
pulmones 105
pulpa 57, 58, 59, 101
púlpito 446, 447
pulpo 72, 157
pulpo, morfología 72
pulsador de llamada 287
pulsera de dijes 264
pulverizador 214, 236, 402
pulverizador de agua 348
puma 88
puño 245, 477, 492, 514
puño de amura 519
puño de escota 519
punta 55, 125, 167, 169, 216, 218, 220, 221, 226, 227, 246, 247, 273, 301, 312, 469, 471, 510, 514, 526, 538
punta cruciforme 221
punta de caja cuadrada 221
punta de diamante 202
punta de hoja plana 221
punta de la plancha 208
punta de plástico 269
punta de sujeción 304
punta del cuello 245
punta del diente de la desterronadora 398
punta del esquí 514
puntal 308
puntal trasero 412
puntales de refuerzo 187
puntas; tipos 221
puntera 229, 511, 514
puntera perforada 240
puntera protectora 459
puntero 533
punto 468
punto de apoyo 70
punto de apoyo variable 518
punto de empulgada 535
punto de información 437, 512
punto de interés 25
punto de mira 533, 534
punto de penalti 480
punto de salida 504
punto de saque 506
puntos 492
punzón 531
pupila 87, 119
pupila vertical 76
pupitre del alumno 444
pupitre del profesor 444
putter 505

Q
Qatar 452
quad 369
quark d 414
quark u 414
quarterback 485
quelicero 70
quemador 174, 210, 529
queroseno 405
queso chèvre 150
queso cottage 150
queso cremoso 150
queso, rallador cilíndrico 170
quesos azules 151
quesos blandos 151
quesos de cabra 150
quesos frescos 150
quesos prensados 151
quiasma óptico 109
quijada 83, 86
quilla 521
química 414
quingombó 128
quinientos 427
quinta 298
quinteto 300
quinto octante 5
quinua 143
quiosco 437
quirófano 464, 465
quitagrapas 341
quitanieves 365
quitapiedras 376, 377

R
rábano 129
rábano blanco 129
rábano daikon 129
rábano negro 129
rabillo 57, 58, 59
rabiza 536
racimo 57, 61
racimo de uvas 62
raclette 151
raclette-grill 179
radar 382, 383, 386, 387
radar de navegación 392
radar meteorológico 38
radiación 415
radiación infrarroja 46, 418
radiación solar 45, 46, 410, 411
radiación solar absorbida 46
radiación solar refleja 46
radiación ultravioleta 418
radiador 350, 358
radiador, manguito 358
radiadores 11
radial externo primero 97
radial externo segundo 97
radícula 53, 63
radio 70, 98, 371, 428, 457
radio blando 74
radio despertador 325
radio espinoso 74
radio medular 63
radio portátil 325
radiocativdad, unidad de medida 426
radiocasete con lector de disco compacto 326
radiocasete portátil personal (Walkman) 326
raíces 53, 62, 129
raíces adventicias 52
raíces superficiales 63
raíles del travelín 290
raíz 54, 101, 118, 167
raíz anterior 110
raíz cuadrada de 427
raíz de la uña 114
raíz motora 109, 110
raíz posterior 110
raíz primaria 53, 63
raíz principal 53
raíz secundaria 53
raíz sensitiva 109, 110
rallador 169, 170
rallador cilíndrico de queso 170
rallador de nuez moscada 170
rallar 170
rally, coche 524
rama 53, 63, 65, 460
rama comunicante 110
rama con fruto 62
rama madre 63

ASTRONOMÍA > 2-25;   TIERRA > 26-71;   REINO VEGETAL > 72-89;   REINO ANIMAL > 90-143;   SER HUMANO > 144-177;   PRODUCTOS ALIMENTARIOS Y DE COCINA > 178-241;   CASA > 242-295;
BRICOLAJE Y JARDINERÍA > 296-333;   VESTIDO > 334-371;   ACCESORIOS Y ARTÍCULOS PERSONALES > 372-391;   ARTE Y ARQUITECTURA > 392-465;   COMUNICACIONES Y AUTOMATIZACIÓN DE
OFICINA > 466-535;   TRANSPORTE Y VEHÍCULOS > 536-643;   ENERGÍA > 644-677;   CIENCIA > 678-705;   SOCIEDAD > 706-785;   DEPORTES Y JUEGOS > 786-920

ramaje 63
ramal de enlace 343
rambután 137
ramificación 62
ramificación colateral 110
ramilla 63
rampa 281, 343
rampa de acceso 279, 344
rampa del muelle 381
rampa plegable 386
rana 75
rana arborícola 75
rana bermeja 75
rana de bosque 75
rana leopardo 75
rana, morfología 75
ranita 261
ranura 169, 221, 274, 359, 473
ranura de depósito 442
ranura de la tarjeta PC 336
ranura de lectura de tarjeta 346
ranura de puesta al día de la cartilla 442
ranura de registro de la transacción 442
ranura de ventilación 336
ranura guía 510
ranura para el pan 178
ranura para toldo 361
Ranvier, nódulo 110
rape 160
raqueta de bádminton 494
raqueta de tenis 492
ras el hanout 139
raspador 400
rasqueta 219, 514
rastrillo 233, 237
rastrillo 292
rata 82
rata, morfología 82
ratón de campo 82
ratón de rueda 332
ratón inalámbrico 332
ratón mecánico 332
ratón óptico 332
raviolis 146
raya 158, 246
raya continua 342
raya discontinua 342, 343
rayo 41
rayo de luz 419
rayo láser 420
rayos gamma 418
rayos X 418
razas de gatos 87
razas de perros 86
re(D) 298
Rea 3
reacción en cadena 415
reactor 408
reactor nuclear, carga 409
rebajo de escalón 191
rebobinado 319
reborde 293, 301, 302
rebosadero 194, 196, 406
rebote 487
rebozuelo 123
recalentamiento global 46
recepción 439, 442, 462, 465
recepción de carga 391
recepción de documentos 328
recepción directa en la casa 316
recepción, nivel 439
receptáculo 51, 56, 59
receptáculo del cepillo 272
receptor 303, 321, 327, 475, 476
receptor 419
receptor alejado 485
receptor de los bajos 303
receptor de los intermedios 303
receptor del sonido 460
receptor sensorial 110
receptor triple 303
receptores gustativos 118
recibo 423
recibo de transacción 443
reciclado 49
reciclado de aluminio, contenedor 49
reciclado de papel, contenedor 49
reciclado de vidrio, contenedor 49
reciclaje, contenedores 49
recinto ferial 430
recipiente 180
recipiente con vertedor 177
recipiente del abrillantador 214
recipiente del detergente 214
recipiente inferior 181
recipiente superior 181
reclamo 535

recogedor 215, 237
recogepelotas 490
recogida de papel, contenedor 49
recogida de vidrio, contenedor 49
recogida diferenciada 49
rectángulo 429
recto 106, 111, 112
recto anterior 96
recto del abdomen 96
recto entallado 252
recto interno del muslo 97
recubrimiento aislante 12
recubrimiento antirreflectante 410
recuperación del documento enviado 328
red 205, 487, 489, 491, 493, 495
red de cables telefónicos 434
red de distribución por cable aéreo 316
red de mano 538
red de transmisión por cable subterráneo
    317
red de transmisión privada 316
red nacional de transmisión 316
red telefónica 317
redonda 299
redondo mayor 97
redondo menor 97
refinado, productos 405
refinería 404, 431
reflector 217, 365, 370, 523
reflectores solares 316
reflexión parcial, espejo 420
reflexión total, espejo 420
refrigeración, torre 402
refrigeración, varilla 420
refrigerante 405, 408
refrigerante caliente 408
refrigerante frío 408
refuerzo 259, 458, 525
refuerzo del talón 240
refugio 345
refugio de montaña 512
refugio en la cima 512
refugio presurizado 345
refugio principal 512
regadera 236
región lumbar 93, 95
región malar 78
región negativa 410
región positiva 410
registro de altos 296
registro de cristal líquido 424
registro sísmico 402
registro, cilindro 27
registros de bajos 296
regla 531
regla graduada 425
regla, escala 425
regulador de entrada de agua 214
regulador de presión 174, 454, 529
regulador de temperatura 365
regulador de velocidad 354
reina 68, 468, 470
Reina Maud, Tierra 15
reina, cámara 278
reino animal 66
Reino Unido de Gran Bretaña e Irlanda del
    Norte 449
reino vegetal 50
reja 217
reja de entrada al pronaos 279
reja de entrada, pronaos 279
reja de seguridad 442
reja metálica de contacto 410
rejilla 174, 178, 210, 211, 296, 318,
    358, 359, 407
rejilla de calefacción 380
rejilla de entrada de aire 270
rejilla de salida de aire 270
rejilla de ventilación 214
rejilla del ventilador 209
rejilla desmontable 174
rejilla protectora 324
religión 446
rellano 191
rellano de la escalera 189
reloj 178, 210, 444, 501
reloj de arena 171
reloj de pulsera 424
reloj de sol 424
reloj digital 424
reloj programador 178
remache 169, 222
remate 191
remate en T 193
remeras primarias 78
remeras secundarias 78
remeras terciarias 78

remo 501
remolacha 129
remolcador 384
remolque 361
remolque rígido trasero 363
reniforme 55
reno 84
repetidor 317
repisa 192
repisa para accesorios 8
repollo 126
repollo verde 126
reposa-mano 332
reposabrazo 353
reposabrazos 467
reposacabezas 353
reposapiés 205, 369
reposapiés 224, 467
reproductor de CD portátil 325
reproductor de disco compacto 325
reproductor de DVD 333
reproductor DVD 318
reproductor/grabador de video VCR 319
reptación 31
reptiles 76
reptiles, ejemplos 77
República Centroafricana 451
República Checa 450
República de Corea 453
República de Malí 451
República de San Marino 450
República Democrática del Congo 451
Republica Democrática Popular de Corea
    453
República Dominicana 449
repuesto 312
repulsión 416
reseña gastronómica 313
resguardo del parachoques 348
residuos domésticos 47, 48
residuos industriales 47, 48
residuos no reciclables 49
residuos nucleares 48
residuos primarios 405
residuos, separación selectiva 49
resistencia 210, 213, 214, 218
resistencia eléctrica, unidad de medida
    426
resistencias 417
resonador 305, 309, 324
resorte 27, 206, 212, 222, 273, 312,
    535
resorte de la válvula 360
resorte de retorno 357
resorte de tensión 500
resorte hidráulico 501
resorte tensor 355
respaldo 200, 201, 205, 353, 369, 467,
    523
respaldo reclinatorio 460
respiradero 182, 367
respiradero lateral 361
resta 427
restador 490, 495
restaurante 386, 432, 435, 436, 438
restaurantes de comida rápida 437
resurgencia 31
retablo 446
retén de la esfera 332
retén imantado 180
retícula 420
retícula, sistema 22
retículo endoplasmático 50, 66
retina 119, 419
retira cutículas 265
retoño 63
retorno 331
retorno a la memoria 337
retrato 441
retroceso 331
retrovisor 368
retrovisor de gran angular 362
retrovisor gran angular 363
revestimiento 357, 493, 505, 534
revestimiento de fósforo 199
revestimiento de la popa 7
revestimiento interior 352
revestimientos textiles del suelo 190
revisor 374
revista sensacionalista 313
revólver portaobjetivos 421
rey 468, 470
rey, cámara 278
ría para la carrera de obstáculos 472
ría, carrera de obstáculos 472
rías 35

remo 501
ribete 238, 240, 244, 262
ribosoma 50, 66
ricotta 150
riel corredizo 214, 521
riel de iluminación 207
riel de rodamiento 397
riel deslizador 353
riel para las rejillas 211
rifle 534
rigatoni 146
rillettes 156
rimaya 30
rímel en pasta 266
rímel líquido 266
rincón 498
rinconera 203
ringside 498
rinoceronte 85
riñón 73, 107
riñón derecho 107
riñón izquierdo 107
riñonera 486
riñones 83, 154
río 24, 25, 32
río Amazonas 17
río Congo 20
río Danubio 18
río Mackenzie 16
río Mississipi 16
río Niger 20
río Orinoco 17
río Paraná 17
río San Lorenzo 16
río Senegal 20
río Vístula 18
río Volga 18
risco 5
rizador de mantequilla 169
rizador de pestañas 266
rizoide 51
rizoma 52
róbalo 160
Roberval, balanza 422
roble 64
robot de cocina 177
roca firme 27
roca impermeable 403
roca madre 54
rocas ígneas 26
rocas intrusivas 26
rocas metamórficas 26
rocas sedimentarias 26
rociador 197
rociadores 408
rocío 41
Rocosas, montañas 16
rodaballo 161
rodamiento 332
rodapié 202
rodilla 83, 86, 92, 94
rodillera 476, 486, 500, 526, 527
rodillo 172, 219
rodillo de pintor 219
rodrigón 230, 231
roedor 82
roedores 82
roedores, ejemplos 82
roja 469
rojo 418
Rojo, mar 14, 19, 20
rollos de la Torá 447
rombo 429
romero 142
rompehielos 384
rompiente 33
ropa 538
ropa de bebé 260
ropa de cama 204
ropa de hombre 244
ropa de mujer 251
ropa de niños 261
ropa deportiva 262
ropa interior 247, 258, 524
ropa para ejercicio 263
ropero 203
roquefort 151
rorcual 90
rosa 56
rosa de los vientos 23, 533
rosca 221, 223, 425
roseta 186, 236, 302
rosetón 285
rosquilla 144
Ross, banquisa 15
rotonda 25, 435
rotor 395, 412, 537
rotor de cola 395

rótula 98
rotulador 340
rough 504
router 334
Ruanda 451
rubí pulsado, láser 420
rubí, varilla 420
rubio 159
rueda 231, 364, 467, 501, 522, 525,
    526, 527
rueda central de enfoque 420
rueda de cadena 523
rueda de corrimiento 327
rueda de desplazamiento 332
rueda de empuje 467
rueda de la dirección 467
rueda de mando 331
rueda de modulación 310
rueda de repuesto 361
rueda de transmisión 523
rueda delantera 401
rueda giratoria 205
rueda guía 398
rueda humedecedora 339
rueda libre 360
rueda motriz 398
rueda para ajustar el tono 310
rueda para graduar el respaldo 353
ruedas de tracción 401
ruedecilla 209, 277, 308
Ruffini, corpúsculo 114
rugby 482
rugby, botas de tacos 483
ruibarbo 125
ruiseñor 80
ruleta de enfoque lejos/cerca 320
ruleta de selección de efectos especiales
    320
rulo 268
rulo para el cabello 268
Rumanía 450
rupia 440
ruqueta 127
rusula verde 123
ruta de servicio 388
ruta pintoresca 25
Ryukyu, fosa 34

S

sábalo 160
sabana 44
sábana 204
sábana ajustable 204
sable 519, 520
sacacorchos 146, 170, 531
sacacorchos con brazos 170
sacapuntas 341
saco de arena 498
saco de Douglas 112
saco de marinero 276
saco de piel 296
saco portabebé 260
saco rectangular 530
saco semirrectangular 530
sacos de dormir, ejemplos 530
sacrificio, piedra 283
sacristía 446
sacro 98, 99
safety débil 484
safety fuerte 484
Sahara, desierto 20
sahariana 255
Saint Kitts and Nevis 449
sal de mesa 141
sal gorda 141
sal marina 141
sala 188, 293
sala de alumnos 445
sala de anestesia 464
sala de audiencias 440, 447
sala de bombeo 384
sala de ceremonias 447
sala de cine 386
sala de clasificación 463
sala de conferencias 442
sala de control 406
sala de curas 465
sala de enyesado 463
sala de equipajes 374
sala de espera 463, 465
sala de espera de embarque 391
sala de espera del centro de extracción de
    sangre 465
sala de espera para la familia 462
sala de espera principal 465

sala de estar 188
sala de esterilización 464, 465
sala de examen de audiometría 465
sala de extracciones 465
sala de máquinas 384, 386, 406, 407
sala de navegación 382
sala de observación psiquiátrica 462
sala de oración 447
sala de preparación quirúrgica 464
sala de profesores 445
sala de proyección 294
sala de reanimación 462
sala de reconocimiento 465
sala de recuperación posoperatoria 464
sala de reposo de enfermeras 465
sala de reuniones 439, 442, 445
sala del jurado 440
sala del personal 443, 463
salamandra 75
salami alemán 156
salami de Génova 156
salas de entrevistas 440
salchicha chipolata 156
salchicha de Frankfurt 156
salchicha de Toulouse 156
salchicha kielbasa 156
salchicha merguez 156
salchow 509
salero 166
salida 343, 469
salida de agua fría 197
salida de aire caliente 192
salida de humo 192
salida de la pista 391
salida de la pista de alta velocidad 388
salida del refrigerante 410
salmón del Atlántico 161
salmón del Pacífico 161
salmonete 159
salmuera, especias 139
salón 188, 439
salón bar 439
salón de baile 387
salón de pasajeros 386
salpicadero 354, 369
salpicadero, equipamiento 457
salsa de ciruelas 141
salsa de soja 140
salsa de tamarindo 140
salsa de tomate 140
salsa hoisin 140
salsa Tabasco 140
salsa Worcertershire 140
salsa, ciruelas 141
salsa, soja 140
salsa, Tabasco 140
salsa, tamarindo 140
salsa, tomate 140
salsa, Worcertershire 140
salsera 166
salsifí 129
saltador 513
saltamontes verde 69
salto de altura 473
salto de espalda 518
salto de esquí 513
salto de longitud 472
salto de pértiga 472
salto en equilibrio 518
salto frontal 518
salto interior 518
salto inverso 518
saltos 518
salud 460
salvavidas 387
salvelino 161
salvia 142
sambal oelek 141
Samoa 453
San Bernardo 86
San Lorenzo, río 16
San Vicente y las Granadinas 449
sandalia 241, 242
sandía 135
sangre desoxigenada 104
sangre oxigenada 104
sangre, composición 104
Santa Lucía 449
Santo Tomé y Príncipe 451
santuario. lámpara 446
sapo común 75
saque 487
sardina 159
sargento 224
sarmiento 62
sarraceno, trigo 61
sartén 175, 531

sartén doble 175
sartén honda 175
sartén para crepes 175
sartén pequeña 175
sartorio 96
satélite 316
satélite artificial 37
satélite de telecomunicaciones 335
satélite meteorológico 38
satélite, comunicación 316
satélite, telecomunicaciones 317
satélites 2
satélites de telecomunicaciones 316
Saturno 2, 3
sauce llorón 64
saxofón 306
schnauzer 86
Schwann, célula 110
secador de mano 270
secadora de ensalada 171
secadora de ropa 213
sección 313
sección articulada 363
sección del cañón 193
sección frontal 459
sección rígida de tracción delantera 363
sección sagital 111, 112
sección transversal de la góndola 413
sección transversal de un observatorio
    astronómico 7
sección transversal de un telescopio
    reflector 9
sección transversal de un telescopio
    refractor 8
sección transversal de una carretera 342
sección transversal de una central
    hidroeléctrica 407
sección vertical 526
secretaría 443, 445
secretario/a de producción 291
sector 428
secuenciador 310
sedal 536
segmento 360
segmento abdominal 67
segmento de marcas 471
segmento intermedio 111
segmento terminal 111
segunda 298
segunda aleta dorsal 74
segunda base 474
segunda línea 482
segundero 424
segundo 428
segundo árbitro 487
segundo aumento de tensión 413
segundo ayudante de cámara 290
segundo espacio 489
segundo jugador 515
segundo molar 101
segundo pistón móvil 307
segundo premolar 101
segundos violines 295
seguridad 454
seguro 178, 209, 222
seguro de inclinación del disco 227
seguro de la base 224
seguro del fuelle 296
seguro del interruptor 228
seis doble 468
selección de cartón 49
selección de metal 49
selección de nivel 2 330
selección de papel 49
selección de vidrio 49
selección manual 49
selección óptica 49
selector 178
selector cuadro-direccional 315
selector de canales 319
selector de corte 271
selector de enfoque 320
selector de entrada 322
selector de focalización 314
selector de la recepción 303
selector de la voz 311
selector de movimiento orbital 227
selector de nivel de agua 212
selector de programa 310, 314
selector de sintonización 325
selector de temperatura 178, 212, 213
selector de tipo de cinta 323
selector de tostado 178
selector de velocidad 176, 228
selector de velocidades 176, 177
selector de volumen 325
selector del modo audio 322

selector del ritmo 311
selectores de funciones 327
selectores de modalidad 326
sellado, tapa 417
sello de goma 338
semáforo 375, 434
semáforo de peatones 434
sembradora de mano 231
semicírculo 428
semicírculo de la zona de tiro libre 488
semicírculo del área 480
semicorchea 299
semieje 351
semifusa 299
semilla 53, 57, 58, 59, 60
semilla, tegumento 57
semillas de adormidera 139
semillas de soja 131
semimembranoso 97
semirremolque frigorífico 365
semirremolque, caja, tipo 365
semisótano 182
semitendinoso 97
semola 144
sémola 144
señal de dirección 379
señal de distancia fija 391
señal de eje de pista 390
señal de identificación de pista 390
señal de zona de contacto de pista 391
señal de zona de espera 390
señal exterior 378
señales de límite de la pista 391
señales laterales de pista 390
Senegal 451
Senegal, río 20
seno 33, 94, 113, 418
seno del pecíolo 62
seno esfenoidal 117
seno frontal 117
seno lateral inferior 62
seno lateral superior 62
sensor de colisión primario 354
sensor de movimiento 286
sensor de seguridad 354
sensor de temperatura 358
sensor de velocidad de las ruedas 357
sensor del mando a distancia 318, 323
sensor óptico 332
sépalo 56, 58, 59
separacables 535
separación cartón 49
separación magnética 49
separación papel 49
separador 274, 384, 402, 409, 417, 467
separador de gas y líquido 359
separador de placas 359
separador electrolítico 417
sepia 157
séptima 298
septum 60
septum pellucidum 109
ser humano 92
serac 30
serie, número 441
serpiente 76
serpiente coral 77
serpiente de cascabel 77
serpiente de jarretera 77
serpiente venenosa, morfología, cabeza
    76
serpollo 62
serrucho 226
serrucho de punta 226
servicio de enlace ferroviario 390
servicio de mesa 166
servicio para fondue 174
servicio, estación 346
servicios de crédito 442
servicios de seguros 442
servicios financieros 442
servicios sociales 465
servidor 334, 335
servidor de acceso 335
servofreno 350, 357
sésamo, aceite 149
sesos 212
set 291
seta enoki 123
seto 183, 230
setos, cizallas 234
sexta 298
sexteto 300
Seychelles 452
shiitake 123
si(B) 298
siamés 87

sien 92
sierra circular de mano 227
sierra de cadena 235
sierra de calar 227
sierra de campo 533
sierra de ingletes 226
sierra de marquetería 226
sierra de podar 234
Sierra Leona 451
sierra para metales 226
sifón 72, 194, 196, 197
silbato 180, 377
silenciador 351, 367, 369
silencio de blanca 299
silencio de corchea 299
silencio de fusa 299
silencio de negra 299
silencio de redonda 299
silencio de semicorchea 299
silencio de semifusa 299
silencios, valores 299
silicua 60
silla alzadora 205
silla cabriolé 200
silla cojín 200
silla de brazos 200
silla de ruedas 467
silla de seguridad para niños 356
silla del director 291
silla escalera 201
silla plegable 201
silla plegable de lona 200
silla poltrona 200
silla porta-niño 372
silla sin brazos 201, 444
silla Wassily 200
sillas apilables 201
sillas de los actores 290
sillas, ejemplos 201
sillín 369, 370
sillín del conductor 369
sillín del pasajero 369
sillón 444
sillón de reposo 464
silo 122
silos 381
símbolos 468
símbolos científicos 426
sinagoga 447
sinapsis 110
sínfisis púbica 111, 112
Singapur 453
síntesis de los colores 418
síntesis de los colores aditivos 418
síntesis de los colores sustractivos 418
sintetizador 310
sintonizador 326
sirena 455
Siria 452
sisa 247
sismógrafo 27
sismógrafo horizontal 27
sismógrafo vertical 27
sismógrafos 27
sismograma 27
sistema antibloqueo de frenos 357
sistema de aire acondicionado 46
sistema de alimentación de gasolina 351
sistema de audio 354
sistema de botones 310
sistema de carreteras 342
sistema de células solares 411
sistema de control del puente de luces
    457
sistema de coordenadas terrestres 21
sistema de dirección 351
sistema de escape 351
sistema de frenado 351
sistema de lentes 420
sistema de refrigeración 351
sistema de restricción del airbag 354
sistema de soporte vital 10
sistema de suspensión 351
sistema de transmisión 351
sistema eléctrico 351
sistema fino de guía 7
sistema hidráulico 396
sistema internacional de unidades de
    medida 426
sistema magnético de amortiguación 422
sistema manipulador remoto 11, 12
sistema nervioso 108
sistema nervioso central 109
sistema nervioso periférico 108
sistema rotativo 403
sistema solar 2

sistemas de sonido portátiles 325
sistemas del automóvil 351
sistro 309
skateboard 526
skimmer 184
slip 247
smash 491
smog/niebla tóxica 47
snooker 503
snowboard 513
snowboarder 513
soba, fideos 147
sobre almohadillado 339
sobrefusión 414
sociedad 430
sofá 200
sofá cama 204
sofá de dos plazas 200, 439
sofá tipo imperio 200
softball 477
Sol 2, 4, 5, 38
sol(G) 298
Sol, estructura 4
solapa 244, 532
solapa autoadhesiva 339
solapa con ojal 248
solapa puntiaguda 244
soldador 218
soldadura, herramientas 218
sóleo 96
solera doble 187
solera inferior 187
solideo 238
solidificación 414
sólido 414, 415
sólido amorfo 414
solitario 264
solsticio de invierno 38
solsticio de verano 38
solución multipropósito 272
Somalia 451
sombra 424
sombra de ojos 266
sombrero 52
sombrero de campana 239
sombrero de fieltro 238, 239
sombrero de hongo 238
sombrero sin alas 239
sombreros 238
sombreros de hombre 238
sombreros de mujer 239
sombreros unisex 239
somen, fideos 147
somier 204
sonda destapacaños 216
sonda espacial 37
sonda térmica 178
sonido, sistemas portátiles 325
sopera 166
soplete 218
soporte 9, 174, 199, 227, 236, 269,
    277, 308, 355, 369, 387, 409, 533
soporte colgante 467
soporte de acoplamiento 337
soporte de la cadena 370
soporte de la mano 297
soporte de la plaqueta 273
soporte de la plataforma 412
soporte de la red 493
soporte del brazo 200
soporte del pie 473, 501
soporte del plano fijo 400
soporte del tablero 489
soporte para el antebrazo 466
soporte para el brazo 352
soporte para el cuello 525
soporte para el sobaco 466
sordina 307
sorgo 61
sorgo : panícula 61
soso 52
sortija de sello 264
sostenido 299
soufflé, molde 172
Sri Lanka 453
stilton 151
stylus 337
Suazilandia 452
subártico 40
subducción 27
subsuelo 54
subterráneo 281
subtítulo 313
subtropical húmedo 40
subtropical mediterráneo 40

ASTRONOMÍA > 2-25;   TIERRA > 26-71;   REINO VEGETAL >72-89;   REINO ANIMAL > 90-143;   SER HUMANO > 144-177;   PRODUCTOS ALIMENTARIOS Y DE COCINA > 178-241;   CASA > 242-295;
BRICOLAJE Y JARDINERÍA > 296-333;   VESTIDO > 334-371;   ACCESORIOS Y ARTÍCULOS PERSONALES > 372-391;   ARTE Y ARQUITECTURA > 392-465;   COMUNICACIONES Y AUTOMATIZACIÓN DE
OFICINA > 466-535;   TRANSPORTE Y VEHÍCULOS > 536-643;   ENERGÍA > 644-677;   CIENCIA > 678-705;   SOCIEDAD > 706-785;   DEPORTES Y JUEGOS > 786-920

sucesos 313
sudadera 262
sudadera con capucha 262
Sudáfrica 452
Sudeste 23
Suecia 450
suela 229, 240, 263, 503, 509
suela antiderrapante 261
suela rígida 511
suelo 48
suelo de cabina 287
suelo, absorción 46
suelo, capa superficial 54
suelo, fertilización 47
suelo, movimiento horizontal 27
suelo, movimiento vertical 27
suelo, revestimiento 190
suero de la leche 150
sueste 239
Suiza 450
sujetador 259, 308, 421
sujetador de aros 259
sujetador de escote bajo 259
sujetador del pabellón 306
sujetador sin tirantes 259
sujetalibros 341
suma 427
sumario 313
sumiller 438
supercross 525
superficie de cocción 179
superficie de deslizamiento 510
superficie de fijación 341
superficie de juego 493
superficie de la piel 114
superficie del agua 518
superficie dura (cemento) 492
superficie lunar 5
superficie sintética 492
superficies 428
superficies de juego 492
supermercado 120, 433, 437
supinador largo 96, 97
suplemento a color 313
suplemento literario 313
suprimir 331
Sur 23
Sur Sudeste 23
Sur Suroeste 23
surco 118
surco medio 118
surco nasolabial 117
surco terminal 118
Surinam 448
Suroeste 23
surtidor 197
surtidor de agua 272
surtidor de gasolina 346
suspensión 376, 380
suspensión trasera 522
suspensión, brazo 351
sustancia blanca 109, 110
sustancia despolarizante 417
sustancia gris 109, 110
sustrato impermeable 402
sutura 60, 73
sutura coronal 100
sutura escamosa 100
sutura lambdoidea 100

T

tábano 69
tabernáculo 446
tabique de contención longitudinal 384
tabique interventricular 104
tabique nasal 117
tabique, cartílago nasal 117
tabla abierta 253
tabla alpina 513
tabla armónica 301, 302
tabla con argollas 340
tabla con pinza 340
tabla de cortar 169
tabla de freestyle 513
tabla de los resultados 518
tabla de surf 519
tabla delantera 253
tabla harmónica 304
tablas 253
tablero 202, 224, 344, 470, 489
tablero de ajedrez 470
tablero de anuncios 341
tablero de damas 470
tablero de distribución 198
tablero de información 374
tablero de instrumentos 366, 368
tablero de juego 469
tablero de llegadas y salidas 391
tablero de operaciónes 455
tableta de resonancia 305
tablillas 461
tablinum 280
tablón de anuncios 444
tabulación a la derecha 330
tabulación a la izquierda 330
taburete 164, 201
taburete de bar 438
taburete escalera 219
tachuela 220
tachuelas para papel 341
tacita de café 166
tackle defensivo derecho 484
tackle defensivo izquierdo 484
tacle derecho 485
tacle izquierdo 485
taco 263, 473, 478, 534
taco de billar 503
taco de salida, atleta 473
tacómetro 355, 368
tacón 509
tacos 473
tacos de rosca 480
tacto 114
Tailandia 453
tailback 485
Tajikistán 452
tajín 140
tajina 174
taladro eléctrico 228
taladro percutor inalámbrico 228
tallarines de espinacas 146
talle corto 259
taller de máquinas diésel 375
taller mecánico 346
tallo 51, 53, 54, 114, 125
tallo principal 62
talo 50, 51
talón 93, 95, 226, 228, 229, 240, 247,
   262, 301, 302, 467, 477, 494, 506,
   536, 537
talón de apoyo 176, 208
talón de la hoja 169
talonario de cheques 274, 275
taloneador 482
talonera 511
talud 342
talud continental 33
tam-tam 308
tamarillo 136
tamarino 91
tambor 170, 212, 213, 286, 357, 425,
   537
tambor giratorio 27
tambor hablante 297
tamboril 308
tamiz 171, 172
tamiz vibratorio para lodos 403
tándem 373
Tanganyika, lago 20
tanque 13, 385, 454, 529
tanque auxiliar 365
tanque de agua de rociado 408
tanque de almacenamiento 405
tanque de gas propano 361
tanque de regulación de presión 404
tanque de techo pontón 404
tanque del combustible 235, 364
Tanzania 451
tapa 174, 176, 177, 178, 179, 180, 181,
   186, 198, 209, 210, 211, 212, 215,
   225, 240, 277, 305, 312, 315, 358,
   417, 454, 533
tapa de cierre 417
tapa de la batería 359
tapa de la cisterna 196
tapa de la culata 350
tapa de sellado 417
tapa del filtro 459
tapa del inodoro 196
tapa del objetivo 314
tapa del tanque 364
tapa deslizante 327
tapa flotante 404
tapa frontal 333
tapa inferior 417
tapa superior 417
tapa terminal 409
tapacubos 349
tapete 502
tapón 196, 267, 532
tapón de registro 194

tapón de rosca 163
tapón de vaciado 360
tapón del depósito de gasolina 349
tapón del depósito de la gasolina 368
tapón del sifón 197
tapón hermético 529
tapones para los oídos 458
taquilla 294
taquilla automática 294
taquilla de venta de billetes 378
taquillas de consigna automática 374
taquillas de los alumnos 445
tarjeta de circuito impreso 417
tarjeta de crédito 441
tarjeta de débito 443
tarjeta de memoria 315
tarjeta, número 441
tarjetero 274
taro 124
tarso 78
Tasmania 15
Tasmania, mar 15
tatami 499
taza 166, 196, 531, 532
tazas medidoras 171
té 148
té negro 148
té oolong 148
té verde 148
té, bolsita 148
teatro 292, 432, 433
teatro griego 278
techo 193, 349, 361
techo a dos aguas 189
techo acústico 293
techo corredizo 349
techo de cabina 287
techo de vidrio 374
techo de vidrio 188, 435
techo ponton, tanque 404
tecla 296, 304
tecla alternativa 330
tecla bloqueo numérico 331
tecla de adición 337
tecla de anular 333
tecla de bloqueo de mayúsculas 330
tecla de cambio de signo 337
tecla de confirmación 443
tecla de división 337
tecla de enter 331
tecla de fijación de pantalla 320
tecla de final de búsqueda 320
tecla de final de llamada 327
tecla de igualdad 337
tecla de impresión pantalla 331
tecla de iniciación 328
tecla de inicio/stop de grabación 320
tecla de llamada 327
tecla de mayúsculas 330
tecla de multiplicación 337
tecla de número 337
tecla de pedal 305
tecla de porcentaje 337
tecla de raíz cuadrada 337
tecla de reinicialización 328
tecla de repetición 323
tecla de retroceso 331
tecla de selección 327
tecla de selección de banda 322
tecla de selección de entrada 322
tecla de selección de modalidad FM 322
tecla de selección del grabador 322
tecla de selección sintonía 322
tecla de servicio 330
tecla de sustracción 337
tecla de visualización del título 320
tecla decimal 337
tecla email 330
tecla escape 330
tecla inicio 330
tecla memoria 322
tecla para limpiar la pantalla 337
tecla para limpiar la pantalla y de acceso
   337
tecla pausa 331
tecla tabulación 330
teclado 304, 310, 327, 330, 336
teclado alfabético 338
teclado alfanumérico 327, 330, 346,
   442, 443
teclado de bajos 296
teclado de funciones 423
teclado del número de identificación
   personal(PIN) 443
teclado del órgano de expresión 305
teclado del órgano mayor 305

teclado del órgano positivo 305
teclado numérico 328, 331, 338, 423
teclado triple 296
teclado, instrumentos 304
teclados manuales 305
teclas 311
teclas de control 328
teclas de cursor 331
teclas de función 328
teclas de funciones 330
teclas de funciones programables 443
teclas de Internet 330
teclas de operación 442, 443
teclas de selección de la sintonía 322
teclas de selección de los altavoces 322
técnica de salto 513
técnicas 487
tee 505, 515
tegumento de la semilla 57
teja 280, 283
tejado 183, 193, 283
tejido adiposo 113, 114
tejido conjuntivo 113
tejido subcutáneo 114
tejón 88
tela de araña 70
tela impermeable 273
telares 292
telecomunicaciones vía satélite 317
telecomunicaciones, satélites 316
teleférico 512
teléfono 327, 439
teléfono celular 327
teléfono público 294, 437, 438, 463
teléfono, comunicación 327
telémetro 315
teleobjetivo 314
teleporte 317
telescopio 7
telescopio espacial Hubble 7
telescopio reflector, sección transversal 9
telescopio refractor 8
telescopio refractor, sección transversal 8
telesilla 512
telesquí 512
televisión 318, 439
televisor 444
televisor 318
televisor de pantalla ancha 321
telón cortafuegos 292
telón de boca 292, 293
telón de fondo 292
telson 71
temperatura ambiente 39
temperatura Celsius, unidad de medida
   426
temperatura del punto de rocío 39
temperatura termodinámica, unidad de
   medida 426
temperatura, medición 424
temperatura, sensor 358
templo azteca 283
Templo de Huitzilopochtli 283
Templo de Tlaloc 283
templo griego 279
templo griego, plano 279
tenacillas 269
tenazas 193
tendencia barométrica 39
tenedor 167, 531
tenedor de ensalada 168
tenedor de fondue 168
tenedor de mesa 168
tenedor de ostras 168
tenedor de pescado 168
tenedor de postre 168
tenedor de trinchar 169
tenedores, ejemplos 168
tenis 490
tenis de mesa 493
tenista 492
tensiómetro 461
tensión, disminución 413
tensor 412, 498, 521, 537
tensor de la fascia lata 96
tensor de las cuerdas 308
tensores pectorales 500
tentáculo 72
tentáculo ocular 72
tentáculo táctil 72
tercelete 284
tercer octante 5
tercer pistón móvil 307
tercera 298
tercera base 474
tercera línea 482

tercera línea derecho 482
tercera línea izquierdo 482
tercero 515
terminación nerviosa 114
terminal 198, 404
terminal de carga 381
terminal de contenedores 430
terminal de granos 381
terminal de mercancías 430
terminal de pago electrónico 121, 443
terminal de pasajeros 381, 389, 390
terminal de petróleo 381
terminal de tierra 198
terminal del control remoto 314
terminal satélite de pasajeros 389
términos familiares 57, 58, 59
términos técnicos 57, 58, 59
termita 69
termo 532
termo con llave de servicio 532
termómetro 404, 424
termómetro clínico 424
termómetro de azúcar 171
termómetro de horno 171
termómetro de medida instantánea 171
termómetro de mercurio 461
termómetro digital 461
termómetro para carne 171
termómetros clínicos 461
termopausa 37
termosfera 37
termostato 178, 211
termostato de seguridad 213
termostato regulable 179
ternera, carne troceada 152
ternera, cortes 152
ternero 84
Terranova, isla 16
terraplén 342
terraza 182, 387
terremoto 27
terreno de juego 479
terrina 174
terrina para mantequilla 163
terrina, mantequilla 163
testículo 111
testículos 71
testigo 472
testigo luminoso 454
testuz 83
tetera 166
Tetis 3
tetra anterior 96
tibia 98
tibial anterior 96
tiburón, morfología 74
tiburones 144
tiempo, medición 424
tienda 280, 432
tienda de animales 436
tienda de artículos de decoración 437
tienda de bricolaje 436
tienda de campaña clásica 529
tienda de campaña tamaño familiar 528
tienda de deportes 437
tienda de discos 436
tienda de electrónica 436
tienda de regalos 436
tienda de ropa 436
tienda interior 528, 529
tienda libre de impuestos 391
tienda para dos 528
tienda rectangular 528
tienda tipo domo 529
tienda tipo iglú 529
tienda tipo vagón 528
tienda unipersonal 529
tiendas de campaña, ejemplos 528
Tierra 2, 3, 4, 5, 14
tierra apisonada 342
tierra batida 492
Tierra de la Reina Maud 15
Tierra de Marie Byrd 15
Tierra de Wilkes 15
Tierra del Fuego 17
Tierra, estructura 26
tifón 43
tigre 89
tijeras 461, 531
tijeras con doble filo para entresacar 270
tijeras con filo simple para entresacar 270
tijeras de cocina 173
tijeras de pedicura 265
tijeras de peluquero 270
tijeras de podar 269
tijeras de punta roma 265
tijeras de uñas 265
tijeras para aves 173

tijeras para cutículas 265
tila 148
timbal 308
timbales 295
timón 13, 383, 384, 386, 393
timón de profundidad 393
tímpano 75, 279, 285
tímpano, membrana 116
tinta 312
tinta de color cambiante 441
tinte para el cabello 267
tintorería 437
tipi 288
tipo de combustible 346
tipo de nube alta 39
tipo de nube baja 39
tipo de nube media 39
tipos de cabeza 221
tipos de eclipses 4, 5
tipos de movimientos 470
tipos de parqué 190
tipos de puntas 221
tipos de varillas 176
tira 286
tirador 163, 210, 286
tirador de la puerta 352
tirante 187, 219, 259, 344
tirante ajustable 260
tirante con botones 261
tirante de la botavara 519
tirante del pescante 397
tirantes 246
tirilla 245, 250
tirilla elástica 247, 250, 261
tirita 461
tirita Velcro® 260
tiro de aire caliente 192
tisanas 148
Titán 3
Titania 3
titi 91
Titicaca, lago 17
titular 313
titular, firma 441
título de propiedad 469
tiza 503
toalla con capuchón 260
toalla de baño 267
toalla de lavabo 267
toalla para la cara 267
toallero 195
tobera de sección variable 394
tobillera 257, 476, 513
tobillo 92, 94
toca 239
tocón 63
Togo 451
toldo 361
toldo de ventana 528
toldo delantero 528
tolva de carga 364
toma 236
toma audio 329
toma de aire 346, 362
toma de aire del motor 362
toma de aire del tejado 194
toma de aire para el ventilador de
    sustentación 383
toma de aire para refrigeración del motor
    525
toma de aire principal 194
toma de alimentación 329
toma de auriculares 329
toma de corriente 361
toma de entrada audio 337
toma de oxígeno 464
toma de salida audio 337
toma para auriculares 310, 311, 326
toma para la boca de riego 455
toma para los auriculares 322
tomas entrada /salida video 322
tomas vídeo 315
tomate 128
tomate en rama 128
tomatillo 128
tómbolo 35
tomillo 142
Tonga 453
tope 224, 270, 375, 459
tope amortiguador 209
tope de la escalera 455
tope de la puerta 211
tope fijo 425
tope móvil 425
toque 487

Torá, rollos 447
tórax 67, 68, 92, 94
torca 31
tornado 43
tornapunta 187
tornillo 219, 221, 223, 301
tornillo cruciforme (Phillips) 221
tornillo de ajuste 206, 222, 224, 461
tornillo de ajuste de ranilla 229
tornillo de ajuste de tensión 341
tornillo de ajuste del condensador 421
tornillo de anclaje 473
tornillo de apriete 224
tornillo de cabeza achaflanada 221
tornillo de cabeza avellanada 221
tornillo de cabeza redonda 221
tornillo de caja cuadrada 221
tornillo de montaje 501
tornillo de sujeción 227
tornillo de un solo sentido 221
tornillo guía 228
tornillo macrométrico 421
tornillo micrométrico 421, 425
tornillo nivelador 423
tornillo sin fin 365
tornillos de bloqueo 425
torniquete de entrada 378
torniquete de salida 378
torno de banco 224
torno de perforación 403
toro 429
toronja 134
torre 284, 397, 412, 413, 470
torre de control 388
torre de oficinas 435
torre de perforación 382, 403, 404
torre de recepción 316
torre de refrigeración 402
torre de saltos 518
torre de señales 375
torre de transmisión 316
torre del homenaje 282
torre esquinera 282
torre flanqueante 282
torre, grúa 397
torrecilla de lavado 214
torrente de montaña 29
Torres, estrecho 15
torreta 282
torsión 228
tortellini 146
tortilla 145
tortuga 76
tortuga, morfología 76
tostador 178
touch pad 336
trabilla 246, 254, 477
trabilla de la pretina 246
trabilla de suspensión 250
trabilla para el pie 501
tracción, coche 380
tracería 285
tracto olfatorio 117
tractor de orugas 398
tractor de ruedas 399
tractor, motor 400
tragadero 31
tragaluz 182
trago 115
trainera 384
traje 454
traje cruzado 252
traje de baño 263, 516
traje de carrera 508
traje de carreras 525
traje de chaqueta 251
traje de entrenamiento 262
traje de esquí 510
traje de esquí 513, 514
traje de esquí de salto 513
traje de judo 499
traje de protección 525
traje espacial 10
traje ignífugo 524
tramo 191
tramo central 344
tramo de elevación 345
tramo giratorio 344
tramo lateral 344
tramo suspendido 344
trampa de agua 504
trampa petrolífera 403
trampas de arena 504
trampilla 281, 292
trampilla de acceso 434

trampolín 184
trampolín de 1 m 518
trampolín de 3 m 518
transacción, recibo 443
transacciones financieras 335
Transantárticos, montes 15
transbordador 381, 386, 391
transbordador espacial 12
transbordador espacial en posición de
    lanzamiento 12
transepto 285
transferencia de calor al agua 408
transformador 207, 407
transformador principal 376
transmisión 212
transmisión de cadena 372
transmisión de calor 415
transmisión de electricidad 408
transmisión de ondas hertzianas 316
transmisión longitudinal, árbol 351
transmisión por cable submarino 317
transmisor 327
transmisor-receptor radar 457
transpaleta 396
transpiración 45
transporte 342
transporte aéreo 388
transporte de electricidad de alta tensión
    402, 413
transporte ferroviario 374
transporte hacia los usuarios 402, 413
transporte marítimo 381
transporte terrestre 342, 381
trapecio 96, 97, 429
tráquea 105
traste 296, 302, 303
tratamiento de datos 38
tratamiento químico 405
travelín 290
travelín, raíles 290
travesaño 187, 201, 202, 219, 297, 412,
    466, 467, 479
travesaño de apoyo 412
travesaño superior 186
travesaño superior de la vidriera 186
trébol 468
tren de alta velocidad 376
tren de aterrizaje delantero 392
tren de aterrizaje principal 393
tren de pasajeros 374
tren subterráneo 378, 380
tren suburbano 375
trenca 249
triángulo 295, 309, 429, 503
tribuna del jurado 440
tribunal 440
tríceps braquial 97
triciclo 373
triclinio 280
trifoliada 55
trifolio 285
trigo 61, 143
trigo : espiga 61
trigo sarraceno 61, 143
trimarán 521
trincha 244
trinchera 248
Trinidad y Tobago 449
trino 299
trinquete 221
trío 300, 468
tripa 154
triple salto 472
trípode 8, 308
tripulantes, vehículo de emergencia 11
triticale 143
Tritón 3
tritón 75
triturador de ajos 170
triturador de basura 197
trituradora 49, 402
trituradora de documentos 341
trocánter mayor 99
troje 122
tromba marina 43
trombarina 43
trombón 307
trombones 295
trompa 75, 295, 307
trompa de Eustaquio 116, 117
trompa de Falopio 112, 113
trompa uterina, ampolla 113
trompeta 307, 342
trompetas 295
trona 205

tronco 52, 62, 63, 75, 93, 95
tronco celiaco 103, 107
tronco, corte transversal 63
tronera 502
tronera central 502
tropical lluvioso 40
trópico de Cáncer 20, 21, 22
trópico de Capricornio 20, 21, 22
tropopausa 37, 46
troposfera 37
trote 83
trucha 161
trufa 123
tuba 295, 307
tubérculos 124
tubería de agua caliente 194, 197
tubería de agua fría 194, 196
tubería de carga 406
tubo 163, 199, 224, 307, 420, 461
tubo ajustable 466
tubo alimentador 180
tubo articulado 355
tubo binocular 421
tubo capilar 424
tubo de aire 270, 454
tubo de aspiración 407
tubo de circulación 410
tubo de cristal 424
tubo de desagüe 197
tubo de destellos 420
tubo de embocadura 305
tubo de empuje 312
tubo de entrada 177
tubo de escape 199, 350, 351, 364, 368,
    395, 398, 401
tubo de extensión 209
tubo de gasolina 351
tubo de irrigación 365
tubo de la hélice 383
tubo de lengüeta 305
tubo de pantalla 318
tubo de perforación 403
tubo de Pitot 525
tubo de presión 409
tubo de subida del agua 181
tubo de suministro de agua 194, 197
tubo de toma de agua 194
tubo de vapor 181
tubo del asiento 370
tubo del manillar 371
tubo del pistón 307
tubo en Y 460
tubo flexible 209, 460
tubo fluorescente 199
tubo inferior del cuadro 371
tubo portaocular 421
tubo principal 8, 9
tubo principal de observación 420
tubo rígido 209
tucán 80
tuerca 222, 223
tuerca cerrada 223
tuerca de ajuste 197
tuerca de bloqueo 425
tuerca de mariposa 223
tuerca de sujeción 536
tuerca hexagonal 223
tuercas 223
tulipán 56
tumbona 201
tundra 40, 44
túnel 378
túnel de carretera 345
túnel de comunicación 13
túnel de desvío 406
túnel de embarque 389
Túnez 451
túnica 252
turbante 239
turbina 402
turbina de viento de eje horizontal 413
turbina de viento de eje vertical 412
turbinas de viento 412
turbo-alternador 402
turborreactor 393
turión 125
turismo de tres puertas 347
turismo, neumático 358
Turkmenistán 452
Turquía 452
Tuvalu 453

U

uapiti 84
ubicación de la estatua 279
Ucrania 450
udon, fideos 147
ued 36
Uganda 451
uke (defensor) 499
umbela 57
umbo 73
umbral 30, 185
Umbriel 3
un par 468
uña 76, 78, 115, 220
uña, cuerpo 114
uña, raíz 114
uñas, esmalte 265
uñas, lima 265
unicelulares 66
unidad astronómica 3
unidad CD/DVD-ROM 336
unidad de casetes 333
unidad de CD/DVD-ROM 329
unidad de control de la temperatura del
    cuerpo 10
unidad de control electrónico 357
unidad de cuidados intensivos 464
unidad de destilación al vacío 405
unidad de disco duro extraíble 333
unidad de discos 310
unidad de disquete 329
unidad de disquete externo 333
unidad de extracción de solventes 405
unidad de medida de cantidad de materia
    426
unidad de medida de carga eléctrica 426
unidad de medida de corriente eléctrica
    426
unidad de medida de energía 426
unidad de medida de frecuencia 426
unidad de medida de fuerza 426
unidad de medida de intensidad luminosa
    426
unidad de medida de la diferencia de
    potencial eléctrico 426
unidad de medida de la temperatura
    Celsius 426
unidad de medida de longitud 426
unidad de medida de masa 426
unidad de medida de potencia eléctrica
    426
unidad de medida de presión 426
unidad de medida de radioactividad 426
unidad de medida de resistencia eléctrica
    426
unidad de medida de temperatura
    termodinámica 426
unidad de pesas 501
unidad de refrigeración 365
unidad del disco duro 333
unidad móvil 316
unidad móvil de rayos X 462
unidad móvil de servicio por control
    remoto 11
unidad para maniobras en el espacio 10
unidades astronómicas 2
unidades de almacenamiento de
    información 333
unidades de entrada de información 330
unidades de medida, sistema
    internacional 426
unidades de salida de información 333
uniforme 456
unión 312, 427
unísono 298
universidad 432
uno 427
Urales, montes 18
uranio en fisión 408
Urano 2, 3
uréter 107
uretra 107, 111, 112
urgencias 462
urinario, aparato 107
URL localizador universal de recursos 334
urna 423
urópodo 71
Uruguay 448
usos de Internet 335
usuario particular 335
utensilios de cocina 169, 174, 531
utensilios diversos 173
utensilios para abrir y descorchar 170
utensilios para la chimenea 193
utensilios para medir 171

ASTRONOMÍA > 2-25;   TIERRA > 26-71;   REINO VEGETAL >72-89;   REINO ANIMAL > 90-143;   SER HUMANO > 144-177;   PRODUCTOS ALIMENTARIOS Y DE COCINA > 178-241;   CASA > 242-295;
BRICOLAJE Y JARDINERÍA > 296-333;   VESTIDO > 334-371;   ACCESORIOS Y ARTÍCULOS PERSONALES > 372-391;   ARTE Y ARQUITECTURA > 392-465;   COMUNICACIONES Y AUTOMATIZACIÓN DE
OFICINA > 466-535;   TRANSPORTE Y VEHÍCULOS > 536-643;   ENERGÍA > 644-677;   CIENCIA > 678-705;   SOCIEDAD > 706-785;   DEPORTES Y JUEGOS > 786-920

657

utensilios para repostería 172
útero 112, 113
útero, ligamento ancho 113
uva 62, 132
uva, corte 59
uvas, racimo 62
úvula 116, 117
Uzbekistán 452

V

vaca 84
vaciador 173
vacuno, carne picada 152
vacuno, carne troceada 152
vacuno, cortes 152
vacuola 50, 66
vacuola contráctil 66
vacuola digestiva 66
vacuola digestiva en formación 66
vagina 112, 113
vagón cisterna 377
vagón comedor 376
vagón de carga 375
vagón de pasajeros 376, 380
vagón frigorífico 377
vagón intermodal 377
vagón máquina 380
vagón para automóviles 377
vagón para contenedores 377
vagón para ganado 377
vagones de pasajeros 376
vagones, ejemplos 377
vaina 55, 60
vaina de mielina 110
vajilla 166
valla 434
valla de madera 506
vallado 182
vallado del campo 475
valle 29, 32
valor 441
valores de las notas musicales 299
valores de los silencios 299
valva 73
válvula 371
válvula aórtica 104
válvula de admisión 360
válvula de control 529
válvula de drenaje 211
válvula de entrada 196
válvula de escape 360
válvula de exhalación 459
válvula de inhalación 459
válvula de liberación de aire 385
válvula de llenado 404
válvula de seguridad 174, 408
válvula de vaciado 404
válvula mitral 104
válvula pulmonar 104
válvula tricúspide 104
Vanuatu 453
vapor 402, 415
vapor, tubo 181
vaporera eléctrica 179
vaporizador 208
vaquería 122
vaqueros 254
vara 301
varano 77
variedades de inflorescencias 57
varilla 199, 259, 273
varilla de acero 309
varilla de batir 176
varilla de carbón (cátodo) 417
varilla de refrigeración 420
varilla de rubí 420
varilla de tensión 308
varilla del pedal 304
varilla reflectante 420
varilla rizadora 269
varillas, tipos de 176
varios aparatos electrodomésticos 180
Varolio, puente 109
vaso 184
vaso capilar 114
vaso corto 165
vaso largo 165

vaso medidor 171
vaso mezclador 176
vaso sanguíneo 104, 114
vástago 220, 221, 371, 502
vástago aislado 217
vástago de arrastre 403
vástago interno 96, 97
vatio 426
vegetación 44
vegetación, distribución 44
vehículo de emergencia 345
vehículo de emergencia para los
    tripulantes 11
vehículo todo terreno 347
vehículos 342
vejiga 107, 111, 112
vela 446, 519, 520
vela mayor 520
velero 520
veleta 413
veleta (grímpola) 520
velo 536
velo del paladar 116, 117
velo del paladar, pilar anterior 116
velocidad del viento 39
velocidad, selector 176
velocímetro 355, 368, 501
vena axilar 102
vena basílica 102
vena cava inferior 102, 103, 104, 107
vena cava superior 102, 103, 104
vena cefálica 102
vena femoral 102
vena hepática 103
vena ilíaca 103
vena ilíaca común 107
vena mesentérica superior 102
vena porta 103
vena pulmonar 102
vena pulmonar derecha 104
vena pulmonar izquierda 104
vena renal 102, 107
vena safena interna 102
vena subclavia 102
vena yugular externa 102
vena yugular interna 102
venas principales 102
vencejo 80
venda de gasa 461
venda elástica 461
venda triangular 461
veneno, conducto 76
veneno, glándula 76
venera 157
Venezuela 448
venta de billetes, taquilla 378
ventalla 60
ventana 178, 179, 186, 189, 361, 519
ventana a la francesa 287
ventana a la inglesa 287
ventana abajo 331
ventana arriba 331
ventana basculante 287
ventana corredera 287
ventana de acceso 333
ventana de celosía 287
ventana de guillotina 287
ventana de la nariz 117
ventana de librillo 287
ventana del semisótano 183
ventana panorámica 435
ventana pivotante 287
ventana protectora 318
ventana-mosquitero 528
ventanas, ejemplos 287
ventanilla 349, 352, 380, 392, 443
ventanilla comercial 443
ventanilla de aterrizaje 395
ventanilla de observación 13
ventanilla de ventilación del techo 361
ventanilla trasera 349
ventilación 354
ventilador 213, 322, 350, 358, 360, 365,
    380
ventilador de césped 237
ventilador de la carcasa 329

ventilador del equipo de alimentación 329
ventosa 72, 75
ventrículo derecho 103, 104
ventrículo izquierdo 103, 104
Venus 2, 3
verano 38
verano fresco 40
verano tórrido 40
verbena 148
verde 418
verdolaga 127
verdura 120
verdura 124
verduras de hojas 126
vereda 504
vermicelli de arroz 147
vernier 425
vértebra lumbar 110
vértebras cervicales 99
vértebras dorsales 99
vértebras lumbares 99
vertedero 431
vertedero autorizado 47
vertedor 180
vertido de hidrocarburos 48
vesícula biliar 106
vesícula seminal 111
vestíbulo 116, 188, 280, 374, 386, 390,
    435, 439
vestido 238
vestido acampanado 252
vestido camisero 252
vestido camisero sin mangas 252
vestido cruzado 252
vestido de camiseta 252
vestido de talle bajo 252
vestido de tirantes 252
vestidos, ejemplos 252
vestuario 290
vestuarios 444
vía 374, 378
vía de tren suburbano 375
vía férrea 25
vía ferroviaria 431, 432
Vía Láctea 6
Vía Láctea (vista desde arriba) 6
Vía Láctea (vista lateral) 6
vía principal 375
vía subsidiaria 375
víbora 77
vibrisas 82
Victoria, lago 20
vid 62
videocámara analógica: vista frontal 320
videocámara analógica: vista posterior
    320
videocinta 319
videojuego 471
vidriera 446
vidrio 186
vidrio, selección 49
vieira 157
viento 47, 48, 528
viento dominante 43
viento, dirección 39
viento, instrumentos 306
viento, molino 412
viento, velocidad 39
vientre 83
vierteaguas 349
vierteguas 185, 186, 193
Vietnam 453
viga 280, 283, 288
viga cantilever 344
viga continua 344
viga de cola 395
viga maestra 11, 187
viga, puente 344
vigueta 190
vigueta del piso 187
vigueta del techo 187
vigueta esquinera 187
vinagre balsámico 141
vinagre de arroz 141
vinagre de malta 141
vinagre de manzana 141
vinagre de vino 141
vinagre, arroz 141

vinagre, malta 141
vinagre, manzana 141
vinagre, vino 141
vino 120
viola 301
violas 295
violeta 56
violín 301
violines, familia 295, 301
violoncelo 301
violoncelos 295
vira 240
virola 503
virola hembra 537
virola macho 537
visera 238, 239, 367, 458, 506, 525
visión 419
visión normal 419
visión, defectos 419
visón 88
visor 210, 315
visor electrónico 320
visor telescópico 420
vista 119
vista anterior 92, 94, 96, 98
vista frontal 478
vista general 186
vista lateral 478
vista lateral del cráneo 100
vista posterior 93, 95, 97, 99, 113
vista transversal de una calle 434
Vístula, río 18
visualización de datos 328
visualización de la información 319
vitrales 285
vitrina 203
vitrinas refrigeradas 120
vivienda 122
viviendas plurifamiliares 289
viviendas tradicionales 288
viviendas urbanas 289
volador 471
volante 350, 354, 385, 525
volante de control 455
volante de plumas 495
volante sintético 495
volantes 260
volcadora 401
volcán 26, 28
volcán efusivo 28
volcán explosivo 28
volcanes, ejemplo 28
volea 490
voleibol 487
Volga, río 18
volt 426
voltio 426
voluta 200, 301
volva 52
vuelo del peldaño 191
vuelta 246
vulva 94, 113

W

wakame 123
walkie-talkie 456
wasabi 141
Weddel, mar 15
wigwam 288
Wilkes, Tierra 15
winch 521
windsurf 519
wok 174

X

xilófono 295, 309

Y

yak 85
yate de motor 385
yema 54, 79, 114
yema axilar 53
yema terminal 53
yembé 297
Yemen 452

yen 440
yeyuno 106
Yibouti 451
yogur 150
Yucatán, península 16
Yugoslavia 450
yunque 116
yurta 288

Z

zaguero 482
zaguero derecho 487
zaguero izquierdo 487
zaguero medio 487
zamarra 249
Zambia 452
zampoña 297
zanahoria 129
zanca 191
zanca de contén 191
zanco 398
zángano 68
zapata 224, 357, 365
zapata antideslizante 219
zapata de goma 219
zapatería 437
zapatilla 473, 478, 488, 500
zapatilla con tacos 476
zapatilla de tenis 242, 492
zapatilla deportiva 262
zapato 522, 524
zapato con cordones 241
zapato con tacos 486
zapato de cordones 240
zapato de correa 241
zapato de salón 241
zapato de tacón con correa 241
zapato de tatón abierto 241
zapato oxford 240
zapatos de golf 500
zapatos de hombre 240
zapatos de mujer 241
zapote 137
zarcillo 62
zarpa 187
Zimbabue 452
zócalo 191
zócalo de la bañera 195
zona comercial 431, 435
zona de anotación 484
zona de ataque 487
zona de atención 475
zona de camillas 462
zona de combate 499
zona de convección 4
zona de defensa 487
zona de defensa protegida 515
zona de entrega 472
zona de espera 442
zona de la portería 507
zona de marca 483
zona de precipitación 39
zona de preparación de productos 120
zona de radiación 4
zona de recepción de mercancías 120
zona de recepción productos lácteos 120
zona de recreo 386
zona de saque 495
zona de seguridad 499
zona de servicio 389
zona de traspaso de carga 385
zona de tres segundos 489
zona del hoyo 504
zona libre 487
zona neutral 484, 507
zona pelúcida 112
zona residencial 431
zona residencial (de las afueras) 25
zona residencial de las afueras 431
zorro 88
zumaque 139